THE
EXPOSITOR'S BIBLE COMMENTARY

with the New International Version

THE

EXPOSITOR'S BIBLE COMMENTARY

with the New International Version

Hebrews through *Revelation*

VOLUME 12

Hebrews - Leon Morris

James - Donald W. Burdick

1 & 2 Peter - Edwin A. Blum

1, 2 & 3 John - Glenn W. Barker

Jude - Edwin A. Blum

Revelation - Alan F. Johnson

Frank E. Gæbelein general editor

GRAND RAPIDS, MICHIGAN 49530 USA

ZONDERVAN™

The Expositor's Bible Commentary, Volume 12

Requests for information should be addressed to:

Zondervan, *Grand Rapids, Michigan 49530*

Library of Congress Cataloging-in-Publication Data
(Revised for Volume 12)

Main entry under title:
The Expositor's Bible commentary.
Includes bibliographies.
Contents: v. 1. Introductory articles.—v. 9. John, Acts.—
v. 10. Romans–Galatians.—v. 11. Ephesians–Philemon.—
v. 12. Hebrews–Revelation.
ISBN 0-310-36540-6 (v. 12)
1. Bible — Commentaries. I. Gaebelein, Frank Ely, 1899–
II. Douglas, James Dixon. III. Bible. English. New International 1976.
BS491.2.E96
220.7'7 76-41334

This edition is printed on acid-free paper.

Printed in the United States of America

03 04 05 06 07 08 /DC/ 42 41 40 39 38 37 36 35 34 33

CONTENTS

CONTRIBUTORS TO VOLUME 12

Hebrews: Leon Morris
B.Sc., University of Sydney; M.Sc., University of Melbourne; B.D., M.Th., London; Ph.D., Cambridge; Th.D. (honorary), Australian College of Theology
Formerly Principal, Ridley College, Melbourne

James: Donald W. Burdick
A.B., Wheaton College; B.D., Th.M., Th.D., Northern Baptist Theological Seminary
Professor of New Testament, Denver Seminary

1, 2 Peter, Jude: Edwin A. Blum
B.S., Bob Jones University; Th.M., Th.D., Dallas Theological Seminary; D. Theol., University of Basel, Switzerland
Associate Professor of Historical Theology, Dallas Theological Seminary

1, 2, 3 John: Glenn W. Barker
A.B., A.M., Wheaton College; Th.D., Harvard University
Provost and Professor of Christian Origins, Fuller Theological Seminary

Revelation: Alan F. Johnson
B.S., William Jennings Bryan College; Th.M., Th.D., Dallas Theological Seminary; Post Doctoral Fellow, Duke University Graduate School of Religion
Professor of Bible and Theology, Wheaton College

PREFACE

The title of this work defines its purpose. Written primarily by expositors for expositors, it aims to provide preachers, teachers, and students of the Bible with a new and comprehensive commentary on the books of the Old and New Testaments. Its stance is that of a scholarly evangelicalism committed to the divine inspiration, complete trustworthiness, and full authority of the Bible. Its seventy-eight contributors come from the United States, Canada, England, Scotland, Australia, New Zealand, and Switzerland, and from various religious groups, including Anglican, Baptist, Brethren, Free, Independent, Methodist, Nazarene, Presbyterian, and Reformed churches. Most of them teach at colleges, universities, or theological seminaries.

No book has been more closely studied over a longer period of time than the Bible. From the Midrashic commentaries going back to the period of Ezra, through parts of the Dead Sea Scrolls and the Patristic literature, and on to the present, the Scriptures have been expounded. Indeed, there have been times when, as in the Reformation and on occasions since then, exposition has been at the cutting edge of Christian advance. Luther was a powerful exegete, and Calvin is still called "the prince of expositors."

Their successors have been many. And now, when the outburst of new translations and their unparalleled circulation have expanded the readership of the Bible, the need for exposition takes on fresh urgency.

Not that God's Word can ever become captive to its expositors. Among all other books, it stands first in its combination of perspicuity and profundity. Though a child can be made "wise for salvation" by believing its witness to Christ, the greatest mind cannot plumb the depths of its truth (2 Tim. 3:15; Rom. 11:33). As Gregory the Great said, "Holy Scripture is a stream of running water, where alike the elephant may swim, and the lamb walk." So, because of the inexhaustible nature of Scripture, the task of opening up its meaning is still a perennial obligation of biblical scholarship.

How that task is done inevitably reflects the outlook of those engaged in it. Every biblical scholar has presuppositions. To this neither the editors of these volumes nor the contributors to them are exceptions. They share a common commitment to the supernatural Christianity set forth in the inspired Word. Their purpose is not to supplant the many valuable commentaries that have preceded this work and from which both the editors and contributors have learned. It is rather to draw on the resources of contemporary evangelical scholarship in producing a new reference work for understanding the Scriptures.

A commentary that will continue to be useful through the years should handle contemporary trends in biblical studies in such a way as to avoid becoming outdated when critical fashions change. Biblical criticism is not in itself inadmissible, as some have mistakenly thought. When scholars investigate the authorship, date, literary characteristics, and purpose of a biblical document, they are practicing biblical criticism. So also when, in order to ascertain as nearly as possible the original form of the text, they deal with variant readings, scribal errors, emendations, and other phenomena in the manuscripts. To do these things is essential to responsible exegesis and exposition. And always there is the need to distinguish hypothesis from fact, conjecture from truth.

The chief principle of interpretation followed in this commentary is the grammatico-historical one—namely, that the primary aim of the exegete is to make clear the meaning of the text at the time and in the circumstances of its writing. This endeavor to understand what in the first instance the inspired writers actually said must not be confused with an inflexible literalism. Scripture makes lavish use of symbols and figures of speech; great portions of it are poetical. Yet when it speaks in this way, it speaks no less truly than it does in its historical and doctrinal portions. To understand its message requires attention to matters of grammar and syntax, word meanings, idioms, and literary forms—all in relation to the historical and cultural setting of the text.

The contributors to this work necessarily reflect varying convictions. In certain controversial matters the policy is that of clear statement of the contributors' own views followed by fair presentation of other ones. The treatment of eschatology, though it reflects differences of interpretation, is consistent with a general premillennial position. (Not all contributors, however, are premillennial.) But prophecy is more than prediction, and so this commentary gives due recognition to the major lode of godly social concern in the prophetic writings.

THE EXPOSITOR'S BIBLE COMMENTARY is presented as a scholarly work, though not primarily one of technical criticism. In its main portion, the Exposition, and in Volume 1 (General and Special Articles), all Semitic and Greek words are transliterated and the English equivalents given. As for the Notes, here Semitic and Greek characters are used but always with transliterations and English meanings, so that this portion of the commentary will be as accessible as possible to readers unacquainted with the original languages.

It is the conviction of the general editor, shared by his colleagues in the Zondervan editorial department, that in writing about the Bible, lucidity is not incompatible with scholarship. They are therefore endeavoring to make this a clear and understandable work.

The translation used in it is the New International Version (North American Edition). To the International Bible Society thanks are due for permission to use this most recent of the major Bible translations. The editors and publisher have chosen it because of the clarity and beauty of its style and its faithfulness to the original texts.

To the associate editor, Dr. J. D. Douglas, and to the contributing editors—Dr. Walter C. Kaiser, Jr. and Dr. Bruce K. Waltke for the Old Testament, and Dr. James Montgomery Boice and Dr. Merrill C. Tenney for the New Testament—the general editor expresses his gratitude for their unfailing cooperation and their generosity in advising him out of their expert scholarship. And to the many other contributors he is indebted for their invaluable part in this work. Finally, he owes a special debt of gratitude to Dr. Robert K. DeVries, executive vice-president of the Zondervan Publishing House; Rev. Gerard Terpstra, manuscript editor; and Miss Elizabeth Brown, secretary to Dr. DeVries, for their continual assistance and encouragement.

Whatever else it is—the greatest and most beautiful of books, the primary source of law and morality, the fountain of wisdom, and the infallible guide to life—the Bible is above all the inspired witness to Jesus Christ. May this work fulfill its function of expounding the Scriptures with grace and clarity, so that its users may find that both Old and New Testaments do indeed lead to our Lord Jesus Christ, who alone could say, "I have come that they may have life, and have it to the full" (John 10:10).

FRANK E. GAEBELEIN

ABBREVIATIONS

A. General Abbreviations

A	Codex Alexandrinus
Akkad.	Akkadian
א	Codex Sinaiticus
Ap. Lit.	Apocalyptic Literature
Apoc.	Apocrypha
Aq.	Aquila's Greek Translation of the Old Testament
Arab.	Arabic
Aram.	Aramaic
b	Babylonian Gemara
B	Codex Vaticanus
C	Codex Ephraemi Syri
c.	*circa*, about
cf.	*confer*, compare
ch., chs.	chapter, chapters
cod., codd.	codex, codices
contra	in contrast to
D	Codex Bezae
DSS	Dead Sea Scrolls (see E.)
ed., edd.	edited, edition, editor; editions
e.g.	*exempli gratia*, for example
Egyp.	Egyptian
et. al.	*et alii*, and others
EV	English Versions of the Bible
fem.	feminine
ff.	following (verses, pages, etc.)
fl.	flourished
ft.	foot, feet
gen.	genitive
Gr.	Greek
Heb.	Hebrew
Hitt.	Hittite
ibid.	*ibidem*, in the same place
id.	*idem*, the same
i.e.	*id est*, that is
impf.	imperfect
infra.	below
in loc.	*in loco*, in the place cited
j	Jerusalem or Palestinian Gemara
Lat.	Latin
LL.	Late Latin
LXX	Septuagint
M	Mishnah
masc.	masculine
mg.	margin
Mid	Midrash
MS(S)	Manuscript(s)
MT	Masoretic text
n.	note
n.d.	no date
Nestle	Nestle (ed.) *Novum Testamentum Graece*
no.	number
NT	New Testament
obs.	obsolete
OL	Old Latin
OS	Old Syriac
OT	Old Testament
p., pp.	page, pages
par.	paragraph
Pers.	Persian
Pesh.	Peshitta
Phoen.	Phoenician
pl.	plural
Pseudep.	Pseudepigrapha
Q	Quelle ("Sayings" source in the Gospels)
qt.	quoted by
q.v.	*quod vide*, which see
R	Rabbah
rev.	revised, reviser, revision
Rom.	Roman
RVm	Revised Version margin
Samar.	Samaritan recension
SCM	Student Christian Movement Press
Sem.	Semitic
sing.	singular
SPCK	Society for the Promotion of Christian Knowledge
Sumer.	Sumerian
s.v.	*sub verbo*, under the word
Syr.	Syriac
Symm.	Symmachus
T	Talmud
Targ.	Targum
Theod.	Theodotion
TR	Textus Receptus
tr.	translation, translator, translated
UBS	The United Bible Societies' Greek Text
Ugar.	Ugaritic
u.s.	*ut supra*, as above
viz.	*videlicet*, namely

vol.	volume
v., vv.	verse, verses
vs.	versus
Vul.	Vulgate
WH	Westcott and Hort, *The New Testament in Greek*

B. Abbreviations for Modern Translations and Paraphrases

AmT	Smith and Goodspeed, *The Complete Bible, An American Translation*
ASV	American Standard Version, American Revised Version (1901)
Beck	Beck, *The New Testament in the Language of Today*
BV	Berkeley Version (The Modern Language Bible)
JB	The Jerusalem Bible
JPS	*Jewish Publication Society Version of the Old Testament*
KJV	King James Version
Knox	R.G. Knox, *The Holy Bible: A Translation from the Latin Vulgate in the Light of the Hebrew and Greek Original*
LB	The Living Bible
Mof	J. Moffatt, *A New Translation of the Bible*
NAB	The New American Bible
NASB	New American Standard Bible
NEB	The New English Bible
NIV	The New International Version
Ph	J. B. Phillips *The New Testament in Modern English*
RSV	Revised Standard Version
RV	Revised Version — 1881–1885
TCNT	Twentieth Century New Testament
TEV	Today's English Version
Wey	*Weymouth's New Testament in Modern Speech*
Wms	C. B. Williams, *The New Testament: A Translation in the Language of the People*

C. Abbreviations for Periodicals and Reference Works

AASOR	*Annual of the American Schools of Oriental Research*
AB	*Anchor Bible*
AIs	de Vaux: *Ancient Israel*
AJA	*American Journal of Archaeology*
AJSL	*American Journal of Semitic Languages and Literatures*
AJT	*American Journal of Theology*
Alf	Alford: *Greek Testament Commentary*
ANEA	*Ancient Near Eastern Archaeology*
ANET	Pritchard: *Ancient Near Eastern Texts*
ANF	Roberts and Donaldson: *The Ante-Nicene Fathers*
ANT	M. R. James: *The Apocryphal New Testament*
A-S	Abbot-Smith: *Manual Greek Lexicon of the New Testament*
AThR	*Anglican Theological Review*
BA	*Biblical Archaeologist*
BASOR	*Bulletin of the American Schools of Oriental Research*
BAG	Bauer, Arndt, and Gingrich: *Greek-English Lexicon of the New Testament*
BC	Foakes-Jackson and Lake: *The Beginnings of Christianity*
BDB	Brown, Driver, and Briggs: *Hebrew-English Lexicon of the Old Testament*
BDF	Blass, Debrunner, and Funk: *A Greek Grammar of the New Testament and Other Early Christian Literature*
BDT	Harrison: *Baker's Dictionary of Theology*
Beng.	Bengel's *Gnomon*
BETS	*Bulletin of the Evangelical Theological Society*
BJRL	*Bulletin of the John Rylands Library*
BS	*Bibliotheca Sacra*
BT	*Babylonian Talmud*
BTh	*Biblical Theology*
BW	*Biblical World*
CAH	*Cambridge Ancient History*
CanJTh	*Canadian Journal of Theology*
CBQ	*Catholic Biblical Quarterly*

CBSC	*Cambridge Bible for Schools and Colleges*
CE	*Catholic Encyclopedia*
CGT	*Cambridge Greek Testament*
CHS	Lange: *Commentary on the Holy Scriptures*
ChT	*Christianity Today*
Crem	Cremer: *Biblico-Theological Lexicon of the New Testament Greek*
DDB	*Davis' Dictionary of the Bible*
Deiss BS	Deissmann: *Bible Studies*
Deiss LAE	Deissmann: *Light From the Ancient East*
DNTT	*Dictionary of New Testament Theology*
EBC	*The Expositor's Bible Commentary*
EBi	*Encyclopaedia Biblica*
EBr	*Encyclopaedia Britannica*
EDB	*Encyclopedic Dictionary of the Bible*
EGT	Nicoll: *Expositor's Greek Testament*
EQ	*Evangelical Quarterly*
ET	*Evangelische Theologie*
ExB	*The Expositor's Bible*
Exp	*The Expositor*
ExpT	*The Expository Times*
FLAP	Finegan: *Light From the Ancient Past*
GR	*Gordon Review*
HBD	*Harper's Bible Dictionary*
HDAC	Hastings: *Dictionary of the Apostolic Church*
HDB	Hastings: *Dictionary of the Bible*
HDBrev.	Hastings: *Dictionary of the Bible*, one-vol. rev. by Grant and Rowley
HDCG	Hastings: *Dictionary of Christ and the Gospels*
HERE	Hastings: *Encyclopedia of Religion and Ethics*
HGEOTP	Heidel: *The Gilgamesh Epic and Old Testament Parallels*
HJP	Schurer: *A History of the Jewish People in the Time of Christ*
HR	Hatch and Redpath: *Concordance to the Septuagint*
HTR	*Harvard Theological Review*
HUCA	*Hebrew Union College Annual*
IB	*The Interpreter's Bible*
ICC	*International Critical Commentary*
IDB	*The Interpreter's Dictionary of the Bible*
IEJ	*Israel Exploration Journal*
Int	*Interpretation*
INT	E. Harrison: *Introduction to the New Testament*
IOT	R. K. Harrison: *Introduction to the Old Testament*
ISBE	*The International Standard Bible Encyclopedia*
ITQ	*Irish Theological Quarterly*
JAAR	*Journal of American Academy of Religion*
JAOS	*Journal of American Oriental Society*
JBL	*Journal of Biblical Literature*
JE	*Jewish Encyclopedia*
JETS	*Journal of Evangelical Theological Society*
JFB	Jamieson, Fausset, and Brown: *Commentary on the Old and New Testament*
JNES	*Journal of Near Eastern Studies*
Jos. Antiq.	Josephus: *The Antiquities of the Jews*
Jos. War	Josephus: *The Jewish War*
JQR	*Jewish Quarterly Review*
JR	*Journal of Religion*
JSJ	*Journal for the Study of Judaism in the Persian, Hellenistic and Roman Periods*
JSOR	*Journal of the Society of Oriental Research*
JSS	*Journal of Semitic Studies*
JT	*Jerusalem Talmud*
JTS	*Journal of Theological Studies*
KAHL	Kenyon: *Archaeology in the Holy Land*
KB	Koehler-Baumgartner: *Lexicon in Veteris Testament Libros*
KD	Keil and Delitzsch: *Commentary on the Old Testament*
LSJ	Liddell, Scott, Jones: *Greek-English Lexicon*
LTJM	Edersheim: *The Life and Times of Jesus the Messiah*

MM — Moulton and Milligan: *The Vocabulary of the Greek Testament*
MNT — Moffatt: *New Testament Commentary*
MST — McClintock and Strong: *Cyclopedia of Biblical, Theological, and Ecclesiastical Literature*
NBC — Davidson, Kevan, and Stibbs: *The New Bible Commentary*, 1st ed.
NBCrev. — Guthrie and Motyer: *The New Bible Commentary*, rev. ed.
NBD — J. D. Douglas: *The New Bible Dictionary*
NCB — *New Century Bible*
NCE — *New Catholic Encyclopedia*
NIC — *New International Commentary*
NIDCC — Douglas: *The New International Dictionary of the Christian Church*
NovTest — *Novum Testamentum*
NSI — Cooke: *Handbook of North Semitic Inscriptions*
NTS — *New Testament Studies*
ODCC — *The Oxford Dictionary of the Christian Church*, rev. ed.
Peake — Black and Rowley: *Peake's Commentary on the Bible*
PEQ — *Palestine Exploration Quarterly*
PNFl — P. Schaff: *The Nicene and Post-Nicene Fathers* (1st series)
PNF2 — P. Schaff and H. Wace: *The Nicene and Post-Nicene Fathers* (2nd series)
PTR — *Princeton Theological Review*
RB — *Revue Biblique*
RHG — Robertson's *Grammar of the Greek New Testament in the Light of Historical Research*
RTWB — Richardson: *A Theological Wordbook of the Bible*
SBK — Strack and Billerbeck: *Kommentar zum Neuen Testament aus Talmud und Midrash*
SHERK — *The New Schaff-Herzog Encyclopedia of Religious Knowledge*
SJT — *Scottish Journal of Theology*
SOT — Girdlestone: *Synonyms of Old Testament*
SOTI — Archer: *A Survey of Old Testament Introduction*
ST — *Studia Theologica*
TCERK — Loetscher: *The Twentieth Century Encyclopedia of Religious Knowledge*
TDNT — Kittel: *Theological Dictionary of the New Testament*
TDOT — *Theological Dictionary of the Old Testament*
Theol — *Theology*
ThT — *Theology Today*
TNTC — *Tyndale New Testament Commentaries*
Trench — Trench: *Synonyms of the New Testament*
UBD — *Unger's Bible Dictionary*
UT — Gordon: *Ugaritic Textbook*
VB — Allmen: *Vocabulary of the Bible*
VetTest — *Vetus Testamentum*
Vincent — Vincent: *Word-Pictures in the New Testament*
WBC — *Wycliffe Bible Commentary*
WBE — *Wycliffe Bible Encyclopedia*
WC — *Westminster Commentaries*
WesBC — *Wesleyan Bible Commentaries*
WTJ — *Westminster Theological Journal*
ZAW — *Zeitschrift für die alttestamentliche Wissenschaft*
ZNW — *Zeitschrift für die neutestamentliche Wissenschaft*
ZPBD — *The Zondervan Pictorial Bible Dictionary*
ZPEB — *The Zondervan Pictorial Encyclopedia of the Bible*
ZWT — *Zeitschrift für wissenschaftliche Theologie*

D. Abbreviations for Books of the Bible, the Apocrypha, and the Pseudepigrapha

OLD TESTAMENT			NEW TESTAMENT	
Gen	2 Chron	Dan	Matt	1 Tim
Exod	Ezra	Hos	Mark	2 Tim
Lev	Neh	Joel	Luke	Titus
Num	Esth	Amos	John	Philem
Deut	Job	Obad	Acts	Heb
Josh	Ps(Pss)	Jonah	Rom	James
Judg	Prov	Mic	1 Cor	1 Peter
Ruth	Eccl	Nah	2 Cor	2 Peter
1 Sam	S of Songs	Hab	Gal	1 John
2 Sam	Isa	Zeph	Eph	2 John
1 Kings	Jer	Hag	Phil	3 John
2 Kings	Lam	Zech	Col	Jude
1 Chron	Ezek	Mal	1 Thess	Rev
			2 Thess	

APOCRYPHA

1 Esd	1 Esdras	Ep Jer	Epistle of Jeremy
2 Esd	2 Esdras	S Th Ch	Song of the Three Children (or Young Men)
Tobit	Tobit	Sus	Susanna
Jud	Judith	Bel	Bel and the Dragon
Add Esth	Additions to Esther	Pr Man	Prayer of Manasseh
Wisd Sol	Wisdom of Solomon	1 Macc	1 Maccabees
Ecclus	Ecclesiasticus (Wisdom of Jesus the Son of Sirach)	2 Macc	2 Maccabees
Baruch	Baruch		

PSEUDEPIGRAPHA

As Moses	Assumption of Moses	Pirke Aboth	Pirke Aboth
2 Baruch	Syriac Apocalypse of Baruch	Ps 151	Psalm 151
3 Baruch	Greek Apocalypse of Baruch	Pss Sol	Psalms of Solomon
1 Enoch	Ethiopic Book of Enoch	Sib Oracles	Sibylline Oracles
2 Enoch	Slavonic Book of Enoch	Story Ah	Story of Ahikar
3 Enoch	Hebrew Book of Enoch	T Abram	Testament of Abraham
4 Ezra	4 Ezra	T Adam	Testament of Adam
JA	Joseph and Asenath	T Benjamin	Testament of Benjamin
Jub	Book of Jubilees	T Dan	Testament of Dan
L Aristeas	Letter of Aristeas	T Gad	Testament of Gad
Life AE	Life of Adam and Eve	T Job	Testament of Job
Liv Proph	Lives of the Prophets	T Jos	Testament of Joseph
MA Isa	Martyrdom and Ascension of Isaiah	T Levi	Testament of Levi
		T Naph	Testament of Naphtali
3 Macc	3 Maccabees	T 12 Pat	Testaments of the Twelve Patriarchs
4 Macc	4 Maccabees		
Odes Sol	Odes of Solomon	Zad Frag	Zadokite Fragments
P Jer	Paralipomena of Jeremiah		

E. Abbreviations of Names of Dead Sea Scrolls and Related Texts

CD	Cairo (Genizah text of the) Damascus (Document)
DSS	Dead Sea Scrolls
Hev	Nahal Hever texts
Mas	Masada Texts
Mird	Khirbet mird texts
Mur	Wadi Murabba'at texts
P	Pesher (commentary)
Q	Qumran
1Q, 2Q, etc.	Numbered caves of Qumran, yielding written material; followed by abbreviation of biblical or apocryphal book.
QL	Qumran Literature
1QapGen	Genesis Apocryphon of Qumran Cave 1
1QH	*Hodayot* (Thanksgiving Hymns) from Qumran Cave 1
1QIsa a, b	First or second copy of Isaiah from Qumran Cave 1
1QpHab	Pesher on Habakkuk from Qumran Cave 1
1QM	*Milhamah* (War Scroll)
1QpMic	Pesher on portions of Micah from Qumran Cave 1
1QS	*Serek Hayyahad* (Rule of the Community, Manual of Discipline)
1QSa	Appendix A (Rule of the Congregation) to 1Qs
1QSb	Appendix B (Blessings) to 1QS
3Q15	Copper Scroll from Qumran Cave 3
4QExod a	Exodus Scroll, exemplar "a" from Qumran Cave 4
4QFlor	Florilegium (or Eschatological Midrashim) from Qumran Cave 4
4Qmess ar	Aramaic "Messianic" text from Qumran Cave 4
4QpNah	Pesher on portions of Nahum from Qumran Cave 4
4QPrNab	Prayer of Nabonidus from Qumran Cave 4
4QpPs37	Pesher on portions of Psalm 37 from Qumran Cave 4
4QTest	Testimonia text from Qumran Cave 4
4QTLevi	Testament of Levi from Qumran Cave 4
4QPhyl	Phylacteries from Qumran Cave 4
11QMelch	Melchizedek text from Qumran Cave 11
11QtgJob	Targum of Job from Qumran Cave 11

TRANSLITERATIONS

Hebrew

א = ʾ	ד = ḏ	י = y	ס = s	ר = r
בּ = b	ה = h	כּ = k	ע = ʿ	שׂ = ś
ב = ḇ	ו = w	כ = ḵ	פּ = p	שׁ = š
גּ = g	ז = z	ל = l	פ = p̄	תּ = t
ג = ḡ	ח = ḥ	מ = m	צ = ṣ	ת = ṯ
דּ = d	ט = ṭ	נ = n	ק = q	

(ה)◌ָ = â (h)	◌ָ = ā	◌ַ = a	◌ֲ = ^{a}
◌ֵי = ê	◌ֵ = ē	◌ֶ = e	◌ֱ = ^{e}
◌ִי = î	◌ֹ = ō	◌ִ = i	◌ְ = ^{e} (*if vocal*)
וֹ = ô		◌ָ = o	◌ֳ = ^{o}
וּ = û		◌ֻ = u	

Aramaic

ʾ b g d h w z ḥ ṭ y k l m n s ʿ p ṣ q r ś š t

Arabic

ʾ b t ṯ ǧ ḥ ḫ d ḏ r z s š ṣ ḍ ṭ ẓ ʿ ġ f q k l m n h w y

Ugaritic

ʾ b g d ḏ h w z ḥ ḫ ṭ ẓ y k l m n s s̀ ʿ ġ ṗ ṣ q r š t ṯ

Greek

α	—	*a*	π	—	*p*	αι	—	*ai*
β	—	*b*	ρ	—	*r*	αὐ	—	*au*
γ	—	*g*	σ,ς	—	*s*	ει	—	*ei*
δ	—	*d*	τ	—	*t*	εὐ	—	*eu*
ε	—	*e*	υ	—	*y*	ηὐ	—	*ēu*
ζ	—	*z*	φ	—	*ph*	οι	—	*oi*
η	—	*ē*	χ	—	*ch*	οὐ	—	*ou*
θ	—	*th*	ψ	—	*ps*	υι	—	*hui*
ι	—	*i*	ω	—	*ō*			
κ	—	*k*				ῥ	—	*rh*
λ	—	*l*	γγ	—	*ng*	‛	—	*h*
μ	—	*m*	γκ	—	*nk*			
ν	—	*n*	γξ	—	*nx*	ᾳ	—	*ā*
ξ	—	*x*	γχ	—	*nch*	ῃ	—	*ē*
ο	—	*o*				ῳ	—	*ō*

HEBREWS

Leon Morris

HEBREWS

Introduction

1. Literary Form
2. Destination
3. Authorship
4. Use of the Old Testament
5. Date
6. Bibliography
7. Outline

This book is unlike any other in the NT, though not without resemblance to 1 John. In subject matter it is distinctive, and its picture of Jesus as our great High Priest is its own. It is not easy to see who wrote it, to whom it was written, or why. It lacks an epistolary opening but has an epistolary conclusion. Difficulties abound, but the profundity of its thought gives it a significant place in the NT.

1. Literary Form

Though we usually call Hebrews an epistle, important features of a letter are lacking for this book. But if we cannot straightforwardly label it a letter, there are at least indications that it was meant for a restricted circle of readers, not the general public or even the general Christian public. The recipients are a group who ought to be teachers (5:12). The writer knows them and looks forward to visiting them (13:19, 23). He has a good opinion of them (6:9). He can ask for their prayers (13:18) and give them news of their mutual friend Timothy (13:23). The writer recalls "earlier days" (10:32) and remembers persecutions his friends had endured (10:32; 12:4), their generosity to other believers (6:10), and their cheerful attitude when their property had been confiscated. He knows their present attitude toward their leaders (13:17). In the light of such statements, it is plain that the writer is addressing a definite, known group, and a small one at that (not many Christians would qualify for the position of teacher).

Moreover, the intended recipients were a group whose needs the writer knew. He wanted them to advance to the level of being teachers (5:12) and to avoid apostasy (6:4ff.). There is a homiletic air about much that he writes; so it is not surprising that many have considered the book a sermon—one the author had preached earlier or one he was now composing for the benefit of his friends. He himself calls his work "my word of exhortation" (13:22; cf. Acts 13:15, where a sermon is similarly styled; NIV has "a short letter" at the end of 13:22, but the Gr. means simply "briefly," *dia bracheōn*). There are oratorical touches, and E.F. Scott calls it "one of the noblest examples of Christian eloquence" (p. 2). The style makes it not unlikely that there is a sermon behind it. But as it stands, the book is addressed to a specific group. So it may be called a letter, though the lack of the usual epistolary framework shows that the writer is paying no attention to conventional niceties. He is concerned for his friends and writes to correct some specific erroneous tendencies he sees in them.

2. Recipients

The title "To the Hebrews" is attested by Pantaenus (Eusebius *Ecclesiastical History* 6.14.4) and in the West by Tertullian (*De Pudicitia* 20). It is in the oldest MSS. It is often said that the title was not original, and this may be the case, though it should be added that we have no knowledge of any other title or any time when it lacked this one. If the title is accurate, then it follows that the letter was written to a group of Jews. However, it would still remain to be determined whether they were Jewish Christians or non-Christians. The traditional view is that the recipients were Christian Jews, but some recent scholars doubt whether there is enough evidence to sustain this position. Some think it better to see the original recipients as Gentiles.

The most persuasive argument for Jewish recipients is the way the book moves so consistently within the orbit of the OT Scriptures and Jewish liturgy. The writer has much to say about the worship of the tabernacle, the priests and the kind of sacrifice they offered, the covenant that meant so much to the Jews, and Jewish worthies like Abraham, Moses, Joshua, and a host of others mentioned in chapter 11. Topics like the sufferings of the Messiah and the replacement of the Levitical priesthood by a priesthood after the order of Melchizedek would interest Jews. Incidental references such as "surely it is not angels he helps, but Abraham's descendants" (2:16) are more likely to appeal to Jews than Gentiles. The argument that Jesus is superior to Moses (3:1ff.) would have more weight with Jews than with anyone else. (What would it matter to Gentiles who was superior to Moses?)

Some have thought that the recipients were a group of Jewish priests—perhaps specifically Essene priests—or members of the Qumran community.[1] Such positions, however, are scarcely tenable. The readers were certainly members of the Christian community (e.g., 3:1; 6:9; 10:23). Jewish Christians they may have been, but we cannot place them as non-Christian Jews.

On the other hand, some argue that the elegant Greek of the epistle indicates that neither the writer nor the recipients were Jews. But this argument is not relevant. The Jews of the Diaspora were familiar with Greek; after all, the LXX had been written for them. So there would be no problem for Jews either to write or to read "elegant" Greek. Furthermore, it is not necessary that the author himself be a Jew. A Gentile could certainly write to Jews. Nor is the argument from the book's use of the LXX decisive, for many Jews used this version instead of the Hebrew OT.

More significant is the appeal to fundamentals in chapter 6. The "elementary teachings" are listed as "repentance from acts that lead to death, . . . faith in God, instruction about baptisms, the laying on of hands, the resurrection of the dead, and eternal judgment" (vv.1–2). It is urged that this is the basis of the Gentile mission, but it would have been necessary in the first stages to teach Jews that Jesus is the

---

[1]W.G. Kümmel, *Introduction to the New Testament* (London: SCM, 1966), p. 279.

Christ and perhaps that God is present in the Holy Spirit. Again, people who turned back to Judaism would not be turning away "from the living God" (3:12), though those who returned to Gentile ways would. Jewish regulations about foods are said to be "strange teachings" (13:9). The epistle never contrasts Jew and Gentile and indeed never mentions either in set terms.

Many do not regard the constant reference to the OT as significant, for from the first the OT was the Bible of Gentile Christians as well as Jewish Christians. The church saw itself as the true Israel, as the heir of the promises of the OT. And while the author makes a good deal of the Jewish priesthood and Jewish practices, it must be borne in mind that he does not take his information and symbolism from the temple that existed in the first century. Rather, he referred to the much earlier tabernacle, about which all the available information is in the OT.

Not all this evidence is equally convincing. The appeal to the OT would be valid for Gentiles only if they were Christians. But if they were falling away from the faith, the OT would hold no authority for them. However, it was authoritative for Jewish readers, whether they were Christians or not. Also, one could fairly argue that 3:12 does not tell against Jewish recipients of the letter because the author sees all apostasy as falling away from the "living God." Indeed, he illustrates this by referring to the Israelites in the wilderness who rejected Moses' leadership and rebelled against God (3:16ff.). The "elementary teachings" of chapter 6 might be taken as being just as applicable to Jews as to Gentiles. So we might go on. And when we are through, we may conclude that it cannot be proved beyond any doubt that Hebrews was written for either Jews or Gentiles.

On the whole, it seems that more is to be said for Hebrews having been written for Jewish rather than Gentile readers. I find it hard to think that a writing that moves so much in the area of Jewish ritual was in the first instance intended for non-Jews, however readily they may have embraced the OT. And it is conjecture that the title "To the Hebrews" was not original. The evidence favors it. While absolute certainty is impossible, it is best, therefore, to see the epistle as written for a group of able Jewish Christians. They seem to have been hesitant about cutting themselves off decisively from the Jewish religion (which was tolerated by the Romans) in favor of the Christian way (which was not).

Many consider the recipients to have been Palestinian Jews. Specifically, some suggest that these Jews had a connection with the Qumran community. But the evidence for this is slight. These people had helped others (6:10), whereas Palestinian Christians were poor (Acts 11:27–30; Rom 15:26; 2 Cor 8–9). They had not seen Jesus (2:3), but many Palestinian Christians must have done so. There is more to be said for indications that point to recipients in Rome. For example, the epistle is first attested in Clement of Rome's letter. The greeting "Those from Italy send you their greetings" (13:24) is perhaps most naturally understood of a group of Italian origin, now living elsewhere, sending greetings back home. The word *hēgoumenos* ("leader") applied to church leaders (13:7, 17, 24) occurs in a similar way in 1 Clement and Hermas, both connected with Rome. Also, there was more hesitation at Rome to regard Hebrews as canonical than there was elsewhere, and a big factor in this hesitation was doubt that Paul wrote the epistle. The argument is that the Romans knew who wrote it and that the author was not Paul. Obviously all this falls far short of proof. Yet there do seem to be more reasons for connecting the letter with Rome than with any other place.

3. Authorship

The epistle was used by Clement of Rome (e.g., 1 Clement 17; 36) probably also by Polycarp (*To the Philippians* 6; 12) and Hermas (*Visions* 2.3.2; 3.7.2; *Similitudes* 9.13.7). Therefore the author was an early Christian. The earliest reference to authorship is a statement of Clement of Alexandria that Paul wrote it in Hebrew and that Luke translated the work into Greek (quoted in Eusebius *Ecclesiastical History* 6.14.2). When it was accepted as part of the NT, this was partly at least because contemporaries held Paul to be the author. This view, however, appears to rest on no reliable evidence but rather to be a deduction from the facts that Paul was a prolific writer of epistles and that Hebrews is a noble writing that must have had a distinguished author. But both the language and thought forms are unlike those of Paul. The Greek is polished; Paul's is rugged, though vigorous. This book moves in the context of Levitical symbolism, about which Paul elsewhere says nothing. The same argument also tells against Clement of Alexandria's view that Luke translated it. While there are some interesting coincidences of language between Hebrews and Luke-Acts, there are also some differences. And it is incredible that if Luke knew Hebrews, he should have made no reference whatever to its teaching either in his Gospel or in the Acts.

None of the early writers who cites the epistle mentions its author. Nor does internal evidence help us much. The author was plainly a teacher, a second generation Christian (2:3). The style is unlike that of any other NT document; consequently, we have nothing more to go on to determine authorship than conjecture. Though many suggestions have been made, it will suffice to mention only a few of them. The allegation that Barnabas was the author is as old as Tertullian (*De Pudicitia* 20), but little can be said in its support. Barnabas was a Levite (Acts 4:36), and there is much about Levitical ritual in the epistle. Again, in Acts 4:36 Barnabas was called *huios paraklēseōs* ("Son of Encouragement"); and in Hebrews 13:22 the epistle refers to itself as *tou logou tēs paraklēseōs* ("my word of exhortation," NIV). But it is hard to see 2:3 as applying to Barnabas.

Luther suggested that Apollos was the author. A number of modern scholars support this view. Apollos was an eloquent man (Acts 18:24), and there is indeed eloquence in this epistle. Apollos came from Alexandria, a center where allegorical interpretation, which might be said to be akin to the method used in Hebrews, flourished (cf. Philo). Apollos had "a thorough knowledge of the Scriptures" (Acts 18:24), a description particularly appropriate for the author, who did not simply use the "proof-text" method but applied a thorough knowledge of Scripture in an original manner. Apollos must remain a possible author, but the evidence is far from conclusive.

Harnack thought that Priscilla probably wrote the epistle.[2] His strong point is that this would account for the suppression of the author's name. It was a man's world, and there would be every reason for keeping it quiet that a woman had written an epistle intended to be authoritative and to have wide circulation. Priscilla and her husband were cultured Hellenistic Jews, and the woman who could instruct Apollos

---

[2]Adolph von Harnack, "Probabilia über die Adresse und den Verfasser des Hebräerbriefes," ZNW, i (1900), 16ff.

in the faith (Acts 18:26) was no mean teacher. The interest in the tabernacle would be natural in a family whose living came from tentmaking (Acts 18:3), and the outlook of a pilgrim would be natural to one who did so much traveling. All this is interesting, but plainly it falls far short of proof. And against it stands the masculine participle *diēgoumenon* ("to tell") used of the author in 11:32.

In the end we must agree that we have no certain evidence about the authorship of Hebrews. Who wrote it remains unknown to us. We can scarcely improve on the words of Origen's conclusion, that "who wrote the Epistle, God only knows the truth" (Eusebius *Ecclesiastical History* 6.25.14).

4. The Use of the Old Testament in Hebrews

There are some interesting features of the author's use of the OT. To begin with, he uses the LXX almost exclusively. Now and then he bases his argument on the LXX where that differs from the Hebrew (e.g., 10:5–7). G. Howard argues that the author seems to have used a variety of Greek texts, some agreeing with our LXX and some differing from it (NovTest 10 [1968], pp. 208–16).

The author's favorite sources are the Pentateuch and the Psalms. Westcott finds him quoting from the Pentateuch twelve times and alluding to it without direct quotation thirty-nine times. The figures for the other parts of the OT are Historical books, one quotation, no allusions; the Prophets, four quotations, eleven allusions; Psalms, eleven quotations, two allusions; Proverbs, one quotation, one allusion. This means twenty-three out of twenty-nine quotations come from the Pentateuch and the Psalms. It is curious that there is so little from the Prophets, especially in view of the author's attitude toward the sacrifices. One would think he would have found much in the Prophets that was applicable to his purpose. There are no quotations from the Apocrypha, though there appears to be an allusion to an event narrated in 2 Maccabees 6–7 (11:35).

The author has an unusual method of citation; he almost always neglects the human author of his OT quotations (exceptions are 4:7; 9:19–20), though throughout the rest of the NT the human author is often noted. Instead, without actually saying "God says," he normally ascribes the passage he quotes to God, except, of course, where God is addressed, as in 2:6. Twice he attributes words in the OT to Christ (2:11–12; 10:5ff.) and twice to the Holy Spirit (3:7; 10:15). No other NT writer shares this way of quoting the OT. Elsewhere in the NT words are normally ascribed to God only when God is the actual speaker in the OT. This is not invariable, but the habit in Hebrews is only the occasional use in the other books. The effect is to emphasize the divine authorship of the whole OT. For the author, what Scripture says, God says.

A further point is that the author sees Scripture as pointing to Jesus. What the ancient writings say is fulfilled in him. This means more than that specific prophecies are fulfilled in Jesus. Rather the thrust of the whole OT is such that it leads inescapably to him. The author writes of Christianity as the final religion, not because he regards the faith of the OT as mistaken, but because he sees it as God's way of pointing men to Jesus. Judaism is not so much abrogated by Christianity as brought to its climax. The fuller meaning of the OT is to be seen in the person and work of Jesus. The OT and the new way are rightly seen only when they are recognized as parts of one whole. And it is Jesus who enables us to discern that whole and its meaning.

5. Date

The mention of Timothy (13:23) shows that the writing must be early, unless the reference is to a Timothy other than Paul's companion. But this is highly improbable. However, as we know nothing about the dates of Timothy's birth and death, this reference to him does little to narrow down our search. The words "you have not yet resisted to the point of shedding your blood" (12:4) points to a date before the persecutions, or at least before the lives of any of the community the letter was written to had been lost in the persecutions. Once again we have an indication of an early date, but one we cannot narrowly tie down.

The principal indication of the date is that the epistle says nothing about the destruction of the temple but leaves the impression that the Jewish sacrificial system, with its ministry of priests and all that that involved, was a continuing reality (cf. 9:6–9). But the author is arguing that Judaism is superseded by Christianity and specifically that the sacrifices of the old system are of no avail now that the sacrifice of Jesus has been offered. It would have been a convincing climax had the author been able to point out that the temple and all that went with it had ceased to exist. "The best argument for the supersession of the old covenant would have been the destruction of the Temple" (Montefiore, p. 3). The author's failure to mention this surely means that it had not yet occurred.

This seems about as far as we can go. A date before A.D. 70 is indicated, but how much before that we cannot say. Some passages in the epistle gain in force if we think of a time not long before, when there was a compelling call to loyal Jews to cast in their lot with those fighting against Rome. So perhaps we should think of a date near or even during the war of A.D. 66–70.

6. Bibliography

Barclay, William. *The Letter to the Hebrews*. Edinburgh: Saint Andrew, 1955.
Bowman, J.W. *Hebrews, James, I and II Peter*. London: SCM, 1962.
Brown, J. *An Exposition of Hebrews*. 1862. Reprint. London: Banner of Truth, 1961.
Bruce, F.F. *The Epistle to the Hebrews*. Grand Rapids: Eerdmans, 1964.
Buchanan, G.W. *To the Hebrews*. New York: Doubleday, 1972.
Calvin, J. *The Epistle of Paul the Apostle to the Hebrews and the First and Second Epistles of St. Peter*. Edinburgh: Oliver and Boyd, 1963.
DuBose, W.P. *High Priesthood and Sacrifice*. London: Longmans, 1908.
Héring, J. *The Epistle to the Hebrews*. London: Epworth, 1970.
Hewitt, T. *The Epistle to the Hebrews*. London: Tyndale, 1960.
Kent, H.A. *The Epistle to the Hebrews*. Grand Rapids: Baker, 1972.
Manson, W. *The Epistle to the Hebrews*. London: Hodder and Stoughton, 1951.
Moffatt, J. *A Critical and Exegetical Commentary on the Epistle to the Hebrews*. ICC. Edinburgh: T. & T. Clark, 1924.
Montefiore, H.W. *A Commentary on the Epistle to the Hebrews*. London: Black, 1964.
Nairne, A. *The Epistle of Priesthood*. Edinburgh: T. & T. Clark, 1913.
Purdy, A.C. *The Epistle to the Hebrews*. New York: Abingdon, 1955.
Robinson, T.H. *The Epistle to the Hebrews*. London: Hodder and Stoughton, 1933.
Scott, E.F. *The Epistle to the Hebrews*. Edinburgh: T. & T. Clark, 1922.
Snell, A. *New and Living Way*. London: Faith, 1959.
Spicq, C. *L'Épître aux Hébreux*. Paris: Gabalda, 1952.

Tasker, R. V. G. *The Gospel in the Epistle to the Hebrews*. London: Tyndale, 1950.
Westcott, B. F. *The Epistle to the Hebrews*. London: MacMillan, 1892.
Williamson, R. *Philo and the Epistle to the Hebrews*. Leiden: Brill, 1970.

7. Outline

I. Introduction (1:1–4)
II. The Excellence of the Christ (1:5–3:6)
   A. Superior to Angels (1:5–14)
   B. Author of "Such a Great Salvation" (2:1–9)
   C. True Man (2:10–18)
   D. Superior to Moses (3:1–6)
III. The Promised Rest (3:7–4:13)
   A. Scriptural Basis (3:7–11)
   B. Some Did Not Enter the Rest (3:12–19)
   C. Christians Enter the Rest (4:1–10)
   D. Exhortation to Enter the Rest (4:11–13)
IV. A Great High Priest (4:14–5:11)
   A. Our Confidence (4:14–16)
   B. The Qualities Required in High Priests (5:1–4)
   C. Christ's Qualifications as High Priest (5:5–11)
V. The Danger of Apostasy (5:12–6:20)
   A. Failure to Progress in the Faith (5:12–14)
   B. Exhortation to Progress (6:1–3)
   C. No Second Beginning (6:4–8)
   D. Exhortation to Perseverance (6:9–12)
   E. God's Promise Is Sure (6:13–20)
VI. Melchizedek (7:1–28)
   A. The Greatness of Melchizedek (7:1–10)
   B. The Royal Priesthood of Melchizedek and of Christ (7:11–14)
   C. Christ's Priesthood Superior Because of:
      1. His life (7:15–19)
      2. The divine oath (7:20–22)
      3. Its permanence (7:23–25)
      4. His better sacrifice (7:26–28)
VII. A New and Better Covenant (8:1–10:39)
   A. Christ's "More Excellent" Ministry (8:1–7)
   B. The Old Covenant Superseded (8:8–13)
   C. The Old Sanctuary and Its Ritual (9:1–10)
   D. The Blood of Christ (9:11–14)
   E. The Mediator of the New Covenant (9:15–22)
   F. The Perfect Sacrifice (9:23–28)
   G. The Law a Shadow (10:1–4)
   H. One Sacrifice for Sins (10:5–18)
   I. The Sequel—the Right Way (10:19–25)
   J. The Sequel—the Wrong Way (10:26–31)
   K. Choose the Right (10:32–39)
VIII. Faith (11:1–40)
   A. The Meaning of Faith (11:1–3)
   B. The Faith of the Men Before the Flood (11:4–7)
   C. The Faith of Abraham and Sarah (11:8–19)

- D. The Faith of the Patriarchs (11:20–22)
- E. The Faith of Moses (11:23–28)
- F. The Faith of the Exodus Generation (11:29–31)
- G. The Faith of Other Servants of God (11:32–38)
- H. The Promise (11:39–40)

IX. Christian Living (12:1–13:19)
- A. Christ Our Example (12:1–3)
- B. Discipline (12:4–11)
- C. Exhortation to the Christian Life (12:12–17)
- D. Mount Sinai and Mount Zion (12:18–24)
- E. A Kingdom That Cannot Be Shaken (12:25–29)
- F. Love (13:1–6)
- G. Christian Leadership (13:7–8)
- H. Christian Sacrifice (13:9–16)
- I. Christian Obedience (13:17)
- J. Prayer (13:18–19)

X. Conclusion (13:20–25)
- A. Doxology (13:20–21)
- B. Final Exhortations (13:22–25)

Text and Exposition

I. Introduction

1:1–4

[1]In the past God spoke to our forefathers through the prophets at many times and in various ways, [2]but in these last days he has spoken to us by his Son, whom he appointed heir of all things, and through whom he made the universe. [3]The Son is the radiance of God's glory and the exact representation of his being, sustaining all things by his powerful word. After he had provided purification for sins, he sat down at the right hand of the Majesty in heaven. [4]So he became as much superior to the angels as the name he has inherited is superior to theirs.

The author begins with a magnificent introduction in which he brings out something of the greatness of Jesus and his saving work. He goes on to point out that Jesus is superior to the angels and thus leads into the first main section of the epistle. In the Greek this is a single, powerful sentence that shows the difference between the old revelation, which is fragmentary and spoken through prophets, and the new, which is complete and comes from one who has all the dignity of being Son of God (cf. v.2 for comment on "being Son").

1 It is significant that the subject of the first verb is "God," for God is constantly before the author; he uses the word sixty-eight times, an average of about once every seventy-three words all through his epistle. Few NT books speak of God so often. Right at the beginning, then, we are confronted with the reality of God and the fact that he has been active. The first divine activity commented on is that God has spoken in a variety of ways. He spoke to Moses in the burning bush (Exod 3:2ff.), to Elijah in a still, small voice (1 Kings 19:12ff.), to Isaiah in a vision in the temple (Isa 6:1ff.), to Hosea in his family circumstances (Hos 1:2), and to Amos in a basket of summer fruit (Amos 8:1). God might convey his message through visions and dreams, through angels, through Urim and Thummim, through symbols, natural events, ecstasy, a pillar of fire, smoke, or other means. He could appear in Ur of the Chaldees, in Haran, in Canaan, in Egypt, in Babylon. There is no lack of variety, for revelation is not a monotonous activity that must always take place in the same way. God used variety.

"In the past" (*palai*) means "of old," rather than simply "formerly." The revelation the writer is speaking of is no novelty but has its roots deep in the past. He is not referring here to what God does continually but to what he did in days of old, in the time of "our forefathers." The expression is usually translated "fathers" and is normally used in the NT of the patriarchs (cf. KJV, John 7:22; Rom 9:5, et al.), but here the contrast to "us" in v.2 shows that the term "forefathers" is a shorthand way of referring to OT believers in general. There is a problem concerning the phrase "through the prophets," for scholars are not agreed on how we should take *en* (translated "through"). Moffatt takes the word as equivalent to "through," though noting that in antiquity Philo saw the prophets as God's interpreters in a way that requires us to see God as really "in" them (in loc.). This latter view is held by a number of exegetes. Westcott, for example, explicitly rejects the rendering "through" in favor of "*in them* . . . as the quickening power of their life . . . they were His messengers, inspired by His Spirit, not in their words only but as men" (in loc.). Kent reminds us that the construction is parallel to that in v.2: God was in Christ and before that he was in the prophets (in loc.). It seems best to see the meaning in some such way as this. God not only used the prophets as his voice but was "in" them. The "prophets" here may mean more than the canonical prophets and may include the men of God, like Abraham, who preceded them.

2 "In these last days" is more literally "on the last of these days." The expression is found in the LXX, where it not infrequently refers in some way to the days of the Messiah (e.g., Num 24:14). Here, in Hebrews, it means that in Jesus the new age, the Messianic Age, has appeared. Jesus is more than simply the last in a long line of prophets. He has inaugurated a new age altogether. In Jesus there is continuity and there is discontinuity. The continuity comes out when we are told that God "has spoken to us by his Son." The verb "spoken" is the same one used in v.1 of the prophets, and there is a grammatical connection: "God, having spoken in the prophets . . . has spoken in the Son" (personal translation). The earlier revelation is not irrelevant to the later one but is continuous with it. The same God has spoken in both. The old prepares the way for the new, a truth that will be brought out again and again in this epistle as the author backs up his arguments with quotations from Scripture. The discontinuity is seen when we come to the reference to the Son. It is noteworthy that in the Greek there is no article or possessive; there is nothing corresponding to NIV's "his." In essence the writer is saying God spoke "in one who has the quality of being Son." It is the Son's essential nature that is stressed. This stands in contrast to "the prophets" in the preceding verse. The consummation of the revelatory process, the definitive revelation, took place when he who was not one of "the goodly fellowship of the prophets" but the very Son of God came. Throughout the epistle we shall often meet such thoughts. The writer is concerned to show that in Jesus Christ we have such a divine person and such divine activity that there can be no going back from him.

This emphasis on the Son leads to a series of seven propositions about him (eight if we include v.4). In the first we find that God "appointed" him "heir of all things." The verb "appointed" is somewhat unexpected. We should have anticipated that the Son would simply *be* heir. Perhaps there is a stress on the divine will as active. In the term "heir" there is no thought of entering into possession through the death of a testator. In the NT the word and its cognates are often used in a sense much like "get possession of" without reference to any specific way of acquiring the property in question. In other words, the term points to lawful possession but without indicating in what way that possession is secured. "Heir of all things," then, is a title of dignity and shows that Christ has the supreme place in all the mighty universe. His exaltation to the highest place in heaven after his work on earth was done did not mark some new dignity but his reentry to his rightful place (cf. Phil 2:6–11).

The second truth about the Son is that it is "through" him that God "made the universe." The "through" (*di'*) preserves the important truth that God is the Creator. But as elsewhere in the NT the thought is that he performed the work of creation through the Son (cf. John 1:3; 1 Cor 8:6; Col 1:16). The term rendered "the universe" is literally "the ages" (*tous aiōnas*) and has a temporal sense. While the universe may well be in mind (it is the natural object of the verb "made"), it will be the universe as "the sum of the periods of time, including all that is manifested in them" (A-S, s.v.). Buchanan thinks that the word here (and in 11:3) means "ages," arguing that it was a Jewish idea that God created the ages (in loc.). This may be so. Yet it seems that in this context "the universe" makes better sense, though the word may be meant to hint at the temporal nature of all things material.

3 The one long sentence (Gr.) continues, but there is a change of subject. NIV has supplied "The Son," which gives the sense of it; but the Greek has simply the relative *hos* ("who"). The Son is described first as "the radiance of God's glory." There is ambiguity in the Greek term *apaugasma,* which may mean "radiance," a shining forth because of brightness within, or "reflection," a shining forth because of brightness from without. Jesus is thus spoken of as the outshining of the brightness of God's glory, or as the reflection of that glory. In either case we see the glory of God in Jesus, and we see it as it really is. "Glory" can be used of literal brightness (Acts 22:11). However, it is more commonly used in the NT of the radiance associated with God and with heavenly beings in general. "Glory" sometimes indicates the presence of God (e.g., Ezek 1:28; 11:23), and, to the extent that man is able to apprehend it, the revelation of God's majesty.

"The exact representation of his being" is the fourth of the statements about the Son. "Exact representation" translates *charaktēr,* a very unusual word (here only in the NT). Originally it denoted an instrument for engraving and then a mark stamped on that instrument. Hence it came to be used generally of a mark stamped on a thing, the impress of a die. It might be used figuratively, for example, of God as making man in his own image (1 Clement 33:4). In its literal sense it was used of the impression on coins; RSV's "bears the very stamp of his nature" brings out something of this meaning. Here the writer is saying that the Son is an exact representation of God. The word *hypostaseōs,* rendered "being," is difficult. Its etymological equivalent in English is "substance," viz., that which stands under a thing, that which makes it what it is. The Son is such a revelation of the Father that when we see Jesus, we see what God's real being is.

"Sustaining" translates *pherōn,* which has a meaning like "carrying along." The author does not see Christ's work in sustaining creation as holding up the universe like a dead weight (as Atlas was supposed to do!). Rather his thought is that of carrying it along, of bearing it toward a goal. The concept is dynamic, not static. "All things" is *ta panta,* the totality, the universe considered as one whole. Nothing is excluded from the scope of the Son's sustaining activity. The author pictures the Son as in the first instance active in creation and then as continuing his interest in the world he loves and bearing it onward towards the fulfillment of the divine plan. And all this he does "by his powerful word," or, as Knox renders it, by "his enabling word." The "word" (*rhēma* here, "command," "order," according to BAG) is thought of as active and powerful. The universe (*aiōnas,* "ages") was created by this "word" (11:3). The "word" is not empty. It has force. It does things. The word for "powerful" (lit., "by the word of his power") is *dynamis,* which may be used of literal physical power or in more metaphorical usages like "capability," "wealth," or the like. Here it has something like the literal meaning.

With the statement about the Son's having effected purification of sins, the author comes to what is for him the heart of the matter. His whole epistle shows that the thing that had gripped him was that the very Son of God had come to deal with the problem of man's sin. He sees him as a priest and the essence of his priestly work as the offering of the sacrifice that really put sin away. The author has an unusual number of ways of referring to what Christ has done for man: The Savior made a propitiation for sins (2:17). He put sins away so that God remembers them no more (8:12; 10:17). He bore sin (9:28), he offered a sacrifice (*thysia*) for sins (10:12), he made an offering (*prosphora*) for sin (10:18), and brought about remission of sin (10:18). He annulled sin by his sacrifice (9:26). He brought about redemption from transgressions (9:15). In other passages the author speaks of a variety of things the former covenant could not do with respect to sin, the implication in each case being that Christ has now done it (e.g., 10:2, 4, 6, 11). It is clear from all this that the author sees Jesus as having accomplished a many-sided salvation. Whatever had to be done about sin he has done.

The word "purification" (*katharismos*) is most often used in the NT of ritual cleansing (e.g., Mark 1:44), but here (and in 2 Peter 1:9) it refers to the removal of sin. It also points to the defiling aspect of sin. Sin stains. But Christ has effected a complete cleansing. The verb "provided" is in the aorist tense; the cleansing in question, being based on a past action, is complete. The purification was accomplished at Calvary. The genitive "of sins" probably means that Christ took the sins away rather than that the person was cleansed "from sins." The word for sin (*hamartia*) occurs in this epistle twenty-five times, a total exceeded only by Romans with forty-eight. The author sees *hamartia* ("sin") as a great problem; and in this epistle "sin appears as the power that deceives men and leads them to destruction, whose influence and activity can be ended only by sacrifices" (BAG, s.v.). But the usual sacrifices could not remove sin, and it is the author's conviction that Jesus Christ was needed to remove it. In him and him alone are sins really dealt with.

The seventh in the series of statements about the Son is that when his work of purification was ended, "he sat down at the right hand of the Majesty in heaven." Sitting is the posture of rest, and the right-hand position is the place of honor. Sitting at God's right hand, then, is a way of saying that Christ's saving work is done and that he is now in the place of highest honor. By contrast, the posture for a priest is standing (10:11). The word translated "Majesty" (*megalōsynē*) appears again in the NT only in 8:1; Jude 25. It means "greatness" and thus came to signify "majesty." Here it is obviously a periphrasis for God himself. "In heaven" is more literally "in the heights," but clearly this means "heaven" (for the thought cf. Eph 4:10; Phil 2:9). Some take the expression with "sat down"; i.e., "sat down in heaven at the right hand." This makes it refer to the exaltation, but this scarcely seems warranted. The Greek word order as well as the general sense make it better to link "in heaven" with "the Majesty."

4 "He became" is again somewhat unexpected (cf. "appointed," v.2). The writer has made some strong statements about the excellence of Christ's person, and so we should expect him to describe Christ as eternally superior to the angels rather than as "becoming" superior to them. But the writer says it this way because he was thinking of what the Son did in becoming man and putting away the sins of men. Of course, the Son was also eternally superior to the angels. That, however, is not what is in mind here. It was because he had put away sins that he sat down on the throne in the place of highest honor, and it is in this aspect that he is seen as greater than any angel.

"Superior" is the translation of *kreittōn*, which is more usually rendered "better." This is one of the author's favorite words. He uses it thirteen out of the nineteen times it appears in the NT (1 Cor, with three occurrences, is the only other book that has the word more than once). So we read in Hebrews that there are better things (6:9) and that the less is blessed of the better (7:7); there is a better hope (7:19) and a better covenant (7:22; 8:6); there are better promises (8:6) and better sacrifices (9:23); there are a better possession (10:34), a better country (11:16), a better resurrection (11:35), something better (11:40), and blood that speaks better (12:24). This strong emphasis on what is "better" arises from the author's deep conviction that Jesus Christ is "better" and that he has accomplished something "better" than anyone else.

Another word that appears frequently in this epistle is "angel." The author uses it thirteen times. The only NT books that use it more often are Matthew, Luke, Acts, and Revelation. While the term can be used of a human messenger (Luke 9:52), sometimes sent by God (Mark 1:2), in the overwhelming number of cases it means a spirit being from the other world. In many cases the idea of a messenger remains. Sometimes, however, the thought is simply that of beings intermediate between God and man. It also may be used of evil beings, but references to good angels are much more common.

In antiquity "the name" meant much more than it does today. We use a name as little more than a distinguishing mark or label to differentiate one person from other people. But in the world of the NT the name concisely sums up all that a person is. One's whole character was somehow implied in the name. Opinions differ as to what is meant here by "the name." Some take this to mean that in his whole character and personality Christ was superior to any angel. Others think the reference is simply to the name "Son," which is a better name than "angel" because it denotes superiority in character and personality. Either interpretation is possible.

The word "superior" as applied to "the name" is *diaphorōteron* (not *kreitton*, which is translated the same way earlier in the verse). *Diaphorōteron* is the comparative of the adjective meaning "different" and, in a derived sense, "excellent." The name of the Son is "more excellent" than that of any angel. "Inherited" (*keklēronomēken*) is not quite the verb we expect, for there is no question of entering into possession as the result of the death of someone. On the contrary the word as used in the NT denotes entering into possession without regard to the means. So here we should think of Christ as obtaining the more excellent name as the result of his atoning work. The main idea is that of an abiding possession in Christ's capacity as heir (see comments on v.2).

Notes

2 Bruce sees ἐπ' ἐσχάτου τῶν ἡμερῶν (*ep eschatou tōn hēmerōn*, "from the last days") as a Septuagintalism that reflects a Hebrew expression meaning literally "in the latter end of the days" and that "according to the context may mean 'hereafter,' 'ultimately' or 'in the end-time.'" Here it "implies an inaugurated eschatology" (p. 3).

3 According to Westcott (in loc.), the Greek fathers unanimously take the sense of ἀπαύγασμα (*apaugasma*) as "effulgence" ("radiance"). This he sees as the preferable sense here, for the truth involved in "reflection" is conveyed also in χαρακτὴρ (*charaktēr*), whereas "effulgence" adds another thought.

4 The perfect κεκληρονόμηκεν (*keklēronomēken*, "inherited") puts some stress on the continuing possession of the more excellent name. The writer is referring to a present fact, not simply to past history.

II. The Excellence of the Christ

In the introduction the author has drawn attention to the excellence of the Christ; now he dwells on the point. He brings out the fact that Christ is possessed of a greater dignity than any other being, so great indeed that he must be classed with God rather than with men. This does not mean any weakening of the doctrine of the Incarnation. On the contrary, in this epistle as high a Christology as is conceivable is combined with an emphasis on the real humanity of Jesus. Nobody insists on the limitations of Jesus' human frame as does the writer of Hebrews. But he unites with this the thought that Jesus is exalted far above all creation.

A. *Superior to Angels*

1:5–14

5For to which of the angels did God ever say,

> "You are my Son;
> today I have become your Father"?

Or again,

> "I will be his Father,
> and he will be my Son"?

6And again, when God brings his firstborn into the world, he says,

> "Let all God's angels worship him."

7In speaking of the angels he says,

> "He makes his angels winds,
> his servants flames of fire."

8But about the Son he says,

> "Your throne, O God, will last for ever and ever,
> and righteousness will be the scepter of your kingdom.
> 9You have loved righteousness and hated wickedness;
> therefore God, your God, has set you above
> your companions
> by anointing you with the oil of joy."

10He also says,

> "In the beginning, O Lord, you laid the foundations
> of the earth,
> and the heavens are the work of your hands.
> 11They will perish, but you remain;
> they will all wear out like a garment.
> 12You will roll them up like a robe;
> like a garment they will be changed.
> But you remain the same,
> and your years will never end."

13To which of the angels did God ever say,

> "Sit at my right hand
> until I make your enemies
> a footstool for your feet"?

14Are not all angels ministering spirits sent to serve those who will inherit salvation?

The discussion of the excellence of the Son begins with a series of seven quotations from the OT, five being from the Psalms. They all stress the superiority of Christ to the angels.

5 The opening question, "For to which of the angels did God ever say . . . ," implies that Christ is to be seen in all the Scriptures because there is no explicit reference to him in the passage cited. In the OT angels are sometimes called "sons of God" (cf. mg., Job 1:6; 2:1); and the term was applied to Israel (Exod 4:22; Hos 11:1) and Solomon (2 Sam 7:14; 1 Chron 28:6). But none of the angels nor anyone else was ever singled out and given the kind of status this passage gives to Christ. The first quotation comes from Psalm 2:7. Among the rabbis, the "Son" is variously identified as Aaron, David, the people of Israel in the messianic period, or the Messiah himself (SBK, pp. 673–77). But clearly our writer is taking the psalm as messianic and sees it as conferring great dignity on Jesus. We should not concern ourselves overmuch with trying to identify the day meant in "today." Since the writer seems to be quoting the text to bring out the greatness of the Son, he could scarcely pass over the word rendered "today." But his interest was not here, and he makes no special reference to the day.

The second quotation comes from 2 Samuel 7:14 (=1 Chron 17:13). Though the words were originally used of Solomon, the writer of Hebrews is applying them to the Messiah, a usage which does not seem to occur among the rabbis (SBK, p. 677). There was, however, a widespread expectation that the Messiah would be a descendant of David (de Jonge, TDNT, 9:511ff.). The quotation points to the father-son relationship as the fundamental relationship between God and Christ. No angel can claim such a relationship. This and 12:9 are the only passages in Hebrews in which the term "Father" is applied to God.

6 This verse is the only place in the NT where "firstborn" (*prōtotokos*) is used absolutely of Christ. Elsewhere it is used with reference to Jesus' birth (Luke 2:7) and it is linked with many brothers (Rom 8:29), all creation (Col 1:15), or the church (Col 1:18; Rev 1:5). It represents Christ in his relationship to others and gives the word a social significance. Here, however, it signifies that he has the status with God that a firstborn son on earth has with his father (cf. reference to "heir" in v.2). Some hold that the bringing of the firstborn into the world should be closely linked with "again" (*palin*). If this is done, there is a reference to the Second Coming. The arguments in support of this are not convincing, however, nor are those that see a reference to the Incarnation. It is probably better to think of Christ's "exaltation and enthronement as sovereign over the inhabited universe, the *oikoumenē*, including the realm of angels" (Bruce, in loc.), without emphasis on when this takes place.

The quotation is from Deuteronomy 32:43 in the LXX; it is absent from our Hebrew text, though attested in the Qumran material. The LXX reads "sons of God" where our quotation has "God's angels," but "angels" occurs later in the verse and again in a similar context in Psalm 97:7. Justin quotes it in the same form as here (*Dialogue* 130), which may indicate that the early Christians had it in their text. "All" shows that this is no small, hole-in-the-corner affair but one in which the worship of all heaven is offered the Son. The one the angels worship is clearly superior by far to them.

7 The Hebrew of Psalm 104:4 can mean either that God makes the winds his messengers and the flames his servants or that he makes his messengers (angels) into winds and his servants into flames. The LXX, which the author quotes, takes the latter view. This means no downgrading of the angels as the Targum quoted by Buchanan (in loc.) shows: "Who makes his messengers swift as the wind, his ministers mighty as flaming fire." But if the angels are immeasurably superior to men, the Son is immeasurably superior to the angels. Whereas he has sonship, they are reducible to nothing more than the elemental forces of wind and fire. Also, the implication is probably that the angels are temporary in contrast to the Son, who is eternal.

8–9 Some translations render the opening words of v.8 as "God is your throne" or the like (cf. RSV, NEB mg.). But it is better to take the Greek as a vocative as NIV: "Your throne, O God." The quotation from Psalm 45:6–7 is referred to the Son who is then addressed as "God." His royal state is brought out by the references to the "throne," "scepter," and "kingdom" and by his moral concern for the "righteousness" that is supreme where he reigns. This concern continues with loving righteousness and hating wickedness (better: lawlessness), which lead to the divine anointing. We should perhaps take the first occurrence of the word "God" as another vocative: "Therefore, O God, your God has set you." Anointing was usually a rite of consecration to some sacred function (e.g., Exod 28:41; 1 Sam 10:1; 1 Kings 19:16). This is in view here as the Son is set above his companions, who are probably the "brothers" of 2:11.

10–12 The author next quotes from Psalm 102:25–27 to bring out the Son's eternality and his supremacy over creation. In the OT these words are applied to God. Here, however, they apply to Christ without qualification or any need for justification. Christ was God's agent in creation, the one who laid the earth's foundations and constructed heaven. All these will in due course perish, but not their maker.

The metaphor of clothing has a twofold reference: the created things will wear out (the process is slow but certain); and the Son deals with them as with clothing, rolling them up and changing them. He began the universe and he will finish it. Clearly the final transformation of all things is in mind (cf. Isa 66:22; Rev 6:14; 21:1). This universe that seems so solid and permanent will be rolled up, changed, and replaced by a totally new heaven and earth. But through it all the Son remains unchanged. Our years come to an end, but his will never do so.

13 The quotation from Psalm 110:1 is introduced with a formula that stresses its inapplicability to angels (see comment on 1:4). This psalm is accepted by the NT writers as messianic. It is repeatedly applied to Christ; and apparently even Jesus' opponents accepted it as messianic (Mark 12:35–37), though, of course, they would not apply it to Jesus. Since the angels stand before God (Luke 1:19; Rev 8:2; cf. Dan 7:10), it is a mark of superior dignity that the Son sits. And the statement that God discharges the task of a servant in preparing a footstool for the Son is a striking piece of imagery. The angels are God's servants. How great then is he whom God deigns to serve! To make the enemies a footstool means to subject them utterly. Consequently, God will render all Christ's enemies utterly powerless.

14 We now consider the angels who are contrasted with the Son. He sits in royal state; they, however, are no more than servants. "All" applies without distinction. Not only are they servants, but they are servants of saved men. "Spirits" preserves their place of dignity, but their function is service (*eis diakonian,* "to serve"). *Diakonia* is the usual NT term for the service Christians render God and man, but nowhere else is it used of the service angels render. "Inherit" is often used in the NT in senses other than the strict one of obtaining something by a will. It can mean "obtain possession of" without regard to the means. It is used of possessing the earth (Matt 5:5), the kingdom of God (1 Cor 6:9–10), eternal life (Mark 10:17), the promises (Heb 6:12), incorruption (1 Cor 15:50), blessing (Heb 12:17), a more excellent name (v.4, where see comments).

"Salvation" is a general word, but among first-century Christians it was used of salvation in Christ, either in its present or, as here, future aspect. The word "salvation" (*sōtēria*) is used in Hebrews seven times, the most of any NT book; so the concept clearly matters to the author. His use of it here without explanation or qualification shows that it was already accepted by the readers as well as the author as a technical term for the salvation Christ brought. And the angels are the servants of those saved in this way.

Notes

---

6 Δὲ (*de,* "and," NIV) has here no strong adversative force, for this quotation reinforces the preceding rather than contrasts with it. The point of the δὲ is possibly the fact that now the relation of the angels to the Son is dealt with, whereas in the previous quotations it was that of the Son to the Father, a different relation.

8 Δὲ (*de,* "but," NIV) certainly has adversative force here: the Son is set in strong contrast with the angels (cf. the *μὲν* [*men,* an untranslatable emphatic particle] in v.7).

12 The words *ὡς ἱμάτιον* (*hōs himation,* "like a garment") are not found in the LXX but are well attested here and are certainly part of the true text.

14 The adjective **λειτουργικὰ** (*leitourgika,* "ministering") is especially appropriate to the service of God and may be used, for example, of ritual (cf. our word "liturgical"). These "ministering spirits" are "spirits in holy service" (BAG, p. 472).

B. *Author of "Such a Great Salvation"*

2:1–9

[1]We must pay more careful attention, therefore, to what we have heard, so that we do not drift away. [2]For if the message spoken by angels was binding, and every violation and disobedience received its just punishment, [3]how shall we escape if we ignore such a great salvation? This salvation, which was first announced by the Lord, was confirmed to us by those who heard him. [4]God also testified to it by signs, wonders and various miracles, and gifts of the Holy Spirit distributed according to his will.

[5]It is not to angels that he has subjected the world to come, about which we are speaking. [6]But there is a place where someone has testified:

"What is man that you are mindful of him,
  the son of man that you care for him?
[7]You made him a little lower than the angels;
  you crowned him with glory and honor
8 and put everything under his feet."

> In putting everything under him, God left nothing that is not subject to him. Yet at present we do not see everything subject to him. [9]But we see Jesus, who was made a little lower than the angels, now crowned with glory and honor because he suffered death, so that by the grace of God he might taste death for everyone.

The second step in the argument for Jesus' superiority shows him to be infinitely great because of the nature of the salvation he won. He who brought about a salvation that involved tasting death "for everyone" (v.9) cannot but be greater by far than any angel. The author precedes the development of this thought with a brief section in which he exhorts his readers to attend to what has been said, a feature we shall notice elsewhere (e.g., 3:7–11; 5:11–14).

1 "Therefore" might refer to what immediately precedes. Because angels are sent to minister to the saved, certain consequences follow. It is more likely that the term refers to the argument as a whole. Since the Son is so far superior to the angels, we should give heed to what he says. His message is superior to theirs. So we must "pay more careful attention" to it. The verb *prosechein* means not only to turn the mind to a thing but also to act upon what one perceives (see its use in Acts 8:6; 16:14). Inaction in spiritual things is fatal. The author does not explain what he means by "what we have heard," but we need not doubt that the whole Christian gospel is in mind. (Notice that his "we" puts him in the same class as his readers, i.e., dependent on others for the message. He was not one of the original disciples. Of course, a writer will sometimes class himself with his readers without actually meaning that he is in quite the same position. But it is difficult to think of Paul or one of those who followed Jesus in the days of his flesh writing exactly these words.) The danger is that we might "drift away" (*pararyōmen*). While this verb may mean "lest we let them slip," the more likely meaning is as in NIV. It is used of such things as a ring slipping off a finger, a vivid figure for the man who lets himself drift away from the haven of the gospel. One need not be violently opposed to the message to suffer loss; one need only drift away from it.

2 "Message" translates *logos,* more commonly rendered "word." It means in the first place a word spoken (as opposed to a deed) and then a series of words, a statement. What the statement is varies with the context. It can mean a message from God, a revelation, and so the Christian gospel (Acts 4:4; 8:4). The final revelation is, of course, Christ. He himself is "the Word" (John 1:1). In Hebrews the "word" is usually God's word (e.g., 2:2; 4:2, 12), though it can also be the writer's own word (5:11, "to say," NIV) or the word the Israelites did not wish to hear (12:19). Or it may be used in the sense of giving account (13:17). Here in v.2 it is the divinely given law. "By angels" is literally "through (*di'*) angels," which stresses the important truth that the law came from God. The OT does not speak of angels in connection with the giving of the law; but their presence is mentioned in other NT passages (Acts 7:53; Gal 3:19), in the LXX of Deuteronomy 33:2, and in Josephus (Antiq. XV, 136). The rabbis also thought of angels as there on that great occasion (SBK, 3:554–56). Thus the author is appealing to this well-attested view for his "how shall we?" argument (v.3). If the law came through angels, how much more should respect be given the message that came, not through angels, but through the Son? The law was "binding," i.e., fully valid. And it had provision for the proper punishment of wrongdoers so that every transgression was dealt with in the proper way.

3 The just penalties meted out under the law show that where God is concerned strict standards apply. This makes it imperative that those to whom a great salvation is offered do something about the offer. The emphatic pronoun "we" (*hēmeis*) is found only five times in Hebrews. Therefore its occurrence here is significant. It probably means "we, in contrast to those who had only the law," though it may be taken to mean "we, with our privileged position." Notice that the disaster that threatens is brought on by nothing more than neglect. It is not necessary to disobey any specific injunction. For had we done nothing when we were offered salvation, we would not have received it. This is the first of a number of warnings to the readers not to surrender their Christian profession. Clearly the writer is determined to guard against that possibility. He distinguishes the salvation he writes about from the many other kinds of salvation offered in the ancient world by calling it "such a great salvation" and then by telling us three things about it. In the first place, it was "announced by the Lord." Once more "by" is literally "through" (*dia*), with the implication that the salvation originates with the Father. The verb rendered "announced" is *laleisthai,* which is unusual in such a connection. But the meaning is plain enough. This is one of the places where this epistle has a point of contact with the Gospel of Luke, for there only does Jesus announce salvation (Luke 19:9, though cf. John 4:22). Luke also calls Jesus "Savior" (Luke 2:11) and tells us that he brings salvation (Luke 1:69, 71, 77). We have already seen that the writer has much to say about salvation (see comments on 1:14). Anything Jesus said is of interest and importance to his followers, but his proclamation of salvation must be regarded as especially important.

The second point about this salvation is that it "was confirmed to us by those who heard him." The author is appealing to the first hearers as those to whom the authentic gospel was entrusted (cf. Luke 1:2). Any later preaching must agree with theirs. If it does not, then it will stand convicted of being an innovation instead of the genuine article. Once more we see an indication that the author of Hebrews was not one of the original disciples. For him as for his readers the message was "confirmed" by the original disciples. The verb "confirm" (*bebaioō*) is used as a legal technical term "to designate properly guaranteed security" and in this context means "the saving message was guaranteed to us" (BAG, p. 138). Its frequent use in a legal sense gives it great force here; i.e., there cannot be the slightest doubt about the salvation offered. It came through Christ and that this is the salvation Christ offered is guaranteed by its apostolic attestation.

4 The third and clinching point is that God himself has also "testified" to our great salvation. The compound "with" (*syn*) shows that the preachers were not left to bear their witness alone. No less a one than God has shared in this. In John's Gospel we have the bold thought that God has borne witness to Christ (John 5:37). Since anyone who bears witness commits himself by that very act, God has gone on record, so to speak, that he too is a witness to the great salvation of his Son.

Here, however, we have an even bolder thought: God has been pleased to commit himself through the original disciples. He gave the signs that attested their preaching. The gospel is not a human creation, and the early hearers were not left in doubt as to its origin. They actually saw the way God attested it. So the author stresses the miraculous accompaniments of the preaching. "Signs" (*sēmeia*), a word used often in John to designate miracles, puts emphasis on the meaning of the miracles. They were not pointless displays of power but, in the literal sense of the word, they were *sign*ificant. They pointed beyond themselves. The miracles were full of spiritual meaning and led those who heeded them to see that they were signs from God and conveyed his message. "Wonders" emphasizes the marvelous aspect of the signs. They were such that no man could produce them and they were not explicable on merely human premises. It is this wonder-producing aspect that comes spontaneously to mind when we think of miracles. Yet to NT people this was far from being the most important aspect, for they never use this term by itself when they speak of Christ's miracles. They always link it with some other word or words, usually with "sign" and commonly in the expression "signs and wonders." "Miracles" is properly "mighty works" and is the term usually employed in the synoptic Gospels. It brings out the truth that in Christ's miracles there is superhuman power. The mighty works prove something about the gospel because they are not of human origin and thus show that the gospel they attest is not human either. "Various" (*poikilais*) means "many-colored" and is a vivid word. There was no flat uniformity about the accompaniments of the preaching of the gospel but a many-hued attestation.

There is a problem about the "gifts of the Holy Spirit" in that it is not clear whether we should take this in the sense of "gifts the Holy Spirit gives" (as in 1 Cor 12:11) or "gifts of the Holy Spirit himself" (as in Gal 3:5). Either way, there were manifestations of the Holy Spirit in believers, and the author sees these as confirming the gospel. But on the whole it seems more likely that he is speaking about God as giving men the gift (and the gifts) of the Holy Spirit. God does this as he wills, the reference to "his will" reminding us of the divine overruling. It is God who is supreme, not man nor angel. When God gives his attestation, it must accordingly be taken with full seriousness.

5 Having looked at "such a great salvation" that Christ won for his own, the author goes on to the further point that the subjection of the world to man spoken of in Psalm 8 is to be seen in Christ, not in mankind at large. "Not to angels" implies that the subjection was made to someone other than the angels, not that it has not been made at all. The world in question was subjected, but not to angels. "The world" (*tēn oikoumenēn*) is a term that normally denotes the inhabited earth. The Greeks often used it of countries occupied by men of their own race as opposed to barbarians. Later it came to be used for the Roman Empire. It is unusual to have it employed of the Messianic Age (BAG, p. 564, notes this usage only here), "age" (*aiōn*) being much more common in this sense (e.g., Matt 12:32).

6 A quotation from Psalm 8:4–6 is introduced by the unusual verb *diamartyromai* ("testify"). Only here in the NT does it introduce a quotation from Scripture. More often it is used in a sense like "adjure" or "testify solemnly." It shows that the words following it are to be taken with full seriousness. The author tells us neither the place where the words are found nor who said them. Consistently he regards all that is in his Bible as coming from God and puts no emphasis on the human author. It is impossible to hold that his general manner of citation here shows that he did not know where the words come from; for he quotes the passage exactly and his whole epistle shows that he was very familiar with the Psalms. His quotation is exact (except that he has omitted one line: "You made him ruler over the works of your hands" [Ps 8:6]).

The psalmist is concerned with both the insignificance and the greatness of man. There is, of course, no difference in meaning between "man" and "son of man" in this verse. The parallelism of Hebrew poetry requires that the two be taken in much the same sense; and in any case it is quite common in Hebrew idiom for "the son of" to denote quality, as, for example, "the son of strength" means "the strong man." So "son of man" means one who has the quality of being man. (We should not be led astray by recollecting that in the Gospels Jesus often calls himself "Son of man"; that usage is quite different.) God is said to be "mindful of" (*mimnēskē*) and to "care for" (*episkeptē*) man. The former thought has the sense of remembering with a view to helping. O. Michel warns against misinterpreting the word as used in the Bible "along historicising or intellectualistic lines. It includes total dedication to God, concern for the brethren, and true self-judgment (Hb. 13:3). It carries with it the thinking in terms of salvation history and the community which the whole of Scripture demands" (TDNT, 4:678). As used with God as subject much of this must be modified, but the word *mimnēskē* is clearly one with far-reaching implications.

Episkeptē may mean "visit in order to punish for wrongdoing," or, as here, "visit in order to 'care for.'" The psalmist asks what there is about man that the great God should stoop to help him. The rabbis endorsed the sentiment, and there is a saying attributed to R. Joshua b. Levi that when Moses came to receive the law the angels objected: "That secret treasure," they said, "which has been hidden by Thee for nine hundred and seventy-four generations before the world was created, Thou desirest to give to flesh and blood! *What is man, that thou art mindful of him?*" (*Shabbath* 88b).

7 Having asked the rhetorical questions that pinpoint man's insignificance, the psalmist goes on to his greatness. God has given man an outstanding position, one but a little lower than that of the angels. In the psalm the meaning may be as in RSV: "Yet thou hast made him little less than God," where the final word translates *'elōhîm*. Some prefer to understand this as "gods," but LXX renders it "angels" (as does the Targum, according to Buchanan). As he usually does, the author follows the LXX. Man's dignity, then, is such that he is placed in God's order of creation only a short way below the angels, and this seems to set him above all else in creation, an impression that the rest of the passage confirms. God "crowned him with glory and honor." "Glory" denotes brightness or splendor and is used of the splendor of God as well as of the glory of earthly potentates. "Honor" is frequently linked with "glory" and the combination stresses the supreme place of man in creation.

8 The dignity of man is further brought out by the fact that God has "put everything under his feet." Man is supreme among the beings of this created world. "Under his feet" shows that he has complete supremacy. Having completed the quotation, the writer goes on to draw out an important implication. In that God put all things in subjection to man, he left nothing unsubjected. It is a picture of a divinely instituted order in which man is sovereign over all creation. A few commentators see "him" as referring in this place to Christ, to whom alone all things are rightly subjected. But grammatically there is no reason for this. The passage is describing the place of mankind in God's order, and we do not come to Christ's place until v.9. While there is a sense in which it is only Christ everything is subject to, there is another sense in which man has his rightful place of supremacy over the other created things. It is this latter sense that is in view here.

From this ideal picture the writer turns his attention to current reality. As things are now, we do not see the subjection of all things to man. The writer's use of *oupō* ("not yet") shows his optimistic outlook. One day this subjection will be fully realized. But for the present there is a difference between what the psalm promises and what we see around us. While man has his powers and dignity, there are many limitations. The full promise of the psalm awaits realization. It is part of the frustration of life that in every part of it there are the equivalents of the "thorns and thistles" (Gen 3:18) that make life so hard for the tiller of the soil. Everyone knows what it is to chafe under the limitations under which he must do his work while he glimpses the vision of what would be possible were it not for those cramping limitations.

9 But if we do not see the fulfillment of this passage from Scripture in the way we might have expected, we do see a fulfillment in another way. We see it fulfilled in Jesus. He has gone through the experience of living out this earthly life, and he is now "crowned . . . with glory and honor" (the very words of the psalm) because of his saving work for man. The writer calls the Savior by his human name, Jesus, a usage we find nine times in this epistle (here, 3:1; 4:14; 6:20; 7:22; 10:19; 12:2, 24; 13:12); and on each occasion he seems to place emphasis on the humanity of our Lord. He was Jesus, the man. In this book the writer uses "Jesus Christ" three times and "our Lord Jesus" once, as well as "Christ" nine times (see comments on 3:6). Clearly, in this epistle there is a high proportion of passages with the name "Jesus." That Jesus was true man meant a good deal to the writer of Hebrews. Here he is saying that we do not see the psalm fulfilled in mankind at large but we do see it fulfilled in the man Jesus. He had a genuine incarnation because he "was made a little lower than the angels." But we do not now see him in this lowly place. Now we see him crowned with glory and honor. He is in the place of supremacy that the psalmist envisaged. And he is there because of his saving work, "because he suffered death."

"So that" looks back to the reference to suffering rather than to "crowned" (which immediately precedes it in the Gr.); and the clause it introduces gathers up "the full object and purpose of the experience that has just been predicated of Jesus" (Moffatt, in loc.). This is one of several places in the NT where someone is said to taste death (Matt 16:28; Mark 9:1; Luke 9:27; John 8:52). The verb means to taste with the mouth, from which the metaphorical sense "come to know" develops. It means here that Jesus died, with all that that entails. There is a problem as to whether we should read "by the grace [*chariti*] of God" or "apart from [*chōris*] God." The latter is read by a few MSS only, but it has strong patristic support. The author has a variety of ways of viewing the atoning work of Christ; and it would not be surprising if at this point he made a passing reference to our Lord's death as one in which the Sin-Bearer was forsaken by God (cf. Matt 27:46; Mark 15:34). Others see "apart from God" to mean that his divine nature was not involved in his death or that he died for all, God excepted. But it seems better to accept the reading of most of the MSS. It was by God's grace that Christ's saving work was accomplished. Grace is one of the great Christian words, and it is not surprising to find it connected with the Atonement here.

Notes

---

1 Μήποτε παραρυῶμεν (*mēpote pararyōmen,* "lest we should drift") is literary rather than vernacular. Μή (*mē,* "not") is used in the negative of apprehension followed by the subjunctive when the meaning is to ward off something that depends on the will (the indicative would be used if the thing had happened or if it was independent of the will; see BDF, par. 370).

4 Θέλησις (*thelēsis,* "will") is found only here in the NT, whereas θέλημα (*thelēma,* "will," "desire") occurs sixty-two times. It is spoken of as a "vulgar word" and it means "the act of willing," whereas θέλημα (*thelēma*) is "what is willed" (BAG, p. 355).

9 Διὰ τὸ πάθημα τοῦ θανάτου (*dia to pathēma tou thanatou*) is more literally "on account of the suffering of death"; and some take it with "made a little lower than the angels," i.e., "Jesus was made man in order to suffer death." It is doubtful whether the Gr. will stand this meaning (διὰ, *dia*, means "on account of" something that is, not "with a view to" something being realized). And in any case this interpretation ignores both the thrust of the present passage and the consistent view throughout Heb that the glory follows the passion.

C. *True Man*

2:10–18

[10]In bringing many sons to glory, it was fitting that God, for whom and through whom everything exists, should make the author of their salvation perfect through suffering. [11]Both the one who makes men holy and those who are made holy are of the same family. So Jesus is not ashamed to call them brothers. [12]He says,

> "I will declare your name to my brothers;
> in the presence of the congregation I will sing
> your praises."

[13]And again,

> "I will put my trust in him."

And again he says,

> "Here am I, and the children God has given me."

[14]Since the children have flesh and blood, he too shared in their humanity so that by his death he might destroy him who holds the power of death—that is, the devil—[15]and free those who all their lives were held in slavery by their fear of death. [16]For surely it is not angels he helps, but Abraham's descendants. [17]For this reason he had to be made like his brothers in every way, in order that he might become a merciful and faithful high priest in service to God, and that he might make atonement for the sins of the people. [18]Because he himself suffered when he was tempted, he is able to help those who are being tempted.

It has been argued that Jesus was greater than the angels and that his greatness is to be seen in the salvation he obtained for us. But he had lived on earth as an ordinary man. There was nothing about the Teacher from Nazareth to show that he was greater than the angels. Indeed, the reverse was true, for he had undergone humiliating sufferings culminating in a felon's death. The author proceeds to show, however, that, far from this being an objection to his greatness, this was part of it. This was the way he would save men. He would be made like those he saves.

10 Usually we do not speak of things as being "fitting" for God, but here the word is appropriate. The way of salvation is not arbitrary but befitting the character of the God we know, the God "for whom and through whom everything exists" (i.e., he is the goal and the author of all that is). The words show that the sufferings of Jesus did not take place by chance. They have their place in God's great eternal purpose. "Many sons" is an unusual expression for the total number of the saved. But sonship is important and so is the fact that the number of the saved will not be few. "Glory" points to what Montefiore calls "the splendour of ultimate salvation" (in loc.). It is no mean state into which we are saved but one actually to be thought of in terms of splendor.

Christ is "the author of their salvation." The word *archēgos*, "author," may be used in more senses than one (just as there are differing meanings for *archē*, "beginning," "first," etc.). It can denote a leader, a ruler, or one who begins something as the first in a series; RSV renders the word "pioneer." Or it might mean the originator or founder. Bowman thinks that "the picture is of one who, as a member of the fellowship, moves ahead, leading the way to ever higher ground of experience" (in loc.). The word contains the thoughts of supremacy, personal participation, and originating something. Any one of these may be prominent. Here it is surely the thought of origination that is stressed, but the choice of word enables the author to see Jesus as one who trod this earthly way before us as he established the way of salvation.

The idea of being made perfect is at first sight a startling one to apply to Jesus, but it is one the author repeats. He is fond of the word *teleioō* ("make perfect") and uses it nine times altogether (five times in John is the next most frequent use of it in the NT). BAG (pp. 817–18) sees the present passage as usually understood in the sense of "the *completion* and *perfection* of Jesus by the overcoming of earthly limitations" and notes the use of the verb in the mystery religions in senses like "consecrate" and in the passive "be consecrated," "become a *teleios*." Neither, however, seems probable. There is nothing to indicate an allusion to the mystery religions. A reference to transcending earthly limitations is more possible. Yet it may be fairly objected that suffering is the means of perfecting, not resurrection, ascension, or the like. What the author is saying is that there is a perfection that results from actually having suffered and that this is different from the perfection of being ready to suffer. The bud may be perfect, but there is a difference between its perfection and that of the flower. There is, of course, no thought of perfecting what was morally imperfect. No imperfection is implied (cf. 4:15).

11 Here the writer has emphasized the link between Jesus and those he saves. He "who makes men holy" is, of course, Jesus. He makes them into God's people by his offering of himself (10:10). The passive, "those who are made holy," coming, as it does, from the same verb, puts some emphasis on the unity of Christ and his own. But the writer does not say they are one; he says they are "of one" (NIV, "of the same family," though the Gr. has nothing corresponding to "family"). If the reference to spiritual unity is pressed, then this "one" will be God. All are "from" him. It is, however, more in keeping with the thrust of the passage to see a reference to earthly descent. In that case the "one" is Adam (as in Acts 17:26). The thought, then, is that Jesus is qualified to be our Priest and Savior because he shares our nature, because he is not some remote being but truly "one of us." Since the entire universe and angels as well as men have their origin in God, it is merely a truism to say that it is he from whom we all come. That gives no reason for Christ's being qualified to save. But that he shares with us a descent from Adam does. This enables him to call us "brothers."

Those who follow Christ are often called "brothers"; rarely, however, are they called his brothers in the NT. Indeed, sometimes the two are differentiated, as when Jesus says, "You have only one Master and you are all brothers" (Matt 23:8). Mostly Jesus' "brothers" refers to those in his immediate family (e.g., Matt 12:46–48; Luke 8:19–20; John 2:12). Sometimes, however, the word is used in a spiritual sense while linking people to Christ (Matt 12:49–50; Mark 3:33–35; Luke 8:21; Rom 8:29). So this passage in Hebrews, while somewhat unusual, is not unparalleled. There is a sense in which Jesus is brother to all who call God "Father." That is why it is important to identify the "them" in "Jesus is not ashamed to call them brothers." It is not people as such he calls brothers but only those who are sanctified.

12 The writer clarifies the point of spiritual brotherhood with an appeal to Scripture. Psalm 22 was regarded as messianic in the early church. As he hung on the cross, Jesus quoted its opening words: "My God, my God, why have you forsaken me?" (Mark 15:34). And the words about dividing garments (Ps 22:18) are seen as fulfilled in what the soldiers did as they crucified Jesus (John 19:24). It was thus the most natural thing in the world for the writer of Hebrews to see Jesus as the speaker in this psalm. He will declare his name to his brothers. In antiquity "name" generally signified more than an identifying label. It stood for the whole character, the whole person. So in this psalm the writer sees Jesus as saying that he will proclaim God's character as he has revealed himself, not simply that he will declare the name of God. The important thing in this quotation is that Jesus will do this "to [his] brothers." Jesus recognizes them as kin. The parallel statement in the next line reinforces the idea.

The word "congregation" (*ekklēsia*) can mean a properly summoned political group (Acts 19:39) or an assembly of almost any kind, including the rioting Ephesians (Acts 19:32, 41). But it is also used of the congregation of ancient Israel (Acts 7:38). In the NT *ekklēsia* ("assembly") became the characteristic word for the gatherings of Christians. Now he who sings God's praises in the midst of God's people is by that very fact showing that he is one of them, their spokesman. The "brothers" are the church.

13 Two further citations from Scripture underline the point. The second of these is from Isaiah 8:18, and this makes it almost certain that the first is from Isaiah 8:17, not Isaiah 12:2 or 2 Samuel 22:3 (all three are identical in LXX). The reason the author cites this first passage is not obvious. The context in Isaiah, however, speaks of difficulties, and the thought may be that just as Isaiah had to trust God to see him through, so was it with Jesus. In this he was brother to all God's troubled saints. The second quotation continues the first, but it is introduced here with "and again he says" because it makes a new point. The author now sees believers as "the children God has given" Christ. The word *paidion,* normally used of literal children, is not infrequent in the NT. This is, however, the one place where it is used of "children" of Christ (though in John 21:5 the risen Christ greets the disciples as "children," *paidia* [NIV, "friends"]). These children are "given" by God as the disciples were given to Jesus (John 17:6).

All three quotations from the OT, then, place the speaker in the same group as God's children. The actual word "brothers" occurs only in the first, but they all locate Christ firmly among people. He had a real community of nature with those he came to save.

14–15 The author now develops the thought of community of nature. Jesus shared "blood and flesh" with the children. (This order is found only in Eph 6:12; NIV for some reason reverses the order of the Gr.) He really came where they are. The word "humanity" is not in the Greek; it is "blood and flesh" that Christ shared with "the children." He did this for the purpose of nullifying the power of the devil, who is described as the one "who holds the power of death." This raises a problem because it is God alone who controls the issues of life and death (Job 2:6; Luke 12:5). But it was through Adam's sin, brought about by the temptation of the devil, that death entered the world (Gen 2:17; 3:19; Rom 5:12). From this it is logical to assume that the devil exercises his power in the realm of death. But the death of Christ is the means of destroying the power of the devil.

The author does not explain how Christ's death does this but contents himself with the fact that it does. In doing so he stresses the note of victory that we find throughout the NT (e.g., 1 Cor 15:54–57). The defeat of the devil means the setting free of those he had held sway over, those who had been gripped by fear of death. Fear is an inhibiting and enslaving thing; and when people are gripped by the ultimate fear—the fear of death—they are in cruel bondage. In the first century this was very real. The philosophers urged people to be calm in the face of death, and some of them managed to do so. But to most people this brought no relief. Fear was widespread, as the hopeless tone of the inscriptions on tombs clearly illustrates. But one of the many wonderful things about the Christian gospel is that it delivers men and women from this fear (cf. Rev 1:18). They are saved with a sure hope of life eternal, a life whose best lies beyond the grave.

16 "Surely" translates *dēpou,* a word used only here in the NT. It makes a strong affirmation and appeals to information shared by the reader. There is a problem about the verb rendered "helps" (*epilambanetai*). It means "to take hold of," "take by the hand," from which sense "helps" is derived. But the statement may also be understood in the following sense: "For it was not the angels that he took to himself" (JB); i.e., he became man. The fact that the Incarnation is in view in v.17 supports the rendering "helps." Furthermore, the verb is thought to mean "take hold with a purpose," i.e., to help. The author has in mind that Jesus came to rescue people. This is not in dispute; yet it is another question whether this is all contained in the verb. On the whole it seems better to see the statement as pointing to the fact of the Incarnation rather than to its purpose. "Abraham's descendants" particularizes the manner of the Incarnation and makes it harder to see the meaning of the verb as "helps," for Jesus helps many more than Jews. But he became incarnate as a Jew. He did not descend to the level of the angels and become one of them. He descended to the level of mankind and became a Jew.

17 The purpose of salvation involved a genuine incarnation. "He had to" means "he owed it" (the verb can be used of financial debts), "he ought." There is the sense of moral obligation. The nature of the work Jesus came to accomplish demanded the Incarnation. In view of this work, he ought to become like the "brothers." "In order that" renders the conjunction *hina,* which expresses purpose. The Incarnation was not aimless; it was for the specific purpose of Jesus' becoming a high priest, another way of saying that it was to save men. "Merciful" receives emphasis from its position (the Gr. word order is "that a merciful he might become and faithful high priest").

There is an interesting contrast in Philo, who thinks of the Jewish high priest as one who will not show his feelings: "He will have his feeling of pity under control" (*De Specialibus Legibus* 1.115). Not so our great High Priest. He is one who is first and foremost merciful. He is also "faithful." This adjective can refer to the faith that relies on someone or something or that on which one can rely, i.e., "relying" or "reliable." Jesus is, of course, both. But here the emphasis is on his relationship to God the Father, and so the first meaning is more probable (cf. Rev. 1:5; 3:14; 19:11).

Only in Hebrews is the term "high priest" applied to Jesus in the NT. This is the first example of its use, and the author does not explain it. He may want us to see

Jesus as superior to all other priests. Or he may be using the term because he sees Jesus' saving work as fulfilling all that is signified by the ceremonies of the Day of Atonement, for which the high priest's ministry was indispensable. Sometimes in this epistle the author calls Jesus simply a "priest," but there seems to be no great difference in meaning.

"In service to God" (i.e., "with respect to the things of God" [*ta pros ton theon*]) shows where Christ's high priestly work is carried out. Some of the service of the high priest was directed toward the people, but this is not in view here. The service Christ was to render was "that he might make atonement for the sins of the people." The introductory conjunction denotes purpose: he became high priest with a view to this.

"Make atonement" is a curious rendering. The word *hilaskesthai* means "to propitiate," not "to make atonement," and relates to putting away the divine wrath (NIV mg.). When people sin, they arouse the wrath of God (Rom 1:18); they become enemies of God (Rom 5:10). One aspect of salvation deals with this wrath, and it is to this the author is directing attention at this point. Christ saves us in a way that takes account of the divine wrath against every evil thing. *Hilaskesthai* ("make atonement") is followed here by the accusative case of "sins" (*tas hamartias*), an unusual construction that means "to make propitiation with respect to the sins of the people." "The people" (*tou laou*) in some contexts indicates the people in contrast to their leaders or their priests. But it is frequently used for the people of God—those Christ died for—and this is the meaning here.

18 The sufferings Jesus endured enable him to help others. "He himself" (*autos*) is emphatic. Contrary to what might have been expected, *he* suffered. The verb *peponthen* ("suffered") naturally applies to the cross, but the context shows that a wider reference is in mind. Throughout his earthly life Jesus suffered. Being what he is, temptation must have been far more distasteful for him than it is for us. The verb *peirastheis* ("tempted") sometimes means "tested," and here it might conceivably apply to the sufferings simply as trials to be endured. But the verb is more often used in the sense of "tempt." The author is saying that Jesus can help the tempted because he has perfect sympathy with them. He too has been tempted and knows what temptation is. The words "he is able" are important and mean more than "he helps." Only he who suffers *can* help in this way. Jesus went all the way for us. He was not only ready to suffer, but he actually did suffer.

Notes

---

10 Δι' οὗ (*di' hou*) would normally be taken of the agent "through" whom a task was accomplished. But it can also denote the originator (1 Cor 1:9; cf. Rom 11:36). The participle ἀγαγόντα (*agagonta*, "bringing") must be taken in sense with αὐτῷ (*autō*, "to him"; NIV, "God"), even though the case is different. Here the aorist is timeless, drawing attention to the act as a simple fact, not as an event in the past.

15 The articular infinitive with an attributive in the same case, διὰ παντὸς τοῦ ζῆν (*dia pantos tou zēn*, "through all of life"; NIV, "all their lives"), is without parallel in the NT (BDF, par. 398). Τὸ ζῆν (*to zēn*) was evidently regarded as equivalent to a noun, "the life" (cf. 2 Cor 1:8).

D. *Superior to Moses*

3:1–6

> [1]Therefore, holy brothers, who share in the heavenly calling, fix your thoughts on Jesus, the apostle and high priest whom we confess. [2]He was faithful to the one who appointed him, just as Moses was faithful in all God's house. [3]Jesus has been found worthy of greater honor than Moses, just as the builder of a house has greater honor than the house itself. [4]For every house is built by someone, but God is the builder of everything. [5]Moses was faithful as a servant in all God's house, testifying to what would be said in the future. [6]But Christ is faithful as a son over God's house. And we are his house, if we hold on to our courage and the hope of which we boast.

The author steadily develops his argument that Jesus is supremely great. He is greater than the angels, the author of a great salvation, and great enough to become man to accomplish it. Now the author turns his attention to Moses, regarded by the Jews as the greatest of men. They could even think of him as greater than angels (SBK, 3:683). Perhaps then he was superior to Jesus? The writer does nothing to belittle Moses. Nor does he criticize him. He accepts Moses' greatness but shows that as great as he was, Jesus was greater by far.

1 The address "holy brothers" is found only here in the NT (though cf. Col. 1:2 and some MSS of 1 Thess 5:27). It combines the notes of affection and consecration. These people are members of the brotherhood and dear to the writer. They are also people who have been set apart for the service of God. The reference to "the heavenly calling" shows that the initiative comes from God. He has called them to be his own. "Therefore" links this section to the preceding. Because Christ has taken our nature and can help us, therefore we are invited to consider him in his capacities as apostle and high priest.

"Apostle" is applied to Jesus only here in the NT, but the idea that God "sent" him is more frequent, especially in the fourth Gospel. The basic idea is that of mission. Jesus was sent by the Father to accomplish his purpose. "High priest" brings before us the sacrificial nature of that mission. In the Greek the verse ends by naming him simply "Jesus." Though he is the most glorious of beings, this name draws attention to his humanity. It is as man that his work as apostle and high priest is accomplished.

2 The point could have been made that there were times when Moses was not as faithful as he might have been. But the writer makes no criticism of the man held in such honor by the Jews. He prefers to accept Moses as "faithful." Yet he sees Jesus' faithfulness as much more comprehensive. Moses was no more than part of the "house," but Jesus made the house. Again, Jesus as Son was over the house, whereas Moses was a servant in it. The "house," of course, is the household, the people, not the building; and it is God's house, the people of God. Moses was a member of that house and proved faithful there (the words are a quotation from Num 12:7). The adjective "all" may point to a concern both Moses and Jesus had for the whole house. Others, such as prophets, kings, or priests, dealt with restricted areas.

3 The first point of comparison pronounces Jesus as "worthy of greater honor than Moses" because he was builder of the house rather than part of it, as was Moses. Incidentally, *doxa,* which is the usual word for "glory," and *timē* are both translated "honor" in this verse by NIV. Though Moses was a glorious person, his glory did not measure up to that of Christ. But the word *doxa* ("glory") is close in meaning to *timē* ("honor"), and the two often occur together (e.g., 2:7, 9). He who makes a house is worthy of more honor than the house, glorious though the house may be. Moses was at all times a member of the people of God, that and no more. He had great honor within that people, but there was no way for him to be any other than one of them. Not so Jesus! He was more. The author has just made the point that Jesus became true man and could truly call men "brothers." But that does not alter his conviction that Christ is also more than man. He is the founder of the church, and the church was continuous with the OT people of God. The author will come back to this thought in v.6.

4 Parenthetically, this verse makes the point that God is over all. The author does not want us to lose sight of this fact. So he points out that the existence of a house is an argument for a builder. Houses do not build themselves. "But" (the adversative *de*) introduces something different. There is, of course, similarity. A house argues for a builder, and all that is argues for God. There is also a difference, because God is not to be put on a level with any builder of a house.

5 Having made his point that God transcends everyone, for he made everything, the writer returns to Moses. He repeats his statement that Moses was faithful in God's house (v.2; in both places and again in v.6 the Gr. reads "his house," but NIV has correctly interpreted it as "God's house"). Now he makes a further point: Whereas Moses was no more than a servant, Jesus was greater, for he was Son over the house. The thought is still that of Moses' faithfulness. There is no criticism of him, but his faithfulness consisted in his discharge of his role as servant.

The word for "servant" (*therapōn*) is found only here in the NT. It denotes an honored servant, one who is far above a slave but still a servant. It can be used for "henchman, attendant . . . companion in arms, squire" (LSJ, p. 793). Here the emphasis is on the subordinate, if honorable, capacity: It is the "squire" rather than the "companion in arms." The writer goes on to say that Moses' faithfulness did not relate to his own day only. He was "testifying to what would be said in the future." Some hold that this means what Moses himself would say and points perhaps to Deuteronomy. But it seems more likely that the thought is that there would be revelations to others. This epistle began with a reference to such revelations and to the importance of what God said (the verb *laleō* ["speak"] is the same as that used in 1:1). And there is a reference to our Lord's speaking about salvation in 2:3 (same verb again).

6 The name "Christ" is used here for the first time in this epistle, without the article (as in 9:11, 24). It has the article six times (3:14; 5:5; 6:1; 9:14, 28; 11:26) and the expression "Jesus Christ" occurs three times (10:10; 13:8, 21). Here, where a name of dignity is called for, it is a proper name. Christ is contrasted with Moses "as a son over God's house." Moses was no more than a member—even though a very distinguished member—of the house. He was essentially one with all the others. Christ has an innate superiority. He is the Son and as such is "over" the household.

The author adds a most important explanation as to the composition of this house. One might easily suppose that he was referring to the Jews or at least to the Jews of the OT. They were, of course, in mind. But he is not thinking of the Jews as a race nor of a group of historical figures. He is thinking of the people of God. In OT days this had been the people Israel. But Israel had rejected the Son of God when he came, and now the people of God is the church. Perseverance is one of the marks of being a Christian. Without it we are not Christ's. As F.F. Bruce puts it, "The doctrine of the final perseverance of the saints has as its corollary the salutary teaching that the saints are the people who persevere to the end" (in loc.).

We are to hold on to "our courage." The word *parrēsia* has about it the feeling of being quite at home when words flow freely and so means "confidence" or "courage." "The hope of which we boast" may perhaps be not quite it. The word for "boast" is *kauchēma*, which means something one can boast about, rather than *kauchēsis*, the act of boasting. Our position as God's "house" is something of which we may be proud. We have a good gift from God. Instead of being ashamed of this gift, we should glory in it. "Boast" is connected with "hope." "Hope" is used in the NT in much the same way as we use it, now in ordinary speech. But more characteristically it is the Christian hope, the certainty that God will carry out his promises, especially those in the gospel. The Christian looks forward eagerly, expecting God's triumph. To be God's house, then, means to persevere in quiet confidence, knowing that one has matter for pride in the Christian hope.

Notes

---

2 Ποιήσαντι (*poiēsanti*) is correctly translated "appointed." It cannot mean "created" since the Son is not a created being (1:3). There might be a reference to the Incarnation, but it seems more probable that it is the Son's appointment as apostle and high priest that is meant. The same verb is used of the appointment of Moses and Aaron (1 Sam 12:6 LXX), the apostles (Mark 3:14), and Christ himself (Acts 2:36).

III. The Promised Rest

The comparison between Christ and Moses leads to one between their followers. The writer uses the conduct of the Israelites as a means of challenging his readers to a closer walk with God. There was a promise in the OT that God's people would enter into rest. The writer sees this promise as fulfilled—not in anything in the OT—but in Christ. In drawing attention to this, he shows from another angle that Christ is God's final word to mankind (cf. 1:2).

A. *Scriptural Basis*

3:7–11

[7]So, as the Holy Spirit says:

"Today, if you hear his voice,
[8] do not harden your hearts
as you did in the rebellion,
during the time of testing in the desert,
[9]where your fathers tested and tried me
and for forty years saw what I did.

> 10That is why I was angry with that generation,
> and I said, 'Their hearts are always going astray,
> and they have not known my ways.'
> 11So I declared on oath in my anger,
> 'They shall never enter my rest.' "

The writer begins this section with a quotation from Psalm 95:7–11. Israel did not walk in fellowship with God but disobeyed and provoked him. Therefore they did not enter his rest. Judaism is not the way of entry into that rest.

7 Some see the quotation as a long parenthesis, "so" being followed by v.12: "So . . . see to it. . . ." But it seems better to take "so" with the quotation "So . . . do not harden your hearts." Do not repeat the mistake the Israelites made. The quotation is ascribed directly to the Holy Spirit (cf. 9:8; 10:15; Acts 28:25; the human author is mentioned in 4:7). The author is fond of the word "today," using it eight times (Luke and Acts are the only NT books that use it more). Here its prominent position gives it emphasis. Immediate action is imperative. The voice of God is sounding now. It must not be neglected.

8 To "harden" the heart is to disobey the voice of God and act in accordance with one's own desires. This is what Israel did in the wilderness. Here the reference is to the incident when there was no water and the Israelites "put the Lord to the test" (Exod. 17:1–7). In the LXX the place names Massah and Meribah are always translated by words such as those here rendered "rebellion" and "testing." Through lack of faith and failure to appreciate God's purposes of grace, the people of Israel put him to the test.

9 The thought of "testing" God continues. NIV may be correct in rendering "tested and tried me," but there is no "me" in the Greek. This opens up the alternative possibility that "my works" (NIV, "what I did") is the object of both the preceding verbs: "Your fathers tested and saw my works for forty years." They ought to have proceeded in faith. Since God had done so much for them, they should have trusted him when they could not see. Instead, they tested his works where they could see ("saw" puts stress on visibility). This faithlessness was no passing phase but something that went on for forty years. In the LXX the "forty years" is connected with God's anger, not with the testing. The author may have had other MSS with this way of taking the words. Or he may have put the words in a new position himself. It may well be that at the time he wrote this epistle, the author reflected on the fact that it was the fourth decade since Jesus' crucifixion. The Israelites had rejected God for forty years, and it was now nearly forty years since their descendants had rejected Jesus—a reason for serious concern.

10 We should not miss the reference to the anger of God. The Bible is clear that God is not impassive or indifferent in the face of human sin. He is a "consuming fire" (12:29), and his inevitable reaction to sin is wrath. "Generation" may mean a "clan" or "race," sometimes those living at a particular time or those who have the characteristics of a particular age. Here it is all the Israelites living at a particular time. They showed constancy in error, "always going astray." "Heart" (*kardia*) as used in the Bible does not stand for the emotions as with us but for the whole inner being—

thoughts, feelings, and will. Often the emphasis is on the mind. Here the thought is that Israel went wholly astray. Their inner state was not right with God. The last line of the verse implies that if people really knew the ways of God, they would walk in them. But these people did not know. Their ignorance was culpable, not innocent. They were not blamed simply for not knowing but for not knowing things they ought to have known and acted on. They did not take the trouble to learn. To neglect opportunity is serious.

11 The seriousness with which God viewed Israel's sin is shown by the divine oath. This points to an unshakable determination. The form of the oath in the Hebrew, reflected in the LXX, is "If they shall enter." This construction implies an ending that occurs only rarely; e.g., "If I have done evil to him who is at peace with me . . . let my enemy pursue and overtake me" (Ps 7:4–5). Here it will be something like "If they shall enter into my rest . . . then my name is not God!" (NIV, "They shall never enter"). The oath refers to the time when the spies had returned from their survey of the Promised Land (Num 14:21ff.).

The psalmist has brought together two incidents, one from the beginning and one from the end of the wilderness period, to make the impressive point that the Israelites of old consistently provoked God. God swore the oath in his "anger." Here the word *orgē* is from a different root from that rendered "angry" in v.10 (*prosōchthisa*). *Orgē* is the usual word for the "wrath" of God and points to the strong and settled opposition of God's holy nature to all that is evil. God is not passive in the face of wrongdoing; he actively opposes it. "Wrath" may not be the perfect word with which to express this (as used of men it implies lack of self-control and the like that do not apply to God). But it seems the best word we have and it does bring out God's passionate opposition to evil and his concern for the right. Those who reject its use are in danger of misrepresenting God as one who does not care. But God does care, and he did not allow the sinning Israelites to enter the rest.

The author has a fondness for the verb "enter" (*eiserchomai*) and uses it seventeen times, more than any other NT book except the Synoptics and Acts. Eleven times in chapters 3–4 he speaks of entering rest. "Rest" (*katapausis*), as used here, points to a place of blessing where there is no more striving but only relaxation in the presence of God and in the certainty that there is no cause for fear. R. Akiba understood Psalm 95 (in conjunction with Num 14:35) to mean that the wilderness generation would have no part in the world to come (Talmud *Sanhedrin* 110b; M *Sanhedrin* 10.3 bases the same thought on Num 14:35). Disobedience cut them off from the blessing. Buchanan thinks of the "rest" as "the promised heritage of the land of Canaan under the rule of the Messiah to be fulfilled for Jesus and his followers" (in loc.). This would give us an easy interpretation to the word "rest," but it is more than difficult to fit it in with what the writer says elsewhere. It is better to take "rest" in a spiritual sense.

B. *Some Did Not Enter the Rest*

3:12–19

[12]See to it, brothers, that none of you has a sinful, unbelieving heart that turns away from the living God. [13]But encourage one another daily, as long as it is called Today, so that none of you may be hardened by sin's deceitfulness. [14]We have come to share in Christ if we hold firmly till the end the confidence we had at first. [15]As has just been said:

> "Today, if you hear his voice,
> do not harden your hearts
> as you did in the rebellion."
>
> [16]Who were they who heard and rebelled? Were they not all those Moses led out of Egypt? [17]And with whom was he angry for forty years? Was it not with those who sinned, whose bodies fell in the desert? [18]And to whom did God swear that they would never enter his rest if not to those who disobeyed? [19]So we see that they were not able to enter, because of their unbelief.

Having shown that Scripture looks for a rest for God's people, the author proceeds to show that Israel of old did not enter that rest. The implication is that it is still available for others. And there is a warning. When God opens up an opportunity, that does not necessarily mean that those who have that opportunity will take it.

12 The writer has a tender concern for every one of his readers. He exhorts them to beware lest any one of them fall away. The "sinful, unbelieving heart" stands in marked contrast to the faithfulness ascribed to both Jesus and Moses (v.2). It is an unusual and emphatic expression. The author stresses the heinousness of this by speaking of turning away from the living God. "Turn away" is perhaps not strong enough; the meaning is rather "rebel against." The author is fond of the expression "the living God" (cf. 9:14; 10:31; 12:22). The rebellion he warns against consists of departing from a living, dynamic person, not from some dead doctrine. Jews might retort that they served the same God as the Christians so that they would not be departing from God if they went back to Judaism. But to reject God's highest revelation is to depart from God, no matter how many preliminary revelations are retained. A true faith is impossible with such a rejection.

13 Contrariwise, they must encourage one another constantly and urgently. The author sees Christian fellowship as very important. It can build people up in the faith and form a strong bulwark against sin and apostasy (cf. 10:25; Matt 18:15–17). "Daily" means that encouragement should be habitual. "As long as it is called Today" adds a touch of urgency, for "Today" does not last forever. The aim of the swift action the writer looks for is that not one of his readers be hardened. Once again we see his concern for every individual reader. The verb "hardened" does not refer only to "the heart" but is quite general. One's whole life may be hard and in that case one is no candidate for spiritual progress. What hardens is "sin's deceitfulness." The readers were tempted to go back to Judaism in the belief that by doing so they would be better off. But sin deceived those who thought like this. Temporal and physical safety would be bought only at the price of spiritual disaster.

14 The expression *metochoi tou Christou* can be understood as "participators in Christ" (NIV, Moff., RSV, etc.) or as "participators with Christ" (NEB, TEV, JB, etc.). The former is supported by the use of the same noun of sharing (*metochoi*) in the Christian calling (v.1) and in the Holy Spirit (6:4), the latter by the use of partnership with Christ in 1:9. It seems to me that there is more to be said for the former rendering. It may be supported by the context, for it is the privilege we have in being Christians that is stressed, not the kind of work Christians do alongside Christ. The two sides of a paradox appear when we have, on the one hand, "we have come" and, on the other hand, "if we hold firmly." What God has done God has done. But it is important that the believer hold firmly to what God has given him (cf. v.6). The word *hypostasis* means literally "that which stands under" and may be used of essential "being" (as in 1:3). Here it will rather be that which undergirds the Christian's profession, and "confidence" is a good translation. "The confidence we had at first" is that experienced when the readers first believed. They had no doubts then, nor should they have any now. "Till the end" may point to the end of the age or the end of the believer's life.

15 The construction is uncertain. This verse may be taken with the preceding one, as in NIV, or with what follows, as NEB, which starts a new paragraph with "When Scripture says . . . who, I ask, were those who heard?" This is attractive, but it ignores the *gar* ("for") at the beginning of v.16. Some link the words with v.13 and regard v.14 as a parenthesis: "Exhort one another while it is called today . . . while it is said. . . ." The question is not an easy one, but it seems best to take things in order, as NIV does. The words, of course, have already been quoted (vv.7–8, where see commentary).

16 The author presses home his point by three questions that emphasize that it was the people who were in a position of spiritual privilege and yet sinned grievously who were in mind in Psalm 95. Some scholars, it is true, take *tines* as the indefinite pronoun and not as an interrogative (as does KJV, "for some . . . did provoke"). But "some" is a strange designation for practically the whole nation, and in any case it is better to see the same construction in all three of these verses. The first question, then, asks, "Who were they who heard and rebelled?" The verb "rebelled" (*parepikranan*) is found only here in the NT (though a cognate noun occurs in v.8). It means "embitter," "make angry," and is a strong expression for the rebellious attitude that characterized the Exodus generation.

The writer answers his question with another, this one phrased so as to expect the answer yes. "All those Moses led out of Egypt" is comprehensive, but that Joshua and Caleb are not mentioned does not invalidate the argument. The nation was characterized by unbelief, and the faithfulness of two men does not alter this. NIV says that Moses "led" the people out of Egypt; but, more literally, the author said that they "came out through [*dia*] Moses"— implying that they acted of their own volition and made a good start.

17 The second question refers to those God was angry with those forty years. (For the anger of God, see comments on vv.10–11.) In the earlier treatment of the incident (vv.7–8), the forty years referred to testing God and seeing his works. Here it refers to the continuing wrath of God (as in the Heb. and LXX). The wrath of God was not something transitory and easily avoided. It lasted throughout the wilderness period. The question "Was it not. . . ?" employs the emphatic *ouchi*, found in only one other place in this epistle (in 1:14). Its use leaves no doubt whatever that God was angry with the sinners in question. Their punishment is mentioned in words taken from or reminiscent of Numbers 14:29, 32. The author may be quoting or he may simply be using scriptural language to add solemnity to his point. He reminds his readers that in the past those who sinned against God had been destroyed, and, indeed (as the verbs in the Numbers passage are future since they were spoken before the event), that they were destroyed as it was prophesied. The word rendered "desert" refers to "deserted" land. It is wilderness country in contrast to cultivated and inhabited land.

It can be used for pasture (Luke 15:4). Here it is the uninhabited area the Israelites passed through on their wanderings.

18 The third question refers to those to whom the oath was sworn (cf. v.11). Those who would not enter God's rest were "those who disobeyed." The verb *apeitheō* means properly "disobey," but some accept the meaning "disbelieve" (as NIV mg.). This is possible since for the early Christians "the supreme disobedience was a refusal to believe their gospel" (BAG, p. 82). But here it seems that we should take the meaning "disobey." God did much for these people. Yet in the end they went their own way and refused to obey him.

19 The depressing conclusion sums up what has gone before. The author does not say that they did not enter but that they "were not able to enter." Sin is self-defeating and unbelief of itself prevents us from entering God's rest. This is not an arbitrary penalty imposed by a despotic God. It is the inevitable outcome of unbelief. In the Greek the final word in this section of the argument, thrown to the end of the sentence for greater emphasis, is *apistia* ("unbelief"). That is what robbed the wilderness generation of the rest they had every reason to expect when they came out of Egypt. The warning to the people of the writer's day is clear. To slip back from their Christian profession into unbelief would be fatal.

Notes

---

12 Ἐν (*en*) with the dative of the articular infinitive τῷ ἀποστῆναι (*tō apostēnai*, "turns away from") is rather more frequent in Heb than in most of the other NT writings. The tense is usually the present and the sense temporal. However, exceptions to both occur, as here where the tense is aorist and the meaning something like "in that." There is probably another nontemporal example, this time with the present, in v.15.

C. *Christians Enter the Rest*

4:1–10

1Therefore, since the promise of entering his rest still stands, let us be careful
that none of you be found to have fallen short of it. 2For we also have had the gospel
preached to us, just as they did; but the message they heard was of no value to
them, because those who heard did not combine it with faith. 3Now we who have
believed enter that rest, just as God has said,

> "So I declared on oath in my anger,
> 'They shall never enter my rest.' "

And yet his work has been finished since the creation of the world. 4For somewhere
he has spoken about the seventh day in these words: "And on the seventh day God
rested from all his work." 5And again in the passage above he says, "They shall
never enter my rest."

6It still remains that some will enter that rest, and those who formerly had the
gospel preached to them did not go in, because of their disobedience. 7Therefore
God again set a certain day, calling it Today, when a long time later he spoke
through David, as was said before:

"Today, if you hear his voice,
do not harden your hearts."

[8]For if Joshua had given them rest, God would not have spoken later about another day. [9]There remains, then, a Sabbath-rest for the people of God; [10]for anyone who enters God's rest also rests from his own work, just as God did from his.

The author argues that the purposes of God are not frustrated because Israel of old disobeyed him and failed to enter the rest he had promised his people. The promise remains. If the ancient Israel did not enter God's rest, then someone else will; namely, the Christians. But this should not lead to complacency. If the Israelites of an earlier day, with all their advantages, failed to enter the rest, Christians ought not to think there will be automatic acceptance for them. They must take care lest they, too, fail to enter the blessing.

1 NIV's "let us be careful" is more strictly "let us fear," and the exhortation comes first in the sentence. It is emphatic because the writer does not want his readers to be complacent. There is real danger. God's promises mean much to the writer, and indeed the word *epangelia* ("promise") occurs more often in Hebrews than in any other NT book (fourteen times; next is Gal with ten). The promise in question "still stands." That is to say, though it has not been fulfilled, it has not been revoked. In one sense, of course, there was a fulfillment, for the generation after the men who died in the wilderness entered Canaan. But throughout this section it is basic to the argument that physical entry into Canaan did not constitute the fulfillment of the promise. God had promised "rest" and that meant more than living in Canaan.

There is a problem about the word translated "be found." The verb is *dokeō,* which means "think," "suppose" if transitive, and "seem," "have the appearance of" if intransitive. Moffatt points out that a meaning like "judge," "adjudge" is also attested in some passages in Josephus, LXX, and Attic. There are two main possibilities. The one accepts "think" as the meaning and sees the writer as reassuring fearful Christians who thought they might miss the rest. (The earlier generation had missed it, and why should not they?) The other interpretation prefers "seem," "be judged," or "be found" and takes the words as a warning to the readers to take care lest they miss the promised rest. ("Seem" is a way of softening the warning so that the writer refrains from saying that any of them actually missed or will miss the promise.) A decision is not easy, but on the whole it seems that this second interpretation fits the context better. The author, then, is reminding his readers that there was a generation to whom the rest was promised and who missed it. They should beware lest they make the same mistake.

2 There is a question about following the rendering "we have had the gospel preached to us" or whether the phrase should be taken as general—i.e., "we have heard the good news as well as they." The verb *euangelizomai* is used of preaching good news in general, but in a Christian context it is much more often used of the specific good news of the gospel; indeed, it becomes the technical term for preaching the gospel. Here everything turns on whether we think that what was preached to Israel of old was what Christians call "the gospel." If it was, then NIV is correct. If we think otherwise, we will follow the rendering "heard the good news." The first half of the verse makes it clear that on the score of hearing God's Good News there was not much to choose between the wilderness generation and the readers: "We also have had the gospel preached to us, just as they did." The stress is on the readers. They have the message. They must act on it in contrast to the men of old who did not.

"The message they heard" (i.e., "the word of hearing," an expression much like that in 1 Thess 2:13) brought them no profit. A difficult problem remains at the end of the verse, where the reason for this is given. While there are several textual variants in the MSS, they boil down to two—whether we take the participle of the verb "to combine" or "unite" as singular, in which case it agrees with "word" (in "word of hearing") or as plural, in which case it goes with "them." Only a few MSS have the singular reading, some of them very old, but many scholars favor it on grammatical grounds. If adopted, it gives this sense: "It [the word] was not mixed with faith in them that heard." On the other hand, if we take the plural, the meaning is, "They were not united by faith with them that heard" (i.e., real believers, men like Caleb and Joshua). The resolution of the question is difficult and may be impossible with the information at our disposal. The main thrust, however, is plain enough. The writer is saying that it is not enough to hear; the message must be acted on in faith.

This is the writer's first use of *pistis* ("faith"), a term he will employ 32 times (out of the 243 times it occurs in the NT), a total exceeded only in Romans (40 times). *Pistis* means "faithfulness" as well as "faith," but the latter preponderates in the NT. Sometimes faith in God is meant and sometimes faith in Christ. In this epistle it is often the former. In the NT, the term is usually used without an object, i.e., as "true piety, genuine religion" (BAG, p. 669). Here the term points to the right response to the Christian message. It is the attitude of trusting God wholeheartedly. The writer speaks of "those who heard" without specifying what it was they heard. But there can be no doubt that he is looking for a right response to what God has done and to what God has made known.

3 "We who have believed" once more stresses the necessity of faith. This is one of only two places where the verb *pisteuō* ("to believe") occurs in Hebrews (the other is in 11:6)—a contrast to the frequency of the noun. It is believers who enter God's rest, not members of physical Israel, and they do so through a right relationship to God, with an attitude of trust. The verb *eiserchomai* ("enter") is in the present tense. Montefiore, for one, regards this as important: "Contrary to some commentators, the Greek means neither that they are certain to enter, nor that they will enter, but that they are already in process of entering" (in loc.). By contrast Bruce complains of translations that "suggest that the entrance is here and now, whereas it lies ahead as something to be attained. The present tense is used in a generalizing sense" (in loc.). Either view is defensible and probably much depends on our idea of the "rest." If it lies beyond death, then obviously "rest" must be understood in terms of the future. But if it is a present reality, then believers are entering it now. Characteristically, the writer supports his position by an appeal to Scripture.

There is nothing in the Greek to correspond to NIV's "God" ("God has said"). Yet this is a correct interpretation because the writer habitually regards God as the author of Scripture. The perfect tense *eirēken* ("has said") puts some emphasis on permanence. What God has spoken stands. The quotation is from Psalm 95:11 (already cited in 3:11, where see comments). Its point appears to be that those to whom the promise was originally made could not enter the rest because of the divine oath. This does not mean any inadequacy on God's part. He had completed his works from of old, in fact from the Creation. The writer is saying that God's rest was available from the time

Creation was completed. The "rest" was thus the rest he himself enjoyed. The earthly rest in Canaan was no more than a type or symbol of this.

4 The writer does not precisely locate his quotation (Gen 2:2) but contents himself with the general "somewhere." Nor does he say who the speaker is, though once again it will be God, the author of all Scripture. Locating a passage precisely was not easy when scrolls were used; and unless it was important, there would be a tendency not to look it up. In the present case the important thing is that God said the words, not where and when they were spoken. The passage speaks of God as resting from his work on the seventh day.

It is worth noticing that in the creation story each of the first six days is marked by the refrain "And there was evening, and there was morning." However, this is lacking in the account of the seventh day. There we simply read that God rested from all his work. This does not mean that God entered a state of idleness, for there is a sense in which he is continually at work (John 5:17). But the completion of creation marks the end of a magnificent whole. There was nothing to add to what God had done, and he entered a rest from creating, a rest marked by the knowledge that everything that he had made was very good (Gen 1:31). So we should think of the rest as something like the satisfaction that comes from accomplishment, from the completion of a task, from the exercise of creativity.

5 The writer adds a second quotation (Psalm 95:11). It is one that is central to his argument at this point. As here, he often uses "again" where a further quotation is added to a preceding one (e.g., 1:5; 2:13; 10:30). In this case, however, it does more than that; it introduces a second point in the argument. The first passage said that God rested (and by implication that the rest was open to those who would enter it); the second passage said that the Israelites did not enter that rest because God's judgment fell on them. So the way is prepared for later steps in the argument.

6–7 "It still remains" misses some of the force of the original, which is rather: "Since therefore it remains. . . ." The argument moves along in logical sequence. Some will enter that rest because it is unthinkable that God's plan should fail of fulfillment. If God prepared a rest for humanity to enter into, then they will enter into it. Perhaps those originally invited would not do so, for there is often something of the conditional about God's promises. This is not to say that one is to fear that these promises will not be kept. It is precisely the force of the present argument that nothing can stop the promises from being kept. But they must always be appropriated by faith. There is no other way of laying hold on them. So if one does not approach the promises by faith, he does not obtain what God offers and the offer is made to others. Some, then, must enter God's rest; but the first recipients of the Good News (cf. comment on v.2) did not.

The writer concentrates on two generations only: the wilderness generation and his contemporaries. There had been other generations who might have appropriated the promise. But the focus is on the first generation who set the pattern of unbelief and then on the writer's generation, who alone at that time had the opportunity of responding to God's invitation. All the intervening generations had ceased to be and could be ignored for the purpose of the argument.

The reason the first group did not enter God's rest was "their disobedience." The word *apeitheia* ("disobedience") is always used in the NT of disobeying God, often with the thought of the gospel in mind; so it comes close to the meaning disbelief (cf. v.11; Rom 11:30). Because the first generation had passed the opportunity by, God set another day. The idea that the wilderness generation was finally rejected was one the rabbis found hard to accept. In their writings we find statements such as the following: "Into this resting-place they will not enter, but they will enter into another resting-place" (Mid *Qoheleth* 10.20.1). The rabbis also had a parable of a king who swore in anger that his son would not enter his palace. But when he calmed down, he pulled down his palace and built another, so fulfilling his oath and at the same time retaining his son (ibid.). Thus the rabbis expressed their conviction that somehow those Israelites would be saved. The author, however, has no such reservations about the wilderness generation. They disobeyed God and forfeited their place. Psalm 95 was written long after that generation had failed to use its opportunity and had perished. Its use of the term "Today" shows that the promise had never been claimed and was still open. The voice of God still called. The author has already used the quotation in 3:7ff. (cf. comments). But its point this time is the word "Today." There is *still* a day of opportunity, even though the fate of the wilderness generation stands as an impressive witness to the possibility of spiritual disaster.

8 The form of the Greek sentence indicates a contrary-to-fact condition: "If Joshua had given them rest [as he did not], God would not have spoken later about another day [as he did]." The name "Joshua" is the Hebrew form of the Greek name "Jesus." "Joshua" is a good way of rendering the text, as it makes clear to the English reader who is in mind. The Greek text, however, says "Jesus"; and both the writer and his original readers would have been mindful of the connection with the name of Christ, even though the emphasis in the passage lies elsewhere. There had been a "Jesus" who could not lead his people into the rest of God just as there was another "Jesus" who could.

9 The sentence begins with the inferential *ara* ("so," "as a result"). What follows is the logical consequence of what precedes. The term "Sabbath-rest" (*sabbatismos*) is not attested before this passage and looks like the author's own coinage. He did not have a word for the kind of rest he had in mind; so he made one up. There were various kinds of "rest." There was, for example, the kind Israel was to get in its own land when it had rest from wars (Deut 25:19). When the psalmist wrote Psalm 95, he knew firsthand what this kind of rest in Palestine meant, and he still looked for "rest." So this is not what the author of Hebrews had in mind.

Buchanan has a long note on rest in which he surveys a number of opinions and rejects all spiritualizing interpretations. He thinks that many scholars read their own ideas into "rest"; and he thinks it impossible for the word to be used in a nonnational, nonmaterial sense: "They were probably expecting a rest that was basically of the same nature as Israelites had anticipated all along" (in loc.). But surely this is precisely what the author is rejecting. He knew that Israel had been in its own land for centuries. There had been quite long periods of peace and independence. Yet the promise of rest still remained unfulfilled.

Jesus spoke of quite another kind of rest—rest for the souls of men (Matt 11:28–30). This is nearer to what the author means. We might also notice an idea of the rabbis. The Mishnah explains the use of Psalm 92 (a psalm headed "A Psalm: A Song for the Sabbath") in these terms: "A Psalm, a song for the time that is to come, for the day that shall be all Sabbath and rest in the life everlasting" (*Tamid* 7:4). This is the kind of rest the author refers to, though his idea is not the rabbinic one. He links rest with the original Sabbath, with what God did when he finished Creation and what Christians are called into. This, then, is a highly original view, not simply an old idea refurbished. The author sees the rest as for "the people of God"—an expression found elsewhere in the NT only in 11:25 (though 1 Peter 2:10 is similar, and expressions like "my people" occur several times). In the OT "the people of God" is the nation of Israel, but in the NT it signifies believers. The rest the author writes about is for such people. Others cannot enter into it. This is not so much on account of a law or rule denying them entrance as that they shut themselves out by disobedience and unbelief.

10 We now have a description of at least part of what the rest means. The writer reverts to the word for rest he has been using earlier instead of the "Sabbath-rest" of v.9. To enter rest means to cease from one's own work, just as God ceased from his. There are uncertainties here. Some think the reference is to Jesus, who would certainly fit the description except for the "anyone" (which is a reasonable interpretation of the Gr.). But the general reference is there, and we must take it to refer to the believer.

The question then arises whether the rest takes place here and now, or (as Kent, for example, holds) after death, as seen in Revelation 14:13: "Blessed are the dead who die in the Lord . . . they will rest from their labor, for their deeds will follow them." Bruce thinks it is "an experience which they do not enjoy in their present mortal life, although it belongs to them as a heritage, and by faith they may live in the good of it here and now" (in loc.). I should reverse his order and say that they live in it here and now by faith, but what they know here is not the full story. That will be revealed in the hereafter. There is a sense in which to enter Christian salvation means to cease from one's works and rest securely on what Christ has done. And there is a sense in which the works of the believer, works done in Christ, have about them that completeness and sense of fulfillment that may fitly be classed with the rest in question.

Notes

---

1 There is a variety of constructions with ἐπαγγελία (*epangelia*, "promise"). The genitive may denote the one who makes the promise (Rom 4:20), the one to whom the promise is given (Rom 15:8), or the thing promised (Heb 9:15). Or the genitive "of promise" may be added to a noun, as in "land of promise" = "promised land" (11:9). This seems to be the only place where a following infinitive gives the content of the promise. The tense of ὑστερηκέναι (*hysterēkenai*, "fallen short") is perfect, which points to a permanent condition. It is not a past defeat or a present momentary failure but a continuing failure.

3 Καίτοι (*kaitoi*) is rare in the NT (John 4:2; Acts 14:17). The use here with a following genitive absolute is not classical. The meaning is "and yet."

The writer does not use κτίσις (*ktisis*), the usual word for "creation," but καταβολή (*katabolē*), which means a "throwing down." Among other things it is used of laying foundations; and in the NT it is generally used, as here, of the foundation of the world and thus the Creation.

7 Ἐν Δαυίδ (*en Dauid*, "in David") is an example of the instrumental ἐν (*en*). God used David as his means or instrument. David is not mentioned as the author of this psalm in the Hebrew, but he is in the LXX.

9 Ἄρα (*ara*) is found in Hebrews only again at 12:8. It does not begin a clause in the classics as it does quite often in the NT. It is an inferential particle meaning "so, as a result."

D. *Exhortation to Enter the Rest*

4:11–13

[11]Let us, therefore, make every effort to enter that rest, so that no one will fall by following their example of disobedience.
[12]For the word of God is living and active. Sharper than any double-edged sword, it penetrates even to dividing soul and spirit, joints and marrow; it judges the thoughts and attitudes of the heart. [13]Nothing in all creation is hidden from God's sight. Everything is uncovered and laid bare before the eyes of him to whom we must give account.

The idea of the rest of God is not simply a piece of curious information not readily accessible to the rank and file of Christians. It is a spur to action. So the writer proceeds to exhort his readers to make that rest their own.

11 It is possible that this verse should be attached to the preceding paragraph but it seems meant to introduce an exhortation based on the penetrating power of the Word of God. Notice that the writer includes himself with his readers in urging a quick and serious effort to enter the rest "so that no one will fall by following their example of disobedience." Paul refers to the same generation to hammer home a similar lesson, and he regards the wilderness happenings as types (1 Cor 10:1–12; cf. *typikōs*, "examples," v.11). These earlier people had perished. Let the readers beware!

12 "The word of God" means anything that God utters and particularly the word that came through Jesus Christ. He is called "the Word" in John 1:1, but that is not the thought here (though there have been exegetes who have taken this line). The comparison with a sharp sword and its penetration into human personality shows that it is not the incarnate Word that is in mind. "Living and active" shows that there is a dynamic quality about God's revelation. It does things. Specifically it penetrates and, in this capacity, is likened to a "double-edged sword" (for the sword, cf. Isa 49:2; Eph 6:17; Rev 19:15; and for the double-edged idea, cf. Rev 1:16; 2:12).

The Word of God is unique. No sword can penetrate as it can. We should not take the reference to "soul" and "spirit" as indicating a "dichotomist" over against a "trichotomist" view of man, nor the reference to "dividing" to indicate that the writer envisaged a sword as slipping between them. Nor should we think of the sword as splitting off "joints" and "marrow." What the author is saying is that God's Word can reach to the innermost recesses of our being. We must not think that we can bluff our way out of anything, for there are no secrets hidden from God. We cannot keep our thoughts to ourselves. There may also be the thought that the whole of man's nature, however we divide it, physical as well as nonmaterial, is open to God. With "judges" we move to legal terminology. The Word of God passes judgment on men's feelings (*enthymēseōn*) and on their thoughts (*ennoiōn*). Nothing evades the scope of this Word. What man holds as most secret he finds subject to its scrutiny and judgment.

13 Here the same truth is expressed in different imagery. This time the impossibility of hiding anything from God is illustrated by the thought of nakedness. "Nothing in all creation," or "no created being" (*ktisis* means "the act of creating" and then "a created being," "a creature"), remains invisible to God. "Uncovered" renders *gymna*, a word used of the soul being without the body (2 Cor 5:3), of a bare kernel of grain (1 Cor 15:37), or of a body without clothing (Acts 19:16). Here it means that all things are truly uncovered before God. The word rendered "laid bare" (*trachēlizō*) is an unusual one, found here only in the NT and not very common outside it. It is obviously connected with the neck (*trachēlos*), but just how is not clear. It was used of wrestlers who had a hold that involved gripping the neck and was such a powerful hold that it brought victory. So the term can mean "to prostrate" or "overthrow." Those who accept this meaning render this verse in this way: "All things are naked and prostrate before his eyes."

Most scholars, however, think a meaning like "exposed" is required. Yet it is not easy to see how it is to be obtained. It has been suggested that the wrestler exposed the face or neck of his foe by his grip. While this may be so, it entails reading something into the situation. Another suggestion is the bending back of the head of a sacrificial victim to expose the throat. Unfortunately, no example of the word used in this way is attested. In the end we must probably remain unsatisfied. Clearly the author is saying that no one can keep anything hidden from God, but the metaphor by which he brings out this truth is not clear.

The verse contains yet another difficulty, namely, the precise meaning of its closing words. KJV renders them "him with whom we have to do," and this may be right. But the expression is used of accounting, and it seems more likely that NIV's "him to whom we must give account" is correct. Nothing is hidden from God, and in the end we must give account of ourselves to him. The combination makes a powerful reason for heeding the exhortation and entering into the rest by our obedience.

Notes

---

13 The problem is that there is no verb in the expression πρὸς ὃν ἡμῖν ὁ λόγος (*pros hon hēmin ho logos*), while both πρός (*pros*) and λόγος (*logos*) can have more than one meaning. "To whom we must give account" takes the most natural meaning of *pros* ("to") and is supported by a good deal of the exegesis of the Greek fathers and by the fact that *logos* is often used in the papyri in the sense "account," "reckoning" (see MM, s.v.). "With whom we have to do" can claim support from LXX (1 Kings 2:14; 2 Kings 9:5).

IV. A Great High Priest

One of the major insights of this epistle is that Jesus is our great High Priest. The author proceeds to reinforce his exhortation to enter the rest with a reminder of the character of our High Priest. Jesus is one with his people and for them he offers the perfect sacrifice. This is seen largely in terms of the Day of Atonement ceremonies in which the role of the high priest (and not simply any priest) was central.

A. *Our Confidence*

4:14–16

[14]Therefore, since we have a great high priest who has gone through the heavens, Jesus the Son of God, let us hold firmly to the faith we profess. [15]For we do not have a high priest who is unable to sympathize with our weaknesses, but we have one who has been tempted in every way, just as we are—yet was without sin. [16]Let us then approach the throne of grace with confidence, so that we may receive mercy and find grace to help us in our time of need.

The first point is that Jesus knows our human condition. It is not something he has heard about, so to speak, but something he knows; for he, too, was man. We may approach him confidently because he knows our weakness.

14 Our confidence rests on Jesus. He is "a great high priest," a title that suggests his superiority to the Levitical priests ("high priest" in Heb. is lit. "great priest"; the author's usage is not common in the OT, though it does occur there). Jesus has "gone through the heavens." The Jews sometimes thought of a plurality of heavens, as in Paul's reference to "the third heaven" (2 Cor 12:2) or the Talmud's reference to seven heavens (*Hagigah* 12b). The thought is that Jesus has gone right through to the supreme place. His greatness is further emphasized by the title "Son of God." All this is the basis for an exhortation to hold firmly to our profession.

15 Our High Priest has entered into our weakness and so can sympathize meaningfully with us. He "has been tempted . . . just as we are" (*kath' homoiotēta*) may mean "in the same way as we are tempted" or "by reason of his likeness to us"; both are true. There is another ambiguity at the end of the verse where the Greek means "apart from sin." This may mean that Jesus was tempted just as we are except that we sin and he did not. But it may also mean that he had a knowledge of every kind of temptation except that which comes from actually having sinned. There are supporters for each interpretation. But it may be that the writer was not trying to differentiate between the two. At any rate his words can profitably be taken either way. The main point is that, though Jesus did not sin, we must not infer that life was easy for him. His sinlessness was, at least in part, an earned sinlessness as he gained victory after victory in the constant battle with temptation that life in this world entails. Many have pointed out that the Sinless One knows the force of temptation in a way that we who sin do not. We give in before the temptation has fully spent itself; only he who does not yield knows its full force.

16 Having this High Priest gives confidence. So the writer exhorts his readers to approach God boldly. The word "us" does away with the mediation of earthly priests. In view of what our great High Priest has done, there is no barrier. *We* can approach God. "The throne of grace" occurs only here in the NT. It points both to the sovereignty of God and to God's love to men. The rabbis sometimes speak of a "throne of mercy" to which God goes from "the throne of judgment" when he spares people (Lev R 29. 3, 6, 9, 10). The idea here is not dissimilar, all the more so since the writer goes on to speak of receiving mercy. We need mercy because we have failed so often, and we need grace because service awaits us in which we need God's help. And help is what the writer says we get—the help that is appropriate to the time, i.e., "timely help." The writer is urging a bold approach. Christians should not be tentative because they have the great High Priest in whom they can be confident. His successful traverse of the heavens points to his power to help, and his fellow-feeling with our weakness points to his sympathy with our needs. In the light of this, what can hold us back?

B. *The Qualities Required in High Priests*

5:1–4

> [1]Every high priest is selected from among men and is appointed to represent them in matters related to God, to offer gifts and sacrifices for sins. [2]He is able to deal gently with those who are ignorant and are going astray, since he himself is subject to weakness. [3]This is why he has to offer sacrifices for his own sins, as well as for the sins of the people.
>
> [4]No one takes this honor upon himself; he must be called by God, just as Aaron was.

The author now directs his readers to the qualities required in the well-known institution of high priests, though he confines his attention to the Aaronic priesthood in the LXX and does not consider contemporary Jewish priests who fell far short of the ideal. He shows that the necessary qualifications include oneness with the people, compassion, and appointment by God. Then he goes on to show that Christ had these qualifications.

1 The author proposes to explore something of the nature of high priesthood and begins by showing that it has both a manward and a Godward reference. It is of the essence of priesthood that the priest has community of nature with those he represents. But his work is "in matters related to God," specifically in offering "gifts and sacrifices for sins." These two are sometimes differentiated as cereal and animal offerings. It seems more likely, however, that the writer is summing up the priestly function of offering.

2 It is not easy to translate *metriopathein* (NIV, "to deal gently with"). It refers to taking the middle course between apathy and anger. A true high priest is not indifferent to moral lapses; neither is he harsh. He "is able" to take this position only because he himself shares in the same "weakness" as the sinners on whom he has compassion. The word may denote physical or moral frailty, and the following words show that in the case of the usual run of high priests the latter is included. The earthly high priest is at one with his people in their need for atonement and forgiveness.

3 The high priest is required to make offerings for himself just as for his people. For the Day of Atonement it was prescribed that the high priest present a bull "for his own sin offering" (Lev 16:11). And in the first century, as he laid his hands on the head of the animal, he would say, "O God, I have committed iniquity and transgressed and sinned before thee, I and my house and the children of Aaron, thy holy people. O God, forgive, I pray, the iniquities and transgressions and sins which I have committed and transgressed and sinned before thee, I and my house" (M *Yoma* 4:2). Only then was he able to minister on behalf of the people. In the matter of sins and of sacrifices the priest must regard himself in exactly the same way he regards the people. His case is identical with theirs.

4 The negative statement immediately refutes any thought that a man can take the initiative in being made high priest. It is an honor to be a high priest (cf. Jos. Antiq. III, 188 [viii. 1]). The only way to be made high priest is by divine appointment, and the appointment of Aaron sets the pattern (Exod 28:1–3). In point of fact, no other call to be high priest is recorded in Scripture, though we might reason that the call to Aaron was not simply personal but also included his family and descendants. At any rate, the Bible records disasters that befell those who took it upon themselves to perform high priestly duties, as in the cases of Korah (Num 16), Saul (1 Sam 13:8ff.), and Uzziah (2 Chron 26:16ff.).

Notes

3 Περί (*peri*) sometimes comes very close in meaning to ὑπέρ (*hyper*), as in the first two instances here. The meaning must be "on behalf of" or "in the place of."

C. *Christ's Qualifications as High Priest*

5:5–11

5So Christ also did not take upon himself the glory of becoming a high priest. But
God said to him,

"You are my Son;
today I have become your Father."

6And he says in another place,

"You are a priest forever,
in the order of Melchizedek."

7During the days of Jesus' life on earth, he offered up prayers and petitions with
loud cries and tears to the one who could save him from death, and he was heard
because of his reverent submission. 8Although he was a son, he learned obedience
from what he suffered 9and, once made perfect, he became the source of eternal
salvation for all who obey him 10and was designated by God to be high priest in
the order of Melchizedek.
11We have much to say about this, but it is hard to explain because you are slow
to learn.

Having made clear what is required in high priests, the author shows that Christ has these qualifications. Moreover, he shows that Christ is both Priest and King, which goes beyond the view expressed in some Jewish writings that there will be two messiahs, one of Aaron and another of David. No other NT writer speaks of Jesus as a high priest. It is a highly original way of looking at him.

5–6 Christ has the qualification of being called by God. There is perhaps a hint at his obedience in the use of the term "the Christ" (*ho Christos*) rather than the human name "Jesus." He who was God's own Christ did not take the glory on himself (cf.

John 8:54). The writer cites two passages, the first being Psalm 2:7 (cf. 1:5). He will later argue that Jesus ministers in the heavenly sanctuary. Accordingly, it is important that Jesus be seen to be the Son, one who has rights in heaven.

The second citation is from Psalm 110:4. The first verse of this psalm is often applied to Jesus (e.g., 1:13), but this appears to be the first time the Melchizedek passage is used in this way. The psalm says, "You are a priest forever," which is the first use of the term "priest" in this epistle (a term the author will use fourteen times, out of thirty-one in NT; next most frequent use is in Luke—five times). The author of Hebrews uses it of priests generally (7:14; 8:4), of the Levitical priests (7:20, etc.), of Melchizedek (7:1, 3), and of Christ (5:6; 7:11, 15, 17, 21; 10:21). When it is used of Christ, it seems to differ but little from "high priest." It is a powerful way of bringing out certain aspects of Christ's saving work for men. All that a priest does in offering sacrifice for men Christ does. But whereas they do it only symbolically, he really effects atonement.

"Forever" is another contrast. Other priests have their day and pass away. Not Christ! His priesthood abides. He has no successor (a fact that will be brought out later). He is a priest "of the same kind as Melchizedek" (J. C. Ward). Most translations render this "of the order of Melchizedek," but this is incorrect. There was no succession of priests from Melchizedek and thus no "order." Jesus, however, was a priest of this kind—not like Aaron and his successors.

7 The author turns to the second qualification—Jesus' oneness with mankind. In realistic language he brings out the genuineness of Jesus' humanity. Commentators agree that the writer is referring to the agony in Gethsemane, but his language does not fit into any of our accounts. It seems that he may have had access to some unrecorded facts. It is also possible that he wants us to see that there were other incidents in Jesus' life that fit into this general pattern. He speaks of "the days of his flesh," which NIV renders "Jesus' life on earth." But the use of the word "flesh" (*sarx*) is probably meant to draw attention to the weakness that characterizes this life.

"Prayers and petitions" (the latter word [*hiketērias*] appears only here in the NT) point to dependence on God, who alone can save from death. The "loud cries and tears" are not mentioned in the Gethsemane accounts, though there is no reason for thinking that they had no part in the incident. Westcott quotes a rabbinic saying: "There are three kinds of prayers, each loftier than the preceding: prayer, crying, and tears. Prayer is made in silence: crying with raised voice; but tears overcome all things ('there is no door through which tears do not pass')" (in loc.).

There are difficulties at the end of v.7. The word "heard" (*eisakoustheis*) is usually taken to mean that the prayer was answered, not simply noted. Most interpreters agree. But they also contend that the prayer must have been answered in the terms in which it was asked. The problem, then, is that Jesus prayed, "Take this cup from me" (Mark 14:36); but he still died. Some see the solution in holding that "from death" (*ek thanatou*) means "out of the state of death," whereas *apo thanatou* would be needed for "deliverance away from dying." This is ingenious; but the usage of the prepositions does not support it. Others draw attention to the word rendered "reverent submission" (*eulabeia,* used again in the NT only at 12:28). As it can mean "fear" as well as "reverence," or "godly fear," it has been suggested that we might understand the verse thus: "He was heard and delivered from the fear of death." This, however, does seem to be reading something into the text. Another solution is that the prayer was not that Jesus should not die but that he should not die in Gethsemane ("If Christ had died in the Garden, no greater calamity could possibly have fallen on mankind," Hewitt, in loc.). This, however, seems artificial and has not gained much support.

All in all, it seems much better to remember that Jesus' prayer was not simply a petition that he should not die, because he immediately said, "Yet not what I will, but what you will" (Mark 14:36). The important thing about answered prayer is that God does what brings about the end aimed at, not what corresponds exactly to the words of the petitioner. In this case the prayer was that the will of God be done, and this has precedence over the passing of the cup from Jesus. Since the cup had to be drunk, it was drunk! But the significant point is that the Son *was* strengthened to do the will of the Father. Yet another solution is to take some of the words over into the next verse. This involves inserting a full stop after "death" and then combining the rest as follows: "Having been heard because of his reverent submission, although he was a son, he learned obedience from what he suffered." This, however, seems unnatural and puts too much weight on v.8.

8 We should take these words in the sense of "son though he was" rather than "although he was *a* son." It is the quality of sonship that is emphasized. Again, it is the fate of sons to suffer (12:7), but the writer does not say "because he was a son" but "although . . . ." Jesus' stature was such that one would not have expected him to suffer. But he did suffer and in the process learned obedience. This, startling though it is, does not mean that Jesus passed from disobedience to obedience. Rather, he learned obedience by actually obeying. There is a certain quality involved when one has performed a required action—a quality that is lacking when there is only a readiness to act. Innocence differs from virtue.

9 Here we must make a similar comment about Jesus' being "made perfect." This does not mean that he was imperfect and that out of his imperfection he became perfect. There is a perfection that results from having actually suffered; it is different from the perfection that is ready to suffer. "He became" indicates a change of relationship that follows the perfecting. The suffering that led to the perfecting did something. It meant that Jesus became "the source of eternal salvation." This expression can be paralleled in Greek literature, though there, of course, "salvation" is understood in very different ways. "Eternal salvation" is not a very common expression (found only here in the NT; cf. Isa 45:17). "Eternal" (*aiōnios*) means "pertaining to an age (*aiōn*)." Normally the word refers to the age to come and so means "without end," though it can also be used of what is without beginning or end (9:14) or simply of what is without beginning (Rom 16:25). It is used of what does not end in connection with redemption (9:12), covenant (13:20), judgment (6:2), and inheritance (9:15). Jesus will bring people a salvation that is eternal in its scope and efficacy, a salvation that brings them into the life of the world to come. It is a nice touch that he who learned to obey brought salvation to those who obey.

10 The writer has forcefully made his point that Jesus shared our human life. He was qualified to be high priest because of his common nature with us and his compassion. Now the writer returns to the thought that Jesus was made high priest by God. What is to become his characteristic designation throughout this epistle is a title not given by men, nor assumed by himself, but conferred on him by God the Father.

11 NIV takes this verse as the opening sentence in a new paragraph, as do some commentators. This is not impossible, but on the whole it seems better to take it as completing the preceding paragraph. The writer points out that there is a good deal that could be said about his subject. It is "hard to explain," not because of some defect in the writer or the intrinsic difficulty of the subject, but because of the slowness of the learners. This leads to a new train of thought that is pursued throughout chapter 6 (we come back to Melchizedek in ch. 7). While "this" is quite general, it might be masculine and so could refer to Melchizedek or Christ. On the whole, it seems best to see a reference here to the way Melchizedek prefigures Christ. "Are" should really be "have become." It is an acquired state, not a natural one. "Slow" renders *nōthros,* which means "sluggish," "slothful." They ought to have been in a different condition. The readers of the epistle were not naturally slow learners but had allowed themselves to get lazy.

V. The Danger of Apostasy

Obviously the author was much concerned lest his readers slip back from their present state into something that amounts to a denial of Christianity. So he utters a strong warning about the dangers of apostasy. He wants his friends to be in no doubt about the seriousness of falling into it.

A. *Failure to Progress in the Faith*

5:12–14

[12]In fact, though by this time you ought to be teachers, you need someone to teach you the elementary truths of God's word all over again. You need milk, not solid food! [13]Anyone who lives on milk, being still an infant, is not acquainted with the teaching about righteousness. [14]But solid food is for the mature, who by constant use have trained themselves to distinguish good from evil.

This little section is of special interest because it shows that the recipients of the letter were people of whom better things might have been expected. They should have been mature Christians. Since they had evidently been converted for quite some time, they ought to have made much more progress in the faith than they in fact had. The author is troubled by their immaturity.

12 The readers had been Christians for long enough to qualify as teachers. This does not necessarily mean that the letter was written to a group of teachers, for the emphasis is on progress in the faith. Those addressed had failed to go on though they had been believers long enough to know more. Christians who have really progressed in the faith ought to be able to instruct others (as 1 Peter 3:15 shows; cf. Rom 2:21). But, far from this being the case, they still need instruction, and that in elementary truths.

"Someone to teach you" stands over against "teachers" and points up the contrast. Their knowledge of the faith is minimal when it ought to have been advanced. "The elementary truths" renders an expression that is equivalent to our "ABC." It points to the real beginnings. The Greek actually means something like "the ABC of the beginning of the oracles of God." There can be no doubt as to the elementary nature of the teaching in question. Yet it is not quite clear what "the oracles of God" are.

Quite possibly the OT is meant, though some think it is the whole Jewish system. Since the expression is quite general, it seems better to take it of all that God has spoken—i.e., the divine revelation in general.

The verse ends with another strong statement about the plight of the readers. "You need milk" renders an expression that literally means "you have become having need of milk," an expression in which "you have become" is important. Once again the writer is drawing attention to the fact that his readers have moved their position. Always in the Christian life, one either moves forward or slips back. It is almost impossible to stand still. These people had not advanced; so the result was that they had gone back and had "become" beginners. The contrast between milk and solid food is found elsewhere (cf. 1 Cor 3:2, though there the word for "food" is different). "Milk" stands for elementary instruction in the Christian way. "Solid food" is, of course, more advanced instruction, the kind of teaching beginners cannot make much of but which is invaluable to those who have made some progress. What is appropriate at the early stages of the Christian life may cease to be suitable as time goes on.

13 The author explains his reference to milk and solids (the Gr. has a *gar* ["for"], which shows he is giving the reason for his preceding statement). "Anyone" (*pas*) is inclusive (*pas* allows no exception). In other words, the author is saying, "This is the way it is." The Christian occupied with elementary truths is spiritually "still an infant" and must be treated as such. He is "unskilled in the word of righteousness" (RSV), to take a translation a little more literal than NIV. The Greek *apeiros* means "without experience of" and so comes to mean "unskilled." It is uncertain what "word of righteousness" means. The problem is that both "word" and "righteousness" may be taken in more ways than one. "Word" may mean the Christian message, in which case we may wish to see "righteousness" in terms of "the righteousness of God" that is made known and made available in Christ. Or we may see "righteousness" as the right conduct God expects believers to follow. Or the author may be following up the previous metaphor and thinking of the prattling speech of the child (cf. G. Schrenk, "There is a most unusual phrase in Hb. 5:13, where *apeiros logou dikaiosynēs* implies that the infant is incapable of understanding correct, normal speech," TDNT, 2:198). The first of these suggestions scarcely seems called for by the context. Therefore I am inclined to favor the second, though agreeing that the third is quite possible.

14 Mature people (*teleioi*) need solid food. The *teleioi* in the mystery religions were the initiates. It is unlikely, however, that this is its meaning here. "But" (*de*) shows the contrast to infants in v. 13. The reference is clearly to the mature who have "trained themselves." The NT makes considerable use of metaphors from athletics and *gymnazō* means "to exercise naked," "to train." It is not easy to find a good equivalent for *hexis* in this place (NIV, "constant use"). The difficulty is that, apart from this passage, *hexis* seems to denote the quality that results from training, not the training itself ("not the process but the result, the condition which has been produced by past exercise and not the separate acts following one on another" [Westcott, in loc.]). But our uncertainty about the detail does not carry over to the main thrust of the passage. The writer is clearly saying that the mature Christian, the eater of solid food, constantly exercises himself in spiritual perception, and the result is manifest. He can "distinguish good from evil" and, therefore, the implication runs, will not be in danger of doing the wrong thing to which the readers find themselves attracted. Lacking this perception, Christian service will always be immature and partial.

B. *Exhortation to Progress*

6:1–3

[1]Therefore let us leave the elementary teachings about Christ and go on to maturity, not laying again the foundation of repentance from acts that lead to death, and of faith in God, [2]instruction about baptisms, the laying on of hands, the resurrection of the dead, and eternal judgment. [3]And God permitting, we will do so.

Since the readers were still in need of milk, we anticipate that this is what the writer will provide. Instead, he says he will leave elementary things and go on to "maturity." We expect him to introduce this with "despite your condition" or the like. Instead, we get "therefore." The reason for this may lie in the nature of what he calls "the elementary teachings." "Practically every item" in his list "could have its place in a fairly orthodox Jewish community" (Bruce, in loc.). He may have felt that to concentrate on this area would be of no help to those slipping back into Judaism. *Therefore* he went on to "solid food."

1 The writer links himself with his readers in his exhortation to leave elementary things behind and go forward. He sees "repentance from acts that lead to death" as basic. Repentance was the first thing required in the preaching of John the Baptist, Jesus, and the apostles; and it remains basic. Here it is repentance "from dead works," a phrase that has been understood to mean legalistic adherence to Jewish ways (works that could never bring life) or genuinely evil actions (actions that belong to death and not life). The latter seems preferable. Linked with this is the positive attitude of "faith in God." Faith matters immensely to the author. Though in other writings in the NT "faith" usually means faith in Christ, in this epistle it is mostly faith in God. But this means more than a conviction that there is a God. It means trusting in that God in a personal relationship. And it is not so different from faith in Christ as some suggest, because it is basic Christian teaching that God was in Christ and because the author emphasizes the reality of the Incarnation.

2 "Instruction" is in apposition to "foundation" and introduces a fresh group of subjects. "Baptisms" (here *baptismōn*) is a word usually used of purification ceremonies other than Christian baptism (9:10; Mark 7:4), and it is plural (which would be unusual for baptism). Thus it is likely that the word refers to something other than baptism. There were such purification ceremonies, or lustrations, in the Jewish religion as in most other religions of the day. Sometimes there was confusion over ritual washings (John 3:25ff.; Acts 19:1–5). It would thus be one of the elementary items of instruction that converts be taught the right approach to the various "baptisms" they would encounter.

The "laying on of hands" was a widespread practice in antiquity. Among Christians, hands were laid on new converts (Acts 8:17), on Timothy by the presbyterate (1 Tim 4:14), and on Timothy by Paul (2 Tim 1:6). This action was sometimes associated with commissioning for ministry and sometimes with the beginnings of Christian service. It seems to have been connected with the gift of the Spirit at least on some occasions (e.g., Acts 8:17–19). It is Christian beginnings, perhaps with the thought of God's gift of the Holy Spirit, that are in mind here.

"The resurrection of the dead . . . and eternal judgment" were topics that went together and were important for Jews and Christians alike. They form a reminder that this life is not everything. We are responsible people, and one day we shall rise from the dead and give account of ourselves to God. This must have been of importance to new converts in a time when many people thought of death as the end of everything.

3 This verse expresses not only a resolute determination to go ahead on these lines but also a recognition that it is only with the help of God that this can be done. We should take the words not simply as a pious nod in the direction of God but as coming out of the author's realization that without divine aid the plan he was suggesting was impossible.

Notes

1 Φερώμεθα (*pherōmetha*) pictures the Christian as "continually carried along" to maturity. God keeps bearing him up. The preposition ἐπί (*epi*, "upon," "on") is sometimes found after the verb πιστεύειν (*pisteuein*, "to believe"), but it is unusual after the noun. It will point to the fact that faith is not a self-sustaining virtue. Faith rests "on" God.

2 Most MSS read διδαχῆς (*didachēs*, "teaching," "instruction"), but a few important ones have διδαχήν (*didachēn*). With the genitive we have six qualities under the heading "foundation," whereas with the accusative (which is to be preferred) repentance and faith are regarded as foundational, and conjoined with that foundation is teaching about the other four. The word for Christian baptism is βάπτισμα (*baptisma*), but we have βαπτισμός (*baptismos*) here. This latter is used of Christian baptism in some MSS at Col 2:12, but elsewhere it is used only of other lustrations.

C. *No Second Beginning*

6:4–8

> [4]It is impossible for those who have once been enlightened, who have tasted the heavenly gift, who have shared in the Holy Spirit, [5]who have tasted the goodness of the word of God and the powers of the coming age, [6]if they fall away, to be brought back to repentance, because to their loss they are crucifying the Son of God all over again and subjecting him to public disgrace.
>
> [7]Land that drinks in the rain often falling on it and that produces a crop useful to those for whom it is farmed receives the blessing of God. [8]But land that produces thorns and thistles is worthless and is in danger of being cursed. In the end it will be burned.

The writer proceeds to underline the seriousness of apostasy from the Christian faith and, indeed, of any failure to make progress. He does this by pointing to the impossibility of making a second beginning. It is impossible for a Christian to stand still. He either progresses in the faith or slips back. And slipping back is serious; it can mean cutting oneself off from the blessings God offers. The writer is not questioning the perseverance of the saints. As he has done before, he is insisting that only those who continue in the Christian way are the saints.

4 "For" (*gar*, omitted in NIV) indicates the reasonableness of what follows: Had they really fallen away, there would be no point in talking to them. Some see in the reference to being "enlightened" a glance at baptism, for this verb was often used of baptism in the second century. But it is not attested as early as this, and so it is better to interpret the term in the light of the general usage whereby those admitted to the Christian faith are brought to that light that is "the light of the world" (John 8:12; cf. 2 Cor 4:6; 2 Peter 1:19). To abandon the gospel would be to sin against the light they had received.

"The heavenly gift" is not closely defined. Some interpret it as the holy communion, though there seems little reason for this. It would fit well with the verb "tasted," but this verb can be used metaphorically; so the point proves little. The word "gift" (*dōrea*) points to freeness but could be used of any one of a variety of gifts. The thought is of God's good gift and we cannot be more precise than this. The Holy Spirit is active among all believers and for that matter to some extent beyond the church, in his work of "common grace." It is clear that some activity of the Spirit is in mind. Yet once more our author does not define it closely.

5 The people in question have "tasted the goodness of the word of God." While some limit this to the gospel, there seems to be no need and no point in doing this. Any word that God has spoken is a good gift to men, and those the writer has in mind here have come to hear something of God's word to men. They have also experienced something of "the powers of the coming age." The age to come is normally the Messianic Age, and the thought is that powers proper to the coming Messianic Age are in some sense realized now for God's people. "Powers" indicates that that age puts at men's disposal powers they do not have of themselves.

6 "If they fall away" means "fall away from Christianity." The verb *parapiptō* is found only here in the NT, and its meaning is clear. The writer is envisaging people who have been numbered among the followers of Christ but now leave that company. Such cannot be brought back to repentance. Notice that he does not say "cannot be forgiven" or "cannot be restored to salvation" or the like. It is repentance that is in mind, and the writer says that it is impossible for these people to repent. This might mean that the repentance that involves leaving a whole way of life to embrace the Christian way is unique. In the nature of the case, it cannot be repeated. There is no putting the clock back. But it seems more likely that the reference is to a repentance that means leaving the backsliding into which the person has fallen. He cannot bring himself to this repentance. The marginal reading "while they are crucifying the Son of God" is attractive, but in the end it really amounts to a truism and scarcely seems adequate. The tense, however, does convey the idea of a continuing attitude.

It is probable that we should take the verb rendered "are crucifying . . . all over again" (*anastaurountas*) simply as "crucifying." Elsewhere it seems always to have this meaning. The author is saying that those who deny Christ in this way are really taking their stand among those who crucified Jesus. In heart and mind they make themselves one with those who put him to death on the cross at Calvary. *Heautois* ("to themselves"; NIV, "to their loss") points to this inward attitude. The final words of v.6 stress what this attitude means.

There has been much discussion of the significance of this passage. Some think that the author is speaking about genuine Christians who fall away and that he denies that they may ever come back. This view sets the writer of the epistle in contradiction with other NT writers for whom it is clear that the perseverance of the saints is something that comes from God and not from their own best efforts (e.g., John 6:37; 10:27–29). Others think that the case is purely hypothetical. Because the writer does not say that this has ever happened, they infer that it never could really happen and that to put it this way makes the warning more impressive. But unless the writer is speaking of something that could really happen, it is not a warning about anything. Granted, he does not say that anyone has apostatized in this way, nevertheless, he surely means that someone could, and he does not want his readers to do so. A third possibility is that the writer is talking about what looks very much like the real thing but lacks something. The case of Simon Magus springs to mind. He is said to have believed, to have been baptized, and to have continued with Philip (Acts 8:13). Presumably he shared in the laying on of hands and the gift given by it. Yet after all this Peter could say to him, "Your heart is not right before God. . . . you are full of bitterness and captive to sin" (Acts 8:21–23). The writer is saying that when people have entered into the Christian experience far enough to know what it is all about and have then turned away, then, as far as they themselves are concerned, they are crucifying Christ. In that state they cannot repent. (For a good discussion of the various interpretations, see Kent, in loc.)

7 The process is illustrated from agriculture. There is land that frequently drinks in rain and as a result brings forth a crop. The rain comes first. The land does not produce the crop of itself. The spiritual parallel should not be overlooked. The word translated "a crop" (*botanē*) is a general term for herbage; it does not mean any specific crop. "Useful to those for whom it is farmed" means that the beneficiaries are people in general and not only those who actually work on the farm. This land, then, receives God's blessing.

8 We should not miss the point that this is the same land as in v.7. We should probably place a comma at the end of v.7 and proceed thus: "but if it produces . . ." or "but when it produces . . . ." The reference to producing "thorns and thistles" reminds us inevitably of the curse of Genesis 3:17ff.—a curse on that very creation of which it had been said, "God saw all that he had made, and it was very good" (Gen 1:31). This land then, producing only what is worthless, awaits the curse. "Is in danger of being cursed" might give the impression that the land came close to being cursed but just escaped. The author seems rather to be saying that at the moment of which he speaks the curse has not yet fallen, certain though it is. Such a field in the end "will be burned." Some commentators think the writer knew little of agriculture, for the burning of the field was not a curse but rather a source of blessing as it got rid of the weeds and so prepared for a good crop. But whatever his knowledge of farming, he had a valid point. Land that produced nothing but weeds faced nothing but fire. The warning to professing Christians whose lives produce only the equivalent of weeds is plain.

Notes

---

6 In the verb ἀνασταυρόω (*anastauroō*) the prefix ἀνα (*ana*) is usually taken in the sense of "up," "to lift up on a cross." In other compounds *ana* sometimes signifies "again," and this is why some take the verb here to mean recrucify. But as this sense is not attested elsewhere, it seems better to take it as "crucify."

D. *Exhortation to Perseverance*

6:9–12

[9]Even though we speak like this, dear friends, we are confident of better things in your case—things that accompany salvation. [10]God is not unjust; he will not forget your work and the love you have shown him as you have helped his people and continue to help them. [11]We want each of you to show this same diligence to the very end, in order to make your hope sure. [12]We do not want you to become lazy, but to imitate those who through faith and patience inherit what has been promised.

The preceding sections have contained salutary warnings about the dangers of apostasy. The readers have had it made clear to them that they must make progress along the Christian way or suffer disaster. There are no other possibilities. Now the writer goes on to indicate that he has confidence in his correspondents. He has felt it necessary to warn them. But he does not really think they will fall away. So he speaks encouragingly and warmly, at the same time using the occasion to exhort them to go forward.

9 For the only time in the epistle the writer here addresses the readers as "beloved" (*agapētoi;* NIV, "dear friends"). He has a tender concern for his correspondents, even though he has had to say some critical things about them. "We are confident" (which is the first word in the Gr.) carries a note of certainty: "We are sure." He is sure that there are "better" things about them than the kind of disaster he has been speaking about. The writer is fond of the word "better" (see commentary on 1:4). He does not say what these good things are better than, but it is clearly implied that it is the cursing and the like that he has been speaking of. So he goes on and says, "And having salvation" (*echomena sōtērias*). This unusual expression might mean "things that lead to salvation" or "things that follow from salvation." Perhaps we should leave it general as NIV: "things that accompany salvation." The words "even though we speak like this" come last in the Greek and they simply look back. The "we" of course is a plural of authorship and means "I." The writer has been giving some solemn warnings and reminds the readers of them again. But he does not think that in the end they will be caught in the condemnation he refers to.

10 "For" (*gar,* which for some reason NIV does not translate) introduces the grounds for his confidence—a confidence that rests basically on God's constancy. In a masterly understatement the writer refers to God as "not unjust." It is the character of God, the perfectly just judge of all, that gives rise to confidence. This God will not forget what the readers have done. The statement about his remembrance of their work is not an intrusion of a doctrine of salvation by works. But the Christian profession of the readers had been more than formal and they had shown in changed lives what that profession meant. This, the writer is saying, would not go unnoticed with God. He adds, "And the love you have shown him" (lit., "to his name"). "Name" in antiquity summed up all that the person was. The following words show that it is deeds of kindness to men that are in mind. Such deeds, proceeding from loving hearts as they do, demonstrate that the doers have a real affection for God. These Christians have served God's people in the past and they continue with this kind of service. Thus they manifest the love for man that is a proof of real love for God (1 John 4:19–21).

11 "We want" translates a verb that refers to strong desire. The writer was passionately concerned for his friends, a concern that has already appeared in v.9 ("dear friends"; lit., "beloved"), and which we see again in his desire for "each" of them. Not one is excluded. He calls on them to show "this same diligence." The past had set a standard, and he looks for it to be maintained "to the very end." Persistently he brings before them the importance of perseverance. "In order to make your hope sure" renders a somewhat unusual expression (lit., "to the fullness of the hope"). The term *plērophoria* can mean "full assurance" (as in 1 Thess 1:5, where NIV has "deep conviction"). But here it is rather the full development of the hope. Notice that in these verses we have love (v.10) and faith (v.12) as well as hope. The three are often joined in the NT (Rom 5:2–5; 1 Cor 13:13; Gal 5:5–6; Col 1:4–5; 1 Thess 1:3; 5:8; Heb 10:22–24; 1 Peter 1:21–22). It was evidently an accepted Christian practice to link just these three. In the twentieth century we would easily think of faith and love for a similar short list. But hope? Clearly it had a greater significance for the early church than it has for us. Hope is important. Probably no movement has ever gripped the hearts of people if it did not give them hope.

12 The Greek does not have the verb "want" (as NIV), but the conjunction *hina* denotes purpose, i.e., "in order that you do not become lazy." The readers are to "imitate" those who get the promises, "imitate" and not simply "follow." Faith is important throughout this epistle, and it is not surprising to have it included here as a most important part of the Christian life. It is probably faith in God, as is usual in this epistle, that is meant here. "Patience," or "longsuffering," points to a quality of being undismayed in difficulties. Faith has a steadfastness about it that sees it through whatever difficulties present themselves.

The verb "inherit" is often used in the NT where there is no strict notion of inheritance, as here. It simply means "to have sure possession of" without specifying the means. It is uncertain whether the allusion is to the great ones of the past (as in ch. 11) or to outstanding contemporaries. Perhaps the present tense tips the scale in favor of those then living. The readers had good examples. Let them follow them.

E. *God's Promise Is Sure*

6:13–20

13When God made his promise to Abraham, since there was no one greater for
him to swear by, he swore by himself, 14saying, "I will surely bless you and give
you many descendants." 15And so after waiting patiently, Abraham received what
was promised.

16Men swear by someone greater than themselves, and the oath confirms what
is said and puts an end to all argument. 17Because God wanted to make the
unchanging nature of his purpose very clear to the heirs of what was promised, he
confirmed it with an oath. 18God did this so that, by two unchangeable things in
which it is impossible for God to lie, we who have fled to take hold of the hope
offered to us may be greatly encouraged. 19We have this hope as an anchor for
the soul, firm and secure. It enters the inner sanctuary behind the curtain, 20where
Jesus, who went before us, has entered on our behalf. He has become a high priest
forever, in the order of Melchizedek.

Abraham is a splendid example of what the author has in mind. Though that patriarch had God's promise, he had to live for many years in patient expectation with nothing to go on except that God had promised. But that was enough. God is utterly reliable. What he has promised he will certainly perform. But we must wait patiently, for he does it all in his own good time, not in ours.

13 The author is fond of Abraham, whom he refers to ten times, a total exceeded only by Luke (fifteen) and John (eleven). Abraham is the supreme example of one who continued to trust God and obey him even though the circumstances were adverse and gave little support to faith. The NT often speaks of God's promise in connection with this man (Acts 3:25; 7:17; Rom 4:13; Gal 3:8,14,16,18). His greatness and the frequency with which God's promise was linked with his name made him a natural example for the author. It is the fact of the promise rather than its content that the author appeals to—especially to the fact that God confirmed it with an oath. Westcott (in loc.) points out that the oath in itself implies delay in fulfilling the promise. If God had been about to fulfill it immediately, there would have been no place for an oath. So from the first Abraham was faced with the prospect of waiting in hope and faith. God swore the oath by himself, a point mentioned by Philo (*Legum Allegoriae* 3.203). In the Talmud we read, "R. Eleazar said: Moses said before the Holy One, blessed be He: Sovereign of the Universe, hadst Thou sworn to them by the heaven and the earth, I would have said, Just as the heaven and earth can pass away, so can Thy oath pass away. Now, however, Thou hast sworn to them by Thy great name: just as Thy great name endures for ever and ever, so Thy oath is established for ever and ever" (*Berakoth* 32a; the oath is that mentioned in Exod 32:13). So here it is significant that God swore by himself. But for the present the author says no more than that there was no one greater to swear by.

14 The quotation is from Genesis 22:17. (That it was an oath is attested in Gen 22:16.) The few slight changes from the LXX do not affect the sense. "I will surely bless you" reflects the Hebrew infinitive absolute, which conveys the ideas of emphasis and certainty. This is the first occurrence of the word "bless" in this epistle. The author will use it seven times in all, as many as in all the Pauline epistles put together (and exceeded in the NT only by Luke [thirteen times]). Sometimes it is used of people, when it means "invoke blessings on" or sometimes "give thanks." But where God is the subject, the meaning is "bless," "prosper." Here the blessing refers to descendants who would form a great nation, possess the land, and in due course be the source of blessing to others.

15 "So" should not be taken too closely with "waiting patiently." It is not so much "waiting thus" as "thus [confident in God's promise] he waited patiently." Abraham was content to await God's time for the fulfillment of the promise. This meant real patience, because Isaac was not born till twenty-five years after the promise was first given (Gen 12:4; 21:5) and long after Sarah could have been expected to bear children. Abraham's grandchildren were not born for another sixty years (Gen 25:26), only fifteen years before his death (Gen 25:7). The complete fulfillment of the promise, of course, could not take place within his lifetime (a nation cannot be born so quickly). But enough happened for the writer to say, "Abraham received what was promised."

We should possibly bear in mind also John 8:56: "Abraham rejoiced at the thought of seeing my day; he saw it and was glad." In that sense Abraham saw the fuller working out of the promise. But the important thing in the present context is that Abraham had to be patient if he was to see anything in the way of fulfillment. He was patient and he did see it. So the readers are encouraged to be patient and await God's action. He does not go back on his promises. He is completely reliable. But he works in his own way and time, not ours.

16 The importance of the oath is now brought out. When a man swears an oath, he makes a solemn affirmation of the truth of his words before a greater who presumably will punish any misuse of his name if a false statement is made. The Greek here could mean "something greater." Yet NIV is surely right in preferring the masculine "someone greater."

Among people an oath "puts an end to all argument." The writer makes use of the expression *eis bebaiōsin*, which Deissmann calls an "Egyptian legal formula, persistent through hundreds of years" and which he says "is still a technical expression for a legal *guarantee*" (Deiss BS, p. 107). It was widely used in the papyri, and there is no doubt that the writer is making use of a well-known expression to bring out his point that an oath, as commonly understood, is the end of a matter. It is an authoritative word guaranteed by the highest authority.

17 We now turn from human oaths to the oath God swore to Abraham. God had no need to swear an oath. Nevertheless, he did it to make absolutely clear to his servant that his promise would be fulfilled. Abbott-Smith says that the verb NIV translates "wanted" (*boulomenos*) implies "more strongly than *thelō* . . . the deliberate exercise of volition" (s. v.). The operation of God's will is stressed and is further brought out by the reference to "the unchanging nature of his purpose" (where *boulē*, "purpose," is cognate with the word "wanted"). God's will does not change. He has his purpose and he works it out. That was what the oath said.

The word rendered "confirmed" is sometimes translated "interposed" or the like. *Mesiteuō* has the idea of "mediate," which often means "interpose," "stand between." But here the idea is rather that of "stand as guarantor." God appears, so to speak, in two characters, the giver of the promise and then its guarantor. "The only possible translation is 'to guarantee,' 'to vouch for.' In giving the promise, God is as it were one of the parties. But with His oath, and as its Guarantor,. . . He puts Himself on neutral ground and pledges the fulfillment of the promise" (Oepke, TDNT, 4:620). We should not miss the reference to "the heirs." The promise was not confined to Abraham or even to him and his immediate family. Since he was to have a mighty multitude of heirs, it was to all those who follow him, which includes not merely physical Israel but also his spiritual descendants (Gal 3:7). The readers of the epistle must number themselves among those to whom the oath referred.

18 "So that" (*hina*) introduces the purpose God had in swearing the oath. It gave men "two unchangeable things," the promise and the oath. Once God had spoken, it was inconceivable that either should alter. It is impossible for God to lie. At the end of the verse the sense may be as NIV, or we could understand it as "so that . . . we who have fled may have strong encouragement to lay hold on the hope." The word order favors NIV, but Héring, for one, prefers something like the second.

The writer does not specify what we have "fled" from, but the context makes it clear that he is thinking of some aspect of life in a sinful world. So far from clinging to that, he and his readers "take hold of the hope offered." Once again we see the importance of hope. It is the very antithesis of the despair that might grip us if we saw no more than a sinful world. But we do see more. We look forward to the consummation of God's great work of salvation. The word translated "offered" (*prokeimenēs*) pictures hope lying before us, spread out like some inviting prospect; and we are encouraged to go in to it.

19 While the metaphor of the anchor is widely used in antiquity, it occurs only here in the NT. The ship firmly anchored is safe from idle drifting. Its position and safety are sure. So hope is a stabilizing force for the Christian. "Soul" (*psychē*) may be the way to understand it, but the term is often used of the life of man and this seems to be the meaning here. The author is not saying simply that hope secures the "spiritual" aspect of man. He is affirming that hope forms an anchor for the whole of life. The person with a living hope has a steadying anchor in all he does. Westcott takes "firm" (*asphalēs*) to mean that hope "is undisturbed by outward influences" and "secure" (*bebaia*) as "firm in its inherent character" (in loc.). Perhaps we should not tie these qualities too tightly to the two words (which many point out are a standard expression in Gr. ethics). But the two aspects are important, and hope embraces them both.

And there is something more: hope "enters the inner sanctuary." The imagery takes us back to the tabernacle, with its "curtain" shutting off the Most Holy Place. That little room symbolized the very presence of God, but people were not allowed to enter it. But hope can, says the author. The Christian hope is not exhausted by what it sees of earthly possibilities. It reaches into the very presence of God.

20 We return to the imagery of the Day of Atonement, when the high priest entered the Most Holy Place on behalf of the people. Our forerunner, Jesus, has entered the holiest for us. This is something more than the Levitical high priest could do. Though he entered the Most Holy Place and made atonement on behalf of the people, at the end he and they were still outside. But to call Jesus our "forerunner" implies that we will follow in due course.

"On our behalf" indicates that Jesus did something for us. He not only showed the way but also atoned for us. So we come to the thought that he has become "a high priest forever, in the order of Melchizedek." The thought had been introduced in 5:6, but the author had gone on to other things. Now he comes back to that thought and proceeds to develop it.

Notes

14 This is the one place in the NT where we have the oath formula εἰ μήν (*ei mēn*) (classical ἦ μήν, *ē mēn*). This formula in oaths gives the meaning "surely," "certainly" (BAG, s. v.).

18 Some MSS have the article before θεόν (*theon*, "God"), but it should be omitted. The anarthrous form gives the thought "it is impossible for one who is God [one with the nature of God] to lie."

VI. Melchizedek

The writer has mentioned Melchizedek before and has spoken of Jesus as a priest of the Melchizedekian kind, but he has done no more than glance at the theme. Now he develops it. This is an understanding of Christ's work that is peculiar to this epistle, and in the author's hands it is very effective. He uses it to show something of the uniqueness of Christ and something of the greatness of the work he accomplished for humanity. For the Jews of his day, it would have been axiomatic that there was no priesthood other than the Aaronic. We are now shown that the Law itself proves that there is a higher priesthood than that.

A. *The Greatness of Melchizedek*

7:1–10

[1] This Melchizedek was king of Salem and priest of God Most High. He met
Abraham returning from the defeat of the kings and blessed him, [2]and Abraham
gave him a tenth of everything. First, his name means "king of righteousness"; then
also, "king of Salem" means "king of peace." [3]Without father or mother, without
genealogy, without beginning of days or end of life, like the Son of God he remains
a priest forever.

[4]Just think how great he was: Even the patriarch Abraham gave him a tenth of
the plunder! [5]Now the law requires the descendants of Levi who become priests
to collect a tenth from the people—that is, their brothers—even though their brothers are descended from Abraham. [6]This man, however, did not trace his descent
from Levi, yet he collected a tenth from Abraham and blessed him who had the
promises. [7]And without doubt the lesser person is blessed by the greater. [8]In the
one case, the tenth is collected by men who die; but in the other case, by him who
is declared to be living. [9]One might even say that Levi, who collects the tenth, paid
the tenth through Abraham, [10]because when Melchizedek met Abraham, Levi was
still in the body of his ancestor.

The writer begins with a brief notice of the one incident recorded in the life of Melchizedek, namely his meeting with Abraham as the patriarch returned from the slaughter of the five kings (Gen 14:18–20; Melchizedek is mentioned again only in Ps 110:4). He draws attention to what is known of this man and reaches some important conclusions for Christians. He sees several reasons for regarding Melchizedek as superior: he took tithes from Abraham; he blessed him; he was "without beginning of days or end of life" (v.3); he "is declared to be living" (v.8, in contrast to the Aaronic priests who die); and Levi, the ancestor of the Levitical priests, paid him tithes (being included in Abraham).

1 The writer begins his explanation of the significance of Melchizedek by referring to the incident in Genesis 14:17ff. His minor changes from the LXX do not affect the sense. First he describes Melchizedek as "king of Salem," which may mean "king of Jerusalem" ("Salem" is another name for Jerusalem in Ps 76:2). But it is curious that if the writer thought that Jerusalem was in fact where Melchizedek ministered, he does not mention the fact that Jesus suffered there. Perhaps he was not particularly interested in geography. But it is also possible that he saw Salem as some other place. Westcott (in loc.) says that in Jerome's time Salem was understood to be near Scythopolis; and, again, the LXX of Genesis 33:18 seems to identify Shechem with Salem.

Melchizedek was not only a king but a "priest of God Most High." It was not uncommon for one person to combine the roles of priest and king in antiquity. It is, however, the special characteristics of this man rather than the dual offices that are noteworthy. In Genesis 14:17–18 we read that the king of Sodom, who had suffered at the hands of the kings Abraham had just routed, went out to meet the triumphant patriarch and that Melchizedek brought out bread and wine; but the author passes over both of these facts. He concentrates on those aspects of the incident that will help him make the points he has in mind about the work of Christ. The first of them is that he "blessed him," a point he will return to in v.7.

2 Abraham gave Melchizedek a tenth of everything, i.e., of the spoils from the battle. This is another point that is elaborated later (in vv.4ff.). So far the author is simply identifying Melchizedek with his reference to the incident after the battle. Now he goes on to the significance of Melchizedek's name and title. The name, he says, means "king of righteousness." (This is a translation of the Heb. name; it might be more accurate to render it "my king is righteous," but NIV gives the sense and brings in the noun "righteousness" that features so largely in the NT vocabulary of salvation.)

Then the writer goes on to the title "king of Salem." The place name comes from the same root as *šālôm,* the Hebrew word for "peace," and it may accordingly be translated in this way. The Greek word "peace" (*eirēnē*) has about it the negative idea of the absence of war; in the NT, however, it picks up something of the fuller meaning of the Hebrew *šālôm,* which it regularly translates in the LXX. So *eirēnē* comes to signify the presence of positive blessing, the result of Christ's work for men. We are reminded of the "Prince of Peace" (Isa 9:6; righteousness in v.7 is among the qualities linked with this messianic figure). The combination of righteousness and peace is seen in Psalm 85:10. As used here, the two terms point to distinctive aspects of Christ's saving work.

3 The terms "without father" and "without mother" (*apatōr, amētōr*) are used in Greek for waifs of unknown parentage, for illegitimate children, for people who came from unimportant families, and sometimes for deities who were supposed to take their origin from one sex only. Some scholars hold that Melchizedek is viewed in the last mentioned way and is being pictured as an angelic being. But it seems much more likely that the author is proceeding along the lines that the silences of Scripture are just as much due to inspiration as are its statements. When nothing is recorded of the parentage of this man, it is not necessarily to be assumed that he had no parents but simply that the absence of the record is significant.

What was true of Melchizedek simply as a matter of record was true of Christ in a fuller and more literal sense. So the silence of the Scripture points to an important theological truth. Melchizedek is also "without genealogy," a term the writer apparently coins. Taken together, the three terms are striking, for in antiquity a priest's genealogy was considered all-important. After the Exile, certain priests whose genealogy could not be established "were excluded from the priesthood as unclean" (Neh 7:64). And just as the record says nothing of Melchizedek's genealogy, so it says nothing of his birth or death. This further silence in Scripture points the writer to another truth about Jesus—viz., that his priesthood is without end. He uses the full title of Jesus—"Son of God"—as in 4:14; 6:6; 10:29 ("my son" in 1:5; 5:5). Since the writer does not use it often, we may sense an emphasis on the high dignity of the Son of God. And it is the Son of God who is the standard, not the ancient priest-king. The writer says that Melchizedek is "made like" (*aphōmoiōmenos*) the Son of God, not that the Son of God is like Melchizedek. Thus it is not that Melchizedek sets the pattern and Jesus follows it. Rather, the record about Melchizedek is so arranged that it brings out certain truths that apply far more fully to Jesus than they do to Melchizedek. With the latter, these truths are simply a matter of record; but with Jesus they are not only historically true, they also have significant spiritual dimensions. The writer is, of course, speaking of the Son's eternal nature, not of his appearance in the Incarnation.

4 The author proceeds to bring out the greatness of Melchizedek with an argument the modern mind may find rather curious but which would have been compelling to his contemporaries. In the ancient world, it was generally recognized that there was an obligation to pay tithes to important religious functionaries. This implies a certain subjection on the part of those paying to those to whom the tithe was paid. So it was significant that Abraham paid to Melchizedek "a tenth of the plunder." This last word means literally "the top of the heap" and was used of the choicest spoils of war. From these spoils an offering would be made to the gods as a thanksgiving for victory. Abraham gave a tenth of the very best to Melchizedek. In the Greek text the subject "the patriarch" comes at the end of the sentence, giving it strong emphasis; i.e., "none less than the patriarch."

5–6a Here the meaning of the payment of the tithe is spelled out. Not only was such a payment widely customary but the law required it to be made. The writer speaks of "the descendants of Levi who become priests" as "collecting a tenth from the people." In the law it was provided that the people were to pay tithes to the Levites (Num 18:21, 24). But the Levites similarly paid tithes to the priests (Num 18:26ff.); so it could well be said that the people paid tithes to the priests. In any case there seems to be some evidence that in the first century the priests carried out the whole tithing operation, and the writer may be glancing at contemporary custom. This tithing was done by divine appointment.

The writer is strongly interested in "the law," which he mentions fourteen times. The word can denote law in general or a principle according to which one acts. But it is specially used for the law of Moses, which is the meaning here. The law required tithes to be taken of people of whom the priests were "brothers." There is a sense in which the priests had no inherent superiority. They were kin to those who gave tithes to them. They owed their ability to collect tithes to the provision made in the law and not to any natural superiority. But with Melchizedek it was different. He "did not trace his descent from Levi." Melchizedek was not simply one among a host of brothers. He was a solitary figure of grandeur. And he exacted tithes not simply from his brothers but from Abraham. His greatness stands out.

6b–7 Not only did Melchizedek exact tithes from Abraham, but he also blessed him. The giving of a blessing was a significant act in antiquity. As Calvin puts it, "Blessing is a solemn act of prayer with which one who is endowed with some outstanding public honour commends to God private individuals who are under his care" (in loc). There are senses of the word "bless" in which men "bless" God, i.e., praise him, or in which an inferior prays that God will prosper some superior. But the word is not used in such a way here. It is rather the official pronouncement given by an authorized person. When that happens, there is no denying that it proceeds from a superior: "The lesser person is blessed by the greater."

In the Genesis account Melchizedek makes no claims nor does Abraham concede anything in words. But the patriarch gave up a tenth of the spoils, thus implicitly acknowledging the superior place of Melchizedek. And Melchizedek proceeded to bless Abraham, accepting the implied superiority. The situation is clear to all parties. There is no need to spell it out. And the author is simply drawing attention to what the narrative clearly implies when he brings out the superior status of Melchizedek. Even when Abraham is seen as the one "who had the promises," Melchizedek is superior.

8 NIV is a trifle free in this verse. Rather, it reads, "And, here, mortal ['dying'] men receive tithes, but, there, one of whom it is testified that he lives." Those who receive tithes are not merely capable of dying; they do die. They are seen to die. (The present tenses of both dying and receiving coupled with the "here" at the beginning may be held to indicate that the temple system was still in operation at the time the words were written. Thus they support a date before A.D. 70 for the writing of the epistle.) "There" puts Melchizedek in strong contrast to the Aaronic priests. He is remote from this scene. The writer does not say that Melchizedek lives on but that the testimony about him is that he lives. Once more he is emphasizing the silences of Scripture to bring out his point. Scripture records nothing about the death of Melchizedek. This must be borne in mind when estimating the significance of the incident and the way the priest-king prefigures Christ.

9–10 "One might even say" translates *hōs epos eipein*, an unusual expression (not found elsewhere in the NT or LXX) that "serves to introduce a statement which may startle a reader, and which requires to be guarded from misinterpretation" (Westcott, in loc). The characteristic of Levi (and his descendants) was not that of paying but of receiving tithes. Of course, there is something of the "in-a-manner-of-speaking" about Levi's collecting of tithes just as there is in his paying of them, because he collects them not in person but through his descendants. But the startling thing is that he should be said to pay tithes at all.

When Abraham paid Melchizedek a tithe, the author sees Levi as paying it, for "Levi was still in the body of his ancestor." This is a way of speaking we find here and there in the Bible when the ancestor includes the descendants. So it was said to Rebekah, not two children but "two nations are in your womb" (Gen 25:23). Again, Paul can say, "In Adam all die" (1 Cor 15:22). Levi was thus included in the payment of the tithe (and, of course, all the priests who descended from him and whom the Hebrews esteemed so highly). The author wants his readers to be in no doubt about the superiority of Christ to any other priests and sees the mysterious figure of Melchizedek as powerfully illustrating this superiority.

Notes

1 The full name "God Most High" is rare apart from the Melchizedek incident (but see Ps 78:35). But the title "Most High" (עליון, *'ēlyôn*) is quite often used as a title for God.

3 "Forever" translates εἰς τὸ διηνεκές (*eis to diēnekes*), which occurs only in Hebrews in the NT (four times). It does not necessarily indicate duration without any end but rather duration which lasts through the circumstances indicated in the particular case. Here, however, no limit is expressed or implied and the expression thus indicates that Melchizedek's priesthood goes right on without cessation.

5 "Descended from Abraham" is rather "come out from the loins of Abraham." Ὀσφῦς (*osphys,* "the waist, "loins") is used of the place where the belt is (Mark 1:6) and hence a number of metaphorical uses emerge, mostly concerned with preparation for activity ("girding up the loins," etc.). It is also used of the place of the reproductive organs and thus, as here, with reference to a man's descendants.

9 "One might even say" renders ὡς ἔπος εἰπεῖν (*hōs epos eipein*) which BDF refers to as "the so-called infinitive absolute after ὡς" and which "is fairly common in Attic in certain formulae" (par.391a). Héring rejects the meaning "so to speak" in favor of "to give the real point"(in loc.).

B. *The Royal Priesthood of Melchizedek and of Christ*

7:11–14

[11]If perfection could have been attained through the Levitical priesthood (for on the basis of it the law was given to the people), why was there still need for another priest to come—one in the order of Melchizedek, not in the order of Aaron? [12]For when there is a change of the priesthood, there must also be a change of the law. [13]He of whom these things are said belonged to a different tribe, and no one from that tribe has ever served at the altar. [14]For it is clear that our Lord descended from Judah, and in regard to that tribe Moses said nothing about priests.

For the Jew there was an air of finality about the law; it was God's definitive word to men. Also, there was for the Jew the presumption that the Aaronic priesthood was superior to that of Melchizedek, for the law came later than Melchizedek and could be thought to be God's way of replacing all previous priesthoods. But the author points out that the priesthood of Melchizedek was spoken of in Psalm 110, well after the giving of the law. That God spoke through David about the Melchizedekian priesthood, while the Aaronic priesthood was a going concern, shows that the priests of the line of Aaron could not accomplish what a priesthood aimed at. And because the priesthood and the law went together, that meant a change in the law as well. The author sees it as significant that Jesus did not come from the priestly tribe of Levi but from the royal tribe of Judah. This fits in with the fact that Jesus' priesthood is of the order of Melchizedek and that he was king as well as priest.

11 Here "perfection" means the condition in which men are acceptable to God. The work of the priests of the line of Levi aimed at bringing about this acceptability, but our author tells us that they failed. That the psalmist speaks of another priest shows that the Levitical priests had not accomplished what they aimed at. The words in parenthesis show that the law and the priesthood were closely connected. Moffatt translates, "It was on the basis of that priesthood that the Law was enacted for the People."

We ought not think of the law and the priesthood as two quite separate things that happened to be operative at the same time among the same people. The priesthood is the very basis of the law. Without that priesthood it would be impossible for the law to operate in its fullness. Thus the declaration by the psalmist (v.17) that there would be another priest was devastating. He looked for a priest "in the order of

Melchizedek, not in the order of Aaron." The Aaronic priesthood was not succeeding and thus had to be replaced by a more effective priesthood.

12 The connection between the priesthood and the law means that a change in the one involves a change in the other. The author is speaking of more than a transference of the office of priest from one person to another. He is speaking of a change from one kind of priesthood to another. Priesthood like that of Melchizedek differs fundamentally from that after the order of Aaron. Christ is not another Aaron; he replaces Aaron with a priesthood that is both different and better. And with the Aaronic priesthood went the law that had been erected with that priesthood as its basis. Lacking that priesthood, that law had to give way. It had lost its basis. So the author says there *must* be a change of law.

13 The change in the law is seen in that Jesus did not belong to the tribe recognized by the law as the priestly tribe. His tribe was "different," which may mean no more than that it was another than the priestly tribe or that that tribe was of a different nature. It was a nonpriestly tribe. In fact, it was a royal tribe. From this tribe no one "has ever served at the altar." There is a change of tense from the perfect in the word translated "belonged" to an aorist in that rendered "served." Zuntz comments, "The differentiation is excellent; it intimates that no one of the tribe of Judah *had ever attended* to the altar (*prosesche*) and that Jesus *'has permanently a share in'* (*meteschēke,* 'belongs to') that tribe" (cited by Bruce, in loc.).

David and Solomon, who were of the tribe of Judah, are said to have offered sacrifice (2 Sam 6:12–13,17–18; 24:25; 1 Kings 3:4; 8:62ff.). But two things should be said about this. In the first place, it is possible that these kings did not do the actual ceremonial. (It is unlikely that Solomon personally offered 22,000 oxen and 120,000 sheep.) David and Solomon may have "offered" in the sense that they provided the sacrificial victims, leaving priests to perform the liturgical function. And in the second place, even if these kings did sometimes perform the actual offering, this was occasional and not their regular function. The author is speaking of the regular ministrations of a priest at the altar, and this none but the sons of Aaron did in the OT period.

14 "For" introduces the explanation of the preceding. The author calls Jesus "our Lord" again only in 13:20. Mostly his use of the term "Lord" (*kyrios*) is for the Father, but there is no doubt as to whom he means here. His verb "descended" (*anatetalken*) is unusual in this sense; and Buchanan can go as far as to say, "In none of the Old Testament usages of the verb *anatellein* was it employed to mean a 'descendant' of a certain tribe or family" (in loc.). *Anatellein* means "rise," "spring up" and may be used of the rising of a star or of the springing up of a shoot from the roots of a plant. The author may have in mind the rising of a star or, more likely, the OT prophecies about the Messiah being a shoot from the root of David (Jer 23:5 uses the cognate noun for this purpose). Here in v.14 Jesus is said to come "from Judah," this and Revelation 5:5 being the only places outside the nativity stories to say explicitly that this was his tribe. And to this tribe Moses had nothing to say about priests; the law did not envisage priests from any tribe other than Levi. That is what made the priesthood like that of Melchizedek so unusual.

Notes

11 There is dispute about the unexpected ἐπ' αὐτῆς (*ep' autēs*). We might have anticipated περὶ αὐτῆς (*peri autēs*) or ἐπ' αὐτήν (*ep' autēn*). Some take it in the sense of περὶ αὐτῆς (*peri autēs*), "about it," but it seems better to understand it as "on the basis of it" (with BAG; BDF, par. 234 [8]; NIV;etc.).

Νομοθετέω (*nomotheteō*) means "to make laws" and the passive here will have the sense "to be furnished with laws" (A-S, s.v.).

12 Ἱερωσύνη (*hierōsynē*) "priesthood" is used only in this ch. in the NT (vv.12, 24). There does not seem special significance in this, but the word is certainly unusual.

13 Ἑτέρος (*heteros*) strictly means "the other of two," and our author may be eliminating from his thinking all priesthoods but these two. But the word also sometimes means "different," and this may be his meaning.

C. *Christ's Priesthood Superior Because of:*

1. *His life*

7:15–19

> [15]And what we have said is even more clear if another priest like Melchizedek appears, [16]one who has become a priest not on the basis of a regulation as to his ancestry but on the basis of the power of an indestructible life. [17]For it is declared:
>
> "You are a priest forever,
> in the order of Melchizedek."
>
> [18]The former regulation is set aside because it was weak and useless [19](for the law made nothing perfect), and a better hope is introduced, by which we draw near to God.

The author pursues his theme of the superiority of Christ. He sees him as superior because of his life, the divine oath, the permanence of his priesthood, and his sacrifice. First, he indicates the importance of the fact that Christ is not limited by death as the Levitical priests were.

15 What it is that is "even more clear" is not said (there is nothing in the Gr. equivalent to NIV's "what we have said"). Westcott thinks it is the ineffectiveness of the Levitical priesthood; Moffatt, that it is the abrogation of the law. More likely the expression is general and is meant to include both—possibly also that Jesus came not from Levi but from Judah. It is the appearance of a priest "like Melchizedek" that is the decisive factor.

16 This priest is distinguished by the quality of his life. "A regulation as to his ancestry" renders an expression that is literally "a law of a fleshly commandment." This includes his ancestry, but it may well be wider. It includes all that is "fleshly" about the law. As Robinson puts it, the command "is one which belongs to the realm of man's physical nature, and bears only indirectly on his spiritual being" (in loc.). By contrast, Christ's priesthood depends on "the power" (which means more than "authority") "of an indestructible life." There is a special quality about the life of

Christ. Neither does it end nor can it end (cf. the description of him as "the prince" or "author of life," Acts 3:15).

17 "For" introduces the clinching testimony of Scripture. The passage cited gives the reason for the foregoing. It is quoted verbatim as in 5:6 (where see commentary). It establishes the special character of Christ's priesthood because of no other priest could it be said that his life was "indestructible." Though it could be said that the Aaronic priesthood was "a priesthood that will continue for all generations" (Exod 40:15), no individual priest is "forever."

18 The opening words might more literally be rendered "For there is an annulling of a foregoing commandment," where "annulling" is a legal term that points to the complete cancellation of the commandment in question. "Regulation" refers as in v.16, to the whole law. The Levitical system in its entirety is set aside by the coming and the work of Christ. At the same time, "former" (*proagousēs*) implies a connection. The Levitical system was not simply earlier in time; it also prepared the way for the coming of Christ. But it had to give way because it was weak and unprofitable. It could not give men strength to meet all the needs of life. It could not bring men salvation.

19 The parenthesis underlines the defects of the law. The writer does not explain what he means by "made perfect" (see comments on 2:10), but clearly he has in mind something like "made fit for God." The law did not give people complete and lasting access to the presence of God. It had its merits, but it did not satisfy their deep needs. For the writer's use of "better," see comments on 1:4; and for his use of "hope," see comments on 3:6; 6:11. The thought of what is better is characteristic of Hebrews, and hope is central to the Christian way. Notice that the hope is said to be better than the regulation or commandment, not better than the hope associated with the commandment. Law and gospel stand in contrast. The gospel is "better" because it enables people to "draw near to God." It was this that the old way could not bring about, but the new way can.

2. *The divine oath*

7:20–22

[20]And it was not without an oath! Others became priests without any oath, [21]but he became a priest with an oath when God said to him:

"The Lord has sworn
and will not change his mind:
'You are a priest forever.' "

[22]Because of this oath, Jesus has become the guarantee of a better covenant.

The argument is now developed with reference to the oath that established the priesthood after the order of Melchizedek. There was no such oath when the Aaronic priesthood was set up, which means that this priesthood lacks the permanence so characteristic of the priesthood after the order of Melchizedek. There was always something conditional about Aaron's priesthood.

20–21 The oath declares the purpose of God in an absolute fashion. It allows of no qualification on account of human weakness or sinfulness or anything else. So the writer contrasts the priesthood that has the security of the divine oath to that which lacked it. Christ is contrasted with the Levitical priests, and the importance of the oath is stressed. It was not simply that an oath was sworn at the same time he was made priest but that the oath was the very essence of what was done. That is the point of the argument. The psalm is quoted once more, this time beginning a little earlier to include the reference to the swearing of the oath and the assurance that the Lord will not change his mind. The new priesthood is permanent. There is no question of its ever being done away.

22 "Guarantee" translates a word found only here in the NT (*engyos*) and it brings before us an unusual idea. The old covenant was established, as Bruce (in loc.) points out, with a mediator (Gal 3:19) but with no one to guarantee that the people would fulfill their undertaking. But Jesus stands as a continuing guarantor and that in two directions. He guarantees to men that God will fulfill his covenant of forgiveness, and he guarantees to God that those who are in him are acceptable.

This is the writer's first use of the term "covenant" (*diathēkē*), a word whose importance for him may be gauged from the fact that he uses it no fewer than seventeen times, whereas in no other NT book is it found more than three times. In nonbiblical Greek it denotes a last will and testament, but in the LXX it is the normal rendering of the Hebrew *beriṯ* ("covenant"). It is agreed that in NT *diathēkē* mostly means "covenant." It also seems, however, that now and then the meaning "testament" is not out of mind (e.g., 9:16). The author may have chosen this word rather than *synthēkē*, the usual word for "covenant," because the latter might suggest an agreement made on more or less equal terms. By contrast, there is something absolute about a will. One cannot dicker with the testator. And in like manner man cannot bargain with God. God lays down the terms. (See further my *Apostolic Preaching of the Cross* 3rd ed. [Grand Rapids: Eerdmans, 1965] ch.2).

Notes

---

20 The periphrastic perfect tense εἰσὶν γεγονότες (*eisin gegonotes*, "became," NIV) is unusual and may be meant to indicate a continuing state. Christ's priesthood lasts eternally whereas theirs terminates, but within that framework there is a certain element of continuance.

21 Ὁ δέ (*ho de*, "but he") sets Christ in contrast to the Levitical priests, answering as it does to the οἱ μέν (*hoi men*, "they") of the previous verse. So also μετά (*meta*, "with") stands over against χωρίς (*chōris*, "without").

22 There is no "oath" in the text, but NIV gives the sense, as κατὰ τοσοῦτο (*kata tosouto*) answers to καθ' ὅσον (*kath' hoson*) in v.20.

---

3. *Its permanence*

7:23–25

[23]Now there were many of those priests, since death prevented them from continuing in office; [24]but because Jesus lives forever, he has a permanent priesthood. [25]Therefore he is able to save completely those who come to God through him, because he always lives to intercede for them.

It matters to the author that Christ's life was different in quality from other lives. He has emphasized this in vv. 15ff. and he comes back to it with the thought that the permanence of Christ's priesthood makes it superior to the Levitical priesthood. His life is such that there is no need and no place for a successor.

23–24 Once more the Levitical priests are set in contrast to Christ. They had to be numerous because like all men they died, and successors were needed to keep the priesthood functioning. Josephus says that there were eighty-three high priests from Aaron to the destruction of the temple in A.D. 70 (Antiq. XX, 227 [x.1]; the Tal says there were eighteen during the first temple and more than three hundred during the second, *Yoma* 9a).

Death was inevitable for the Aaronic priests and it meant the cessation of their exercise of the high priesthood. But with Christ it is different. He remains forever and thus his priesthood never has to be continued by another. The word rendered "permanent" (*aparabatos*) is found nowhere else in the NT. It is often understood to mean "without a successor," but this meaning does not seem to be demonstrated. The word means "that cannot be transgressed," or, as Abbott-Smith puts it, "*inviolable*, and so unchangeable" (s.v.). Christ lives through eternity, and his priesthood lives with him. The quality of his life means a quality of priesthood that cannot be matched by the Levitical priests.

25 From Christ's unchanging priesthood the author draws an important conclusion about the salvation Christ accomplishes. The verb "to save" (*sōzō*) is used absolutely, which means that Christ will save in the most comprehensive sense; he saves from all that humanity needs saving from. The expression rendered "completely" (*eis to panteles*) is an unusual one, used again in the NT only in Luke 13:11 of the woman who could not straighten herself "completely" ("at all," NIV). This may well be the sense of it here, too. Christ's salvation is a complete deliverance, no matter what the need of the sinner. Some take the word *pantelēs* in a temporal sense and see it as scarcely differing from "forever" or "always." There is more to be said for the former meaning, though the latter is not impossible. The verb "is able" (*dynatai*) refers to power. Christ's inviolable priesthood, a priesthood that can never be put away, means that he has the capacity (as others have not) of bringing a complete salvation to all who approach God through him.

At the end of the verse we find that Christ intercedes for those who come to him (cf. Rom 8:34). This is sometimes made the vehicle of strange theories, such as the one that says that Christ is always pleading his sacrifice in heaven while worshipers on earth do the same thing in the Holy Communion. It must be stressed that there is no thought of Christ as a humble suppliant. Rather, he is supreme and his very presence in heaven in his character as the one who died for mankind and rose again is itself an intercession. As Snell puts it, "We must be careful not to infer from this verse, or from the last phrase of 9:24, that the author thought of our Lord as having to maintain a kind of continuous liturgical action in heaven for our benefit . . . the meaning is that our Lord's presence in heaven, *seated* at God's right hand, and awaiting the full manifestation of his already achieved victory, itself constitutes his effective intercession for us" (in loc.).

Notes

24 Μένειν (*menein*, "remain"; NIV, "lives") takes up παραμένειν (*paramenein*, "remain with"; NIV, "continuing") of the previous verse: the Levitical priest could not "remain with" men but he does "remain."

4. *His better sacrifice*

7:26–28

[26]Such a high priest meets our need—one who is holy, blameless, pure, set apart from sinners, exalted above the heavens. [27]Unlike the other high priests, he does not need to offer sacrifices day after day, first for his own sins, and then for the sins of the people. He sacrificed for their sins once for all when he offered himself. [28]For the law appoints as high priests men who are weak; but the oath, which came after the law, appointed the Son, who has been made perfect forever.

This section of the study is rounded off with a glowing description of Christ as our High Priest, better qualified than the Levitical priests, and one who offered a better sacrifice than they did.

26 NIV omits the important word "for" (*gar*) that links this proposition to the preceding one. It is because Christ is what he is that he intercedes as he does. "Meets our need" is literally "is fitting for us" (*hēmin eprepen*). Even our human sense of the fitness of things is able to recognize Christ's suitability for his saving work.

There are two Greek words for "holy," one (*hagios*) refers to the quality of separateness, of belonging to God, and the other (*hosios*) signifies rather the character involved in that separation. *Hosios* is used here. He is also "blameless" (*akakos*, "without evil," "innocent") and "pure" (*amiantos*). "Pure" contains the thought of being undefiled, and there may be a contrast between the ritual purity the Levitical high priest must be careful to maintain and the complete moral purity of Jesus.

There is probably another contrast in the words "set apart from sinners," for the Levitical high priest was required to leave his home seven days before the Day of Atonement and live in such a manner as to ensure that he avoided ritual defilement (M *Yoma* 1.1). But Jesus' separation was not ritual. Some think the words refer to his spotless character and think he is being contrasted with sinful men. It is more likely that we should take the words closely with the following. His work on earth is done. He has accomplished his sacrifice. He has been "exalted above the heavens." This makes him the perfect intercessor.

27 There is a problem in the reference to offering sacrifices "day after day" for, while there were daily sacrifices in the temple, the high priest was not required to offer them personally; and the sacrifices that did demand his personal action, those on the Day of Atonement, took place once a year not once a day, a fact the author well knows (9:7,25; 10:1). Some have thought that we should understand the words to mean not that the high priest offered every day but that he felt the need to offer every day. Others think that Christ's high priestly office, unlike that of the Levitical high priests which involved repeated offerings, is fulfilled daily by his one sacrifice. Such solutions have their attraction. Yet it is not easy to reconcile them with the actual words used. Bruce (in loc.) reminds us that it was always possible for the high priest, as for other people, to commit inadvertent sin, which required the offering of a sin offering (Lev 4:2–3) and that thus the high priest needed to offer daily (to ensure his fitness for ministry). We should also bear in mind that Leviticus requires the high priest to offer the cereal offering each day (Lev 6:19–23; notice that it is "the son [not all the priests] who is to succeed him [Aaron] as anointed priest" who is required to offer this offering [v.22]). This was regarded as expiatory (Lev R 3:3).

Jesus stands in contrast to the earthly priests. He has no need to offer for his own sins because he has none (4:15). And he has no need to keep offering for the sins of the people, for his one sacrifice has perfectly accomplished this. They were sinful men and had to provide for the putting away of their own sin before they were in a fit condition to do anything about the sins of the people. What they did for themselves, they then proceeded to do for others. But Christ's offering is different. There is none for himself. And for others, he offered "once for all" (*ephapax*). There is an air of utter finality about this expression. It is characteristic of the author that he introduces the thought of Christ's sacrifice but does not elaborate. He will return to the thought later and develop it.

28 Here the contrast between men with all their infirmities and the Son with his eternal perfection is further brought out. "The law" brings us back to the law of Moses, the law of divine origin indeed, but the law that necessarily operates among men with all their weakness. And when the law appoints high priests, they must be limited as all men are limited. There is no other possibility. The "weakness" (*astheneia*) refers to "the frailty to which all human flesh is heir" (BAG, s.v.). Priests are not made from some super race but from ordinary men, with all the frailty that characterizes ordinary men.

"But" introduces the contrast: the oath makes the difference. This, we are reminded, "came after the law" and so cannot be thought of as superseded by it. The oath has the last word, not the law. And the oath appointed the Son. Actually Psalm 110, which speaks of the oath, does not mention the Son, who is referred to in Psalm 2. But the author sees both psalms as referring to Jesus; so he has no difficulty in applying terminology taken from the one to a situation relating to the other. And the Son "has been made perfect forever." He has been made perfect through those sufferings (2:10) that bring people to God.

Notes

---

26 We should notice the transition from the perfect participle κεχωρισμένος (*kechōrismenos*, "set apart from") to the aorist γενόμενος (*genomenos*, "having been"; untranslated in NIV). Christ continues in his state of separation, after the single event of his exaltation.

VII. A New and Better Covenant

Throughout the OT period the relationship of the people of God to their God was characteristically viewed in terms of covenant. Indeed, it would not be too much to say that covenant was fundamental to the thinking and outlook of the men of the old way. "It included every aspect of the relation of Israel to Yahweh" (Robinson, MNT, *Hebrews*, p. 112). It is accordingly something radically new and daring to maintain that this whole system has been done away and replaced by a new covenant. And central to the new covenant is the death of Jesus, the sacrifice that established the new covenant. The demonstration of what all this means spells out the end of the Mosaic system. The author shows that once the Christian way is understood, there is no place for the old system.

A. *Christ's "More Excellent" Ministry*

8:1–7

1The point of what we are saying is this: We do have such a high priest, who sat
down at the right hand of the throne of the Majesty in heaven, 2and who serves in
the sanctuary, the true tabernacle set up by the Lord, not by man.
3Every high priest is appointed to offer both gifts and sacrifices, and so it was
necessary for this one also to have something to offer. 4If he were on earth, he
would not be a priest, for there are already men who offer the gifts prescribed by
the law. 5They serve at a sanctuary that is a copy and shadow of what is in heaven.
This is why Moses was warned when he was about to build the tabernacle: "See
to it that you make everything according to the pattern shown you on the mountain."
6But the ministry Jesus has received is as superior to theirs as the covenant of
which he is mediator is superior to the old one, and it is founded on better promises.
7For if there had been nothing wrong with that first covenant, no place would have
been sought for another.

The author leads on from his treatment of the priesthood after the order of Melchizedek to emphasize the point that Christ's ministry far surpasses that of the Levitical priests. The readers of the epistle would be familiar with this priesthood, and the writer wants it to be clear that Jesus has a ministry far excelling it.

1 The problem in this verse is whether we should understand *kephalaion* in the sense of "the chief point" or "to sum up." While the word could have either meaning, here it seems that something like "the chief point" is required. The words that follow are not a summary of what has gone before (nor do they summarize the argument that is to be developed). The present participle *legomenois* (NIV, "what we are saying") does not suit a summary, and the same must be said of the introduction of new material (e.g., "the true tabernacle" [v.2]). The writer is rather picking out the principal point and proceeding to develop it. There is also something of an ambiguity with "such," which might be taken with the preceding ("such as we have just described") or with the following ("such that he sat down . . ."). The stress on his high place perhaps favors the latter. We have, then, a high priest who is so great that he took his seat at God's right hand. "The Majesty in heaven" is a reverent way of referring to God, and to be at his right hand is to be in the place of highest honor (see comments on 1:3). The posture of sitting points to a completed work. "Heaven" can be used in a variety of ways, but here it clearly means the dwelling place of God.

2 "The sanctuary" renders *tōn hagiōn*, which might mean "of holy men," but in this context almost certainly means "of holy things," i.e., the sanctuary. NIV has taken the noun *leitourgos* ("minister," "servant") and made it into a verb—"who serves."

The word is used of one who engages in any one of a variety of forms of public service. In the Bible, however, it seems to be confined to the service of God, though it includes what is done by pagan officials (Rom 13:6). It is used also of angels (1:7) and of men (Rom 15:16; Phil 2:25). It speaks of Christ in his capacity as servant, which is striking, as it immediately follows the reference to his high place in heaven.

The "tabernacle" takes us back to the wilderness days. The word means no more than "tent" and could be used of tents that people lived in. But it was also used of the tent used for worship during the wilderness wanderings (e.g., Exod 27:21). That earthly tent corresponds to a heavenly reality, and it is in the heavenly reality that Christ's ministry is exercised. "True" (*alēthinos*) means true "in the sense of the reality possessed only by the archetype, not by its copies" (BAG, s.v.). This is further brought out with the statement that the Lord pitched it, not man. Sin is dealt with in the way and in the place determined by God.

3 The author has already said in 5:1 that high priests are appointed to offer sacrifices. "For" (which NIV omits) links the argument to the preceding. Christ is ministering in the real tabernacle because to offer sacrifice is of the essence of being high priest. So the writer finds it "necessary" that Christ have something to offer. The Greek has no verb here and some understand the phrase in the sense of "it *is* necessary." NIV is, however, surely right. The author is referring to one offering made once for all, not a continuous offering always being made in heaven. Christ is eternally High Priest, for he never loses his status. But to say that he is eternally offering is quite another thing and one to which this epistle lends no support. It is characteristic of the author that he does not say what is offered at this point; having introduced the subject, he will explain it more fully later (9:14; cf. also 7:27).

4 We must be clear that Christ's priesthood is not one of this earth (though his offering of himself took place here). There are divinely appointed earthly priests, and Jesus has no place among them. On earth Jesus was a layman. He performed no priestly functions in any earthly sanctuary. Those functions were performed by the priests to whom God had entrusted them. Christ's priestly functions must obviously, then, be exercised elsewhere, in the true sanctuary in heaven.

5 The earthly priests serve in a sanctuary they value highly, though it is no more than "a copy and shadow of what is in heaven." There has been much discussion as to how "Platonic" this idea is. Some remind us that Plato thought of heavenly "ideas" as the archetypes of all things earthly. They think that the author has used the thought of an earthly sanctuary as no more than the imperfect actualization of a Platonic heavenly sanctuary. Others point out that the idea of heavenly counterparts of earthly objects was widespread. For example, we read of the heavenly temple in the Testament of Levi 5:1 and in Wisdom of Solomon 9:8, which says, "Thou hast given command to build a temple on thy holy mountain, and an altar in the city of thy habitation, a copy of the holy tent which thou didst prepare from the beginning."

There can be no question but that there is enough of the heavenly counterpart concept in Jewish sources for us to maintain that the author need not have been dependent on Plato. However, he does not say that the earthly was an exact copy of the heavenly, as the rabbis apparently did. There is a good deal to be said for the idea that his language is that of the Alexandrian modification of Platonism. This does not mean that he is using the distinction out of strong philosophic views but that he is using popular terminology with such associations. His main thought accords with the OT model, though he adds the idea that the earthly is but imperfect. It is the heavenly that is real. Inevitably the ministry of the Levitical priests was defective; they could serve only the "copy and shadow." So we are reminded of the Lord's words to Moses that he must make everything "according to the pattern shown [him] on the mountain" (Exod 25:40). The rabbis often appealed to the Mosaic example (see SBK pp. 702–4). For example, they said, "An ark of fire and a table of fire and a candlestick of fire came down from heaven; and these Moses saw and reproduced" (Tal *Menahoth* 29a; the passage goes on to affirm that Moses did this "after their pattern" and not merely "according to the fashion thereof").

6 The ministry of priests in a sanctuary made according to the heavenly pattern is obviously one of great dignity. But the author's point is that Jesus' ministry in the heavenly archetype is of incomparably greater dignity and worth. He chooses to bring this out by using a comparison of the two covenants. Jesus is the mediator of a better covenant. "Mediator" is a legal term for one who arbitrates between two parties. The thought is that Christ mediates between men and God; it is he who establishes the new covenant (for this latter term see comments 7:22). This new covenant is better than the old because it is "founded on better promises." Calvin reminds us that "the same salvation" was promised to the ancients (in loc.). But the new covenant is explicitly based on the forgiveness of sins, as the author goes on to show; and the better promises may be held to refer to the concentration on spiritual things in the new covenant (there is a good deal about possessing the land and the like in the old covenant) and in its unconditional nature.

7 The author brings out the superiority of the new covenant by referring to the supersession of the old one. If there had been "nothing wrong" with the old covenant, there would have been no place for the new. That the new covenant has now been established is itself evidence that the old one was not adequate. (For the line of argument, cf. 7:11ff.) The old covenant was lacking not so much in what its terms spelled out as in the fact that it was weak and unable to bring men to God (cf. 7:18f.; Rom 7:10f.).

Notes

1 "Heaven" is plural (*οὐρανοῖς*, *ouranois*), as in seven instances out of the ten in Hebrews. But there seems to be no distinction between singular and plural in this epistle (we have the plural in 9:23 and the singular in 9:24 with no apparent change in meaning). The preference for the plural probably does not indicate a belief in a plurality of heavens but is a stylistic feature. In Rev the singular is used in every case but one, whereas in Eph the word is always plural.

2 "The Lord" is ὁ κύριος (*ho kyrios*). In this epistle the form with the article seems usually to mean Christ, whereas that without the article means the Father. It is hard to see a reason for the variation here and in v.11.

B. *The Old Covenant Superseded*

8:8–13

8But God found fault with the people and said:

"The time is coming, declares the Lord,
when I will make a new covenant
with the house of Israel
and with the house of Judah.
9It will not be like the covenant
I made with their forefathers
when I took them by the hand
to lead them out of Egypt,
because they did not remain faithful to my covenant,
and I turned away from them,
declares the Lord.
10This is the covenant I will make with the house of Israel
after that time, declares the Lord.
I will put my laws in their minds
and write them on their hearts.
I will be their God,
and they will be my people.
11No longer will a man teach his neighbor,
or a man his brother, saying, 'Know the Lord,'
because they will all know me,
from the least of them to the greatest.
12For I will forgive their wickedness
and will remember their sins no more."

13By calling this covenant "new," he has made the first one obsolete; and what is obsolete and aging will soon disappear.

This long quotation from Jeremiah 31:31–34 makes the point that the old covenant under which Israel has had its religious experience is now superseded by a new covenant. The author's interest is in the fact that under the new covenant forgiveness of sins is brought about. As soon as he comes to the words about forgiveness, he breaks off his quotation.

8 The writer proceeds to show that a place was indeed sought for a new covenant. He begins by telling us that God found fault with the men of old, and this leads to the quotation from Jeremiah 31:31ff., which differs only slightly from the LXX reading. The Greek says only "he says." But NIV is correct in inserting "God" as subject. It is the author's habit to ascribe what is found in Scripture to God. "I will make" (*synteleso͞*) is not the usual word for making a covenant but one with a meaning like "I will bring a new covenant to accomplishment" (BAG, s.v.). There may be the thought that the covenant is all of God. Men do not bargain with God and come to an acceptable compromise. In any covenant with God, it is God who lays down the terms (for "covenant," cf. comments on 7:22). The prophet looks for the unification of "the house of Israel" and "the house of Judah." They had long been separated when Jeremiah wrote, but his vision was large enough to take in both and to look for the day when they would be one.

9 The new covenant is contrasted with the old one. Calvin points out that the prophet does not say, "I will renew the covenant which has failed by your fault," but "he says expressly that it will be different" (in loc.). It will not be simply the old one patched up and renewed. The differences will be those mentioned in the following verses, especially the way the new covenant brings forgiveness of sins. But first the kindness and the love of God are brought out by the reference to taking the people "by the hand" to bring them out of Egypt. The metaphor is that of a father or mother taking a little child by the hand to lead him safely to the place where he is going (cf. Hos 11:1–4). Egypt had been a place of slavery. Yet God had brought Israel out of it to set up the old covenant. But Israelites lacked perseverance. The emphatic pronouns set "they" and "I" over against each other. They refused to remain faithful but found no less a one than God ranged against them. "I turned away from them" is a strong expression (*emelēsa autōn*), with a meaning like "I ignored them" (Buchanan, in loc.) or perhaps "I abandoned them" (NEB).

10 From the failures of the past, Jeremiah turns his vision to the future. Again he sees a united people as he thinks of the covenant being made with "the house of Israel." It will be made "after that time," which clearly refers to the future but does not locate it with any precision. The repeated "declares the Lord" keeps before the reader the truth that a divine and not a human act is in mind. The first point is that the new covenant is inward and dynamic: it is written on the hearts and minds of the people. A defect in the old had been its outwardness. It had divinely given laws, indeed; but it was written on tablets of stone (Exod 32:15–16). The people had not been able to live up to what they knew was the word from God. It remained external. Jeremiah looked for a time when people would not simply obey an external code but would be so transformed that God's own laws would be written in their inmost beings. We should probably not distinguish too sharply between "minds" and "hearts," for in poetic parallelism such expressions are close in meaning. But if there is a difference, "hearts" is the more inclusive term, standing for the whole of the inner life.

The second point in the new covenant is that there will be a close relationship between the God who will be "their God" and the people who, he says, will be "my people." There is nothing really new in the terms of this promise, for in connection with the old way it was said, "I will take you as my own people, and I will be your God" (Exod 6:7). But Bruce is certainly correct in saying, "While the 'formula' of the covenant remains the same from age to age, it is capable of being filled with fresh meaning to a point where it can be described as a *new* covenant. 'I will be your God' acquires fuller meaning with every further revelation of the character of God" (in loc.). The life, death, resurrection, and ascension of Jesus mean that God has acted decisively to save a people. The God who saves people in Christ is the God of his redeemed in a new and definitive way. And when people have been saved at the awful cost of Calvary, they are the people of God in a way never before known.

11 The third significant feature of the new covenant is that all who enter it will have knowledge of God. There will be no need for a person to instruct his neighbor. The word rendered "neighbor" (*politēs*) means a "citizen" (as in Luke 15:15), and thus a "fellow-citizen." Jeremiah moves from the wider relationship in the community to the narrower relationship in the family and says that in neither case will there be the need for exhorting anyone to know God. For "from the least of them to the greatest," all will know God. This does not mean that in the conditions of the new covenant there will be no place for a teacher. There will always be the need for those who have advanced in the Christian way to pass on to others the benefit of their knowledge. Rather, the meaning is that the knowledge of God will not be confined to a privileged few. All those in the new covenant will have their own intimate and personal knowledge of their God.

12 The fourth significant thing about the new covenant is that in it sins are forgiven. "For" shows the important point that it is God's forgiveness that is the basis of what has gone before. It is because sins are really dealt with that the blessings enumerated earlier become possible. And those sins really are dealt with. God's wrath no longer rests on the sinner and God does not bear his sins in mind. They are completely forgotten. We might get some of the force of all this by reflecting that the men of Qumran saw themselves as the men of the new covenant. But for them that meant looking forward to a day when the corrupt priesthood in Jerusalem would be deposed and replaced by those they regarded as the true priests and when the whole temple ritual with its never-ceasing round of sacrifices would be carried on in the way they approved in a kind of ritualist's paradise! For the writer of this epistle, there was no more sacrifice. The one sacrifice that avails has been offered once and for all. Therefore sin has been completely and finally dealt with; it is a problem no longer.

13 The author picks out the word "new" (cf. v. 8) and sees it as making his essential point. It implies that something else is "old" and that the old is to be replaced. When God speaks of a "new" covenant, then, it means that the old one is obsolete. And that in turn means that it is close to disappearing. It is not something people should go back to with nostalgia. The words used of it emphasize that it is ineffective, unable to meet people's needs, outworn.

The idea of the new covenant is not confined to this epistle. It is implied in the narratives of the institution of the Lord's Supper in the first two Gospels (Matt 26:27–28; Mark 14:23–24). What is the meaning of "covenant" in these passages unless the new covenant is in mind? And it is explicit in Luke's longer narrative (Luke 22:20) and in Paul's account (1 Cor 11:25). Paul also saw Christian ministers as "ministers of a new covenant" (2 Cor 3:6). The new covenant is thus one of the strands in the NT teaching about what Christ has done for us. While it emphasizes radical novelty, we should not overlook the fact that it also points to continuity. The new arrangement retains the term "covenant" and it is established on the basis of sacrifice. It refers to the fulfillment of what is superseded rather than outright opposition to it.

Notes

8 The verb for "making" the covenant is συντελέω (*synteleō*) used only here in the NT in this sense. The usual word is διατίθημι (*diatithēmi*) (8:10; 10:16; Acts 3:25), but ποιέω (*poieō*) (8:9) and ἐντέλλομαι (*entellomai*, "command") (9:20) are also used. The thought conveyed is that God is in charge. He dictates the terms.

10 It is not certain whether we should take ἐπὶ καρδίας (*epi kardias*, "on their hearts") as genitive singular or accusative plural. The corresponding word in the original is singular, which favors the singular here. But most take the similar expression in 10:16 to be plural. The sense is not greatly affected.

C. *The Old Sanctuary and Its Ritual*

9:1–10

[1]Now the first covenant had regulations for worship and also an earthly sanctuary. [2]A tabernacle was set up. In its first room were the lampstand, the table and the consecrated bread; this was called the Holy Place. [3]Behind the second curtain was a room called the Most Holy Place, [4]which had the golden altar of incense and the gold-covered ark of the covenant. This ark contained the gold jar of manna, Aaron's rod that had budded, and the stone tablets of the covenant. [5]Above the ark were the cherubim of the Glory, overshadowing the place of atonement. But we cannot discuss these things in detail now.

[6]When everything had been arranged like this, the priests entered regularly into the outer room to carry on their ministry. [7]But only the high priest entered the inner room, and that only once a year, and never without blood, which he offered for himself and for the sins the people had committed in ignorance. [8]The Holy Spirit was showing by this that the way into the Most Holy Place had not yet been disclosed as long as the first tabernacle was still standing. [9]This is an illustration for the present time, indicating that the gifts and sacrifices being offered were not able to clear the conscience of the worshiper. [10]They are only a matter of food and drink and various ceremonial washings—external regulations applying until the time of the new order.

The author proceeds to bring out the superiority of the new covenant by pointing to the significance of the way of worship in the old one. Interestingly, he concentrates his attention not on the temple but on the long-vanished tabernacle, which would have had a wider appeal to Jews than the temple had. The temple was accessible only to those in Jerusalem; but wherever Jews were, their Scriptures told them all about the tabernacle. And in any case it was the synagogue rather than the temple that was the center of worship for most Jews. Even in Palestine there were some, like the men of Qumran, who repudiated the temple. But the tabernacle was different. The attention it received in Scripture meant that wherever Jews were it was known and esteemed. It is also not unimportant that the account of the setting up of the old covenant is recounted in Exodus 24, while the description of the tabernacle follows in the very next chapter. So when the author wants to show the greatness of the new covenant, it is natural for him to draw attention to the ineffectiveness of the old as reflected in the way the tabernacle was set up and used.

1 The writer has no noun with his adjective "first," but NIV is almost certainly correct in inserting "covenant." Buchanan argues on grammatical grounds that we should read "the first Tent" (in loc.). Few, however, have followed him. The thrust of the argument at this point is to contrast the old and the new covenants. It is true that this involves the "Tent," but it means much more. The author is contrasting two whole ways of approach to God. Some press the past tense "had" as though it means that the temple had been destroyed. Yet this is illegitimate. The writer is not talking about the temple but about the old covenant that has been superseded now that Jesus has established the new one. But the old one, the writer points out, had been set up with a full set of regulations for worship and the like. The method of worship was not left haphazard but was divinely prescribed. The old way must be seen as originating in the divine initiative. Then the new is its fulfillment, not its contradiction.

The old way not only had regulations but also a sanctuary described as "earthly" (*kosmikon*). The adjective is unusual and in its only other NT occurrence signifies "worldly" (Titus 2:12). NIV is certainly correct here. The meaning is not that the sanctuary is worldly in the bad sense but simply that it belonged to this world in contrast to the heavenly sanctuary where Jesus ministers (v.11). The first covenant, then, was established with its due regulations for worship and its holy place of this earth where worship could be carried on. The author will go on to stress the "earthly" nature of it all.

2 NIV uses the traditional term "tabernacle," no doubt to remind readers of the wilderness sanctuary of the Israelites of old. But the word is the ordinary word for "tent" and it is thus translated elsewhere (e.g., NEB, JB, TEV). Usually it is described as a tent with two compartments. Here, however, the writer speaks instead of two tents (there is nothing in the Gr. to correspond to NIV's "room"; that "tent" is to be supplied with "first" is clear from the specific use of this word in v.3, where NIV has translated *skēnē* by "room").

The term rendered "was set up" (*kateskeuasthē*) is not the usual word for the pitching of a tent but has rather the meaning of "prepare." It may be used not only of the erection of a building but also of its furnishings and equipment. This is in mind here as is shown by the list of furnishings that follows. In the first tent there was "the lampstand," i.e., the seven-branched lampstand (Exod 25:31ff.; 37:17ff.; Solomon's temple had ten lampstands [1 Kings 7:49], but our author is referring to the tabernacle, not the temple).

"The table and the consecrated bread" is a hendiadys for "the table of the consecrated bread." There were twelve loaves, each baked from two-tenths of an ephah of fine flour, arranged in two rows of six, pure frankincense being put with each row. Every Sabbath day Aaron was bidden to set them up, and it was prescribed that they were to be eaten only by the priests (Lev 24:5–9). Scripture does indeed record an exceptional occasion when they were eaten by David and his men (1 Sam 21:1–6), and Jesus referred to the incident (Mark 2:25–26). The loaves were called "the continual bread" (Num 4:7), a name that brings out the fact that there were always to be such loaves in the Holy Place. They were put on a table specially constructed for the purpose (Exod 25:23–30; 37:10–16). The tent in which these objects were placed was called "the Holy Place."

3 The "second curtain" is that which screened off the Most Holy Place from the Holy Place (Exod 26:31–33; 36:35–36; Lev 24:3). It is called the "second" to distinguish it from the curtain between the outer court and the Holy Place (Exod 26:36–37; 36:37–38). Behind this curtain was a tent (*skēnē*) called the "Most Holy Place" (*Hagia Hagiōn*). This was the very special place where God dwelt between the cherubim; and, as the author will presently emphasize, it was never to be entered by anyone other than the high priest, and by him only on the Day of Atonement.

4 The author says some things about the furnishings of the Most Holy Place. There are problems about the expression translated "the golden altar of incense." The word *thymiatērion* denotes something connected with the burning of incense (*thymiama*), and in the LXX it is always used of a censer. Some (e.g., KJV, RV, Snell) favor this meaning here. But the word is also used by Symmachus, Theodotion, and others of the altar on which incense was offered (Exod 30:1–10); and most agree that this is the meaning here. There seems no reason for referring to the censer and much reason for referring to the far more significant altar.

A further problem arises from the fact that the author appears to locate this altar inside the Most Holy Place, though its place was really "in front of the curtain" (Exod 30:6). Indeed, it *had* to be outside the Most Holy Place, for it was in daily use (Exod 30:7–8). Some have thought that this altar was in the Most Holy Place (2 Baruch 6:7). But it seems more likely that the author has in mind the intimate connection of the incense altar with the Most Holy Place. So it "belonged to the inner sanctuary" (1 Kings 6:22), as is shown by its situation "in front of the curtain that is before the ark of the testimony—before the atonement cover [mercy seat] that is over the Testimony" (Exod 30:6).

On the Day of Atonement, the high priest was to offer incense, using coals of fire from this altar (Lev 16:12–13). Notice the warning "so that he will not die" (Lev 16:13). The incense was indeed important. We should also notice that the writer does not say that his altar was "in" the Most Holy Place but only that that Place "had" it. It is true that the same verb covers the ark that was undoubtedly inside the veil, but the indefinite term may be significant. Montefiore comments, "In any case our author does not actually commit himself to the view that the altar of incense is situated in the sanctuary: he merely says that it belonged to the sanctuary" (in loc.).

There is no question that the "gold-covered ark of the covenant" was in the Most Holy Place (Exod 25:10ff.; 26:33; 40:21). That is to say, it was there in the time of the tabernacle. It was placed in the Most Holy Place in the temple of Solomon (1 Kings 8:6); but evidently it was taken out for some reason, and the last time it appears is when Josiah told the priests to put it into the temple (2 Chron 35:3). According to the rabbis, the ark disappeared at the time of the early prophets (Mishnah, *Yoma* 5:2; *Shekalim* 6:1f.); and there was a tradition that Jeremiah hid it (2 Macc 2:4ff.).

The author goes on to inform us that the ark contained "the golden jar of manna" (cf. Exod 16:33–34). MT does not say what the jar was made of, but LXX says it was golden. Aaron's rod that had budded was also there (Num 17:1–11). Neither of these is said in the OT to be "in" the ark; rather, they were "in front of" it (Exod 16:34; Num 17:10). We are told in 1 Kings 8:9 that in Solomon's temple there was nothing in the ark but the tables of stone. But the author is not concerned with the temple. He is writing about the tabernacle, and it is possible that a different arrangement held there; though, if that was so, we have no information about it. Also in the ark were "the stone tablets of the covenant" (cf. Exod 25:16; 31:18; Deut 9:9ff.; 10:3ff.). They represented the permanent record of the terms of the old covenant and were kept in the most sacred place.

5 Above the ark were "the cherubim of the Glory." The exact form of these is not known, but most interpreters hold that they had bodies of animals. They were certainly winged (Exod 25:18–20; 37:7–9). Moreover, they were especially associated with the presence of God (Ps 80:1; 99:1), which is why they are here called the cherubim "of the Glory" (NEB, "of God's glory"; others, however, prefer the sense "the glorious cherubs," JB). They overshadowed the lid of the ark, which is here called "the place of atonement." The justification for this translation is that on the Day of Atonement this object was sprinkled with the blood of the sin offering whereby sins were atoned. The word is from the word group meaning "propitiate," and it may be that there is a recognition that it was the place where God's wrath against sin was put away. But as our author is taking the term from the LXX, we cannot press the point. As with the other articles mentioned, details of its construction are given in the account of the tabernacle (Exod 25:17ff.; 37:6ff.). Doubtless the writer would have been glad to dwell on the significance of all these objects. He points out, however, that it is not the time for him to do this. His argument proceeds on other lines.

6 From the sanctuary the author moves to the ritual. He is particularly interested in what was done on the Day of Atonement, and he uses the limitations attached to the high priest's entry into the Most Holy Place to bring home the inferiority of the whole Levitical system. But he begins with the ministry of the lower priests. When the tabernacle system was established, the priests did their work in "the first tent" ("outer room," NIV). This included such things as burning incense (Exod 30:7–8), setting out the holy loaves (Lev 24:8–9), and trimming the lamps (Exod 27:20–21; Lev 24:3–4). There was a sharp distinction between the duties and place of service of the priests and those of the Levites (Num 18:1–7).

7 "But" (*de*) marks the contrast. We move from the priests to the high priest and from ministry in the Holy Place to that in the Most Holy Place. Into "the inner room" (i.e., "second tent," v.3) only the high priest might go and then "only once a year." The reference is to the ceremonies of the Day of Atonement (Lev 16). We should understand "once" to mean "on one day," because the high priest made more than one entrance into the room beyond the curtain. He certainly went in twice (Lev 16:12, 15), and a third entrance may be meant for the sprinkling of the blood of the bull (Lev 16:14). The rabbis thought there were four entrances of the high priest into the Most Holy Place, the three just mentioned and a final one to retrieve the ladle and the fire pan he had left there when he offered the incense (M *Yoma* 5:1, 3, 4; 7:4).

To go into the Most Holy Place was dangerous; so the high priest had to safeguard himself by offering blood in the prescribed manner. The rabbis were conscious of the danger and spoke of the high priest as praying when he came out the first time, "but he did not prolong his prayer lest he put Israel in terror" (*Yoma* 5:1). They also said that when he emerged safely from the hazards of the Day, he made a feast for his friends (*Yoma* 7:4). His offering was "for himself and for the sins the people had committed in ignorance." Being a sinner himself, he had to atone for himself before he could minister on behalf of others. The sins "committed in ignorance" point to the truth that there is ignorance that is culpable. Sins of this kind do matter, and we should be on our guard against minimizing their seriousness. In Ecclesiasticus 23:2 the son of Sirach asks not to be spared discipline for these sins of ignorance (he uses the same word that appears here), lest they multiply and bring him low.

8 The author sees the Holy Spirit as using the pattern of the tabernacle to teach important truths. The limited access into the Most Holy Place was meant to bring home the fact that ordinary men had no direct access to the presence of God. NIV is almost certainly correct in its translation, "the way into the Most Holy Place." Yet we should notice that *hagiōn*, which is usually taken as neuter ("holy things" and thus "the Holy Place") might be masculine. In that case the meaning would be "the way for the saints." Now while we should probably not accept this translation, it does point us to the fact that it is the saints who are to travel the way. This was was not revealed while "the first tabernacle was still standing." Some take "the first tabernacle" to mean the Holy Place (as in v.6), but this yields a difficult sense. It seems much more likely that the writer means the whole tabernacle ("the way into the Most Holy Place was not disclosed while the Holy Place still stood" would be strange). The final words do not bear on the problem of whether the temple was still standing. The author is saying that people get direct access to God through the finished work of Christ and that before that work was accomplished there was no such access.

9 "This is an illustration" ("All this is symbolic," NEB). But the precise application of the symbolism is not quite clear. Bruce (in loc.) points out that "the present time" might mean "the time then present" (i.e., in OT days the way to God was not yet revealed) or "the time now present" (i.e., "the real meaning of the tabernacle can only now be understood, in the light of the work of Christ"). In either case the writer is contrasting the limited access that was all that could be obtained in OT days with the free access to the presence of God that Christ has made possible for his people. The trouble with the sacrificial offerings of the old covenant was that they could not "clear the conscience of the worshiper." The reference to conscience is significant. The ordinances of the old covenant had been external. They had not been able to come to grips with the real problem, that of the troubled conscience. This does not mean, of course, that no OT saint ever had a clear conscience, but he did not obtain it by the sacrifices as such.

10 The externality of the old way is brought out from another viewpoint. It concerned only matters like "food and drink and various ceremonial washings." There is no problem about the mention of food, for there were some strict food laws (Lev 11). But drink is not so prominent. Priests were to abstain from alcoholic drinks while engaged in their ministry (Lev 10:8–9) and there were limitations on the Nazarites (Num 6:2–3). No one was allowed to drink from an unclean vessel, one into which a dead animal had fallen (Lev 11:33f.). And, of course, there were libations accompanying some of the sacrifices (e.g., Num 6:15, 17; 28:7f.). There were several ceremonial lustrations in the OT, such as those performed by the priests in their ministry (Exod 30:20), and a variety of washings for defiled people (Lev 15:4–27; 17:15–16; Num 19:7–13). All such things the author dismisses as "external regulations." They have their place, but only "until the time of the new order." Though he does not explain this, the drift of his argument shows that he has in mind the new covenant Christ brought. It replaced all the merely external regulations of the old way.

Notes

---

2 Unexpectedly we have ἡ πρόθεσις τῶν ἄρτων (*hē prothesis tōn artōn*, "the setting out of the loaves") where we might have had οἱ ἄρτοι τῆς προθέσεως (*hoi artoi tēs protheseōs*) as in Matt 12:4. The expression is used figuratively to denote the table on which the bread was set out. Ἅγια (*Hagia*) is taken by NIV, probably rightly, as a neuter plural, "holy things," and thus "the Holy Place." But Montefiore sees it as feminine singular, pointing out that the use of this adjective without the article in such a sense is unparalleled and, further, that our author uses this expression of the Most Holy Place, not the Holy Place. He prefers to take it in the sense "this Tent is called Holy." This is possible, but NIV is to be preferred.

3 This is the one example in the NT of μετά (*meta*) with the accusative in the local sense, "behind."

4 JB has a note that our author "may be following a different liturgical tradition, or the sense may be that the place of the altar of incense was immediately in front of the curtain of the inner sanctuary."

6 "Regularly" translates διὰ παντὸς (*dia pantos*), which according to Westcott denotes "the continuous, unbroken permanence of a characteristic habit, while πάντοτε marks that which is realised on each several occasion" (in loc.).

D. *The Blood of Christ*

9:11–14

[11]When Christ came as high priest of the good things that are already here, he went through the greater and more perfect tabernacle that is not man-made, that is to say, not a part of this creation. [12]He did not enter by means of the blood of goats and calves; but he entered the Most Holy Place once for all by his own blood, having obtained eternal redemption. [13]The blood of goats and bulls and the ashes of a heifer sprinkled on those who are ceremonially unclean sanctify them so that they are outwardly clean. [14]How much more, then, will the blood of Christ, who through the eternal Spirit offered himself unblemished to God, cleanse our consciences from acts that lead to death, so that we may serve the living God!

The argument moves a stage further as the author turns specifically to what Christ has done. The sacrifices of the old covenant were ineffectual. But in strong contrast Christ made an offering that secures a redemption valid for all eternity. In the sacrifices, a good deal pertained to the use of blood. So in accord with this, the author considers the significance of the blood of animals and that of Christ.

11–12 The MSS are divided as to whether we should read "the good things that are already here" or "the good things that are to come." The resolution of the point is not easy. On the whole it seems that NIV is correct in preferring the former. Scribes would be tempted to alter the past into the future, but scarcely the reverse. All the more would they do this in view of the similar expression in 10:1 and the frequency of the verb (*mellō*) that expresses the future in this epistle. The author does not explain what the "good things" are, but the expression is evidently a comprehensive way of summing up the blessings Christ has won for his people. The past tense points us to the Cross and all it means. At the same time, we should bear in mind Héring's point that the aorist is probably ingressive and means "The good things have begun to come into existence." There is more to come than we now see. Because the new covenant has been established, the past tense is fitting. Yet the full realization of what this means is yet to come.

There is another difficult problem in the meaning of the "greater and more perfect tabernacle" (v.11) and with it the meaning of "through" (*dia*), which relates to this tabernacle. Also, in the same Greek sentence (v.12) *dia* relates negatively to the blood of animals and positively to the blood of Christ. Many commentators see a reference to heaven in "a greater and more perfect tabernacle"; and still others think of Christ's flesh, his glorified body, or his people (cf. 3:6). Some suggestions seem negated by the words "not man-made, that is to say, not a part of this creation" (v.11). Perhaps we should take notice of the similar expression in v.24, where the author is saying that it was by means of the heavenly sanctuary, and by means of his own blood (not that of animals), that Christ entered the holiest of all, into the presence of God. This is an emphatic way of saying that he has won for his people an effective salvation and that this has nothing to do with earthly sacrifices.

Some translations import the idea of Christ as taking his blood into heaven, e.g.,

RSV, "taking not the blood of goats and calves but his own blood" (similar are TEV, JB). This is quite unwarranted. The Greek does not say this. The translation is objectionable because it implies that Christ's atoning work was not completed on the cross but that he still had to do some atoning act in heaven like the earthly high priest who took the blood into the Most Holy Place on the Day of Atonement. In this epistle, what Christ did on the cross was final. It needs no supplement. There may be another glance at the Day of Atonement ceremonies in the listing of "goats and calves," for these were the animals used on that day. "Once for all" (*ephapax*) is an emphatic expression underlining the decisive character of Christ's saving work. There can be no repetition. "Redemption" (*lytrōsis*) is the process of setting free by the payment of a ransom price, in this case the death of Jesus.

13 The author turns again to the Levitical sacrifices. In them he finds the power to effect an external purification, a cleansing from ritual defilement. He refers to the blood "of goats and bulls," which means much the same as that of "goats and calves" in v.12 (the calf now being seen as a young adult). "The ashes of a heifer" point to the ceremony for purification described in Numbers 19:1–10. A red heifer was killed, the carcass was burned (together with "cedar wood, hyssop and scarlet wool"), and the ashes used "in the water of cleansing; it is for purification from sin." When anyone was ceremonially unclean because of contact with a dead body or even by entering a tent where a dead body lay (Num 19:14), he was made clean by the use of these ashes. The verb "sanctify" is often used of the moral and spiritual process of "sanctification." Here, however, a ritual matter is plainly in mind. The Levitical system is not dismissed as useless. It had its values and was effective within its limits. But those limits were concerned with what is outward.

14 The "how much more" argument stresses the incomparable greatness of Christ and his work for us. "The blood of Christ" means Christ's death regarded as a sacrifice for sin. Though some have suggested that we should see in references to "the blood" allusions to life rather than death, this does not seem soundly based. The word "blood" points to death (see my *Apostolic Preaching of the Cross*, 3rd ed. [Grand Rapids: Eerdmans, 1965], ch. 3). In this context "blood" is not death in general but death seen as a sacrifice. Christ offered himself in sacrifice to God. "Unblemished" (*amōmos*) is the word used technically of animals approved for sacrifice, animals without defect of any kind. The idea of Christ as an offering to God is not popular these days and can, of course, be stated in a crude and totally unacceptable way. But we must never forget that atonement must be seen in the light of God's demand for uprightness in a world where people sin constantly. No view of atonement can be satisfactory that does not regard the divine demand.

There is a problem in the way we should understand "the eternal Spirit." Spelled with capital "S," it appears to be another name for the Holy Spirit (cf. NIV, KJV, RSV, JB, et al.). But the Holy Spirit is not elsewhere referred to in this way. Thus many commentators, feeling that such a reference would be out of place here, prefer to see the "spirit" as Christ's own spirit. For example, Snell sees the words as possibly "a rather odd way of saying that he put his whole human self into it," but he prefers the meaning "by virtue of his own Personal nature as being Spirit" (in loc.). Probably most modern commentators take the words in some such way. Bruce (in loc.), however, points out that we ought to see the "Servant of the Lord" imagery behind this whole passage and he reminds us that the Servant is introduced in Isaiah with "I will put my Spirit on him" (Isa 42:1). Just as the prophet sees the Servant as accomplishing his entire ministry in the power of the divine Spirit, so we should see Christ as winning men's salvation by a mighty act performed in the power of the Spirit of God.

Yet, despite the modern disinclination to see a Trinitarian reference here, it does seem as though something of the kind is needed if we are to do justice to the writer's thought. While Christ's own spirit is involved in his sacrifice, the divine Spirit is involved, too. It seems that the writer has chosen this unusual way of referring to the Holy Spirit to bring out the truth that there is an eternal aspect to Christ's saving work.

Christ, then, offered himself in sacrifice, the aim being to "cleanse our consciences." It is important to be clear that Christ's saving work operates on quite a different level from that of the Levitical sacrifices. These were but external and material, as the author repeatedly emphasizes. But Christ was concerned with the sins that trouble the consciences of men. So his sacrifice was directed to the cleansing of conscience, something the sacrifices under the law could never do (10:2). NIV speaks of a cleansing "from acts that lead to death," where the Greek is more literally "from dead works." This might mean "either those which end in death or which are the fruits of death" (Calvin, in loc.). So far from engaging in works of that kind, those purified by Christ "serve the living God" (see comments on 3:12). The Christian way is positive, not negative.

Notes

11–12 Διά (*dia*) is used with σκηνῆς (*skēnēs*, "tent") and in the same sentence with both examples of αἵματος (*haimatos*, "blood"). It is not easy to see why it should be used with different meanings in expressions so close; so a meaning like "by means of" is favored. But many favor "through" in the case of the tabernacle and "by means of" in the later places.

13 "Outwardly clean" translates πρὸς τὴν τῆς σαρκὸς καθαρότητα (*pros tēn tēs sarkos katharotēta*) "to the purifying of the flesh."

E. *The Mediator of the New Covenant*

9:15–22

[15]For this reason Christ is the mediator of a new covenant, that those who are
called may receive the promised eternal inheritance—now that he has died as a
ransom to set them free from the sins committed under the first covenant.
[16]In the case of a will, it is necessary to prove the death of the one who made
it, [17]because a will is in force only when somebody has died; it never takes effect
while the one who made it is living. [18]This is why even the first covenant was not
put into effect without blood. [19]When Moses had proclaimed every commandment
of the law to all the people, he took the blood of calves, together with water, scarlet
wool and branches of hyssop, and sprinkled the scroll and all the people. [20]He said,
"This is the blood of the covenant, which God has commanded you to keep." [21]In
the same way, he sprinkled with the blood both the tabernacle and everything used
in its ceremonies. [22]In fact, the law requires that nearly everything be cleansed with
blood, and without the shedding of blood there is no forgiveness.

The author has introduced the thought of the death of Christ and proceeds to develop it. This death is the means of redeeming people from the plight they found themselves in as the result of their sin. It brings them an eternal inheritance. With a play on the double meaning of *diathēkē* (both "a covenant" and "a testament"), the author goes on to bring out the necessity for the death of Christ just as the death of the testator is required if a will is to come into force.

15 "For this reason" may refer to the preceding: because Christ really cleanses from dead works by his blood, he mediates the new covenant. But it is also possible that the words look forward: Christ mediates the new covenant so that the called might receive the inheritance. "Those who are called" preserves the divine initiative, as does "promised." Both expressions remind us of the freeness of salvation and of God's will to bless his people. "Inheritance" originally denoted a possession received through the will of someone who died; then it came to denote anything firmly possessed without regard to the way it was obtained. "Eternal" points to the fact that the believer's possession is no transitory affair. The salvation Christ won is forever.

Christ's death is viewed, then, as "a ransom," the price paid to set free a slave or a prisoner or a person under sentence of death. While the idea of redemption is widespread in the ancient world, the actual word used here (and the most common one in the NT) is a rare word—a fact that may point to the conviction that the redemption Christians know is not simply another redemption among many. It is unique. And this redemption avails for those who sinned under the old covenant as well as for those who are embraced in the new covenant. The author insists that the sacrifices offered under the old covenant cannot take away sins. So it is left to Christ to offer the sacrifice that really effects what the old offerings pointed to but could not accomplish.

16 The argument is not easy to follow in English because we have no single word that is the precise equivalent of *diathēkē*. This Greek word denotes something like an authoritative laying down of what is to be done and is the normal word for a last will and testament. But it is also suited to covenants God makes with people. These are not the result of a process of negotiation in which God talks things over with people and they come to a mutually acceptable arrangement. God lays down the terms. The result is a covenant characterized by the same kind of finality as we see in a testament. (One cannot dicker with a testator!) The author moves easily from the idea of covenant to that of testament. It might help us follow him if we render the first clause in v.15 (with NEB) as "he is the mediator of a new covenant, or testament." This gives two translations for the one Greek word but helps us retain something of the continuity of thought. The death of the testator is necessary for a *diathēkē* (taking the term in the sense "testament") to come into effect. The will may be perfectly valid but it does not operate till death takes place.

17 The point is emphasized. The author uses a technical legal term to indicate that the will is "in force" only (as Moffatt puts it in loc.) "in cases of death." "It never takes effect" makes use of another legal term. It is only the death of the testator that brings the provisions of a will into force.

18 From this the author reasons to the necessity for Christ's death. It was not, so to speak, an option God happened to prefer. The writer will go on to show from the Law that for sin to be forgiven the rule is that blood must be shed. But first he argues that the necessity for death if a *diathēkē* is to be effective (it is plainly needed in the case of a testament), applies just as much when a covenant is in mind. This kind of *diathēkē* also demands that blood be shed if it is to be "put into effect."

19 When the first covenant was made, Moses did two things. First, he "proclaimed every commandment of the law to all the people." That is to say, he set out the terms and conditions of the covenant; he made plain the requirements the covenant laid on the people so they were left in no doubt as to what covenant membership demanded of them. They were now God's people, and that meant they must obey God's laws.

Second, Moses performed certain ritual actions. In what follows the author includes some details not mentioned in Exodus 24. There Moses threw blood on the altar and on the people and read the book to the people. But there is no mention of the water, scarlet wool, hyssop, or the sprinkling of the book. Water and scarlet (whether wool or other material is not said) and hyssop were used in the rite of cleansing healed lepers (Lev 14:4–6; cf. 49–51). Hyssop is mentioned also in connection with the Passover (Exod 12:22) and the cleansing rites associated with the ashes of the red heifer (Num 19:6, 18). It was the natural thing to use hyssop in cleansing (Ps 51:7). The sprinkling of the scroll is not mentioned in Exodus 24. But the book was written by men, and thus it must be cleansed of any defilement they might have conveyed to it. While we do not know where this information came from, there is nothing improbable about any of it.

20 The author has changed the LXX's "Behold, the blood of the covenant" to "This is the blood of the covenant" (which may be meant as a reminiscence of the words used by Jesus at the Last Supper [Mark 14:24]). The verb, too, is different, and the change to "commanded" is highly suitable in the case of a covenant where God lays down the terms. This is no negotiated instrument.

21 "In the same way" does not imply "at the same time." When the covenant was made, the tabernacle had not been constructed. But the cleansing with blood that marked the solemn inauguration of the covenant marked also the solemn inauguration of the place of worship when that took place in due course. Perhaps we are meant to see the dedication of the tabernacle as a kind of renewal of the covenant. Certainly there is continuity. The sprinkling with blood at the consecration of the tabernacle is not specifically mentioned in the OT. It is, however, attested also by Josephus, who says that Aaron's garments, Aaron himself, and apparently the tabernacle and its vessels were sprinkled with blood (Antiq. III, 205–6 [viii. 6]). Under the old covenant sprinkling with blood was the accepted way of cleansing.

22 Cleansing, then, meant blood, though the qualification "nearly [*schedon*] everything" shows that the author is well aware that there were exceptions. Thus the worshiper who was too poor to offer even little birds might instead make a cereal offering (Lev 5:11–13). Some purification could be effected with water (e.g., Lev 15:10), and there might be purification of metal objects by fire and "the water of impurity" (Num 31:22–23). On one occasion gold made atonement for the warriors (Num 31:50), while on another occasion incense atoned (Num 16:46). But such ceremonies were all exceptional. As a whole the Levitical system looks constantly for blood as the means of putting away sin and impurity. The author does not ask why this should be so, though it is clearly the teaching of the OT, as the rabbis also recognized (see, for example, Tal *Yoma* 5a).

Notes

16 It is not said that he who makes the testament must die but that his death must be "brought forward" (*φέρεσθαι*, *pheresthai*). Bruce cites P Oxy ii.244 for the verb used in the technical sense "be registered" and Wettstein for the meaning "be produced as evidence" (in loc.).

17 There is a problem in the use of *μήποτε* (*mēpote*) with an indicative. The best suggestion seems to be that the expression should be taken as a question expecting the answer no; i.e., "Does it ever take effect while the testator lives?"

19 After *μόσχων* (*moschōn*, "calves"), a number of MSS add *καὶ τῶν τράγων* (*kai tōn tragōn*, "and goats"). Some argue that the longer reading is to be preferred, the words being left out by scribes because they do not occur in Exod 24. This is possible, but it seems better to take the shorter reading as original. The reference to goats may have been added because "calves and goats" was a common expression or because goats were so prominent in the Day of Atonement ritual.

22 *Αἱματεκχυσία* (*haimatekchysia*, "shedding of blood") is not attested before this time, and the writer may have coined the word himself.

F. *The Perfect Sacrifice*

9:23–28

[23]It was necessary, then, for the copies of the heavenly things to be purified with these sacrifices, but the heavenly things themselves with better sacrifices than these. [24]For Christ did not enter a man-made sanctuary that was only a copy of the true one; he entered heaven itself, now to appear for us in God's presence. [25]Nor did he enter heaven to offer himself again and again, the way the high priest enters the Most Holy Place every year with blood that is not his own. [26]Then Christ would have had to suffer many times since the creation of the world. But now he has appeared once for all at the end of the ages to do away with sin by the sacrifice of himself. [27]Just as man is destined to die once, and after that to face judgment, [28]so Christ was sacrificed once to take away the sins of many people; and he will appear a second time, not to bear sin, but to bring salvation to those who are waiting for him.

From the sanctuary and what is needed to purify it the author turns to the sacrifice that perfectly cleanses, a sacrifice that was offered once and for all. That one sacrifice, once offered, has effectively put away sin. And the author looks forward briefly to the time when our Lord will come back again, this time not to do anything in connection with sin (all that is necessary has been done) but to bring salvation.

23 "It was necessary" points to something more than expediency or the selection of one among a number of possible courses of action. There was no other way. "Therefore" (rather than "then"; the Greek is *oun*) introduces the necessary inference. The writer has made it clear that blood must be shed in purification according to the law. Specifically the rule is that "without the shedding of blood there is no forgiveness" (v.22). This cannot be ignored as merely Jewish, for the Mosaic system was set up by divine command.

It is true, the author reasons, that the Mosaic system was concerned only with "the copies of the heavenly things"; it was taken up with the external. But the fact that God commanded the system to be set up means that there must be something analogous in it to the way the forgiveness that would really put away sin was brought about. What is stressed is that where atonement really matters—i.e., in the heavenly sphere—better sacrifices are needed than were provided under the old system.

There is a problem in seeing in what sense things in heaven—where God is (v.24)—need purification. Some deny outright that they need it, regarding the expression as a way of referring to God's people. Thus Bruce (in loc.) reminds us that the author tells us repeatedly that it is people's consciences that need to be cleansed; and so the author can speak of God's people as his dwelling, his house (cf. 3:6). Others make essentially the same point and hold that it is not something material but spiritual that is seen as needing cleansing—a fact meaning that Christ's work is effective in the spiritual life of men, not in some material sanctuary. The difficulty with such interpretations is that, while what they say is true, "the heavenly things themselves" is a strange way of referring to men and women here on earth. Other commentators see in v.23 a reference to Satan's rebellion and think of that as somehow defiling heaven so that heaven itself needs cleansing. Still others think of purification in the sense in which it is used here as meaning not so much the removal of impurity as a consecratory or inaugural process. This, they feel, is not out of place with "the heavenly things" any more than with an earthly sanctuary. Akin to that is the view that the earthly sanctuary needed cleansing, not so much because it was unclean, as because it was the place where sinners were restored. So with heaven.

On the whole, it seems best to recall that in the NT there are references to "the spiritual forces of evil in the heavenly realms" (Eph 6:12); the "rulers of this age" (1 Cor 2:8); the "powers" like "height" and "depth" (Rom 8:38–39), as well as "angels" and "demons." Such references seem to indicate wickedness beyond this earth. And when Christ performed his atoning work, he "disarmed the powers and authorities, . . . triumphing over them by the cross" (Col 2:15). It was God's will "through him to reconcile to himself all things, whether things on earth or things in heaven, by making peace through his blood, shed on the cross" (Col 1:20). This strand of teaching is not prominent in Hebrews. Nevertheless, the language used here seems to accord with it better than with other views. The author is fond of the word "better" (see comments on 1:4), but it is unexpected for him to use the plural "sacrifices," since he is insistent that there was but one sacrifice and that Christ suffered "once for all" (v.26). Probably we should take "sacrifices" as the generic plural that lays down the principle fulfilled in the one sacrifice.

24 Christ's work for mankind was done where it really counted. "For" introduces an explanation of what precedes. We have already had the idea that Christ's ministry was not in a sanctuary that is "man-made" (v.11), and here we come back to it. Not in such sanctuaries can the Atonement be made that really deals with sin. Here such a sanctuary is described as a "copy" (*antitypa*) of the true one. The word *typos* "type" is ambiguous and may mean the original or a copy. Thus *antitypos*, "corresponding to the *typos*," is also ambiguous. It may mean the fulfillment of what is foreshadowed in the type, as in 1 Peter 3:20–21, where the Flood is no more than a foreshadowing and baptism the *antitypos*, the significant thing. Here it seems the other way around. The *antitypos* is the copy, the shadow, of the real thing that is in heaven. The earthly antitype points us to the heavenly reality, "the true one."

What he entered is "heaven itself." The word for "heaven" is usually plural in this epistle. Here, however, it is singular. There seems no difference in meaning. The important point is that heaven itself is regarded as the true sanctuary, not some structure within it to which the earthly tabernacle corresponded. "Now" points to present activity. After his atoning work done once for all, Christ now appears before God. We are not fit to stand before God and plead our case, and in any event we are on earth and not in God's heaven. But Christ is there in our stead and in his capacity as the one who died as a better sacrifice (v.23) for sins.

25 "Nor" carries on the negative at the beginning of v.24: "Christ did not enter a man-made sanctuary . . . nor did he . . . offer himself again and again." While there is nothing in the Greek corresponding to NIV's "did he enter heaven," the words seem required. The author is concerned in this verse to repudiate the idea that Christ might have made an offering from time to time in the manner of the high priests. It was basic to their ministry to offer sacrifices repeatedly, just as it was basic to Christ's ministry that he did not do so. The reference in v.25 to entering "the Most Holy Place every year" shows that the sacrifices mainly in mind are those of the Day of Atonement.

Two things call for comment. The first is the clear implication that only Christ's offering can put away sin. The sins of those who lived in old times were dealt with by Christ's one offering. The reasoning is that if that offering had not been sufficient, Christ would have had to offer himself "again and again." That is to say, no other offering is in view when it is a matter of really putting sin away. The other point is that when the high priest entered the Most Holy Place he did so "with blood that is not his own." The superiority of Christ's offering is seen in that he does not press into service some external means, like the blood of some noncooperating, noncomprehending animal. He uses his own blood and with it makes the one sufficient offering.

26 What is implied in v.25 is made explicit here. "Then" is perhaps not the best translation of *epei,* which, as often, introduces an elliptical construction, with a meaning like "for [if it were different]" or, as BAG (s.v.) puts it, "for otherwise he would have had to suffer many times." Again, the implication is that there is no other way of dealing with sin than Christ's own offering of himself. If his one offering was not enough, he would have had to suffer over and over. "Suffer," of course, is used in the sense of "suffer death." The reference to "creation" carries the idea right back to the beginning. No one would ever have been saved without the offering made by Christ.

"Now" (*nyni*) is not temporal; this is an example of its use "introducing the real situation after an unreal conditional clause or sentence, *but, as a matter of fact*" (BAG, s.v.). Once again the author emphasizes the decisive quality of Christ's sacrifice with his "once for all." It matters a great deal to the author that Christ made the definitive offering and that now that it has been made there is no place for another. Many take "at the end of the ages" to mean that the author thought he was living in the last days and that Christ would return very speedily to bring this world to an end. So his sacrifice on the cross was made in the world's last days. But whatever he thought about the imminence of the end of all things, the author says little about it. We should probably understand the words here rather in the sense of "the consummation of the ages," or perhaps with NEB, "at the climax of history." If we take it in the sense of "the close of the age," it would mean that the first coming of Christ—and more particularly his offering of himself on the cross—ushered in the final state of affairs.

It is a common thought of the NT writers that God's decisive action in Christ has altered things radically. The Messianic Age has come—the age that all the preceding ages have led up to.

The purpose of Christ's coming was "to do away with sin." Here the expression *eis athetēsin* is a strong one, signifying the total annulment of sin. The word "is used in a technical juristic sense" (Deiss BS, pp. 228–29) with the meaning "to annul" or "cancel." Sin, then, is rendered completely inoperative and this was done "by the sacrifice of himself." It is the self-offering of Christ that is the decisive thing. For the author this is the truth that must be grasped.

27 This phase of the argument is rounded off with a reference to the one death men die and the one death Christ died. There is a finality about both but very different consequences. Men are "destined to die once." This is not something within their control. A condition of life here on earth is that it ends in death. The "once for all" (*hapax*) so often used of Christ's sacrifice is here used of man's death. There is a finality about it that is not to be disputed. But if it is the complete and final end to life on earth, it is not, as so many in the ancient world thought, the complete and final end. Death is more serious than that because it is followed by judgment. Men are accountable, and after death they will render account to God.

28 "So" introduces a correspondence with the "just as" at the beginning of the previous verse. The passive "was sacrificed" is interesting because it is much more usual for the author to say that Christ offered himself (cf. v.26). Some see the thought here that Christ's enemies were in a sense responsible for his death, but it seems more likely that it is the divine purpose that is in mind. Once more we have the adverb "once-for-all" (*hapax*) applied to the death of Christ. This means a good deal to the author, and he comes back to it again and again.

It is a little difficult to follow NIV in this verse, for an expression meaning "to bear sins" is here rendered "to take away the sins" while later in the verse "not to bear sin" is the translation of an expression that signifies "apart from sin" and has nothing to do with the bearing of sin at all. Sin-bearing is a concept found in the NT only here and in 1 Peter 2:24, but it is quite frequent in the OT, where it plainly means "bear the penalty of sin." For example, the Israelites were condemned to wander in the wilderness for forty years as the penalty for their failure to go up into the land of Canaan: "For forty years—one year for each of the forty days you explored the land—you will suffer for your sins" (Num 14:34; cf. Ezek 18:20, et al.). Many see here an echo of the fourth Servant Song: "He will bear their iniquities" (Isa 53:11); "he bore the sin of many" (Isa 53:12). So the author is saying that Christ took upon himself the consequences of the sins of the many (cf. Mark 10:45).

But this is not the whole story. Christ will come back a second time and then he will not be concerned with sin. The thought is that sin was dealt with finally at his first coming. There is nothing more that he should do. The second time he will come "to bring salvation." There is a sense in which salvation has been brought about by Christ's death. But there is another sense in which it will be brought to its consummation when he returns. Nothing is said about unbelievers. At this point the writer is concerned only with those who are Christ's. They "are waiting for him," where the verb *apekdechomai* expresses the eager looking for the Lord's coming so characteristic of the NT.

Notes

24 Ἅγια (*hagia*, "holy things") is used in the sense "sanctuary" as in 8:2 and elsewhere.

After "the true one" NIV omits "but." The Greek is ἀλλ' (*all'*), the strong adversative, which sets the following in firm contrast to the preceding. The adversative idea comes out in the NIV translation, however.

"For us" renders ὑπὲρ ἡμῶν (*hyper hēmōn*). The preposition in such contexts signifies "on behalf of" or "in the place of."

26 The ἐπεί (*epei*, "since," "then") construction is classed under "the imperfect (without ἄν) in expressions of necessity, obligation, duty, possibility, etc." This "denotes in classical something which is or was actually necessary, etc., but which does not or did not take place" a construction which "is retained in the NT" (BDF, par.358[1]).

"The end of the ages" ἐπὶ συντελείᾳ τῶν αἰώνων (*epi synteleia tōn aiōnōn*) is found in this form here only, though there are some similar expressions in Matt 13:39, 40, 49; 24:3; 28:20.

On ἁμαρτία (*hamartia*, "sin") BAG (s.v.) has the following note: In Hebrews "sin appears as the power that deceives men and leads them to destruction, whose influence and activity can be ended only by sacrifices."

G. *The Law a Shadow*

10:1–4

[1]The law is only a shadow of the good things that are coming—not the realities themselves. For this reason it can never, by the same sacrifices repeated endlessly year after year, make perfect those who draw near to worship. [2]If it could, would they not have stopped being offered? For the worshipers would have been cleansed once for all, and would no longer have felt guilty for their sins. [3]But those sacrifices are an annual reminder of sins, [4]because it is impossible for the blood of bulls and goats to take away sins.

The preceding sections have brought out the efficacy of the blood of Jesus as a prevailing sacrifice, and now stress is laid on the once-for-all character of that sacrifice. First, the author contrasts the substance and the shadow. He sees the ancient system that meant so much to the Jews as no more than an unsubstantial, shadowy affair. The real thing is in Christ. To leave Christ in favor of Judaism would be to forsake the substance for the shadow. The sacrificial system practiced by the Jews could not deal effectually with sin. Since it was no more than a shadow, that was quite impossible.

1 "The law" means strictly the law of Moses, but here it stands for the whole OT, with particular reference to the sacrificial system. This is dismissed as no more than "a shadow" (*skia*). The word is used in conjunction with "copy" (*hypodeigma*) in 8:5 and in opposition to "body" (*sōma*) in Colossians 2:17. It points to something unsubstantial in opposition to what is real. This is not the Platonic thought of a copy of the heavenly "idea" but rather that of a foreshadowing of what is to come. Here the contrast is with "image" (*eikōn*), which is surprising, as *eikōn* normally means "a *derived* likeness and, like the head on a coin or the parental likeness in a child, implies an archetype" (A-S, s.v.).

NIV renders a Greek expression meaning "the image itself of the things" as "the realities themselves." Perhaps those exegetes are right who see a metaphor from painting (e.g., Calvin, in loc.). The "shadow" then is the preliminary outline that an artist may make before he gets to his colors, and the *eikōn* is the finished portrait. The author is saying that the law is no more than a preliminary sketch. It shows the shape of things to come, but the solid reality is not there. It is in Christ. The "good things that are coming" are not defined, but the general term is sufficient to show that the law pointed forward to something well worthwhile.

There is a problem in the second half of v.1. Should we take the expression *eis to diēnekes,* rendered as "endlessly," with what precedes it in the Greek (as NIV) or with what follows, as NEB: "It provides for the same sacrifices year after year, and with these it can never bring the worshippers to perfection for all time [*eis to diēnekes*]"? Technically, the former is possible, but there are reasons for preferring NEB here. The expression *eis to diēnekes* marks "an act which issues in a permanent result" (Westcott, in loc.), a meaning we see when it is repeated in v.12 (where NIV has "for all time") and v.14 (NIV, "forever"). The Greek word order also favors NEB (Montefiore [in loc.] thinks that this, along with vv.12, 14, "forbids" taking the word otherwise).

The author is saying, then, that the Levitical sacrifices continue year by year, but they are quite unable to bring the worshipers into a permanent state of perfection. The yearly sacrifices mark another reference to the Day of Atonement ceremonies—ceremonies of which the author makes a good deal of use. "Can never" points to an inherent weakness of the old system: the animal sacrifices are quite unable to effect the putting away of sin. The yearly repetition repeats the failure. The same rites that were unavailing last year are all that the law can offer this year. There is an inbuilt limitation in animal sacrifice. "Make perfect" is used, of course, in a moral and spiritual sense.

2 The rhetorical question emphasizes the truth that the very continuity of the sacrifices witnesses to their ineffectiveness. Incidentally, the way it is put seems to accord more naturally with a situation in which the sacrifices were still being offered in the temple than with one in which they had ceased. This may be a pointer to the date of the epistle. Had the sacrifices really dealt with sins, the author reasons, the worshipers would have been cleansed and that would have been that. There would have been no need and no place for repeating them (cf. 9:9). The very necessity for repetition shows that the desired cleansing has not been effected. "An atonement that needs constant repetition does not really atone; a conscience which has to be cleansed once a year has never been truly cleansed" (Robinson, in loc.). The translation "would no longer have felt guilty for their sins" obscures the reference to "conscience." It may be that this rendering gives much the right sense, but we should not miss this further reference to conscience, which means so much in this epistle (see 9:9, 14; 10:2, 22; 13:18; in the NT only 1 Cor uses the term more often). A really effectual atonement would mean the permanent removal of the worshipers' sins. There would be no need for anything like the annual Day of Atonement ceremonies.

3 The strong adversative "but" (*all'*) puts the truth in sharp contrast with false estimates of what sacrifices might do. Perhaps the flavor of the Greek word *anamnēsis* is better caught with "remembrance" instead of "reminder"; i.e., "in them is a remembrance of sins." *Anamnēsis* is used in the NT only in the accounts of the institution of the Lord's Supper (Luke 22:19; 1 Cor 11:24–25) and here. Where the Bible has the idea of remembrance, as Bruce points out (in loc.), action appears to be involved. When people remember sins, they either repent (Deut 9:7) or else persist in sin (Ezek 23:19). When God remembers sin, he usually punishes it (1 Kings 17:18; Rev 16:19); when he pardons, he can be said not to remember sin (Ps 25:7). The author then is using an expression that reminds us that Jesus said, "Do this in remembrance of me" (Luke 22:19), as he established a covenant in which the central thing is that God says, "[I] will remember their sins no more" (Jer 31:34). The Day of Atonement ceremonies each year reminded people of the fact that something had to be done about sin. But the ceremonies did no more than that.

4 The yearly ceremonies were ineffective because "it is impossible for the blood of bulls and goats to take away sins." The word "impossible" is a strong one. There is no way forward through the blood of animals. "Take away" (*aphaireō*) is used of a literal taking off, as of Peter's cutting off the ear of the high priest's slave (Luke 22:50), or metaphorically as of the removal of reproach (Luke 1:25). It signifies the complete removal of sin so that it is no longer a factor in the situation. That is what is needed and that is what the sacrifices could not provide.

Notes

1 Instead of *οὐκ αὐτὴν τὴν εἰκόνα* (*ouk autēn tēn eikona*, "not the image itself"), P[46] reads *καὶ τὴν εἰκόνα* (*kai tēn eikona*, "and the image"), which solves some problems by making the text read, "For the law, having a shadow and the image of the good things. . . ." But support for this reading is slight and the construction of the sentence seems to imply that *εἰκών* (*eikōn*, "image") is contrasted with *σκιά* (*skia*, "shadow"), not joined with it as of similar meaning. It seems an attempt to remove a difficulty and should be rejected.

Another textual problem is whether to take the singular *δύναται* (*dynatai*, "it can") or the plural *δύνανται* (*dynantai*, "they can"). NIV is almost certainly correct in favoring the singular, for the plural involves leaving *νόμος* (*nomos*, "law") as a *nominativus pendens*, which the author normally avoids.

Εἰς τὸ διηνεκὲς (*eis to diēnekes*) is found in NT only in 7:3; 10:1, 12, 14. A-S derives the adjective from *διήεγκα* (*diēnenka*), the aorist of *διαφέρω* (*diapherō*), and gives it the meaning "unbroken, continuous." The present expression he sees as meaning "continually, perpetually, forever" (s.v.). Westcott distinguishes it from *εἰς τὸν αἰῶνα* (*eis ton aiōna*, "forever") in that "it expresses the thought of a continuously abiding result. The former phrase looks to the implied absence of limit while *εἰς τὸ διηνεκές* affirms uninterrupted duration in regard to some ruling thought" (in loc.).

Προσέρχομαι (*proserchomai*) has a curious distribution. It is found in NT eight-seven times, of which no less than fifty-two are in Matt, ten in Luke, ten in Acts, and then seven in Heb. It occurs but once in all the Pauline corpus and similarly once in all the Catholic Epistles. The word means "approach," "draw near," and may be used of drawing near to God (7:25; 11:6) or to the throne of grace (4:16). Here, as in v.22, we have the absolute use, with "God" understood. The participle "those who draw near" means "the worshipers."

2 We must understand an ellipsis after *ἐπεί* (*epei*) to give the meaning "since [if it were not so]," "otherwise," "if it could."

H. *One Sacrifice for Sins*

10:5–18

5Therefore, when Christ came into the world, he said:

"Sacrifice and offering you did not desire,
but a body you prepared for me;
6with burnt offerings and sin offerings
you were not pleased.
7Then I said, 'Here I am—it is written about me
in the scroll—
I have come to do your will, O God.' "

8First he said, "Sacrifices and offerings, burnt offerings and sin offerings you did
not desire, nor were you pleased with them" (although the law required them to be
made). 9Then he said, "Here I am, I have come to do your will." He sets aside the
first to establish the second. 10And by that will, we have been made holy through
the sacrifice of the body of Jesus Christ once for all.
11Day after day every priest stands and performs his religious duties; again and
again he offers the same sacrifices, which can never take away sins. 12But when
this priest had offered for all time one sacrifice for sins, he sat down at the right
hand of God. 13Since that time he waits for his enemies to be made his footstool,
14because by one sacrifice he has made perfect forever those who are being made
holy.
15The Holy Spirit also testifies to us about this. First he says:

16"This is the covenant I will make with them
after that time, says the Lord.

I will put my laws in their hearts,

and I will write them on their minds."

17Then he adds:

"Their sins and lawless acts
I will remember no more."

18And where these have been forgiven, there is no longer any sacrifice for sin.

It is the author's habit to clinch his argument by appealing to Scripture. In the preceding sections, however, he has been arguing without such appeals. Now he rounds off this stage of his theme by showing that the Bible proves the correctness of the position he has advocated. Animal sacrifices could not take away the sins of the people. But it was the will of God that sin be atoned for. Christ's perfect sacrifice of himself fulfills God's will as animal sacrifices could never do. This the author sees foretold in Psalm 40. Then, as he goes on to bring out something of the utter finality of the offering of Christ, he returns to the quotation from Jeremiah he had used in chapter 8 to initiate his discussion of the new covenant. His argument up till now has been the negative one that the animal sacrifices of the old covenant were unavailing. Now he says positively that Christ's sacrifice, which established the new covenant, was effectual. It really put away sin. And it was foreshadowed in the same passage from Jeremiah.

5–7 The inferential conjunction "therefore" (*dio*) introduces the next stage of the argument: Because the Levitical sacrifices were powerless to deal with sin, another provision had to be made. The writer does not say who the speaker is nor whom he spoke to, but TEV gives the sense of it with "When Christ was about to come into the world, he said to God. . . ." The words of the psalm are regarded as coming from Christ and as giving the reason for the Incarnation. The preexistence of Christ is assumed. The quotation is from Psalm 40:6–8 (LXX, Ps 39:7–9), with some variations that, however, do not greatly affect the sense. This psalm is not quoted elsewhere in the NT, and this reminds us once more that the writer of this epistle has his own style of writing and his own way of viewing Holy Writ.

In the passage quoted, the LXX reads "a body you prepared for me," whereas the Hebrew has "ears you have dug for me." Some MSS of the LXX, it is true, read "ears." Moreover, some scholars hold that this reading is original and that the reading "body" arose from accidental error in the transmission of the text. But it seems more probable that the LXX gives an interpretative translation (with "ears" substituted in some MSS by scribes who knew the Hebrew). Some see a reference to the custom of piercing the ear of a slave who did not wish to avail himself of the opportunity to be set free, preferring to remain enslaved to his master for life (Exod 21:6; Deut 15:17). But the language makes this unlikely. It is more probable that the LXX translators are giving us a somewhat free rendering. They may wish to express the view that the body is the instrument through which the divine command, received by the ear, is carried out (so, for example, Westcott). Or, taking the part for the whole, they may be reasoning that "the 'digging' or hollowing out of the ears is part of the total work of fashioning a human body" (Bruce, in loc.). The verb "prepare" is an unusual one to use of a body, but in this context it is both intelligible and suitable.

The words "sacrifice" and "offering" are both quite general and might apply to any sacrificial offering, whereas the "burnt offering" and the "sin offering" are both specific. Actually, in the Hebrew the first two are a trifle more precise and may be differentiated as the sacrifice of an animal (*zebaḥ*) and the cereal offering (*minḥāh*). The four terms taken together are probably meant as a summary of the main kinds of Levitical sacrifice. The classification is not exhaustive, but the ones listed sufficiently indicate the main kinds of sacrifices under the old covenant.

The psalmist says that God did not "will" (so rather than "desire," *ēthelēsas*) or "take pleasure in" such offerings. This does not mean that the offerings were against the will of God or that God was displeased with them. The meaning rather is that, considered in themselves as simply a series of liturgical actions, they were not the product of the divine will nor did they bring God pleasure. They might have done so if they had been offered in the right spirit, by penitent people expressing their state of heart by their offerings. But the thrust of the quotation emphasizes the importance of the will.

"Then" means "in those circumstances" rather than "at that time." Since sacrifice as such did not avail before God, other action had to be taken. That action means that Christ came to do the will of God. In his case, there was no question of a dumb animal being offered up quite irrespective of any desires it might have. He came specifically to do the will of God, and his sacrifice was the offering of one fully committed to doing the will of the Father.

The reference to the "scroll" is not completely clear, but probably the psalmist meant that he was fulfilling what was written in the law. The author sees the words as emphasizing that Christ came to fulfill what was written in Scripture. The words that immediately follow in the psalm are "your law is within my heart," and they show what this expression implies. The author uses the word "will" (*thelēma*) five times, always of the will of God. It was important to him that what God wills is done. Christ came to do nothing other than the will of God.

8 "First," that is, "above," "as he said above," refers to what came earlier, not to what was spoken first of all. It is not clear why the references to sacrifices are all plural here. In v.5 both "sacrifice" and "offering" are singular and while "burnt offerings" in v.6 is plural, in most MSS of the LXX it is singular, as is the underlying Hebrew throughout. Probably all we can say is that the plural makes it all very general. Multiply them how you will and characterize them how you will, God takes no pleasure in sacrifices as such. Indeed, this is so even though the law requires them to be offered and the law is from God. Westcott sees a significance in the absence of the article "the" with "law" (*nomos*), which indicates to him that the stress is on the character of the sacrifices as legal rather than Mosaic (in loc.). But even if the grammatical point be sustained, it is not easy to see how this helps.

We should see the statement concerning the necessity of sacrifice as another illustration of the attitude consistently maintained by the author that the OT system is divinely inspired but preliminary. He holds it to be effective but only within its own limited scope. The sacrifices were commanded in God's law and therefore must be offered. But they were not God's final will nor God's answer to the problem of sin. They were partial and they pointed the way. Even though they came as part of the law, we are to recognize their limitation.

9 "He said" (*eirēken*) is perfect, whereas "I said" (*eipon*) in v.7, to which it refers, is aorist; the change of tense emphasizes the permanence of the saying ("the perfect of a completed action = the saying stands on record," Moffatt, in loc.). The words about doing the will of God are there for all time. On this occasion the omission of the parenthesis means that they stand out in their simplicity and strength. The verb "sets aside" (*anairei*) is used only here in Hebrews. It means "take away" and is used sometimes in the sense of taking away by killing, that is, murdering, and this shows that it is a strong word. It points to the total abolition of the former way. By contrast the second way is "established," "made firm." Neither "the first" nor "the second" is defined, but clearly the way of the Levitical sacrifices and the way of the sacrifice of Christ are being set over against each other. These are not complementary systems that may exist side by side. The one excludes the other. No compromise is possible between them.

10 We must translate *en ho thelēmati* in some such way as "by that will." But the preposition *en* is "in," and it may be that our author sees the sanctified as "in" the will of God. That will is large enough and deep enough to find a place for them all. We should notice a difference between the way the author uses the verb "to sanctify" (NIV, "made holy") and the way Paul uses it. For the apostle, sanctification is a process whereby the believer grows progressively in Christian qualities and character. In Hebrews the same terminology is used of the process by which a person becomes a Christian and is therefore "set apart" for God. There is no contradiction between these two; both are necessary for the fully developed Christian life. But we must be on our guard lest we read this epistle with Pauline terminology in mind. The sanctification meant here is one brought about by the death of Christ. It has to do with making people Christian, not with developing Christian character. It is important also to notice that it is the offering "of the body" of Christ that saves.

Some exegetes have been so impressed by the emphasis on doing the will of God over against the offering of animal sacrifice that they suggest that the actual death of Jesus mattered little. What was important, they say, is the yielded will, the fact that Jesus was ready to do his Father's will at whatever cost to himself. The death was incidental; the will was primary. But this is not what the author is saying. The will is certainly important, and unless we see this we misunderstand the author's whole position. Yet it is also important to realize that the will of God in question was that "the body of Jesus Christ" be offered. Calvary, not Gethsemane, is central, important though the latter certainly was. The contrast is not between animal sacrifice and moral obedience. It is between the death of an uncomprehending animal and the death in which Jesus accepted the will of God with all that it entails.

The offering of Jesus' body was made "once for all." Here again we have the emphatic *ephapax*. It matters immensely that this one offering, once made, avails for all people at all times. This contrasts sharply with the sacrifices under the old covenant as the author has been emphasizing. But it contrasts also with other religions. Héring (in loc.), for example, points out that this distinguishes Christianity from the mystery religions, where the sacrifice of the god was repeated annually. In fact, there is no other religion in which one great happening brings salvation through the centuries and through the world. This is the distinctive doctrine of Christianity.

11 The author brings out the finality of Jesus' sacrifice from another angle as he considers once more the continuing activity of the Levitical priests. Actually he does not confine the continual activity to those priests, for he uses the quite general expression "every priest." It is characteristic of the activity of a priest that he stands and ministers day by day. But of course the writer has the Levitical priests especially in mind. And it is true of them (as of other priests) that they keep offering sacrifices that can never take sins away. Standing is the posture appropriate to priestly service, and in the tabernacle or temple the priests of Aaron's line never sat during the course of their ministry in the sanctuary.

The word translated "performs his religious duties" (*leitourgōn*) is that from which we derive our word "liturgy." Originally it meant "perform a public service" and was used of a wide variety of activities. In the Bible, however, it is confined to service of a religious character. Here it clearly applies to all the services a priest performs. Yet despite all their activity, priests cannot deal with the basic problem—that of removing sin.

12 Jesus' work is contrasted to that of priests. He offered one sacrifice—just one alone (there is emphasis on "one"). Then he sat down. The author mentioned this before (e.g., 1:3; 8:1), but he put no emphasis on it. Now he stresses Jesus' posture, contrasting it to that of the Levitical priests, and the contrast brings out an important point for understanding the work of Christ. Levitical priests stand, for their work is not done but goes on. Christ sits, for his work is done. Sitting is the posture of rest, not of work. That Christ is seated means that his atoning work is complete; there is nothing to be added to it. The expression "for all time" (*eis to diēnekes*) is so situated in the Greek that it can be taken either with "offered" (as NIV) or with "sat down" (as Moffatt, in loc.). There is no grammatical reason for either course, but on the whole it seems best to take it with the words about offering. This seems more consistent with the way the author is unfolding his thought.

We should notice further that to be seated at God's right hand is to be in the place of highest honor. Even angels are not said to have attained to this; they stand in God's presence (Luke 1:19). When Jesus claimed this place for himself, the high priest tore his robe at what he regarded as blasphemy (Mark 14:62–63). The author is combining with the thought of a finished work the idea that our Lord is a being of the highest dignity and honor.

13 His work accomplished, the Lord now waits. The remaining words of this verse are a quotation from Psalm 110:1, with slight alterations to fit the grammatical context. The "enemies" are not defined, and the meaning appears to be that Christ rests until in God's good time all evil is overthrown. In other parts of the NT we read of God's enemies as being defeated at the end time (notably in Rev), but this is not a feature in Hebrews; and we have no means of knowing precisely what enemies he has in mind. There is possibly a hint of warning to the readers—viz., they should take care that they are not numbered among these enemies.

14 Once more the writer emphasizes that Christ has offered one offering that saves men. Clearly this is of the utmost importance for him. So he comes back to it again and again. The conjunction "because" introduces the reason for the statement in v.13. As in v.12, "one" is in an emphatic position; the perfecting of the saints came by one offering and by one alone. The writer does not say that Christ's sacrifice perfects the people but that Christ does this. His salvation is essentially personal. We have seen a number of times that the author is fond of the idea of "perfecting." He applies it to Christ (see comments on 2:10) and also to his people. The process of salvation takes people who are far from perfect and makes them fit to be in God's presence forever. It is not temporary improvement he is speaking of but improvement that is never ending.

As in v.10, the author uses the concept of sanctifying, or making holy, to characterize the saved. The present tense (*hagiazomenous*, "those being made holy") poses a small problem that has been solved in more than one way. Some see it as timeless; others think of it as indicating a continuing process of adding to the number of the saved, others again of those who in the present are experiencing the process of being made holy. The last-mentioned view is not likely to be correct because, as we have noticed, the idea of sanctification as a continuing process does not seem to appear in Hebrews. But either of the other two views is possible. Those Christ saves are set apart for the service of God and that forever. The writer, then, is contemplating a great salvation, brought about by one magnificent offering that cannot and need not be repeated—an offering that is eternal in its efficacy and that makes perfect the people it sanctifies.

15–17 The writer consistently regards God as the author of Scripture and, as we have seen, ascribes to God words uttered by Moses and others. He does not often speak of the Holy Spirit as responsible for what is written. (See 3:7 and here; in 9:8 he sees the arrangement of the tabernacle, which of course is recorded in Scripture, as due to the Spirit.) But this is consistent with the writer's general approach, and we should not be surprised at it here. The Spirit, he says, "testifies." The choice of word implies that there is excellent testimony behind what he has been saying about Christ. There is a small grammatical problem because the quotation is introduced with "First he says," though there is nothing to follow this up. NIV supplies the lack with "Then he adds" in v.17; and this seems to be the sense of it, even though there is nothing in the Greek corresponding to these words.

Once more the writer quotes from Jeremiah 31:33ff. (words he quoted at length in 8:7ff.). This time he does not begin his quotation so early (in ch. 8 it began at Jer 31:31), and there is a big gap (with the omission of the end of Jer 31:33 and most of 34). The reason for this appears to be that he quotes enough to show that it is the "new covenant" passage he has in mind and then goes straight to the words about forgiveness. Since his real interest lies here, he omits all else. The quotation has a considerable number of minor differences from the LXX, though none that greatly affects the sense. But there are so many of them that most commentators think the writer is here quoting from memory and giving the general sense of Jeremiah's words. The effect of all this is to emphasize the fact that Christ has established the new covenant and that he has done so by providing for the forgiveness of sins.

18 This short verse emphatically conveys the utter finality of Christ's offering and the sheer impossibility of anything further. Where sins have been effectively dealt with, there can be no further place for an offering for sin. The author sees this as established by Scripture, and this is consistent with his normal use of the OT. He cites the Bible to show that since the new covenant is established, there is no room for any further sacrifice. This is the word of the prophet and must be accepted by any who see the OT as Scripture. So, the author reasons, now that the new covenant spoken of by the prophet is a reality, the prophetic word itself rules out the possibility of any further sacrifice.

Notes

5 Προσφορά (*prosphora*) is found nine times in the NT, five of them in this chapter (vv.5, 8, 10, 14, 18). The word means originally "the act of bringing" and thus "what is brought," or "offering." Here it is practically equivalent to "sacrifice."

6 This is one of the few cases in which the verb εὐδοκέω (*eudokeō*, "be pleased") takes a direct object (v.8; Matt 12:18).

7 Κεφαλίς (*kephalis*), here only in NT, is a diminutive of κεφαλή (*kephalē*) and it is used for such things as the capital of a column. It is often said that its use here comes from its application to the little knobs at the end of the sticks on which scrolls were wound. Though this is not improbable, Westcott points out that no example of this usage of κεφαλίς (*kephalis*) is cited (in loc.). Be that as it may, here the word must mean "scroll." The genitive of the articular infinitive, τοῦ ποιῆσαι (*tou poiēsai*, "to do"), normally denotes purpose, as here.

13 This is the one occurrence of λοιπός (*loipos*) in Hebrews (55 times in NT). The word means "remaining" and the neuter singular is used adverbially with or without the article in the sense of "from now on," "in the future," "henceforth" (BAG [s.v.] translates here as "then waiting"). From the time that Christ sat down, his saving work completed, he waited.

15 Some regard ἡμῖν (*hēmin*) as a dative of advantage, "bears witness for us" rather than "to us." But the difference is not great.

I. *The Sequel—The Right Way*

10:19–25

[19]Therefore, brothers, since we have confidence to enter the Most Holy Place
by the blood of Jesus, [20]by a new and living way opened for us through the curtain,

that is, his body, [21]and since we have a great priest over the house of God, [22]let us draw near to God with a sincere heart in full assurance of faith, having our hearts sprinkled to cleanse us from a guilty conscience and having our bodies washed with pure water. [23]Let us hold unswervingly to the hope we profess, for he who promised is faithful. [24]And let us consider how we may spur one another on toward love and good deeds. [25]Let us not give up meeting together, as some are in the habit of doing, but let us encourage one another—and all the more as you see the Day approaching.

We have now concluded the solid doctrinal section that constitutes the main section of the epistle. As Paul often does, the writer of Hebrews exhorts his readers on the basis of the doctrine he has made so clear. Because the great teachings he has set forth are true, it follows that those who profess them should live in a manner befitting them. There are resemblances between the exhortation in this paragraph and that in 4:14–16. But we must not forget that the intervening discussion has made clear what Christ's high priestly work has done for his people. On the basis of Christ's sacrifice, the writer exhorts his readers to make the utmost use of the blessing that has been won for them.

19 The address "brothers" is affectionate, and the writer exhorts them on the basis of the saving events. "Therefore" links the exhortation with what has preceded it. These saving events give the Christian a new attitude towards the presence of God. Nadab and Abihu died while offering incense (Lev 10:2), and it had become the custom for the high priest not to linger in the Most Holy Place on the Day of Atonement lest people be terrified (M *Yoma* 5:1). But Christians approach God confidently, completely at home in the situation created by Christ's saving work. They enter "the Most Holy Place," which, of course, is no physical sanctuary but is, in truth, the presence of God. And they enter it "by the blood of Jesus," i.e., on the basis of his saving death.

20 The way to God is both "new" and "living." It is "new" because what Jesus has done has created a completely new situation, "living" because that way is indissolubly bound up with the Lord Jesus himself. The writer does not say, as John does, that Jesus is the way (John 14:6), but this is close to his meaning. This is not the way of the dead animals of the old covenant or the lifeless floor over which the Levitical high priest walked. It is the living Lord himself. This way to God he "dedicated" (NIV, "opened"; the word is that used of dedicating the old covenant with blood, 9:18), which hints again at his sacrifice of himself. The "curtain" goes back once more to the imagery of the tabernacle, for it was through the curtain that hung before the Most Holy Place that the high priest passed into the very presence of God.

There is a problem as to whether we take "that is, his flesh" (NIV, "body") with "curtain," which is the more natural way of taking the Greek, or whether we take it with "way." The difficulty in taking it with "curtain" is that it seems to make the flesh of Christ that which veils God from men. There is a sense, however, in which Christians have always recognized this, even if in another sense they see Christ's body as revealing God. As a well-known hymn puts it, "Veiled in flesh the Godhead see." The value of this way of looking at the imagery of the curtain is that it was by the rending of the veil—the flesh being torn on the cross—that the way to God was opened. The author is saying in his own way what the Synoptists said when they spoke of the curtain of the temple as being torn when Christ died (Matt 27:51; Mark 15:38;

Luke 23:45). The flesh (NIV, "body") here is the correlate of the blood in v.19. The alternative is to see in the equation of "flesh" and "way" the thought that the whole earthly life of Jesus is the way that bring us to God. This is not impossible, but the grammar favors the former view.

21 The term "great priest" is a literal rendering of the Hebrew title we know as "high priest" (see, e.g., Num 35:25, 28; Zech 6:11). We have had references to Jesus as "a son over God's house" (3:6) and as a high priest. Now the two thoughts are brought together. The author does not forget Jesus' high place. He has taken a lowly place (cf. the reference to his flesh, v.20), and he has died to make a way to God for men. But this assumption of the role of a servant should not blind us to the fact that Jesus is "over" God's household. Once again we have the highest Christology combined with the recognition that Jesus rendered lowly service.

22 Now come three exhortations: "Let us draw near," "Let us hold unswervingly" (v.23), and "Let us consider" (v.24). The contemplation of what Christ has done should stir his people into action. First, we are to draw near to God "with a sincere heart." The "heart" stands for the whole of the inner life of man, and it is important that as God's people approach him, they be right inwardly. It is the "pure in heart" who see God (Matt 5:8). In view of what Christ has done for us, we should approach God in deep sincerity. The "full assurance of faith" stresses that it is only by trust in Christ, who has performed for us the high priestly work that gives access to God, that we can draw near at all.

The references to the sprinkled hearts and the washed bodies should be taken together. The washing of the body with pure water is surely a reference to baptism, despite the objection of Calvin, who sees it as meaning "the Spirit of God" (in loc.). But the thing that distinguished Christian baptism from the multiplicity of lustrations that were practiced in the religions of the ancient world was that it was more than an outward rite cleansing the body from ritual defilement. Baptism is the outward sign of an inward cleansing, and it was the latter that was the more important. So here it is mentioned first. The sprinkling of the hearts signifies the effect of the blood of Christ on the inmost being. Christians are cleansed within by his shed blood (cf. the sprinkling of the priests, Exod 29:21; Lev 8:30).

23 The second exhortation is to hold fast the profession of hope. The author has already used the verb *katechō* in urging his readers to "hold on to" their confidence and their glorying in hope (3:6) and the beginning of their confidence (3:14). With a different verb (*krateō*), he has told them to "hold firmly" to the confession (4:14). Now he wants them to retain a firm grasp on "the confession of the hope," or, as NIV puts it, "the hope we profess." This is an unusual expression, and we might have expected "faith" rather than "hope" (this is actually the reading in a few MSS). But there is point in referring to hope. It has already been described as an "anchor for the soul" (6:19). Westcott comments, "Faith reposes completely in the love of God: Hope vividly anticipates that God will fulfill His promises in a particular way" (in loc.). Christians can hold fast to their hope in this way because behind it is a God in whom they can have full confidence. God is thoroughly to be relied on. When he makes a promise, that promise will infallibly be kept. He has taken the initiative in making the promise, and he will fulfill his purposes in making it.

24 The third exhortation is to consider one another. This is the only place where the author uses the expression "one another" (*allēlous*), though it is frequently found in the NT. He is speaking of a mutual activity, one in which believers encourage one another, not one where leaders direct the rest as to what they are to do. The word rendered "spur" is actually a noun, *paroxysmos,* which usually has a meaning like "irritation" or "exasperation." It is most unusual to have it used in a good sense, and the choice of the unusual word makes the exhortation more striking.

Christians are to provoke one another to love (*agapē*), a word found again in Hebrews only in 6:10. It is the characteristic NT term for a love that is not self-seeking, a love whose paradigm is the Cross (1 John 4:10). This is a most important Christian obligation, and believers are to help one another attain it. It is interesting that this kind of love is thus a product of community activity, for it is a virtue that requires others for its exercise. One may practice faith or hope alone, but not love. (For the conjunction of faith, hope, and love, see comments on 6:11.) The readers are to urge one another to "good deeds" as well as to love. The contemplation of the saving work of Christ leads on to good works in the lives of believers. The expression is left general, but the writer selects as especially important love and (in the next verse) the gathering together of believers—an interesting combination.

25 Though NIV might give the impression that this is a fourth exhortation, this is not so. The construction is a participial one, carrying on the thought of the previous verse, not giving up "meeting together." "Some" were doing this. The word is quite general, and we have no way of knowing who these abstainers were. Though it would be interesting to know whether they were from the same group as the readers, we know no more than that the early church had its problems with people who stayed away from church. It was a dangerous practice because, as Moffatt says, "Any early Christian who attempted to live like a pious particle without the support of the community ran serious risks in an age when there was no public opinion to support him" (in loc.). The attitude may mean that the abstainers saw Christianity as just another religion to be patronized or left alone. They had missed the finality on which the author lays such stress.

The writer goes on to suggest that Christians ought to be exhorting one another, and all the more as they see "the Day" getting near. Some think this Day was that of the destruction of Jerusalem, signs of which may have been evident even as this letter was being written. But it is more in accordance with NT usage to see a reference to the Day of Judgment, though, as many commentators point out, it must have been difficult for Christians in those early days to separate the two. The main thing, however, is that the writer is stressing the accountability of his readers. They must act toward their fellow believers as those who will give account of themselves to God.

Notes

---

19 The construction *παρρησίαν εἰς τὴν εἴσοδον* (*parrēsian eis tēn eisodon,* "confidence to enter") is unusual, and Héring refers to it as "rather strained." Eἰς (*eis*) apparently denotes the end or aim, "confidence leading to."

23 Strictly *ἀκλινῆ* (*aklinē,* "unswervingly") refers to *ὁμολογίαν* (*homologian,* "confession"), but NIV and most translations transfer it to those who do the confessing, a reasonable procedure, for it is the people who must hold unwaveringly to the confession.

25 "Meeting together" here is ἐπισυναγωγή (*episynagōgē*), a very unusual word used again in the NT only at 2 Thess 2:1. Some argue that the ἐπί (*epi*) is important and means "in addition." They think that some Jewish Christians worshiped in the synagogue and also in the Christian "episynagogue." In that case, ceasing to attend the "episynagogue" would leave them simply as Jews. But this is reading a lot into the prefix, and the word does not seem to be used in this way elsewhere. The Jews held firmly to the importance of meeting together; there is a well-known saying of Hillel's, "Keep not aloof from the congregation" (M *Aboth* 2:5). There is also a less-well-known one in which he says that God said, "To the place that I love, there My feet lead me: if thou wilt come into My House, I will come into thy house; if thou wilt not come to My House, I will not come to thy house" (Tal *Sukkah* 53a).

J. *The Sequel—the Wrong Way*

10:26–31

[26]If we deliberately keep on sinning after we have received the knowledge of the truth, no sacrifice for sins is left, [27]but only a fearful expectation of judgment and of raging fire that will consume the enemies of God. [28]Anyone who rejected the law of Moses died without mercy on the testimony of two or three witnesses. [29]How much more severely do you think a man deserves to be punished who has trampled the Son of God under foot, who has treated as an unholy thing the blood of the covenant that sanctified him, and who has insulted the Spirit of grace? [30]For we know him who said, "It is mine to avenge; I will repay," and again, "The Lord will judge his people." [31]It is a dreadful thing to fall into the hands of the living God.

The issues are serious. While the writer continues to express confidence that his friends will do the right thing, he leaves them in no doubt as to the gravity of their situation and the terrible consequences of failing to respond to God's saving act in Christ. God is a God of love. But he is implacably opposed to all that is evil. Those who persist in wrong face judgment.

26 It is clear that the writer has apostasy in mind. He is referring to people who "have received the knowledge of the truth," where "truth" (*alētheia*) stands for "the content of Christianity as the absolute truth" (BAG, s.v.), as it frequently does in the NT. The people in question, then, know what God has done in Christ; their acquaintance with Christian teaching is more than superficial. If, knowing this, they revert to an attitude of rejection, of continual sin (cf. the present participle *hamartanontōn* rendered "keep on sinning"), then there remains no sacrifice for sins. Such people have rejected the sacrifice of Christ, and the preceding argument has shown that there is no other. If they revert to the Jewish sacrificial system, they go back to sacrifices that their knowledge of Christianity teaches them cannot put away sin (v.4). The writer adopts no pose of superiority, but his "we" puts him in the same class as his readers. While he emphasizes the danger of others, he does not forget that he too is weak and liable to sin.

27 Far from any sacrifice to put away the sins of the apostates, "only a fearful expectation of judgment" awaits such people. The nature of this expectation is not defined, and the fact that the fate of these evil persons is left indefinite makes the warning all the more impressive. The adjective *phoberos* ("fearful") is unusual; it occurs elsewhere in the NT only in v.31 and 12:21 and conveys the idea of "frightening." The judgment of the person still bearing his sins is a terrible one. The writer describes it as "raging fire" (possibly borrowed from Isa 26:11), which is a vivid expression for "the fire of judgment that, with its blazing flames, appears like a living being intent on devouring God's adversaries" (BAG, p. 338). The word "enemies" (*hypenantious*) shows that the apostates were not regarded as holding a neutral position. They have become the adversaries of God.

28–29 An argument from the greater to the lesser brings out the seriousness of the situation. To despise the law of Moses was a very serious matter, but this is more serious still. The law of Moses was held by Jews to be divinely given: anyone who rejected it rejected God's direction. When this happened, no discretion was allowed: the man must be executed. In such a serious matter the charge had to be proved beyond doubt. The testimony of one witness was not sufficient; there had to be two or three. But when there were the required witnesses to say what the man had done, then justice took over. There was no place for mercy. He must be executed (Deut 17:6; 19:15).

The writer invites the readers to work out for themselves how much more serious is the punishment of the man who apostatizes from Christ. It must be more severe than under the old way because Jesus is greater than Moses (3:1ff.); the new covenant is better than the old, founded on better promises (8:6) and established by a better sacrifice (9:23).

There are three counts in the indictment of the apostate. First, he has "trampled the Son of God under foot." It is most unusual to have the verb *katapateō* used with a personal object (elsewhere in the NT it is the literal treading under the feet of things that the verb denotes). "To trample under foot" is a strong expression for disdain. It implies not only rejecting Christ but also despising him—him who is no less than "the Son of God."

The second count is that the apostate takes lightly the solemn shedding of covenant blood. "The blood of the covenant" is an expression used of the blood that established the old covenant (Exod 24:8; cf. Heb 9:20) and also of the blood of Jesus that established the new covenant (Matt 26:28; Mark 14:24; cf. also Luke 22:20; 1 Cor 11:25). The author regards it as a dreadful thing to take lightly the shedding of the blood of one who is so high and holy and whose blood moreover is the means of establishing the new covenant that alone can bring men near to God. The apostate regards that blood as "a common thing" (*koinon*). That is to say he treats the death of Jesus as just like the death of any other man. The word "common" can also be understood over against the holy and it thus comes to mean "unhallowed." So NIV has the translation "an unholy thing." This stands out all the more sharply when it is remembered that that blood has "sanctified" him. The person who accepts Christ's way is set apart for God by the shedding of Christ's blood. As elsewhere in this epistle, the idea of being sanctified refers to the initial act of being set apart for God, not the progressive growth in grace it usually means in the other NT writings. To go back on this decisive act is to deny the significance of the blood, to see it as a common thing.

The third count in the indictment of the apostate is that he has "insulted the Spirit of grace." The author does not often refer to the Holy Spirit, being occupied for the most part with the person and the work of the Son. Nevertheless, he esteems the person of the Spirit highly as this passage shows. It also implies that he saw the Spirit as a person, not an influence or a thing, for it is only a person who can be insulted. His word for "insulted" is *enybrizō*, from *hybris*, which Westcott sees as "that insolent self-assertion which disregards what is due to others. It combines arrogance with wanton injury" (in loc.). In the NT there is a variety of ways of referring to the Spirit, but only here is he called "the Spirit of grace" (cf. Zech 12:10). The expression may mean "the gracious Spirit of God" or "the Spirit through whom God's grace is manifested." Willful sin is an insult to the Spirit, who brings the grace of God to man.

30 The appeal to knowledge ("we know") reminds us of Paul who is fond of appealing to his readers' understanding. The author calls God "him who said" words of Scripture. He uses this word for "said" (*eipon*) six times, four of them being with quotations from Scripture. He is sure that God speaks to men. The author's first quotation here is from Deuteronomy 32:35. It agrees exactly neither with the MT nor the LXX, though it is quoted in the same form in Romans 12:19. It is unlikely that either the Deuteronomy or Romans passage is dependent on the other, and much more probably the authors were both using a Greek text form that happens not to have survived. We usually speak of "the" LXX as though there was but one translation of the OT into Greek, but it is highly probable that there were a number of such translations.

The quotation here emphasizes that vengeance is a divine prerogative. It is not for men to take it into their own hands. But the emphasis is not on that. It is rather on the certainty that the Lord will act. The wrongdoer cannot hope to go unpunished because avenging wrong is in the hands of none less than God. The second quotation, from Deuteronomy 32:36, agrees with the LXX (see also Ps 135[134]:14). It leaves no doubt whatever about the Lord's intervention, for he is named and so is his activity.

The word "judge" may mean "give a favorable judgment" as well as "condemn." In both Deuteronomy 32:36 and Psalm 135:14, it is deliverance that is in mind; and both times RSV, for example, translates it as "vindicate." But in the OT God does not vindicate his people if they have sinned. Vindication implies that they have been faithful in their service and that God's intervention recognizes this. But where they have not been faithful, that same principle of impartial judgment according to right demands that intervention bring punishment. It is this that the author has primarily in mind. That a man claims to be a member of the people of God does not exempt him from judgment. God judges all. Let not the apostate think that he, of all people, can escape.

31 The sinner should not regard the judgment of God calmly. It is "a dreadful thing" to fall into God's hands ("dreadful" renders the word *phoberos*, which is translated "fearful" in v.27—i.e., it is frightening). David chose to fall into God's hands (2 Sam 24:14; 1 Chron 21:13; cf. Ecclus 2:18). But David was a man of faith; he committed himself in trust to God, not man. It is different with one who has rejected God's way. He must reckon with the fact that he will one day fall into the hands of a living, all-powerful deity. Such a fate is a daunting prospect, not to be regarded with equanimity.

Notes

---

27 The word ἐκδοχή (*ekdochē*), found here only in the NT, usually seems to mean "receiving from or at the hands of another" (LSJ, s.v.). The context here shows that a meaning like NIV's "expectation" is required, but this is not found elsewhere. Héring commends Spicq's translation "prospect," adding, "The question is less of a psychological fact than of an objective future which is drawing nearer" (in loc.).

The expression rendered "raging fire" (πυρὸς ζῆλος, *pyros zēlos*) is more literally "zeal of fire." "Zeal" may be used in a good sense or in the bad sense of "jealousy," "envy." To Montefiore its use here "suggests the passionate jealousy of wounded love" (in loc.).

K. *Choose the Right*

10:32–39

32Remember those earlier days after you had received the light, when you stood your ground in a great contest in the face of suffering. 33Sometimes you were publicly exposed to insult and persecution; at other times you stood side by side with those who were so treated. 34You sympathized with those in prison and joyfully accepted the confiscation of your property, because you knew that you yourselves had better and lasting possessions.

35So do not throw away your confidence; it will be richly rewarded. 36You need to persevere so that when you have done the will of God, you will receive what he has promised. 37For in just a very little while,

"He who is coming will come and will not delay.
38But my righteous one will live by faith.
And if he shrinks back,
I will not be pleased with him."

39But we are not of those who shrink back and are destroyed, but of those who believe and are saved.

As he has done before, after a section containing stern warnings, the author expresses his confidence in his readers and encourages them to take the right way. He reminds them of the early days of their Christian experience. Then they had experienced some form of persecution and had come through it triumphantly. This should teach them that in Christ they had blessings of a kind they could never have had if they had given way to persecution.

32 "But" (which NIV omits) sets the following section over against the preceding one. The author does not class his friends among those who go back on their Christian profession. He begins by inviting them to contemplate the days just after they had become Christians. The verb translated "received the light" (*phōtisthentes*) was sometimes used in the early church in reference to baptism. But it is difficult to find it used with this meaning as early as this, and in any case it is not required by the context. It is the enlightenment the gospel brought that is in mind. This had resulted in some form of persecution that the readers had endured in the right spirit. There should be no going back on that kind of endurance now. The word rendered "contest" (*athlēsis*) is used of athletic competition and is, of course, the term from which we get our word "athletics." It became widely used of the Christian as a spiritual athlete and so points to the strenuous nature of Christian service. On this occasion, the athletic performance had been elicited by a period of suffering they had steadfastly endured.

33–34 This suffering is further explained. "Sometimes . . . at other times" (so also RSV) is often taken to mean that the one group of people had had two experiences.

But it seems more likely that we should take it to mean two groups: "Some of you . . . others of you." The first group had been subjected to verbal attack ("insult") and also to other forms of trouble (*thlipsis* points to severe pressure and thus to trouble or "persecution" of various kinds). The word "publicly exposed" (*theatrizomenoi*) is not a common one; its connection with *theatron* "a theatre" makes it clear that it connotes publicity. The readers had been made a spectacle by being exposed to insult and injury.

The second group had suffered by being associates of the former group. This is explained as sympathizing with prisoners. In the world of the first century the lot of prisoners was difficult. Prisoners were to be punished, not pampered. Little provision was made for them, and they were dependent on friends for their supplies. For Christians visiting prisoners was a meritorious act (Matt 25:36). But there was some risk, for the visitors became identified with the visited. The readers of the epistle had not shrunk from this. It is not pleasant to endure ignominy, and it is not pleasant to be lumped with the ignominious. They had endured both. Attempts have been made to identify the persecution behind these words, but there is not enough information for such attempts to be successful. None of them had been killed (12:4), a fact that rules out Jerusalem, where James had been put to death quite early (Acts 12:2), and Rome after the Neronian persecution. We have no means of knowing what the persecution referred to was.

In addition to identifying with prisoners, the readers had had the right attitude to property. There is a question whether the word rendered "confiscation" (*harpagē*) means official action by which the state took over their goods, or whether it points rather to mob violence. A third possibility is the readers' voluntary surrender of their goods to some Christian community when they joined it (as Buchanan holds possible). But the word *harpagē* makes this unlikely. It is also an unlikely term for the action of officials (unless they were acting in a very "unofficial" manner; the scope for petty officialdom to tyrannize over Christians was immense). On the whole, it looks like mob violence or the like. The readers had taken this in the right spirit. It would not be a surprise if they endured all this with fortitude, but that they accepted it "joyfully" is another thing altogether. So firmly had their interest been fixed on heavenly possessions that they could take the loss of earthly goods with exhilaration.

The reason for their cheerful attitude is not quite clear. NIV gives a very plausible understanding of the Greek. But "yourselves" might be the object and not the subject of the verb, in which case it means "knowing that you had yourselves as a better and lasting possession." This would be in the spirit of Luke 21:19: "By standing firm you will save yourselves." Whichever way we take it, the possession (the word is singular in the Gr.) was both better and longer lasting. The possession in Christ is not subject to petty depredations like the earthly possessions of which they had been robbed. It is an abiding possession.

35 "So" connects what follows with what precedes. There is a reason for the conduct suggested. "Throw away" (*apoballō*) seems a fairly vigorous verb and perhaps conveys the thought of a reckless rejection of what is valuable. Because the earlier conduct of the readers showed that they knew the value of their possession in Christ, the writer can appeal to them not to discard it. As Christians they had a confidence that was based firmly on Christ's saving work and that would be the height of folly to throw away. What they had endured for Christ's sake entitled them to a reward. Let them not throw it away. The NT does not reject the notion that Christians will receive rewards, though, of course, that is never the prime motive for service.

36 The Greek has the equivalent of "you have need of perseverance"; the word *hypomonē* denotes an active, positive endurance or steadfastness. Christianity is no flash in the pan. "Need" means something absolutely necessary, not merely desirable. This leads to the thought that doing the will of God has its recompense. The author has spoken of Christ as occupied with doing the will of God (vv.7ff.). Now he makes the point that Christ's people must similarly be occupied in doing that will. He describes the result in terms of receiving the promise, and this safeguards against any doctrine of salvation by works. God's good gift is in mind, and it is secured—though not merited—by their continuing to the end.

37–38 Now the writer encourages his readers by drawing their attention to passages in Scripture that point to the coming of God's Messiah in due course. The "very little while" (cf. Isa 26:20) points to a quite short period. The argument is that the readers ought not let the "very little while" rob them of their heavenly reward. The writer goes on to a quotation from Habakkuk 2:3–4, but he makes a few significant changes from the LXX. The first of them is to precede his quotation with the definite article so that it is "the," not "a," coming one. In other words, the reference to the Messiah is unmistakable (cf., e.g., Matt 11:3; 21:9; John 11:27 for this expression used of the Messiah). The rabbis could interpret this passage messianically as when it was held to teach people patience and warn them against calculating the date when the Messiah would come: "Blasted be the bones of those who calculate the end. For they would say, since the predetermined time has arrived, and yet he has not come, he will never come. But (even so), wait for him, as it is written, *Though he tarry, wait for him*" (Tal *Sanhedrin* 97b).

The author has reversed the order of the clauses. He thus finishes with the words about shrinking back, and this enables him to apply them immediately to his readers. We should notice also a difference between the Hebrew and the Greek of this quotation. In the original Hebrew the point is that the faithful must await God's good time for the destruction of their enemies, the Chaldeans. This cannot be hastened, and they must patiently await it. Meanwhile, the faithful man is preserved by his trust in God. In the LXX, however, it is not so much for the fulfillment of the vision that the prophet waits as for a person, a deliverer. If someone appears and draws back, he is not God's deliverer. The author is using the LXX to bring out the truth that Christ will come in due course. In the intervening time, the readers must patiently await him.

The words about the "righteous one" living by faith are used again in Romans 1:17 and Galatians 3:11. In those passages the emphasis appears to be on how the man who is righteous by faith will live, whereas here the author seems to be using the words to convey the meaning that the person God accepts as righteous will live by faith. Paul is concerned with the way a man comes to be accepted by God; the author is concerned with the importance of holding fast to one's faith in the face of temptations to abandon it.

The mention of faith (*pistis*) leads us into the most sustained treatment of the subject in the NT. The term is mentioned again in the next verse and then throughout chapter 11. The first point made is that faith and shrinking back are opposed to each other.

The passage does not say from what the shrinking back is. In the context, however, it must relate to proceeding along the way of faith and salvation. The quotation from Habakkuk makes it clear that God is not at all pleased with the one who draws back. It is important to go forward in the path of faith.

39 The chapter closes with a ringing affirmation of confidence in which the writer identifies himself with his readers. He takes no position of superiority but sees himself as one with them. He sees two possibilities: on the one hand, drawing back and being destroyed; on the other hand, persevering in faith to salvation. The end result of shrinking back he sees as total loss (*apōleia*). But that will not be the fate of his readers. Far from being lost, they will go on in faith and be saved.

Notes

34 The reading δεσμίοις (*desmiois*, "prison") should be accepted, even though it is not read by many MSS. Δεσμοῖς (desmois, "bonds") is read by a few MSS, but it is hard to accept. Most MSS have inserted μου (*mou*, "my"), perhaps under the influence of the view that Paul was the author.

37 The expression translated "just a very little while" is μικρὸν ὅσον ὅσον (*mikron hoson hoson*), which is sufficiently unusual for us to identify it with the words of Isa 26:20 with some confidence.

38 The author puts μου (*mou*, "my") after δίκαιός (*dikaios*, "righteous one"), though there are some MSS that omit it (which seems to be an assimilation to the quotations in Rom 1:17; Gal 3:11, neither of which has the possessive). In this he follows the "A" text of the LXX, while the "B" text places it after πίστεως (*pisteōs*, "*faith*"). There is no reason for thinking that our author has put the pronoun there himself.

VIII. Faith

The preceding section introduced the thought of faith, and the subject is now continued in one of the classic treatments of the topic. In a passage of great eloquence and power, the author unfolds some of his thoughts on this most important subject for Christians. He is sometimes criticized for failing to convey the idea of warm personal faith in Jesus Christ that means so much to Paul. Such criticisms are, however, beside the point. Granted that the author does not follow the thoughts of Paul, yet what he says is both true and important in its own right. Nor is it of any less value because it is not what another would have said had he written at the same length on the same subject. The writer does not contrast faith with works as Paul sometimes does, nor does he treat it as the means of receiving justification. Instead, he treats faith not so much with reference to the past (what God has done in Christ) as to the future. He sees faith as that trust in God that enables the believer to press on steadfastly whatever the future holds for him. He knows that God is to be relied on implicitly. So the writer's method is to select some of the great ones in the history of the people of God and to show briefly how faith motivated all of them and led them forward, no matter how difficult the circumstances. The result is a great passage that not only encouraged his readers but also has encouraged hosts of Christians through the ages.

A. *The Meaning of Faith*

11:1–3

[1]Now faith is being sure of what we hope for and certain of what we do not see. [2]This is what the ancients were commended for. [3]By faith we understand that the universe was formed at God's command, so that what is seen was not made out of what was visible.

The chapter begins with some general observations on the nature of faith. They do not constitute a formal definition; rather, the writer is calling attention to some significant features of faith. Then he proceeds to show how faith works out in practice.

1 In the Greek the verb "is" (*estin*) is the first word. Faith is a present and continuing reality. It is not simply a virtue sometimes practiced in antiquity. It is a living thing, a way of life the writer wishes to see continued in the practice of his readers. Faith, he tells us, is a *hypostasis* of things hoped for. The term has evoked lively discussion. Sometimes it has a subjective meaning, as in 3:14 where NIV translates it as "confidence." But it may also be used more objectively, and KJV understands it that way in this passage by translating it as "substance." This would mean that things that have no reality in themselves are made real (given "substance") by faith. But this does not seem to be what the writer is saying. Rather, his meaning is that there are realities for which we have no material evidence though they are not the less real for that. Faith enables us to know that they exist and, while we have no certainty apart from faith, faith does give us genuine certainty. "To have faith is to be sure of the things we hope for" (TEV). Faith is the basis, the substructure (*hypostasis* means lit. "that which stands under") of all that the Christian life means, all that the Christian hopes for.

There is a further ambiguity about the word *elenchos,* which usually signifies a "proof" or "test." It may be used as a legal term with a meaning like "cross examining" (LSJ, s.v.). Some take it here as "test" and some see its legal use, while many prefer to understand it in much the same sense as the preceding expression (e.g., NIV). This may well be the right way to take it, though "test" is far from impossible. The meaning would then be that faith, in addition to being the basis of all that we hope for, is that by which we test things unseen. We have no material way of assessing the significance of the immaterial. But Christians are not helpless. They have faith and by this they test all things. "What we do not see" excludes the entire range of visible phenomena, which here stand for all things earthly. Faith extends beyond what we learn from our senses, and the author is saying that it has its reasons. Its tests are not those of the senses, which yield uncertainty.

2 "The ancients" more strictly means "the elders" (*hoi presbyteroi*), a term that may be used of age or dignity. Here it refers to the religious leaders of past days and means much the same as "the forefathers" in 1:1. These men had witness borne to them (*emartyrēthēsan*) on account of their faith. As this chapter unfolds, the writer will go on to bring out some of that testimony and link the heroes of old specifically with faith. This is an example of a type of literature that recurs in antiquity. A well-known example is the passage in Ecclesiasticus, which begins, "Let us now praise famous men" (44:1–50:21). But this chapter in Hebrews is distinguished from all others by its consistent emphasis on faith. Other writers see a variety of reasons for the success of those they describe. Here in Hebrews one thing and one thing only is stressed—faith. Single-mindedly the author concentrates on that one splendid theme.

3 "By faith" runs through the chapter with compelling emphasis. For the most part it is attached to the deeds of the great ones of previous generations. Here, however, the writer and his readers are involved in the "we." Faith is a present reality, not exclusively the property of past heroes. Faith gives us convictions about creation. Belief in the existence of the world is not faith, nor is it faith when men hold that the world was made out of some preexisting "stuff." (In the first century there were people who did not believe in God but who held to some kind of "creation.") But when we understand that it was the Word of God ("God's command," NIV) that produced all things, that is faith. The emphasis on God's word agrees with Genesis 1, with its repeated "And God said." The point is emphasized with the explicit statement that the visible did not originate from the visible. For the author the visible universe is not sufficient to account for itself. But it is faith, not something material, that assures him that it originated with God. His view is none the less certain because it is based on faith, and he does not qualify his statement as though any doubt were possible. This world is God's world, and faith assures him that God originated it.

Notes

1 On ὑπόστασις (*hypostasis,* "confidence"), MM (s.v.) note a variety of uses of the word in the papyri and conclude: "These varied uses are at first sight somewhat perplexing, but in all cases there is the same central idea of something that *underlies* visible conditions and guarantees a future possession." They suggest that we translate here "Faith is the *titledeed* of things hoped for." This translation may not commend itself, but the word as used here does seem to point to certainty.

B. *The Faith of the Men Before the Flood*

11:4–7

4By faith Abel offered God a better sacrifice than Cain did. By faith he was commended as a righteous man, when God spoke well of his offerings. And by faith he still speaks, even though he is dead.

5By faith Enoch was taken from this life, so that he did not experience death; he could not be found, because God had taken him away. For before he was taken, he was commended as one who pleased God. 6And without faith it is impossible to please God, because anyone who comes to him must believe that he exists and that he rewards those who earnestly seek him.

7By faith Noah, when warned about things not yet seen, in holy fear built an ark to save his family. By his faith he condemned the world and became heir of the righteousness that comes by faith.

The author proceeds to demonstrate the universality of faith in those God approves. He selects a number of men and women universally regarded among the Jews as especially outstanding (though we cannot always see why he has chosen one and not another). He begins by looking to remote antiquity and showing that faith was manifested in the lives of certain great men who lived before the Flood.

4 The first example of faith is Abel, who brought God a more acceptable sacrifice than did his brother Cain (Gen 4:3–7). Bruce (in loc.) canvasses a number of opinions as to the reasons for the superiority of Abel's offering: it was living, whereas Cain's was lifeless; it was stronger, Cain's weaker; it grew spontaneously, Cain's by human ingenuity; it involved blood, Cain's did not. But all such suggestions seem wide of the mark. Scripture never says there was anything inherently superior in Abel's offering. It may be relevant that there are some references to Abel as being a righteous man (Matt 23:35; 1 John 3:12), while the author of Hebrews insists on the importance of Abel's faith. Abel was right with God and his offering was a demonstration of his faith.

Once again, NIV's "commended" represents the passive of the verb "to witness": "it was witnessed" or "testified" that he was righteous (cf. v.1). This is explained as that God "bore witness" to (NIV, "spoke well of") his offerings. This indicates the importance the author attached to Abel's sacrifice offered in faith, for very rarely is God said to have borne witness. The meaning may be either that on the basis of Abel's sacrifice God testified to his servant or that God bore witness about the gifts Abel offered. We should probably accept NIV's "And by faith he still speaks," though the Greek is simply "through it," where "it" might refer either to "sacrifice" or to "faith." Whichever way we resolve this problem, the main point is that Abel is not to be thought of as one long-since dead and of no present account. He is dead, but his faith is a living voice.

5 In Jewish apocalyptic thought, Enoch was a very popular figure, and several books are ascribed to him. But in the NT he figures only in Luke 3:37, Jude 14, and here. The Hebrew OT says nothing of the manner of his departure from this life, only that God "took" him (Gen 5:24). But the author follows LXX in speaking of him as "transferred," which indicates that he did not die, a truth made explicit in the words "he did not experience death."

The passive of the verb "to find" (*heuriskō*) is sometimes used with the meaning "no longer be found, despite a thorough search = *disappear*" (BAG, s.v.). The author follows this up with the active *metethēken* (lit., "God transferred him") instead of the passive *metetethē* he used previously, a change that brings out the divine initiative. There is an air of permanence about the use of the perfect of this verb. There was no going back on it. For the fourth time in this chapter NIV avoids translating the verb *martyreō* with "witness" or "testify," preferring "he was commended." But this must be understood to mean that testimony was borne to him, the content of the testimony being that he was "one who pleased God" (Gen 5:22, 24, LXX).

6 Though the OT does not say that Enoch had faith, the author goes on to explain why he can speak of it so confidently. It is impossible to please God without faith, and Enoch pleased God. Thus it is clear that he had faith. Notice that the author lays it down with the greatest of emphasis that faith is absolutely necessary. He does not say simply that without faith it is difficult to please God; he says that without faith it is impossible to please him! There is no substitute for faith. He goes on to lay down two things required in the worshiper ("anyone who comes to him" renders the participle of the verb *proserchomai,* used, as in 10:1, of one who comes near in worship). First, he must believe that God exists. This is basic. Without it there is no possibility of faith at all. But it is not enough of itself. After all, the demons can know that sort of faith (James 2:19). There must also be a conviction about God's moral character, belief "that he rewards those who earnestly seek him." As Barclay puts it,

"We must believe, not only that God exists, but also that God cares" (in loc.). Without that deep conviction, faith in the biblical sense is not a possibility.

7 Attention moves to Noah. He was "warned," a verb that is used frequently of divine communications, the pronouncements of oracles, and the like. Noah was not acting on a hunch or on merely human advice. It was the voice of God that carried conviction to him. The warning concerned things "not yet seen," i.e., events of which there was no present indication, nothing that could be observed. At the time Noah received his message from God, there was no sign of the Flood and related events. His action was motivated by faith, not by any reasoned calculation of the probabilities based on the best available evidence.

In the expression "holy fear" (*eulabētheis*), some put the emphasis on "holy" and some on "fear." While it is true that this verb may convey the notion of fear, it is not easy to see it in this context. The author is not telling us that Noah was a timid type but that he was a man of faith. He acted out of reverence for God and God's command. So he "built" (*kateskeuasen*) an ark. Though the verb may be used of preparing or building in a variety of senses, it is a "favorite word for construction of ships" (BAG, p. 419) and so is relevant to this reference to the ark. The purpose of building the ark was "to save his family" (lit., "for the salvation of his house"). In the NT the noun "salvation" (*sōtēria*) usually refers to salvation in Christ. Here, however, as in a few other places, it is the more general idea of salvation from danger—deliverance from disaster—that is in mind. Noah's faith led to the preservation of his entire household during the Flood.

There is a problem here similar to that in v.4, and NIV solves it exactly the same way. The Greek relative pronoun *di' hēs* ("through which"; NIV, "by") might refer back either to "faith," "ark," or "salvation." NIV inserts "faith" and removes the ambiguity. This is probably the correct way to understand the passage, though we should bear in mind that some notable exegetes think that the ark is meant (e.g., Calvin). Westcott (in loc.) refers it to the ark as the outward expression of faith. Noah's faith in action was a condemnation of the men of his day who failed to respond to the example of that godly man and presumably to the reasons he gave for his conduct. (Noah must have told them why he was doing such an extraordinary thing as building an ark there on dry land.) Upright conduct will always stand in condemnation of wickedness (cf. Matt 12:41–42; Luke 11:31–32; 1 John 3:12).

"The world" signifies the totality of mankind of that day who did not obey God. "Heir" is used in the sense of "possessor," not strictly of one who enters a possession as a result of a will. Here in v.7 we have the author's one use of the term "righteousness" in the Pauline sense of the righteousness that is ours by faith. In the Bible Noah was the first man to be called righteous (Gen 6:9). He was right with God because he took God at his word; he believed what God said and acted on it.

Notes

3 NIV is surely correct in understanding τοὺς αἰῶνας (*tous aiōnas*) as "the universe," though we should bear in mind that the term strictly means "the ages." The author prefers to use a word that has a time reference.

4 The use of πλείονα (*pleiona*) of Abel's sacrifice has puzzled commentators. Usually it is taken in the sense of "better" and support for such an understanding may be found in passages such as Luke 12:23: "Life is more than food" (cf. Luke 11:31–32). But some conjecture that there was an early textual error with ΗΔΕΙΟΝΑ being misread as ΠΛΕΙΟΝΑ. This is possible, but there is no MS evidence to support such a reading. If such a corruption did occur, it must have been very early. Some prefer to take the expression literally and think of Abel as giving God "more" in the literal sense. Some such sense as in NIV seems right.

In the second occurrence of the word "God," some MSS read the dative τῷ θεῷ (*tō theō*) instead of the genitive τοῦ θεοῦ (*tou theou*). With this reading the meaning is that Abel bore witness to God on the basis of his gifts. But the reading should probably be rejected. It is not strongly supported in the MSS, and it looks like an attempt to make a hard reading easier. Héring further points out that it demands an unusual sense for the preposition ἐπί (*epi*), "by his offerings" (in loc.).

C. *The Faith of Abraham and Sarah*

11:8–19

[8]By faith Abraham, when called to go to a place he would later receive as his
inheritance, obeyed and went, even though he did not know where he was going.
[9]By faith he made his home in the promised land like a stranger in a foreign country;
he lived in tents, as did Isaac and Jacob, who were heirs with him of the same
promise. [10]For he was looking forward to the city with foundations, whose architect
and builder is God.
[11]By faith Abraham, even though he was past age—and Sarah herself was
barren—was enabled to become a father because he considered him faithful who
had made the promise. [12]And so from this one man, and he as good as dead, came
descendants as numerous as the stars in the sky and as countless as the sand on
the seashore.
[13]All these people were still living by faith when they died. They did not receive
the things promised; they only saw them and welcomed them from a distance. And
they admitted that they were aliens and strangers on earth. [14]People who say such
things show that they are looking for a country of their own. [15]If they had been
thinking of the country they had left, they would have had opportunity to return.
[16]Instead, they were longing for a better country—a heavenly one. Therefore God
is not ashamed to be called their God, for he has prepared a city for them.
[17]By faith Abraham, when God tested him, offered Isaac as a sacrifice. He who
had received the promises was about to sacrifice his one and only son, [18]even
though God had said to him, "It is through Isaac that your offspring will be reckoned." [19]Abraham reasoned that God could raise the dead, and figuratively speaking, he did receive Isaac back from death.

The great progenitor of the race and his wife are now singled out as examples of faith. The Jews prided themselves on their descent from Abraham, and the great patriarch is mentioned a number of times in the NT as one who had faith and who acted on his faith (Acts 7:2–8; Rom 4:3; Gal 3:6; James 2:23). It is in line with this that the author gives more space to Abraham than to any other individual on his list. He sees Abraham as an excellent example of what he has in mind, for the author does not see faith as making a good guess based on the best human estimate of the possibilities. Abraham's faith accepted God's promises and acted on them even though there was nothing to indicate that they would be fulfilled. He "went, even though he did not know where he was going." This faith is seen in his acceptance of the promise of a child when Sarah was old and even more in his readiness to sacrifice that child—the one through whom the promise was to be fulfilled—when God commanded. Consistently, Abraham believed God and acted on his faith. He obeyed God implicitly, though there was nothing tangible he could rely on.

8 Abraham is mentioned ten times in Hebrews, a total exceeded only by Luke (fifteen) and John (eleven). The author of Hebrews shows a strong interest in this patriarch. "When called" translates a present participle that indicates a very prompt obedience. "He obeyed the call while (so to say) it was still sounding in his ears" (Westcott, in loc.). His prompt obedience took him out to a region as yet unknown to him but which he would later receive "as his possession" (*klēronomia;* strictly, "inheritance"). The last half of this verse is a classical statement of the obedience of faith. Men like to know where they are going and to choose their way. But the way forward can be obscure. Abraham was one who could go out, knowing that it was right to do so, but not knowing where it would all lead. God told him to go "to the land that I will show you" (Gen 12:1). Yet it was not till some time after he reached Canaan that he was informed that this was the land God would give his descendants (Gen 12:7; later on Abraham himself was included in the same promise, Gen 13:15). To leave the certainties one knows and go out into what is quite unknown—relying on nothing other than the Word of God—is the essence of faith, as the author sees it.

9 Paradoxically, when he got to the land of Canaan that God had promised to him, Abraham lived in it, not as its owner, but as a resident alien. The verb translated "made his home" (*parōkēsen*) is not normally used of permanent residence but, as BAG (s.v.) says, it means to "inhabit . . . as a stranger" (BAG also sees "migrate" as possible here). "The promised land" (more lit. "land of the promise") is an expression found only here in the Bible. As the context plainly shows it means Canaan, but v.10 indicates that heaven is meant, too. The earthly Canaan is a foretaste of God's heavenly country. Though Canaan was to be his own land in due course, Abraham had to live there as though "in a foreign country." He had no rights. He and his household lived in tents, in temporary dwellings. The whole land had been promised to him. Yet Abraham did not even have a proper house in it.

The verb rendered "lived" (*katoikēsas*) has the notion of settling down. It is normally used of a continuous, permanent dwelling. But Abraham's permanent dwelling place in Canaan was a temporary tent! Right to the end of his life the only piece of the country he owned was the field he purchased as Sarah's burial place (Gen 23). God "gave him no inheritance here, not even a foot of ground" (Acts 7:5). Nor was it any better with Isaac and Jacob. They shared the same promises. They were the descendants through whom God's purpose would be worked out. But all their lifetimes they had no more share in Canaan than Abraham did. Toward the end of Jacob's life the clan went down to Egypt, and when they came back many years later, it was not as sojourners but as a mighty people who made the land their own. The lives of the three patriarchs thus cover the whole time of the temporary dwelling in the land.

10 The reason for Abraham's patient acceptance of his lot was his forward look in faith to "the city with foundations" (actually, "the foundations"). To cultured men in the first century, the city was the highest form of civilized existence. Nothing served so well as the pattern for the ideal community. Buchanan argues that the city in mind was probably Jerusalem, and he cites a good deal of evidence to show the high regard in which Jews held their holy city (in loc.). But it is difficult to see God as the "architect and builder" of the earthly Jerusalem, and we should also bear in mind the author's reference to "the heavenly Jerusalem" (12:22). Buchanan's evidence shows how congenial to Jew as well as Gentile the present reference to the city would have been.

The thought of the heavenly city recurs in v.16; 12:22; 13:14 and it is found elsewhere in the NT; e.g., in Philippians 1:27 (*politeuesthe,* "act as members of a city") and 3:20 and described in Revelation 3:12; 21:10, et al. The description the "city with foundations" raises the question as to what the "foundations" are. We should not look for anything literal; the expression probably means that the city is well based—i.e., a "city with permanent foundations" (TEV). It is eternal, more lasting than earth's ephemeral edifices.

The city owes everything to God, who is its "architect and builder." The first of these words, *technitēs,* means a craftsman or designer. As applied to a city, it may mean an architect or point to what we would call a "city planner." The thought is that the city is entirely designed by God. The second word, *dēmiourgos,* points rather to one who does the actual work. God built the city as well as designed it; it owes nothing to any inferior being. Neither term is applied to God anywhere else in the NT (3:4 uses another word of God's activity in building all things). The thought of this verse shows clearly that more than Canaan was in Abraham's mind when he went out in faith. These words cannot be limited to an earthly place. God is not the "architect and builder" of Canaan any more than he is of any other land.

11 This verse presents us with a problem so difficult that Héring speaks of it as a "cross which is frankly too heavy for expositors to bear" (in loc.). The difficulty is that on the face of it the verse ascribes to Sarah an activity possible only to males: *dynamin eis katabolēn spermatos* ("power for the depositing of semen"). The simplest solution is to delete the words "and [or 'even'] Sarah herself," and this is favored by some commentators. It would give a good connection with the preceding and carry forward the story of Abraham's faith. But there is no MS authority for this reading, and it looks suspiciously like a way of getting rid of the problem, not of solving it. A second suggestion is that we see the words "Sarah herself" as dative and not nominative. The meaning would then be "By faith he, together with Sarah herself, received power. . . ." The whole of the rest of the section is about Abraham's faith, and this would bring this verse into line. It would also agree with "from this one man" in v.12 and with the fact that the promise was made to Abraham, not Sarah. A third possibility is to take the words about Sarah as a parenthesis, as NIV does. For good measure this translation also inserts "Abraham" into the text and makes the rest of the verse refer unambiguously to a male. A fourth approach is to take the word *katabolē* in the sense of "foundation." The word means basically a "throwing down" (LSJ, s.v.), and it is from this that it gets the sense of depositing semen. But it is also used of depositing what it used at the beginning of a building and thus "foundation." It is used in much this sense in 4:3; 9:26 (NIV renders "creation" both times). If it is taken in this sense here, the word for "semen" would be understood in the sense of "descendants," and Sarah would be regarded as having received power for the foundation of a posterity. A decision is not easy, but I incline to the second view (with Bruce [in loc.]; BDF, par. 194 [1]; et al.). Abraham then had faith in connection with the birth of Isaac, and Sarah is linked with him.

There is a further problem in that in Genesis Sarah was anything but an example of faith, for she laughed incredulously at the suggestion that she should bear a son in her old age (Gen 18:9ff.). The author appears to mean that, despite her initial skepticism, Sarah came to share Abraham's faith (otherwise she would not have cooperated with her husband to secure the birth of the boy). The aged couple lacked the physical ability to cause birth, but faith introduced them to the power that brought about the birth of Isaac. "Past age" (which could refer to either of the two but applies to Abraham if the view I am taking is correct) draws attention to the area in which faith had to operate. On the merely human level, there was no hope. But for Abraham there was hope. He knew that God had made a promise and he knew that God is "faithful." As in 10:23, God is described with reference to his promise; and, again as in that passage, he is said to be faithful. Faithfulness to his word is a characteristic of God.

12 "And so" introduces the inevitable result. Because God promised and Abraham believed him, the consequence necessarily followed. The smallness of the beginning is brought out. Abraham was but "one man." Moreover, he was not one from whom a numerous progeny might be anticipated because he was "as good as dead" (an expression referring to his capacity for begetting offspring, not to his general state). By contrast his descendants would be as numerous as the stars in the sky or the sand on the seashore. This part of the verse is not a quotation from a specific OT passage. The words are reminiscent of a number of passages (e.g., Gen 15:5; 22:17; Exod 32:13; Deut 1:10; 10:22; Dan 3:36, LXX). Both the stars and the sand were proverbial for multitude; so the general meaning is that Abraham's descendants would be too many to count. God's blessing is beyond human calculation.

13 The author breaks off his treatment of Abraham for a moment to engage in some general remarks about "all these people," i.e., those he had dealt with thus far. They lived out their lives and died still exercising faith, without having possessed what was promised. "All" allows no exceptions. What is said applies to every one of them. They knew that God had promised certain blessings, but they did not receive them. We must be careful how we understand this, for the author has already said that Abraham "received what was promised" (6:15). Humanly speaking, when there was no hope of having a son, he saw Isaac born. The promise, however, meant far more than that. Actually, it is the fullness of the blessing that is in mind in v.13. The best that happened to the saints of old was that they had glimpses of what God had for them.

Perhaps it will help us to see something of what is meant if we recall Moses' view of the Promised Land. He prayed that God would let him enter the land (Deut 3:23–25), but the most God would permit was for him only to see it (Deut 3:26–28; 34:1–4). The patriarchs did no more than "see" their equivalent of the Promised Land. "See" can be used of various kinds of sight. Here it is plainly an operation of faith that is in mind, and the word points to an inner awareness of what the promises meant. In their attitude, the patriarchs showed that they knew themselves to be no more than "aliens and strangers." The latter term means those living in a country they do not belong to, i.e., resident aliens.

The combination "aliens and strangers" reminds us of Abraham's description of himself as "an alien and a stranger" (Gen 23:4) and Jacob's words to Pharaoh (Gen 47:9). The psalmist could also describe himself as "an alien, a stranger," and add, "as all my fathers were" (Ps 39:12). It is true that Isaac once sowed "crops" (Gen 26:12) and Jacob at one time "built a place for himself" (Gen 33:17). But neither really settled down in the land, and to the end of their lives they were pilgrims rather than residents. The author sees that it was faith that enabled all these great men of old to recognize their true position as citizens of heaven and thus as aliens everywhere on earth.

14–15 To acknowledge the things stated in v.13 has further implications; namely, that the kind of people spoken of are looking for "a country [*patris*] of their own." If they had regarded themselves only as earthlings, they would not have retained the vision of faith with their attention squarely fixed on what is beyond this earth.

There is some difficulty in translating the verb *mnēmoneuō* (NIV, "thinking"). The usual meaning is "remember." Some, however, point out that in v.22 it must mean something like "make mention of," "speak about." So they think that a similar meaning will suit this passage. Others prefer to keep the term in the region of thought. Perhaps NEB's "If their hearts had been in the country they had left" gives the fuller sense. The patriarchs could have gone back had they so chosen, whether we understand this to mean "going back to Mesopotamia" or "going back to the things of this world." There was nothing physical to stop them. But their attitude excluded the possibility.

When Abraham wanted a wife for Isaac, he wanted her to be from his homeland. But he did not go back there himself. Instead, he sent a servant to get the bride and said to him, "Make sure that you do not take my son back there" (Gen 24:6). After Jacob had spent twenty years in Mesopotamia, he still regarded Canaan as "my own homeland" (Gen 30:25); and he heard God say, "Go back to the land of your fathers" (Gen 31:3). Abraham buried Sarah in Canaan, not Mesopotamia, and in due course he was buried there himself (Gen 23:19; 25:9–10), as were Isaac (Gen 35:27–29) and Jacob (Gen 49:29–33; 50:13), Jacob being brought up from Egypt for the purpose. Joseph commanded that the same be done for him (Gen 50:24–26; cf. Exod 13:19; Josh 24:32). All these men wholeheartedly accepted God's word. Had they been earthly minded, they could have gone back to Mesopotamia. But their hearts were set on their heavenly home, and they did not go back. Singlemindedly they walked the path of faith.

16 "Instead" contrasts the actuality with what might have been. The people's longing was for the heavenly country. The adjective "heavenly" connects country with God and with all it means to belong to God. So firm was their commitment to their heavenly calling that God was not ashamed of them. Indeed, he is spoken of again and again as "the God of Abraham, the God of Isaac, and the God of Jacob." Sometimes God uses these very words of himself (Exod 3:6, 15–16). Jesus used the same expression to show the truth that the patriarchs still live (Mark 12:26–27). Not only is God not ashamed of those servants of his, he honored their faith by preparing a city for them (see comments on v.10). The use of the past tense should not be overlooked. It is not that God will one day prepare their city but that he has already done so.

17–18 The writer returns from the patriarchs in general to Abraham in particular. In doing so he brings out something of the significance of the greatest trial that that great man had to endure: God demanded that he sacrifice his son Isaac. We are apt to see this as a conflict between Abraham's love for his son and his duty to God. But for the author the problem was Abraham's difficulty in reconciling the different revelations made to him. God had promised him a numerous posterity through Isaac; yet now he called on him to offer Isaac as a sacrifice. How then could the promise be fulfilled?

Though he did not understand, Abraham knew how to obey. His faith told him that God would work out his purpose, even if he himself could not see how that could be. So he "offered Isaac as a sacrifice." The perfect tense of the Greek verb *prospherō* ("offered") indicates that as far as Abraham was concerned the sacrifice was complete. In will and purpose he did offer his son. He held nothing back. But immediately the same verb is used in the imperfect tense, which means that the action was not in fact completed. Abraham did not fail in his obedience, for God did not require him to slay his son.

Isaac is called *monogenēs* here, which NIV renders "one and only." The term has a meaning like "unique." Abraham had other sons (Gen 25:1–2, 5–6); so *monogenēs* does not mean "only." Yet he had no other born in the way Isaac was and bearing the kind of promises that were made about Isaac. The word for "received" (*anadechomai*) is an unusual one, found again in the NT only in Acts 28:7. MM find many examples of its use in the papyri in the legal sense of "undertake," "assume," and say, "The predominance of this meaning suggests its application in Heb 11[17]. The statement that Abraham had 'undertaken,' 'assumed the responsibility of' the promises, would not perhaps be alien to the thought" (s.v.). If we accept this, Abraham's faith is highlighted.

Abraham was not passive; he took the responsibility of being the man through whom God would work out his promise. Yet he was ready to offer the required sacrifice. His dilemma is brought out with the quotation of God's promise from Genesis 21:12. God's promise was to be fulfilled in Isaac, not in another of Abraham's sons. The words "through Isaac" are placed in an emphatic position. The quotation from Genesis underlines the truth that the divine call had singled out the line through Isaac as the line through which God would fulfill his promise.

19 Now comes an explanation of why Abraham, who believed that God was going to fulfill his promises through Isaac, was nevertheless ready to offer up his son. He calculated (*logisamenos*) that God could raise the dead. This would fit in with the Genesis narrative, for as Abraham went off with the boy to sacrifice him—and as we have seen he was fully determined to go through with the program—he said to the servants, "Stay here with the donkey while I and the boy go over there. We will worship and then we will come back to you" (Gen 22:5).

The rest of v.19 probably should be understood as NIV has it: "And figuratively speaking, he did receive Isaac back from death." Abraham had had to reconcile himself to the death of the son in whom he had thought the promises of God would be realized. To have Isaac alive was like getting someone back from the dead. Abraham's unswerving faith in God was vindicated. We should, however, notice that some take "figuratively speaking" (*en parabolē*) to mean "in a way that prefigured the resurrection" (Moffatt, in loc.). Again, some commentators relate "from death" to Isaac's birth, coming from one "as good as dead" (v.12). But neither of these seems likely. We should rather see the words as meaning that Abraham "did not bind the power of God to the life of Isaac but was persuaded that it would be effective in his ashes when he was dead no less than when he was alive and breathing" (Calvin, in loc.).

Notes

8 NIV takes the infinitive ἐξελθεῖν (*exelthein*, "went") with καλούμενος (*kaloumenos*, "called"). But it is also possible to see it as epexegetic and take it with ὑπήκουσεν (*hypēkousen*, "obeyed") to give the meaning "went out obediently."

10 Δημιουργὸς (*dēmiourgos*, "builder") is used a good deal by the philosophers to denote the Creator of the universe, but it is unlikely that the author is influenced by such usage. As I. H. Marshall puts it, "The writer here uses a fine, rhetorical phrase to stress the excellence and abiding quality of the heavenly city as one built on firm foundations by God himself; the thought is metaphorical and non-philosophical" (DNTT, 1:387).

11 In uncial MSS there would have been no iota subscript so that ΑΥΤΗ ΣΑΡΡΑ (*AUTE SARRA*, "Sarah herself") might be either dative or nominative. Most MSS do not read στεῖρα (*steira*, "barren"), and the word is rejected in the critical editions of Nestlé, Kilpatrick, etc. NIV's "was enabled" translates δύναμιν ἔλαβεν (*dynamin elaben*, "received power"). The verb will have a passive sense. The power was not something natural to Abraham or within his grasp but something God gave him.

13 The standard πίστει (*pistei*, "by faith") is here replaced by κατὰ πίστιν (*kata pistin*, "according to faith"). Some find significance in the change and see a meaning "according to the spirit of faith" or the like. But it is probably a stylistic change with no real difference in meaning.

D. *The Faith of the Patriarchs*

11:20–22

[20]By faith Isaac blessed Jacob and Esau in regard to their future.
[21]By faith Jacob, when he was dying, blessed each of Joseph's sons, and worshiped as he leaned on the top of his staff.
[22]By faith Joseph, when his end was near, spoke about the exodus of the Israelites from Egypt and gave instructions about his bones.

What impresses the author about these patriarchs was that they had a faith that looked beyond death. It was when he thought he was near death that Isaac blessed Jacob and Esau (Gen 27:2, 4). Jacob gave blessings and Joseph gave instructions in the light of the nearness of death. With all three the significant thing was their firm conviction that death cannot frustrate God's purposes. Their faith was such that they were sure God would work his will. So they could speak with confidence of what would happen after they died. Their faith, being stronger than death, in a way overcame death, for their words were fulfilled.

20 Just as Abraham acted in view of things to come, so did Isaac. He blessed his two sons in terms that looked into the distant future (Gen 27:27–29, 39–40). The author says nothing about Jacob's deception of his old father. It might perhaps be objected that the words Isaac spoke with reference to Jacob he thought he was speaking to Esau so that what he said did not really apply and was not an example of soundly based faith. But Isaac quickly recognized that the blessing belonged to Jacob (Gen 27:33), and later he specifically blessed Jacob with full knowledge of what he was doing (Gen 28:1–4). In any case, the author is not interested in such details; it is enough that both blessings concerned "their future." His concern is with the faith that undergirded the patriarch's blessing. On each occasion Isaac spoke out of a firm conviction that a blessing given in accordance with God's purposes could not possibly fail. Though there were marked differences in the two blessings, these are passed over. They are not relevant. The important thing is Isaac's faith, seen in the fact that the patriarch spoke of blessings that would not be fulfilled until the distant future. Isaac trusted God. Fittingly, the sons are listed in the order in which they received the blessings, not that of their birth.

21 Jacob's claim for inclusion in the list rests on his blessing of his grandsons Ephraim and Manasseh (Gen 48). As with Isaac, the blessing went against the natural order of birth. In fact, when Jacob was dying, Joseph tried to have the major blessing given to Manasseh, the firstborn. But Jacob crossed his hands to pick out Ephraim as the greater. God is not bound by human rules like those that give pride and benefit of place to the firstborn. He fulfills his purposes as he chooses. The incident, like the preceding one, again illustrates the theme of the patriarchal blessing with its fulfillment far distant. At the time the words were spoken, fulfillment could be known only by faith.

To the words about the blessing of the boys, the author adds a reference to a previous incident in which Jacob "worshiped as he leaned on the top of his staff." There is an ambiguity in the text in Genesis 47:31 because the Hebrew was originally written without vowels. The reader supplied them as he went along. Usually this presents no difficulty, but in Genesis 47:31 there is a word that with one set of vowels means "bed" and with another, "staff." The text behind the RSV accepts the former, giving the meaning "Israel bowed himself upon the head of his bed." As he usually does, the author of Hebrews follows the LXX, which takes the word to mean "staff." Some have thought that we should understand the text to mean that Jacob worshiped the top of his staff (there is no "leaning" in the Gr.). But quite apart from the improbability of Jacob's doing any such thing, the linguistics are against it. There is an "on" (*epi*) with the "staff," and we must supply "leaning" or the like to make sense of it. The author, then, speaks of Jacob as adopting a worshipful attitude as he blessed the sons of Joseph.

22 Joseph's faith, like that of the others, looked beyond death, though his words referred to nothing more than his burial arrangements. But the charge to carry his bones to Canaan (Gen 50:24–25; Exod 13:19; Josh 24:32) give evidence of his deep conviction that in due course God would send the people back to that land. Joseph's wish to be buried in Canaan is all the more striking when we remember that, apart from his first seventeen years, he spent all his life in Egypt. But Canaan was the land for the people of God. So despite his short acquaintance with it, Joseph wanted to be buried there. His speaking about the "exodus" of the Israelites from Egypt and his concern about the proper disposal of his bones reflect his high faith that in due course God would act.

E. *The Faith of Moses*

11:23–28

[23]By faith Moses' parents hid him for three months after he was born, because they saw he was no ordinary child, and they were not afraid of the king's edict.

[24]By faith Moses, when he had grown up, refused to be known as the son of Pharaoh's daughter. [25]He chose to be mistreated along with the people of God rather than to enjoy the pleasures of sin for a short time. [26]He regarded disgrace

for the sake of Christ as of greater value than the treasures of Egypt, because he was looking ahead to his reward. [27]By faith he left Egypt, not fearing the king's anger; he persevered because he saw him who is invisible. [28]By faith he kept the Passover and the sprinkling of blood, so that the destroyer of the firstborn would not touch the firstborn of Israel.

No OT character ranked higher in popular Jewish estimation than Moses. He was the great lawgiver, and the law was central to Jewish life. Legend made free with his name, and many astonishing feats were attributed to him. (For example, Josephus says that when Pharaoh's daughter brought the child to the king he put his royal crown on the boy's head, but little Moses flung it to the ground and trod on it [Antiq. II, 233f. (ix. 1)].) Moses is highly honored in the NT, but the references to him there are much more sober (e.g., Acts 7:20–44). The author has a just appreciation for the greatness of Moses but shows none of the extravagances so typical of the Judaism of his time. We may fairly say that both Christians and Jews honored both Abraham and Moses; but whereas the Jews tended to put Moses in the higher place and to see Abraham as one who kept the law before Moses, the Christians, with their emphasis on faith, preferred to put Abraham in the more exalted place and see Moses as one who followed in the steps of Abraham's faith. The author is certainly interested in the way Moses exercised faith, and he gives five instances of faith in connection with the great lawgiver.

23 Moses is mentioned eleven times in Hebrews, which is more than in any other NT epistle (though not so many times as in John and Acts). Like the others in this chapter, he lived by faith. But here the reference to him begins with the faith exercised when he was too young to know what was going on—the faith of his parents. In the account in Exodus the role of Moses' mother receives all the attention, his father not being mentioned. In the LXX, however, the plural verbs in Exodus 2:2–3 show that both parents were involved, and the author follows his customary practice of depending on LXX. In any case, the mother could not have hidden the child without the father's agreement. So both parents were necessarily involved.

NIV says both parents hid Moses "because they saw he was no ordinary child." However, the Greek *asteios* means "beautiful" or perhaps "well-pleasing" rather than "not ordinary." The meaning appears to be that the child was so exceptionally beautiful that his parents believed that God had some special plan for him. The king's edict was for every male Hebrew child to be thrown into the Nile (Exod 1:22). Presumably, anyone who disobeyed would be severely punished. But Moses' parents were people of faith. They hid their beautiful baby for three months, trusting God rather than fearing Pharaoh.

24 The author passes over the putting of the baby in the ark of bulrushes, the finding of the child by Pharaoh's daughter, and the rearing of Moses in Pharaoh's house. He comes at once to Moses' faith as a grown man. "When he had grown up" is probably the best way to understand *megas genomenos* ("having become great"), though the suggestion has been made that there is a reference to the social and political position the man Moses found himself in. Stephen tells us that Moses was about forty years old at the time (Acts 7:23). The author appears to be saying that the decision Moses reached was that of a mature man—not the decision of a child or rebellious adolescent. In full knowledge of what he was doing, Moses "refused to be known as the son of

Pharaoh's daughter," which, as Bruce puts it, "must have seemed an act of folly by all worldly standards" (in loc.). He had open to him a place of great prestige and he could have lived comfortably among the Egyptian aristocracy. But he gave it all up. Some have tried to identify "Pharaoh's daughter," but we lack sufficient information to do this.

25 Moses' decision involved the ready acceptance of oppression as he cast in his lot with God's people instead of the pleasures he could have had at the court. The full expression "the people of God" is not frequent, though it is often implied. Its use here rather than something like "the people of Israel" seems to indicate a religious rather than nationalistic commitment. Moses is seen not as a revolutionary but as a man of faith deliberately classing himself with God's own, even though doing that meant ill treatment. "The pleasures of sin" does not mean Moses saw himself as a dissolute rake while at court. It implies rather that once he saw where God's call lay, it would have been sin for him to turn away from it and align himself with the Egyptians. There would have been pleasures, but they would have been enjoyed only at the expense of disobeying God. Moreover, they would have been purely temporary. Moses had a sense of values. He could estimate at their true worth the suffering and rejection involved in aligning himself with God's people as contrasted with the transitory pleasures of the godless court.

26 Here the point made in v.25 is seen from another angle. While Moses knew what "the treasures of Egypt" were worth, he counted "the disgrace for the sake of Christ" as great riches. This may mean that he received the same kind of reproaches Christ was later to receive. More probably, however, the author thought of Christ as identified in some way with the people of God in OT times. The prophet could say of God, "In all their distress he too was distressed" (Isa 63:9). Similarly, Christ could be said to be involved with the people. Some suggest that we should bear in mind that "the Christ" is equivalent to "the Anointed," and thus this could be a reference to the people of God rather than to an individual. To support this view Psalm 89:51 is sometimes used. But this does not seem to be what the author means. He saw Christ to be the same yesterday as he is today (13:8); so it is much more probable that he thought of him as identified with Israel in OT times (cf. 1 Cor 10:4).

When Moses suffered, he suffered with Christ—the same Christ whom the writer is encouraging his readers to identify with. It no doubt carried great weight with them to realize that they were being called to participate in the same kind of experiences and attitudes the great Moses had. Moses looked forward to the "reward." He bore in mind the just consequences of his actions and was not deceived by the glitter of the Egyptian court. History, of course, has vindicated him. We do not so much as know the name of the Pharaoh of his time; and even if we did, he would be of interest to us chiefly because of his link with Moses. But the choice Moses made resulted in his influence still being felt. It is not "realistic" to opt for the security of worldly safety. Moses did not do this, and he was right. It is faith that finally emerges triumphant, not worldliness.

27 This verse poses a problem because Moses left Egypt on two occasions: he fled to Midian after he had slain the Egyptian oppressor (Exod 2:11–15) and he went out with the rest of the Israelites at the Exodus. There would be little doubt that the former is meant here were it not for the fact that it was fear that led Moses to flee to Midian after killing the Egyptian (Exod 2:14), whereas here in v.27 he is said not to have feared the king's anger. That this reference to Moses' leaving Egypt is to his flight to Midian is supported by the following:

1. The order of events. The Passover is mentioned in v.28. Therefore, Moses' flight seems to have preceded this event.
2. "He" left Egypt seems a strange way of referring to the Exodus of an entire nation.
3. The Exodus was the result of Pharaoh's request (Exod 12:31–32). Yet it is possible to suppose that Pharaoh's anger was not far away.

Those who see Moses' departure in v.27 as referring to the Exodus draw attention to the following:

1. It is hard to reconcile "not fearing the king's anger" with "Then Moses was afraid" (Exod 2:14). So strong does this appear to some that they call any other view special pleading. Yet we should notice that the flight is not connected with fear in Exodus or anywhere else. Other options were open to Moses, such as leading a slaves' revolt. While his fear was real, his flight appears to have been because he did not think it was God's time for action, or, as the writer of Hebrews puts it, he went out "by faith."
2. The word for "left" (*katelipen*) is best understood of a permanent abandonment. (But would this not also apply to the flight to Midian? After it Moses paid only a short visit to Egypt.)
3. Moses must have expected Pharaoh would get angry at the Exodus, and he apparently did (Exod 14:5).

On the whole it seems best to take the words as referring to the flight to Midian. The author goes on to give the reason for Moses' perseverance in a fine paradox: "He saw him who is invisible." The OT has a good deal to say about Moses' close relationship with God: "The Lord would speak to Moses face to face, as a man speaks with his friend" (Exod 33:11; cf. Num 12:7–8). This close walk with God sustained Moses through all the difficult days.

28 The final example of faith in connection with Moses concerns the Passover. The verb *pepoiēken* may be translated "kept" as in NIV, but some feel that a meaning like "instituted" is required (cf. TEV, "It was faith that made him establish the Passover"). Whichever translation we prefer, the striking thing is Moses' provision for its continuance: "For the generations to come you shall celebrate it as a festival to the Lord—a lasting ordinance" (Exod 12:14). The author's use of the perfect tense agrees with this. He adds a reference to "the sprinkling of blood" (cf. Exod 12:7), which is a further illustration of faith. There was nothing in the previous experience of either Moses or the Israelites to justify this action, but their faith was vindicated when "the destroyer of the firstborn" passed over them. Moses had nothing to go on but the conviction that God had directed him. Clearly, faith was his mainspring.

Notes

27 Ὡς ὁρῶν (*hōs horōn*) might be understood in the sense "as though he saw" (TEV), but better is NIV's "because he saw": ὡς (*hōs*) with the participle "gives the reason for an action" (BAG, s.v.).

F. *The Faith of the Exodus Generation*

11:29–31

[29]By faith the people passed through the Red Sea as on dry land; but when the Egyptians tried to do so, they were drowned.
[30]By faith the walls of Jericho fell, after the people had marched around them for seven days.
[31]By faith the prostitute Rahab, because she welcomed the spies, was not killed with those who were disobedient.

The author moves naturally enough from Moses to those associated with him. For some reason he does not mention Joshua, nor does he recount any example of faith during the wanderings in the wilderness. Since the wilderness generation was not noteworthy for faith (though there were some conspicuous exceptions), their omission is understandable. But the omission of Joshua is puzzling. Perhaps we should think of him in connection with the destruction of Jericho.

29 NIV supplies "the people" to bring out the force of the plural verb. Some of those who went out of Egypt with Moses were anything but shining examples of faith. But they must have had some faith to follow Moses through the sea, and it is on this that attention is focused. The crossing of the Red Sea is attributed to God (Exod 14:14) and to the east wind that God sent (Exod 14:21); but the author prefers to concentrate on the faith that enabled the people to respond to what God had done. That their faith and not merely their courage was important is shown by the fate of the Egyptians. The Egyptians were just as courageous as the Israelites, for they attempted to cross in the same way. But they lacked faith, and the result was disaster. Their fate shows that the faith of Moses and his followers was real and not just a formality.

30 That the falling of the walls of Jericho should be ascribed to faith is not surprising (see Josh 6:1–21). What else could account for it? The author does not say whose faith he discerned in the story, though it was probably that of both Joshua and those who followed him. The taking of Jericho is a striking example of the power of faith. Apart from the conviction that God would act, nothing could have been more pointless than the behavior of those warriors. They did not attack. Instead, they simply walked around the city once a day for six days and then seven times on the seventh. But once more faith was vindicated, for the walls tumbled down.

31 "The list of the champions of Faith whose victories are specially noticed is closed by a woman and a gentile and an outcast" (Westcott, in loc.). Rahab the prostitute seems at first sight an unlikely example of faith. But she was highly regarded among both Jews and Christians. According to Jewish tradition, she married Joshua and became the ancestress of eight priests (Tal *Megillah* 14b). She is also listed as one of the four women of surpassing beauty (ibid. 15a; the others were Sarah, Abigail, and Esther).

Rahab is mentioned favorably in James 2:25, and she is listed in the genealogy of the Lord as the wife of Salmon (Matt 1:5). She came from outside Israel and was one who might not be expected to believe in Yahweh, but she acted decisively out of her deep convictions. She put her life at risk, for she would undoubtedly have been destroyed by her countrymen had they known what she was doing. So Rahab did exercise a faith that might have been very costly (Josh 2:1–21). She is contrasted to the "disobedient," which appears to be a general term for those who do not walk in God's ways. No specific act of disobedience is mentioned. Rahab "welcomed" the spies, or, more exactly, "received" them "with peace." She did not act in the spirit of a combatant but looked after Yahweh's men.

Some have tried to soften the description of Rahab and have understood her to be a hostess or an innkeeper. Also certain MSS have inserted the word "called" in another whitewash attempt. But she is designated as "the harlot" (the Heb. word signifies a secular prostitute, not a temple prostitute). It is significant that a woman from such a background could become an example of faith.

G. *The Faith of Other Servants of God*

11:32–38

32And what more shall I say? I do not have time to tell about Gideon, Barak,
Samson, Jephthah, David, Samuel and the prophets, 33who through faith conquered kingdoms, administered justice, and gained what was promised; who shut
the mouths of lions, 34quenched the fury of the flames, and escaped the edge of
the sword; whose weakness was turned to strength; and who became powerful in
battle and routed foreign armies. 35Women received back their dead, raised to life
again. Others were tortured and refused to be released, so that they might gain a
better resurrection. 36Some faced jeers and flogging, while still others were chained
and put in prison. 37They were stoned; they were sawed in two; they were put to
death by the sword. They went about in sheepskins and goatskins, destitute,
persecuted and mistreated—38the world was not worthy of them. They wandered
in deserts and mountains, and in caves and holes in the ground.

From particular cases the author moves to generalities. To continue in such detail would require writing at great length, and the author has no time for that. On the other hand, there are many shining examples of faith, and it would be a pity not to notice them in some way. So the author names a few outstanding men of faith without detailing what their faith led them to do and then goes on to mention certain groups of the faithful. Sometimes men and women of faith did similar things quite independently of one another. It is doubtless some of these whom the author lists.

32 With a neat rhetorical flourish, the author shows that his subject is far from exhausted, even though he does not propose to continue his list. His rhetorical question may be understood as "What more shall I say?" (NIV, Moffatt, in loc.) or "Is there any need to say more?" (JB), depending on whether we take the *ti* to mean "what?" or "why?" Not having time to go through them all, the author lists a half dozen faithful men: Gideon, Barak, Samson, Jephthah, David, and Samuel. The first four of these are mentioned only here in the NT. Samuel is mentioned only twice elsewhere in the NT. David, of course, is mentioned frequently. The reason for the order of these names is not clear. It is neither that of the OT, nor is it chronological. In fact, if we arrange them in pairs, the second of the two in each case is the earlier in time. Samuel might well be placed last as heading up the prophets who came after him, but we can only guess at the reasons for the way the rest are placed.

The writer does not go into detail about what these men did. But if we examine the OT record, we find that each man battled against overwhelming odds so that, humanly speaking, there was little chance of his coming out on top. For men in such positions faith in God was not a formality. It meant real trust when the odds seemed stacked against them. They set worthy examples for the readers in their difficult circumstances. Calvin points out that there were defects in the faith of four of them. Gideon was slow to take up arms; Barak hesitated and went forward only when Deborah encouraged him; Samson was enticed by Delilah; and Jephthah made a foolish vow and stubbornly kept it. Calvin comments, "In every saint there is always to be found something reprehensible. Nevertheless although faith may be imperfect and incomplete it does not cease to be approved by God" (in loc.).

33 Up till now, the writer has characteristically used the dative "by faith" (with an occasional *kata pistin*, "according to faith"). Now there is a change of construction to "through faith" (*dia pisteōs*), though there is probably no great difference in meaning. In the list that follows, there are three groups of three. Westcott (in loc.) points out that we may see them as indicating, first, the broad results of the believers' faith: material victory, moral success in government, spiritual reward; second, forms of personal deliverance: from wild beasts, from physical forces, from human tyranny; third, the attainment of personal gifts: strength, the exercise of strength, and the triumph of strength. In each case it is possible to see OT examples, perhaps the very ones the writer has in mind.

First, the author speaks of those who "conquered kingdoms" (as did Joshua and others), then of men who "administered justice." The Greek word *dikaiosynē* may mean "righteousness" as well as "justice" and some have found the meaning here as "did deeds of righteousness." But NIV is probably correct. The reference seems to be to men like the Judges. The next group may be, as in NIV, those who "gained what was promised," or possibly those who obtained words of promise from God. Either way they were men of faith. In the OT there were a number of men who could be said to have "shut the mouths of lions," notably Daniel (Dan 6:17–22). David also was delivered from a lion (1 Sam 17:34–37), and Benaiah killed one in a pit on a snowy day (1 Chron 11:22; cf. also Samson, Judg 14:5–6).

34 When he speaks of those who "quenched the fury of the flames," the writer probably has in mind the three whom Nebuchadnezzar had cast into the furnace and who then emerged unharmed (Dan 3:23–27). Buchanan takes the words about escaping "the edge of the sword" to refer to people who ran away; "they had successfully escaped when they were forced to flee" (in loc.), but JB translates it as "emerge unscathed from battle." Probably the writer is thinking of people like Elijah, who was not killed by Jezebel (1 Kings 19:2ff.). The OT contains many examples of those "whose weakness was turned to strength," such as Gideon, who also "became powerful in battle and routed foreign armies." It might fairly be said that the typical deliverance of Israel in OT times came about when a small number of Israelites (like Gideon's three hundred [Judg 7:7] or the tiny armies of Israel "like two little flocks of goats" [1 Kings 20:27]) fought at God's direction against vastly superior forces and defeated them. It was God's power that prevailed; he made these puny forces strong enough to defeat mighty enemies.

35 A number of times in Scripture women are said to have received their dead back to life, as Elijah's hostess (1 Kings 17:17–24) and the Shunammite who befriended

Elisha (2 Kings 4:18–37). In the NT there are the son of the widow of Nain (Luke 7:11–14), Lazarus (John 11), and Dorcas, the friend of widows (Acts 9:36–41). Sometimes, however, faith worked in another way. Some accepted torture rather than release in order that "they might gain a better resurrection," i.e., be raised to the life of the age to come with God and not simply be restored to the life of this age (cf. 2 Macc 7:23, 29). A "better" resurrection perhaps implies that all will be raised but that the prospects for apostates are grim. It is better to endure suffering and even torture now in order that the resurrection may be joyous.

36 Others were harshly treated in different fashion. NIV takes *empaigmos* in the sense "mockery" with its translation "jeers." This may well be right, for there is no doubt that other words from this root are used in the NT in such ways. But *empaigmos* itself is found only here in the NT. Outside the NT it may mean something like "derisive torture," as when it is used in 2 Maccabees of the second of the seven brothers who died for their religion. NEB translates, "The second was subjected to the same brutality [*empaigmon*]. The skin and hair of his head were torn off—"(2 Macc 7:7). "Jeers" may well be the way we should translate the word here, but it is not gentle mockery that is meant. Other forms of ill-treatment are added: floggings, chains, and imprisonment.

37 Stoning was a characteristic Jewish form of execution. Some of the men of faith had suffered at the hands of their fellow-countrymen. To be "sawed in two" was a most unusual form of killing. According to tradition this was the way the prophet Isaiah was killed (*The Martyrdom of Isaiah* 5:1ff.). The statement that some were put to death "by the sword" is important, lest it be deduced from v.34 that men of faith were safe from this fate. While God could deliver them from it, his purpose might be for some believers to be slain in this way. It is not for men of faith to dictate. They trust God and know that, whether in life or death, all will ultimately be well. From the various ways men of faith died, the writer turns to consider the hardships they had to endure in their lives. Their clothing had been the simplest. Apparently the prophets sometimes wore sheepskins (cf. the reference to Elijah's "garment of hair," 2 Kings 1:8). The reference here is not, however, so much to a definite class (like the prophets) as it is to men of faith in general who were roughly clad. That they were "destitute" is in accord with this, for the author is speaking of men without earthly resources. Misery pressed on them as they were "persecuted and mistreated."

38 To all outward appearance, these people of faith were insignificant and unimportant. But the true situation was very different. They were worth more than the whole world, though they lacked everything. The author appeals to deep realities, not apparent on the surface of things. The despised and ill-treated group of servants of God was of greater real worth than all the rest of humanity put together. Their description is rounded off with the reminder that they had no settled homes. They wandered in lonely places, and their shelters were "caves and holes in the ground" (i.e., underground caves). The heroes of the faith had no mansions; they cared for other things than their own comfort.

Notes

34 The plural στόματα (*stomata*, "mouths") is linked with the singular μαχαίρης (*machairēs*, "sword"). From this some have deduced that the writer had a two-edged sword in mind. This, however, seems not to be the thought. It is rather that there were many examples of sword-type violence.

35 "Tortured" renders ἐτυμπανίσθησαν (*etympanisthēsan*). The τύμπανον (*tympanon*) was a drum; the meaning appears to be that the victims of this kind of torture were stretched (on a rack or a wheel?) tight as the skin on a drum and then beaten to death.

"Refused to be released" renders οὐ προσδεξάμενοι τὴν ἀπολύτρωσιν (*ou prosdexamenoi tēn apolytrōsin*, "not having accepted the redemption"). It is important that "redemption" be given its full force. These people were not offered unconditional freedom. The writer had more than release in mind—viz., release on payment of a price and that price apostasy.

37 A number of MSS read ἐπειράσθησαν (*epeirasthēsan*, "they were put to the test") either before or after ἐπρίσθησαν (*epristhēsan*, "they were sawed in two"). But this appears to be an error due to dittography.

H. *The Promise*

11:39–40

39These were all commended for their faith, yet none of them received what had been promised. **40**God had planned something better for us so that only together with us would they be made perfect.

The author rounds off this section with a reminder of the great privilege Christians have. The giants of the faith had done great things for God in their times, and there is no question regarding God's approval of them. Nevertheless, they would not be "made perfect" apart from the humble followers of Jesus.

39 "These" refers to the preceding heroes of the faith; "all" omits none of them. God never forgets any of his faithful servants. The characteristic now singled out is that they had "witness" borne to them (*martyrēthentes;* NIV, "were commended") on account of their faith. The importance of faith, which has been stressed throughout the chapter, continues to the end. But for all their greatness and for all the blessing God gave them, these heroes of the faith did not receive "the promise" (*tēn epangelian*). Verse 33 tells us that they "gained what was promised." Indeed, Abraham was cited as an example of that as far back as Hebrews 6:15. But here it is not a question of "the promises" but of "the promise." God made many promises to his people and kept them. So there were many blessings that they received along the way. But the ultimate blessing (which the author characteristically sees in terms of promise) was not given under the old dispensation. God kept that until Jesus came.

40 God's plan provided for "something better for us." The indefinite pronoun leaves the precise nature of the blessing undefined. The important thing is not exactly what it is but that God has not imparted it prematurely. "Us" means "us Christians"; we who are Christ's have our place in God's plan. And that plan provides that the heroes of the faith throughout the ages should not "be made perfect" apart from Christians.

Salvation is social. It concerns the whole people of God. We can experience it only as part of the whole people of God. As long as the believers in OT times were without those who are in Christ, it was impossible for them to experience the fullness of salvation. Furthermore, it is what Christ has done that opens the way into the very presence of God for them as for us. Only the work of Christ brings those of OT times and those of the new and living way alike into the presence of God.

IX. Christian Living

The last main section of the epistle is largely devoted to the practical business of living out the Christian faith. In it there are exhortations to a variety of Christian duties.

A. *Christ Our Example*

12:1–3

> Therefore, since we are surrounded by such a great cloud of witnesses, let us throw off everything that hinders and the sin that so easily entangles, and let us run with perseverance the race marked out for us. [2]Let us fix our eyes on Jesus, the author and perfecter of our faith, who for the joy set before him endured the cross, scorning its shame, and sat down at the right hand of the throne of God. [3]Consider him who endured such opposition from sinful men, so that you will not grow weary and lose heart.

The writer begins by pointing to what Christ has done for us. In one of the great, moving passages of the NT, he points to the Cross as the stimulus that nerves Christ's people to serious and concentrated endeavor as they face the difficulties involved in living out their faith.

1 "We" links the writer to his readers. He is a competitor in the race as well as they and writes as one who is as much caught up in the contest as they are. The word "cloud" (*nephos,* only here in the NT) may be used of a mass of clouds in the sky (the more common *nephelē* means a single cloud). But it is also used from time to time of a throng of people, when it emphasizes the number. The witnesses are a vast host.

There is a question whether we should understand "witnesses" as those who have witnessed to the faith or as spectators witnessing the present generation of Christians. Normally the word is used in the former sense, and it is doubtful whether it ever means simply "a spectator." Still it is difficult to rid the word of this idea in 1 Timothy 6:12 (perhaps also in Heb 10:28), and the imagery of the present passage favors it. The writer is picturing athletes in a footrace, running for the winning post and urged on by the crowd. He speaks of the runners as "surrounded," which makes it hard to think of them as looking to the "witnesses" and all the more so since they are exhorted to keep their eyes on Jesus (v.2). Both ideas may be present. Perhaps we should think of something like a relay race where those who have finished their course and handed in their baton are watching and encouraging their successors.

With the great gallery of witnesses about us, it is important for us to run well. So we are exhorted, "Let us throw off everything that hinders." "Everything that hinders" translates *onkos* (only here in the NT), a word that may mean any kind of weight.

It is sometimes used of superfluous bodily weight that the athlete sheds during training. Here, however, it seems to be the race rather than the training that is in view. Athletes carried nothing with them in a race (they even ran naked), and the writer is suggesting that the Christian should "travel light." He is not referring to sin, for that follows in the next clause. Some things that are not wrong in themselves hinder us in putting forward our best effort. So the writer tells us to get rid of them.

Christians must also put off every sin. There is a problem relating to the adjective rendered "that so easily entangles" (*euperistatos*), for it is found nowhere else. The word is made up of three parts that mean respectively "well," "around," and "standing." Most scholars accept some such meaning as "easily surrounding" or "easily entangling." Sin forms a crippling hindrance to good running. Christians then, are to lay aside all that could hinder them in their race and are to "run with perseverance." The author is not thinking of a short, sharp sprint but of a distance race that requires endurance and persistence. Everyone has from time to time a mild inclination to do good. The author is not talking about this but about the kind of sustained effort required of the long-distance runner who keeps on with great determination over the long course. That is what the heroes of faith did in their day, and it is that to which we are called.

2 We are to run this race "with no eyes for any one or anything except Jesus" (Moffatt, in loc.). It is he toward whom we run. There must be no divided attention. The "author and perfecter of faith" (there is no "our" in the Gr.) may mean that Jesus trod the way of faith first and brought it to completion. Or it may mean that he originated his people's faith and will bring it to its perfection. Since it is not easy to think that the author sees the faith by which Jesus lived as essentially the same as our own, perhaps it is better to see the emphasis on what he does in his followers. (Yet the thought of example will not be entirely absent, for we should bear in mind that Jesus' kinship with men has been stressed in this epistle.) As the heroes of faith in chapter 11 are OT characters, there is the thought that Jesus led all the people of faith, even from the earliest days.

The expression rendered "for the joy set before him" is problematic. The preposition *anti* strictly means "in the stead of," "in the place of." Accordingly the meaning may be that in place of the joy he might have had Jesus accepted the cross. The "joy" is then the heavenly bliss the preincarnate Christ surrendered in order to take the way of the Cross. He replaced joy with the Cross. But *anti* sometimes has a meaning like "for the sake of" (F. Büchsel sees this in Eph 5:31 etc.; TDNT, 1:372). So with this understanding of the term the meaning is that Jesus went to the Cross because of the joy it would bring. He looked right through the Cross to the coming joy, the joy of bringing salvation to those he loves. The latter meaning is preferable. For this joy, then, Jesus "endured the cross" (or, perhaps, "endured a cross").

The "cross" is not as common a way of referring to the death of Jesus as we might have expected. Actually, this is the one occurrence of the word outside the Gospels and Pauline Epistles. If one "scorns" a thing, one normally has nothing to do with it; but "scorning its shame" means rather that Jesus thought so little of the pain and shame involved that he did not bother to avoid it. He endured it. Then, having completed his work of redemption, he "sat down at the right hand of the throne of God" (see comments on 1:3). The perfect tense in the verb "sat down" points to a permanent result. The work of atonement ended, Christ is at God's right hand forevermore.

3 "Consider" (*analogisasthe,* used only here in the NT) is a word used in calculations. The readers are invited to "take account of" Jesus. He is described as one who "endured" (the perfect tense points to the abiding result). The example he set remained before the readers. He endured "opposition from sinful men" and thus was in the same kind of position the readers found themselves in. They must not think their situation unique. They were not called upon to put up with something their Master had not first endured. Several commentators point out that the two verbs used at the end of this verse, "grow weary and lose heart," are both used by Aristotle of runners who relax and collapse after they have passed the finishing post. The readers were still in the race. They must not give way prematurely. They must not allow themselves to faint and collapse through weariness. Once again there is the call to perseverance in the face of hardship.

Notes

1 "Therefore" translates τοιγαροῦν (*toigaroun*), found again in the NT only in 1 Thess 4:8. It is an inferential particle meaning "wherefore then, so therefore" (A-S, s.v.).

Notice that in this verse the words τοσοῦτον (*tosouton*) and ὄγκον (*onkon*) are thrust forward for emphasis.

A number of commentators accept the reading of P[46], εὐπερίσπαστον (*euperispaston,* "easily distracting"). This is attractive, but it is not easy to see why, if it was original, it has left so little mark on the textual tradition. "Race" translates ἀγῶνα (*agōna*), the technical expression for a contest in the games.

2 Ἀφοράω (*aphoraō*) means "to look away from all else at, fix one's gaze upon" (A-S, s.v.). It is no casual glance but a firmly fixed gaze that is meant.

3 There is a difficult textual problem posed by the fact that most of the oldest authorities read the plural εἰς ἑαυτούς (*eis heautous,* "against themselves"). The singular "against him" is obviously superior; in fact, a number of commentators maintain that it alone makes sense. But precisely because it makes so much better sense many argue that the plural—the more difficult reading—must be accepted. If it is, then the meaning is that Jesus received opposition "from sinners against themselves"; i.e., sinners doing hurt to themselves (cf. Num 16:38; Prov 8:36; Jude 11).

B. *Discipline*

12:4–11

4In your struggle against sin, you have not yet resisted to the point of shedding
your blood. 5And you have forgotten that word of encouragement that addresses
you as sons:

> "My son, do not make light of the Lord's discipline,
> and do not lose heart when he rebukes you,
> 6because the Lord disciplines those he loves,
> and he punishes everyone he accepts as a son."

7Endure hardship as discipline; God is treating you as sons. For what son is not
disciplined by his father? 8If you are not disciplined (and everyone undergoes
discipline), then you are illegitimate children and not true sons. 9Moreover, we have
all had human fathers who disciplined us and we respected them for it. How much

more should we submit to the Father of our spirits and live! [10]Our fathers disciplined us for a little while as they thought best; but God disciplines us for our good, that we may share in his holiness. [11]No discipline seems pleasant at the time, but painful. Later on, however, it produces a harvest of righteousness and peace for those who have been trained by it.

Suffering comes to all; it is part of life, but it is not easy to bear. Yet it is not quite so bad when it can be seen as meaningful. The author has just pointed out that Christ endured his suffering on the cross on account of the joy set before him. His suffering had meaning. So for Christians all suffering is transformed because of the Cross. We serve a Savior who suffered, and we know he will not lead us into meaningless suffering. The writer points to the importance of discipline and proceeds to show that for Christians suffering is rightly understood only when seen as God's fatherly discipline, correcting and directing us. Suffering is evidence, not that God does not love us, but that he does. Believers are sons and are treated as sons.

4 The "struggle [*antagōnizomai* retains the imagery of athletic games] against sin" seems to refer not to sin the readers might be tempted to commit (though some think apostasy is in mind) but to the sin of oppressors who tried to terrorize them into abandoning their faith. Shedding blood would not accompany the normal course of temptation, but it was a very real possibility for those facing persecution. Jesus had been killed, and many of those honored in chapter 11 had likewise been killed for their faithfulness to God. The words "not yet" show that there was real danger and that the readers must be ready for difficult days. But they had not had to die for their faith. The comparative mildness of their sufferings must not be overlooked, the writer is saying. They were evidently concerned at the prospect facing them, and he points out that their experience is not nearly so difficult as that of others.

5–6 They had forgotten an important point: Scripture links suffering and sonship, as Proverbs 3:11–12 shows. The address "My son" is normal for a maker of proverbs who assumes a superior but caring position. The author, however, sees a fuller meaning in these words than that, for they are words from God to his people. When God speaks of discipline and rebuke, it is sons that he addresses. It is interesting that this warning is called "that word of encouragement." The certainty of suffering encourages the believer rather than dismays him because he knows that it is God's discipline for him. Incidentally, it seems not improbable that the words might perhaps be taken as a question: "Have you forgotten?"

The word for discipline combines the thoughts of chastening and education. It points to sufferings that teach us something. In v.4 the striving was against sin, but somehow the hand of God was in it, too. No circumstances are beyond God's control, and there are none he cannot use to carry out his purpose. So the believer is not to belittle the significance of his sufferings nor lose heart in the face of God's correction. "Those he loves" comes first in the Greek, which gives it a certain emphasis. God disciplines people he loves, not those he is indifferent to. The readers should see the sufferings they were experiencing as a sign of God's love, as Scripture already assured them. It is the son that is punished and "every son" (*panta huion*) at that.

In the ancient world it was universally accepted that the bringing up of sons involved disciplining them. Therefore, we should not read back modern permissive attitudes into our understanding of this passage. The Roman father possessed absolute authority. When a child was born, he decided whether to keep or discard it. Throughout its life he could punish it as he chose. He could even execute his son and, while this was rarely done, the right to do it was there. Discipline was only to be expected.

7 NIV takes the verb "endure" as imperative. This may well be correct, though it could be an indicative. The important thing here is the emphatic position of the words "as discipline" in the Greek sentence. It is not as misery, accident, or the like that Christians should understand suffering but as discipline. God uses it to teach important lessons. It shows that "God is treating you as sons." The rhetorical question appeals to the universality of fatherly discipline. It was unthinkable to the writer and his readers that a father would not discipline his sons. Perhaps we should notice in passing that while the author clearly sees believers as children of God, he does not specifically call God father (except in a quotation in 1:5; cf. also "the Father of spirits," v.9).

8 The hypothetical possibility of being without chastisement is looked at and a devastating conclusion drawn. "Everyone," he says, "undergoes discipline" (*hēs metochoi gegonasin pantes;* lit., "of which all are sharers"), which recalls the "everyone" of v.6. It is the universal experience of children that life means discipline. If anyone does not receive discipline, then, the author says, he is "illegitimate." The word *nothos* is used of one born of a slave or a concubine, or of the illegitimate in general (see LSJ, s.v.). The point is that they are not heirs, not members of the family. For them the father feels no responsibility. Their freedom from discipline is not evidence of a privileged position. Rather the reverse is true. They are bastards—"not-sons" (*ouch huioi*).

9 The writer appeals to the practice and result of discipline exercised in the human family. He and his readers have had experience of discipline; they have had fathers who were *paideutai,* "correctors," "discipliners." Fathers are seen in their capacity as chastisers, trainers of their children by punishing them when they go wrong. The effect of such paternal chastisement is to arouse respect, not resentment. How much more, then, should believers submit to God's discipline! "The Father of spirits" (there is no "our" in the Gr.) is a most unusual expression found only here in Scripture, though a similar expression occurs in Numbers 16:22; 27:16. The spirits might be those of "righteous men made perfect" (v.23), but there seems no reason for limiting it in this way. But likewise there is no reason why we should press the expression to mean a universal fatherhood. A number of translations render this phrase "our spiritual Father" (TEV, NEB, JB), and something like this seems meant. The verb "live" (*zaō*) is used here of "the glory of the life to come" (BAG, s.v.). When people subject themselves to God, accepting life's sufferings as discipline from his fatherly hand, they enter the life that is alone worthy of the name.

10 There is a difference in the quality of the discipline we have received from our earthly fathers and that which comes from God. They disciplined us "for a little while," i.e., the comparatively brief days of childhood; and they did it "according to their lights" (NEB). They did their best, but the phrase seems to imply that they made mistakes. But God's discipline is always "for our good." There is nothing of the "hit or miss" about it. It is aimed at our good and the aim is "that we may share in his holiness." The word "holiness" (*hagiotēs*) is not common (elsewhere in the NT it occurs only in a variant reading in 2 Cor 1:12). It points to God's holy character. The aim of God's chastisement of his people is to produce in them a character like his own.

11 At the time it takes place, chastisement is never a happy, joyous affair. On the contrary, sorrow (*lypē*) goes with it. But while it does not "seem pleasant," it does produce a result the writer calls a "harvest of righteousness and peace." The adjective *eirēnikos* (tr. "peace" in NIV) is interesting. Moffatt comments, "The writer might be throwing out a hint to his readers, that suffering was apt to render people irritable, impatient with one another's faults. The later record even of the martyrs, for example, shows that the very prospect of death did not always prevent Christians from quarreling in prison" (Moffatt, in loc.). It is important that suffering be accepted in the right spirit; otherwise it does not produce the right result. So the author goes on to speak of those who have been "trained" by it, where the word *gegymnasmenois* (once more the metaphor from athletics) points to those who have continued to exercise themselves in godly discipline. It is not a matter of accepting a minor chastisement or two with good grace; it is the habit of life that is meant. When that is present, the "peaceable fruit" follows.

Notes

5 Ὀλίγος (*oligos*, "little") connects with ὤρα (*ōra*, "care") to give ὀλιγωρέω (*oligōreō*, "think little of").

10 The construction εἰς τό (*eis to*) plus an infinitive expresses purpose. It is found eight times in Hebrews. Here it indicates that God does not discipline his people aimlessly but with a definite end in view.

C. *Exhortation to the Christian Life*

12:12–17

12Therefore, strengthen your feeble arms and weak knees. 13"Make level paths for your feet," so that the lame may not be disabled, but rather healed.

14Make every effort to live in peace with all men and to be holy; without holiness no one will see the Lord. 15See to it that no one misses the grace of God and that no bitter root grows up to cause trouble and defile many. 16See that no one is sexually immoral, or is godless like Esau, who for a single meal sold his inheritance rights as the oldest son. 17Afterward, as you know, when he wanted to inherit this blessing, he was rejected. He could bring about no change of mind, though he sought the blessing with tears.

From the acceptance of life's discipline in general, the writer turns to the way this discipline is applied in Christian experience. It is important that God's people live as God's people. They are not to take their standards from the ungodly.

12 "Therefore" links this exhortation to what has gone before. Because of what they now know of God's loving discipline, they must put forward their best effort. The "hands" (not "arms" as NIV) are pictured as "limp" (JB) and thus useless. They accomplish nothing. The knees are "weak." There is a reference to similar hands and knees in Isaiah 35:3 (cf. Ecclus 25:23), and the writer may have taken his imagery from there. "Strengthen" is NIV's translation of *anorthōsate* ("make upright" or "straight"). The picture is of someone whose hands and legs are for some reason out of action but are put right. The exhortation implies that the readers are acting as though spiritually paralyzed. They are urged to put things right and get moving.

13 A quotation from Proverbs 4:26 is added. NIV takes the words *orthas poieite* to mean "make level," though they are usually understood as "make straight." Clearly the idea is to put the paths into better order in order to facilitate travel, specifically for the lame. The writer is mindful of the fact that Christians belong together. They must have consideration for the weak among their members, i.e., the "lame." There is a problem relating to the verb rendered "be disabled" (*ektrapē*, more lit., "turned away"). It might mean that the lame are not to be turned from the right way (so Snell, for example, in loc.). BAG (s.v.) note that linguistically there is another possibility—"that what is lame might not be avoided"—but this meaning is obviously unsuitable to the context. The following reference to healing makes it certain that it is something like dislocation that is meant (as in RSV, NEB, etc.). By taking care for the defective members of the congregation, the stronger members can help them along the way. Where the Christian life is in any way "out of joint," steps should be taken to revitalize it.

14 The NT contains a number of exhortations to believers to be at peace, either with one another or with people in general (cf. Matt 5:9; Mark 9:50; Rom 12:18). People are often selfish and abrasive, but this is not the way Christians should be. For them peace is imperative, and they must "make every effort" to attain it. Commentators differ as to whether "all men" is to be taken in its widest sense or whether the writer means "all fellow believers." Granted that it is especially important for Christians to live in harmony with one another, there seems to be no reason for taking "all" in anything other than its normal meaning. The readers are to make every effort to live at peace with all people. We need not doubt that the writer is especially interested in harmony in the Christian community, but he has so worded his exhortation that it covers all relations and not only those among believers.

Coupled with peace is "holiness." The rendering "to be holy" (NIV, TEV) misses the point that "holiness" is a noun set alongside "peace" as the object of the verb. Holiness means being set apart for God. It is characteristic of the believer. As Barclay puts it, "Although he lives in the world, the man who is *hagios* must always in one sense be different from the world and separate from the world. His standards are not the world's standards" (in loc.). Without this readiness to belong to God, this being separated to God, no one will see God. Jesus said that the pure in heart see God (Matt 5:8), and no one has a right to expect that vision without that qualification.

15 The verb rendered "see to it" (*episkopountes*) is an unusual one. It conveys the idea of oversight (the verb is connected with the noun we translate as "bishop"). In this context the thought is that believers must have care for one another. The writer speaks of three things in particular the readers must avoid. The first is coming short of God's grace. Paul could speak of receiving God's grace in vain (2 Cor 6:1) and of falling from grace (Gal 5:4). It is something like this that is in mind here. God is not niggardly in offering grace. He gives his people all they will take. Accordingly, it is important for them not to fail to make use of their opportunities.

The second contingency to guard against is the springing up of a "bitter root." The expression is reminiscent of Deuteronomy 29:17. But if it is a quotation from the LXX, it is fairly free. A "bitter root" is a root that bears bitter fruit. The metaphor is taken from the growth of plants. Such growth is slow, but what is in the plant will surely come out in time. So it is possible for a seed of bitterness to be sown in a community and, though nothing is immediately apparent, in due time the inevitable fruit appears. It will certainly "cause trouble." The effects of bitterness cannot be localized: it "can poison a whole community" (JB). "Defile" in the first instance refers to ceremonial defilement (John 18:28), but it is also used of moral defilement. Bitterness defiles people and makes them unfit to stand before God. When bitterness is allowed to grow, it has wide-ranging effects. It defiles "many."

16 The third warning begins with a reference to the "sexually immoral" (*pornos*, "fornicator"). The OT has passages that use sexual sin as a metaphor for idolatry and the like. Some have felt that this is the way the word should be taken here. But there seems nothing in the context to demand it, so it is better to take the word literally. A further question is whether *pornos* is meant to apply to Esau. There is no evidence in the OT that Esau was a fornicator, though some have taken the fact that he married Hittite wives (Gen 26:34) to be the object of the allusion. In Jewish legend Esau was accused of many sins including this one. But there seems no reason for thinking that the writer of the epistle has this in mind. He seems to be warning his readers against two things: fornication and being "godless" like Esau.

The word rendered "godless" (*bebēlos*) means "unhallowed," "profane." The author is saying that Esau was not spiritually minded but rather a man taken up with the things of the here and now. This is apparent in the incident referred to, when Esau for just one meal bargained away "his inheritance rights as the oldest son" (cf. Gen 25:29–34). He could not recognize its true value. His insistence on the gratification of his immediate needs led him to overlook the importance of his rights as the firstborn. For a small immediate gain, he bartered away what was of infinitely greater worth. So with the apostates.

17 The opening word (*iste*) may be imperative "know" or indicative "as you know," as NIV takes it. The writer appeals to knowledge common to his readers and himself. Nothing is known about Esau's change of mind other than what we read here. It appears that in due course Esau came to realize he had made a mistake. He wanted to go back but found he could not. Some take the second part of the verse to mean that he could not change Isaac's mind, but this has to be read into the text. Isaac is not mentioned. The meaning is, rather, "he could not find a way to change what he had done" (TEV). There is a finality about what we do. Barclay points out that "if a young man loses his purity or a girl her virginity, nothing can ever bring it back. The choice was made and the choice stands" (in loc.). Notice that it is not a question of forgiveness. God's forgiveness is always open to the penitent. Esau could have come back to God. But he could not undo his act.

D. *Mount Sinai and Mount Zion*

12:18–24

[18]You have not come to a mountain that can be touched and that is burning with fire; to darkness, gloom and storm; [19]to a trumpet blast or to such a voice speaking words, so that those who heard it begged that no further word be spoken to them, [20]because they could not bear what was commanded: "If even an animal touches

the mountain, it must be stoned." [21]The sight was so terrifying that Moses said, "I am trembling with fear."

[22]But you have come to Mount Zion, to the heavenly Jerusalem, the city of the living God. You have come to thousands upon thousands of angels in joyful assembly, [23]to the church of the firstborn, whose names are written in heaven. You have come to God, the judge of all men, to the spirits of righteous men made perfect, [24]to Jesus the mediator of a new covenant, and to the sprinkled blood that speaks a better word than the blood of Abel.

The writer proceeds to contrast the Jewish and Christian ways by contrasting the terrors associated with the giving of the law on Mount Sinai with the joys and the glory associated with Mount Zion. He sounds the note of warning that great privilege means great responsibility.

18 The older MSS omit "mountain." The meaning might then be thus: "You have not come to a fire that can be touched." It is better, however, to see it as quite general: "You have not come to anything that can be touched." There can be no doubt that the events on Sinai are in mind, though the writer chooses not to refer to the mountain specifically but to what it represented—the outward, the physical, and the material (cf. JB, "What you have come to is nothing known to the senses"). The phenomena listed are all associated with the Sinai event (see Deut 4:11). Elsewhere they are all linked with the presence of God: fire (Judg 13:20; 1 Kings 18:38), darkness (1 Kings 8:12), and tempest (Nah 1:3); the trumpet (v.19) being associated with the end time when God will manifest himself (Matt 24:31; 1 Cor 15:52; 1 Thess 4:16). The picture is one that strikes terror into the heart.

19 The trumpet is spoken of repeatedly in connection with Sinai (Exod 19:16, 19; 20:18). And on that occasion the people heard the voice of God (Deut 5:24). But the effect of it all was to terrify them, and they asked that they should hear God's voice no more (Exod 20:19; Deut 5:25–27). They were overcome with awe and wanted no further part in the wonderful events.

20 The fearfulness of the giving of the law on Sinai is brought out with reference to one of the commands laid on the people, namely, that neither man nor beast should even touch the mountain under penalty of death. The writer uses a present participle in saying "what was commanded," which makes it all terrifyingly present. The command that nothing touch it indicates the holiness and separateness of the mountain. The quotation is from Exodus 19:13. Killing by stoning (Exod 19:13 also permitted shooting, i.e., with darts or arrows) was prescribed so that those taking part in it would not need to touch the mountain themselves.

21 There is a further indication of the awesomeness of it all. At the time of the giving of the law, Moses was the leader of the people. He was known as one who had an especially close relationship with God (Exod 33:11). Yet even he was terrified. The words quoted are not found in the Sinai narrative but do occur at the time of the golden calf (Deut 9:19). The author may have had access to a tradition that recorded these words on this occasion. Or he may be including Moses in the general fear spoken of in Exodus 20:18. Or possibly he is taking words spoken on one occasion and applying them to another to which they also refer. At any rate, he is picturing an awe-inspiring occasion, one that affected all the people and terrified even Moses, the man of God.

22 "But" is the strong adversative (*alla*) and introduces a marked contrast. It is not a Sinai type experience that has befallen Christians. They "have come" (the perfect tense points to an accomplished and continuing state) to Mount Zion. This is one of the hills on which the city of Jerusalem was built. It sometimes stands for that city (Matt 21:5), and stands here, of course, for that city as the home of God's people. It is also called "the heavenly Jerusalem" and "the city of the living God." Elsewhere in the NT there is the thought of the Jerusalem above (Gal 4:26, where again there is a contrast with Mount Sinai; cf. also Rev 3:12; 21:2, 10).

The author has already spoken of "the city with foundations, whose architect and builder is God" (11:10). He is bringing out the thought of the ideal, heavenly city. His mention of "the living God" (see comments on 3:12) emphasizes the thought that this city is no static affair; it is the city of a vital, dynamic, living Being, one who is doing things. Its inhabitants include large numbers of angels. NIV says that there are "thousands upon thousands" of them, which is the translation of the one word *myriasin*. Originally this meant ten thousand, but it came to be used for a very large number. (For angels at Sinai, see Deut 33:2. The heavenly city is not deficient on this score.)

Scholars differ as to whether we should take the expression "joyful assembly" with angels (as NIV) or with the following verse (as TEV, "you have come to the joyful gathering of God's oldest sons"). While it cannot be proved to be the only way, NIV's understanding of it fits the Greek better and should probably be accepted. The word meant originally a national festive assembly to honor a god, then more generally any festal assembly.

23 "The church of the firstborn" is another difficult expression. Does it mean the angels just spoken of? They are not usually called a "church," but the word basically means an assembly and so could be applied to angels. If it refers to people, it is not easy to see it as the church triumphant because that is the same as "the spirits of righteous men made perfect" at the end of the verse. Nor is it easier to see it of the church here and now, for (1) the readers would be included and would be "coming" to themselves, and (2) it would give a strange sequence—angels, the church on earth, God, the departed. Angels are not normally described as having their "names . . . written in heaven," whereas there are references to the recording of the names of the saved (e.g., Luke 10:20; Rev 21:27). Perhaps the best solution is to see a reference to the whole communion of saints, the church on earth and in heaven. Believers not only come *to* it but *into* it. This would follow naturally on the reference to angels, after which there is the thought of God as Judge and those who have been vindicated by his judgment.

Montefiore (in loc.) objects to the usual translations like "God, the Judge of all" partly because they do not take account of the Greek word order and partly because they miss the force of the argument. God is not third on the list of the inhabitants of heaven; rather, the author's concern is "with the Judge (who is God) who has rewarded the spirits of righteous men." It is unusual to have the departed referred to as "spirits." The expression is probably used to give emphasis to the spiritual nature of the new order the "righteous men" find themselves in. There is a sense in which they are not made perfect without Christians (11:40). But there is also a sense in which they have been brought to the end for which they were made.

24 The climax is reached with the reference to Jesus, seen here as "the mediator of a new covenant." The word for "new" (*neas*) is applied to the covenant only here. It refers to what is recent. The covenant involves "sprinkled blood" (cf. 9:19–22), which reminds us of the cost of the covenant. The idea of blood speaking is not common, and there is undoubtedly a reference to Genesis 4:10 where Abel's blood cried from the ground for vengeance on his killer. Jesus' blood speaks "a better word" than that. His blood opens up a way into the holiest for people (10:19): Abel's blood sought to shut out the wicked man.

Notes

---

18 The use of the perfect tense προσεληλύθατε (*proselēlythate,* "you have come") should be noted. It may mean that the position once taken up by the Jews is retained. For them there is still nothing but the equivalent of Sinai. Ὄρει (*orei,* "mountain") is read by many MSS but omitted by the oldest authorities. There would be every tendency for a scribe to insert it but none to omit it. It can scarcely be original.

22 It is striking that in vv.22–24 there is no article until we come to τὸν Ἄβελ (*ton Abel*). "The thoughts are presented in their most abstract form" (Westcott, in loc.).

E. *A Kingdom That Cannot Be Shaken*

12:25–29

> [25]See to it that you do not refuse him who speaks. If they did not escape when they refused him who warned them on earth, how much less will we, if we turn away from him who warns us from heaven? [26]At that time his voice shook the earth, but now he has promised, "Once more I will shake not only the earth but also the heavens." [27]The words "once more" indicate the removing of what can be shaken —that is, created things—so that what cannot be shaken may remain.
>
> [28]Therefore, since we are receiving a kingdom that cannot be shaken, let us be thankful, and so worship God acceptably with reverence and awe, [29]for our God is a consuming fire.

Earthly, material things (things that can be "shaken") will not last forever. By contrast, God's kingdom is unshakable, and the author uses the contrast as an exhortation to right conduct. He has made it plain that God will not trifle with wrongdoing. The persistent sinner can reckon only on severe judgment. God will bring all things present to an end. Accordingly, the readers should serve him faithfully.

25 Several times in this epistle Judaism and Christianity have been contrasted, and here the contrast concerns the way God speaks. Some feel there is a contrast between Moses and Christ. This may be so, but the basic contrast is between the way God spoke of old and the way he now speaks. Israel of old "refused" him, which means that in their manner of life they rejected what God said and failed to live up to what he commanded (cf. Deut 5:29; the writer cannot be referring to Israel's refusal to hear God's voice because they were praised for this, Deut 5:24–28). What God said was a warning "on earth" because it was connected with the revelation made at Sinai. If, then, the Israelites of old did not escape the consequences of their refusal of a voice on earth, the readers ought not to expect that they will escape far worse consequences if they "turn away from him who warns us from heaven."

26 Here the solemnity of Sinai is recalled. Repeatedly we are told that then the earth shook (Exod 19:18; Judg 5:4–5; Ps 68:8; 77:18; 114:4, 7). The writer has already spoken of the awe-inspiring nature of what happened when the law was given. Now the reference to the shaking of the earth brings it all back. At the same time it enables him to go on to speak of a promise that involved a further shaking, that recorded in Haggai 2:6. The prophet looked forward to something much grander than Sinai. Then God shook the earth, but Haggai foresaw a day when God would shake "not only the earth but also the heavens." This will be no small event but one of cosmic grandeur. The reference to heaven and earth may be meant to hint at the concept of the new heaven and the new earth (Isa 66:22). At any rate, it points to the decisive intervention that God will make at the last time.

27 The writer picks out the expression "once more" (*eti hapax;* lit., "yet once more") to point out the decisive significance of the things of which he is writing. There is an air of finality about it all. This is the decisive time. The word rendered "the removing" (*metathesin*) can mean a "change" (as in 7:12 of a change of law). But "removal" is also possible and seems better in this context. What can be shaken will be removed in that day. NIV renders *hōs pepoiēmenōn* as "that is, created things" (RSV, "as of what has been made"), and this is the sense of it (*poieō* is often used of God's creative activity). This physical creation can be shaken, and it is set in contrast to what cannot be shaken. These are the things that really matter, the things that have the character of permanence. The author does not go into detail about the precise nature of the ultimate rest. But whatever it may be, it will separate the things that last forever from those that do not. "So that" introduces a clause of purpose. It is God's will for this final differentiation to be made so that only what cannot be shaken will remain.

28 The "kingdom" is not a frequent subject in this epistle (the word occurs in a quotation in 1:8 and in the plural in 11:33). This is in contrast to the synoptic Gospels, where the "kingdom" is the most frequent subject in the teaching of Jesus. But this passage shows that the author understood ultimate reality in terms of God's sovereignty. This reality contrasts with earthly systems. They can be shaken and in due course will be shaken. Not so God's kingdom! The author does not simply say that it will not be shaken but that it cannot be shaken. It has a quality found in nothing earthly. The kingdom is something we "receive." It is not earned or created by believers; it is God's gift.

It is not quite certain how we should understand the expression "let us be thankful" (*echōmen charin*). A strong argument for this rendering is that it is the usual meaning of the expression. But *charis* means "grace"; and, as Montefiore (in loc.) points out, elsewhere in this epistle it signifies "grace" rather than "gratitude." He thinks that the duty of thanksgiving is not inculcated elsewhere in Hebrews nor is it particularly appropriate here. So he prefers to translate it, "Let us hold on to God's grace" (JB is similar). Montefiore's position is favored by the following "through which" (*di' hēs*), which NIV renders "and so." The writer appears to be saying that we must appropriate the grace God offers and not let it go, because it is only by grace that we serve as we should. "Worship" may be too narrow for *latreuōmen,* for the word can be used of service of various kinds. KJV renders it "serve." Whether the meaning is service in general or worship in particular, it must be done "with reverence and awe." The combination stresses the greatness of God and the lowly place his people should take in relation to him.

29 In an expression apparently taken from Deuteronomy 4:24, the writer emphasizes that God is not to be trifled with. It is easy to be so taken up with the love and compassion of God that we overlook his implacable opposition to all evil. The wrath of God is not a popular subject today but it looms large in biblical teaching. The writer is stressing that his readers overlook this wrath at their peril. Baillie speaks of the wrath of God "as being identical with the consuming fire of inexorable divine love in relation to our sins" (D.M. Baillie, *God Was in Christ* [London: Faber & Faber, 1955], p. 189). It is something like this to which the writer directs his readers' attention.

Notes

---

26 There are several rabbinic passages that show that Hag 2:6 was frequently considered in discussing messianic questions, notably the date of the coming of the Messiah (Tal *Sanhedrin* 97b; Exod R, 18.12; Deut R, 1.23; etc.)

27 The writer uses participles that strictly mean "the things being shaken . . . the things not being shaken." But verbal adjectives were not a prominent feature of Gr. during the NT period, and this use of passive participles in the sense of verbal adjectives was not uncommon (see BDF, par. 65 [3]).

28 Some MSS read the indicative ἔχομεν (*echomen,* "we have") instead of the subjunctive ἔχωμεν (*echōmen,* "let us have"). But most scholars hold that support for the latter and its suitability to the context demand that it be preferred. There would have been little difference in pronunciation, and it would have been easy for a scribe to confuse them.

The first twelve chapters of Hebrews form a closely knit argument. Chapter 13 is something of an appendix dealing with a number of practical points. Some commentators find the difference so striking that they think it an addition by someone other than the author of the first twelve chapters. This is going too far. There is no linguistic difference, and, while the argument is not so tight, it is in the manner of the author, especially the section on the cross (vv.9–14).

F. *Love*

13:1–6

1Keep on loving each other as brothers. 2Do not forget to entertain strangers, for by so doing some people have entertained angels without knowing it. 3Remember those in prison as if you were their fellow prisoners, and those who are mistreated as if you yourselves were suffering.

4Marriage should be honored by all, and the marriage bed kept pure, for God will judge the adulterer and all the sexually immoral. 5Keep your lives free from the love of money and be content with what you have, because God has said,

"Never will I leave you;
never will I forsake you."

6So we say with confidence,

"The Lord is my helper; I will not be afraid.
What can man do to me?"

Christians are to be concerned for the needs of others. Those Christ has died for cannot live for themselves. Christianity is faith in action and that means love at work. So the writer draws attention to something of what it means to live in love.

1 "Brotherly love" (*philadelphia*) is a most important virtue in the NT. Those who are linked in the common bond of having been saved by the death of Jesus cannot but have warm feelings toward one another (cf. Rom 12:10; 1 Thess 4:9; 1 Peter 1:22; 2 Peter 1:7; in the OT see Ps 133:1). Calvin comments, "We can only be Christians if we are brethren" (in loc.).

2 To "brotherly love" the author adds "hospitality" (*philoxenia,* "love of strangers"). Entertaining angels unawares reminds us of Abraham (Gen 18:1ff.) and Lot (Gen 19:1ff.). The writer is not advocating hospitality on the off chance that one might happen to receive an angel as guest but rather because God is pleased when believers are hospitable. Sometimes unexpectedly happy results follow acts of hospitality. It was highly esteemed in the ancient world and was certainly very important for Christians. Accommodation at inns was expensive, and in any case inns had a bad reputation. But as Christian preachers traveled around, believers gave them lodging and so facilitated their mission. Without hospitality in Christian homes, the spread of the faith would have been much more difficult.

3 The writer takes a further step in turning his attention to prisoners. Guests may come unbidden, but prisoners must be actively sought out. In the first century prisoners were not well treated, and they depended—often even for necessities like food—on sympathizers. Sometimes people withheld help for fear of identifying themselves with the prisoners and suffering similar punishment. But Christians should have compassion on those in prison "as if you were their fellow prisoners." "If one part suffers, every part suffers with it," wrote Paul (1 Cor 12:26); and there is something of the same thought here. Believers should feel so much for their friends in prison and for "those who are mistreated" that they become one with them. Compassion is an essential part of Christian living.

4 From love for the badly treated the author turns to love within the marriage bond. We should probably understand the opening expression as an imperative: "Let marriage be held in honor" (RSV). "By all" (*en pasin*) might be masculine, "among all men," or neuter, "in all circumstances," probably the latter. Some ascetics held marriage in low esteem, but the author repudiates this position. "The marriage bed" is a euphemism for sexual intercourse. He considers the physical side of marriage important and "pure." Contrary to the views of some thinkers in the ancient world, there is nothing defiling about it. Over against honorable marriage he sets "sexual immorality" (*pornous;* the word is usually rendered "fornicators") and "adulterers" (*moichous,* used where violation of the marriage bond is involved).

All forms of sexual sin come under the judgment of God. This was a novel view to many in the first century. For them chastity was an unreasonable demand to make. It is one of the unrecognized miracles that Christians were able not only to make this demand but to make it stick. The word "God" comes last in the Greek and is emphatic. Sexual sinners are likely to go their way, careless of all others. But in the end they will be judged by none less than God.

5 Sins of impurity and covetousness are also linked elsewhere in the NT (e.g., 1 Cor 5:10–11; Eph 4:19; 5:3–5; 1 Thess 4:3–6). The covetous man pursues his selfish aims, whether sexual or financial, without regard to the rights of others. So the writer warns against the love of money and urges contentment with what one has. In any case covetousness is needless, for the believer has the promise that God will never leave him nor forsake him. The origin of this quotation is not clear; the words do not correspond exactly to any OT passage, though there are several statements that are rather like it (e.g., Gen 28:15; Deut 31:6, 8; Josh 1:5; 1 Chron 28:20; Isa 41:17; perhaps closest is Josh 1:5). It is interesting that Philo has the same quotation in the same words (*On the Confusion of Tongues* 166). Accordingly, it seems that both Philo and the writer of Hebrews are quoting from a version of the LXX that has not survived. Be that as it may, the words point to the complete reliability of God. Since he has promised to help his own, covetousness in all its forms is useless. God's people are secure no matter what comes, because he is with them. Beside this great fact, the petty securities of worldly possessions, position, and the like do not matter at all.

6 Despondency is foreign to Christians. They can speak "with confidence" (*tharrountas,* a participle that indicates an attitude of courage and trust). "We" once more links the writer with his readers. He sees his lot as bound up with theirs. The quotation from Psalm 118:6 is exact, agreeing with the LXX (117:6). There are three points in this confidence. First, the Lord is the psalmist's (and our) helper. This carries on the argument of the previous verse, sharpening a little the thought of the assistance that the believer may count on. Second, there is the ringing declaration of confidence as the psalmist renounces fear. With the Helper he has at his side, there is no reason for fear, and he has none. Third, there is the rhetorical question that underlies man's insignificance. The question is "What will man do to me?" rather than "What can man do to me?" as in NIV, JB, NEB, RSV, and TEV. It is performance rather than capacity the psalmist is speaking of. He is not thinking theoretically but of what will happen. Man will not succeed in anything he attempts to do against one who trusts in God.

Notes

---

2 The present imperative *μὴ ἐπιλανθάνεσθε* (*mē epilanthanesthe,* "do not forget") may indicate that the readers of this epistle were in fact forgetting this duty. The most natural way of taking it is of an action already in progress.

3 NIV is a trifle free at the end of this verse where the Gr. means rather "as being yourselves in [the] body" and the question is "What does 'in body' [*en sōmati*] mean?" Some have taken it to mean "in the body of Christ" (e.g., Calvin). But it seems rather to be an unusual way of referring to life here and now, in bodies like ours. With such bodies imprisonment like that suffered by the friends was always possible and the thought should promote compassion.

6 Of the construction introduced by ὥστε (*hōste*, "so"), E.A. Abbott says that it "rather suggests what we *may* say than states what we *do* say" (*Johannine Grammar* [A. & C. Black, London, 1906], 2203*b*).

G. *Christian Leadership*

13:7–8

> [7]Remember your leaders, who spoke the word of God to you. Consider the outcome of their way of life and imitate their faith. [8]Jesus Christ is the same yesterday and today and forever.

The concluding section of the epistle contains a number of small, disconnected units. From love the writer passes to a few thoughts about Christian leaders. This is important, for there is not much in the NT about the way Christians should treat their leaders. There is, however, more about how leaders themselves should behave.

7 Three times in this chapter the present participle of the verb *hēgeomai* occurs in the sense of "leader" (here, vv. 17, 24). The term is a general one and is used of leaders of religious bodies as well as of princes, military commanders, etc. This makes it difficult to say precisely who these leaders were or what they did. They may have been "elders," but that word is not used of them and so we cannot be sure that they were elders. They "spoke the word of God" so that one of their principal functions was preaching or teaching. But again the word is a general one. The aorist tense may well point to a specific time—that of the original proclamation of the gospel to these readers (cf. 2:3). "The word of God" is the totality of the Christian message, and the expression reminds the readers that this is no human invention but of divine origin.

The word translated "outcome" (*ekbasis*, again in the NT only in 1 Cor 10:13) is understood by many as a euphemism for death, often as a martyr's death (so Héring, Westcott, Moffatt). "Martyr's death" does seem to be stretching the word a bit. On the whole, however, it seems as though past leaders were in mind (though TEV is much too definite with "Remember your former leaders . . . . Think back on how they lived and died"). The past tenses and the word *ekbasis* support this, though it is not impossible to see the meaning as "consider the result of their manner of life." They are held up as examples to be imitated and, specifically, their faith is singled out. Faith is the important thing, and the readers were being tempted to unbelief in falling back from the Christian way. They should instead follow these good examples of faith.

8 In this profound and wonderfully succinct verse, the writer's thoughts turn again to Christ. Earthly leaders come and go, but he is always there. The full name "Jesus Christ" (again in Hebrews only in 10:10; 13:21) adds solemnity to this pronouncement. *Echthes* ("yesterday") should probably not be taken to refer to Christ's preexistence or the Incarnation. It stands for the past as a whole and is part of an expression taking up past, present, and future into an impressive statement of Christ's unchanging nature. The readers need not fear that Christ is different now or will be different in the future from what he has been in the past. Past or present makes no difference to the eternal Savior. "Forever" (*eis tous aiōnas*, "into the ages," "to eternity") takes the continuity as far into the future as it will go. No matter what ages lie ahead, Christ will be unchanged through them. Christian conduct is based on this certainty. Christ will never be superseded.

H. *Christian Sacrifice*

13:9–16

[9]Do not be carried away by all kinds of strange teachings. It is good for our hearts to be strengthened by grace, not by ceremonial foods, which are of no value to those who eat them. [10]We have an altar from which those who minister at the tabernacle have no right to eat.

[11]The high priest carries the blood of animals into the Most Holy Place as a sin offering, but the bodies are burned outside the camp. [12]And so Jesus also suffered outside the city gate to make the people holy through his own blood. [13]Let us, then, go to him outside the camp, bearing the disgrace he bore. [14]For here we do not have an enduring city, but we are looking for the city that is to come.

[15]Through Jesus, therefore, let us continually offer to God a sacrifice of praise—the fruit of lips that confess his name. [16]And do not forget to do good and to share with others, for with such sacrifices God is pleased.

The writer has put strong emphasis on the centrality of Christ's sacrifice and keeps this steadily in view as he approaches the end of his letter. He has some erroneous teaching in mind, but we cannot define it with precision. He and his readers both knew what it was; so there was no need for him to be specific. Whatever it was, the unchangeability of Christ should inspire them to refuse its curious diversities and novel teaching.

Once more the writer draws attention to Christ's sacrifice, using the ceremonies of the Day of Atonement as the basis. Some may have thought the Christian way an impoverished one, lacking the sacrifices that were central to religion in the ancient world. But Christians do have sacrifices, none the less real for being spiritual and not material.

9 The writer warns against being carried away by "all kinds of strange teachings." "All kinds of" renders *poikilais;* literally, "many-colored." Since it points to a great variety of teaching, it is difficult to identify specifically what is in mind. There was not one straightforward piece of wrong teaching but a variety of wrong teachings. "Strange" renders *xenais* ("foreign," i.e., foreign to the gospel). The readers should know better than to go after such teachings, for they have known the grace of God. The heart, as often, stands for the whole of the inner life; and this is sustained, not by anything material, such as food, but by grace. God is the source of the believer's strength as he lives out the Christian life.

Though there is nothing in the Greek to correspond to the adjective "ceremonial," which NIV prefixes to "foods," this is probably a correct gloss. Most religions of the day had food regulations, as did the Jews; but usually this meant that some foods were regarded as "unclean." The foods were not regarded as "good for our hearts." So it seems likely that what the worshipers took to be the beneficial effects of some sacrificial meal are in mind. The author denies it. The real life of man is not sustained on the level of things to eat. It requires the grace of God. The end of the verse means something like "in which those who walk are not profited" (NIV has paraphrased). This points to a way of life in which "foods" are a dominant element.

10 Some see the "altar" as the communion table (from which Christians, but not others, eat). But this is a curious way of interpreting the passage in the light of the point just made. This would simply be substituting one material thing for another, and the whole argument would fall to the ground. Instead, the writer is saying that the cross is distinctive to the Christian way. It was on a cross that the Christian sacrifice was offered. Thus it may not improperly be spoken of as an "altar." In a Christian context the sacrifice must be on the cross as the author has made abundantly clear in a number of places. "Those who minister at the tabernacle" are often understood to be the Jewish priests. But the word *latreuontes* ("those who minister") may be used of the service of others than priests, and the participle is used of worshipers in 9:9; 10:2. The writer seems to be speaking of Jewish worshipers in general. Those who worship at the tent have, as such, no rights in the altar of the cross. The crucified Savior means nothing to them. The writer is pointing his readers to the privilege Christians have and warning them against losing it.

11 "For" (*gar,* which NIV omits) leads from the general idea of serving the altar to a specific example, one taken from the Day of Atonement ceremonies in all probability. The doubt is caused by the fact that the expression that NIV renders "the Most Holy Place" (*ta hagia*) may be used of the "Holy Place" (as in 9:2); and there were sin offerings other than those of the Day of Atonement when the bodies were burned outside the camp (Lev 4:12, 21). But there have been references to the Day of Atonement earlier in the epistle, which also seems to fit the present passage better than the other sin offerings. On that Day the high priest brought the blood of the victims into the Most Holy Place (Lev 16:14–15), but the bodies of the animals were burned outside the camp (Lev 16:27). The word used here for "animals" (*zōōn*) is not common in the Bible and does not appear to be used elsewhere of sacrificial victims. The bodies of the animals used on the Day of Atonement were burnt up—totally consumed—in the fire. This was "outside the camp," the word drawing attention to the wilderness situation ("camp," *parembolē,* basically a military term, was readily applied to such situations as that of Israel in the wilderness).

12 "And so" (*dio*) introduces an inference. The Day of Atonement typologically foreshadowed the atoning work of Jesus. The author apparently is reasoning that because the type involved an activity "outside the camp," there will be an equivalent with the antitype. The parallel is not complete because in the case of the sin offerings the animal was actually killed inside the camp and only the carcass disposed of outside the camp (though the red heifer, "which was a kind of sin-offering, was slaughtered outside the camp," Bruce, in loc.). The type was clear enough. The human name Jesus brings before us the picture of the Man, suffering for us. The conjunction *hina* introduces a clause of purpose. His suffering was not aimless but was designed with a specific object in mind, "to make his people holy."

The verb *hagiazō* means "to set aside for God"; and it is applied both to things used for ritual purposes and to people who are thus taken out of the circle of the merely worldly and brought into the number of the people of God. This process was effected "through his own blood." The expression puts some emphasis on the fact that Christ did not need an external victim (as did the high priests) but brought about the sanctification in question by the sacrifice of himself. "Blood" clearly signifies "death," as is commonly the case in the NT—and, for that matter, in the OT. There are some scholars who think the meaning is "life," but this seems untenable (cf. my discussion in ch. 3 of my *Apostolic Preaching of the Cross,* 3rd ed. [Grand Rapids: Eerdmans, 1965]).

"People" can mean people in general; but more characteristically it means "the people of God," a meaning that suits this passage. To effect this purpose, then, Jesus suffered "outside the gate." Though not stated elsewhere in the NT, this is implied in John 19:17; and, anyway, crucifixions took place outside cities. Snell argues from Leviticus 10:1–5; 24:14, 23 that "*people* were taken 'outside the camp' when they were accursed under the Law and rejected, as much as the ritually useless bodies were after the sacrifice was finished" (in loc.). He goes on to argue that "our Lord's offering has been first compared with that on the Day of Atonement . . . and is next said to have involved formal rejection by the authorities of the old Judaism" (ibid.). That does seem to be the point of the reference. Jesus was rejected by Jewish authorities, and his death outside Jerusalem symbolized this.

13 This leads to an appeal to the readers to "go to him outside the camp" (the compound verb *exerchomai,* "to go out," and the adverb *exō,* "outside," emphasize the thought of "out," "outside"). Christ is outside the camp of Judaism, and the readers are encouraged to go to him where he is. To remain within the camp of Judaism would be to be separated from him. Here there may be an allusion to Moses' pitching "the tent of meeting" outside the camp and to the people's going out to it (Exod 33:7). But in the case of Christ, there was a price to pay—that of sharing in the rejection he had undergone, "bearing the disgrace he bore." In 11:26 Moses was said to have accepted "disgrace for the sake of Christ" (the same expression as here). To align oneself with Christ is to subject oneself to scorn, reproach, and perhaps more. But consistently throughout this epistle the writer has argued, as he does here, that it is well worth it. Furthermore, his readers must have a different outlook from that of contemporary Judaism. The Jews held that the way Christ died proved him to be accursed (Deut 21:23; Gal 3:13). The readers must be ready to stand outside Judaism with the Christ who bore the curse for them "outside the camp."

14 The writer reinforces his appeal to go to Jesus by reminding Christians that they have no stake in any earthly city, Jewish or otherwise. For people with such an outlook it is no great matter to be "outside the camp." As in 11:10 (where see the comments) the "city" will stand for the highest and best in community life, the heavenly city. That is not to be found "here," i.e., "here on earth." In this sense no earthly city is "enduring." All earthly cities are transient, temporary. But Christians are looking for a city to come. People love to look for earthly security. But the best earthly security is insecure. The readers should pursue that which is really lasting. They should put earnest endeavor (*epizēteō;* NIV, "we are looking") into striving for the abiding city, not into maintaining their grip on any fleeting earthly one.

15 The verse begins with an emphatic "through him" (NIV apparently tries to add force by substituting "Jesus" for "him"). It is through Jesus and not the Jewish priests (or any other priests) that men offer to God acceptable sacrifice. The verb *anapherō* is the technical one for the offering of sacrifices of animals and the like. The author uses it of the only sacrifices Christians offer, spiritual sacrifices. So he urges them to offer "a sacrifice of praise" (the expression occurs in LXX in Lev 7:13, 15 and with the definite articles in Lev 7:12), i.e., a sacrifice consisting of praise. The thought that the sacrifice Christians offer is spiritual occurs elsewhere, as in Romans 12:1 (cf. the similar thought that the essence of religion is ethical and spiritual, James 1:27). This sacrifice is to be offered "continually." In systems like Judaism sacrifices were offered at set times, but for Christians praise goes up all the time. Since a loving God is working out his purposes all the time, there are no circumstances in which praise should not be offered (cf. 1 Thess 5:18). The sacrifice is further explained in an expression from Hosea 14:2 (LXX 14:3; cf. Prov 18:20), "the fruit of lips that confess his name." In the light of the Cross, there is no room for sacrifices such as those the Jews offered. Now believers offer the sacrifice of praise and acknowledge Christ.

16 The writer gives two more examples of the sacrifices Christians offer. "To do good" (*eupoiia,* only here in the NT and not in the LXX) is a general term, while "fellowship" or "sharing" (*koinōnia*) is more specific. It signifies sharing with others such things as we have: money, goods, and, of course, those intangibles that make up "fellowship." Animal sacrifices were the almost universal religious practice. Christians had nothing of the sort, but the writer is making the point that this did not mean they had nothing to offer. They had their sacrifices, some of which he has listed, and it is "with such sacrifices" that God is well pleased. Christ's suffering "outside the camp" has altered everything. Now God looks to people to take Christ's way. And that means they offer no animals but make their response to what Christ has done for them in praise, good deeds, and works of love and charity.

Notes

---

10 Some understand "we have an altar" to mean "we Jews have an altar." The Jews did have an altar, and even so there were some sacrifices of which the priests did not eat, such as those on the Day of Atonement. But this is not a very natural way of reading the passage. In any case, the author writes as a Christian to people who have made a Christian profession. (Whether he or they were in fact Jews we do not know for certain.)

14 There is a play on words with the participles μένουσαν (*menousan,* "enduring"), and μέλλουσαν (*mellousan,* "is to come").

I. *Christian Obedience*

13:17

[17]Obey your leaders and submit to their authority. They keep watch over you as men who must give an account. Obey them so that their work will be a joy, not a burden, for that would be of no advantage to you.

The author is mindful of the responsibility of Christian leaders to whom he has already referred (v.7). In due course they must give account to God for their flock. So he urges his readers to keep this in mind and not make things hard for their leaders.

17 The readers are to be obedient to their leaders. In v.7 the leaders were men who had died. Here, however, those alive and currently in places of authority are meant. (At the same time we should perhaps notice that there is nothing in the Gr. to correspond to NIV's "their authority"; *hypeikete* means simply "yield" or "submit," i.e., to them.) NIV omits "for" (*gar*), which introduces the reason for the submission. The pronoun *autoi* puts some emphasis on the subject: "They and no one else." The verb "keep watch" (*agrypneō*) means literally "keep oneself awake, be awake" (BAG, s.v.). There is the imagery of the leaders keeping awake nights in their concern for their people.

"They keep watch over you" is more literally "they keep watch for your souls," where it is a question whether NIV (also NEB) is right and "souls" (*psychōn*) is simply a periphrasis for "you," or whether, as a number of commentators think, the thought is of the spiritual life. In view of the similar use of *psychē* in 10:39 (lit., "of faith, to the saving of the soul"), it may well be that we are to see here a reference to spiritual well-being. The leaders are concerned for the deep needs of their people, not simply for what lies on the surface. They are concerned, because they must render account. Leaders are responsible, and God will call them to account one day. The writer pleads that the readers will so act that keeping watch will be a thing of joy for the leaders (Paul could speak of the Thessalonians as his "glory and joy": 1 Thess 2:20; cf. Phil 2:16; 3 John 4). The alternative is for them to do it with "groaning" (*stenazontes;* NIV, "a burden"), which, he says, would be "of no advantage" for the readers.

J. *Prayer*

13:18–19

> [18]Pray for us. We are sure that we have a clear conscience and desire to live honorably in every way. [19]I particularly urge you to pray so that I may be restored to you soon.

A short appeal for prayer reveals both the writer's conviction that prayer is a powerful force and his hope that he will soon see his correspondents again. Following immediately on the reference to the leaders, this leads a number of commentators to see the writer as one who had once been a leader in the group. His desire to "be restored to you" (v.19) shows clearly that he had once worked among them in some capacity.

18 The present imperative "Pray" (*proseuchesthe*) looks for a continuous activity and implies that they had already been doing this. "Keep praying for us" is its force. There is a question whether we should take the plural "us" as a genuine plural or as epistolary, meaning "I" (as in 5:11; 6:9, 11). The plural in this verse is followed by a singular in v.19, and exactly opposite conclusions have been drawn from this. Westcott and Kent (in loc.), for example, think the plural genuine and that the writer associates others with him (for a similar transition from plural to singular, cf. Gal 1:8–9; Col 4:3). But Bruce and Hewitt (in loc.) think that the singular shows the plural to be no more than literary. I see no reason for thinking that others are associated with the writer; so I incline to this latter view.

The writer has rebuked his readers from time to time; he has warned them of the dangers in their conduct and exhorted them. But he depends on them, too, and looks to them now to support him with their prayers. At the same time there is a problem arising from the way he puts his request. He says, "Pray for us, for we are persuaded that we have a good conscience" (NIV omits the "for" [*gar*]; this makes it a separate statement and thus eliminates the problem). Having a good conscience is a most unusual reason for requesting prayer. We could understand it if the writer spoke of his difficulties or the like. Lacking knowledge of the circumstances, we cannot be sure. Yet it seems that the readers have been accusing the writer of some fault. Moffatt suggests that they may have attributed his absence from them to unworthy motives (in loc.). Something had gone wrong. The writer protests that he has a clear conscience and that this is a reason for asking for their fellowship in prayer.

The adjective "good" (*kalēn*) is applied to conscience only here in the NT (elsewhere we find *agathē*). The writer is not aware of having committed any sin. He goes on to affirm his determination "to live honorably" (the adverb is *kalōs*) and that "in every way." He allows no exceptions but expresses wholeheartedness. "Desire" is perhaps a little weak for *thelontes,* for the verb expresses the set of the will, not merely a wish. The writer professes a firm determination to live in the way indicated.

19 The author underlines the importance of the readers' doing as he asks. He appeals (*parakalō,* NIV, "urge") strongly, where the adverb *perissoterōs* (which NIV renders "particularly") means something like "more abundantly," "beyond measure." What it was that prevented him from being "restored" to them is not said, but evidently the obstacle was considerable. Some have suggested that he had been imprisoned for his faith. We know too little of the circumstances to rule this out, but there is nothing to indicate it. Others think it was sickness. We simply do not know. The language seems to show that it was something outside the writer's control and that it needed a good deal of prayer. The problem was with the writer, not the readers, because he specifically asks for prayer for himself.

Notes

19 The adverb τάχιον (*tachion*) is comparative in form and may be used in the sense "more quickly." But the comparative had lost some of its force and the word may mean no more than "soon."

X. Conclusion

The writer has finished what he has to say. It remains for him only to round off his letter, and he does so with a magnificent doxology and a few greetings.

A. *Doxology*

13:20–21

> [20]May the God of peace, who through the blood of the eternal covenant brought back from the dead our Lord Jesus, that great Shepherd of the sheep, [21]equip you with everything good for doing his will, and may he work in us what is pleasing to him, through Jesus Christ, to whom be glory for ever and ever. Amen.

This doxology gathers up a number of the themes that have meant so much as the argument of the epistle has unfolded: the blood, the eternal covenant, the lordship of Jesus, the importance of doing his will. It also introduces some things not yet dealt with. This is the only place in the epistle, for example, where Jesus is seen as our Shepherd or where the Resurrection is specifically referred to. The whole forms a superb doxology that has meant much to Christians throughout the centuries.

20 God is called "the God of peace" a number of times in the Pauline writings (Rom 15:33; 16:20; 2 Cor 13:11; Phil 4:9; 1 Thess 5:23). "Peace" connotes the fullest prosperity of the whole man, taking up as it does the OT concept of the Hebrew *šālôm* (see comments on 7:2). Here it reminds us that it is God in whom all our prosperity is centered. There is no well-rounded life that does not depend on him. The expression is especially suitable in view of what the epistle discloses of the condition of the readers. They have had to cope with some form of persecution and were still not free from opposition. They were tempted to go back from Christianity and have had to be warned of the dangers of apostasy. They may have had doubts about who their true leaders were. It is well for them to be reminded that real peace is in God.

The doxology goes on to characterize God in terms of the Resurrection. In the NT, Jesus is occasionally said to have risen. It is, however, much more common in the NT for the Resurrection to be ascribed to God, as here (though the verb *anagō* is not common in this connection). The one whom God brought up from the dead is now described as "the great Shepherd of the sheep." The language seems to be derived from Isaiah 63:11. "Where is he who brought them through the sea, with the shepherd of his flock?"—though the thought here is, of course, quite different. Christ is called a shepherd in the great treatment of the shepherd theme in John 10 and again in 1 Peter 2:25 (cf. also Matt 26:31; Mark 14:27). It is a piece of imagery that stresses the care of our Lord for his own, for sheep are helpless without their shepherd. But an aspect we in modern times sometimes miss is that the shepherd has absolute sovereignty over his flock (cf. Rev 2:27; 12:5; 19:15; in each case the verb rendered "rule" in NIV means "to shepherd"). The adjective "great" is used because Christ is not to be ranked with other shepherds. He stands out.

The Resurrection is linked with "the blood of the eternal covenant" (cf. Isa 55:3; Zech 9:11). It is interesting to see how the thought of covenant persists to the end. It has been one of the major themes of this epistle. The adjective again brings out the point that this covenant will never be replaced by another as it replaced the old covenant. It is perpetual in its validity. And it was established by blood. The author never forgets that. For him the death of Jesus is central. At the same time, his linking it with the Resurrection shows that he did not have in mind a dead Christ but one who, though he shed his blood to establish the covenant, lives for ever. Last in this verse in the Greek (and with some emphasis) come the words "our Lord Jesus." The expression is unusual outside of Acts, where it occurs a number of times. It combines the lordship of Christ and his real humanity, two themes of continuing importance.

21 The prayer is that God will "equip" the readers "with everything good for doing his will." The verb "equip" (*katartizō*) is often used of mending what is broken and torn, and some see a reference to putting right what was amiss in the spiritual life of the readers. A prayer that God would put things right would be quite in place. But in this context perhaps the meaning is "supply you with what you need to live the Christian life"; so NIV gives the right meaning. "Everything good" is comprehensive. The writer wants nothing to be lacking. Notice the emphasis on doing the will of God, a thought we have had before in this epistle.

It is also interesting to notice the juxtaposition of "doing his will" and "may he work in us." From one point of view a deed is the deed of man, but from another it is God working in and through his servant. We should not overlook the significance of the word "us." As he has done so often, the writer links himself with his readers. He looks for God to do his perfect work in them and in him alike. He is not aloof and a special case; he needs the grace of God as much as they do. He wants God to do in us "what is pleasing to him," where "pleasing" (*euarestos*) renders a word used only here in

Hebrews but eight times elsewhere in the NT. In Titus 2:9 it refers to slaves being pleasing to their masters; elsewhere it always refers to people being acceptable to God. But men can do what is acceptable to God only through Jesus Christ. Therefore, the prayer includes this point.

Whether "to whom" refers to the Father or to Christ poses a problem. Grammatically it could be either. A number of commentators take it to refer to God on the ground that *ho theos* is the subject of the main verb and that in any case doxologies mostly refer to him. Others point out that "Jesus Christ" immediately precedes the word in question and that in any case this epistle puts emphasis on Christ and his work for men. So it seems that a good case can be made for either. I do not see how the question can be resolved. Perhaps the writer was not making a sharp distinction.

The doxology concludes with "for ever and ever. Amen." A number of important MSS omit the words "and ever." It is the kind of addition scribes would naturally insert if it was lacking in the text before them. There seems, however, to be no reason for anyone to omit it if it were original; so the shorter reading should probably be preferred. It is curious that doxologies should include "Amen," as this one does, for the word was normally the response of a congregation. Perhaps initially a doxology was spoken by the leader of a congregation and the people responded with their "Amen." In time the response was added to the doxology, as being the normal thing. Be that as it may, the "Amen" makes a satisfying close.

B. *Final Exhortations*

13:22–25

22Brothers, I urge you to bear with my word of exhortation, for I have written you only a short letter.

23I want you to know that our brother Timothy has been released. If he arrives soon, I will come with him to see you.

24Greet all your leaders and all God's people. Those from Italy send you their greetings.

25Grace be with you all.

The author now rounds off the whole epistle with a final appeal and a brief section of greetings. The greetings show that the epistle was being sent to a definite, known group of Christians with whom the author had ties.

22 "I urge" (NIV, NASB) may be the right way to translate *parakalō;* but it seems to mean something more like "I beg you" (TEV, NEB; cf. "I do ask you, brothers, to take these words of advice kindly" [JB]). There is appeal in it, but also encouragement. The letter has had its share of rebukes and stern warnings, and the writer now softens the impact a little with this appeal and with the affectionate address "Brothers." He calls his epistle the "word of exhortation" ("my" is inserted by NIV, RSV). A similar expression is found in Acts 13:15, where it clearly means a homily. So the point of it here may be that this letter is rather like a written sermon. "Exhortation" (*paraklēseōs*) includes the note of encouragement as elsewhere in the letter. It contains a good deal of exhortation here; but the writer means it as encouragement, not as rebuke.

The author goes on to say that he has written only briefly. Some commentators think that such a description can scarcely apply to an epistle as long as this one and so suggest that perhaps chapter 13 (or part of it) was added to some previously existing writing and that this expression refers only to the "addition." Against that it is hard to see why anyone would bother to apologize for writing anything as short as this chapter. It is better to see it as applying to the whole. For the letter *is* short, considering the subject matter. Some of the subjects could have been dealt with at much greater length. There has been some straight speaking. So before he finishes, the writer adds this brief section inviting the readers to take it in the right spirit. It would all be much worse if they did not.

23 "I want you to know" renders the word *ginōskete,* which could be either indicative, "you know," or imperative, "Know!" On the whole it seems more likely to be the latter (as implied by "I want you to know"), for the writer is evidently giving some new information, whereas the indicative would mean that he was repeating something they already knew (why would he do so?). Timothy is no doubt the companion of Paul (no other Timothy is known to us from those times) and he seems to have had some ties with both the readers and the writer. Otherwise we would expect a general expression instead of "our brother Timothy."

It is not clear what "released" means, for the word can refer to starting off on a journey (as in Acts 13:3; 28:25) or making other beginnings. Timothy may have started on a journey or he may have been released from some obligation. But on the whole it seems most likely that the term, used absolutely as it is, means that he had been released from imprisonment. All that we can say for certain is that Timothy had left the place where he was. The writer now expected that he would come to the place where Timothy was and hoped that then the two of them might go on to visit the readers. But evidently he intended moving fairly soon, whether or not Timothy came.

24 For the third time in the chapter, the leaders come to our attention. That they are to be greeted by the recipients of the letter makes it clear that the "leaders" were not the recipients and, furthermore, that the letter was not sent to the whole church. That greetings were to be sent shows that the recipients were on good terms with the leaders. The words "and all" may be significant—viz., there are no exceptions. "The saints" (*hoi hagioi;* NIV, "God's people") is a common NT description of the people of God, but it is found in this epistle again only in 6:10. It means God's people as those consecrated to him, set apart to do him service. The greeting from "those from Italy" raises the question whether they were Italians living abroad or in their own country. The words could mean either. (Acts 10:23 has a similar expression for those still living in their homeland and Acts 21:27 for those living away from their homeland.) There seems no way of determining the point.

25 The NT letters normally end with a prayer for grace for the recipients. Grace is a fitting note on which to end a letter like this one, so full of what God has done for people in Christ. There are some variant readings, but NIV has the text that most agree is correct. The author then closes by praying for God's grace for all his friends. He omits none from his concern or from God's.

Notes

21 Καταρτίσαι (*katartisai*) is apparently the only example of the optative in the epistle (BDF, par. 384). It expresses a wish: "May he equip. . . ."

A number of MSS read ὑμῖν (*hymin*, "in you") instead of ἡμῖν (*hēmin*, "in us"), and a few scholars favor it because of the sense and the preceding ὑμᾶς (*hymas*, "you"). But these are precisely the reasons that would induce scribes to change from ἡμῖν (*hēmin*), which has better support. There seems little doubt that we should accept it.

JAMES

Donald W. Burdick

JAMES

Introduction

1. **Authorship**
2. **Date**
3. **Destination**
4. **Occasion and Purpose**
5. **Canonicity**
6. **Relation to Other Writings**
7. **Theological Values**
8. **Bibliography**
9. **Outline**

1. Authorship

Even though this epistle names its author, it does not specify his actual identity. James was a common name in the first century. Indeed, there are in the NT four men called James. Of these, only two have ever been seriously suggested as possible authors of this epistle. A very few scholars have understood the writer to be James the son of Zebedee, one of the twelve apostles. Most scholars, however, have recognized that he was martyred too early (A.D. 44) to have written the epistle (Acts 12:1–2).

Since at least the third century, the most prominent view has been that James, the Lord's brother (Mark 6:3), wrote the book. This was the belief of Origen (c. A.D. 185–253), Eusebius (c. 265–340), and Jerome (c. 340–420). In more recent times other views have been advanced, such as that the designation "James" (1:1) is a pseudonym, that the epistle was originally anonymous, that it was written by an unknown James, or that it was the product of a disciple of the Lord's brother and thus represented the teaching of James.

However, the evidence of the epistle itself favors the traditional identification of the Lord's brother as author. The characteristics of James the brother of the Lord as seen in Acts 21:17–25, in Galatians 2:12, and in the description of "James the Just" by Hegesippus (Eusebius *Ecclesiastical History* 2.23) all are in harmony with the heavy emphasis on genuine religious practice and ethical conduct apparent in the epistle. The vocabulary of James's speech and letter in Acts 15:13–29 reveals significant similarity to that of the epistle (Mayor, pp. iii–iv). The authoritative tone of the epistle (forty-six imperatives) agrees well with the authority exercised by James in Acts 15:13ff.; 21:18.

2. Date

Some writers, not accepting the view that James the Lord's brother wrote the epistle, have dated it either late in the first century or some time between A.D. 100

and 150. But if the Lord's brother is identified as author, the book must have originated prior to A.D. 62, when, according to Josephus, James was martyred.

Among those who hold the traditional view of authorship, there are two general opinions. Some argue for a date near the end of James's life, perhaps in the early sixties; others insist that the epistle was written before A.D. 50. If the latter date is correct, James may have been the first NT book written.

Several considerations make it probable that James wrote between A.D. 45 and 50.

1. The Jewish orientation of the epistle fits the earlier period much more naturally than the later. That the author does not refer to Gentiles or related subjects may well point to the time in the history of the early church when Gentiles were only beginning to be reached with the gospel.
2. The absence of any reference to the controversy concerning the Judaizers and their insistence on Gentile circumcision is best explained by the earlier date.
3. The close affinity of the teaching of James to that of the OT and Christ is significant. If the epistle were later, one might expect to find a greater similarity to the writings of Paul, such as is apparent in 1 Peter, for example.
4. Furthermore, the evidence of a simple church order favors the early date. The leaders are "teachers" (3:1) and "elders" (5:14).
5. Finally, the use of the Greek term *synagōgē* (synagogue; NIV, "meeting") to describe the church assembly or meeting place (2:2) points to the early period when Christianity was largely confined to Jewish circles.

3. Destination

The epistle is addressed to "the twelve tribes scattered among the nations" (1:1). Although this is quite indefinite, it does reveal something about the recipients. The expression "twelve tribes" is clearly Jewish and no doubt was intended to identify the readers as Jews. The description of their congregation or meeting place as a *synagōgē* (2:2) also supports this interpretation. Another indication that the recipients were Jews is the use in 5:4 of the Hebrew title *kyriou sabaōth* ("Lord Almighty"; lit., "Lord of hosts").

The author further limits his intended readership by statements that assume the recipients are Christians. The most explicit statement of this kind is the pointed imperative of 2:1: "My brothers, as believers in our glorious Lord Jesus Christ, don't show favoritism." Here James clearly assumes that the Jews he is addressing are followers of Christ. The same fact is less explicitly indicated in the insistence of 5:7, that the brothers should be patient until the Lord comes, and in the further instruction that they "stand firm, because the Lord's coming is near" (5:8). It would seem, then, that the epistle was addressed to Jewish believers in Jesus as Messiah.

The geographical location of these Jewish Christians is not specifically identified. They are merely described as "scattered among the nations" (1:1), which means they were not centered in one locality. Beyond this the biblical text does not take us. It is possible, however, to theorize about the identity of the addressees. Some have suggested that they were the believers who were forced to leave Jerusalem during the persecution that followed Stephen's death. These Jewish Christians spread out over Judea and Samaria (Acts 8:1) and even as far as Phoenicia, Cyprus, and Syrian Antioch (Acts 11:19).

It is most reasonable to assume that James, the leading elder of the Jerusalem church, would feel responsible for these former "parishioners" and attempt to instruct them somewhat as he would have done had they still been under his care in Jerusalem. The epistle reveals his intimate knowledge of their circumstances and characteristics. And he writes with the note of authority expected of one who had been recognized as a spiritual leader in the Jerusalem church.

4. Occasion and Purpose

If it is correctly assumed that James, the leader of the Jerusalem church, wrote this epistle to believers who had been dispersed from Jerusalem in the persecution following Stephen's death, the occasion for writing is fairly clear. These Jewish Christians, scattered throughout the area east of the Mediterranean Sea, no longer had contact with the apostles; nor was James among them to instruct and exhort them.

Difficulties—perhaps persecutions—were confronting them (1:2–4); the ungodly rich were oppressing them (5:1–6); the religion of some was becoming a superficial formality (1:22–27; 2:14–26); discriminatory practices revealed a lack of love (2:1–13); and bitterness in speech (3:1–12) and attitude (3:13–4:3) marred their fellowship. Apparently reports of such problems among the scattered brothers had reached James in Jerusalem. In response, he wrote as pastor *in absentia* to urge his people to make the needed changes in their lives and in their corporate relationships.

5. Canonicity

The epistle was not readily received into the collection of writings that were viewed as being on a par with the OT Scriptures. It was rejected by some as late as the time of Eusebius (c. 265–340). Few early Christian writers refer to it. The Muratorian Canon (c. 170) omits it, as does the OL version.

Such negative evidence could be taken as ground for doubting the authority of the book if it were not that, after a period of questioning, the churches finally granted unanimous recognition to it as canonical. It had successfully passed the test. Furthermore, there are reasonable explanations for the late acceptance of the epistle. Eusebius himself explained that some denied the book because few ancient writers had quoted from it (*Ecclesiastical History* 2.23). It was not questioned because any fault was found with its teaching, but merely because it had not been widely used. There are reasons why this condition existed. Among these are its untheological nature, its brevity, the question of James's identity, the fact that it was not written by one of the twelve apostles, and its general address (sent to no specific person or church).

In due time, such authorities as Eusebius and Jerome (c. 340–420) placed their stamp of approval on the book, and the Council of Carthage (397) recognized its canonicity. Ultimately, churches everywhere were reading it as authoritative Scripture.

6. Relation to Other Writings

Many attempts have been made to trace a connection between the Epistle of James and numerous biblical and extrabiblical writings (e.g., Prov, the synoptic Gospels,

Rom, 1 Cor, Gal, 1 Peter, Ecclus, Philo). In a number of cases it is uncertain who influenced whom. In other instances, the similarities prove no literary reliance of any kind.

There are, however, two areas where the literary relationships seem relatively well defined and significant. The similarity between the Epistle of James and the teachings of Jesus in the Sermon on the Mount has often been noted. A clear example of this connection is seen in James 5:12: "Above all, my brothers, do not swear—not by heaven or by earth or by anything else. Let your 'Yes' be yes, and your 'No,' no, or you will be condemned." This teaching was obviously derived from the words of Jesus recorded in Matthew 5:34–37. Jesus said, "But I tell you, Do not swear at all: either by heaven, for it is God's throne; or by the earth, for it is his footstool; or by Jerusalem, for it is the city of the Great King. . . . Simply let your 'Yes' be 'Yes,' and your 'No,' 'No'; anything beyond this comes from the evil one." Other related statements include James 2:5 (Luke 6:20), James 3:10–12 (Matt 7:16–20), and James 3:18 (Matt 5:9). From such parallels we may conclude that James reflects the thoughts and often the very words of Christ.

Another possible literary relationship is that between James and the wisdom writings. Some, in fact, have described James as NT wisdom literature. Ropes, on the other hand, writes, "In the Wisdom-literature, as a literary type, it is impossible to place James" (p. 17).

It is true that James was not written in the same style as Proverbs, where one finds long series of proverbial statements structured in the parallel form characteristic of Hebrew poetry. Nevertheless, the two have noteworthy affinities. For example, the pithy, proverbial style of James should be noted (1:8, 22; 4:17), as well as the juxtaposition of good and evil (3:13–18). Also James's use of the word "wisdom" is significant (1:5; 3:13–17). In James 1:5 wisdom is the understanding that enables a person to face trials, and in 3:13–17 it is an attitude that determines how one lives. The Book of Proverbs abounds with references to wisdom, always viewing it as the kind of understanding that produces a sensible and an upright life. And in Proverbs as in James wisdom has its source in God.

Another evidence of affinity between James and Proverbs appears in the area of quotation and allusion. James 4:6 is a direct citation of Proverbs 3:34. In addition, there are numerous concepts or expressions in James that may be traced back to Proverbs (cf. James 1:5 with Prov 2:6; 1:19 with Prov 29:20; 3:18 with Prov 11:30; 4:13–16 with Prov 27:1; and 5:20 with Prov 10:12). Parallels to other wisdom literature could also be cited.

7. Theological Values

The Epistle of James is without doubt the least theological of all NT books, with the exception of Philemon. In fact, one of the reasons for the delay in canonical recognition of the epistle was its lack of theological content.

Having recognized this, however, one must hasten to insist that the book is not without theological value. The practical emphases of James rest on a solid theological foundation, which is often explicitly revealed and perhaps more often assumed or implied.

Three doctrines come to the surface more often than any others, and of these the most prominent is the doctrine of God. In keeping with the ethical nature of the epistle is the repeated stress on the doctrine of sin. And, surprisingly, the third most prominent theological theme is eschatology.

God is seen as being generous (1:5) and holy (1:13), the unchanging source of good (1:17). He is the one and only God (2:19), the Father of his people and the prototype in whose likeness men were created (3:9). Furthermore he is sovereign (4:15) and just (5:4), filled with pity and tender mercy (5:11).

James views sin as universal (3:2), indwelling all persons (1:14–15) and resulting in death (1:15). It expresses itself in anger (1:20), moral filth (1:21), blasphemy (2:7), discrimination (2:9–11), bitterness and lust (4:1–3), intimate ties with the evil world (4:4), pride (4:6), and theft and oppression (5:4).

In the third area of theological emphasis, James sees the end time as the day of rewards (1:12), the day when God's kingdom will be introduced (2:5), the day of judgment (2:12; 3:1), and the day when the Lord will return (5:7–8).

Several other doctrines receive limited mention. Christ is described as Lord (1:1; 2:1), but the Holy Spirit is not referred to unless it be in 4:5. In the area of soteriology, James speaks of regeneration (1:18), salvation of the soul (1:21), and justification (2:21–25). He promises the believer forgiveness of sins (5:15). He discusses the relation of saving faith and resultant good deeds (2:14–26). And he makes incidental reference to church order when he speaks of elders (5:14).

8. Bibliography

Adamson, James. *The Epistle of James,* NIC. Grand Rapids: Eerdmans, 1976.

Barclay, William. *The Letters of James and Peter. The Daily Study Bible.* Philadelphia: Westminster, 1960.

Blackman, E.C. *The Epistle of James. Torch Bible Commentaries.* London: SCM, 1957.

Carr, A. *Epistle of St. James.* CGT. Cambridge: Cambridge University Press, 1895.

Easton, B.S. *The Epistle of James.* IB. Vol. 12. New York: Abingdon, 1957.

Hort, F.J.A. *The Epistle of James.* London: Macmillan, 1909.

Lenski, R.C.H. *The Interpretation of the Epistle to the Hebrews and of the Epistle of James.* Columbus, Ohio: Wartburg, 1946.

Mayor, J.B. *The Epistle of St. James.* 3rd. ed. Grand Rapids: Zondervan, 1954.

Metzger, Bruce M. *A Textual Commentary on the Greek New Testament,* A Companion Volume to the United Bible Societies' *Greek New Testament.* 3rd ed. New York: UBS, 1971.

Mitton, C. Leslie. *The Epistle of James.* Grand Rapids: Eerdmans, 1966.

Moffatt, James. *The General Epistles of James, Peter, and Judas.* MNT. Garden City, N.Y.: Doubleday, 1928.

Plummer, Alfred. *The General Epistles of St. James and St. Jude.* ExB. London: Hodder & Stoughton, 1897.

Ropes, James H. *A Critical and Exegetical Commentary on the Epistle of St. James.* ICC. New York: Charles Scribner's Sons, 1916.

Ross, Alexander. *The Epistles of James and John.* NIC. Grand Rapids: Eerdmans, 1954.

Tasker, R.V.G. *The General Epistle of James.* TNTC. Grand Rapids: Eerdmans, 1956.

9. Outline

I. Salutation (1:1)
II. Trials and Temptations (1:2–18)
  1. The Testing of Faith (1:2–12)
  2. The Source of Temptation (1:13–18)
III. The Practice of the Word (1:19–27)
IV. The Condemnation of Partiality (2:1–13)
V. The Relation of Faith and Action (2:14–26)
VI. The Control of the Tongue (3:1–12)
VII. Two Kinds of Wisdom (3:13–18)
VIII. The Worldly Attitude (4:1–10)
IX. Faultfinding (4:11–12)
X. Arrogant Self-Sufficiency (4:13–17)
XI. Denunciation of the Wicked Rich (5:1–6)
XII. Miscellaneous Exhortations (5:7–20)
  1. Concerning Patience (5:7–11)
  2. Concerning Oaths (5:12)
  3. Concerning Prayer (5:13–18)
  4. Concerning the Wanderer (5:19–20)

Text and Exposition

I. Salutation

1:1

> [1]James, a servant of God and of the Lord Jesus Christ, To the twelve tribes
> scattered among the nations: Greetings.

1 In the discussion of the authorship of the epistle (cf. Introduction), James was identified as the brother of Jesus. More specifically, since Jesus was virgin born, James was his half brother. In the Book of Acts this same James appears as the leader of the Jerusalem church (Acts 15:13ff.; 21:18).

The author describes himself as "a servant [*doulos*] of God and of the Lord Jesus Christ." The *doulos* was neither a free man nor a hired servant; he was a slave, the rightful property of his master. The term "slave," however, did not necessarily carry the degrading connotation attached to the word today. James was a servant who was proud to belong—body and soul—to God and to Jesus Christ.

The letter is addressed to "the twelve tribes," a designation intended to identify the readers as Jews. They were not residents of Palestine but were "scattered among the nations" as part of the Jewish Dispersion (*diaspora*). James's designation of his readers as "believers in our glorious Lord Jesus Christ" (2:1) makes it clear that not all dispersed Jews are included. It is probable that the recipients were the members of the Jerusalem church who had been driven out of Jerusalem at the time of Stephen's martyrdom (Acts 8:1, 4; 11:19–20). If this identification is correct, James had formerly been their spiritual leader. As such, he wrote to them with rightful spiritual authority and with full knowledge of their needs.

II. Trials and Temptations (1:2–18)

1. *The Testing of Faith*

1:2–12

> [2]Consider it pure joy, my brothers, whenever you face trials of many kinds,
> [3]because you know that the testing of your faith develops perseverance. [4]Persever-
> ance must finish its work so that you may be mature and complete, not lacking
> anything. [5]If any of you lacks wisdom, he should ask God, who gives generously
> to all without finding fault, and it will be given to him. [6]But when he asks, he must
> believe and not doubt, because he who doubts is like a wave of the sea, blown and
> tossed by the wind. [7]That man should not think he will receive anything from the
> Lord; [8]he is a double-minded man, unstable in all he does.
>
> [9]The brother in humble circumstances ought to take pride in his high position.
> [10]But the one who is rich should take pride in his low position, because he will pass
> away like a wild flower. [11]For the sun rises with scorching heat and withers the plant;
> its blossom falls and its beauty is destroyed. In the same way, the rich man will fade
> away even while he goes about his business.
>
> [12]Blessed is the man who perseveres under trial, because when he has stood
> the test, he will receive the crown of life that God has promised to those who love
> him.

2 In vv.2–4 James explains that trials are reason for rejoicing because of the wholesome effects they produce. The word "trials" (*peirasmois*) describes things that put a person to the test. They may be difficulties that come from without, such as persecution, or they may be inner moral tests, such as temptations to sin. James uses the word in the former sense in vv.2–4 and in the latter sense in vv.13–18. The outward trial, rather than being a reason for unhappiness, can be a ground for "pure joy." The expression is *pasan charan,* which speaks of full and complete joy. And it is not merely the coming of a single trial that is described; James speaks of the experience of "trials of many kinds." The verb *peripesēte,* translated "face," speaks of falling into the midst of people, objects, or circumstances, such as trials (as here) or robbers (as in Luke 10:30). The picture is that of being surrounded with "trials of many kinds." The primary meaning of *poikilois* is "many-colored," and thus, "variegated," "of many kinds." Being surrounded by all kinds of trials should be viewed as reason for genuine rejoicing.

3 The reason that trials are to be considered grounds for joy is that they are capable of developing "perseverance." They put the believer's faith to the test, and this experience produces the desired result. The question answered by the testing of faith is whether or not faith will persevere. If it is genuine faith, testing serves to develop its persistence. *Hypomonēn* is translated "patience" in KJV, but it is a much more active and forceful word. It speaks of tenacity and stick-to-it-iveness. Barclay explains that it is not the patience that passively endures; instead, it is the quality that enables a man to stand on his feet facing the storm (William Barclay, *New Testament Words* [London: SCM, 1964], pp. 144–45). It is in struggling against difficulty and opposition that spiritual stamina is developed.

4 "Perseverance" has a work to do, and this can be accomplished only by persistence in trials. If perseverance is to "finish its work," faith must not falter or give up. The goal in view is that believers "may be mature and complete" (*teleioi kai holoklēroi*). *Teleioi* can mean "perfect" (KJV), "complete," or "mature." There are three reasons, however, for understanding the word as referring here to maturity.

1. Scripture does not indicate that believers reach perfection in this life.
2. Since *holoklēroi* describes that which has all its parts, it is most natural when it occurs with *teleioi* to reserve the meaning of completeness for *holoklēroi*.
3. The statement that "perseverance must finish its work" indicates progress and development, the result of which may well be described as maturity. Thus, perseverance in facing trials develops maturity of character and a balance of all the graces and strengths needed for the Christian life.

5 Verses 5–8 contain God's offer of help for those who are facing trials. The repetition of the word "lack" shows that James is still discussing the subject of trials. In v.4 he assures his readers that when perseverance has finished its work, the believer will lack none of the needed virtues and strengths. In v.5, however, James speaks of the period of testing before perseverance has completed its work. During such testing, if anyone "lacks wisdom," he may have it by asking. The type of Greek conditional sentence found here assumes that people facing trials do lack wisdom. What they need is not the speculative or theoretical wisdom of a philosophical system. It is the kind of wisdom that plays such a large part in the Book of Proverbs (1:2–4; 2:10–15; 4:5–9). It is the God-given understanding that enables a person to avoid the paths of wickedness and to live a life of righteousness. In this context wisdom is understanding the nature and purpose of trials and knowing how to meet them victoriously. Such wisdom is available to the one who will "ask God" for it, not once only, but repeatedly (Gr., present tense). The promise is that "it will be given to him." There is nothing in God that keeps him from giving. It is his practice to give "generously" and "without finding fault." He does not scold his children for asking nor berate them for their deficiency.

6 Although there is nothing in God that prevents him from giving wisdom to his people, a barrier may exist in them. When they ask, they "must believe and not doubt." Their faith must be more than mere acceptance of a creed. To believe is to be confident that God will give what is requested; it is to expect him to do so. The extent of faith that God looks for is emphasized by the words "not doubt" (*mēden diakrinomenos*). The true force of this expression is "and not doubt at all" (BAG, p. 520). *Diakrinomenos* describes one who is divided in his mind and who wavers between two opinions. One moment he voices the yes of faith; the next moment it is the no of disbelief. Such an attitude is graphically illustrated by "a wave of the sea." Completely lacking in stability, it is "blown and tossed by the wind." First there is the crest, then the trough. Instead, prayer that moves God to respond must be marked by the constancy of unwavering faith.

The reference to the sea is the first of James's illustrations from nature. See also 1:10–11, 17–18, 26; 3:3–5, 7, 11–12; 5:7, 17–18. As Jesus drew numerous illustrations from life around him, so James revealed his love for nature by his repeated use of it for illustrative purposes.

7–8 "That man" is a somewhat derogatory reference to the doubter, whom James has just compared to the tossing wave. Here he is further characterized as "double-minded" and "unstable." The Greek *dipsychos* in strictest literalness means "double-souled." It is as though one soul declares, "I believe," and the other in turn shouts, "I don't!" This sort of instability is not only apparent when the man prays, it marks "all he does." In his personal life, his business life, his social life, as well as in his spiritual life, indecisiveness negates his effectiveness. A person like this will not "receive anything from the Lord." But one may wonder how this man is different from the anguished father who cried, "I do believe; help me overcome my unbelief!" (Mark 9:24). Such an exclamation seems to suggest that the father was "a double-minded man." But there is a difference. The father was not oscillating between belief and unbelief. He desired to believe—and even asserted his belief—but because he felt keenly the inadequacy of his faith, he asked for help in believing. He was not facing in both directions at the same time like the "double-minded man" of James 1:8. In spite of his conscious weakness, the father had set his heart to believe. And Christ responded to his faith and healed his son (Mark 9:25–27). In response to this kind of faith, God will give wisdom to those who ask for it, and will enable them to persevere in times of trial.

9 Verses 9–11 are thought by some to introduce an entirely new subject (EGT, 4:424). However, since v.12 explicitly deals with persevering "under trial," it is best to understand vv.9–11 to be related to the same general subject. James seems to be indicating that trials erase any superficial distinctions that may be thought to separate the rich brother from the poor one.

"Brother" shows that James is referring to a believer. To describe the "circumstances" of this brother, the author uses the word *tapeinos,* which has the basic meaning of "lowly," "mean," "insignificant," "weak," "poor" (TDNT, 8:1). In view of the constrast with the rich (*plousios*) man in v.10, it is best to understand that the man in v.9 is one who is financially poor, and thus "in humble circumstances." The "high position" in which this brother is to take pride has reference first of all to his position in Christ. In saving him, God lifts him up and gives him new dignity and worth. In this context, however, it seems most likely that James also has in mind the privilege of "suffering disgrace for the Name [Jesus]" (Acts 5:41). To endure persecution for Christ's sake lifts the believer to a position of honor that more than offsets his poverty.

10 The text does not explicitly state that "the one who is rich" is a believer, and for that reason some have insisted that he is unsaved. It would seem most natural, however, for James to omit the word "brother" in v.10 and assume that it would be carried over from v.9. The wealthy believer, then, is exhorted to glory "in his low position." Since the context deals with trials, the low position may be a description of the humbling experience of suffering persecution for Christ's sake. The very same treatment that exalts the poor man and gives him a new sense of worth also humbles the rich man. Suffering shows him that, instead of having a lasting lease on life, his life on this earth is no more permanent than "a wild flower" (cf. Isa 40:6–8.) Some interpreters understand James to say that it is the rich man's wealth that passes away, not the man himself (Ropes, p. 148). But it should be noted that the subject of the verb "pass away," is not riches but "the *one* who is rich." Again, in v.11b it is the rich man who will "fade away." Suffering and persecution reveal how tentative and short life really is.

11 The phenomenon James speaks of was a familiar one. Green grass and plants do not last long under the "scorching heat" of the Palestinian summer sun. More specifically, the reference may be to the sudden coming of a hot, searing wind known as the sirocco, which quickly withers and burns the vegetation. The withering of the plant and falling of its blossom are taken almost verbatim from Isaiah 40:7 (LXX). It may be that the "beauty" of the blossom is suggestive of the fine clothes that the rich wear. As impressive and attractive as the garments may be, they soon fade and wear out. And, what is even more important, "the rich man" himself "will fade away." Here again Ropes refers the wasting away to the loss of wealth (p. 149), but it should be noted that it is the man who fades away. Nothing is said about his wealth. This fading takes place "even while he goes about his business." Unexpectedly, in the midst of a busy life, the end comes. These are sobering thoughts that tend to reduce the rich to the level of men in general, just as the privilege of suffering for Christ lifts the poor man to a new plane of dignity and worth.

12 James concludes his discussion of the testing of faith with a promise of the reward to be given to the one who successfully stands the test. This verse is seen to be related to the preceding verses, rather than those that follow, by the repetition of terminology ("trials," v.2; "testing," "perseverance," v.3) and also from the fact that testings are to be endured ("perseveres"), whereas temptations are to be resisted (Ropes, p. 150). The expression "Blessed is the man" reveals the author's familiarity with the language of the OT (cf. Pss 1:1; 32:2; 34:8; 84:12; Prov 8:34; Isa 56:2; Jer 17:7) and the beatitudes (Matt 5:3–11). It is not sufficient to translate the word *makarios* as "happy." Even in secular Greek the word described "the transcendent happiness of a life beyond care, labour and death" (TDNT, 4:362). In biblical usage it speaks of "the distinctive religious joy" which is one of the benefits of salvation (ibid., p. 367). James uses the term to describe the enviable state of the man who does not give up when confronted with trying circumstances but remains strong in faith and devotion to God. The word *dokimos*, which indicates that the man "has stood the test," was used to describe the successful testing of precious metals and coins. It referred to the process of testing and also to the consequent approval of the tested object as genuine. Perseverance under trial results in approval, and approval results in "the crown [*stephanon*] of life." Although this term may designate a kingly crown, it more often refers to the crown given to a victorious athlete—a wreath of laurel, oak, or even celery. For James, the word refers to the reward to be given the believer who is victorious in his struggle against trials. It is evident that this "life that God has promised" is more than the eternal life given to every believer at the time of his salvation (John 5:24). Since it is a reward for an accomplishment subsequent to initial faith, it must refer to a still higher quality of life.

Notes:

---

3 The classical Gr. meaning of δοκίμιον (*dokimion*) is "a means of testing," but the papyri reveal that the word came to refer to that which is tested and approved. Adolf Deissmann has shown that the word is in reality the neuter of the adjective δοκίμιος (*dokimios*, "proved," "tried") and is here used substantively (*Bible Studies* [Edinburgh: T. & T. Clark, 1909], pp. 259ff.). Thus it is not the mere fact of testing that "develops perseverance;" it is faith that has been put to the test and approved.

10 KJV reads "flower of the grass," which is the literal rendering of ἄνθος χόρτου (*anthos chortou*). But James apparently borrowed this expression from the LXX of Isa 40:6, where it translates the Heb. ציץ השׂדה (*ṣîṣ haśśāḏeh*), "flower of the field," and thus "a wild flower."

---

2. *The Source of Temptation*

1:13–18

13When tempted, no one should say, "God is tempting me." For God cannot be tempted by evil, nor does he tempt anyone; 14but each one is tempted when, by his own evil desire, he is dragged away and enticed. 15Then, after desire has conceived, it gives birth to sin; and sin, when it is full-grown, gives birth to death.
16Don't be deceived, my dear brothers. 17Every good and perfect gift is from above, coming down from the Father of the heavenly lights, who does not change like shifting shadows. 18He chose to give us birth through the word of truth, that we might be a kind of firstfruits of all he created.

In these verses James declares that no one should assume that enticement to sin comes from God (v. 13a); he then proceeds to give a series of reasons for his assertion (vv. 13b–18).

13 The Greek noun *peirasmos* can refer either to an outward circumstance of trial or to a temptation to sin. The same is true of the verb form as well. Whereas the noun is used in vv.2–3 of "trials" and "testing," in vv.13–15, where the verb occurs, the obvious reference is to temptation. That this is the meaning is indicated by the words "evil" (v.13), "evil desire" (v.14), and "sin" (v.15).

The first reason why temptation does not come from God is that God "cannot be tempted by evil." That is, he cannot be successfully tempted. His omnipotent, holy will fully resists any invitation to sin. Furthermore, in him there is not the slightest moral depravity to which temptation may appeal. Therefore, it is inconsistent to think that God could be the author of temptation.

14 Instead, the source of temptation lies within man himself. He is tempted "by his own evil desire." James personifies man's sinful desire and identifies it as the efficient cause of temptation (RHG, p. 635). He does not blame any external person or object. It is by man's own sinful nature that "he is dragged away and enticed." These two verbs are taken from the sphere of fishing and hunting. Although "dragged away" is a possible translation of *exelkomenos* (BAG, p. 273), when it is coupled with *deleazomenos* ("enticed"), it may better be rendered by "drawn out." Mayor lists a number of examples where the word describes the "drawing of the fish out of its original retreat" (p. 51). James pictures man's "evil desire," first, as attracting his attention and persuading him to approach the forbidden thing and, second, as luring him by means of bait to yield to the temptation. Robertson entitles this verse "*Snared by One's Own Bait*" (A.T. Robertson, *Practical and Social Aspects of Christianity* [New York: Hodder & Stoughton, 1915], p. 76).

15 James changes his figure from a snare to conception and birth. The genealogy of evil desire is traced for three generations, as it were. A chronological order is suggested by the words "then" and "after." First, temptation comes (v.14); then desire, like a human mother, conceives and "gives birth to sin." In this graphic manner the author portrays the experience of yielding to temptation. Then sin, the child of evil desire, develops till it "is full-grown" and ready to produce offspring. When it conceives, it "gives birth to death." James is not suggesting that only when sin has reached its full development does it result in death. The penalty of sin of any kind or extent is spiritual death. The details of the illustration must not be pressed too far. The author's intention is simply to trace the results of temptation when one yields to it. The order is evil desire, sin, death.

16 "Don't be deceived" is an expression employed as a pointed introduction for a significant statement (cf. 1 Cor 6:9; 15:33; Gal 6:7; and a similar construction in 1 John 3:7). The warning in this passage is against being deceived into thinking that God is the author of temptation. In fact, the Greek construction used here (*mē* with the present tense imperative) often implies that the addressees have been engaging in the practice being prohibited. In that case James would be saying, "Stop being deceived."

17 Here follows the significant statement that the prohibition of the previous verse was intended to introduce. Instead of sending temptation, God is the giver of "every good and perfect gift." The concept of goodness rules out the possibility that God would send an influence as destructive as temptation. God's gifts are marked by kindness and helpfulness, not destructiveness. They are "perfect," which in this context excludes any possibility of moral evil, such as tempting his people to commit sin. The point of James's statement is that nothing but good comes from God. The second half of the verse shows that this is invariably true.

Here God is designated as "the Father of the heavenly lights." NIV has inserted the word "heavenly," even though it is not found in the Greek text. The context seems to indicate that the lights referred to are the stars and planets. "Father" probably has a twofold significance, pointing on the one hand to the creation of the lights and on the other to God's continuing sovereignty over them.

Unlike the "shifting shadows" that are caused by the sun, moon, and stars, God "does not change." With him there is no variation at all (*ouk eni parallagē*). The shadows cast by the sun are minimal at noon, but just before sunset they stretch out for yards across the landscape. God is not like that. He does not change. He is always the giver of good gifts, never a sadistic being who would entice his creatures to destroy themselves in sin.

18 James advances his final reason for denying that God is the author of temptation. Rather than acting destructively, God acts constructively. "He chose to give us birth." Inasmuch as this birth is "through the word of truth," that is, through the gospel, the birth referred to here must be spiritual rather than natural. God accomplishes this action by his own deliberate choice (*boulētheis*). His purpose in regeneration is "that we might be a kind of firstfruits." The figure the author has in mind is drawn from such OT passages as Exodus 34:22 and Leviticus 23:10. The term "firstfruits" referred to the first portion of the harvest given to God, a foretaste of that which was to come. So it was that the early Christians were a preliminary indication of the great host of people (*tōn autou ktismatōn,* "his creatures") who through subsequent centuries would be born again.

Notes

---

17 UBS has adopted the reading *παραλλαγὴ ἢ τροπῆς ἀποσκίασμα* (*parallagē ē tropēs aposkiasma*) following ℵ[c] A C, numerous miniscules, and several versions. A straightforward translation would be "variation or shadow of [from] turning," referring to a shadow caused by the turning of an object such as a heavenly body. If this was the original text of James, he might well have been speaking of an eclipse.

However, a second reading has significant textual support. Three sources have *παραλλαγὴ ἢ τροπῆς ἀποσκιάσματος* (*parallagē ē tropēs aposkiasmatos*): ℵ* B P[23], all representatives of the Alexandrian text. Inasmuch as ancient Gr. MSS had few accents or breathing marks, *η* (*ē*) may originally have been the article *ἡ* (*hē*). In that case the translation would be "variation which is [consists in] the turning of a shadow." This reading is adopted by Ropes (pp. 162–64), Tasker (pp. 48–49), Edgar J. Goodspeed (*Problems of New Testament Translation* [Chicago: University of Chicago, 1945], pp. 189–90), RSV mg., NEB, and NIV.

Whereas the first-listed reading is more specifically astronomical, the second reading is more general. It may refer to any changing shadow. Although most translations are based on the former reading, the more general reading has much in its favor and is the one represented in the commentary above.

III. The Practice of the Word

1:19–27

[19]My dear brothers, take note of this: Everyone should be quick to listen, slow to speak and slow to become angry, [20]for man's anger does not bring about the righteous life that God desires. [21]Therefore, get rid of all moral filth and the evil that is so prevalent, and humbly accept the word planted in you, which can save you.

[22]Do not merely listen to the word, and so deceive yourselves. Do what it says. [23]Anyone who listens to the word but does not do what it says is like a man who looks at his face in a mirror [24]and, after looking at himself, goes away and immediately forgets what he looks like. [25]But the man who looks intently into the perfect law that gives freedom, and continues to do this, not forgetting what he has heard, but doing it—he will be blessed in what he does.

[26]If anyone considers himself religious and yet does not keep a tight rein on his tongue, he deceives himself and his religion is worthless. [27]Religion that God our Father accepts as pure and faultless is this: to look after orphans and widows in their distress and to keep oneself from being polluted by the world.

Verses 19–21 may seem at first glance to be an isolated section of miscellaneous exhortations. Further examination, however, reveals significant links to the preceding and following contexts. The term "word" is found in vv.18, 21–25 and refers to the Scriptures, the Word of God. Verse 18 indicates that regeneration comes through the instrumentality of the Word; v.21 contains a call to receive the Word; and vv.22–25 discuss the doing of the Word. It would seem, then, that vv.19–21 emphasize listening to and receiving the Word, while vv.22–25 stress the doing of the Word.

19 In vv.19–21a, James is attempting to clear the way for the reception of God's truth (v.21b). He begins by calling for the readers' attention: "Take note of this." (KJV's "Wherefore" is based on an inferior Gr. text.) The reception of the Word demands a readiness "to listen." Reluctance at this point will block the acceptance of truth. It also demands restrained speech. A continual talker cannot hear what anyone else says and by the same token will not hear when God speaks to him. Finally, the restraint of anger is demanded. Anger will close the mind to God's truth. Ross explains, "Ceaseless talkers may easily degenerate into fierce controversialists" (p. 38). And a fiercely argumentative attitude is not conducive to the humble reception of truth.

20 The connective "for" indicates that this verse gives the reasoning that lies behind the last exhortation. Anger does not produce "the righteous life that God desires." An angry attitude is not the atmosphere in which righteousness flourishes. James stresses this from the positive side when he says, "Peacemakers who sow in peace raise a harvest of righteousness" (3:18).

21 In further preparation for the reception of the Word, one must "get rid of all moral filth." The Greek word translated "get rid of" (*apothemenoi*) was primarily used of taking off garments. Hebrews 12:1 speaks of throwing off any excessive weight, such as unnecessary clothing, to make ready for the race of faith. The "moral filth" and the evil that is so abundant are to be stripped off like dirty clothes in preparation for "accept[ing] the word." The reception of truth must of necessity be marked by humility or meekness (Gr., *praytēti*). This is not to be construed as spineless weakness. Instead, it is the quality of a strong man that makes him docile and submissive rather than haughty and rebellious. Only in such a spirit can one fully receive God's truth. That the Word is described as "planted in you" suggests the readers were believers who already possessed the truth. The phrase "which can save you" simply describes the truth as saving truth. James is not calling for an initial acceptance of that message, but for a full and intelligent appropriation of the truth as the Christian grows in spiritual understanding.

22 The author next discusses putting the Word into practice. It is not enough merely to "listen to the word" or, by the same token, merely to read it. Those who congratulate themselves on being hearers of the truth are deceiving themselves. If they assume that this is all that is needed, they are sadly mistaken. If they think that merely listening to the message earns them a position of special favor with God, they are duped by their own faulty reasoning. In reality, the responsibility of those who hear is far greater than that of those who have never heard. If they do not combine doing with hearing, they put themselves in a most vulnerable position.

The call to "do what it says" lies at the center of all that James teaches. It sums up the message of the whole book: Put into practice what you profess to believe. Indeed, 1:22 may well be the key verse of James's epistle.

23 After urging the practice of the Word in v.22, the author proceeds to explain why people should do more than merely listen to the truth. Here he uses the illustration (vv.23–24) of a man who "looks at his face in a mirror." The Greek verb *katanoeō* does not describe a hasty glance as some have suggested. Instead, it refers to careful observation. It is "attentive scrutiny of an object" (TDNT, 4:975). So the man carefully studies his face and becomes thoroughly familiar with its features. This illustrative act is paralleled by the person who listens to the Word, apparently not momentarily but attentively, and at length, so that he understands what he hears. He knows what God expects him to do. Any failure to respond cannot be blamed on lack of understanding.

24 James further explains that upon going away the man "immediately forgets what he looks like." For him it is "out of sight, out of mind." In spite of thoroughly scrutinizing his face, he forgets what it was like. This is, of course, ludicrous, but no less ludicrous is the believer who listens carefully to God's truth and does not remember to put into practice what he has heard. Listening to truth is not an end in itself any more than gazing at one's face in a mirror is an end in itself. The purpose of listening to truth is to act upon it. Theoretical knowledge of spiritual truth is never commended in Scripture. In fact, it is discouraged and condemned. In the Judeo-Christian context, knowledge is inseparably tied to experience. The believer gains knowledge through experience, and his knowledge is intended to affect subsequent experience.

25 In contrast to the person who listens to the Word but does not do what it says, this verse describes one who both listens and puts what he hears into practice. "He will be blessed in what he does." The reason is fourfold. First, he "looks intently" into God's truth. This Greek verb (*parakyptō*) "denotes penetrating absorption" (TDNT, 5:815). It is the word used to describe John's act of stooping and peering into the tomb of Jesus (John 20:5). Here in James 1:25 it is as though a person stoops over the Scripture, zealously searching for its message. The second reason why this man is blessed is that "he continues to do this." He is the blessed man of Psalm 1 who meditates in God's law day and night. The third reason for his blessedness is that he does not forget "what he has heard." And the fourth and most important reason is that he puts the truth into practice.

James's use of the term "law" deserves special attention. He calls it "the perfect law of freedom" (Gr.). The use of the word "law" reveals his Jewish orientation and that of his readers. But James qualifies the word to make sure his readers do not misunderstand. He describes this law as "perfect" and as characterized by "freedom." It is not merely the OT law, nor is it the Mosaic law perverted to become a legalistic system for earning salvation by good works. When James calls it the "perfect law," he has in mind the sum total of God's revealed truth—not merely the preliminary portion found in the OT, but also the final revelation made through Christ and his apostles that was soon to be inscripturated in the NT. Thus it is complete, in contrast to that which is preliminary and preparatory. Furthermore, it is the "law of liberty" (Gr.), by which James means that it does not enslave. It is not enforced by external compulsion. Instead, it is freely accepted and fulfilled with glad devotion under the enablement of the Spirit of God (Gal 5:22–23). For similar uses of the term "law" in James, see 2:8, 12.

26 Verses 26–27 point out three specific areas where truth should be put into practice. The first is speech. James introduces a hypothetical case. The person involved "considers himself religious." The word *thrēskos* ("religious") occurs only here in the NT; and the corresponding noun *thrēskeia* ("religion") appears but four times in the NT, two of which are in James 1:26–27. The adjective *thrēskos* describes a person who performs the external acts of religion, such as public worship, fasting, or giving to the needy. The person James is referring to is the one who "does not keep tight rein on his tongue." Lenski says that he lets "his tongue go like an unbridled horse" (in loc.). He exerts no controlling restraint on his speech. Exactly how his speech offends is not indicated, whether it be by the cutting criticism of others, by uncleanness, by dishonesty, or by other ways. His uncontrolled tongue reveals that "his religion is worthless," being merely external sham. Such a person has been playing the part of one who is religious and has convinced himself that he really is religious, but in so doing "he deceives himself." This is the second instance of self-deception in this chapter. In v.22 the person who hears the truth but does not put it into practice is self-deceived. In v.26 the self-deceived person is the one whose religious acts do not make a difference in the way he lives.

27 The kind of "religion that God our Father accepts" is the kind that exerts a positive influence on one's life. Notice that this verse does not give us a definition of religion. Instead, it presents a concrete way of insisting that genuine religion is a life-changing force. One's religion, then, should be more than external; it must spring from an inner spiritual reality that expresses itself in love to others and holiness before God. James next describes a specific example of love—the care of "orphans and widows." The verb *episkeptesthai* also appears in Matthew 25:36, 43 with reference to visiting the sick, not merely to make a social call, but in order to care for their needs. This is "faith expressing itself through love" (Gal 5:6). One whose religion is genuine will also avoid "being polluted by the world." "World" describes the total system of evil that pervades every sphere of human existence and is set in opposition to God and to righteousness.

To summarize, vv.22–27 insist that a person's religion must consist of more than superficial acts. It is not enough to listen to the statement of spiritual truth (vv.22–25), nor is it sufficient to engage in formal religious activity (v.26). The person whose religious experience is genuine will put spiritual truth into practice, and his life will be marked by love for others and holiness before God.

IV. The Condemnation of Partiality

2:1–13

1My brothers, as believers in our glorious Lord Jesus Christ, don't show favoritism. 2Suppose a man comes into your meeting wearing a gold ring and fine clothes,
and a poor man in shabby clothes also comes in. 3If you show special attention to
the man wearing fine clothes and say, "Here's a good seat for you," but say to the
poor man, "You stand there" or "Sit on the floor by my feet," 4have you not
discriminated among yourselves and become judges with evil thoughts?
5Listen, my dear brothers: Has not God chosen those who are poor in the eyes
of the world to be rich in faith and to inherit the kingdom he promised those who
love him? 6But you have insulted the poor. Is it not the rich who are exploiting you?
Are they not the ones who are dragging you into court? 7Are they not the ones who
are slandering the noble name of him to whom you belong?
8If you really keep the royal law found in Scripture, "Love your neighbor as
yourself," you are doing right. 9But if you show favoritism, you sin and are convicted
by the law as lawbreakers. 10For whoever keeps the whole law and yet stumbles
at just one point is guilty of breaking all of it. 11For he who said, "Do not commit
adultery," also said, "Do not murder." If you do not commit adultery but do commit
murder, you have become a lawbreaker.
12Speak and act as those who are going to be judged by the law that gives
freedom, 13because judgment without mercy will be shown to anyone who has not
been merciful. Mercy triumphs over judgment!

In 1:19–27 James has shown the importance of putting spiritual truth into practice. It is not too much to say that these verses comprise the bedrock on which the whole epistle rests. In each of the following sections James discusses at some length the application of the Word of truth to a specific aspect of life. In 2:1–13 he shows how partiality or discrimination violates the standard of God's truth.

1 James begins his discussion of partiality by a prohibition: "Don't show favoritism." The Greek construction here (*mē* with the present tense imperative) is used of forbidding a practice already in progress. That the recipients of this epistle were guilty of practicing discrimination is apparent from the context (v.6, "But you have insulted the poor"). Thus the prohibition means "Stop showing favoritism." The point James is making is that partiality is inconsistent with faith "in our glorious Lord Jesus Christ." To say that practicing favoritism contradicts one's profession of faith is another way of saying that one's action does not measure up to the truth he professes to believe. The stress on Christ as "glorious" heightens the gross inconsistency of allowing favoritism and discrimination to be associated with faith in such an exalted person as Christ.

2 A hypothetical illustration follows: "Suppose a man comes into your meeting." The word translated "meeting" is the Greek *synagōgē*, which had primary reference to the Jewish synagogue. The term need not be taken literally, however, as an indication that the Jewish Christians were still meeting in synagogue buildings. Even after leaving the synagogue, Jewish Christians no doubt continued to refer to their church meeting as a *synagōgē*.

James pictures two men entering this early assembly. The first one is "wearing a gold ring and fine clothes." The Greek word *lampra* ("fine") was a term used to describe the clothing of a rich person or a dignitary. In the Roman world it was the proper description for the toga of a candidate for public office. In sharp contrast are the "shabby clothes" of the "poor man." The word *rhypara* ("shabby") normally means "dirty" or "filthy." It is the adjective form of the noun in 1:21 that NIV translates as "moral filth." Inasmuch as this "poor man" is in reality a beggar (*ptōchos*), it seems most natural that his clothes should be described as filthy.

3 The rich man is shown "special attention." The Greek *epiblepsēte* means "to look with favor on" someone. This was the plea of the father of the demon-possessed boy: "I beg you to look at my son" (Luke 9:38). The verb refers not only to the favorable look but also to the consequent assistance. The rich man of James 2 is the object of solicitous attention as he is shown to "a good seat." It is possible, however, that the word *kalōs* does not refer to the proffered seat but should be translated "please" ("Sit here, please"). In contrast, "the poor man" is abruptly told to "stand there," perhaps in the back of the assembly or in some other out-of-the-way place. His other alternative is to "sit on the floor." The Greek text actually says, "Sit under my footstool," which probably means "by my footstool." The contrast between the speaker who has a stool for his feet and the beggar who must sit on the floor heightens the discrimination.

4 The expressed condemnation of this practice is put in question form. However, the Greek construction leaves no doubt as to James's opinion. The negative particle *ou* ("not") shows that he expects his readers to agree with his conclusion: "Have you not discriminated?" The practice illustrated in vv.2–3 rests on an unjustified distinction. The basis for showing favor is terribly wrong. Those acting in this way "become judges with evil thoughts." Here the play on words in the Greek is not apparent in the English translation. The word translated "discriminated" (*diekrithēte*) is built on the same root as the word for "judges" (*kritai*). In so judging between men, the readers had become unjust judges.

5 Verses 5–11 advance two arguments against the practice of favoritism. The first may be called the social argument (vv.5–7). The importance the author attaches to these arguments is seen in the imperative "Listen, my dear brothers." The early church was not drawn from the wealthy or ruling classes. It was largely made up of poorer people, those who are "poor in the eyes of the world." This is apparent in the gospels (e.g., Matt 11:5); Paul implies it (1 Cor 1:26–29); and James declares it (2:5). By saying that the believers' poverty is poverty "in the eyes of the world," James is suggesting that they are not really poor. They are "rich in faith" and heirs of the kingdom. The aspect of the kingdom James has in mind is yet future. It is the eternal kingdom that Christ equated with eternal life (Matt 25:34, 46). So James has shown us that the social snobbery of the world is short-sighted and superficial. And the favoritism James's readers practiced was based on this same shallow kind of evaluation.

James's concept of the blessed poor may be misunderstood. He does not say that all poor people are "rich in faith," nor does he exclude the rich from the ranks of the saved. Furthermore, God's choice of the poor must not be taken as based on any merit inherent in poverty. One reason God "has chosen those who are poor" may be seen in the account of the rich young ruler (Mark 10:17–27). There Jesus indicated that those who have riches find it exceedingly difficult to enter God's kingdom (vv.23–25), apparently because their wealth stands in the way. God blesses those who willingly recognize their spiritual bankruptcy (Matt 5:3). A second reason why God chooses the poor is explicitly stated in 1 Cor 1:26–29. God selects those who have nothing or are nothing in themselves "so that no one may boast before him" (v.29).

6 In sharp contrast to God's choice of the poor (v.5) is the way James's readers had treated them. God had chosen them, but they had "insulted" them! The incongruity of such treatment is dramatized by three pointed questions. Question number one: The rich are the ones "who are exploiting you," are they not? The word *katadynasteuō* ("exploit") is a strong term describing the brutal and tyrranical deprivation of one's rights. It occurs in a number of pasages in the LXX that speak of oppression of the poor, the widow, and the stranger (Ezek 22:29; Zech 7:10).

Question number two: Is it not the rich "who are dragging you into court?" Although *helkō* ("drag") may sometimes mean nothing more than "to draw or attract" (John 6:44; 12:32), in other situations it describes the act of forcibly dragging a person (Acts 16:19; 21:30), as seems to be the case here. The presence of the third personal pronoun *autoi* ("they") suggests that the rich men themselves ("with their own hands"—Mayor) dragged the poor into the courts.

7 Question number three: The rich "are slandering the noble name" of Christ, aren't they? Where God or his name are being spoken against, it is better to translate the Greek *blasphēmeō* by the English word "blaspheme," which has come to refer to speaking irreverently and disrespectfully of Deity. Christ's name is described as *kalon*, that is, "noble," "excellent," "honorable," rather than as *agathon*, which refers to that which is kind or morally good. NIV explains that this "noble name" is the name of "him to whom you belong." The word-for-word translation of James's Greek would read "the noble name that was called upon you." This expression clearly reveals its OT background (Deut 28:10; 2 Chron 7:14; Amos 9:12). A man was dedicated to God by calling God's name over him. The act indicated that he belonged to God. So Christians bear the worthy name of Christ as indication that they are his people. To show favoritism to those who blaspheme that wonderful name is the greatest incongruity of all.

8 James now proceeds to his moral argument in refutation of the practice of showing favoritism (vv.8–11). Here it is not a question of mere incongruity but of the rightness or wrongness of showing partiality. The commandment to love one's neighbor as oneself (Lev 19:18) is not described as "the royal law" simply because of its lofty character. Numerous commentators (Ropes, Mayor, Tasker, Ross, Lenski) agree that it is called "royal" because it is the supreme law to which all other laws governing human relationships are subordinate. It is the summation of all such laws (Matt 22:36–40). The one who keeps this supreme law is "doing right." NIV has translated *kalōs* ("well") as "right," since it seems to be contrasted with committing sin in v.9. The right course of action is to show favor to everyone, whether he is rich or poor. Love overlooks such superficial distinctions as wealth and quality of clothing. It shows kindness to a person in spite of any distasteful qualities he may have.

9 Whereas v.8 depicts the positive example of one who fully keeps the law, v.9 sets forth the negative example of one who breaks it. To "show favoritism" is not merely to be guilty of an insignificant fault or social impropriety; it is sin. Such a conclusion is based on solid legal ground rather than general human opinion. Those engaging in partiality "are convicted by the law as lawbreakers." Some understand this as a reference to the law in general; others assert that the law referred to is stated in Leviticus 19:15 or Deuteronomy 16:19. James, however, has already cited the law he is referring to. It is the "royal law" quoted in v.9. Anyone who shows favoritism breaks the supreme law of love for his neighbor, the law that comprehends all laws governing one's relationships to one's fellowmen.

10 By beginning this verse with the word "for" (*gar*), James indicates that he is going to explain how an act of favoritism makes a person a lawbreaker (v.9). It is obvious that he has set up a special case when he speaks of someone who "keeps the whole law" except for "one point," for in 3:2 he insists that "we all stumble in many ways." However, for the sake of his argument he imagines a person who "stumbles at just one point." Although *ptaisē,* ("stumbles") may describe an insignificant offense or error, it was also used as a synonym for the verb "to sin," but with no indication of the degree of seriousness. So James's reasoning is that to commit one act of sin, which breaks one commandment of the law, makes a person "guilty of breaking" the whole law.

11 Like v.10, this verse also opens with the explanatory "for," showing that the author is continuing his explanation. He does so with a simple illustration based on the unity of law. Although God's law has many facets, it is essentially one, being the expression of the character and will of God himself. To violate the law at any one point is not to violate one commandment only; it is to violate the will of God and to contradict the character of God. The same God who said, "Do not commit adultery," also said, "Do not murder." It is also the same God who gave the royal law of love for one's neighbor. The person who breaks just one of these laws has "become a lawbreaker." Although but one commandment is broken, the entire law of God has been flouted. When viewed like this, an act of favoritism is far from insignificant.

12 The section (2:1–13) is concluded with an urgent exhortation and warning (vv.12–13). The commands "Speak and act" are stronger in the Greek text than in the English. James says, "So speak and so act." His repetition of "so" (*houtōs*) is emphatic and also serves to distribute the emphasis equally between the two verbs. The present tense in both verbs calls for continuing action. James would have his readers continue to speak and act in light of the fact that they "are going to be judged." Since he is speaking to believers, the judgment to which he refers must be the judgment of believers at the judgment seat of Christ (2 Cor 5:10). The standard of judgment will be "the law that gives freedom," rather than the enslaving legalistic system developed by the scribes and Pharisees. It is the royal law of love (v.8), which the believer is enabled to keep by the Holy Spirit (Gal 5:22–23).

13 The reason for responding to the exhortation of v.12 is that "judgment without mercy" will be the lot of the unmerciful. No doubt mercy is singled out because James has the poor man of v.2 in mind. Instead of the mercy the man needed, he received cruel discrimination, and that at the hands of professing Christians. The basic principle that underlies v.12a was stated by Christ himself (Matt 18:33). The recipient of mercy should likewise be merciful. In fact, mercy should be the mark of the regenerated person. If it is present in the believer's life, he will have nothing to fear at the judgment. It is in this sense that "mercy triumphs over judgment." The believer will be able to smile triumphantly in the time of judgment. In the same vein John declares, "Love is made complete among us so that we will have confidence on the day of judgment, because in this world we are like him" (1 John 4:17). The presence of love (or mercy) shows that God has performed a work of grace in the believer's heart, making him like Christ. As a result, he can have confidence when he is judged.

Notes

---

4 A decided difference of opinion exists concerning the correct translation of **διεκρίθητε** (*diekrithēte*, NIV, "discriminated"). Most commentators point out that the common NT meaning of this verb in the passive voice is "to waver," "to doubt." It is to be divided within oneself as in James 1:6 (cf. Alford, Lenski, Mayor, Ropes, and Tasker). This view is also supported by TDNT (3:947–49) and is expressed in NEB and the translations of Goodspeed and Beck. The reasoning of James is usually explained as follows: The persons showing favoritism are wavering between worldly standards and true spiritual values. They take their place in the congregation as believers, but they judge men as the world views them.

On the other hand, a number of translations view the verb as meaning "to make a distinction." This is to treat the passive form as though it were active, a practice justified with certain verbs (RHG, p. 817). For example, NASB translates v.4a, "Have you not made distinctions among yourselves?" Similar renderings are found in ASV, RSV, Wms, Mof, *Centenary Translation*, Ph, TEV, and NIV. Several commentators agree (A.T. Robertson, *Practical and Social Aspects of Christianity* [New York: Hodder & Stoughton, 1915], p. 114; Ross). Although there is no parallel usage of this particular verb to support this interpretation, it is the most natural one in the light of the immediate context. The fault James was aiming at was discrimination against one person and favoritism toward another. To engage in such practices is clearly "to make distinctions." The view that the verb means "to waver" between worldly and spiritual standards is more contrived and thus less obvious to the average reader than the view just presented. The obvious sense of the passage argues that in this case there is a variance from the normal usage of the passive voice.

V. The Relation of Faith and Action

2:14–26

14What good is it, my brothers, if a man claims to have faith but has no deeds?
Can such faith save him? 15Suppose a brother or sister is without clothes and daily
food. 16If one of you says to him, "Go, I wish you well; keep warm and well fed,"
but does nothing about his physical needs, what good is it? 17In the same way, faith
by itself, if it is not accompanied by action, is dead.
18But someone will say, "You have faith; I have deeds."
Show me your faith without deeds, and I will show you my faith by what I do. 19You
believe that there is one God. Good! Even the demons believe that—and shudder.
20You foolish man, do you want evidence that faith without deeds is useless?
21Was not our ancestor Abraham considered righteous for what he did when he
offered his son Isaac on the altar? 22You see that his faith and his actions were
working together, and his faith was made complete by what he did. 23And the

scripture was fulfilled that says, "Abraham believed God, and it was credited to him as righteousness," and he was called God's friend. [24]You see that a person is justified by what he does and not by faith alone.

[25]In the same way, was not even Rahab the prostitute considered righteous for what she did when she gave lodging to the spies and sent them off in a different direction? [26]As the body without the spirit is dead, so faith without deeds is dead.

This section has sometimes been misunderstood as conflicting with Paul's doctrine of justification by faith alone. No less a scholar than Martin Luther thought he saw an inconsistency between the teachings of James and Paul. However, careful study reveals that there is no disagreement between a Pauline statement like that in Ephesians 2:8–10 and the declaration of James 2:24.

The passage at hand (2:14–26) divides itself into three sections: the proposition (vv. 14–17); the argument (vv. 18–25); and the concluding statement (v. 26). Here the author makes another application of the bedrock principle set forth in 1:19–27. As in that passage hearing must be accompanied by doing, so in 2:14–26 faith must be attended by action. This epistle leaves no place for a religion that is mere mental acceptance of truth.

14 James first states his proposition interrogatively. The two questions posed in this verse actually declare that faith not accompanied by good deeds is of no saving value whatsoever. The questions set up the hypothetical case of a person who "claims to have" genuine saving faith. Notice that James does not say that the person actually has faith. The question "Can such faith save him?" is so structured in the Greek text (using the negative particle *mē* interrogatively) that it expects a negative answer. The word "such" is the translation for the Greek article that appears before *pistis*, "faith." James is asking, "This faith can't save him, can it?" The article refers to the faith described in the preceding question—faith not accompanied by deeds. Faith without works cannot save; it takes faith that proves itself in the deeds it produces. James is not speaking of deeds performed to earn merit before God (as Paul uses the term in Rom 3:20). Genuine faith is a concomitant of regeneration and therefore affects the believer's behavior. Faith that does not issue in regenerate actions is superficial and spurious.

15 In vv. 15–16 the proposition is illustrated by a supposition bordering on the ludicrous. It is the case of a believer ("brother or sister") who is in dire need ("without clothes and daily food"). The Greek *gymnoi* actually means "naked" and is probably to be understood as hyperbole. The purpose of the overstatement is to emphasize the drastic need of this believer. His is no mild case of need. He is desperate.

16 The statement "Go, I wish you well" is a modern idiom used to represent James's Greek *Hypagete en eirēnē* ("Go in peace"). This was a standard Hebrew farewell. The translation "keep warm and well fed" may be somewhat misleading in suggesting that the person is already warm and fed, which is not the case, as v. 15 indicates. The two verbs are identified as passives by numerous commentators, with the understanding that they are commands to someone else to clothe and feed the unfortunate person. A.T. Robertson's suggestion that they are to be taken reflexively (as Greek middle voices) is more natural (*Word Pictures in the New Testament* [New York: Harper, 1933], 6:34–35). The meaning would be "get some warm clothes and eat your fill."

The preposterousness of such a command is no doubt intentional. "What good is it?" James asks. Its seeming concern for the welfare of the poor person is a worthless façade.

17 Here James states the proposition he intends to demonstrate in the following verses: "Faith . . . not accompanied by action is dead." Action is the proper fruit of living faith. Because life is dynamic and productive, faith that lives will surely produce the fruit of good deeds. Therefore, if no deeds are forthcoming, it is proof that the professed faith is dead. Notice that James does not deny that it is faith. He simply indicates that it is not the right kind of faith. It is not living faith, nor can it save.

18 James next proceeds to develop the argument in support of his proposition. His first point is that works are necessary to prove that a person has faith. There is some question as to the end of the quotation introduced by the words "But someone will say." Some translations, such as NASB and Wms, include all of v.18 in the quotation. It seems preferable, however, to limit the statement to the words "You have faith; I have deeds," as do RSV, TEV, NIV, and Beck. The problem of identifying the persons referred to by the pronouns "you" and "I" is not easily resolved. Perhaps it is best to paraphrase the quotation as follows: "One person has faith; another has deeds." The statement then becomes an assertion that faith and works are not necessarily related to each other and that it is possible to have either one without the other (Tasker, pp. 64–66). To this assertion James responds with a challenge: "Show me your faith without deeds." The implication is that faith cannot be demonstrated apart from action. Faith is an attitude of the inner man, and it can only be seen as it influences the actions of the one who possesses it. Mere profession of faith proves nothing as to its reality; only action can demonstrate faith's genuineness. Hence James declares, "I will show you my faith by what I do."

19 The second argument offered in support of the proposition stated in v.17 concerns the nature of saving faith. All faithful Jews believed the creed known as the Shema found in Deuteronomy 6:4: "Hear, O Israel: The LORD our God, the LORD is one." James commends his Jewish Christian readers for believing "that there is one God." This is "good!" That God is one was a basic truth of Jewish orthodoxy, but such acceptance of a creed is not enough to save a person. To prove his point, James declares that "even demons believe" the Shema. They know that there is but one God, and as a result they "shudder." The Greek term *phrissō* describes a shudder that results from fear. That the demons so respond to the fact of God is evidence that their belief is a thorough conviction. However, their response is also evidence that their faith is not saving faith, for they are terrified at the thought of God. Belief has not brought them peace with God. Saving faith, then, is not mere intellectual acceptance of a theological proposition. It goes much deeper, involving the whole inner man and expressing itself outwardly in a changed life.

20 James introduces the next argument in support of his proposition (v.17) with the question "Do you want evidence?" His manner of addressing his imagined opponent is blunt, to say the least. The Greek adjective translated "foolish" means "empty." It refers to a deficiency that is intellectual, but in the theological and moral context of the NT the term also has a moral and spiritual flavor. So James addresses his opponent as one who has no comprehension of spiritual truth. He does not see "that faith without deeds is useless." In v.17 such faith is called "dead." Here it is described as something that does not work (*argē*); it accomplishes nothing. The evidence James offers his opponent is found in vv.21–25 and consists of two OT examples—Abraham and Rahab.

21 The designation of Abraham as "our ancestor" (*patēr,* "father") agrees with evidence found elsewhere in the epistle (e.g., 1:1) that James wrote for a Jewish readership. The Greek word *edikaiōthē* ("considered righteous") is the term the older versions translate as "justified." Its standard meaning is "to declare righteous." It is a forensic term, never referring to making a person subjectively righteous, but always describing the act of declaring a person righteous. So James states that Abraham was declared righteous "for what he did." It was a pronouncement that found its source (*ek,* "out of") in Abraham's obedient offering of his son (Gen 22:1–14). The explanation of this statement is given in the following verses.

22 Here James makes it clear that he is not talking about works as the sole source of Abraham's justification, as v.21 taken out of its context might lead one to believe. Instead, Abraham's "faith and his actions were working together." Faith and works are inseparable. It is not possible for one person to have valid faith without works and for another to have genuine works without faith, as James's opponent argued in v.18. But this may sound as if Abraham's justification resulted from a mixture of faith and works, each being equally efficacious. If this is what James meant, he is in conflict with Paul, who insists that faith is the only means of justification. However, it is not necessary to take James's statement in this way. Other NT passages show plainly that a person is justified by faith alone. James, assuming this fact, declares that this justifying faith has a certain quality, a vitality that makes it the producer of good deeds. It is an action-producing faith. Mayor wrote, "Abraham's faith was not mere profession but an extremely active principle" (p. 95). Paul described this quality of faith when he spoke of "faith expressing itself through love" (Gal 5:6). Faith, then, is the means of obtaining justification, but by its very nature it is faith that produces deeds. In this sense Abraham's faith was validated by his deeds. If there had been no good deeds following, faith would have been incomplete (v.22), dead (v.17), and useless (v.20). In this sense also Abraham was "considered righteous for what he did." If there had been no good deeds forthcoming, his faith would not have been genuine; and therefore it could not have been counted to him for righteousness.

23 "The scripture" to which James refers as "fulfilled" is Genesis 15:6. The account of the offering of Isaac on the altar appears in Genesis 22:1–14. Thirty years may have intervened between the events of these two chapters. In the former passage Abraham's faith is said to have been "credited to him as righteousness." The obedient offering of Isaac in the latter passage "fulfilled" the statement of the former passage. This is not to be understood as the fulfillment of a prophecy. Rather, it is fulfillment in the sense of completion (cf. v.22). What Abraham did in Genesis 22 was the outworking of the faith described in chapter 15. That it was the kind of faith that justifies is shown in chapter 22. God's act of crediting Abraham with righeousness because of his faith was vindicated by Abraham's act of obedience in offering his son. In this way Genesis 22:1–14 fulfilled Genesis 15:6. James adds, as a parallel description of Abraham's standing with God, that "he was called God's friend" (see 2 Chron 20:7; Isa 41:8). This is another way of saying that he was right with God. It was not that Abraham earned the favor of God by obeying him; instead, he acted as a friend of God should act and thus showed that he was in reality God's friend.

24 In this summary statement James assumes that a person is justified by faith but "not by faith alone." It is by faith *and* "by what he does." Taken by itself, this declaration may seem blatantly contradictory to such Pauline statements as that of Ephesians 2:8–9. If both passages are studied in context, however, the seeming contradiction disappears. James has indicated that deeds complete faith (v.22). They are the outworking of genuine faith. Thus deeds are the evidence that saving faith is present in a person's life (v.18). James was combating a superficial faith that had no wholesome effect in the life of the professed believer. Paul, on the other hand, was combating legalism—the belief that one may earn saving merit before God by his good deeds. Consequently Paul insisted that salvation is not by works but by faith alone. However, the following context of the Ephesians passage (2:10) reveals that Paul did not depreciate good works. He declared, "We are God's workmanship, created in Christ Jesus to do good works." In Paul, therefore, as well as in James, good deeds are the product of genuine faith. In both writers faith that produces no good deeds is incapable of saving a person.

25 The second OT person cited as an example of genuine faith is "Rahab the prostitute." She too was "considered righteous for what she did." Although her faith was like that of Abraham, she was unlike the patriarch in almost every other way. She had been a pagan; she was a woman; and she was a prostitute. Nevertheless, she chose to become identified with the people of Israel, a decision based on faith (cf. Josh 2:8–13; Heb 11:31). Far from being dead or worthless, her faith moved her to risk her life to protect the spies. As a result, "even" (*kai*) the prostitute was declared righteous. James does not give approval to Rahab's former life; it is her living faith, seen against the background of her previous immorality, he commends.

26 The argument of vv. 18–25 concludes with a statement that cites the human body as an illustration. "The body without the spirit" is nothing but a corpse. "Faith without deeds" is as dead as a corpse, and equally useless. James does not imply that deeds are the actual life principle that gives life to faith, but only that faith and deeds are inseparable. If there are no acts springing from faith, that faith is no more alive than "the body without the spirit."

Notes

---

19 The variant readings of the reference to Deut 6:4 can be divided into two categories: those that have the article before θεός (*theos*, "God") and those that do not. The articular reading adopted by UBS is tr. "there is one God" by NIV. But more literally it is "God is one," since the article identifies θεός (*theos*, "God") as the subject of the copulative sentence. The anarthrous reading εἷς θεός ἐστιν (*heis theos estin*, "there is one God") has good MS support (B), but it is the least conventional (Ropes, p. 215).

20 KJV translates the latter part of this verse "faith without works is dead," basing its rendering on the external evidence of the majority of MSS. However, since the word ἀργή (*argē*, "barren"; NIV, "useless") is supported by B and C, and since νεκρά (*nekra*, "dead") may well be a harmonization with vv.17, 26, ἀργή (*argē*) seems to be the best reading. A possible play on words (ἔργων–ἀργή, *ergōn–argē*, "works–useless") is pointed out by Metzger (p. 681).

VI. The Control of the Tongue

3:1–12

[1]Not many of you should presume to be teachers, my brothers, because you know that we who teach will be judged more strictly. [2]We all stumble in many ways. If anyone is never at fault in what he says, he is a perfect man, able to keep his whole body in check.

[3]When we put bits into the mouths of horses to make them obey us, we can turn the whole animal. [4]Or take ships as an example. Although they are so large and are driven by strong winds, they are steered by a very small rudder wherever the pilot wants to go. [5]Likewise the tongue is a small part of the body, but it makes great boasts. Consider what a great forest is set on fire by a small spark. [6]The tongue also is a fire, a world of evil among the parts of the body. It corrupts the whole person, sets the whole course of his life on fire, and is itself set on fire by hell.

[7]All kinds of animals, birds, reptiles and creatures of the sea are being tamed and have been tamed by man, [8]but no man can tame the tongue. It is a restless evil, full of deadly poison.

[9]With the tongue we praise our Lord and Father, and with it we curse men, who have been made in God's likeness. [10]Out of the same mouth come praise and cursing. My brothers, this should not be. [11]Can both fresh water and salt water flow from the same spring? [12]My brothers, can a fig tree bear olives, or a grapevine bear figs? Neither can a salt spring produce fresh water.

In this section the author picks up a subject first mentioned in 1:19 and reiterated in 1:26. Genuine religion should exert a controlling influence over a person's tongue. James's treatment of the topic may be broken into three subdivisions: the weighty responsibility of teachers (vv.1–2); the powerful influence of the tongue (vv.3–6); and the perversity of the tongue (vv.7–12).

1 James's first concern in this passage has to do with those who desired to be "teachers" in the scattered Jewish Christian congregations. A somewhat similar situation is reflected in 1 Timothy 1:7. The KJV "masters" is an Old English term for teachers (e.g., schoolmaster). The Greek construction (*mē* with the present imperative *ginesthe*) probably suggests that it had been a common practice for many of the readers to seek to become teachers. So James warns that they should stop becoming teachers in such large numbers. No doubt many who were not qualified by natural ability or spiritual gift were coveting the prestige of teaching. They are warned that teachers "will be judged more strictly." It is apparent from the words "we who teach" that James includes himself as a teacher. The KJV translation "we shall receive the greater condemnation" is unfortunate. The Greek word *krima* refers to the decision of a judge, whether it be favorable or unfavorable. In this context the term is neutral. James merely says that the judgment of teachers will be especially strict because greater responsibility rests on teachers. The reason for this is that the teacher's essential instrument—the tongue—which is so easily misused, has great influence.

2 In the Greek text this verse begins with *gar* ("for"), indicating an explanation for the previous statement. The teacher's responsibility is weighty because the tongue is the most difficult member of the body to control. To say that "we all stumble" is not merely to declare that everyone makes mistakes (RSV). The literal meaning of *ptaiō* is "to stumble," but in both biblical and extrabiblical writings it was also used figuratively to refer to acts of sin (cf. 2:10). Thus the author declares the universality of sin, even among believers. The person who "is never at fault" in his speech (i.e., never commits sins of speech) "is a perfect man." If anyone could be found who never sins with his tongue, he would never sin in any other way, either. Since sins of the tongue are hardest to avoid, anyone who could control his tongue would surely be able to "keep his whole body in check"—i.e., keep it from being used as an instrument of sin.

3 James illustrates the powerful influence of the tongue by the practice of putting "bits into the mouths of horses to make them obey us." A very small bit "can turn the whole animal." So a man who controls his tongue can control his whole being.

4 The next illustration of the influence of the tongue is the rudder of a ship. James vividly introduces the illustration: "Take ships as an example." Three factors made ships of that day difficult to control: they were "so large"; they were "driven by strong winds"; and they were "steered by a very small rudder." The rudder was a small blade on the end of a tiller, extending through a form of oarlock from the rear of the ship. Compared to the size of the vessel and the power of the gale, the rudder was but a minute part; yet it guided the ship "wherever the pilot [wanted] to go."

5 With the words "likewise the tongue," the application of the two preceding verses is introduced. Like bits (v.3) and rudders (v.4), the tongue also is a small item. Yet, also like them, it exerts a powerful influence. "It makes great boasts," and these are not empty claims. The tongue is able to sway multitudes. It can alter the destinies of nations. Since *megala auchei* ("makes great boasts") is usually employed in a derogatory sense, it may be that the author uses the expression to apply the first two illustrations of the tongue's influence (vv.3–4) and also to introduce the third one (vv.5b–6). The destructive potential of the tongue is graphically pictured by a forest fire. Thousands of acres of valuable timber may be devastated by a "small spark." In the two former illustrations, animals and ships are controlled by small objects; in this last illustration, a huge forest is destroyed by a tiny spark. The tongue likewise can either control or destroy.

6 So, James says, "The tongue also is a fire." The inflammatory tongue has turned brother against brother, neighbor against neighbor, nation against nation. The tongue is also "a world of evil." It is as though all the wickedness in the whole world were wrapped up in that little piece of flesh. There are few sins people commit in which the tongue is not involved.

James describes the tongue's influence as both destructive and as corrupting "the whole person." The Greek word translated "person" by NIV is *sōma* ("body"). Since the person resides in the body and uses the body as his instrument, James seems to use "body" to refer to the whole man. In reality, he is not referring to the tongue of flesh but to the intelligent, communicating mind that uses the tongue as its instrument. So the mind corrupts the whole person. But the corrupting influence of the tongue reaches out in widening circles, for it "sets the whole course of his life on fire." The pronoun "his" in the NIV is not in the Greek text and therefore might better be omitted. It limits the sphere of influence to the speaker, whereas James seems to refer to the whole of human existence. Finally, James traces the inflaming nature of the tongue back to its source. It is, he says, "set on fire by hell," a way of saying that it comes from the devil. The term *geennēs* or *gehenna* comes from the Greek form of the Hebrew name of the valley of Hinnom (*gê-hinnōm*), a spot just south of Jerusalem where the rubbish of the city was deposited and burned. This continual burning of rubbish became a figure for eternal punishment.

7 James shifts almost unnoticeably from discussing the power of the tongue (vv.3–6) to a discussion of its perversity (vv.7–12). Actually v.6, in depicting the tongue's influence, is already describing its perversity. According to vv.7–8, man's inability to tame his tongue shows the perversity of the tongue. At creation God gave man the dominion over the animals that he has exercised ever since (Gen 1:28). "All kinds" of creatures of land, sea, and air have been subdued by mankind. To emphasize the continuing aspect of man's dominance over the animals, James uses both the present and the perfect tenses—"are being tamed and have been tamed."

8 But even though man has retained his dominion over all kinds of animals, Tasker says, "Because of the fall man has lost dominion over himself" (p. 77). When he says, "No man can tame the tongue," James is stating that no man by himself can subdue the tongue. This is not to say that God cannot bring it under control. While the tongue cannot be controlled by man, the tongue of the regenerate person can be controlled by the indwelling Holy Spirit. In its natural state the tongue "is a restless evil," like a ferocious beast that will not be subdued. It is "full of deadly poison," like a serpent ready to inject venom into its victim.

9 James goes on to speak of inconsistency as an aspect of the tongue's perversity (vv.9–12). We use the same instrument to "praise our Lord and Father" and to "curse men." But praising God and cursing men is tantamount to praising and cursing the same person, for in v.9 James describes man as "made in God's likeness" (cf. man's having been created in the image of God [Gen 1:26–27]). Although marred by sin, that image is still very much a reality; and man's intellect, emotion, and will show that he bears God's likeness. Obviously, James is not referring to such words as those of Paul when he invoked a curse on anyone who perverts the gospel (Gal 1:6–9). Instead, it is the cursing that grows out of bitterness and hatred that he speaks of.

10 Again, James stresses the inconsistency of the tongue in that it is the source of such direct opposites as "praise and cursing." He does not have only the unsaved in mind because he introduces his rebuke with the words "my brothers," the term used throughout the epistle to address believers (1:2, 16, 19; 2:1, 5, 14; 3:1; et al.). Although the believer has in the indwelling Holy Spirit the potential for controlling the tongue, he may not be appropriating this potential. Hence, James insists that "this should not be." The mouth should be used consistently to praise God and to express love and kindness to men.

11 James again turns to nature for his illustrations. He asks, "Can both fresh water and salt water flow from the same spring?" The word *bryei* ("flow") is a poetic term describing water that pours out, almost as being under pressure. The water is sweet (*glyky;* NIV, "fresh") and bitter (*pikron;* NIV, "salt"). "Sweet" describes fresh water that is good for drinking; "bitter" refers to water so brackish or even salty as to be unfit for drinking. James may have had the Dead Sea in mind.

12 James concludes his discussion of the tongue by going behind the physical organ to the real source of speech. He asks, "Can a fig tree bear olives?" A plant produces according to its nature, whether figs, grapes, or any other fruit. So with "a salt spring." It cannot "produce fresh water" because it is not a fresh water spring. Therefore, out of the mouth of a good man come good words, and out of the mouth of a sinful man come sinful words.

Notes

---

6 The question of punctuation in this verse is a difficult one. It is clear from the repetition of ἡ γλῶσσα (*hē glōssa,* "the tongue") that καὶ ἡ γλῶσσα πῦρ (*kai hē glōssa pyr,* "the tongue also is a fire") is a complete clause, with the verb ἐστίν (*estin,* "is") being assumed. It is possible that this clause should be followed by a comma and that ὁ κόσμος τῆς ἀδικίας (*ho kosmos tēs adikias,* "a world of evil") is a second predicate nominative after the assumed ἐστίν (*estin,* "is"). This, however, makes the following clause to be a rather pointless statement: ἡ γλῶσσα καθίσταται ἐν τοῖς μέλεσιν ἡμῶν (*hē glōssa kathistatai en tois melesin hēmōn,* "the tongue is placed among our members"). It seems best, therefore, to assume a period after πῦρ (*pyr,* "fire") and to take ὁ κόσμος τῆς ἀδικίας (*ho kosmos tēs adikias,* "a world of evil") as the predicate nominative after καθίσταται (*kathistatai,* "is placed"). The verse would then read, "The tongue also is a fire. The tongue is constituted a world of evil among the parts of the body, which corrupts. . . ." For a parallel use of καθίσταται (*kathistatai,* "is placed") followed by a predicate nominative, see Rom 5:19.

The expression τὸν τροχὸν τῆς γενέσεως (*ton trochon tēs geneseōs,* "the course of nature") is both difficult and interesting. Tροχός (*trochos*), when accented on the ultima, means "wheel," or when accented on the penult, τρόχος (*trochos*), means "course" (from τρέχειν [*trechein,* "to run"]). Γενέσεως (*geneseōs*) may mean "birth" or "origin." BAG (s.v.) also gives "existence" as a meaning in certain extrabiblical passages. In Judith 12:18 (LXX) it is used in the expression πάσας τὰς ἡμέρας τῆς γενέσεώς μου (*pasas tas hēmeras tēs geneseōs mou,* "all the days of my existence"). Since extensive research has yielded no exact parallel for the phrase employed by James, it seems best to assume that he did not borrow it from any pagan philosophical or religious source, but rather coined the expression himself. Whether we understand τροχόν (*troch'on*) to mean "wheel" or "course" makes little difference. James refers to the whole of existence, which is set on fire by the tongue.

VII. Two Kinds of Wisdom

3:13–18

[13]Who is wise and understanding among you? Let him show it by his good life, by deeds done in the humility that comes from wisdom. [14]But if you harbor bitter envy and selfish ambition in your hearts, do not boast about it or deny the truth. [15]Such "wisdom" does not come down from heaven but is earthly, unspiritual, of the devil. [16]For where you have envy and selfish ambition, there you find disorder and every evil practice.

[17]But the wisdom that comes from heaven is first of all pure; then peace loving, considerate, submissive, full of mercy and good fruit, impartial and sincere. [18]Peacemakers who sow in peace raise a harvest of righteousness.

This passage is a natural outgrowth of the discussion of the tongue. The six verses divide into three sections: an exhortation (v.13); earthly wisdom (vv.14–16); and wisdom from heaven (vv.17–18).

13 James addresses the person who is "wise and understanding." The word *sophos* ("wise") was the technical term among the Jews for the teacher, the scribe, the rabbi (TDNT, 7:505). It appears that the author is still speaking to those who would be teachers (cf. 3:1); here it is not what they say that he is concerned with, but rather how they live. The term *epistēmōn* describes one who is expert, who has special knowledge or training. Thus anyone who would be a teacher, who claims to be an expert with special understanding, is under obligation to "show it by his good life." He should possess "knowhow" and be skilled in applying God's truth to practical, everyday living. The KJV term "conversation" is not to be restricted to speech. In 1611 it possessed the much broader meaning of "conduct," "manner of life," and was at that time a good translation of *anastrophēs* (NIV, "life").

The particular characteristic stressed in this verse is "humility that comes from wisdom." The word translated "humility" in NIV is *prautēti*, more commonly rendered "meekness." "Humility" may not be the best translation, since it confuses *prautēs* with the word *tapeinophrosynē*, more normally translated "humility." A better translation might be "gentleness," but even this does not adequately render the Greek word (see remarks on 1:21). *Prautēs* is gentleness, but not a passive gentleness growing out of weakness or resignation. It is an active attitude of deliberate acceptance (TDNT, 6:645). The word was used to describe a horse that had been broken and trained to submit to the bridle (William Barclay, *New Testament Words* [London: SCM, 1971], pp. 241–42). So this gentleness is strength under control, the control of the Spirit of God (Gal 5:22–23). It is a gentleness "that comes from wisdom" or is characteristic of wisdom (see remarks on 1:5). James does not have in mind the Greek concept of speculative or theoretical wisdom but the Hebrew idea of practical wisdom that enables one to live a life of godliness.

14 Apparently some of James's readers were harboring "bitter envy and selfish ambition" in their hearts. The Greek simple conditional sentence assumes the existence of the situation described. The determinative word is *eritheian* ("selfish ambition"), which speaks of a self-seeking attitude bent on gaining advantage and prestige for oneself or one's group. This forceful term colors the word *zēlon* ("envy"), so that *zēlon* here means "selfish zeal." The word is often used to describe fanatical zeal for a cause (1 Kings 19:10 [3 Kings 19:10 LXX]; Ps 69:9 [68:10 LXX]; Isa 9:7), either in a good or a bad sense. James makes it clear by the adjective "bitter" that he is referring to a sinful zeal. Because this condition existed among his readers, he insists that they must "not boast about it or deny the truth." The phrase "about it," which has been added by the translators, could be taken to mean "Do not boast about your bitter zeal and selfish ambition." James's readers may have been priding themselves in their partisan defense of the truth—a defense that was to their own advantage and advancement. Through such bitter and partisan defense, they were in reality denying the very truth they were attempting to defend.

15 Though James refers to the attitude described in v.14 as "wisdom," he obviously does not mean that it is genuine wisdom. On the contrary, it is the wisdom claimed by the would-be teachers of v.14 whose lives contradict their claims. Such "wisdom" evaluates everything by worldly standards and makes personal gain life's highest goal. Yet even this spurious use of the term reflects the Hebrew concept of wisdom as practical rather than theoretical. God is the source of genuine wisdom (Prov 2:6), but this pseudo-wisdom is not from him, because, as James declares, "such 'wisdom' does not come down from heaven." Instead of being from above (*anōthen*), it is "earthly" in source as well as kind. It views life from the limited viewpoint of this world rather than from heaven's vantage point. Its mind is set on earthly things (Phil 3:19).

James also calls wisdom *psychikē* ("unspiritual"). In 1 Corinthians 2:14–15 *psychikos* ("unspiritual") is contrasted to *pneumatikos* ("spiritual"). The *pneumatikos* ("spiritual") man has received the Spirit of God (1 Cor 2:12), but the *psychikos* ("unspiritual") man does not have the Spirit (Jude 19). Thus "wisdom" that is *psychikē* ("unspiritual") characterizes unregenerate human nature. James also says that it is "of the devil" (more lit., "demonic" [*daimoniōdēs*]).

16 The conjunction "for" (*gar*) indicates that bitter zeal and selfish ambition always result in "disorder and every evil practice." *Akatastasia* ("disorder") is a common word for anarchy and political turmoil. Luke uses it to refer to political uprisings (Luke 21:9). James is no doubt speaking of disturbance and turmoil in the church. The "evil practice" refers specifically to worthless activity, to deeds that are bad because they are good for nothing and cannot produce any real benefit (Trench, pp. 305–6). Selfish zeal and ambition, then, always tend to destroy spiritual life and work.

17 In contrast to the denial of v.15—"Such 'wisdom' does not come down from heaven"—James next turns to a description of "the wisdom that comes from heaven." It is "first of all pure." This is its basic characteristic. The reference is not to sexual purity but to the absence of any sinful attitude or motive. It is the opposite of the self-seeking attitude of vv.14–16. From this inner quality flow the outward manifestations given in the rest of the verse. James describes this wisdom as "peace loving" in contrast to the bitter spirit of competitiveness and selfish ambition described in v.14.

Next, this godly wisdom is "considerate" (*epieikēs*). This is one of the great words of character description in the NT. In the LXX it is used mostly of God's disposition as King. He is gentle and kind, although in reality he has every reason to be stern and punitive toward men in their sin. God's people also are to be marked by this godlike quality, not insisting on their rights according to the letter of the law, but exercising love's leniency instead.

Likewise, "the wisdom that comes from heaven is . . . submissive." This quality is the opposite of obstinacy and self-seeking; it is a readiness to yield. The attitude that comes from God is "full of mercy and good fruit." Altogether compassionate, heavenly wisdom is always ready to help those who are in need. Furthermore, it is "impartial," showing no favoritism, and discriminating against no one. Finally, this wisdom is "sincere" (*anhypokritos*, "without hypocrisy"). Far from being theoretical and speculative, James's concept of wisdom is thoroughly practical. It is the understanding and attitude that result in true piety and godliness.

18 James concludes his discussion of "the wisdom that comes from heaven" by reiterating the second quality listed in v.17. To "raise a harvest of righteousness" demands a certain kind of climate. A crop of righteousness cannot be produced in the climate of bitterness and self-seeking. Righteousness will grow only in a climate of peace. And it must be sown and cultivated by the "peacemakers." Such persons not only love peace and live in peace but also strive to create conditions of peace.

VIII. The Worldly Attitude

4:1–10

[1]What causes fights and quarrels among you? Don't they come from your desires
that battle within you? [2]You want something but don't get it. You kill and covet, but
you cannot have what you want. You quarrel and fight. You do not have, because
you do not ask God. [3]When you ask, you do not receive, because you ask with
wrong motives, that you may spend what you get on your pleasures.
[4]You adulterous people, don't you know that friendship with the world is hatred
toward God? Anyone who chooses to be a friend of the world becomes an enemy
of God. [5]Or do you think Scripture says without reason that the spirit he caused
to live in us tends toward envy, [6]but he gives us more grace? That is why Scripture
says:

"God opposes the proud
but gives grace to the humble."

[7]Submit yourselves, then, to God. Resist the devil, and he will flee from you.
[8]Come near to God and he will come near to you. Wash your hands, you sinners,
and purify your hearts, you double-minded. [9]Grieve, mourn and wail. Change your
laughter to mourning and your joy to gloom. [10]Humble yourselves before the Lord,
and he will lift you up.

In 3:14–16 James has discussed a philosophy of life that is characteristic of the unregenerate mind and is a major ingredient of worldliness. In 4:1–10 he examines this worldly attitude in greater detail. First he identifies the source of worldly antagonisms (4:1–3); next, he reproves spiritual unfaithfulness (4:4–6); and, finally, he pleads for submission to God (4:7–10).

1 Instead of the climate of peace necessary for the production of righteousness (3:18), James's readers were living in an atmosphere of constant "fights and quarrels." These two nouns (*polemoi* and *machai*) were normally used of national warfare, but they had also become common, forceful expressions for any kind of open antagonism. James asks, "What causes fights and quarrels among you?" His answer, with which he expects his reader to agree, is "Don't they come from your desires?" The term *hēdonōn* (NIV, "desires") means "pleasures." It is the source of the English word "hedonism," the designation of the philosophy that views pleasure as the chief goal of life. James pictures these pleasures as residing within his readers, there carrying on a bitter campaign to gain satisfaction. Pleasure is the overriding desire of their lives. Nothing will be allowed to stand in the way of its realization.

2 The NIV translation "You want something" is not quite forceful enough to fit the context or to represent the Greek verb. *Epithymeite* expresses longing and eager desire. Buchsel says, "*Epithymia* is anxious self-seeking" (TDNT, 3:171). And in Exodus 20:17 (LXX) and Romans 7:7 *ouk epithymēseis* is the Greek translation of the tenth commandment, "Do not covet." So James says, "You eagerly desire something, but you don't get it." So strong is the desire that "you kill and covet."

This last statement has aroused much discussion. First, it is difficult to believe that James's readers, whom he elsewhere addresses as Christians (2:1), were actually guilty of murder. Some, insisting that the word must be taken literally, say that James is not referring to any specific occurrences but is indicating what happens when men desire pleasure rather than God (Ropes, p. 255). This interpretation, however, does not do justice to the pointed accusation "You kill." In the context of forceful words such as *polemoi* ("wars") and *machai* ("battles"), it seems better to take *phoneuete* ("you kill") as hyperbole for hatred. This also resolves the problem of seeming anticlimactic word order. To say "You hate and covet" is a much more natural order than to say "You murder and covet." Furthermore, Matthew 5:21–22 and 1 John 3:15 show that hatred is equal to murder. James repeats his assertion that, with all their consuming desire and bitter antagonism, his readers were not able to obtain what they wanted. The reason was that they were going after it in the wrong way. They did "not ask God" for it. They were lusting and fighting rather than praying.

3 And even when James's readers did ask God for things, they did "not receive" what they requested. Why? They asked "with wrong motives." Their purpose was to "spend" (*dapanēsēte*) what they got for pleasure. The prodigal son exemplifies one who spent (same Gr. verb) his money in this way (Luke 15:14). "Pleasures" (*hēdonais*) is the same word translated "desires" in v.1. It was the desire of James's readers for pleasures that was battling within them for satisfaction (v.1) and even leading them to try to use prayer as a means of gratification (v.3). They were not actually asking for gratification but for things, such as money, that they intended to use for pleasure. They wanted to gratify themselves rather than help others and please God.

4 Having identified the source of the bitter fighting as being the desire for pleasure (4:1–3), James next rebukes his readers for spiritual unfaithfulness (4:4–6). The noun translated "adulterous people" is feminine, meaning "adulteresses." The people of God in the OT are considered the wife of the Lord (Jer 31:32), and in the NT, the bride of Christ (Eph 5:23–32). It is reasonable, therefore, to understand "adulteress" as a figure of speech for spiritual unfaithfulness. It is a blunt and shocking word, intended to jar the reader and awaken him to his true spiritual condition. The concept of spiritual adultery was no doubt taken from the OT (cf. Hos 2:2–5; 3:1–5, 9:1).

For the believer, however, there are two objects for affection: the world and God, and these two are direct opposites. James uses the word *kosmos* ("world"), as do Paul and John, to refer to the system of evil controlled by Satan. It includes all that is wicked and opposed to God on this earth. James is thinking especially of pleasures that lure men's hearts from God. By its very nature, then, "friendship with the world is hatred toward God." To have a warm, familiar attitude toward this evil world is to be on good terms with God's enemy. It is to adopt the world's set of values and want what the world wants instead of choosing according to divine standards. The person who deliberately "chooses [*boulēthē*] to be a friend of the world" by that choice "becomes an enemy of God."

5 This verse is one of the most difficult in the epistle. Various translations have been suggested, but there is good reason to believe that the translation given in the NIV footnote for the last part of the verse is correct, "that God jealously longs for the spirit that he made to live in us." This rendering fits the immediate context better than the

NIV text, "that the spirit he caused to live in us tends toward envy." Verse 4, which is closely tied to v.5 by the conjunction "or," indicates that the believer who is a friend of the world is guilty of spiritual adultery. Although his love and devotion belong to God, he has fallen in love with the world. It is natural, therefore, to expect v.5 to speak of God's jealous longing for his people's love, rather than of their envious spirit. And there are OT passages that refer to God as jealously desiring the devotion of his people. Since there is no passage of which James 4:5 is a verbatim quotation, it is best to understand it as giving the gist of such passages as Exodus 20:5 and 34:14.

A second reason for preferring the NIV footnote rendering is that it more accurately represents the Greek text. It is true that the words *pros phthonon* can literally mean "to envy," but BAG indicates that this phrase was a Greek adverbial idiom meaning "jealously" (p. 718; cf. Ropes, p. 262). Furthermore, the Greek verb *epipothei* is not adequately represented by "tends." *Epipothei* means "to long for," "to yearn for" something or someone. It is much better, therefore, to translate *pros phthonon epipothei* as "longs jealously for." Thus, in v.4 James has accused his readers of spiritual unfaithfulness. If they are not willing to accept this indictment, he asks in v.5 what they think about the OT passages dealing with God's jealous longing for his people. This is the significance of the introductory conjunction "or." Do they think Scripture speaks "without reason" or emptily? Of course they don't think this. Consequently, it is necessary to believe that friendship with the world is enmity toward God, and thus it is spiritual unfaithfulness.

6 NIV makes the words "but he gives more grace" a part of the question of v.5. However, this arrangement is contrary to almost all other current translations of the verse. It should be noted that the words "he gives more grace" are not found in the OT in connection with any statement about the jealousy of God. Instead, they are taken from Proverbs 3:34, which is quoted in the latter part of James 4:6. It is better, therefore, to end v.5 with a question mark and to make the clause "but he gives more grace" a new sentence. The meaning of vv.4–6 would then be that God has set a high standard for wholehearted love and devotion on the part of his people, but he gives grace that is greater than the rigorous demand he has made. This assurance is documented with a quotation from the OT. The point of the quotation, as James uses it, is in the second clause. The reference to the gift of grace looks back to God's demand for loyalty (vv.4–5). God in grace gives his people the help they need to resist the appeal of the world and to remain loyal to him. The reference to "the humble" constitutes the theme for vv.7–10, where James pleads for submission to God. "The humble" are the people who willingly submit to God's desire for them rather than proudly insisting on satisfying their own desires for pleasure (cf. vv.1–3).

7 The command to submit to God is the logical response to the quotation from Proverbs 3:34. This is indicated by the word "then" (*oun*), which has the inferential meaning of "therefore." Since "God opposes the proud" but helps "the humble," believers should submit to him. Submission is not the same as obedience. Instead, it is the surrender of one's will, which leads to obedience.

James issues a series of ten commands in vv.7–10 ("submit," "resist" [v.7]; "come near," "wash," "purify" [v.8]; "grieve," "mourn," "wail," "change" [v.9]; "humble" [v.10]). In each instance the Greek aorist imperative calls for immediate response. It is a pointed and forceful way to demand action. Rather than resisting God's will for us, we should "resist the devil." James seems to suggest that the spiritual unfaithfulness of v.4 was the result of the devil's influence. The promise "he will flee from you" gives assurance that, as powerful as he may be, Satan can be resisted.

8 The series of imperatives continues with the command "Come near to God." In setting their hearts on pleasure, James's readers had drifted away from God. Though still his people, they had become estranged from him. But the assurance that God will welcome them back accompanies the command to return. God jealously yearns for their devotion (v.5). The call to "wash your hands" is a command to make one's conduct pure. Similarly, the call to "purify your hearts" insists on purity of thoughts and motives. The eager quest for pleasure (vv.1–5) had resulted in sins of heart and hand. So James bluntly addresses them as "you sinners," a strong term, showing the extent of their involvement in worldly attitudes and actions. The designation "double-minded" is used somewhat differently than in 1:8. Here it describes the attempt of the readers to love God and the pleasures of the world at the same time.

9 Four of the ten imperatives of vv.7–10 occur in this verse, and all four are calls to repentance. *Talaipōrēsate* ("grieve") is a strong word meaning "to be miserable," "to be wretched." In contrast to the worldly pleasures they had sought so eagerly, James's readers are to repent in misery. They also are commanded to "mourn." This verb (*pentheō*) usually depicts passionate grief that cannot be hidden. Similar outward grief is called for in the verb *klausate* ("wail"). In the past, when the readers had pursued pleasure, their lives had been marked by "laughter" and "joy"; but now they are to change their "laughter to mourning" and their "joy to gloom." Some have imagined that the attitude expressed in this verse is to be the constant characteristic of the Christian. Such an interpretation, however, overlooks the situation that gave rise to these commands. It was the burning desire for pleasures that led James to issue this powerful call to all-out repentance.

10 With the words "humble yourselves," James returns to the text quoted from the OT (cf. v.6). God graciously gives aid to the humble; therefore "humble yourselves." Here the specific form of humbling is that of repentance for the sin of transferring affections from God to pleasures of the world. However, the principle stated in this verse is much more comprehensive in its application. That God exalts those who humble themselves is a consistent biblical principle (cf. Matt 23:12; Luke 14:11; 18:14; Phil 2:5–11; 1 Peter 5:6.)

Notes

---

2 This verse has been punctuated in several ways. Many have a semicolon, a comma, or no punctuation after ἔχετε (*echete,* "you have"; NIV, "get") and a period or a semicolon after φονεύετε (*phoneuete,* "you kill") (RSV, NASB, NEB, TEV, Wms, Beck, AmT). This seems to necessitate a translation similar to the following: "You desire and do not have; so you kill. And you covet and cannot obtain; so you fight and wage war" (RSV). A number of others place a period or a semicolon after ἔχετε (*echete,* "you have") and a comma or no punctuation after φονεύετε (*phoneuete,* "you kill") (TR, WH, UBS, KJV, ASV, Mof, NIV). Three factors argue in favor of the latter punctuation. First, the necessity to supply the word "so" makes the former punctuation questionable. Second, the καὶ (*kai,* "and") before ζηλοῦτε (*zēloute,* "you covet") would no doubt have been omitted if the former punctuation had been intended. Third, the identification of φονεύετε (*phoneuete*, "you kill") as hyperbole for hatred removes the seeming anticlimax that gave rise to former punctuation in the first place.

4 The KJV reads, "Ye adulterers and adulteresses," following the TR. The MS support for this reading comes from the eighth and ninth centuries, with a host of minuscules from the ninth century on. The reading adopted by the NIV and most modern versions is μοιχαλίδες (*moichalides*, "adulteresses"), omitting the masculine μοιχοί (*moichoi*, "adulterers"). The textual evidence strongly favors the latter reading. In addition, Metzger explains the probable origin of the reading that includes μοιχοί (*moichoi*, "adulterers"). It apparently was inserted at a time when the words were understood literally. Being puzzled by the omission of reference to men, the copyists inserted μοιχοί (Metzger, p. 683).

IX. Faultfinding

4:11–12

> [11]Brothers, do not slander one another. Anyone who speaks against his brother or judges him speaks against the law and judges it. When you judge the law, you are not keeping it, but sitting in judgment on it. [12]There is only one Lawgiver and Judge, the one who is able to save and destroy. But you—who are you to judge your neighbor?

11 The prohibition introducing this verse would more accurately be translated "Do not speak against one another" rather than "Do not slander." Although the verb *katalaleite* may be used of "slander," it is a broader term than that. To slander is to make false charges or misrepresentations that damage a person's reputation. *Katalaleite* refers to any form of speaking against a person. What is said may be true in its content but harsh and unkind in the manner of its presentation. The grammatical construction used here (*mē* with the present imperative) usually forbids the continuation of a practice already in progress. James's readers had fallen into the habit of criticizing one another, and so he says, "Stop speaking against one another." The reason he gives is that the one who criticizes or judges his brother "speaks against the law and judges it." The law referred to is probably the command of Leviticus 19:18: "Love your neighbor as yourself." To speak against your neighbor is to violate this law. The person who does so places himself above the law and, by his action, declares that law to be a bad or unnecessary statute. Rather than submitting to it and "keeping it," he passes judgment on its validity and sets it aside.

12 In passing judgment, this critic of his brother has usurped a position of authority that is reserved for God alone. God is the "one Lawgiver and Judge." Since he gave the law, he is qualified to judge those who are responsible to keep it. That he is "able to save and destroy" is proof that he is in a position to enforce the law, rewarding those who keep it, and punishing those who violate it. God stands supreme as giver of the law and as its judge. The NIV's "But you—who are you?" catches the full force of the Greek construction. With shattering bluntness, James crushes any right his readers may have claimed to sit in judgment over their neighbors. This is not to rule out civil courts and judges. Instead, it is to root out the harsh, unkind, critical spirit that continually finds fault with others.

X. Arrogant Self-Sufficiency

4:13–17

[13]Now listen, you who say, "Today or tomorrow we will go to this or that city, spend a year there, carry on business and make money." [14]Why, you do not even know what will happen tomorrow. What is your life? You are a mist that appears for a little while and then vanishes. [15]Instead, you ought to say, "If it is the Lord's will, we will live and do this or that." [16]As it is, you boast and brag. All such boasting is evil. [17]Anyone, then, who knows the good he ought to do and doesn't do it, sins.

13 This section gives another example of the "wisdom" that characterizes the world (cf. 4:15). James addresses businessmen, probably Christians, since v.17 seems to suggest that the readers know that their practice is wrong. "Now listen" (*age nyn*) is a pointed call for attention that indicates the seriousness of what follows. The present tense *legontes* ("say") seems to indicate that the situation under consideration was not an isolated instance. It was something that occurred frequently. Business travel in the first century was very common, and Jews, especially, traveled widely for business purposes; NT examples are Aquila and Priscilla (Acts 18:2, 18; Rom 16:3) and Lydia (Acts 16:14). Notice the well-laid plan: (1) "go to this or that city," (2) "spend a year there," (3) "carry on business," and (4) "make money." The starting time is arranged—"today or tomorrow." The city has been selected—the Greek text simply says "this city" (*tēnde tēn polin*). But God has no place in the plans.

14 No allowance is made for unforeseen circumstances. These businessmen are confident that they will be able to carry their plans through to completion. And so James points out their fallacy. They "do not even know what will happen tomorrow," to say nothing about a year from now. They have been planning as if they know exactly what the future holds or even as if they have control of the future. Not only is their knowledge limited, but their very lives are uncertain. They may not be here next year. To point up the transitory nature of life, James employs another illustration from nature—"You are a mist." In the morning it covers the countryside; before noon it is gone. But some of James's readers had been planning as if they were going to be here forever!

15 Instead of saying, "Today or tomorrow we will go to this or that city . . . and make money" (v.13), the Christian businessman "ought to say, 'If it is the Lord's will.' " No Christian can safely assume that he can live independently of God. For a believer to leave God out of his plans is an arrogant assumption of self-sufficiency, a tacit declaration of independence from God. It is to overlook reality. Whether men recognize it or not, they "will live and do this or that" only "if it is the Lord's will." A study of the use of this conditional clause in the NT makes it clear that we are not to repeat it mechanically in connection with every statement of future plans. Paul, for example, employs it in Acts 18:21 and 1 Corinthians 4:19, but he does not use it in Acts 19:21; Romans 15:28; or 1 Corinthians 16:5, 8. Yet it is obvious that whether Paul explicitly stated it or not, he always conditioned his plans on the will of God.

16 Some of James's readers, however, rather than subjecting their plans to God's will, made it their practice to "boast and brag." To make plans without considering God's plan is the same thing as arrogantly claiming to be in full command of the future. The Greek text literally means "You are boasting in your arrogant pretentions" (*kauchasthe en tais alazoneiais hymōn*). *Alazoneia* refers to proud confidence in one's own knowledge or cleverness, hence, arrogance. It implies that these qualities are not really possessed (so Mayor, in loc.). The businessmen addressed by James were proud of their arrogant assumption that they could foresee and control the future. Some interpreters, however, have taken *en tais alazoneiais hymōn* to be adverbial, describing the manner of the boasting. But the verb *kauchaomai* ("to boast") followed by the preposition *en* ("in") occurs in sixteen other NT passages, and in every instance the prepositional phrase expresses the ground of the boasting (cf. Rom 2:17, "brag about your relationship to God"; 2:23, "you brag about the law"). Thus it is best to understand that it was about their arrogant pretentions concerning the future that James's readers were boasting. "Such boasting," says James, "is evil." It not only lacks the quality of being good, it is aggressively and viciously wicked.

17 Although this statement may apply to any number of situations, James intended it to refer to the immediately preceding context. He says, "Anyone, then, who knows." The word "then" (*oun*) introduces a concluding summary statement. Ropes suggests that it is a maxim that means something like "You have been fully warned" (p. 281). It is like saying, "Now that I have pointed the matter out to you, you have no excuse." Knowing what should be done obligates a person to do it.

Notes

14 Whether the text reads τῆς αὔριον ποία ἡ ζωὴ ὑμῶν (*tēs aurion poia hē zōē hymōn*, "what your life will be tomorrow") or τὸ τῆς αὔριον. Ποία ἡ ζωὴ ὑμῶν (*to tēs aurion. Poia hē zōē hymōn*, "what will be tomorrow. What is your life?") affects the meaning of the verse. NIV follows the latter as the best reading, which Metzger says is supported by "a wide diversity of witnesses" (p. 684). It should also be noted that a third variant has τὰ τῆς αὔριον (*ta tēs aurion*, "the things of tomorrow"), which may argue for the presence of an article, whether singular or plural. If τῆς αὔριον (*tēs aurion*) is adopted, the tr. of the verse must be somewhat as follows: "You do not know what your life will be like tomorrow. You are just a vapor" (NASB). This reading, however, has a built-in inconsistency, as Ropes points out (p. 278). It is not a question of what the conditions of life will be tomorrow, but of whether you will still be alive tomorrow. This is indicated by the statement "You are a mist that appears for a little while and then vanishes." The best reading, therefore, seems to be τὸ τῆς αὔριον (*to tēs aurion*, "what will be tomorrow").

XI. Denunciation of the Wicked Rich

5:1–6

[1]Now listen, you rich people, weep and wail because of the misery that is coming upon you. [2]Your wealth has rotted, and moths have eaten your clothes. [3]Your gold and silver are corroded. Their corrosion will testify against you and eat your flesh like fire. You have hoarded wealth in the last days. [4]Look! The wages you failed

to pay the workmen who mowed your fields are crying out against you. The cries of the harvesters have reached the ears of the Lord Almighty. [5]You have lived on earth in luxury and self-indulgence. You have fattened yourselves in the day of slaughter. [6]You have condemned and murdered innocent men, who were not opposing you.

In these six verses James first declares the fact of coming judgment (v.1) and then lists the crimes against which this judgment will be meted out (vv.2–6). Those crimes are four in number: hoarded wealth (vv.2–3); unpaid wages (v.4); luxury and self-indulgence (v.5); and the murder of innocent men (v.6).

There is good reason to believe that the persons referred to in this section are not believers. It might be argued that they are personally addressed in the same way other groups are addressed in previous sections (3:1; 4:13). Since the epistle in general is written to Christians, it might be assumed that the rich of 5:1–6 are Christians just as the rich of 1:9–11 are. However, there are significant differences between 5:1–6 and the rest of the epistle. These individuals are not addressed as "brothers" (cf. 1:2, 16, 19; 2:1, 5, 14; 3:1, 10, 12; 4:11; 5:7, 9, 10, 12). Furthermore, they are not called on to repent and change their ways but only to "weep and wail" because of the judgment they are going to undergo. It is, therefore, more reasonable to understand the section as similar to OT prophetic declarations of coming judgment against pagan nations. It will be noted that the latter also are interspersed among sections addressed to God's people (e.g., Isa 13–21, 23; Ezek 25–32).

1 That this verse begins a new section is indicated by the repeated call for attention: "Now listen" (cf. 4:13). The rich are to "weep and wail." While the first word, *klausate,* may describe audible weeping, the second term, *ololyzontes*, most certainly does. It is an onomatopoeic word that sounds like howling. In 4:9 James's readers are commanded to make themselves miserable (*talaipōrēsate,* "grieve") in all-out repentance. But here in 5:1 the rich are told that God will send the miseries (*tais talaipōriais*) of judgment upon them.

2 The first crime charged against the wicked rich is that of hoarding various forms of wealth. They have so much wealth stored up that it "has rotted"; their clothes also are moth eaten. Wealth in those days consisted of both money and such commodities as grain, oil, and costly garments. Evidence that costly garments were stored as wealth and used as payment for services rendered occurs in such passages as 2 Kings 5:5, 22; 1 Maccabees 11:24; and Matthew 6:19. Thus it was the commodities that had rotted and the stored garments that had been invaded by moths. There is no reason to take these happenings as figurative or as predictive of the future. The tragic fact was that the rich had hoarded so much food and clothing that it was going to waste. Their crime was uncontrolled greed that resulted in oppression of the poor (v.4).

3 An obvious form of wealth was "gold and silver," and this is said to have become "corroded." The Greek word *katiōtai* may refer to rust, tarnish, or corrosion. Since gold and silver do not rust or even corrode, James must refer to tarnished metal. The tarnish was indication of how long the hoarded wealth had lain idle. He warns the rich, "Their corrosion will testify against you." It witnessed to the greed and selfishness of these wicked men, who had far more than they could ever use, while their workers were deprived of their wages. The idea that the corrosion will eat the flesh of the rich "like fire" is a graphic way of declaring that their greed will result in their own destruction, as if the corrosion that ate their riches actually will eat their very flesh.

James's statement that the rich had "hoarded wealth in the last days" shows that he had the future judgment in mind. The NT regards the whole period between Christ's first and second comings as the last time or last days (Heb 1:1–2; 1 John 2:18). In comparison with the preparatory days of the OT, this is the last period before Christ comes to set up his kingdom and to judge all men. It was even in the last hour, as it were, before Christ comes to judge, that the rich "hoarded wealth."

4 The second crime the rich are charged with is that they "failed to pay the workmen" who harvested their crops. Here James vividly pictures the unpaid wages, still in the possession of the unscrupulous rich farmers, as continually accusing them of their dishonesty. It was as though the very coins cried out the guilt. The harvesters complained about their treatment, and their complaints "reached the ears of the Lord Almighty." God heard their cries as he always hears the voice of his suffering people (cf. Exod 3:7). The designation "the Lord Almighty" represents a Hebrew expression that literally means "Lord of hosts" or "Lord of the armies." In 1 Samuel 17:45 it refers to the armies of Israel. The word "host" is also used to refer to God's angels (2 Chron 18:18) and to all the stars (Deut 4:19). God is Lord of the armies of earth, of the angelic armies, and of all the starry host. This is a graphic way of declaring that God is almighty. The God who hears the cries of his suffering people is "the Lord Almighty," and he will vindicate them in due time.

5 The third charge against the rich is that they have lived "in luxury and self-indulgence." These two words (*etryphēsate* and *espatalēsate*) are synonyms, but there is a shade of difference between them. The first refers to a soft, enervating luxury that tends to demoralize. The second word describes extravagant and wasteful self-indulgence. Ropes says that in its secular use it seems to have had certain immoral associations (p. 290). In their unrestrained indulgence, the rich had "fattened" themselves. The Greek text says that they had fattened their hearts (*kardias*). The heart is viewed as desiring luxury and pleasure, and the rich are pictured as giving their hearts everything they desired. The "day of slaughter" is a designation of the day of judgment (Jer 12:3). James uses graphic imagery to indicate that the rich are on the brink of judgment. On the very day when judgment was due to come, they were fattening themselves, like cattle completely unaware of their impending destruction.

6 The final crime of the wicked rich was that they had "murdered innocent men." In 2:6 the rich are accused of dragging believers into court; here they are charged with murder. This is not to be taken figuratively but literally. Examples were Christ, Stephen, James the son of Zebedee, and, later, the author himself. The word *dikaion*, here translated "innocent men," literally means "righteous." It is that class of people who were known as the righteous that James had in mind. More than being "innocent," they were believers. And they came largely from the ranks of the poor. (cf. 2:5–7). The NIV translation "who were not opposing you" misses the bluntness of James's indictment. The Greek text abruptly declares, *ouk antitassetai hymin* ("He does not oppose you"). The rich were guilty of attacking not merely a righteous man but a man who was defenseless or who refused to fight back.

Notes

3 WH, RSV^mg, and Ropes place a period after τὰς σάρκας ὑμῶν (*tas sarkas hymōn*, "your flesh") and no punctuation after πῦρ (*pyr*, "fire"). Both RSV^mg and Ropes then tr. as follows: "And will eat your flesh, since you have stored up fire." Ropes argues that ἐθησαυρίσατε (*ethēsaurisate*, "you have hoarded") without an object is impossible (p. 287). However, the verb does occur without any possible object in Luke 12:21 and 2 Cor 12:14. Furthermore, "since" is not a normal meaning of ὡς (*hōs*); and the phrase ὡς πῦρ (*hōs pyr*, "like fire") goes with the preceding clause more naturally than with the one that follows. Consequently, the UBS punctuation is preferable.

XII. Miscellaneous Exhortations (5:7–20)

1. *Concerning Patience*

5:7–11

[7]Be patient, then, brothers, until the Lord's coming. See how the farmer waits for the land to yield its valuable crop and how patient he is for the autumn and spring rains. [8]You too, be patient and stand firm, because the Lord's coming is near. [9]Don't grumble against each other, brothers, or you will be judged. The judge is standing at the door!

[10]Brothers, as an example of patience in the face of suffering, take the prophets who spoke in the name of the Lord. [11]As you know, we consider blessed those who have persevered. You have heard of Job's perseverance and have seen what the Lord finally brought about. The Lord is full of compassion and mercy.

This exhortation concerning patience is built around three illustrations: the farmer (vv.7–9); the prophets (v.10); and Job (v.11).

7 The exhortation is addressed to the "brothers," indicating that James is turning his attention from the unbelieving rich back to the believing Jews to whom the epistle was sent. The word "then" (*oun*) suggests that the oppression of the righteous poor described in vv.1–6 is what gives rise to the call for patience in vv.7–11. In the former section James warns the oppressing rich of coming judgment; in the latter section he encourages the oppressed poor to "be patient." The verb *makrothymēsate* ("be patient") describes the attitude of self-restraint that does not try to get even for a wrong that has been done (so J.B. Lightfoot, *St. Paul's Epistles to the Colossians and to Philemon* [London: Macmillan, 1890], p. 138). It usually represents long-suffering patience toward persons rather than things (so Trench). So James calls for a patience toward the rich oppressors that will last "until the Lord's coming." The word *parousias* ("coming") was a common term used to describe the visit of a king to a city or province of his kingdom and thus depicts Christ as a royal personage.

The first illustration of patience is that of the farmer who waits patiently "for the fall and spring rains" (KJV, "the early and latter rain"). In Palestine the early rains came in October and November soon after the grain was sown, and the latter rains came in April and May as the grain was maturing. Both rainy seasons were necessary for a successful crop. Knowing this, the farmer was willing to wait patiently until both rains came and provided the needed moisture.

8 With the words "You too, be patient," James applies the illustration of the patient farmer. In addition, he urges his readers to "stand firm." The clause *stērixate tas kardias hymōn* literally means "strengthen your hearts," that is, be strong in the inner man. The verb has the idea of providing solid support, of establishing a person, and thus enabling him to stand unmoved by trouble. The reason given for standing firm is that "the Lord's coming is near." The day when things will be set right is imminent. This confident expectation will undergird the faint heart and make it strong.

9 The believers are to be patient toward both outsiders who oppress them and insiders who irritate them. Christians are not to "grumble against each other." *Stenazete*, translated "grumble," commonly means "to sigh," "to groan." It speaks of inner distress more than open complaint. What is forbidden is not the loud and bitter denunciation of others but the unexpressed feeling of bitterness or the smothered resentment that may express itself in a groan or a sigh. James uses the Greek *mē* with the present imperative to prohibit the continuation of this hateful practice. To continue it would result in judgment. And the Judge is represented as "standing at the door," as if his hand is on the latch, ready to enter at any time.

10 The second illustration of patience is that of "the prophets who spoke in the name of the Lord." In their position as his representatives, they experienced affliction (*kakopatheias*) and responded to it with long-suffering patience (*makrothymias*). Although James refers to "the prophets" as a group, Jeremiah certainly stands out as one who endured mistreatment with patience. He was put in the stocks (Jer 20:2), thrown into prison (32:2), and lowered into a miry dungeon (38:6); yet he persisted in his ministry without bitterness or recrimination. Such men constitute a model (*hypodeigma*) for believers who are oppressed and mistreated.

11 The third illustration is Job. "Those who have persevered" are considered blessed. No doubt James has in mind his words in 1:12, where he points out the enviable joy of the person who does not cave in under trial. In 5:7–10 the plea is for patience (*makrothymia*), the self-restraint that does not retaliate; but here in 5:11 it is *hypomonē*, perseverance in difficult circumstances. (For a brief discussion of this word, see the comments on 1:3.) It is significant that James does not speak of Job's patience, for despite the popular phrase "the patience of Job," he hardly exemplified that quality (cf. Job 12:2; 13:3–4; 16:2). He was, however, an outstanding example of perseverance in the most trying situations (cf. Job 1:21–22; 2:10; 13:15; 19:25–27). His experience also was proof that "the Lord is full of compassion and mercy," as we see in "what the Lord finally brought about" for him. Because Job persevered, God gave him "twice as much as he had before" (Job 42:10–17). To sum up, in James 5:7–11 the author is urging his readers not to fight back but to exercise long-suffering patience toward the rich who oppress them; and he is calling for stout-hearted perseverance in the trying circumstances that confront them.

2. *Concerning Oaths*

5:12

[12]Above all, my brothers, do not swear—not by heaven or by earth or by anything else. Let your "Yes" be yes, and your "No," no, or you will be condemned.

12 In addition to the preceding exhortations to patience and perseverance, James next places special emphasis on the prohibition of oaths: "Above all, . . . do not swear." As in v.9, the grammatical construction shows that the use of oaths was an existing practice that ought to be discontinued. James is echoing the words of Jesus in Matthew 5:34–37, which forbid swearing altogether. It should be obvious that what is referred to in Matthew and James is the light, casual use of oaths in informal conversation—not formal oaths in such places as courts of law. God himself is said to have taken an oath (Ps 110:4), and Paul sometimes called God to witness (2 Cor 1:21; Gal 1:20). Rather than employing an oath to convince people that a statement is true, the Christian should let his " 'Yes' be yes," and his " 'No,' no." That is, he should be honest in all his speech so that when he makes an affirmation or denial people will know it is unquestionably the truth. In the careless use of oaths a person is in danger of taking God's name in vain, for which he will come under judgment (cf. Exod 20:7).

3. *Concerning Prayer*

5:13–18

13Is any one of you in trouble? He should pray. Is anyone happy? Let him sing
songs of praise. 14Is any one of you sick? He should call the elders of the church
to pray over him and anoint him with oil in the name of the Lord. 15And the prayer
offered in faith will make the sick person well; the Lord will raise him up. If he has
sinned, he will be forgiven. 16Therefore confess your sins to each other and pray
for each other so that you may be healed. The prayer of a righteous man is powerful
and effective.

17Elijah was a man just like us. He prayed earnestly that it would not rain, and
it did not rain on the land for three and a half years. 18Again he prayed, and the
heavens gave rain, and the earth produced its crops.

This passage on prayer falls into two sections. Verses 13–16 constitute a call for prayer in every circumstance of life; vv.17–18 illustrate the effectiveness of sincere prayer.

13 One circumstance that calls for prayer is the experience of being "in trouble." Here James has used the verb form (*kakopathei*) of the noun *kakopatheias,* which he employed in v.10 to describe the trouble experienced by the prophets. When such an experience comes, the Christian needs patience. He is not to grumble in bitter disgust (v.9), nor is he to express himself in oaths (v.12). Instead, "he should pray." Patience comes from God, and prayer is an effective way to obtain it. James also urges anyone who is in good spirits to "sing songs of praise." This too is prayer.

14 Sickness is another circumstance where prayer is needed, and concerning such prayer James gives detailed instructions. The sick person "should call for the elders of the church." In Titus 1:5, 7 and Acts 20:17, 28 elders and bishops (or overseers) are equated. In Acts 20:28 the elders are instructed to shepherd (*poimainein*) the church of God; that is, to do the work of an overseer or pastor. That "elder," "bishop," "pastor" refer to the same office is also suggested in 1 Peter 5:1–4. Thus, the sick person is to call the pastors of the church "to pray over him and anoint him with oil." Prayer is the more significant of the two ministries performed by the elders. "Pray" is the main verb, while "anoint" is a participle. Moreover, the overall emphasis of the paragraph is on prayer. So the anointing is a secondary action. There are a number of reasons for understanding this application of oil as medicinal rather than sacramental. The word *aleipsantes* ("anoint") is not the usual word for sacramental or ritualistic anointing. James could have used the verb *chriō* if that had been what he had in mind. The distinction is still observed in modern Greek, with *aleiphō* meaning "to daub," "to smear," and *chriō* meaning "to anoint." Furthermore, it is a well-documented fact that oil was one of the most common medicines of biblical times. See Isaiah 1:6 and Luke 10:34. Josephus (Antiq. XVII, 172 [vi. 5]) reports that during his last illness Herod the Great was given a bath in oil in hopes of effecting a cure. The papyri, Philo, Pliny, and the physician Galen all refer to the medicinal use of oil. Galen described it as "the best of all remedies for paralysis" (*De Simplicium Medicamentorum Temperamentis* 2.10ff). It is evident, then, that James is prescribing prayer and medicine.

15 The assurance is given that prayer "will make the sick person well." In the final analysis this is what effects the healing. In answer to "the prayer offered in faith," God uses the medicine to cure the malady. The statement "the Lord will raise him up" means that the sick man will be enabled to get up from his sick bed. If it was sin that occasioned his sickness, "he will be forgiven." This suggests the possibility that, because of persistence in sin, God sent sickness as a disciplinary agent (cf. 1 Cor 11:30). The conditional clause "if he has sinned" makes it clear that not all sickness is the result of sin.

16 From the promise of v. 15 an inference is drawn ("therefore"). Since confession of sin and the prayer of faith bring healing, Christians should confess their "sins to each other and pray for each other." It is not merely the elders who are told to pray, but Christians in general. If a person has sinned against a brother, he should confess the sin to him. This will no doubt result in mutual confession—"to each other." Then the two believers should "pray for each other." If the sin has caused sickness, healing will follow confession and prayer. James proceeds to add the assurance that prayer "is powerful and effective." The "righteous man" here referred to is the man whose sins have been confessed and forgiven. His prayer is fully able to secure results, such as healing of the sick.

17–18 Verses 17 and 18 offer illustrative proof that a righteous man's prayer is "powerful and effective." "Elijah," James says, "was a man just like us." He had no superhuman powers; he was by nature a human being and nothing more. However, when he prayed "that it would not rain, . . . it did not rain" (cf. 1 Kings 17:1; 18:42–45). The explanation of his power in prayer is twofold: he was a righteous man, and "he prayed earnestly." So James assures his readers that such answers to prayer are within the reach of any believer. It is true that 1 Kings 17–18 does not explicitly say that Elijah prayed, but this may be assumed from 17:1 and especially from 18:42. The three and one-half years is a round number based on 18:1.

4. *Concerning the Wanderer*

5:19–20

[19]My brothers, if one of you should wander from the truth and someone should bring him back, [20]remember this: Whoever turns a sinner from the error of his way will save him from death and cover over a multitude of sins.

19–20 It is clear from the words "my brothers" that James addresses this last exhortation to believers. It is also apparent that he speaks of the possibility that one of them may "wander from the truth." Verse 20 gives reason to believe that the truth from which the wanderer turns is the saving truth of the gospel. James's purpose in these closing verses is to encourage Christians to make an effort to bring the wanderer back. Two worthy results of such an accomplishment are cited. First, it will "save him from death." That this cannot be physical death may be inferred from the literal translation of the Greek text: it "shall save his soul from death." So it would seem that spiritual death is in view. Since Scripture teaches that once a person is regenerated he can never be lost, it may be assumed that his hypothetical wanderer is not a genuine believer. He would be one who had been among the believers and had made a profession of faith, but his profession had been superficial. To bring him to genuine faith in the truth is to save his soul from eternal death. The result of bringing the wanderer back is that "many sins" will be covered. Genuine faith brings full forgiveness of the wanderer's sins; and they are covered, never to be held against him again. As difficult as it may be to win such a person to saving faith, the eternal results make it infinitely worthwhile. For a similar situation see Hebrews 6:4–8.

1 PETER

Edwin A. Blum

1 PETER

Introduction

1. Simon Peter
2. Authorship
3. Date and Place of Origin
4. Destination
5. Occasion and Purpose
6. Literary Form
7. Theological Values
8. Canonicity
9. Text
10. Bibliography
11. Outline

1. Simon Peter

According to the four Gospels, Peter was the leader and spokesman for the early disciples (Matt 15:15; 18:21; Mark 1:36–37; 8:29; 9:5–6; Luke 12:41; John 6:68). Peter's original name in Hebrew was "Simeon" (*šim*^{e}*ʿon*). James called Peter by this name at the Jerusalem Council (Acts 15:14; cf. v.7). The only other NT usage of Simeon is in 2 Peter 1:1. The Greek name "Simon" (*Simōn*), however, is applied to Peter forty-nine times in the NT. A third name "Cephas" (*Kēphas*) is a Greek transliteration of the Aramic word *kêpāʾ* ("rock"), which is the same as "Peter" (*Petros*). The NT, therefore, has four names for Peter. The combination "Simon Peter" (Matt 16:16) and the phrase "Simon who was known as Peter" (Acts 10:18) indicate that his new name (Peter) became his common designation.

Simon was one of the first disciples called into the service of Jesus (Mark 1:16–18). He was a fisherman from Bethsaida of Gaulanitis (John 1:44). Gaulanitis was the portion of the Transjordan immediately east of Galilee. Peter had a home in Capernaum (Mark 1:21, 29), which is about five kilometers west of Bethsaida, in Galilee. Peter was married (Matt 8:14; Mark 1:30; Luke 4:38) and took his wife on journeys to churches (1 Cor 9:5). His strong north-country accent marked him as a Galilean (Mark 14:70). Doubtless he was influenced by the preaching of John the Baptist; his brother Andrew was one of the Baptist's disciples (John 1:35–42).

Andrew introduced Peter to Jesus (John 1:42). Peter quickly became the leader of the twelve disciples, and his name always stands first in lists of them in the Synoptics. Of the twelve, Peter was one of the inner three (along with James and John) closest to Jesus (Mark 5:37; 9:2; 14:33). His preaching in the early days of the church (Acts 1–10) shows his great ability. The risen Lord appeared especially to him (1 Cor 15:5) and gave him a special commission (John 21:15–19).

Peter's leadership in the early church is not matched by his literary output. The NT contains only two letters that bear his name. Papias (c.60–c.130) (cited by

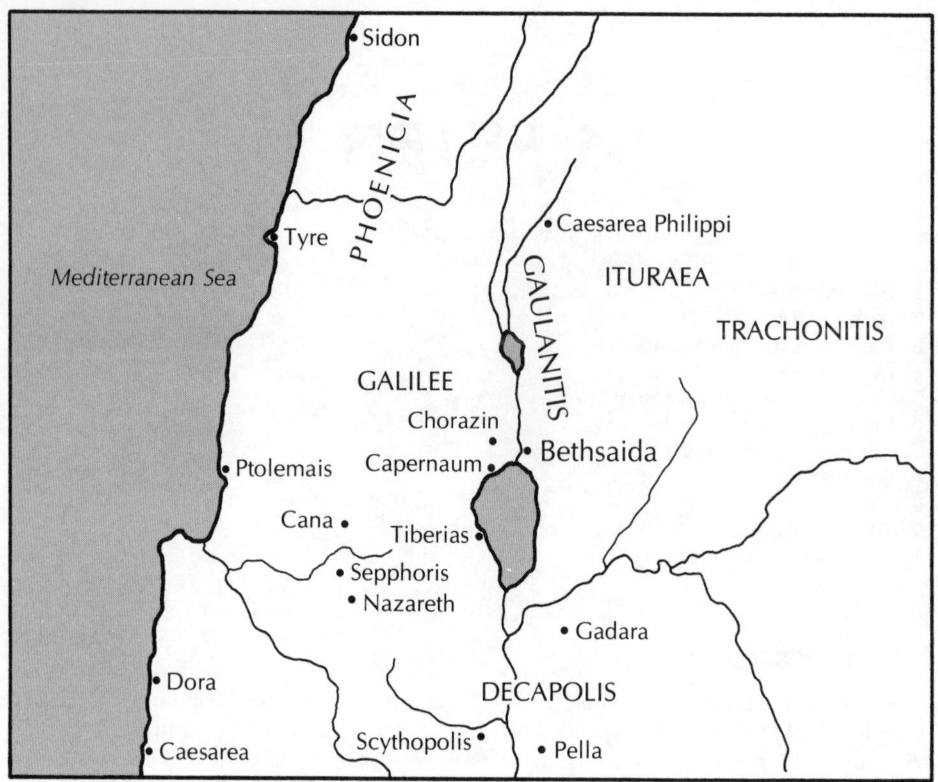

Eusebius *Ecclesiastical History* 3.39.15) and Irenaeus (fl. c.175–c.195) (*Contra Haereses* 3.1.2) state that Mark was the disciple and interpreter of Peter and that he transmitted in writing the things preached by Peter.

2. Authorship

This first letter claims to be from "Peter, an apostle of Jesus Christ" (1:1), who says he was "a witness of Christ's sufferings" (5:1). In addition, it states that he wrote it "with the help of Silas, . . . a faithful brother" (5:12). The reference is undoubtedly to "Silas" of Acts 15:22 and 1 Thessalonians 1:1. Also, the "Mark" mentioned in 1 Peter 5:13 appears to be the same man mentioned in Acts 12:12. Both such references as these together and the strong, early reception of the letter by the church (cf. Bigg, p. 15) led to the almost universal acceptance of it as from Peter, till recent years.

In 1945, F.W. Beare said, "The English reader is here offered for the first time a commentary based upon the thesis, now widely accepted, that First Peter is a pseudonymous work of the post-Apostolic Age" (p. vii). Beare followed the lead of the German commentators Gunkel, Knopf, and Windisch (ibid.). In his third edition (1970), Beare is more dogmatic, claiming that "there can be no possible doubt that 'Peter' is a pseudonym" (p. 44). He bases this claim mainly on his identification of the persecutions mentioned in the book with those of the reign of Trajan (98–117). Since Peter died under Nero's reign (54–68), he could not have written the letter. The dating of the persecutions depends on the commentator's judgment. As Beare says, "The justification of the thesis must depend upon the commentary" (ibid.). In other words, unless there are clear references to dated events in the letter, its dating must depend on (1) evidences of the dependence of 1 Peter on other NT writings, (2) evidences of the use of 1 Peter by later Christian writers, and (3) what sense the letter itself makes when viewed against a specific historical setting. The third factor involves the writing of a whole commentary to determine whether the data fit the supposition. The first two factors are discussed here.

1. E.G. Selwyn finds a variety of materials current in the mid-first-century church: creedal elements, hymns, sermonic forms, catechetical paradigms, and sayings of Jesus—these form a rich traditional deposit behind 1 Peter and other NT books (pp. 365–466). Beare holds that the literary relationship of 1 Peter to the Pauline letters "including the Deutero-Pauline Ephesians" (p. 28) is patent. Bigg (pp. 15–24) prints the parallels with the rest of the NT and concludes his discussion with the remark that "the evidence of style, vocabulary, phraseology does not appear to afford any conclusive evidence of either the absolute or relative date of 1 Peter" (p. 24). The parallels with Ephesians are notable, but what are the correct inferences from them? Beare calls Ephesians "Deutero-Pauline." If this were a fact, and if 1 Peter clearly quotes Ephesians, then a late date would be indicated. But according to Markus Barth, "Rome, about 62, is the best guess for the origin" of Ephesians.[1] It is possible that Peter read Paul's letters. (Second Peter 3:15–16 states that he did.) Did Peter, then, depend on Paul's letters? This is not probable in light of the fact that both Paul and Peter shared the heritage of the oral teaching of the early church. And even if Peter did utilize Paul's wisdom, this is no strong argument against Peter's authorship of 1 Peter. Paul's gifts were well known in the church (Acts 15:1–21; Gal 2:11–24). A good shepherd like Peter would give his sheep the best spiritual food.

2. The evidence for the use of 1 Peter by later writers is helpful but not decisive in fixing its date. The earliest attestation to 1 Peter is 2 Peter 3:1: "This is now my second letter to you." Since 2 Peter is commonly dated late by NT scholars, or since the reference to a "second letter" might not refer back to 1 Peter but to a lost epistle (so Spitta, Zahn), 2 Peter 3:1 does not solve the case. Bigg (pp. 7–9) gives lists of similarities between 1 Peter, the Epistle of Barnabas (c.130), and the writings of Clement of Rome (fl. c.90–100). Once again, the evidence is not clear enough to demonstrate that Barnabas and Clement used 1 Peter. It was not until Polycarp of Smyrna wrote to the Philippians (c.135) that actual citations of 1 Peter demonstrate that it must have been written some time earlier.

Another consideration that led Beare to the dogmatic position that Peter could not have written 1 Peter is that he finds it "scarcely imaginable" that Peter could develop the knowledge of the LXX, the Greek version of the OT (p. 45). In addition, the author of the letter was a master of Greek prose, while Peter, according to Acts 4:13, was "unlearned" (*agrammatos*). Beare (p. 47) argues that this word means "illiterate." But though *agrammatos* means "unable to write," "illiterate," in early Greek, it seems

[1]Markus Barth, *Ephesians: Introduction, Translation, and Commentary on Chapters 1–3* (Garden City, N.Y.: Doubleday, 1974), p. 51.

to have a wider meaning in later Greek. Here it can mean "uneducated" and perhaps "lacking in expertise concerning the law" in a Jewish context (cf. BAG, p. 13).

In response to Beare's objections, the following points are offered in support of Peter's authorship of this First Epistle. It is impossible to know to what extent Peter's home was bilingual. It is also very difficult to determine how much fluency in Greek a man like Peter could have achieved. Since use of Greek was widespread in the Middle East, one who was addressing Gentile converts would naturally use the LXX. As to the good literary style of 1 Peter, the book itself states that Peter used Silas as his secretary (5:12), and Silas might have had a part in shaping its style.

The positive case for Peter's authorship rests on these considerations: (1) The self-witness of the book is clear in claiming Petrine authorship. (2) The alternative of a pseudonymous letter is not without serious problems.[2] (3) The church's early and strong reception of the letter as Peter's cannot be overlooked. (4) The letter reveals none of the telltale marks of a late pseudepigraphon. (5) The letter makes good sense when taken at face value as by Peter. Kelley, while noncommittal about the letter's authorship, states that if certain arguments are accepted, "both contents and tone are fully consistent with apostolic times" (p. 31).

3. Date and Place of Origin

First Clement 5:4–7 names Peter and Paul as victims of persecution. The common understanding is that the passage refers to the persecution by Nero at Rome (cf. IDB, 3:755), which began after the disastrous fire in the city of Rome on 19 July 64. First Peter is written from "Babylon" (5:13). This is most likely a code word for Rome (cf. the commentary in loc.; cf. also the similar usage of "Babylon" in Rev 14:8; 17:5) as "the great city that rules over the kings of the earth" (Rev 17:18). If 1 Peter is a genuine letter of Peter, then it was probably written from Rome shortly before Nero's great persecution—that is, in 62–64.

4. Destination

First Peter is addressed to "God's elect, strangers in the world, scattered throughout Pontus, Galatia, Cappadocia, Asia and Bithynia" (1:1)—places in northern Asia Minor or modern Turkey (see map). Peter may have evangelized the northern region of Asia Minor while Paul founded churches in the southern and the western areas of Asia Minor. It is possible that Silas may have ministered in these northern provinces. The churches were no doubt composed of Christians from both Jewish and Gentile backgrounds. But the Christians outnumbered the Jews in these places. Jewish blindness to the gospel was a common phenomenon (cf. Acts 4:17–18; 28:25–28; Rom 10–11; 2 Cor 3:13–15). First Peter 4:3–4 (cf. commentary) supports the thesis that the majority of the Christians had been converted out of paganism rather than out of Judaism.

---

[2]Cf. D. Guthrie, *New Testament Introduction* (Downers Grove, Ill.: InterVarsity, 1970), pp. 786–90, esp. Appendix C: "Epistolary Pseudepigraphy," pp. 671–84.

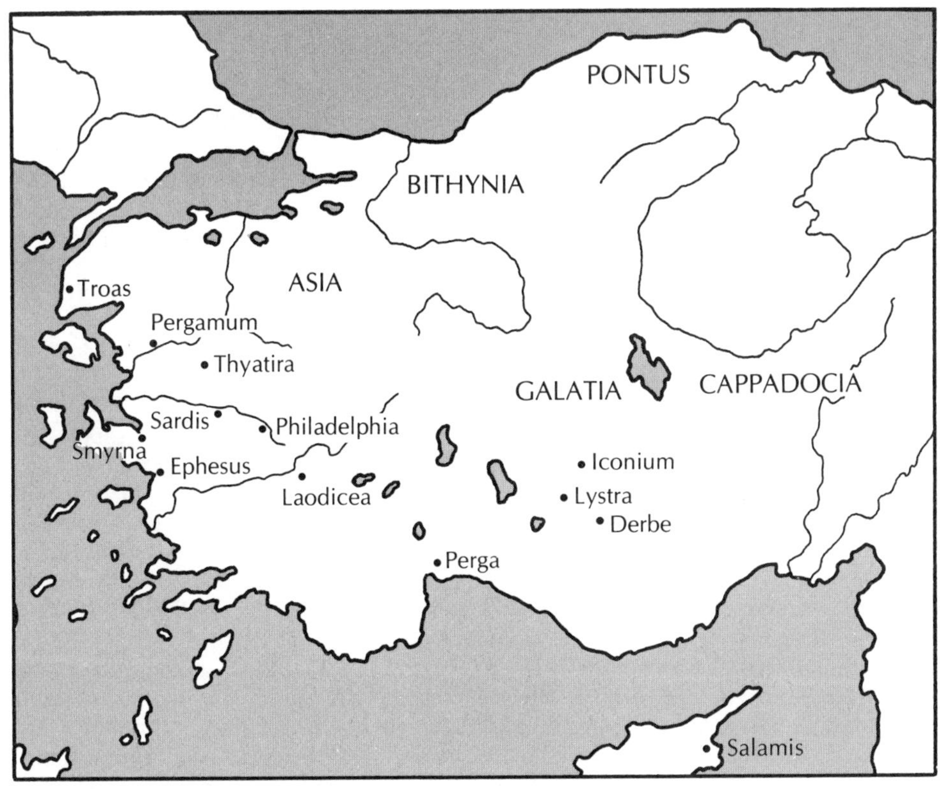

5. Occasion and Purpose

The tone of 1 Peter is a warm pastoral one, full of encouragement. The exhortations are addressed to Christians who are scattered over a wide area. They share a common faith with Christians everywhere and face common problems. Their basic problem is to live for God in the midst of a society ignorant of the true God. Because they are Christians, they are misunderstood and subjected to cruel treatment. Peter's pastoral purpose is to help these early believers see their temporary sufferings in the full light of the coming eternal glory. In the midst of all their discouragements, the sovereign God will keep them and enable them by faith to have joy. Jesus Christ by his patient suffering and glorious future destiny has given them the pattern to follow and also a living hope. Life in a pagan society is difficult and requires humility and submission. The immediate future for the church is an increase in the conflict with the world (*kosmos*) (4:7–18). But God will provide the grace to enable the community of the faithful to grow into maturity. They must help one another and show loving concern lest the members of God's flock be injured (4:8, 10; 5:1–2).

6. Literary Form

First Peter is an epistle, or letter, written in the normal letter form of the NT world. Many scholars have worked to isolate or identify creedal or hymnic fragments in 1 Peter. It has been viewed as a sermon or homily (e.g., a baptismal homily), a paschal liturgy, or even as an early Christian catechesis. (For a survey of these views, cf. Dalton, pp. 62–71.) The rhetorical and didactic nature of the letter may reflect the fact that it was intended to be read aloud to congregations (cf. Col 4:16; 1 Thess 5:27; Rev 1:3 for evidence of the practice).

This commentary takes the view that while Peter may have used material that existed in other forms (possibly material from his past teaching and preaching activity), yet these materials now form a letter the author intends to be intelligible apart from the knowledge of previously existing forms.

7. Theological Values

Although it is not a theological treatise, 1 Peter abounds with valuable theological implications. It presupposes a biblical world view based on God's sovereignty. This is God's world; yet the devil "prowls around like a roaring lion looking for someone to devour" (5:8). People who live in this world are subject to evil desires, ignorance, false gods, and all forms of sinful living (1:14; 4:3–4). God allows people time to repent of their sins, but the time for repentance is limited. He is gracious (5:2, 10), but he is also a righteous and holy Judge who will visit all people, living and dead, with their just deserts (1:17; 2:12, 23; 4:5–6, 17–19).

In common with the rest of the NT, 1 Peter presents a new eschatological perspective. With the coming of Jesus as Messiah, the age-old plan of God is on the way to its consummation (1:20). The writings of the prophets have found fulfillment in the death and resurrection of Jesus (1:11–12). Two major themes of prophetic teaching in 1 Peter are the messianic sufferings and the subsequent messianic glory. The first phase of the messianic times has already occurred! Jesus is the Suffering One who has died and has now been raised. The time is short, and Jesus must soon enter into his full glory. Already God has glorified him in heaven (1:21). All that remains is the final manifestation of the glorious Lord from heaven (1:7, 13; 4:13).

Christians are God's chosen people in an ignorant and rebellious world. In God's grace, the Triune God (1:2) is accomplishing in history a plan of redemption (1:20). The Father's role is extensive (1:1–3, 5, 15, 20–21, et al.) and is neither impersonal nor remote. The Spirit's participation in the salvation of humanity is also shown (1:2, 11–12; 4:14); but as in the other NT writings, the focus in 1 Peter is on the Messiah.

Peter regularly speaks of Jesus as "Jesus Christ" (1:1, 2, 3, 7, 13; 2:5, et al.), indicating his confession and that of the church (cf. Matt 16:16ff.). He also calls Jesus "Lord" (*kyrios*) (1:3; 2:13, 3:15) and recognizes the exaltation of Jesus (cf. Acts 2:36, where Peter, at the conclusion of his sermon on the Day of Pentecost, said, "Therefore let all Israel be assured of this: God has made this Jesus, whom you crucified, both Lord and Christ"). Peter does not develop the idea of the preexistence of Messiah.[3] Yet he declares that the Spirit of Messiah inspired the prophets (1:11) and that the Messiah was "foreknown" before the creation of the world (1:20). Peter implies the deity of Messiah (2:3) by applying Psalm 34:8 to him, where Messiah is called "LORD," which is the Hebrew "Yahweh." The ascription of a doxology to Jesus in 5:11 (if 5:11

[3]Cf. R.G. Hamerton-Kelly, *Pre-Existence, Wisdom, and the Son of Man* (Cambridge: Cambridge University Press, 1973), pp. 258–62.

is taken as referring to Jesus rather than to "the God of all grace" [v.10]) reveals his dignity and deity. Jesus is also called "a lamb" (1:19), "the living Stone" (2:4), "the Shepherd and Overseer of your souls" (2:25), and "the Chief Shepherd" (5:4).

In his sufferings, Jesus fulfills the OT Scriptures in types and prophecies. He is the spotless Passover lamb of Exodus (1:16–21), the Suffering Servant of Isaiah 53 (2:24–25), and the scapegoat of Leviticus (2:24a). He carries away the sins of people, takes the punishment on himself, and provides a new life of righteousness. Not only is his death a substitutionary atonement (2:24), but at the same time it provides a pattern for Christian living. Since Jesus was the Suffering Servant, his followers also have a vocation of suffering (2:21).

The key vocabulary in 1 Peter provides insight into one of the letter's distinctive contributions. Peter uses the word *anastrophē* ("way of life," "conduct," "behavior") six times; *paschō* ("suffer"), twelve times; *hypotassō* ("subject," "subordinate"), six times, and *agathopoieō* ("do good"), four times. When we consider these words together, we see that 1 Peter emphasizes the godly life of submission and good deeds in the midst of suffering. By their noble deeds, Christians may glorify God in difficulties (2:12). The sovereign Lord sustains them in adversity and has all power (5:10–11). Thus faith, submission, and trust provide the basis for Christian living.

Commentators have often discerned the close theological unity of 1 Peter with Paul's epistles (cf. Beare, p. 44; Selwyn, p. 363f.)—a unity ought to be expected in view of 2 Peter 3:15–16, which states that Peter knew and respected Paul's letters. Yet the unity between Peter and Paul should not be exaggerated as Beare does (p. 44–45) so as to make Peter dependent on Paul. For 1 Peter has none of the great Pauline emphases on justification by faith and the relation of the Jewish law and circumcision to Gentile Christians. First Peter has a distinctively pastoral tone with a strong emphasis on godly behavior in suffering. It is of great value for Christians today, who are still in a hostile world and many of whom in certain lands are suffering for Christ. A faithful witness for him can be costly, not only under repressive regimes but also in our more open society.

8. Canonicity

Eusebius of Caesarea (c.265–c.339) in his *Ecclesiastical History* (3.25.2) places 1 Peter among the books that were accepted by the church without any doubt (the *homologoumena*) and says that Papias (c.60–c.130) "used witnesses from the first epistle of John and similarly from Peter" (ibid., 3.39.17). There are probably traces of 1 Peter in 1 Clement (c.96) and even more in Ignatius, Hermas, and Barnabas (all in the early second century A.D.).

In his Epistle to the Philippians, Polycarp (c.70–150/166) unmistakably refers to 1 Peter. Though it is not in Marcion's (d.c.160) canon, this is hardly significant since Marcion's mention of letters is limited to the Pauline ones. It is not mentioned (by accident, as some—e.g., Zahn—think) in the Muratorian Fragment (c. late second century), which is in any case an incomplete document. Yet "it is reflected in the *Gospel of Truth*, which seems to use the books regarded as authoritative in Rome c. A.D. 140."[4] After the Polycarp reference, Irenaeus, Clement of Alexandria, Tertullian, and Origen all attest Peter's authorship of the book.

[4](A.F. Walls, NBD, p. 974; cf. p. 883).

There is no question of the canonicity of 1 Peter. It was accepted by the church because the church universally recognized its worth and authority. As Bigg (p. 7) states, "There is no book in the New Testament which has earlier, better or stronger attestation, though Irenaeus is the first to quote it by name."

9. Text

F.W. Beare, in the third edition of his commentary on 1 Peter, deals with the text of the epistle (pp. 1–24). It must be remembered that each book of the Bible circulated independently, and therefore each has a different textual history. The text of 1 Peter is reliable and is attested by 3 papyri, 16 uncials, about 550 minuscules, and a fair number of lectionaries. Until some more definitive work on the theory of textual criticism than UBS's eclectic text finds general assent, and until progress is made in the utilization of the mass of material, the commentator on 1 Peter can do little more than use the third edition of the UBS Greek text and its companion work by Metzger.[5] The earlier work of Tischendorf and von Soden should be supplemented by the materials in Beare's Introduction (pp. 1–24). Most notable is Beare's claim that there is no evidence for a "Western" text type in 1 Peter (p. 24).

10. Bibliography

For extensive bibliography, see Dalton, xv–xxiv, Goppelt, 11–26, Reicke, *Disobedient Spirits*, pp. 249–69, or Schelkle, pp. 249–55.

Balz, Horst, and Schrage, Wolfgang. *Die "Katholischen" Briefe*. DNTD. Göttingen: Vandenhoeck & Ruprecht, 1973.

Barnett, Albert E. *The Second Epistle of Peter*. Vol. 12. IB. New York: Abingdon, 1957.

———. *The Epistle of Jude*. Vol. 12. IB. New York: Abingdon, 1957.

Beare, Francis W. *The First Epistle of Peter*. 3d ed. Oxford: Basil Blackwell, 1970.

Best, Ernest. *I Peter*. NCB. London: Oliphants, 1971.

Bigg, C. *The Epistles of St. Peter and St. Jude*. ICC. Edinburgh: T. & T. Clark, 1901.

Blenkin, G.W. *The First Epistle General of Peter*. CGT. Cambridge: Cambridge University Press, 1914.

Calvin, John. *Calvin's Commentaries: The Epistle of Paul The Apostle to the Hebrews and The First and Second Epistles of St. Peter*. Translated by W.B. Johnston. Edited by D.W. and T.F. Torrance. Grand Rapids: Eerdmans, 1963.

———. *Calvin's Commentaries: A Harmony of the Gospels Matthew, Mark and Luke and The Epistles of James and Jude*. Translated by A.W. Morrison. Edited by D.W. and T.F. Torrance. Grand Rapids: Eerdmans, 1972.

Chaine, Joseph. *Les Épitres Catholiques*. 2d ed. Etudes Bibliques. Paris: J. Gabalda, 1939.

Clark, Gordon H. *Peter Speaks Today*. Philadelphia: Presbyterian and Reformed, 1967.

———. *II Peter: A Short Commentary*. Nutley, N.J.: Presbyterian and Reformed, 1972.

Cranfield, C.E.B. *I & II Peter and Jude*. TBC. London: SCM, 1960.

———. *The First Epistle of Peter*. London: SCM, 1950.

Cross, F.L. *I Peter: A Paschal Liturgy*. London: Mowbray, 1954.

---

[5](Bruce M. Metzger, *A Textual Commentary on the Greek New Testament*, corrected ed. [New York: UBS, 1975]).

Dalton, William J. *Christ's Proclamation to the Spirits*. Rome: Pontifical Biblical Institute, 1965.

Goppelt, Leonhard. *Der Erste Petrusbrief*. 8th ed. Edited by Ferdinand Hahn. KEK. Göttingen: Vandenhoeck & Ruprecht, 1978.

Green, E.M.B. *2nd Peter Reconsidered*. London: Tyndale, 1961.

______. *The Second Epistle General of Peter and the General Epistle of Jude*. TNTC. London: Tyndale, 1968.

Hort, F.J.A. *The First Epistle of St. Peter*. I.1–II.17. London: Macmillan, 1898.

Hunter, A.M. *The First Epistle of Peter*. Vol. 12. IB. New York: Abingdon, 1957.

James, Montague R. *The Second Epistle General of Peter and the General Epistle of Jude*. CGT. Cambridge: Cambridge University Press, 1912.

Kelly, J.N.D. *A Commentary on the Epistles of Peter and of Jude*. HNTC. New York: Harper and Row, 1969.

Lawlor, George L. *The Epistle of Jude*. Nutley, N.J.: Presbyterian and Reformed, 1972.

Leaney, A.R.C. *The Letters of Peter and Jude*. Cambridge: Cambridge University Press, 1967.

Mayor, Joseph B. *The Epistle of St. Jude and the Second Epistle of St. Peter*. 1907. Reprint. Grand Rapids: Baker, 1965.

Moffatt, James. *The General Epistles. James, Peter, and Judas*. MNTC. London: Hodder and Stoughton, 1928.

Reicke, Bo. *The Disobedient Spirits and Christian Baptism*. Copenhagen: Ejnar Munksgaard, 1946.

______. *The Epistles of James, Peter, and Jude*. AB. Garden City, N.Y.: Doubleday, 1964.

Schelkle, Karl H. *Die Petrusbriefe der Judasbriefe*. 4th ed. HTK. Freiburg: Herder, 1976.

Schlatter, Adolf. *Petrus und Paulus nach dem ersten Petrusbrief*. Stuttgart: Calwer, 1937.

Schneider, Johannes. *Die Briefe des Jakobus, Petrus, Judas und Johannes*. NTD. Göttingen: Vandenhoeck & Ruprecht, 1967.

Selwyn, Edward G. *The First Epistle of St. Peter*. 2d ed. London: Macmillan, 1947.

Sidebottom, E.M. *James, Jude and 2 Peter*. CB. London: Nelson, 1967.

Stibbs, Alan M. *The First Epistle General of Peter*. TNTC. Grand Rapids: Eerdmans, 1959.

Wand, J.W.C. *The General Epistles of St. Peter and St. Jude*. WC. London: Methuen & Co., 1934.

Windisch, Hans. *Die Katholischenbriefe*. HzNT. 3d ed. Revised by H. Preisker. Tübingen: J.C.B. Mohr, 1951.

11. Outline

I. Salutation (1:1–2)
II. The Privileges and Responsibilities of Salvation (1:3–2:10)
  A. God's Plan of Salvation (1:3–12)
    1. The praise of God for salvation (1:3–9)
    2. The prophecy of salvation (1:10–12)
  B. The Lifestyle of Salvation (1:13–25)
    1. A life of hope and holiness (1:13–16)
    2. A life of reverence before God (1:17–21)
    3. A life of love (1:22–25)
  C. Growth in Salvation (2:1–10)
    1. Growth through the pure milk (2:1–3)
    2. Participation in the temple and priesthood (2:4–10)
      a. Christ the Rock and the Christian living stones (2:4–8)
      b. The nation of priests (2:9–10)
III. Christian's Submission and God's Honor (2:11–3:12)
  A. The Noble Life and God's Glory (2:11–12)
  B. The Duty of Christian Submission (2:13–3:7)
    1. The submission to civil authority (2:13–17)
    2. The submission of slave to master (2:18–25)
      a. The submission of household slaves (2:18–20)
      b. The example of Christ's submission (2:21–25)
    3. The submission of Christian wives (3:1–6)
    4. The obligation of Christian husbands (3:7)
  C. The Call to Righteous Living (3:8–12)
IV. The Suffering and Persecution of Christians (3:13–5:11)
  A. The Blessing of Suffering for Righteousness (3:13–17)
  B. The Pattern of Christ's Suffering and Exhaltation (3:18–22)
  C. Death to the Old Life (4:1–6)
  D. The Life for God's Glory (4:7–11)
  E. Consolations in Suffering (4:12–19)
  F. The Shepherd's Suffering Flock (5:1–4)
  G. Humility and Watchfulness in Suffering (5:5–9)
  H. The Sustaining Grace of God (5:10–11)
V. Final Words (5:12–14)
  A. Silas's Role Writing the Letter (5:12)
  B. The Greeting From Rome (5:13)
  C. A Final Exhortation and a Prayerful Wish (5:14)

Text and Exposition

I. Salutation

1:1–2

[1]Peter, an apostle of Jesus Christ,
To God's elect, strangers in the world, scattered throughout Pontus, Galatia, Cappadocia, Asia and Bithynia, [2]who have been chosen according to the foreknowledge of God the Father, through the sanctifying work of the Spirit, for obedience to Jesus Christ and sprinkling by his blood:

Grace and peace be yours in abundance.

1 Peter begins by using his name in its most common NT form. His name in Hebrew was probably "Simeon" (Acts 15:14; 2 Peter 1:1 [Gk.]), the Greek equivalent of which was "Simon." He also had the Aramaic nickname of "Cephas" (John 1:42; Gal 2:11 [Gk.]). "Peter" is the Greek translation of "Cephas" or "rock." Cullmann suggests that to bring out the power of the nickname and to follow the common NT practice ("Simon Peter"), Peter should be called "Simon Rock" (TDNT, 6:101). "An apostle of Jesus Christ" indicates the dignity and authority as one selected by Jesus and given unique responsibilities of ministry in the establishment of the Christian church (Matt 16:18–19; Mark 1:16f.; 3:16; John 1:42; John 21:15–19).

As is common in Greek letters of the NT era, the writer first identifies himself, then identifies the recipient, and finally gives a word of greeting. Peter begins by designating those he is writing to as "God's elect." In biblical teaching, election is a central theme and the foundation of spiritual blessing (cf. Deut 4:37; 7:6; 14:2; Ps 105:6, 43; Isa 45:4; Eph 1:4–5). No believer should ever feel threatened by the doctrine of election, because it is always presented in Scripture as the ground of comfort. So here the designation of "elect" reminds the scattered Christians in danger of persecution that God's purposes for them are certain and gracious. "Strangers in the world" (*parepidēmoi*) points to the fact that Christians are "pilgrims" who do not reside permanently on earth. They belong to the heavenly realm (cf. Eph 2:19; Phil 3:20; Heb 11:13–16). The destination of the letter is "Pontus, Galatia, Cappadocia, Asia and Bithynia." These were the Roman provinces north of the Taurus Mountains in what is today Turkey.

2 Peter next announces some basic themes of his letter ("foreknowledge of God the Father," "sanctifying work of the Spirit," and "obedience to Jesus Christ and sprinkling by his blood") that will later be expanded and developed. Here he reminds his readers of their Triune faith and of the Triune work of God. While Peter does not go into the developed theological form of the Trinitarian faith, the triadic pattern of the Christian faith is already evident in his words. The "foreknowledge of God" is more than God's simply knowing what will take place in the future, for it includes God's special relations with mankind even before creation (cf. 1:20; Amos 3:2; Acts 2:23; Rom 8:29–30; 11:2). The "special relations" include God's election and his special plans for his people (cf. TDNT, 1:714). The "sanctifying" of the Spirit is his operation of applying the work of redemption to the Christian, purifying him and setting him to tasks of service. The goal of election and redemption is obedience that grows out of faith (cf. Paul's reference to "the obedience that comes from faith" in Rom 1:5). The salutation closes with the wish for the multiplication of God's grace and peace to the believers.

II. The Privileges and Responsibilities of Salvation (1:3–2:10)

A. *God's Plan of Salvation* (1.3–12)

1. *The praise of God for salvation*

1:3–9

> [3]Praise be to the God and Father of our Lord Jesus Christ! In his great mercy he has given us new birth into a living hope through the resurrection of Jesus Christ from the dead, [4]and into an inheritance that can never perish, spoil or fade—kept in heaven for you, [5]who through faith are shielded by God's power until the coming of the salvation that is ready to be revealed in the last time. [6]In this you greatly rejoice, though now for a little while you may have had to suffer grief in all kinds of trials. [7]These have come so that your faith—of greater worth than gold, which perishes even though refined by fire—may be proved genuine and may result in praise, glory and honor when Jesus Christ is revealed. [8]Though you have not seen him, you love him; and even though you do not see him now, you believe in him and are filled with an inexpressible and glorious joy, [9]for you are receiving the goal of your faith, the salvation of your souls.

The first major section of Peter's letter concerns salvation (*sōtēria*), the key term of this unit that occurs at 1:5, 9–10 and 2:2 but nowhere else in the book. Its basic meaning is "deliverance," "preservation," or "salvation" (BAG, p. 808–9). In 1:9 Peter defines his use of it as "the salvation of your souls" (cf. below). The section closes with an OT quotation, as the next major division also does (cf. 3:10–12).

3–4 The nature of this salvation as a new birth according to the mercy of God evokes praise to God the Father, who is the source of salvation. The new birth is the work of the Holy Spirit, as Jesus taught in John 3:3–8. The Christian has a "living hope" because Jesus has been raised by the Father (cf. Titus 2:13). This hope is further described in v.4 as an inheritance "that can never perish, spoil or fade." The concept of inheritance is one of the major Bible themes and stresses family connection and gift. As Paul wrote to the Galatians, "God in his grace gave it [the inheritance] to Abraham through a promise" (3:18; cf. 1 Peter 3:9; Matt 5:5; 19:29; 25:34; see also DNTT, 2:295–303). The inheritance is kept (*tetērēmenēn,* perfect tense) or reserved by God for his people in "heaven."

5 God's people are described as "the ones being guarded" (*tous phrouroumenous,* present passive; NIV, "who are shielded"). This stresses the continued activity of God in their lives, while the phrase "through faith" stresses the believers' activity. The divine protection and the final salvation are only for believers. The salvation "ready to be revealed in the last time" looks at the final aspects or realization of what Christians already have and enjoy.

6 "In this" (*en hō*) probably refers to anticipation of the future deliverance. As the Christian longs for his inheritance, he can "rejoice" (*agalliasthe,* which is best taken as a present indicative). Bultmann says, "God's help is always the theme of [*agalliaē*] which is a jubilant and thankful exultation" (TDNT, 1:20). The participle *lypēthentes* (grieve) is concessive, as the translation "though now for a little while you may have had to suffer grief" shows. The Greek emphasizes that the suffering is brief, for the present time (*arti*), and necessary (*ei deon*). The aorist participle also plays down the duration of the grief of the believer. That Peter uses *peirasmoi* ("trials") instead of *diōgmoi* ("persecutions") or *thlipseis* ("tribulations") is significant. While they are not technical terms (cf. BAG, s.v.), *diōgmoi* or *thlipseis* are not found in Peter's epistles. Peter is thinking in terms of the broadest category of the pagans' attitude toward Christians rather than of specific actions, and this may be an evidence of the early dating of the book.

7 Gold is one of man's most prized objects. When it is refined, its impurities are removed by a fiery process. Though extremely durable, gold belongs to the perishing world-order. Faith, which is more valuable than gold because it lasts longer and reaches beyond this temporal order, is purified in the tests of life. Gold, not faith, is presently valued by men. But God will set his stamp of approval on faith that has been tested and show this when Christ is revealed. Then the believer will openly share in the praise, glory, and honor of God.

8 Faith is directed toward Jesus Christ and produces love and joy in Christians. Without seeing Jesus (either because they were second-generation believers or because they were geographically removed), Peter's readers have come to love Jesus because they believe he has loved them enough to die for them. Christians do not rejoice because of sufferings but because of the glorious expectation of their future with Christ. "This is a mystery of faith contradicting everyday experience, and so the *joy* is *inexpressible*" (italics his) (Kelly, p. 57).

9 "For you are receiving" (*komizomenoi,* a present causal participle) gives the reason for the paradoxical joy while stressing that the anticipated salvation is even now in the process of realization. The "goal" (*telos*) or consummation of faith is "the salvation of your souls." No soul-and-body dichotomy of Greek thought is implied. The "soul" is used in the Semitic biblical sense of "self" or "person." Therefore the thought of this section closes with the believers' enjoyment of the future salvation in this present age.

Notes

3–13 A.B. du Toit has an instructive article on the argument here (cf. "The Significance of Discourse Analysis for New Testament Interpretation and Translation: Introductory Remarks with Special Reference to 1 Peter 1:3–13," *Neotestamentica* 8 [1974], 54–79).

6,8 Ἀγαλλιᾶσθε (*agalliasthe,* "you rejoice") may be taken as a command or as a future present. The indicative seems to fit the argument best.

---

2. *The prophecy of salvation*

1:10–12

[10]Concerning this salvation, the prophets, who spoke of the grace that was to come to you, searched intently and with the greatest care, [11]trying to find out the time and circumstances to which the Spirit of Christ in them was pointing when he predicted the sufferings of Christ and the glories that would follow. [12]It was revealed to them that they were not serving themselves but you, when they spoke of the things that have now been told you by those who have preached the gospel to you by the Holy Spirit sent from heaven. Even angels long to look into these things.

10–11 This salvation was the subject of the OT prophecies of the messianic sufferings and glories. The prophets not only spoke to the situation of their contemporaries, but they also spoke of the longed-for messianic times. In predicting the future, they did not always understand their utterances. The clearest example is Daniel and his visions (8:27; 12:8) and his study of other prophets (9:2ff.). The prophets longed to see the messianic time and so searched into what they could know of it (cf. Luke 10:24). The motivating force in prophecy is not the human will (cf. 2 Sam 23:2: "The Spirit of the Lord spoke through me; his word was on my tongue"; cf. also 2 Peter 1:21); it is the Holy Spirit. The content of the prophecies embraced both the "sufferings" and the "glories" of Christ (cf. Luke 24:26). Both words are plural. The gospels list various aspects of the predicted sufferings of Christ—e.g., hatred by his people, betrayal by his friend, being forsaken by his flock, his scourging and crucifixion, etc. His glories include his transfiguration (2 Peter 1:17), his resurrection (1:21), his glorious return, and his reign.

12 Through revelation the prophets learned that some of their utterances related to future generations. The writings of the prophets contain both "near" and "far" aspects. Yet the prophets were unable to understand the time significance of their prophecies or to understand fully the relation of the sufferings of the Messiah to his glory. Denial or ignorance of these things has led to denial of supernatural predictive prophecy. The word translated "serving" (*diēkonoun*) is significant, for it points to the fact that the writings of the OT are of service to the new community—the church. The unity of the OT and NT writings centers in Christ and his salvation. This message of salvation has come to humanity through men under the power of the Holy Spirit, who has come from heaven.

The last statement of v.12 is especially significant—"even angels long to look into these things." The Scriptures reveal that the angels have intense interest in human salvation. They rejoice at the conversion of a sinner (Luke 15:10); they observed Jesus in his early life (1 Tim 3:16); they will rejoice in songs of praise at the completion of redemption (Rev 5:11–14).

The verb *parakyptō* (NIV, "long to look") means "to stoop over to look." It implies willingness to exert or inconvenience oneself to obtain a better perspective. Here the present tense gives it a continuous aspect. The verb is also used in Luke 24:12; John 20:5, 11; and James 1:25. It means continuous regard rather than a quick look.

The Bible says nothing about salvation for angels. On the contrary, they learn about it from the church (Eph 3:10); and they serve the church (Heb 1:14).

B. *The Lifestyle of Salvation* (1:13–25)

1. *A life of hope and holiness*

1:13–16

[13]Therefore, prepare your minds for action; be self-controlled; set your hope fully on the grace to be given you when Jesus Christ is revealed. [14]As obedient children, do not conform to the evil desires you had when you lived in ignorance. [15]But just as he who called you is holy, so be holy in all you do; [16]for it is written: "Be holy, because I am holy."

13 "Therefore" (*dio*) relates this section to the former one, which is the basis of the commands in these verses. The general meaning is that the reception of salvation must issue in a life of holiness, reverence, and love. Moreover, since the prophets and the angels take great interest in this salvation, how much more should Christians pay careful attention to its results. The Greek syntax is significant. Peter used the indicative mood in stating the nature of the Christian faith in vv.3–12. In this section (1:13–2:5) he changes to the imperative. Most of these commands are in the aorist tense, and NIV correctly reflects their significance—e.g., "Set your hope" (1:13). The alternation of the indicative and imperative moods throughout Peter's writing differs from Paul's style. Paul tends to group his indicatives first and follow them with imperatives in the last portions of his letters (cf. Rom 12:1ff.; Eph 4:1ff.).

"Prepare your minds for action" (NIV) replaces KJV's literal translation "Gird up the loins of your mind." The figure is of a man gathering the folds of his long garment and tucking it into his belt so that he can move freely and quickly (cf. 1 Kings 18:46; Jer 1:17; Luke 17:8). Related uses of the figure occur in Luke 12:35 and Ephesians 6:14. Selwyn (p. 140) offers "Pull yourselves together" as a comparable English idiom. "Be self-controlled" renders the Greek present participle *nēphontes* and implies another figure. The original meaning of *nēphō* related to abstaining from excessive use of wine. In the NT its sense broadens to "live soberly"—a meaning that embraces sound judgment in all areas of life (TDNT, 4:936–38).

The main emphasis of v.13 is on putting one's hope wholly in the eschatological consummation of the grace of God in Jesus Christ. At the present time, we enjoy only a beginning of that grace. Now we are God's children, John wrote, but when Christ returns, we will be like him (1 John 3:2–3). This longing for the Parousia permeates the NT writings (cf. Acts 1:11; Rom 11:26; 1 Cor 15:51; 1 Thess 4:13ff.; Heb 9:28; James 5:8; 2 Peter 3:12–13; Rev 1:7; 19:11ff.; 22:7–20). For Christians, the consummation of this grace occurs at the unveiling of Jesus the Messiah at the second coming (1 Thess 4:13ff.).

14 The Christians' lifestyle is not to conform to the base desires that formerly dominated them and kept them from God. The imperatival participle *syschēmatizomenoi* ("do not conform") is passive (BAG, p. 803) and is found only here and in Romans 12:2 in the NT. (Ph's tr. of Rom 12:2 is a happy one: "Don't let the world around you squeeze you into its own mold, but let God remold your minds from within.") Peter exhorts Christians to control their desires rather than to be controlled by them. Formerly Christians were in ignorance; now they have come to know God and his will. They are to be "children of obedience"—a Semitic expression describing not only their quality but also their nature.

15–16 God is first described as the one who "called." Here the Greek verb *kaleō* ("call") implies the divine calling or what theologians term "efficacious grace" (cf. DNTT, 1:275). God is described as "holy." Holiness embraces purity and moral integrity. Those called to be God's children are to be like him. Peter reinforces this command by citing Leviticus (cf. 11:44–45; 19:2; 20:7). The basic idea of holiness in the Bible is that of separation from all that is profane. The developed sense of holiness includes various meanings translated into English as "purify," "sanctify," "separate from," "dedicate," etc. The simplest understanding of holiness is that of loving conformity to God's commands and to his Son (cf. 1 John 2:4–6).

2. *A life of reverence before God*

1:17–21

17Since you call on a Father who judges each man's work impartially, live your
lives as strangers here in reverent fear. 18For you know that it was not with
perishable things such as silver or gold that you were redeemed from the empty
way of life handed down to you from your forefathers, 19but with the precious blood
of Christ, a lamb without blemish or defect. 20He was chosen before the creation
of the world, but was revealed in these last times for your sake. 21Through him you
believe in God, who raised him from the dead and glorified him, and so your faith
and hope are in God.

17 In the Greek, this verse begins with *kai* ("and"), which links it with vv.13–16 and carries on the call to a lifestyle that is different from that of non-Christians. Peter reminds Christians that they invoke God as "Father" and that as his children (v.14) they should indeed call on him constantly in prayer. But God is Judge as well as Father, and those who call on his name must remember that he is impartial in judgment. Simply because some people call themselves Christians does not mean that all will be well for them in the Judgment. Justified persons are persons changed by grace and they must walk in good works as the evidence of grace (Eph 2:10).

As for sinners, they "will not stand in the judgment" (Ps 1:5–6). This means that at the Last Judgment the unregenerate will be doomed. The regenerate will have their lives evaluated by God also (Rom 14:10–12; 1 Cor 3:13–17; 2 Cor 5:10) and will receive according to what they have done. Justified persons, however, cannot be condemned (Rom 8:1, 34). But only the Lord who knows the hearts knows who the justified are.

Since judgment is certain, Christians are to live in reverential awe of God—yet not in terror, for peace is one of their prerogatives (1 Peter 1:2). The Christian life is a temporary stay on this earth (cf. comments on 1:1). So the brief time granted us should be used carefully (cf. TDNT, 5:848–53).

18–19 "For you know" translates the Greek participle *eidotes* and is grammatically subordinate to the command "Live your lives" (*anastraphēte*) of v.17. The logic is "Live . . . because you know!" That is, the Christian life is lived out of knowledge of the redemption that Christ has accomplished. What do Christians know? Peter reminds his readers of the cost of redemption. The value of redemption is the value of the Person of the righteous Messiah himself.

The Greek word *lytroō* ("redeem") goes back to the institution of slavery in ancient Rome. Any representative first-century church would have three kinds of members:

slaves, freemen, and freed men. People became slaves in various ways—through war, bankruptcy, sale by themselves, sale by parents, or by birth. Slaves normally could look forward to freedom after a certain period of service and often after the payment of a price. Money to buy his freedom could be earned by the slave in his spare time or by doing more than his owner required. Often the price could be provided by someone else. By the payment of a price (*lytron, antilytron*), a person could be set free from his bondage or servitude. A freed man was a person who formerly had been a slave but was now redeemed. (See A.A. Rupprecht, "The Cultural and Political Setting of the New Testament," EBC, 1:483ff.) Jesus described his ministry in Mark 10:45: "The Son of Man . . . [came] to serve, and to give his life as a ransom [*lytron*] for [*anti,* 'in the place of'] many."

The redemption of Christians is from the "empty" (*mataios*) lifestyle of their ancestors. This implies a pagan lifestyle rather than a Jewish one because the NT stresses the emptiness of paganism (cf. Rom 1:21; Eph 4:17; TDNT, 4:521–24).

Verse 19 stresses the value of the purchase price of redemption and at the same time identifies the blood as that of a spotless lamb—the Messiah. When Israel was in bondage in Egypt, the Passover lamb was killed and the blood provided release from bondage and judgment. Because Jesus is without sin, he is unique and his life is of infinite value as the Sacrificial Lamb of the Passover (cf. Exod 12:46; John 19:36; 1 Cor 5:7).

20 "He was chosen before the creation of the world." The Greek word for "chosen" is *proegnōsmenou,* often translated "know before." The meaning, however, must be more than "foresight." For why would Peter at this point make the obvious statement that God knew before about Jesus and his death? The word connotes purpose (cf. Rom 11:2). Kelly (p. 75) translates this clause as "predestined before the foundation of the world." The redemption was in the plan of God before Creation occurred. And now this redemption has been "revealed" in Jesus of Nazareth "in these last times." With the coming of Jesus, the last age has come (cf., e.g., Acts 2:17; Heb 1:2; 9:26). The salvation in Christ purposed from eternity is now made plain, Peter tells his readers, "for your sake." He personalizes it so as to spur them to a life of response to God.

21 The paragraph (vv. 17–21) closes with a statement about the believers' faith in God. Their faith in (*eis*) God comes through the work of Jesus because he is the one who reveals the Father (John 1:18) and because he is the means of reconciliation (2 Cor 5:19; cf. Kelly, p. 77). Peter identifies the Father (v. 17) as the God who raised Jesus and glorified him with the result that believers have faith and hope in God. Jesus' resurrection is the foundation of our faith, and his glorification is the pledge of the hope of our new future (cf. Rom 8:17–30; 1 Cor 15:1–11; Heb 2:10).

Notes

18 On redemption, cf. the following for the various words used in the NT: Acts 20:28; Gal 3:13; 4:4; 1 Cor 6:19–20; Eph 1:7,14; 1 Tim 2:6; Titus 2:14; Heb 9:12. See also, B.B. Warfield, "The New Testament Terminology of Redemption," PTR, 15 (1917), 201–49; Leon Morris, *The Apostolic Preaching of the Cross* (Grand Rapids: Eerdmans, 1955), pp. 9–59; and TDNT, 4:328–56.

For valuable background on slavery, cf. J. Scott Bartchy, ΜΑΛΛΟΝ ΧΡΗΣΑΙ" *First-Century Slavery and the Interpretation of 1 Corinthians 7:21* (Missoula, Mont.: Society of Biblical Literature, 1973).

---

3. *A life of love*

1:22–25

22 Now that you have purified yourselves by obeying the truth so that you have
sincere love for your brothers, love one another deeply, from the heart.
23 For you
have been born again, not of perishable seed, but of imperishable, through the
living and enduring word of God.
24 For,

"All men are like grass,
and all their glory is like the flowers of the field;
the grass withers and the flowers fall,
25 but the word of the Lord stands forever."

And this is the word that was preached to you.

22 In the third subdivision of this section on the Christian way of life, Peter adds to the command to be holy and to reverence God the command to love. This command is supported by two participles—one before and one after—that explain the reasons for Christians to love one another. The first participle (*hēgnikotes*, "now that you have purified yourselves") is in the perfect tense, stressing the state that results from regeneration. The word itself is not common in the NT nor in the LXX, but its sense is clear. It denotes the moral purity that comes to Christians through the gospel.

The means of this purification is "by obeying the truth," or obeying the gospel (cf. Acts 15:9: "He purified their hearts by faith"; Rom 10:16; 2 Thess 1:8). The Good News carries with it a command to repent and believe. In the early church, this was commonly tied to baptism. Not that the church believed that baptism itself saved; rather, it was the focal point of decision (cf. Acts 2:38). Being purified from sin enables Christians to show genuine family love for God's children. Yet this love is not entirely a foregone conclusion, because it can be and is commanded. Here the command is in the aorist tense, which often expresses "the coming about of conduct which contrasts with prior conduct; in this case it is ingressive" (BDF, par. 337).

This love is to be "from a pure heart" (NIV mg.). So Peter exhorts Christians—because they are purified—to love fellow Christians purely and fervently. Love for non-Christians is not in view here, but of course it is also part of Christians' obligations (cf. Matt 5:44; Luke 6:27, 35). The NT teaches that there are different kinds of love and different emotions of love. Yet Christians are enabled to love all people with agape love—viz., a self-sacrificing desire to meet the needs of others that finds expression in concrete acts (cf. 1 John 3:14–18).

23 The second reason for Christians to love others is expressed by the second participle (*anagegennēmenoi*, "for you have been born again"). This participle is also in the perfect tense and stresses the state into which Christians come at conversion. What is the "seed" that gives the new birth? Schulz claims that it is "the living and abiding divine word of baptism by which Christians are born again" (TDNT, 7:546). Others connect it with "the word" (cf. Luke 8:11: "The seed is the word of God") or with the "seed" of the divine life (1 John 3:9). Perhaps it is best explained as the life-giving message about Jesus' death and resurrection. Peter explains that the new birth comes through the living and abiding word of God. By the "word" (*logos*), he probably means "God's self-revelation," which would include both his spoken message and his written one. God's word is living because it imparts life (cf. Ps 33:9; Isa 55:10–11; Heb 4:12). His word endures because the God who speaks it is the eternal, faithful, powerful one who keeps his promises.

24 The quotation from Isaiah 40:6–8 supports the assertion of the character of God, with its stress on the abiding faithfulness of the Lord's statements. The quotation comes from the "Book of Comfort" in Isaiah as the prophetic message of God to an exiled and oppressed people. How fitting the application is to pilgrim Christians (cf. 1 Peter 1:1) in the light of their oppression by the pagan world! (And what Christian is not in some sense a pilgrim?) The theme of Isaiah's prophecy is the perishable nature of all flesh and the imperishable nature of the Word of God. To the exiles in Babylon, the message was that "human help is weak and perishable, but God's promise of restoration can never fail" (Blenkin, p. 41).

25 Here Peter gives us the application of Isaiah's words. In the Hebrew and in the Greek of the LXX, it is the "word of *God*" that is spoken of. Peter says it is the utterance (*rhēma*, not *logos*) of the Lord (*kyrios*) that endures. So he stresses the specifically Christian application, for Jesus is *kyrios*. The message about Jesus was proclaimed to Peter's readers, and it is utterly reliable. This message gives life and transforms life so that Christians are able to love.

Notes

---

22 After τῆς ἀληθείας (*tēs alētheias*, "the truth") most minuscules add διὰ πνεύματος (*dia pneumatos*, "through the Spirit"). If this reading is accepted, the idea of how a person is purified would be expanded to state the Spirit's divine working in regeneration-conversion. But most textual critics regard the reading as a later theological expansion introduced by a copyist (cf. Bruce M. Metzger, *A Textual Commentary on the Greek New Testament*, corrected ed. [New York: UBS, 1975], p. 688).

C. *Growth in Salvation* (2:1–10)

1. *Growth through the pure milk*

2:1–3

> [1]Therefore, rid yourselves of all malice and all deceit, hypocrisy, envy, and slander of every kind. [2]Like newborn babies, crave pure spiritual milk, so that by it you may grow up in your salvation, [3]now that you have tasted that the Lord is good.

This section (2:1–10) flows logically ("therefore," *oun*) out of the previous section. Peter uses a variety of images to describe the Christian life. He begins by speaking of "stripping off" habits like garments and then compares Christians to babies. Next he likens them to stones in the temple and finally to a chosen, priestly people.

1 "Therefore" points directly to the conversion of Peter's Christian readers, when they obeyed the truth of the gospel and were purified (1:21). "Rid yourselves" represents the aorist participle *apothemenoi,* not an imperative. This translation may be misleading because it implies that Peter is assuming that the Christians he is addressing have made a real break with pagan vices. But he is probably reminding them of their baptism, which was the focal point of their commitment to Christ, when they stripped off the old life and made a new beginning in repentance and faith. Vice lists such as this were common in the ancient world and also in the NT (cf. Mark 7:21–22; Rom 1:29–31; 13:13; 1 Cor 5:10; Gal 5:19–20; 2 Peter 2:10–14; and the appendix to Eric H. Wahlstrom's *New Life in Christ* [Philadelphia: Muhlenberg, 1950], pp. 281–87).

2 The young Asian Christians whom Peter addresses were, in the main, new converts, i.e., "new born" (*artigennēta*). A major characteristic of a healthy new baby is its instinctive yearning for its mother's milk. Christians are to crave what is "pure" (*adolos*) in contrast to the "deceit" (*dolos,* v.1) of the old life. The "spiritual milk" (*logikos gala*) is probably a reference to the Word of God (*logos*). Therefore the translation might be expanded to "crave the unadulterated spiritual milk of the word." The continuous nourishment from the "milk" causes the newborn to "grow up in [their] salvation." Salvation is the present possession of Christians as well as their future goal (cf. 1 Peter 1:5, 9). After conversion, their lives should be marked by continuous growth (cf. 1 Cor 3:1–4; Heb 5:11–14). This growth comes from the teaching about Christ and God the Father that is at the core of the Word, or the Bible.

3 "Now that you have tasted" has the Greek *ei* or *eiper* (lit., "if") introducing a first-class conditional sentence, which implies that they have tasted the goodness of the Lord. The image of "tasting" the Lord goes back to Psalm 34:8: "Taste and see that the Lord is good." In the psalm, the Lord is Yahweh. In his writings, Peter applies *kyrios* ("Lord") to Jesus, who is the exalted Lord. Once a person has come to taste the graciousness or goodness of the Lord, he should have a continuing appetite for spiritual food.

2. *Participation in the temple and priesthood* (2:4–10)

a. *Christ the Rock and the Christian living stones*

2:4–8

4As you come to him, the living Stone—rejected by men but chosen by God and precious to him— 5you also, like living stones, are being built into a spiritual house to be a holy priesthood, offering spiritual sacrifices acceptable to God through Jesus Christ. 6For in Scripture it says:

"See, I lay a stone in Zion,
a chosen and precious cornerstone,
and the one who trusts in him
will never be put to shame."

[7]Now to you who believe, this stone is precious. But to those who do not believe,

> "The stone the builders rejected
> has become the capstone,"

[8]and,

> "A stone that causes men to stumble
> and a rock that makes them fall."

They stumble because they disobey the message—which is also what they were destined for.

4 This section (2:4–8) is connected to the previous one by the relative clause *pros hon proserchomenoi* ("to whom coming"; NIV, "As you come to him"), by the continued use of Psalm 34, and by the concept of Christians' finding in Christ great value. So the figure changes. Now Peter presents Christ not as food but as a rock or a stone. The "rock-stone" imagery is common in Scripture. As Hillyer says, "There is, for example, the stumbling stone of Isaiah 8:14, the foundation-stone of Isaiah 28:16, the parental rock of Isaiah 51:1f., the rejected but vindicated building-stone of Psalm 118:22, the supernatural stone of Daniel 2:34, and the burdensome stone of Zechariah 12:3" (Norman Hillyer, " 'Rock-Stone' Imagery in 1 Peter," *The Tyndale Bulletin*, 22 [1971], 58). There is fair evidence that "Rock/Stone" was a messianic title among the Jews as well as among Christians (cf. Selwyn, p. 158–59; TDNT, 4:274–77).

"As you come to him" (*pros hon proserchomenoi*) probably reflects Psalm 34:5 (LXX 33:6, *proselthate pros auton*, "come to him"). Christians "come" to Christ in salvation, but their continual "coming" may also be included in the present tense. Jesus Christ is identified as the "living Stone," which refers to his stability as the risen Lord. God's raising of Jesus from the dead shows Jesus' value and God's choice of him. The "rejection" of Christ is, first, the valuation of Jesus by the nation (Matt 26:14–15; Acts 2:22–24; 3:13–15; 4:10–11) and, second, the current rejection of him by the disobedient in every land.

5 Jesus' great prophecy to Peter (Matt 16:18f.) concerned Jesus' building of his church. Peter sees, in the coming of individuals to Jesus the Rock, the building of a new spiritual edifice. Solomon was amazed at the thought of God's gracious condescension in dwelling among his people and in a house (temple) that Solomon built (1 Kings 8:27). Now the localized manifestation of God's presence on earth is replaced by his indwelling of all believers (1 Cor 3:17; 6:19).

"Are being built" (*oikodomeisthe*) is best taken as an indicative (NIV) rather than an imperative: "Be yourselves built" (RSV). The verb is to be understood as customary or timeless. Thus the thought is that when anyone comes to Christ, a new stone is added to the "spiritual" house. The use of the word "spiritual" does not mean that what Peter is speaking of is less "real" than a material house or material sacrifices. Rather, the material sacrifices and temples that were shadows of the reality to come are now superseded. The OT spoke of the offerings of prayer, thanksgiving, praise, and repentance (Pss 50:14; 51:19; 107:22; 141:2) in addition to the material sacrifices and offerings. The NT speaks of the offering of "faith" (Phil 2:17), gifts as "a fragrant offering" (Phil 4:18), "your bodies as living sacrifices" (Rom 12:1), "a sacrifice of praise"

(Heb 13:15), the conversion of the Gentiles as "an offering acceptable to God" (Rom 15:16), and Paul's coming death as "a drink offering" (2 Tim 4:6; cf. Schelkle, pp. 58–59).

The great new truth Peter states here is the revelation that "through Jesus Christ," i.e., through his work on the Cross, every Christian is part of a new priestly order. This truth of the "priesthood of all believers" was rediscovered and restressed during the Reformation. It means that every Christian has immediate access to God, that he serves God personally, that he ministers to others, and that he has something to give. It does not mean that each Christian has public gifts of preaching or teaching. In this verse Peter is stressing the reassuring fact that through Christ the believer is able to worship and serve God in a manner pleasing to him.

6 Next Peter cites Scripture to support his teaching. The quotation of Isaiah 28:16 refers to God's foundation stone, carefully chosen and very costly, placed in position in Zion. The picture is from the building of a temple. At great cost and care the corner foundation stone was obtained, moved, and laid. Hillyer mentions one stone in a quarry that was sixty-nine feet by twelve feet by thirteen feet ("'Rock-Stone' Imagery," p. 66, n.34). There are similar large foundation stones in many sites in the Middle East—e.g., Baalbek. Once this large foundation corner stone was in place, the rest of the building was determined. Isaiah uses this figure to encourage his people to build on the Lord himself, the one who is immovable and unchangeable, rather than on lies and falsehood. The applications of Peter's use of the figure are self-evident. God has set Jesus forth in Jerusalem as the foundation of the new temple. Whoever builds on this foundation will be established and will never be ashamed (cf. 1 Cor 3:10; Eph 2:20).

7 "Now to you who believe, this stone is precious." Here the Greek literally reads, "For you, therefore, who believe [is] the honor" (*timē*, cf. BAG, p. 825, 2b). The honor for Christians is linked to their union with Christ. Since Christ is honored by God, so will all who participate in Christ. But for unbelievers two other "stone" citations from the OT are strong warnings. The first is from Psalm 118:22, where the builders rejected a building block that later turned out to be the final stone in the building (cf. Mark 12:10–12; TDNT, 1:792; 4:278). In the same way, Jesus, who was rejected by men, has been exalted by God.

8 The second warning quotation is from Isaiah 8:14, where the disobedient are portrayed as stumbling over the stone. So Peter warns that those who refuse to believe in Jesus as Messiah stumble—"which is also what they were destined for." What is "destined"? The unbelief of men or the stumbling that is the result of the unbelief? It is common to argue that only the result or stumbling was ordained (so Beare, p. 126; Bigg, p. 133). Peter probably means to say that the appointment of God embraces both the setting forth of Christ and his work and the rejection by men. Peter's preaching in Acts 2:14–40 makes the same emphasis (cf. esp. v.23). Scripture in other places teaches that human disobedience is within the plan of God (cf. Rom 11:8, 11, 30–32). Yet it must be recognized that though human disobedience is within God's plan, it does not become less blameworthy (cf. Acts 2:23). It is important to recognize also that human disobedience is not necessarily final or irretrievable (cf. Hort, p. 123; Selwyn, p. 164–65). Paul says, "God has bound all men over to disobedience so that he may have mercy on them all" (Rom 11:32).

b. *The nation of priests*

2:9–10

[9]But you are a chosen people, a royal priesthood, a holy nation, a people belonging to God, that you may declare the praises of him who called you out of darkness into his wonderful light. [10]Once you were not a people, but now you are the people of God; once you had not received mercy, but now you have received mercy.

9 "But you" marks the contrast with the disobedient who were mentioned in vv.7–8. Peter applies to the church various terms originally spoken concerning Israel (cf. Exod 19:5–6; Deut 4:20; 7:6; Isa 43:20–1). But this does not mean that the church is Israel or even that the church replaces Israel in the plan of God. Romans 11 should help us to guard against that misinterpretation. Why then does Peter apply OT terminology to the church? He does so chiefly because of the conviction of the church that the OT writings are for it (2 Tim 3:16) and that these writings speak of Jesus and his times. The functions that Israel was called into existence to perform in its day of grace the church now performs in a similar way. In the future, according to Paul, God will once again use Israel to bless the world (cf. Rom 11:13–16, 23–24).

The title "chosen people" stresses God's loving initiative in bringing the church to himself. "Royal priesthood" may be understood as "a royal house," "a body of priests" (see Notes). Both titles stress the dignity of the church because of its union with Christ. Jesus is King, and all in his "house" belong to a royal house. Calling the church "a body of priests" emphasizes its corporate role in worship, intercession, and ministry. "Holy nation" shows that God has "set apart" the church for his use. The title "a people belonging to God" stresses ownership (cf. Titus 2:14: "A people that are his very own"). "That you may declare the praises" gives the purpose of grace to men. "The praises" (*aretai*) often mean his "self-declarations" or his manifestations to men (cf. TDNT, 1:457–61). So then the church is to "advertise" (Selwyn, p. 167) the noble acts of God in history and thus make him known. Specifically, the Father ("him who called" [cf. 1:15]) is revealed by Jesus in his death and resurrection. Light–darkness is a common dualism in the Bible to describe God–evil, good–bad, revelation–ignorance, new age–old age (e.g., Isa 8:21–9:2; John 1:4, 8–9; Eph 5:8; 1 John 1:5–2:2). Christians are once again reminded of God's action in bringing them out of darkness into his marvelous light (cf. Ps 34:5: "Those who look to him are radiant").

10 Peter closes this section with another free use of the OT. This time the words of Hosea (1:6, 9–10; 2:23) are put together. In their original context they describe God's rejection of disobedient Israel followed by future restoration to grace. Here Peter applies them to the salvation that has come to the Asian Christians. Once they were not a people (*laos* is used for Israel; the nations were *ethnē*), now they are "God's people" (lit. Gr.).

Notes

2:1–10 is extremely rich theologically, and a great amount of literature has been devoted to it in recent years. The most important is J.H. Elliott, *The Elect and the Holy* (Supplements to N.T. XII) (Leiden: Brill, 1966). See also Norman Hillyer's "'Rock-Stone' Imagery," pp. 58–81. Ernest Best, "1 Pet. II:4–10—A Reconsideration," NovTest, 11 [1969], 270–93.

III. Christian's Submission and God's Honor (2:11–3:12)

A. *The Noble Life and God's Glory*

2:11–12

> [11]Dear friends, I urge you, as aliens and strangers in the world, to abstain from sinful desires, which war against your soul. [12]Live such good lives among the pagans that, though they accuse you of doing wrong, they may see your good deeds and glorify God on the day he visits us.

11 This division of the letter deals with some practical implications of what it means to be God's people in a hostile world. Peter begins by reminding them of their position. He calls them "Dear friends" (*agapētoi,* "beloved") because they are bound together by Christ's love. Next he exhorts them as "foreigners and strangers." These titles are rich in content, going back to Abraham (cf. Gen 23:4; cf. also Ps 39:12; Heb 13:14; 1 Peter 1:1, 17). Christians are only in the world, not of it, for their true destiny is the renewed and redeemed earth in which righteousness will dwell. Therefore, they are not to derive their values from what is transitory. So Peter warns of the "passions" (*sarkikōn epithymiōn*) or "sinful desires."

The body's desires are not wrong or sinful in themselves, but sin perverts these desires; and the Christian is tempted to satisfy the bodily desires in ways contrary to God's will. "Which war against your soul" speaks of the warfare that is a mortal threat against the self (cf. TDNT, 7:712; 9:639). Schweizer calls this use of *psychē* in 2:11 "the most strongly Hellenized *psychē* passage in the NT" (TDNT, 9:653). The issue is whether we are to understand Peter as teaching that the sinful desires war against a part of a person (his soul) or against the whole person. Peter's usage of *psychē* elsewhere favors the understanding "against the person" in this location (contra Schweizer) (cf. 1:9 and comments). Peter's exhortation means that the Christian is not to participate in pagan immorality.

12 Instead, Christians are to have a "noble lifestyle" (*kalē anastrophē*) among the pagans. The purposes of the godly life of Christians are twofold. First, as the pagans take careful notice of our good works, they will not slander us. Second, in the future they will glorify God. What kind of charges did non-Christians make in Peter's time? Some of the more common were disloyalty to the state or Caesar (John 19:12), upsetting trade or divination (Acts 16:16ff.; 19:23ff.), teaching that slaves are "free" (cf. 1 Cor 13:13; Gal 3:20), not participating in festivals because of "hatred of mankind" (cf. Col 2:16), holding "antisocial" values, and being "atheists" because they had no idols (cf. Acts 15:29).

The meaning of "on the day he visits us" (*en hēmera episkopēs*) is problematic. Does Peter mean "on the return of the Lord" or "on God's gracious visitation of salvation that may come to the non-Christian?" In favor of the latter is the word "see" (*epopteuontes*), which suggests that the pagans will continuously observe the good works and perhaps God will grant them repentance unto life.

B. *The Duty of Christian Submission* (2:13–3:7)

1. *The submission to civil authority*

2:13–17

> [13]Submit yourselves for the Lord's sake to every authority instituted among men: whether to the king, as the supreme authority, [14]or to governors, who are sent by him to punish those who do wrong and to commend those who do right. [15]For it is God's will that by doing good you should silence the ignorant talk of foolish men. [16]Live as free men, but do not use your freedom as a cover-up for evil; live as servants of God. [17]Show proper respect to everyone: Love the brotherhood of believers, fear God, honor the king.

13–14 Submission (*hypotassō*; cf. 2:13, 18; 3:1) is the key theme of this section of the letter. The word in general means to "subject oneself." In this location, it is the acquiescence in the divinely willed order of society. NIV translates *anthrōpinē ktisei* as "every authority instituted among men." There seems, however, to be better reasons for understanding the phrase as "every human creature" (cf. TDNT, 1:366; 3:1034; Kelly, p. 130; Goppelt, p. 182). The noun *ktisis* in the NT always means "creature" or "creation." The thought is that of a Christian who does not seek his own interests but rather assumes a "voluntary ordination of [himself] to others" (Kelly, p. 109).

The reason for this submission is expressed in the phrase "because of the Lord" (*dia ton kyrion*). Is "the Lord" the Creator or Christ? The question does not seem to be correctly put, since the NT sets Christ forth as the Creator (John 1:1–4; Col 1:16; Heb 1:2). But if we ask whether the reference is to Christ in his creative activity or in his humiliation or exaltation, then the answer would appear to be that Christ in his lordship order as manifest in his creative activity is in mind.

Peter then mentions the rulers of the time. The "king" (*basileus*) is the title used in the East for the emperor who had the "supreme authority" among people. The governors (*hēgemones*) are the legates, procurators, or proconsuls charged with carrying out the imperial will of punishing the disobedient and rewarding the good.

15 Peter is speaking of ordinary situations and not of persecutions (cf., e.g., Acts 4:18ff.; 5:18ff.) when he speaks of governors as commending the good. Later in this epistle, Peter deals with the more difficult situation of governmental persecution of those who do good (3:14, 17; 4:1, 12–19). No government that consistently rewards evil and punishes good can long survive, because evil is ultimately self-destructive. It is God's will for Christians by their submission to the state authorities to "silence" (*phimoun*) the "ignorance" (*agnōsia*)—a kind description—of "foolish" men. The word *aphronōn* ("foolish") is a common biblical adjective for an obstinate sinner. Three different Hebrew words are commonly translated in the LXX by this Greek word (cf. Derek Kidner, *The Proverbs: An Introduction and Commentary* [London: Tyndale, 1964], pp. 39–42).

16 Christians are free because the service of God is freedom (cf. John 8:32; Rom 6:15; Gal 5:13). It is freedom from bondage to sin, Satan, and selfish desires. Christians are not to misuse their freedom in Christ and invoke "freedom" as a covering for wickedness. Christ himself said, "I tell you the truth, everyone who sins is a slave to sin"

(John 8:34). In Plato's *Gorgias* (491), the question is asked, "How can a man be happy who is the servant of anything?" The Christian response is that the service of God, who is the source of joy, is indeed perfect freedom, because Christ frees us from the bondage of sin.

17 Peter next sums up the social obligations of Christians in four succinct commands: (1) "Honor all men" ("Show proper respect to everyone," NIV). Here *timēsate* ("honor") is a constative aorist and is not to be taken as a general heading to be completed by the present tenses that follow (BDF, par. 336[2]). The honor is the recognition of the value of each man in his place as the creature of God. (2) "Love the brotherhood." Special love is due to others within the family of believers because they are brothers and sisters. (3) "Fear God." (4) "Honor the king" (*basileus*). God is to be feared, but the emperor was only to be honored. Christ taught, "Do not be afraid of those who kill the body but cannot kill the soul. Rather, be afraid of the one [i.e., God] who can destroy both soul and body in hell" (Matt 10:28). Normally duties to God and Caesar do not conflict, and Christians can obey both (Matt 22:15–21); but in special cases their higher loyalty is clear: "We must obey God rather than men!" (Acts 5:29).

2. *The submission of slave to master* (2:18–25)

a. *The submission of household slaves*

2:18–20

> 18Slaves, submit yourselves to your masters with all respect, not only to those who are good and considerate, but also to those who are harsh. 19For it is commendable if a man bears up under the pain of unjust suffering because he is conscious of God. 20But how is it to your credit if you receive a beating for doing wrong and endure it? But if you suffer for doing good and you endure it, this is commendable before God.

18 (On slavery, see the literature cited at notes, 1:18.) It is difficult for twentieth-century Christians to understand the slavery of the ancient world. During the time of the NT writings, slavery was not as bad as that practiced in America before the Civil War. Ancient slaves had fairly normal marital lives. Often people sold themselves into slavery (for a period of time) as a way to get ahead in the world. Nevertheless the lot of a slave could be very hard if the master was unkind. Here "slaves" (*oiketai*) means "house-servants"—i.e., domestic slaves. Their Christian duty was submission and loyalty to their master, even if he was harsh (*skolios*, "perverse").

19 Peter now motivates this. "For it," he writes, "is commendable"—i.e., a grace (*charis*). It is an attractive quality in the sight of God when because of conscience (or perhaps "consciousness" of God) a Christian slave puts up with pain as he suffers unjustly. (On the conscience, cf. DNTT, 1:348–53.)

20 To endure a well-deserved beating is nothing extraordinary. The word "beating" (*kolaphizomenoi*, "strike with the fist") is used in Mark 14:65 of Christ's treatment at his trial. However, it is "commendable" (*charis*) in the sight of God to do good and to endure suffering. The "commendable" thing is not the suffering but being so committed to God's will (the "good") that devotion to him overrides personal comfort.

b. *The example of Christ's submission*

2:21–25

[21]To this you were called, because Christ suffered for you, leaving you an example, that you should follow in his steps.

> [22]"He committed no sin,
> and no deceit was found in his mouth."

[23]When they hurled their insults at him, he did not retaliate; when he suffered, he made no threats. Instead, he entrusted himself to him who judges justly. [24]He himself bore our sins in his body on the tree, so that we might die to sins and live for righteousness; by his wounds you have been healed. [25]For you were like sheep going astray, but now you have returned to the Shepherd and Overseer of your souls.

21 Peter's exhortation for Christians to be submissive now receives a christological foundation. The "calling" (*kaleō*) is God's grace that brings them to salvation (cf. comments on 1:15) and includes the divine ordination in all aspects of their life (Rom 8:28–30), "because [*hoti*] Christ also [*kai*] suffered for you." The sufferings of Christ referred to here are exemplary as well as expiatory on behalf of Christians. "Leaving you an example" (*hypogrammon*, lit., "model, pattern to be copied in writing or drawing," BAG, p. 851) shows that Christ is the pattern for believers to copy in their lives. Just as in his life Christ suffered unjustly for doing God's will, so Christian slaves may have this calling. Servants are to follow their Master's tracks (cf. Matt 10:38; Mark 8:34; John 13:15).

22–23 The preeminent OT passage on the suffering of the Messiah is Isaiah's fourth Servant Song (Isa 52:13–53:12). Peter quotes Isaiah 53:9 to stress the submission of the innocent Sufferer. Other echoes of Isaiah 53 sound in the next verses—viz., 53:12 in v.24a; 53:5 in v.24b; 53:6 in v.25.

Throughout his earthly ministry, Jesus was reviled (cf. Matt 11:19; 26:67; 27:30, 39–44; Mark 3:22). In all these situations, he was ever the patient sufferer who was able to control his tongue. He committed his case to the heavenly Judge whom he trusted to give a just judgment. "Entrusted" (*paredidou*) is an imperfect tense in Greek, describing continual activity in the past.

24–25 Peter explores the sufferings of the Messiah more deeply. Peter has stated that Christ was patient and innocent. Moreover, his sufferings for us are indeed expiatory and substitutionary. He did no sin (v.22) and he "bore *our sins*"(v.24; cf. John 1:29). The exact figure is not clear. Some commentators see a reference to the scapegoat (Lev 16) and others to Levitical sacrifices (cf. Lev 14:20 LXX; Isa 53:12). Peter is probably looking at the basic ideas involved in the sacrificial system. The location of the expiatory offering was "in his body on the tree" (*xylon*, lit., "wood"; cf. Deut 21:23; Gal 3:13; Col 1:22). The purpose of the death of Christ is to produce new life in the believer. By means of Christ's death on the cross, whoever comes to him ends his old life and begins a new one devoted to righteousness (cf. Rom 6:1–14, 18–19; 2 Cor 5:14–15; Gal 2:20; 6:14).

"By his wounds you have been healed" is Peter's application of this precious truth from Isaiah to Christian slaves who had received lashes unjustly. Formerly they were straying sheep (Isa 53:6; Luke 15:3–7) but now they "have returned." The aorist (*epestraphēte*) looks at the decisive action in contrast to their former habitual wandering (*planōmenoi*, present participle; NIV, "going astray"). Jesus is now described as the "Shepherd and Overseer of your souls." (For Jesus as shepherd, cf. TDNT, 6:486–98.)

3. *The submission of Christian wives*

3:1–6

> [1]Wives, in the same way be submissive to your husbands so that, if any of them do not believe the word, they may be won over without talk by the behavior of their wives, [2]when they see the purity and reverence of your lives. [3]Your beauty should not come from outward adornment, such as braided hair and the wearing of gold jewelry and fine clothes. [4]Instead, it should be that of your inner self, the unfading beauty of a gentle and quiet spirit, which is of great worth in God's sight. [5]For this is the way the holy women of the past who put their hope in God used to make themselves beautiful. They were submissive to their own husbands, [6]like Sarah, who obeyed Abraham and called him her master. You are her daughters if you do what is right and do not give way to fear.

1 "In the same way" (*homoiōs*) in both v.1 and v.7 points back to 2:13. Christian wives are not to be in subjection like slaves but rather the principle of Christian subjection to God's will relates to every class and every situation. Rules for wives occur in other locations in the NT (Eph 5:22; Col 3:18; 1 Tim 2:9–15; Titus 2:4–5). The order for family life in NT times was still clearly patriarchal. Yet in religious matters women are coheirs with men (v.7) when both come to faith.

The phrase translated "so that" (*hina kai*) introduces the purpose of the command. Literally the translation is "in order that *also*." Here the evangelistic motivation is added to the general necessity of the divine order. As the gospel was proclaimed, it was always possible for a wife to be converted before the husband. In such a situation where the man is disobedient to the gospel message (*tō logō*, lit., "the word"; cf. 1:23–25), he may be "won over" (*kerdainō*, "a missionary term," TDNT, 3:672–3) for the faith "without talk" (lit., "without a word") by the way his wife lives.

2 The husband will then observe purity of life (on purity, see TDNT, 1:122–24) lived in the "fear" (NIV, "reverence") of God. Kelly (p. 128) aptly cites Augustine's account of how his mother influenced his father. "She served her husband as her master, and did all she could to win him for you, speaking to him of you by her conduct, by which you made her beautiful. . . . Finally, when her husband was at the end of his earthly span, she gained him for you" (*Confessions* 9.19–22).

3–4 The divinely intended manner of life for wives is inward, not outward. Mankind constantly makes superficial value judgments: "Man looks at the outward appearance, but the LORD looks at the heart" (1 Sam 16:7). Many have taken Peter's words to be an absolute prohibition of any outward adornment. The early fathers Tertullian and

Cyprian did this, and many rigorists have followed them. But Peter's emphasis is not on prohibition but on a proper sense of values.

The "inner self" is literally the "hidden person [man] of the heart," or the character of a person. In biblical psychology the "heart" is the central psychological term and refers to the faculty where man relates to God and makes his basic decisions (cf. Prov 3:5; 4:23; 21:1; DNTT, 2:180–84). The Christian woman is to cultivate an inner disposition (*pneuma*, "spirit") of a submissive (*praeōs*, "meekness," as of Christ; cf. Matt 11:29) and quiet sort that is imperishable or "unfading"—an attitude God highly values. Today, when the world's values governed by materialism, self-assertion, and sex obsession are seeping into the church, Peter's words need to be taken seriously (cf. Isa 3:16–24).

5–6 Next Peter turns to the OT in support of his exhortation—first broadly and then from the example of Sarah. The major characterization of these women who were "holy" because they were set apart to God was their hope in God. They trusted the promises of God and longed for the messianic salvation (cf. 1:3, 13; 3:15; Heb 11:13). In so doing, they were habitually adorning themselves with an inner beauty.

The great model of womanly submission is Sarah, whose respect and obedience to Abraham extended to her speech—she "called him her master." Such terminology was not uncommon in the ancient world (cf. Gen 18:12). Peter does not hesitate to apply Sarah's example to his readers: "You are her daughters if you do what is right." The norm for wifely conduct should be submission to God and devotion to the development of Christian character. Moreover, wives are "not [to] give way to fear"; their submissive trust in the living God will keep them from undue apprehension.

4. *The obligation of Christian husbands*

3:7

> 7Husbands, in the same way be considerate as you live with your wives, and treat them with respect as the weaker partner and as heirs with you of the gracious gift of life, so that nothing will hinder your prayers.

7 Peter's instructions for the Christian husband are brief, probably because the family normally followed the husband's religious choice. Yet the husband needs instruction concerning the care of his wife for several reasons. The phrase "in the same way" does not refer to subjection to the wife but rather that the husband "likewise" in the relationship of marriage is to do everything possible to foster the spiritual life of the home. A harsh or unthinking Christian husband could cause a hindrance to the family's spiritual growth. The woman is called the "weaker partner" (*skeuos*, lit., "vessel"); but this is not to be taken morally, spiritually, or intellectually. It simply means that the woman has less physical strength. The husband must recognize this difference and take it into account. "As you live with" probably refers to sexual intercourse in addition to the broader aspects of living together. The husband is to show his wife "respect" (*timēn*, "honor") and not despise her physical weakness.

Men are also to remember that women are coheirs of "the gracious gift of life." The sexual function and sexual distinctions are only for this age. Women will have an equal share in the new age; and even now in the life of the new age, they experience the grace of God equally with men (cf. Gal 3:28). Men must also remember that selfishness and egotism in the marriage relationship will mar their relationship with God.

Notes

7 The exact metaphorical meaning of σκεύει (*skeuei*, "vessel") is disputed. In Gr. usage, it is a common term for the body as the container of the soul. In the rabbinic background, a Heb. equivalent of this word was used for "wife" or "sexual partner." The dispute regarding it extends to the exegesis of 1 Thess 4:4 as well as 1 Peter 3:7. For an extended discussion, cf. TDNT, 7:358–67.

C. *The Call to Righteous Living*

3:8–12

[8]Finally, all of you, live in harmony with one another; be sympathetic, love as brothers, be compassionate and humble. [9]Do not repay evil with evil or insult with insult, but with blessing, because to this you were called so that you may inherit a blessing. [10]For,

"Whoever would love life
and see good days
must keep his tongue from evil
and his lips from deceitful speech.
[11]He must turn from evil and do good;
he must seek peace and pursue it.
[12]For the eyes of the Lord are on the righteous
and his ears are attentive to their prayer,
but the face of the Lord is against those who do evil."

8 Peter brings his treatment of the duties of Christians, considered in various groupings, to a close with general practical advice for the whole community. His use of "Finally" (*to telos*) and his citation of Psalm 34:12–16 show the concluding character of this passage. In v.8 he gives several imperatives for Christians' getting along together; in v.9 he gives them a basic imperative for dealing with those who are hostile to them. The five virtues in v.8 have many illustrations in the life of Jesus and parallels in the other epistles. They are normative qualities every person united to Christ should manifest. (On "harmony," see Rom 12:16; Phil 1:27; 2:2; on "be sympathetic," Rom 12:15; 1 Cor 12:26; on "love as brothers," 1 Thess 4:9–10; for "be compassionate," see Christ's example in Matt 11:29; and concerning "humble," see Christ's example as set forth in Phil 2:6ff.)

9 Here Peter turns to Christ as the pattern for relating to a hostile pagan society. The natural response to hostility is retaliation. But Jesus in his teaching (Matt 5:44) and in his practice responded to hostility with grace (Luke 23:34; 1 Peter 2:21–22). What does it mean to "bless" our enemies? "Bless" translates *eulogountes,* which literally means "to speak well [of someone]." The word occurs over four hundred times in the LXX, often in opposition to cursing. H.G. Link suggests that "blessing here [1 Peter 3:9] means simply a friendly disposition towards enemies" (DNTT, 1:215). But the instruction and practice of Jesus and the apostles goes beyond a "friendly disposition" to active prayer and intercession (cf. Acts 7:60; 1 Cor 4:12). The great desire of Christians must not be revenge but for God to grant the gift of repentance to those who do not know him. The phrase "because to this" is not immediately clear. Does

Peter mean that intercession will bring rewards to Christians? Or that the calling of Christians to grace should make them gracious to others? The second seems best in this context.

10–12 "For" (*gar*) introduces an explanatory quotation that reinforces the teaching of non-retaliation. The source is Psalm 34:12–16, which Peter has already alluded to in 2:3. In the psalm, the "life" and the "good days" refer to earthly life and joys. Peter's use of these terms is not limited to this life but goes beyond it to eschatological salvation. Yet it is still true in this age that being gracious to others may lead to longer life and better days. On the contrary, a life of evil and strife may be shortened and marred. "The way of transgressors is hard" (Prov 13:15 KJV).

Christians should desire life in its goodness. Therefore, they must guard their ways and their tongues. Most importantly, they are to overcome evil with the good (cf. Rom 12:21). Since peace between people is elusive and hard to achieve, Christians must actively seek and pursue it. The fear (reverential awe) of the Lord provides a rationale for godly living and a warning to the wicked. Our "eyes," our "ears," and our "face" speak of our personal relation to God. The "eye" of the Lord over the righteous reminds us of his providential care for his people (cf. Exod 2:25), and his "ear" is open to our cries for help in prayer (cf. Exod 3:7). The "face" of the Lord is a Hebrew expression for "God's countenance, i.e., the side he turns to man" (TDNT, 6:772). Here it relates to his anger against evil doers.

IV. The Suffering and Persecution of Christians (3:13–5:11)

A. *The Blessing of Suffering for Righteousness*

3:13–17

> [13]Who is going to harm you if you are eager to do good? [14]But even if you should suffer for what is right, you are blessed. "Do not fear what they fear; do not be frightened." [15]But in your hearts set apart Christ as Lord. Always be prepared to give an answer to everyone who asks you to give the reason for the hope that you have. But do this with gentleness and respect, [16]keeping a clear conscience, so that those who speak maliciously against your good behavior in Christ may be ashamed of their slander. [17]It is better, if it is God's will, to suffer for doing good than for doing evil.

Peter's major emphasis in this letter is on Christian conduct under persecution (cf. Introduction: Occasion and Purpose). Especially from now on (3:13–5:11), this is Peter's chief concern. Dalton divides his treatment of 3:13–5:11 into two main sections (each with three subdivisions)—"Persecution viewed in calm detachment," 3:13–4:11; "Persecution faced realistically," 4:12–5:11 (pp. 72–86). These two headings capture the essence of the rest of the letter.

13 While suffering and unjust treatment have been in the background (1:6–7; 2:12, 15, 19ff.; 3:9), now they come to the fore. In the Greek, v.13 begins with "and" (*kai*), which shows the connection with the preceding section. If Christians have the zeal for good that Psalm 34 speaks of, who will do them harm? The "harm" Peter alludes to must be understood in the light of Paul's rhetorical question "If God is for us, who can be against us?" (Rom 8:31) and his reference to Christians as being like "sheep to be slaughtered" and yet being "more than conquerors" (Rom 8:36–37). Kelly (p. 140) cites an interesting parallel from Plato (*Apology* 41d) concerning Socrates before his judges: "No harm can befall a good man, either when he is alive or when he is dead, and the gods do not neglect his cause."

14 "But even if you should suffer" (*all' ei kai paschoite*) is a conditional clause in the Greek (fourth class) that has a "future less probable" sense. The use of this construction (optative) points to the fact that suffering is not the expected outcome of zeal for good. The suffering Peter is considering is that which results from righteousness—i.e., from the kind of life that conforms to God's standard. If this should happen to his readers, they are "blessed" (*makarioi*). This blessedness or happiness is the certainty that comes from belonging to God and his kingdom with the promises of future vindication (cf. Matt 5:3–10; "blessing" in DNTT, 1:215–17). The last part of v.14 and the beginning of v.15 are built on the words of Isaiah 8:12b–13:

> Do not fear what they fear,
>   do not dread it.
> The LORD Almighty is the one you are to
>   regard as holy.

In the Isaiah passage, the prophet admonishes the godly in Israel not to fear the impending invasion as the unbelievers in the nation do. Instead, godly reverence is to be their concern (cf. Matt 10:28).

15–16 So Peter admonishes his readers not to be afraid of men but acknowledge "Christ as Lord." This passage is important for Peter's Christology. The "Lord" as applied to Christ refers to "Yahweh of armies" in Isaiah 8:13. The literal Hebrew of "Yahweh of armies" is "LORD Almighty" in NIV. (See Preface to NIV [p. ix] for an explanation of the principle involved in its translation of "Yahweh of armies.") The Christians Peter is writing to are to acknowledge in their hearts Christ as the Holy One. In biblical revelation, the heart is the religious center of man (cf. DNTT, 2:180–84). When the center of one's life is rightly related to God, he is able to respond properly to the vicissitudes of life.

One of the distinguishing marks of Christians is their possession of hope (*elpidos*, cf. 1:3, 21; Rom 4:18; Eph 2:12; Titus 2:13; DNTT, 2:238–44). Christian hope is so real and distinctive that non-Christians are puzzled about it and ask for a "reason" (*logos*, "account"). The type of questioning could be either official interrogations by the governmental authorities—the word for "answer" (*apologia*) can relate to a formal inquiry (cf. Acts 25:16; 26:2; 2 Tim 4:16)—or informal questioning.

Christians should respond with care. "Gentleness" (or "meekness") is the quality that trusts God to do the work of changing attitudes (cf. 2 Tim 2:24–25; cf. also Prov 15:1: "A gentle answer turns away wrath, but a harsh word stirs up anger"). The "respect" (*phobos*, "fear") is reverential awe of God (cf. 1:17; 2:17; 3:2). The "clear conscience" relates to the liberty and boldness that come from living before God in purity (cf. Acts 24:16; 1 Tim 1:19). So in the case in which non-Christians slander believers the statement of the truth may shame them into silence (cf. Luke 13:17). "Speak maliciously" (*epēreazontes*) is a word classical writers used of false accusations; in the NT papyri it is used of "treating wrongfully" (MM, p. 232).

17 Peter next states that it is better to suffer for doing good than for doing evil. Suffering is a just recompense for doing evil. But if one does good and still suffers, there is no disgrace—if his conscience is clear before God—for he can have confidence that his suffering was not caused by his sin. There must be a providential reason for it—perhaps to prick the conscience of some and bring them to salvation. Or suffering may be a necessary prelude to glorification.

B. *The Pattern of Christ's Suffering and Exhaltation*

3:18–22

[18]For Christ died for sins once for all, the righteous for the unrighteous, to bring
you to God. He was put to death in the body but made alive by the Spirit, [19]through
whom also he went and preached to the spirits in prison [20]who disobeyed long ago
when God waited patiently in the days of Noah while the ark was being built. In it
only a few people, eight in all, were saved through water, [21]and this water symbolizes baptism that now saves you also—not the removal of dirt from the body but
the pledge of a good conscience toward God. It saves you by the resurrection of
Jesus Christ, [22]who has gone into heaven and is at God's right hand—with angels,
authorities and powers in submission to him.

18 This section contains some of the most difficult exegetical problems in the NT. (For more extensive treatment, see the literature cited in the Notes.) Before giving the exposition of the passage, a brief view of the major types of interpretations is in order. The three main groups of interpretation may be easily differentiated if the following questions are kept in mind: (1) Who are the "spirits" to whom Christ made a proclamation? (2) When was this proclamation made? (3) What was its content?

1. In the first group of interpretations, Christ during the interval between his crucifixion and resurrection went down to the realm of the dead and preached to Noah's contemporaries. This group is subdivided by various opinions on the nature of the proclamation. (1) Christ's soul ministers an offer of salvation to the spirits. (2) He announces condemnation to the unbelievers of Noah's time. (3) He announces good tidings to those who had already been saved.

2. In the second interpretation group, the pre-existent Christ is viewed as preaching in the time of Noah to Noah's sinful generation.

3. In the third interpretation group, Christ proclaimed to the disobedient spirits (fallen angels) his victory on the cross. This proclamation took place either (1) during the three days in a descent into hell or (2) during his ascension. The writer takes the position that after Christ's death, he made a victorious proclamation to the fallen angels during his ascension. The exposition of 3:18–4:6 develops and defends this position.

The main purpose of the first subsection (3:18–22) is fairly clear. "For Christ died" (v.18) translates *hoti kai Christos . . . epathen* (UBS 3d ed., see Notes) (lit., "because Messiah also . . . suffered"). Dalton says, "The development beginning with 3:18 has for its purpose the doctrinal justification of the main topic of the preceding section (3:13–17), which is Christian confidence in the face of persecution" (p. 84). Thus the example of Christ's experience through suffering into victory gives assurance that those joined to him will share the same destiny. "For Christ died for sins once for all" stresses the definitive and final work of Jesus in salvation (cf. Rom 6:10). "For sins" is a phrase describing the reason for his death (cf. Rom 4:25; 1 Cor 15:3; Gal 1:4; Heb 10:12). "The righteous for the unrighteous" points to Jesus as the Righteous Servant of Isaiah 53 (cf. Acts 3:13f.), who suffers in the place of the sinners (cf. Isa 53:5–6, 11–12) and thus dies a substitutionary death. The purpose of his death is "to bring you [other MSS read 'us'] to God." For the verb "bring" (*prosagagē*), see Luke 9:41; Acts 16:20. The noun form (*prosagōgē*) is used by Paul of Christ's work of opening the way to God (Rom 5:2). BAG (p. 718) cites a parallel from Xenophon "of admission to an audience with the Great King" (cf. also TDNT, 1:131–34).

"He was put to death in the body but made alive by the Spirit." Behind the NIV translation stand a number of problems. The antithesis is between "flesh" and "spirit." "Flesh" and "spirit" do not refer to two "parts" of Christ, i.e., his body and his soul; nor does the "spirit" refer to the Holy Spirit or Christ's human spirit. Rather, "flesh" refers to Christ in his human sphere of life and "spirit" refers to Christ in his resurrected sphere of life (cf. Dalton, pp. 124–34; TDNT, 6:417, 447; 7:143). (For similar "two sphere thinking," cf. Rom 1:3–4; 1 Tim 3:16.) If this view is adopted, the exegesis makes good sense. The Greek is literally "put to death in flesh, made alive in spirit." To translate one member of the antithesis as a dative of sphere or reference and the other as a dative of cause or instrument is inconsistent. It is best to take both as datives of reference (or "adverbial" or even "of sphere") and to translate both "in the sphere of" (cf. Dalton, p. 134).

19 "Through whom" translates *en hō* ("in which"). But the way v.18b is interpreted is determinative. "Once we take πνεύματι [*pneumati*] as 'in the sphere of the spirit,' then we should take ἐν ᾧ [*en hō*] as 'in this sphere,' 'under this influence,' or even 'as one now made alive in the spirit.' In other words, the person who does the preaching in 3:19 is the risen Lord" (Dalton, p. 140). So the NIV translation might be corrected to read, "in which state [of resurrection] he went and preached."

To whom did he preach? What did he preach? The "spirits" have been understood as the souls of men, fallen angels, or both. The best explanation is that the "spirits" (*pneumata*) are fallen angels (BAG, p. 682; Dalton, p. 150; Kelly, p. 153; Reicke, *Disobedient Spirits*, pp. 90–91 [with possible addition of offspring of fallen angels]; idem. AB, p. 109; Selwyn, p. 353). Jesus, then, in his resurrection "goes" to the place of angelic confinement. Since this is in another realm, we cannot locate it spatially. However, there does not seem to be good evidence for seeing here a "descent into hell." The same word *poreutheis* ("went") is used in v.22 of his ascension.

The content of the proclamation is not stated. The verb *kēryssō* means "to proclaim" or "to announce." The choice of this verb rather than *euangelizō* ("to proclaim good news"), which is used in 4:6, appears to be significant. Christ does not announce the gospel or Good News to the fallen angels. The thought of salvation for angels is foreign to the NT (Heb 2:16) and also to Peter (cf. comments on 1:12). The announcement is of his victory and of their doom that has come through his death on the cross and his resurrection.

To sum up, the thought of vv.18–19 may be paraphrased as follows: "He was put to death in the human sphere of existence but was made alive in the resurrection sphere of existence, in which state of existence he made a proclamation of his victory to the fallen angels." As for the pastoral significance of these verses, it is one of comfort because through suffering Christians go to victory. Those who oppose Christians will be defeated (Col 2:15; 2 Thess 1:6–8).

20 The fallen angels (spirits) are identified as those who were disobedient at the time of Noah. This connects with the rebellion of Genesis 6:1–4, which is referred to in Jude 6 and 2 Peter 2:4. Verse 20 makes a connection between the disobedience of the spirits and the Flood-judgment. The Flood-judgment is a warning to humanity of God's coming eschatological judgment on the disobedient world (cf. Matt 24:37–41; 2 Peter 3:3–7). The ark that saved a few through water portrays the salvation now available in Christ.

21 Although the parallel between the OT deliverance of Noah's family and NT salvation through Christ is not precise in every detail, Peter says that the water of the Flood-judgment portrays the water of baptism: "And this water symbolizes baptism." Baptism is an antitype (Gr. *antitypos*) or counterpart of the type (*typos*, cf. TDNT, 8:246–59). Baptism is the "copy," the "representation," or even the "fulfilment" (BAG, p. 75) of the OT deliverance from judgment. How does baptism "save"? Peter says it does not concern an external washing from filth but relates to the conscience. In the proclamation of the gospel, salvation from sin and its punishment is announced through Jesus' death and resurrection. The announcement of the penalty for sin stirs the conscience and the spirit brings conviction (John 16:8–11; Acts 2:37f.; 13:37–41).

"The pledge of a good conscience toward God" renders a difficult expression in Greek. The thought appears to be as follows: The conviction of sin by the Spirit in the mind calls for a response of faith or commitment to Christ and his work. This is concretely and 'contractually" done in the act of baptism. Saving faith ("saving" because of its object—Christ) is expressed in baptism (cf. Acts 2:38–39). Salvation comes to men because Christ has risen from the dead.

22 Not only has Christ been raised from the dead, but in his victory he "has gone" (*poreutheis*, the same verb tr. "went" in v. 19) into heaven to the place of power and authority (cf. Ps 110:1; Rom 8:34). "With angels, authorities and powers" now under him, he is the supreme Lord. Therefore, the oppressed Christians in Asia Minor to whom Peter is writing need not fear anyone. Psalm 110:1 speaks of Messiah sitting at God's right hand "until I [God] make your enemies a footstool for your feet." So now even the fallen angels are subject to Jesus the Messiah (cf. Rom 8:38–39; 1 Cor 15:24ff.).

Notes

18ff. The literature on the problem passages from 3:18–4:6 is extensive, perhaps because of the article in the Apostle's Creed that states, "He descended into hell." Roman Catholic scholars have done excellent work in this area. Dalton's work is outstanding. For later literature, cf. A. Grillmeier, "Der Gottessohn im Totenreich," in *Mit ihm und in ihm: Christologische Forschungen und Perspektiven* (Freiburg: Herder, 1975) pp. 76–174.

18 Ἔπαθεν (*epathen*, "suffered"; NIV, "died") is the reading of the UBS 3d ed. text, which lists nine variants in the apparatus. The translation and meaning, however, are not seriously affected. Πάσχω (*paschō*, "I suffer") is commonly used for death when applied to Christ (TDNT, 5:913, 917).

C. *Death to the Old Life*

4:1–6

[1]Therefore, since Christ suffered in his body, arm yourselves also with the same attitude, because he who has suffered in his body is done with sin. [2]As a result, he does not live the rest of his earthly life for evil human desires, but rather for the will of God. [3]For you have spent enough time in the past doing what pagans choose to do—living in debauchery, lust, drunkenness, orgies, carousing and detestable idolatry. [4]They think it strange that you do not plunge with them into the same flood of dissipation, and they heap abuse on you. [5]But they will have to give account to him who is ready to judge the living and the dead. [6]For this is the reason the gospel was preached even to those who are now dead, so that they might be judged according to men in regard to the body, but live according to God in regard to the spirit.

1 NIV renders *pathōn sarki* ("suffered in his body") in both clauses in v.1 (cf. BV, NEB, and others). But it may be better to be more literal and follow KJV, RSV, and NASB with "suffered in the flesh." *Sarki* ("flesh," "body") is the same as in 3:18 (cf. comments there). The suffering of Christ was "unto death" as in 3:18. The thought appears to be this: Since Christ suffered to the extent of death in the realm of fleshly existence, Christians are to arm themselves with the same attitude that guided Christ.

"He who has suffered in his body is done with sin" (*ho pathōn sarki pepautai hamartias*) is often taken as a proverbial expression (Beare, p. 179) and linked in thought to Romans 6:7. It is also possible to refer this statement to Christ and the finality of his work against sin (Kelly, p. 166). Many commentators see the purging effects of suffering in the sanctification process (Selwyn, p. 209). But the expression "is done with sin" (*pepautai hamartias*) is a perfect tense and looks to a definite past act. So this difficult statement is probably best understood in the Pauline sense of Romans 6. By union with Christ, the Christian is to understand that his conversion is a death to sin. Thus he is "done with sin" (BAG, p. 643; cf. Gal 5:24; 6:14).

2 Peter gives a twofold purpose for Christians' arming themselves with Christ's attitude. (For the "arming" metaphor, cf. Rom 13:12; 2 Cor 10:4; Eph 6:11–17; 1 Thess 5:8.) First, "he does not live the rest of his earthly life for evil human desires." "His earthly life" is *en sarki;* the word *sarki* ("flesh") is found twice in v.1 and once in 3:18. The rest of life after conversion is not to be lived according to human passions (flesh), but the ruling principle is the will of God. Christ is the doer of God's will (John 8:29: "I always do what pleases him"; cf. John 4:34; 5:30; 6:38–40; 7:16–17); and he taught his disciples to pray, "Your will be done" (Matt 6:10; cf. TDNT, 3:55–62).

3 The counsel of the pagans (*boulēma tōn ethnōn*) is now contrasted with the will of God. (For comments on the catalogs of pagan vices, cf. comments on 2:1.) This verse clearly supports the position that the recipients of the letter had, before their conversion, been pagans. The "detestable idolatry," or "illicit idolatries," distinguished the Jews from their pagan neighbors. The other items listed are the common excesses of drink, sex, and wild parties found among the non-Christians then and also now.

4–5 The Christian lifestyle of sober, godly living is a condemnation of the values of pagan society. The pagan response will be one of astonishment when Christians refuse to plunge into the "flood of dissipation" (*tēs asōtias anachysis;* cf. the prodigal son's "wild living" [*asōtōs*] in Luke 15:13). Christians are expected by pagans to "run with them" (*syntrechontōn;* NIV, "plunge with them") into the pleasures of the satisfaction of the flesh. But Peter's denial is at once a warning and a judgment on the life lived in such a fashion. The pagan amazement will often turn to hatred and evil speaking (cf. John 3:19–21, esp. v.20: "Everyone who does evil hates the light").

The Christian is supported in his stand against the ungodly life by the basic truth of the coming judgment. In the OT and the NT, God is the Judge (cf. DNTT, 2:362–67). Yet the NT also shows that the Father has given judgment into Jesus' hands (John 5:22–23). This judgment is near (4:7); and it will be universal, for it will embrace all the living and all the dead. In it unbelievers will have to give an account of their lives and will not be able to withstand the divine scrutiny (cf. Ps 1:5–6).

6 The interpretation of this verse is often linked to 3:19, but the vocabulary of the text and its context differ. (See the Notes for other views.) This verse makes good sense in its own setting. "For this is the reason" (*eis touto gar*) is not retrospective but prospective. The coming judgment not only will bring sinners into account (v.5) but will also reverse the judgments of men (v.6). The Good News was proclaimed (*euēngelisthē*) to those (Christians) who are now dead (*nekrois,* same word as in v.5). Even though pagans might condemn Christians and put them to death in the realm of the flesh (*sarki*), yet in God's judgment there will be a reversal. Christians will live (*zōsi*) in a new realm—namely, in the spiritual realm.

Notes

---

6 Dalton (p. 42) outlines the history of the interpretation of this passage and finds four main solutions:

1. Christ, while in his three-day death, went and preached salvation to all the dead, offering salvation to those who lived in pre-Christian times.
2. Christ, while in his three-day death, went and preached salvation to the just of OT times.
3. The theme is the preaching of the gospel by the apostles and others on this earth to those who were spiritually dead.
4. The dead are Christians, who had the gospel preached to them and who then died (or were put to death). In the judgment of God, the opinions of men will be reversed and they will live in the new resurrection realm. I have adopted view 4, which is held by Dalton, Kelly, Moffatt, and Selwyn. The main advantages are (1) it takes "dead" in vv.5–6 in the same physical sense. (2) The terms σαρκὶ (*sarki,* "flesh") and πνεύματι (*pneumati,* "spirit") are taken in the same sense as in 3:18. (3) It solves the problem of a "second chance" (or opportunity after death) for conversion, which seems quite contrary to NT theology. (4) The μὲν (*men,* "on the one hand") and the δὲ (*de,* "on the other") are given full weight as contrasting man's view with God's judgment.

D. *The Life for God's Glory*

4:7–11

[7]The end of all things is near. Therefore be clear minded and self-controlled so that you can pray. [8]Above all, love each other deeply, because love covers over

a multitude of sins. [9]Offer hospitality to one another without grumbling. [10]Each one should use whatever gift he has received to serve others, faithfully administering God's grace in its various forms. [11]If anyone speaks, he should do it as one speaking the very words of God. If anyone serves, he should do it with the strength God provides, so that in all things God may be praised through Jesus Christ. To him be the glory and the power for ever and ever. Amen.

7 As is common in the NT, the end or final salvation is set before Christians to stimulate their faith and to encourage them in difficulty. Most translations (including NIV) miss the connective *de* that joins this unit to the previous one, with its statement of God's readiness to judge. It should be translated as "now" or "but." "Is near" is in the Greek a perfect tense, which has the sense "has drawn near." All is in readiness. "Therefore" (*oun*) introduces the ethical implications of eschatology. Jesus taught responsible living in the light of his return (cf. Luke 12:35–43; 17:26–27). Christians are not to give way to "eschatological frenzy" but to practice self-control and be active in prayer. (Peter had set a negative example in his failure to watch and pray in the Garden [Matt 26:40–41].)

8 "Above all" (*pro pantōn*) reminds us of the primacy of agape love among fellow Christians. This love is to be "eager," "earnest" (*ektenē*, lit., "strained," BAG, p. 245; NIV, "deeply"). Agape love is capable of being commanded because it is not primarily an emotion but a decision of the will leading to action. (On the necessity of Christians' loving one another, see Mark 12:30–33; John 13:34f.; 15:12–17.) The reason for us to show love is that "love covers over a multitude of sins." This quotation from Proverbs 10:12 does not mean that our love covers or atones for our sins. In the proverb the meaning is that love does not "stir up" sins or broadcast them. So the major idea is that love suffers in silence and bears all things (1 Cor 13:5–7). Christians forgive faults in others because they know the forgiving grace of God in their own lives.

9 Hospitality between Christians was an important, concrete expression of love in a world without our modern inns and hotels. This virtue was required of the bishops and widows (1 Tim 3:2; 5:10; Titus 1:8) and is commanded for us all (Matt 25:35ff.; Rom 12:13; 3 John 5–8; cf. TDNT, 5:20–36). Hospitality is to be "without grumbling"—a phase that connotes the difficulty of carrying out this command. In certain cultures that are strongly family-orientated, the bringing of strangers into a house may be somewhat shocking. Yet Christians overcome these conventions because God's love has made them into a single great family.

10–11 Hospitality is not a one-way virtue; every Christian is in some way capable of ministering to others. Every Christian has a gift (Rom 12:6–8; 1 Cor 12:12–31) that he has received from God—whether at birth, rebirth, or sometime after is not stated. Since every Christian has a gift, his being equipped with it apparently takes place with the indwelling of the Holy Spirit at regeneration. That the Holy Spirit can take "natural" talents and abilities and redirect them for Christ was most dramatically shown in Paul's ministry. The believer is not only to view himself as gifted but also as a steward (*oikonomos*, "a responsible slave"; cf. TDNT, 5:149–51) and a minister (*diakonountes*). One of the longstanding misconceptions in church practice is the idea that only one person is to "minister" in the local church. The biblical principle is that all can and should minister in one way or another.

The grace of God is "variegated" (*poikilēs*), or "manifests itself in various ways" (BAG, p. 690).

Peter puts these manifestations of grace in two broad categories: "speaking" and "serving" (v.11). Speaking (*lalein*) covers all forms of oral service—teaching, preaching, prophecy, perhaps even tongues. "The very words of God" translates *logia* or "oracles," which are utterances from God's mouth. So what one says is to be as God says it (cf. 2 Cor 5:20; 1 Thess 2:13). As for service it is to be empowered "with the strength God provides," which means by dependence on God's help by the Spirit (cf. Eph 3:16). The verb translated "provides" (*chorēgei*) originally meant to "supply a chorus" and later was used of lavish provision (cf. MM, pp. 689–90).

The purpose of mutual Christian service is that through Jesus Christ God will be glorified. Serving fellow Christians does glorify God because people will praise him for his grace that comes to them through Jesus and through his followers.

Peter adds a doxology—something that is not uncommon in Christian letters at various places besides the end (cf. Rom 11:33–36; Eph 3:20–21). In "To him be the glory and the power," "be" is supplied; the sentence is elliptical (i.e., without a verb). Perhaps "is" would be better, since God possesses the glory (cf. Isa 6:1ff.) and the power (cf. Isa 46:9–10). The "Amen" signifies assent—"So it is!"

E. *Consolations in Suffering*

4:12–19

12Dear friends, do not be surprised at the painful trial you are suffering, as though
something strange were happening to you. 13But rejoice that you participate in the
sufferings of Christ, so that you may be overjoyed when his glory is revealed. 14If
you are insulted because of the name of Christ, you are blessed, for the Spirit of
glory and of God rests on you. 15If you suffer, it should not be as a murderer or thief
or any other kind of criminal, or even as a meddler. 16However, if you suffer as a
Christian, do not be ashamed, but praise God that you bear that name. 17For it is
time for judgment to begin with the family of God; and if it begins with us, what will
the outcome be for those who do not obey the gospel of God? 18And,

> "If it is hard for the righteous to be saved,
> what will become of the ungodly and the sinner?"

19So then, those who suffer according to God's will should commit themselves
to their faithful Creator and continue to do good.

12 "Dear friends" (*agapētoi*, "beloved," as at 2:11; cf. its use in 2 Peter 3:1, 8, 14–15, 17) marks the beginning of a new section. Some scholars have argued that since the situation revealed in 4:12–5:14 is so different ("distress and terror occasioned by an actual persecution," so Beare, p. 188) from the general tenor of the letter, 4:12–5:14 is the real letter. The preceding section (1:3–4:11) was, they assume, only hypothetical and was perhaps general baptismal instruction. But the letter makes good sense as a whole, and 4:12–5:14 makes a fitting climax to its argument. There are also a number of unifying items that reveal connections between this section and the previous one. See, for example, the use of *xenizein* ("be surprised") in 4:4 and 4:12. This verb is uncommon in the NT and only occurs in Acts (seven times) and in Hebrews (once). The idea of the glory of God occurs in 4:11 and 4:14, 16. Eschatology and the judgment of evildoers are also common to both units (cf. Kelly, pp. 183–84).

Suffering is not to be regarded as something foreign to Christian experience but rather as a refining test. Peter has already mentioned the necessity of faith being refined through suffering and testing (1:6–7). Here the idea of refining is found in the word "painful" (*pyrōsis,* lit., "burning"), which occurs in the Greek OT (LXX) in the metaphor of the refining of metals (TDNT, 6:951). Jesus said, "If the world hates you, keep in mind that it hated me first" (John 15:18); and John writes, "Do not be surprised, my brothers, if the world hates you" (1 John 3:13). In the light of Jesus' experience and teaching, his followers should expect troubles, but troubles should only encourage them (cf. John 16:33).

13 In contrast to the usual response of sorrow and shock to suffering and persecution, the Christian is to rejoice because he is participating in Christ's sufferings. (For the idea of suffering with Christ in other NT writings, cf. Rom 8:17; 2 Cor 1:5–7; Phil 3:10.)

For illustrations of Christians' rejoicing because they had been counted worthy of suffering disgrace for the name of Christ, see Acts 5:41 (of all the apostles) and Acts 16:22–25 (of Paul and Silas). Christian rejoicing rests on the fact that as Christians share in Christ's suffering, so they will share in his glory with great joy. The prospect of Christ's full manifestation in all his glory fills the believer with joy and comfort.

14 Jesus said, "Blessed are you when people insult you, persecute you and falsely say all kinds of evil against you because of me. Rejoice and be glad" (Matt 5:11–12). Here in 1 Peter we have a fulfillment of the Lord's own promises to his disciples. In Matthew the cause for happiness is the reward in heaven. Here it is the possession of the messianic Spirit: "For the Spirit of glory and of God rests on you." (Many ancient MSS add "and of power" after "glory.") Verse 14 is based on Isaiah 11:2 (and perhaps Ps 89:50–51). One of God's great characteristics is his glory (Acts 7:2; Eph 1:17), and in Jesus his glory is revealed (John 1:14, 18).

The Spirit of the Father and of the Son now rest on and in every believer. The martyrdom of Stephen illustrates this. He is described as "a man full of faith and of the Holy Spirit" (Acts 6:5, cf. v.8). In his defense his face was like that of an angel (Acts 6:15), and he saw the "glory of God" (7:55; cf. DNTT 2:44–51).

15 The promise of the blessing of the Spirit resting on believers is not universal. Not all who suffer are sharing in Christ's sufferings. Much suffering is the punishment or consequence of sin. Christians must have really broken with sin (4:1–3; cf. Rom 6:1ff.; 1 Cor 6: 9–11). If they suffer, it should be because of their union with Jesus, not with evil. The sins mentioned here characterize a pagan, not a Christian, lifestyle. Yet it is possible for Christians to fall in times of weakness. The NIV choice of "meddler" to translate *allotriepiskopos* (a rare word that may have been coined by Peter) is a happy one. Other scholars have taken *allotriepiskopos* to mean "spy," "informer," "false guardian," or "revolutionist" (cf. discussions in BAG, p. 39; TDNT, 2:620–22).

16 But to suffer as a "Christian" is no shame. The title *Christianos,* which is now so common, was just coming into use when Peter wrote. At first Christians were known as "Jews," "disciples," "believers," "the Lord's disciples," and those "who belonged to the Way" (cf. Acts 1:15; 2:44; 6:1; 9:1–2). It was not till the church took root in Antioch that the use of "Christians" for believers began (Acts 11:26). "Christian" is a Latinism of pagan origin (cf. IDB, 571–72). Goppelt (p. 309) lists its NT, patristic, and classical usage: Acts 11:26; 26:28; 1 Peter 4:16; *Didache* 12.4; Ignatius *Ephesians*

11.2; idem, *Romans* 3.2f.; idem, *Polycarp* 7.3; Tacitus *Annales* 15.44; Suetonius *Vita Nero* 16.2; Pliny *Epistolae* 10.96.1–3; Lucian *Alexander* 25.38.

"Do not be ashamed"—i.e., to suffer as a Christian—recalls Peter's own shame at his betrayal of Jesus (Mark 14:66–72). "That you bear that name" (lit., "in this name") could refer to (1) Christ (v.14), (2) the name "Christian," or (3) in "this category" or "under the heading of" (Kelly, pp. 190–91). Most commentators take the second view.

17–18 Paul said, "We must go through many hardships to enter the kingdom of God" (Acts 14:22). Before the full unfolding of the messianic kingdom, there are to be judgments. In the Prophets, mention is made of judgment coming first upon the people of God (Ezek 9:6; Zech 13:7–9; Mal 3:1–5) before coming upon the nations. Here in 1 Peter the idea seems to be that the coming of the Lord in his eschatological judgment has, as a harbinger, a beginning of "birth pains" that will purify believers (cf. 1:7). (This judgment is not, of course, a punishment for the believers' sins, which were laid on Jesus.) Now if the preliminary judgment (Christian suffering) is already taking place, the final doom on the disobedient is certain to follow shortly. Peter cites Proverbs 11:31 (LXX) to reinforce this thought. The righteous are *just* saved. The rest come far short, and only a great disaster awaits them.

19 The conclusion to this section is that the Christians who are suffering according to the divine will (1:6; 3:17) are to "commit [*paratithesthōsan*] themselves" to God. In his seventh word from the Cross, Jesus used *paratithemai* in committing his Spirit to God (Luke 23:46, which probably reflects a Jewish evening prayer in Ps 31:5; so TDNT, 8:163). Peter described God as the "faithful Creator"—an unusual designation because only here in the NT is God called *ktistēs* ("Creator," cf. TDNT, 3:1000–1035). The combination of "faithful" and "Creator" reminds the believer of God's love and power in the midst of trials so that they will not doubt his interest or ability. The continuation in good works or action is a concrete sign of the faith that is the essence of being a Christian (cf. 2:15, 20; 3:6, 17).

F. *The Shepherd's Suffering Flock*

5:1–4

1To the elders among you, I appeal as a fellow elder, a witness of Christ's sufferings and one who also will share in the glory to be revealed: 2Be shepherds of God's flock that is under your care, serving as overseers—not because you must, but because you are willing, as God wants you to be; not greedy for money, but eager to serve; 3not lording it over those entrusted to you, but being examples to the flock. 4And when the Chief Shepherd appears, you will receive the crown of glory that will never fade away.

1 The "elders" are the leaders of the local congregations. The institution of a group of older and wiser men providing direction and rule goes back to the early days of Israel as a people. This was done both nationally and locally. Thus there were "elders" of the Sanhedrin in Jerusalem as well as "elders" of local synagogues (cf. TDNT, 6:651–83; DNTT, 1:188–201). The institution of eldership was adopted by the Jerusalem church (Acts 11:30; 21:18), and Paul and Barnabas applied it to the local congregations they founded on their missionary journeys (Acts 14:23; 1 Tim 3:1–7; Titus 1:5ff.). Peter, therefore, addresses the elders because of their vital role in the life of the congregation. NIV does not translate the *oun* ("therefore") in v.1 that links this section and the preceding one. Because of suffering and persecution, the need of pastoral leadership was important for the local churches. According to Titus 1:5, 7, the words *presbyteros* ("elder") and *episkopos* ("bishop," or "overseer," cf. v.2 here) are interchangeable. The early church utilized more people than the church today does (see comments on 4:10; cf. Eph 4:12) and so put the spiritual leadership in the hands of a plurality.

The basis of Peter's exhortation to the elders (*presbyteroi*) is threefold: (1) He is their fellow elder. In John 21:15–19, Jesus charged Peter with the care of his sheep. (2) He is a witness (a giver of testimony) of Christ's sufferings. (3) He is a sharer of the coming glory. It is notable that he does not command as an apostle (much less as a "pope") but views himself as an elder, as does John also (2 John 1, 3 John 1). As a "witness" (*martys*), it is possible Peter is referring to the sufferings of Jesus that he had seen. But the stress is on the testimony he gives (cf. Luke 24:45–48; Acts 1:8).

2–3 Peter's command is to "shepherd" (*poimanate*) God's "flock" (*poimnion*). The comparison of God's people to a flock of sheep and the Lord to a shepherd is prominent in Scripture. (Sec, for example, Jacob's words: "The God who has been my Shepherd all my life" [Gen 48:15]; David's Shepherd Psalm [Ps 23]; Ps 100:3: "We are his people, the sheep of his pasture"; Isa 53:6–7; Luke 15:3–7, the parable of the lost sheep; and John 10:1–16.)

The verb *poimainō* ("shepherd") occurs in Christ's command to Peter (John 21:16) and Paul's charge to the Ephesian elders (Acts 20:28). Its meaning embraces protecting, leading, guiding, feeding, etc. (cf. BAG, p. 690). Peter reminds the elders that the flock is God's and that they are responsible for its loving care. "Serving as overseers" (*episkopountes*) reveals the interchangeability of the terms "overseer" and "bishop." Elder (*presbyteros*) denotes the dignity of the office; "bishop" (*episkopos*) denotes its function—"to oversee."

Peter's exhortation to the elders "Be shepherds of God's flock" is followed by three contrasting statements that tell how this responsibility is not to be carried out and how it should be carried out: "Serving as overseers . . . because you are willing . . . eager to serve." These words remind us of what Paul wrote to Timothy: "If anyone sets his heart on being an overseer, he desires a noble task" (1 Tim 3:1).

Since the responsibilities of the office of elder are great and since elders will be required to give account of their work (Heb 13:17), no one should be forced into this position ("not because you must," v.2). God will work in men's lives and make them willing to do his will. The motivation of elders will be divine, not human. It is not to be financial, though elders were evidently paid in the early church and handled the finances of the congregations (cf. 1 Cor 9:7–11; 1 Tim 5:17). Not money but enthusiasm and zeal for God and his work will motivate elders. They are not to be "lords" over "those entrusted to" (*kleroi,* "allotted to") them. Probably in each congregation, individual elders had portions of the congregation for which they were particularly responsible. Elders should endeavor to be patterns for Christ's sheep.

4 For faithfulness, elders will receive a "crown of glory that does not fade away." The "crown" could be a "garland" or "wreath" made of leaves or of gold. (In Christ's suffering it was ironically made of thorns [Matt 27:29].) The unfading "crown of glory" makes a striking contrast to the "use of *withered* parsley for the crown at the Isthmian games" (DNTT, 1:406). The glorification will take place at the manifestation of the True Shepherd or Chief Shepherd (cf. Rom 8:17ff.; 1 John 3:2).

G. *Humility and Watchfulness in Suffering*

5:5–9

> [5]Young men, in the same way be submissive to those who are older. Clothe yourselves with humility toward one another, because,
>
> "God opposes the proud
> but gives grace to the humble."
>
> [6]Humble yourselves, therefore, under God's mighty hand, that he may lift you up in due time. [7]Cast all your anxiety on him because he cares for you.
>
> [8]Be self-controlled and alert. Your enemy the devil prowls around like a roaring lion looking for someone to devour. [9]Resist him, standing firm in the faith, because you know that your brothers throughout the world are undergoing the same kind of sufferings.

5 "Young men," or "younger members," may refer only to young men in general, to an office of younger men (cf. Acts 5:6, 10), or to all the younger people (spiritually) in the congregation. The first is the most likely interpretation. The women are not mentioned because their activity in the churches was very limited in Peter's time. "In the same way" (*homoiōs*) indicates a new unit of instruction (cf. 3:1, 7). The exhortation to submission is not limited to a few, but all (*pantes*) Christians are to manifest this quality.

"Clothe yourselves" (*egkombōsasthe*) is a rare word that refers to a slave putting on an apron before serving. So Christians are to imitate their Lord, who girded himself and served (John 13:4–17). The reason for humility is based on a text from Proverbs (3:34; cf. James 4:6) that states God's provision of grace to the submissive and God's opposition to the proud. The verbs are present tenses, with something of the timeless character of a proverb, and stress that these actions are God's constant activity.

6 Christians should, therefore, submit themselves to God's "mighty hand." In the OT, God's hand symbolizes discipline (Exod 3:19; 6:1; Job 30:21; Ps 32:4) and deliverance (Deut 9:26; Ezek 20:34). Both meanings are appropriate in view of the sufferings of the Asian Christians. Once more Peter ties his exhortation to humility to eschatology. The "due time" (*en kairō*) is the time God sets for Christ's appearing. Thus the whole destiny of Christians—whether suffering or glory—is God-ordained.

7 "Cast all your anxiety on him." Here the verb *epiripsantes* is aorist and means "to throw upon," indicating a decisive act on our part. Peter does not say what the anxiety is; perhaps he had persecution in mind. The application of his exhortation embraces all the difficulty a believer who wants to live godly in a fallen world must face. The "casting" entails an act of the will and would be done prayerfully and in obedience to Jesus' teaching about anxiety (Matt 6:25–34). "He cares for you" means that God is not indifferent to our sufferings. This conception of God's concern for human affliction is one of the peculiar treasures of the Judeo-Christian faith; though Greek philosophy at its highest could formulate a doctrine of God's perfect goodness, it could not even imagine his active concern for mankind (cf. Beare, p. 204). The Incarnation reveals a caring God, and Christ's teaching about his heavenly Father stresses his intimate concern for his children (Matt 10:29–31).

8–9 Belief in the sovereignty of God and in his fatherly concern for us (vv.6–7) does not permit us to sit back and do nothing. We are to "work out [our] salvation" because "it is God who works in [us]" (Phil 2:12–13). So here Peter warns his flock of the danger of making the fact of God's sovereign care an excuse for inactivity. "Be sober, be watchful" perhaps reflects Peter's own experience in which Satan had "sifted" him (Luke 22:31) and he had failed to "watch" (Matt 26:38; Mark 14:34). God's sovereignty does not preclude peril to the Christian life. Peter calls Satan "your enemy the devil" and likens him to a lion in search of prey. The word "enemy" (*antidikos*, "adversary") meant an opponent in a lawsuit (BAG, p. 73; cf. Job 1:6ff.; Zech 3:1; Rev 12:10). "Devil" (*diabolos*) is the Greek translation of the Hebrew "Satan" (1 Chron 21:1; Job 2:1), which means "slanderer" (cf. TDNT, 2:71–81; 7:151–65). According to Scripture, he has great power on earth, "being the prince of this world" (John 14:30) and "the ruler of the kingdom of the air" (Eph 2:2). But God has limited his activity. Through his captive subjects (Eph 2:2; 2 Tim 2:25–26), the devil attempted to destroy the infant church by persecution.

The Christian response to satanic opposition is not panic or flight but firm resistance in faith (v.9). "Resist" (*antistēte*) is the same word as that found in Ephesians 6:11–13 and James 4:7 in contexts of struggle against hostile spiritual forces. This implies a common "resist-the-devil" formula in the early church (cf. Selwyn, p. 238). Stibbs illustrates the idea of resistance "in the faith" from Revelation 12:10–11 (where Satan is overcome): "They overcame him by the blood of the lamb and by the word of their testimony; they did not love their lives so much as to shrink from death." "In the faith" (*tē pistei*) is not so much then "the Christian faith" or "your faithfulness" but rather "your positive faith and trust in God" (Kelly, p. 210).

Support in the struggle also comes from the realization that the sufferings of the Asian Christians were not unique (cf. 1 Cor 10:13). The same kinds of sufferings (unusual in Gr.; cf. Selwyn) are afflicting "your brothers." The word *adelphotēs* ("brothers") stresses the solidarity of the Christian body. All who are in union with Christ may expect suffering (John 15:18–20; 16:33), and the whole body is joined together in suffering (1 Cor 12:26). The "world" (*kosmos*) is that orderly system under Satan that is opposed to God and his Messiah (cf. Ps 2:1–12). Verse 9, then, relates to the common lot of believers in Christ (cf. John 16:33).

H. *The Sustaining Grace of God*

5:10–11

> [10]And the God of all grace, who called you to his eternal glory in Christ, after you have suffered a little while, will himself restore you and make you strong, firm and steadfast. [11]To him be the power for ever and ever. Amen.

10–11 "And" (*de*) might well be translated "but" to show the contrast between satanic opposition and God's purpose and enablement. For Christians God has as his gracious purpose bringing his children himself to share in his glory (cf. Ps 73:23–24; John 17:22, 24; Rom 8:30—"called . . . glorified"). "Called" (*kaleō*) in the Pauline and Petrine writings stresses God's sovereign working (DNTT, 1:275–76). The eternal glory contrasts with the temporal trials Christians suffer. "Restore you and make you strong, firm and steadfast" translates four future indicative verbs in the best-attested reading. (Some MSS have these verbs in the optative.) The four verbs emphatically promise divine aid. "Restore" (*katartisei*) means "make complete" or "put in order." "Make you strong" (*stērixei*) means "strengthen one so he can stand fast in persecution." "Strengthen" (*sthenōsei;* NIV, "make you . . . firm") is found only once in the NT but more often in the papyri. (The exact difference between *stērixei* and *sthenōsei* is difficult to determine.) "Settle" (*themeliōsei;* NIV, "make you . . . steadfast") is to put on a firm foundation.

With this brief doxology, Peter closes the main part of his letter. Since the verb is not expressed, it may be either "is" (NIV) or "be" (RSV and others).

V. Final Words (5:12–14)

A. *Silas's Role Writing the Letter*

(5:12)

12With the help of Silas, whom I regard as a faithful brother, I have written to you briefly, encouraging you and testifying that this is the true grace of God. Stand fast in it.

12 Silas (or "Silvanus," here Gr. text has *dia Silouanou* ["with the help of Silvanus"]) is undoubtedly the same person as the one mentioned in Acts 15:22–33; 15:40–18:5; 1 Thessalonians 1:1; 2 Thessalonians 1:1 (on *Silas, Silouanos,* see BAG, p. 758). As Selwyn says, "There is no reason for disputing the identity" (p. 10). If this is correct, Silas was one of the leading men in the early church. What help he gave Peter in writing this letter is uncertain. If he was the amanuensis, it would have been normal for him to have a significant part in writing. Sometimes the amanuensis took shorthand and at other times he used his own words to convey his employer's message.

Peter says this letter is brief (*di' oligōn*), and he characterizes it as exhortation and testimony ("encouraging you and testifying"). The reference to exhortation (*parabaleō*) reminds us of the commands for ethical living he has given his readers while the reference to testimony stresses the reliability of what he has borne witness to. His final exhortation "Stand fast in it" relates to the "grace of God," which no Christian earns or merits but which all Christians are obligated to abide in.

B. *The Greeting From Rome*

5:13

13She who is in Babylon, chosen together with you, sends you her greetings, and so does my son Mark.

13 Who is "she" whom Peter calls "chosen together [*syneklektē*, 'coelect'] with you"? Who is the Mark referred to? What and where is Babylon? "She" could be Peter's wife (Mark 1:30; 1 Cor 9:5), and "Mark" his own son. Most, however, think "she" refers to the church (which is feminine in Gr.) and "Mark" to John Mark (cf. Acts 12:12, 25; 15:36–39; 2 John 1, 13). Strong early tradition links John Mark with Peter and his Gospel. "Babylon" could be (1) in Mesopotamia, (2) a town in Egypt, or (3) a cryptic reference to Rome. The last view is best because (1) according to early church tradition Peter was in Rome; (2) there is no evidence for Peter's having been in Egypt or Mesopotamia; and (3) the reference may be cryptic because of persecution, or it may be an allusion to the "exile" of God's people on the pattern of the exile of ancient Israel in Babylon.

C. *A Final Exhortation and a Prayerful Wish*

5:14

[14]Greet one another with a kiss of love. Peace to all of you who are in Christ.

14 The formal kiss was common among early Christians as an expression of agape love in the church. From the third century A.D., the sexes were separated (TDNT, 9:143) in the practice of the "kiss of love." But we do not know how old the practice of the formal kiss was. Peter ends his letter with a wish that all his readers who are believers—i.e., who are "in Christ"—may have God's peace. Such a wish is also a prayer. "Peace" reflects the common Hebrew blessing "Shalom." Peter's first letter begins (1:2) and ends with peace.

2 PETER

Edwin A. Blum

2 PETER

Introduction

1. **Authorship and Canonicity**
2. **Date**
3. **Place of Origin**
4. **Destination**
5. **Occasion**
6. **Bibliography**
7. **Special Problem**
8. **Outline**

1. Authorship and Canonicity

Among all the books of the NT, none has been more disputed as to canonicity and authorship than 2 Peter. There is no assured reference to it in the early Christian writings till Origen (c.185–c.254), who first attributed it to Peter. Doubt about it persisted into the fourth century. It may, however, be reflected in Clement of Rome, the Epistle of Barnabas, and in noncanonical Petrine writings, though this is only a possibility (cf. INT, pp. 387–89). The Gospel of Truth and the Apocryphon of John probably quote or allude to 2 Peter, and this might imply acceptance of it in the second century.[1] Also, "the very early (third-century) Bodmer papyrus designated P^{72} shows acceptance of 2 Peter as canonical, for in that manuscript 2 Peter shares with 1 Peter and Jude a blessing on the readers of these sacred books and receives even more elaborate support than the other two epistles."[2]

Yet while early support of 2 Peter may not be entirely lacking, it is less well attested than the other NT writings. However, it was admitted to the canon[3] and, despite widespread questioning of its Petrine authorship, it still speaks with the authority of Scripture.

Canonicity and authorship, though not synonymous, are often related. In the early church, one of the main reasons for acceptance of a book as authoritative was its apostolic authorship or authorization. The canonicity of 2 Peter was questioned primarily because of doubts about its Petrine authorship. These doubts about the authorship, and therefore the authority, of 2 Peter reappeared at the time of the Reformation. Today they are widespread among contemporary scholars, many of whom deny that the apostle Peter wrote the letter. Kelly, for example, rejects the Petrine authorship (p. 235) but still accepts the letter as revealing "remarkable spiritual insight and power" (p. 225). His attitude is not unusual, for rarely does one

---

[1]Cf. R.H. Gundry, *A Survey of the New Testament* (Grand Rapids: Zondervan, 1970), p. 353.
[2]Ibid.
[3]EBC, 1:631–43.

hear a call to excise 2 Peter from the NT canon. Yet rejection of the Petrine authorship of the letter is very common.

There are approximately eleven arguments against Petrine authorship. Eusebius[4] and Jerome[5] give us the first two: (1) No long line of tradition for 2 Peter could be traced to their day. (2) Its style is different from that of 1 Peter, which was strongly accepted by the church as Petrine.

Two other arguments also stem from the time of the ancient church: (3) Peter's name was used in connection with some Gnostic literature. (4) Knowledge of 2 Peter was geographically limited.

In addition, modern scholars have added these arguments: (5) Petrine authorship is forbidden by its literary dependence on Jude. (6) The conceptual and rhetorical language is too Hellenistic for a Galilean fisherman. (7) The problem of the delay of the Parousia is a second-century one. (8) The collection of Pauline Letters referred to in 2 Peter 3:15–16 was made in the second century. (9) Second Peter is not mentioned by Christian writers in the second century. (10) The letter sounds like "early Catholicism" rather than first generation Christianity. (11) If Peter wrote it, why is there all the doubt about it and reluctance to accept it? In the light of these arguments, the majority of NT scholars today reject 2 Peter as authentic.

Yet there is more to be said. As the following discussion seeks to show, there is another side to the case against 2 Peter; and no single argument is conclusive enough to finally rule out its apostolic authorship.

1. Because of the letter's brevity, governmental persecutions of the early churches, and communication problems in the ancient world, the lack of a long tradition for 2 Peter is hardly surprising. If the letter had been sent to an area not in the main travel routes or one that suffered sudden persecutions, normal circulation patterns may have been hindered.

2. The style does differ from that of 1 Peter, but this may be explained by the use of a different amanuensis (cf. 1 Peter 5:12). If 1 Peter was written by Peter with the assistance of Silvanus, 2 Peter could either be in Peter's own style or in his style with the assistance of a different amanuensis. Moreover, stylistic arguments are hard to evaluate because the criteria for the identity and distinctiveness of writers are not settled. Bruce discusses the interplay of personality, subject, and the freedom of the scribe as a possible solution to stylistic problems within the Pauline corpus.[6]

The work of the Spirit in inspiration may well extend to the amanuensis who in certain cases may even be termed a coauthor. For example, Timothy is associated with Paul's name in the salutations of 1 and 2 Thessalonians, Philippians, Colossians, and Philemon. The stylistic differences in the Pastoral Epistles have long been recognized. In 2 Timothy 4:11, Paul says, "Only Luke is with me." Perhaps Luke served as Paul's amanuensis. So the Pastorals would have a different style from other of Paul's letters. Yet their authority would not be inferior because the superintendence of the Spirit would be over the amanuensis as well as over Paul. The same factors may apply to Peter's letters. Strangely, Morton has argued on the basis of various data, including cumulative sum analysis on a computer, that 1 and 2 Peter are "linguistically

---

[4]*Ecclesiastical History* 3.3.1–4; 25.3–4.

[5]*Scriptorium Ecclesiasticorum* 1, *Letter to Hedibia* (*Epist*. 120.11).

[6]F.F. Bruce, *The Letters of Paul: An Expanded Paraphrase* (Grand Rapids: Eerdmans, 1965), pp. 10–11.

indistinguishable."[7] Such a conclusion, which can only cause most NT Greek scholars to shake their heads in wonder, should at least call for scholarly caution in making dogmatic statements based on stylistic considerations.

3. The argument that the appearance of Peter's name on certain Gnostic writings led to some hesitation in the acceptance of 2 Peter by the early church has a factual basis. But that the early church accepted 2 Peter in spite of the circulation of spurious works bearing the apostle's name shows that it recognized a difference in character between the two epistles and the other works bearing his name.

4. As for the contention that knowledge of 2 Peter was geographically limited, it could be that persecution, the brevity of 2 Peter, or its remote destination resulted in its not being widely circulated in the first hundred years of the church.

5. The literary dependence of 2 Peter on Jude is not conclusively settled (see below, Special Problem). But even if Peter quoted or utilized a substantial part of Jude's letter, this would neither preclude Peter's authorship of the second letter nor its inspiration. For scholars to accept Mark's priority and Matthew's use of Mark is not incompatible with a high view of biblical inspiration and authority.

6. In answer to the claim that the language of the letter is too Hellenistic for a man of Peter's background, we may reply that the extent of Hellenistic influence Peter had in his life is not known. He lived about five miles from the region of the Greek league of ten cities known as Decapolis. We do not know whether he was bilingual or how much he learned between the Resurrection and his martyrdom. Nor do we know whether Peter had help in writing his letters. Just as today a high government official uses a speech writer, though the final product is the official's responsibility, so 2 Peter may have been drafted by an amanuensis as has been suggested under 2 above.

7. The problem of the delay of the Parousia was most certainly a first-century problem as well as a second-century one. John 21:20–23 shows that Christ's return was a live issue at the time of writing of the Gospel of John. Other texts show a similar interest at an earlier time (cf. Matt 25:1–13; Acts 1:6–11; 2 Thess 2:1–4; Heb 9:28).

8. The reference in 2 Peter 3:15–16 to Paul's letters need not refer to the complete corpus of his letters but only to those known to the writer of these verses. The collecting of Paul's letters would have begun as soon as a church or some influential person recognized their value. Paul's instruction about exchanging letters (cf. Col 4:16) and their public reading (1 Thess 5:27) would have facilitated the collection of his letters. That Luke or Timothy were traveling companions of Paul makes them likely collectors of his writings.

9. Although it is true that 2 Peter is not mentioned by name by writers in the second century, several things may account for this. For one thing, the brevity of 2 Peter, its remote destination, and the persecution of its recipients could have led to the lack of any second-century reference to it. Also we need to remember that much of the literature of the early church has not survived. For example, many, if not most, of the writings of Origen (c.185–c.254) are not extant. The odds against writings of the second century perishing were very high. Again, there is, as already has been said, some evidence of traces of 2 Peter in second-century writers. On this point, see also Bigg (pp. 199–210) and Warfield.[8]

---

[7]A.Q. Morton, *The Authorship and Integrity of the New Testament* (London: SPCK, 1965).

[8]B.B. Warfield, "The Canonicity of Second Peter," reprinted in *Selected Shorter Writings*, 2 vols., ed. by Joan E. Meeter, (Nutley, N.J.: Presbyterian and Reformed, 1970, 1973), 2:49–79.

10. The "early-Catholicism" argument, which affirms that the stress on good works and orthodoxy in the letter points to a late date, though often repeated (cf. Kelly, p. 235), entails some questionable assumptions. Why should not Peter have been concerned about the orthodox interpretation of Scripture? Why should he not have been concerned about tradition? Paul stressed tradition (cf. 1 Cor. 11:2; 15:3). The stress on good works and orthodoxy that some see as marks of "early Catholicism" appears in James, which was undoubtedly written early.

11. If, as has already been suggested, Peter wrote this letter to Christians in a remote place or an early persecution hindered its circulation, these things would have delayed its acceptance and led to doubts about it. Moreover, the existence and circulation of heretical books under Peter's name may have fed doubts about the letter and hindered its acceptance.

But there is still more to be said in favor of the Petrine authorship:

1. The book clearly claims to have been written by the apostle Peter ("Simon Peter," 1:1). It recalls how the Lord spoke to Peter about his imminent death (1:14) and refers to Peter's presence as an eyewitness at Jesus' transfiguration (1:16–18). It claims to be his second letter (3:1), a claim most commentators interpret as referring back to 1 Peter, and says that Paul is his "beloved brother" (3:15). Such indications of apostolic authorship are not easily set aside. If the book is unreliable in these statements, how can its teaching be accepted? Either 2 Peter is a genuine work of Simon Peter the apostle or it is an unreliable forgery.

2. Instead of making this choice, writers often accept 2 Peter as a pseudepigraphic work that has value for the church today (cf. Kelly, p. 225) and should be retained in the canon. Sidebottom (p. 100) justifies the acceptance of 2 Peter as pseudonymous by asserting that "the custom of a disciple writing under the name of a famous teacher or leader was well established in the ancient world . . . our conventions about copyright were not those of the first century." The last assertion is true, but what about the former one? Did the first-century Christians adopt the practices of the pagan world as to pseudonymity, or did their concern for truth cause them to repudiate it? This issue is sharply debated. Evangelical Christians have as a whole rejected the view that there are pseudonymous works in the canonical Scriptures. Baldwin concludes her study of OT pseudonymity by saying that "we contend that there is no clear proof of pseudonymity in the Old Testament and much evidence against it."[9] Guthrie argues that pseudonymity was not acceptable among Christians.[10] And Walls refers to Tertullian's statement that the presbyter who wrote the apocryphal *Acts of Paul and Thecla* pseudonymously was deposed.

> This suggests that deliberate pseudepigraphy was not, as is often stated, an established and acceptable convention. To this day, though hundreds of writings of a pseudepigraphic nature from the early Christian centuries have survived, the overwhelming majority of them are more or less affected by Gnostic or other tendentious influences, and many were clearly written to propagate such views. Most of the rest of them are works of what one might call "popular religion"—cheap

[9]Joyce Baldwin, "Is there pseudonymity in the Old Testament?" *Themelios* 4 (September 1978): 12.

[10]Donald Guthrie, *New Testament Introduction*, 3rd ed. (Downers Grove, Ill.: Intervarsity, 1970), pp. 671–84.

> devotional literature, not intentionally deviant in theology but using expressions theologians would abhor and concentrating on the miraculous and the bizarre. The contrast with the works in the emergent canon is unmistakable.[11]

If epistolary pseudepigraphy was rejected by Christians, then who would have written this letter? Hardly a good man! If it had been a false teacher, what was his motivation? After all, the book does not seem to have any distinctive views that would require presentation under an assumed name.

3. We should also remember that pseudonymous works bearing Peter's name were circulated in the early church. The following are known to us: The Apocalypse of Peter (c.135), The Gospel of Peter (c.150–75), The Acts of Peter (c.180–200), The Teaching of Peter (c.200), The Letter of Peter to James (c.200), and The Preaching of Peter (c.80–140). That none of these was accepted into the canon is noteworthy. Second Peter won its way by its intrinsic worth. As Calvin (*Epistles of Peter*, p. 363) puts it: "At the same time, according to the consent of all, it [the second letter] has nothing unworthy of Peter, as it shows everywhere the power and grace of an apostolic spirit." The internal evidence of 2 Peter—viz., the quality of its teaching—should not be underestimated. In contrast to the Petrine apocrypha, one does not detect false notes in reading 2 Peter. The book rings true. The author's zeal for truth (1:12), his rejection of clever fables (1:16), and his concern for righteousness (2:7–9) are impressive.

4. The letter gives no hint of a second-century environment or of problems such as the monarchical bishop, developed Gnosticism, or Montanism.

5. The most serious problem (style) is not insuperable if we give due consideration to the use of an amanuensis (cf. Silvanus, NIV mg., 1 Peter 5:12) for 1 Peter. Selwyn (pp. 9–15) argues that Silvanus was the coauthor of the first letter. If this was so, the different style of 2 Peter might mean that Peter used a different secretary or assistant in its composition. Also, the argument from style is sometimes exaggerated (cf. Kelly, p. 236), and Green (*Peter and Jude*, pp. 16–19) cites a number of studies that show the clear limitations of style arguments.

As mentioned above, authorship and canonicity were closely related in the ancient church's decisions about canonicity. Seven NT books—Heb, James, Jude, 2 Peter, 2 and 3 John, and Rev—were recognized as canonical only after a certain amount of discussion. The other twenty books had almost universal early acknowledgment. But many other books were known and widely circulated in the early church. Some were highly regarded (e.g., The Shepherd of Hermas) but were never recognized by the church as Scripture.

Second Peter was acknowledged as Scripture by Origen (c.240) who said, "Peter . . . has left one acknowledged epistle, and, it may be, a second also; for it is doubted."[12] Eusebius placed it among the disputed books rather than among the spurious writings.[13] By the time of Cyril of Jerusalem (c.315–86), 2 Peter was considered canonical; and Cyril's acceptance of it as well as its acceptance by Athanasius, Augustine, and Jerome settled the issue for the early church. These leaders acknowledged 2 Peter to be Scripture because the evidence, both internal and external, showed its solid worth.

---

[11] Andrew F. Walls, "The Canon of the New Testament," EBC, 1:638–39.

[12] *Ecclesiastical History* 6.25.8.

[13] *Ecclesiastical History* 3.3.1.

2. Date

From 2 Peter 3:15–16 it is clear that the letter could not have been written until a good number of the Pauline Epistles had been written and gathered together. This means that the earliest possible date would be A.D. 60. If the reference in 3:1 ("Dear friends, this is now my second letter to you") refers to 1 Peter (though this is not entirely certain; cf. comments at 3:1), then the earliest possible date for 2 Peter would be about 63–64, i.e., around the time of the writing of 1 Peter. The latest possible date (for those who hold a non-Petrine authorship) is shortly before 135, because 2 Peter is used in the Apocalypse of Peter.[14]

If the apostolic authorship of 2 Peter is accepted and the letter was published while Peter was still alive, the date would be shortly before his death (cf. 2 Peter 1:12–15) or A.D. 64–68. Some evangelical writers view 2 Peter as "the testament of Peter" and favor a posthumous publication by one or more of the apostle's followers.[15] This would make the date about 80–90. Those who reject the letter's apostolic authorship or any connection of the letter with the apostle date it anywhere from 135 (Harnack dated it 150–75). Our conclusion is that to date the letter 64–68 is reasonable and best fits its self-witness.

3. Place of Origin

We have no reliable information for fixing the place where the letter was written, though Rome is a favorite choice because Peter is known to have been there. But since he traveled widely (Palestine, Asia Minor, Corinth [?], and Rome), it is impossible to determine where 2 Peter was written unless new information comes to light.

4. Destination

The only clues to the destination are in the letter itself. It is addressed "to those who through the righteousness of our God and Savior Jesus Christ have received a faith as precious as ours" (1:1). This contrasts with the provinces in Asia Minor mentioned in 1 Peter 1:1 and may imply that 2 Peter was written to Christians in various places. In 2 Peter 3:1 the writer says, "Dear friends, this is now my second letter to you." If this refers to 1 Peter, then the letter is addressed to Christians in Pontus, Galatia, Cappadocia, Asia, and Bithynia. But if 3:1 refers to a lost letter of Peter's (cf. 1 Cor 5:9; Col 4:16b for probable lost letters of Paul), then we have no firm information about the destination of 2 Peter. Asia Minor or Egypt have been favorite choices of commentators. From the warnings in the letter concerning the false teachers (2:1–20), it seems that their vices were more typical of Gentiles than Jews.

---

[14]So C. Maurer, "Apocalypse of Peter" in *New Testament Apocrypha*, 2 vols., edd. E. Hennecke and W. Schneemelcher (London: Lutterworth, 1963–65), 2:664.

[15]Cf. G. Barker, W. Lane, and J.R. Michaels, *The New Testament Speaks* (New York: Harper & Row, 1969), pp. 32, 349–52.

5. Occasion

The occasion for writing 2 Peter may be inferred from its contents. The immediate occasion was Peter's knowledge that his time was short and that God's people were facing many dangers (1:13–14; 2:1–3). Just as sheep are prone to wander, so Christians are prone to forget the basic truths of the faith. The gift of exhortation in the church was a means of correcting this tendency (cf. Rom 12:8). Peter himself mentions this need in his first letter (5:1 [NIV, "appeal"], 12). So 2 Peter is a reminder of the basis for Christian faith (cf. 1:12–13). Faith in Jesus as Messiah is not grounded on myths or clever stories (1:16). It is based on sure revelation from God (1:16–21). The Christian's personal faith should not be static but ever growing. Continual growth in the Christian graces gives a certainty of election to the believer (1:8–10).

Christians must beware of false teachers (2:1–22) who deny the soon return of the Lord (3:3–4) and live immoral and greedy lives. These teachers are clever and claim scriptural support from Paul's Epistles for their views of liberty, but they pervert the letters and are headed for damnation (3:15–16). The church is to be alert to error and growing in the grace and knowledge of God (3:17–18).

6. Bibliography

(See Bibliography for 1 Peter, pp. 216–17.)

7. Special Problem

There are so many similarities between 2 Peter (mainly ch. 2) and Jude that some kind of literary or oral dependence seems necessary. Mayor writes at length about this problem (pp. i–xxv, 2–15).[16]

The common material almost entirely relates to the description and denunciation of false teachers. The majority view is that 2 Peter is dependent on Jude (so Mayor, Feine, Behm). Some scholars use this apparent dependence on Jude to deny Petrine authorship.[17] But the use of Jude by the author of 2 Peter would pose a problem for Petrine authorship of the letter only if (1) the dependence of 2 Peter on Jude were conclusively proved, (2) the composition of Jude were definitely dated later than A.D. 64, or (3) it could be shown that an apostle such as Peter would not have used so much material from another writer.

Some students of 1 Peter find a large amount of catechetical material within it (cf. Selwyn, pp. 363–466). If Peter in the composition of his first letter used material common within the church, there is no reason why he should not have done the same thing in writing his second letter. However, the dependence of 2 Peter on Jude is not a certainty. Mayor (pp. i–ii) holds that 2 Peter uses Jude while Bigg (p. 218) finds that Jude borrows from 2 Peter. It is also quite possible that both letters used a common source.

Since the date of Jude is not fixed by any firm internal or external data, it might

---

[16]See also E.F. Harrison, INT, pp. 396–98.

[17]E.g., "Petrine authorship is forbidden by the literary relation to Jude" (Paul Feine and Johannes Behm, *Introduction to the New Testament*, 14th ed., ed. W. Kümmel [New York: Abingdon, 1966], p. 303).

have been written by A.D. 60. In that case Peter could have used Jude. But would an apostle of the stature of Peter make use of material by one who was not an apostle? The utilization of material by ancient authors cannot be judged by today's standards of citation in writing. Tradition played a much larger role in the thoughts of writers and speakers then than it does today. This is evident (to go back to an OT example) from parallel accounts of Kings and Chronicles and also from the synoptic gospels. To sum up, the special problem of the relation between Jude and 2 Peter or their relation to some common source remains unsolved. The adoption of a particular position—viz., Jude as prior, 2 Peter as prior, or both Jude and 2 Peter used an earlier source—does not necessarily affect the authenticity, authorship, or inspiration of these letters. Any of the three views is compatible with an evangelical theology, and conservative scholars generally leave the question open.[18]

---

[18]Cf. Guthrie, *New Testament Introduction*, pp. 925–27, esp. p. 926, n. 3.

8. Outline

I. Salutation and Blessing (1:1–4)
II. The Essential Christian Virtues (1:5–15)
   1. The Efforts for Christian Fruitfulness (1:5–9)
   2. The Confirmation of Election (1:10–11)
   3. The Need for Reminders (1:12–15)
III. Christ's Divine Majesty (1:16–21)
   1. Attested by Apostolic Eyewitnesses (1:16–18)
   2. Attested by Divinely Originated Prophecy (1:19–21)
IV. False Prophets and Teachers (2:1–22)
   1. Warning Against False Teachers (2:1–3)
   2. Three Examples of Previous Judgments (2:4–10a)
   3. The Insolence and Wantonness of the False Teachers (2:10b–16)
   4. The Impotence of Their Teaching (2:17–22)
V. The Promise of the Lord's Coming (3:1–18)
   1. The Certainty of the Day of the Lord (3:1–10)
   2. The Ethical Implications of the Day of the Lord (3:11–16)
   3. The Need to Guard Against Error and to Grow in Grace (3:17–18)

Text and Exposition

I. Salutation and Blessing

1:1–4

[1]Simon Peter, a servant and apostle of Jesus Christ, To those who through the righteousness of our God and Savior Jesus Christ have received a faith as precious as ours:

[2]Grace and peace be yours in abundance through the knowledge of God and of Jesus our Lord.

[3]His divine power has given us everything we need for life and godliness through our knowledge of him who called us by his own glory and goodness. [4]Through these he has given us his very great and precious promises, so that through them you may participate in the divine nature and escape the corruption in the world caused by evil desires.

1 The author identifies himself as "Simon Peter." Some MSS have *Simōn*, which is the common Greek form of the name. The best-attested reading, however, is the Hebraic *Symeōn*, which is the more difficult spelling and is used of Peter only in Acts 15:14—a detail that supports the Petrine authorship of the letter, for a pseudonymous author would probably have used the more common spelling. *Symeōn*, an old Hebrew name, goes back to the second son of Jacob and Leah and became the tribal name of one of the twelve tribes of Israel.

The disciple *Symeōn* (Simon) also had the nickname "Cephas." This is the Greek transliteration of an Aramaic word for stone (cf. TDNT, 6:100–112) and *Petros* ("Peter") is its Greek translation. As Cullmann suggests, "In order to bring out the power of the nickname as the authors and early readers of the NT felt it, we ought perhaps to follow the NT practice and reproduce the name as Simon Rock" (ibid., 6:101). (See also Introduction to 1 Peter: Simon Peter.)

Peter gives a twofold identification of himself: "a servant and apostle of Jesus Christ." As a "servant" (*doulos;* lit., "slave"), he belongs to Jesus by right of purchase (so 1 Peter 1:18–19. "It was not with perishable things such as silver or gold that you were redeemed, . . . but with the precious blood of Christ"; cf. 1 Cor 6:19–20: "You are not your own; you were bought at a price"). As a servant of Christ, Peter is to obey his commands and do his will. The "servant" has status by virtue of the Lord he serves (cf. TDNT, 2:273–74). Moreover, as an "apostle" Peter has an authoritative commission and speaks God's words (cf. DNTT, 1:133–34).

Those whom Peter is addressing are described only in general terms that can apply to any Christian. The letter itself, however, contains a few clues concerning the people Peter is writing to. A relationship of some duration between author and recipients is implied by 1:12–15. From 3:15 we learn that Paul also wrote to them. In 3:1 Peter says, "This is now my second letter to you." Many scholars believe that the reference is to 1 Peter. If so, the recipients of 2 Peter are clearly identified in 1 Peter 1:1. But others have argued against this identification (cf. comments on 3:1) and posited a lost first letter (cf. 1 Cor 5:9 for a similar situation). If this is the case, we know practically nothing about those to whom 2 Peter was addressed.

The recipients are described as possessing "a faith as precious as ours." Is this "faith" the objective faith or "body of truth" committed to an individual? (so Schrage, Kelly,

Schelkle). Or should we take it in a subjective sense of the ability to trust God? (so Green). In favor of the latter are (1) the omission of the article before *pistin* ("faith"), (2) the fact that when faith is clearly objective (e.g., Jude 3, 20) the article is often present, and (3) that the only other use of faith (*pistis*) in this letter (cf. 1:5) is most likely subjective in sense. It is also possible that Peter combines the objective and subjective senses of faith much as we do when we sometimes speak of "our faith" (i.e., in Christ). In my judgment, the personal side of faith is clearly here. That Peter describes the faith of those he is writing to being as "precious" (*isotimon;* lit., "equally privileged") as "ours" underlines the fact that every Christian has equal access to God (Rom 5:2); every Christian has the same heavenly Father and the same prospect of glory.

The statement that those the letter is addressed to "have received" (*lachousin;* lit., "have been granted") their faith clearly implies that faith (whether objective, subjective, or both) is a gift of God. God's bestowal is through his "righteousness" (*dikaiosynē*) or, better, "justice." *Dikaiosynē* is a central biblical word, and Paul used it in stating the theme of Romans (1:1–16)—viz., justification by faith—and then in developing it. But here *dikaiosynē* means "justice," either in the sense of the impartiality of God's justice in giving all believers an equally privileged faith or in the sense of God's granting of salvation being compatible with his justice.

The phrase "of our God and Savior Jesus Christ" raises a well-known problem. Is Peter speaking of one person or two? Is Jesus called God here? The grammar leaves little doubt that in these words Peter is calling Jesus Christ both God and Savior (see Notes).

2 The first seven words of this verse are identical with 1 Peter 1:2b (see comment there), but here the words "through the knowledge of God and of Jesus our Lord" are added. As in other NT letters, the basic theme of the letter is quickly sounded. For 2 Peter it is the "knowledge" (*epignōsis*) of God. *Epignōsis* (lit., "full knowledge") also occurs in vv.3, 8 and in 2:20. The related verb *epiginōskō* occurs twice in 2:21. *Gnōsis* ("knowledge") occurs at 1:5, 6; 3:18; and *ginōskō* ("know") occurs at 1:20 and 3:3. This makes a total of eleven occurrences of these related words in this short letter (on these words, cf. Notes). The knowledge of God is a central biblical theme (cf. Jer 9:23–24; John 17:3; 1 John passim [42 occurrences of "knowing" in its 105 verses]; cf. Calvin *Institutes* 1.1). The knowledge of God was also claimed by the false teachers of the apostolic and postapostolic times. As Paul warned in Titus 1:16, "They claim to know God, but by their actions they deny him." In postapostolic times a developed "gnosticism" was the great challenge to the Christian church (cf. DNTT, 2:392–409).

3 The connection of this verse with v.2 is a problem. The English translation obscures the fact that in v.3 a genitive absolute (*dedōrēmenēs;* NIV, "has given") serves as the main verb. This either ties it to v.2 as the way in which the multiplication of the knowledge of God takes place or else it begins a new paragraph. NIV, RSV, and NEB take the latter position; KJV, RV, ASV, and NASB, the former one. Either position makes sense, but on balance the former one—namely, having vv.3–4 explain what is contained or conveyed in the knowledge of God—seems preferable.

God has called believers "by his own glory [*doxa*] and goodness [*aretē*]"—that is, God in salvation reveals his splendor (*doxa*) and his moral excellence (*aretē*), and these are means he uses to effect conversions. In bringing people to the knowledge of himself, God's divine power supplies them with everything they need for life and godliness. Probably what is in view is the work of the Spirit of God in believers, providing them with gifts and enabling them to use these gifts.

4 "Through these" refers to God's "glory and goodness" or "more generally [to] his saving intervention in the incarnation" (Kelly, p. 301). So when Jesus Christ came in his first advent, God made certain promises ("very great and precious") of the new Messianic Age (cf. 3:9, 13) to be brought in by the return of Christ. These promises of the coming Christological Age enable Christians to "participate in the divine nature."

How does this participation come about? In at least two ways, this verse implies. First, the promises themselves have a purifying effect on the believer's life (cf. 1 John 3:3). Second, conversion entails a definite break with the corruption caused by evil desire. The NIV rendering "and escape the corruption" might better be translated "since you have escaped" in order to bring out the force of the aorist participle (*apophygontes,* "have escaped"). Thus, in coming to know God through Christ, the believer escapes the corruption of sin; and Christ renews and restores the image of God in him.

Notes

1 Bigg (pp. 251–52) gives two forms of argumentation to support the view that "God" and "Savior" both refer to Jesus: grammatical and historical. The grammatical support is that (1) the use of one article with two substantives strongly suggests that these are names of the same Person; (2) if Peter intended to distinguish two Persons, it is doubtful whether he could have omitted the article before σωτῆρος (*sōtēros,* "Savior"); (3) Peter's usage of *sōtēr* is to couple it under the same article with another name (cf. 1:11; 2:20; 3:2, 18). Under historical support, Bigg finds analogous material in the NT for calling Jesus "God" (cf. John 1:1; 20:28); the doxologies addressed to Christ; the meaning of "Lord" in 1 Peter; and the language of the Apocalypse (cf. also A.T. Robertson, RHG, pp. 785–86).

2 Γνῶσις (*gnōsis*) is the noun for "knowledge"; γινώσκω (*ginōsko*) is the verb; ἐπιγινώσκω (*epiginōskō*) is the same verb with the prepositional prefix *epi*. Both verb forms are commonly translated "know," "learn," "notice," "understand." When emphasis is placed on the prepositional prefix, the meaning is "know exactly, completely, through and through" (BAG, pp. 290–91).

3–4 The vocabulary of 2 Peter contains a number of distinctive terms (e.g., θεῖος [*theios,* "divine"] and ἀρετή [*aretē,* "goodness," "virtue"]) and expressions (e.g., that "you may participate in the divine nature") that seem "unusual" for a Galilean fisherman. These "Hellenistic features" are commonly used as a major argument against Petrine authorship (cf. Werner G. Kümmel, *Introduction to the New Testament,* tr. H. Kee, rev. ed. [Nashville: Abingdon, 1975], p. 423). But we do not know how much "Hellenization" Peter was exposed to in Palestine, how much he learned after his conversion, or if he is picking up key terms in the false teachers' vocabulary and using them against them.

II. The Essential Christian Virtues (1:5–15)

1. *The Efforts for Christian Fruitfulness*

1:5–9

> [5]For this very reason, make every effort to add to your faith goodness; and to goodness, knowledge; [6]and to knowledge, self-control; and to self-control, perseverance; and to perseverance, godliness; [7]and to godliness, brotherly kindness; and to brotherly kindness, love. [8]For if you possess these qualities in increasing measure, they will keep you from being ineffective and unproductive in your knowledge of our Lord Jesus Christ. [9]But if anyone does not have them, he is nearsighted and blind, and has forgotten that he has been cleansed from his past sins.

5 Because of the new birth and the promises associated with it, Christians participate in the divine nature (v.4). But the new birth does not rule out human activity. Berkhof defines sanctification as "a work of God in which believers co-operate" (L. Berkhof, *Systematic Theology* [Grand Rapids: Eerdmans, 1939], p. 534). This definition fits the biblical pattern of ethical imperatives built on dogmatic indicatives (cf. Rom 6:11–14; 12:1f.; Phil 2:12–13; 1 Peter 1:13–21) and is in accord with biblical statements of how God works (cf. Rom 8:13b; Phil 2:13). So Peter urgently calls for a progressive, active Christianity. It is by faith alone that we are saved through grace, but this saving faith does not continue by itself (Eph 2:8–10). Peter's chain of eight virtues (vv.5–7) starts with faith and ends in love (cf. 1 Tim 1:5; Ignatius *To the Ephesians* 14.1: "Faith is the beginning and love is the end").

Christians are told to "make every effort to add to [their] faith." In NT times the word "add" (*epichorēgein*) was used of making a rich or lavish provision. Originally it referred to a person who paid the expenses of a chorus in staging a play. To "make every effort" (*spoudē*) requires both zeal and seriousness in the pursuit of holiness. "Goodness" (*aretē*) is an attribute of Christ himself (1:3) and therefore is to be sought by his people. It is excellence of achievement or mastery in a specific field—in this case virtue or moral excellence (cf. Phil 4:8; 1 Peter 2:9). The "knowledge" (*gnōsis*) that is to be added to faith is the advance into the will of God. The false teachers (the soon-to-come Gnostics) claimed a superior knowledge. The apostles stressed the necessity for those who know God to live a godly life (cf. 1 John 2:3–4; 5:18) and that Christ taught them the will of the Father (John 15:15).

6 The next virtue in Peter's chain is "self-control" (*egkrateia*). The concept of self-control played a great role in the philosophical ethics of classical Greece and Hellenism (TDNT, 2:340–41). But in NT ethical discussions it is not generally used, perhaps because the normal biblical emphasis is on God at work in us by the Spirit rather than on man's self-mastery. Self-control is the exact opposite of the excesses (2:3, 14, *pleonexia*, "greed") of the false teachers and the sexual abuses in the pagan world. The NT use of the noun *egkrateia* and the verb *egkrateuomai* ("control oneself," "abstain"), though limited, is instructive. Paul uses *egkrateuomai* of the unmarried—"But if they cannot control themselves, they should marry" (1 Cor 7:9)—and of his own self-discipline for the gospel (1 Cor 9:25). In preaching to Felix and Drusilla (Acts 24:25), Paul speaks of "self-control" (*egkrateia*). In the only other use of the noun besides 2 Peter 1:6, Paul lists it as one facet of the fruit of the Spirit (Gal 5:23). So while the biblical ethic does include "self-control," it sees self-control as the manifestation of the Spirit's work in man resulting in the human activity Paul speaks of in Romans 8:13.

Following self-control is patience (*hypomonē;* NIV, "perseverance"). This virtue views time with God's eyes (3:8) while waiting for Christ's return and for the punishment of sin. Perseverance is the ability to continue in the faith and resist the pressures of the world system (cf. Luke 8:15; Rom 5:3; Heb 12:2). "Godliness" (*eusebeia*) is piety or devotion to the person of God. Green defines it as "a very practical awareness of God in every aspect of life" (*Peter and Jude*, p. 70).

7 "Brotherly kindness" (*philadelphia*) and love (*agapē*) complete the list. The knowledge of God issues into the love of other believers (1 John 4:7–20). *Philadelphia* denotes the warmth of affection that should characterize the fellowship of believers. *Agapē* is the queen of the virtues (cf. 1 Cor 13) and denotes self-sacrificing action in behalf of another. This love flows from God who is himself love (*agapē* in 1 John 4:8) and reaches the world (John 3:16; 1 John 3:16). Godly people who participate in the divine nature must abound in love.

8 The knowledge of God is the beginning, the continuance, and the goal of the Christian life (cf. Phil 3:10). Peter is saying that if Christians possess in ever-increasing measure the eight virtues he has just listed, they will not be "ineffective and unproductive" (like the false teachers he describes in ch. 2). Progressive growth in the Christian graces is a sign of spiritual vitality and prevents "sloth" and unfruitfulness (Matt 13:22; John 15:1–7).

9 Not to have these virtues is to be "nearsighted and blind." In the NT "blind" (*typhlos*) is commonly used in a metaphorical as well as a literal sense (cf. John 9:39–41). The problem at this point is that in the Greek text "nearsighted" (*myōpazōn*) follows "blind." NIV solves it by reversing the order—viz., "nearsighted and blind." Perhaps the Greek construction can be taken as a causal participle—i.e., a person is blind because he is so nearsighted. Such a defect of vision (Peter is obviously speaking metaphorically) leads one to forgetfulness of cleansing from old sins. Perhaps Peter had in mind those who turn away from their commitment at baptism.

2. *The Confirmation of Election*

1:10–11

[10]Therefore, my brothers, be all the more eager to make your calling and election sure. For if you do these things, you will never fall, [11]and you will receive a rich welcome into the eternal kingdom of our Lord and Savior Jesus Christ.

10 In view of the dangers spoken of in v.9 and the possibility of a fruitful knowledge of God (v.8), Peter exhorts Christians "to make [their] calling and election sure." The word "make" (*poieisthai*) is in the middle voice and thus implies "to make for oneself." "Sure" (*bebaian*) is a word used of confirming something as in the legal terminology of validating a will. So a Christian by growing in grace becomes assured of having been called and elected by God. Bigg (p. 261) prefers a corporate sense of election here and in 1 Peter 1:1. In favor of a corporate or general election is the fact that "calling" (*klēsin*) and "election" (*eklogēn*) are bound together by the one Greek article (*tēn*) and that "calling" can have a general application (cf. Matt 22:14). Nevertheless, in the Pauline epistles calling and election are normally used in a particular sense (cf. Rom 8:28–30). Man responds in faith to God's gracious working. Likewise Peter's emphasis is clearly on human response. Many commentators see an influence of Paul on Peter (cf. comments on 2 Peter 3:15).

If Christians are continually advancing in the virtues mentioned in vv.5–7, they will never "stumble" or "fall" (*ptaiō*). Some have argued that "the loss of salvation" is in view here (BAG, p. 734). But the meaning of "suffer a reverse, misfortune" (TDNT, 6:884) fits the context well. Strong warnings about unfaithfulness to Christ and emphasis on the necessity of perseverance are common in the letters of Paul. See, for example, Colossians 1:22–23: "He has reconciled you by Christ's physical body through death to present you holy in his sight, without blemish and free from accusation—if you continue in your faith, established and firm, not moved from the hope of the gospel"; and 2 Timothy 2:12–13:

> If we endure,
> we will also reign with him.
> If we disown him,
> he will also disown us;
> If we are faithless,
> he will remain faithful,
> for he cannot disown himself.

11 Eschatology provides a motivation for ethics. Present difficulties are easier to go through because of bright prospects for the future, when "the kingdom of our Lord and Savior Jesus Christ" will be inaugurated. In one sense, Christians are already in the kingdom (Col. 1:13). Yet, as Paul and Barnabas said, "We must go through many hardships to enter the kingdom of God" (Acts 14:22). The kingdom is seen as temporally limited in 1 Corinthians 15:24 and Revelation 20:1–6. But in this verse, Peter speaks of it as "the eternal kingdom." A kingdom is where a king exercises his rule and authority. The diversity of statements about the kingdom in the Bible reflects the many facets of the rule of the triune God over humanity (both saved and lost) and also over angels (both fallen and unfallen) (cf. Pss 22:28; 145:11–13; Dan 4:35; Acts 17:24).

Jesus Christ is now the Lord (Acts 2:36), and as such he rules. In his coming to earth, his rule or kingdom will be visibly manifested and imposed (Matt 13:40–43). This will mark the end of this age and inaugurate the earthly messianic phase of the kingdom (Rev 20:1–6), which will last for a thousand years. Yet the kingdom does not end, for God's reign is eternal (Rev 11:15); and the mediatorial kingdom becomes the eternal kingdom of the triune God. Here, then, Peter looks to the future aspects of the kingdom of Jesus Christ that the believer enters at death or at the imposition of the kingdom.

The future for the Christian who diligently pursues holiness is very bright. He will be welcomed "richly" (*plousiōs;* NIV, "receive a rich welcome") "into the eternal kingdom." He will not barely "make it" into the kingdom or "be saved, . . . only as one escaping through the flames" (1 Cor 3:15); but he will receive his Lord's "Well done, good and faithful servant!" (Matt 25:21). Green (*Peter and Jude*, p. 75) suggests that perhaps Peter's words in v.11 allude to the honors paid to winners of the Olympic games. When a winner came back to his home town, he would be welcomed by a special entrance built in the town or city wall in his honor.

3. *The Need for Reminders*

1:12–15

[12]So I will always remind you of these things, even though you know them and are firmly established in the truth you now have. [13]I think it is right to refresh your memory as long as I live in the tent of this body, [14]because I know that I will soon put it aside, as our Lord Jesus Christ has made clear to me. [15]And I will make every effort to see that after my departure you will always be able to remember these things.

12 Truth needs to be repeated. The future hope is indeed well known to Christians. Yet reminders of it and exhortations regarding its application to life and service are essential. "So" (*dio*) links what Peter now says about reminding his readers with his statements about the need for possessing Christian virtues in increasing measure (v.8), participating in the divine nature (v.4), and the eschatological hope. Peter declares that he knows that they have a settled conviction of "the truth [they] now have" (*tē parousē alētheia*). The last statement implies a relatively fixed body of truth (cf. Jude 3: "the faith that was once for all entrusted to the saints"). This, however, is not necessarily to be taken as a sign of a late date or of "early Catholicism" since as far back as Acts 2:42 there is in the NT a body of recognizable apostolic truth.

"Firmly established" renders the perfect passive participle *estērigmenous*. Jesus used the related word *stērizō* ("establish," "strengthen") when he exhorted Simon Peter to "strengthen [his] brothers" (Luke 22:32). The teaching of the body of apostolic truth leads to spiritual strength; when one has received this teaching, he is established. But this does not obviate warnings of spiritual pitfalls, exhortations to pursue truth, and prayer for divine strengthening (1 Peter 5:10).

13–14 That Peter knows that he will not always live in "the tent of this body" (*skēnōmati*) underlines what he has been saying. The cognate word *skēnos* ("tent") was used of a body either living or dead. Paul, for example, uses it in 2 Corinthians 5:1, 4: "If the earthly tent we live in is destroyed. . . ." Although it is possible that Peter was influenced by Paul's usage, it is also possible that they shared a common linguistic and conceptual heritage. Peter knows that he will soon die and refers to a special revelation Jesus gave him (TDNT, 2:61–62). The most common interpretation links Peter's words to John 21:18–19, but this connection is uncertain. In that passage Jesus spoke of a violent death for Peter. So it is possible that Peter is speaking of some other revelation Jesus gave him.

For Christians death should hold no terrors; it is like putting off old clothes (*apothesis*) or an exit (*exodos*, v.15) from old age. According to Paul, to die is to "be with Christ" (Phil 1:23) in a new way. So in view of his approaching death, Peter wants "to refresh [his readers'] memory" (v.13). The verb rendered "refresh" (*diegeirō*) literally means "to wake up" or "arouse."

15 "And I will make every effort" translates *spoudasō* (future tense of *spoudazō*). See the use of the noun *spoudē* in v.5 and the verb in v.10. To use an educational term, Peter wants his readers to "overlearn" the basic truths so that after his death they will never forget them. Much discussion has centered around this sentence and the nature of what Peter is promising. Is he referring to the written form of his teaching or perhaps to the Gospel of Mark (so Green, *Peter and Jude*, p. 80; contra Kelly, p. 314)?

Probably Peter means that he intends to continue his ministry with all diligence until his death so as to strengthen the church. Apparently no specific writings are in view.

III. Christ's Divine Majesty (1:16–21)

1. *Attested by Apostolic Eyewitnesses*

1:16–18

> [16]We did not follow cleverly invented stories when we told you about the power and coming of our Lord Jesus Christ, but we were eyewitnesses of his majesty. [17]For he received honor and glory from God the Father when the voice came to him from the Majestic Glory, saying, "This is my Son, whom I love; with him I am well pleased."[18]We ourselves heard this voice that came from heaven when we were with him on the sacred mountain.

16 Here Peter links himself with the other apostles ("we"—cf. comment on v.18) in certifying that their message is based on their own eyewitness experience of Jesus and on hearing of God's attestation of him. Peter denies that they have followed "cleverly invented stories" (*sesophismenois mythois,* "stories," "myths"). The words refer to fables about the gods.

The NT always uses *mythos* in a negative sense and in contrast to the truth of the gospel (1 Tim 1:4; 4:7; 2 Tim 4:4; Titus 1:14). (On myth, cf. F.F. Bruce in DNTT, 2:644–47). It is likely that the false teachers claimed that the Incarnation, Resurrection, and coming kingdom the apostles spoke about were only stories. These teachers may have been men like Hymenaeus and Philetus, who said that "the resurrection has already taken place" (2 Tim 2:17–18). Apparently they denied a future aspect of eschatology or else reinterpreted it so as to lose its intended meaning.

The specific point in view was the second coming of Jesus (*tēn dynamin kai parousian,* "the power and coming"). Peter sees his preaching of the Second Coming as being based on his eyewitness observation of the transfiguration of Jesus (cf. vv.17–18 with Matt 16:28–17:5). In the return of Jesus, the kingdom will be visibly inaugurated in power. The dead will be raised, and judgment will occur. The "power" he will manifest in his coming embraces destruction of the lawless one (2 Thess 2:8) and his hosts (Rev 19:11–16), calling out the dead by his voice (John 5:28), judgment (John 5:27), and the consummation of the kingdom (Rev 11:15–18).

"Eyewitness" (*epoptai*) occurs only here in the NT. BAG (p. 305) defines it as a "t.t. [technical term] of the mysteries, to designate those who have been initiated into the highest grade of the mysteries" (cf. Kelly, p. 318; Green, *Peter and Jude,* p. 83). (Michaelis, TDNT, 5:375, denies any such usage of *epopteuō* [the related verb] here "to the usage in the mysteries.") Peter probably takes up a favorite term of some false teachers and uses their vocabulary against them. *Epopteuō* ("observe," "see") occurs in the NT only in 1 Peter 2:12; 3:2. This lends support to the view of the common origin of the two letters or of dependence of the second letter on the first one.

17 Verses 17–18 explain how and when Peter was an eyewitness of the majesty of Jesus Christ. God the Father gave honor and glory to Jesus. The "honor" is the public acknowledgment of his sonship (cf. Ps 2:6–7; Matt 3:17; Luke 3:22), and the "glory" is the transfiguration of the humiliated Son into his glorious splendor. On the Mount of Transfiguration, Jesus' face "shone like the sun," his clothes "became as white as the light" (Matt 17:1–9; Mark 9:2–10; Luke 9:28–36), a unique (*toiasde*, lit., "such as this") voice sounded from a bright cloud that covered them and said, "This is my Son, whom I love; with him I am well pleased." The scene showed Jesus as Messiah and was a preview of his glory as King.

18 Peter emphatically says, "We [*hēmeis;* NIV, 'we ourselves,' i.e., Peter, James, and John] heard this voice that came from heaven," while they were with Jesus "on the sacred mountain." It was the Transfiguration that transformed the mountain from a common one into a "sacred" (*hagios*) one. As for the place of the Transfiguration, Mount Hermon (over nine thousand feet high and near Caesarea Philippi, where the event that preceded the Transfiguration took place) or one of its spurs is the most likely choice. Traditionally, Mount Tabor, a steep eminence in the Plain of Jezreel, is identified as the Mount of Transfiguration. But its modest height makes it a less likely site than Hermon.

2. *Attested by Divinely Originated Prophecy*

1:19–21

[19]And we have the word of the prophets made more certain, and you will do well to pay attention to it, as to a light shining in a dark place, until the day dawns and the morning star rises in your hearts. [20]Above all, you must understand that no prophecy of Scripture came about by the prophet's own interpretation. [21]For prophecy never had its origin in the will of man, but men spoke from God as they were carried along by the Holy Spirit.

19 By saying "And we have the word of the prophets made more certain," Peter indicates that the OT prophets spoke of the same things he did and that their words are made more certain because the Transfiguration is a foreview of their fulfillment. Green (*Peter and Jude,* p. 87) adopts the interpretation that the Scriptures confirm the apostolic witness—viz., "We have also a more sure word of prophecy" (KJV). The critical term is *bebaioteron,* which BAG (p. 137) cites as meaning in this context "we possess the prophetic word as something altogether reliable." But if this meaning is adopted, there is no point of comparison between the OT prophecies and the apostles' testimony or that of the Voice at the Transfiguration. The comparative would be used for the superlative, and Peter would merely be giving additional reasons to cling to the message. On the whole, NIV is to be preferred to KJV and BAG.

After affirming the reliability of the OT Scriptures, Peter exhorts his readers to continue to pay careful attention to the prophetic message. He compares it to "light shining in a dark place" (cf. Ps 119:105: "Your word is a lamp to my feet and a light to my path"). The "dark place" is the whole world, which has turned from God the Light (cf. Isa 9:2; Eph 6:12). Christians are to ponder and keep the word of God "until the day dawns." The "day" is the day of the Parousia (cf. Rom 13:12). The "morning star" (*phōsphoros*) appears only here in the NT, but the use of "star" for the Messiah occurs in Numbers 24:17 ("a star . . . out of Jacob"). Related expressions—"the rising sun" (Luke 1:78) and "the bright Morning Star [*astēr*]" (Rev 22:16)—support the view that Peter is referring to Christ in his advent.

The phrase "rises in your hearts" is difficult. Green (*Peter and Jude,* p. 89) suggests the possibility of reading this phrase as part of v.20 rather than v.19. But the word order in Greek is against this. The idea that the Second Coming is only subjective (that is, only "in your hearts") is clearly contrary to the eschatology of the book (cf. 3:4, 10) and to the rest of the NT (cf. Acts 1:11; 1 Thess 4:13–18; 2 Thess 2:8). The best interpretation sees "in your hearts" as the subjective results of Christ's actual coming. When he comes, an illuminating transformation will take place in believers.

20 Peter continues his exhortation with the expression "above all" (*touto prōton ginōskontes;* lit., "knowing this first"). The primary thing to be known is that the prophetic Scriptures did not come into being through the prophet's "own interpretation" (*idias epilyseōs;* lit., "of one's now unloosing"—though *epilysis* is the regular word for "interpretation"). What exactly does Peter mean by this expression? The major views are that (1) no prophecy is a matter of one's own interpretation—so either the church must interpret prophecy, the interpretation must be that intended by the Holy Spirit, or the individual's interpretation is not to be "private" but according to the analogy of faith; (2) the NIV translation, "No prophecy of Scripture came about by the prophet's own interpretation"—i.e., no prophecy originated through the interpretation of the prophet himself; and (3) *epilysis* is not to be taken as meaning the interpretation but refers to the origination of Scripture. The sense of the verse is probably that of the first view, that no prophecy of Scripture is to be interpreted by any individual in an arbitrary way. This fits the problem of the false teachers' distorting Paul's writings and other Scripture mentioned at 3:16, and the next verse clarifies that the prophecy originated with the Holy Spirit.

21 Each prophecy originated in God (*apo theou*), not in the will of man. To understand each prophecy, one must interpret it not according to one's own "private" ideas. Verse 21 is notable for the light it sheds on how Scripture was produced. Peter's statement "men spoke from God" implies the dual authorship of Scripture. This is also implied in the OT. For example, David said, "The Spirit of the Lord spoke through me; his word was on my tongue" (2 Sam 23:2); or as Jeremiah was told, "You must . . . say whatever I command you. . . . Now, I have put my words in your mouth" (Jer 1:7, 9). Men spoke, but God so worked in them so that what they said was his word. It was not through a process of dictation or through a state of ecstasy that the writers of Scripture spoke but through the control of the Spirit of God—"as they were carried along by the Holy Spirit." (For other texts on Inspiration, cf. 1 Cor 14:37; 2 Tim 3:16.)

Notes

21 NIV's "men spoke from God" follows the UBS text. The KJV "holy men" has good support but the insertion of ἅγιοι (*hagioi*, "holy") is easier to explain than its omission.

IV. False Prophets and Teachers (2:1–22)

1. *Warning Against False Teachers*

2:1–3

[1]But there were also false prophets among the people, just as there will be false teachers among you. They will secretly introduce destructive heresies, even denying the sovereign Lord who bought them—bringing swift destruction on themselves.

> [2]Many will follow their shameful ways and will bring the way of truth into disrepute. [3]In their greed these teachers will exploit you with stories they have made up. Their condemnation has long been hanging over them, and their destruction has not been sleeping.

1 Although Israel had a notable succession of true prophets, she was often plagued by false or lying prophets (cf. Deut 13:1–5; 18:20; 1 Kings 18:19; 22:6ff.; Jer 5:31; 23:9–18). "The people" (*laos*) is a common designation for Israel (cf. TDNT, 4:52–54). The church also must expect false teachers to come in (cf. Acts 20:29). They "secretly introduce" (*pareisaxousin*) or "smuggle in" their doctrines. Similar warnings occur in Galatians 2:4, concerning the entrance of false brothers into a Christian gathering, and in 2 Corinthians 11:13–15, concerning Satan's masqueraders. The "destructive heresies" are teachings that lead to darkness and damnation. The focal point of their error was christological; they were "denying the sovereign Lord who bought them." The "sovereign Lord" (*despotēs*) is Christ (so BAG, p. 175; DNTT, 2:509; TDNT, 2:48–49), as in the parallel in Jude 4.

"Who bought them" is a difficult phrase. It seems to some to raise questions about the Calvinistic doctrine of the perseverance of the saints (i.e., eternal security). The theological problem lies in the fact that persons bought by Christ appear to be lost. Clark writes, "The meaning of 2:1 is . . . that the false teachers even deny the God who delivered the Israelites from Egypt" (*II Peter*, pp. 38–39). For him the words "denying the sovereign Lord who bought them" refer to the God of the Exodus who is denied rather than to Jesus Christ and what he did on the cross for the false teachers. This requires understanding the antecedent of "them" to be "the people" in the first part of the sentence. While this is grammatically possible, it is very unlikely because of the distance between the pronoun and its antecedent noun. The natural sense of the verse is that "they" (the false teachers) deny the Lord who bought them (the false teachers).

Other solutions to the theological problem have been advanced. Among them are the following:

1. The false teachers were redeemed but fell away or lost their salvation. But to many Christians, including many who are not strict Calvinists, the idea that a redeemed person can lose his salvation contradicts clear passages that state the contrary (e.g., John 10:28–29; Rom 8:28–39). Moreover, v.2 says nothing about the application of redemption to the false teachers or their appropriation of it.

2. The word "redeem" (*agorazō;* NIV, "bought") is to be taken in the sense of "temporal deliverance" or "sovereign creation"—viz., that the word is not used soteriologically (Gary Long, *Definite Atonement* [Nutley, N.J.: Presbyterian and Reformed, 1976], pp. 67–78).

3. Some Calvinistic interpreters argue that Peter is speaking not in terms of the reality of the false teachers' faith but in terms of their profession. They profess to be those who have been bought by the blood of Christ, but they are lying.

4. Calvin, speaking of the false teachers, said, "Those who throw over the traces and plunge themselves into every kind of license are not unjustly said to deny Christ, by whom they are redeemed" (*Epistles of Peter*, p. 346).

In my judgment, v.2 asserts that Christ "bought" the false teachers; but this does not necessarily mean that they were saved. Salvation in the NT sense does not occur till the benefits of Christ's work are applied to the individual by the regeneration of the Spirit and belief in the truth. To put it in other words, Christ crucified is the propitiation for the sins of the whole world (1 John 2:2). Yet the wrath of God is on all sinners—elect and nonelect (John 3:36; Eph 2:3)—till the work of the Cross is applied to those who believe.

"Bringing swift destruction on themselves" is "not a simple extinction of existence . . . but an everlasting state of torment and death" (TDNT, 1:397). It will be "swift" because it will descend on them suddenly either at their death or at the return of the Lord.

2 The false teachers will be popular with many followers. John speaks of the same phenomenon when, speaking of the false prophets who do not acknowledge that Jesus is from God, he says, "The world listens to them" (1 John 4:5). Moreover, Peter says that the many adherents of the false teachers "will follow their shameful ways" (*aselgeiais*, "vices," "sexual debaucheries"; cf. 1 Peter 4:3; 2 Peter 2:7, 18). Their disciples will be like the false teachers and, bringing their sexual immorality into the churches, will cause "the way of truth" to be defamed. "The way" (*hē hodos*) was a common early name for the Christian faith (cf. Acts 9:2; 19:9, 23; 22:4; 24:14, 22). The thought of ungodly conduct bringing reproach on the name of God or Christ occurs in Romans 2:23–24; 1 Timothy 6:1; and Titus 2:5.

It is important to understand that the Christian faith is "the way of truth." It is not only correct thought or "truth" but it is the "way" of life that responds to and is determined by the truth. True doctrine must issue in true living. The knowledge of God should lead to a godly life.

3 Christian teachers have the right to financial support (cf. 1 Cor 9:1–14; Gal 6:6; 1 Tim 5:17–18), but their motivation in the ministry should not be mercenary. For false teachers, however, religion will be commercialized—they will "buy and sell, trade in" (cf. *emporeuomai*, BAG, p. 256) and exploit people. With fabricated stories they fleece the sheep. In the light of the commercialism of religious cults today, Peter's warning is clear enough.

The popularity and prosperity of the errorists will certainly come to an end (3b). Their judgment and doom has been announced long ago (cf. Ps 1:5–6). Destruction (*apōleia*, used twice in v.1), is now personified as "not sleeping" (*ou nystazei*). NEB translates it "perdition waits for them with unsleeping eyes." The only other NT use of *nystazo* ("become drowsy") occurs in Matthew 25:5 in the parable of the wise and foolish virgins.

2. *Three Examples of Previous Judgments*

2:4–10a

[4]For if God did not spare angels when they sinned, but sent them to hell, putting them into gloomy dungeons to be held for judgment; [5]if he did not spare the ancient world when he brought the flood on its ungodly people, but protected Noah, a preacher of righteousness, and seven others; [6]if he condemned the cities of Sodom and Gomorrah by burning them to ashes, and made them an example of what is going to happen to the ungodly; [7]and if he rescued Lot, a righteous man, who was distressed by the filthy lives of lawless men [8](for that righteous man, living among them day after day, was tormented in his righteous soul by the lawless deeds he saw and heard)— [9]if this is so, then the Lord knows how to rescue godly men from trials and to hold the unrighteous for the day of judgment, while continuing their punishment. [10]This is especially true of those who follow the corrupt desire of the sinful nature and despise authority.

Syntactically, vv.4–9 are a single sentence, one of the longest in the NT. The protasis (the "if" part of a conditional sentence) is extended by the use of three examples of divine judgment. The apodosis (the conclusion) is delayed until v.9. In the NIV, the "if" (*ei*) is repeated four times (vv.5, 6, 7, 9); in the Greek text it occurs only in v.4. The cumulative examples of the first part of the sentence make the main point (v.9) stand out with force and emphasis.

4 The first example of divine judgment is that which came upon the fallen angels. The literal word order from the Greek is instructive—"For if God angels who sinned did not spare"—stressing that if angels are judged, then certainly men will also be judged. Of which judgment of angels does Peter speak? Jesus said, "I saw Satan fall like lightning from heaven" (Luke 10:18); and John in Revelation 12:7–9 describes a war in heaven after which Satan and his angels were cast down to the earth. The most common interpretation is to relate the judgment Peter speaks of with the mention of angels in Genesis 6:1–4 (where "sons of God" apparently means "fallen angels"; cf. Job 1:6; 2:1; 38:7). Another interpretation relates this judgment to the original sin of the angels. But the explanation in relation to Genesis 6:1–4 is best because (1) it was common in Jewish literature (Enoch 6:2; 1 QapGen col. 2), (2) the three examples (angels, Flood, and cities of the plain) all come one after another in the early chapters of Genesis, and (3) the angels referred to here in 2 Peter are confined to "gloomy dungeons." Apparently some fallen angels are free to plague mankind as demons while others such as these are imprisoned. The connection with Genesis 6:1–4 provides a reason for this phenomenon.

Peter uses the verb *tartaroō* ("to hold captive in Tartarus") to tell where the sinning angels were sent. "Tartarus, thought of by the Greeks as a subterranean place lower than Hades where divine punishment was meted out, was so regarded in Jewish apocalyptic as well" (BAG, p. 813). The usual translation of *tartaroō* as "sent" or "cast into hell" (so KJV, RSV, NASB, NIV, et al.) only approximates the idea of a special place of confinement until the final judgment. Though "gloomy dungeons" (*seirais zophou*) may be correct, "chains of darkness" (KJV) is an equally possible translation (cf. Jude 6). *Seira* ("a chain"), *seiros* ("a pit"), and *siros* ("a pit," "a cave") all occur in the MSS.

5 Peter's second example is the Flood. He has referred to it in his first letter (3:18–22) and will do so again in the next chapter of this one (3:5–6). Noah was the "eighth" (*ogdoos*) meaning there were seven others saved with him (wife, three sons, and daughters-in-law). They were guarded or protected by God during the Flood that wiped out the ungodly antediluvian civilization. Noah was a herald (*kēryx*) of righteousness. This could refer to his preaching activity not recorded in the OT or to the fact that his lifestyle condemned sin and proclaimed righteousness to his contemporaries (Gen 6:9).

6 The third example of judgment is the destruction of the cities of Sodom and Gomorrah. According to Genesis 19:24–28, "the LORD rained down burning sulfur on Sodom and Gomorrah—from the LORD out of heaven." The area is rich in bitumen, salt, and sulfur and has been geologically active in historical times. The Lord may have used volcanism as the means of his judgment. Peter says he "condemned" them "by burning them to ashes." The rare word *tephrōsas* means either "reduce to ashes" or "cover with ashes." This word is cited in MM (p. 632) as being used in Dio Cassius (66.1094) of Vesuvius's erupting and Lycophron's "being overwhelmed with ashes." This total destruction is an example (*hypodeigma*) to the ungodly of the things that are going to happen to them.

7–8 In the midst of God's judgment of the cities of the plain, he delivered Lot, whom Peter calls "righteous." This is puzzling because in Genesis Lot is hardly notable for his righteousness. He seems worldly and weak and had to be dragged out of Sodom (Gen 19:16). Yet Abraham's intercession in Genesis 18:16–33 may imply that he considered Lot to be righteous. Peter's characterization of Lot may reflect extrabiblical revelation or tradition such as Wisdom of Solomon 10:6, where Lot is called "the just one." It is also possible that Peter inferred Lot's righteousness from his deliverance from the destruction of Sodom and from his being "tormented" and "distressed by the filthy lives" of his fellow citizens. The contemporary application is plain. To what extent are Christians living today in a godless society "tormented" (*ebasanizen*) by what they see?

9 Peter states the main point next. It is one of abiding comfort. "The Lord knows how to rescue godly men from trials." Suffering Christians anywhere and at any time can find consolation in the fact that their Lord knows all about their plight. Furthermore, "the Lord knows how . . . to hold the unrighteous for the day of judgment, *while continuing their punishment*" (italics mine). Immediate judgment of sinners is only the beginning. Temporal judgments, death, and "being in torment" in Hades (Luke 16:23) do not exhaust the divine wrath. A great Judgment is yet future (Rev 20:11–15), followed by the "second death" (Rev 20:14)—the lake of fire.

10a God's wrath is especially certain to fall on the false teachers of Peter's day. He characterizes them as "indulging the flesh" (i.e., as "those who follow the corrupt desire of the sinful nature"). This refers to sexual profligacy. They also "despise authority." "Authority" translates *kyriotētos*, which may refer to the rejection of angelic powers (cf. Eph 1:21; Col 1:16). Most likely, however, it refers here to their rejection of the rule of the Lord (*kyrios*) Jesus Christ over them.

3. *The Insolence and Wantonness of the False Teachers*

2:10b–16

Bold and arrogant, these men are not afraid to slander celestial beings; [11]yet even angels, although they are stronger and more powerful, do not bring slanderous accusations against such beings in the presence of the Lord. [12]But these men blaspheme in matters they do not understand. They are like brute beasts, creatures of instinct, born only to be caught and destroyed, and like beasts they too will perish.

[13]They will be paid back with harm for the harm they have done. Their idea of pleasure is to carouse in broad daylight. They are blots and blemishes, reveling in their pleasures while they feast with you. [14]With eyes full of adultery, they never stop sinning; they seduce the unstable; they are experts in greed—an accursed brood! [15]They have left the straight way and wandered off to follow the way of Balaam son of Beor, who loved the wages of wickedness. [16]But he was rebuked for his wrongdoing by a donkey—a beast without speech—who spoke with a man's voice and restrained the prophet's madness.

10 The false teachers are "bold and arrogant"—i.e., presumptuous and self-willed. They respect no one, and nothing restrains them. "They are not afraid to slander celestial beings [*doxai*]." *Doxai* has been interpreted to mean (1) the imperial and magisterial power (so Calvin, *Epistles of Peter,* p. 401, but few follow this view), (2) rulers of the church (Bigg, p. 280), (3) good angels, or (4) fallen angels. As *doxai* seems highly unusual as a term for church leaders or magistrates, most interpreters think it refers to celestial beings of some kind. Because v.11 implies that these beings bring slanderous accusations in the presence of the Lord, it seems best to think of them as fallen angels. As to when they slandered or what kind of slander was involved, one can only surmise. Perhaps the false teachers were accused of being in league with Satan, and their reply was to disparage and mock him (cf. Jude 8–9).

11 In contrast to these audacious errorists, angels, even though they are stronger and more powerful, do not indict "such beings" (i.e., the "celestial beings"—perhaps the fallen angels of v.4) in the presence of the Lord. The good angels are more powerful than the fallen ones (cf. Rev 12:7–8).

12 The false teachers act like irrational animals without the restraint that angels and righteous men have. They may claim a *gnōsis* (a special knowledge), but they blaspheme out of their ignorance. Like wild beasts who are slaves to their instincts and are born to be slaughtered, they too are destined for destruction (lit., "in their destruction, they shall be destroyed").

13 "They will be paid back with harm for the harm they have done" translates three Greek words (*adikoumenoi misthon adikias*). The verb *adikeō* commonly means "to suffer injustice," which may account for the variant reading *komioumenoi* ("receiving"). Perhaps a scribe thought that the reading *adikoumenoi* implies that God was treating them unjustly. But the UBS text makes good sense and preserves a word play in Greek that is quite characteristic of Peter's style in this epistle. So the errorists "suffer harm" as a "wage" of "injury."

Normally one thinks of carousing as a nighttime activity (1 Thess 5:7), perhaps because of the shame involved. But these people carouse in broad daylight. Peter sees them as "feasting together" with the recipients of his letter. Perhaps Peter has in mind the love feasts or communal meals of the church (cf. NIV mg.). "Reveling in their pleasures" translates *en tais apatais autōn,* which literally means "reveling in their deceptions." *Apatais* in later Greek means "pleasure" or "lusts" (BAG, p. 81).

14 In the Greek text vv.12–16 are one sentence. So the vivid phrase "with eyes full of adultery" (*ophthalmous echontes mestous moichalidos;* lit., "having eyes full of an adulteress," meaning to desire every woman they see) implies that the false teachers desired to turn church gatherings into times of dissipation. They are, Peter says, "never at rest from sin" (NEB), or their eyes unceasingly look for sin. They "seduce" (*deleazō,* "lure," "bait," "entice") "unstable souls" (*psychai;* NIV, "unstable"). Here "soul" means "person" as in 1 Peter 3:20. The unstable are those with no foundation (*astēriktous*). In 1:12 of this letter Peter has spoken of his readers as being "firmly established [*estērigmenous*] in the truth," and in 3:16 he will warn them of "unstable" (*astēriktos*) people and of the danger of falling "from [their] secure position" (*stērigmos*) in 3:17 (cf. comments on 1:12).

"They are experts in greed" is literally "having a heart exercised in greed." The word "exercised" (*gegymnasmenos*) relates to athletic training (cf. our English word "gymnasium"). In biblical thought the "heart" denotes the center of human personality (cf. Prov 4:23). Deep within them, the thoughts of the false teachers are of *pleonexia* ("greediness, insatiableness, avarice, covetousness, lit. 'a desire to have more' " [BAG, p. 673]). Of them Peter exclaims, "An accursed brood!" (lit., "children of a curse"), meaning that God's curse is on them.

15–16 The false teachers resemble Balaam, the son of Beor (Bosor in most MSS), in that Balaam loved money and was willing to pursue it instead of obeying God (Num 22:5–24:25). Balaam also taught immorality (Num 31:16; Rev 2:14). So the false teachers have left the biblical way and have gone into Balaam's error—mercenary greed and sexual impurity. As Balaam went to curse the children of Israel for money (if he could) "he was rebuked for his wrongdoing by a donkey—a beast without speech." Actually, according to the account in Numbers 22:27–35, the rebuke is twofold: first from the donkey, then from the angel of the Lord. Ironically the dumb animal had more "spiritual" perception than the prophet! The utterance (*phthenxamenon*, "to utter a loud sound") restrained the prophet's "insanity" (*paraphronia*—a "hapax legomenon," [occurring only here, though a related verb is found in 2 Cor 11:23]).

Notes

15 Balaam is the son of Beor (Βεώρ, *Beōr;* Heb. בְּעוֹר, *b^e ṣôr*) according to Num 22:5; 31:8; Deut 23:4. Yet most MSS spell his name Βοσόρ (*Bosor*) in 2 Peter 2:15. No good reason is known for this. Green (*Peter and Jude*, p. 113) suggests that *Bosor* may represent "the Galilean mispronunciation of the guttural in the Hebrew name."

4. *The Impotence of Their Teaching*

2:17–22

> [17]These men are springs without water and mists driven by a storm. Blackest darkness is reserved for them. [18]For they mouth empty, boastful words and, by appealing to the lustful desires of sinful human nature, they entice people who are just escaping from those who live in error. [19]They promise them freedom, while they themselves are slaves of depravity—for a man is a slave to whatever has mastered him. [20]If they have escaped the corruption of the world by knowing our Lord and Savior Jesus Christ and are again entangled in it and overcome, they are worse off at the end than they were at the beginning. [21]It would have been better for them not to have known the way of righteousness, than to have known it and then to turn their backs on the sacred commandment that was passed on to them. [22]Of them the proverbs are true: "A dog returns to its vomit," and, "A sow that is washed goes back to her wallowing in the mud."

17 Whatever else may be said about this chapter, it is a powerful piece of writing that gains momentum as it reaches its climax. In vivid words, Peter goes on to describe the false teachers as "springs without water." Christ provides "a spring of water welling up to eternal life" (John 4:13–14), and from those who believe in him flow "streams of living water" (John 7:37–38). But the false teachers give nothing because they have nothing to give. They are "mists driven by a storm," a metaphor of their instability and transcience. The "blackest darkness . . . reserved for them" (*ho zophos tou skotous*) may refer to hell, for *zophos* is used especially of "the darkness of the nether regions" (BAG, p. 340).

18 These heretics "mouth [*phthengomenoi*, same word as in v.16] boastful [*hyperonka*, 'swollen,' 'of excessive size'] words." Kelly (p. 345) says, "In plain language, their propaganda consists of declaiming bombastic futilities (lit. 'bombastic words of vanity')." By their sensual propaganda, they ensnare (*deleazō*, same word as v.14) "people who are just escaping from those who live in error." So they take for their targets new converts to Christianity from paganism.

19 They promise "freedom," perhaps from any law or restraint of the flesh. Paul ran into similar error—"Everything is permissible for me" (1 Cor 6:12f.)—among false teachers in Corinth, and possibly in Galatia also (cf. Gal 5:14). Yet, Peter says, the very ones who speak of freedom are "slaves of depravity—for a man is a slave to whatever has mastered him." To this the best parallel is Jesus' words: "Everyone who sins is a slave to sin" (John 8:34; cf. Rom 6:16; 1 Cor 6:12b). So though the false teachers talk of religion and freedom, they do not know the Son; for as Jesus said, "If the Son sets you free, you will be free indeed" (John 8:36).

20 Of whom is Peter speaking in vv.20–22—i.e., who does the pronoun "they" refer to? Does it refer (1) to the false teachers of v.19, (2) to the unstable people of v.18, or (3) more generally to both but particularly to the false teachers (cf. Balz and Schrage, p. 140)? In my opinion, it refers basically to false teachers because (1) proximity makes the false teachers (spoken of in v.19) the normal antecedent of "they," (2) the conjunction *gar* (untranslated in NIV) in v.20 (*ei gar*, "for if") logically connects v.20 with v.19, (3) "mastered" (*hēttētai*) in v.19 is verbally linked to "overcome" (*hēttōtai*) in v.20, and (4) the teachers are the main subject of the whole chapter. (For arguments supporting view 2, see Kelly, pp. 347–48.)

Verse 20 mentions the possibility of reverting to the old paganism after having "escaped the corruptions of the world" through knowing Jesus Christ as Lord and Savior. Is it possible, then, for Christians to lose their salvation? Many would answer affirmatively on the basis of this and similar texts (e.g., Heb 6:4–6; 10:26). But this verse asserts only that false teachers who have for a time escaped from worldly corruption through knowing Christ and then turn away from the light of the Christian faith are worse off than they were before knowing Christ. It uses no terminology affirming that they were Christians in reality (e.g., "sons of God," "children," "born again," "regenerate," "redeemed"). The NT makes a distinction between those who are in the churches and those who are regenerate (cf. 2 Cor 13:5; 2 Tim 2:18–19; 1 John 3:7–8; 2:19: "They went out from us, but they did not really belong to us. . . . but their going showed that none of them belonged to us"). So when Peter says, "They are worse off at the end than they were at the beginning," the reference is to a lost apostate.

21 This verse underlines the seriousness of apostasy. The "sacred commandment that was passed on to them" evidently refers to the authoritative, apostolic message; *paradotheisēs* ("that was passed on") is an important NT term for the transmission of the Christian faith (cf. 1 Cor 15:3; TDNT, 2:171–73). The "sacred commandment" is the whole Christian message with emphasis on its ethical demands (DNTT, 1:339).

22 Peter concludes his strong denunciation of the false teachers by citing two proverbs. The first is a biblical one (Prov 26:11); the second is extrabiblical. Both dogs and pigs were considered vile by the Jews. (For background information on "dogs" in Scripture and Jewish culture, cf. TDNT, 3:1101–4.) So the false teachers are unclean and return to the pagan corruption. Significantly, Jesus used the designations "dogs" and "pigs" in speaking of those opposed to God and his Word. Though it may be overinterpretation, many have observed that the nature of the "unclean" animals does not change. So the "dog [that] returns to its vomit" or the sow that "is washed" (*lousamenē;* lit., "washed itself," an aorist middle participle) portrays the person who has a religious "profession" or outward change without a regenerating inner change that affects his nature. Such a person soon reverts to his true nature.

Notes

---

18 The evidence in relation to ὀλίγως (*oligōs,* "scarcely," "barely"; NIV, "just") and ὄντως (*ontōs,* "really," "certainly," "in truth") is fairly evenly divided. In Gr. capitals (ΟΛΙΓΩΣ, ΟΝΤΩΣ) the readings are easily confused. *Oligōs* is a rare word and, if genuine here, this is its only NT usage.

V. The Promise of the Lord's Coming (3:1–18)

1. *The Certainty of the Day of the Lord*

3:1–10

1Dear friends, this is now my second letter to you. I have written both of them
as reminders to stimulate you to wholesome thinking. 2I want you to recall the words
spoken in the past by the holy prophets and the command given by our Lord and
Savior through your apostles.
3First of all, you must understand that in the last days scoffers will come, scoffing
and following their own evil desires. 4They will say, "Where is this 'coming' he
promised? Ever since our fathers died, everything goes on as it has since the
beginning of creation." 5But they deliberately forget that long ago by God's word
the heavens existed and the earth was formed out of water and with water. 6By
water also the world of that time was deluged and destroyed. 7By the same word
the present heavens and earth are reserved for fire, being kept for the day of
judgment and destruction of ungodly men.
8But do not forget this one thing, dear friends: With the Lord a day is like a
thousand years, and a thousand years are like a day. 9The Lord is not slow in
keeping his promise, as some understand slowness. He is patient with you, not
wanting anyone to perish, but everyone to come to repentance.
10But the day of the Lord will come like a thief. The heavens will disappear with
a roar; the elements will be destroyed by fire, and the earth and everything in it will
be laid bare.

1 "Dear friends" (*agapētoi,* "beloved") is repeated in vv.8, 14, and 17 in this chapter. "This is now my second letter to you." Does this refer to 1 Peter? Most commentators say yes. But this is not certain because (1) it has not been established that the recipients of the two letters are the same, (2) 1:12, 16 may imply a personal ministry to the recipients of this second letter that 1 Peter gives no indication of, (3) the description of the two letters ("both of them as reminders") here in 3:1 does not fit 1 Peter very well, and (4) other letters of apostles have not been preserved (cf. 1 Cor 5:9; Col 4:16). None of these points is in itself very strong; yet taken together and when coupled with the lack of use of 1 Peter in 2 Peter, they raise a doubt that leaves the question open.

"As reminders to stimulate you" (*diegeirō hymōn en hypomnēsei*) is almost identical with the phrase in 1:13 that NIV translates "to refresh your memory" (*diegeirein hymas en hypomnēsei*). "To wholesome thinking" translates *eilikrinē dianoian* (lit., "pure minds"). *Dianoia* is commonly used in the LXX for "heart" (Heb. *lēb*). Behm thinks that "in 2 Pt. 3:1 the [*eilikrinēs dianoia*] which the author seeks to maintain in his readers through the epistle is a 'pure disposition' " (TDNT, 4:967).

2 In the Greek text, v.2 continues the sentence begun in v.1 and is notable for the succession of words in the genitive case. NIV smooths out the rough construction by reversing the order of words. The sense is fairly plain, but a few points need clarification. The "words spoken in the past" are the prophetic oracles with special reference here to the day of the Lord. The "commandment" is a way of referring to the moral demands of the Christian faith (cf. 2:21 and comments there) and primarily to the command of love.

Kelly claims that "the expression *your apostles* could not of course have been penned by the historical Peter; it inadvertently betrays that the writer belongs to an age when the apostles have been elevated to a venerated group who mediate Christ's teaching authoritatively to the whole church" (p. 354). Kelly's claim, however, is unfair. If Peter had written "my command" or "from us," the same objection would doubtless be raised. The premise on which Kelly's claim rests is that the apostles were not so conscious of their authority as v.2b implies. If this premise is adopted, the apostolicity of many sections of the NT must be rejected, for they claim more than Peter does here (cf. Rom 1:1, 5; 1 Cor 14:37; 1 John 1:1–5; 4:6; Rev 22:18). To place the prophets and apostles on the same level is not "postapostolic" (cf. Eph 2:20) but it is simply to recognize that the Spirit used them both.

3 Peter next states a primary thing to be remembered from the prophetic and apostolic deposit: the appearance of scoffers in the last days, who deny biblical truths and live in an ungodly way (cf. Dan 7:25; 11:36–39; Matt 24:3–5, 11, 23–26; 1 Tim 4:1ff.; 2 Tim 3:1–7; Jude 17–18). The "last days" are the days that come between the first coming of the Messiah and his second coming. The "scoffers" are the false teachers of chapter 2 who deny a future eschatology. Bertram suggests that they were "possibly Gnostic libertines" (TDNT, 5:636). On the subject of mockery, see TDNT, 5:630–36, for the antithesis between the mockers and the righteous in the biblical revelation (cf. Ps 1:1, 6).

4 Part of the early church proclamation was the announcement of the return of Jesus to complete the work of salvation and to punish the wicked (cf., e.g., Matt 24:3ff.; John 14:1–3; Acts 1:11; 17:31; Rom 13:11; 1 Cor 15:23; 1 Thess 4:13–18; 5:1–11; 2 Thess 1:7–10; Heb 9:28; Rev 1:7). The false teachers ask, "Where is this 'coming' he promised?" Mocking the faith of Christians, they support their own position by claiming, "Ever since our fathers died, everything goes on as it has since the beginning of creation." Who are the persons Peter calls "our fathers"? Kelly (p. 355) and Schelkle (p. 224) argue that they were first-generation Christians. But Bigg (p. 291) and Green (*Peter and Jude,* p. 128–29) consider this unlikely. "Fathers" are much more likely to be OT fathers as in John 6:31, Acts 3:13, Romans 9:5, and Hebrews 1:1. This is the normal NT usage, and the other view requires a clumsy forger to have missed so obvious a blunder. "Our fathers died" (lit., "fell asleep") is a lovely metaphor for the death of believers (cf. Acts 7:60; 1 Thess 4:13–14). The argument of the false teachers is essentially a naturalistic one—a kind of uniformitarianism that rules out any divine intervention in history.

5–6 But they "deliberately [*thelontas,* 'willingly'] forget" the great Flood, when God intervened in history by destroying the antediluvian world. What they forget is not only the Flood but also God's prior activity by his word—the existence of the heavens and the watery formation of the earth (Gen 1:2–10). It seems unlikely that Peter is seeking to affirm that water was the basic material of creation, though many commentators claim this. He does not use the verb *ktizō* ("create") but says that "long ago by God's word the heavens existed [*ēsan*] and the earth was formed [*synestōsa*] out of water and with water." In Genesis the sky (firmament) separates the waters from the waters by the word of God and the land appears out of the water by the same word.

At the beginning of v.6, NIV renders the Greek *di' hōn* ("through which," a plural form) as "by water." The antecedent may be "water," "waters," "word" and "water," or "heavens." Probably both water and the word are to be understood as the agents for destroying the former world (v.6), as the word and fire will be the destructive agents in the future (v.7). "The world of that time" translates the Greek *ho tote kosmos*. The globe was not destroyed, only its inhabitants and its ordered form.

7 Peter's reference to a future conflagration to destroy the present cosmos is highly unusual. Some, indeed, would contend that it shows the influence of Stoic or Iranian (Persian) eschatology (TDNT, 6:928–52). Yet the OT speaks of fire in the day of the Lord (Ps 97:3; [possibly Isa 34:4]; Isa 66:15–16; Dan 7:9–10; Mic 1:4; Mal 4:1). And Matthew 3:11–12 speaks of the future baptism of fire by the Messiah in which he will destroy the "chaff" (cf. 2 Thess 1:7). Peter argues that just as in the past God purged the then-existing *kosmos* by his word and by waters, so in the future he will purge the *kosmos* by his word and by fire. Whether this will take place before the Millennium or after, Peter does not say. Matthew 3:11–12 supports the former, while the sequence of Revelation 20–21 puts the new heaven and new earth after the thousand years (cf. 2 Peter 3:13).

8 Peter's second argument against the false teachers' scoffing at the "delay" of the Lord's coming stems from Psalm 90:4: "For a thousand years in your sight are like a day that has just gone by, or like a watch in night." They overlooked God's time perspective. The admonition "Do not forget" is addressed to believers and uses the same word (*lanthanō*) that is used in v.5 of the false teachers' deliberate forgetfulness. Christians must be careful lest the propaganda of the scoffers distort their thinking.

9 The third argument against the scoffers grows out of the second one. God's "delay" is gracious; it is not caused by inability or indifference. The scoffers argued that God was slow to keep his promise of the new age, and evidently some Christians were influenced by this ("as some understand slowness"). God's time plan is influenced by his patience (*makrothymei*), an attribute prominent in Scripture (cf. Exod 34:6; Num

14:18; Ps 86:15; Jer 15:15; Rom 2:4; 9:22). In Romans 9:22 Paul says that God "bore with great patience the objects of his wrath." Here in v.9 God's patience is directed *eis hymas* ("to you"—NIV, "He is patient with you"). Other MSS read "to us" (*eis hēmas*) or "because of you" (*di' hymas*).

With whom is God patient and whom does he desire to come to repentance? This verse has been a battleground between some Arminian and some Calvinistic interpreters. One of the latter argues, "It is not his [God's] will that every man without exception should repent. . . . Peter therefore is saying simply that Christ will not return until every one of the elect has come to repentance" (Clark, *II Peter*, p. 71). This view, if rigorously applied, is obviously incompatible with premillennialism, whose adherents normally teach that some will be saved during the millennial period following Christ's return.

Calvin's comment shows his moderation and exegetical wisdom: "*Not willing that any should perish*. So wonderful is his love towards mankind, that he would have them all to be saved, and is of his own self prepared to bestow salvation on the lost" (italics his) (*Epistles of Peter*, p. 419). Thus the "you" is addressed to mankind and the "not wanting" (*mē boulomenos*) is of his "desirative" will, not of his decretive will (cf. ibid., pp. 419–20 and Ezek 18:23; 1 Tim 2:4).

10 Peter's fourth argument against the false teachers reaffirms the early church teaching—viz., the day of the Lord will come suddenly. Jesus taught that his coming would be as unexpected as the coming of a thief (Matt 24:42–44). This analogy is commonly repeated in the NT (cf. Luke 12:39; 1 Thess 5:2; Rev 3:3; 16:15). The "Lord" in these texts is Jesus in his exaltation and should so be understood here in 2 Peter. In that catastrophic day "the heavens will disappear with a roar." The "roar" (*rhoizēdon*, only here in NT) is an adverb related to *rhoizos*, "the noise made by something passing swiftly through the air" (BAG, p. 744). Revelation 6:14 says, "The sky receded like a scroll, rolling up," and 20:11 portrays the earth and sky as fleeing from the presence of God.

"The elements" (*stoicheia*) could be stars (heavenly bodies) or the basic materials that make up the world (cf. TDNT, 7:666–87). The "elements" commonly thought of in NT times were air, earth, fire, and water. It is possible that in this verse Peter is looking at three realms (the heavens, that of the heavenly bodies, the earth); so the "heavenly bodies" (*stoicheia*) affected would be those mentioned in other eschatological passages (Joel 2:10; Mark 13:24–26; Rev 6:12–13). Some have seen the splitting of the atom or atomic fusion in this verse, but that is certainly eisegesis. On "the earth and everything in it will be laid bare," see note below.

Notes

10 Ἔργα εὑρεθήσεται (*erga heurethēsetai*, "everything in it will be laid bare") is very uncertain and the meaning difficult. (1) It could mean that all human products will be destroyed (if κατακαήσεται [*katakaēsetai*, "shall be burned."] is accepted). (2) It could mean that all that man does will be known in the judgment (1 Cor 3:13–15). (3) Kelly translates it, "And the earth and the works it contains—will they be found?" (pp. 364f.). NIV (v.11) accords with the first view.

2. *The Ethical Implications of the Day of the Lord*

3:11–16

[11]Since everything will be destroyed in this way, what kind of people ought you to be? You ought to live holy and godly lives [12]as you look forward to the day of God and speed its coming. That day will bring about the destruction of the heavens by fire, and the elements will melt in the heat. [13]But in keeping with his promise we are looking forward to a new heaven and a new earth, the home of righteousness.

[14]So then, dear friends, since you are looking forward to this, make every effort to be found spotless, blameless and at peace with him. [15]Bear in mind that our Lord's patience means salvation, just as our dear brother Paul also wrote you with the wisdom that God gave him. [16]He writes the same way in all his letters, speaking in them of these matters. His letters contain some things that are hard to understand, which ignorant and unstable people distort, as they do the other Scriptures, to their own destruction.

11 Peter here makes the impending disintegration of the universe the ground for a personal challenge to his readers. The present tense of *lyomenōn* (NIV, "destroyed") may be taken either as emphasizing the certainty of imminent destruction or as implying the process of disintegration (cf. 1 John 2:17) "in this way" (i.e., as in v.10). In view of what is in store for the world, Peter asks his readers, "What kind of people ought you to be?" Since the day of the Lord will soon come to punish the wicked and reward the righteous, believers should live "holy and godly lives." Holiness entails separation from evil and dedication to God; godliness relates to piety and worship.

12 Another element of godly living is expectation of the future day. Peter relates this to the idea of "speed[ing] its coming." But how can Christians hasten what God will do? Peter would probably answer by saying that prayer (Matt 6:10) and preaching (Matt 24:14) are the two principal means to bring people to repentance. To the crowd that gathered after the healing of the lame beggar at the Beautiful Gate in Jerusalem Peter proclaimed, "Repent, . . . so that your sins may be wiped out, that times of refreshing may come from the Lord, and that he may send the Christ" (Acts 3:19–20). Once more Peter describes the coming as a fiery disintegration of the very heavens (cf. comment on v.10). Again, the "elements" probably refers to the "celestial bodies" on fire. *Tēketai* ("melt") occurs in the LXX (mg.) of Isaiah 34:4.

13 Through his prophets God promised righteousness. Jeremiah sees the Righteous One bringing in righteousness, and his name is "The LORD Our Righteousness" (23:5–7; 33:16; cf. Ps 9:8; Isa 11:4–5; 45:8; Dan 9:24). This promise of righteousness will be fulfilled ultimately in the new heavens and the new earth of which Isaiah spoke (65:17–25) and which Peter refers to here. John also saw "a new heaven and a new earth" in which there was nothing impure (Rev 21:1, 8, 27).

14 Since there will be perfect righteousness in the new heaven and new earth, Christians must now be righteous in their lives. "So, then" (*dio*) makes the transition to their conduct. "Make every effort" (*spoudasate*) is a favorite word of Peter's (cf. 1:10, 15 and the related noun in 1:5). Christians are to make intense efforts to be morally pure ("spotless, blameless") like Christ. The two words *aspiloi* and *amomētoi* used here occur in reverse order in 1 Peter 1:19 ("without blemish or defect"), where they refer to Jesus. Their appearance in both letters, though pointing to a connection between the letters, does not prove anything regarding their common authorship. In 2:13 Peter has called the false teachers "blots and blemishes" (*spiloi kai mōmoi*). When the Lord comes, all will appear before him. Believers should aim to live so as "to be found . . . at peace with him"—i.e., having the peace that results from their efforts to please the Lord. In Revelation 2:16, the risen Christ warns the church to repent or he will "fight against them with the sword of his mouth." Those who are "found at peace with him" have put out of their lives the things he hates.

15–16 Again Peter stresses the purpose of the Lord's "patience" (*makrothymia*, "longsuffering," KJV)—that it is designed for salvation. Some confuse the divine patience with slackness. But Christians should esteem (*hēgeisthe*—the same verb occurs in v.9) it as salvation.

"Just as our dear brother Paul also wrote you" is very significant in the light of Paul's rebuke of Peter (Gal 2:11–14). Peter had recognized the ministry of Paul and Barnabas to the Gentiles. But what did Paul write to the recipients of 2 Peter? It is impossible to answer that question. Nor is it necessary to do so in view of Peter's general statement: "He [Paul] writes the same way in all his letters." Green (*Peter and Jude*, p. 145) suggests that Peter may have alluded to a copy of Romans sent out as a circular letter. In Romans 2:4 Paul says that "God's kindness leads you toward repentance." Many commentators (e.g., Kelly, p. 370) argue that vv.15–16 reveal clearly that the apostolic age is past and that the writer is trying to pass himself off as an apostle but fails to do so. The presuppositions one brings to these verses are determinative. If one accepts the Petrine authorship, they make good sense.

Peter affirms that Paul's letters contain "some things that are hard to understand" (*dysnoēta*). This word is found only here in the NT, twice in the classics (so LSJ, p. 459), and a few times in the patristic writings (cf. G.W.H. Lampe, *A Patristic Lexicon* [Oxford: Clarendon, 1961], p. 393). The difficulty in Paul's letters stems from the profundity of the God-given wisdom they contain. Apparently false teachers were seeking to use Pauline support for their opposition to Peter. Paul's letters contain things—e.g., slogans and arguments—that can be given meanings far beyond what Paul intended. (For examples of this, see esp. Rom 3:8; 5:20–6:1; 7:25; 1 Cor 6:12–13; 8:4.)

The unlearned (*amatheis;* NIV, "ignorant") are those who have not learned the apostolic teaching (Acts 2:42) nor have they been taught by the Father (John 6:45). They are "unstable" (*astēriktoi*) because they are without a foundation (cf. comments on 2:14). They "distort" the things in Paul's letters as they do the "other Scriptures." The word "distort" (*strebloō*, "twist," "torment") is used in the papyri of torture. Like Satan, the false teachers and their followers can quote Scripture out of context for their purpose (cf. Matt 4:6).

Does Peter's expression "the other Scriptures" (*tas loipas graphas*) imply that Paul's writings were already considered Scripture by this time (c.A.D. 64)? This is the normal understanding of the Greek (BAG, p. 481; cf. Introduction: Authorship and Canonicity). Bigg (pp. 301–2) cites some evidence that the expression could be translated "the Scriptures as well" or "the Scriptures on the other hand," but his NT example from 1 Thessalonians 4:13 is not parallel because it contains a distinguishing phrase ("who have no hope"). That Paul's writings should be considered "Scripture"—authoritative writing—is not surprising, for from the moment of composition they had the authority of commands of the Lord through his apostle (Rom 1:1; 1 Cor 14:37; Gal 1:1).

Twisting the Scriptures leads to "destruction" (*apōleia*, cf. comments at 2:1, 3) because it is the rejection of God's way and the setting up of one's own way in opposition to God (cf. Rom 8:7). In a time when the Christian church is plagued by heretical cults and false teaching, Peter's warning about the irresponsible use of Scripture is important. Correct exegesis must be a continuing concern of the church.

3. *The Need to Guard Against Error and to Grow in Grace*

3:17–18

17Therefore, dear friends, since you already know this, be on your guard so that you may not be carried away by the error of lawless men and fall from your secure position. 18But grow in the grace and knowledge of our Lord and Savior Jesus Christ. To him be glory both now and forever! Amen.

17–18 With an affectionate reference to his readers—"Therefore, dear friends" (*hymeis oun agapētoi;* lit., "You, therefore, beloved")—Peter begins his conclusion. These two verses touch on the main themes of the letter and summarize its contents. First, there is the reminder for his readers to watch out lest the false teachers lead them astray. Second, there is the exhortation to grow in Christ. The dominant motivation for writing this letter was Peter's love and concern for the flock (cf. the repeated use of *agapētoi*). Since he has told the believers beforehand about the false teachers, they are able to be on guard.

The "lawless" (*athesmoi*) men will attempt by their error to shift the believers off their spiritual foundation. The noun *stērigmos* ("secure position," NIV) occurs only here in the NT, but the related verb and adjective are important in Peter's life (cf. Luke 22:32 of Jesus' command to Peter) and also in this letter (cf. 2:14; 3:16). The Christians' guarding against false teachers includes (1) prior knowledge of their activities, (2) warning against their immoral lives (2 Peter 2; Matt 7:16: "By their fruit you will recognize them"), (3) reminders of the historicity of the apostolic message (2 Peter 1:16–18), (4) the prophetic teaching of the past (2 Peter 1:19; 3:1–2), and (5) the warning of judgment, e.g., the Flood.

Now Peter speaks positively: "But grow in the grace and knowledge of our Lord and Savior Jesus Christ." In 1:3–11 he has already stressed the necessity for progress in Christian living. Green (*Peter and Jude,* p. 150) says, "The Christian life . . . is like riding a bicycle. Unless you keep moving, you fall off!" John says that the knowledge of God and Christ is "eternal life" (John 17:3). But as Paul says, Christians never in this life attain all there is in Christ; so their goal is to know Christ in a fuller, more intimate way (Phil 3:10–13; cf. Eph 1:17).

The closing doxology is notable for its direct ascription of "glory" (*hē doxa;* lit., "the glory") to Christ. For a Jew who has learned the great words in Isaiah 42:8—"I am the LORD; that is my name! I will not give my glory to another"—this doxology is a clear confession of Christ (cf. John 5:23: "that all may honor the Son just as they honor the Father"). This supreme honor belongs to Jesus Christ today ("now") and "forever" (lit., "unto the day of the age"). So Peter finally points his readers to the new age, "the day of the Lord," when Christ will be manifested in all his glory.

1 JOHN

Glenn W. Barker

1 JOHN

Introduction

1. **Background**
2. **Occasion and Purpose**
3. **Structure**
4. **Authorship**
5. **Date**
6. **Relation to Other Writings**
7. **Bibliography**
8. **Outline**

The Epistles of John are foundational to what is known in the NT as Johannine Christianity. Even as his gospel account is distinct from the others in content, structure, and theological emphasis, so John's epistles differ in style and content from the other NT letters. Although numbered among the Catholic or General Epistles, John's epistles have little in common with them. His are not concerned with the problem of institutionalizing the Christian Movement, nor do they fit easily into any historical reconstruction of the growth and development of the Christian church in the world.

If John's epistles address the problem of heresy, they do so in unconventional terms. They insist that true Christian faith requires knowing that Jesus the Christ came in human flesh, lived a human life, and died in the flesh. But the evidence of that faith is measured by the genuineness of one's Christian lifestyle, not so much by what one "knows." The knowledge that God is light is tested by whether one walks in that light and obeys God's commands. The knowledge that God is righteous is tested by whether one lives righteously as befits one born of God. The knowledge that God is love is tested by whether one loves fellow believers even as one loves God. The single but radical requirement for love and obedience in the Johannine Epistles recalls the simplicity of Jesus' own teaching and the radical response he required of those who would follow him. The ability of these letters to recall to the church its origins and cause it to hear afresh the word of him who came in the flesh has preserved a special place for them in the life and devotion of the church.

1. Background

Establishing the background for the Johannine Epistles is at best speculative. Whereas for the Pauline Epistles we have the Book of Acts with its treatment of the origin of the church, the conversion of the apostle, and a record of his subsequent journeys to provide background for understanding his epistles, we have nothing similar for the Johannine material. While Paul's epistles fairly bristle with historical allusions that we can readily identify from other sources, those of John contain almost no references to known persons or places. Nonetheless, traditions relating to the origin of these writings did develop in the church. And since there are no alternatives, it is these traditions that have been largely responsible for providing the historical background for interpreting these letters. Traditions that existed uncontested from the third to the eighteenth centuries connected them and the fourth Gospel with the apostle John, recognized Asia as the place of their publication, and identified Cerinthianism as the heresy troubling the Johannine churches.

The tradition concerning authorship is preserved in the writings of Irenaeus and in the Muratorian Canon. The assumption is that 1 John and John's Gospel have a common origin. Irenaeus quotes copiously from 1 John and attributes it to John the disciple of the Lord.[1] The Muratorian Canon includes the following testimony:

> The fourth of the Gospels, that of John, [one] of the disciples. When his fellow disciple and bishops urged him, he said: Fast with me from today for three days, and what will be revealed to each one let us relate to one another. In the same night it was revealed to Andrew, one of the apostles, that whilst all were to go over [it], John in his own name should write everything down. . . . For so he confesses [himself] [in 1 John 1:1] not merely an eye and ear witness, but also a writer of all the marvels of the Lord in order.[2]

Regarding John's Epistles, the Muratorian Fragment testifies that two are received by the Catholic Church. Whether 1 John is omitted because of its previous inclusion in the missing opening portion of the Fragment, as Gregory maintained, is not of great significance. All agree that the Muratorian Canon certainly meant to testify to the full authority of 1 John and that it clearly supports Irenaeus's view of its authorship.

Asia as the place of the epistle's publication finds support from two lines of tradition. First, there is the direct statement of Irenaeus: "Afterward John, the disciple of the Lord, who also had leaned upon his breast, himself published his gospel, while he was living at Ephesus in Asia" (*Contra Haereses* 3.1.1). Second, the earliest-known references to the epistle are by church leaders from Asia. Polycarp of Smyrna appears to have been depending on 1 John when he asserted that whoever does not confess that Jesus Christ has come in the flesh is antichrist. Polycarp likewise urges a return to the message handed down from the beginning.[3] Eusebius testifies that Papias of Hierapolis quoted from 1 John.[4]

The tradition identifying Cerinthus as the opponent of 1 John also depends on Irenaeus. He preserved a description from Polycarp of an encounter between the apostle and Cerinthus in a public bathhouse, which John hurriedly left so that he would not have to bathe in the same place with such an enemy of the truth.[5] Irenaeus also described in some detail the heresy of Cerinthus.[6] Cerinthus, he said,

> represented Jesus as having not been born of a virgin, but as being the son of Joseph and Mary according to the ordinary course of human generation, while he

[1] *Contra Haereses* 3.16.5, 8.

[2] E. Hennecke and W. Schneemelcher, *New Testament Apocrypha*, trans. R. McL. Wilson et al., 2 vols. (London: Lutterworth, 1963–65), vol. 1, *Gospels and Related Writings* (1963), pp. 941–42.

[3] *To the Philippians* 7.1–2; cf. 1 John 2:24; 3:8; 4:2–3.

[4] *Ecclesiastical History* 3.39.

[5] *Contra Haereses* 3.4.

[6] Ibid., 1.26.1.

> nevertheless was more righteous, prudent and wise than other men. Moreover, after his baptism, Christ descended upon him in the form of a dove from the Supreme Ruler, and that then he proclaimed the unknown Father, and performed miracles. But at last Christ departed from Jesus, and that then Jesus suffered and rose again, while Christ remained impassible, inasmuch as he was a spiritual being.[7]

Traditional critics see strong evidence that Cerinthus was the opponent of the apostle in the insistence in 1 John that Jesus was the Son of God; that he came as the Christ in the flesh; and that his baptism, his suffering, and his dying make up the redemptive event.

The conclusions Westcott drew from this traditional material, and which have been followed by many of the earlier exegetes, are that (1) the Epistle is "addressed primarily to a circle of Asiatic Churches, of which Ephesus was the centre" (p. xxxii), (2) the false teaching with which John is involved "is Docetic and specifically Cerinthian" (p. xxxiv), and (3) the false teaching was a "condensed moral and practical application of the gospel" (p. xxx).

While there remains some general support for the reconstruction advanced by Westcott among the modern exegetes, there are also some significant departures from it. Asia continues as the clear choice of modern scholars for the place of publication. Comparison of the problems presented in 1 John with the more complete description of the heresies of the second century now available from recent finds provides additional support for Asia as the place where 1 John originated.

It is not absolutely certain, however, that Cerinthus was the opponent of John or that the heresy in view in the Epistle resulted from a Gnostic theological movement that had infiltrated the church. The internal evidence strongly suggests that the heresy arose within the church and was propogated by respected and able teachers in the community who had defected from the true faith and fellowship (2:19). Indeed, the seriousness of the situation probably derived from the fact that past leaders had become "false prophets," teaching untruths and becoming embodiments of Antichrist. That they were able to lead the community astray (2:26; 3:7) gives strong support to the idea they were secessionists, not intruders. Moreover, while they held some ideas in common with Cerinthus, it is clear that they also differed from him in significant ways. There is no reflection in 1 John of Cerinthus's distinctions between the supreme God and the series of divine emanations proceeding downward to the aeon who was Christ and who created the material universe. (For further discussion on Gnosticism, see introduction to commentary on Colossians in EBC, 11:166–67.) Furthermore, the false teachers in 1 John appear to draw theological conclusions that have no parallels in Cerinthian Gnosticism. The espousal of sinlessness (1:8, 10), their claim to know God through inspiration (2:4; 4:1–3), their loss of "fellowship" with God (1:6), and their life in the light (2:9) seem to be independent of Cerinthus's teaching. The attempt to identify the false teachers with Cerinthus or his followers is therefore dubious.

Alternate suggestions for the identity of the false teachers have lacked scholarly consensus. Schnackenburg (pp. 20ff.) suggests that a better case can be made for the Docetic heretics attacked by Ignatius. They were known for resisting belief in the validity of Jesus' suffering and for denying the reality of his flesh. Moreover, they are

---

[7]Ibid., 28.1.

described as being without love or compassion for the oppressed and afflicted. Yet Schnackenburg acknowledges that the false prophets of 1 John differ at numerous points from the Docetics of Ignatius and concludes that it is impossible to identify the heretics in 1 John with any who are known to us historically.

Marshall (p. 21) identifies the opponents with Christians

> who felt that they had moved beyond the elementary stages of orthodox theology to a new position which called affirmations into question. . . . Relying on their belief that they were inspired by the Spirit and claiming a direct knowledge of God, they thought that they no longer needed Jesus or his teaching. Under the influence of Docetism they argued against a real incarnation of the Son of God in Jesus, and probably adopted a view like that of Cerinthus or Basilides, that the Christ or Son of God inhabited Jesus only for a temporary period.

Although Marshall's reconstruction is essentially acceptable, it does leave unanswered the question of how the heresy happened to develop in such a distinctive form within the church and why it grew into such a powerful movement.

At this point Dodd's theory provides some help. He sees the root of the problem in the confrontation of Christianity with the "evangelistic and pietistic religious movements" developing within the "higher paganism" characteristic of the Hellenistic world but especially present in Asia. When the missionaries of the Christian faith first came into contact with the representatives of these movements, they undoubtedly received, at least initially, a warm welcome. The eclectic character of these advocates of "higher paganism" would make sure that they would be prepared "to adopt Christianity as they had already tried to adopt Judaism" (pp. xvi–xvii).

As Dodd shows, the Johannine community already reflected some of the language style of this world. He believes therefore that one could expect the Johannine community to be unusually successful in its missionary effort among such persons. Converts from this particular milieu would inevitably bring philosophical and religious verbiage with them into the community that would require an extensive theological response by the teachers. The Gospel of John may in itself represent not only a missionary document for these persons but some response to the questions raised by the converts. Inevitably, however, a significant number of the faithful would prove vulnerable to pagan reinterpretation that borrowed from Christian categories.

In his First Epistle John seems to recognize this pull and seeks to help those trying not to fall back into non-Christian speculation. On the other hand, as Dodd points out, the community would inevitably contain some "enthusiastic but ill-informed converts to Christianity," who would be eager to reinterpret their new found faith "in terms of modern thought" (ibid., p. xvii). The false teachers who previously had been in the community and had then departed, proving that they had not really belonged to the community, may well have been representatives of such a movement. They would be presenting themselves as preserving the best of both traditions.

Furthermore, the false teachers' motive, at least in the beginning, may have been prompted only by the desire to translate the gospel into the terms of another culture. Their enthusiasm would likely blind them to the fact that their reinterpretation would ultimately lead to the dissolution of what was central to the Christian faith: Jesus as the Son of God through whose death the bonds of sin had finally been destroyed. If this reconstruction is valid, it would help explain why these new "false teachers" had such a strong position in the community. Originally they had belonged to those who had been most involved in the missionary activity of the community. That they no longer were true to the faith and were to be classed as antichrists would certainly be hard for some of the community to accept.

2. Occasion and Purpose

It is clear from the internal evidence of 1 John that a developing schism within the Christian community led to its writing. The difficulty had already reached a point where some members, including teachers, had separated themselves from the others and were in the process of setting up their own community (1 John 2:19). Although the breach was complete, the dissidents continued to keep in touch with the rest of the membership and were actively trying to entice them to join the new group (2:26). With the breach of fellowship, there came also a breach in understanding the faith. What earlier may have been hypothetical questions now became tenets of the rival community, identified in John's epistles primarily by what the false teachers denied. They denied that Jesus was the Christ, the Son of God (2:22; 5:1, 5). They denied that the Christ had come in the flesh (4:2; 2 John 7). They denied authority to Jesus' commands (2:4). They denied their own sinfulness (1:8, 10). They denied salvation through the work of Christ (2:2). They denied the absolute demand that believers love one another (2:9). They denied righteous conduct as a requirement of fellowship with God (1:6; 2:29; 3:6, 10). They denied the responsibility to live as Jesus had lived (2:4, 6; 3:7). They denied the nature of the company of believers as a community of fellowship with the Father, with his Son, and with one another (1:3; 2:11). They denied the authority of the writer of the Epistles as the proclaimer of the message that had been from the beginning (1:5; 3 John 10). They denied that the members of the community who did not follow them were in the truth (2:20–21).

It is harder to reconstruct the points at which the false teachers agreed with the community of faith. Apparently they believed in God as light (1:5). They seemed to have believed that the truth of the gospel released them from the power of sin (1:8). They also seemed to have believed in the Christ as a philosophical concept, though denying his existence in the flesh (4:2). They believed in the mission to the world (2 John 10). They apparently held to the anointing of the Spirit (2:27). They probably believed in the devil as an anti-God (3:8–10; 4:2–3).

The writer responded to the false teachers by recognizing them as a supreme danger threatening the very life and faith of the community. He saw that what was called for was a positive reaffirmation of the cardinal doctrines of the faith that have been from the beginning and a clear and explicit exposure of the heresies the dissidents were promoting. He also sensed the need for reassuring the faithful. So he gave his letter a strong pastoral flavor. Its contents are marked by strong affirmations and words of encouragement for the community—viz., that the nature of the fellowship is one of love and righteousness (1:3, 7), that its origin is from the beginning (1:1), that in the community there is genuine forgiveness of sins (1:9) and a walk of obedience not unlike Jesus' own example (2:6), that walking in the light is living in love (2:10), that members of the community will not be ashamed at Jesus' coming (2:28), and that they may have complete confidence in his answering their prayers (3:22). Warnings are addressed to the community against the seduction of the world (2:15), against the present antichrist, (2:18), and against false spirits and false prophets (3:22; 4:1–2). Reminders to the members of their anointing (2:20) as being sufficient to enable them to remain in God (4:13) are provided as well as promises that belong to them as the children of God (3:1). Jesus Christ as the epitome and example of love to the community becomes a critical theme (3:16–18) just as the proclamation that God himself is love (4:16), that love derives from him, and that the Christian life is lived in him (4:12–13) are also critical themes. Again and again the letter returns to the primary confession that Jesus is the Christ, the one who has come in the flesh and has overcome the world. He is the true God and eternal life (5:20).

3. Structure

The development of the Epistle is fascinating. In some places it seems intricately structured; in others it seems rambling and disconnected. Outlines offered by various commentators reflect this.[8] R. Law represents those who see the Epistle as significantly structured. He is impressed with its recurring themes and thinks the ideas develop in the form of an ascending spiral. His outline is as follows:

Prologue. 1:1–4
1. First Cycle. 1:5–2:28. The Christian life as fellowship with God (walking in the Light), tested by righteousness (1:8–2:6), love (2:7–17), and belief (2:18–28).
2. Second Cycle. 2:29–4:6. Divine sonship tested by righteousness (2:29–3:10a), love (3:10b–24a), and belief (3:24b–4:6).
3. Third Cycle. 4:7–5:21. Closer correlation of righteousness, love, and belief.

P.R. Jones also sees the Epistle as significantly structured but thinks the structure develops from statements about the nature of God.

Prologue. 1:1–4.
- I. God is light. 1:5–2:27.
  1. Communion with God and confession of sin. 1:5–2:2.
  2. Communion with God and obedience. 2:3–11.
  3. Attitude toward the world. 2:12–17.
  4. Warning against the antichrists. 2:18–27.
- II. God is righteousness. 2:28–4:6.
  1. The righteous children of God. 2:28–3:10.
  2. The righteous love of the children of God. 3:11–18.
  3. Confidence before God. 3:19–24.
  4. Warning against the spirit of antichrist. 4:1–6.
- III. God is love. 4:7–5:12.
  1. The nature of true agape. 4:7–21.
  2. Cruciality of faith in Jesus. 5:1–12.

Epilogue. 5:13–21.

On the other hand, Marshall represents those who see the Epistle as primarily unstructured. He thinks the organization of the Epistle is "governed by association of ideas rather than by a logical plan."

---

[8]The following three outlines are from Marshall, pp. 22–26.

Prologue—the Word of life. 1:1–4.
Walking in the light. 1:5–2:2.
Keeping his commands. 2:3–11.
The new status of believers and their relation to the world. 2:12–17.
A warning against antichrists. 2:18–27.
The hope of God's children. 2:28–3:3.
The sinlessness of God's children. 3:4–10.
Brotherly love as the mark of the Christian. 3:11–18.
Assurance and obedience. 3:19–24.
The spirits of truth and falsehood. 4:1–6.
God's love and our love. 4:7–12.
Assurance and Christian love. 4:13–5:4.
The true faith confirmed. 5:5–12.
Christian certainties. 5:13–21.

In the outline presented in section 8, the writer of this Epistle is seen as following a somewhat structured approach without being bound by it. He is quite willing to depart from the structure in order to allow room for the introduction of divergent themes as well as overlapping ones. As the exposition will show, the writer of the Epistle deals with the problems raised by the schismatic actions of the "false teachers." He does this within the context of a general exposition that focuses on the nature and life of the community of God. His deepest concern is pastoral. He desires to reassure, protect, alert, and teach the faithful members about their life together as the people of God. To accomplish this the writer shows that "from the beginning" the basis of the believing community is Jesus Christ. He is the one through whom fellowship with the Father and with the members of the community becomes possible. This fellowship is further defined as life in him and as eternal life.

The writer asserts that the fellowship of believers draws its character from God, who is light, righteousness, and love. It is these attributes of God, shown by Jesus our example, that in turn become criteria for the standard of conduct expected of the children of God. Obedience to him thus becomes a primary obligation of the community.

The writer makes clear that the fellowship is exclusive. It consists of those born of God who are committed to obedience to his Son's commands and example; who confess Jesus as the Christ, the incarnate Son of God; and who depend on him for forgiveness and for overcoming the evil one. So the writer provides tests by which the false teachers can be exposed and the faithful members of the community reinforced in their own confidence that they truly are the children of God. Over and over he stresses the fact that the test of true faith and practice for those born of God is to love one's brother. This becomes the final test for walking in the light, living in truth and righteousness, and loving God. Into all this the writer also weaves his pastoral concern for the flock entrusted to his care.

4. Authorship

The author of 1 John never identifies himself in the Epistle. Apparently his identity was so well known to his "children" that he knew they would recognize him by what he wrote. We do get an ambiguous clue in 2 and 3 John when he uses the title "elder" to address them. The fourth Gospel is likewise unidentified as to authorship except that in the epilogue there is the enigmatic statement about "the disciple whom Jesus loved" (21:20; cf. 13:23): "This is the disciple who testifies to these things and who wrote them down" (21:24).

For those who recognize common authorship for the Gospel of John and John's epistles, it is possible through a process of elimination to identify the "beloved" disciple as John the son of Zebedee. Since this identity is also attested by the universal witness from the traditions of the church from the end of the second century forward, a large number of critics have accepted Johannine authorship for both the Gospel of John and the Epistles. A more detailed presentation of this evidence is given by Merrill C. Tenney in the Introduction to his commentary on the Gospel of John in volume 9 of this Commentary. See also Morris's comprehensive treatment.[9]

Strong objections to this identification have been made by critical investigators. Many modern exegetes eliminate the apostle John as author on stylistic and linguistic grounds ("The Gnostic language of the Johannine Jesus discourses make impossible the composition of John by an apostle") and because the Gospel "was able to make its way along so slowly and against opposition" into the mainstream of the church.[10]

These objections, however, are largely based on a reconstruction of events that see the Gospel and the Epistle written in response to "Gnostic" influence. These events have traditionally been located outside Palestine and generally assigned a date in the second century. But the Qumran writings certainly indicate that what has been called "Gnostic" language was already in use in Palestine before Jesus' birth. For a gospel to use this kind of language does not necessarily prove it to be non-Palestinian.

Second, Gnosticism may owe its later development—rather than its origin (cf. Brown, pp. 145–46)—to those who seceded from the Johannine community. If that is so, it is easy to see why the Johannine writings would cause difficulty for the main body of the church. That the fourth Gospel was known and cited by the defectors, that they used thought forms similar to those in the Gospel and in the Johannine Epistles, would cast a shadow on these writings. There would certainly be reluctance on the part of the church to cite them in debate with the Gnostics and their predecessors lest the church appear to concede the argument. Nevertheless the church was able to distinguish the two bodies of literature, accepting the Johannine literature as belonging to the apostolic witness, while rejecting the Gnostic materials. On balance and in view of what is now known, the best answer to the question of the authorship of the fourth Gospel and the Johannine Epistles is that the apostle John wrote them.

5. Date

The date for the Epistles of John is at best very problematic. It depends largely on our ability to reconstruct the history of the Johannine community. This community

---

[9]Leon Morris, *The Gospel According to St. John*, NIC (Grand Rapids: Eerdmans, 1971), pp. 8–30.

[10]Paul Feine and Johannes Behm, *Introduction to the New Testament*, ed. W. Kümmel (Nashville: Abingdon, 1966), p. 174.

may have begun about the same time as the church at Antioch. Persecution may have finally driven the leaders from Jerusalem, and John may have gathered with some of the Samaritan converts along with the former followers of the Baptist. They probably located somewhere in southern Palestine and continued their mission to the Jews.

Sometime before A.D. 70 (Brown thinks closer to 80), perhaps as a result of increased hostility from the Jews, the Johannine community migrated to Asia Minor and initiated what became a very successful mission to those Gentiles whose religious orientation was in the direction of "higher paganism."

The need for a gospel that would double as a missionary document for these converts became evident, and the Gospel of John was published somewhere around A.D. 75–80 to meet this challenge. It expresses its own purpose clearly: "These are written that you may believe that Jesus is the Christ, the Son of God, and that by believing you may have life in his name" (20:31).

The heretical developments discussed elsewhere in this Introduction took place during the next ten years and finally resulted in the secession of some members of the community in order to found a rival one. First John was written as a response to this crisis somewhere around 85–90. That it was written to reassure the faithful is also clear from its author's own testimony: "I write these things to you who believe in the name of the Son of God so that you may know that you have eternal life" (5:13). The letter is addressed to a single community but probably was meant to circulate throughout the geographical area where Johannine churches had been established.

The Second and Third Epistles of John are brief letters written to what appear to be member churches in other places. These churches also appear in danger of problems created by the secessionists. So the two letters were apparently written in anticipation of these problems.

The perspective of 1 John is clearly reflected in 2 John. The community addressed in it has been faithful to "the truth" (i.e., the gospel) as the "elder" has proclaimed it (v.4). He warns, however, against traveling missionaries whom he expects to visit this locality soon (v.10). Evidently they will present themselves as emissaries of the secessionists and continue to spread their false teaching (v.7). The elder warns the church neither to extend hospitality to such emissaries nor even to welcome them into the community (v.11). Second John was probably written not long after 1 John.

The background of 3 John is more obscure, despite its personal references. It seems best to consider that the situation was the same for 3 John as for 1 and 2 John. If so, still another community is addressed—a community in which there appear to be several groups of Christians in "house" churches as well as one larger group or church led by one Diotrephes (v.9). The smaller house churches, one led by Gaius and another apparently led by Demetrius, have remained faithful to the elder. They remain "in the truth" and "in love." They have received missionaries from the elder's faithful community and have shown them the proper hospitality (vv.5–8). But the elder complains against Diotrephes, the description of whom shows that he has been affected by the secessionists. He "gossips" maliciously against the elder and refuses to receive his message. He even goes so far as to throw out of the church anyone who welcomes the faithful "brothers" from the elder's community (v.10).

There would appear to be an interval of time between 2 John and 3 John. The situation has grown decidedly worse in the place where Gaius ministers than in that where the "chosen lady" is. Probably one would do well to think of an interval of a year or more between the two Epistles. Their date may be placed around A.D. 90.

6. Relation to Other Writings

With a few notable exceptions, modern critics agree that the evidence points to a common author for 1, 2, and 3 John. They also concur that there is a strong connection between 1 John and the Gospel of John, though they do not all agree as to the best explanation of this connection.

Historically, the relationship between the Gospel and the First Epistle has been explained in accord with tradition—viz., on the basis of common authorship. Internal evidence strongly supports this conclusion. Among modern critics, Brooke (pp. i–xv) best presents this view. He includes the lists originally developed by Holtzmann with even a more complete citing of the parallel passages from the Greek text. His material provides graphic evidence of the relationship between the two writings. He demonstrates their common vocabulary, similar style, overlapping ideas, a singular point of view, and a shared theology. Though he raises the question of imitation, he shows that the nature of the relation between the Gospel and the First Epistle makes common authorship a far more likely possibility than imitation.

Nevertheless, a significant number of modern critics dissociate themselves from that conclusion. The relationship they propose is not one of literary dependence but common style and vocabulary resulting from membership in a common or Johannine school. Thus they surmise a coterie of teachers who lived, taught, and ministered within a common theological heritage. Members of this coterie traced their roots to the apostle John and remained within their particular theological milieu. They were responsible for the different layers and development of sources associated with the Gospel of John as well as for certain redactional activity connected with that writing. The sources for the Gospel of John and its redactions, the Epistles of John, and the bulk of Revelation are believed by these critics to owe their existence to members of this Johannine school. The only external evidence, however, for someone other than the apostle John as author is drawn from this difficult-to-interpret testimony of Papias, quoted by Eusebius:

> If anyone came who had followed the presbyters, I was accustomed to inquire about the sayings of the presbyters, what Andrew or what Peter had said, or Philip or Thomas or Jacob or John or Matthew or any other of the Lord's disciples, and what Aristion and the presbyter John, the disciple of the Lord, say.[11]

Papias's statement certainly allows the possibility that there were two disciples named John. However, it does not establish beyond all doubt that the presbyter John whom he identifies as a disciple of the Lord may not also have been one of the Twelve. The link with Aristion may indicate that Aristion and the presbyter John were "personal disciples" of the Lord other than the Twelve. Nevertheless, Papias's chief intention was to distinguish between what had been said by disciples (known to others) and what these two disciples were saying. In either instance, according to Papias's statement, we are dealing only with persons who were historical disciples of the Lord. Thus the eyewitness factor is not changed, nor does the age of the persons enter into the question. Moreover, we have no historical evidence connecting the writing of either the Gospel of John or 1 John with any John other than the son of Zebedee.

---

[11]*Ecclesiastical History* 39.4.

The most extensive argument based on internal evidence for different authors of the Epistle and the Gospel was worked out by Dodd. As evidence for his hypothesis, he lists linguistic differences—viz., omission of key words, phrases, or ideas; words or phrases used in different ways or with different meanings; and altered theological perspectives.[12] Other modern supporters for different authors include Bultmann, Haenchen, Conzelmann, G. Klein, and, more recently, R.E. Brown and Schnackenburg.

Supporters for common authorship maintain that the difference between John's Gospel and the First Epistle can be accounted for on the ground of differing purposes and an interval of time between the two publications. They argue that none of the differences requires a different author and say that the likenesses are so indisputable that they require the hypothesis of a complex Johannine school for which no historical evidence exists.

On balance and on the basis of present evidence, single authorship appears to be the simpler explanation of the data. As Kümmel points out, "There hardly exists adequate reason to suppose another author."[13] But if another author is proposed, this requires a person with a viewpoint so similar to that of the author of the Gospel that it makes little difference in the end whether one holds to one or two authors.

7. Bibliography

Books

Alexander, J.N.S. *The Epistles of John*. Torch Bible Commentaries. London: SCM, 1962.

Barclay, William. *The Letters of John*. Daily Study Bible Series. Philadelphia: Westminster, 1976.

Barker, Glenn; Lane, W.L.; and Michaels, J.R. *The New Testament Speaks*. New York: Harper & Row, 1969.

Boice, James Montgomery. *The Epistles of John*. Grand Rapids: Zondervan, 1979.

Brooke, A.E. *A Critical and Exegetical Commentary on the Johannine Epistles*. ICC. Edinburgh: T. & T. Clark, 1912.

Brown, R.E. *The Community of the Beloved Disciple*. New York: Paulist, 1979.

Bruce, F.F. *The Epistles of John: Introduction, Exposition, and Notes*. Grand Rapids: Eerdmans, 1970.

Brunner, Emil. *The Misunderstanding of the Church*. Translated by H. Knight. Philadelphia: Westminster, 1953.

Bultmann, Rudolf. *The Johannine Epistles*. Hermeneia Series. Translated by R. Phillip O'Hara, et al. Philadelphia: Fortress, 1973.

Dodd, C.H. *The Johannine Epistles*. MNT. London: Hodder and Stoughton, 1946.

Haas, C.; deJonge, M.; and Swellengrebel, J.L. *A Translator's Handbook on the Letters of John. Helps for Translators, Volume XIII*. London: United Bible Societies, 1972.

Harrison, E.F. *Introduction to the New Testament*. Grand Rapids: Eerdmans, 1964.

Houlden, J.L. *A Commentary on the Johannine Epistles*. Black's New Testament Commentaries. London: Black, 1973.

Johnston, G. "I, II, III John." *Peake's Commentary on the Bible*. Edited by Matthew Black and H.H. Rowley. New York: Nelson, 1962.

---

[12]C.H. Dodd, "The Johannine Epistles" BJRL, 21 (April 1972), ix.

[13]Feine and Behm, *Introduction to the NT*, p. 312.

Law, R. *The Tests of Life: A Study of the First Epistle of St. John*. Edinburgh: T. & T. Clark, 1914.
Marshall, I.H. *The Epistles of John*. NIC. Grand Rapids: Eerdmans, 1978.
Marxsen, Willi. *Introduction to the New Testament: An Approach to its Problems*. Translated by G. Buswell. Philadelphia: Fortress, 1968.
Morris, Leon. "1 John, 2 John, 3 John." *New Bible Commentary Revised*. Edited by D. Guthrie, et al. Grand Rapids: Eerdmans, 1970.
O'Neill, J.C. *The Puzzle of 1 John*. London: SPCK, 1966.
Ross, A. *The Epistles of James and John*. NIC. Grand Rapids: Eerdmans, 1954.
Ryrie, C.C. "Commentary on 1, 2, 3 John." *Wycliffe Bible Commentary*. Edited by C.F. Pfeiffer and E.F. Harrison. Chicago: Moody, 1962.
Schnackenburg, R. *Die Johannesbriefe*. Herders Theologische Kommentar zum Neuen Testament. Freiburg: Herder, 1973.
Stott, J.R.W. *The Epistles of St. John*. TNTC. Grand Rapids: Eerdmans, 1964.
Wengst, K. *Häresie und Orthodoxie im Spiegel des ersten Johannesbriefes*. Gutersloh: Mohn, 1976.
Westcott, B.F. *The Epistles of St. John: The Greek Text with Notes and Essays*. London: Macmillan, 1883.

Articles

Feuillet, A. "The Structure of First John. Comparison with the Fourth Gospel. The Pattern of Christian Life." *Biblical Theology* 3 (1973), 194–216.
Filson, F.V. "First John: Purpose and Message." *Interpretation* 23 (1969), 259–76.
Funk, R.W. "The Form and Structure of II and III John." *Journal of Biblical Literature* 86 (1967), 424–30.
Horvath, T. "3 John 11b: An Early Ecumenical Creed?" *Expository Times* 85 (1974), 339–40.
Hunter, A.M. "Recent Trends in Johannine Studies." *Expository Times* 71 (1960), 164–67, 219–22.
Minear, P.S. "The Idea of Incarnation in First John." *Interpretation* 24 (1970), 291–302.
Moody, Dale. "The Theology of the Johannine Letters." *Southwestern Journal of Theology* 13 (1970), 7–22.
Ward, R.A. "The Theological Pattern of the Johannine Epistles." *Southwestern Journal of Theology* 13 (1970), 23–39.

8. Outline

I. Preface (1:1–4)

II. Requirements for Fellowship With God Who Is Light (1:5–2:28)
   1. Walking in the Light (1:5–2:2)
   2. Obeying His Commands (2:3–11)
   3. Knowing the Father and Abiding Forever (2:12–17)
   4. Warnings Against Antichrists (2:18–28)

III. Requirements for Fellowship With God Who Is Righteous (2:29–4:6)
   1. Doing What Is Right (2:29–3:10)
   2. Loving One Another (3:11–24)
   3. Warning Against the False Spirits (4:1–6)

IV. Requirements for Fellowship With God Who Is Love (4:7–5:12)
   1. Brotherly Love (4:7–12)
   2. Living in God and Living in Love (4:13–16)
   3. Love Displaces Fear (4:17–18)
   4. Love Summarized (4:19–21)
   5. Love for the Father and Faith in the Son (5:1–5)
   6. The Spirit, the Water, and the Blood (5:6–12)

V. Concluding Remarks (5:13–21)

Text and Exposition

I. Preface

1:1–4

[1]That which was from the beginning, which we have heard, which we have seen with our eyes, which we have looked at and our hands have touched—this we proclaim concerning the Word of life. [2]The life appeared; we have seen it and testify to it, and we proclaim to you the eternal life, which was with the Father and has appeared to us. [3]We proclaim to you what we have seen and heard, so that you also may have fellowship with us. And our fellowship is with the Father and with his Son, Jesus Christ. [4]We write this to make our joy complete.

1 The unusual nuance of feeling and thought present in the Greek of this Preface to the letter is difficult to catch in translation. Even to untangle its syntactical structure takes special effort. The four verses represent a single periodic sentence in Greek. But the main verb and subject "we proclaim" (*apangellomen*), which controls the whole sentence, does not appear until v.3, though in the NIV the translators have introduced it at the end of v.1 in order to help the English readers. Instead the Preface opens with the object of the verb. This consists of four relative clauses—"That which was from the beginning, which we have heard, which we have seen with our eyes, which we have looked at"—and is followed by a parenthesis in v.2 enlarging on "the Word of life." Only then are the subject and main verb introduced, with a restatement of the object "what we have seen and heard." Two purpose clauses, indicating the direction of the author's thinking—"that you also may have fellowship with us" and "to make our joy complete"—conclude the Preface.

This grammatical tangle should not lead us to infer that the author is careless in his written expression. Actually it is the main instance in the Epistle where such complexity occurs. What does confront us here is the intensity of the author's feeling when he reflects on the nature of the Christian message in the light of its very beginnings. Although the events the message is founded on occurred many years earlier, the immensity of their implication and the abiding mystery they represent retain the power to overwhelm his thinking and extend his literary skills as he witnesses to them. This first paragraph could be described as the author's language of ecstasy.

The reader is clearly pointed back to John 1:1—"In the beginning was the word"—and from there to Genesis 1:1—"In the beginning God"—with this difference: The Gospel deals with the "personal word" (*ho logos*), of his eternity and his entrance into time. The Epistle centers on the life heard and in turn proclaimed (cf. Acts 5:20; Phil 2:16). This message, the gospel, is from the beginning because it is of God. It precedes creation, time, and history. NEB perhaps strikes the right note in saying, "It was there from the beginning." But in God the message of life also draws near to humanity and finds its culmination in Jesus. In him the Word of life becomes incarnated, manifested, and hence can be seen, touched, and even handled.

According to Dodd (*Johannine Epistles*, p. 5), the author's stress is twofold. He is stating what has always been true about the gospel. His witness, unlike that of his opponents, represented neither innovation nor afterthought. Moreover his witness was based on the immediate evidence of the senses. It does not represent "airy speculation or *fabricated fable*" (emphasis his).

The use of the pronoun "we" assures the reader that the message is being proclaimed by those who had heard the gospel with their own ears and who had touched him with their own hands (perhaps a reference to the Resurrection appearances—Luke 24:39, John 20:24–29—but see Notes). Already the writer is mounting his polemic against the heretics who denied that Christ came in a human body.

2 Because this is the nub of John's argument, he takes pains to restate it: The life to which he bears witness, the life that was with the Father, is precisely the life manifested in the historical person of Jesus. That is why John can say he has seen it (*heōrakamen*), can bear personal witness to it (*martyroumen*), and can make an apostolic declaration concerning it (*apangellomen*). Westcott (p. 9) says, "The three verbs give in due sequence the ideas of personal experience, responsible affirmation, authoritative announcement, which are combined in the apostolic message." The phrase "eternal life" underscores the divine character of the life described, not its length.

3 This verse introduces the purpose of the Epistle: "that you also may have fellowship with us. And our fellowship is with the Father and with his Son, Jesus Christ." The Greek word rendered "fellowship" (*koinōnia*) occurs here and in v.6. It is not easily put into English. It has been translated "fellowship," "communion," "participation," "share a common life," and "partnership"; its root meaning is "common" or "shared" as opposed to "one's own." Hellenistic literature uses it to describe partners in business, joint owners of a piece of property, or shareholders in a common enterprise. In the NT it refers to Christians who share a common faith (Philem 6), who share possessions (Acts 2:44; 4:30), or who are partners in the gospel (Phil 1:5).

Koinōnia, with its derivatives, occurs over sixty times in the NT in reference to the supernatural life that Christians share. This supernatural life is disclosed in the incarnate Christ. It is the eternal life that comes from the Father and becomes the life shared individually and corporately by the company of believers. It is what causes the oneness of faith. "The Koinonia ('fellowship') is the union in common faith brought about by the proclamation" (Bultmann, p. 12). Brunner (p. 12) says of this "fellowship" that it is its combining of the vertical with the horizontal, "the divine with the human," that constitutes its "utterly unparalleled life."

That the words "fellowship with us" precede in the text the words "fellowship is with the Father and with his Son, Jesus Christ" may be significant. Westcott (in loc.) sees here a reminder that there can be no fellowship with the Father or with the Son that is not based on apostolic witness. So John stresses "fellowship with us" as having priority in time. Brunner (p. 11) states it this way: "Therefore the community as bearer of the Word and Spirit of Christ precedes the individual believer. One does not first believe and then join the fellowship: but one becomes a believer just because one shares in the gift [the Holy Spirit] vouchsafed to the fellowship."

4 The author links his concern for his readers to his own standing as an apostolic witness. Their obedience will result in the completion of joy in him, and therefore also in them and in the whole fellowship. The joy he refers to is mentioned in his gospel: "I have told you this so that my joy may be in you and that your joy may be complete" (John 15:11). "Now is your time of grief, but I will see you again and you will rejoice, and no one will take away your joy. In that day you will no longer ask me anything. . . . Ask and you will receive, and your joy will be complete" (John

16:22–24). "I say these things while I am still in the world, so that they may have the full measure of my joy within them" (John 17:13).

Clearly this joy is inseparable from the salvation that is present in the Son, but it is directly bound up with the person of the Son, who is himself present in the fellowship. Joy is a gift of the Father, even as the Son is a gift of the Father, and is present wherever the fellowship truly appears. But joy can never be perfectly known or fully complete because the fellowship itself, though real, is imperfectly realized. The present joy in the fellowship is a token of the ultimate expression of joy, which depends on the final revelation of the Son. In the Gospel, this final revelation required Jesus' "going away" so that he may "come again" (cf. John 16:16).

Notes

1 Bultmann's dating of the Johannine literature makes its composition by an eyewitness impossible. His first alternative in dealing with the "we" is to distinguish contemporaneity with the historical event from contemporaneity with the eschatological event. The "we" of 1 John is for Bultmann those who were "eschatological contemporaries" of Jesus. Though the verbs used in the text indicate sense perception, Bultmann sees them as used against the gnosticizing Christians who sever the present eschatological relationship from the historical. But would this not place the writer in an impossible position? Would his enemies allow him to represent himself as an eyewitness to an event of which he himself had no more information than they did?

Bultmann's second alternative has more merit, though it is equally difficult. Those who bore witness, he says, are the "bearers of the tradition," and as such they have personal authority over the congregation. But if there is no correspondence between the author's claim to being an eyewitness and the facts of history, would the author's enemies allow him this platform from which to launch an attack? Would they permit him to describe himself as an eyewitness? The better explanation still appears to be that the author is building his case on the fact that he is one who bears the tradition precisely *because* the manifestation of the truth of the gospel included him! (For Bultmann's interpretation, see pp. 7–13 of his commentary.)

2 "Thus one cannot enter into His self-revelation merely by believing in a dogma, but only insofar as one has communion with Him through the Son, and therewith ceases to be an isolated individual. Insofar as one learns to know God, who gives Himself for us and wills to dwell with us, inasmuch as one learns to know Him in such wise that to know Him and to dwell with Him are one and the same, one is brought into the life of self-impartation for and communion with, mankind. Fellowship with Christ and fellowship with men are correlative, the one cannot exist without the other" (Brunner, p. 14).

II. Requirements for Fellowship With God Who Is Light (1:5–2:28)

1. *Walking in the Light*

1:5–2:2

5 This is the message we have heard from him and declare to you: God is light;
in him there is no darkness at all. 6 If we claim to have fellowship with him yet walk
in the darkness, we lie and do not live by the truth. 7 But if we walk in the light, as
he is in the light, we have fellowship with one another, and the blood of Jesus, his
Son, purifies us from all sin.

[8]If we claim to be without sin, we deceive ourselves and the truth is not in us.
[9]If we confess our sins, he is faithful and just and will forgive us our sins and purify
us from all unrighteousness. [10]If we claim we have not sinned, we make him out
to be a liar and his word has no place in our lives.
[2:1]My dear children, I write this to you so that you will not sin. But if anybody does
sin, we have one who speaks to the Father in our defense—Jesus Christ, the
Righteous One. [2]He is the atoning sacrifice for our sins, and not only for ours but
also for the sins of the whole world.

If the readers are to have fellowship with the Father and with the Son (v.3), they must understand what makes this possible. They must know who God is in himself and, consequently, who they are in themselves as creatures of God. So the author first describes the moral character of God in terms of light (v.5) and then goes on to deny three claims made by those who falsely boast of their knowledge and fellowship with God. The false positions are (1) moral behavior is a matter of indifference in one's relationship to God (v.6); (2) immoral conduct does not issue in sin for one who knows God (v.8); and (3) the knowledge of God removes sin as even a possibility in the life of the believer (v.10). True "tests" or evidence of fellowship with God or walking in the light are (1) fellowship with one another (v.7), with subsequent cleansing by the blood of Christ; (2) confession of sin, (v.9) which brings both forgiveness and cleansing; and (3) trusting that if we sin we have Jesus Christ as an advocate and sacrifice for our sins (2:2).

5 John begins his exposition by referring to the message "heard from him," that is, from Jesus. The allusion is probably not to a specific word of Jesus (though it may include reference to the sum of his teaching) but to Jesus himself as the one sent, the Son in whose life and death the Father manifested himself. Again, in contrast to the false teachers he opposes, the author shows the authority that lies behind his own apostolic witness.

The message that "God is light" needs to be compared with the declarations elsewhere by John that "God is spirit" (John 4:24) and that "God is love" (1 John 4:8). All three stress the immateriality of God and the "Godness" of God—viz., God in his essence. Light emphasizes especially the splendor and glory of God, the truthfulness of God, and his purity.

Certain OT ideas dominate the Christian concept of "light" as a description of God. Light stresses the self-communicative nature of God. It is his nature to impart himself without limit. It stresses the action of God for man and for his salvation. The psalmist catches this with such utterances as "In your light we see light" (Ps 36:9) or "The LORD is my light and my salvation" (Ps 27:1). John expounds this in vv.5–7 (cf. John 1:9).

Light also accents God's empowering activity. God as light not only shines downward for man's salvation but enables him to walk in the light. Jesus said, "I am the light of the world. Whoever follows me will never walk in darkness, but will have the light of life" (John 8:12; cf. also 12:35). Likewise, in Ephesians 5:8–14, Paul exhorts believers to live as children of light. John similarly encourages his readers to walk in the light. Light, then, is the presence of God's grace.

God's light also has the character of a demand. That is certainly the meaning here in vv.5–6. Light defines the mode of human existence. If men turn from the light or love darkness rather than light, it is because their deeds are evil (John 3:19–21). In the world of first-century religious thought, the word "light" described ultimate realities. But there the weight was on the metaphysical implications. John is far removed from that type of speculation. He is concerned with the goodness of God and also the goodness of man. The heretical form of Christianity that prospered later showed all too clearly the folly of dividing moral seriousness from philosophic or theological speculation.

Even some pagans had a greater sensitivity to the ethical than did some expressions of the Christian faith. But as Dodd says, "There is no religion in the Christian sense of the word unless it includes moral endeavour and the criticism of conduct. . . . [Christians] believing in a God of pure goodness, accept the obligation to be good like Him" (*Johannine Epistles*, p. 20; cf. Matt 5:48). The latter part of v.5—"in him [i.e., in God] there is no darkness at all"—is a negative corollary specially emphasizing the statement that God is light. As darkness has no place in God, so all that is of the darkness is excluded from having fellowship with God. This idea stands out as the author approaches the behavior pattern of his opponents.

6 John introduces the first of three antithetic tests of Christian faith by the clause "If we claim." He apparently uses this device to refer to "boasts" made by the false teachers. The first false claim—to have fellowship with God and yet to walk in darkness—probably belongs, as Bultmann asserts (p. 17), to Gnostics who, as John describes them, have no love for one another (v.7), hate their brothers (2:9, 11), claim sinlessness (v.8), and deny that Jesus came in the flesh (2:22). To "walk in the darkness" is the same as "abiding" in darkness or "living in darkness." In each case the meaning is that of allowing darkness to define one's life.

It is not to be assumed that the opponents agreed with the author that they did indeed walk in darkness. Far from it! They claimed to walk in the light while they practiced the deeds of darkness. This is what made their actions so pernicious. Inevitably they, like all persons in similar situations, began to call their "darkness" light and to claim righteousness without becoming righteous or doing righteousness. In such situations, the author says, we lie and do not live by the truth. He also links lying to the life of darkness (cf. note on v.2).

"Do not put the truth into practice" translates *ou poioumen tēn alētheian* (lit., "we do not the truth," or "we do not live out the truth"). For the author the test of truth is not belief—though that is not excluded—but action, deeds, and conduct. As Brooke (p. 14) says, " 'Speaking' the truth is only one part of 'doing' the truth and not the most important. To 'do the truth' is to give expression to the highest of which one is capable in every sphere of his being. It relates to action, and conduct and feeling, as well as to word and thought."

7 The positive test of knowing God is to live (*peripateō*, "walk") in the light as he himself is in the light. It would not be different if he had said here, as he did in v.5, "as he is the light" (cf. Bultmann, p. 20, n. 21). He is simply reiterating the fact that light is God's sphere. It is his nature, and he wills that it should become ours.

The consequence of obedience is to have fellowship with one another. Although life with God should indeed have wholesome effects on our relationship with all human beings, Bultmann wrongly sees this as the primary meaning of the text. Those who walk in the light are also those who have fellowship with one another. The author is combating the heresy that boasts of knowledge of and communion with God but neglects fellowship with other Christians. As Westcott (p. 20) states, "True fellowship with God comes through men. Love of the brethren is the product of the love of God: fellowship with the brethren is the proof of fellowship with God."

A second consequence of walking in the light is that the blood of Jesus keeps on cleansing us from every defilement due to sin. The language is, as Westcott has shown, ritualistic and reminds us of the OT sacrificial system, as well as of the interpretation of Christ's death given us in the Epistle to the Hebrews. The present tense of the verb stresses Christ's work as an ongoing provision against present and future contingencies. Without it enduring fellowship would be impossible, for the guilt resulting from sin destroys fellowship. The cleansing John speaks of results in forgiveness, restoration, and the reestablishment of love. Stott's summary is excellent: "What is clear is that if we walk in the light, God has made provision to cleanse us from whatever sin would otherwise mar our fellowship with Him or each other" (p. 76). Similarly, the use of the singular "sin" reminds us that the emphasis is not on sinful acts but on the work of God in Christ that meets and deals with the sin principle itself.

8 The second denial is against the false assertion that a Christian has no sin. The opponents probably did not claim that they had never committed wrong (sinful acts), but they denied that the sin principle (*hamartian echein*, "to have sin") had lasting power over them or even had a presence in them. It is not surprising that Gnostics, whether Christian or otherwise, should have denied sin. No human being, ancient or modern, wishes to understand his existence under that rubric.

The Gnostic rationalization, though ingenious, was not unique. Some, according to Dodd's reconstruction, held that

> Christians have been given a new nature superior to that of other men. . . . Christians are already sinless beings; or if not all Christians, at least those who have attained to superior enlightenment. They have no further need for moral striving: they are already perfect. . . . if the enlightened do things which in other men would be counted sinful, they are not sinners. Their mystical communion with God in itself removes them from the category of sinful men" (*Johannine Epistles*, pp. 21–22).

Law (in loc.) has argued that the phrase *hamartian echein* pertains especially to the guiltiness of the sin. This would certainly pertain to the Gnostics since they evidently chose to accept no responsibility for moral action.

Others may have argued, like some in Corinth, that sin was a matter of the flesh and had nothing to do with the spirit, or that since they possessed the spirit, they were beyond the categories of good and evil and therefore moral principles no longer applied to them.

Whatever the shape of the argument, and regardless of whether it is an affirmation from the ancient world or a modern restatement, it remains true that whenever the principle of sin is denied as an ongoing reality, there follows a denial of responsibility for individual actions. Gossip, defiling of persons, hatred of the brethren, jealousy, and boasting become sanctioned as non-sins; walking in the light is denied; and the fellowship to which we are called is never permitted to exist.

The implications of the denial of the sin principle are momentous. First, there is the matter of personal responsibility. Brooke (p. 18) points out that the fact that we have deceived ourselves "emphasizes the agent's responsibility for the mistake. The evidence is there; only willful blindness refuses to accept it." Bultmann (p. 21), commenting on the same phrase, says that "self-deception does not mean a simple mistake, but rather that misdirected self-identity which is not aware of its nothingness."

Second, we recognize that the truth is simply not in us or with us. When the principle of sin is denied, truth as an inner principle of life cannot exist. The futility and irony of our predicament then becomes evident: In God's name, we make God's presence and power an impossibility.

9 In what follows we are confronted with our second definite test of obedience. Walking in the light is demonstrated not by the denial of sin but by confessing and abandoning it. This action links us to God's mercy. " 'He who confesses and condemns his sins,' says Augustine, 'already acts with God. God condemns thy sins: if thou also dost condemn them, thou art linked on to God' " (Ross, p. 146). And we can confess our "sins" (note the plural) to God and before man fearlessly and in confidence because God is both faithful and just.

The plural "sins" makes clear that we affirm our sinfulness by "confessing our sins." The forgiveness that comes is related to God's faithfulness and justice. God is faithful in himself, that is, to his own nature (cf. 2 Tim 2:13), and faithful to his promises (cf. Rom 3:25; 1 Cor 10:13; Heb 10:23; 11:11). Everywhere he promises forgiveness to his children—e.g., "I will forgive their wickedness and will remember their sins no more" (Jer 31:34; cf. Mic 7:19–20). And in keeping this promise, God reveals his faithfulness and justice.

Commentators disagree as to the force of *dikaios* ("just") in v.9. Does it point to the Cross (Stott, Ross), to the covenant (Brooke), to God's eschatological rule (Bultmann), or to the attributes of God from which forgiveness flows (Dodd)? Probably the use ought not to be forced in any single direction. And certainly God's mercy must not be set against his justice. The phrase "he is faithful and just" includes all those things. It is a corollary of the fact that God is light and love.

The word the author uses for forgiveness (*aphiēmi*) has at its roots the idea of the "cancellation of debts" or the "dismissal of charges." The verb used for purification is *katharizō*. It pictures an act of cleansing from the pollution of sin so that a new life of holiness may begin. The sinner is perceived as cleansed from moral imperfections and from the injustices that separate him from God.

10 The third and final false claim begins with the assertion "If we claim we have not sinned." But is this a different assertion from that in v.8 or just a restatement of the same issue with an even more dramatic conclusion: "We make him [God] out to be a liar and his word has no place in our lives"?

In favor of the former possibility is the change in the verbal construction of *hamartian ouk echomen* ("we have no sin," present tense) (v.8) to *ouch hēmartēkamen* ("we have not sinned," perfect tense) (v.10). To be sure, the latter statement is more inclusive. The persons involved could be saying, "Whatever is true about the sin principle in others, we as Gnostic believers have transcended it all. We do not sin! We have not sinned! Sin has gained no foothold in us." Probably we should understand that both statements had their adherents among the Gnostic believers. Some may have said it one way, some the other. Some may have claimed that through their "knowledge" derived from the Christian proclamation they were removed from the possibility of sin. Others may have boasted that they had entered a sinless state through "knowledge" before the gospel had even come to them.

Although the assertions made in v.8 and v.10 are more alike than unlike, the latter statement is far more blatant and defiant. It makes a mockery of the gospel. It states that the reason God acted in grace and mercy toward us for the sake of our sins is false, that God first deceived us about ourselves and then becomes himself the Deceiver. The author's statement "his word has no place in our lives" means that the Word proclaimed, the tradition received, or the witness from the OT Scriptures has no place in those who deny their sin. The most elemental presence of the Word of God in the heart and conscience has been denied. Consequently the possibility of hearing a redemptive Word is denied. The ability to live by the Word is removed (see note on v.10). The possibility of receiving the forgiveness offered by God is lost.

2:1 As John resumes his discourse on sin and forgiveness, we see a striking change of mood. Whereas earlier he was focusing on his opponents and their false teaching, now he specifically speaks about these things as they affect his followers. The note of endearment—"my dear children"—in no way minimizes the seriousness of the discussion. Lest any conclude from his previous statements that sin must be considered inevitable in the life of the believer and not a matter of urgent concern since forgiveness is present by confession and the blood of Christ, John hastens to add, "I write this to you so that you will not sin." There is no question at all in his mind that sin and obedience to God are irreconcilable. Sin is the enemy. It removes the believer from the light. It prevents fellowship with God and it destroys fellowship with the children of light. The principle of sin as the power of darkness must be excluded from the believer's life, and individual acts of sin must be resisted. Where failure occurs, the sin must be confessed before the body and the Lord and then abandoned. And always the intent of the believer remains the same—not to commit sin!

If any of his children should fail and commit sin, the author is anxious that they neither deceive themselves about it nor lie about their action nor give up walking in the light. The answer to lapsing into sin is not self-deceit but the forgiveness of God made available through Jesus Christ. He has been designated the believer's advocate, the counsel who speaks in our defense. His worthiness to perform this function rests on the fact that even as God is righteous (1:9), so Jesus Christ also merits the title "The Righteous One."

2 The advocate does not maintain our innocence but confesses our guilt. Then he enters his plea before the Father on our behalf as the one who has made "atoning sacrifice for our sins." The word describing this activity is *hilasmos*. It is used elsewhere in the NT only in 4:10 (cognates appear in Luke 18:13; Rom 3:25; Heb 2:17; 9:5).

Notes

---

6 Περιπατεῖν (*peripatein*, "to walk"), which describes the manner of one's life, is a standard expression in the Johannine writings (cf. John 8:12; 11:9; 12:35; 1 John 1:6–7; 2:11; 2 John 4, 6; 3 John 3–4).

Concerning ψευδόμεθα (*pseudometha*, "lie") Conzelmann says, "In accordance with the Johannine meaning of ἀλήθεια . . . the lie is not just error but an active contesting of the truth, i.e., unbelief. . . . The demand that we do the truth and not lie is based on the statement that God is light. . . . Lying is also a denial of the confession, 2:21f. The liar is a historical manifestation of antichrist" (TDNT, 9:602).

10 Westcott (p. 26) says, "The word, like the truth, can be regarded both as the moving principle which stirs the man and as the sphere in which the man moves. The word abides in him (John v.38, comp. viii.37), and conversely he 'abides in the word' (John viii.3)."

2:2 The normal use of the word ἱλάσκομαι (*hilaskomai,* "propitiation") in Greek literature carries the idea of an offering made by a guilty person in order to placate or appease the person (God) who has been offended. The English word "propitiate" is used to render this meaning. But Westcott argues, and Dodd agrees, that "the scriptural conception . . . is not that of appeasing one who is angry . . . but of altering the character of that which from without occasions a necessary alienation, and interposes an inevitable obstacle to fellowship" (Westcott, p. 85; cf. C.H. Dodd, "*Hilaskomai,* Its Cognates, Derivatives, and Synonyms in the Septuagint," JTS 32 [1931], 352–60). If this is the correct emphasis, then the word is better rendered by the English word "expiation."

Modern translations reflect the difficulty; there is no clear consensus. NEB offers the translation "remedy for defilement," which suggests the idea of expiation. TEV reflects a related stance with its "means by which our sins are forgiven," as does JB in "the sacrifice that takes our sins away." In support of NIV's "atoning sacrifice," Marshall (p. 18) argues that "both concepts—propitiation and expiation—must be included . . . The one action has the double effect of expiating the sin and thereby propitiating God."

Surely the text makes clear that God is not over against man as the opponent since God is the one who sends the Son in order that as Father he may grant forgiveness to the confessor. It is sin that is the offense. It must be atoned for so that the just punishment due the sinner can be averted. The blot of the sin must also be removed so that the believer will not rest under the burden of guilt and defilement. Both actions are necessary for the restoration of the child to the Father.

The sacrifice is "also for the sins of the whole world." This statement asserts two things: Christ's sacrifice is sufficient for all, and it is necessary for all.

---

2. *Obeying His Commands*

2:3–11

[3]We know that we have come to know him if we obey his commands. [4]The man who says, "I know him," but does not do what he commands is a liar, and the truth is not in him. [5]But if anyone obeys his word, God's love is truly made complete in him. This is how we know we are in him: [6]Whoever claims to live in him must walk as Jesus did.

[7]Dear friends, I am not writing you a new command but an old one, which you have had since the beginning. This old command is the message you have heard. [8]Yet I am writing you a new command; its truth is seen in him and you, because the darkness is passing and the true light is already shining.

[9]Anyone who claims to be in the light but hates his brother is still in the darkness. [10]Whoever loves his brother lives in the light, and there is nothing in him to make him stumble. [11]But whoever hates his brother is in the darkness and walks around in the darkness; he does not know where he is going, because the darkness has blinded him.

The first section (1:1–2:2) dealt with fellowship, primarily fellowship with God. Three false claims made by the opponents were denied (vv.6, 8, 10), and each false claim was used as an occasion for the presentation of what are true "tests" or evidences of living in fellowship with God. The second section (2:3–11) is concerned with knowledge of God. Again the false claims to knowledge by the opponents are stated first, this time introduced by the clause "he who says" (cf. vv.4, 6, 9). Each of these claims is again denied and the evidence or "tests" of the true knowledge of God is set forth: obeying his commands (v.5), walking in his likeness (v.6), and loving one's brother (v.10).

3 There appears to be a break in subject matter with what precedes as the author now turns to the topic of knowing God. For him to know God is, however, a natural corollary to the idea of walking in the light and of having fellowship with God. It is simply another way of speaking of the reality of God. In this instance the language probably is a response to the opponents for whom knowledge (*gnōsis*) was a key term. These "Gnostic" opponents, though not sharing the full-blown ideas reflected among the second-century Gnostics, naturally shared some of their essential thoughts. Knowledge of God, they said, came through "mystical insights" or by a "direct vision of God." *Corpus Hermetica* 10.5–6 is an example of Gnostic thought:

> Not yet are we able to open the eyes of the mind and to behold the beauty, the imperishable, inconceivable beauty, of the Good. For you will see it when you cannot say anything about it. For the knowledge of it is divine silence and annihilation of all senses. . . . Irradiating the whole mind, it shines upon the soul and draws it up from the body, and changes it all into divine essence (cited in Dodd, *Johannine Epistles,* p. 30).

Such thinking is clearly devoid of interest in moral conduct and unconcerned about human behavior. For the Hebrew or Christian mind, however, knowledge of God is not separable from the experience of righteousness. Consequently there is no greater claim one can make in knowing God than to obey him. "We can be sure we know him," the author says, "if we obey his commands." For John, therefore, the test of knowledge of God is moral conduct (cf. also Titus 1:16). It is keeping God's commandments. Bultmann (p. 25) appropriately observes that " 'keeping the commandments' (like fellowship with one another, 1:7) is not the condition, but rather the characteristic knowledge of God. There is no knowledge of God which as such would not also be 'keeping the commandments.' "

4 In v.3 the author dealt with the general question of how we may have assurance that we know God. Here he deals with those who claim that they know God but at the same time break his commandments. For John knowledge of God is clearly not perceived as academic, theoretical, or speculative but as practical and experiential. It is "a relationship to God, in which the one knowing is determined in his existence (and thus also in his 'walking,' his conduct) by God" (Bultmann, p. 25). To claim to know God and at the same time to be disobedient to his commandments is, the author asserts, to lie and be devoid of all truth.

5 Next John states the positive side of knowledge. He who "obeys his word" (a way of speaking of the gospel that is more comprehensive—including the promises as well as the commandments) finds God's love "made complete" in him. The true knowledge of God does not end with speculative ideas, as for the Gnostics, but with obedience to the moral law and with the presence of God's love in the believer. The term "made complete" (*teleioō*) carries with it the idea of continuous growth and development.

It describes both state and process. As obedience is practiced, so also God's love matures in us.

6 "To live in him" ("abideth," KJV) introduces another way the opponents described their relationship to God. What they claimed by this experience we do not know; probably they boasted of mystical experiences, visions of the light, and the like. What they did not claim was any new ethical seriousness as a consequence of their life in God. The author's comment is direct and forceful: "Whoever claims to live in him [either the Father or the Son, but in the context the Father is more likely] must walk [live] as Jesus did." The uniqueness of Christian ethics comes again to the surface. Relationship to God requires moral behavior worthy of God. And as the revelation of God in Christ is accepted as the high point of divine self-disclosure, so the human life of Jesus becomes the measuring stick of true moral and ethical behavior. The author is not claiming that the walk of Jesus can be perfectly imitated but that there is a divine imperative—which must be taken seriously—for believers to live according to the way Jesus lived. Also included is the true test for those who want to know whether their life in God is real or mere fantasy: To claim a relationship to God necessitates a commitment to moral standards expressed positively (to love as God himself loves) and negatively (to obey commandments and not to sin).

7 The introduction of the affectionate term "dear friends" (*agapētoi*, "beloved") reminds us that the author is looking in two directions at once. On the one hand, he is setting forth tests that will expose the false teachings and claims of his opponents; on the other hand, he is providing tests by which his own spiritual children will know they are walking in the light.

In addition, John may be dealing with a serious charge against his own teaching. The opponents may have claimed that he has in fact distorted the gospel by adding to it. For his opponents the knowledge of God available in the gospel was itself the end of the religious quest. The knowledge was freedom from the world. To the author, the gospel is fulfilled in the knowledge of God that is revealed in Jesus, and this in turn requires obedience to his commands and results in a new relationship with God expressed in a life of love. The point of view reflects Jesus' words as recorded in John's gospel: "A new command I give you: Love one another. As I have loved you, so you must love one another" (John 13:34). The new command John speaks of here in v.7 sums up what it means to "walk in the light" and to "walk as Jesus did." Thus it stands at the heart of the gospel. Moreover, what John was proclaiming to his "dear children" was not "a new command but an old one" they had had since the beginning." So he denies that there ever was "a message" that did not have this command at its heart, despite his opponents' claims.

8 In view of v.7, how can the author assert that this command is also at the same time "a new command"? Its newness lies at the point of its realization and fulfillment. Jesus lived a life of divine love. He also extended this life to his disciples as a new command. But certainly for them this requirement had to be received in an eschatological framework, as a command yet to be fulfilled in them (John 15:12ff.). After Jesus' death and resurrection, however, they discovered that as they obeyed his commands, his promise found fulfillment. What had been true in Jesus' own life now became part of the reality of their lives. They too began to know what it was to "love." Luke and Paul also experienced this realized eschatology. For Paul the old had passed away;

in Christ all had become new (2 Cor 5:17). For Luke the gift of the Holy Spirit marked the beginning of fulfillment of the promise (Acts 2). Here in v.8 John expresses the realized fulfillment by simply saying that "the darkness is passing and the true light is already shining." Paul also used this imagery of light (cf. Eph 5:8–14; 1 Thess 5:4–8).

9 This verse brings us to the third false claim that the author denies. Whereas obedience to the new command leads to love among the brethren, among the opponents who claim to "be in the light" there is hate. This hate for one's brother shows that the light they follow is nothing but darkness.

How does John understand hate? Does he think in conceptual terms or concrete ones? Undoubtedly the answer for him lies primarily in what one does. Hate is the absence of the deeds of love. To walk in the light is to love one's brother, and God's love will express itself in concrete actions. If these are missing, it is not because love can be neutral or can exist unexpressed. Love unexpressed is not love at all. Love has no neutral capabilities. When it is absent, hate is present.

In this instance, then, hate is the failure to deny oneself, the unwillingness to lay down one's life for a brother (John 15:13). It considers its own plight first (1 Cor 13:5); disregards the robbed and afflicted (Luke 10:30–37); despises the little ones (Matt 18:10); withholds the cup of cold water from the thirsty (Matt 25:42); and makes no effort to welcome the stranger, clothe the naked, or help the sick (Matt 25:43). Whenever a brother has need and one does not help him, then one has despised and, in fact, hated his brother.

Does the word "brother" refer here to one's neighbor or to one who belongs to the community of faith? In this instance it probably refers to a member of the community of faith. It is not that John lacks concern for those outside the faith; rather, in this letter he has the community of believers in view. Moreover, if a believer cannot love his brother, it is doubtful whether he can love his neighbor.

10 The author now gives us a positive test of living in the light. Unlike his opponents, his concern is with deeds, not claims. "Whoever loves," he says, is "in the light." Conversely, it follows that one who does not live "in the light" will not manifest God's love.

The uncertain antecedents of the Greek pronouns leads to some ambiguity in the rest of the sentence. The pronouns could be rendered in the following ways: "There is nothing in him to make him [his brother] stumble" or "There is nothing in him to cause his [own] stumbling" or "There is nothing in it [the light] to cause him to stumble" or "There is nothing in it [the light] to cause him [his brother] to stumble." In view of the author's aim, it is probable that he is saying that the one who loves and abides in the light will never cause the offense the opponents do.

11 Now the author picks up the concept of darkness from 2:9 and gives it a final elaboration and conclusion. He who "hates his brother" is not simply "in the darkness" but is condemned to walk or spend his life in darkness. Though he has eyes, he can see nothing. And the darkness so blinds his eyes that he has no idea "where he is going." Life is a search, but for him it is without direction. He never knows whether he is closer or further from his destination. The only certainty is that he is without hope of reaching it. So hate destroys any window for light from God. To live without loving one's brother is, for the author, to live in total meaninglessness, denying oneself the presence of God and the reality of fellowship with the brothers.

Notes

3 "Knowledge" is a characteristic concept in this Epistle. Two verbs for "knowing" are used in the Greek for the concept: *οἶδα* (*oida*) and *γινώσκω* (*ginōskō*). The latter, a common word in the Johannine Epistles (twenty-five times), emphasizes knowledge by experience; the former, that which is immediate and absolute.

Αὐτόν (*auton*, "him"), though ambiguous here, probably refers to God the Father. When Jesus is referred to, the writer generally uses *ἐκεῖνος* (*ekeinos*) (cf. Schnackenburg, p. 75).

5 The author develops this idea in 4:12, 17–20. "In this" most likely refers to obeying the commandments (v.3) and keeping God's word (v.5). Whether "the love of God" is to be understood as a subjective genitive, "the love that God gives" (so NIV, Bultmann, Houlden, Westcott), or as an objective genitive, "our love for God" (so RSV, Brooke, Bruce, Dodd, Marshall, Ross, Stott), or as a descriptive or qualitative genitive, "God's kind of love" (so Schnackenburg), is disputed. NIV is probably correct because (1) generally in the NT *ἀγάπη* (*agapē*, "love") is followed by a subjective genitive; (2) it is certainly a subjective genitive in 1 John 4:9; (3) the subjective idea is what dominates the author's mind (cf. 1 John 3:1: "The Father has given to us love"; cf. also 4:7, 16); (4) it agrees best with the context (see Westcott, p. 49).

Τελειόω (*teleioō*, "perfected") is a favorite Johannine word (cf. John 4:34; 5:36; 17:4; 19:28, 30).

6 Μένειν (*menein*, "abide"; NIV, "live in him") occurs twenty-four times in 1 John, three times in 2 John, and forty times in the Gospel of John. Bultmann points out that "abide" always contains a negative implication: Do not yield, Do not leave, Stay where you are (p. 26, n.9). In 1 John and the Gospel of John, "abide" means "faithfulness" and reciprocity (cf. John 15:1–17). (For an extended treatment of "abide," see Schnackenburg, pp. 105–10.)

7 Ἀγαπητοί (*agapētoi*, "beloved") also occurs in 3:2, 21; 4:7, 11. The singular form occurs in 3 John 2, 5, 11 (cf. Rom 12:19; 2 Cor 7:1).

8 "Its truth" does not refer to the truthfulness of the new command but to the fact that there is something that must "properly" and "truly" be understood as a new command (cf. Marshall, p. 129; for a different position, see Westcott, p. 53).

"True" as applied to "light" (cf. John 1:9; 1 John 1:5–7; 5:20) should be understood in contrast to the "false" light in which the Gnostic opponents walk. The adjective *ἀληθινός* (*alēthinos*, "true") is common in Johannine literature; it occurs four times in 1 John, nine times in the Gospel of John, and ten times in Revelation.

10 Σκάνδαλον (*skandalon*) occurs twenty-five times in the NT, but only here in John. It means literally "trap" or "snare" (cf. Westcott, p. 56). (For a different conclusion, see Brooke, p. 39; Bultmann, p. 28; Schnackenburg, p. 115.)

11 Σκοτία (*skotia*, "darkness") is an important theme in the Gospel of John (see 8:12; 9:39–41; 11:9–10; 12:35–36, 40).

Ἀδελφός (*adelphos*, "brother") is consistently used in the NT to refer to a member of the church, Bultmann's opinion (p. 28) notwithstanding (see Westcott, p. 55).

---

3. *Knowing the Father and Abiding Forever*

2:12–17

[12]I write to you, dear children,
because your sins have been forgiven on account
of his name.
[13]I write to you, fathers,
because you have known him who is from
the beginning.

I write to you, young men,
  because you have overcome the evil one.
I write to you, dear children,
  because you have known the Father.
14 I write to you, fathers,
  because you have known him who is from
    the beginning.
I write to you, young men,
  because you are strong,
  and the word of God lives in you,
  and you have overcome the evil one.

15 Do not love the world or anything in the world. If anyone loves the world, the
love of the Father is not in him. 16 For everything in the world—the cravings of sinful
man, the lust of his eyes and the boasting of what he has and does—comes not
from the Father but from the world. 17 The world and its desires pass away, but the
man who does the will of God lives forever.

The first part of the Epistle (1:5–2:11) involved untrue assertions made by the author's Gnostic-type opponents and provided "tests" for exposing the false claims as well as for assuring those who walked in the light. The next section is in two parts. The first (2:12–14) contrasts the position of the believer who walks in the light with that of the Gnostics who walk in darkness. The second part (2:15–17) warns the believer not to fall into the trap of worldliness, as the false teachers did.

The first section is rhythmical, almost lyrical. Two sets of three statements introduced by the words "I write" and "I have written," or "I wrote" (NIV does not bring out this distinction) are addressed in turn to "children," "fathers," and "young men." We do not know why the author changes tenses. Most commentators agree that the change is stylistic and is added for emphasis. Nor do we know the significance of the various forms of address. It is possible that John's intention was to address his entire congregation from two standpoints—that of chronological age ("children," "young men," "fathers") and that of spiritual age (novices in the faith, those whose faith is vigorous and who are responsible for the work of the gospel, and those whose knowledge and experience in the faith are the foundation on which the community exists).

The alternative suggestion that the categories of "children," "young men," and "fathers" represent offices in the Johannine community comparable to those of deacons, elders, and bishops (if indeed the last two are to be distinguished) in the Pauline church is attractive but speculative (cf. Houlden, pp. 70–71). What is clear in any instance is that John wanted to speak representationally to the entire church. As members of the new covenant, their sins are forgiven, they know the truth, and they have overcome the world.

12 "Dear children" (*teknia*) is the author's favorite term for the congregation of believers as a whole. Under this rubric he offers the most basic and universal words of assurance he can give: "Your sins have been forgiven on account of his name" (see Notes). They have confessed their sins (1:9) and, on account of his name, or by faith in his name (3:23; 5:13), or by faith in him (5:1, 5)—the meaning is the same—forgiveness that was bought through the covenant of his blood (1:7) has become their possession. In this knowledge they may stand firm. Because they are forgiven, they may also have fellowship with God and true knowledge of him (13c). Whether the author is speaking to new converts or to old ones is unimportant. Knowledge of God begins with conversion in which sin, known and confessed, is forgiven.

13a "Fathers" is an unusual form of address for senior members of a congregation. According to Jewish custom, it would refer to those who had responsibility for authority. Many times it is used to refer to the leaders of the past, the fathers of Israel, the patriarchs, etc. If it refers to members of the congregation who were mature both in years and in faith, it was indeed a solemn designation, one entailing assumption of responsibility in the community of believers. The secondary address to the "fathers" in v. 14—"because you have known him who is from the beginning"—is peculiarly appropriate to older members of the community. It stresses the historic origins of the faith and the growth of the personal knowledge of Christ that comes only with experience.

Although the pronoun "him" is ambiguous and could refer to God (so Bruce, Stott), it is more likely in view of the reference to the Father in 13c that here it refers to Christ. In any instance, it looks back to 1:1–3, where both God and Christ are equally represented, and reminds the readers that they have come to know Jesus as the One who is and who was from the beginning. Dodd (*Johannine Epistles*, pp. 36–37) points out that this "knowing" God and the Son that looms so large in the Epistle and the Gospel of John reflects a special interest of the prophets: "Isaiah (xi. 1–9) forecasts the reign of a Messiah, upon whom rests the spirit of knowledge," as one in which the earth shall be full of the knowledge of God. Isaiah says, "Therefore my people will know my name; therefore in that day they will know that it is I who foretold it" (Isa 52:6). Jeremiah (31:34) says, "They will all know me, from the least of them to the greatest. . . . For I will forgive their wickedness and will remember their sins no more."

13b The description of the community as "young men" who "are strong" (14b) and "have overcome" adds a new dimension. Believers are to see themselves as not only in conflict with the enemy but as having perceived the victory in Christ's name and by his power. The victory obviously was gained through Christ's death, and now his followers have the task under his leadership of establishing his reign over the world and the devil (14b). This victory, seen as already realized, does not promise that believers shall be removed from the heat and peril of the battlefield. But it does assure them that if they are faithful they will overcome the "evil one." As Christ has been victorious over the evil one, so they too may commit themselves to the conflict without fear (cf. John 16:33; Rom 8:31–39; Col 2:15; 1 John 3:8). This idea will be expanded on in 4:4 and 5:4–5. It is clear that "the evil one" is but another way to refer to the devil (3:12; 5:18; cf. John 17:15; Eph 6:16; 2 Thess 3:3).

13c This time the "children" are addressed as *paidia*. If a difference in emphasis is intended, the use of *teknia* emphasizes more the relationship, the dependence or weakness of the infant, while *paidia* stresses the immaturity (subordination) of the child, the need to be under instruction or direction. The author is saying that as children under teachers or instructors in the faith his readers have come to know God as the Father. Second only to forgiveness in importance for the new community of faith is the relationship to God as Father that came through the gospel of Jesus Christ.

14 After referring again to the "fathers," the author concludes by addressing the young men as those in whom "the word of God lives." They were indeed "strong" as the children of faith, but the author reminds them that their strength ultimately depends on one fact alone—the Word of God abiding or living in them.

Six times the author uses the perfect tense (rendered by "have" in NIV) to describe the action expressed in the subordinate clauses. In each instance, what is described has been initiated or established in the past (i.e., the Cross and/or their conversion) and continues to be true into the present.

15 Having assured the believers of their position before God—viz., their sins are forgiven, they know the Father, and they have overcome the evil one—John moves to application. He warns them not to love the world and gives two reasons: Love of the world precludes love for the Father, and the investment of love in the world is without meaning because the world is passing away (v.17). The love of the world versus the love of the Father provides yet another "test" of walking in the light.

The word for world (*kosmos*) occurs six times in vv.15–17. It obviously means something quite different here than in John 3:16. There the Father's love of the world is apparently based on God's having willed the world into existence. It is his creation; he created it to be good, beautiful, and worthy of giving glory to him. Likewise those who live in the world are his creatures; he created them, loves them, and, even in their desperate state of living in darkness and the shadow of death, remains constant in desiring to rescue them from eternal death.

Here, however, the world is presented as the evil system totally under the grip of the devil (cf. 1 John 5:19; John 12:31; 14:30). It is the "godless world" (NEB), the world of "emptiness and evil" (Bultmann, p. 33), the world of enmity against God (James 4:4).

Love also means something different in this passage. Here it is not the selfless love for one's brother (cf. 2:10) but the love that entices by evil desire or base appetite that is forbidden (John 3:19; 12:43). It is the world's ability to seduce the believer, to draw him away from love of the Father, that concerns John. "Anything in the world" is not a reference to "natural" phenomena, as v.16 makes clear.

16 What love for the world or worldliness entails is now spelled out by John in a memorable triad: "the cravings of sinful man, the lust of his eyes and the boasting of what he has and does." The phrase "the cravings of sinful man" (lit., "the desire of the flesh [*sarkos*]") describes the principle of worldliness from which love of the world flows. "Flesh" refers to "the outlook orientated towards self, that which pursues its own ends in self-sufficient independence of God" (DNTT, 1:680) and in self-sufficient independence of one's fellow man. The "flesh" not only becomes the basis for rebellion against God and for despising his law but also connotes all that is materialistic, egocentric, exploitative, and selfish. It is at the root of racism, sexism, love of injustice, despising the poor, neglecting the weak and helpless, and every unrighteous practice.

The "lust of the eyes," according to Bultmann (p. 34), "can refer especially to sexual lust, but can also mean everything that entices the eyes." Marshall (p. 145) sees it as "the tendency to be captivated by outward, visible splendor and show, but more probably the basic thought is of greed and desire for things aroused by seeing them." Stott (p. 100) gives "Eve's view of the forbidden tree as 'a delight to the eyes,' Achan's covetous sight among the spoil of a 'goodly Babylonish garment,' and David's lustful looking after Bathsheba as she bathed" as obvious examples. Law sees it as "the love of beauty divorced from the love of goodness" (cited in Stott, p. 100).

The key term in the third phrase, "pride of life," is *alazoneia;* it occurs only here and in James 4:16. The corporate adjective *alazōn* is used in Romans 1:30 and 2 Timothy 3:2. It describes a pretentious hypocrite who glories in himself or in his possessions. He is a person of ostentatious pride in "his own non-existent importance." (Barclay, in loc.). Bruce (p. 61) says, "If my reputation, my 'public image,' matters more to me than the glory of God or the well-being of my followers, the 'pretentiousness of life' has become the object of my idol-worship."

"Pride of life" will be reflected in whatever status symbol is important to me or seems to define my identity. When I define myself to others in terms of my honorary degrees, the reputation of the church I serve, my annual income, the size of my library, my expensive car or house, and if in doing this I misrepresent the truth and in my boasting show myself to be only a pompous fool who has deceived no one, then I have succumbed to what John calls the pride of life.

The following is an ancient caricature of the self-important fool, the "*Alazon*":

> The *Alazon* is the kind of person who will stand on the mole and tell perfect strangers what a lot of money he has at sea, and discourse of his investments, how large they are, and what gains and losses he has made, and as he spins his yarns he will send his boy to the bank—his balance being a shilling. If he enjoys company on the road, he is apt to tell how he served with Alexander the Great, how he got on with him, and how many jewelled cups he brought home; and to discuss the Asiatic craftsmen, how much better they are than any in Europe—never having been away from Athens. He will say that he was granted a free permit for the export of timber, but took no advantage of it, to avoid ill-natured gossip; and that during the corn-shortage he spent more than fifteen hundred pounds in gifts to needy citizens. He will be living in a rented house, and will tell anyone who does not know the facts that this is the family residence, but he is going to sell it because it is too small for his entertainments (Plutarch's *Characters*, quoted in Dodd, *Johannine Epistles*, p. 42).

17 All the vanity of this evil world with its devices is passing away. It has already begun to putrify. It is a corpse not yet buried. But the person who really does the will of God has the breath of eternal life.

Notes

12 For the origin and use of the expression "his name," see Ezek 20:8–9; 36:22; in the NT see Matt 10:22 (Gk.); Luke 24:47; Acts 4:12, 30; 13:38; 1 Cor 1:10. Elsewhere in Johannine literature, see John 20:31; 1 John 3:23; 5:13.

12–14 The change from the present tense, γράφω (*graphō*, "I write"), in vv.12–13 to the aorist tense, ἔγραψα (*egrapsa*, "I wrote"), goes unnoticed in NIV. Schnackenburg (pp. 125ff.) says that *egrapsa* can be used to describe something being written in the present as well as of the past (cf. 1 John 2:21; Gal 6:11; Philem 19, 21). Brooke (p. 41) prefers to think that the writer used the aorist tense in referring to that part of the letter already finished. The possibility that these are epistolary aorists, in which the writer has projected himself forward to the readers' time, for whom the event would already be past, does not seem to offer any real value here. Most likely the author changed tenses for the sake of emphasis.

15 In the choice between "love for the Father" or "the kind of love manifested in the Father," I would take the former (cf. Bultmann, p. 33; Marshall, p. 143).

4. *Warnings Against Antichrists*

2:18–28

18Dear children, this is the last hour; and as you have heard that the antichrist
is coming, even now many antichrists have come. This is how we know it is the last
hour. 19They went out from us, but they did not really belong to us. For if they had
belonged to us, they would have remained with us; but their going showed that none
of them belonged to us.
20But you have an anointing from the Holy One, and all of you know the truth.
21I do not write to you because you do not know the truth, but because you do know
it and because no lie comes from the truth. 22Who is the liar? It is the man who
denies that Jesus is the Christ. Such a man is the antichrist—he denies the Father
and the Son. 23No one who denies the Son has the Father; whoever acknowledges
the Son has the Father also.
24See that what you have heard from the beginning remains in you. If it does,
you also will remain in the Son and in the Father. 25And this is what he promised
us—even eternal life.
26I am writing these things to you about those who are trying to lead you astray.
27As for you, the anointing you received from him remains in you, and you do not
need anyone to teach you. But as his anointing teaches you about all things and
as that anointing is real, not counterfeit—just as it has taught you, remain in him.
28And now, dear children, continue in him, so that when he appears we may be
confident and unashamed before him at his coming.

In the first three sections of his letter, the author has been directly presenting his followers with "tests" by which they could know they were truly in union with the Father. At the same time, he was dealing with his opponents by showing that they failed each of these tests of discipleship. In this section he reverses his method. He no longer uses indirection against his opponents but now confronts them and their teaching by openly labeling them for what they are: antichrists (vv.18–19). He exposes their method: they lie and deny Jesus as Christ (vv.20, 23). He teaches his followers how to cope with this: they are to remain in what they were taught (vv.24–26); and, finally, he assures his followers of their power to overcome: "His anointing teaches you" (vv.27–28).

18 The reference to the transitoriness of the world—viz., "it is passing away" (v.17)—provides the link to what has preceded. One of the signs of the end of this transitory world is the appearance of false teaching and of the Antichrist. What the apostles warned of is now being fulfilled. The spirit of antichrist is present in the world, evidenced by the fact that many antichrists have already appeared. This is no surprise, however, but only further confirmation that the company of believers are living in the last hour, an hour that draws its significance from the appearance of the true Christ in the flesh.

The term "last hour" occurs only here in the NT. Like the similar terms "the last days" and "the last times," it owes much to OT expectations (cf. Joel 2:28; Mic 4:1) and later Jewish speculation. Jesus called the present age an evil age and looked forward to the age to come, which would be ushered in by God's own intervention. Some Jewish theologians believed this "golden age" would be inaugurated by a special personage, namely God's Messiah.

The NT writers thought of the "last days" in two ways. Theologically they connected this period to the new age that they associated with the advent of Jesus. In the Gospel of John this new age is designated by the statement "the hour is come" and is marked by Jesus' death and resurrection (John 4:23; 5:25). In Acts the new age is referred to as the "days to come" and is signaled by the pouring forth of the Spirit (2:17) and salvation through calling on the name of the Lord (2:21). The NT writers did not believe the new age had completely come. They recognized it as being present provisionally in Christ and in the Holy Spirit. But because of this dawning of the new age, they saw the present age as already doomed and passing away.

They also used the term "last days" eschatologically to designate the last days before Christ's return (cf. 2 Tim 3:1ff.; 2 Peter 3:3). In the Gospel of John, the last day refers to the last resurrection and judgment (cf. 6:39–40, 44, 54; 11:24; 12:48).

How should the term "last hour" in 1 John be understood? The majority of commentators see it eschatologically, indicating "the last period of the interval between the first and second coming of Christ" (Brooke, p. 51; cf. Dodd, *Johannine Epistles*, pp. 48ff.). Some commentators therefore conclude that the author was mistaken.

Westcott (p. 68) translates the Greek literally—"it is a last hour"—and observes that, since no definite article is used with "last hour," the term describes "the general character of the period" rather than its temporal nature. Stott (pp. 108–9) agrees that it refers to "the last hours of the last days," which the author could say on theological grounds "had struck." He understands, however, that the words involve no chronological or temporal assertions.

Against any exclusively eschatological interpretation stands the Gospel of John, which uses "hour" theologically to indicate the fulfillment of time, the time of redemption and salvation (John 2:4; 4:21; 7:30; 8:20; 12:23).

19 The "departure" may have had a greater effect on the congregation than the reason for it. The early church obviously had severe debates with significant differences of opinion being expressed. Yet as far as we know, no one thought that "separation from the congregation" was an option for anyone professing belief. Departure, like Judas's going out from the community of disciples, pointed to betrayal, denial of faith, and separation from God's grace. That is why John acknowledges that those false teachers he now designates as antichrists had been regular members of the congregation. "They went out from us," he says, but hastens to add, "they did not really belong to us." Like Judas, they had been nominal members of the community and had never truly shared its fellowship.

John now goes on to teach the congregation the significance and abiding nature of life in the community. "If they had belonged to us, they would have remained with us." Those who have actually been a part of the divine life will without fail persevere in the community. But in order that the true nature of the false teachers might be exposed, "they went out from us," so that the community might know that "none of them belonged to us" (cf. Matt 24:24).

Expulsion from the Christian community for misdeeds is a serious act, and hopefully it lasts only so long as to allow for repentance and restoration (cf. 1 Cor 5:2–5; 2 Cor 2:5–11). The case at hand is unique; apparently the going out was neither expulsion nor excommunication but the voluntary departure of those involved. Yet their departure is taken as absolutely serious. It shows that they were never truly one with the community. If they had been true disciples, their nonperseverance with the community would never have occurred. Here Stott (pp. 105–6) cites Calvin: "Future and final perseverance is the ultimate test of a past participation in Christ (cf. Heb iii.14). 'Those who fall away,' on the other hand, 'have never been thoroughly imbued with the knowledge of Christ but only had a slight and passing taste of it.' "

20 The author now returns to the heretical claims of his opponents. They probably claimed superior knowledge because they had received an exclusive ritual anointing that gave them knowledge (*gnōsis*). Dodd (*Johannine Epistles,* p. 61) suggests that their attitude may have been similar to that of the " 'Gnostic' sect known as Naassenes," who much later also boasted of a special sacrament of anointing: " 'We alone of all men are Christians, who complete the mystery at the third portal, and are anointed there with speechless chrism' (*Philosophumena* V. 9.121–2)." Schnackenburg (p. 152, nn. 3 and 4) also refers to the Gnostic ritual of anointing with oil.

The author combats his opponents' claim by reminding his readers: "But you have an anointing from the Holy One, and all of you know [because all of you received it] the truth." This is probably an allusion to the coming of the Holy Spirit as set forth in the Gospel of John: "But when he, the Spirit of truth, comes, he will guide you into all truth" (16:13; cf. also 14:17; 15:26). The early Christians connected this with their baptism. Although "anointing" is used only infrequently in the NT, both Luke and Paul do use it with reference to the Holy Spirit (Luke 4:18; Acts 10:38). "He anointed us, set his seal of ownership on us, and put his Spirit in our hearts as a deposit, guaranteeing what is to come" (2 Cor 1:21–22).

The messengers of God proclaimed the gospel, but God himself by his Spirit taught the heart, from which true knowledge was then manifested. When this divine teaching was truly recognized, Christians were genuinely protected against false teaching or unbelief. Paul has this same emphasis in his epistles: "Now about brotherly love we do not need to write to you, for you yourselves have been taught by God to love each other" (1 Thess 4:9); "I myself am convinced, my brothers, that you yourselves are full of goodness, complete in knowledge and competent to instruct one another" (Rom 15:14).

The statement "you have an anointing from the Holy One" may refer to God, but it more likely refers to Christ (cf. John 6:69).

21 Lest there be any doubt among the faithful as to John's perception of their understanding and orthodoxy, he says that he has not written because they did not know the truth—he is not providing new information or teaching—but because they know it so certainly. They know the character of truth, and therefore they know that "no lie comes from truth." The author aims his remarks precisely at the innate knowledge of the gospel that he knows his followers possess. Lies cannot come from God. The antichrists and their followers, the false teachers, are liars. So they do not come—in fact, cannot come—from God who is the truth.

22 "Who is the liar?" v.22 asks and then rhetorically answers by pointing to those antichrists who promulgate the particularly pernicious falsehood that Jesus is not the Christ. This falsehood should not be linked to the Jewish opponents who denied that Jesus was the Messiah but rather to the Gnostic opponents who denied that Christ came in the flesh. (For more explicit references, see 1 John 4:2–3 and 2 John 7.)

The exact kind of Gnostic denial in view is uncertain. Commentators have traditionally favored a Gnosticism like that of Cerinthus, who held that "after Jesus' baptism, the Christ, coming down from that power which is above all, descended upon him in a form of a dove. . . . In the end, however, the Christ withdrew again from Jesus. . . . The Christ, being spiritual, remained unable to suffer" (Brown, p. 112).

However, since the opponents came out of the Johannine community, it is more likely that their Christology would not be as extreme as that of Cerinthus. Yet it probably did include the ideas that the true Christ, who was preexistent, merely appeared in human form to bring eternal life, that his human existence was without real significance, and that his human presence was not essential to his true being. The revelations he brought came not through any of his actions as Jesus of Nazareth or through any of the events connected to his life—especially not through his sufferings or his death on the cross. It was not in his human life as Jesus of Nazareth that eternal life came but in his divine glory as the preexistent and eternal Christ.

Obviously such a denial of Jesus' humanity struck at the very heart of the Incarnation. Denying Jesus' true sonship, these opponents of John denied the Father as well. Because they denied Jesus' human life, they rejected the community of love he established. It is likely that the false teachers in the name of orthodoxy and purism mocked the commands of Jesus as taught by the apostles. Little wonder that John designates them "antichrists." They rejected Jesus. They rejected their own sinfulness, their need of forgiveness, the life of love, and the "fellowship" with the Father and the Son.

23 The statement "No one who denies the Son has the Father; whoever acknowledges the Son has the Father also" makes clear the singular dependence of the Christian faith on the reality of God available through the Son. Those who claim they have a Father but exclude the Son have neither the Father nor the Son. Consequently, when Jesus is acknowledged as the Son and as the eternal Christ, the Father has also truly been lifted up, known and honored, confessed and possessed. The words "has the Father" probably are meant to stress this relationship. John is not talking about having a creed but possessing a person. A person is confessed or believed when we accept or acknowledge our relationship to him. So also we deny God by denying him his proper relationship with us.

24 At this point John shifts his attention to his readers. They, in contrast to the antichrists, are exhorted to make certain that what they heard "from the beginning," that is, the true apostolic declaration concerning Jesus as Son and Christ, "remains" in them. If it "remains" in them, they may be assured that they will also "remain" in the Son and in the Father.

The use of the special Johannine word "remain" (*menō,* "abide") gives weight to the warning. The Word of the gospel must not only be heard but it must be given a vital place in one's life. The power of the gospel depends on the freedom permitted it. The Word is not present simply as a matter of course but only where a person is committed to receive it and unite with it. Marshall (p. 161) says, "It is not enough merely to have heard it and assented to the message in time past. The message must continue to be present and active in the lives of those who have heard it. They must continually call it to mind and let it affect their lives."

If the gospel "abides" in them, Christians may be assured they will also "abide" in the Son and in the Father. While the exhortation is clearly to faithfulness to the Word, it is an exhortation with an assured promise of fulfillment. Where the Word abides, there also the Son and Father abide. Fellowship with the Father and the Son, which is of such concern to the author, is assured those in whom the Word of God abides. The Word is not the goal of the fellowship but rather a means through which the fellowship with the Son and the Father occurs. The listing of the Son before the Father may emphasize the fact that access to the Father becomes possible only through the

Son (John 10:10; 17:2; 20:31). This is why denial of the Son has such fearful consequences.

25 What is promised in the gospel is the everlasting knowledge of Father and Son (John 17:3). It is a promise the community has already received. Eternal life has begun, but its eschatological fulfillment is also promised. What dimension this fellowship with the Son and the Father will assume in the "life to come" is yet unknown (3:2). But the hope is certain. All that is now known about it is only a foretaste of the glory that will be revealed. If the author shows concern about emphasizing the present possibilities of fellowship with the Son and the Father, he does not do so at the expense of the future.

26–27 The author concludes his attack on the false teachers with a warning and a word of encouragement for his followers. He has identified the heretical beliefs of those who have deserted the community of believers (v.22). He has properly labeled his opponents antichrists (v.18) and has described them as "those trying to lead you astray" (cf. 4:6; 2 John 7). This description is the more significant because it reveals the actual intent of those who have deserted the community. Not only have they forsaken the true faith, but they intend to lead many of the faithful astray. Their aim is to assume leadership over the community. They are enemies who are not content to spread new teaching but "invaders" and "deceivers" who seek to win the whole community over to their position.

Against their threat, John once more expresses his supreme confidence in the power of the divine anointing. The Son's gift of the Spirit, who accompanied the apostolic word "from the beginning," abides in them (cf. John 14:16). If they abide in the teaching and in the anointing, they need neither new teaching nor new teachers. Since they have received their "teaching" from the Son through those who were his witnesses from the beginning and have his "anointing," they have in fact no need for anyone more to teach them, not even John himself. Does he think of this letter as "teaching"? Probably not. He is simply reminding them to keep to the teaching they received from the beginning. His opponents are, however, false teachers, antichrists, deceivers, because they teach that which was not from the beginning. This definition of teachers differs from that found in the Pauline epistles, but the result is much the same. Though teaching in the Pauline church is a gift of ministry, what is taught can only be what was received from the beginning (Gal 1:6; 1 Tim 6:3; 2 Tim 1:13; 4:3–5; Titus 1:9; cf. also 2 Peter 3:2).

The last part of v.27 summarizes the threefold reason to trust the anointing already received from Jesus (2:20). First of all, his anointing teaches all things. "All things" seemingly means everything necessary and possible for them to know concerning the Word of Life. He does not mean to advance the idea, perhaps favored by some of his opponents, that the Spirit will add new revelation to what has already been given.

Second, this anointing is real (true) and not counterfeit (cf. John 15:26; 16:3), a reference to the gnosticizing opponents who claim as the source of their teaching a special anointing not commonly received by the company of believers. But the test of the anointing is its fidelity to that which is from the beginning. Since the opponents' teaching fails precisely at this point, their anointing is exposed as false or "counterfeit."

Third, the community has in its history experienced the teaching from the anointing

—i.e., they have known the confirming work of the Spirit in their lives. The gospel has taken root in them and has brought forth its fruit (cf. 2:12–14). Therefore John concludes with his most important word to them: "Remain [abide] in him [Christ]."

28 This verse makes the transition from concern about false teachers to concern for the children of God. It joins the admonition developed in the previous paragraph ("remain in him") to the confidence and unashamedness that should be the possession of the children of God when Christ appears. In some sense, John now explains what it means to remain or abide in Christ by the tests he now develops. *Mē aischynthēnai* can be either middle ("to be ashamed") or passive ("to be put to shame," "to be disgraced") in sense.

Parrhēsian ("confidence") in Acts and in Paul's writings especially denotes the boldness given through the Spirit for witnessing. It is also a favorite word of John's to describe the freedom that belongs to the Christian before God in prayer (3:21; 5:14; cf. Heb 4:16; 10:19) and at Christ's coming. "Confidence" is too weak a word to translate the Greek, but there is no suitable alternative.

Parousia ("coming") occurs only here in 1 John and not at all in John's Gospel. The combination of *phanerōthē* ("appears"), used in 1:2 to describe Jesus' historical appearance in the flesh, with *parousia*, the technical term to refer to Jesus' second coming, makes it certain that the author held in common with other early Christians that Jesus would return in visible splendor. Historically *parousia* was used to describe the festivities attendant on a monarch's arriving for a state visit. The early Christians anticipated the Lord's return as being no less joyous and majestic.

Notes

---

19 It is inescapable that the false teachers not only went out to establish their own teaching but also physically departed from fellowship with the community. Although Bultmann (p. 36) sees them as still claiming membership in the community, the language of "leaving and remaining" seems to imply a final separation.

20 The object of οἴδατε πάντες (*oidate pantes*, "you all know") is to be supplied from v.2, where *oidate* occurs again, followed by the object ἀλήθειαν (*alētheian*, "truth"). The author draws again on the innate knowledge his followers have as Christians. Lies cannot come from God. The antichrists are liars. Therefore they do not come from God who is the truth.

21 "Because" renders ὅτι (*hoti*) in the text. It may be understood as a simple causal dependent on ἔγραψα (*egrapsa*, "I wrote"; so NIV) or as an explanatory conjunction dependent on οἴδατε (*oidate*, "you know") (so RSV), which is far preferable. RSV reads "*and know that no lie* is of the truth" (italics mine).

27 The Greek allows the verb μένετε (*menete*) to be either indicative ("you abide") or imperative ("abide"). In view of the context, however, the imperative seems to be correct.

The Greek pronoun αὐτῷ (*autō*) here can mean either "in him" (the Father, the Son, or the Holy Spirit) or "in it" (the "anointing," which may be a reference to what has been taught). Again, the context seems to support "in him."

III. Requirements for Fellowship With God Who Is Righteous (2:29–4:6)

The main theme of this second main division of the epistle is to provide assurance that even as the believers "continue in Jesus" they can know they are the children of God. The "tests" for knowing this are (1) doing what is right (2:29–3:10), (2) loving one another (3:11–24), and (3) testing the spirits (4:1–6). Obedience will guarantee confidence before Jesus at his coming (2:28) and before God in prayer (3:21).

1. *Doing What Is Right*

2:29–3:10

[29]If you know that he is righteous, you know that everyone who does what is right has been born of him.

[3:1]How great is the love the Father has lavished on us, that we should be called children of God! And that is what we are! The reason the world does not know us is that it did not know him. [2]Dear friends, now we are children of God, and what we will be has not yet been made known. But we know that when he appears, we shall be like him, for we shall see him as he is. [3]Everyone who has this hope in him purifies himself, just as he is pure.

[4]Everyone who sins breaks the law; in fact, sin is lawlessness. [5]But you know that he appeared so that he might take away our sins. And in him is no sin. [6]No one who lives in him keeps on sinning. No one who continues to sin has either seen him or known him.

[7]Dear children, do not let anyone lead you astray. He who does what is right is righteous, just as he is righteous. [8]He who does what is sinful is of the devil, because the devil has been sinning from the beginning. The reason the Son of God appeared was to destroy the devil's work. [9]No one who is born of God will continue to sin, because God's seed remains in him; he cannot go on sinning, because he has been born of God. [10]This is how we know who the children of God are and who the children of the devil are: Anyone who does not do what is right is not a child of God; neither is anyone who does not love his brother.

John begins this section with a promise of future likeness to Jesus (2:29–3:3), followed by a warning that a life of sin is not compatible with a life of fellowship with God but evidences the presence of the devil. Christ came to destroy the devil's work, prominent in which is hatred of one's brother.

29 There is a clear break in thought and a new topic—"tests for knowing the children of God"—introduced here. Attention naturally focuses on the Father (3:1) and the significance of being "born of him." Since John never speaks of being "born of Jesus," it makes more sense to conclude that the subject from the beginning of v.29 is the Father and that John depended on his readers to get the meaning from the total context.

Neither God's righteousness nor that of the Son appears to be the subject of dispute between John and his opponents (cf. 1:5; 2:1, 20; 3:7) but rather the significance of this righteousness. For John, who reflects the teaching that is "from the beginning," to be born of God and to become his child means to accept as the standard for Christian conduct the Father's righteousness as revealed through the Son (2:6; 3:7; cf. also Matt 5:48). Therefore, one must keep Jesus' commands, foremost of which is the command to love, which also becomes the test for distinguishing who is truly born of God. Those who obey his commands, who do his righteous will, should know (imperative force) that they have been born of him. Righteous conduct is not a condition for rebirth but a consequence of it.

On the other hand, the opponents of the author, who presumably also claimed rebirth, apparently thought of it not in ethical or moral terms but in terms of nature (*physis*). They may have said that because they possessed the divine nature they could not sin (1:8) and were consequently removed from any obligation to the commandments (2:3–4). For them the proof that they were born of God or had fellowship with God lay in their new teaching, which freed them from commandments; in their knowledge, which enabled them to reject the fact that Christ had come in the flesh; and in their exclusivism, which allowed them to hate their brothers (3:17–20), forsake the community (2:19), and deny the commandment to love (3:10).

From the tone of the epistle, we conclude that the denial of the necessity to keep the commandments had not yet led to flagrant immoral conduct among the dissidents but that the implications of their theological method were seen by John as allowing—if not encouraging—that possibility. The willingness of the antagonists to destroy the community, to refuse the admonition of love, and to deny the significance of the message heard from the beginning certainly gave him no reason for optimism about the future.

3:1 The phrase "born of him [God]" (2:29) leads the author to marvel at the wonder of God's redemptive activity. See how great the gift of his love really is! Why he has identified us as being his very own children! And this is exactly what we have become through his acts. We have really been born of him. Clearly the author means to encourage his readers by reminding them of the grace of God they have received through the lavishness of God's own love. Such grace and love are missing from his opponents' lives. Love appears to be of no concern to them. They fail to recognize God's love and feel no obligation to express it. But apart from love, there would have been no children of God.

Because the believers are the children of God, the author warns them that the world is unable to recognize them or relate to them. That should not surprise them because neither did the world recognize God. The failure of the world to know God is one of the basic themes of the Gospel of John (5:37; 7:28; 16:3). Those who belong to the world live in darkness. They cannot come to the light but must inevitably hate it. This "belonging to the world" becomes also a matter of their choice; i.e., they refuse to acknowledge God in their hearts.

The author wants his readers to know that approval by the world is to be feared, not desired. To be hated by the world may be unpleasant, but ultimately it should reassure the members of the community of faith that they are loved by God, which is far more important than the world's hatred.

2 Though they are now God's children, the unveiling of their identity or the complete revelation of their nature still lies in the future. Moreover, "has not yet been made known" probably means that it is a "mystery" to be revealed only at the last time. The author encourages no speculation in these matters. His concern is to reiterate the "tradition" from which the promise comes. He (Jesus) will appear. We will see him as he truly is; his full glory will be revealed (cf. John 17:1, 5, 24). We will become like him. That the author is once more presenting the teaching shared in the church "from the beginning" seems clear from its similarity to Paul's teaching: We shall "be conformed to the likeness of his Son" (Rom 8:29; cf. 1 Cor 15:49); we are being transfigured into his likeness—from one degree of glory to another (2 Cor 3:18); with unveiled face we will behold the glory of the Lord (Phil 3:4).

3 All who have their hope in Jesus, i.e., their hope of being like him (3:2) when he appears (2:28), will also be committed to keeping themselves from sin. They will put away every defilement; they will aim to be like him in purity and righteousness. Once more we have the pattern of the incarnate Jesus being held up as an example to believers (cf. 2:6; 3:7, 16; 4:17). Those who claim likeness to him must be conformed to his earthly life, even as they wait for his coming. To live in sin or disobedience to his commands is to abandon any hope in him. It is the pure in heart who will see God (cf. Matt 5:8).

4 Here John uses two words to describe sin: *hamartian* and *anomian* (translated here "lawlessness"). In the OT as well as the NT, these two words are used frequently as synonyms (cf. Pss 32:1; 51:3; Rom 4:7; Heb 10:17). In John's community, however, they were used apparently with different meanings. "Sin" (*hamartian*) was used to describe the transgression of the law, the breaking of the commandments of God. "Lawlessness" (*anomian*) defined sin as rebellion against God and was connected with Satan's rebellion against God. This latter concept had its origin early in the teaching of the church (Matt 7:22; 24:11–13; 2 Cor 6:14–16; 2 Thess 2:1–12). Apparently the false teachers and John agreed that "lawlessness" was incompatible with being born of God. What they did not agree on was that sin, defined as transgression of the moral law, was "lawlessness." Indeed, as those "born of God" they claimed themselves "morally" to be sinless, or guiltless. Either they believed that they were by nature incapable of violating the law or that sinful deeds done in the flesh were of no concern to God, and they were therefore "sinless" in his sight.

John decries such a dichotomy. That his opponents hate their brothers (2:11) shows that their claim to sinlessness is a lie, which along with their failure to love stems from one source, their lawlessness. And their lawlessness shows that they do not belong to God but to the devil (3:10). They are part of the evil soon to be revealed (2:18).

5 In this verse John turns again to the teaching received "from the beginning" in order to raise two additional arguments against sin as a principle of life. First, not only is sin lawlessness (v.4), but Jesus appeared in history in order to remove it (cf. John 1:29; Heb 9:26). Second, Jesus lived a sinless life (cf. 2:1; 3:3; 2 Cor 5:21). In this latter statement the author probably is looking in two directions. Because Jesus was sinless, the devil had no hold on him (cf. John 14:30). Therefore Jesus was able to destroy the works of the devil, one of which is sinning (3:8).

But in addition, Jesus' sinlessness reveals what kind of lifestyle is proper for those who abide in him. John uses the present tense ("in him is no sin") to emphasize that sinlessness is characteristic of Jesus' eternal nature. He was sinless in his preexistence, in his life in the flesh, and in his eternal position as Son.

6 This verse seems to contradict 1:8, 10. However, as we have reconstructed the situation (see comment on 3:4), the author simultaneously faced two different problems with these precursors of Gnosticism. There were those who apparently claimed to be sinless by nature; i.e., they were unable to sin because they were "born of God."

There were others who claimed a standing with God apart from a life of righteousness. They believed that the commandments had no authority over them, i.e., over their flesh, and taught that it was a matter of indifference to God whether they sinned or not. Therefore they could hate their brothers without guilt or concern (cf. Dodd, *Johannine Epistles*, p. 80; Stott p. 126).

In opposition to the latter opponents, the author states that those who "live" in the "sinless one" will, like him, live a life of righteousness. They commit themselves not to sin. And if they sin, they will confess it as lawlessness and abandon it.

John acknowledges the life of righteousness, or sinlessness, as being possible only in Christ. By "living" in him, in his "sinlessness," one can expect conformity to his righteousness. On the other hand, those who continue to sin make it certain that they have never had their eyes opened spiritually to see him, nor have they ever known him (cf. John 5:37–38; 8:19; 14:7, 9; 3 John 11).

7 The warning "do not let anyone lead you astray" appears to have been directed against the false teachers in the community. The author, by using the address "dear children" (cf. 2:1), places his own position in the community on the line.

8 There is clearly a progression in the author's thought on sin in this section. He begins with the "sinfulness" of sin—viz., "it is lawlessness," rebellion against God (v.4). Next he shows its incompatibility with Christ: "He appeared so that he might take away our sins" (v.5). Then he shows its incompatibility for anyone who lives in Christ: "No one who lives in him keeps on sinning" (v.6). Now he shows the diabolic nature of sin—its source is the devil who "has been sinning from the beginning" (v.8). The statement that the Son of God appeared "to destroy the devil's work" is an elaboration of what John said in v.5.

John sees the enmity of God against the devil as absolute. It lies at the heart of God's commitment to rescue man from the devil's clutches. It is a battle without quarter. God will destroy the devil and all his works, including those children of the devil who accept sinning as a way of life. The statement "the devil has been sinning from the beginning" probably refers to the Genesis account of the Fall and includes an identification of the devil with the serpent. He was, from the beginning, evil. "He was a murderer from the beginning, not holding to the truth" (John 8:44). The force of the statement is that the character, the very being of those like the false teachers, derives from the devil. His desires become their desires (John 8:44). Like him they become liars and seducers. Those who continue in sin prove themselves to be the children of sin and the children of the devil (3:10).

9 John summarizes what he has said. In v.6 he stated that no one who "lives in him" can practice a life of sin. Here he adds that "no one who is born of God" or has "God's seed" in him can "continue to sin." Both elements are necessary for understanding John's theology of community. The believers must abide or "live" in him. The Father in turn must dwell in the believers (3:24; 4:12; cf. John 14:20; 17:21–23). If we live in him, "we are removed" from "life in the world," or life under the dominion of Satan. If he lives in us, then our life will be his life in us and we will live even as he lived.

10 This verse reveals the heart of the entire section and furnishes a transition to the next one. It is not a theoretical consideration of the nature of sinfulness or the possibility of sinlessness that occupies the author but the issue of the community. How are the children (community) of God to be recognized and how are the children (community) of the devil to be discerned?

"Anyone who does not do what is right is not a child of God." And what is the "right" he does not do? He "does not love his brother." "Love for one's brother" is the true test of righteous behavior. This requirement of love helps explain the absolute requirement that those who are born of God "cannot go on sinning" (vv.6, 9). For if God is love, and if God lives in us and we in him, then love for the brethren will occur as an expression of righteousness without exception. Bruce (p. 93) comments on this connecting of love with righteousness: "For him, righteousness and love are inseparable; since they are inseparable in the character of God and in His revelation in Christ, so they must be inseparable in the lives of His people."

"Righteousness involves the fulfillment of all law, of relation to God and to man, both personally and socially. The love of Christian for Christian, resting on the sense of a divine fellowship (cf. 1:3) carries forward to its loftiest embodiment the righteousness which man can reach" (Westcott, p. 106).

The author, then, is not stressing absolute moral conformity or "sinless perfection" but the one requirement by which all other requirements are measured—love for one's brother. For this there is no substitute, its violation allows for no excuse, its application permits no compromise. Here there are no gray areas, no third possibilities. One either loves his brother and proves he is God's child or does not love his brother and proves he belongs to the devil.

Notes

29 Γινώσκετε (*ginōskete*, "know") has the same Greek form in the indicative and the imperative. Γεγέννηται ἐξ αὐτοῦ (*gegennētai ex autou*, "born of him") is a favorite concept of the author (cf. 3:9; 4:7; 5:1, 4, 18; cf. also John 1:13; 3:3–8).

3:1 Bultmann (p. 41) notes that in the Gnostic literature "there is no mention of brotherly love."

3 The phrase "everyone who has" is used characteristically by John to refer "to someone who had questioned the application of a general principle in particular cases" (Westcott, p. 98). In this situation his opponents probably claimed likeness to God for themselves though they refused to be obedient to the commandments, especially the commandment of love.

The *Translator's Handbook* gives the following helpful analysis for hope: "There are to be distinguished four main semantic components which combine in various ways to represent the concept of "hope." These are (1) time, for hope always looks to the future; (2) anticipation, for there is always some goal to the time span; (3) confidence, namely, that the goal hoped for will occur; and (4) desire, since the goal of hoping is a valued object or experience" (Haas, deJonge, and Swellengrebel, p. 79).

7 Note the interchangeable character of certain key words in this context. The author can say "that everyone who does what is right has been born of him" as in 2:29, or that everyone "who does what is right is righteous." (For the phrase "just as he is righteous," see comments on 2:6, 29; 3:3).

9 The use of "seed" to describe the divine life in believers is common in the later Gnostic literature. John clearly means the term figuratively. It may refer to the Spirit (cf. John 3:6; so Schnackenburg), his offspring (so Moffatt), Jesus as the Word (John 1:12), the Word of God (cf. Luke 8:11; 1 Peter 1:23, 25; so Dodd), or God's nature (Goodspeed). In any instance, it is not the means of the divine presence that is the issue but the fact of that presence.

2. *Loving One Another*

3:11–24

11This is the message you heard from the beginning: We should love one
another. 12Do not be like Cain, who belonged to the evil one and murdered his
brother. And why did he murder him? Because his own actions were evil and his
brother's were righteous. 13Do not be surprised, my brothers, if the world hates you.
14We know that we have passed from death to life, because we love our brothers.
Anyone who does not love remains in death. 15Anyone who hates his brother is a
murderer, and you know that no murderer has eternal life in him.

16This is how we know what love is: Jesus Christ laid down his life for us. And
we ought to lay down our lives for our brothers. 17If anyone has material possessions and sees his brother in need but has no pity on him, how can the love of God
be in him? 18Dear children, let us not love with words or tongue but with actions
and in truth. 19This then is how we know that we belong to the truth, and how we
set our hearts at rest in his presence 20whenever our hearts condemn us. For God
is greater than our hearts, and he knows everything.

21Dear friends, if our hearts do not condemn us, we have confidence before God
22and receive from him anything we ask, because we obey his commands and do
what pleases him. 23And this is his command: to believe in the name of his Son,
Jesus Christ, and to love one another as he commanded us. 24Those who obey
his commands live in him, and he in them. And this is how we know that he lives
in us: We know it by the Spirit he gave us.

As the knowledge of God is tested by conduct—whether one walks in the light (1:5–2:11)—so being "born of God" (2:29) is tested by righteous action and love of the brethren. The command to love the brethren was first introduced in 2:9–11 as a test of whether one was walking in light, i.e., had true knowledge. Here it is the sum of the new life in God. In the former instance it was primarily leveled as a charge against the heretics. Here it is addressed to the community of faith both for encouragement and for admonition. It is likely that the disregard for the principle of love by the heretics had caused a lessening of the emphasis of love within the community. The author's procedure is to present the case for love first by the negative example of Cain (vv. 12–15) contrasted with the positive example of Jesus (v. 16).

11 The admonition that "we should love one another" is highlighted by the return to the critical formula "This is the message you heard from the beginning," an almost identical reminiscence of 1:1 and 1:5. Since the nature of God as light is the foundation of the gospel that was received from the beginning, so the command to "love one another" has the same origin. Love is not the application of the "message" but the goal established "from the beginning." As Westcott (pp. 100–101) says, "The whole aim of the gospel is the creation and strengthening of love. . . . The words ['love one another'] do not simply give the content of the message, but its aim, its purpose."

12 The mention of Cain points back to 3:8 and reminds us that hatred is also from the beginning. The choice between the children of God and the children of the devil, between "hatred and love, life and death, murder and self-sacrifice" stems from the earliest moment of man's existence (Stott, p. 139). It also probably points to John 8:37–47, where some Jewish opponents of Jesus had exhibited the same kind of hatred toward Jesus that Cain expressed toward Abel (8:59). There Jesus says to them, despite their claim to be Abraham's children: "As it is, you are determined to kill me. . . . If God were your Father, you would love me. . . . You belong to your father, the devil, and you want to carry out your father's desire. He was a murderer from the beginning, not holding the truth" (John 8:40, 42, 44). The overlap of language and ideas between the two passages supports Dodd's contention that John 8 was probably in the author's mind when he wrote this section.

The sequence of thought in this section of 1 John is probably significant. It is not that Cain by murdering his brother became the child of the devil; but, being a child of the devil, his actions were evil and culminated in the murder of his brother. The reason given for the murder is that his brother's acts were righteous. Righteousness draws hatred from the devil and hatred from the children of the devil. Darkness cannot tolerate light; immorality, morality; hatred, love; or greed, sacrifice. All the words of darkness are shown to be what they really are by the light; hatred that can lead to such brutality as Cain's slaughter of Abel. *Sphazō,* the verb for "murder" (used twice in v.12), has the meaning of "butcher" or "slaughter" (BAG, p. 803). This verse is the only direct reference to the OT in the epistle.

13 The hatred of the world for the community of faith must not surprise the believers. The author does not say that the world always hates believers. It did not always hate Jesus. But whenever the community of faith acts so as to expose the greed, the avarice, the hatred, and the wickedness of the world, it must expect rejection; and if it should go so far as to interfere with its evil practices, as Jesus did in the temple, it may expect suffering and brutal death (cf. John 15:18–19, 25; 17:14).

"Brothers" (*adelphoi*) occurs only here in 1 John. At this most critical point, the author appears to step past his relationship to them as "little children" and to openly proclaim them his peers. Perhaps they have already experienced persecution with him. Or perhaps he associates himself with them this way because he knows that if they receive his letter and obey it, persecution will soon come because they have identified themselves with him rather than with his opponents.

14 This verse looks back to v.10 and answers the question How do we know who have been "born of God"? or Who are the children of God? by saying, "We know that we have passed from death to life, because we love our brothers" (cf. John 5:24). This conviction is not based on self-judgment or self-justification but on the certainty that love is the basis for life in the believing community. As Bultmann (p. 55) observes, "The arrogant 'we know' makes the congregation aware of its real character, against which each individual member is to measure himself. In this sense, therefore, v.14 is also an indirect admonition as was the case of v.6a. The question is therefore posed for each individual, whether he belongs to the Christian congregation." Love will not cause the passage to spiritual life but will give evidence of it. Conversely, to be unable to love means that a person is without life from the Father and remains in death.

15 Here John links hatred with murder. We are reminded of Matthew 5:21–22, where Jesus made the two equivalent. In the heart there is no difference; to hate is to despise, to cut off from relationship, and murder is simply the fulfillment of that attitude. Cain, because he murdered his brother, was cut off from the covenant community. He received no promise. So no murderer is within the community, nor anyone who "hates his brother." He has no life of God, no rebirth, no fellowship with the faithful.

16 The test of true love is identified as willingness to sacrifice one's life for one's brother. The demonstrative "this" that begins the statement points backward to the negative example of Cain and forward to the positive example of Christ (cf. Westcott, p. 110). Love is used absolutely and its reference point is Christ's death. The demand for love thus arises from his command, and the meaning of love is found in his example.

In the Greek "we know" (*egnōkamen*) is in the perfect tense. It shows that the knowledge that is involved belongs to the historical event of Jesus Christ. It was the same knowledge that was transmitted through those who saw it and heard it from the beginning (1:1; 3:11). *Agapē* ("love") cannot be derived from some intuitive grasp of an idea but is known in the historical event in which Jesus Christ laid down his life for us. His sacrificial death thus distinguishes *agapē* love from all other loves by its costliness, its unconditional acceptance of another, and its "accomplishment." Its costliness is expressed in the Gospel of John by the image of the Good Shepherd who lays down his life for his sheep (John 10:11).

The personal commitment of Christ is expressed in the words of John 15:12–13 (cf. 13:1): "Love each other as I have loved you. Greater love has no one than this, that one lay down his life for his friends." Its accomplishment as a "for us" kind of love is reflected in Jesus' work. "I give them eternal life" (John 10:28). It is clear that Jesus understood his death as an effectual, accomplishing act—the only method open to him to fulfill his Father's will (cf. John 10:11–18; 27–30; 15:9–18; 17:19). (That John's understanding is held in common with early apostolic witness is shown by Mark 10:45; Rom 5:8; Gal 1:4; Titus 2:14; 1 Peter 3:18.)

Since *agapē* love is grounded in Jesus' death "for us," it is clear that knowledge of it can be received only where his "death" is appropriated into our experience. Bultmann points out that only when we have "experienced" love can we know love. "From his love for us we learn what love is" (p. 55).

The dramatic conclusion we are irresistibly led to is this: "And we ought to lay down our lives for our brothers." We are to do this not simply because that is what Jesus did, but because that is what Jesus revealed to be the demand of *agapē* love. Love is denial of self for another's gain. It is doing what Jesus himself would do.

17 Again John's penchant for providing practical "tests" of the validity of one's faith comes to the fore. How can we know whether we would sacrifice our life for a brother? We can know by being compassionate toward him in his present need. If we are unable or unwilling to sacrifice material advantage for the sake of our brother, we know the love of God is not in us. What are the conditions for our involvement with our brother? If we are in a position to see (*theōreō*) with our own eyes his need, as, for example, the good Samaritan did, and can offer help, then we cannot do otherwise than act. To withhold help from a brother in need, to shut off compassionate action, is to deny the presence of God's love in one's own heart. As Dodd says, "If such a minimal response to the law of charity, called for by such an everyday situation, is absent, then it is idle to pretend that we are within the family of God, the realm in which love is operative as the principle and the token of eternal life" (*Johannine Epistles*, p. 86).

18 The vocative "little children" gives this admonition the tone of a spiritual father pleading for the heart-felt response of his children. Love requires more than idle talk or exalted theology. It demands simple acts, which anyone can see, that meet the needs of brothers and sisters in distress. Any expression of love that fails here is not only empty but blasphemous. "Suppose a brother or sister is without clothes and daily food. If one of you says to him, 'Go, I wish you well; keep warm and well fed,' but does nothing about his physical needs, what good is it?" (James 2:15; cf. 1 Cor 13:1).

19–20 John began this section (2:29–4:6) by addressing the question How may we be confident and unashamed at Christ's coming? (cf. 2:28). The answer expressed in the phrases "continue in Jesus" and "doing what is right" (2:29; 3:7, 10) is tested by our love for our brothers. Now the author addresses the question of assurance—i.e., confidence before God. How may "we know that we belong to the truth" (3:19) and how do we deal with our own condemning hearts (3:20–21)? The anxious note in the first part of the question should probably be attributed at least in part to the unrelenting attack of opponents on the "teaching" and "beliefs" of the Christian community. The whole section, however, may also simply be explaining the nature of "fellowship" with the Father (1:3).

The passage itself is complex in the Greek and allows several translations and interpretations. "This" (v.19) may be taken to point backward to the absolute demand of love introduced in 3:14ff. If we know that we love truly, with actions and not mere words, that knowledge will not only assure us "that we belong to the truth" but will also act to "set our hearts at rest in his presence whenever our hearts condemn us."

It is possible, however, in the Greek text to make a full stop after "presence" and then read v.20 as follows: "If our hearts should condemn us, God is greater than our hearts, and he knows everything."

Another possibility is that the "this" in v.19 points not only backward to 3:14ff. but forward to v.20b. The meaning would be as follows: There are two ways we know that we "belong to the truth": First, because we love in deed; second, God himself assures us that we belong to the truth—he "is greater than our hearts, and he knows everything." The latter possibility is preferable because it allows a more connected argument.

In any instance, what is stressed is *agapē* love, which always expressed first in deeds, is reassuring evidence that we are of God. Why our hearts should condemn us is not discussed by the author. Apparently it is not important. His readers, like all others, know how easily the conscience can render us ineffective. Doubt, guilt, and failure are never far from any of us. Sometimes our misgivings are the result of our own actions or inactions. Sometimes it is the "accuser" who seizes our weaknesses and shortcomings and so elevates them that we wonder whether we can really be in the truth. What then can we do? We can remember that God understands everything. His word and his truth are greater than our feelings or our conscience. We may rest ourselves in his love for us and live in that love and by that love. We will not excuse ourselves of any sin, but neither will we needlessly accuse ourselves (cf. 1 Cor 4:3–5).

21 Christians are called to fellowship with God (1:3; 2:24). But if they are guilt-ridden and conscience-stricken, rather than seeking that fellowship or enjoying it, they will flee the presence of God. They will be unable to abide in him or claim their position as "his children." Nor will they dare seek answers to prayer that he alone can provide. On the other hand, those who have his peace in their hearts will have "confidence" not only at his appearing but in the ordinary here-and-now relationship to the Father, especially as it involves prayer. Believers will stand in his presence "naturally" as those who are supposed to be there, because he has so provided for them.

22 The fruit of this boldness is God's own openness to his children. He will never withhold any good thing from those who ask. The author does not give the basis for his assurance, but his words "because we obey his commands and do what pleases him" point directly to Jesus' own words in John 8:28–29: "I do nothing on my own but speak just what the Father has taught me . . . for I always do what pleases him." Jesus, who always did his Father's will, knew that his Father heard him: "I knew that you always hear me" (John 11:42), he says to the Father. Likewise Jesus assures his disciples, "In that day you will ask in my name. I am not saying that I will ask the Father on your behalf. No, the Father himself loves you" (John 16:26–27).

23 This verse specifies what command it is that the children must obey in order to receive whatever they ask of him (v.22). It is "to believe in the name of his Son, Jesus Christ, and to love one another."

"Belief," which occurs here for the first time in 1 John, will be seen more and more as the issue between John and the "heretics." The "false teachers" do not "love"—that is clear—but the reason they do not love is that God's love is not in them, for they have not truly believed in Jesus Christ, the Son of God. To believe in Jesus Christ means in this context to believe the gospel about Jesus—that he is God's Son, that he came to save men and women from their sins, and that by believing in him they can have eternal life (John 3:16–18). The joining of belief and love in a single command shows how inextricably connected the two are in John's mind. Belief comes first because it is the basis for love (cf. 3:16), but love is the only expression of true faith.

The end of the command—"and to love one another as he commanded us"—recalls Jesus' own command given in the Gospel of John (13:34; 15:12, 17). The practice of the author to make no attempt to distinguish the subjects of verbs or the antecedents of pronouns as to whether Jesus or the Father is in view is characteristic of his writing. It is also characteristic of his theology. God is revealed in Christ Jesus. To see the Son is to see the Father; to know the Father is to know the Son. The deeds of the one are the deeds of the other. So completely are the wills of the Father and the Son joined that it is many times a matter of indifference as to which one is in view.

24 In this summary verse the author states for the first time in this epistle the mutual reciprocity involved in "living" in God. Obedience issues in the perfection of the "fellowship" between God and us. We "live" in him. He "lives" in us. We come to our "fellowship" with the Father through the "fellowship" the Son has with the Father (John 14:20; 17:21–23). The Son also enters into fellowship with us (15:4–5); and through him we have fellowship with the Father and with one another, just as the sign of our fellowship with the Father and with the Son is our love for them (cf. John 17:23–26). Clearly, Jesus' words in the Gospel of John are the basis for this expansion of the relation of love to "living" in God in 1 John.

The latter part of v.24 characteristically furnishes the transition to the next section. The evidence that we abide in him is our obedience to his commands. The evidence that he abides in us is the presence of his Spirit, whom he gave to us (cf. Rom 5:5; 8:14–16). This is the first mention of the Spirit in 1 John. The author presupposes knowledge about the Spirit in his readers. He does not rehearse the teaching about the Spirit from his Gospel but only applies it to the particular problem at hand—distinguishing the true Spirit from false spirits (4:1–3) and receiving the Spirit's witness (5:6–7). The reference to the Spirit as the one "he gave us" is not an appeal to their existential experience of the Spirit but to their knowledge of the gospel as it had come to them from the eyewitnesses. The Father's giving or the Son's sending the Spirit to the disciples (John 14–16; 20:22) was a well-known event in the church (cf. Acts 1–2; Rom 8; Gal 4:6).

Notes

11 The phrase "to love one another" (cf. 3:23, 4:7, 11–12) is not essentially different in 1 John from the command "to love one's brother" (2:10; 3:10; 4:20–21) or "to love our brothers" (3:14). The reference is to the community of faith where Christian love must always begin and "abide."

14 The plural ἀδελφοί (*adelphoi*, "brothers") is used here "to show that the reference is to individual persons, whereas the singular is used when the reference is to the group viewed as a collectivity" (Haas, deJonge, and Swellengrebel, p. 90).

17 The Greek allows the genitival expression "love of God" to be descriptive, "the divine love," or possessive, "God's love," or objective, "love for God." But the subjective use, "love that comes from God," fits the context best.

21 "Confidence" translates παρρησία (*parrēsia*). "The word rendered **confidence** stood in ancient Greece for the most valued right of a citizen in a free state, the right to 'speak his mind' . . . unhampered by fear or shame. In our relationship to God such freedom of speech is not an inherent right, but is strictly dependent upon an equally frank and straightforward obedience to the divine will (verse 22)" (Dodd, *Johannine Epistles*, p. 93).

23 Πιστεύω (*pisteuō*, "believe") occurs in 4:1, 16; 5:1, 5, 10, 13. Πίστις (*pistis*, "faith") appears only in 5:4. In contrast to ἀγαπῶμεν (*agapōmen*, "we should love"), which is in the present tense, πιστεύσωμεν (*pisteusōmen*, "we should believe") is aorist, which stresses faith as an event, as when one "confesses" his faith in Christ (cf. 4:3) and acknowledges him as the Son of God (2:23).

3. *Warning Against the False Spirits*

4:1–6

[1]Dear friends, do not believe every spirit, but test the spirits to see whether they
are from God, because many false prophets have gone out into the world. [2]This
is how you can recognize the Spirit of God: Every spirit that acknowledges that
Jesus Christ has come in the flesh is from God, [3]but every spirit that does not
acknowledge Jesus is not from God. This is the spirit of the antichrist, which you
have heard is coming and even now is already in the world.

[4]You, dear children, are from God and have overcome them, because the one
who is in you is greater than the one who is in the world. [5]They are from the world
and therefore speak from the viewpoint of the world, and the world listens to them.
[6]We are from God, and whoever knows God listens to us; but whoever is not from
God does not listen to us. This is how we recognize the Spirit of truth and the spirit
of falsehood.

This passage parallels 2:18–27, where the author warned against the presence of antichrists among those who had "gone out" from them. Now he directs a second warning to his followers, this time against the spirit of antichrist, who even now inspires false prophets among the dissenters (v.1). The false spirit can be detected because he will deny that Jesus Christ came in the flesh (v.3). The community of faith will overcome the false prophets because believers belong to God, and the Spirit in them is greater than the false spirit (v.4). The world listens to the false prophets (v.5), but the children of God listen to the apostolic declaration. Belief of the gospel is the true test of the Holy Spirit's presence and work (v.6).

1 The opponents not only lay claim to God but boast of their "inspiration" by the "spirit." Likely they gave evidence of their "inspiration" through "prophetic utterings" and perhaps even other signs such as ecstasies and glossolalia. Such "signs" were present in the religious milieu of the Greeks and Romans and most persons took them seriously. That they sometimes caused special problems in the early church is attested by Paul (cf. 1 Cor 12:3; ch. 14; 1 Thess 5:21). The warning is not against those who "feign" the Spirit's presence but against genuine evil spirits' inspiring the existence of false prophets—i.e., those who had left the community. By outward token these people were no less inspired than members of the faithful community. They were zealous in proclamation (cf. 2 John 7) and may have been even more successful than the faithful community in making converts from the world (4:5). Likely John saw in them the fulfillment of Jesus' warnings (cf. Mark 13:22) against false prophets in the "end times" (cf. 2:18).

The false prophets' success would itself be a problem and was probably used as an authenticating sign by them. Therefore, the need for some test to discern the presence of false prophets was all the more critical.

2 The test itself appears to hinge on the words "that Jesus Christ has come in the flesh." The false prophets may well have believed that Christ was the Savior of the world, but they probably denied the connection between the divine Christ with Jesus of Nazareth. At least they clearly denied that "the Christ" ever had come "in the flesh." This denial makes them not only precursors of Gnosticism but also of Docetism. The confession John urges speaks not only against those heresies but against any form of adoptionism as well. The clause "that Jesus Christ has come" reflects the author's clear view of the preexistence of the Son, who came from the Father and from the moment of his historical birth was Jesus Christ in the flesh.

How does this confession give evidence of the Spirit? For John, as for Paul, the truth of the Christian gospel is hid from the world (cf. 1 Cor 2:7–16). Only because there is a divine intervention and the darkness is removed can the light of the gospel be recognized (cf. 4:6).

3 Here a negative confession gives the counterpart of that in v.2, and the source of this denial is seen to be the spirit of antichrist. John reminds his followers that Jesus had warned that the Antichrist would come. It is now John's painful duty to announce that in the false teachers (2:18ff.) the spirit of antichrist is already present. By this the community was warned that the conflict between the false teachers and John was not a "leadership" or "personality" one. The Gospel itself was at stake. The struggle in the controversy was not against flesh and blood but against principalities and powers (Eph 6:12). Hence, whatever success the opponents had had within the community resulted from satanic inspiration.

4 The use of "dear children" shows the author's desire to address all the faithful in the community once more (cf. 2:1). They have indeed overcome the false prophets, because they resisted their teaching (v.5). So they establish the fact that they are "from

God"—that is "born of him" (2:29)—and that the one who is in them is "greater than the one who is in the world" (v.4). The false teachers do not have the Spirit of Christ living in them because "living" involves "fellowship," which is possible between God and his children only by the Holy Spirit. The false teachers are without this fellowship. Therefore they do not love because they do not know love. The antichrist can be "in the world" and evil spirits can be "in the false teachers," but "living in God" is possible only for the children of God.

5 In contrast to the "dear children" who "are from God" are the false teachers who "are from the world." The false teachers are successful "in the world" because their thinking, their theology, is accomodated to the world's beliefs. So their teaching is philosophically congenial to the prevailing currents of the day. Naturally the world hears such teachers gladly. The term "world" (*kosmos*) is probably to be understood in two ways: as a system of thought antithetical to Christian belief and as a description of those members of the community who were led astray by the false teachers. That some members of the community were easily persuaded to forsake the truth of the gospel should not bewilder the faithful. Although these members appeared to belong to the community, their willingness to hear and follow the false teachers showed their true colors.

6 The author repeats the description of the true followers as "we [who] are from God." The "we" probably is meant to include all the faithful but has particular reference to the true teachers. Whoever "knows" God, (i.e., has knowledge through fellowship with him by loving him and abiding in him and his Word) "listens to us"—not just to any words we may speak, but "listens to us" as we proclaim the word "heard from the beginning." The argument is parallel to that of Jesus in John 8:47: "He who belongs to God hears what God says. The reason you do not hear is that you do not belong to God" (cf. John 10:4–5; 18:37). So a second test for discerning the presence of the Spirit of God is added to the one developed in v.2. When people confess that Jesus came in the flesh, when they hear God speak to them in the gospel of his Son and are obedient to it, then the "Spirit of truth" has been present and active. When people deny the gospel, when they will not hear it as God's Word and will not confess that Jesus Christ has come in the flesh, then "the spirit of falsehood" has been at work.

Notes

3 An alternate reading to μὴ ὁμολογεῖ (*mē homologei,* "not acknowledge," "not confess") is λύει (*lyei,* "destroy," "annul"). Commentators are divided about which is the original and which is the explanatory gloss. It does not affect the meaning, because to "annul" that Jesus is from God, that he, the Son of God, has indeed come in human flesh into the world, would be an even more drastic way of referring to this denial (cf. Brooke, pp. 111–14; Bultmann, p. 62; Marshall, p. 207).

4 Here, as in vv.11, 18–27, protection against evil or victory over evil is ascribed both to an objective standard of doctrine and to the indwelling Spirit who illumines our minds to grasp and apply this victory; for "unless the Spirit of wisdom is present, there is little or no profit in having God's Word in our hearts" (Calvin, cited in Stott, p. 157).

6 The "Spirit of truth" occurs only here in 1 John, but see the Gospel of John 14:17; 15:26; 16:13. The phrase "the spirit of error" is unique in the NT but is comparable to "the spirit of the world" in 1 Cor 2:12. For reference to the two spirits in Jewish literature, see IQS 3.18 and Testament of Judah 20.1.

IV. Requirements for Fellowship With God Who Is Love (4:7–5:12)

The third main division of the epistle has as its major thesis an analysis of love. Love of one's brother was first introduced as a test of living in God who is light (2:9–11). The command to love received an even more significant treatment as a test of being born of God who is righteous (3:10–24). Here love of fellow believers finds its most complete representation in the Father's own being and activity.

1. *Brotherly Love*

4:7–12

> [7]Dear friends, let us love one another, for love comes from God. Everyone who loves has been born of God and knows God. [8]Whoever does not love does not know God, because God is love. [9]This is how God showed his love among us: He sent his one and only Son into the world that we might live through him. [10]This is love: not that we loved God, but that he loved us and sent his Son as an atoning sacrifice for our sins. [11]Dear friends, since God so loved us, we also ought to love one another. [12]No one has ever seen God; but if we love each other, God lives in us and his love is made complete in us.

7 The vocative "dear friends" (cf. 2:7; 4:1; lit., "beloved") and the imperative force of the verb make clear that the author is speaking primarily to the community itself. His intention is to provide final assurance that the community's commitment to mutual love is the explicit requirement of the gospel as revealed in God himself. Love for one's brother comes "from God." It is evidence of our being "born of God" that is as important as righteous behavior is (2:29). It is not a virtue innate in us nor is it learned behavior. It is "from God." He is the originator—the giver of love. Furthermore, whoever truly loves "his brother" not only is born of God (2:28; 3:24) but also "knows God."

8 Conversely, whoever does not love does not "know" God at all, for God in his very nature is love. To the statements, then, that God is light (1:5) and God is righteous (2:29), John adds the supreme statement "God is love" (4:8, 16). Love so conceived is not to be understood as one of God's many activities but rather that "all His activity is loving activity. If He creates, He creates in love; if He rules, He rules in love; if He judges, He judges in love. All that He does is the expression of His nature, is—to love" (Dodd, *Johannine Epistles,* p. 110). Since this is true of God, our failure to love can only mean that we have no true knowledge of God, we have not really been born of him, we do not have his nature.

9 The simple but profound statement "God is love" is explained by what God did. He "showed his love among us: He sent his one and only Son into the world that we might live through him" (cf. John 3:16–17). The author makes clear that the love he speaks of involves concrete and objective acts. God's love required him to send his Son. God's love in us requires deeds by which we show our love for one another.

The phrase "among us" (*en hēmin*) may be translated "in us," indicating the medium in which God revealed his Son and for whom the revelation was effective (cf. Brooke and Westcott), or "to us" (cf. Schnackenburg) or "for us" (cf. Bultmann).

"One and only" translates *monogenēs*, a word that both serves as "a predicate of value and designates the unique one as beloved at the same time" (Bultmann, p. 67).

The purpose of God's act is "that we might live through him. Death is man's present condition (cf. 3:14). God's act has as its intention not just our salvation (Gospel of John 3:17) but our 'living.' And it is to be a 'living' in love so that God's love is seen 'visibly working' in us and through us" (Westcott, p. 141).

10 "This" has as its point of reference God's act for us as stated in vv.9–10. In v.10 the author distinguishes *agapē* love from any love claimed by the false teachers. It is not that "we loved God" (3:17; 4:20) as his opponents claimed but that "he loved us." For the author, *agapē* love can be given to God only when it has first been received from God. It exists only as response to his initial love for us. Moreover, it is God's love for us that defines what true love requires, which is the commitment to sacrifice one's most beloved possession for another's gain. So for God, love required that he send "his Son as an atoning sacrifice for our sins."

The difference in understanding between John and the false teachers is never greater than in their understanding of love. The false teachers claimed to love God but understood love not in Christian terms but in those of Greek philosophy. As Dodd (*Johannine Epistles*, p. 111) points out, love in the Hellenistic world became a "cosmic principle, and the mystical craving for union with the eternal is given a metaphysical basis." In religious terms, love is perceived as "essentially the love of man for God—that is to say, the insatiable craving of limited, conditional, and temporal beings for the infinite, the Absolute, the Eternal" (ibid.). Two things derive from this understanding of love. First, love for God as it was expressed by the false teachers becomes primarily an exercise in self-gratification. As such, it expresses the vanity of those teachers. Second, one can never attribute love to God and say, for example, that God loves us. God as the Absolute is always passionless and unmoved. (On the meaning of *hilasmos*, see note on 2:2.)

11 The author continues to show that the true nature of love is unselfish and sacrificial. In 3:16 he appealed to Jesus, who laid down his life for his brothers, as the example for believers to follow. Now he directs attention to God's own example: "Since God so loved us, we also ought to love one another." The nature of the argument is not properly deductive but analogical, as Bruce (p. 109) has shown: "If the children of God must be holy because He is holy (Lev 11:44f; 1 Pet 1:15f) and merciful because He is merciful (Lk 6:36), so they must be loving because He is loving—not with the 'must' of external compulsion but with the 'must' of inward constraint: God's love is poured into their hearts by the Holy Spirit whom they have received (Rom 5:5)."

12 Here most commentators see a reference to the false teachers who may have claimed "visions" of God—visions from which their own knowledge was mediated to them (cf. Bultmann, p. 68; Schnackenburg, pp. 240–41). John's response is the blanket rejection: "No one has ever seen God." But the conclusion he moves toward is different from that expected from the Gospel of John. Instead of saying, "God the only Son, who is at the Father's side, has made him known" (John 1:18), he turns rather to love: "If we love each other," we know that God is present with us. As God was once present in his Son, so now he is present through the community of faith. And it is in this community that love has its ultimate fulfillment.

Stott (p. 164) warns against weakening this assertion: "We must not stagger at the majesty of this conclusion. God's love which originates in Himself (7, 8) and was manifested in His Son (9, 10) is perfected in His people (12). . . . God's love for us is perfected only when it is reproduced in us or (as it may mean) 'among us' in the Christian fellowship." Similarly, Westcott (p. 144) says, "It is through man that the 'love of God' finds its fulfillment on earth." With this conclusion, we can begin to understand a little better John's urgent concern for the "fellowship" of the community of believers. It was not an optional "blessing" or "fruit" of belief that so deeply concerned him but the basic question of God's presence and manifestation in the world.

The genitive in "love of God" is best taken as subjective—viz., the love that has its origin in God.

Notes

7 "The initial imperative, 'let us love one another,' leaves no doubt that πᾶς ὁ ἀγαπῶν *pas ho agapōn* ('he who loves') means the love of neighbor, even though no object is apprehended. . . . There is certainly no love without a *vis-a-vis*. The *vis-a-vis* of God is the world, as indicated in Jn 3:16. . . . If the love of God has as its object the world and thereby 'we', the object of those loved by God is accordingly the neighbors" (Bultmann, pp. 15, 66).

2. *Living in God and Living in Love*

4:13–16

[13]We know that we live in him and he in us, because he has given us of his Spirit. [14]And we have seen and testify that the Father has sent his Son to be the Savior of the world. [15]If anyone acknowledges that Jesus is the Son of God, God lives in him and he in God. [16]And so we know and rely on the love God has for us.

God is love. Whoever lives in love lives in God, and God in him.

In v. 12 the author linked living in God to loving one another. In 3:24 he linked living with God to obeying his commands. There, as here, the primary evidence for this relationship with God is the Holy Spirit. And it is the Spirit who enables us to testify that "the Father has sent his Son to be the Savior of the world" (4:14; cf. 4:2). Whoever confesses this also knows that God (by his Spirit) is present in them and that they live "in God" (v. 15). And those who know they live in God know also that they live in his love (v. 16).

13 Reciprocal abiding (2:24; 4:13, 15—God in us, we in God) is the final expression of fellowship with God. It is possible only through the gift of his Spirit, by whom the relationship with the Father and with the Son is sealed eternally. Reciprocal abiding makes possible God's love for us and our love for him. It is also the reason we can love one another. No longer do we need to regard ourselves as "orphans" in the world (John 14:18).

14 To whom does the "we" refer in the statement "we have seen and testify"? The "we" certainly refers to all those, especially the apostles, who had direct knowledge of Jesus' earthly life; but it probably ought not to be limited to them. It is the Spirit working in them and in us who permits us to "see" in the historic event of Jesus' death God's act for our salvation. Although "no one has ever seen God" (v. 12) at any time (the same Greek word *theaomai* is used), we do "see" by faith that the cross lifted up in Palestine was for our sins and for our salvation. We do "see" in Jesus our own Savior and Lord. We do "see" in the fellowship of faith the presence of his love. And because his Spirit in us gives us this "seeing" experience, we are commissioned to bear witness to the event. "When the counselor comes, whom I will send to you from the Father, the Spirit of truth who goes out from the Father, he will testify about me; but you also must testify, for you have been with me from the beginning" (John 15:26). Therefore, since there is such a close connection between seeing and testifying and the gift of the Holy Spirit, it is likely that the author meant his words to include his readers and to be applied to all Christians now as well as in the past.

15 The author goes on to state that "anyone" who "acknowledges" (*homologēsē*, lit., "confesses") God's act in his Son is included in the divine fellowship in which the Father is in the believers and the believers in the Father. Initially John connected the fellowship with obedience to the command to love one another (3:24). Then he showed its dependence on the gift of the Spirit (4:13). Here he shows that the fellowship is built on Jesus, who must be acknowledged as being one with the Father (2:23), as the one who came in the flesh (4:2), and as the Son of God who was sent to be the Savior of the world (4:14–15).

16 The same combination of knowing and believing is found in Peter's confession of Jesus in John 6:69, except that there the order is reversed: "We believe and know that you are the Holy One of God." The fact is that faith may lead to knowledge and knowledge may lead to faith. Here knowledge of God's love necessarily precedes the ability to "rely" on that love. The sequence of thought is this: First, we must know and rely on the fact that God loves us. Second, we come to realize through relying on his love (or having faith in his Son—the meaning is the same) that in his very nature God is love. Third, we discover that to live in God means to live in love. The fellowship we have with the Father and with the Son (1:3), the fellowship in which he lives in us and we live in him, is perceived as nothing other than a fellowship of love.

3. *Love Displaces Fear*

4:17–18

> [17]Love is made complete among us so that we will have confidence on the day of judgment, because in this world we are like him. [18]There is no fear in love. But perfect love drives out fear, because fear has to do with punishment. The man who fears is not made perfect in love.

The perfection or completeness of love is confidence. This confidence relates especially to the time of judgment (cf. 2:28), though John probably believed that "confidence" was the mark of a believer in every relationship to God (cf. 3:21; 5:14). He may have introduced the judgment theme in the context of the commandment to love because Jesus himself made this command so specific and established love as the basis for judgment. Not to love, therefore, is to disobey Jesus and to spurn the Father's own love in sending Jesus. To live in love, however, is to live in God; and this results in complete confidence for prayer and judgment.

17 The meaning of "because in this world, we are like him" is uncertain. The Greek literally says, "Because even as that one is, so also we are in the world." It is possible to understand this as an appeal to be like Jesus, the Holy One of God—viz., that "even as he is" refers to his eternal purity, love, righteousness, and perfect fellowship with the Father (Brooke, p. 124; Westcott, in loc.). Another possibility is to see it primarily in terms of the Incarnation (Marshall—"we live as Jesus lived"—p. 233). The appeal would then be to his example, as elsewhere in the epistle (e.g., 2:6). In view of the context, however, it is preferable to understand the words to mean that just as Jesus "abides" in the love of the Father (cf. John 15:10), an abiding that already marked his earthly existence and gave him "confidence" before God in the face of temptation, trial, and death, so "in this world" we also may abide in the Father's love and share in that same confidence (Bultmann, p. 73).

18 The other side of confidence is fear. If we truly abide in the Father's love, it follows that we will be without fear. "Perfect love drives out fear." The statement probably should be taken almost as a Christian truism as well as an allusion to the fear of God in judgment. Love and fear are incompatible. They cannot coexist. For the Christian love is first an experience of the Father's love for us. That "love" is so powerful and life changing that when we know it we are forever removed from the "fear" of God.

The fear spoken of here is not to be confused with reverence for God. Reverence will only deepen through the experience of God's love. The experience of the holiness of God's love makes us desire to be even more obedient to his commands. But it also removes us from the power of fear. Whatever may take place in this world cannot nullify the power of his love nor separate us from it. Similarly, if we experience fear in any portion of our life, to that extent we deny God's love and fail to trust him.

Notes

18 Ὁ φόβος κόλασιν ἔχει (*ho phobos kolasin echei*) may be rendered "fear brings its own punishment." Luther's translation—"fear has its own agony"—is based on this interpretation. Bultmann also prefers it.

4. *Love Summarized*

4:19–21

[19]We love because he first loved us. [20]If anyone says, "I love God," yet hates his brother, he is a liar. For anyone who does not love his brother, whom he has seen, cannot love God, whom he has not seen. [21]And he has given us this command: Whoever loves God must also love his brother.

19 In summarizing the command to love one's brother, the author begins with his most important truth. Love must never be conceived of as a "natural" experience of the natural man. There is such a "natural" love, but it must not be confused with the divine love (*agapē*). The love John speaks of originates with the Father. It became manifest in and through the Son and now characterizes the life of the children of God. Therefore he begins this summary by saying, "We love." Although the Greek verb form expresses either exhortation or description, here it is better to understand it descriptively: as the Father loves, and as the Son loves, so also will we love.

The love with which we love is not our own. We do not create it, nor do we even have the power to express it. It is always God's love or Jesus' love in us. But because we abide in the Father and in the Son, the love becomes also our own love. It is not that God reveals his love apart from us, or in spite of us, but that he invites us to love even as he loves. So we return to him his own love and love him with the gift of his love. So also we love our brother with the love God has loved us with.

20 The confidence we have in knowing that God loves us delivers us from fear but not from responsible action. In fact, God's love for us and in us sets us free to love our brother even as God loves him. To fail this test of love proves that one's claim to love God is a lie—just as the previous claims to have fellowship with God while walking in darkness (1:6), to know him while disobeying his commands (2:4), or to possess the Father while denying his Son were lies—and establishes the one making this claim as a liar. Bultmann (p. 76) shows that "liar" has a double sense: "The liar does not speak the truth" in that what he claims is false; and, second, his action shows that he has divorced "himself from the reality of God." The liar's life is a lie because it betrays the being and essence of God.

The second part of the verse is problematic. It can mean that if one is not able to love his brother, whom he can see, he certainly will not be able to love God, whom he cannot see. Or, if one does not practice the life of love by loving his brother, whom he can see, he will certainly be unable to express love for God, who is not even visible to him. Or, preferably, if one fails the test of loving his visible brother, he makes it certain that he does not love the invisible God and thus proves that there is no true love in him.

21 The final warrant of the life of love is obedience to the teaching of Christ. He gave the command that "whoever loves God must also love his brother." The quotation presents an unmistakable echo of Jesus' words in Mark 12:30–31, in answer to the question "Which is the most important commandment?" Jesus answered, "The most important one is this: 'Hear, O Israel, the Lord our God, the Lord is one. Love the Lord your God with all your heart and with all your soul and with all your mind and with all your strength.' The second is this: 'Love your neighbor as yourself' " (cf. John 13:34).

John makes clear that obedience expresses itself in a single command. Love for God and love of neighbor are inseparable. The one is not possible apart from the other. If one loves God, he cannot refuse love to the image of God that meets him in his brother. Dodd puts it thus: "Being the object of God's love, we are to love our neighbor in Him and Him in our neighbor; and that is what it is to remain in His love" (*Johannine Epistles*, p. 124).

Notes

21 The "he" mentioned may be taken as a reference to God who has given his command through his Son. Westcott (p. 155) argues, "The commandment was given in substance by Christ (John xiii. 34), but it came from God (ἀπό) as its final source." However, since the quotation represents so closely Jesus' own word, it seems likely that the NEB is right in concluding that it was Jesus' command the author had in mind.

5. *Love for the Father and Faith in the Son*

5:1–5

[1]Everyone who believes that Jesus is the Christ is born of God, and everyone who loves the father loves his child as well. [2]This is how we know that we love the children of God: by loving God and carrying out his commands. [3]This is love for God: to obey his commands. And his commands are not burdensome, [4]for everyone born of God overcomes the world. This is the victory that has overcome the world, even our faith. [5]Who is it that overcomes the world? Only he who believes that Jesus is the Son of God.

The author now focuses on the relationship of the three fundamental elements so important to him in the knowledge of God: faith, love, and obedience. *Pisteuō* ("to believe," "to have faith"), first introduced at 3:23, becomes the primary term and pervades the section. In John *pisteuō* is "always connected with an object" (Bultmann, p. 59). Faith requires not only that something is held true, but that someone has entered into one's life. A commitment has been made and a relationship has been established that one can then only "confess" (cf. 3:23; 4:2, 4, 15).

1 The argument parallels 4:19. Even as we love only because God first loved us, so also our belief is possible only because we have first been "born of God." The author is not addressing the question of incorporation into the family of God but rather looks only at its result. "Believing" in Jesus (present tense in Gr.) is a direct consequence of our "having been born" (perfect tense in Gr.) of God and therefore becomes a "test" or proof of that birth. From this the author moves to a truism from nature: whoever loves his progenitor (*ton gennēsanta*, KJV, "him that begat"; NIV, "the father") will also love those similarly born, even his brothers and sisters.

2 This statement troubles commentators because it reverses what is expected. One anticipates a conclusion like this: "And this is how we know that we love God: by loving his children and obeying his commands." Instead the author concludes: "This is how we know that we love the children of God: by loving God and carrying out his commands." But as elliptical as this verse may be, it is probably best to assume that the author is saying exactly what he intends to say. Even as one cannot love God without loving his children, so also it is impossible to truly love the children of God without loving God also. If one claims he loves his brother and not God, he has not truly recognized his brother as one born of God and has not offered him the true love that comes from the Father. "If love to men proves the worth of our love to God, love to God proves the worth of our love to men" (G.G. Findley, cited in Bruce, p. 117).

The author cannot really talk of loving God, however, without also linking his words to obedience (i.e., "carrying out his commands").

3 The connection between love for God and obedience is meant as a protection against thinking of love for God as "emotional feelings" about God. True love (*agapē*) requires action. In respect to humankind, it means willingness to lay down one's life. In respect to God, it means a life of willing obedience, a relation of sonship with God, and service on behalf of God. It requires laying down one's life as being one's own possession and taking up a new life in response to a Lord and Master.

John now qualifies what he has just said by adding "And his commands are not burdensome." To the natural man the will of God is strange; the requirement for righteousness, foreign and hard. Even the law of love is a burden. But when God has entered into us and when we trust God's Son, then his yoke becomes gentle and the burden light (cf. Matt 11:30). We who have been born of God have within us a desire and a yearning for the Father. Seeking and hungering after righteousness becomes our joy. Living the life of love becomes our delight. The commands of God bring us the freedom and the liberty we so ardently long for.

4 "Everyone born of God overcomes the world." Here NIV personalizes the Greek word *pan*. Literally, however, *pan* has the sense of "whatever" or "everything"—viz., "everything born of God" (KJV, RSV). "It is not the man but his birth from God, which conquers" (Alfred Plummer, *Commentary on the Epistles of St. John*, CGT [Cambridge: Cambridge University Press, 1894], in loc.). Our being born of God is God's act on our behalf, the event through which he moves to overcome the world. The supernatural act by which human beings are being translated (the verb here is in the present tense) out of the kingdom of death into the kingdom of life through the Son—all this is in view.

The victory that overcomes the world is now identified with "our faith." The Greek literally says, "The victory that is victorious over the world." The participial form (*nikēsasa*, "that has overcome") is in the aorist tense. It may be taken as a simple statement of fact as NIV suggests or more likely as a reference to a past event. If the latter, the author would be emphasizing that the victory he refers to has already been won. By faith we now have access to what was once accomplished by and through the appearance of Jesus on earth.

5 Observe the progression of thought in what John says about how victory over the world is gained. It begins with the new birth, the begetting act of God (5:4a). It moves on to the believer's experience and act of faith (v.4b). It culminates in the confession that Jesus is the Son of God (v.5). The victory requires the whole process. The victory assures us that we too can love God and the children of God and that we too can obey his commands (v.3). Belief, love, and obedience are the marks of the new birth. And the life lived in the new birth is not a burden but a life of celebration. This was the experience of the apostles and also that of the early church. The Book of Acts is full of references to the victorious power of God against every principality and power. Paul's cry that "in all these things we are more than conquerors" (Rom 8:37) echoed throughout the Roman world. Whereas at first the victories were thought of in terms of alien powers on the outside, Christian consciousness soon perceived that the victory included the internal enemies that confront the conscience, assail Christian beliefs and standards, corrupt the soul, and negate the life of love and obedience to God.

The confession with which the victory is linked is again the confession that "Jesus is the Son of God" (cf. 2:22—4:15). This is where the author began. It is also where he will end. Every single tenet of belief in God, of knowledge about him, depends on the revelation and obedient confession and commitment that Jesus is the eternal life that was with the Father (1:2). He is the Son of God. The confession has in view the false teachers who acknowledge Christ the Redeemer but deny his historical identity, his true humanity. Verse 5 makes the transition to the final exposition regarding the Son and provides the base on which the final section develops: the witness of the Father to the Son.

6. *The Spirit, the Water, and the Blood*

5:6–12

6This is the one who came by water and blood—Jesus Christ. He did not come by water only, but by water and blood. And it is the Spirit who testifies, because the Spirit is the truth. 7For there are three that testify: 8The Spirit, the water and the blood; and the three are in agreement. 9We accept man's testimony, but God's testimony is greater because it is the testimony of God, which he has given about his Son. 10Anyone who believes in the Son of God has this testimony in his heart. Anyone who does not believe God has made him out to be a liar, because he has not believed the testimony God has given about his Son. 11And this is the testimony: God has given us eternal life, and this life is in his Son. 12He who has the Son has life; he who does not have the Son of God does not have life.

6a Jesus, who is the Son of God (5:5) and the Christ (5:1), came not just by water, but "by water and blood." This enigmatic statement has given rise in the church to many interpretations. Augustine linked the reference to John 19:34, where the piercing of Jesus' side produced water and blood. Calvin and Luther connected it to John 4 and 6 and saw in it a reference to the sacraments. Plummer and Candlish related it to OT sacrificial symbolism, the water of purification and the blood of the sacrifice. More commentators today, however, agree with Tertullian and see the water referring to Jesus' baptism and the blood to his death on the cross. Even though John's Gospel does not describe the water baptism of Jesus, the Johannine community could not have been ignorant of it.

The purpose of the statement seems clear. The author once more affirms that it is the historical Jesus who is the Christ, the Son of God. Although the false teachers may have acknowledged Christ as the Savior, the divine Son of God, they denied his true human existence. Like Cerinthus, they probably held that the Christ came on the man Jesus at his baptism and remained till the time of the Crucifixion. In this way they could deny that the Christ had ever been truly human and subject to suffering and death. The author rightly regards this as a denial of the redemptive activity of God. It was the Son of God who came into the world. It was this same divine Son who was baptized and received the Spirit. It was the Son who, with the Father's approval and in fulfillment of the Father's intention, shed his blood on the cross to redeem humanity. God would not be involved in man's redemption apart from the Christ's true humanity, suffering, and dying. Water and blood become, therefore, the key words of the true understanding of the Incarnation.

It is likely that once the author had arrived at his primary understanding, he saw in the incident of John 19:34 a divine confirmation of it. He may also have seen the reference to the water in John 4:10, 14 and the reference to drinking his blood in John

6:53 as confirmatory testimony. But these flow from the facts that are the historic base for them all. Jesus, the Son of God, came. He came through the water of baptism. He came also through the Cross. It is this coming by water and blood that is the basis of humankind's salvation.

6b "And it is the Spirit who testifies" (present tense; cf. John 14:26; 15:26; 16:8, 12), because the Spirit, as ultimate truth, is the only one capable of so bearing witness (cf. 1 John 3:24; 4:13). Man cannot receive the witness by himself. There are no human categories available to him through which he can understand it. God's redemptive act in Christ is not a bit of data humankind can deduce for itself by analogical reasoning. Like the Resurrection, it can only be announced. And this time it is not made known by angels (cf. Luke 24:6) but by the Spirit of God.

The Spirit bore witness historically in Jesus' baptism by coming down from heaven as a dove and remaining on him (John 1:32). At Jesus' death on the cross, the "blood and water" that flowed from his side bore witness and led to the following statement: "The man who saw it has given testimony, and his testimony is true. He knows that he tells the truth, and he testifies so that you also may believe" (John 19:35). But here in v.6 the present tense of the verb indicates that the author wants to show that the Spirit continues in his witness to the community of believers.

7–8 "For there are three that testify: the Spirit, the water and the blood." Does the author mean that the Spirit still witnesses through the biblical Word in which Jesus' baptism and death are recounted, or that the Spirit gives witness to the community of the efficacy of the historic baptism and death through the rites of water baptism and communion? Probably the author is pointing to the former as having priority but not so as to exclude the latter. Dodd says,

> The Spirit is, as we have seen, both a factor in the historical life of Jesus, and a continuing factor in the experience of the Church. Similarly, the baptism and the crucifixion are authenticated facts in history, and as such bear witness to the reality of the incarnate life of the Son of God; but further, the Church possesses a counterpart to the baptism of Christ, in the sacrament of Baptism, and a counterpart to His sacrificial death, in the sacrament of the Eucharist. Both sacraments attest and confirm to believers the abiding effect of the life and death of Christ. It seems likely that our author is thinking of these two sacraments as providing a continuing witness to the truth of Christ's incarnation and redemptive death. Their value as evidence lies precisely in their being concrete, overt, "objective" actions, directly recalling (or "representing") historical facts of the Gospel, while at the same time they are the vehicles of a suprahistorical life in the Church. As *verba visibilia*, they confirm the prophetic word, inspired by the Spirit. Thus the apostolic faith is authenticated against all false teaching by a threefold testimony: the living voice of prophecy, and the two evangelical sacraments; and **the three of them are in accord**" (emphasis his) (*Johannine Epistles*, pp. 130–31; cf. Bultmann and Westcott in Notes below).

But how does the Spirit give witness in the "living voice of prophecy"? Presumably he does it inwardly and supernaturally. The Spirit opens eyes and ears to perceive what God is declaring through his proclaimed word (cf. 1 Cor 12:3). He does not declare his own words but through inward conviction confirms the proclamation as being indeed the truth (cf. Acts 5:32). The Spirit provides what humanity is unable to acquire for itself. This witness of the Spirit accompanies every presentation of the word whether that presentation comes as a personal message or as the apostolic or inscripurated word.

9 The divine witness is not limited to the Spirit but includes the witness of the Father as well. His witness is greater than even the authenticated witness of man because of the nature of the one who gives it and of its greater trustworthiness (cf. John 5:36–37; 1 John 3:20). It was his voice that confirmed that Jesus' "passion" was an act in which God would glorify himself (John 12:28–30). So also it is God's own voice that is being heard again in the threefold witness.

10a Here the fact that the incarnate and crucified Jesus is God's own Son is clearly set forth. He who believes this testimony receives the Father's own witness in his heart—"that is, he is given a yet deeper assurance by the inward witness of the Spirit that he was right to trust in Christ" (Stott, p. 82). The inward witness is not a "small voice speaking within, but is the inbreaking of faith within the soul. It is the testimony becoming the possession of faith" (Schnackenburg, p. 265). Faith itself is God's own gift to the believer to lay hold of the Father. "Believing" becomes a "receiving," and the work of God in Christ results in cleansing from sin and forgiveness of sins and inward establishment of the love of God. Faith in the Son immediately becomes faith in the Father: "Whoever acknowledges the Son has the Father also" (1 John 2:23).

10b The gravity of receiving this witness is now demonstrated by the corollary: "Any one who does not believe [the witness borne by] God [about the Son] has made him out to be a liar." To receive the Son is to receive the Father. To deny the Son is to deny the Father. "The witness has been borne, once for all; it cannot be ignored or set aside. It has been borne by God Himself, in a case where His word alone can be final, as it concerns His own Son" (Brooke, p. 139).

The writer, then, cannot allow that one can profess belief in God, as did his opponents, and yet reject God's testimony to his own Son. Such rejection cannot be excused on the basis of ignorance. The evidence is too clear and too weighty. Rather, it is deliberate unbelief, the character of which in the end impugns the very being and character of God. If Jesus is not God's own Son in the flesh, then God is no longer the truth. He is the liar.

11–12 The witness is that through his Son God gave us eternal life. That Jesus is God's Son is established by God's own testimony from the time of Jesus' baptism up to and including his suffering and death. It is a testimony given through the Spirit and confirmed in the heart of the person who believes in the Son. The consequence of accepting this testimony from God is the fulfillment of the promise John made in 1:2 to bear witness and to testify to that eternal life that was with the Father and has now appeared to us in the Son. The witness has been given. Eternal life—which is nothing less than fellowship with the Father, with the Son, and with his people—is present in his Son. He who has the Son has this life. He who is without the Son is without life. It is not an idea nor a system of belief nor even a fact that is the ultimate object of faith; it is a Person. That Person is Jesus Christ. He is to live in us (3:24). His love is to abide and be made complete in us (4:12). We are to live in him (4:13). And this is life eternal.

Notes

7–8 KJV has in 5:7–8 the following: "For there are three that bear record in heaven, the Father, the Word, and the Holy Ghost: and these three are one. And there are three that bear witness in earth." NIV places these verses in a footnote. They are obviously a late gloss with no merit (see Marshall, p. 236). Some connect the "threefold witness" to Deut 19:15, which serves as a basis for the rabbinic law that no charge may be made against someone unless it is confirmed by two or three witnesses.

8 " 'Water' and 'Blood' therefore must have a different meaning than in v.6. What they now mean can scarcely be in doubt: they are the sacraments of baptism and the Lord's supper, which bear testimony for Jesus Christ as God's Son, since they mediate the salvation of the community imparted through him. This may also serve to explain why the 'spirit' as witness is combined into a unity with the two other witnesses. If this combination was initially prompted by the fact that the 'spirit' was called 'witness' in v.6, it nevertheless has a special meaning for the redactor: the two sacraments, baptism and the Lord's supper, 'are witnesses out of the power of the Spirit' " (Bultmann, p. 81). Similarly, Westcott (p. 176) says, "The witness here is considered mainly as the living witness of the Church and not as the historical witness of the Gospels. Through believers, these three, 'the Spirit and the Water and the Blood,' perform a work not for believers only but for the world" (cf. John 17:20–23).

V. Concluding Remarks

5:13–21

13I write these things to you who believe in the name of the Son of God so that you may know that you have eternal life. 14This is the assurance we have in approaching God: that if we ask anything according to his will, he hears us. 15And if we know that he hears us—whatever we ask—we know that we have what we asked of him.

16If anyone sees his brother commit a sin that does not lead to death, he should pray and God will give him life. I refer to those whose sin does not lead to death. There is a sin that leads to death. I am not saying that he should pray about that. 17All wrongdoing is sin, and there is sin that does not lead to death.

18We know that anyone born of God does not continue to sin; the one who was born of God keeps him safe, and the evil one does not touch him. 19We know that we are children of God, and that the whole world is under the control of the evil one. 20We know also that the Son of God has come and has given us understanding, so that we may know him who is true. And we are in him who is true—even in his Son Jesus Christ. He is the true God and eternal life.

21Dear children, keep yourselves from idols.

13 This verse makes the transition from the main argument to the Epilogue. It reminds us of John 20:31, where the author said he had written his Gospel so that his readers might believe in Jesus and receive eternal life in his name. John's first epistle is addressed to those who have accepted this belief but still need assurance that through this name they have indeed received eternal life. So the author refers six times (in addition to v.13) to what we believers know:

> We know that he hears us—whatever we ask.
> We know that we have what we asked.

> We know that anyone born of God does not continue to sin.
> We know that we are children of God.
> We know also that the Son of God has come.
> We . . . know him who is true.
>
> (vv.15, 18–20)

The false teachers present a different "knowledge" as well as a different lifestyle. The author counters with a series of tests by which the believers can evaluate the false teachers' claims and practices. Walking in the light, obeying his commands, loving one's brother, being steadfast in the community of faith, doing what is right—these serve as tests of whether the life that is from God has been received. When it has been received, it is only because God's witness to his own Son as the source of that life has been accepted and believed. On this basis, we can expect God to hear us in prayer, free us from the presence and power of sin, and forgive our transgressions. Those who know these things know also that they have received eternal life.

14 The confidence we have in our life with Christ belongs not only in the future time of his coming (2:28) and of judgment (4:17) but also in the present and especially in the fellowship of prayer. We know that we have access to him (3:21) and that "he hears us." In John "hearing" does not mean simply to be listened to but to be heard favorably (cf. John 11:41–42). The expectation is, of course, linked to the qualifying clause "if we ask according to his will." This seems to reflect a natural dependence on Jesus' own teaching—"Thy will be done" (Matt 6:10)—and his example in Gethsemane—"Not what I will, but what you will" (Mark 14:36).

It is not "any" prayer that is answered but the prayer of the disciple who is in fellowship with the Father, who asks in Jesus' name (John 14:13; 15:16), who "remains" in him (15:7), and who obeys his commands (1 John 3:22). This is not meant to dampen the expectation we may have in prayer, but the condition for addressing God is to know he will hear and act. He who is in "fellowship" with God, who has received life from the Father, knows that he may address God in confidence. Prayer becomes not only a time for petitioning but of yielding one's life to the will and work of God. Prayer made in these circumstances is always heard because it is God's will that is being done and his intention for humankind that is being met. "When we learn to want what God wants, we have the joy of receiving his answer to our petitions" (Marshall, p. 245).

15 The author now goes on to state that the "assurance" for approaching God and asking him anything is absolute. A paraphrase of the text is as follows: "If we know that he hears us whenever we ask in his will, and we certainly do know this, then we may also know with equal certainty that we '*possess* the requests we have made' [Dodd, *Johannine Epistles*, p. 135] the moment we have prayed." Brooke (p. 144) sees the answer to prayer as fulfilled prophetically: "In the certainty of anticipation there is a kind of possession of that which has been granted, though our actual entering upon possession may be indefinitely delayed." This, however, seems to understate the author's position. That our petition is answered is not dependent on whether or not we have personally observed the answer.

Some answers to prayer are recognized immediately, others later, and some are not recognized in our lifetime. But this is not the author's point. When we pray as Jesus prayed, in full accord with the Father's will, we can know that we have our requests, because God has made them his own and his will must be done. What is required of us is simply the faith to believe that this is so, that his will will be done on earth as it is in heaven, and then decide to live accordingly. The author is exalting faith in the will of God and its relation to our privilege to pray. He is echoing Jesus' own words: "Therefore I tell you, whatever you ask in prayer, believe that you have received it, and it will be yours" (Mark 11:24).

16a The author now turns from assurance in prayer to the ministry of prayer. Although he does not give the basis for his statement, what he says about intercessory prayer follows logically from the tenor of his teaching. If love requires the willingness to lay down one's life for a member of the community (3:16), then it follows that if one sees a brother commit sin, he is obligated to intercede for him in prayer. For John it would be obvious that not to pray for a brother would be as much a betrayal of God's love as to withhold material aid from him if he hungered or thirsted (3:17). Moreover, when we pray for a brother or a sister who commits sin, we can know that the prayer we are praying is "according to his [God's] will" because Christ is the atoning sacrifice for sins; and "if we confess our sins," he is committed to "forgive us our sins and purify us from all unrighteousness" (1:9).

But why should a brother need such intercession? Why does he not pray for himself and make his own confession? We can only speculate as to John's answer. Perhaps here again it is a matter of assurance. The brother may need to be forgiven through intercessory prayer as an expression of the community's forgiveness. Because the sin was presumably committed after entrance into the community, the need to confess the sin to another and to have received assurance of forgiveness may have had special significance. Also, there might be an allusion here to Jesus' words in the Gospel of John: "If you forgive anyone his sins, they are forgiven; if you do not forgive them, they are not forgiven" (20:23).

16b The author comments that intercession is not required if it involves a "sin that leads to death." This is puzzling. We do not know exactly what the author has in mind. Judaism distinguished between deliberate or presumptuous sins—sins of open rebellion against God that are punishable by death—and sins of ignorance or inadvertence that can be atoned for (Lev 4; Num 15:22–29—cf. vv.30–31). First-century Judaism retained this pattern (see Notes). In the Johannine community some such distinction was presumably made, hence the limitation "sin that leads to death."

Conjecture as to whether there was one such sin—e.g., blasphemy against the Holy Spirit—or several—e.g., apostasy, murder, etc.—is fruitless. Nor is it the author's concern. He desires that intercessory prayer be made in all instances with the exception of sins that lead to death. Why does he make this exception? Presumably because he is speaking of spiritually efficacious prayer—prayer that will lead to eternal life. Such prayer can be made only for those who are rooted in God's life and love.

Who then is excluded from efficacious prayer? The text offers no clues. As has just been said, it might refer to the blasphemy against the Holy Spirit (Mark 3:29). But the content of the epistle may point to the surmise that the sin John has in mind may be that of false teaching. For life to be given to those who deny Jesus Christ, hate their brother, and refuse the witness of God would be a contradiction. Since such persons deny the mercy of God, prayer for them would appear to be limited to asking for their repentance and conversion to God's truth.

17 Earlier John defined sin as "lawlessness" (3:4). Now he adds "unrighteousness" (NIV, "wrongdoing"). Possibly some in the community, knowing that the children of God were not to sin (3:9–10), attempted to deal with the problem of Christians' sinning by limiting sin to deliberate or lawless acts. If so, John will have none of it. All wrongdoing (*adikia*) is sin, even when done by the children of God. But not all sin results in death. The author aims first at honesty (cf. 1:8) and only then at resolution. Sin is not dealt with by denial but by confession and by community intercession for one another (5:16). Where this intercession occurs, the divine life of God is present and fellowship with God takes place. Within this life and fellowship, the blood of Jesus Christ purifies believers from all sin (1:7).

18 John concludes by stating three certainties that characterize his own position and that of his followers over against the false teachers: (1) We know that anyone born of God does not continue in sin (v.18). (2) We know that we are the children of God (v.19). (3) We know that the Son of God has come and has given us certain, definite knowledge about himself (v.20). Never has John wavered from the priority of the ethical requirement, nor does he do so now. Christians must not walk in darkness (1:7). They must not hate their fellow believers (2:10). They must not live of a sin (3:6).

However noble the sentiments expressed by the false teachers, the test of the truth of God is conduct. A sinful life is totally incompatible with the life received from God. John is not unaware of the difficulties involved in living the new life nor of the quality of the opposition from the evil one. John knows the wiles of the evil one and expects them. Nonetheless, the author has been adamant in his confidence that the evil one need not prevail. It is not the quality of strength in the life of the believer that gives him hope of prevailing but the presence of the power of God.

Already John has shown that if he who lives in him will not sin (3:6), no one born of God possessing the divine life of God will fall victim to the life of sin (3:9). To this he now adds that the Son of God himself will keep him safe from the evil one. NIV renders the article *ho* as an indefinite pronoun—"the one who"—but NEB supplies the subject and RSV capitalizes "he" to make clear that the reference is to Christ. John may first have used "born of God" for believers generally and then also for Christ to emphasize the relation between the two somewhat after the pattern of the Epistle to the Hebrews.

The phrase "keeps him safe" recalls Jesus' words in John's Gospel: "While I was with them, I protected them and kept them safe. . . . None has been lost. . . . My prayer is . . . that you protect them from the evil one" (John 17:12, 15). (For the evil one, see comment on 2:13b.) The phrase "touch him" obviously means "harm."

19 The second affirmation builds on the first one (v.18), but emphasizes the positive consequence: "We know that we are children of God" (lit., "we are of God"). The author now openly identifies himself with the community of faith and stresses the personal quality of the relationships involved in fellowship (*koinōnia*, 1:3) with the Father. We know we "belong to him," i.e., are "his children." And how is this known? It is not by boastful claims, like those made by the false teachers, but on the basis of the "tests of eternal life" that are substantiated by life and action. As Bruce (p. 127) says, "To claim to belong to the family of God is one thing; to exhibit the marks of His family, in the light of the criteria of obedience, love, and preseverance, is another thing. In the case of John and his 'little children,' these criteria have been met." In contrast to the true community that belongs to God (cf. John 8:47) is the rest of the world, which lies under the control of the evil one (cf. 2:15–17). Clearly there is no middle ground for the author. To be born of God is to be safe from the power of the evil one. Not to be born of God is to be wholly under the power of the evil one.

20 The third and final affirmation of John is in fact the summary of the epistle. It affirms the point of dispute with the false teachers. Christian faith has to do with Jesus Christ. He is the "Word of life" (1:1), "the eternal life" (v.2) that was with the Father and through the Incarnation came into human history. By his coming, humankind is enabled to know the true God and to have fellowship with him. But the false teachers said that this relationship was apart from the Son. Fellowship with God as they taught it came through divine knowledge of the subject. It was received through a process of speculative inquiry. From the beginning John denied this teaching. The reality of God can be known only through apprehending the reality that is in the Son. This comes through revelation, but it is a revelation grounded in the facts of history. It requires that one know Jesus Christ as God's Son and that one live his life entirely in him. One knows by this experiential life in the Son that he is also in the Father and that the Son is none other than the true God, the author of eternal life.

"He" in 20b is literally "this one" (*houtos*); RSV has "This is the true God." Grammatically the pronoun most naturally refers to Jesus Christ. Westcott, (p. 187) however, argues that in terms of subject emphasis it more naturally refers backwards to God, who earlier in the text was designated as the one who is true (20a): "This Being—this One who is true, who is revealed through and in His Son, with whom we are united by His Son—is the true God and life eternal." Stott supports Westcott, noting that all "three references to 'the true' are to the same Person, the Father, and the additional points made in the apparent final repetition are that it is *this* One, namely the God made known by Jesus Christ, who is *the true God*, and that, besides this, He is *eternal life*. As He is both light and love (i.5, iv.8), so He is also life" (italics his) (Stott, p. 196; cf. Brooke, pp. 152–53; Dodd, *Johannine Epistles*, p. 140). It is just as defensible, however, to argue that here at the climax of the epistle the author should ascribe full deity to Jesus. After all, this is the crux of his argument and the basis for his statement that he who is in Jesus is in the Father (cf. Bultmann, p. 90; Marshall, p. 254). (For Jesus Christ as the author of eternal life, see John 11:25; 14:6; 1 John 5:11.)

21 John closes on an affectionate note and with a final admonition. The phrase "dear children" (cf. 3:7; 4:4) serves to remind his readers of his genuine commitment to them. The exhortation "keep yourselves from idols" at first glance seems out of place. Idolatry has not so much as been mentioned in the epistle. Although the warning may be understood as a general admonition to "avoid any contact with paganism" (Dodd, *Johannine Epistles*, p. 141), it is more likely that the warning represents a final characterization of the "heresy" represented by the false teachers. False teaching is ultimately "apostasy from the true faith." To follow after it is to become nothing better than an idol worshiper, especially if it is a matter of the truth of one's conception of God. The author is blunt. The false teachers propose not the worship of the true God, made known in his Son Jesus, but a false god—an idol they have invented.

Notes

16a The Qumran community distinguished between sins requiring expulsion and those requiring penance. "Every man who enters the Council of Holiness and who deliberately or through negligence transgresses one word of the Law of Moses, on any point whatever, shall be expelled. . . . But if he has acted inadvertently, he shall be excluded from the pure mind and the Council. . . . For one sin of inadvertence (above) he shall do penance for two years. But as for him who has sinned deliberately, he shall never return; only the man who has sinned inadvertently shall be tried for two years that his way and counsel may be made perfect according to the judgment of the Congregation" (1 QS 8f., quoted from Houlden, p. 135).

16b In *δώσει αὐτῷ ζωήν* (*dōsei autō zōēn*, "he will give him life"), the subject of the verb *dōsei* may refer either to God (NIV, Marshall, Schnackenburg, Stott, Westcott) or to the one who prays (Bultmann, Brooke, Dodd).

19 Ἐν *τῷ πονηρῷ* (*en tō ponērō*, "in the evil one" (may be masculine (so NIV) or neuter ("under the domination of evil"). For Satan's power over the world, cf. John 12:31; 14:30; 16:11; Eph 2:2; 6:12.

20 Ἥ*κει* (*hēkei*, "has come"; cf. John 8:42) clearly refers to Jesus' appearance in history (cf. 1:2; 3:5, 8).

Διάνοιαν (*dianoian*, "understanding") appears only here in the Johannine writings (cf. Eph 4:18; Col 1:21).

In *γινώσκωμεν τὸν ἀληθινόν* (*ginōskōmen ton alēthinon*, "we may know him who is true"), *ginosōkōmen* is in the present tense and emphasizes "a continuous and progressive apprehension" (Westcott, in loc.).

Ἀ*ληθινόν* (*alēthinon*, "true") has the force of "real" (NEB, "genuine") contrasted with the "idols" (v.21), which are false.

21 The command *φυλάξατε ἑαυτὰ* (*phylaxate heauta*, "keep yourselves") does not appear elsewhere in 1 John or in the NT, but comparable phrases are in 2 Cor 11:9; 1 Tim 5:22; James 1:27; Jude 21.

Ε*ἰδώλων* (*eidōlōn*, "idols") is used frequently in the literature of the period to refer to "false gods" (cf. 1 Cor 8:4, 7; 1 Thess 1:9).

2 JOHN

Glenn W. Barker

Outline

I. Introduction (1–3)
II. A Formal Word of Instruction (4–11)
   1. An Exhortation (4–6)
   2. A Warning (7–11)
III. Conclusion (12–13)

Text and Exposition

I. Introduction

1–3

[1]The elder,

To the chosen lady and her children, whom I love in the truth—and not I only, but also all who know the truth— [2]because of the truth, which lives in us and will be with us forever:

[3]Grace, mercy and peace from God the Father and from Jesus Christ, the Father's Son, will be with us in truth and love.

The introduction is a normal epistolary salutation. The author is identified as "the elder" (cf. 3 John 1); the recipients are identified as "the chosen lady and her children"; and an appropriate Christian greeting is extended: "Grace, mercy and peace from God the Father and from Jesus Christ, the Father's Son" (v.3).

1 The word that designates the author as "elder" is *presbyteros,* which can mean an old man, a senior person deserving respect, or a senior official of a local church (cf. Acts 11:30; 14:23; 1 Tim. 5:17). A special use of the word in the early church was to designate a church officer who had been a personal follower of one of the apostles (Eusebius *Ecclesiastical History* 3.39.3–4; Irenaeus *Contra Haereses* 5.33.3, 36.2). The author of this brief letter must have been so well known to those he was writing to that the title "elder" immediately identified him. That he assumes authority over them, though he is obviously not a member of their church, suggests that he was more than a local pastor. He probably held an influential position (like that of a bishop) in the region where his readers lived. Also he was probably so well established with his audience that he could simply call himself "the elder." That "the elder" was also the writer of the first epistle and that he was the apostle John is a valid inference (cf. Introduction to 1 John: Authorship and Date).

The designation of the letter's addressee raises questions. From ancient times opinion has been divided as to whether this letter was addressed to an anonymous noble lady, though she might have actually been called "Eclecta" (from the Gk. *eklekta,* "chosen"), as Clement of Alexandria supposed, or even "Kyria" (a direct transliteration from the Gk. *kyria,* "lady"), or whether it was addressed to a Christian community metaphorically identified as "the chosen lady and her children." Some commentators (Plummer, Ross, Ryrie) favor a person as the designee, while other commentators (Brooke, Bruce, Marshall, Stott, Westcott) favor a local church.

While a strict interpretation of the text supports an individual person as the addressee, the context supports an enigmatic reference to a community. Such a veiled allusion may have been, as Dodd suggests, a device for shielding the identity of the community from adverse action by public officials who opposed the Christian community. If the letter fell into unfriendly hands, it would seem to be nothing more than a private message to a friend. The reference to the elder's children would be a veiled way of referring to the members of the community; and the greetings extended to her from the children of her "chosen sister" (v.13) would be understood as being from the members of the community of the elder. The statement "whom I love in the truth—and not I only, but also all who know the truth" seems more appropriate as a reference to a church than to an individual. No dogmatic conclusion about the addressee is possible, however, because of the ambiguity of the text.

The linking of "truth" and "love" is of great importance. Because John's readers are in the truth—i.e., they know Jesus as the Christ, the Father's Son—they are also the recipients of God's love as it is known and manifested in the community of faith. And the love received by the community comes from all who know the truth. The community of love is as encompassing as the truth that is believed and lived.

The author is speaking in clear contrast to the heretics. They do not have the truth nor do they know what it means to be in the community of love.

2 John goes on to explain why the community of love can be so inclusive. Love relates to the truth, which lives in us and will be with us forever. Truth, for him, is more than what is objectively known. It is that which indwells the believer, permeating his whole existence. Because it is the truth of God, it also has no temporal limitation. It exists without end. Love and truth are themselves not passing sentiments; nor are they dependent on depths of emotional feeling or the strength of personal commitment that some believers might or might not possess. Love and truth originate in God. Like him, they endure without changing, and their splendor never fades.

3 At the time John's epistles were written, the salutation of a letter, according to secular practice, ended with a greeting. Most of the NT epistles follow this custom but give it a special Christian character, such as "grace and peace to you" (Rom 1:7; cf. 1 Peter 1:2) or "grace, mercy and peace from God the Father and Christ Jesus our Lord" (1 Tim 1:2). Here, however, John adds a significant variation to this custom. Rather than wishing or praying that God would grant them his peace, he turns it into a promise that God's mercy and grace will be ours if we truly remain in his truth and love. The words "truth and love" provide the transition to the next section, where they become the chief topic.

II. A Formal Word of Instruction (4–11)

1. An Exhortation

4–6

[4]It has given me great joy to find some of your children walking in the truth, just as the Father commanded us. [5]And now, dear lady, I am not writing you a new command but one we have had from the beginning. I ask that we love one another. [6]And this is love: that we walk in obedience to his commands. As you have heard from the beginning, his command is that you walk in love.

4 The author continues to follow the custom of his time by expressing his pleasure in writing to his readers. Like other Christian writers, John relates this note of joy to their spiritual state; for they are in this instance faithful to the truth.

The force of "some" in v.4 is disputed. Bruce and Stott do not understand its usage as pejorative. According to their reconstruction, the elder had met only some members of the community; and it is to them he refers. It seems more likely, however, that the news of the church had been brought to the elder and that part of this news was that the church had suffered division as a consequence of the work of the heretics. Brooke speculates that the majority had been led astray. Be that as it may, the author rejoices that some of the children remained true to the faith he had delivered to them.

Since the word for "truth" (*alētheia*) is not accompanied by the article, it is more normal for it to be rendered with almost adverbial force—"walking in truth" or "truthfully," meaning "authentically" (see Notes). However, NIV may be right in disregarding that possibility here in view of the usage of the word in v.2, where it occurs with the article and refers to the truth as the "divine reality." The following clause—"just as the Father commanded us"—seems more natural if it is "the truth" heard "from the beginning" (v.5) to which the author is referring (contra Bultmann). The commandment received from the Father is explained in v.5 as the commandment of love and in v.7 as belief in the Son (cf. 1 John 3:23: "And this is his command: to believe in the name of his Son, Jesus Christ, and to love one another as he commanded us").

5 It is clear that for the author the commandment of love has precedence here as it does in 1 John 4:21: "And he has given us this command: Whoever loves God must also love his brother." It is not that love precedes truth or belief but that love offers the clearest test of the truthfulness of the confession and the sincerity of the obedience given to God's commands. Belief may be feigned and confession only of the lips, but love is harder to counterfeit. The elder is not requiring something new but that which has been the supreme and final word "from the beginning." What the Father required (1 John 4:7), the Son manifested (1 John 3:16), and the Spirit makes available through life in him (1 John 4:13–15), the elder now asks for—viz., "that we love one another."

6 Four times in vv.4–6 the author uses the noun "command" (*entolē*). This is his way of making clear that what he is saying is a direct expression of God's will. And how does one know that he fulfills the will of God? The test of love is obedience to God's commands, and the test of obedience is whether one "walks in love." The argument is intentionally circular. Love of God that does not result in obedience to the Word of God cannot be the love that is God's gift in Jesus Christ. Jesus' own love was manifested by his obedience even to death. Love of God can finally be expressed only in action and truth (1 John 3:18). Do we love our brother? Are we prepared to die for him? Obedience that does not lead to the life of love in which we love one another even to death is not obedience offered to God. Not to love means to remain in darkness (1 John 2:11) and in death (1 John 3:14). Hatred of one's brother can never be defended as obedience to God. It is rather obedience and gratification of one's own sin—one's own evil nature (cf. 1 John 3:12).

2. *A Warning*

7–11

[7]Many deceivers, who do not acknowledge Jesus Christ as coming in the flesh, have gone out into the world. Any such person is the deceiver and the antichrist. [8]Watch out that you do not lose what you have worked for, but that you may be rewarded fully. [9]Anyone who runs ahead and does not continue in the teaching of Christ does not have God; whoever continues in the teaching has both the Father and the Son. [10]If anyone comes to you and does not bring this teaching, do not take him into your house or welcome him. [11]Anyone who welcomes him shares in his wicked work.

7 This verse is reminiscent of 1 John 2:18, 27, and 4:1–3. The "deceivers" are those who have left the believing community for the world. It is unlikely that those who went out were members of the "lady's" community. More likely they were members of the original community of the elder. Nonetheless, they may have been known to the community here addressed and were therefore a risk to that community also. What distinguishes them is their unwillingness to acknowledge that Jesus Christ is come in the flesh. Curiously the tense is changed from the past tense "has come [*elēluthota*] in the flesh" (1 John 4:2) to the present participle "as coming [*erchomenon*] in the flesh." It would be possible, therefore, to interpret this as a reference to Jesus' return: he is coming (i.e., will come) in the flesh (cf. 1 John 2:28; 3:2). But since we know of no controversy in this area, this seems unlikely. Dodd obscures the sense by translating the participle *erchomenon* in the past tense, as if its meaning were simply identical with 1 John 4:2, and then offers the surprising explanation that "our author is not skilled in the niceties of the Greek idiom" (*Johannine Epistles*, p. 149).

It is far safer, however, to assume that the writer does know the difference between a present participle and a perfect (past tense) and that his intention is to say something beyond what he was saying in 1 John 4:2. What the present tense would emphasize normally in such a case is the timeless character of the event. As Bultmann suggests, this would be in line with the gospel's presentation in John 3:31; 6:14; 11:27. It is seen not simply as an event in history but as an "abiding truth" defining the union between humanity and deity that is present in Jesus' person. This union is not limited to Jesus' historical manifestation but remains true of him as the one at the right hand of the Father. As Brooke (p. 175) states it: "The incarnation was more than a mere incident, and more than a temporary and partial connection between the Logos and human nature. It was the permanent guarantee of the possibility of fellowship, and the chief means by which it is brought about."

8 There is a difficult textual problem here that allows for two quite different meanings. NIV reads "Watch out that you do not lose what you have worked for," as does RSV. But RV, NEB, and JB accept the alternative reading: "Watch out that you do not lose what we have worked for." Bultmann and Schnackenburg support the reading, whereas NIV, Brooke, Marshall, and Westcott support that of the NEB. The textual evidence is so divided that it is difficult to make a choice. On balance the more difficult reading "we" is preferable and, in fact, coincides with similar feelings expressed by Paul in writing to the Galatians: "I fear for you, that somehow I have wasted my efforts on you" (4:11; cf. v.19: "My dear children, for whom I am again in the pains of childbirth until Christ is formed in you").

As messengers of Christ, the apostles could not help but feel completely involved in the lives of their charges (cf. Phil 2:16). Whether or not they actually planted all the churches or whether missionaries were responsible for some of them is beside the point. Paul did not establish the Christian communities in Rome and Colosse. Yet he accepted full responsibility for them in terms of the apostolic message. As one in charge of the message that was "from the beginning," all the apostle John's labors were directed to the maintenance of the truth of Jesus Christ as one come in the flesh. If anyone failed to continue in this message, then in a real sense John's apostolic mission had failed. That the reader would lose was self-evident. But so would the community of faith and "the elder" himself.

A "full reward" (*misthon plērē*, NIV, "rewarded fully") suggests that John envisions two possibilities. Verse 8 appears to address the situation when a reader is partially deceived and so loses some of his reward for faithfulness and perseverance. One receives according to his labor. (For the concept of "rewards," see Matt 5:12; John 4:36; 1 Cor 3:8; Rev 11:18; 22:12.)

9 This verse, which is John's second possibility, suggests a more radical departure from the faith: "Anyone who goes too far." NIV's translation—"Anyone who runs ahead"—may be too weak for the verb *proagōn* in this context. The NEB rendering—"Anyone who runs ahead too far"—is supported by Westcott's paraphrase: "Everyone that advances in bold confidence beyond the limits set to the Christian Faith" (p. 219). The situation here in v.9 implies not a loss of reward but of God himself, the loss or nonattainment of eternal life as promised in 1 John 2:25.

The "teaching of Christ" can be construed as an objective genitive—i.e., the teaching about Christ—as Bultmann and Marshall read it. The reference would then be to the teaching that Jesus Christ has indeed come in the flesh. But it is equally possible that the genitive is subjective and refers to Jesus' teaching in v.5 that "we love one another" (cf. Brooke, Schnackenburg, Stott, Westcott). It is of little importance, however, which alternative is accepted, because the author holds equally to both positions. For Jesus Christ to be acknowledged as the one come in the flesh is fundamental to the faith, and for us to love one another is equally fundamental. To confess the former requires that we do the latter. To have the Father and the Son is to have precisely what the false teachers have lost. To give up the Son is to lose the Father (cf. John 5:23; 14:6–7).

10–11 The last warning extended to the reader is both the most objective and the most final. "If anyone comes to you and does not bring this teaching, do not take him into your house or welcome him." The author is not certain what will happen in the lady's community. Probably he expects that the false teachers will soon arrive with their pernicious propaganda. If so, the situation is dangerous. The false teachers must not be shown hospitality, as if they were brothers in the faith. Because they are deceivers, it would be a mockery of the Father and a sin against Christ to give those who deny the Son and hate the brethren a place of respect within the community of faith. To do so would be to become a partaker in their unbelief and hatred of the truth.

The statement is all the more remarkable since it comes from the "apostle of love." Moreover, the command to extend hospitality is deeply rooted in the tradition (Rom 12:13; 1 Tim 3:2; 5:3–10; Titus 1:8; Heb 13:2; 1 Peter 4:8–10). It was an absolute demand that brothers in Christ be supported, fed, and housed by the local congregations they visited. Nevertheless, the elder invokes a higher principle here. False prophets, antichrists, and deceivers are not to share in the provision of hospitality. Even the Christian greetings that might be given ever so casually are forbidden in the case of the false teachers. One cannot serve God and mammon simultaneously (Matt 6:24). One cannot be a partner of God and a partner of the devil (1 Cor 10:20).

Clearly the elder's words are an offense to some today and are not considered "a sufficient guide to Christian conduct" (Dodd, *Johannine Epistles*, p. 152) or worthy of the church. Admittedly great care should be exercised before applying such a radical withholding of hospitality from anyone. For the elder it was applied only to antichristians who were committed to destroying the faith of the community. The issue involved more than disagreements in interpretation or personal misunderstandings among members of the body of Christ. It was radical and clearly defined unbelief, and it involved active and aggressive promotion of perversions of truth and practice that struck at the heart of Christianity.

But ought not persons who had gone so far astray be dealt with all the more in love? Do they not require even more by way of grace, mercy, and forgiveness of Christ? At the personal level, Christians should always be prepared to turn the other cheek and seek tirelessly to be reconciled with others. But only those whose own faith is secure and whose understanding beyond corruption can do this. Unfortunately, the community of the elect lady was not yet in this position. It was not mature enough to deal with such deadly deviations; in fact, it was more likely that it might be destroyed by them. The responsibility of parents may furnish an analogy. Parents must discriminate as to whom even among their relatives they entertain in their home. Some relatives might be of such questionable character as to menace the moral, spiritual, and physical welfare of the children. Such relatives must be excluded. Parents must balance their concern for their relatives with their responsibility for their children. Notice that John does not suggest that the elect lady and her children deal with the false teachers in hatred or retaliate against them. Instead, he counsels that the false teachers be kept at a distance lest their heresy destroy the young church.

We today can only be grateful that the infant church took heresy regarding the person of Christ seriously. Christianity stands or falls with its Christology. From the human point of view, if John and other apostolic leaders had tolerated the "antichrists" who denied the basic truth of the Incarnation, the church might never have survived. We today are the beneficiaries of the spiritual discernment and moral courage of John and others like him.

III. Conclusion

12–13

[12]I have much to write to you, but I do not want to use paper and ink. Instead, I hope to visit you and talk with you face to face, so that our joy may be complete.

[13]The children of your chosen sister send their greetings.

12–13 The epistle closes with a quite normal wish. The elder acknowledges that there is much more he might say, but he recognizes that it will be more effective if he were to say it in person. The phrase "face to face" (lit., "mouth [*stoma*] to mouth") suggests an intimacy that requires personal presence. When the community of believers enjoys fellowship in Christ, one of the results of their fellowship is the joy of the Lord.

The children who sent greetings were doubtless members of the elder's community who understood the plight of the community of the chosen lady; and they wished to share the elder's concern to strengthen the bonds of love that unite all saints.

Notes

---

1 Ἐν ἀληθείᾳ (*en alētheia,* NIV, "in the truth") is anarthrous (without an article) here and therefore should be understood as having an adverbial force—viz., "truly," as in John 1:47;

7:26; 8:31; 17:8. Marshall (p. 61), however, argues that "in view of the significant role which 'truth' plays in these letters, a deeper sense may already be present here." But if this were the author's intent, how natural it would have been to include the article as he did in v. 1b! A more judicious decision would be to follow the example of NEB and not supply the article where none is present. The practice of supplying the article (so RSV, JB, NIV) almost inevitably obscures any difference in the text and encourages what might well be over-interpretation, particularly in the case of 2 John 1 and 3 John 1.

4 Compare Paul's words in Rom 1:8: "First, I thank my God through Jesus Christ for all of you, because your faith is being reported all over the world" (cf. 1 Cor 1:4; Phil 1:3; Col 1:3; 1 Thess 1:2; 3 John 3–4).

7 The question has been raised as to whether John's view contradicts Paul's statement that "flesh and blood cannot inherit the kingdom of God" (1 Cor 15:50). Paul thinks of the flesh as that which must die and be transformed. The "fleshly" body must become a "spiritual body." John, however, as well as Luke, thinks of flesh as defining the human reality of a person. When Jesus' disciples were startled when he appeared to them after the Resurrection, he said to them, "Look at my hands and my feet. It is I myself! Touch me and see; a ghost does not have flesh and bones, as you see I have" (Luke 24:39). John understands that Jesus arose from the dead in his physical body (John 20:27) and that his glorification was in that same body (John 20:17). Both John and Paul recognize the need of the transformation of the flesh but used different terms to define it.

(For "deceiver and the antichrist," see comment at 1 John 2:18ff.)

3 JOHN

Glenn W. Barker

Outline

I. Salutation (1)
II. Personal Words to Gaius (2–4)
III. Commendation for Gaius's Hospitality (5–8)
IV. Complaints Against Diotrephes (9–10)
V. Exhortation and Endorsement of Demetrius (11–12)
VI. Personal Remarks and Farewell Greetings (13–15)

Text and Exposition

I. Salutation

1

[1]The elder,

To my dear friend Gaius, whom I love in the truth.

Third John is a genuine letter written by "the elder" to a man named Gaius in another community. Although the letter is highly personal, it is also clearly official. The elder expresses thoughts that are meant to be shared with other members of the community. Concern for the situation in the church is the occasion for writing. The letter implies that Gaius was in a specially influential position and commends and supports him.

1 The elder (cf. comment on 2 John 1 and Introduction to 1 John: Authorship and Date) addresses Gaius as "my dear friend," and his warm affection for Gaius permeates the entire letter. Although the name Gaius occurs elsewhere in the NT (cf. Acts 19:29; 20:4; Rom 16:23; 1 Cor 1:14) and is common enough in the literature of the time, his identity, aside from what is said of him in this letter, is unknown to us. He may have been a member of the church Diotrephes appears to have headed. But whether he held any official position in it is uncertain. The pronoun in the phrase "whom I love in the truth" is emphatic but probably not, as Westcott suggests, in contrast to the attitude of some other detractors of Gaius.

On NIV's rendering of *en alētheia* as "in the truth," see note on 2 John 1.

II. Personal Words to Gaius

2–4

[2]Dear friend, I pray that you may enjoy good health and that all may go well with you, even as your soul is getting along well. [3]It gave me great joy to have some brothers come and tell about your faithfulness to the truth and how you continue to walk in the truth. [4]I have no greater joy than to hear that my children are walking in the truth.

2 The elder, wishing good health to Gaius does not mean that Gaius was ill. The wish was a conventional one and though it does not rule out the possibility of particular concern for Gaius's health, it does not necessitate it. Here the elder commends him by praying that things will be well for his physical health as they have proved to be for his spiritual health. Implied in this verse is a tribute to the wholesome state of Gaius's spiritual life. Of how many Christians could their physical health be equated with their spiritual health? But the elder knew his man!

3 Behind this verse we see the flow of Christians between the early churches as well as between the Johannine ones. And it went on in the second century also. It may have been occasioned in some instances by a change in personal circumstances and in others because of opposition and persecution. However, it may have been more intentional than this and may have represented, particularly among the Johannine churches, a commitment to live as a fellowship of Christians deeply concerned for one another.

Traveling missionaries and evangelists may have indeed swelled the ranks of those who moved back and forth. Yet it would probably be too much to read into the term "brothers" an exclusive reference to them. In any event there was a lively flow of persons between the church where Gaius was a member and the elder's community. Moreover, these men appear to be reporting to the elder as a normal and expected activity. They tell him about Gaius's faithfulness to Christian truth as well as about his sincerity and faithfulness in his daily living. In vv.5–8 the elder specifies the conduct he has in mind. Nowhere in this letter, however, does he refer to the theological issue before the church. Westcott's (p. 226) comment may well be correct. "The words evidently point to some difficulties from false teaching which Gaius had boldly met, though as yet the issue of his work was uncertain."

4 The importance for the church of Gaius's stand for the truth is seen in the elder's next comment. There is no more important news he can receive, no greater joy he can experience, than that his own "children" (i.e., his own converts to the faith) are living in fidelity "to the truth." The word "children" could of course designate less specifically all for whom John feels pastoral responsibility. Westcott sees the possessive pronoun *ema* ("my") used here as indicating a stronger relationship (cf. Bultmann also).

III. Commendation for Gaius's Hospitality

5–8

5Dear friend, you are faithful in what you are doing for the brothers, even though they are strangers to you. 6They have told the church about your love. You will do well to send them on their way in a manner worthy of God. 7It was for the sake of the Name that they went out, receiving no help from the pagans. 8We ought therefore to show hospitality to such men so that we may work together for the truth.

5 Again the writer's warm feeling shines through as for the third time he addresses Gaius as his "dear friend" (cf. vv.1–2). Now he commends him for his hospitality to Christian brothers who came from the elder to visit the church, even though they were at the time unknown to Gaius. It is likely that Gaius's actions were quite in contrast to what others in the church did. As Westcott (p. 227) surmises, Gaius may have incurred the displeasure of some in his church. Although hospitality was required of all Christians (Matt 10:10; Rom 12:13; 1 Tim 3:2; 5:10; Heb 13:2), it was sometimes necessary to refuse it (2 John 10).

6 Part of what the traveling brothers had reported to the elder was the wholehearted way—involving, perhaps, risk to his standing in the community—in which Gaius had entertained them. On returning, they had testified to this before the whole church, and this increased the elder's pride in "his son in the faith." He had not only entertained the traveling brothers but had shown them *agapē* love.

It seems that these brothers had returned, perhaps carrying letters from the elder;

and they again needed Christian hospitality. The admonition to send them on their way "in a manner worthy of God" shows the supreme importance assigned to hospitality. The phrase probably means that the traveling brothers were to be recognized as servants of God and supported as such. In such instances, Christians were to provide hospitality as if the Lord himself were being welcomed (cf. John 13:20; Gal 4:14–15; Heb 13:2).

7 That they went out "for the sake of the Name" shows that they were missionaries. Assuredly "the Name" is Jesus Christ (cf. Acts 5:41), and the sending body is either the elder's community or a company of believers known to the elder and Gaius. That they could make no preparation and accept nothing from pagans shows how strongly the Johannine community depended on the word of Jesus: "Take nothing for the journey except a staff—no bread, no bag, no money in your belts. . . . Whenever you enter a house, stay there until you leave that town" (Mark 6:8, 10). Whether it was Jesus' words "Freely you have received, freely give" (Matt 10:8), as Marshall conjectures, or simply common sense that forbade them to take support from pagans, we do not know. What we do know is that wandering preachers and missionaries of pagan deities were common in the Roman world. Deissmann also recounts how profitable it became for some of them and what distrust it occasioned (*Light from the Ancient East* quoted in Dodd, *Johannine Epistles,* p. 160).

It was difficult enough accepting gifts from the church, as Paul showed, let alone taking help from unbelievers (cf. 1 Cor 9:14–18; 2 Cor 12:16–18; 1 Thess 2:6–9). Although Paul acknowledged the right of the traveling missionaries to be supported by the church (2 Cor 9:14), he was well aware of the risks this entailed. Nonetheless, for the mature Christian community such support was encouraged and gladly received (cf. Phil 4:10–18). Both for the giver and receiver there was a blessing to be received. In the Johannine community such support was certainly a part of the sacrifice one Christian owed another. Even a Christian's life was not beyond the limit love required (1 John 3:16–17).

8 Whether this call to practice hospitality is based on the principle that by their support church members may be fellow laborers with missionaries in proclaiming the gospel (cf. 2 Cor 8:23; Col 4:11) or whether such support guarantees participation in the truth is not clear. In the Johannine community, *koinōnia* ("fellowship") required the former, while obedience to the commands of Christ demanded the latter. The author could be ambiguous if he desired because both alternatives were involved. However, the preferable understanding would support the NIV rendering.

IV. Complaints Against Diotrephes

9–10

[9]I wrote to the church, but Diotrephes, who loves to be first, will have nothing to do with us. [10]So if I come, I will call attention to what he is doing, gossiping maliciously about us. Not satisfied with that, he refuses to welcome the brothers. He also stops those who want to do so and puts them out of the church.

9 This paragraph brings us to the nub of the problem the elder is writing about. He had already addressed a letter to the church through its leader Diotrephes. That letter is lost, perhaps destroyed by Diotrephes himself. Its contents are not, however, difficult to imagine. On the basis of what the elder wrote Gaius, we can surmise that he had written the church asking them to extend hospitality to the traveling missionaries he had sent out. It may also have included a request for support that would speed them on their way. Diotrephes chose to thwart the elder's intention either by suppressing the letter or opposing the request before the congregation. He also had threatened the expulsion of any in the church who were considering offering hospitality to the elder's emmissaries. In fact, some may already have been forced out of the church.

Why Diotrephes was opposing the elder is not clear. The elder's statement that Diotrephes "loves to be first" could simply reflect personal rivalry. Or it could reflect an inflated and dictatorial ego. The elder's prominence in the community was obviously longstanding. Diotrephes may have been troubled by the elder's continued influence over the church Diotrephes was leading. If Diotrephes was a younger man, the elder's age may have been a problem. That there was a deeper split, perhaps involving theological differences, is not supported by the text.

The elder commends Gaius for his faithfulness to the truth and for living according to the truth. Does this indicate that the elder suspected Diotrephes of wavering in opposition to the false teachers in the area? Does the statement that he "will have nothing to do with us" and that he is "gossiping maliciously about us" and "refuses to welcome the brothers" indicate that he is not really committed to the commandment of love the elder contends so unremittingly for? If so, Diotrephes had as yet shown no theological deviation regarding the person of Christ. If he had, we can, in view of his other actions, be quite certain that the elder would have exposed him and pronounced judgment on him. But quite apart from doctrinal deviation, the opposition of Diotrephes would have the effect of weakening the elder's position in the community and making the work of the false teachers that much easier.

Another cause for the problem may have been that the elder may have expanded the activity of the missionary emissaries in order to stem the tide of false teaching flooding the area. The presence of these missionaries would have been an effective deterrent to schism and would have strengthened the hand of the elder in dealing with this threat to the gospel. But his actions may have been resented by Diotrephes as eroding the local autonomy of the churches. The "malicious gossip" referred to may have been that the elder was using the presence of false teachers as a pretext for establishing his own authority more completely over the churches.

Exactly how Gaius fits into all this is unclear. Dodd surmises that he was the leader of another local church in the area and on that basis the elder writes to him. Dodd senses the difficulty of placing Gaius in the same church as Diotrephes. Why should he be telling Gaius about what Diotrephes is doing when presumably Gaius would already know about it firsthand? Marshall conjectures that Gaius may have lived in a nearby village—perhaps a day's journey away—and therefore did not know all that was taking place in the church. If so, that would explain how Gaius could be a member of the same church, as the letter implies, and yet not know all its workings.

A commonly accepted reconstruction of the situation is that the letter reflects the circumstances of the transition from the apostolic period to a time of more rigid, episcopal church government (Adolph Harnack, *Über die dritten Johanesbrief,* T.U. 15:3b [Leipzig: Hinrichs, 1897], in loc.). The tension between Diotrephes and the elder is then seen as a conflict between one of the first monarchical bishops and one of the last of those possessing immediate apostolic authority (cf. Dodd, Houlden, Marshall). (The idea is given a perverse twist by Käsemann, who sees the elder himself as a heresiarch and Diotrephes the episcopal representative of the orthodox party [E. Käsemann, "Ketzer und Zeuge," ZTK 48 (1951), 292–311]!)

Although Harnack's theory is not implausible, it goes beyond the evidence. The elder does not object that Diotrephes should have authority, but he does object to its misuse to the detriment of the truth. The real conflict is not between two types of belief. It is between two levels of commitment to the work of God: Diotrephes is more interested in furthering his own position than in furthering the work of God (cf. Stott, pp. 226–27).

10 Exactly how the elder intended to deal with Diotrephes is unclear. John's statement that he "will call attention to what he [Diotrephes] is doing" suggests that John planned to confront Diotrephes, perhaps personally, and expose his conduct before the whole church, unless he completely repented. There seems to be an implication that Diotrephes' misdeeds were not yet fully known to the congregation; and perhaps it was the elder's hope that once they were revealed, the church would either censure or expel Diotrephes from his position.

How are we to explain the sharp words and drastic response on the part of the apostle of love? Do they not represent a contradiction to his teaching? More probably they represent the response of one who sensed that the very nature of the gospel was threatened by such hypocritical conduct on the part of one of its ministers. Diotrephes' actions against the elder were reprehensible by any standard; but they were even more so on the part of one who probably had been of the fellowship of the elders, who knew the message of love that had been received, and who had pledged to live a life according to the commandment given by the Son of God. For such a leader of the church to give way to personal pique and selfish ambition was unthinkable.

Moreover, the wickedness involved spread beyond the vicious innuendos and lies directed against the elder. It extended to those wholly innocent of possible wrongdoing. The hospitality due the missionary "brothers" in order to speed them on their way in their service of the gospel had also been singled out for abuse; and they were denied the welcome due them as members of the household of faith. Because they came from the elder, they suffered the consequences of guilt by association. The harshest treatment of all had been directed against those whose conscience required them to extend hospitality to the brethren. Because they dared to disobey Diotrephes on this matter, they had been cast out of the congregation.

Such contradiction to the gospel by word and deed as done by Diotrephes could not be condoned, and indeed it was not. It was no longer Diotrephes who was on trial for his action but the elder and all those who believed like him. Silence on their part in the face of such total rejection of the truth and the life of the gospel would have been as hypocritical as Diotrephes' earlier action.

It was no pleasant experience that awaited the elder, but "truth" without love is no truth at all. Diotrephes was condemned not because he violated sound teaching regarding the person and nature of Jesus Christ but because his "life" was a contradiction to the truth of the gospel. This condition required action by John and by the congregation.

V. Exhortation and Endorsement of Demetrius

11–12

[11]Dear friend, do not imitate what is evil but what is good. Anyone who does what is good is from God. Anyone who does what is evil has not seen God. [12]Demetrius is well spoken of by everyone—and even by the truth itself. We also speak well of him, and you know that our testimony is true.

11 That the elder admonishes Gaius not to "imitate what is evil but what is good" need not imply that he fears for Gaius's character. It is rather for his encouragement in continuing to do good. He may have expected Diotrephes and his supporters to exert intense pressure on Gaius to give up his support of the elder and his missionaries. In that event, Gaius would have no option but to take his stand on principle. To give in to pressure against one's convictions is to submit to evil. Whatever its source or whoever its advocates, evil can never be reconciled to God. Even to contemplate giving in to evil means that loyalty to God's revealed will is jeopardized.

Why does the elder appeal to imitators? Because it is the nature of God's revelation that truth (vv.1, 3), love (v.6), and righteousness (v.11) have been modeled first in Jesus Christ and then by those who are faithful to his commandments. Humankind does not have in its nature a dependable standard by which to judge itself. It must always measure its understandings and actions by God himself, for whom love, truth, and righteousness are absolute attributes. In Christ these same attributes have become available to all who love God and desire to obey his commands. To show them forth in our lives proves that we are "from God." All goodness proceeds from him; our perseverance in goodness demonstrates that in Jesus Christ we have seen God.

12 The elder now commends Demetrius, of whom we know no more than what is said of him here. For some reason John felt it important for Gaius to know and trust him. Apparently he was also a supporter of the elder. Some have conjectured that Demetrius was the bearer of the letter or that he was a traveling missionary. The elder honors him with a threefold tribute: (1) He "is well spoken of by everyone." (2) He is well spoken of "by the truth iself." (3) The elder also "speaks well of him." This strong backing of Demetrius leads us to think he had been given a special mission that required unusual trust, but one that the elder did not choose to describe here.

How the truth could speak well of Demetrius is somewhat puzzling. Bultmann sees "the truth" as a personification. If so, it could stand for God, Christ, the gospel, the revelation. It seems more likely, however, that it is the truth of the gospel in Demetrius's life the elder is referring to. Like Gaius, Demetrius is "walking in the truth." His life matches his confession. In Pauline terms, he manifests the fruit of the Spirit. In Johannine terms, he lives the life of love. The clause "and you know that our testimony is true" reminds us of John 21:24.

VI. Personal Remarks and Farewell Greetings

13–15

[13]I have much to write you, but I do not want to do so with pen and ink. [14]I hope to see you soon, and we will talk face to face.

[15]Peace to you. The friends here send their greetings. Greet the friends there by name.

13-14 John's statement that he wished to write more parallels not only 2 John 12 but also John 20:30. It is characteristic of his style as is also his expressed desire to see Gaius soon and talk with him "face to face" (cf. comment on 2 John 12).

15 The closing word again bears the mark of the warm relationship existing between John and Gaius. John extends "peace" to him, knowing that his situation may become very difficult in the days ahead. He also reminds him that all who are with John are also Gaius's friends. Then he concludes by asking Gaius to greet his friends in the church. This last remark supports the assumption that the elder's real desire is that Gaius will in fact share this letter with the members of the church.

Notes

1 On this form of epistolary address, see Funk, p. 425.

2 Marshall's statement (p. 83) that "there is some probability that Gaius was not in the best of health" based on v.9 is only conjectural. If Gaius's health were really a problem, it seems unlikely that he would be able to exercise the hospitality he is commended for; and it might be even less likely that in such a warm personal note his health would have been referred to in such a perfunctory way.

3 Καθὼς (*kathōs,* "and how") may be understood as introducing the author's own personal knowledge. "The brothers came and told about your faithfulness just as indeed you are faithful" (Bultmann, p. 98, n.6).

11 Ὁ ἀγαθοποιῶν (*ho agathopoiōn,* "one who does what is good") occurs only here in the Johannine writings. "To be from God" reminds us of 1 John 2:3–5; 33:4–10; 4:7.

JUDE

Edwin A. Blum

JUDE

Introduction

1. Authorship
2. Date
3. Canonicity
4. Place of Origin
5. Destination
6. Purpose
7. Special Problems
8. Bibliography
9. Outline

1. Authorship

The first verse identifies the author of this letter as "Jude, a servant of Jesus Christ and a brother of James." "James," an English form of the Hebrew name "Jacob," was a popular name among the Jews in NT times because of its patriarchal connection. Likewise popular was "Judah," the name of Jacob's fourth son, founder of the tribe of Judah. "Jude" is an English form of "Judas" (*Ioudas*), the Greek form of "Judah." The name gained added luster from Judas Maccabaeus, a national hero of the Jews, who led the revolt against Antiochus Epiphanes in the second century B.C. But the perfidy of Judas Iscariot may perhaps have led practically all major English versions (except the RV) to use the form "Jude" rather than "Judas" in translating this letter.

Can Jude be identified with any certainty among the number of men in the NT named Judas? BAG lists eight possibilities (pp. 380–81). The link of Jude with James provides the best clue for identifying the author of the letter. After the martyrdom of James the son of Zebedee under Herod Agrippa I (c. A.D. 44; cf. Acts 12:2), the only James who is well enough known in the early church that the unspecified use of his name would be generally recognizable was James of Jerusalem. Paul called him "James, the Lord's brother" (Gal 1:19). Later, according to Hegesippus, he became known as "James the Just."[1]

If the James of Jude 1:1 can be so identified, Jude was the brother of the leader of the Jerusalem church (Acts 12:17; 15:13; 21:18; 1 Cor 15:7; Gal 1:19; 2:9, 12) and the half-brother of Jesus of Nazareth (Matt 13:55; Mark 6:3). If the Jude of this letter was the half-brother of Jesus, he did not believe in the messiahship of Jesus until after the Resurrection (John 7:5; cf. Acts 1:14 ["his brothers"]). This probably explains the humility with which Jude introduces himself in 1:1 as a servant (slave) of the brother (now recognized as the Messiah) he had denied.

In a story that comes from Hegesippus and is related by Eusebius, this trait of

[1]Eusebius, *Ecclesiastical History* 2.23.

humility was shown by the grandsons of Jude, "said to have been the Lord's brother according to the flesh."[2] (This is "the only mention of Jude [the man] in ecclesiastical history" [HDB, s.v.].) The story tells how the grandsons were brought before Domitian, the Roman emperor (A.D. 81–96), and accused of belonging to the royal house of David. The emperor questioned them about the Christ and his kingdom, and they explained that it was a heavenly kingdom that would come at the end of the age. So the emperor dismissed them as simple peasants with no royal pretensions.

Modern objections to the authorship of the letter by a half-brother of Jesus include the fact that its language seems very Hellenistic for an author who grew up in Galilee. In addition, the vocabulary abounds in ornate and rare words (there are thirteen words not found elsewhere in the NT). Yet it is unreasonable to dogmatize about what facility in the Greek language and literature or what knowledge of Jewish apocalytic writings (cf. the possible use of the Assumption of Moses in v.9 and the Apocalypse of Enoch in v.14) the half-brother of Jesus might have had. Greek was the lingua franca of the Mediterranean world, and the presence of the Decapolis to the east and to the south of the Sea of Galilee provided ample opportunity for Greek influence on nearby Nazareth.

Hughes has surveyed the evidence regarding the languages Jesus used in his ministry and concludes that, while more work needs to be done in this field, it is certainly probable that Jesus spoke Greek fluently.[3] His half-brother Jude grew up in a multilingual environment. Turner describes the language of Jude as revealing a Jewish Christian author who had a distinctly Hellenistic style. In addition, Turner finds evidence of biblical Greek in Jude's vocabulary.[4]

Schrage opposes the authorship of the letter by the Lord's half-brother on the ground that it bears the marks of the beginning of early Catholicism (*Frühkatholizismus*). "Early Catholicism" is a step in the development of the Catholicism of the later Roman church. Schrage finds support for his view in the "Catholic" salutation of the letter as well as in the letter's artistic style and its appeal to tradition (v.3). From this slender evidential base, he alleges a late date of composition that would rule out the possibility that Jude the half-brother of Jesus wrote the letter (Balz and Schrage, pp. 219–20).

None of these objections are weighty, since the appeal to tradition is common in Paul's letters (cf. 1 Cor 11:23ff.; 15:3ff.).[5] The salutation and artistic style of the letter do not prove a late date. Christianity spread rapidly in the ancient world; so a "polished" work may well have been sent to the church at large in Jude's time.

2. Date

The letter is so short that it contains little to help fix its date of composition other than the points mentioned above and inferences that can be drawn from the heresy

[2]2 Ibid., 3.20.

[3]Philip Edgcumbe Hughes, "The Languages Spoken by Jesus," *New Dimensions in New Testament Study*, edd. R.N. Longenecker and M.C. Tenney (Grand Rapids: Zondervan, 1974), pp. 127–43.

[4]Nigel Turner, James H. Moulton's *A Grammar of New Testament Greek*, vol. 4, *Style* (Edinburgh: T. & T. Clark, 1976), p. 139.

[5]See also F.F. Bruce, "Scripture and Tradition in the New Testament," *Holy Book and Holy Tradition*, edd. F.F. Bruce and E.G. Rupp (Grand Rapids: Eerdmans, 1968), pp.68–93.

the author opposes. If the author was the younger half-brother of Jesus (the older half-brother being the influential James of Jerusalem), the most probable time of writing would be between A.D. 40 and 80. If the letter was used by Peter in 2 Peter, the writing would have to be sometime prior to Peter's death or before A.D. 65. However, Peter's use of Jude is not certain (cf. Introduction to 2 Peter: Special Problem). Guthrie thinks Jude could have been written in the period between 65 and 80. The heresy of the false teachers could have developed quite early. So all things considered, the letter may most probably be dated about 60 to 65.

3. Canonicity

If 2 Peter utilized Jude and if Peter wrote 2 Peter (both positions are disputed), then 2 Peter is the oldest witness to Jude, and its "apostolic" character or canonicity is, in principle, settled at a very early date. In the early church fathers, a number of allusions to Jude have been identified (cf. Bigg, pp. 305–9). The Muratorian Canon (c.200) states that an epistle of Jude was accepted in the Catholic church.[6] Tertullian, Clement of Alexandria, and Origen all knew the book.

Eusebius, in speaking of the Epistle of James, says, "It is to be observed that its authenticity is denied since few of the ancients quote it, as is also the case with the epistle called Jude's which is itself one of the seven called Catholic; nevertheless we know that these letters have been used publicly with the rest in most churches."[7] Eusebius later ranks Jude as a book of the church that has been spoken against (*Antilegomenōn*) and distinguishes it from the spurious books (*Notha*).[8] Schelkle (p. 144) says that Jude was considered canonical by the end of the second century in Rome, Africa, and Egypt.

On the other hand, there were doubts about the letter. Those who spoke against it objected to its use of noncanonical writings and noted also the limited number of citations of the letter in the literature of the early church. These doubts were overcome, and the worth of the book was recognized by the church. Didymus of Alexandria (c.395) defended the book, and since then little objection to its canonicity has been voiced.

4. Place of Origin

The lack of internal clues makes determining the letter's place of origin a problem. Egypt and Palestine are common guesses.

5. Destination

Since the address is so general—"To those who have been called, who are loved by God the Father and kept by Jesus Christ" (v.1)—it is quite possible that the author

[6]Cf. English text in E. Hennecke and W. Schneemelcher, edd., *New Testament Apocrypha*, 2 vols. [London: Lutterworth, 1963–65], 1:44–45).

[7]*Ecclesiastical History* 2.23.25.

[8]Ibid., 3.25.3.

intended the letter to be circulated to a number of churches. Against this are the internal indications that the author knows the conditions within the church or churches to whom he writes (v.4). It is possible, however, that Jude itinerated and thus knew the dangers affecting the churches of a region or a circuit of churches within a region. The fixing of the destination remains speculative. Asia Minor, Syrian Antioch, or even Palestine are common suggestions.

6. Purpose

Jude had desired to write on the subject of the church's teaching ("the salvation we share," v.3). But he found it necessary to warn his readers concerning innovators who were smuggling false teaching into the churches. Quite likely, these teachers had an itinerant ministry in imitation of the apostles. Both Paul (cf. Gal, Col) and John (cf. 1 and 2 John) faced the problem of false teachers who promoted a different gospel and erroneous instruction.

Jude's purpose is to give a strong denunciation of the errorists. He evidently hopes that by his concise but vigorous exposure of them, the church will see the danger of their error and be alert to the coming judgment on it. Jude also wants to reassure the church by showing that the fact that such scoffers would come was part of the content of apostolic prophecy. In his last paragraphs, he calls the Christians to exercise their faith within the received common instruction. He also praises God as the one who is able to keep both the church and individuals from falling. Christians may have confidence that the God who began a good work of salvation within them (Phil 1:6) will keep them (v.1) and finally bring them safely into his glorious presence (v.24).

The Book of Jude has been called "the most neglected book in the New Testament."[9] There may be various reasons for its neglect, e.g., its brevity, its citation of noncanonical Jewish writings, and its burning denunciation of error. Yet Christians and the church today need to listen to Jude's contribution to biblical revelation. The emphasis on a "fixed" core of truth known as "the faith" needs to be pondered. Jesus is God's Word to man (cf. Rom 6:17; Heb 1:1–4). "God is light; in Him there is no darkness" (1 John 1:5ff.) is the apostle John's summary of the revelation of God in Jesus. God is righteous and true and he hates sin and error.

Contemporary culture is becoming indifferent to the question of truth. Christians have found truth in Jesus (Eph 4:21). Jude warns of the dangers in the mixture of error with this truth. So his eloquent tract for maintaining the purity and truth of the Christian faith is needed in view of the relativity and syncretism so common today. While it must be granted that some Christians have been and are still intolerantly dogmatic about relatively minor theological issues, there is also the great danger of accepting uncritically all teaching or positions as valid and thus compromising God's once-and-for-all self-disclosure in Jesus.

---

[9]Douglas J. Rowston, "The Most Neglected Book in the New Testament," NTS, 21 (July 1975), pp. 554–63.

7. Special Problems

At least two special problems confront the student of Jude: the identity of the heretics and the relation of Jude to 2 Peter. For a discussion of the second problem, see the Introduction to 2 Peter.

Regarding the first problem, the identity of the heretics, Rowston[10] states "that Hermann Werdermann[11] is the only modern scholar to investigate the matter fully." Werdermann called the error "libertine gnosis" and did not identify it with any known system. But since 1913, the time of Werdermann's work, the amount of knowledge concerning Gnosticism has greatly increased.[12] While the exact historical background of Jude is still uncertain, much more information is available (e.g., from Nag Hamadi in Egypt [ancient Chenoboskion]) to supplement previous sources (e.g., Plotinus, Irenaeus, Tertullian, Hippolytus, Origen, Epiphanius, and Clement of Alexandria.[13]

The emerging picture of the world of Gnosticism is very complicated. Generally speaking, the Gnostic world-view was hostile toward the world and all worldly ties. From this perspective, Gnosticism branched into ascetic and libertine divisions. For the libertine Gnostic the idea of "thou shalt" or "thou shalt not" does not come from God (who is absolutely transmundane) but from the Archons (or the demiurges) who are related to this world. Salvation (pneumatic freedom) involves the intentional violation of the rules of the Archons. Gnosticism also could cause a nihilism. In some systems, the Gnostic despaired of this world to such an extent that body and soul were meaningless. Only the acosmic pneuma would transcend this universe to reach the unknown God.

Against this kind of thinking, Jude's strong polemic becomes understandable. The heretics were antinomian; they did not observe Christian moral instruction. Though the false teachers spoke about the pneuma (spirit) and claimed to be spiritual, they were really *psychikoi* ("soulish,' "psychic," "unspiritual") and did not have the "Spirit" (v.19). Their lives gave evidence of bondage to the world, not liberation from it (v.8). Their rejection of Jesus (v.4), their blaspheming of angels (v.8, 10), their complaining and cynicism (v.16) all fit libertine Gnosticism.

The ultimate threat of this Gnostic faith to Christianity lay in its denial of God's revelation in Christ. To follow the Gnostic path led to a radical rejection of all God's Word to man and to a substitution of a different salvation. The means of salvation became an esoteric teaching, and salvation did not free the whole person (body, soul, spirit) from the bondage of sin. This world was negated and the knowledge of the one, true God hidden. Jude's vehement opposition to this kind of error was justified in the light of the significant issues that were involved.

8. Bibliography

(See Bibliography for 1 Peter, pp. 216–17.)

[10] Ibid., p. 554.

[11] "*Die Irrlehrer der Judas und 2 Petrusbriefs* (Gutersloh: C. Bertelsmann, 1913).

[12] Cf. Hans Jonas, *The Gnostic Religion* (Boston: Beacon, 1970).

[13] Ibid., pp. 37–42.

9. Outline

I. The Salutation (1–2)
II. The Reason for the Letter (3–4)
III. The Warning Against the False Teachers (5–16)
   1. Examples of God's Judgment in History (5–7)
   2. The Description and Doom of the False Teachers (8–13)
   3. Enoch's Prophecy of the Coming Judgment (14–16)
IV. The Exhortations to the Believers (17–23)
V. The Doxology (24–25)

Text and Exposition

I. The Salutation

1–2

[1]Jude, a servant of Jesus Christ and a brother of James,

To those who have been called, who are loved by God the Father and kept by Jesus Christ:

[2]Mercy, peace and love be yours in abundance.

1 This brief letter begins with the customary self-identification of the author. He is "Jude" (cf. Introduction: Authorship). There were eight different individuals in the NT with that name; but a process of elimination makes it probable that the Jude of this letter is the brother of Jesus and James (cf. Matt 13:55; Mark 6:3). Modestly he calls himself a "servant" (*doulos;* lit., "slave") of Jesus Christ, and as such he belongs to him. While Jude's being Christ's servant is not without distinction (e.g., "Moses my servant," Josh 1:2), it is probably mentioned here to imply that what he is about to write is what his Master wants him to say. He also calls himself "a brother of James." The self-identification of linking himself to his brother makes sense only if the brother is well known to the recipients of the letter. The James (*Iakōbos*) spoken of here is one of six persons of that name mentioned in the NT and, on the basis of NT evidence, is "the Lord's brother" (cf. Jos. Antiq. XX, 200 [ix. 1]). He was the author of the Epistle of James and became the head of the church in Jerusalem (cf. Introduction: Authorship).

The readers are "the called" (*klētois;* cf. DNTT, 1:271–76), which in Pauline theology stresses the sovereign activity of God's grace in summoning to salvation. The term "the called" is almost synonymous with "a Christian" (Kelly, p. 243). Second, they are "loved by God the Father" (*tois en theō patri ēgapēmenois;* lit., "beloved in God the Father"). Many MSS read "sanctified" (*hēgiasmenois*), which is close in appearance to *ēgapēmenois* and occurs in 1 Corinthians 1:2. These factors may have caused an accidental substitution of the latter for "beloved in God the Father." This reading makes good sense; for the Father, who is love (1 John 4:16), has set his love on his people (cf. Deut 7:6–8). Third, those to whom Jude is writing are "kept [*tetērēmenois*] by Jesus Christ." There is no "by" in the Greek text. Some have argued that the "in" (*en:* NIV, "by") with "God the Father" was displaced (Mayor, EGT, 5:253) and should be taken with Jesus Christ. As the text stands, it could be translated "kept for Jesus Christ," with the thought that God the Father preserves the Christian for his Son (cf. vv.24–25; John 17:15).

2 "Mercy, peace and love be yours in abundance" is typical of the greeting, or prayer, that was customary in ancient letters. Jude omits the word "grace," which is used in the salutations of practically all the other NT letters. Perhaps his reference to "mercy," "peace," and "love" is a way of showing facets of God's grace to men. It seems correct to understand all three as indicative of what God does for us. Mercy is his compassion, peace is his gift of quiet confidence in the work of Jesus, and love is his generosity in granting us his favors and meeting our needs.

II. The Reason for the Letter

3–4

> [3]Dear friends, although I was very eager to write to you about the salvation we share, I felt I had to write and urge you to contend for the faith that was once for all entrusted to the saints. [4]For certain men whose condemnation was written about long ago have secretly slipped in among you. They are godless men, who change the grace of our God into a license for immorality and deny Jesus Christ our only Sovereign and Lord.

3 Jude tells his "dear friends" (*agapētoi;* lit., "loved," "beloved"; cf. vv.17, 20) how he came to write this letter. He had to write a positive statement of the Christian faith. Whether he was actively engaged in writing or only in the process of thinking about it is not clear from the Greek *pasan spoudēn poioumenos graphein* (present participle and infinitive—i.e., "making every effort to write").

"The salvation we share" (*tēs koinēs hēmōn sōtērias;* lit., "our common salvation") is that which all Christians now participate in. First Peter 1:5 speaks of a "salvation that is ready to be revealed in the last time." Both are true. Christians have been saved (Titus 3:5), they now possess salvation (Jude 3; cf. Heb 6:9), and they long for Christ who "will appear a second time, . . . to bring salvation to those who are waiting for him" (Heb 9:28).

By saying "I felt I had to write," Jude explains that a compelling obligation to the people of God prompted him to write for their spiritual good. His letter is intended to exhort the readers to struggle for "the faith that was once for all entrusted to the saints." "To contend" or "struggle" translates *epagōnizesthai,* a word that occurs only here in the NT. However, related words do occur in the NT (cf. TDNT, 1:135–40). The basic meaning of this word is that of the intense effort in a wrestling match (cf. *agōnizomenos* in 1 Cor 9:25). The verb form is a present infinitive, showing that the Christian struggle is to be continuous.

"The faith" is the body of truth that very early in the church's history took on a definite form (cf. Acts 2:42; Rom 6:17; Gal 1:23). Without doubt, the form of the faith as a body of recognized truth became clearer as time passed. Jude stresses that this faith has been entrusted "once for all" (*hapax*) to the "saints" (*tois hagiois*—the ones set apart by God for himself). Basically the Christian faith cannot be changed; its foundation truths are not negotiable. (This conviction is not, of course, peculiar to Jude; see the similar emphasis in Gal 1:6–9 and in 2 John 9.)

4 Jude goes on to explain the reasons why he was compelled to write. Ungodly men had "secretly slipped in" (*pareisedysan,* "crept in unawares") among the believers. Paul uses the related word *pareisaktos* of Judaizers who had "infiltrated" Christian congregations to spy on their freedom in Christ Jesus (Gal 2:4). Concerning these men, the Greek says *hoi palai progegrammenoi eis touto to krima,* which KJV translates as "who were before of old ordained to this condemnation," while NIV has "men whose condemnation was written about long ago." The word *prographō* means to "write before," either in the same document or in a previous one. The reference could be to God's writing down from eternity the destiny (i.e., the reprobation or punishment) of the wicked. But it is more likely that it refers to previously written predictions about the doom of the apostates (so Mayor, p. 24; BAG, p. 711; contra Schrenk, TDNT, 1:772).

After stating the destiny of these men, Jude describes them as "impious" or "ungodly" (*asebeis*), a term often used of notorious sinners. This general word is made more specific by the two specific charges that follow. First, they "change the grace of our God into a license for immorality." Evidently their understanding of grace and perhaps of the forgiveness of sins led them to feel free to indulge in all forms of sexual depravity (*aselgeian*, cf. comments at 2 Peter 2:2). Second, they "deny Jesus Christ our only Sovereign and Lord." Exactly how they deny Jesus Christ, Jude does not say. Certainly they denied him by their immoral living that ran counter to his commands. Perhaps also they denied him in their teaching of a Christology that denied either his full humanity or his full deity. NIV's translation of *ton monon despotēn kai kyrion hēmōn Iēsoun Christon* ("Jesus Christ our only Sovereign and Lord") is defensible because of the one article (*ton*) with two nouns and the use of *despotēs* in 2 Peter 2:1 in reference to Christ. However, *despotēs* is commonly used of the Father (Luke 2:29; Acts 4:24; and LXX), and the word "only" (*monon*) makes it more difficult to apply *despotēs* to Jesus. Thus the translation would be "the only Sovereign [the Father] and our Lord Jesus Christ." If this is adopted, then the error of the godless men was more likely a moral rather than a theological one (cf. Titus 1:16; "They claim to know God, but by their actions they deny him").

III. The Warning Against the False Teachers (5–16)

1. *Examples of God's Judgment in History*

5–7

[5]Though you already know all this, I want to remind you that the Lord delivered his people out of Egypt, but later destroyed those who did not believe. [6]And the angels who did not keep their positions of authority but abandoned their own home—these he has kept in darkness, bound with everlasting chains for judgment on the great Day. [7]In a similar way, Sodom and Gomorrah and the surrounding towns gave themselves up to sexual immorality and perversion. They serve as an example of those who suffer the punishment of eternal fire.

5 As did Peter in 2 Peter 1:12, Jude states that his readers already know what he is about to say but that he will remind them of it. So he gives them three examples of the Lord's judgments: on the unbelievers at the time of the Exodus, on the fallen angels, and on Sodom and Gomorrah. In each instance the objects of judgment are notable rebels against the Lord. In v.5 there is a difficult textual problem (cf. Notes). However, NIV gives the sense.

The first example is that of Israel, who experienced the great display of God's grace in the Exodus, saw and heard his revelation at Sinai, and received his care in the wilderness; yet a number of them disbelieved and rebelled. Obviously this is not an instance of people being saved and then losing their salvation. Jude describes the rebels as "those who did not believe" (*tous mē pisteusantas*). The Israelites were physically delivered from bondage, not by their faith as a nation, but by God's covenant love and mercy. The warning in this judgment is against unbelief and rebellion.

6 The second example is of the fallen angels. The most likely reference here is to the angels ("sons of God," cf. Gen 6:4; Job 1:6; 2:1) who came to earth and mingled with women. This interpretation is expounded in the pseudepigraphical Book of Enoch (7; 9.8; 10.11; 12.4), from which Jude quotes in v.14, and is common in the intertestamental literature and the early church fathers (e.g., Justin *Apology* 2.5). These angels "did not keep their positions of authority" (*tēn heautōn archēn*). The use of the word *archē* for "rule," "dominion," or "sphere" is uncommon but appears to be so intended here (cf. BAG, p. 112). The implication is that God assigned angels stipulated responsibilities (*archē*, "dominion") and a set place (*oikētērion*). But because of their rebellion, God has kept or reserved (*tetērēken*—perfect tense) these fallen angels in darkness and in eternal chains awaiting final judgment. Apparently some fallen angels are in bondage while others are unbound and active among mankind as demons.

7 The third example of judgment is that of the cities of the plain, Sodom and Gomorrah. In v.7 NIV is so concise that it slides over the significance of the pronoun "these" (*toutois*). Kelly (p. 253) translates this verse thus: "Just as Sodom and Gommorah and the surrounding cities, which practiced immorality in the same way as these and lusted after different flesh, stand out as an example, undergoing as they do a punishment of everlasting fire." The key factors are "these" (*toutois*—masculine, referring to "angels" [v. 6], not cities [feminine], and the words "different flesh" (*sarkos heteras*). Thus the sin of Sodom and Gomorrah was seeking union with "different flesh" in a way similar to what the "sons of God" (angels?) did (Gen 6:2) when they mingled with "the daughters of men" (humans).

Normally angels do not marry, nor do they have substantial bodies, though at times they have assumed bodies or appeared in a bodily form as divine messengers (Gen 19:1ff.; Zech 1:9ff.; 2:1ff.; Matt 28:2ff.; Mark 16:5; Luke 24:4ff.; John 20:12ff.; Acts 1:10f.). In Genesis 19 angelic messengers in the form of men visited Sodom; and the men of the city, motivated by their homosexuality and supposing the messengers to be men, desired them. So they "went after different flesh." God destroyed the cities of the plain by raining fire and brimstone from heaven on the cities (Gen 19:24)—possibly the divine use of a natural catastrophe associated with the volcanic activity of the area.

Notes

5 This verse has suffered confusion in the history of the transmission. UBS (3d ed.) lists nine different readings and gives its choice as πάντα, ὅτι ὁ κύριος ἅπαξ (*panta, hoti ho kyrios hapax*, "all things, that the Lord once"). Nestle (26th ed.) follows UBS. Other readings replace κύριος (*kyrios*, "Lord") with θεὸς (*theos*, "God"), Ἰησους (*Iēsous*, "Jesus"), or even θεὸς Χριστός (*theos Christos*, "God Christ"). The Byzantine tradition has ἅπαξ τοῦτο ὅτι ὁ κύριος (*hapax touto, hoti ho kyrios*, "once this, that the Lord"). It appears that *kyrios* is correct, that *panta* ("all things") is to be accepted above *touto* ("this"), and that *hapax* ("once") is being used in a series with τὸ δεύτερον (*to deuteron*, "second," "second time").

2. The Description and Doom of the False Teachers

8–13

[8]In the very same way, these dreamers pollute their own bodies, reject authority and slander celestial beings. [9]But even the archangel Michael, when he was disputing with the devil about the body of Moses, did not dare to bring a slanderous accusation against him, but said, "The Lord rebuke you!" [10]Yet these men speak abusively against whatever they do not understand; and what things they do understand by instinct, like unreasoning animals—these are the very things that destroy them.

[11]Woe to them! They have taken the way of Cain; they have rushed for profit into Balaam's error; they have been destroyed in Korah's rebellion.

[12]These men are blemishes at your love feasts, eating with you without the slightest qualm—shepherds who feed only themselves. They are clouds without rain, blown along by the wind; autumn trees, without fruit and uprooted—twice dead. [13]They are wild waves of the sea, foaming up their shame; wandering stars, for whom blackest darkness has been reserved forever.

8 Jude now links the examples of God's judgment (vv.5–7) to the false teachers whom he calls "dreamers" (*enypniazomenoi*). Though this word might refer to pretensions of prophecy, it more likely refers to their carnal sin that leads them to live in a dream world. "In the very same way" (*homoiōs mentoi kai houtoi*) points back to the sins of Sodom and Gomorrah (v.7). The false teachers pollute "their own bodies" (lit., "flesh") in various forms of sexual excess, doubtless including homosexuality. Their rejection of authority (*kyriotēta,* "lordship") implies that they repudiated Jesus as Lord (*kyrios*) over their lives.

The third sin of these false teachers is that they "slander celestial beings." How and why, Jude does not say. Perhaps their materialistic and fleshy bent led them to deny all spiritual forces—good or evil.

9 The false teachers should have learned from the example of the archangel Michael. Oral tradition and apocryphal literature tell of a struggle over Moses' body. According to Clement of Alexandria (*Adumbr. in Ep. Judae*), Origen (*De princ.* 3.2.1), and Didymus of Alexandria (*In Ep. canon brevis enarr.*), Jude is quoting from the apocyphal Assumption of Moses, only small portions of which have survived. Accordingly, the devil, it seems, claimed the right to the body because of Moses' sin of murder (Exod 2:12) or because he (the devil) considered himself the Lord of the earth. Michael is mentioned in Revelation 12:7, and 1 Thessalonians 4:16 refers to "the voice of the archangel." In Daniel 10:13, 21 and 12:1, Michael is a great prince or mightly angel for Israel. Yet in spite of Michael's power and dignity, he dared not bring a "slanderous accusation" against the devil but referred the dispute to the sovereignty of God. So if he, a mighty archangel, had respect for celestial powers, Jude is saying, how much more should the mere human false teachers do so? (On the struggle over Moses' body, cf. TDNT, 4:866, n. 211.)

10 "Yet these men" (*houtoi de*) connotes contempt. They, unlike Michael, presume to speak evil against what they know nothing about. (Later, in v.19, Jude explains that they do not have the Spirit.) These "dreamers," however, do have knowledge, but only on the instinctual level of animal passion. So like the "unreasoning animals" (*aloga zōa*), they are destroyed (by God) through the things they practice.

11 Again Jude turns to the OT—this time for another triad of examples. Because of their coming judgment, he pronounces "woe" (*ouai*) on the false teachers as Jesus did on the scribes and Pharisees (Matt 23:13, 15–16, 23, 25, 27, 29).

1. The false teachers have "taken [*eporeuthēsan*] the way of Cain." The verb *poreuomai* connotes a moral or religious "walk" (cf. TDNT, 6:575). Cain's way was the religion of his own works without faith (Heb 11:4) and led to the hatred and murder of his brother (1 John 3:12–13). Like Cain, these men belong to the evil one, manufacture religion, and kill the souls of men by error.

2. They have abandoned themselves to Balaam's error (cf. comments on 2 Peter 2:15–16). Balaam was the prototype of all greedy religionists who lead God's people into false religion and immorality (cf. the events at Baal-Peor, Num 31:16–19). The combination of *exechythēsan* (passive from *ekcheō*, "pour on," here, "abandoned themselves"; NIV, "they have rushed") and *planē* ("error") indicates that the false teachers were wholly consumed by their love of money.

3. "They have been destroyed in Korah's rebellion." Numbers 16:1–35 tells of the drastic punishment inflicted on Korah, Dathan, Abiram, and 250 other rebels against Moses' authority. So, with a bold disregard of anachronism, Jude says of the false teachers, "They have been destroyed [*apōlonto*, the aorist tense, i.e., completed action] in Korah's rebellion." It is a striking way of saying that their doom is certain and settled.

12–13 Now, with burning eloquence, Jude piles figure upon figure (six of them in all) to describe the errorists:

1. The false teachers are "blemishes at your love feasts." Translators are divided on which of the two usages of *spilas* (cf. BAG, MM) is preferable here. Some (e.g., Alford, Weymouth, NASB, Kelly [p. 269]) render it "rocks" or "hidden rocks"; others (e.g., KJV, RSV, NEB, NIV, TEV) render it "spots" or "blemishes." In either case, the metaphor is a striking one. The rendering "hidden rocks" connotes the danger of shipwreck of the faith; "spots" or "blemishes" parallels 2 Peter 2:13 and connotes defilement. The "love feasts" were communal meals in which the early church ate together and observed the Lord's Supper. "Eating with you" is too tame a translation of *syneuōchoumenoi*; with its connotation of sumptuous eating, it might better be translated "feasting with you." "Without the slightest qualm" (*aphobōs*, lit., "without fear") means that the false teachers do not recognize the terror of the Lord against those who mock his Son's death shown in the Supper (cf. 1 Cor 11:27–32; Heb 10:26–31).

2. Jude goes on to depict the false teachers as "shepherds who feed only themselves"—a figure that points to all the biblical warnings against the false shepherds who care nothing for the flock (e.g., Ezek 34:8; John 10:12–13).

3. They are like clouds that promise rain but are "blown along by the wind" and "without rain" (*anydroi*, lit., "waterless"). Thus the false teachers are wind, devoid of refreshment, promise, and performance.

4. They are, Jude says, like fruit trees in late autumn, long past the harvest, bearing no fruit. Furthermore, they are trees not only fruitless but also uprooted—thus "twice dead."

5. Next is the metaphor of the restless sea (v.13). For modern man, the sea is often a thing of beauty; to ancient man, less able to cope with the sea's fury, it was a terror. (Rev 21:1, with its promise of no more sea, reflects this attitude.) Isaiah (57:20) compares the wicked to the sea: "The wicked are like the tossing sea, which cannot

rest, whose waters cast up mire and mud." The errorists are busy, restless, untamed. Their product is like the foam or scum at the seashore. "Foaming" (*epaphrizō*) is another of Jude's words that occur in the NT only in his book.

6. The final metaphor (*asteres planētai*, "wandering star") is astronomical. The ancients called the planets "wandering stars" because of their movements. The reference here could be to meteors, shooting stars, comets, or planets; but planets is the most likely meaning. An unpredictable star would provide no guidance for navigation; so false teachers are useless and untrustworthy. Their doom is the eternal darkness that is reserved for them (cf. 2 Peter 2:4).

3. *Enoch's Prophecy of the Coming Judgment*

14–16

[14]Enoch, the seventh from Adam, prophesied about these men: "See, the Lord is coming with thousands upon thousands of his holy ones [15]to judge everyone, and to convict all the ungodly of all the ungodly acts they have done in the ungodly way, and of all the harsh words ungodly sinners have spoken against him." [16]These men are grumblers and faultfinders; they follow their own evil desires; they boast about themselves and flatter others for their own advantage.

14 Enoch, who "walked with God; then he was no more, because God took him away" (Gen 5:24), is not specifically called "the seventh from Adam" in the OT. But in Genesis 5 and also in 1 Chronicles 1:1–3, he is the seventh in order (counting Adam as the first). Here, however, Jude quotes not Genesis but the Book of Enoch (also called "The Ethiopic Book of Enoch")—the longest of the surviving Jewish pseudepigraphical writings and a work that was highly respected by Jews and many Christians. Those who wonder about the propriety of Jude's quotation of this noncanonical book should note that he does not call it Scripture. Paul also quoted from noncanonical writers statements he considered true. See Acts 17:28, where he quoted Cleanthes and Aratus (*Phaenomena* 5); 1 Corinthians 15:33, where he quoted Menander (*Thais* 218); and Titus 1:12, where he quoted Epimenides (*De oraculis*). Lawlor (p. 102) argues that Jude is not quoting the Book of Enoch but a prophecy of his given to Jude by inspiration. This is possible, of course, but unnecessary. The prophecy does not give any startling new information but is simply a general description of the return of the Lord in judgment (cf. Deut 33:2; Dan 7:10–14; Zech 14:5; Matt 25:31).

15–16 The stress is on two words, each used four times: "all" (*pantōn*) and "ungodly" (*asebeia, asebeō, asebēs;* cf. v.4). Jude finds Enoch's prophecy a good summary of the universal divine judgment on the impious and all their deeds.

Verse 16 completes Jude's denunciation of the false teachers as "grumblers" (*gongystai*). In 1 Corinthians 10:10 the related verb *gongyzō* is used by Paul of the rebels in the wilderness (cf. LXX Exod 16–17; Num 14–17; cf. also TNDT, 1:728–37). Jude also calls the false teachers "faultfinders" (*mempsimoiroi*), a term that underlines their critical attitude and habitual complaining. (Both *gongystai* and *mempsimoiroi* occur only here in the NT.) "They follow their own evil desires" might be translated "they live by their passions." "They boast about themselves" is literally "and their mouth speaks haughty [or bombastic] words," which reminds one of Antiochus Epiphanes (cf. Dan 7:8–11; 11:36). "Flatter others for their own advantage" reinforces Jude's stress on the venality of the false teachers. Here the literal sense of the Greek text ("honoring faces for the sake of advantage") is highly picturesque.

IV. The Exhortations to the Believers

17–23

[17]But, dear friends, remember what the apostles of our Lord Jesus Christ foretold.
[18]They said to you, "In the last times there will be scoffers who will follow their own
ungodly desires." [19]These are the men who divide you, who follow mere natural
instincts and do not have the Spirit.
[20]But you, dear friends, build yourselves up in your most holy faith and pray in
the Holy Spirit. [21]Keep yourselves in God's love as you wait for the mercy of our
Lord Jesus Christ to bring you to eternal life. [22]Be merciful to those who doubt;
[23]snatch others from the fire and save them; to others show mercy, mixed with
fear—hating even the clothing stained by corrupted flesh.

17–18 "But, dear friends" (*hymeis de, agapētoi;* lit., "but you, beloved") makes the transition from the burning denunciation in vv.8–16 to the preparation of the believers for their necessary struggles. They must remember (cf. v.5; 2 Peter 1:12–15) the previously spoken words of the apostles. The apostles (the Twelve plus Paul) must have had a wide ministry of which we have little knowledge, and their preaching was part of the oral deposit of faith for the early churches. One of their prophecies was a prediction of mockers in the last time who would live ungodly lives. So the church was to be vigilant, for the last time was seen to be at hand and the ungodly mockers on the scene. The "last time" (Gr., singular) is the age of messianic salvation and judgment that culminates in the judgments of the Second Advent. Since the apostles have predicted this time, the church should not be surprised or discouraged but prepare itself for action.

19 Again Jude returns to his triadic pattern of describing the false teachers.

1. He calls them "men who divide you" (*apodiorizontes*). This extremely rare word (only here in the NT) may mean that "they made distinctions," perhaps as the later Gnostics divided Christians by classifying them into groups of initiates ("spiritual") and lesser ones, which translates the word *psychikoi*.

2. Next he calls them men "who follow mere natural instincts," *psychikoi* (lit., "soulish," "psychic," "unspiritual"; cf. BAG, p. 902; TDNT, 9:656–63). *Psychikoi* was very likely used by the Gnostics as a slander of the orthodox when the fact was that they themselves were living on the natural level. Here Jude turns the word against the false teachers. The church today is plagued by false teachers claiming superior knowledge and experience; yet their lives are often worse than those of the average pagan.

3. Finally he says that they "do not have the Spirit" (*pneuma*). *Pneuma* is without the definite article (*ho*) in Greek—a fact that has led some to translate this as "they do not have a spirit" and teach that man is dichotomous until conversion, when he becomes trichotomous. But this view is without biblical support. The use of *pneuma* without the article for the Holy Spirit is common in the NT (cf. John 3:5; 7:39; Gal 5:16). In spite of all their vaunted claims and teaching, the false teachers are devoid of the Holy Spirit.

20–21 The repetition of "beloved" (*agapētoi;* NIV, "dear friends") personalizes the message and redirects attention back to the believers. (In v.17 Jude had started his exhortations to the faithful but returned to one final salvo against his opponents.) Now he gives them a fourfold exhortation for their spiritual profit.

1. Christians are to be "building themselves up" (*epoikodomountes*, present participle) in their "most holy faith." In the NT "the faith" is the orthodox body of truth and practice from the apostles (cf. Acts 2:42; 20:32; Rom 6:17). It is "most holy" because the Spirit gave it concerning God's "holy servant Jesus" (Acts 4:27, 30). Christians build themselves by having fellowship with the Lord and his people, by continuing in the gospel and in the Word of God, and by worship—especially by remembering the Lord at his table.

2. Christians are to be praying (present participle) in the Holy Spirit (cf. Rom 8:26–27; Gal 4:6; Eph 6:18). Because all believers have the Spirit, they are to pray according to the Spirit's will (set forth in the written Word and made known by inner promptings) to accomplish God's work by God's power.

3. Christians are to keep themselves in God's love (v.21; cf. vv.1–2). The realm of God's love is in Jesus Christ; those who depart from Christ depart from the love of God. Those who reject the commands of Jesus reject his love (cf. John 15:10: "If you obey my commands, you will remain in my love").

4. Christians are to keep their attention fixed on the "mercy of our Lord Jesus Christ [that brings them] to eternal life." True eschatology keeps present reality in focus. The mention of mercy reminds Christians that salvation is never a matter of good works and that only in Christ is their hope of salvation (cf. comments on v.3). "Eternal life" in this verse refers to the future aspects of the presently enjoyed salvation.

22–23 These verses contain certain minor textual problems. The most important is whether three groups are in view (NIV, UBS 3d ed., Nestle 26th ed.) or only two (Nestle 25th ed., B, Clement of Alexandria). The shorter reading of B is split against other good members of its family (e.g., 1739). The stronger MS support for the longer reading is also reinforced by the triadic pattern of Jude's thought. Accepting the longer text, the three groups are (1) those who are hesitating (according to most texts), (2) those who need to be saved from the fire, and (3) those who need pity because of contamination.

The first command is to show mercy to those who are doubting (or hesitating). This group of people are "at odds with themselves" (reading *diakrinomenous* and understanding this verb as "doubt" or "waver" rather than "dispute"). The teaching and example of the false teachers have caused them to be uncertain about the truth of Christianity. They must be dealt with patiently and mercifully by showing them Christian love. The second group needs to be dealt with directly and vigorously. Salvation is God's work, and here Christians are portrayed as God's instruments for snatching brands out of the fire (cf. Zech 3:3). The picture is of a person slipping into the eternal fire but rescued from error by the grace and truth of God.

The final group of people appears to be deep in the immorality of the false teachers. Their very clothing is "stained by corrupted flesh." Perhaps the figure is that their depravity has made them infectious. Christians are to show mercy as in the first case, but now they are to be fearful lest the infection spread to them. Yet even here God's wondrous grace can exchange the excrement-covered garments (cf. Zech 3:3, Heb. text) for festive garments of righteousness. For no one, not even the most defiled sinner, is beyond salvation through faith in Christ's redeeming work.

V. The Doxology

24–25

[24]To him who is able to keep you from falling and to present you before his glorious presence without fault and with great joy— [25]to the only God our Savior be glory, majesty, power and authority, through Jesus Christ our Lord, before all ages, now and forevermore! Amen.

24 Jude's message of warning and doom might have depressed and discouraged his readers. Beset by so much false teaching and immorality, how can Christians ever reach heaven? The answer lies only in the power of God. So this doxology, surely one of the greatest in the NT, reminds us of God's ability to bring every one of his own safely to himself. God "is able to keep [us] from falling" (or "stumbling"). Furthermore, he is able "to present [us] before his glorious presence [lit., 'his glory'] without fault" (*amomos,* used of Christ as a faultless lamb in 1 Peter 1:19; cf. comments there). "With great joy" (*agalliasei*) is the response of Christians for their completed salvation (cf. DNTT, 2:354).

25 "To the only God our Savior" points to the monotheistic nature of the faith by showing that the Father is the Savior as well as the Son. Whatever the false teachers may say, there is only one God and Savior. To "God our Savior . . . through Jesus Christ our Lord" (notice the intimate pronouns "our . . . our") belong four attributes: (1) "glory" (*doxa*), a word with many associations and connotations difficult to capture in a few words—perhaps "radiance" or "moral splendor" comes close to its meaning (cf. DNTT, 2:44–48; TDNT, 2:232–55); (2) "majesty" (*megalōsynē*), which refers to God's greatness (Kelly [p. 293] suggests "awful transcendence"); (3) "power" (*kratos*); and (4) "authority" (*exousia*)—the last two stressing his might and "the sovereign freedom of actions He enjoys as Creator" (Kelly, p. 293). The solemn time notation "before all ages, now and forevermore" indicates that these attributes of God suffer no change and that therefore his divine plan will surely be carried out. Salvation is completely secure because God's own purpose stands and because he is able to do all that he wills (Isa 46:9–10).

REVELATION

Alan Johnson

REVELATION

Introduction

1. General Nature and Historical Background

The Book of Revelation fascinates and also perplexes the modern reader. For the present generation, it is the most obscure and controversial book in the Bible. Yet those who study it with care agree that it is a unique source of Christian teaching and one of timeless relevance. Accordingly, Swete says, "The Apocalypse offers to the pastors of the church an unrivaled store of materials for Christian teaching, if only the book is approached with an assurance of its prophetic character, chastened by a frank acceptance of the light which the growth of knowledge has cast and will continue to cast upon it" (p. viii). Indeed, it may well be that with the exception of the Gospels, the Apocalypse is the most profound and moving teaching on Christian doctrine and discipleship found anywhere in Holy Scripture.

Neither the fanaticism of some who have fixed their attention on prophecy but not on Christ, nor the diversity of interpretative viewpoints should discourage us from pursuing Christian truth in the marvelous book.

The title of the last book of the NT sheds light on its character. Revelation differs in kind from the other NT writings. The difference is not in doctrine but in literary genre and subject matter. It is a book of prophecy (1:3; 22:7, 18–19) that involves both warning and consolation—announcements of future judgment and blessing. For communicating its message, the Lord uses symbol and vision.

Why did the Lord use a method that seemingly makes his message so obscure? The answer is twofold. First, the language and imagery were not so strange to first-century readers as they are to many today. Faced with the apocalyptic style of the book, the modern reader who knows little about biblical literature and its parallels is like a person who, though unfamiliar with stocks and bonds, tries to understand the Dow-Jones reports. Therefore, familiarity with the prophetic books of the OT (especially Dan and Ezek), apocalyptic literature current during the first century, the

DSS, and the Targums (paraphrases of the OT into Aram. and Gr.) will help the reader grasp the message of the Apocalypse. (See the commentary for references to these cognate materials.)

Second, the subject matter, with its glimpses into the future and even into heaven itself, required the kind of language John used. Only through symbolism and imagery can we gain some understanding of the things the Lord was unveiling through the writer John. Moreover, while the symbolic and visionary mode of presentation creates ambiguity and frustration for many of us, it actually conduces to evocative description of unseen realities with a poignancy and clarity unattainable by any other method. For example, "evil" is an abstract term, but a woman "drunk with the blood of the saints" graphically sets forth the concrete and more terrible aspect of this reality. Such language can trigger all sorts of ideas, associations, existential involvement, and mystical responses that the straight prose found in much of the NT cannot attain.

The letters to the seven churches in the Roman province of Asia, modern Turkey, specifically locate the recipients of the book and give some broad indication of the historical situation. Some of the churches were experiencing persecution (2:10, 13). From this it has been customary to assume that persecution was quite intense and widespread. Revelation is then viewed as a "tract for the times" document, warning Christians against emperor worship and encouraging them to be faithful to Christ even to death. Recent studies, however, question how intense, widespread, or sustained the persecution was, even under Domitian.[1] Thus the primary occasion for the writing of the book must be sought elsewhere than in the persecution of that time.

The letters to the churches imply that five of the seven had serious problems. The major problem seemed to be disloyalty to Christ. This may indicate that the major thrust of Revelation is not sociopolitical but theological. John is more concerned with countering the heresy that was creeping into the churches toward the close of the first century than in addressing the political situation. Newman suggests that this heresy could well have been Gnosticism, an idea he derives from a critical study of Irenaeus's statements in the second century about the Book of Revelation.[2]

Revelation is also commonly viewed as belonging to the body of nonbiblical Jewish writings known as apocalyptic literature. The name for this type of literature (some nineteen books) is derived from the word "revelation" (*apocalypsis*) in Revelation 1:1 (q.v.). The extrabiblical apocalyptic books were written in the period from 200 B.C. to A.D. 200. Usually scholars stress the similarities of the Apocalypse of John to these noncanonical books—similarities such as the use of symbolism and vision, the mention of angelic mediators of the revelation, the bizarre images, the expectation of divine judgment, the emphasis on the kingdom of God, the new heavens and earth, and the dualism of this age and the age to come. Although numerous similarities exist, John's writing also has some clear differences from these writings, and these differences must not be overlooked.[3]

---

[1]F.F. Bruce, *New Testament History* (New York: Doubleday, 1972), pp. 412–13; Barclay Newman, "The Fallacy of the Domitian Hypothesis," NTS, 10 (1963), 133–39; G. Edmundson, *The Church in Rome in the First Century* (London: Longmans, Green, 1913).

[2]Newman, "Domitian Hypothesis," pp. 133–39; also his "A Consideration of the Apocalypse as an Anti-Gnostic Document" (Th.D. diss., Southern Baptist Theological Seminary, 1959) and *Rediscovering the Book of Revelation* (Valley Forge: Judson, 1968); also W. Foerster, TDNT, 3:135, n.11; Minear, *I Saw a New Earth*, pp. 250–56; cf. discussion at ch. 13 introduction.

[3]The literature on recent apocalyptic discussion is extensive. See esp. D.S. Russell, *The Method and Message of Jewish Apocalyptic* (Philadelphia: Westminster, 1964); idem, *Apocalyptic Ancient and Modern*

Unlike the Jewish and Jewish-Christian apocalyptic books, the Apocalypse of John clearly claims to be a book of prophecy (1:3; 22:7, 10, 18–19), the effect of which is to identify the message, as in the OT prophetic tradition, with the Word of God (1:2; 19:9). The Jewish apocalyptists used the literary form of prophecy to trace the course of history from ancient times down to their own day. John does not follow this method. He clearly places himself in the contemporary world of the first century and speaks of the future eschatological consummation in much the same way as Ezekiel and Jeremiah did. While extrabiblical apocalypses are clearly pseudonymous (e.g., Enoch, Abraham, Ezra, Baruch, et al.), the last book of the NT is plainly attributed to John. It does not, however, explicitly identify him as being well known or an apostle. Many of the noncanonical apocalyptic works are ethically passive; they blame the immediate plight of God's people, not on their unfaithfulness, but on the pervasive presence of evil in the world. While Revelation is not lacking in words of encouragement to the faithful, it also strongly urges the churches to repent.

Finally, and importantly, these apocalypses are pessimistic concerning the outcome of God's present activity in the world; and for hope they look wholly to the eschatological end, when God will once again intervene and defeat the evil in the world. Though Revelation is often read in this manner, there are great differences between it and the noncanonical apocalypses. In the latter, the turning point of history is the future event of the Messiah's coming as a conquering warrior-king. In Revelation the climactic event has already occurred in the victory of the slain Lamb (ch. 5). Now, however, the Lamb's victory is being worked out in history in the obedient suffering of his followers (12:11; 15:2). Their deaths are seen in Revelation as a part of the victory over evil that God is already effecting in the world. This partial victory through the suffering of the saints is combined with the hope of the final unambiguous victory of God at the end of history.

By viewing history in this way, the book makes clear that the source of Christian hope is not imminent in history itself but relates to a transcendent future. For John, there is no evolutionary progress of righteousness in history. Therefore, any identification of the Apocalypse with the writings of the extrabiblical apocalyptists must be

---

(Philadelphia: Fortress, 1978); Klaus Koch, *The Rediscovery of Apocalyptic*, Second Series, no. 22 (Naperville, Ill.: Allenson, 1972); Paul D. Hanson, *The Dawn of Apocalyptic* (Philadelphia: Fortress, 1975); idem, "Apocalypse," "Apocalyptic," IDB, 5:27–34; John J. Collins, who takes the position that the difference between Revelation and the Jewish apocalyptic writings are superficial except in the former's reference to the earthly Jesus, "Pseudonymity, Historical Reviews and the Genre of the Revelation of John," CBQ, 39 (March 1977), 329–43; idem, ed., *Apocalypse: The Morphology of a Genre*, Semeia 14 (Missoula, Mont.: Scholar's, 1979; J.H. Charlesworth, *The Pseudepigrapha in Modern Research* (Missoula, Mont.: Scholar's, 1976). For the primary documents, see R.H. Charles, *The Apocrypha and Pseudepigrapha of the Old Testament*, 2 vols. (Oxford: Clarendon, 1913) and J.H. Charlesworth, ed., *The Pseudepigrapha of the Old Testament* (Garden City, N.Y.: Doubleday, 1980). Those who point out the difference between the Apocalypse of John and other apocalyptic literature are G.E. Ladd, "The Revelation and Jewish Apocalyptic," EQ, 29 (1957), 95–100; idem, "Why Not Prophetic-Apocalyptic?" JBL, 76 (1957), 192–200; idem, "Apocalyptic and NT Theology," in *Reconciliation and Hope*, ed. Robert Banks (Grand Rapids: Eerdmans, 1974), pp. 285–96; James Kallas, "The Apocalypse—An Apocalyptic Book?" JBL, 86, (1967), 69–80; Leon Morris, *Apocalyptic* (Grand Rapids: Eerdmans, 1972), pp. 78–81; idem, *Revelation of St. John*, TNTC (Grand Rapids: Eerdmans, 1969), pp. 23–25. See esp. Elisabeth S. Fiorenza, *The Apocalypse* (Chicago: Franciscan Herald, 1976), who emphasizes that the book is a "Christian Prophetic-Apocalyptic Circular letter" (pp. 14–26). See also idem, "Composition and Structure of the Book of Revelation," CBQ, 39 (March 1977), 344–66. For a good survey of recent Roman Catholic views on Revelation, see John J. Pilch, *What Are They Saying About the Book of Revelation?* (New York: Paulist, 1978).

severely qualified. Indeed, the reader would do well to reexamine every method of interpreting Revelation that rests on this assumed similarity. For example, is it truly a "tract for the times" as other apocalyptic books, or should this supposed connection be questioned and the book freed to speak its own message about realities that are far more determinative of world events than immediate political powers?

John was no doubt quite familiar with the Jewish apocalyptists of the intertestamental period, and in some instances there seems to be a direct allusion to them (cf. comments at 2:7). But the relation is in general superficial. Only twice is an interpreting angel involved in the explanation of a vision (chs. 7 and 17), a feature constantly present in the other kind of apocalyptic writing. In no case can it be demonstrated that John depends on the assumed knowledge among his readers of the Jewish apocalyptists for clarity of meaning.[4] On the other hand, he is everywhere dependent on the OT canonical books, especially those where symbol and vision play a dominant role, such as portions of Isaiah, Ezekiel, Daniel, and Zechariah.

Although throughout the following pages frequent references to noncanonical apocalyptic literature appear, they are given as aids in understanding the background of John's writing and should not be taken as sources of his thought or method in the same way that the inspired canonical Scriptures influenced him.

Ladd's suggestion that we create a new category called "Prophetic-Apocalyptic" to distinguish canonical materials from the late Jewish apocalyptics, if not so much in form, certainly in world view, has much merit. Thus, in Ladd's view, the beast of chapters 13 and 17 is historical Rome, but it is far larger than the ancient city and is also the future Antichrist. The references to the persecution of Christians likewise go far beyond the known historical situation of John's day. Evil at the hands of Rome is realized eschatology. Recently this view has been held also by others.[5] The commentary on chapters 13 and 17 will reveal sympathy for Ladd's break with the dominant preterist interpretation while at the same time arguing that the preterist-futurist viewpoint, like that of the preterist, rests on the questionable assumption that John's Apocalypse is describing historical-political entities rather than theological archetypes (see Introduction: Interpretative Schemes; cf. also the introductions to chs. 13 and 17).

Much more important than the late Jewish apocalyptic sources is the debt John owes to the eschatological teaching of Jesus, such as the Olivet Discourse (Matt 24–25; Mark 13; Luke 21). The parallelism is striking and certainly not accidental. In the commentary, these connections are dealt with in more detail (cf. introduction to 6:1ff.). In short, we believe that the ultimate source of John's understanding of the future as well as his interpretation of the OT lies not in his own inventive imagination but definitely in Jesus of Nazareth.[6]

---

[4]J. Julius Scott, Jr., likewise arrives at the same conclusion for the connection between Paul and the apocalyptists: "Paul and Late-Jewish Eschatology—A Case Study, 1 Thess 4:13–18 and 2 Thess 2:1–12," JETS, 15 (1972), 3:133–43. See also Mounce, *Revelation*, pp. 18–25.

[5]See n.4; see also Ladd, *Commentary on Revelation*, pp. 8–10; idem, BDT, p. 53; Morris, *Revelation of St. John*, p. 24; Beasley-Murray, "The Revelation," pp. 1279ff.

[6]The development of this parallelism with the Olivet Discourse has been noted by Austin Farrer, *The Revelation of St. John the Divine* (Oxford: Clarendon, 1964), pp. 31–32; Swete, pp. cli-clii; Beckwith, pp. 139–40 and most recently by Louis A. Vos, *The Synoptic Traditions in the Apocalypse* (Kampen: J.H. Kok, 1965).

2. Unity

The question of the unity of Revelation is a relative one. Even Charles, who consistently advances a fragmentary approach to the book, recognizes the pervading unity of thought in the majority of the material (*Commentary on Revelation*, 1:lxxxviiif.). Likewise Ford, who views the book as originating from three different authors, nevertheless insists that it displays an amazing and masterly literary unity that she ascribes to the work of still another person, an editor (p. 46).

The evidence that allegedly argues against a single author revolves around a number of internal difficulties. These fall into four categories: (1) the presence of doublets—the same scene or vision described twice; (2) sequence problems—persons or things introduced seemingly for the first time when in fact they had already been mentioned; (3) seeming misplaced verses and larger sections; and (4) distinctive content within certain sections that does not fit the rest of the book. In each case, however, there are satisfying alternative explanations. In fact, the difficulties just named stem more from the reader's presuppositions than from the text itself. Dissection of the text has been notoriously unfruitful in yielding further light on the book itself. We are more likely to discover the author's original intent if we approach Revelation with the assumption of its literary integrity than if we attempt at every turn to judge it by our modern and Western mentality.[7]

There is also a certain artificiality about interpolation theories that claim unity for the book until a passage is encountered that does not fit in with preconceived views, by which, without the slightest evidence, "interpolation" is cited to alleviate the embarrassment. Some of the best interpreters have succumbed to this temptation.[8]

Yet without belaboring the argument, we may affirm that the book everywhere displays both the literary and conceptual unity to be expected from a single author. This does not eliminate certain difficult hermeneutical problems nor preclude the presence of omissions or interpolations encountered in the extant MSS of the book. Nor does the view of single authorship preclude that John in expressing in written form the revelation given to him by Christ used various sources, whether oral or written (cf. comments at 1:2). Yet, under the guidance of the Holy Spirit, who is of course the primary author, John has everywhere made these materials his own and involved them with a thoroughly Christian orientation and content.

---

[7]This is precisely the point of three recent studies that look critically but fairly at the general trends of form and redaction criticism of NT documents: Northrop Frye, *Anatomy of Criticism: Four Essays* (Princeton: Princeton University, 1957); Walter Wink, *The Bible in Human Transformation* (Philadelphia: Fortress, 1973); and Leland Ryken, "Literary Criticism of the Bible: Some Fallacies," ch. 2 in *Literary Interpretations of Biblical Narratives*, edd. Louis, Ackerman, and Warshaw (Nashville: Abingdon, 1974). G. Mussies's recent and detailed work on the language of the Apocalypse has reaffirmed the unity of the entire book (*The Morphology of Koine Greek as Used in the Apocalypse of St. John* [Leiden: E.J. Brill, 1971], p. 351); as has also Vos, *Synoptic Tradition*.

[8]Thus Eller (pp. 159, 165–66), following M. Rissi ("The Kerygma of the Revelation to John," Int, 22 [1968], 4), chooses to dismiss John's number 666 as an interpolation mainly because it is unlike John to be a "calenderizer," which is contrary to his overall view of the Apocalypse. The issue, however, is not whether interpolations have crept into the text but the method of approach to determining interpolations. If there is no evidence to support such a view, there is no way of distinguishing whether an actual interpolation has occurred anywhere except in the mind of the commentator.

3. Authorship and Canonicity

The question of the authorship of Revelation is the same as that of the authorship of the other Johannine writings (the Gospel and the Epistles). The earliest witnesses ascribe Revelation to John the apostle, the son of Zebedee (Justin Martyr [d. 165]; Clement of Alexandria [d.c.220]; Hippolytus [d.c.236]; Origen [d.c.254]) (Swete, pp. clxxif.). Not until Dionysius, the distinguished bishop of Alexandria and student of Origen (d.c.264), was any voice raised within the church against its apostolic authorship.[9] Dionysius questioned the apostolic origin of Revelation because the advocates of an earthly eschatological hope ("Chiliasts"), whom he opposed, appealed to Revelation 20. He based his arguments on four main comparisons between the First Epistle of John and the Gospels at points where these differ from Revelation: (1) the Gospel and First Epistle do not name their author but Revelation does; (2) the Gospel and First Epistle contain parallels to each other but not to Revelation; (3) no reference to Revelation appears in the Gospel or First Epistle and no reference to the Gospel or First Epistle is found in Revelation; and (4) the Greek in which Revelation is written is faulty and entirely different from that of the Gospel and First Epistle (ANF, 6:82–84).

From the time of Dionysius, the apostolic origin of the book was disputed in the East until Athanasius of Alexandria (d.373) turned the tide toward its acceptance. In the West the story was different. From at least the middle of the second century, the book held its own, being widely accepted and listed in all the principal canon enumerations. The Reformation period witnessed a renewal of the earlier questions concerning its apostolic authorship and canonical status. Thus Luther, offended by the contents of Revelation, declared that he regarded it as "neither apostolic nor prophetic."[10]

Typical of current views is that of Moule, who claims that "few can now believe that the John of the Apocalypse is the same as the author (or authors) of what are commonly called the Johannine writings—the Gospel and the three epistles."[11] The chief

---

[9]Kümmel mentions certain heretical parties ("Alogoi") who opposed the Montanists as tracing the authorship of the book to the Gnostic Cerinthus. Gaius, the Roman anti-Montanist, likewise held such a view (Feine, Paul, and Behm, Johannes, *Introduction to the New Testament,* ed. W. Kümmel [Nashville: Abingdon, 1966], p. 330). Dionysius refers to these earlier views in his treatise against the apostolic authorship of the Apocalypse (ANF, 6:82). For the most extensive treatment of the canon evidence, see Ned. B. Stonehouse, *The Apocalypse in the Ancient Church* (Goes, Holland: Oosterboon and LeCointre, 1929).

[10]Feine-Behm, *Introduction to NT,* p. 330.

[11]C.F.D. Moule, *An Idiom Book of New Testament Greek,* 2d ed. (Cambridge: Cambridge University, 1960), p. 3; also Mussies, *Morphology,* p. 352: "The linguistic and stylistic divergence of the Apc. on the one hand and the Gospel and Letters of St. John on the other, proves beyond any reasonable doubt that all these works as we have them before us were not phrased by one and the same man." While Mounce (*Revelation,* pp. 28–30) probably underestimates the negative linguistic evidence against a common authorship of Gospel and Apocalypse, he does cite an early Gnostic text, the *Apocryphon of John,* which credits the passage in Revelation 1:19 to "John, the brother of James, these who are the two sons of Zebedee" (see also the review of Mounce by Alan F. Johnson, "A New Standard on the Apocalypse," CT [January 5, 1979], pp. 36–37). Elisabeth S. Fiorenza argues for a Johannine school as the explanation of the origin of both Gospel and Revelation: "The Quest for the Johannine School: The Apocalypse and the Fourth Gospel," NTS, 23 (April 1977), 402–27. Thus, recent NT scholarship is tending more toward the view that the writing of NT books was more located in "schools" or "communities" of disciples in various locations. Thus, a school of Matthew, or a school of John, Paul, or Peter, may account for the diversity

obstacle is the barbarous Greek style of Revelation as compared to that of the other Johannine writings. Of course, there is no good reason why the John of the Apocalypse could not have been the apostle John, while another John wrote the Gospel and the epistles.

However, despite the linguistic problem, a number of scholars have been convinced of the similarities between Revelation and the other Johannine books. So a group of dissenting scholars attribute the Apocalypse to the apostle, the son of Zebedee, or lean in that direction (e.g., most of the Roman Catholic scholars, Alford, Feine-Behm, Guthrie, Mounce, Stauffer, Swete, Zahn). Others leave the question open but do not deny apostolic authorship (Beasley-Murray, Beckwith, Bruce, Morris). Ford's view, that the book was not written by the apostle but was a composite writing by John the Baptist (chs. 4–11), a disciple of John the Baptist (chs. 12–22), and a later unknown Christian author (chs. 1–3), rests on conjectural evidence and has little to commend it to serious scholarly acceptance (pp. 28–40). Her arguments, instead, could be used to support the traditional view that the apostle, the son of Zebedee, who was a disciple of John the Baptist, was the author.

From the internal evidence, the following things can be said about the author with some confidence.

1. He calls himself John (1:4, 9; 22:8). This is not likely a pseudonym but instead the name of a well-known person among the Asian churches. Other than the apostle, John the Baptist, and John Mark, the only John we know about is the disputed "John, the presbyter" Papias spoke of (Eusebius *Ecclesiastical History* 3.39.1–7). (The John mentioned in Acts 4:6 would obviously not be a serious candidate.)

2. This John of the Apocalypse identifies himself as a prophet (1:3; 22:6–10, 18–19) who was in exile because of his prophetic witness (1:9). As such, he speaks to the churches with great authority.

3. His use of the OT and Targums make it virtually certain that he was a Palestinian Jew, steeped in the temple and synagogue ritual.[12] He may also have been a priest.[13]

To sum up, it must be admitted that the question of authorship of Revelation is problematic. On the one hand, the language and grammatical style are incompatible with the Gospel and the epistles; yet, on the other hand, in imagery, literary forms, liturgical framework, and symbolism, there are notable similarities to the Gospel and the epistles. Early and widespread testimony attributes the book to the apostle John, and no convincing argument has been advanced against this view. Perhaps we must be satisfied at present with a similar judgment for this book that Origen suggested for the authorship of Hebrews: "Who wrote the letter, God really knows."[14] Regardless of the problem of authorship, the church universal has come to acknowledge the Apocalypse as divinely authoritative, inspired Scripture.

---

in style and emphasis among the writings in the NT attributed to the same author. See E. Earl Ellis's "Further Reflections on John A.T. Robinson and the Dating of the New Testament," NTS, 26, no. 4 (1980): 487–502; also K. Stendahl, *The School of St. Matthew (Uppsala: Gleerup, 1954)* and Raymond E. Brown, *The Community of the Beloved Disciple* (New York: Paulus, 1979).

[12]L. Paul Trudinger, "Some Observations Concerning the Text of the Old Testament in the Book of Revelation," JTS, 17 (1966), 1:82–88.

[13]Ethelbert Stauffer, *New Testament Theology* (London: SCM, 1965), pp. 40–41.

[14]Daniel J. Theron, *Evidence of Tradition* (Grand Rapids: Baker, 1958), pp. 40–41.

4. Date

Only two suggested dates for Revelation have received serious support. An early date, shortly after the reign of Nero (A.D. 54–68), is supported by references in the book to the persecution of Christians, the "Nero redivivus" myth (a revived Nero would be the reincarnation of the evil genius of the whole Roman Empire), the imperial cult (ch. 13), and the temple (ch. 11), which was destroyed in A.D. 70 (so Westcott, Hort, Lightfoot, Ford). Some external evidence for the early date exists in the Muratorian Fragment (170–190) and the Monarchian Prologues (250–350). These documents claim that Paul wrote to seven churches following the pattern of John's example in Revelation.[15] But this would date the book before the Pauline Epistles!

The alternate and more generally accepted date rests primarily on the early witness of Irenaeus (185), who stated that the apostle John "saw the revelation . . . at the close of Domitian's reign" (A.D. 81–96) (*Contra Haereses* 5.30.3; ANF, 1:559–60). Both views appeal to the book's witness to persecution because of refusal to comply with emperor worship. On the other hand, if most of the persecution referred to in the book is anticipatory, and if the exegesis that sees in the book references to the succession of the emperors (ch. 17) and enforced emperor worship (ch. 13) is questionable, then no substantial argument can be advanced for either date. Therefore, though the slender historical evidence on the whole favors the later date (81–96), in the light of the present studies, the question as to when Revelation was written must be left open.[16]

---

[15]Ibid., pp. 59, 111; cf. Krister Stendahl, "The Apocalypse of John and the Epistles of Paul in the Muratorian Fragment," *Current Issues in New Testament Interpretation*, ed. W. Klassen and G.F. Snyder (New York: Harper, 1962), pp. 239–45. Stendahl argues that in addition to apostolic inspiration, a canonical book also needed to be universal in nature, i.e., written for the whole church. Apparently the Apocalypse served as a standard for including other books into the canon of the NT. Thus, the canon of Mommsen (c. early fourth century) states: "But as it is said in the Apocalypse of John, 'I saw twenty-four elders presenting their crowns before the throne,' so our fathers approved that these books are canonical and that the men of old have said this" (Theron, *Evidence of Tradition*, p. 121).

[16]See chs. 13 and 17, where the dating schemes are discussed in more detail and questioned. Kümmel suggests that since the congregation of Smyrna had been tried for a long time (2:8–11) and according to Polycarp (*Philippians* 11) the church did not exist in Paul's day, and since 3:17 describes the church at Laodicea as rich, though this city was almost completely destroyed by an earthquake in A.D. 60/61, the later date for the book is to be preferred (Feine-Behm, *Introduction to NT*, p. 329). However, John A.T. Robinson (*Redating the New Testament* [Philadelphia: Westminster, 1976], pp. 229–30) has recently challenged the above objection to the early date and favors a date prior to A.D. 70. He has effectively shown that this evidence is misinterpreted by Kümmel and others. Robinson's early date for the Apocalypse is conceded by D. Moody Smith ("A Review of John A.T. Robinson's *Redating the New Testament*," *Duke Divinity School Review*, 42 [1977], 193–205). Robinson claims that in addition to J.M. Ford and R.M. Grant, F.F. Bruce now inclines in the same direction (*Redating the New Testament*, p. 225, n.27). Morris correctly concludes that "the date of John is far from certain and there are some grounds for holding that it is to be dated before the destruction of Jerusalem in A.D. 70" (*Revelation of St. John*, p. 39). Albert A. Bell, Jr., has argued that the Domitian dating is not credible since the only direct evidence comes from Irenaeus ("The Date of John's Apocalypse. The Evidence of Some Roman Historians Reconsidered," NTS, 25 [1978], 93–102). Bell says, "Second-century traditions about the apostles are demonstrably unreliable, and Irenaeus' testimony is not without difficulties." Bell argues against the persecution theory as a backdrop to Revelation by refuting the evidence of Cassius Dio. He places the date of Revelation between June 68 and January 69!

5. Purpose

Swete captured the basic thrust of the book when he remarked, "In form it is an epistle, containing an apocalyptic prophecy; in spirit and inner purpose, it is a pastoral" (p. xc). As a prophet, John is called to separate true belief from false—to expose the failures of the congregations in Asia. He desires to encourage authentic Christian discipleship by explaining Christian suffering and martyrdom in the light of how Jesus' death brought victory over evil. John is concerned to show that the martyrs (e.g., Antipas [2:13]) would be vindicated. He also discloses the end both of evil and of those who follow the beast (19:20–21; 20:10, 15); he also describes the ultimate issue of the Lamb's victory and of those who follow him. John himself is centrally concerned with God's saving purpose and its implementation by Jesus. John writes to the church universal in every age so that they too might join him in confirming this witness of Jesus (1:9; 22:16).[17] Sadly, because of the sometime overemphasis on either the symbolic or the literal, and because of the theological problems (see below), the church has often been deprived of the valuable practical thrust of this book as through it God seeks to lead us into authentic Christian discipleship.

6. Theological Problems

From earliest times, certain theological emphases in Revelation are cited as objections to the whole book or to certain parts that are considered unworthy and sub-Christian. Among these are (1) its eschatological view of history, which includes an earthly Millennium (ch. 20); (2) the cry for vengeance in 6:10; (3) its "weakly Christianized Judaism";[18] and (4) its overuse of visions and symbols, according to Luther, who said that Christ is neither taught nor accepted in this book, and who considered it neither apostolic nor prophetic.

To sum up, Revelation is alleged to be sub-Christian in its Christology, eschatology, and doctrine of God, all three of which are thought to obscure or to contradict outright the central message of the NT.[19] While none of the above problems should be glossed over, it is becoming apparent that prior commitment to a certain viewpoint on these three areas, rather than the intrinsic incompatibility of John's ideas with the central NT message, often determines the negative judgments that some scholars pass on Revelation. A recent study by Beasley-Murray points out the basic difference in John's views from standard Jewish apocalyptic thought and wisely argues for the necessity to read Revelation in conjunction with the NT books that preceded it, not as contradictory, but as complementary to them.[20]

---

[17]Cf. Minear, *I Saw a New Earth,* pp. 213–17, for an excellent discussion of the prophet's motives in writing the book.

[18]Rudolph Bultmann, *Theology of the New Testament,* 2 vols. (New York: Scribner, 1951), 2:175.

[19]Cf. Kümmel (Feine-Behm, *Introduction to NT*), pp. 331–32. Even the conservative Morris complains that apocalyptic is not a good medium for expressing the "cruciality of the cross," and he believes that it does not express it: "Apocalyptic fails us at the heart of the faith" (*Apocalyptic,* p. 86). Yet the Book of Revelation seems to capture splendidly this cruciality of the Cross in its own unique way (cf. chs. 5 and 12) and provides a needed complement to the other NT descriptions of the Cross (see Beasley-Murray, n.20, below).

[20]G.R. Beasley-Murray, "How Christian Is the Book of Revelation?" in *Reconciliation and Hope, New Testament Essays on Atonement and Eschatology,* ed. Robert Banks (Grand Rapids: Eerdmans, 1974), pp.

7. Text

The MSS of Revelation are few compared to those of other NT literature. Thus, of the important early witnesses, only three papyri and scarcely half a dozen uncials of the Apocalypse are extant. While there are over a thousand minuscule MSS for each of most of the other books, Revelation has a total of only about 250.[21] Thus we have P^{18} (third-fourth century), P^{24} (fourth century), P^{47} (late third century), ℵ (fourth century), A (fifth century), C (fifth century), P (ninth century), and a few minuscules cited in Metzger's apparatus and commentary.[22] In the Notes throughout this commentary, only those textual variants are discussed where, in my opinion, the sense of the passage is affected. I have also followed the practice of not citing all the textual evidence, since those who understand such technicalities have ready access to the standard critical editions of the Greek NT and works such as Metzger's (*Textual Commentary*) and Hoskier's collations (*Text of the Apocalypse*). In general, MSS A, ℵ, C, P^{47} weigh heavily in the external evidence, especially where they agree. A alone is sometimes the preferred reading. Most of the cases must be settled on intrinsic probability and context. I have given Metzger's conclusions throughout but have occasionally dissented when the internal evidence seems to warrant it.

8. Interpretative Schemes

Four traditional ways of understanding Revelation 4–22 have emerged in the history of the church. In our day, additional mixed views have been developed by combining elements from these four traditions.

a. Futurist

This view is that, with the exception of chapters 1 to 3, all the visions in Revelation relate to a period immediately preceding and following the second advent of Christ at the end of the age. Therefore, the seals, trumpets, and bowls refer to events still in the future; the beasts of chapters 13 and 17 are identified with the future Antichrist, who will appear at the last moment in world history and will be defeated by Christ in his second coming to judge the world and to establish his earthly millennial kingdom.

Variations of this view were held by the earliest expositors, such as Justin Martyr (d.165), Irenaeus (d.c.195), Hippolytus (d.236), and Victorinus (d.c.303). After nearly a ten-century eclipse, during which time the allegorical method prevailed, the futurist view was revived in the late sixteenth century by Franciscus Ribeira, a Spanish Jesuit. He held that the beast was the Antichrist of the end time and that Babylon was not Rome under papal rule but a degenerate Rome of a future age. Unlike many modern futurists, Ribeira founded his views on a thorough appreciation of the historical

---

275–84. See also Carl E. Braaten, *Apocalyptic Themes in Theology and Culture: Christ and Counter-Christ* (Philadelphia: Fortress, 1972), esp. ch. 1, "Apocalyptic Interpretation of History"; also G.E. Ladd, "The Theology of the Apocalypse," GR, 7 (1963–64), 73–86.

[21]H.C. Hoskier's monumental work has collated afresh all the uncial and minuscule witnesses to the book and is the best source for variants (*Concerning the Text of the Apocalypse,* 2 vols. [London: Bernard Quaritch, 1929]).

[22]Bruce M. Metzger, *A Textual Commentary on the Greek New Testament* (New York: UBS, 1971).

backgrounds of Revelation and its language. Thus he understood the first five seals to depict various elements of early Christianity. The white horse was the apostolic age; the red, the early persecutors; the black, heresies; the pale, the violent persecutions by Trajan. But when Ribeira came to the sixth seal, he took this to indicate the signs that would precede the return of Christ; he also understood the seven trumpets and seven bowls to follow the three and a half years. This futurist approach to the book has enjoyed a revival of no small proportion since the nineteenth century and is widely held among evangelicals today. The chief problem with it is that it seems to make all but the first three chapters of Revelation irrelevant to the contemporary church. This objection is pressed more strongly when adherents to the futurist view affirm, as many do today, that the church will be removed from the earth before the events described in 6:1ff. occur.[23]

b. *Historicist*

As the word implies, this view centers on history and its continuity as seen in Revelation. It started with Joachim of Floris (d. 1202), a monastic who claimed to have received on Easter night a special vision that revealed to him God's plan for the ages. He assigned a day-year value to the 1,260 days of the Apocalypse. In his scheme, the book was a prophecy of the events of Western history from the times of the apostles (in some varieties, from the Creation) until Joachim's own time. A short time after his death, the Franciscans considered themselves the true Christians of his vision. They interpreted Babylon not only as pagan Rome but also as papal Rome. In the various schemes that developed as this method was applied to history, one element became common: the Antichrist and Babylon were connected with Rome and the papacy. Later, Luther, Calvin, and other Reformers came to adopt this view. That this approach does not enjoy much favor today is largely because of the lack of consensus as to the historical identification it entails. The distinguished exegete Henry Alford (1810–71) held a guarded version of this view.

c. *Preterist*

According to this view, Revelation is to be seen as related to what happened in the time of the author; as to the time of its writing, it is a contemporary and imminent historical document. So the main contents of chapters 4–22 are viewed as describing events wholly limited to John's own time. This approach identifies the book with the Jewish apocalyptic method of producing "tracts for the times" to encourage faithfulness during intense persecution. The beasts of chapter 13 are identified respectively as imperial Rome and the imperial priesthood. This is the view held by a majority of contemporary scholars, not a few of whom are identified with the liberal interpretation of Christianity. As a system, it did not appear till 1614, when a Spanish Jesuit named Alcasar developed its main lines. Today some commentators argue that the events were imminent but not yet realized when John wrote; hence, they suggest an imminent historical view (so Caird). While they do not ignore the importance of the historical setting, those who accept Revelation as a book of genuine prophecy concerning events extending beyond the first six centuries are little attracted by this view.

---

[23]Some good sources for the history of interpretation are the works by Beckwith, Elliott, and Swete cited in the Bibliography.

d. *Idealist*

This method of interpreting Revelation sees it as being basically poetical, symbolic, and spiritual in nature. Indeed, it is sometimes called the spiritualist view—not, of course, in reference to the cult of spiritualism, but because it "spiritualizes" everything in the book. Thus Revelation does not predict any specific historical events at all; on the contrary, it sets forth timeless truths concerning the battle between good and evil that continues throughout the church age. As a system of interpretation, it is more recent than the three other schools and somewhat more difficult to distinguish from the earlier allegorizing approaches of the Alexandrians (Clement and Origen). In general, the idealist view is marked by its refusal to identify any of the images with specific future events, whether in the history of the church or with regard to the end of all things.[24] Undoubtedly, the book does reflect the great timeless realities of the battle between God and Satan and of divine judgment; undoubtedly, it sees history as being ultimately in the hand of the Creator. But certainly it also depicts the consummation of this battle and the triumph of Christ in history through his coming in glory.

Which view is the right one? Since there have been evangelicals who have held to each of the four views, the issue is not that of orthodoxy but of interpretation. In recent years many expositors have combined the stronger elements of the different views. The history of the interpretation of Revelation should teach us to be open to fresh approaches to it, even when this attitude goes contrary to the prevailing interpretations. Nothing short of the careful exegesis of the text uninhibited by prior dogmatic conclusions is required for the fullest understanding of the Apocalypse.

This commentary will pay close attention to the historical situation of first-century Christianity in its Judeo-Greco-Roman world setting. I do not, however, take the position that this emphasis necessarily leads to the conclusion that John's language and visions describe the political entities of imperial Rome or the imperial priesthood. Thus we feel that the preterist and to a lesser extent the preterist-futurist's views are misled.[25] On the other hand, we believe that John is describing the final judgment and the physical, bodily return of Christ to the world. This means that in every age Revelation continues to encourage the church in persecution as well as to warn the church of the beast's satanically energized, multifaceted deception. Its language describes the deeper realities of the conflict of Christ's sovereignty with satanic power rather than the mere temporary historical-political entities, whether past (such as Rome) or future.

Revelation may then be viewed, on the one hand, as an extended commentary on Paul's statement in Ephesians 6:12: "For our struggle is not against flesh and blood, but against the rulers, against the authorities, against the powers of the dark world and against the spiritual forces of evil in the heavenly realms." On the other hand,

---

[24]Recent interpreters who favor this view are Calkins, Hendriksen, and Milligan; see Bibliography, also.

[25]Beasley-Murray, Bruce, Ladd, Morris, Mounce, among others, are recent evangelical interpreters who have endeavored to combine the preterist and futurist schools. The key issue seems to be this: To what extent does the Apocalypse fit the literary genre of apocalyptic at the point of its view of history? The Jewish apocalyptists related their messages to the immediate historical-political entities. But does John in fact do this? Our answer is no. His language about the beast and Babylon describes more a theological than a political entity (see at chs. 13, 17). While the preterist-futurist view is a big step in the right direction away from the purely preterist or nonhistorical futurist views, in our opinion it falls short of the actual sense of the language throughout the book.

it also reveals the final judgment upon evil and the consummation of God's kingdom in time and eternity.

9. Use of the Old Testament

While Revelation does not have a single direct quotation, there are hundreds of places where John alludes in one way or another to the OT Scriptures. Swete mentions that of the 404 verses of the Apocalypse, 278 contain references to the Jewish Scriptures (p. cxxxv). UBS's Greek NT (2d ed.) cites over five hundred OT passages in connection with the book (pp. 897–920). In any case, the author's use of the OT is unique (e.g., Paul's epistles contain ninety-five direct quotations and possibly an additional one hundred allusions to the OT).

The OT used by John is primarily Semitic rather than Greek, agreeing often with the Aramaic Targums and occasionally reflecting Midrashic background materials to the OT passages; and it can be shown that he used a text other than the Masoretic that has a close affinity with the Hebrew text of the Qumran MSS.[26] From the Prophets, John refers quite frequently to Isaiah, Jeremiah, Ezekiel, and Daniel. John also refers repeatedly to the Psalms, Exodus, and Deuteronomy. Especially important are John's christological reinterpretations of OT passages he alludes to. He does not simply use the OT in its pre-Christian sense but often recasts the images and visions of the OT. While there is an unmistakable continuity in Revelation with the older revelation, the new emerges from the old as a distinct entity.[27]

10. Structure

The main contents of Revelation are given in terms of a series of sevens, some explicit, some implied: seven churches (chs. 2–3); seven seals (chs. 6–7); seven trumpets (chs. 8–11); seven signs (chs. 12–15); seven bowls (chs. 16–18); seven last things (chs. 19–22). It is also possible to divide the contents around four key visions: (1) the vision of the Son of man among the seven churches (chs. 1–3); (2) the vision of the seven-sealed scroll, the seven trumpets, the seven signs, and the seven bowls (4:1–19:10); (3) the vision of the return of Christ and the consummation of this age (19:11–20:15); and (4) the vision of the new heaven and new earth (21–22). Commendable attempts have also been made to show that the literary structure of the Apocalypse is patterned after the Easter liturgy of the early church.[28] All such schemes must, however, be subordinate to the exegesis of the book.

---

[26]DSS have shown that there were many text types in the first century, including a Masoretic-like text. John's use of the OT reflects some of the Qumran text types rather than the MT. See Trudinger, "Text of OT in Relevation," pp. 83–88; cf. D. Moody Smith, Jr., "The Use of the Old Testament in the New" in *The Use of the Old Testament in the New and Other Essays*, ed. James M. Efird (Durham: Duke University, 1972), pp. 58–63. See also Vos's excellent chapter "The Apocalyptist's Manner of Using Pre-Existent Material As Illustrated from His Employment of the Old Testament" (*Synoptic Traditions*, pp. 16–53).

[27]Austin Farrer (*A Rebirth of Images: the Making of St. John's Apocalypse* [London: Darce, 1949]) has opened my eyes to this dimension of the Apocalypse. The chief difficulty with Farrer is that his own book is more difficult to understand than Rev itself.

[28]Massey H. Shepherd, Jr., *The Paschal Liturgy and the Apocalypse* (Richmond: John Knox, 1960).

11. Bibliography

Space allows the mention of only representative books. Some defy exact categories and it may be unfair to classify them. We have used the interpretation of the beast (ch. 13) and Babylon (ch. 17) as the chief indicators of the nature of the books listed.

A. *Futurist*

1. *Dispensational*

Smith, J.B. *A Revelation of Jesus Christ*. Scottdale, Pa.: Herald, 1961.
Tenney, Merrill C. *Interpreting Revelation*. Grand Rapids: Eerdmans, 1957.
Walvoord, John F. *The Revelation of Jesus Christ*. Chicago: Moody, 1966.

2. *Purely Eschatological*

Eller, Vernard. *The Most Revealing Book of the Bible: Making Sense Out of Revelation*. Grand Rapids: Eerdmans, 1974.
Lilje, Hanns. *The Last Book of the Bible: The Meaning of the Revelation of St. John*. Philadelphia: Muhlenberg, 1955.

3. *Preterist-Futurist*

Beasley-Murray, G.R. "The Revelation." NBC rev. Edited by D. Guthrie, et al. Grand Rapids: Eerdmans, 1970.
Beckwith, Isbon T. *The Apocalypse of John*. New York: Macmillan, 1922.
Bruce, F.F. "The Revelation to John." In *A New Testament Commentary*. Edited by G.C.D. Howley, F.F. Bruce, and H.L. Ellison. Grand Rapids: Zondervan, 1969.
Ladd, George E. *A Commentary on the Revelation of John*. Grand Rapids: Eerdmans, 1972.
Morris, Leon. *The Revelation of St. John*. Grand Rapids: Eerdmans, 1969.
Mounce, Robert H. *The Book of Revelation*. NIC. Grand Rapids: Eerdmans, 1977.

B. *Historicist*

Alford, Henry. *The Revelation*. Alf. London: Cambridge, 1884.
Elliott, E.B. *Horae Apocalypticae*. 4 vols. Eng. tr. 3d ed. London: Seeley, Burnside, and Seeley, 1828.

C. *Preterist*

Barclay, William. *The Revelation of John*. 2 vols. The Daily Study Bible Series. Philadelphia: Westminster, 1959.
Caird, G.B. *The Revelation of St. John the Divine*. *Harper's New Testament Commentaries*. New York: Harper, 1966.
Charles, R.H. *A Critical and Exegetical Commentary on the Revelation of St. John*. 2 vols. ICC. Edinburgh: T. & T. Clark, 1920.
Ford, J. Massyngberde. *Revelation*. AB. New York: Doubleday, 1975.
Glasson, T.F. *The Revelation of John*. *The Cambridge Bible Commentary on the New English Bible*. New York: Cambridge at the University, 1965.
Harrington, Wilfred J. *The Apocalypse of St. John: A Commentary*. London: Geoffrey Chapman, 1969.
Heidt, William G. *The Book of the Apocalypse*. *New Testament Reading Guide*. Collegeville, Minn.: Liturgical, 1962.
Pieters, Albertus. *Studies in the Revelation of St. John*. Grand Rapids: Eerdmans, 1954.
Summers, Ray. *Worthy Is the Lamb*. Nashville: Broadman, 1951.

Sweet, J.P.M. *Revelation*. Philadelphia: Westminster, 1979.
Swete, Henry Barclay. *The Apocalypse of St. John*. New York: Macmillan, 1906.

D. *Idealist*

Calkins, Raymond. *The Social Message of the Book of Revelation*. New York: Woman's, 1920.
Carrington, Philip. *The Meaning of the Revelation*. New York: Macmillan, 1931.
Hendriksen, W. *More Than Conquerors*. Grand Rapids: Baker, 1940.
Kiddle, Martin. *The Revelation of St. John*. MNT. New York: Harper, 1940.
Milligan, William. *The Book of Revelation*. ExB. Hodder & Stoughton, 1909.
Minear, Paul S. *I Saw a New Earth: An Introduction to the Visions of the Apocalypse*. Cleveland: Corpus Books, 1968.
Rissi, Mathias. *Time and History*. Richmond: John Knox, 1966.

12. Outline and Map

- I. Introduction (1:1–8)
  - A. Prologue (1:1–3)
  - B. Greetings and Doxology (1:4–8)
- II. Vision of the Son of Man Among the Seven Churches of Asia (1:9–3:22)
  - A. The Son of Man Among the Lampstands (1:9–20)
    1. Introduction and voice (1:9–11)
    2. The sight of the vision (1:12–20)
  - B. The Letters to the Seven Churches (2:1–3:22)
    1. To Ephesus (2:1–7)
    2. To Smyrna (2:8–11)
    3. To Pergamum (2:12–17)
    4. To Thyratira (2:18–29)
    5. To Sardis (3:1–6)
    6. To Philadelphia (3:7–13)
    7. To Laodicea (3:14–22)
- III. Vision of the Seven-Sealed Scroll, the Seven Trumpets, the Seven Signs, and the Seven Bowls (4:1–19:10)
  - A. The Seven-Sealed Scroll (4:1–8:1)
    1. Preparatory: the throne, the scroll, and the Lamb (4:1–5:14)
       - a. The throne (4:1–11)
       - b. The scroll and the Lamb (5:1–14)
    2. Opening of the first six seals (6:1–17)
    3. First interlude (7:1–17)
       - a. The 144,000 Israelites (7:1–8)
       - b. The great white-robed multitude (7:9–17)
    4. Opening of the seventh seal (8:1)
  - B. The Seven Trumpets (8:2–11:19)
    1. Preparatory: The angel and the golden censer (8:2–5)
    2. Sounding of the first six trumpets (8:6–9:21)
    3. Second interlude (10:1–11:14)
       - a. The little book (10:1–11)
       - b. The two witnesses (11:1–14)
    4. Sounding of the seventh trumpet (11:15–19)
  - C. The Seven Signs (12:1–14:20)
    1. The woman and the dragon (12:1–17)
    2. The two beasts (13:1–18)
    3. The Lamb and the 144,000 (14:1–5)
    4. The harvest of the earth (14:6–20)
  - D. The Seven Bowls (15:1–19:10)
    1. Preparatory: The seven angels with the seven last plagues (15:1–8)
    2. Pouring out of the seven bowls (16:1–21)
    3. The woman and the beast (17:1–18)
    4. The fall of Babylon the Great (18:1–24)

5. Thanksgiving for the destruction of Babylon (19:1–5)
6. Thanksgiving for the marriage of the Lamb (19:6–10)

IV. Vision of the Return of Christ and the Consummation of This Age (19:11–20:15)
   A. The Rider on the White Horse and the Destruction of the Beast (19:11–21)
   B. Binding of Satan and the Millennium (20:1–6)
   C. Release and End of Satan (20:7–10)
   D. Great White Throne Judgment (20:11–15)

V. Vision of the New Heaven and the New Earth and the New Jerusalem (21:1–22:5)
   A. The New Jerusalem (21:1–27)
   B. The River of Life and the Tree of Life (22:1–5)

VI. Conclusion (22:6–21)

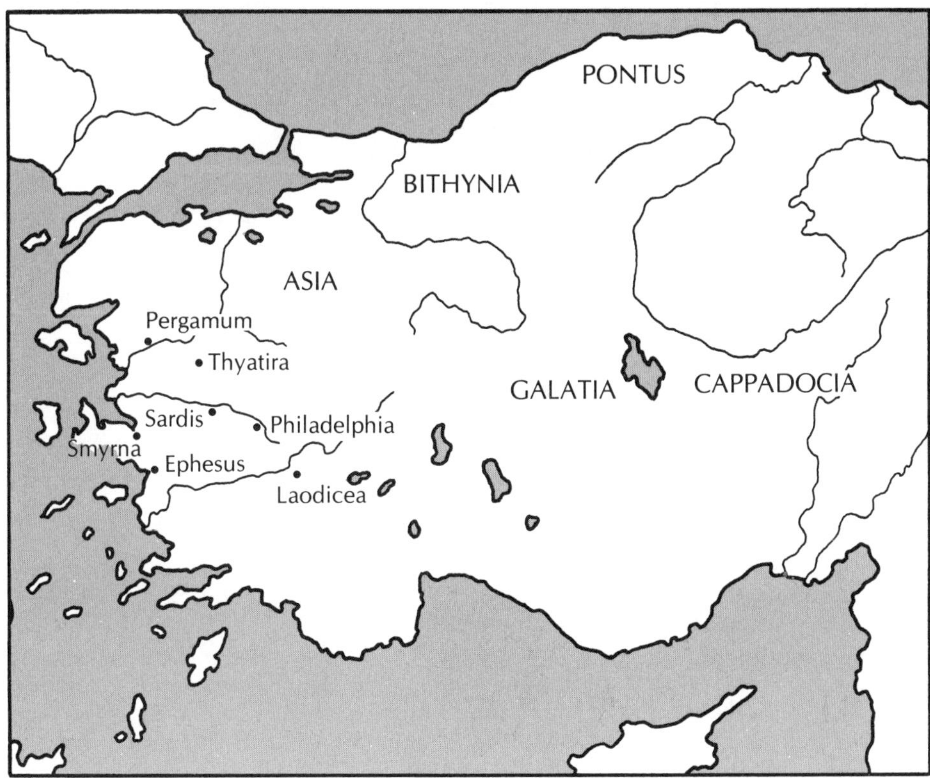

Text and Exposition

I. Introduction (1:1–8)

A. *Prologue*

1:1–3

[1]The revelation of Jesus Christ, which God gave him to show his servants what must soon take place. He made it known by sending his angel to his servant John, [2]who testifies to everything he saw—that is, the word of God and the testimony of Jesus Christ. [3]Blessed is the one who reads the words of this prophecy, and blessed are those who hear it and take to heart what is written in it, because the time is near.

The Prologue contains a description of the nature of the book, a reference to the author, and a statement that the book was meant for congregational reading. Probably vv. 1–3 were written last.

1 The book is called the "revelation of Jesus Christ." "Revelation" (*apokalypsis*) means to expose in full view what was formerly hidden, veiled, or secret. In the NT the word occurs exclusively in the religious sense of a divine disclosure. "Revelation" may refer to either some present or future aspect of God's will (Luke 2:32; Rom 16:25; Eph 3:5) or to persons (Rom 8:19) or especially to the future unveiling of Jesus Christ at his return in glory (2 Thess 1:7; 1 Peter 1:7, 13). In this single occurrence of *apokalypsis* in the Johannine writings, the meaning is not primarily the appearing or revealing of Christ—though certainly the book does this—but rather, as the following words show, the disclosure of "what must soon take place."

The content of the book comes from its author, Jesus Christ. Yet even Christ is not the final author but a mediator, for he receives the revelation from God the Father ("which God gave him to show"). John is the human instrument for communicating what he has seen by the agency of Christ's messenger or angel (cf. 22:6, 8, 16). Through John the revelation is to be made known to the servants of God who comprise the churches (cf. 22:16).

"What must soon take place" implies that the revelation concerns events that are future (cf. Dan 2:28–29, 45; Mark 13:7; Rev 4:1, 22:6). But in what sense can we understand that the events will arise "soon" (*en tachei*)? From the preterist point of view (the events are seen to be imminent to the time of the author; cf. Introduction), the sense is plain: all will "soon" take place—i.e., in John's day. Others translate *en tachei* as "quickly" (grammatically this is acceptable) and understand the author to describe events that will rapidly run their course once they begin. However, it is better to translate *en tachei* as "soon" in the light of the words "the time is near" in v.3 (cf. 22:10).

Yet, if we adopt this sense, it is not necessary to follow the preterist interpretation of the book. In eschatology and apocalyptic, the future is always viewed as imminent without the necessity of intervening time (cf. Luke 18:8). That *en tachei* does not preclude delay or intervening events is evident from the Book of Revelation itself. In chapter 6 we hear the cry of the martyred saints: "How long, Sovereign Lord, holy and true, until you . . . avenge our blood?" They are told to "wait a little longer" (vv.10–11). Therefore, "soonness" means imminency in eschatological terms. The church in every age has always lived with the expectancy of the consummation of all things in its day. Imminency describes an event possible any day, impossible no day. If this sense is followed, we are neither forced to accept a "mistaken apocalyptic" view as Schweitzer advocated nor a preterist interpretation (Albert Schweitzer, *The Quest of the Historical Jesus* [New York: Macmillan, 1968]).

Two more focal points of the book are introduced by the words "by sending his angel to his servant John." First, they introduce us to the significance of angels in the worship of God, in the revelation of God's Word, and in the execution of his judgments in the earth. Angels are referred to sixty-seven times in Revelation.

The second focal point is the word "servant" (*doulos*). All of God's people are known in Revelation as his servants. No less than eleven times in the book are they so described (e.g., 2:20; 7:3; 22:3). John is one servant selected to receive this revelation and communicate it to other servants of God. "Servant," used throughout the NT to describe those who are so designated as the special representatives of the Lord Christ himself, becomes a beautiful title of honor for God's people. Here, then, in the Prologue are five links in the chain of authorship: God, Christ, his angel, his servant John, and those servants to whom John addressed his book.

2 Two elements in the book are of chief importance: "The word of God and the testimony of Jesus Christ." In referring to his visions as the "word of God," John emphasizes his continuity with the prophets in the OT as well as the apostles in the NT. The following passages show us John's concept of the Word of God: 1:9; 3:8, 10; 6:9; 12:11; 17:17; 19:9; 20:4. In 19:13 Jesus is himself identified with the name "the Word of God." Here, in chapter 1, the reference is not directly to Christ but to the promises and acts of God revealed in this book that are realized through Jesus, the Word of God incarnate (cf. John 1:1–2; 1 John 1:1). The church needs to be reminded that the neglected Book of Revelation is the very Word of God to us. While John's literary activity is evident throughout, he claims that what he presents he actually "saw" in divinely disclosed visions. And in the book God himself bears witness to the readers that these things are not the product of John's own mind (1:1–2; 21:5; 22:6; cf. 2 Peter 1:21).

"Testimony" translates the Greek *martyria*, another important term for the author. It is variously rendered as "witness," "attestation," "validation," "verification." "The testimony of Jesus" grammatically could be the testimony "to" Jesus—i.e., John's own testimony about Jesus (objective genitive). However, the alternate grammatical sense —the testimony or validation "from" Jesus (subjective genitive)—is to be preferred. John testifies both to the Word of God received in the visions and also to the validation of his message from Jesus himself. The important range of possible implications of the term in the following references is worthy of study: 1:9; 6:9; 12:11, 17; 19:10; 20:4; 22:16–20.

3 "The one who reads" reflects the early form of worship where a reader read the Scriptures aloud on the Lord's Day. "Those who hear" are the people of the congregation who listen to the reading. "This prophecy" is John's way of describing his writing and refers to the entire Book of Revelation (10:11; 19:10; 22:7, 9–10, 18). Prophecy involves not only future events but also the ethical and spiritual exhortations and warnings contained in the whole writing. Thus John immediately sets off his writing from the late Jewish apocalyptic literature (which did not issue from the prophets) and at the same time puts himself on a par with the OT prophets (cf. 10:8–11; David Hill, "Prophecy and Prophets in the Revelation of St. John," NTS, 18 [1971–72], 401–18).

The twofold benediction "blessed" (*makarios*) pronounced on the reader and the congregation emphasizes the importance of the message in that they will be hearing not only the word of John the prophet but actually the inspired word of Christ (Rev contains six more beatitudes: 14:13; 16:15; 19:9; 20:6; 22:7, 14). John wrote in anticipation of the full and immediate recognition of his message as worthy to be read in the churches as the Word of God coming from Christ himself. In the ancient Jewish synagogue tradition in which John was raised, no such blessing was promised on anyone who recited a mere human teaching, even if from a rabbi, while one who read a biblical text (Scripture) performed a *mitzvah* (commanded act) and was worthy to receive a divine blessing.

All must listen carefully and "take to heart what is written" (*tērountes,* "observe," "watch," "keep") because "the time is near," the time or season (*kairos*) for the fulfillment of the return of Christ (v.7; cf. Luke 11:28, 21:8) and for all that is written in this book (cf. 22:10). The season (*kairos*) for Christ's return is always imminent—now as it has been from the days of his ascension (John 21:22; Acts 1:11).

A comparison of the Prologue (1:1–3) with the Epilogue (22:7–21) shows that John has followed throughout Revelation a deliberate literary pattern. This should alert us to the possibility that the entire book was designed to be heard as a single unit in the public worship service. As Minear says, "The student should not be content with his interpretation of any passage unless and until it fits into the message of the book as a whole" (*I Saw a New Earth,* p. 5). This should not in any way detract from the fact that John claims to have seen real visions ("saw," v.2), which we may assume were arranged by John in their particular literary form for purposes of communication.

Notes

1 Ἀποκάλυψις Ἰησοῦ Χριστοῦ (*apocalypsis Iēsou Christou,* "the revelation of Jesus Christ") raises two questions: (1) What is the relation of this book to the late Jewish apocalyptic literature (Enoch, T 12 Pat, etc.)? "Apocalyptic," as applied to this body of literature comes from the Gr. title of the Revelation (*apocalypsis*) of John (see p. 402). (2) Is "Jesus Christ" an objective or subjective genitive? If the latter, as most commentators suggest, the sense is the "revelation from Jesus Christ"; if the former, the meaning would be the "revelation about Jesus Christ." Grammatically, either is possible.

2 Τὴν μαρτυρίαν Ἰησοῦ Χριστοῦ (*tēn martyrian Iēsou Christou,* "the testimony of Jesus Christ") involves the same problem as above—viz, whether "Jesus Christ" is in an objective or subjective genitive relation to "witness." If the former, the sense is "the witness to Jesus Christ"; if the latter, it is "the witness received from Jesus Christ," i.e., attested by him (so TDNT, 4:500–501).

3 This is the first place in the book where synoptic parallels to the Apocalypse can be noted (cf. Luke 11:28; 21:8). No less than twenty-five direct and indirect uses of the sayings of Jesus can be identified in the Apocalypse. See the excellent work on this subject by Louis A. Vos, *The Synoptic Traditions in the Apocalypse* (Kampen: J.H. Kok, 1965).

B. *Greetings and Doxology*

1:4–8

[4]John,

[1]To the seven churches in the province of Asia:

Grace and peace to you from him who is, and who was, and who is to come, and from the seven spirits before his throne, [5]and from Jesus Christ, who is the faithful witness, the firstborn from the dead, and the ruler of the kings of the earth.

To him who loves us and has freed us from our sins by his blood, [6]and has made us to be a kingdom and priests to serve his God and Father—to him be glory and power for ever and ever! Amen.

[7]Look, he is coming with the clouds,
and every eye will see him,
even those who pierced him;
and all the peoples of the earth will mourn
because of him.

So shall it be! Amen.

[8]"I am the Alpha and the Omega," says the Lord God, "who is, and who was, and who is to come, the Almighty."

John now addresses the recipients of his book: "To the seven churches in the province of Asia" (cf. v.11; 2:1–3:22). Almost immediately he introduces an expanded form of the Christian Trinitarian greeting that merges into a doxology to Christ (vv.5b–6) and is followed by a staccato exclamation calling attention to the return of Christ to the world (v.7). The Father concludes the greeting with assurances of his divine sovereignty.

4 The epistolary form of address immediately distinguishes this book from all other Jewish apocalyptic works (cf. Introduction). None of the pseudepigraphical works contain such epistolary addresses. John writes to actual, historical churches, addressing them in the same way the NT epistles are addressed. These churches he writes to actually existed in the Roman province of Asia (the western part of present-day Turkey), as the details in chapters 2 and 3 indicate. But the question is this: Why did John address these churches and only these seven churches? There were other churches in Asia at the close of the first century. The NT itself refers to congregations at Troas (Acts 20:5–12), Colosse (Col 1:2), and Hierapolis (Col 4:13). There might also have been churches at Magnesia and Tralles, since Ignatius wrote to them less than twenty years later.

At present it is difficult to say why the Lord selected these seven churches. Some have suggested that the churches selected were prophetic of the church ages throughout history (J.A. Seiss, *The Apocalypse* [Grand Rapids: Zondervan, 1957], p. 64; the Scofield Reference Bible adopts this view in its notes). For example, Ephesus would represent prophetically the apostolic period until the Decian persecution (A.D. 250), followed by Smyrna, which represents the church of martyrdom extending until the time of Constantine (A.D. 316). However, after this initial agreement identifications become more difficult except for the last church. All agree that Laodicea is the final period of lukewarm apostasy. Yet there is no reason from the text itself to hold this view. The churches are simply churches found in every age. If the churches were genuinely prophetic of the course of church history rather than representative in every age, those who hold to the imminent return of Christ would have been quickly disillusioned once they realized this.

The reason seven churches were chosen and were placed in this order seems to be that seven was simply the number of completeness, and here it rounds out the literary pattern of the other sevens in the book (cf. Introduction: Structure). These seven churches contained typical or representative qualities of both obedience and disobedience that are a constant reminder throughout every age to all churches (cf. 2:7, 11, 17, 29; 3:6, 13, 22; esp. 2:23). Mounce suggests that the seven were possibly chosen because of some special relationship to emperor worship (*Revelation*, p. 68). As for the order of their mention (1:11), it is the natural ancient travel circuit beginning at Ephesus and arriving finally at Laodicea (see a map of the area).

"Grace and peace" are the usual epistolary greetings that represent the bicultural background of the NT—Greek (*charis*, "grace") and Hebrew (*šālôm*, "peace"; here the Gr. *eirēnē*). The source of blessing is described by employing an elaborate triadic formula for the Trinity:

"From him who is, and who was, and who is to come," i.e., the Father;
"From the seven spirits before his throne," i.e., the Holy Spirit;
"From Jesus Christ," i.e., the Son (v.5).

Similarly there follows a threefold reference to the identity and function of Christ: "the faithful witness, the firstborn from the dead, and the ruler of the kings of the earth"; and three indications of his saving work: "who loves us and has freed us from our sins . . . and has made us to be a kingdom and priests."

The descriptive name of the Father is "him who is [*ho ōn*], and who was [*ho ēn*], and who is to come [*ho erchomenos*]." Each name of God in the Bible is replete with revelatory significance. This particular title occurs nowhere else except in Revelation (4:8; cf. 11:17; 16:5). It is generally understood as a paraphrase for the divine name represented throughout the OT by the Hebrew tetragrammaton *YHWH*. In Exodus 3:14 the LXX has *ho ōn* for the Hebrew tetragrammaton, and in the LXX of Isaiah 41:4 the Lord is described as the one "who is to come." The complete combination of the three tenses does not occur in our Bibles but can be found in a Palestinian Targum on Deuteronomy 32:39. A case can be made that John has made a literal translation here of that Aramaic Targum (L. Paul Trudinger, "Some Observations Concerning the Text of the Old Testament in the Book of Revelation," JTS, 17, [1966], 87). The force of the name has been widely discussed. In 1:8 and 4:8 it is parallel with the divine name "Lord God, the Almighty." The tenses indicate that the same God is eternally present to his covenant people to sustain and encourage them through all the experiences of their lives.

"And from the seven spirits before his throne" seems clearly to focus on the Holy Spirit, not on angels. But why "seven spirits"? Some understand John to mean the "sevenfold spirit" in his fullness (NIV mg. and Ladd, *Commentary on Revelation*, in loc.). Borrowing from the imagery of Zechariah 4, where the ancient prophet sees a lampstand with seven bowls supplied with oil from two nearby olive trees, John seems to connect the church ("lampstands" [v.20]) to the ministry of the Holy Spirit (3:1; 4:5; 5:6). The "seven spirits" represent the activity of the risen Christ through the Holy Spirit in and to the seven churches. This figure brings great encouragement to the churches, for it is " 'not by might nor by power, but by my Spirit,' says the LORD Almighty" (Zech 4:6), that the churches serve God. Yet the figure is also a sobering one because the history of each church (chs. 2–3) is an unfolding of that church's response to the Holy Spirit—"He who has an ear, let him hear what the Spirit says to the churches" (2:7, 11, et al.).

Mounce opts for the view that the seven spirits are perhaps "part of the heavenly entourage that has a special ministry in connection with the Lamb" (*Revelation*, p. 70). However, to identify the seven spirits with angels is highly unlikely because (1) such reference to angels would break the symmetry of the Trinitarian address in 1:4–5 by the intrusion of an angelic greeting and (2) "spirit(s)" in the Book of Revelation refers only to the Spirit of God or to demons, with the exception of 11:11 and 13:15, neither of which refers to angels (for further objections to Mounce's view, see F.F. Bruce, "The Spirit in the Apocalypse," in *Christ and the Spirit in the New Testament*, edd. B. Lindars and S. Smalley [Cambridge: Cambridge University, 1973], pp. 333–37).

5 Finally, greetings come from the *Son*—"from Jesus Christ." John immediately adds three descriptive epithets about Christ and a burst of doxology to him. He is first the "faithful witness." His credibility is proved by his earthly life of obedience in the past; it is proved in the present by his witness to the true condition of the churches; and it will be proved in the future by the consummation of all things in him. In the past he was loyal to the point of death (cf. John 7:7; 18:37; 1 Tim 6:13), as was his servant Antipas (2:13). That Christ was a reliable witness to God's kingdom and salvation—even to the point of suffering death at the hands of the religious-political establishment of his day—is an encouragement to his servants who also are expected to be loyal to him—even to their death (2:10).

The fact that he is "the firstborn from the dead" brings further encouragement. As Christ has given his life in faithfulness to the Father's calling, so the Father has raised Christ from the dead, pledging him as the first of a great company who will follow (cf. 7:13–14). John nowhere else refers to Christ as the "firstborn" (*prōtotokos*), though Paul uses it in Romans 8:29 and Colossians 1:15, 18; and it also occurs in Hebrews 1:6. The same expression is found in Colossians 1:18, where it is associated with words of supreme authority or origin such as "head," "beginning" (*archē*, cf. Rev 3:14), and "supremacy." In Colossians 1:15 Paul refers to Christ as the "firstborn over all creation." This cannot mean that Christ was the first-created being but rather that he is the source, ruler, or origin of all creation (cf. EBC, 11:183). So for Christ to be the "firstborn" of the dead signifies not merely that he was first in time to be raised from the dead but also that he was first in importance, having supreme authority over the dead (cf. 1:18). In the LXX of Psalm 89:27 the same word is used of the Davidic monarch: "I will also appoint him my firstborn, the most exalted of the kings of the earth." Rabbinic tradition believed this reference was messianic (LTJM, 2:719).

The further title for Jesus, "the ruler of the kings of the earth," virtually connects John's thought with the psalm just quoted. Christ's rulership of the world is a key theme of John (11:15; 17:15; 19:16). Jesus Christ is the supreme ruler of the kings of the earth. But who are the "kings of the earth" over whom Jesus Christ rules? John could mean the emperors such as Nero and Domitian, the territorial rulers such as Pilate and Herod, and their successors. In that case John was affirming that even though Jesus is not physically present and the earthly monarchs appear to rule, in reality it is he, not they, who rules over all (6:15; 17:2). Another approach holds that Jesus rules over the defeated foes of believers, e.g., Satan, the dragon, sin, and death (1:18). A third possibility sees believers as the kings of the earth (2:26–27; 3:21; cf.

11:6). Support for this view comes from the reference to Christ's redeeming activity in the immediate context as well as by the reference to believers in v.6 as a "kingdom." All three ideas are true; so it is difficult to decide which was uppermost in John's mind. We should be careful, however, not to read into the term "king" our own power concepts but to allow the biblical images to predominate.

The mention of the person and offices of Christ leads John to a burst of praise to his Savior: "To him who loves us . . . be glory and power." In the present, Christ is loving us. Through all the immediate distresses, persecutions, and even banishment, John is convinced that believers are experiencing Christ's continual care. Moreover, in the past Christ's love was unmistakably revealed in his atoning death, by which he purchased our release from the captivity of sin. Christ's kingly power is chiefly revealed in his ability to transform individual lives through his "blood" (i.e., his death; cf. 5:9; 7:14). Through his death on the cross, he defeated the devil; and those who follow Christ in the battle against the devil share this victory. "They overcame him [the devil] by the blood of the Lamb and by the word of their testimony" (12:11).

6 This transformation simultaneously involves the induction of blood-freed sinners into Christ's "kingdom" and priesthood. Of Israel it was said that they would be a "kingdom of priests and a holy nation" (Exod 19:6; cf. Isa 61:6). The OT references as well as John's probably refer to both a "kingdom" and "priests" rather than a "kingdom of priests" (RSV). As Israel of old was redeemed through the Red Sea and was called to be a kingdom under God and a nation of priests to serve him, so John sees the Christian community as the continuation of the OT people of God, redeemed by Christ's blood and made heirs of his future kingly rule on the earth (5:10; 20:6). Furthermore, all believers are called to be priests in the sense of offering spiritual sacrifices and praise to God (Heb 13:15; 1 Peter 2:5). While John sees the church as a kingdom, this does not mean that it is identical with the kingdom of God. Neither do the new people of God replace the ancient Jewish people in the purpose of God (cf. Rom 11:28–29).

7 What Christ will do in the future is summed up in the dramatic cry: "Look, he is coming." This is a clear reference to the return of Christ (22:7, 12, 20). The preceding affirmation of Christ's rulership over the earth's kings and the Christians' share in the messianic kingdom leads to tension between the believers' actual present condition of oppression and suffering and what seems to be implied in their royal and priestly status. So the divine promise of Christ's return is given by the Father, and the response of the prophet and congregation follows in the words "So shall it be! Amen." Or we might think of Christ as saying, "So shall it be!" and the prophet and the congregation responding, "Amen" (cf. 22:20). The promise combines Daniel 7:13 with Zechariah 12:10 (taken from the Heb. text rather than LXX, as in John 19:37; cf. Matt 24:30, which also refers to the coming of Christ). Daniel 7 provides a key focus for John throughout the whole book (there are no fewer than thirty-one allusions to it).

Christ's coming will be supernatural ("with the clouds") and in some manner open and known to all ("every eye"), even to those who "pierced" him, i.e., put him to death. "Those who pierced him" might be those historically responsible for his death—such as Pilate, Annas, and Caiphas—and those Jewish leaders of the Sanhedrin who pronounced him guilty. And yet, when he comes, there will be mourning among "all the peoples of the earth." From the NT point of view, Pilate, Annas, Caiaphas, and the others were acting as representatives for all mankind in crucifying

Jesus. While it is possible to see this mourning as a lament of repentance and sorrow for putting the Son of God to death, more probably the mourning results from the judgment Christ brings upon the world. The expression "peoples of the earth" (*phylai;* lit., "tribes") is normally used throughout the LXX and NT of the tribes of Israel (7:4ff; 21:12; cf. Matt 19:28; 24:30). John, however, uses *phylai* in a number of places to refer more broadly to the peoples of all the nations (5:9; 7:9; 11:9; 13:7; 14:6)—a usage that seems natural here, also.

8 Such a stupendous promise requires more than the prophet's own signature or even Christ's "Amen." God himself speaks and, with his own signature, vouches for the truthfulness of the coming of Christ. Of the many names of God that reveal his character and memorialize his deeds, there are four strong ones in this verse: "Alpha and Omega," "Lord God," "who is, and who was, and who is to come," and "the Almighty" (cf. v.4 for comments on the second title). Alpha and omega are the first and last letters of the Greek alphabet. Their mention here is similar to the "First" and "Last" in v.17 and is further heightened by the "Beginning" and the "End" in 21:6 and 22:13. Only the Book of Revelation refers to God as the "Alpha and the Omega." God is the absolute source of all creation and history. Nothing lies outside of him. Therefore, he is the "Lord God" of all and is continually present to his people as the "Almighty" (*pantokratōr,* lit., "the one who has his hand on everything"; cf. 4:8; 11:17; 15:3; 16:7, 14; 19:6, 15; 21:22; 2 Cor 6:18).

Notes

---

4 Ἀπὸ (*apo,* "from") plus the nominative in the divine name presents a problem. G. Mussies (*The Morphology of Koine Greek as Used in the Apocalypse of St. John* [Leiden: E.J. Brill, 1971], p. 93) takes the nominative as an appositional nominative and not as an instance of *apo* with the nominative case.

5 Textual problems exist as to whether λύσαντι (*lysanti,* "freed") or λούσαντι (*lousanti,* "washed") is correct and whether ἀγαπῶντι (*agapōnti,* present tense, "loves") or ἀγαπήσαντι (*agapēsanti,* aorist tense, "loved") is the correct reading. In both cases the evidence is divided, but more diverse witnesses favor the adoption of the readings "freed" and "loves."

II. Vision of the Son of Man Among the Seven Churches of Asia (1:9–3:22)

A. *The Son of Man Among the Lampstands* (1:9–20)

1. *Introduction and voice*

1:9–11

9I, John, your brother and companion in the suffering and kingdom and patient endurance that are ours in Jesus, was on the island of Patmos because of the word of God and the testimony of Jesus. 10On the Lord's Day I was in the Spirit, and I heard behind me a loud voice like a trumpet, 11which said: "Write on a scroll what you see and send it to the seven churches: to Ephesus, Smyrna, Pergamum, Thyatira, Sardis, Philadelphia and Laodicea."

9 This verse begins a third introduction in which the author again identifies himself as John and adds further significant information about where and when the visions took place together with their divinely appointed destination. John stresses his intimate identification with the Asian Christians and the reason for his presence on Patmos.

One of the Sporades Islands, Patmos lies about thirty-seven miles west-southwest of Miletus, in the Icarian Sea. Consisting mainly of volcanic hills and rocky ground, Patmos is about ten miles long and six miles wide at the north end. It was an island used for Roman penal purposes. Tacitus refers to the use of such small islands for political banishment (*Annals* 3.68; 4.30; 15.71). Eusebius mentions that John was banished to the island by the emperor Domitian in A.D. 95 and released eighteen months later by Nerva (*Ecclesiastical History* 3.20. 8–9).

John indicates that it was "because of the word of God and the testimony of Jesus" that he was formerly on Patmos (cf. 1:2; 6:9; 20:4). He was not there to preach that Word but because of religious-political opposition to his faithfulness to it. John sees his plight as part of God's design and says he is a partner with Christians in three things: "suffering" ("ordeal," "tribulation," "distress," "agony"), "kingdom," and "patient endurance" (or "faithful endurance"). John and the Asian believers share with Christ and one another the suffering or agony that comes because of faithfulness to Christ as the only true Lord and God (John 16:33; Acts 14:22; Col 1:24; 2 Tim 3:12). Also, they share with Christ in his "kingdom" (power and rule). In one sense they already reign (1:6), though through suffering. Yet, in another sense, they will reign with Christ in the eschatological manifestation of his kingdom (20:4, 6; 22:5).

Finally, John sees the present hidden rule of Christ and his followers manifested through their "patient endurance." As they look beyond their immediate distresses and put their full confidence in Christ, they share now in his royal dignity and power. Whether those distresses were imprisonment, ostracism, slander, poverty, economic discrimination, hostility (both violent and nonviolent by synagogue, marketplace, and police), disruption of the churches by false prophets, and the constant threat of death from mob violence or judicial action, believers are to realize their present kingship with Christ in their faithful endurance.

Endurance is "the spiritual alchemy which transmutes suffering into royal dignity" (Charles, *Commentary on Revelation*, 1:21). It is the Christians' witness and their radical love in all spheres of life. It produces the conflict with the powers of the world, and it calls for long-suffering as the mark of Christ's kingship in their lives (2:2, 19; 3:10; 13:10; 14:12; cf., e.g., Luke 8:15; 21:19; Rom 2:7; 1 Cor 13:7; Col 1:11). Christ's royal power does not now crush opposition but uses suffering to test and purify the loyalty of his servants. His strength is revealed through their weakness (2 Cor 12:19). Christians are called, as was John, to reign now with Christ by willingly entering into suffering conflict with the powers of this age.

10 "I was in the Spirit" describes John's experience on Patmos. The words imply being transported into the world of prophetic visions by the Spirit of God (4:2; 17:3; 21:10; cf. Ezek 3:12, 14; 37:1; Acts 22:17). At least the first vision—if not the whole Book of Revelation—was revealed on "the Lord's Day" (*kyriakē hēmera*). Since this is the only place in the NT where this expression is used, its identification is difficult. Paul uses *kyriakē* as an adjective in 1 Corinthians 11:20 in reference to the "Lord's supper" (*kyriakon deipnon*). Some feel that John was transported into the future day of the Lord, the prophetic day of God's great judgment and the return of Christ (E.W.

Bullinger, *The Apocalypse,* 2d ed. [London: Eyre & Spottiswoode, 1909], p. 152). The major objection to this is that John does not use the common expression for the eschatological "day of the Lord" (*hēmera kyriou*). Others find a reference here to Easter Sunday and base it on the tradition reported in Jerome's commentary on Matthew 24, that Christ would return on Easter Eve (Friedrich Bleek, *Lectures on the Apocalypse,* ed. and trans. L.T. Hossbach and S. Davidson [London: Williams & Norgate, 1875], p. 156).

More recently a convincing attempt has been made to link the literary form of Revelation with the paschal (Easter) liturgy of the ancient church (Massey H. Shepherd, Jr., *The Paschal Liturgy and the Apocalypse* [Richmond: John Knox, 1960]). Most commentators, both ancient and modern, have, however, taken the expression to mean Sunday, the first day of the week (W. Stott, "A Note on *kyriakē* in Rev 1:10," NTS, 12 [1965], 70–75). This usage occurs early in the apostolic fathers (*Didache* 14; Ignatius *To the Magnesians* 9). Tendencies toward recognizing Sunday as a day designated by Christ to celebrate his redemption occur even in the earlier parts of the NT (Acts 20:7; 1 Cor 16:2). Such a reference would bind the exiled apostle to the worshiping churches in Asia through his longing to be with them on Sunday. It is not impossible, however, that the day referred to here was an Easter Sunday.

11 The "voice" John heard could be Christ's or, more likely, that of the angel who appears frequently to John (4:1; 5:2). What John sees (visions and words), he is to write down in a papyrus scroll and send to the seven Asian churches (v.4). This writing would include the substance of the whole book, not just the first vision. (For a map of the seven churches, see page 415.)

Notes

---

9 Newman, in defending his thesis that Revelation is an anti-Gnostic document, proposes that 1:9 should be repunctuated as follows: "I John, . . . was on the island called Patmos. On account of the Word of God and the testimony of Jesus, I was in the Spirit on the Lord's day." John's words would, then, "indicate that the revelation which he received was given to him while he was *in the Spirit*. This revelation would be a direct rebuttal against his Gnostic opponents, who claimed to possess revelations which came to them while they were under the influence of the Spirit" (italics his) (Barclay Newman, *Rediscovering the Book of Revelation* [Valley Forge: Judson, 1968], p. 15).

---

2. *The sight of the vision*

1:12–20

[12]I turned around to see the voice that was speaking to me. And when I turned
I saw seven golden lampstands, [13]and among the lampstands was someone "like
a son of man," dressed in a robe reaching down to his feet and with a golden sash
around his chest. [14]His head and hair were white like wool, as white as snow, and
his eyes were like blazing fire. [15]His feet were like bronze glowing in a furnace, and
his voice was like the sound of rushing waters. [16]In his right hand he held seven
stars, and out of his mouth came a sharp double-edged sword. His face was like
the sun shining in all its brilliance.

[17]When I saw him, I fell at his feet as though dead. Then he placed his right hand on me and said: "Do not be afraid. I am the First and the Last. [18]I am the Living One; I was dead, and behold I am alive for ever and ever! And I hold the keys of death and Hades.

[19]"Write, therefore, what you have seen, what is now and what will take place later. [20]The mystery of the seven stars that you saw in my right hand and of the seven golden lampstands is this: The seven stars are the angels of the seven churches, and the seven lampstands are the seven churches.

Certain important literary features of John's first vision are noted:

1. Beginning with v. 12, the vision extends as a unit through chapter 3. The quotation that begins in v. 17 is not closed till the end of chapter 3.

2. The introductory section (1:12–20) can be divided into two sections—the sevenfold features in the description of the glorified Christ (vv. 12–16) and the address to John (vv. 17–20).

3. In this symbolic picture the glorified Lord is seen in his inner reality that transcends his outward appearance. The sword coming out of his mouth (v. 16) alerts us to this. In words drawn almost entirely from imagery used in Daniel, Ezekiel, and Isaiah of God's majesty and power, John uses hyperbole to describe the indescribable reality of the glorified Christ. These same poetic phrases reappear in the letters to the churches in chapters 2 and 3 as well as throughout the rest of the book (14:2; 19:6, 12, 15).

4. The words of Christ give his absolute authority to address the churches. And the vision (vv. 12–16) leads to John's transformed understanding of Jesus as the Lord of all through his death and resurrection (vv. 17–18).

12 For the OT tabernacle, Moses constructed a seven-branched lampstand (Exod 25:31ff.). Subsequently this lampstand symbolized Israel. Zechariah had a vision of a seven-branched golden lampstand fed by seven pipes—explained to him as the "eyes of the Lord, which range through the earth" (4:10). Thus the lampstand relates directly to the Lord himself. Since other allusions to Zechariah's vision of the lampstand appear in the Revelation—e.g., "seven eyes, which are the seven spirits of God" (5:6) and the "two witnesses" that are "the two olive trees" (11:3–4)—it is logical to assume here a connection with that vision as well.

But there are problems in any strict identification. In v. 20 Christ tells John that the "seven lampstands are the seven churches" and in 2:5 that it is possible to lose one's place as a lampstand through a failure to repent. Therefore, the imagery represents the individual churches scattered among the nations—churches that bear the light of the divine revelation of the gospel of Christ to the world (Matt 5:14). If Zechariah's imagery was in John's mind, it might mean that the churches, which correspond to the people of God today, are light bearers only because of their intimate connection with Christ, the source of the light, through the power of the Holy Spirit (1:4b; 3:1; 4:5; 5:6).

13 Evidently the words "someone 'like a son of man' " are to be understood in connection with Daniel 7:13 as a reference to the heavenly Messiah who is also human. Jesus preferred the title Son of Man for himself throughout his earthly ministry, though he did not deny, on occasion, the appropriate use of "Son of God" as well (John 10:36; cf. Mark 14:61). Both titles are nearly identical terms for the

Messiah. The early church, however, refrained from using "Son of Man" for Jesus except rarely, such as when there was some special connection between the suffering of believers and Christ's suffering and glory (e.g., Acts 7:56; Rev 14:14; cf. Richard N. Longenecker, *The Christology of Early Jewish Christianity* [London: SCM, 1970], p. 92).

"Dressed in a robe" begins the sevenfold description of the Son of Man. The vision creates an impression of the whole rather than of particular abstract concepts. John saw Christ as the divine Son of God in the fullest sense of that term. He also saw him as fulfilling the OT descriptions of the coming Messiah by using terms drawn from the OT imagery of divine wisdom, power, steadfastness, and penetrating vision. The long robe and golden sash were worn by the priests in the OT (Exod 28:4) and may here signify Christ as the great High Priest to the churches in fulfillment of the OT Aaronic priesthood or, less specifically, may indicate his dignity and divine authority (Ezek 9:2, 11). In Ecclesiasticus 45:8, Aaron is mentioned as having the symbols of authority: "the linen breeches, the long robe, and the ephod."

14 In an apparent allusion to Daniel, Christ's head and hair are described as "white like wool, as white as snow" (Dan 7:9; cf. 10:5). For John, the same functions of ruler and judge ascribed to the "Ancient of Days" in Daniel's vision relate to Jesus. In Eastern countries, white hair commands respect and indicates the wisdom of years. This part of the vision may have shown John something of the deity and wisdom of Christ (cf. Col. 2:3). Christ's eyes were like a "blazing fire," a detail not found in Daniel's vision of the Son of man (Dan 7) but occurring in Daniel 10:6. This simile is repeated in the letter to Thyatira (2:18) and in the vision of Christ's triumphant return and defeat of his enemies (19:12). It may portray either his penetrating scrutiny or fierce judgment.

15 "His feet were like bronze glowing in a furnace" (cf. 2:18). The Greek is difficult (see Notes). His feet appeared like shining bronze, as if it were fired to white heat in a kiln. A similar figure of glowing metal is found in Ezekiel 1:13, 27; 8:2; Daniel 10:6. In both Ezekiel and Daniel the brightness of shining metal like fire is one of the symbols connected with the appearance of the glory of God. Revelation 2:18ff. might imply that the simile of feet "like burnished bronze" represents triumphant judgment (i.e., treading or trampling down) of those who are unbelieving and unfaithful to the truth of Christ.

"His voice was like the sound of rushing [lit., 'many'] waters" describes the glory and majesty of God in a way similar to that in Ezekiel (1:24; 43:2). Anyone who has heard the awe-inspiring sound of a Niagara or Victoria Falls cannot but appreciate this image of God's power and sovereignty (Ps 93:4). The same figure occurs in 14:2 and 19:6 (cf. also the Apocalypse of Ezra, a late Jewish book written about the same time or slightly earlier than Revelation; it similarly refers to the voice of God [4 Ezra 6:17]).

16 "In his right hand he held seven stars." The right hand is the place of power and safety, and the "seven stars" Christ held in it are identified with the seven angels of the seven churches in Asia (v.20). This is the only detail in the vision that is identified. Why the symbolism of stars? This probably relates to the use of "angels" as those to whom the letters to the seven churches are addressed (chs. 2–3). Stars are associated in the OT and in Revelation with angels (Job 38:7; Rev 9:1) or faithful witnesses to God (Dan 12:3). The first letter (that to Ephesus) includes in its introduction a reference to the seven stars (2:1), and in 3:1 they are associated closely with the "seven spirits of God."

John sees a "sharp double-edged sword" going forth from the mouth of Christ. Originally this was a large broad-bladed sword used by the Thracians (HDB, 4:634). The metaphor of a sword coming from the mouth is important for three reasons: (1) John refers to this characteristic of Christ several times (1:16; 2:12, 16; 19:15, 21); (2) he uses a rare word for sword (*rhomphaia*) that is found only once outside Revelation (Luke 2:35); and (3) there is no scriptural parallel to the expression except in Isaiah 11:4, where it is said that the Messiah will "strike the earth with the rod of his mouth" and "with the breath of his lips he will slay the wicked."

The sword is both a weapon and a symbol of war, oppression, anguish, and political authority. But John seems to intend a startling difference in the function of this sword, since it proceeds from the mouth of Christ rather than being wielded in his hand. Christ will overtake the Nicolaitans at Pergamos and make war with them by the sword of his mouth (2:12, 16). He strikes down the rebellious at his coming with such a sword (19:15, 21). The figure points definitely to divine judgment but not to the type of power wielded by the nations. Christ conquers the world through his death and resurrection, and the sword is his faithful witness to God's saving purposes. The weapons of his followers are loyalty, truthfulness, and righteousness (19:8, 14).

Finally, the face of Christ is likened to "the sun shining in all its brilliance." This is a simile of Christ's divine glory, preeminence, and victory (Matt 13:43; 17:2; cf. Rev 10:1; 1 Enoch 14:21).

17–18 These verses identify Christ to John and connect the vision of the glorified Christ (vv.13–16) with his existence in history. The vision is seen in the light of the Eternal One who identifies himself in these verses. "I fell at his feet as though dead" indicates that in the vision John actually saw a supernatural being and was stricken with trembling and fear, as had the prophets before him (Ezek 1:28; Dan 8:17; 10:9). Immediately Christ placed his hand on John and assured him that he would not die: "Do not be afraid" (cf. 2:10; 19:10; 22:8; Matt 17:6–7). The title "the First and the Last," which belongs to God in Isaiah 44:6 and 48:12 (where it means that he alone is God, the absolute Lord of history and the Creator), shows that in John's Christology Christ is identified with the Deity.

Christ is also "the Living One" in that he, like God, never changes. Probably this expression is a further elaboration of what it means to be "the First and the Last," i.e., he alone of all the gods can speak and act in the world (Josh 3:10; 1 Sam 17:26; Ps 42:2; Rev 7:2). These divine qualities of his person are now linked to his earthly existence in first-century Palestine—"I was dead, and behold I am alive for ever and ever!" This passage is sufficient to counter the claim that John's view of Christ does not revolve around atonement theology. On the contrary, his whole view of Jesus and his kingdom revolves around the Cross and resurrection—an interpretation that should serve to set the tone for all the visions that follow.

It was through Jesus' suffering, death, and resurrection that he won the right to have the "keys of death and Hades." Keys grant the holder access to interiors and their contents, and in ancient times the wearing of large keys was a mark of status in the community (cf. 3:7; 9:1; 20:1; 21:25). "Hades" translates the Hebrew term *šᵉʾôl* ("death," "grave") almost everywhere in the LXX. In the NT the word has a twofold usage: in some cases it denotes the place of all the departed dead (Acts 2:27, 31); in others, it refers to the place of the departed wicked (Luke 16:23; Rev 20:13–14). Since

Christ alone has conquered death and has himself come out of Hades, he alone can determine who will enter death and Hades and who will come out of these. He has the "keys." For the Christian, death can only be seen as the servant of Christ.

19 John is told to "write, therefore, what you have seen." This verse faces us with an important exegetical problem concerning the sense of the words and the relationship of the three clauses: "what you have seen, what is now and what will take place later." Does Christ give John a chronological outline as a key to the visions in the book? Many think he does. If so, are there three divisions: "seen," "now," and "later"? Or are there two: "seen," i.e., "now" and "later"? In the latter case, where does the chronological break take place in the book? For others, v.19 simply gives a general statement of the contents of all the visions throughout the book as containing a mixture of the "now" and the "later" (Moffatt, EGT, 5:347; Caird, p. 26).

While no general agreement prevails, the key to the problem may lie in the middle term "what is now." The Greek simply reads "which [things] are" (*ha eisin*). There are two possibilities. First, the verb can be taken temporally ("now") as NIV has done. This would refer to things that were present in John's day, e.g., matters discussed in the letters to the churches (2–3). Or second, the verb can be taken in the sense of "what they mean" (Alf, 4:559). This later explanation agrees with John's usage of the verb *eisin* throughout the book (cf. 1:20; 4:5; 5:6, 8; 7:14; 17:12, 15). "What they are [mean]" would immediately be given in the next verse, i.e., the explanation of the mystery of the lamps and stars. The change from the plural verb *eisin* in the second term to the singular *mellei* ("will") in the third tends to distinguish the last two expressions from both being time references.

Again, most commentators understand the phrase "what you have seen" as referring to the first vision (1:12–16); but it may refer to the whole book as the expression "what you see" in v.11 does (EGT, 5:347). In this case the translation could be either "what you saw, both the things that are and the things that will occur afterwards," or "what you saw, both what it means and what will occur afterwards." "What will take place later" clearly refers to the future, but to the future of what? Some have taken the similar but not identical phrase in 4:1 (q.v.) to mean the same as here and have rendered it "what shall take place after these present things," i.e., after the things relating to the seven churches (2–3). This results in either the historicist view of chapters 4–22 or in the futurist view of them. But if the future is simply the future visions given to John after this initial vision, then the statement has little significance in indicating chronological sequence in the book. While v.19 may provide a helpful key to the book's plan, on careful analysis it by no means gives us a clear key to it (see Notes).

John is told to write down a description of the vision of Christ he has just seen, what it means, and what he will see afterward, i.e., not the end-time things, but the things revealed later to him—whether they are wholly future, wholly present, or both future and present depends on the content of the vision. This leaves the question open concerning the structure of the book and its chronological progression, as John may have intended.

20 The first vision is called a "mystery" (*mystērion*). In the NT a "mystery" is something formerly secret but now revealed or identified. Thus John identifies the "mystery" of the harlot in chapter 17 by indicating that she is the "great city" that rules over the kings of the earth (vv.7, 18; cf. 10:7). The seven stars represent the "angels of the seven churches." Who are the angels? There is no totally satisfactory answer to this question. The Greek word for angels (*angeloi*) occurs sixty-seven times in Revelation and in every other instance refers to heavenly messengers, though occasionally in the NT it can mean a human messenger (Luke 7:24; 9:52; James 2:25 [Gr.]).

A strong objection to the human messenger sense here is the fact that the word is not used that way anywhere else in apocalyptic literature. Furthermore, in early noncanonical Christian literature no historical person connected with the church is ever called an *angelos*. Mounce and others (Beckwith, Morris) following Swete, who claims the idea comes from the Spanish Benedictine Beatus of Liebana (c.785) (p. 22), identify the angels as a "way of personifying the prevailing spirit of the church" (Mounce, *Revelation*, p. 82). Though this is an attractive approach to our Western way of thinking, it too lacks any supporting evidence in the NT use of the word *angelos* and especially of its use in Revelation. Therefore, this rare and difficult reference should be understood to refer to the heavenly messengers who have been entrusted by Christ with responsibility over the churches and yet who are so closely identified with them that the letters are addressed at the same time to these "messengers" and to the congregation (cf. the plural form in 2:10, 13, 23–24).

As stated in v.16, the stars are clearly linked in 3:1 with the seven spirits of God. Whatever may be the correct identification of the angels, the emphasis rests on Christ's immediate presence and communication through the Spirit to the churches. There is no warrant for connecting the seven stars with the seven planets or with images on Domitian's coins (Stauffer). In some sense, the reference to angels in the churches shows that the churches are more than a gathering of mere individuals or a social institution; they have a corporate and heavenly character (cf. 1 Cor 11:10; Eph 3:10; Heb 1:14). (See H. Berkhof, *Christ and the Powers* [Scottdale, Penn.: Herald, 1962] for further insight on the angelic ministries.) That the "seven lampstands are the seven churches" not only shows that the churches are the earthly counterpart of the stars but links the vision of Christ with his authority to rule and judge his churches.

Notes

11 The words "I am the Alpha and Omega, the first and the last" found in KJV have very little MS support, though the expression is represented in vv.8, 11.

13 Rowland has recently argued that the elements in this vision are not only taken from the angelophany of Dan 10:5ff. and the "son of man" image in Dan 7:15ff. but that these texts also can be traced to a theological history within Judaism that stretches back to the call-vision of the prophet Ezekiel (1:4–28). Apparently a trend developed in Jewish angelology that separated the human figure from the throne chariot in Ezekiel 8:2. Rowland suggests that Revelation 1:13ff. reflects this history and attempts to develop a Christology based on the "angel of the Lord" figure in the Old Testament. (C. Rowland, "The vision of the Risen Christ in Rev. 1:13ff.: The Debt of an Early Christology to an Aspect of Jewish Angelology" JTS, N.S., 31/1 (1980), 1–11.)

15 While πεπυρωμένης (*pepyrōmenēs*, "glowing") is supported by only A C, Bruce M. Metzger favors the reading (*A Textual Commentary on the Greek New Testament* [New York: UBS, 1971], p. 732). This ending would modify καμίνῳ (*kaminō*, "furnace"), which is feminine, but Mussies says it could just as well go with χαλκολιβάνῳ (*chalkolibanō*, "brass") (*Morphology*, p. 98).

19 W.C. VanUnnik argues from early Christian and Gnostic literature, especially from the Apocryphon of John, that this threefold expression was a standing formula to identify the true Christian prophet (NTS, 9:86–94).

B. *The Letters to the Seven Churches* (2:1–3:22)

1. *To Ephesus*

2:1–7

1"To the angel of the church in Ephesus write:
These are the words of him who holds the seven stars in his right hand and walks
among the seven golden lampstands: 2I know your deeds, your hard work and your
perseverance. I know that you cannot tolerate wicked men, that you have tested
those who claim to be apostles but are not, and have found them false. 3You have
persevered and have endured hardships for my name, and have not grown weary.
4Yet I hold this against you: You have forsaken your first love. 5Remember the
height from which you have fallen! Repent and do the things you did at first. If you
do not repent, I will come to you and remove your lampstand from its place. 6But
you have this in your favor: You hate the practices of the Nicolaitans, which I also
hate.
7He who has an ear, let him hear what the Spirit says to the churches. To him
who overcomes, I will give the right to eat from the tree of life, which is in the
paradise of God.

The letters are more in the nature of messages than letters. Each message to an individual church was apparently also intended for the other six churches (2:7, 11, 17, etc., esp. 2:23). By reading and comparing each similar component of all the letters, one may gain a fuller insight into the messages. Each message generally follows a common literary plan consisting of seven parts:

1. The addressee is first given. This pattern occurs in the same way at the beginning of each letter; viz., "To the angel of the church in Ephesus write," etc.

2. Then the speaker is mentioned. In each case, some part of the great vision of Christ and of his self-identification (1:12–20) is repeated as the speaker identifies himself; e.g., "him who holds the seven stars in his right hand and walks among the seven golden lampstands" (2:1; cf. 1:13, 16). This identification is preceded in each case with the significant declaration "These are the words of him"—a declaration strongly reminiscent of the OT formula for introducing the words of God to the congregation of Israel.

3. Next, the knowledge of the speaker is given. His is a divine knowledge. He knows intimately the works of the churches and the reality of their loyalty to him, despite outward appearances. Each congregation's total life is measured against the standard of Christ's life and the works they have embraced. In two cases that assessment proves totally negative (Sardis and Laodicea). In the message to Philadelphia, the speaker designates himself as "holy and true" (3:7); to the Laodiceans, he is "the faithful and true witness" (3:14). The enemy of Christ's churches is the deceiver, Satan, who seeks to undermine the churches' loyalty to Christ (2:10, 24).

4. Following his assessment of the churches' accomplishments, the speaker pronounces his verdict on their condition in such words as "You have forsaken your first love" (2:4) or "You are dead" (3:1). While two letters contain no unfavorable verdict

(Smyrna, Philadelphia) and two no word of commendation (Sardis, Laodicea), yet since all seven letters would be sent to each church together with the entire Book of Revelation (cf. 1:11), we may assume that Christ intended that all the churches hear words of both commendation and blame. In the letters all derelictions are viewed as forms of inner betrayals of a prior relation to Christ. Each congregation is responsible as a congregation for its individual members and for its leaders; each leader and each individual believer is at the same time fully responsible for himself and for the congregation. This responsibility especially involves the problem of self-deception concerning good and evil, the true and the false, in situations where they are easily confused. The evil appears under the cloak of good; the good appears as apparent evil. Christ's verdict sets before each church the true criteria for leading it out of self-deception into the truth.

5. To correct or alert each congregation, Jesus issues a penetrating command. These commands further expose the exact nature of the self-deception involved. We are mistaken if we believe that the churches readily identified the heretics and heresies involved in Christ's descriptions. Because they were deceptions, they would not easily be identified; thus there is the use of OT figures such as Balaam, Jezebel, etc., to alert the churches to the deceptiveness of the error. The greater the evil, the more deceptive the cloak. In the exposition of the letters, the commands must be carefully considered so as to determine precisely the particular nature of the various errors. The thrust of the commands is not in the direction of consolation for persecuted churches. It is rather the opposite—viz., that John, like Jesus, was concerned to bring not peace but a sword.

6. Each letter contains the general exhortation "he who has an ear, let him hear what the Spirit says to the churches" (2:7, et al.). Seven exactly identical exhortations occur with only the position in the letter as a variable. The words of the Spirit are the words of Christ (cf. 19:10). Actually, the commands of Christ in the letters are somewhat ambiguous. Therefore, they require the individual and the congregation to listen also to the Spirit's voice that accompanies the words of Jesus if they are truly to realize the victory he considers appropriate for them. The exhortations provide warnings about apathy as well as words of challenge and encouragement. Even though the words of Christ refer initially to the first-century churches located in particular places, by the Spirit's continual relevance they transcend that time limitation and speak to all the churches in every generation.

7. Finally, each letter contains a victor's promise of reward. These promises are often the most metaphorical and symbolic portions of the letters and thus in some cases present interpretative difficulties. Each is eschatological and is correlated with the last two chapters of the book (21–22). For example, "the right to eat from the tree of life, which is in the paradise of God" (2:7) is parallel to "the tree of life" in 22:2; protection from "the second death" (2:11) finds its counterpart in 21:4: "There will be no more death," etc. Furthermore, the promises are echoes of Genesis 2–3: what was lost originally by Adam in Eden is more than regained in Christ. The expression "I will give" or "I will make" identifies Christ as the absolute source and donor of every gift. Probably we are to understand the multiple promises as different facets that combine to make up one great promise to believers, that wherever Christ is, there will the overcomers be. Who are the "overcomers"? Certainly it is those who are fully loyal to Christ as his true disciples, those who are identified with him in his suffering and death (1 John 5:4–5). Compare those who do not overcome in 21:8 with those

referred to in the letters, e.g., the "cowardly" (2:10, 13), the "sexually immoral" (2:14, 20), the "idolaters" (2:14, 20), and the "liars" (2:2, 9, 20; 3:9).

The church at Ephesus is addressed in the first letter. Ephesus was a crossroads of civilization. Politically, it had become the de facto capital of the province, known as "Supreme Metropolis of Asia." The Roman governor resided there. It was a "free" city, i.e., self-governed. Located on the western coast of Asia Minor, at the convergence of three great highways, from the north, east, and south, Ephesus was the trade center of the area. It has been called "The Vanity Fair of the Ancient World" (William Barclay, *Letters to the Seven Churches* [New York: Abingdon, 1957], p. 12).

Religiously, Ephesus was the center for the worship of the fertility "bee" goddess known in Greek as "Artemis," or Romanized as "Diana" (Acts 19:23ff.). The temple with its statue of Artemis was one of the wonders of the ancient world. Thousands of priests and priestesses were involved in her service. Many of the priestesses were dedicated to cult prostitution. (This may be related to the "practices of the Nicolaitans" in v.6.) The temple also served as a great bank for kings and merchants, as well as an asylum for fleeing criminals. To what extent the temple phenomena contributed to the general moral deterioration of the population cannot be assessed, but one of Ephesus' own citizens, the weeping philosopher Heraclitus, said that the inhabitants of the city were "fit only to be drowned and that the reason why he could never laugh or smile was because he lived amidst such terrible uncleanness" (ibid., p. 17). The church at Ephesus was probably founded jointly by Aquila, Priscilla, and (later) Paul (Acts 18:18–19; 19:1–10). The Ephesians were cosmopolitan and transient, and their city had a history of cultural-political change; these factors may have influenced the apostasy of the congregation at Ephesus from its first love (cf. 2:4).

1 The speaker identifies himself by a reference to the vision of chapter 1: "Him who holds the seven stars in his right hand" (cf. 1:16). These words strike both a note of reassurance signaling Christ's strong protection and control of the church and his vital concern. On the other hand, there is a note of warning in the description of Christ as the one who "walks [travels] among the seven golden lampstands," since he may journey to Ephesus to remove their lampstand (2:5).

2–3 The speaker's knowledge includes awareness of their activity, their discernment of evil, and their patient suffering. Their "deeds," their "hard work" (*kopos,* "wearisome toil"), and their "perseverance" are underlined by the phrase "you have . . . endured hardships for my name, and have not grown weary" (v.3). The Ephesian Christians did not lack serious and sustained activity, even to the point of suffering for Christ's name. Paul attributes the same threefold activity to the Thessalonians and there adds to each quality its motivating source: "faith," "love," and "hope" (1 Thess 1:3).

Christ also knows that doctrinal discrimination accompanies the toil and patience of the Ephesians. They "cannot tolerate wicked men." These were not the pagans in Ephesus but false brethren who "claim to be apostles but are not." It is not easy, however, to determine precisely who these people were, what they taught, or how the church tested them. An "apostle" is one who is sent as a representative of another and bears the full authority of the sender (TDNT, 1:421). The word is applied first in the NT to the original circle of the Twelve (Mark 3:14; Acts 1:2, 26), who had a special place historically in the foundation of the church (Eph 2:20; Rev 21:14). But the NT further broadens this original circle to include others such as Paul (Gal 1:1), Barnabas (Acts 14:14), James the brother of Jesus (Gal 1:19), and still others (cf. Rom 16:7). The name was applied to those who were authentically and specially called by Christ to be his authoritative spokesmen.

Miracles were the signs of apostolic authority (2 Cor 12:12; Heb 2:4), but miracles may also accompany false prophets (Mark 13:22; 2 Thess 2:9; 2 Tim 3:8; Rev 13:13–14). Thus it was necessary to "test the spirits to see whether they are from God, because many false prophets have gone out into the world" (1 John 4:1). Beyond their denial of Jesus as Lord, these self-proclaimed apostles also sought selfish advantage through their claims (2 Cor 11:5, 13; 12:11).

As to whether the authoritative function of apostles continued after the first century, the apostolic fathers are instructive. In no case do the many references to apostles in the writings of Clement of Rome, Ignatius, Barnabas, and the Shepherd of Hermas relate to any recognized apostles other than those associated with the NT. The Fathers apparently understood the special apostolic function to have ceased with the end of the apostolic era.

About fifteen years later than John's writing of Revelation, Ignatius wrote to the church of Ephesus and commended them for refusing to give a "home" to any heresy (*To the Ephesians* 6, 7, 9, 16). Thyatira had failed (2:20ff.), but the Ephesians had won the victory over false teachers. They had heeded Paul's earlier warning (Acts 20:28–30).

4 The speaker's verdict shows, on the other hand, that however much had been gained at Ephesus by resisting the false apostles, not all was well there. They had "forsaken," or "let go" (*aphiēmi*), their "first love." This was a serious defect. If uncorrected, it would result in their loss of light bearing (v.5). The majority of commentators take the first love to refer to the original Christian love the Ephesians had for one another. Paul's exhortation to the Ephesian elders to "help the weak" (Acts 20:35) and the warm commendation he gives them in their early years for their fervent love of one another (Eph 1:15) may lend support to this view.

Other commentators, however, see the "first love" as a reference to their inner devotion to Christ that characterized their earlier commitment, like the love of a newly wedded bride for her husband (John R.W. Stott, *What Christ Thinks of the Church* [Grand Rapids: Eerdmans, 1958], p. 27; Alf, 4:563). This interpretation is supported by the fact that the letters to the other churches reveal problems of inner betrayal to Christ as subjects of his complaint. Neither view necessarily eliminates the other. Loving devotion to Christ can be lost in the midst of active service, and certainly no amount of orthodoxy can make up for a failure to love one another. "First" (*prōtos*) love would suggest that they still loved, but with a quality and intensity unlike that of their initial love.

5 The speaker's command further exposes the problem and offers a way to correct the fault. The imperatives are instructive: "Remember. . . . Repent . . . do." The Ephesians are called on to reflect on their earlier works of fervent love (like the Sardians [3:3]), to look in comparison at the present situation, to ponder how far they have fallen from their former devotion and enthusiasm, to humbly "repent" (totally change) before God, and to do the former works motivated by love. These imperatives are all part of a single action designed to keep the Ephesians from the judgment of Christ, which would effectively remove them as his representatives in the world.

How many churches today stand at this same crossroads? Do we sense the importance to Christ of not only honoring his name by our true confession but also reflecting his life by our loving relationship to others? This threat of loss of light bearing (or witness) applies doubtless equally to the other four churches, to whom a similar exhortation to repent is given (Pergamos, Thyatira, Sardis, and Laodicea).

6 Christ adds a further commendation concerning the Ephesians' hatred of the practices of the Nicolaitans (cf. 2:15)—a hatred directed at the practices of the Nicolaitans, not the people themselves (cf. Ps 139:21). It is difficult to determine exactly who the Nicolaitans were and what they taught. Etymologically the name means "to conquer [or 'consume,' *nikao*] the people [*laos*]." Did they call themselves by this name or is it a derogatory title Christ applied to them? The close association of the name with the Balaamites in 2:14–15 may suggest either identity with this group or similarity to their teachings (see comments on 2:14–15).

Information about the Nicolaitans is limited, ambiguous, and based on John's references here in Revelation. Irenaeus claims that John wrote the Gospel to thwart the teaching of the Gnostic Cerinthus whose error was similar to the earlier offshoot of the same kind of teaching known as Nicolaitanism (*Contra Haereses* 3.11.7, cited by Daniel J. Theron, *Evidence of Tradition* [Grand Rapids: Baker, 1958], p. 73). Eusebius mentions that the Nicolaitans lasted only a short time (*Ecclesiastical History* 3.29.1). Seeing the sect as a heresy would agree with the reference in 2:14 and 2:20, which warns against mixing Christian faith with idolatry and cult prostitution. Fiorenza identifies the group as Gnostics and summarizes the problem well: "The Nicolaitans are according to Revelation a Christian group within the churches of Asia Minor and have their adherents even among the itinerant missionaries and the prophetic teachers of the community. They claim to have insight into the divine or, more probably, into the demonic. They express their freedom in libertine behavior, which allows them to become part of their syncretistic pagan society and to participate in the Roman civil religion" (Elisabeth S. Fiorenza, "Apocalyptic and Gnosis in the Book of Revelation," JBL, 92 [1973], 570; see also Barclay Newman, *Rediscovering the Book of Revelation* [Valley Forge: Judson, 1968], pp. 11–30, who sees the entire Book of Revelation as an anti-Gnostic polemic rather than a political-religious persecution document). Others understand the Nicolaitans as Christians who still showed devotion to the emperor by burning incense to his statue or image (William M. Ramsay, *The Letters to the Seven Churches of Asia* [London: Hodder & Stoughton, 1904], pp. 300–301). (See also the letters to Pergamum and Thyatira.)

7 On the general exhortation and the meaning of "overcomes," see the introduction to this section (2:1). The overcomer is promised access to the "tree of life, which is in the paradise of God." The "tree of life" is first mentioned in Genesis 2:9 as one of the many trees given to Adam and Eve for food and was off bounds after their fall into sin (Gen 3:22, 24). It is last mentioned in Revelation 22:19.

Rabbinic and Jewish apocalyptic works mention that the glorious age of the Messiah would be a restoration to Edenic conditions before the Fall (see also Isa 51:3; Ezek 36:35; cf. Ezek 28:13; 31:8–9). Jewish thought joined the concepts of the renewed city of God, the tree of life, and the paradise of God. In the apocalyptic book the Testament of Levi it is promised that God (or Messiah) "shall open the gates of Paradise, and shall remove the threatening sword against Adam, and he shall give the saints to eat from the tree of life, and the spirit of holiness shall be on them" (18:10–11).

"Paradise" (*paradeisos*) is a Persian loan word meaning "a park" or "a garden." The LXX uses it to translate the Hebrew expression the "garden" of Eden (Gen 2:8–10). John seems to reinterpret the Jewish idea of Paradise. First, Jesus Christ is the restorer of the lost Paradise (22:1–4, 14). He gives access to the tree of life. Paradise means to be with him in fellowship rather than the idea of a hidden paradise with its fantastic sensual delights (TDNT, 6:772). The tree of life conveys symbolically the truth of eternal life or the banishment of death and suffering (22:2). Those at Ephesus who truly follow Christ in deep devotion and thus experience the real victory of Christ will share the gift of eternal life that he alone gives.

Notes

1 In addition to Ramsay's and Barclay's work on the seven churches, see also Otto F.A. Meinardus, *St. John of Patmos and the Seven Churches of the Apocalypse* (Athens, Greece: Lycabettus, 1974); idem, "The Christian Remains of the Seven Churches of the Apocalypse," BA, 37 (March 1974), 69–82; Minear, *I Saw a New Earth;* Ramsay, *Seven Churches;* R.C. Trench, *Commentary on the Epistles to the Seven Churches in Asia: Revelation II and III* (New York: Scribner's, 1862); J.R.W. Stott, *What Christ Thinks of the Church*. Two very detailed and accurate treatments of the historical interpretation and archaeological research regarding the cities of the seven churches, with extensive bibliographies, are Edwin Yamauchi's *Archaeology of New Testament Cities in Western Asia Minor* (Grand Rapids: Baker, 1980) and Colin Hemer's four excellent articles on the seven churches in *Buried History*, 11 (1975), 4–27; 56–83; 110–35; 164–90. In 1969 Hemer wrote a dissertation at Manchester University entitled "A Study of the Letters to the Seven Churches of Asia with Special Reference to Their Local Background," which in revised form is to be published in the New Testament Monographs series by Cambridge University.

2. *To Smyrna*

2:8–11

8 "To the angel of the church in Smyrna write:

These are the words of him who is the First and the Last, who died and came
to life again. 9 I know your afflictions and your poverty—yet you are rich! I know the
slander of those who say they are Jews and are not, but are a synagogue of Satan.
10 Do not be afraid of what you are about to suffer. I tell you, the devil will put some
of you in prison to test you, and you will suffer persecution for ten days. Be faithful,
even to the point of death, and I will give you the crown of life.
11 He who has an ear, let him hear what the Spirit says to the churches. He who
overcomes will not be hurt at all by the second death.

Smyrna (modern Izmir) lay almost due north of Ephesus, a distance of about forty miles. The city was exceptionally beautiful and large (c. 200,000 pop.) and ranked with Ephesus and Pergamum as "First of Asia." Known as the birthplace of Homer, it was also an important seaport that commanded the mouth of the Hermus River valley. Smyrna was a wealthy city where learning, especially in the sciences and medicine, flourished. An old city (third millennium B.C.), allegedly founded by a mythical Amazon who gave her name to it, Smyrna repeatedly sided with Rome in different periods of her history, and thus earned special privileges as a free city and assize (self-governed) town under Tiberius and successive emperors. Among the beautiful paved streets traversing it from east to west was the "Golden Street," with the temples to Cybele and Zeus at either end and along which were temples to Apollo, Asclepius, and Aphrodite.

Smyrna was also a center of the emperor worship, having won the privilege from the Roman Senate in A.D. 23 (over eleven other cities) of building the first temple in honor of Tiberius. Under Domitian (A.D. 81–96) emperor worship became compulsory for every Roman citizen on threat of death. Once a year a citizen had to burn incense on the altar to the godhead of Caesar, after which he was issued a certificate. Barclay (*Seven Churches,* p. 29) quotes a request for such a certificate, and the certificate itself.

> To those who have been appointed to preside over the sacrifices, from Inares Akeus, from the village of Theoxenis, together with his children Aias and Hera, who reside in the village of Theadelphia. We have always sacrificed to the gods, and now, in your presence, according to the regulations, we have sacrificed and offered libations, and tasted the sacred things, and we ask you to give us a certification that we have done so. May you fare well.
>
> We, the representatives of the Emperor, Serenos and Hermas, have seen you sacrificing. (*Seven Churches,* p. 29).

Such an act was probably considered more as an expression of political loyalty than religious worship, and all a citizen had to do was burn a pinch of incense and say, "Caesar is Lord [*kyrios*]." Yet most Christians refused to do this. Perhaps nowhere was life for a Christian more perilous than in this city of zealous emperor worship. About sixty years later (c. 156), Polycarp was burned alive at the age of eighty-six as the "twelfth martyr in Smyrna" (IDB, 4:393). His words have echoed through the ages: "Eighty-six years have I served Christ, and he has never done me wrong. How can I blaspheme my King who saved me?" (Eusebius *Ecclesiastical History* 4.15.25). There was a modern-day parallel to the predicament of Christians under Roman emperor worship when the Japanese occupied Korea in 1937–40 and ordered Christians to worship at their Shinto shrines. Many Christians refused and were imprisoned and tortured (Keun, Han Woo, *History of Korea,* ed. G.K. Muntz, tr. Lee Kyuen-Shik [Seoul: Eul-Woo, 1970], p. 496). A large and hostile Jewish community at Smyrna was prominent in Polycarp's death and no doubt troubled the church also in John's day (2:9) (Barclay, *Seven Churches,* p. 31). Concerning the founding of the Smyrna church, we have no information other than this letter to it.

8 The speaker identifies himself as "him who is the First and the Last, who died and came to life again" (cf. comments on 1:17–18). The "First and Last" might remind those suffering persecution and rejection from their countrymen (vv.9–10) that the one they belong to is the Lord of history and the Creator. He is in control regardless of appearances of evil. Ramsay suggests that the term may allude by contrast to Smyrna's claim to be the "first" of Asia in beauty and emperor loyalty (*Seven Churches,* pp. 269–70). But Christians at Smyrna were concerned with him who was truly first in everything.

He who is "the First and the Last" is also the one "who died" (lit., "became a corpse") and "came to life again." To a congregation where imprisonment and death impend, the prisoner who died and came back to life again can offer the crown of life to other executed prisoners and protect them from the second death (vv.8, 10–11).

There might also be an allusion here to the history of the city of Smyrna, which had been destroyed in the seventh century B.C. and rebuilt in the third century B.C. (ibid., p. 269).

9 The speaker's knowledge is threefold: (1) He knows their "afflictions" (*thlipsis*)—a word later translated "persecution" (v.10). (2) He knows their "poverty." This can only mean material poverty because the speaker (Christ) immediately adds, "Yet you are rich" (toward God). Why was this church so poor in such a prosperous city? We do not know. Perhaps the high esteem of emperor worship in the city produced economic sanctions against Christians who refused to participate. In Smyrna, economic pressure may have been the first step toward persecution. Sometimes, even today, for Christians to be loyal to their Lord entails economic loss (cf. 3:17). (3) The risen Lord also knows "the slander of those who say they are Jews and are not, but are a synagogue of Satan." Trouble arose from the Jewish community (cf. commentary on v.8). Certain Jews (not all of them) used malicious untruths ("slander") to incite persecution to the impoverished saints in Smyrna. They "say they are Jews but are not" shows that even though these men claimed descent from Abraham, they were not his true descendants because they did not have faith in Christ, the "Seed" of Abraham (Gal 3:16, 29). These unbelieving and hostile Jews probably viewed the Jewish Christians at Smyrna as heretics of the worst sort, deserving ridicule and rejection. Whether Christians in general were now the "true" Jews, or whether it is those Jews in Smyrna who became Christians who are the "true" Jews is debatable (cf. comments on 7:4).

"But are of the synagogue of Satan" reveals for the first time in Revelation the ultimate source of the persecution of Christians—Satan. Many further references to the archenemy of the followers of Christ are found throughout the book (2:13; 3:9; 9:11; 12:9–10, 12; 13:4; 20:2, 7, 10). In fact, he is one of the principal actors in the apocalyptic drama. While Satan is the author of persecution and wicked men are his instruments, God remains sovereign in that he will give "the crown of life" to those who are "faithful, even to the point of death" (v.10). "Synagogue of Satan" refers, then, to certain Jews in ancient Smyrna who, motivated by Satan, slandered the church there. The term should never be indiscriminately applied to all Jewish synagogues.

10 The speaker's command immediately follows since no word of verdict or fault is spoken of. The prospect of further and imminent suffering may have made the believers at Smyrna fearful: "Do not be afraid of what you are about to suffer" (lit., "Stop being afraid . . ."). The risen Christ reveals that some of them will be imprisoned by the devil in order to test them, and they will have ten days of persecution. Who will do this—whether Jew or pagan—is not stated. The testing will show where their true loyalty lies. For a faithful and suffering church, Christ offers further trial and suffering, even "to the point of death." The "ten days" may be ten actual days. Or it may be a Semitism for an indeterminate but comparatively short period of time (cf. Neh 4:12; Dan 1:12). In the first-century Roman world, prison was usually not punitive but the prelude to trial and execution, hence the words "Be faithful, even to the point of death."

For those who would face martyrdom out of loyalty to Christ, there was to be a "crown of life" given by Christ himself. Those at Smyrna would be very familiar with the term "the crown of Smyrna," which no doubt alluded to the beautiful skyline formed around the city by the "hill Pagos, with the stately public buildings on its rounded sloping sides" (Ramsay, *Seven Churches*, p. 256). The "crown" usually referred to a garland of flowers worn chiefly in the worship of the pagan gods such as Cybele or Bacchus, who was pictured on coins with a crown of battlements. Faithful servants of the city appeared on coins with laurel wreaths on their heads (Barclay, *Seven Churches*, p. 39). As the patriots of Smyrna were faithful to Rome and to their crown city, so Christ's people are to be faithful unto death to him who will give them the imperishable crown of life (James 1:12; 1 Peter 5:4).

11 The general exhortation to all the churches is identical to the parallel passages in the other letters (cf. introduction to letters). For those who overcome, the promise is that they "will not be hurt at all by the second death." Death was a real possibility for these believers. But greater than the fear of physical death should be the fear of God's eternal judgment (Luke 12:4–5). The "second death" is a well-known Targumic expression, but it does not occur elsewhere in Jewish literature. Moses prays, "Let Reuben live in this world, and not die in the second death, in which death the wicked die in the world to come" (paraphrase of Deut 33:6 found in the Paris MS 110, cited by M. McNamara, *Targum and Testament: Aramaic Paraphrases of the Hebrew Bible; A Light on the New Testament*, [Grand Rapids: Eerdmans, 1962], p. 148). Even though death was the outcome of Adam's sin, in Christ there is a complete reversal for man (Gen 2:16–17; Rom 5:15ff.). Since the messianic believers at Smyrna were under attack by some in the Jewish community, it was reassuring indeed to hear the Lord himself say that his followers would not be harmed by the second death—viz., the lake of fire (20:14; 21:8).

Notes

8 Besides Ramsay's studies already cited, cf. C.J. Cadoux, *Ancient Smyrna* (Oxford: Blackwell, 1938), esp. pp. 228–366.

3. *To Pergamum*

2:12–17

[12]"To the angel of the church in Pergamum write:

These are the words of him who has the sharp, double-edged sword. [13]I know
where you live—where Satan has his throne. Yet you remain true to my name. You
did not renounce your faith in me, even in the days of Antipas, my faithful witness,
who was put to death in your city—where Satan lives.
[14]Nevertheless, I have a few things against you: You have people there who hold
to the teaching of Balaam, who taught Balak to entice the Israelites to sin by eating
food sacrificed to idols and by committing sexual immorality. [15]Likewise you also
have those who hold to the teaching of the Nicolaitans. [16]Repent therefore! Otherwise, I will soon come to you and will fight against them with the sword of my mouth.
[17]He who has an ear, let him hear what the Spirit says to the churches. To him
who overcomes, I will give some of the hidden manna. I will also give him a white
stone with a new name written on it, known only to him who receives it.

The inland city of Pergamum lay about sixty-five miles north of Smyrna along the fertile valley of the Caicus River. Pergamum held the official honor of being the provincial capital of Roman Asia, though this honor was in fact also claimed by Ephesus and Smyrna. Among its notable features were its beauty and wealth; its library of nearly two hundred thousand volumes (second only to the library of Alexandria); its famous sculpture; its temples to Dionysus, Athena, Asclepius, and Demeter and the three temples to the emperor cult; its great altar to Soter Zeus; and its many palaces. The two main religions seem to have been the worship of Dionysus, the god of the royal kings, symbolized by the bull, and Asclepius, the savior god of healing, represented by the snake (Ramsay, *Seven Churches*, p. 284). This latter feature made Pergamum the "Lourdes of the ancient world" (Charles, *Commentary on Revelation*, 1:60). Tradition also records that in Pergamum, King Eumenes II (197–159 B.C.) planned to build a library to rival the one in Alexandria. Ptolemy Epiphanes of Egypt (205–182 B.C.) took action to stop this venture by cutting off the export of papyrus sections. It was this embargo that forced Eumenes to develop vellum or parchment (*pergamēnē*, "from Pergamum"), a writing material made from animal skins. Josephus mentions a Jewish community at Pergamum (Antiq. XIV, 247 [x. 22]).

12 The speaker identifies himself as "him who has the sharp, double-edged sword" (cf. comments on 1:16 and cf. Isa 49:2). In dealing with the Pergamum congregation, divided by deceptive teaching, the risen Lord will use this sword to fight against the Balaamites and the Nicolaitans (v.16). It is interesting that Pergamum was a city to which Rome had given the rare power of capital punishment (*ius gladii*), which was symbolized by the sword. The Christians in Pergamum were thus reminded that though they lived under the rule of an almost unlimited *imperium*, they were citizens of another kingdom—that of him who needs no other sword than that of his mouth (Caird, p. 38).

13 The speaker's knowledge is searching: he knows that they live in a hostile and difficult place—"where Satan has his throne." This certainly refers to the fact that Pergamum was a center for worship of the pagan gods, especially the emperor cult. The first temple in the empire was established in honor of Augustus in A.D. 29 at Pergamum because it was the administrative capital of Asia. In succeeding years the city boasted of being the official *neokoros* ("temple sweeper") of the "temple where Caesar was worshiped" (Barclay, *Seven Churches*, p. 45). Others see the reference to the altar of savior Zeus or the center of worship of Asclepius, the snake god of healing. Pergamum was an idolatrous center; and to declare oneself in that place a Christian who worships the one true God and Savior, Jesus Christ, would certainly provoke hostility.

Furthermore, the risen Lord knew their loyalty to him in all that he is revealed to be ("my name") even when "Antipas, my faithful witness, . . . was put to death in [their] city." Nothing further is known about Antipas than the meaning of his name—viz., "against all." The proximity of the name "Satan" before and after Antipas in v.13 makes it virtually certain that his death was instigated by the enmity of pagans in Pergamum. He may have been the first or most notable of martyrs. Christ pays this hero of the faith a noble tribute: "faithful witness"—words that John applies to Christ himself in 1:5. Satan tries to undermine loyalty to Christ by persecution; Christ strengthens that loyalty by commending those who are true to him and by exposing those who are deceitful.

14–15 The speaker's verdict reveals that the church in Pergamum was divided. Some had followed Antipas and did not deny Christ's name or his faith (v.13). Others held to the teaching and practice of the Balaamites and Nicolaitans that Christ hates (2:6). Since the name "Balaam" can mean to "conquer the people" (Heb. *ba'al 'am*), which means the same as "Nicolaitans," and since they are mentioned together in this letter, both groups may be closely related (see Notes, v.15). In fact, the error in the church at Thyatira through the teaching of the woman Jezebel may also be similar to this one. In that letter and this one, the more deadly effects of the error are described as "eating food sacrificed to idols and committing sexual immorality" (2:14, 20).

The OT names Balaam and Jezebel serve to alert the church community to the insidious nature of the teaching that was not until now recognized as overtly evil. Since Satan's chief method is deception, his devices are not known until they are clearly pointed out. Christ exposes error here by identifying the false teaching in Pergamum with clear-cut evil such as that of Balaam and Jezebel. Balak, king of Moab, could not succeed in getting the venial prophet Balaam to curse Israel directly. But Balaam devised a plan whereby the daughters of the Moabites would seduce the Israelite men and lead them to sacrifice to their god Baal-peor and worship him (Num 25:1ff.; 31:16; cf. 2 Peter 2:15; Jude 11). So God's judgment fell on Israel because of fornication and idolatry. What Balak was not able to accomplish directly, he got through Balaam's deception. While the Ephesians recognized the Nicolaitan error (v.6), apparently Pergamum and Thyatira were deceived by it; it was an unconscious subversion. What Satan could not accomplish at Smyrna or Pergamum through intimidation, suffering, and death from outside the church, he achieved from within.

The combination of "food sacrificed to idols" with "sexual immorality" may refer to the common practice of participating in the sacrificial meal of the pagan gods (cf. 1 Cor 10:19–22) and indulging in sexual intercourse with temple priestesses in cult prostitution. This is the more normal way to understand the term "sexual immorality" in the context of the pagan gods. Some feel, however, that the term refers to spiritual unfaithfulness and apostasy from Christ (cf. Isa 1:21; Ezek 23:37). But the prevalence of sexual immorality in first-century pagan society makes it entirely possible that some Christians at Pergamum were still participating in the holiday festivities and saw no wrong in indulging in the "harmless" table in the temples and the sexual excitement everyone else was enjoying (cf. 1 John 5:21). Will Durant made the following observation on the pagan festivities:

> At the center and summit of [each Greek] city was the shrine of the city god; participation in the worship of the god was the sign, the privilege, and the requisite of citizenship. In the spring, the Greek cities celebrated the Athesterion, or feast of flowers, a three-day festival to Dionysus [a chief deity at Pergamum!] in which wine flowed freely and everybody was more or less drunk. At the end of March came the great Dyonysia, a widely observed series of processional and plays accompanied by general revelry. At the beginning of April various cities in Greece celebrated [Aphrodite's] great festival, the Aphrodisia; and on that occasion, for those who cared to take part, sexual freedom was the order of the day (*The Story of Civilization* [New York: Simon and Schuster, 1939], vol. 2, *Life of Greece*, pp. 75, 185).

16 The speaker's command includes both a call to the whole congregation to repent and a special threat to the heretical members if they do not repent. Since those who did not indulge in these things tolerated their practice by some of the church's members, they, along with the guilty, needed to repent. If those at Pergamum will not heed the word of Christ's warning, that word from his mouth will become a "sword" to fight against the disloyal. (Curiously, Balaam himself was slain by the "sword" [Num 31:8].) The words "I will soon come to you" should be understood as a coming "against" the congregation in judgment, as in v.5, and not as a reference to Christ's second coming.

17 The promise to the overcomer includes three difficult symbols: "hidden manna," "a white stone," and "a new name." The "hidden manna" is reminiscent of the manna hidden in the ark of the covenant by Moses (Exod 16:33–34; Heb 9:4). Since Moses' pot of manna was designed to remind the Israelites of God's grace and faithfulness in the wilderness (Ps 78:24), there may be a similar thought here. In apocalyptic Jewish teaching, however, the messianic era will see the restoration of the hidden wilderness manna: "And it shall come to pass at that self-same time (in the days when the Messiah comes) that the treasury of manna shall again descend from on high, and they will eat of it in those years" (2 Baruch 29:8; Sib Oracles 7:149). To those at Pergamum who refused the banquets of the pagan gods, Christ will give the manna of his great banquet of eternal life in the kingdom (John 6:47–58).

The "white stone" is a puzzle. It has been thought of in relation to voting pebbles, an inscribed invitation to a banquet, a victory symbol, an amulet, or a counting pebble. It seems best to link the stone to the thought of the manna and see it as an allusion to an invitation that entitled its bearer to attend one of the pagan banquets.

The "new name . . . known only to him who receives it" is either the name of Christ himself, now hidden from the world but to be revealed in the future as the most powerful of names (3:12; 14:1), or the believer's new name or changed character through redemption (Isa 62:2; 65:15). Pritchard cites an Egyptian text concerning the goddess Isis plotting to learn the secret name of the supreme god Re to gain his hidden power for herself. The one who knew the hidden name received the power and status of the god who revealed it (ANET, p. 12). Hence the name was jealously guarded by the god. This background would fit the context here in Revelation—viz., to Christians tempted to compromise their loyalty to Christ to gain the favor of the pagan gods, Christ generously offers himself and the power of his name so that those who have faith in him may overcome.

Notes

13 The reading *καὶ ὅπου ὁ θρόνος τοῦ Σατανᾶ* (*kai hopou ho thronos tou Satana,* "even the throne of Satan") in the TR and reflected by KJV seems warranted on good MS evidence (046 plus many late MSS). *Καὶ* (*kai,* "even") modifies the sense slightly by broadening the faithfulness of those in Pergamum beyond Antipas's time. Copyists probably omitted the word, not recognizing its ascensive use in the sentence (Bruce M. Metzger, *A Textual Commentary on the Greek New Testament,* [New York: UBS, 1971], p. 733).

Wood has argued that the reference to "Satan's throne" may be "topographical" rather than merely religious: "The actual shape of the city-hill towered, as it still does, like a giant throne above the plain" (Peter Wood, "Local Knowledge in the Letters of the Apocalypse," ET, 73 [1962], 264).

15 The TR has ὃ μισῶ (*ho misō,* "which I hate") instead of ὁμοίως (*homoiōs,* "likewise"). However, *homoiōs* agrees with οὕτως (*houtōs,* "also," "in this way") to call attention to the strong similarity of the two teachings—possibly to imply their identity. The sentence might then read, "In fact, you have people there who similarly hold the teaching of the Nicolaitans."

---

4. *To Thyatira*

2:18–29

[18]"To the angel of the church in Thyatira write:

These are the words of the Son of God, whose eyes are like blazing fire and whose feet are like burnished bronze. [19]I know your deeds, your love and faith, your service and perseverance, and that you are now doing more than you did at first.
[20]Nevertheless, I have this against you: You tolerate that woman Jezebel, who calls herself a prophetess. By her teaching she misleads my servants into sexual immorality and the eating of food sacrificed to idols. [21]I have given her time to repent of her immorality, but she is unwilling. [22]So I will cast her on a bed of suffering, and I will make those who commit adultery with her suffer intensely, unless they repent of her ways. [23]I will strike her children dead. Then all the churches will know that I am he who searches hearts and minds, and I will repay each of you according to your deeds. [24]Now I say to the rest of you in Thyatira, to you who do not hold to her teaching and have not learned Satan's so-called deep secrets (I will not impose any other burden on you): [25]Only hold on to what you have until I come.
[26]To him who overcomes and does my will to the end, I will give authority over the nations—

[27]'He will rule them with an iron scepter;
he will dash them to pieces like pottery'—

just as I have received authority from my Father. [28]I will also give him the morning star. [29]He who has an ear, let him hear what the Spirit says to the churches.

On the inland route about forty-five miles due east of Pergamum was the city of Thyatira. Although not a great city, it was nevertheless important through commerce in wool, linen, apparel, dyed stuffs, leatherwork, tanning, and excellent bronzework. Associated with its commerce was an extensive trade guild or labor union network, which must have played a prominent role in the social, political, economic, and religious life of the city. Each guild had its own patron deity, feasts, and seasonal festivities that included sexual revelries. Religiously, the city was unimportant, though worship of Apollo and Artemis (Diana) was prominent. Acts 16:14 mentions that Lydia, a proselyte of the gate, came from the Jewish settlement at Thyatira. She was a distributor of garments made of the purple dye substance known as "Turkey red" and no doubt a member of the dyers' guild. It has been suggested that some of Paul's converts at Ephesus went out and evangelized Thyatira (Acts 19:10).

18 The speaker of this fourth letter, the longest of the seven, identifies himself as "the Son of God, whose eyes are like blazing fire and whose feet are like burnished bronze" (cf. comments on 1:14–15). The expression "Son of God" appears only here in the book. It is a designation for the Messiah and is almost equivalent to the more frequently used title "Son of Man" and probably anticipates the quotation from the messianic second Psalm in v.27, which implies the term. But the name might also have captured the attention of those who were enticed by the emperor cult into calling Caesar the Son of God. That Christ's eyes are here described as blazing fire might be an allusion to the sun god, Apollo, worshipped at Thyatira. More likely, however, it refers to his penetrating discernment of the false prophetess Jezebel (v.23). The feet of Christ, which are like burnished bronze, would no doubt have special significance to the bronze-workers at Thyatira.

19 The speaker's knowledge of the Thyatirans' works is essentially twofold: he knows their love and faithfulness. Their love manifests itself in "service" and their faithfulness in "perseverance" during trial. Their present state reflects outstanding progress, but there is a perilous flaw in the church there.

20 The speaker's verdict reveals that the congregation had allowed a woman prophetess (a false one, according to Christ's assessment) to remain in the church and to continue to teach the saints to indulge in "sexual immorality" and to "eat food sacrificed to idols." The genuine gift of prophecy was highly respected in the early church. Along with apostles, teachers, and elders, prophets were often elevated to leadership (1 Cor 12:28; Eph 4:11). Women also received the genuine gift of prophecy (Luke 2:36; Acts 21:9; 1 Cor 11:5). Prophets generally brought direct revelation from God in the form of teaching as well as occasional predictions of the future (Acts 11:27). Tests for a true prophet, as for the true apostle (2:2), were available but often difficult to apply.

This supposedly Christian woman at Thyatira had claimed to be a "prophetess," gifted as such by the Holy Spirit. She must have been elevated to prominence in the church because of her unusual gifts. But only a small minority saw through her pious deception (v.24); the rest either followed her or ignored her views without objecting to her presence in the church. In order to expose her true character, she is labeled "Jezebel"—the name of the Canaanite wife of Israel's King Ahab. Jezebel had not only led Ahab to worship Baal but through Ahab had promulgated her teachings of idolatry throughout all Israel (1 Kings 16:31–33; 2 Kings 9:22).

We must not, however, press the similarity too far. As this wicked and deceptive woman in the OT led Israel astray and persecuted the true prophets of God, so this woman at Thyatira was enticing the servants of God to abandon their exclusive loyalty to Christ. Her teaching was no doubt similar to that of the Nicolaitans and Balaamites at Ephesus and Pergamum. While most commentators prefer to see the "sexual immorality" as spiritual adultery (i.e., idolatry), the possibility of cultic fornication should not be ruled out for reasons cited above (cf. 2:14). The distinction between the woman and those who follow her (v.22) may argue against the view that she is symbolic of a group in the church, unless the "woman" represents the false prophets and her "children" are those who follow the teaching. In 2 John the "chosen lady" is probably a reference to the faithful congregation, while "her children" refers to individuals in the congregation who represent her.

21–22 Christ's verdict continues with his strongest accusation directed against, not Jezebel's perversion, serious as that is, nor even against her successful deception of fellow Christians, but against her refusal to repent. Although Christ has dealt with her over a period of time, she will not change her ways or her thinking. The Lord, therefore, will judge Jezebel by two swift acts. She will be "hurled" (NIV, "cast") into a bed, and her children will be put to death. The "bed" or "couch" (*klinē*) can mean a bed used for resting, for guild-banqueting, or for sickness. Ramsay adopts the banqueting sense and relates it to the idol-feast couches (*Seven Churches*, p. 352). Others suggest a bed of sickness or suffering, seen as an act of God's visitation or judgment. On a bed she sinned, on a bed she will suffer; and those who committed adultery with her will also suffer intensely.

As in the case of Jezebel, Christ's strongest threat to the offenders is not in regard to their sin, serious as that is, but to their reluctance to repent. The Lord is walking among his churches. He judges evil; but he also offers deliverance to those who have fallen, if they repent and stop doing Jezebel's deeds.

23 For those who follow Jezebel ("her children") and refuse to repent, a fatal judgment will be meted out by the Lord Christ: "I will strike her children dead" (lit., "I will kill her children with death"—perhaps a Heb. idiom denoting "pestilence" [6:8]). Some understand "her children" to refer to her actual children, born of the sexual sins, rather than to her followers (Beckwith, p. 467). This cannot be decided with certainty. Whatever the exact nature of the judgment, it is announced beforehand by Christ so that when it occurs not just Thyatira but "all the churches will know that I am he who searches hearts and minds," since they too will read the same letter and will later hear of the historical outcome. OT references ascribe omniscience to God alone (Ps 7:9; Prov 24:12; Jer 17:10). "Heart" is literally "kidneys" (Heb., *kᵉlāyôṯ;* Gr., *nephroi*), which in Semitic thought represented the moral center of the life, while "mind" is literally "heart" (Heb., *lēḇ;* Gr., *kardia*), which represents the totality of the feelings, thoughts, and desires traced back to one's deepest inner life. There is nothing in our thoughts or desires that is hidden from Christ's penetrating gaze (Heb 4:12–13). Our only safety from judgment is in repentance. The risen Lord does not stop with searching hearts and minds but brings recompense according to deeds: for faithfulness, reward; for unfaithfulness, judgment.

24–25 Christ's only command to the church at Thyatira was probably for the minority who had sufficient insight to penetrate Jezebel's deception. They are to simply "hold on to what you have" (i.e., their insight into Jezebel's teaching and evil deeds) till Christ returns (v.25). This small group may have been nearer his standard than any other group mentioned in Revelation because they could discriminate between authentic and spurious worship.

The reference to "Satan's so-called deep secrets" is ambiguous (cf. "the deep things of God" [1 Cor 2:10]). It may mean the "deep things," i.e., the secret knowledge of God reserved only for the initiates into the heretical teaching. This would suggest a form of Christian Gnosticism, an early heretical teaching. The words "so-called" would then be a mocking remark of John's—"the so-called deep things of God, which are in fact of Satan" (Bruce, "Revelation," p. 639).

However, this view rests on the doubtful thesis of a developed Christian Gnosticism in the first century (cf. Edwin Yamauchi, *Pre-Christian Gnosticism* [Grand Rapids: Eerdmans, 1973], pp. 55, 185) and strains the normal sense of the Greek. Therefore, another sense is preferable—viz., that the "deep secrets of Satan" is the actual phrase Jezebel used. But could she lure Christians by using such a term? The reasoning of some in the early church (the Nicolaitans) might have gone something like this: The only effective way to confront Satan was to enter into his strongholds; the real nature of sin could only be learned by experience, and therefore only those who had really experienced sin could truly appreciate grace. So by experiencing the depths of paganism ("the deep secrets of Satan"), one would better be equipped to serve Christ, or be an example of freedom to his brothers (cf. 1 Cor 8:9–11). Thus the sin of Jezebel was deadly serious because of the depths of its deception. Only a few perceived where the teaching was leading.

"Until I come" is the first of several references to the second coming of Christ in these letters (cf. 1:7).

26–27 The promise to the overcomers is twofold: "authority over nations" and the gift of "the morning star." It contains one important modification of the regular overcomer's formula. Added to the words "to him who overcomes" is "and does my will to the end" (lit., "who keeps my works until the end"). It reminds us of Jesus' statement in his great eschatological discourse, that "he who stands firm to the end will be saved (Matt 24:13), and of Paul's words to the Colossians about continuing in the faith "established and firm" (Col 1:23). The proof of authentic trust in Jesus is steadfastness of belief and continuance in the will of God till Christ returns or death comes.

The first promise is a fulfillment of Psalm 2, which is messianic and tells how the Father gave the Messiah the rule over the nations of the world. This psalm plays an important part in thinking about Christ (11:18; 12:5; 19:15). The coming reign of the Messiah over the world is to be shared with his disciples (1:6; 3:21; 20:6; 1 Cor 6:2). In the pre-Christian apocryphal Psalms of Solomon, the same psalm is used with reference to the Messiah and the Jews who will reign with him (17:23–24). Here in vv.26–27 its use seems to indicate that the overcomers will participate with Christ in fulfilling the promise of Psalm 2:9. There is a paradox in the combination of the mild word "rule" (*poimainō*, lit., "to shepherd") with the harsh words "with an iron scepter; he will dash them to pieces like pottery" (cf. comments on 19:11ff.). The prospect of such a reversal of their present experience of oppression and persecution would be a constant encouragement for suffering Christians.

28 Second, the overcomers in Thyatira are promised "the morning star" (*astera ton prōinon*). Some link this expression to Christ himself as in 22:16. Believers would then receive Christ as their very life. Or it may refer to the Resurrection in the sense that the morning star rises over the darkness of this world's persecution and offers victory over it. Perhaps a combination of the two thoughts may be intended. The promise of Christ's return is like the "morning star [*phōsphoros*]" (2 Peter 1:19). (See 22:16, where Jesus calls himself "the bright Morning Star" [*ho astēr ho lampros ho prōinos*], in apparent reference to his return.)

29 In this fourth letter and in the three that follow it, the general exhortation comes at the very end; in the first three letters, however, it precedes the promise (cf. comments at introduction to the seven letters).

Notes

---

20 Alexandrinas (A), generally a good witness in Rev, and a number of other witnesses include the word σου (*sou*, "your") after γυναῖκά (*gynaika*, "woman"), giving the sense "your wife." This implies taking "angel" in 1:18 and elsewhere in chs. 2–3 as the bishop or overseer of the church. This inferior reading probably arose through scribal confusion with other frequent references to *sou* in the letters.

The TR has ὀλίγα (*oliga*, "a few things") included in the verdict words, thus reading,

"I have a few things against you." NIV rightly follows the numerous and varied witnesses that omit *oliga*.

27 According to Trudinger's analysis (L. Paul Trudinger, "Some Observations Concerning the Text of the Old Testament in the Book of Revelation," JTS, 17 [1966], 84–85), the text that John follows in the OT quotation from Ps 2:9 is closer to a Semitic original than to the LXX, from which it is generally thought to be derived. He finds at least thirty-nine direct quotations and as many allusions in Rev that go against the LXX in favor of a Semitic text.

---

5. *To Sardis*

3:1–6

1"To the angel of the church in Sardis write:

These are the words of him who holds the seven spirits of God and the seven
stars. I know your deeds; you have a reputation of being alive, but you are dead.
2Wake up! Strengthen what remains and is about to die, for I have not found your
deeds complete in the sight of my God. 3Remember, therefore, what you have
received and heard; obey it, and repent. But if you do not wake up, I will come like
a thief, and you will not know at what time I will come to you.
4Yet you have a few people in Sardis who have not soiled their clothes. They will
walk with me, dressed in white, for they are worthy. 5He who overcomes will, like
them, be dressed in white. I will never erase his name from the book of life, but will
acknowledge his name before my Father and his angels. 6He who has an ear, let
him hear what the Spirit says to the churches.

Sardis was about thirty miles south of Thyatira. Its location commanded the trade of the Aegean Islands and the military road through the important Hermus River valley. Sardis enjoyed prominence as a commercially prosperous and militarily strategic city throughout its history. The city's topography was notable for the acropolis, the temple of Artemis, and the necropolis. The acropolis rose about eight hundred feet above the north section of Sardis and was virtually impregnable because of its rock walls, which were nearly vertical, except on the south side. Formerly the site of the original city, the acropolis became a refuge for the inhabitants in time of siege.

Only twice in the history of Sardis was its fortress ever captured, though attacks on it were frequent. When Cyrus attacked it in the sixth century B.C., a shrewd Persian soldier observed a Sardian descending the southern winding path to retrieve his fallen helmet. Unknown to the soldier, the Persians followed his path back up to the summit and captured the whole city, taking them quite by surprise. There was a similar occurrence when Antiochus attacked Sardis about two hundred years later.

The temple to Artemis (possibly Cybele) equaled in size the famous temple of Artemis in Ephesus. However, the temple at Sardis was never finished.

A third feature of Sardis was the impressive necropolis, or cemetery, of "a thousand hills" (modern Bin Tepe), so named because of the hundreds of burial mounds visible on the skyline some seven miles from Sardis.

Sardis retained its wealth into the first two centuries of the Christian Era. But its political brilliance as the capital city of Asia for Persia lay in the past. Ramsay aptly remarks, "No city of Asia at that time showed such a melancholy contrast between past splendor and present decay as Sardis" (William M. Ramsay, *The Letters to the Seven Churches of Asia* [London: Hodder & Stoughton, 1904], p. 375). In A.D. 26, Sardis begged the Roman Senate to grant it the coveted honor of building a temple to Caesar. The distinction, however, went to Smyrna. The luxurious living of the Sardians led to moral decadence. Herodotus (fifth century B.C.) wrote despairingly of Sardis and its people as "the tender-footed Lydians, who can only play on the cithara, strike the guitar, and sell by retail" (William Barclay, *Letters to the Seven Churches* [New York: Abingdon, 1957], p. 71). Sardis was a city of peace, not the peace won through battle, but "the peace of the man whose dreams are dead and whose mind is asleep, the peace of lethargy and evasion" (ibid., p. 72). A great wool industry flourished at Sardis, and this may account for Christ's reference to clothing (v.4).

1 The speaker identifies himself as "him who holds the seven spirits of God and the seven stars" (cf. comments on 1:4 and 1:16, 20; 2:1). To the Sardians, Christ reveals himself as the one who controls the seven spirits of God. If the Sardian church is strong, it is because Christ has sent his Spirit to encourage and quicken the Sardian believers; if they are dead like Sardis, it is because in judgment he has withdrawn his Spirit from them. Yet the faithful minority at Sardis (v.4) can count on that divine power of Christ to sustain, give life, and mobilize them to do his will even though the majority are dead. (On the "seven stars," cf. comments at 2:1.)

The speaker's knowledge of the church in Sardis reveals their true condition. He knows their "deeds." It is not clear whether this alludes to their past accomplishments, which gave them their reputation of being alive, or whether the reference is to their present deeds, which were not those Christ sought from them. This latter view is supported by v.2, where he mentions their deeds again and says they are incomplete. He also knows that though they claim to be a healthy Christian church, in reality they are "dead."

How does a church die? Why does Christ use this expression for Sardis even though the churches in Thyatira and Laodicea also had serious problems? Sardis had had significant fame as a royal city, but now it was nothing. The citizens were living off past fame. Apparently the same spirit had affected the church. Their loyalty and service to Christ was in the past. Now they were nothing. It may be that they had so made peace with the surrounding society that the offense of the Cross had ceased, and they were no longer in jeopardy of life or vulnerable to suffering. Further facts emerge when we consider the series of commands in vv.2–3. Death was a special preoccupation of the Sardians, as witnessed by the impressive necropolis seven miles from the city. What had been a part of the pagan rites had also crept into the church. But again this work of the enemy came through deception. The Sardian church was for the most part a duped church.

2 The command "Wake up!" or "Be watchful" (present tense, "Be constantly alert") is a call to reverse their attitudes radically. The congregation must be alerted to the seriousness of the situation. Their complacency led them to give up their identification with Christ and their mission for him. The situation was dire but not totally hopeless. Immediate steps were to be taken to "strengthen what remains." Some persons and things were salvageable if quick and decisive action were taken. Otherwise, death would follow.

The Sardians' deeds are in danger of judgment because Christ has not found them "complete [*peplērōmena*, 'full,' 'fulfilled,' 'filled up to measure'] in the sight of my God." Though this could refer to incompleteness in the number of their deeds, more likely it describes the quality of their deeds—they do not measure up to the standard

Christ sets. In the other letters, works acceptable to Christ are love, faithfulness, perseverance, keeping Christ's words, and not denying his name.

3 Like those in Ephesus, the Sardians must remember what they "have received and heard." What they "received" was the apostolic tradition of the gospel; what they "heard" probably were the teachings of the apostles and prophets who brought the gospel to them. Unlike the church at Philadelphia (v.8), the Sardians were not holding to the word of Christ. For them repentance was the only way out of certain and final death. So they were to repent by restoring the gospel and the apostolic doctrine to its authority over their lives. This would mean they would once more start obeying (*tēreō*, "keep," "watch") the truth of Christ's word. Today's church needs to hear this challenge to take the word of Christ seriously. Unless the church at Sardis repents, Christ says that he will come to them in judgment "as a thief"—i.e., by surprise—just as Sardis had been attacked and defeated by Cyrus long before. "As a thief" should probably not be taken as referring to the Second Coming but to Christ's coming against them (opposing them) in judgment (cf. his threat to the church in Ephesus in 2:5).

4 While the majority had departed from faithful obedience to Christ, a few at Sardis remained true. Here an allusion to the wool industry at Sardis intensifies the image of soiled and defiled garments. Those with soiled garments were removed from the public lists of citizens in Sardis. In the pagan religions it was forbidden to approach the gods in garments that were soiled or stained (Barclay, *Seven Churches*, p. 77). Soiling seems to be a symbol for mingling with pagan life and thus defiling the purity of one's relation to Christ (14:4; 1 Cor 8:7; 2 Cor 7:1; 11:2; Jude 23). To "walk with Christ" symbolizes salvation and fellowship with him—something the others at Sardis had forfeited through their sin (1 John 1:6–7). "White" garments are symbolic of the righteousness, victory, and glory of God (3:18; 6:11; 7:9, 13f.; 19:14). As Caird (p. 49) observes, this passage shows that not all faithful Christians were martyrs, nor can we make emperor worship the sole source of the problems of the early Christians. Ironically, the Sardians were occupied with their outward appearance, but they were not concerned with inner purity toward Christ and their outward moral life in a pagan society.

5 The overcomer's promise is threefold and grows out of the reference to white clothing.

1. "Like" the faithful Sardian Christians who would receive white clothes from Christ, the others there who overcame the stains of pagan society would similarly be dressed in white.

2. Furthermore, the pure relationship to Christ is permanently guaranteed: "I will never erase his name from the book of life." In ancient cities the names of citizens were recorded in a register till their death; then their names were erased or marked out of the book of the living. This same idea appears in the OT (Exod 32:32–33; Ps 69:28; Isa 4:3). From the idea of being recorded in God's book of the living (or the righteous) comes the sense of belonging to God's eternal kingdom or possessing eternal life (Dan 12:1; Luke 10:20; Phil 4:3; Heb 12:23; Rev 13:8; 17:8; 20:15; 21:27). For Christ to say that he will never blot out or erase the overcomer's name from the book of life is the strongest affirmation that death can never separate us from Christ and his life (Rom 8:38–39). A person enrolled in the book of life by faith remains in

it by faithfulness and can be erased only by disloyalty. There is some evidence that a person's name could be removed from the city register before death if he were convicted of a crime. In the first century, Christians who were loyal to Christ were under constant threat of being branded political and social rebels and then stripped of their citizenship. But Christ offers them an eternal, safe citizenship in his everlasting kingdom if they only remain loyal to him.

3. Finally, to the overcomer Christ promised to "acknowledge his name before [the] Father and his angels." "Acknowledge" (*homologeō*) is a strong word for confession before the courts. It is Christ's confession of our name before the Father and his angels (implying our fellowship with him) that assures our heavenly citizenship (Matt 10:32; Luke 12:8).

What ultimately counts, then, is not our acceptance by this world's societies but that our relationship to Christ is genuine and hence will merit his approbation in the coming kingdom.

6 Again, the general exhortation comes last, as in the previous letter (cf. comments in the introduction to the seven letters).

Notes

1 See also John G. Pedley, *Ancient Literary Sources on Sardis* (Cambridge, Mass.: Harvard University Press, 1972).

2 The imperfect tense in *ἃ ἔμελλον ἀποθανεῖν* (*ha emellon apothanein,* "what is about to die") probably looks back from the reader's point of view to the time when John saw the vision. At the same time, it expresses the conviction of the writer that the worst would soon be past (Swete, p. 48; Ernest Burton, *Syntax of the Moods and Tenses of New Testament Greek,* 3d ed. [Edinburgh: T. & T. Clark, 1898], par. 73).

4 S. David Garber argues that the white robes mentioned throughout the Book of Revelation refer to the divine gift of salvation that can be preserved only through continued discipleship. He also sees a possible allusion to the idea of a heavenly or spiritual body of glory that accompanies the resurrection—an idea that occurs frequently in the Jewish apocalyptic literature but which is different than the white-clothing imagery found among the Gnostic religions ("Symbolism of Heavenly Robes in the New Testament in Comparison with Gnostic Thought" [Ph.D. diss., Princeton Theological Seminary, 1974], pp. 307–14).

5 The reading *οὕτως* (*houtōs,* "like them") over *οὗτος* (*houtos,* "this one") is by no means certain. While Metzger et al. argues for the first reading on superior MS evidence (Bruce M. Metzger, *A Textual Commentary on the Greek New Testament* [New York: UBS, 1971], p. 736), Alford (Alf, in loc.) and Beckwith (in loc.) have a point in suggesting that the author would have used *ὁμοίως* (*homoiōs,* "likewise"), not *houtōs* to express similarity.

6. *To Philadelphia*

3:7–13

7 "To the angel of the church in Philadelphia write:

These are the words of him who is holy and true, who holds the key of David.
What he opens, no one can shut; and what he shuts, no one can open. 8 I know

your deeds. See, I have placed before you an open door that no one can shut. I know that you have little strength, yet you have kept my word and have not denied my name. [9]I will make those who are of the synagogue of Satan, who claim to be Jews though they are not, but are liars—I will make them come and fall down at your feet and acknowledge that I have loved you. [10]Since you have kept my command to endure patiently, I will also keep you from the hour of trial that is going to come upon the whole world to test those who live on the earth.

[11]I am coming soon. Hold on to what you have, so that no one will take your crown. [12]Him who overcomes I will make a pillar in the temple of my God. Never again will he leave it. I will write on him the name of my God and the name of the city of my God, the new Jerusalem, which is coming down out of heaven from my God; and I will also write on him my new name. [13]He who has an ear, let him hear what the Spirit says to the churches.

About twenty-five miles southeast of Sardis, along the Hermus River valley, lay the important high plateau city of Philadelphia, modern Alasehir. A main highway that ran through the city connected Smyrna (about a hundred miles due west) to northwest Asia, Phrygia, and the east. Furthermore, the imperial post road of the first century A.D., which came from Rome via Troas, Adramyttium, Pergamum, and Sardis, passed through this valley and Philadelphia on the way to the east. So situated, Philadelphia became a strong fortress city. To the northeast was a great vine-growing district, which, along with textile and leather industries, contributed greatly to the city's prosperity.

Philadelphia was established by the Pergamenian king Attalus II (159–138 B.C.), who had been given the epithet "Philadelphus" ("brother lover") because of his love for his brother. The city was to be a mission city for disseminating Greco-Asiatic culture and language in the eastern part of Lydia and in Phrygia. Its success is attested by the fact that the Lydian language ceased to be spoken in Lydia by A.D. 19 and Greek took over (Ramsay, *Seven Churches*, p. 391). But beyond this language achievement, Philadelphia had not been successful in converting the Phrygians (Barclay, *Seven Churches*, p. 80).

According to Strabo, the whole region was earthquake prone (*Geography* 12.579; 13.628). In A.D. 17 an earthquake that destroyed Sardis and ten other cities also destroyed Philadelphia. Consequently, many people preferred to live in the rural area surrounding the city. The fear of earthquakes caused those who continued to live in the city to leave it at the slightest sign of a tremor.

After the devastating earthquake, Tiberius came to the peoples' aid and had the city rebuilt. In gratitude the citizens renamed it Neocaesarea ("New Caesar"). Later the name was changed to Flavia (A.D. 70–79), and this, along with Philadelphia, continued to be its name through the second and third centuries A.D. Later, the establishment of the emperor cult in the city earned it the title "Neokoros," or "Temple Warden" (c. 211–17). In the fifth century, it was nicknamed "Little Athens" because of its proliferation of festivals and pagan cults. Whether this indicates something of its early period is uncertain. Since wine was one of the city's important industries, some have assumed that the worship of Dionysus was a chief pagan cult in it (Swete, p. 52).

Although nothing is known about the origin of the Philadelphian church, in A.D. 100–160 the church prospered under the ministry of a prophetess named Ammia, who was universally recognized as ranking with Agabus and the four daughters of Philip in her possession of the gift of prophecy (Eusebius *Ecclesiastical History* 5.17.2). Long after all the surrounding country had succumbed to Muslim control under

Turkey, Philadelphia held out as a Christian populace till 1392. Even Gibbon admired its fortitude (Ramsay, *Seven Churches,* p. 400).

7 The letter to the church in Philadelphia begins with the speaker's identifying himself as "him who is holy and true, who holds the key of David. What he opens, no one can shut; and what he shuts, no one can open." Each of these identifications calls attention to Jesus as the true Messiah. "Holy and true" relate to God himself and describe aspects of his presence among us (cf. 6:10). Holiness is the attribute of God whereby we sense the presence of the "Wholly Other," the one who says, "I am God, and not man—the Holy One among you" (Hos 11:9). He is the "True One" in that he is wholly trustworthy and reliable in his words and actions. For this congregation for whom Christ has only commendation, these titles would bring encouragement, despite their "little strength" (v.8) to go on in their faithfulness, in contrast to those described in v.9.

The reference to the "key of David" alludes to Isaiah 22:20ff. and the incident of transferring the post of secretary of state in Judah from the unfaithful Shebna to the faithful Eliakim. The "key" signifies the power of the keys that were normally held by the king himself, unless delegated to another. The use of the name "David" points to Christ as the Messiah, who alone determines who will participate in his kingdom and who will be turned away: "He opens, no one can shut; . . . he shuts, no one can open." This may allude to the false claims of certain Jews at Philadelphia who argued that they, not the heretical Nazarenes, would inherit the kingdom of David (v.9) and thus excluded the followers of Jesus. But the true Messiah, Jesus, will exclude them!

8 Here the knowledge of the speaker and his verdict blend together in untarnished praise as in the letter to Smyrna. Between the declaration "I know your deeds" and the words "you have little strength, yet you have kept my word and have not denied my name" is the somewhat awkward interjection "See, I have placed before you an open door that no one can shut."

Since Christ has absolute authority from the Father, he has opened a door for the Philadelphians that even their enemies cannot close. But an open door to what? Swete (in loc.) sees an inference here to Philadelphia as a missionary city. As the easternmost of the seven cities and an outpost on the high tableland of upper Asia, it was effective in evangelizing the area with Hellenism. So the witness of the church in Philadelphia will be effective despite its small strength (1 Cor 16:9; Col 4:3). Others feel that v.8 refers to Christ's opening the door to his kingdom for those who love him and thus reinforces the statement in v.7 about opening and shutting.

Beckwith protests against the first view: "Such a reference to future missionary activity of the church is singularly out of place, thrust in as a parenthesis between the parts of a sentence concerned with commendation of the church for its steadfastness in the past" (p. 430). The context strongly favors the second view (so Ladd, *Commentary on Revelation,* in loc.). What became a serious problem at Sardis (v.3) was not the case with the Philadelphian congregation, to whom the risen Christ said, "You have kept my word." They had been faithful to the Gospel and the apostles' teaching even during the trial of their faith alluded to in the words "and have not denied my name" (cf. 2:13).

9 Here those opposing the witness of the congregation are characterized as "those who are of the synagogue of Satan, who claim to be Jews though they are not, but are liars." The words are like those spoken to the church in Smyrna (cf. comments on 2:9). A "synagogue of Satan" appears to describe a Jewish element that vehemently denied Jesus as the Messiah and that actively persecuted others who made this claim. A true Jew in the view of Jews like John and Paul is one who has found forgiveness and life in Jesus the Messiah, while a false Jew is one who rejects those who believe in Jesus and openly persecutes them; such a one is an antichrist (1 John 2:22).

In writing to the church in Philadelphia a few years later, Ignatius warned them not to listen to "any one propounding Judaism unto you" (*To the Philadelphians* 6.1)—a warning that might refer to certain Christians who tried to lead others into Judaism as did the Judaizers of Paul's day (Acts 15:1; Gal 3:4). Perhaps the words "have not denied my name" in v.8 relate to this. But Christ will make those who have persecuted the followers of Jesus as heretics acknowledge that God is indeed with the church in Philadelphia and that they are not heretics but are God's people.

We catch a glimpse here of the ever-widening gap between Judaism and Christianity toward the end of the first century. The church is the true people of God, loved by Christ, and in some real sense inheritors of the covenant promises in the OT made to the people of God (Isa 43:4; 45:14; 49:23; 60:14). In these OT passages it is the Gentiles, or heathen nations, who bow before Israel and acknowledge that God is with them. In this letter Christ reverses these roles: his followers are the people of God, and Jewish unbelievers are the pagans who come and acknowledge the love of the Messiah for the church! There is, however, no indication of when such acknowledgment will come or of what nature it will be. Ladd (*Commentary on Revelation*, p. 61) sees this as a fulfillment of Paul's expectation of the conversion of "all Israel" (i.e., of the majority of the Jewish people) at some time in the future (Rom 11:25–26; cf. esp. v.28). Most commentaries evade this issue.

Against Ladd's view, however, is the fact that the context seems to require retribution on Christ's enemies, not their conversion. Be that as it may, underlying v.9 is the same truth Paul expressed in Philippians 2:10–11: "At the name of Jesus every knee should bow, . . . and every tongue confess that Jesus Christ is Lord, to the glory of God the Father." Some will do this joyfully and some remorsefully—not penitently (cf. 6:12–17). Mounce (*Revelation*, p. 118) calls this the eschatological interpretation and refers to Isaiah 60:14 ("the sons of your oppressors will come bowing before you"), where Israel in the eschatological future will receive the acknowledgment from the pagan nations that their God is indeed the true Lord. What the Jews expected from the pagans, they themselves will be forced to render to the followers of Jesus.

10 This is another promise given the church in Philadelphia. Though not part of the promise to the overcomers in Philadelphia (v.12), like the special promises to Smyrna and Sardis (2:10; 3:4), it may be taken as a promise to all the churches. The words "since you have kept my command to endure patiently" (lit., "kept the word of my patience") refer to the condition under which the promise is valid. Some translate the phrase as in NIV, inferring that the "word of my patience" means the command of Christ to endure suffering, or to endure till he returns (Luke 21:19; cf. Heb 10:36). Others translate it as "the word enjoining Christ's patient endurance" (Ladd, *Commentary on Revelation*, p. 61). In that case it would refer to an apostolic teaching (such as Paul's) encouraging Christians to endure the contrariness of a sinful world after the pattern of Christ's own endurance (2 Thess 3:5; Heb 12:3). The Greek text slightly favors the latter translation, though the former is also possible.

Related to the promise "I will also keep you from the hour of trial that is going to come upon the whole world to test those who live on the earth" are two problems: the identification of the "hour of trial" and the precise sense of the phrase "keep you from the hour of trial." Both involve the ongoing debate among evangelical eschatologists over the Tribulation-Rapture question.

We can dismiss the view that the "hour of trial" refers to some general or personal distress that will come upon the Philadelphian community and from which the church will be delivered (so J. Barton Payne, *The Imminent Appearing of Christ* [Grand Rapids: Eerdmans, 1962], pp. 78–79). Though the universality of the expression "the whole world" is reason enough to refute Payne's view, the phrase "those who live on the earth" is repeated in Revelation a number of times and refers not to believers but to unbelievers who are the objects of God's wrath—i.e., the "beast-worshipers" (6:10; 8:13; 11:10; 12:12; 13:8, 12, 14; cf. Isa 24; Jer 13:12–14; IQH 8.19–36).

According to some interpreters (Ladd, Mounce, Walvoord), the "hour of trial" (*hōras tou peirasmou,* "time of temptation") is better understood as the time known to the Jews as the "messianic woes," a time of intense trouble to fall on the world before the coming of Christ and known as the eschatological "day of the Lord," or the "Great Tribulation" (Dan 12:1; Joel 2:31; Mark 13:14; 2 Thess 2:1–12; Rev 14:7). This "hour of trial," then, will be the one described in such detail in the following chapters of the book. In that case what, then, is the effect of the promise "I will also keep you from the hour of trial"? There are two possibilities. Some argue, with reference to the same Greek expression (*tēreō ek,* "keep from") in John 17:15, that the sense is preservation while in the trial, since to be kept from evil or the evil one does not mean to be removed from his presence but simply to be kept from his harmful power. Therefore, the church universal will experience preservation from harm in the trial of persecution and suffering and will not be raptured till the end of the period (Ladd; cf. 1 Thess 4:13ff.).

On the other hand, some writers offer these objections to this exegesis: (1) The "hour of trial" John describes is a judgment from God on the unbelieving inhabitants of the world, not a form of evil such as John 17:15 describes. (2) It is not true that the saints of the Tribulation period are exempt from harm during this period; a great group of them will be martyred (6:9–11; 7:9–14, etc.). (3) In the Gospel of John, preservation is from the devil; in Revelation, from a time period—the "hour" of trial (J.B. Smith, pp. 88–89).

Ladd offsets some of this criticism by advocating that the hour of trial has two aspects—the fierce persecution of believers by the beast and the outpouring of divine judgments on a rebellious world represented in the trumpet and bowl plagues. Believers are kept from the harm of the latter but not the former (*Commentary on Revelation*, p. 62). The difficulty in this view lies in Ladd's failure to identify clearly the hour of trial in this verse. It cannot refer to both the Great Tribulation (7:14) on believers and the wrath of God.

In our opinion, this confusion may be avoided by clearly identifying "the hour of trial" as the wrath of God, deliverance from which is promised to every one of Christ's overcomers. As a matter of fact, the expression *tēreō ek* ("keep out of") cannot be proved exegetically to be different from *tēreō apo* ("keep from"). In the LXX of Proverbs 7:5 the sense of this latter expression is to deliver the man from contact with or the presence of the harlot. In James 1:27 the same expression means to be kept from the pollution of the world. In both instances the sense is that of exemption from something. Can one, then, be exempt from the "hour of trial" that will try the whole world by famines, earthquakes, wars, floods, etc., and still be present on the earth? Yes, but removal is still a possible method of protection.

The above discussion shows that v.10 does not settle the question of the time of the Rapture in relation to the Tribulation. Rather, it remains ambiguous. One might be on the earth and yet be exempt from the "hour of trial" if (1) the "hour of trial" is an equivalent derived from the briefer term "trial" and (2) if this "trial" is directed only at the unbelievers in the world while the believers are divinely immune, not from trial or persecution in general, but from a specific type of trial (God's wrath) that is aimed at the rebellious on the earth. To this writer, the most natural way to understand the expression to be "kept from the hour" of something that is universal in the world is not to be preserved through it but to be kept from being present when it happens. In any event, we have here a marvelous promise of Christ's protection (*tēreō*, "keep") for those who have protected (*tēreō*) his word by their loving obedience.

11 Here the words of Christ "I am coming soon" (cf. 22:7, 12, 20) are not a threat of judgment but a promise of Christ's second coming, such as the promise the faithful Christians in Thyatira received (2:25). The testing that faced the Philadelphians was not the same as that facing the unbelieving earth dwellers (v.10). Loyal disciples must face one type of conflict, the world with its earth dwellers quite another (Minear, *I Saw a New Earth,* in loc.). Some such conflict is envisioned when Christ says, "Hold on to what you have, so that no one will take your crown." They had kept his word and had not denied his name in the face of persecution. Either Satan or men could rob them of their crown by diverting them from exclusive loyalty to Jesus (on crown, see comments on 2:10).

12 The promise to the overcomer is again twofold and related to the experience and memory of the inhabitants of the city. First, Christ will make the overcomer a "pillar in the temple of my God." As has already been noted, the city was constantly threatened with earthquakes. Often the only parts of a city left standing after a severe quake were the huge stone temple columns. Christ promises to set believers in his temple (the future kingdom?) in such a secure fashion that no disturbance can ever force them out.

Moreover, a faithful municipal servant or a distinguished priest was sometimes honored by having a special pillar added to one of the temples and inscribed with his name (Barclay, *Seven Churches*, p. 89). This may well be the sense of the second promise, "I will write on him the name of my God and the name of the city of my God, the new Jerusalem, . . . and . . . my new name." The inscribed name signifies identification and ownership. To those who have "little strength" (little influence) because of being ostracized, Christ promises recognition in his kingdom worthy of the most noble hero of any society.

Remembering how in days past the changes of name their city received (e.g., Neocaesarea; see comments on v.7), the Philadelphians would be impressed that God himself (not the emperor) had chosen to identify himself with them and to insure their citizenship in the New Jerusalem (cf. 21:2ff.; Ezek 48:35). Christ's "new name" could be either the unknown name that he alone knows, signifying his absolute power over all other powers (19:12), or the new name of Christ given to the believer, i.e., his possession by Christ through redemption (Isa 62:2; 65:15).

13 The general exhortation follows the promise. (See comments in the introduction to the seven letters.)

Notes

10 A recent addition to the whole debate is Robert Gundry's *The Church and the Tribulation* (Grand Rapids: Zondervan, 1973), pp. 53–61. Gundry follows closely Ladd's views on this question, yet with much more elaborate weaponry.

Commenting on Rev 15:1, Victorinus (d.c.303) says, "For the wrath of God always strikes the obstinate people with seven plagues, that is, perfectly, as it is said in Leviticus; and these shall be in the last time, *when the Church shall have gone out of the midst*" (italics mine) (ANF, 7:357).

7. *To Laodicea*

3:14–22

14"To the angel of the church in Laodicea write:

These are the words of the Amen, the faithful and true witness, the ruler of God's
creation. 15I know your deeds, that you are neither cold nor hot. I wish you were
either one or the other! 16So, because you are lukewarm—neither hot nor cold—I
am about to spit you out of my mouth. 17You say, 'I am rich; I have acquired wealth
and do not need a thing.' But you do not realize that you are wretched, pitiful, poor,
blind and naked. 18I counsel you to buy from me gold refined in the fire, so you can
become rich; and white clothes to wear, so you can cover your shameful nakedness; and salve to put on your eyes, so you can see.

19Those whom I love I rebuke and discipline. So be earnest, and repent. 20Here
I am! I stand at the door and knock. If anyone hears my voice and opens the door,
I will go in and eat with him, and he with me.

21To him who overcomes, I will give the right to sit with me on my throne, just
as I overcame and sat down with my Father on his throne.

22He who has an ear, let him hear what the Spirit says to the churches."

Laodicea was about forty-five miles southeast of Philadelphia and about one hundred miles due east of Ephesus. Along with Colosse and Hierapolis, it was one of the cities in the fertile Lycus valley. The great Roman road stretching to the inland of Asia from the coast at Ephesus ran straight through its center, making Laodicea an important center of trade and communication. In addition, its wealth came from the production of a fine quality of famous glossy black wool—whether dyed or natural in color is not known. That the city's banking assets were noteworthy is evidenced by the fact that Cicero cashed huge bank drafts in Laodicea. So wealthy was Laodicea that after the great earthquake of A.D. 17, which destroyed it, the people refused imperial help in rebuilding the city, choosing rather to do it entirely by themselves.

Laodicea had a famous school of medicine; and a special ointment known as "Phrygian powder," famous for its cure of eye defects, was either manufactured or distributed there, as were ear ointments also. Near the temple of the special god associated with healing, Men Karou (who later became identified with Asclepius), there was a market for trading all sorts of goods (Ramsay, *Seven Churches*, p. 417). Zeus, the supreme god, was also worshiped in the city.

Ramsay notes that Laodicea is difficult to describe because no one thing stands out. There were no excesses or notable achievements to distinguish it. It was a city with a people who had learned to compromise and accommodate themselves to the needs and wishes of others (ibid., p. 423). They did not zealously stand for anything. A six-mile-long aqueduct brought Laodicea its supply of water from the south. The water came either from hot springs and was cooled to lukewarm or came from a cooler source and warmed up in the aqueduct on the way. For all its wealth, the city had poor water. A large and influential Jewish population resided there. As for the church in Laodicea, it may have been founded by Epaphras (Col 4:12–13).

14 The speaker identifies himself by a threefold affirmation: "The Amen, the faithful and true witness, the ruler of God's creation." The normal Hebrew adverb that is rendered by the Greek *amēn* means the acknowledgment of that which is sure and valid. It is a word of human response to the divine verity or action. Jesus is the "Amen" in the sense that he is the perfect human, obedient response to the divine promises (cf. Isa 65:16; TDNT, 1: 337). Jesus' response to God's will was the perfect response of obedience and suffering: he is the "faithful and true witness" (cf. comments on 1:5, 9; 2:13). The same thought is expressed by Paul in 2 Corinthians 1:20: "For no matter how many promises God has made, they are 'Yes' in Christ. And so through him the 'Amen' is spoken by us to the glory of God." In one sense, all Christians are called to be "little amens" after the example of Christ.

The "ruler" (*archē*, "source," "origin") further amplifies the Amen statement. Paul used *archē* in Colossians 1:18 to describe Christ as the source or origin of all creation (not the first created; cf. Prov 8:22; John 1:3), no doubt to correct a heresy. Since Colosse was a neighboring city of Laodicea, it is not improbable that the same heresy was also affecting the sister church at Laodicea. But this is not explicit. What is plain is this: When Christ addresses a church that is failing in loyalty and obedience, he is to them the "Amen" of God in faithfulness and in true witness, the only one who has absolute power over the world because he is the source and origin of all creation (1:17; 2:8; 22:13).

15–16 Sadly, the speaker's knowledge reveals an unqualified condemnation of the Laodicean church. The verdict is the exact opposite of the church's own evaluation and expectations. Their deeds were "neither cold nor hot." The expression "cold nor hot" may refer to their lack of zeal (v.19) or their uselessness, for Christ says, "I wish you were either one or the other" (lit., "either cold or hot"). There is good reason why we should not try to take both of these words as if Christ meant I wish you were either spiritually cold (i.e., unsaved or hostile) or spiritually hot (i.e., alive and fervent). In the first place, it is inconceivable that Christ would wish that people were spiritually cold, or unsaved and hostile. Furthermore, the application of "hot" and "cold" to spiritual temperature, though familiar to us, would have been completely foreign to first-century Christians. The two adjectives in "neither hot nor cold" should be understood together as equivalent to "lukewarmness" (v.16). That is to say, they were useless to Christ because they were complacent, self-satisfied, and indifferent to the real issues of faith in him and of discipleship.

Since the city of Hierapolis, seven miles north of Laodicea, had famous "hot springs," it may be that similar springs were located south of Laodicea and affected the temperature of the water supply. "I am about to spit [*emesai*, 'vomit'] you out of my mouth" seems to allude to the lukewarm water. "Cold" could refer to the useful cool water located at Colosse, less than ten miles away. "Hot" would remind the Laodiceans of the beneficial "hot springs" to the north of Hierapolis. Yet Laodicea, for all its wealth, had an insipid water supply—one that induced vomiting! Christ detests a Laodicean attitude of compromise, one that seeks easy accommodation and peace at any cost. With such a condition, he must deal harshly. To be a Christian means to be useful to Christ.

17 The deeper problem in the Laodicean church was not simply their indifference. It was their ignorance of their real condition: "You say, 'I am rich; I have acquired wealth and do not need a thing.' " Observe the way this indictment is related to the general condition of the populace at large—rich in material possessions and self-sufficient. The spirit of the surrounding culture had crept into the congregation and had paralyzed their spiritual life. But did they actually claim to be materially rich or spiritually rich? Since it is difficult to see how a Christian community would boast of material wealth, many prefer the latter interpretation. Yet the Laodiceans may have interpreted their material wealth as a blessing from God and thus have been self-deceived as to their true spiritual state. In any case, they had misread their true condition.

Christ's revelation of the Laodiceans' actual situation shatters their illusions and calls them to repentance: "But you do not realize that you are wretched, pitiful, poor, blind and naked." Probably the first two characteristics—"wretched" and "pitiful"—are to be linked together, while the latter three explain this twofold condition in more detail (cf. v.18). They are not, as they thought, rich and without need; they are pitifully wretched and in great need, being "poor, blind and naked." Conversely, Jesus said to the church at Smyrna, "I know . . . your poverty—yet you are rich!" (2:9).

To be "wretched" physically describes life when everything one owns has been destroyed or plundered by war (Ps 137:8 LXX). Here it refers to the Laodiceans' spiritual destitution and pitiableness before God. "Poor, blind and naked" refer to the three sources of their miserable condition. "Lukewarmness," then, does not refer to the laxity of Christians but the condition of not really knowing Christ as Savior and Lord and thus being useless to him. Origen likewise understood the passage to refer not to lapsed Christians but to the unregenerate (*Principiis* 3.4.3).

18 The commands of Christ correspond exactly to the self-deceptions of the Laodiceans. Gold, a source of the wealth of the city, was to be bought from Christ and to become the spiritually poverty-stricken's true wealth. Their shameful nakedness was to be clothed, not by purchasing the sleek, black wool of Laodicea, but by buying from Christ the white clothing that alone can cover shameful nakedness (16:15). For those who were blind to their true condition, the "Phrygian powder" was useless (cf. comments on v.14). They needed to buy salve from Christ so that they could truly see. The reference to buying would recall the famous market near the temple of Men Karou, where the commodities manufactured at Laodicea could be bought, along with imports from other areas. But to what do gold, white clothes, and salve symbolically refer? Minear suggests the following:

> The only cure for poverty-stricken disciples was to purchase from Christ gold which is refined in the agonies of the shared passion. For their nakedness (did Hans Christian Andersen find here the theme of "The Emperor's New Clothes"?) the only recourse was to buy such clothes as the naked Christ had worn on the cross. The blindness of self-deception could be cured only by understanding the correlation between Christ's love and his discipline. These three purchases constitute a substantial definition of the kind of zeal and repentance which was the burden of all John's prophecies. The thrust of these commands moves in the direction of

> rigorous warning. They are tantamount to saying "Open your eyes" and "Carry your cross." This letter argues against the widespread assertion of many interpreters to the effect that John's chief concern was to provide consolation to a persecuted church. Nearer the mark would be the opposite assertion; that John, like Jesus, was concerned to bring not peace but a sword (*I Saw a New Earth*, p. 57).

The three figures all point to the Laodiceans' need of authentic salvation through Christ.

19 Even though the state of a church, such as that in Laodicea verges on disaster, all is not lost if there are those in it who will receive Christ's loving rebuke and come back to him. "I love" is the Greek *phileō* ("to have affection for"). This verb does not necessarily connote a lower level of love than *agapaō*. Sometimes it has the force of *agapaō* (e.g., John 5:20; 16:27; 20:22; cf. BAG, s.v.). Christ's statement "I rebuke and discipline" speaks of his love (Prov 3:12; 1 Cor 11:32; Heb 12:6). He spits out those he does not love and "rebukes" (*elenchō*, "reproves," "convicts") and disciplines those who hear his voice. The difference between the expelled and the disciplined lies in their response: "So be earnest [*zeleuō*, 'zealous,' 'enthusiastic'] and repent." The Laodiceans' repentance would come from a rekindling of their loyalty to Christ.

20 To those who hear the words of rebuke, Christ extends an invitation to dine with him. Some older commentators find the reference to the "door" as parallel to the new age that will dawn at the advent of Christ (Swete, Beckwith; cf. Matt 24:33; James 5:9). So the challenge is to be ready to enter the banquet of Christ at his return. This view, however, does not seem to fit the immediate context, nor does it agree with other NT teaching on the Lord's return.

Others hold that the figure represents Christ standing at the door to the hearts of the members of the congregation at Laodicea. Christ will come and have fellowship with anyone who hears his voice of rebuke and thus proves himself Christ's friend by zeal and repentance. The "eating" (*deipneō*) refers to the main meal of the day, which in Oriental fashion was a significant occasion for having intimate fellowship with the closest of friends. It is through the Holy Spirit that Christ and the Father come to have fellowship with us (John 14:23).

While most commentators have taken this invitation as addressed to lapsed, half-hearted Christians, the terminology and context (v.18) suggest that these Laodiceans were for the most part mere professing Christians who lacked authentic conversion to Christ, which is the essential prerequisite for true discipleship. Verse 20 is, therefore, more evangelistic than admonitory. Those who find in it an allusion to the Lord's Supper may be right. Cullman sees v.20 as a response to the old eucharistic prayer: Maranatha (*marana tha*, "Our Lord, come!") (Oscar Cullmann, *Early Christian Worship* [London: SCM, 1953], in loc.).

21 The promise to the overcomers concerns the sharing in Christ's future reign in the eschatological kingdom: "I will give the right to sit with me on my throne." Such a joint reign with Christ has already been referred to earlier in the book (1:6, 9; 2:26–27) and appears later on (5:10; 20:4–6). The kingdom reign is also a theme in other NT writings (Luke 22:28–30; Rom 8:17; 2 Tim 2:12). As Christ overcame through his suffering and death (John 16:33) and entered into the highest honor God could bestow, that of being seated at his "right hand" of sovereignty (Mark 16:19; Acts

2:22ff.; Rev 22:1), so believers who suffer with Christ even to the point of death will share in the honor of Christ's exalted position. The distinction between the Father's throne and Christ's throne is no mere rhetoric. On the contrary, it differentiates aspects of God's program in history (1 Cor 15:24–28). Christ is reigning now, for there is a sense in which the eschatological or messianic kingdom of God was inaugurated in Christ's earthly ministry, death, and resurrection. But the promise here, as elsewhere in the NT, foresees a final earthly consummation of the kingdom that awaits the return of Christ.

22 The general exhortation closes the seventh letter (cf. comments in the introduction to the seven letters).

Notes

15–16 On the meaning of "hot" and "cold" and "lukewarm" as related to the city water supply and the consequent reinterpretation this suggests, see the helpful article by M.J.S. Rudwick and E.M.B. Green, "The Laodicean Lukewarmness," ET, 69 (1958), 176–78.

III. Vision of the Seven-Sealed Scroll, the Seven Trumpets, the Seven Signs, and the Seven Bowls (4:1–19:10)

A. *The Seven-Sealed Scroll* (4:1–8:1)

1. *Preparatory: the throne, the scroll, and the Lamb* (4:1–5:14)

a. *The throne*

4:1–11

1 After this I looked, and there before me was a door standing open in heaven.
And the voice I had first heard speaking to me like a trumpet said, "Come up here,
and I will show you what must take place after this." 2 At once I was in the Spirit,
and there before me was a throne in heaven with someone sitting on it. 3 And the
one who sat there had the appearance of jasper and carnelian. A rainbow, resembling an emerald, encircled the throne. 4 Surrounding the throne were twenty-four
other thrones, and seated on them were twenty-four elders. They were dressed in
white and had crowns of gold on their heads. 5 From the throne came flashes of
lightning, rumblings and peals of thunder. Before the throne, seven lamps were
blazing. These are the seven spirits of God. 6 Also before the throne there was what
looked like a sea of glass, clear as crystal.

In the center, around the throne, were four living creatures, and they were
covered with eyes, in front and in back. 7 The first living creature was like a lion, the
second was like an ox, the third had a face like a man, the fourth was like a flying
eagle. 8 Each of the four living creatures had six wings and was covered with eyes
all around, even under his wings. Day and night they never stop saying:

"Holy, holy, holy
is the Lord God Almighty,
who was, and is, and is to come."

9Whenever the living creatures give glory, honor and thanks to him who sits on the throne and who lives for ever and ever, 10the twenty-four elders fall down before him who sits on the throne, and worship him who lives for ever and ever. They lay their crowns before the throne and say:

11"You are worthy, our Lord and God,
to receive glory and honor and power,
for you created all things,
and by your will they were created
and have their being."

In view of the elaborate use of imagery and visions from 4:1 through the end of Revelation and the question of how this material relates to chapters 1–3, it is not surprising that commentators differ widely regarding them. One problem is that of interpretation: What do the imagery and visions mean? Another problem involves chronology: When do the things spoken of occur? Furthermore, how does John use his frequent OT images? Does he interpret them in exact accordance with their OT sources, or does he freely reinterpret these images and figures? What is symbolic and what is literal? Answers to such questions will determine the interpreter's approach. Since few of these questions are capable of dogmatic answers, there is a need for tolerance of divergent approaches in the hope that the Spirit may use open-minded discussion to bring us further into the meaning of the Apocalypse.

Chapters 4–5 form one vision of two parts—the throne (ch. 4) and the Lamb and the scroll (ch. 5). In actuality, the breaking of all seven seals (chs. 6–8:1) together with the throne vision (chs. 4–5) form a single, continuous vision and should not be separated. Indeed, the throne pictures (chs. 4–5) should be viewed as dominating the entire seven-seal vision (4:1–8:1).

1 Seeing a "door standing open in heaven," John is told to "come up here" (cf. Ezek 1:1, where the prophet says he saw the heavens opened). A new view of God's majesty and power (throne) is disclosed to John so that he can understand the events on earth that relate to the seven-seal vision (cf. 1 Kings 22:19). For the first time in Revelation, the reader is introduced to the frequent interchange between heaven and earth found in the remainder of the book. What happens on earth has its inseparable heavenly counterpart.

Chapter 4 focuses on the throne vision that provides the setting for the dramatic action of the slain Lamb in chapter 5. There is a connection between this throne vision and the vision of the glorified Christ in 1:10–16. Here we are told that John heard the same voice speaking to him that he "had first heard speaking . . . like a trumpet" (cf. 1:10). The words of the messenger relate to what has just transpired: "I will show you what must take place after this" (*meta tauta*, "after this," "next"; i.e., after the time of the historical churches in Asia [cf. 1:19]).

There is no good reason for seeing the invitation for John to come up into the opened heaven as a symbol of the rapture of the church. Some have so interpreted it and have inferred that the absence of the word "church" (*ekklēsia*) from Revelation till 22:16 and the continued references to the "saints" indicate that at this point the church departs from the earth. But the word "church" or "churches" always stands in Revelation for the historic seven churches in Asia and not just for the universal body of Christ. Since 4:1–22:15 concerns the believing community as a whole, it would be inappropriate at least for John's usage to find the narrower term "church" in this section (cf. 3 John 6, 9–10).

Finally, it is significant that in the visions that continue to the end of the book, there are references to the throne, the book, the crowns, the four living creatures, the twenty-four elders, and the victory of the Lamb. In all this, the center of focus appears to be the five hymns of praise that begin in 4:8 and continue through chapter 5.

2–3 Chapter 4 is above all a vision of the royal throne of God. The prophet ascends "in the Spirit" to see the source of all that will happen on earth (cf. 1:10). It will all be an expression of the throne's purpose; nothing happens, nothing exists in the past, present, or future apart from God's intention. Whatever authority is given to an angel or to a horseman is given by God. The throne symbolizes God's majesty and power. Yet his majestic transcendence is fully safeguarded—John does not attempt to describe the "someone sitting on" the throne (cf. 1 Kings 22:19; 2 Chron 18:18; Ps 47:8; Isa 6:1ff.; Ezek 1:26–28; Ecclus 1:8).

The minerals "jasper" and "carnelian" portray the supernatural splendor of God, while the "rainbow, resembling an emerald" conveys the impression of God's encircling brilliance (cf. Ezek 1:27–28). But we need not find symbolism in each element of the vision; it is enough to allow the archetypical imagery to create the impression of transcendant glory. Whether John intends God's judgment to be part of the symbolism of the throne vision (cf. Ps 9:4, 7) is not clear. What is unmistakably clear is that all—whether elders, angels, lamps, sea of glass, or living creatures—centers on the throne and the one who sits on it, "who lives for ever and ever" (v.9).

It is significant that the earliest Jewish mysticism is throne mysticism (Merkabah Mysticism). Its essence is not absorbed contemplation of God's true nature but perception of his appearance on the throne, as described by Ezekiel, and cognition of the mysteries of the celestial throne world (Gershorn G. Scholem, *Major Trends in Jewish Mysticism* [New York: Schocken Books, 1961], esp. ch. 2).

4 John also sees "twenty-four elders." It would be helpful if we could ask an interpreting angel, "Who are the elders?" There are at least thirteen different views of their identity, ranging from the twenty-four ruling stars (or judges) in the heavens to the simple figure of wholeness and fullness (cf. *I Saw a New Earth*, p. 83). Part of the discussion hinges on the correct text in 5:10 (cf. Notes). The following passages are pertinent to the elders' identification: 4:9–11; 5:5–14; 7:11–17; 11:16–18; 12:10–12; 14:3; 19:4.

The elders are always associated with the "four living creatures" (4:6ff.) and engage in acts of worship of God and the Lamb. While not entirely ruling out the elders' possible representative or symbolic significance (a view held by many good expositors), the arguments of Stonehouse, Mounce (*Revelation*, p. 135), and others who have argued that the elders are a class of heavenly spirit-beings belonging to the general class of angels and living creatures seem more compelling (Ned B. Stonehouse, *Paul Before the Areopagus* [Grand Rapids: Eerdmans, 1957], pp. 88–108). From this viewpoint, the "angels," the "twenty-four elders," and "the four living creatures" all designate actual supernatural beings involved with the purpose of God on earth and his worship in heaven. They are always distinguished from the "saints" (5:8; 11:17–18; 19:1–4), and the text of 5:10 is uncertain.

In the Bible twelve appears to be the number of divine government—twelve months in a lunar year, twelve tribes of Israel, twelve apostles, twelve gates in the

New Jerusalem, twelve angels at each gate, twelve foundations, twelve thousand sealed from each tribe, twelve thousand stadia (the length of the New Jerusalem), etc. Multiples of twelve—such as twenty-four, etc.—probably have a similar significance. Thrones are related to the heavenly powers in Colossians 1:16. In Revelation "white" clothing generally belongs to the saints but relates to angelic beings elsewhere in the NT (e.g., John 20:12). While the "crowns of gold" are likewise usually related to the redeemed, here they refer to the royal dignity of those so closely associated with the throne of God (cf. 1 Kings 22:19; Ps 89:7). Golden crowns are referred to in 4:4, 10; 9:7; 14:14.

5 "Flashes of lightning, rumblings and peals of thunder" coming from the throne are symbolic of God's awesome presence and the vindication of the saints and occur with slight variation four times in Revelation (4:5; 8:5; 11:19; 16:18; cf. Exod 19:16; Ezek 1:13; Ps 18:13–15). On the expression "seven blazing lamps," see comments on 1:4 (cf. Ezek 1:13).

6–8 "A sea of glass, clear as crystal" simply adds to the magnificence of the scene (15:2). Caird considers the "sea of glass" identical to the "sea" in Revelation 13:1 and 21:1 and identifies it as "a reservoir of evil" (p. 65). But a sea of "glass" may be an intentional reversal of this sea imagery (cf. Exod 24:10; Ezek 1:22, 26). The mirrorlike reflecting quality could symbolize the fact that before the sight of God all is revealed; i.e., "Everything is uncovered and laid bare before the eyes of him to whom we must give account" (Heb 4:13).

The "four living creatures" should be linked with Isaiah's seraphim and Ezekiel's cherubim (cf. Isa 6:3; Ezek 1:5–25; 10:1–22). They, like the elders and angels, are heavenly creatures of the highest order involved with the worship and government of God. "Covered with eyes" may give the impression of their exceeding knowledge of God, while the faces of a "lion," "ox," "man," and a "flying eagle" suggest qualities that belong to God, such as royal power, strength, spirituality, and swiftness of action. Each of the creatures mentioned is the chief of its species. Together they embody the reflection of God's nature as the fullness of life and power. Their six wings (cf. Isa 6:2) give the impression of unlimited mobility in fulfilling God's commands. Their position "in the center, around the throne" suggests that one might be before and one behind the throne with one on either side (Beckwith). The four living creatures appear throughout Revelation (cf. 5:6, 8, 14; 6:1ff.; 7:11; 14:3; 15:7; 19:4).

The four living creatures ceaselessly proclaim the holiness of God: "Holy, holy, holy" (v.8; Isa 6:3). In Hebrew, the double repetition of a word adds emphasis, while the rare threefold repetition designates the superlative and calls attention to the infinite holiness of God—the quality of God felt by creatures in his presence as awesomeness or fearfulness (Ps 111:9: "Holy and awesome is his name"). The living creatures celebrate God's holiness and power as manifested in his past, present, and future activity. Such holiness cannot tolerate the presence of evil (21:27). (On these titles of God, see comments on 1:4, 8.) The trisagion ("Holy, holy, holy") is a liturgical expression used in both ancient Jewish and Christian worship. Its use does not, however, reach back to the first century.

This hymn is the first not only of the five sung by the heavenly choirs in chapters 4–5 but also of a number of others in Revelation (4:8, 11; 5:9–10, 12, 13; 7:12, 15–17; 11:15, 17–18; 12:10–12; 15:3–4; 16:5–7; 18:2–8; 19:2–6). These hymns relate to the interpretation of the visions and provide a clue to the literary structure of Revelation.

In these two chapters, the sequence of hymns shows that the first two are addressed to God, the next two to the Lamb, and the last one to both. There is also a gradual enlargement in the size of the choirs. The internal movement also builds as the last hymn is sung by "every creature in heaven and on earth and under the earth" to "him who sits on the throne and to the Lamb" (5:13).

9–11 The second hymn is sung by the twenty-four elders. When the living creatures confess the truth of God's holy deeds, the response of the highest order of God's heavenly creatures is to relinquish their crowns of honor before the feet of him who alone is "worthy" of "glory and honor and power" because he alone (no man, not even the emperor) is the source and stay of every created thing (Ps 33:6–9; 102:25; 136:5ff.).

The expression "by your will they were created and have their being" (v.11) presents a translation difficulty because the Greek text has two different tenses (*ēsan*, "they were" [NIV, "have their being"], imperfect; *ektisthēsan*, "they were created," aorist). Although a number of possible explanations have been advanced, Alford's remains the best: the imperfect tense describes the *fact* of their existence while the aorist captures the sense of the *beginning* of their existence (Alf, 4:602–3). Consequently, the phrase might be translated thus: "Because of [not 'by'] your will they continually exist and have come into being."

Notes

1 The expression ἃ δεῖ γενέσθαι μετὰ ταῦτα (*ha dei genesthai meta tauta* "what must take place after this") is found in the LXX of Dan 2:29, 45, where it has the sense of "next" in historical sequence from the time of the writer. "After this" does not mean "at some future time" but refers to what is after that which is at present (KD, *Daniel* p. 111).

8 John's Gr. text of this verse agrees with 1QIsa at Isa 6:2 against both the MT and the LXX (L. Paul Trudinger, "Some Observations Concerning the Text of the Old Testament in the Book of Revelation," JTS, 17 [1966], 88).

b. *The Scroll and the Lamb*

5:1–14

1Then I saw in the right hand of him who sat on the throne a scroll with writing
on both sides and sealed with seven seals. 2And I saw a mighty angel proclaiming
in a loud voice, "Who is worthy to break the seals and open the scroll?" 3But no
one in heaven or on earth or under the earth could open the scroll or even look
inside it. 4I wept and wept because no one was found who was worthy to open the
scroll or look inside. 5Then one of the elders said to me, "Do not weep! See, the
Lion of the tribe of Judah, the Root of David, has triumphed. He is able to open the
scroll and its seven seals."

6Then I saw a Lamb, looking as if it had been slain, standing in the center of the
throne, encircled by the four living creatures and the elders. He had seven horns
and seven eyes, which are the seven spirits of God sent out into all the earth. 7He
came and took the scroll from the right hand of him who sat on the throne. 8And
when he had taken it, the four living creatures and the twenty-four elders fell down
before the Lamb. Each one had a harp and they were holding golden bowls full of
incense, which are the prayers of the saints. 9And they sang a new song:

"You are worthy to take the scroll
and to open its seals,
because you were slain,
and with your blood you purchased men for God
from every tribe and language and people and nation.
10You have made them to be a kingdom and priests to
serve our God,
and they will reign on the earth."

11Then I looked and heard the voice of many angels, numbering thousands upon
thousands, and ten thousand times ten thousand. They encircled the throne and
the living creatures and the elders. 12In a loud voice they sang:

"Worthy is the Lamb, who was slain,
to receive power and wealth and wisdom and strength
and honor and glory and praise!"

13Then I heard every creature in heaven and on earth and under the earth and
on the sea, and all that is in them, singing:

"To him who sits on the throne and to the Lamb
be praise and honor and glory and power,
for ever and ever!"

14The four living creatures said, "Amen," and the elders fell down and worshiped.

1 This chapter is part of the vision that begins at chapter 4 and continues through the opening of the seven seals (6:1–8:1; cf. comments in introduction to ch.4). Its center of gravity lies in the three hymns (vv.9, 12, 13). These are addressed to the Lamb. They beautifully combine the worship of the Lamb (hymns one and two) with the worship of the one who sits on the throne (hymn three, which is addressed to both God and the Lamb). The movement of the whole scene focuses on the slain Lamb as he takes the scroll from the hand of the one on the throne. The actions of all other participants are described in terms of worship directed to the Lamb and the one on the throne. The culminating emphasis is on the worthiness of the Lamb to receive worship because of his death.

John sees "in the right hand of him who sat on the throne a scroll with writing on both sides and sealed with seven seals." This raises a problem involving the phrase "with writing on both sides." Papyrus codices (which were like books as we know them) did not originate until the second century A.D., or perhaps the late first century (Bruce M. Metzger, *The Text of the New Testament* 2d ed. [Oxford: Clarendon, 1964], p. 6). In ancient times, papyrus rolls were used for public and private documents. Usually the writing was on one side only—the inside part, arranged in successive vertical columns. Occasionally a scroll was written on both sides; in that case it was called an "opisthograph." Such double-sided writing was for private, nonsalable use in contrast to the usual scrolls written on only one side, which were sold (Edward Maunde Thompson, *An Introduction to Greek and Latin Paleography* [Oxford: Clarendon, 1912], pp. 49–50). In the context of chapter 5, an opisthograph would signify a scroll full of words. The importance of establishing the scroll rather than codex character of the document lies in the interpretation of the opening of the seals. If the book was a codex, the seals could have been opened one at a time and portions of the book disclosed; a scroll, however, could be opened only after *all* the seals were broken.

Scrolls, or folded sheets, were sealed with wax blobs impressed with a signet ring to protect the contents or guarantee the integrity of the writing. Only the owner could open the seals and disclose the contents. Original documents were usually sealed; copies were not. Sealed documents were kept hidden while unsealed copies were made public (Rev 22:10) (TDNT, 7:941ff.).

The phrase "with writing on both sides" (*gegrammenon esōthen kai opisthen*) is literally "written inside and on the back side," where "on the back side" (*opisthen*) is generally understood as going with "written" (*gegrammenon*). Zahn, however, argues that "back side" (*opisthen*) should go with the verb "sealed" (*katesphragismenon*) and not with "written" (Theodore Zahn, *Introduction to the New Testament*, 3 vols. [Grand Rapids: Kregel, 1953], 3.405–6). While tempting and grammatically possible, Zahn's view has not found acceptance among exegetes; and the adverbial use of *opisthen* in the rest of Revelation and the NT favors taking it always with a preceding rather than a following verb.

As to the identity and significance of the scroll, there are a number of different views.

1. Ancient Roman wills or "testaments" were sealed with six seals, each of which bore a different name of the sealer and could only be opened by him (TDNT, 7:941). This has led some to identify the scroll as the testament of God concerning the promise of the inheritance of his future kingdom (Zahn, *NT Introduction*, 3:395–96). A slight variation of this view refers the scene to the Roman law of *mancipatio*. Under this law an heir received either an inheritance at the death of the testator or the use of *mancipatio* in connection with transference of the inheritance to an executor, known as the *familiae emptor*. The executor could use the property till the death of the testator, at which time he was obligated to distribute the possessions in accordance with the instructions of the testator (Emmet Russell, "A Roman Law Parallel to Revelation Five," BS, 115 [1958], 258–64).

2. Others find the scroll containing, like Ezekiel's scroll, "words of lament and mourning and woe" (Ezek 2:9–10) and depicting the future judgment of the world (Walvoord, p. 113).

3. Still others find the significance to be the progressive unfolding of the history of the world. As each successive seal is opened, the further contents of the book are revealed. J.A. Seiss (*The Apocalypse* [Grand Rapids: Zondervan, 1957], p. 112) connects the scroll with a "title-deed" (Jer 32:10–14). It is the "title-deed" to creation that was forfeited by sin in Genesis. By his redeeming death Christ has won the authority to reclaim the earth.

4. A more recent study finds the scroll to be the OT Torah (Law) (Lucetta Mowry, "Revelation 4–5 and Early Christian Liturgical Usage," JBL, 71 [1952], 75–84).

Each of these views has merit and may provide elements of truth for the background of the striking imagery in these chapters. Yet each view is vulnerable to criticism. Only from Revelation itself can the content and nature of the scroll be determined. Since the seals hinder the opening of the scroll till they are all broken, we may assume that the seals are preparatory to the opening of the scroll and the disclosure of its contents. This means that the seals have the effect of hiding the contents of the scroll till they are broken (Isa 29:11).

The following internal evidence relating to the contents of the scroll may be noted:

1. Just prior to the opening of the seventh seal, in connection with the events under the sixth seal, we read, "For the great day of their [i.e., of the One sitting on the throne and the Lamb] wrath has come, and who can stand?" (6:17).

2. When the seventh seal is opened (8:1–5), no immediate events as such follow on earth—except for the earthquake—as in the first six seals, unless the opening of the seventh seal includes among its events the blowing of the seven trumpets of judgment (8:6–11:15). This appears to be precisely the case.

3. The seventh trumpet likewise is not immediately followed by any specific events on earth (11:15ff.), except for an earthquake and a hailstorm (11:19). However, just before the seventh trumpet is sounded, we read, "The second woe has passed; the third woe is coming soon" (11:14). When the seven angels prepare to pour out "the seven last plagues," symbolized by the bowls, we read that with these bowls God's wrath is completed" (15:1, 7). Thus it seems reasonable to identify the content of the seventh trumpet with the seven bowls of judgment (chs. 16–19).

Furthermore, frequent references to the events of the seals, trumpets, and bowls appear throughout the remaining visions in Revelation (cf. 19:19ff.; 20:4; 21:9), indicating that the content of the seven-sealed scroll ultimately includes the unfolding of the consummation of the mystery of all things, the goal or end of all history, for both the conquerors and the worshipers of the beast. In 10:7 we are told that in the days of the sounding of the seventh trumpet "the mystery of God will be accomplished, just as he announced to his servants the prophets." From this it may be concluded that the scroll contains the unveiling of "the mystery of God" that OT prophets foretold (cf. comments at 10:7). Thus the "seals" conceal the mystery, which only Christ can disclose (Dan 12:9; Rev 10:4), of how God's judgment and his kingdom will come. In 11:15, when the final trumpet sounds, heavenly voices say, "The kingdom of the world has become the kingdom of our Lord and of his Christ," indicating that the scroll also contains the announcement of the inheritance of Christ and the saints who will reign with him (5:10).

The scroll, then, is not only about judgment or about the inheritance of the kingdom. Rather, it contains the announcement of the consummation of all history—how things will ultimately end for all people: judgment for the world and the final reward of the saints (11:18). Christ alone, as the Messiah, is the executor of the purposes of God and the heir of the inheritance of the world. He obtained this by his substitutionary and propitiatory death on the cross (5:9).

2–4 A mighty angel shouts out a challenge for anyone to come forth who is "worthy" to open the great scroll and its seals. All creation in heaven and earth and under the earth stood motionless and speechless. No one was worthy to open the scroll; i.e., no one had the authority and virtue for such a task. If the scroll contains both the revelation and the carrying out of the final drama of history, then John's despair can be appreciated. In this vision, the execution of events on earth is ascribed to the Lamb. As the seals are broken and the roll opened, salvation history unfolds till history culminates in the kingdom reign of the Messiah over the whole earth. History, then, has its center in Jesus Christ and its goal in his triumphant reign over all the powers of the world.

5 John's sorrow is assuaged. One of the elders announces that there is one who has "triumphed" (*nikaō*, "overcome," "conquer," "win a victory"—same word as 2:7; 3:21; et al.). He has triumphed because of his death (v.9). Two figurative titles are used of the one who is worthy—"the Lion of the tribe of Judah" and "the Root of David." Both are familiar OT messianic titles (Gen 49:9–10; cf. Isa 11:1, 10; Jer 23:5; 33:5; Rev 22:16). But they are linked together only here and in the Qumran literature (cf. 4Q Patriarchal Blessings; L. Paul Trudinger, "Some Observations Concerning the Text of the Old Testament in the Book of Revelation," JTS, 17 [1966], 88). In Jewish apocalyptic literature contemporary with John, the figure of a lion was used to designate the conquering Messiah who would destroy Rome (4 Ezra 11:58). Close attention should be paid to John's understanding of the role and function of the Messiah, observing where it is similar to the Jewish understanding of the Messiah and where it differs from it.

6 As John looked to see the mighty Lion (the conquering warrior-Messiah from the Root of David), he saw instead the striking figure of a "Lamb" (*arnion*, "a young sheep") as if it had been slaughtered, standing in the center of the throne court. This new figure portrays sacrificial death and links the Messiah to the OT passover lamb (Exod 12:5f.; Isa 53:7; John 1:29, 36; Acts 8:32; 1 Peter 1:19). Here John joins the OT royal Davidic Messiah with the Suffering Servant of Isaiah (Isa 42–53). Both prophetic themes come together in Jesus of Nazareth, the true Messiah. "As if it had been slain" (*esphagmenon*, "with its throat cut") could refer to the "marks of death" the living Lamb still bore or to his appearance "as if being led to the slaughter," i.e., "marked out for death" (Minear, *I Saw a New Earth*, in loc.). The "lamb" metaphor dominates John's thought in the rest of the book (e.g., 6:1ff.; 7:9ff.; 12:11; 13:8; 21:9).

John notices that the Lamb who bears the marks of death is also the ruler who bears the signs of the fullness of divine omnipotence, dominion, and omniscience ("seven horns and seven eyes"). Following Charles, Mounce (*Revelation*, p. 145) suggests that the figure of a lamb with seven horns is undoubtedly drawn from the apocalyptic tradition, citing 1 Enoch 90.9 (the Maccabees are symbolized by "horned lambs") and the Testament of Joseph 19.8–9 (a *lamb* destroys the enemies of Israel). However, the Enoch passage bears little relationship to the messianic Lamb as portrayed in Revelation, and the Testament of Joseph is notorious for Christian interpolations. Since the lamb image is used by the fourth Gospel to depict the Suffering Messiah in passages where apocalyptic connections would be quite remote, it may still be better to connect the lamb vocabulary to the OT Passover motif and Isaiah's Suffering Servant (Isa 53:7), especially in light of the author's interest in the Passover theme elsewhere in the book (e.g., 19:1ff.).

The "eyes" are more explicitly identified as the "seven spirits of God sent out into all the earth," probably a symbolic reference to the divine Holy Spirit who is sent forth by Christ into the world (1:4; 4:5). The teaching of the fourth Gospel is similar, where the Spirit is sent forth to exalt Christ and convict the world of sin (John 14:26; 15:26; 16:7–15).

7 Next the Lamb acts: "He came and took the scroll." The Greek conveys a dramatic action in the tense of the verb "took" (perhaps a dramatic perfect?): "He went up and took it, and now he has it." Symbolically, the one on the throne thus authorizes the slain messianic King to execute his plan for the redemption of the world because in and through the Lamb, God is at work in history for the salvation of humanity. Observe that this dramatic act of seizing the scroll is not itself the act of victory referred to in v.6 and later in v.9. Christ's victorious death on the cross is the basis of his authority to redeem the world by taking and opening the seven-sealed scroll.

8 The Lamb's act calls forth three hymns of praise (vv.9, 12, 13) from the living creatures and elders. John sees them fall down in worship before the Lamb as they had earlier done before the one on the throne (4:10), thus acknowledging the deity of the Lamb. They have "harps", which are the "lyres" used for the older psalmody (cf., e.g., Pss 33:2; 98:5) but will now be used for the "new song" of praise to the Lamb (v.9; 15:2–3).

The "bowls full of incense" represent the "prayers of the saints" (8:3–4). Prayer (*proseuchē*) in this scene is not praise but petition. Why would John mention the saints on earth as petitioning God? In 6:10 the martyrs are seen as calling to God for his judgment on those who killed them, and in 8:3–4 the prayers of the saints are immediately connected with the trumpets of God's judgment. These prayers, then, are evidently for God's vindication of the martyred saints. And since v.10 refers to the coming kingdom, it may be that the prayers are petitions for God to judge the world and to extend his kingdom throughout the earth (Luke 18:7–8). "Saints" here, as elsewhere in the NT and the rest of Revelation, is simply the normal term for the rank and file of Christians, i.e., those set apart for God's purposes (2 Cor 1:1; Phil 1:1; Rev 11:18; 13:7, 19; 19:8; 22:21).

9 The three hymns interpret the symbolism of the scroll and the Lamb. The number of singers increases from twenty-eight in v.8 to every creature in all creation in v.13. The first two hymns are songs of praise to the Lamb, whereas the last is praise to both the one on the throne and the Lamb (v.13). The first hymn (vv.9–10) is called a "new" song because there was never any like it before in heaven (cf. comments on 14:3).

"You are worthy" (*axios*, "comparable," "equal to," "deserving") refers to the qualifications of this person who alone has won the right to take the scroll and open its seals. His worthiness for this task was won by his loving sacrifice on the cross—"because you were slain." This must be understood as a direct reference to the earthly death of the human Jesus of Nazareth (the Gr. aorist tense supports this). It is no mythological death or salvation. Like other NT writers, John views the death of Jesus as a redeeming death—"and with your blood [or 'by the price of your blood'] you purchased [or 'redeemed,' *agorazo*] men for God."

The death of Jesus broke the stranglehold of the "powers and authorities" over the creation and produced a great victory of liberation for mankind (Col 2:15). It is this victory, obtained through suffering and death, that entitles Christ to execute the unfolding of the mystery of God's consummation of history. The centrality of the Cross and its meaning as a redemptive act comes repeatedly to the fore and should dominate our understanding throughout Revelation. (1:5; 5:12; 7:14; 12:11; 13:8; 14:4; 15:3; 19:7; 21:9, 23; 22:3, et al.). Jesus' death secured a salvation universally applied to all classes and peoples of the earth—"every tribe and language and people and nation" (cf. 7:9).

10 The Lamb's right to open the scroll rests also on the fact that he has made the ransomed into a "kingdom" and made them "priests" (to serve God in praise; cf. Heb 13:15–16). Christians "will reign on the earth" with Christ because they have been given "kingly authority" through his death (1:6; 20:4–6). While not excluding the present reign of believers, the reference to "the earth" is best taken to refer to the future eschatological kingdom reign of Christ (see Notes for various problems in this verse).

11–12 Now John sees a new feature in th. vision: "thousands upon thousands, and ten thousand times ten thousand" angels surrounding the throne. The vision is similar to Daniel's vision of the countless multitude before the Ancient of Days (Dan 7:10). The imagery suggests the infinite honor and power of the one who is at the center of it all. The angels shout out their song of praise to the Lamb who was slain (cf. Heb 1:6). Their sevenfold shout rings out like the sound from a huge bell—"power . . . wealth . . . wisdom . . . strength . . . honor . . . glory . . . praise." All these are intrinsic qualities of Christ except the last, which is the expression of the creatures' worship: "praise" (lit., "blessing"). Elsewhere the same qualities are ascribed to God himself (5:13; 7:12). The sevenfold multiplication of these attributes by angel choirs is a Qumran liturgical method for creating the feeling of God's majesty and glory (7:12; 4QSL).

13–14 Finally, far beyond the precincts of the throne, there arises an expression of praise and worth from the whole created universe to the one on the throne and to the Lamb. John beautifully blends the worship of the Father (ch. 4) and the worship of the Son (5:8–12) together. In appropriate response, the living beings utter their "Amen" (cf. comments on 3:14), and the elders fall down in worship.

Notes

1 The difficult expression ὄπισθεν (*opisthen*, "behind," "back of") has textual variants here. A strongly supported tradition in the versions and Fathers has the reading ἔξωθεν (*exōthen*, "outside"), which probably arose when codices replaced scrolls in the Christian community, making the expression "back side" sound strange (Bruce M. Metzger, *A Textual Commentary on the Greek New Testament*, [New York: UBS, 1971], p. 737).

5 While evidence supporting a pre-Christian Jewish understanding of a suffering Messiah is meager, there do exist some traces of it. Edersheim points out that Isaiah 53 was applied to the Messiah in the Targum and in the Midrash on Samuel, "where it is said that all sufferings are divided into three parts, one of which the Messiah bore" (LTJM, 2:727).

6 The word for "lamb" or young sheep used in Rev some twenty-eight times is ἀρνίον (*arnion*), which occurs only once outside in John 21:15 (pl.). The alternate word elsewhere is ἀμνός (*amnos*), which occurs only four times and is used of Christ (John 1:29, 36; Acts 8:32; 1 Peter 1:19). Both words occur in the LXX and are used in Exod 12 to refer to the Passover sacrificial lamb. No distinction between *arnion* and *amnos* should be pressed; their use merely reflects the author's preference. The diminutive ending ιον (*ion*) has lost its diminutive force (G. Mussies, *The Morphology of Koine Greek as Used in the Apocalypse of St. John* [Leiden: E.J. Brill, 1971], p. 109).

9–10 Here the chief problem is whether the text should read "redeemed us [ἡμᾶς (*hēmas*, 'us')] to God" or simply "redeemed to God," omitting *hēmas* (NIV, "purchased men"). The reading is crucial to the identification of the elders. If *hēmas* is original, it would be difficult to argue that the elders are angelic beings. The evidence for the shorter reading consists of one Gr. MS (A) and one version (Ethiopic), while all other versional and Gr. evidence has the word *hēmas*. Unless unusual weight is given to A (it is considered the best witness), the most reasonable conclusion is to charge A at this point with an omission. On the other hand, Metzger argues that the reading of A best accounts for the origin of the longer variations since scribes were unsatisfied with a less-direct object for ἠγόρασας (*ēgorasas*, "redeemed"; NIV, "purchased") and supplied the awkward *hēmas*, which does not fit the αὐτοὺς (*autous*, "them") of v.10 (*Textual Commentary*, p. 738). It is a difficult question to settle with certainty, but this commentary follows the shorter reading (like NIV) and views the elders as angels.

More difficult are the readings βασιλεύουσιν (*basileuousin*, "they reign" [present tense]) or βασιλεύσουσιν (*basileusousin*, "they will reign" [future tense]). Both have nearly equal MS support. Although NIV has the future tense here, it would seem better to adopt—with reservations—the present-tense reading and understand it as a "future present," in keeping with John's other references to the future reign of the saints (20:4). Mounce concurs (*Revelation*, p. 149, n.27). For a helpful inductive discussion of the whole chapter, see also Robert H. Mounce, "Worthy is the Lamb," ch. 5 in *Scripture, Tradition, and Interpretation*, edd. W. Ward Gasque and William Sanford LaSor, (Grand Rapids: Eerdmans, 1978).

John's expression "a kingdom and priests" is a combination of the LXX rendering of Exod 19:6 and that of the Targum's (M. McNamara, *Targum and Testament: Aramaic Paraphrase of the Hebrew Bible; A Light on the New Testament* [Grand Rapids: Eerdmans, 1962], p. 156). The source of this idea of the saints' reign could well be Dan 7:10ff., though no direct verbal allusion appears in Rev (R.T. France, *Jesus and the Old Testament* [Downers Grove, Ill.: InterVarsity, 1971], p. 204).

---

2. *Opening of the first six seals*

6:1–17

1I watched as the Lamb opened the first of the seven seals. Then I heard one
of the four living creatures say in a voice like thunder, "Come!" 2I looked, and there
before me was a white horse! Its rider held a bow, and he was given a crown, and
he rode out as a conqueror bent on conquest.

3When the Lamb opened the second seal, I heard the second living creature say,
"Come!" 4Then another horse came out, a fiery red one. Its rider was given power
to take peace from the earth and to make men slay each other. To him was given
a large sword.

5When the Lamb opened the third seal, I heard the third living creature say,
"Come!" I looked, and there before me was a black horse! Its rider was holding a
pair of scales in his hand. 6Then I heard what sounded like a voice among the four
living creatures, saying, "A quart of wheat for a day's wages, and three quarts of
barley for a day's wages, and do not damage the oil and the wine!"

7When the Lamb opened the fourth seal, I heard the voice of the fourth living
creature say, "Come!" 8I looked, and there before me was a pale horse! Its rider
was named Death, and Hades was following close behind him. They were given
power over a fourth of the earth to kill by sword, famine and plague, and by the wild
beasts of the earth.

9When he opened the fifth seal, I saw under the altar the souls of those who had
been slain because of the word of God and the testimony they had maintained.
10They called out in a loud voice, "How long, Sovereign Lord, holy and true, until
you judge the inhabitants of the earth and avenge our blood?" 11Then each of them
was given a white robe, and they were told to wait a little longer, until the number
of their fellow servants and brothers who were to be killed as they had been was
completed.

12I watched as he opened the sixth seal. There was a great earthquake. The sun
turned black like sackcloth made of goat hair, the whole moon turned blood red,
13and the stars in the sky fell to earth, as late figs drop from a fig tree when shaken
by a strong wind. 14The sky receded like a scroll, rolling up, and every mountain
and island was removed from its place.

15Then the kings of the earth, the princes, the generals, the rich, the mighty, and
every slave and every free man hid in caves and among the rocks of the mountains.
16They called to the mountains and the rocks, "Fall on us and hide us from the face
of him who sits on the throne and from the wrath of the Lamb! 17For the great day
of their wrath has come, and who can stand?"

1 The opening of the seals continues the vision begun in chapters 4 and 5. Now the scene shifts to events on earth. Before the exposition of each of the seals, it will be helpful to consider their overall meaning. As we have already seen (cf. comments on 5:1), the scroll itself involves the rest of Revelation and has to do with the consummation of the mystery of all things, the goal or end of history for both the overcomers and the beast worshipers. But what relationship do the seals have to this mystery? Are the events of the seals representative and simultaneous world happenings that occur throughout the church age (Minear)? Do they occur sequentially? Are they part of the final drama (Bruce) or merely preparatory to it (Ladd)? One thing is certain: the Lamb has the scroll and he himself opens the seals (6:1, 3, 5, et al.).

With the opening of the fifth seal, the martyrs cry out, "How long, . . . until you judge the inhabitants of the earth?" and are told to wait "a little longer" (vv.10–11). And when the sixth seal is opened, the judgment appears to be imminent (v.17), and this seems to indicate that there is a time progression in the seals. The writer of this commentary tentatively suggests that the seals represent events preparatory to the final consummation. Whether these events come immediately before the end or whether they represent general conditions that will prevail throughout the period preceding the end is a more difficult question.

The seals closely parallel the signs of the approaching end times spoken of in Jesus' Olivet Discourse (Matt 24:1–35; Mark 13:1–37; Luke 21:5–33). In these passages the events of the last days fall into three periods: (1) the period of false Christs, wars, famines, pestilences, earthquakes, and death, called "the beginning of birth pains" (Matt 24:8); (2) the period of the Great Tribulation (Matt 24:21; NIV, "great distress") and, (3) finally, the period "immediately after the distress of those days," when the sun, moon, and stars will be affected and Christ will return (Matt 24:29–30). This parallel to major parts of Revelation is too striking to be ignored. Thus the seals would correspond to the "beginning of birth pains" found in the Olivet Discourse. The events are similar to those occurring under the trumpets (8:2–11:19) and bowls (15:1–16:21) but they should not be confused with those later and more severe judgments. In Jewish apocalyptic literature (cf. 2 Baruch 25–30), the Great Tribulation precedes the age to come and is divided into twelve parts of various trials lasting possibly a week of seven weeks, or forty-nine years (C.K. Barrett, *The New Testament Background: Selected Documents* [New York: Harper and Row, 1961], pp. 245–48). Moreover, in the eschatological reckoning of time (cf. comments on 1:1), the events immediately preceding the end can stretch out over the whole age of the church, from John's time until now, and can still be viewed as "next" (4:1) in the sense that the "last days" began in the first century and are still continuing (cf. 1 John 2:18).

The first four seals are distinct from the last two in that they describe four horses of different colors with four riders who are given different powers over the earth. Background for the imagery of these four seals reflect Zechariah 1:8ff. and 6:1–8. In Zechariah's visions the horsemen and chariots are divine instruments of judgment on the enemies of God's people, while the colors represent geographical points of the compass. This may also be the best interpretation of the horses and their riders in Revelation 6, where each is sent by Christ through the instrumentality of the living creatures. The emphatic call "Come!" (vv.1, 3, 5, 7) should not be viewed as addressed either to John (some ancient Gr. MSS and many commentators, cf. Notes, v.1) or to Christ (Alford, Swete) but, rather, to the horsemen in each case. An analogy may be a first-century amphitheater or circus with various charioteers being summoned forth into the arena of the world by the call "Come!" or "Go forth!"

2 The identification of the first rider seated on a white horse has given interpreters great difficulty. Essentially, the difficulty is whether the rider on the white horse represents Christ and the victory of the gospel (Alford, Ladd) or whether he represents the Antichrist and the forces of evil (Beckwith, Bruce, Caird, Mounce, Swete, Walvoord). In favor of the first identification is the striking similarity of this rider to the portrayal of Christ in 19:11–16, the symbolism of white throughout Revelation always being associated with righteousness and Christ (e.g., 1:14; 2:17; 3:4–5, 18; 4:4; 7:9, 13–14; 20:11), and the references in the Olivet Discourse to the preaching of the gospel throughout the world before the end.

Support for the identification of the white horse with the Antichrist and his forces is the parallelism with the other three horses, which are instruments of judgment. The references in 19:11–16 to the rider on the white horse as "Faithful and True" and of whom it is said that "with justice he judges and makes war" may stand in contrast to the rider in 6:2 who is not faithful or true and who wages war for unjust conquest. As for the Lamb, he opens the seals and would not be one of the riders. Moreover, it would be inappropriate to have an angelic being call forth Christ or his servants. Again, the "bow" would most naturally be connected with the enemy of God's people (Ezek 39:3; cf. Rev. 20:7–8). Finally, the parallelism to the Olivet Discourse shows that the first events mentioned are the rise of "false Christs and false prophets" (Matt 24:24).

It must be admitted that the problem of the identity of the rider on the white horse may be solved either way, depending on the presuppositions one brings to the passage. The evidence, however, seems to favor slightly the second solution, which identifies the white horse with the Antichrist and his forces that seek to conquer the followers of Christ. John sensed that these persecutions were already present in his day and that they would culminate in a final, more severe form (1 John 2:18; Rev 13:7).

Each of the first four seals, then, represents conflict directed at Christians to test them and to sift out false disciples (6:10). This interpretation need not necessarily eliminate the fact that the seals may also refer to judgments on mankind in general. Yet since the fifth seal stresses the cry of the martyred Christians, probably the thought of Christian persecution belongs also in the first four seals (Minear, *I Saw a New Earth*, pp. 78, 266–69). Each of them unleashes events that separate false belief from true. The destruction of Jerusalem is a case in point (Luke 21:20ff.). The white horse is released to conquer. As he goes forth, judgment falls on the unbelief of Israel (Luke 21:22–23), while at the same time there is a testing of believers to separate the chaff from the wheat (cf. Luke 21:12–19).

Although the bow could be a symbol of either the Parthian or Cretan invaders bent on the conquest of Rome, in this context it suggests forces opposed to Christians (cf. Matt 24:5). A "crown" refers to victorious conquest in 19:12, where Christ wears "many crowns." "He was given" is the formula for the sovereign permission to carry out acts that, from a human viewpoint, seem contrary to God's character but nevertheless accomplish his will (cf. 13:5, 7, 15). Thus the rider on the white horse may also point to the attacks of the false Jews (2:9; 3:9) and to the affront to Christians from pagan religionists and the persecutions from Rome as well as all future, limited victories over the church by Satan (cf. 2:13; 12:17).

While v.2 would be sobering for first-century believers, at the same time it would encourage them, provided they understood that the Lamb had, for his own beneficent ends, permitted their testing and suffering. So they could trust that in the midst of seeming defeat from their enemies, he would ultimately be the victor (17:14).

3–4 The second horseman is war and bloodshed. He rides on a "fiery red steed," whose color symbolizes slaughter (2 Kings 3:22–23). Therefore, he is given the "large sword" because the number of those he kills is so great (cf. 13:10, 14). John might have thought of Nero's slaughter of Christians, the martyrdom of Antipas (2:13), or perhaps those slain under Domitian's persecutions (cf. Matt 10:34; 24:9).

5–6 The third horseman is poverty and famine. He rides on a "black horse" and symbolizes the effects of war and bloodshed: sorrow, mourning, and desolation (Isa 50:3; Jer 4:28; Lam 5:10 KJV). In the rider's hand there is a "pair of scales." A voice is heard interpreting its significance in economic terms: "a quart of wheat . . . and three quarts of barley for a day's wage" (lit., "for a denarius," a Gr. coin). This amount suggests food prices about twelve times higher than normal (Beckwith, p. 520) and implies inflation and famine conditions (Matt 24:7). A quart of wheat would supply an average person one day's sustenance. Barley was used by the poor to mix with the wheat. The expression "Do not damage the oil and wine" is less clear. Some view oil and wine as luxuries not necessary for bare survival, and the rich would have them while the poor were starving (cf. Prov 21:17). Others take oil and wine as showing the extent of the famine, since a drought affecting the grain may not be severe enough to hurt the vines and olive trees (ibid., p. 521). Moreover, oil and wine are staple foods in the East, both in dearth and in prosperity (e.g., Deut 7:13; Hos 2:8, 22). So in this view the third seal brings poverty and partial, though not severe, famine. As Mounce notes, "This interpretation is in harmony with the increasing intensity of the three cycles of judgment. The fourth seal affects 'the fourth part of the earth' (6:8), the trumpets destroy a third (8:7, 8, 10, 12), and the destruction by the bowls is complete and final (16:1ff.)" (*Revelation*, p. 155).

7–8 The fourth seal reveals a rider on a "pale horse." "Pale" (*chlōros*) denotes a yellowish green, the light green of a plant, or the paleness of a sick person in contrast to a healthy appearance (cf. BAG, p. 890). This cadaverous color blends well with the name of the rider—"Death" (*thanatos*). This probably refers to the death brought by pestilence, or plague, which often follows famine (cf. Jer 14:12; Ezek 5:17; 14:21; Luke 21:11). "Hades was following close behind him [Death]." But how? On foot? On the back of the same horse? On a separate horse? Scripture does not say. (On "Hades," cf. comments on 1:18.) There seems to be a growth of intensity in the judgments as they are carried out by various agencies—the sword (human violence), famine, plague, and now the wild beasts of the earth.

9–11 The fifth seal changes the metaphor of horsemen and discloses a scene of martyred saints under the altar crying out for justice upon those who killed them. They are told to wait a little longer till their fellow servants are also killed. Who are these martyrs? They are referred to again in 18:24 as "all who have been killed on the earth" and in 20:4 as "those who had been beheaded." In 13:15 they are referred to as those who refused to worship the image of the beast and were "killed." Others also take the group seen in 7:9ff. as martyred saints in heaven. At any rate, the question arises as to why the martyrs alone receive so much attention rather than all suffering or persecuted Christians. One solution understands John to be referring to all those who so faithfully follow Christ as to form a group that may be characterized as the slain of the Lord. They may or may not actually suffer physical death for Christ, but they have (like John) so identified themselves with the slain Lamb that they have in effect already offered up their lives ("because of the word of God and the testimony they had maintained" [cf. 1:2, 9]); and they are seen as a group (cf. Rom 8:36).

John says that he saw the "souls" (*psychas*) of those slain (v.9). This is generally understood to mean the disembodied souls of these saints. However, the Greek word *psychē* has various meanings and probably stands here for the actual "lives" or "persons" who were killed rather than for their "souls." They are seen by John as persons who are very much alive though they have been killed by the beast. "Under the altar" sets the scene as occurring in the temple of heaven. Depending on which altar is meant, one of two different ideas is connoted. In 8:3, 5 and 9:13 the altar is the golden altar of incense that stood in the tabernacle either in or before the Most Holy Place (Exod 30:1ff.; Heb 9:4). Likewise, the other references in Revelation to "altar" also can be understood as referring to this altar of incense (11:1; 14:18; 16:7). In accord with this sense, the prayers of the saints would be for God's vindication of the martyrs of Christ (cf. Luke 18:7–8). On the other hand, some understand this as the brazen altar of sacrifice and see in the imagery the blood of the martyrs at the base or "under the altar" (Ladd, *Commentary on Revelation*, in loc.). But if the symbolism was sacrificial, it would be more natural to read "on" the altar, not "under" it.

The martyred address God as "Sovereign Lord" (*despotēs*) (v.10). This term implies "ownership" (TDNT, 2:44) and is used elsewhere in the NT to denote slave masters (1 Tim 6:1; Peter 2:18), God (Luke 2:29; Acts 4:24), or Jesus Christ (2 Peter 2:1; Jude 4). (On the phrase "holy and true," cf. comments on 3:7.) The martyrs cry for God's vengeance on the evildoers. The word "avenge" (*ekdikeō*) relates everywhere in the OT (LXX) and in the NT to the idea of punishment or retribution (TDNT, 2:442ff.). These saints are following the teaching of Paul in Romans 12:19: "Do not take revenge, my friends, but leave room for God's wrath, for it is written: 'It is mine to avenge, I will repay,' says the Lord." Though believers are forbidden to take revenge, God will vindicate his elect by punishing those who killed them (Luke 18:7f.; 2 Thess 1:8).

The martyrs were each given a "white robe" as an evidence of their righteousness and victory before the Judge of all the earth, who will speedily avenge their deaths. The wait of a "little longer" is in God's estimate but a fleeting moment, though for us it may stretch out for ages (cf. 12:12; 20:3). The DSS refer to the final reward of the righteous as "the garment of honour in everlasting light" (1QS 4.8). The expression "until the number of their fellow servants . . . was completed" presents a slight exegetical difficulty (cf. Notes). It is usually taken to mean that the number of either the martyred or their companions on earth who will be killed will be completed (so NIV). However, another sense may be possible. The verb "completed" (*plēroō*) may mean "until their fellow servants complete their course," or "fulfill their Christian calling," which will involve also martyrdom. In any event, what constitutes the essence of Christian discipleship in John's eyes should not be overlooked. As Lilje says, "Every believer in Christ ought to be prepared for martyrdom; for Christians . . . cannot express their priestly communion with their Lord more perfectly than when they accept the suffering and the glory of martyrdom" (p. 130).

12–14 The sixth seal is broken by the Lamb, and John witnesses certain eschatological signs heralding the imminent, final day of the Lord so often described in Scripture (e.g., Isa 2:10, 19, 21; 13:10; 34:4; Jer 4:29; Ezek 32:7–8; Joel 2:31; 3:15; Zeph 1:14–18; Matt 24:29; Luke 21:11, 25–26). The signs are threefold: (1) the great earthquake and its storm affecting the sun and moon, (2) the stars falling, and (3) the terror on earth

(vv. 15–17). It is difficult to know how literally the whole description should be taken. Some of the events are described from the standpoint of ancient cosmology—e.g., the falling of the stars to earth like figs from a shaken tree, or the sky rolling up like a scroll. The firmament suspended like a roof over the earth is shaken by the great earthquake.

The scene, whether taken literally or figuratively, is one of catastrophe and distress for the inhabitants of the earth. As later biblical authors seized on the earlier imagery of the theophany on Sinai to describe appearances of God to man (e.g., Hab 3:3ff.), so John utilizes the archetypal imagery of the OT to describe this terrible visitation of God's final judgment to the earth. In much the same manner as we would describe a chaotic situation by saying "all hell broke loose" (though not intending to be taken in a strictly literal sense), so the biblical writers use the language of cosmic turmoil to describe the condition of the world when God comes to judge the earth (v. 17). "Earthquakes" are mentioned in Revelation 8:5; 11:13, 19; 16:18 and sun, moon, and/or stellar disturbances in 8:12; 9:2; 16:8. Of course, actual physical phenomena may also accompany the final judgment.

15–17 These verses record the terror of all classes of people at these events and at the wrath of God and the Lamb. "The kings of the earth, the princes [dignitaries], the generals" describe the powerful; "the rich, the mighty" describe the affluent and the heroes. Finally, political distinctions of the widest kind—"every slave and every free man"—are referred to. Since all kinds of people are included, we cannot say that God's wrath is directed only at the powerful, at the rich, or at false Christians. His judgment will fall on all who refuse to repent and instead worship demons and idols and persecute Christ's followers (9:20–21; 16:6, 9).

The plea of people for the rocks and mountains to fall on them (v. 16) occurs in OT contexts of God's judgment (Isa 2:19, 21; Hos 10:8). It expresses the desire to be buried under the falling mountains and hills so as to escape the pains and terrors of the judgment (K D, *Minor Prophets*, 1:131). Jesus said that in this way the inhabitants of Jerusalem would cry out when God's judgment fell on the city, in A.D. 70 (Luke 23:30).

The "wrath" (*orgē*, "anger") of the Lamb is not only a new metaphor but a paradoxical one. Lambs are usually gentle. But this Lamb shows "wrath" against those who have refused his grace (cf. John 5:27). Henceforth in Revelation the wrath of God and of the Lamb is a continuing theme and is described under the figures of the trumpets and bowls (11:18; 14:7, 10, 19; 15:1, 7; 16:1, 19; 19:15). Moreover, God's wrath is a present historical reality as well as an eschatological judgment (cf. Rom 1:18ff.; 2:5). So great is the day of destruction that "who can stand?" (cf. Joel 2:11; Nah 1:6; Mal 3:2).

Notes

1 Ἔρχου (*erchou*) can mean "go forth" rather than "come," thus clearly showing that the horseman rather than John is being addressed. In 16:1, however, John uses a different word, Ὑπάγετε (*hypagete*), for "go forth." ℵ understands *erchou* as addressed to John and adds καὶ ἴδε (*kai ide*, "and see") here and also in vv. 3, 5, 7 (as does the TR). "Come and see" could be understood as a rabbinic invitation to enlightenment (cf. John 1:46). There is,

however, stronger MS support for the abbreviated readings that also agree with the sense given in the exposition. When John himself is addressed, another word is used, Δεῦρο (*deuro*, "come"; 17:1; 21:9).

On the problem of the identification of the white horse and its rider, see Mathias Rissi, "The Rider on the White Horse," Int, 18 (1964), 407–18, who argues for antichristic forces; Zane Hodges, "The First Horseman of the Apocalypse," BS, 119 (October 1962), 324–34, who argues for the Christ identification following the early father Irenaeus.

11 Πληρωθῶσιν (*plērōthōsin*, "was completed"), an aorist passive subjunctive, is supported by A C et al. and is followed by NIV. An alternative reading, πληρώσωσιν (*plērōsōsin*, "was complete"), the plain aorist subjunctive, is supported ℵ P et al. The passive would mean that the "number" was complete, while the plain aorist subjunctive reading favors either the sense that the fellow servants will be complete (rare intransitive sense for the verb, cf. BAG, pp. 677–78, pars. 5 and 6) or that they will complete their course.

---

3. *First Interlude* (7:1–17)

Indications that chapter 7 is a true interlude are the change in tone from the subject matter referred to in the sixth seal as well as the delay until 8:1 in opening the seventh seal. Two main subjects may be distinguished in the chapter. John first sees the angels who will unleash destruction on the earth restrained until the 144,000 servants of God from every tribe of Israel are sealed (vv.1–8). Then he sees an innumerable multitude clothed in white standing before the throne of God, who are identified as those who have come out of the "great tribulation" (vv.9–17). As Charles remarks, this chapter is in many respects one of the most difficult and yet most important in the book (*Commentary on Revelation*, 1:189). Lilje calls the whole picture one of the most glorious in the entire Apocalypse. It probably functions both prospectively and retrospectively.

The principal exegetical difficulty in chapter 7 centers around the identification of the 144,000 (vv.1–8) and the identification of the innumerable multitude (vv.9–17). Is the reference to the tribes of Israel symbolic, representative, or literal? What is the "great tribulation" (v.14)? Are those described in 7:9ff. martyrs? There is considerable divergence of opinion about these questions. The dialogue can be traced only briefly.

a. *The 144,000 Israelites*

7:1–8

[1]After this I saw four angels standing at the four corners of the earth, holding back the four winds of the earth to prevent any wind from blowing on the land or on the sea or on any tree. [2]Then I saw another angel coming up from the east, having the seal of the living God. He called out in a loud voice to the four angels who had been given power to harm the land and the sea: [3]"Do not harm the land or the sea or the trees until we put a seal on the foreheads of the servants of our God." [4]Then I heard the number of those who were sealed: 144,000 from all the tribes of Israel.

[5]From the tribe of Judah 12,000 were sealed,
from the tribe of Reuben 12,000,
from the tribe of Gad 12,000,
[6]from the tribe of Asher 12,000,
from the tribe of Naphtali 12,000,
from the tribe of Manasseh 12,000,

7from the tribe of Simeon, 12,000,
from the tribe of Levi 12,000,
from the tribe of Issachar 12,000,
8from the tribe of Zebulun 12,000,
from the tribe of Joseph 12,000,
from the tribe of Benjamin 12,000.

1–3 The "four angels" at "the four corners of the earth" hold "the four winds of the earth" from blowing on the earth until the servants of God are sealed on their foreheads. The expression "the four corners of the earth" was used in antiquity among the Near-Eastern nations much as we use "the four points of the compass." Since nowhere in Revelation do we read of the four winds actually blowing, they may be taken as representing the earthly catastrophes that occur under the trumpets and bowls.

Another angel comes from the "east" (possibly from Jerusalem or Zion, to emphasize its mission of salvation?) and calls to the four others not to release their destruction until the servants of God have a "seal" on their foreheads. Such a seal surely indicates ownership by God and the Lamb (14:1). Furthermore, a seal may offer protection or security for the bearers. Such seems to be the emphasis in 9:4, where the demonic forces are told to harm "only those people who did not have the seal [*sphragis*] of God on their foreheads." Charles believes that only protection from demonic forces is involved in the sealing rather than escape from physical harm from the plagues, from the Antichrist, or protection from spiritual apostasy (R.H. Charles, *Studies in the Apocalypse* [Edinburgh: T. & T. Clark, 1913], p. 124f.).

By examining references to events that happened to those who, by contrast, have the "mark" (*charagma*) of the beast (13:16–17), Charles's view may be evaluated. In 13:16–17, those who do not have the mark of the beast face severe socio-economic sanctions. Those who have the mark of the beast are not only identified as beast worshipers but become the objects of the irreversible wrath of God (14:9, 11). This implies, by contrast, that those who have "the seal [*sphragis*] of God" are God worshipers and will be the objects of his abiding grace. In 16:2, the bowl of God's wrath appears to be directed exclusively toward those who have the mark of the beast, thus excluding those with the seal of God (cf. 16:6). Those having the mark of the beast are deluded by the beast (19:20), this statement implying that the sealed of God are not thus deceived. Finally, a martyred group is seen just prior to their resurrection and thousand-year reign with Christ and are described as not having the mark of the beast or worshiping him (20:4).

In the light of these passages, we may say that the "sealed" are the people of God and that their sealing must be related to their salvation as in the comparable figure used by Paul (2 Cor 1:22; Eph 1:13; 4:30; cf. 4 Ezra 6:5). This is also evident in 14:3–4, where the sealed are described as those who were redeemed from the earth as firstfruits to God (cf. Rom 8:23; James 1:18). In fact, "baptism" was considered a "seal" of salvation in the early church (cf. BAG, p. 804, s.v. *sphragis*).

Furthermore, while the seal may not protect the sealed against harm inflicted by human agency (13:7; 20:4), they are protected from the divine plagues (16:2). It is clear that the protection from famine, pestilence, and sword afforded the sealed in the apocryphal Psalms of Solomon (15:6, 9) cannot also apply to John's sealed, since they are beheaded (20:4). As for OT background for the problem, Ezekiel 9:4–7 may well be primary. In this passage a divine messenger with stylus in hand was to go through the apostate Jerusalem of Ezekiel's day and put a mark upon the foreheads of those who deplored the faithless idolatry of the Israelites. Those so marked were the faithful and true servants of God in contrast to the professed but false servants who had abandoned him. The sealed would be spared the divine slaughtering of the rebellious inhabitants of the city. Interestingly, the "mark" (*taw*) in the Phoenician script looked like a cross (𐤕) and was later adopted by early Jewish Christians as a symbol of their faith in Jesus ("The Chi-Rho-Sign-Christogram and/or Staurogram," Matthew Black, *Apostolic History and the Gospel*, ed. W. Gasque and R.P. Martin [Grand Rapids: Eerdmans, 1970], pp. 319–27).

The sealing language would have the effect of assuring the people of God of his special concern and plan for them. Even when facing persecution and martyrdom at the hand of the beast, they can be certain that no plague from God will touch them but that they will be in his presence forever because they are his very own possession. Therefore, the seal on the forehead is equivalent to the divine mark of ownership on them that elsewhere in the NT is referred to the presence of the Holy Spirit (2 Cor 1:22; Eph 1:13; 4:30). This act of God will fulfill the promise to the Philadelphian church: "Since you have kept my command to endure patiently, I will also keep you from the hour of trial that is going to come upon the whole world to test those who live on the earth" (3:10). Consequently, those thus sealed must be Christians and not unconverted Jews or Gentiles (contra Robert Gundry, *The Church and the Tribulation* [Grand Rapids: Zondervan, 1973], p. 83).

4 John next gives the number of those sealed—144,000—and their identification: "From all the tribes of Israel." There are two principal views regarding the identification of this group: (1) The number and the tribal identifications are taken literally and refer to 144,000 Jewish Christians who are sealed (to protect them from destruction) during the time of the Great Tribulation (J.A. Seiss, *The Apocalypse* [Grand Rapids: Zondervan, 1957], pp. 160f.; Walvoord, pp. 140f.). (2) According to another viewpoint, John is understood to use the language of the new Israel and thus refers to the completed church composed of Jew and Gentile (Alf, p. 624; Beckwith, p. 535; Caird, p. 95; Swete, pp. 96–97).

In support of the first view is the normal usage of "Israel" in the NT as referring to the physical descendants of Jacob. Galatians 6:16 is no exception, as Peter Richardson observes: "Strong confirmation of this position [i.e., that 'Israel' refers to the Jews in the NT] comes from the total absence of an identification of the church with Israel until A.D. 160; and also from the total absence, even then, of the term 'Israel of God' to characterize the church" (*Israel in the Apostolic Church* [Cambridge: Cambridge University, 1969], pp. 74–84). Reference to the Twelve Tribes (vv.5–8) would most naturally be understood to refer to the ancient historic Israel and not to the church. The view that the Ten Tribes were "lost" in the first-century, though it is popular, hardly needs refuting (cf. IDB, 4:699f.; F.F. Bruce, *The Book of Acts*, NIC [Grand Rapids: Eerdmans, 1954], p. 489, n.13). Thus, in this first view, John would symbolically be describing the beginning of what Paul foretold in Romans 11:25–29 as the salvation of "all Israel."

In support of the second view, which identifies Israel with the church, is the fact that the NT identifies the followers of Christ as "Abraham's seed" (Gal 3:29), as "the true circumcision" (Phil 3:3) and as the "Israel of God" (Gal 6:16; though disputed, cf. above). Furthermore, John himself earlier in Revelation makes a distinction between the true Jew and the false (cf. 2:9; 3:9) and that could imply that here in chapter 7 he intends also to designate the true Israel or the church (Ladd, *Commentary on Revelation*, p. 116). Additional support for this view is found if there is a unity between the first and second groups in chapter 7, groups that otherwise must be treated as different and unconnected.

Without discussing at length the disputed issue of the Jew as Israel versus the church as Israel (though it obviously bears on the interpretation of this passage), we may agree with Walvoord, who says, "The decision as to who are included in the term 'Israel' should be reached on the basis of exegesis and usage" (p. 143). Those who argue that the term "Israel" in other NT books refers exclusively to Jews are in our opinion correct (so Richardson). Strict exegesis, however, must also ask whether the author of Revelation wishes the term to have this same more restricted usage or whether he uses it differently. It is possible that the usage of the term "Jew" among Christians had undergone a historic change from the earlier days when Paul wrote Romans (A.D. 56) until Revelation was written toward the close of the century.

By the middle of the first century, Paul made a distinction between the true, spiritual Jew and the physical descendants of Abraham (Rom 2:28–29; 9:8). Only those Jews who recognized Jesus as Messiah could rightly be called "Israel" in the strictest sense (Rom 9:6), though the term might be used with qualifications to refer to the historic descendants of Jacob ("Israel after the flesh" [1 Cor 10:18 Gr.]). Peter likewise described the church (Jew and Gentile) in terms drawn from the OT that historically describe the true people of God among the Jewish descendants ("holy priesthood . . . chosen people . . . royal priesthood . . . holy nation" [1 Peter 2:4, 9]). Moreover, even Gentiles who received Jesus as the Messiah and Lord were considered "Abraham's seed" (Gal 3:29) and the true "circumcision" (Phil 3:3).

Already in Revelation there has been the distinction between Jews who were Jews in name only and not true Jews because they did not acknowledge Jesus as Lord (2:9; 3:9). Also, the OT image of the people of Israel as a kingdom and priests to God is used by John of the followers of Jesus (1:6). Similarly, many of the promises to the victors in the churches of Asia (chs. 2–3) are fulfillments of OT promises given to the true people of Israel. In Christ's rebuke to the churches, we have the OT imagery of "Balaam" and "Jezebel" describing error that had influenced not the OT Israel but the NT church. In chapter 12, it is again difficult to distinguish whether the "woman" represents the ancient Jewish covenant people or the NT followers of Jesus. In Revelation 21:9–12, the church is called the "bride, the wife of the Lamb"; she is identified with the New Jerusalem, and on its twelve gates are inscribed the "names of the twelve tribes of Israel." Even in the Gospel of John (assuming the apostle wrote it as well as Revelation), Jesus is the "true vine," which many commentators understand to be an allusion to the vine that decorated the temple entrance and stood as a symbol for Israel (cf. Isa 5:1ff. with John 15:1ff.). Jesus is claiming to be the true Israel and his followers, then, the branches, would be related to the true Israel (cf. Rom 11:17–24).

The usage seems evident in the NT itself; the only question is whether John takes the final step in Revelation and, in the context of a largely Gentile church, uses the OT terminology to speak of the church. Richardson's summary is provocative:

> As long as the church was viewed as a community gathered from Gentiles and Jews, it could not readily call itself "Israel." But when it was sharply separated from both, and when it had a theory that Judaism no longer stood in continuity with Israel *ante Christum*, and when Gentiles not only could take over other titles but in some

> cases could claim exclusive rights to them, then the church as an organizational entity could appropriate "Israel" (*Apostolic Church,* p. 204).

All this simply suggests the possibility that in John's mind the followers of Jesus (14:4) are the true servants of God, the Israel of God (cf. John 11:51–52). Richardson also observes that in Qumranic and late Jewish apocalyptic literature the term "Israel" was jealously and exclusively restricted to members of certain Jewish groups who even denied its use to other Jews and claimed that only they were the true Israel of God (ibid., pp. 217ff.).

The identification of the 144,000 with the whole elect people of God, including both Jews and Gentiles, does not negate Paul's teaching to the effect that the majority of the Jews themselves will one day be brought back into a relationship of salvation before God. John simply is not dealing with Paul's emphasis at this point in Revelation (but cf. at 11:2f.).

Mounce has a further suggestion on the identity of the two groups in the chapter. He states:

> The position taken in the following pages is that in both visions it is the church which is in view, but from two vantage points. Prior to the trumpet judgments the last generation of believers is sealed so as to be saved from the destruction coming upon the earth and to be brought safely into the heavenly kingdom. The second vision is anticipatory of the eternal blessedness of all believers when in the presence of God they realize the rewards of faithful endurance (*Revelation,* p. 164).

But Mounce later identifies the "great tribulation" (7:14) through which the second group passes as "that final series of woes which will immediately precede the end" (ibid., p. 173). This seems to contradict the earlier statement that the second group represents "all believers." Confessedly this is a difficult chapter. Perhaps the confusion revolves around our inability to understand John's precise perspective on "the great tribulation."

The number 144,000 is obviously obtained by combining 12,000 for each of the twelve tribes of Israel (vv.5–8). Earlier in Revelation (cf. 4:4), twenty-four (a multiple of twelve) serves as a symbolic number. The "thousand" multiple appears again—this time in relation to the size of the Holy City: "He measured the city with the rod and found it to be 12,000 stadia in length, and as wide and high as it is long" (21:16). Thus, 12,000 is symbolic of completeness and perfection. Even the wall is "144 cubits" (twelves times twelve) (v.17). The tree of life bearing "twelve crops of fruit, yielding its fruit every month" (i.e., twelve months) (22:2) further supports the view that John intends the number twelve to be taken symbolically and not literally. By 144,000, he signifies the sealing of *all* or the *total* number of God's servants who will face the Great Tribulation.

Those who are sealed come from "all the tribes of Israel," and this emphasizes even more the universality and comprehensiveness of the Christian gospel. Whereas in first-century Judaism there were many sects with exclusive tribal claims to being the true Israel, for the followers of Jesus all such sectarianism is broken down and all groups, regardless of race, culture, religious background, or geographical location, are accepted before God (7:9; 14:4). There is an exclusivism in Revelation, but it is based on loyalty to Christ, not on historical or liturgical continuity.

5–8 John goes even further. He enumerates each of the twelve tribes and their number: "From the tribe of Judah 12,000 were sealed," etc. Why was it necessary to provide this detailed enumeration? And why the particular tribal selection? In answering these difficult questions, some facts about the list should be noted. John places Judah first, evidently to emphasize the priority of the messianic King who came from the tribe of Judah (Rev 5:5; Heb 7:13–14). Nowhere in the tribal listings of the OT except in the space arrangement of the wilderness camp (Num 2:3ff.) does Judah come first. This exception may itself be linked with the messianic expectation through Judah (Gen 49:10; 1 Chron 5:2). John's priority of Judah is comparable to the emphasis placed in late Judaism on the tribe of Levi (the priestly tribe). It is significant that John includes Levi among the other tribes, and thus gives no special place to the Levitical order, and that he also places Levi in the comparatively unimportant eighth place.

The particular order and names of the tribes as given here by John is unique. The OT has no fewer than twenty variant lists of the tribes, and these lists include anywhere from ten to thirteen tribes, though the number twelve is predominant (cf. Gen 49; Deut 33; Ezek 48). The grouping of twelve may be a way of expressing the corporate identity of the elect people of God as a whole and may be maintained—even artificially at times—to preserve this identity (cf. the need to make up the "twelfth" apostle when Judas fell [Act 1:25–26]). John omits Dan (which elsewhere is always included) and Ephraim. In order to maintain the ideal number twelve with these omissions, he must list both Joseph and Manasseh as tribes. This is peculiar because the tribe of Joseph is always mentioned in the other lists by either including Joseph and excluding his two sons, Ephraim and Manasseh (Gen 49), or by omitting Joseph and counting the two sons as one tribe each (Ezek 48). It is not until the Levitical priesthood gains more prominence that the tribe of Levi is omitted from the lists and is replaced by the two sons of Joseph.

Various efforts have been made to solve the enigma of John's list and especially to explain the absence of the tribe of Dan. As yet, we have no completely satisfactory solution. Ladd's proposal is interesting: "John intends to say [by the irregular list] that the twelve tribes of Israel are not really literal Israel, but the true, spiritual Israel—the church" (*Commentary on Revelation*, p. 115). While this may be true, whether the mere irregularity of the list is intended to convey it is questionable. It might be more helpful to seek some satisfactory reason why John specifically omitted Dan and Ephraim.

The early church held that the Antichrist would arise from the tribe of Dan. Charles has argued that this belief is in fact pre-Christian Jewish tradition, first mentioned in Christian sources in Irenaeus (d. second century A.D.) (R.H. Charles, *The Apocrypha and Pseudepigrapha of the Old Testament*, 2 vols. [Oxford: Clarendon, 1913], 2:334). Furthermore, Dan was associated in the OT with idolatry (Judg 18:18–19; 1 Kings 12:29–30). This may be the clue. If John sought to expose Christian idolatry and beast worship in his day by excluding Dan from the list of those sealed, it may also be possible to explain, on the same basis, why Manasseh and Joseph were chosen to fill up the sacred number rather than Manasseh and Ephraim. In the OT Ephraim was also explicitly identified with idolatry (Hos 4:17). Qumran literature is of little help because in it both Ephraim and Manasseh are apostate tribes (4Qp Nah 7; 4Qp Ps 37:3—cited by Richardson, *Apostolic Church*, p. 227 and A. Dupont-Sommer, *The Essene Writings from Qumran*, tr. G. Vermes [Cleveland: World, 1962], p. 269, n.2; p. 273, n.2).

If idolatry, then, seems to be the reason for omitting both Dan and Ephraim, the readjustment of the list to include Joseph and Manasseh to complete the twelve can be understood. Since Dan will be reckoned first in the tribal listing of the restored eschatological Jewish community (Ezek 48) and John's list puts Judah first, it may be that John's listing describes the church rather than ethnic Israel.

It is important to note that John does not equate the 144,000 with all in the tribes. Rather, his repeated use of the preposition *ek* ("from") in vv.4–8 implies that the sealed were an elect group chosen out of the tribes: "144,000 from all the tribes of Israel. . . . From the tribe of Judah 12,000 were sealed," etc. If John had the actual Jewish Israel in view, this use of "from" would indicate an election from the whole nation. On the other hand, if he intended to imply something about the church, his language might indicate God's selecting the true church out "from" the professing church. This thought has been mentioned earlier (cf. 2:14ff., 20ff.; 3:16ff.) and is supported by Ezekiel 9:4–7, where the seal identified the true servants of God from the false ones among the professing people of God (see above under vv.2–3). Paul stated the same thought when he wrote, "Nevertheless, God's solid foundation stands firm, sealed with this inscription: 'The Lord knows those who are his,' and 'Everyone who confesses the name of the Lord must turn away from wickedness' " (2 Tim 2:19).

The description of the judgments under the sixth seal (6:12ff.) ends with the question "The great day of their wrath has come, and who can stand?" (6:17). Chapter 7 answers this question by implying that only the true servants of God, who are divinely sealed, can be protected from the wrath of God and the Lamb.

Notes

4–8 For a more thorough discussion of the various views on the identification of the 144,000, see Gundry, *Church and the Tribulation*, pp. 81ff.; Charles *Studies in the Apocalypse*, pp. 114–15; Elliott, 1:226ff.

---

b. *The great white-robed multitude*

7:9–17

9After this I looked and there before me was a great multitude that no one could
count, from every nation, tribe, people and language, standing before the throne
and in front of the Lamb. They were wearing white robes and were holding palm
branches in their hands. 10And they cried out in a loud voice:

"Salvation belongs to our God,
who sits on the throne,
and to the Lamb."

11All the angels were standing around the throne and around the elders and the
four living creatures. They fell down on their faces before the throne and worshiped
God, 12saying:

"Amen!
Praise and glory
and wisdom and thanks and honor
and power and strength
be to our God for ever and ever.
Amen!"

[13]Then one of the elders asked me, "These in white robes—who are they, and where did they come from?"
[14]I answered, "Sir, you know."
And he said, "These are they who have come out of the great tribulation; they have washed their robes and made them white in the blood of the Lamb.
[15]Therefore,

"they are before the throne of God
  and serve him day and night in his temple;
and he who sits on the throne will spread his tent
    over them.
[16]Never again will they hunger;
  never again will they thirst.
The sun will not beat upon them,
  nor any scorching heat.
[17]For the Lamb at the center of the throne will be
    their shepherd;
  he will lead them to springs of living water.
And God will wipe away every tear from their eyes."

John now sees a great multitude from every nation and cultural background, standing before the throne of God and clothed in white robes. They are identified by the angel as those "who have come out of the great tribulation" (v.14). Again, the question is that of identity. Are they the Gentiles who are saved in the Tribulation in contrast to the Jews in vv.1–8? Beckwith answers no because they are described as coming from every nation and tribe and language, and this would mean both Jews and Gentiles (p. 539). Are they, then, martyrs who have given their lives in the Great Tribulation and have been slain by the beast? If martyrs, are they the remainder of those to be killed referred to when the fifth seal is opened (6:11)? Are they the complete group of martyrs? Or do they represent the whole company of the redeemed in Christ as seen in glory?

Although there is no direct evidence that the great multitude are martyrs, there are some indications of this: (1) they are seen in heaven "before the throne" (v.9) and "in his temple" (v.15); (2) they are described as those "who have come out of the great tribulation" (v.14). Thus it is assumed that, since they have died in the Great Tribulation, they have most likely been martyred because the Tribulation will be a time of great killing of the saints (17:6; 18:24; 19:2; 20:4, etc.).

The multitude would not be the whole company of the martyred throughout history but only those who were victims of the beast persecution during the Great Tribulation. The group is probably those future martyrs referred to under the fifth seal as those "who were to be killed as they had been" (6:11). Neither, then, would they be the whole redeemed church as Beckwith and Eller suggest, unless all Christians are to be identified with the martyrs.

The identification of this second group is related to the identification of the first one (vv.1–8). Some argue that the two groups must be different because the first is numbered, the second innumerable; the first is limited to Jews, the second refers to every nation (Gundry, *Church and the Tribulation,* p. 81). These objections are not serious if we recall the exposition of vv.1–8, where it was noted that (1) the number of the sealed was symbolic and not literal and that (2) the delineation of the Twelve Tribes was seen as John's deliberate attempt to universalize the election of God. Thus, what some have seen as contrasts may actually be designed to complement each other and show the continuity of the first group with the second. Furthermore, we should bear in mind that John does not see any group at all in vv.1–8 but merely hears the number of the sealed, whereas in vv.9–17 he actually sees a group and describes what he sees and hears. Therefore, the unity of both groups can be maintained and vv.9–17 understood as the interpretative key to the 144,000. John's vision then leaps ahead to a scene in heaven after the Great Tribulation has run its course and views the glorified Tribulation saints as being in God's presence, at rest from their trial, and serving him continually.

Two slightly different variations of the more literal Jewish identity of those in vv.1–8 and the relationship of this first group to the second (vv.9ff.) are quite popular today. Some see the 144,000 as a select group of Jews who will be converted to Jesus shortly after the rapture of the church to heaven. These Jewish evangelists will preach the gospel to the world during the Tribulation. As a result of their preaching, a great multitude of Gentiles will be converted to Christ (A.C. Gaebelein, *The Revelation,* [New York: Our Hope, 1915], pp. 58–59).

Others, accepting a posttribulational view of the church's rapture, understand the 144,000 as a literal Jewish remnant preserved physically through the Tribulation and converted immediately after the Rapture. They will be the people who will constitute the beginning of the restored Jewish Davidic Kingdom at the inception of the millennial reign of Christ on the earth (Gundry, *Church and the Tribulation,* pp. 82–83).

The Bible speaks of three different types of tribulation or distress, and it is important to distinguish between them:

1. There is tribulation that is inseparable from Christian life in the world (John 16:33; Acts 14:22; Rom 5:3; 2 Tim 2:11–12; 1 Peter 4:12; Rev 1:9; 2:10, etc.). All Christians during all ages participate in tribulation. Thus they share in the continuing sufferings of Christ (Col 1:24).

2. The Bible also speaks of an intense tribulation that will come on the final generation of Christians and climax all previous persecutions. Daniel 12:1 refers to such a time: "There will be a time of distress [*thlipseōs,* LXX] such as has not happened from the beginning of nations until then." Likewise, Jesus predicts such an unprecedented persecution: "For then there will be great distress [*thlipsis*], unequaled from the beginning of the world until now—and never to be equaled again" (Matt 24:21). Paul's mention of "the rebellion" (*apostasia*) and "the man of lawlessness" surely refers to this same period (2 Thess 2:3ff.). In Revelation this more intense persecution is mentioned in 7:14; 11:7–10; 13:7; 16:6, and possibly the events under the fifth seal should be included here (6:9–11; so J. Barton Payne, *The Imminent Appearing of Christ* [Grand Rapids: Eerdmans, 1962], p. 115). This future tribulation is distinguished from previous persecutions of the church in its intensity, in its immediate connection with Christ's second coming, and in the presence of Antichrist during it.

3. Scripture also speaks of a future time of God's intense wrath on unbelievers. Revelation refers to this as "the great day of their wrath" (6:17) and "the hour of trial that is going to come upon the whole world to test those who live on the earth" (3:10). Such wrath from God comes especially under the trumpets and bowls (8:2ff.; 16:1ff.). Probably drawing on the teaching of Jesus in the Olivet Discourse (Matt 24), Paul refers to this punitive action of God in 2 Thessalonians 1:6–10 and even uses the word *thlipsis* ("trouble"). While for Christians the Great Tribulation may be concurrent with a portion of the period of God's wrath on the rebellious, the final and more intense judgment of God seems to *follow* the Great Tribulation itself and is directly connected with the coming of Christ (Matt 24:29; Rev 6:12ff.; 19:11ff.).

9 "A great multitude . . . from every nation, tribe, people and language" pictures what Swete calls a "polyglot cosmopolitan crowd" (p. 97). The words might well describe the crowds common to the agora or the quay of a seaport in first-century Asia. (Similar fourfold descriptions of the members of the Christian community or of the inhabitants of the world also occur in Rev 5:9; 11:9; 13:7; 14:6; 17:15.) "Standing before the throne and in front of the Lamb" signifies their position of acceptance and honor as God's true servants (cf. v.15) and reminds us of the continuity of this vision with the earlier vision of the throne and the Lamb (chs.4–5). This group seems to complete the full circle of participants before the throne begun in chapter 4.

Their "white robes" impress John and are an important feature of the vision (vv.9, 13–14). We cannot fail to connect them with the white robes given the martyrs under the fifth seal (6:11). The white robes symbolize salvation and victory (v.10), and their possessors obtained them by "[washing] their robes and [making] them white in the blood of the Lamb" (v.14). This implies that they were true recipients of Christ's redemption in contrast to others who, though professing belief in Christ, were not genuine overcomers (cf. 3:5–6, 18).

"The blood of the Lamb" connotes here more even than the profound reference to the sacrificial death of Jesus (5:9); it also suggests faithful witness in following Jesus in his death (2:13; 12:11).

"Palm branches" are referred to only one other time in the NT (John 12:13), where they are connected to the Passover celebration. Moses provided that palms should be used at the Feast of Tabernacles (Lev 23:40). Later they were used on other festal occasions (1 Macc 13:51; 2 Macc 10:7). Jewish coins of the period 140 B.C. to A.D. 70 frequently contain palms and some have the inscription "the redemption of Zion" (IDB, 3:646). Palms were emblems of victory. In John 12 they denote the triumph of Christ, while here in Revelation the reference is to the victory of the servants of Christ (Deiss BS, pp. 368–70).

10 In accord with the literary symmetry of chapters 4–7, this group also expresses their worship of the King and the Lamb. Their praise to God is for his "salvation" (*sōtēria*), not their own accomplishments. Since the same word is associated with the final manifestation of God's power and kingdom (12:10; 19:1), here it may also denote God's final victory over sin and the principalities of this world that crucified Christ and that kill his true disciples (cf. Isa 49:8; 2 Cor 6:2).

11–12 Finally, the angelic hosts respond to the cry of the redeemed (v.10) with "Amen" and voice their praise and worship of God for the salvation given to men (cf. Luke 15:10). Compare this doxology with 5:12–13.

13–14 After the manner of the OT apocalyptic passages, the interpreting angel asks concerning the white-robed throng, "Who are they, and where did they come from?" (cf. Dan 7:15–16; Zech 1:9, 19; 4:1–6). Here and in 5:5 are the only references in Revelation to an elder speaking individually, a fact that supports the view that the elders in Revelation are angels and not a symbolic group representing the church.

The reference to the washed robes should be viewed in relation to 3:4, where soiled clothes represent defection from Christ through unbelief and worship of false gods (cf. 21:8). On the "great tribulation," see the introduction to this section.

15 This and the following verses describe the activity and condition of the true servants of God in their future and eternal relation to the Lamb. The scene is one of the most beautiful in the Bible. In it those who have washed their robes in the blood of the Lamb are described as being before the throne of God without fear or tremor, fully accepted by the divine Majesty. What are they doing? Theirs is no state of passivity but of continual service of God in praise and worship.

The reference to the "temple" of God raises the question whether the scene describes the final state of the saints or an intermediate state, as 21:22 tells us that the New Jerusalem has no temple. However, the language used in vv.15–17 (esp. v.17) seems to depict the same condition as that of the saints in chapters 21 and 22 (cf. 21:3–4, 6; 22:1). Since 7:15 relates to worship, it would be appropriate to refer to the presence of God and the Lamb as "in" the temple. In 21:22, however, the future existence of the people of God is described as a city; and in that glorious city, unlike the pagan cities of the present world, there will be no special temple in which to worship God because God himself and the Lamb will be present everywhere.

To "spread his tent [*skēnoō*] over them," or to "reside permanently" (TDNT, 7:385), calls to mind the shekinah presence in the OT tabernacle or temple (Exod 40:34–38; 1 Kings 8:10–11; cf. Ezek 10:4, 18–19) and later in Jesus (John 1:14) and also the idea of a permanent residence (Rev 21:3). Never again will these people endure torment. They have the supreme protection of the living God himself.

16 The condition described here contrasts to the earthly experience of those who suffered much for their faith (cf. Heb. 11:37–38). For them, starvation, thirst, and the burning desert are forever past. There may be allusion here to Isaiah 49:10, which places the time of relief from such distresses in the days of Messiah's kingdom. There may also be an allusion to what the four horsemen bring (6:1–8; cf. Matt 24:7).

17 We now have a beautiful pastoral figure—that of the Lamb shepherding his people (cf. John 10:1–8; Heb 13:20; 1 Peter 2:25). It is not through some perfect environment but through the presence and continual ministry of the Lamb that their sufferings are forever assuaged. Whereas on earth their enemies may have tormented them, now the Lamb guides them: "He will lead [*hodēgēsei,* the same verb is used of the Holy Spirit in John 16:13] them to springs of living water." In contrast to the burning thirst experienced in their tribulation, now they will enjoy the refreshing waters of life. Thus in the future life the saints will not know stagnation, boredom, or satiation (Ps 23:1f.; Jer 2:13; Ezek 47:1–12; Zech 14:8).

Finally, even the sorrowful memory of the pain and suffering of the former days will be mercifully removed by the Father: "God will wipe away every tear from their eyes" (cf. 21:4). Tribulation produces tears. Like a tenderhearted, devoted mother, God will wipe each tear from their eyes with the eternal consolations of glory itself. Never again will they cry out because of pain or suffering. Only through the Resurrection can all this become real (Isa 25:8; 1 Cor 15:54).

Notes

---

14 The correct translation of the nominative participle *οἱ ἐρχόμενοι* (*hoi erchomenoi,* "they who have come out of") is a problem. Grammatically, present participles depend on the main verb for their time of action and are generally coincident in time with it. But is the time of action here the time of John's writing or, for John, some future time? If it is present time for John, the translation would be "they who are coming out of the great tribulation." If future, two possibilities arise: (1) The time is in the future when the vision is to be fulfilled. In this case, the description looks back to the earthly scene that preceded the heavenly bliss: "They who have come [or 'were coming'] out of the great tribulation" (NIV). (2) The time is in the present of John's writing. In this case, the words predict what will happen: "They who will come out of the great tribulation" (cf. 1 Thess 1:10). Charles understands the construction as a Semitism and favors the idea of an imperfect participle—"were coming" (*Commentary on Revelation,* 1:213). One's theology and general exegesis of Rev will determine which rendering is preferred.

---

4. *Opening of the seventh seal*

8:1

When he opened the seventh seal, there was silence in heaven for about half an hour.

1 After the long interlude of chapter 7, the sequence of the opening of the seals is resumed by the opening of the final or seventh seal. This action provides both a conclusion to the seals and a preparation for the seven trumpets. The praises ordinarily heard uninterruptedly in heaven (4:8) now cease in order to allow the prayers of the suffering saints on earth to be heard: "There was silence in heaven for about half an hour." Even heaven's choirs are subdued to show God's concern for his persecuted people in the Great Tribulation (8:4; cf. Luke 18:2–8). A Jewish teacher states, "In the fifth heaven are companies of angels of service who sing praises by night, but are silent by day because of the glory of Israel," i.e., that the praises of Israel may be heard in heaven (Charles, *Commentary on Revelation,* 1:223). But in John's view heaven is quieted, not to hear praises, but to hear the cries for deliverance and justice of God's persecuted servants (6:10). Most interpreters, however, understand the silence to refer to the awesome silence before the great storm of God's wrath on the earth. A kind of Sabbath pause might be thought of here. (The relation between the seals, trumpets, and bowls is discussed at 8:6.)

B. *The Seven Trumpets* (8:2–11:19)

1. *Preparatory: the angel and the golden censer*

8:2–5

2And I saw the seven angels who stand before God, and to them were given seven trumpets.

3Another angel, who had a golden censer, came and stood at the altar. He was given much incense to offer, with the prayers of all the saints, on the golden altar before the throne. 4The smoke of the incense, together with the prayers of the saints, went up before God from the angel's hand. 5Then the angel took the censer, filled it with fire from the altar, and hurled it on the earth; and there came peals of thunder, rumblings, flashes of lightning and an earthquake.

2 While the seven seals are opened by the Lamb himself, the judgments of the seven trumpets and the seven bowls (15:1) are executed by seven angels. In 1 Enoch 20:2–8, reference is made to seven angels who stand before God and are named Uriel,

Raphael, Raguel, Michael, Saraqael, Gabriel (cf. Luke 1:19), and Remiel. John may not have these in mind, but the offering up of the prayers of the saints was in Jewish thought connected with archangels (Tobit 12:15; Levi 3:7).

3–4 Before the trumpet judgments are executed, another angel enacts a symbolic scene in heaven. He takes a golden censer filled with incense and offers the incense on the altar in behalf of the prayers of all God's people. Earlier, in connection with the martyred saints (6:9), John mentioned the altar that was near God's presence. Likewise, a strong assurance is here given to the suffering followers of Christ that their prayers for vindication are not forgotten because God will speedily vindicate them from their enemies' assaults. So close is the altar to God that the incense cloud of the saints' prayers rises into his presence and cannot escape his notice (cf. Ps 141:2).

5 The censer or firepan is now used to take some of the burning coals from the altar and cast them to the earth. Symbolically, this represents the answer to the prayers of the saints through the visitation on earth of God's righteous judgments. God next appears on earth in a theophany. The language, reminiscent of Sinai with its thunder, lightning, and earthquake, indicates that God has come to vindicate his saints (Exod 19:16–19; Rev 4:5; 11:19; 16:18).

2. *Sounding of the first six trumpets*

8:6–9:21

6Then the seven angels who had the seven trumpets prepared to sound them.
7The first angel sounded his trumpet, and there came hail and fire mixed with
blood, and it was hurled down upon the earth. A third of the earth was burned up,
a third of the trees were burned up, and all the green grass was burned up.
8The second angel sounded his trumpet, and something like a huge mountain,
all ablaze, was thrown into the sea. A third of the sea turned into blood, 9a third
of the living creatures in the sea died, and a third of the ships were destroyed.
10The third angel sounded his trumpet, and a great star, blazing like a torch, fell
from the sky on a third of the rivers and on the springs of water—11the name of
the star is Wormwood. A third of the waters turned bitter, and many people died
from the waters that had become bitter.
12The fourth angel sounded his trumpet, and a third of the sun was struck, a third
of the moon, and a third of the stars, so that a third of them turned dark. A third
of the day was without light, and also a third of the night.
13As I watched, I heard an eagle that was flying in midair call out in a loud voice,
"Woe! Woe! Woe to the inhabitants of the earth, because of the trumpet blasts
about to be sounded by the other three angels!"
9:1The fifth angel sounded his trumpet, and I saw a star that had fallen from the
sky to the earth. The star was given the key to the shaft of the Abyss. 2When he
opened the Abyss, smoke rose from it like the smoke from a gigantic furnace. The
sun and sky were darkened by the smoke from the Abyss. 3And out of the smoke
locusts came down upon the earth and were given power like that of scorpions of
the earth. 4They were told not to harm the grass of the earth or any plant or tree,
but only those people who did not have the seal of God on their foreheads. 5They
were not given power to kill them, but only to torture them for five months. And the
agony they suffered was like that of the sting of a scorpion when it strikes a man.
6During those days men will seek death, but will not find it; they will long to die, but
death will elude them.
7The locusts looked like horses prepared for battle. On their heads they wore
something like crowns of gold, and their faces resembled human faces. 8Their hair

was like women's hair, and their teeth were like lions' teeth. 9They had breastplates
like breastplates of iron, and the sound of their wings was like the thundering of
many horses and chariots rushing into battle. 10They had tails and stings like
scorpions, and in their tails they had power to torment people for five months.
11They had as king over them the angel of the Abyss, whose name in Hebrew is
Abaddon, and in Greek, Apollyon.
12The first woe is past; two other woes are yet to come.
13The sixth angel blew his trumpet, and I heard a voice coming from the horns
of the golden altar that is before God. 14It said to the sixth angel who had the
trumpet, "Release the four angels who are bound at the great river Euphrates."
15And the four angels who had been kept ready for this very hour and day and
month and year were released to kill a third of mankind. 16The number of the
mounted troops was two hundred million. I heard their number.
17The horses and riders I saw in my vision looked like this: Their breastplates
were fiery red, dark blue, and yellow as sulfur. The heads of the horses resembled
the heads of lions, and out of their mouths came fire, smoke and sulfur. 18A third
of mankind was killed by the three plagues of fire, smoke and sulfur that came out
of their mouths. 19The power of the horses was in their mouths and in their tails;
for their tails were like snakes, having heads with which they inflict injury.
20The rest of mankind that were not killed by these plagues still did not repent
of the work of their hands; they did not stop worshiping demons, and idols of gold,
silver, bronze, stone and wood—idols that cannot see or hear or walk. 21Nor did
they repent of their murders, their magic arts, their sexual immorality or their thefts.

6 Two questions confront the interpreter at this point: What is the relationship of the trumpets to the preceding seals and the following bowls? Are the events described symbolic or more literal? In answer to the first question, there are two basic options: either the series are parallel and simultaneous or they are sequential or successive. It is not possible to decide with certainty for either of these views. Each contains elements of truth. Both sequential factors and parallel ingredients are evident. This commentary has already argued for the chronological priority of the first five seals to the events of the trumpets and bowls (see comments at 6:1). But the sixth seal seems to take us into the period of the outpouring of God's wrath that is enacted in the trumpet and bowl judgments (6:12–17).

The sequential factors are as follows: (1) There is a rise in the intensity of the judgments (only a part of earth and men are affected in the trumpets, but all are affected under the bowls). (2) There is a difference in sequence and content of the events described in each series. (3) The reference to those not sealed in 9:4 (fifth trumpet) presupposes the sealing of 7:1–8. (4) The explicit statement in 8:1–2 implies a sequence between seals and trumpets—"When he opened the seventh seal, . . . And I saw the seven angels . . . to them were given seven trumpets"—on which Tenney remarks, "The vision of the angels with the trumpets follows the seals directly, and conveys the impression that the seals and the trumpets are successive" (Merrill C. Tenney, *Interpreting Revelation* [Grand Rapids: Eerdmans, 1957], p. 71). (5) The bowl judgments are directly called the "last plagues" because with them God's wrath is "completed" (15:1), indicating the prior trumpet judgments. When the seventh bowl is poured out, the words "It is done" are spoken (16:17).

On the other hand, there are parallelisms. The sixth-seventh seal, the seventh trumpet (11:15ff.), and the seventh bowl (16:17ff.) all seem to depict events associated with the second coming of Christ. This last event parallelism may indicate that all these series (seals, trumpets, bowls) are parallel in their entirety or that there is a partial recapitulation or overlap in the three series. This is especially evident in connection with the sixth-seventh seal (6:12ff.), the seventh trumpet (11:15ff.), and the seventh bowl (16:17ff.). The text seems to demand some type of sequential understanding and hence rules out a complete parallelism.

The main question is whether the parallelism indicates that the events described under the sixth-seventh seal, seventh trumpet, and seventh bowl are identical or merely similar and hence really sequential and not exactly parallel. Here the following points are relevant: (1) The sixth seal brings us into the period of God's wrath on the beast worshipers but does not actually advance beyond that event to refer to the coming of Christ (6:12–17). (2) The seventh seal introduces the trumpet judgments, which run their course, and the seventh trumpet seems to bring us into the kingdom of Christ (11:15–18). (3) The seventh bowl likewise brings us to the consummation and return of Christ, that is, if we keep in mind that the incident of Babylon's destruction is an elaboration of events under the seventh bowl (16:17ff.; 19:11ff.).

But are all three series parallel in their last events (for the affirmative, see Dale Ralph Davis, "The Relationship Between the Seals, Trumpets, and Bowls in the Book of Revelation," JETS, 16 [Summer 1973], 149–58) or only parallel in the last trumpet and last bowl (so Ladd and Mounce)? Ladd and Mounce, following Beckwith, have correctly noted that the "third woe" (9:12, 11:14) is never fulfilled by the seventh trumpet, unless, that is, the content of the seventh trumpet is the seven bowls, which is also the "third woe." This is another way of saying that there is some limited recapitulation or overlap with the seventh seal and the first trumpets and in the seventh trumpet with the first bowls. This might be called a telescopic view of the seals, bowls, and trumpets. Further support for this view is also found in observing that interludes come between the sixth and seventh seals and between the sixth and seventh trumpets but not between the sixth and seventh bowls, which would be expected if the trumpets were strictly parallel to the bowls.

The second problem concerns the literalness of the events described under each trumpet. The important but hard question is not literal versus nonliteral but what did John intend? Some things may need to be understood more literally and others quite symbolically. For example, the reference to the army of 200 million (9:16–19) can hardly be literal (cf. comments on 9:16). Either the number is figurative or the army refers to demonic powers rather than human soldiers. It is also difficult to handle literally the reference to the eagle that speaks human words (8:13). While there is no way to settle this problem finally, the exposition will attempt to steer between a literal approach and a totally symbolic one.

As in the seals, there is a discernible literary pattern in the unfolding of the trumpets. The first four trumpets are separated from the last three, which are called "woes" (8:13; 9:12; 11:14), and are generally reminiscent of the plagues in Exodus. While John refers in 15:3 to the Song of Moses (Exod 15:1–18), he does not follow out the plague parallelism precisely, and the connections should not always be pressed.

Shofar trumpets (usually made of a ram's horn) were used in Jewish life as signaling instruments. They sounded alarms for war or danger as well as for peace and announced the new moon, the beginning of the Sabbath, or the death of a notable. Trumpets were also used to throw enemies into panic (Judg 7:19–20). Their use as eschatological signals of the day of the Lord or the return of Christ is well established in the OT and NT (Isa 27:13; Joel 2:1; Zeph 1:16; Matt 24:31; 1 Cor 15:52; 1 Thess 4:16). The Dead Sea community had an elaborate trumpet signal system patterned after Joshua 6 (cf. 1QM).

7 The first trumpet. Hail and fire are reminiscent of the fourth Egyptian plague of the Exodus (Exod 9:23–26), with added intensity suggested by the reference to hail and fire mixed with blood (cf. Ezek 38:22). A "third" refers to a relative fraction of the total and should not be construed as a specific amount (cf. Ezek 5:2; Zech 13:8–9).

8–9 The second trumpet. A huge blazing mass like a mountain is thrown into the sea and turns part of the sea into blood. This suggests the first plague, when the Nile was turned blood red and the fish destroyed (Exod 7:20–21; cf. Zeph 1:3). Reference to the destruction of ships shows the intense turbulence of the sea.

10–11 The third trumpet. John next sees a huge fiery star fall on the rivers and springs of water and turn a part of these fresh-water supplies into very bitter water. The star's name is "Wormwood," which refers to the quite bitter herb *Artemesia absinthium* found in the Near East and mentioned elsewhere in the Bible (Jer 9:15; 23:15; Lam 3:15, 19; Amos 5:7). It is not clear whether John intended the star to be understood as an angel as in 9:1 and in 1:20. Here is the first reference in the plagues to the loss of human life (cf. 9:15, 20). This plague, aimed at the fresh water, is a counterpart of the preceding one, which was aimed at the sea.

12 The fourth trumpet. The heavens are struck with partial darkness, reminiscent of the ninth plague (Exod 10:21–23). The references to "a third of . . ." refer to a partial impairment of the ordinary light from these bodies. In the OT the darkening of the heavens appears in connection with the theophany of God in judgment (cf. Isa 13:10; Ezek 32:7–8; Joel 2:10; 3:15; cf. Matt 24:29). An unusual darkness also attended the crucifixion of Christ (Matt 27:45).

13 Before the last three trumpets sound, John hears a flying eagle call out "woe" three times. His cry announces the especially grievous nature of the last three plagues, which kill a third part of the population of the earth (9:18). Two of the woes are identified with the fifth and sixth trumpets (9:12; 11:14). (See the comments at 8:6, which argue that the third woe should be seen as the seven bowl judgments (in 16:1ff.) The "inhabitants of the earth" distinguishes the Christ rejectors of the world from the true, faithful followers of the Lamb (cf. comments at 3:10). A flying "eagle" announces these words. This must be taken symbolically. In Revelation there are two other references to eagles (4:7; 12:14). Since 4:7 relates to the description of one of the four living beings, it may be that John intends the eagle mentioned here to have the same significance.

9:1–11 The fifth trumpet. John now focuses attention on the fifth and sixth trumpets (first and second woes) by giving more than twice the space to their description that he gives the previous four trumpets together. The fifth trumpet releases locusts from the Abyss. For five months these locusts torment the inhabitants of the earth who do not have the seal of God. John sees a "star" that has fallen to the earth. Since this star is given a key to open the Abyss, it is reasonable to understand it as being a symbolic reference to an angel. This is supported by v.11, where "the angel of the Abyss" is mentioned and named "Abaddon," as well as 20:1, where reference is also made to "an angel coming down" (i.e., stars "fall") and having the key to the Abyss, where Satan is thrown.

The Abyss is also referred to in 11:7 and 17:8 as the place from which the beast arises. The word *abyssos* ("Abyss") refers to the underworld as (1) a prison for certain demons (Luke 8:31; cf. 2 Peter 2:4; Jude 6) and (2) the realm of the dead (Rom 10:7; TDNT, 1:9). When the Abyss is opened, huge billows of smoke pour out, darken the sky, and release horselike locusts on the earth.

Locust plagues are one of the severest plagues of mankind. The imagery of locusts, appearing like armies, advancing like a cloud, darkening the heavens, and sounding like the rattle of chariots, goes back to Joel's vision of the locust army that came on Israel as a judgment from God (Joel 1:6; 2:4–10). But the locusts of the Apocalypse inflict agony like scorpion stings (vv.3, 5, 10). This, together with the fact that they do not eat grass (v.4), shows that these locusts are something other than ordinary earthly insects. Indeed, they have the special task of inflicting a nonfatal injury only on the beast worshipers, who do not have the seal of God on their foreheads (v.4); (cf. comments on 7:3). This may imply that these locustlike creatures are not simply instruments of a physical plague such as that in Moses' or Joel's day or under the first four trumpets but are demonic forces out of the Abyss from whom the true people of God are protected (cf. John's use of frogs to represent demonic powers in 16:13). The five months of agony (vv.5, 10) may refer to the life span of the locust (i.e., through spring and summer [Charles, *Commentary on Revelation*, 1:243]). So severe is the torment they inflict that their victim will seek death (v.6; cf. Job 3:21; Jer 8:3; Hos 10:8).

John describes the locusts as an army of mounted troops ready for the attack (v.7). The heads of the locusts resemble horses' heads. John does not say that the locusts had crowns of gold on their heads but that they wore "something like crowns of gold" on their heads. Charles suggests that this might refer to the yellow green of their breasts (ibid., 1:244). This, combined with their resemblance to human faces, suggests something unnatural, hence demonic. The comparison of their "hair" with that of women may refer (as in other ancient texts) to the locusts' long antennae, while their lionlike teeth suggest the terrible devastation they can bring (cf. Joel 1:6–7). The "breastplates of iron" refer to their scales, which appeared as a cuirass of metal plates across the chest and long flexible bonds of steel over the shoulders. Their sound was like the rushing of war chariots into battle (v.9; cf. Joel 2:5).

This description creates an image of the fearful onslaught of demonic powers in the last days. Therefore, their leader is called "Abaddon" in Hebrew and "Apollyon" in Greek. The Hebrew term *'ᵃḇaddôn* means "destruction" or "ruin" (Job 26:6 mg.; Prov 27:20 mg.), and more often "the place of ruin" in Sheol (Job 26:6 mg.; Prov 15:11 mg.; 27:20 mg.), or "death" (Job 28:22 mg.), or "the grave" (Ps 88:11 mg.). In late Jewish apocalyptic texts and Qumran literature, it refers to the personification of death (IQH 3.16, 19, 32; IQ ap Gen 12:17 [TDOT, 1:23]).

The Greek term *apollyōn* means "exterminator" or "destroyer" and does not occur elsewhere in the Bible, though it can be readily understood as John's way of personifying in Greek what is personified in the Hebrew word *'ᵃḇaddôn* (LXX *apōleia*). Some understand Apollyon as a separate angel entrusted with authority over the Abyss. Attempts to identify Apollyon with the Greek god Apollo, who in some Greek texts of Revelation is connected with the locusts, or another Greco-Roman deity have not met with much success. The creature, his name, and his responsibility seem to be original with the author of the Apocalypse.

Why John names the king of the Abyss in both Hebrew and Greek is open to question. Perhaps his readers' background in Hebrew, on which John's names and thoughts seem to turn (cf. 16:16), was so slender that an additional help here and there was necessary. This stylistic trait of giving information in bilingual terms is peculiar to Revelation and the fourth Gospel (John 6:1; 19:13, 17, 20; 20:16). It may also reveal a mind steeped in the Targum tradition of the ancient synagogue, where it was customary to render Scripture in Hebrew and then in either Aramaic or Greek for those who did not understand Hebrew.

12 This seems to be a transitional verse, indicating that the "first woe" (fifth trumpet) is finished and two woes are yet to come (presumably the sixth and seventh trumpets; cf. 8:13 with 11:14). There may be in this verse a resumption of the eagle's words (cf. 8:13).

13–19 The sixth trumpet: The second woe. Here we find a description of disasters that reach to the death of a third of mankind (vv.15, 18; cf. 8:7). "Four angels," the instruments of God's judgment, are held at the river Euphrates, whence traditionally the enemies of God's ancient people often advanced on the land of Israel (Jer 2:18 mg.; 13:4f. mg; 51:63; Rev 16:12) and which was recognized as its eastern extremity (Gen 15:18). John here makes use of the ancient geographical terms to depict the fearful character of the coming judgment of God on a rebellious world. While the language is drawn from historical-political events of the OT, it describes realities that far transcend a local geographical event. God's dealings are not accidental but planned and precise in time as to a definite hour of a definite day of a definite month of a definite year. By a reference to the "golden altar" of incense, the release of these angels is again connected with the prayers of God's saints for vindication (6:9; 8:3).

At v.16 a mounted army of some 200 million horses and riders is rather abruptly introduced. While some (e.g., Walvoord) argue for a literal human army here, several factors point to their identity as demonic forces. First, the horsemen are not in themselves important but wear brightly colored breastplates of fiery red, dark blue, and sulfurous yellow, more suggestive of supernatural than natural riders. More important are the horses, which not only have heads resembling lions but are, rather than their riders, the instruments of death by the three plagues of fire, smoke, and sulfur that come from their mouths. Furthermore, these horses have tails like snakes that are able to kill (vv.17–19), unlike the locusts' scorpionlike tails that do not inflict death but only injury (v.5). Finally, according to General William K. Harrison (an expert in military logistics), an army of 200 million could not be conscripted, supported, and moved to the Middle East without totally disrupting all societal needs and capabilities ("The War of Armageddon," xerographic copy of unpublished, undated article). As General Harrison brings out on this aspect of Revelation, God has made men with certain limitations; and the actual raising and transporting of an army of the size spoken of in v.16 completely transcends human capability. All the Allied and Axis forces at their peak in World War II were only about 70 million (*The World Almanac, 1971*, ed. L.H. Long [New York: Newspaper Enterprise Association, 1970], p. 355).

Thus it seems better to understand the vast numbers and description of the horses as indicating demonic hordes. Such large numbers do occasionally indicate angelic hosts elsewhere in Scripture (Ps 68:17; Rev 5:11; cf. 2 Kings 2:11–12; 6:17). This would not eliminate the possibility of human armies of manageable size also being involved. But the emphasis here (vv.16–19) is on their fully demonic character, utterly cruel and determined, showing no mercy to man, woman, or child. These demons might also be manifest in pestilences, epidemic diseases, or misfortunes as well as in armies. Such would explain the use of "plagues" to describe these hordes (vv.18, 20; cf. 11:6; 16:9, 21).

20–21 God's purpose for the plagues is first of all a judgment on man for his willful choice of idolatry and the corrupt practices that go with it (v.21). John had earlier called the churches to "repent" of their faithless tendencies lest they too should share in God's judgment (2:5, 16, 21–22; 3:19). In these verses we see the end result of refusing to turn to God. This stubbornness leads to worship of demons as well as worship of cultic objects made by human hands (gold, silver, bronze, stone, and wood; cf. Pss 115:4–7; 135:17; Jer 10:1–16; Dan 5:23). "Demons" may mean either pagan deities (Deut 32:17; Ps 106:37) or malign spirits (1 Cor 10:20–21; 1 Tim 4:1). But since the Greek here in Revelation distinguishes the cultic objects from the demons, John no doubt shared Paul's concept of demons as evil spirits (Rev 16:14; 18:2). Hence, there is a twofold evil in idol worship: it robs the true God of his glory (Rom 1:23) and it leads to consorting with evil spirits that corrupt man.

This demonic corruption is manifest in the inhuman acts of those who have given up God for idols—acts of murder, sexual immorality, and thefts (cf. Rom 1:24; 28–31). In general, these are violations of the ten commandments. "Magic arts" (*pharmakōn*) means "a practice of sorceries" or "witchcraft" (LXX Exod 7:11; 9:11; Gal 5:20; Rev 21:8; 22:15). Usually drugs were involved in these arts. Sometimes the word *pharmakōn* means "to poison," as in a Jewish prayer from the first century B.C.: "I call upon and pray the Most High, the Lord of the spirits and of all flesh, against those who with guile murdered or poisoned [*pharmakōn*] the wretched, untimely lost Heraclea, shedding her innocent blood wickedly" (MM, p. 664).

The second purpose of God revealed in the agonizing plagues described in chapters 8 and 9 is to bring societies to repentance (cf. 16:9, 11). God is not willing that any person should suffer his judgment but that all should repent and turn to him (Luke 13:3, 5; 2 Peter 3:9). But when God's works and words are persistently rejected, only judgment remains (Eph 5:6; Heb 10:26–31).

Notes

8:13 In place of ἀετός (*aetos*, "eagle") read by ℵ A B and most MSS and versions, other texts read ἄγγελος (*angelos*, "angel") (P and some minuscules). Metzger suggests *aetos* was corrupted to *angelos* by scribal concerns "to harmonize what is done by the eagle into line with what is ascribed to angels elsewhere" (Bruce M. Metzger, *A Textual Commentary on the Greek New Testament* [New York: UBS, 1971], p. 743).

9:1 Ἄβυσσος (*abyssos*, "Abyss") (from Heb. תְּהוֹם [*tᵉhôm*, "the deep"]) is referred to in 1 Enoch in the sense of both an intermediate and a final abode for fallen angels, Satan, demons, and fallen men (1 Enoch 18:12–16; 21:7–10; 108:3–6; Charles, *Commentary on Revelation*, 1:240–41).

11 Ἑβραϊστί (*Hebraisti*) has generally been understood here and elsewhere in the NT to mean "Aramaic," but recent studies are questioning this identification and arguing for the sense "in Hebrew" rather than "in Aramaic" (Philip Edgcumbe Hughes, "The Language Spoken by Jesus," *New Dimensions in New Testament Study*, ed. R.N. Longenecker and M.C. Tenney [Grand Rapids: Zondervan, 1974], pp. 127–28).

16 The words διςμυριάδες μυριάδων (*dismyriades myriadōn*, "200 million") are Heb. and not Aram. in background (G. Mussies, *The Morphology of Koine Greek as Used in the Apocalypse of St. John* [Leiden: E.J. Brill, 1971], p. 353).

---

3. *Second interlude* (10:1–11:14)

a. *The little book*

10:1–11

[1]Then I saw another mighty angel coming down from heaven. He was robed in
a cloud, with a rainbow above his head; his face was like the sun, and his legs were
like fiery pillars. [2]He was holding a little scroll, which lay open in his hand. He
planted his right foot on the sea and his left foot on the land, [3]and he gave a loud
shout like the roar of a lion. When he shouted, the voices of the seven thunders
spoke. [4]And when the seven thunders spoke, I was about to write; but I heard a
voice from heaven say, "Seal up what the seven thunders have said and do not
write it down."

[5]Then the angel I had seen standing on the sea and on the land raised his right
hand to heaven. [6]And he swore by him who lives for ever and ever, who created
the heavens and all that is in them, the earth and all that is in it, and the sea and
all that is in it, and said, "There will be no more delay! [7]But in the days when the
seventh angel is about to sound his trumpet, the mystery of God will be accomplished, just as he announced to his servants the prophets."

[8]Then the voice that I had heard from heaven spoke to me once more: "Go, take
the scroll that lies open in the hand of the angel who is standing on the sea and
on the land."

[9]So I went to the angel and asked him to give me the little scroll. He said to me,
"Take it and eat it. It will turn your stomach sour, but in your mouth it will be as sweet
as honey." [10]I took the little scroll from the angel's hand and ate it. It tasted as sweet
as honey in my mouth, but when I had eaten it, my stomach turned sour. [11]Then
I was told, "You must prophesy again about many peoples, nations, languages and
kings."

1–4 As in the seals, the sequences of the sixth and seventh trumpets is interrupted to provide additional information bearing on the previous events and to prepare the reader for further developments. The author sees a mighty angel (possibly Michael, "the great prince" [Dan 12:1]) whom he describes in such dazzling terms (cloud, rainbow, sun, fiery pillars) that some have identified him with Christ. But angels are always angels in the Apocalypse, as well as in the rest of the NT, and should not be identified with Christ. The voice that speaks in vv.4, 8 could, however, be that of Jesus.

The angel has in his hand a small scroll (v.2). This scroll should not be confused with the Lamb's scroll of chapters 5–7. It should be connected with the symbolic scroll of Ezekiel (Ezek 2:9–3:3; cf. Jer 15:15–17). This prophet was told to "eat" the scroll just as John was told to eat the scroll given him (vv.9–10). Such an action symbolized the reception of the Word of God into the innermost being as a necessary prerequisite to proclaim it with confidence. John could see the words on the scroll because it "lay open" in the angel's hand. The angel standing on both land and sea symbolizes that the prophetic message is for the whole world.

When the angel shouted (v.3), seven thunders spoke, and John proceeded to write down their words. But he is interrupted and is commanded, "Seal up what the seven thunders have said and do not write it down" (v.4). Conceivably, this might have been another series of sevens. Either the seven thunders were intended for John's own illumination and were not essential to the main vision of the seven trumpets or the reference is designed to strike a note of mystery with reference to God's revelatory activities (cf. 2 Cor 12:4). As the visible portion of an iceberg is only a small part of the iceberg, most of which is hidden from man's sight, so God's disclosures reveal only part of his total being and purposes.

5–7 The angel's action of raising his right hand to heaven doubtless alludes to the Jewish oath-swearing procedure (Deut 32:40; Dan 12:7). He swears that "there will be no more delay" (v.6). Clearly there is some type of progression in the seals, trumpets, and bowls that nears its conclusion as the seventh trumpet is about to sound (v.7). When the seventh trumpet is finally sounded, there is an announcement that "the kingdom of the world has become the kingdom of our Lord and of his Christ" and that the time has come to judge the dead, to reward the saints, and to destroy the earth destroyers (11:15, 18). These events are recorded in the remaining chapters of the book, which include the seven bowl judgments and the new heavens and the new earth. Thus here in 10:7 it is announced that "the mystery of God" is accomplished. "The mystery of God" is his purposes for man and the world as revealed to both OT and NT prophets.

The way NIV translates v.7 suggests that the consummation comes before the blowing of the seventh trumpet: "when the seventh angel is about to sound his trumpet. . . ." While this is grammatically possible, it is also possible to render the expression "about to sound" as "when he shall sound." Thus understood, the meaning is that "in the days of" (i.e., during the period of) the sound of the seventh trumpet, when the angel sounds, the final purposes of God will be completed. This rendering clarifies the statement in 11:14, "The second woe has passed: the third woe is coming soon," a statement made just before the seventh trumpet sounds. Hence, the seventh trumpet will reveal the final judgments of the bowls and the final establishment of God's rule on the earth (cf. Notes).

8–11 John, like Ezekiel, is now commanded to take the prophetic scroll and eat it. The scroll tasted "as sweet as honey" but was bitter to the stomach. Receiving the Word of God is a great joy; but since the Word is an oracle of judgment, it results in the unpleasant experience of proclaiming a message of wrath and woe (cf. Jer 15:16, 19). The symbolic act of eating the scroll might also mean that the prophetic message was mixed with joy and comfort as well as gloom. Mounce, following Bruce, argues that the content of the scroll is

> a message for the believing church and is to be found in the following verses (11:1–13). . . . It is *after* the eating of the book that John is told he must prophesy again, this time concerning many peoples, nations, tongues, and kings (Rev. 10:11). This begins with chapter 12. The sweet scroll which turns the stomach bitter is a message for the church. Before the final triumph believers are going to pass through a formidable ordeal. . . . So the little scroll unveils the lot of the faithful in those last days of Satanic opposition (*Revelation*, p. 216).

In any case, the sweetness should not be taken to refer to the joy of proclaiming a message of wrath, for to all God's prophets this was a sorrowful, bitter task (Jer 9:1).

The chief import of chapter 10 seems to be a confirmation of John's prophetic call as v. 11 indicates: "You must prophesy again about many peoples, nations, languages and kings." This prophesying should not be understood as merely a recapitulation in greater detail of the previous visions but a further progression of the events connected with the end. Notice the use of the word "kings" instead of "tribes" (as in 5:9; 7:9; 13:7; 14:6). This may anticipate the emphasis on the kings of the earth found in 17:9–12 and elsewhere.

Notes

---

6 The Gr. word χρόνος (*chronos;* "delay," NIV) can refer to time in a number of aspects. Other verses where *chronos* means "delay" are Matt 25:5 and Heb 10:37.

7 There are two possibilities for rendering μέλλω (*mellō*) plus the infinitive: (1) imminence ("about to," NIV) or (2) strong future certainty ("shall"). I have opted for the second sense to throw the action into the time of the blowing of the seventh trumpet and not to the time *before* its sound.

11 The preposition ἐπί (*epi*) translated correctly "about" in NIV may, with the dative, also mean "upon," "over," "against," "near," "to," "with." The KJV rendering "before" would not be accurate unless the genitive were used (BAG, p. 287).

---

b. *The two witnesses*

11:1–14

[1]I was given a reed like a measuring rod and was told, "Go and measure the temple of God and the altar, and count the worshipers there. [2]But exclude the outer court; do not measure it, because it has been given to the Gentiles. They will trample on the holy city for 42 months. [3]And I will give power to my two witnesses, and they will prophesy for 1,260 days, clothed in sackcloth." [4]These are the two olive trees and the two lampstands that stand before the Lord of the earth. [5]If anyone tries to harm them, fire comes from their mouths and devours their enemies. This is how anyone who wants to harm them must die. [6]These men have power to shut up the sky so that it will not rain during the time they are prophesying; and they have power to turn the waters into blood and to strike the earth with every kind of plague as often as they want.

[7]Now when they have finished their testimony, the beast that comes up from the Abyss will attack them, and overpower and kill them. [8]Their bodies will lie in the street of the great city, which is figuratively called Sodom and Egypt, where also their Lord was crucified. [9]For three and a half days men from every people, tribe, language and nation will gaze on their bodies and refuse them burial. [10]The inhabitants of the earth will gloat over them and will celebrate by sending each other gifts, because these two prophets had tormented those who live on the earth.

[11]But after the three and a half days a breath of life from God entered them, and they stood on their feet, and terror struck those who saw them. [12]Then they heard a loud voice from heaven saying to them, "Come up here." And they went up to heaven in a cloud, while their enemies looked on.

[13]At that very hour there was a severe earthquake and a tenth of the city collapsed. Seven thousand people were killed in the earthquake, and the survivors were terrified and gave glory to the God of heaven.

[14]The second woe has passed; the third woe is coming soon.

Some have considered this chapter one of the most difficult to interpret in the Book of Revelation (Lilje, p. 159). Alford agrees: "This passage may well be called . . . the *crux interpretum;* as it is undoubtedly one of the most difficult in the whole Apocalypse" (Alf, 4: 655). In it John refers to the temple, the Holy City, and the two prophets who are killed by the beast and after three and one-half days are resurrected and ascend to heaven. Does John intend all this to be understood simply as it is given—viz., the literal temple in Jerusalem; two people prophesying for 1,260 days, who are killed by the Antichrist, raised from the dead, and ascend to heaven; a great earthquake that kills seven thousand people and the survivors of which glorify God? Or does he intend all or part of these as symbols representing something? Most commentators take at least part of these things as symbolic. Furthermore, how does this section (11:1–13) relate to the total context (10:1–11:19)?

While details of interpretation vary, there are but two main approaches to the chapter: (1) the temple, altar, worshipers, and Holy City have something to do with the Jewish people and their place in the plan of God; or (2) John is here referring to the Christian church. As in chapter 7, John's references to particular Jewish entities create the chief source of the problem. Does he use these references in a plain, one-to-one sense, or does he use them representatively or symbolically?

At the outset, it may be helpful to state why the Jewish view is less preferable. Actually, this approach has two slightly different aspects. One school of commentators, generally dispensational, understands the "temple" and the "city" to refer to a rebuilt Jewish temple in Jerusalem. While in this view elements in the description may be symbolic, the main import of the passage is seen as depicting a future protection of the nation of Israel prior to her spiritual regeneration. The Antichrist (beast) will permit the rebuilding of the temple in Jerusalem as well as the restoration of Jewish worship for three and a half years; but then he will break his covenant and trample down a part of the temple and the Holy City until Christ returns to deliver the Jewish people (cf. Dan 9:27; so J.B. Smith, Seiss, Walvoord).

More recently Ladd, following Beckwith, Zahn, and perhaps Swete, has argued for a modified Jewish view. He contends that John is prophetically predicting the "preservation and ultimate salvation of the Jewish people" much in the manner of Paul in Romans 11:26 ("And so all Israel will be saved") (*Commentary on Revelation,* pp. 150ff.). Unlike those who hold the strict dispensational view, Ladd believes that the temple and the city of Jerusalem are not the literal Jewish restored temple or the city located in Palestine. Rather, they represent, on the one hand, the believing Jewish remnant (temple, altar, and worshipers) and, on the other hand, the Jewish people or nation as a whole who are now under Gentile oppression (outer court and city) (ibid.). Both Jewish views suffer from their inability to relate this chapter to the context of chapter 10, to the parallelism in the seal interlude (ch. 7), to the ministry and significance of the two witnesses, or to the further chapters in Revelation (esp. chs. 12–13). Therefore, it is better to understand John as referring in chapter 11 to the whole Christian community.

1 John is given a "reed" (*kalamos*), or "cane," long and straight like a "rod," and thus suitable for measuring a large building or area. (The measuring rod referred to in Ezek 40:5 was about ten feet long.) The purpose of the reed is to "measure the temple of God and the altar." Most agree that the principal OT passage in John's mind was Ezekiel's lengthy description of the measuring of the future kingdom temple (Ezek

40:3–48:35). Since interpreters are confused about what Ezekiel's vision means, the ambiguity extends also to John's description. In the ancient world, measuring was accomplished for shorter lengths by the reed cane (Ezek 40:2ff.) or, for longer distances, with a rope line (1 Kings 7:23; Isa 44:13). Measuring with a line may have various metaphorical meanings. It may refer to the promise of restoration and rebuilding, with emphasis on extension or enlargement (Jer 31:39; Zech 1:16). Measuring may also be done to mark out something for destruction (2 Sam 8:2; 2 Kings 21:13; Isa 28:17; Lam 2:8; Amos 7:7–9). In Ezekiel 40:2ff., this latter sense would be inappropriate. But what does John's measuring mean?

Since John is told in v.2 not to measure the outer court but to leave it for the nations to overrun, it may be that here in chapter 11 the measuring means that the temple of God, the altar, and the worshipers (who are to be counted) are to be secured for blessing and preserved from spiritual harm or defilement. So in 21:15–17, John similarly depicts the angel's measuring of the heavenly city (with a golden rod), apparently to mark off the city and its inhabitants from harm and defilement (21:24, 27). As a parallel to the sealing of 7:1–8, the measuring does not symbolize preservation from physical harm but the prophetic guarantee that none of the faithful worshipers of Jesus as the Messiah will perish even though they suffer physical destruction at the hand of the beast (13:7). Such seems also to be the sense of the measuring passage in 1 Enoch 62:1–5 (Charles, *Commentary on Revelation,* 1:276).

In Ezekiel 43:10, the prophet is told to "describe the temple to the people of Israel, that they may be ashamed of their sins." The purpose of the elaborate description and temple measurement in Ezekiel is to indicate the glory and holiness of God in Israel's midst and convict them of their defilement of his sanctuary (43:12). Likewise, John's prophetic ministry calls for a clear separation between those who are holy and those who have defiled themselves with the idolatry of the beast.

John is to measure "the temple of God." There are two Greek words used in the NT for temple. One (*hieron*) is a broad term that refers to the whole structure of Herod's temple, including courts, colonnades, etc. (e.g., Matt 4:5; John 2:14). The other (*naos*) is narrower and refers to the sanctuary or inner house where only the priests were allowed (Matt 23:35; 27:51; and always in Rev). While the distinction between the two words is not always maintained (TDNT, 4: 884), yet in this context (11:1) it may be appropriate since the next verse mentions the outer precinct as a separate entity.

Does John mean the heavenly temple often mentioned in Revelation (cf. 11:19; 15:5, 8; 16:17), or does he refer to the Christian community as in 3:12: "Him who overcomes I will make a pillar in the temple of my God"? In the postapostolic Epistle of Barnabas (16:1ff.), the temple is the individual Christian or alternately the community of Christians as it is in Paul (1 Cor 3:16; 6:19; 2 Cor 6:16). Since John refers to the "outer court" in v.2, which is trampled by the nations, it is quite likely that he has in mind not the heavenly temple of God but an earthly one—either the (rebuilt?) temple in Jerusalem or, symbolically, the covenant people.

The word for temple (*naos*) always refers to the Jerusalem temple in the Gospels with the single exception of John's Gospel, where it refers to Jesus' own body (John 2:19–21; cf. Rev 21:22). Outside the Gospels it refers either to pagan shrines (Acts 17:24; 19:24) or, in Paul's letters, metaphorically to the physical bodies of Christians or to the church of God (1 Cor 3:16; 6:19; 2 Cor 6:16; Eph 2:21). In only one case is it debatable whether Paul means the literal Jerusalem temple or the church (2 Thess 2:4).

While to take the temple in this verse (11:1) as representing the church in the Great Tribulation is not without problems, this seems the best view. Other NT usage outside the Gospels, the figurative usage of temple in John 2:19–21, and his usage in Revelation all point to the image of the temple representing the messianic community of both Jews and Gentiles, comparable to his symbol of the woman in chapter 12 (so Alf, 4:657).

The "altar" would then refer to the huge stone altar of sacrifice in the court of the priests, and the expression "the worshipers" would most naturally indicate the priests and others in the three inner courts (the court of the priests, the court of Israel, the court of the women). These represent symbolically the true servants of God and the measuring symbolizes their recognition and acceptance by God in the same manner as the numbering in chapter 7. The writer of Hebrews likewise speaks of an "altar" that Christians eat from, but that Jewish priests who serve in the temple are not qualified to eat from (Heb 13:10). By this language he speaks of the once-for-all sacrifice of Christ on the cross utilizing the background of the temple images, as does John.

2 As the "outer court" in the Jerusalem temple was frequented by a mixed group including Gentiles and unbelievers, so in John's mind the earthly temple or community of God may involve a part where those who are impure or unfaithful will be (21:8; 22:15). The effect of not measuring this part of the temple is to exclude it and those in it from spiritual security and God's blessing, in contrast to the way the measuring secured these things for the true community. So in measuring the temple, Ezekiel is instructed to exclude from the sanctuary "the foreigners uncircumcised in heart and flesh" (Ezek 44:5–9)—viz., pagans who do not worship the true God and whose presence would desecrate the sanctuary. Previously, John has shown concern over those who were associated with the local churches but were not true worshipers of Christ (cf. 2:14–16, 20–25; 3:1–5, 16). When the great test comes, they will join the ranks of the beast and reveal their true colors.

On the other hand, while Swete (in loc.) suggests that the outer court is perhaps the rejected synagogue (cf. 2:9; 3:9), it may be better to understand the desecration of the outer court as a symbolic reference to the victory of the beast over the saints, which is described in v.7. Thus by using two slightly different images, the "temple-altar-worshipers" and the "outer court-Holy City," John is viewing the church under different aspects. Though the Gentiles (pagans) are permitted to touch the "outer court" and to trample on the "Holy City" for a limited time ("42 months"), they are not able to destroy the church because the "inner sanctuary" is measured or protected in keeping with Christ's earlier words: "And the gates of Hades will not overcome it" (Matt 16:18) (so Morris, *Revelation of St. John*, p. 146; Mounce, *Revelation*, p. 220).

Since John says the outer court will be "given to the Gentiles," it is important to establish the best translation of *ethnē* ("Gentiles"). *Ethnē* may have, in the NT, the more general sense of "nations," describing the various ethnic or national groups among mankind (e.g., Matt 24:9, 14; Luke 24:47; Rom 1:5; 15:11). In other contexts, it may be used as a narrower technical term to denote "Gentiles" in contrast to the Jewish people (e.g., Matt 4:15; 10:5; Luke 2:32; Acts 10:45; Rom 11:11). In many cases the broader sense may shade off into the narrower, producing ambiguity.

But there is another usage of *ethnē*. Just as the Jews referred to all other peoples outside the covenant as "Gentiles," so there gradually developed a similar Christian usage of the term that saw all peoples who were outside of Christ as *ethnē*, including also unbelieving Jews (1 Cor 5:1; 12:2; 1 Thess 4:5; 1 Peter 2:12; 3 John 7). Our word "heathen" may parallel this usage of the word (TDNT, 2: 370, n.19). When the sixteen cases of the plural form (*ethnē*) in Revelation are examined, not once is the sense "Gentiles" appropriate. Everywhere the *ethnē* are the peoples of the earth, either in rebellion against God (11:18; 14:8; 19:15; 20:3) or redeemed and under the rule of Christ (2:26; 21:24, 26; 22:2). There is no good reason why John does not intend the same sense in 11:2. Nevertheless, the versions reflect the uncertainty of the translators: "Gentiles" (KJV, Knox, NEB, NIV) or "nations" (RSV, NASB, Ph).

To sum up, John's words "given to the Gentiles" refer to the defiling agencies that will trample down the outer court of the church, leading either to defection from Christ or physical destruction, though all the while the inner sanctuary of the true believers will not be defiled by idolatry. This spiritual preservation of the true believers will be accomplished by John's prophetic ministry, which distinguishes true loyalty to Christ from the deception of the beast.

The nations will "trample on the holy city for 42 months." Opinion varies between the literal and the symbolic significance of the term "the holy city." The more literal viewpoint sees "the holy city" as the earthly city of Jerusalem. Support for this is found (1) in the OT's use (Neh 11:1; Isa 48:2; 52:1; Dan 9:24) and Matthew's use of "holy city" for Jerusalem (Matt 4:5; 27:53), (2) the proximity of the term "the holy city" to the temple reference (v.1), and (3) the mention in v.8 of the "great city" that is "where also their Lord was crucified."

Since Jerusalem was destroyed in A.D. 70, and since Revelation was presumably written about 95 (cf. Introduction), the more literalistic interpreters hold two views about the meaning of this reference to the city. Some believe it to refer to the rebuilt city and temple during the future Tribulation period (Walvoord, p. 177). Others see the city as merely a representative or symbolic reference to the Jewish people without any special implication of a literal city or temple (Beckwith, p. 588; Ladd, *Commentary on Revelation*, pp. 152–53; Rissi, *Time and History*, pp. 96f.). But if John does in fact differentiate here between believing Jews (inner court) and the nation as a whole (outer court), this would be the only place in the book where he does so. Furthermore, such a reference at this point in the context of chapters 10 and 11 would be abrupt and unconnected with the main themes in these chapters, the subject of which is the nature of the prophetic ministry and the great trial awaiting Christians.

Far more in keeping with the emphasis of the whole book and of these chapters in particular is the view that in the mind of John "the holy city," like the temple, refers to the church. The consistent usage of the expression "holy city" means the community of those faithful to Jesus Christ, composed of believing Jews and Gentiles (21:2, 10; 22:19; cf. 3:12; 20:9). It should also be noted that the name Jerusalem nowhere appears in chapter 11 but that there is a circumlocution for it in v.8, "where also their Lord was crucified," which is prefaced with the word "figuratively" (*pneumatikōs*, lit., "spiritually"). While the vision of the future Holy City (chs. 21–22) describes the condition of the city when she has completed her great ordeal and is finally delivered from the great deceiver, the present reference is to the people as they must first endure the trampling of the pagan nations for "42 months."

Does the trampling (*pateō*) indicate defilement and apostasy, or does it instead mean persecution? The word "trample" can metaphorically mean either of these (BAG, p. 640).

Two factors favor the latter sense. The time of the trampling is "42 months," which is the exact time John attributes to the reign of the beast (13:5–7). Furthermore, in

Daniel's prophecy the trampling of the sanctuary and host of God's people by Antiochus Epiphanes (Dan 8:10, 13; 2 Macc 8:2, *katapateō*, LXX) is clearly a persecution of the people of God. The apocryphal Psalms of Solomon relate that the trampling of Jerusalem by the pagans will be reversed by the Messiah (Pss Sol 17:24, 42–47).

But what of the term "42 months"? This exact expression occurs in the Bible only here and in 13:5, where it refers to the time of the authority of the beast. Mention is also made of a period of 1,260 days (i.e., 42 months of 30 days each) in 11:3 and 12:6. In 12:14 a similar length of time is referred to as "a time, times [i.e., two times] and half a time." All these expressions equal a three-and-one-half-year period.

In the various usages of the terms, "42 months" refers to the period of oppression of the Holy City and the time of the authority of the beast (11:2; 13:5). As for the "1,260 days," this is the period the two witnesses prophesy and the time the woman is protected from the dragon's reach (11:3; 12:6). "Time, times and half a time" seems to be used synonymously for the 1,260 days during which the woman will be protected in the desert (12:14). We cannot assume that because these periods are equal, they are identical. On the other hand, the three different expressions may well be literary variations for the same period. Daniel is generally taken to be the origin of the terms.

In Daniel 9:27 a week is spoken of ("seven," NIV), and the context makes it clear that this is a week of years, i.e., seven years (Glasson, p. 67). Further, the week is divided in half—i.e., three years and a half for each division. These half weeks of years are spoken of in Daniel 7:25 as "a time, times and half a time." Early Jewish and general patristic interpretation followed by the early Protestant commentators referred this to the period of the reign of the Antichrist (James A. Montgomery, *A Critical and Exegetical Commentary on the Book of Daniel,* ICC [Edinburgh: T. & T. Clark, 1964], p. 314).

In Daniel 12:7 the identical expression refers to the period "when the power of the holy people has been finally broken"; in 12:11 the equivalent period expressed in days (1,290) refers to the time of the "abomination" and defilement of the temple. Whether or not these references refer to the second-century B.C. activities of Antiochus Epiphanes must be left to the exegetes of Daniel; but it is known that the Jews and later the Christians believed that these events at least foreshadow, if not predict, the last years of world history under the Antichrist (Glasson, p. 68). Thus John would have a ready tool to use in this imagery for setting forth his revelation of the last days.

Glasson, following the early fathers Victorinus, Hippolytus, and Augustine, suggests that the first three and a half years is the period of the preaching of the two witnesses, while the second half of the week is the time of bitter trial when Antichrist reigns supreme (p. 70). Others believe the expressions are synchronous and thus refer to the identical period (Swete, p. 131). With some reservations, the view of Glasson may be followed. The 1,260-day period of protected prophesying by the two witnesses (11:3–6) synchronizes with the period of the woman in the desert (12:6, 14). When the death of the witnesses occurs (11:7), there follows the forty-two-month murderous reign of the beast (13:5, 7, 15), which synchronizes with the trampling down of the Holy City (11:2). This twofold division seems to be also supported by Jesus' Olivet Discourse, where he speaks of the "beginning of birth pains" (Matt 24:8) and then of the period of "great distress" shortly before his Parousia (Matt 24:21).

Finally, are the two periods of three and a half years symbolic or do they indicate calendar years? Not all will agree, but a symbolic sense that involves a real period but understands the numbers to describe the kind of period rather than its length is in keeping with John's use of numbers elsewhere (cf. 2:10; 4:4; 7:4). Hence, if we follow the twofold division of Daniel's seventieth week of seven years, the preaching of the two witnesses occupies the first half, while the second half is the time of bitter trial when the beast reigns supreme, and during which time the fearful events of chapters 13–19 take place. Since these time references are by no means clear, any explanation must be tentative.

3 Perhaps more diversity of interpretation surrounds these two personages than even the temple in the previous verses. They are called "two witnesses" (v.3), "two prophets" (v.10), and, more figuratively, "two olive trees and the two lampstands who stand before the Lord of the earth" (v.4). Identifications range all the way from two historic figures raised to life, to two groups, to two principles, such as the law and the prophets. Tertullian (d.220) identified the two with Enoch and Elijah.

On the other hand, Jewish tradition taught that Moses and Elijah would return, and this view is followed by a number of Christian interpreters. According to Jochanan ben Zakkai (first century A.D.), God said to Moses, "If I send the prophet Elijah, you must both come together" (Charles, *Commentary on Revelation,* 1: 281; also Seiss, J.B. Smith, Gundry; cf. Mark 9:11–13). Beckwith believes they are two prophets of the future who will perform the functions of Moses and Elijah (p. 595). Others understand the figures to represent the church (Primasius [d.552]). In the words of Swete, "The witness of the church, borne by her martyrs and confessors, her saints and doctors, and by the words and lives of all in whom Christ lives and speaks, is one continual prophecy" (p. 132; also Beasley-Murray). Ladd cannot make up his mind between the witnessing church to Israel and two historical eschatological prophets (*Commentary on Revelation*, p. 154). Bruce believes they are symbolic of the church in its royal and priestly functions ("Revelation," p. 649). Others identify them as representative of the martyrs (Morris, *Revelation of St. John*, p. 147; Caird, p. 134).

More recently Munck has identified them with the Christian prophets Peter and Paul (cited by Bruce, "Revelation," p. 649). Rissi sees them as representatives of the Jewish believers and Gentile believers in the church (Mathias Rissi, "The Kerygma of the Revelation to John," Int, 22 [January 1968]: 16). Minear understands the two to represent all the prophets (*I Saw a New Earth,* p. 99).

Since opinion varies so greatly at this point, it may be wise not to be dogmatic about any one view. Minear's arguments, however, seem more persuasive than the others. The two witnesses represent those in the church who are specially called, like John, to bear a prophetic witness to Christ during the whole age of the church. They also represent those prophets who will be martyred by the beast. Indications that they are representative of many individuals and not just two are that (1) they are never seen as individuals but do everything together—they prophesy together, suffer together, are killed together, are raised together, and ascend together—and all this is hardly possible for two individuals; (2) the beast makes war on them (v.7), which is strange if they are merely two individuals; (3) people throughout the whole world view their ignominious deaths (v.9)—something quite impossible if only two individuals are involved; (4) they are described as two "lamps" (v.4), a figure applied in chapters 1 and 2 to local churches comprised of many individuals. They are "clothed in sackcloth" because they are prophets (cf. Isa 20:2; Zech 13:4) who call for repentance and humility (Jer 6:26; 49:3; Matt 11:21); it was the most suitable garb for times of distress, grief, danger, crisis, and humility. That God himself will appoint, or "give power," to them would encourage the church to persevere even in the face of strong opposition.

4 The reference to the "two olive trees and the two lampstands" is an allusion to Joshua and Zerubbabel in Zechariah's vision, who were also said "to serve the Lord of all the earth" (Zech 4:1–6a, 10b–14). The whole import of Zechariah's vision was to strengthen the two leaders by reminding them of God's resources and to vindicate them in the eyes of the community as they pursued their God-given tasks. Thus John's message would be that the witnesses to Christ who cause the church to fulfill her mission to burn as bright lights to the world will not be quenched (cf. Rev 1:20; 2:5).

Why there should be two olive trees and two lampstands has been variously answered. Some suggest that "two" is the number of required legal witnesses (Num 35:30; Deut 19:15; cf. Matt 18:16; Luke 10:1–24); others suggest that "two" represents the priestly and kingly aspects of the church or the Jewish and Gentile components, etc. Perhaps the dualism was suggested to John by the two olive trees from Zechariah and the two great prophets of the OT who were connected with the coming of the Messiah in Jewish thought, i.e., Moses and Elijah (v.6); cf. Matt 17:3–4). What Joshua (the high priest) and Zerubbabel (the prince) were to the older community and temple, Jesus Christ is to the new community. He is both anointed Priest and King, and his church reflects this character especially in its Christian prophets (1:6; 5:10; 20:6).

5 Here the prophets' divine protection from their enemies is described in terms reminiscent of the former prophets' protection by God (2 Kings 1:10; Jer 5:14). Fire is understood symbolically as judgment from God; and since it proceeds from the witnesses' mouths, we understand that their message of judgment will eventually be fulfilled by God's power (Gen 19:23f.; 2 Sam 22:9; Ps 97:3). Their Lord gives them immunity from destruction until they complete their confirmation of God's saving deed in Christ. This assures the people of God that no matter how many of its chosen saints are oppressed and killed, God's witness to Christ will continue until his purposes are fulfilled.

6 The words "power to shut up the sky . . . and power to turn the waters into blood" clearly allude to the ministries of the prophets Elijah and Moses (1 Kings 17:1; Exod 7:17–21). There is, however, no need for the literal reappearing of these two if it is understood that the two witnesses come in the same spirit and function as their predecessors. Thus Luke interprets the significance of John the Baptist as a ministry in the "spirit and power of Elijah" (Luke 1:17). The author of Revelation is simply describing the vocation of certain Christian prophets, indicating that some follow in the same tradition as the former prophets of Israel. According to Luke 4:25 and James 5:17, Elijah's prophecy shut up the heaven for "three and a half years," a curious foreshadowing, perhaps, of the span of time that these prophets witness (i.e., 1,260 days [v.3]).

7 When they finish their witness, the witnesses are killed by the beast from the Abyss. This is the first reference to the "beast" in the book. The abruptness with which it is introduced seems not only to presuppose some knowledge of the beast but also to anticipate what is said of him in chapters 13 and 17. Only here and in 17:8 is the beast described as coming "up from the Abyss" (cf. 9:1), showing his demonic origin. He attacks the prophets (lit., "makes war with them," *polemon;* cf. 9:7; 12:7, 17; 13:7; 16:14; 19:19; 20:8). This possibly reflects Daniel 7:21: "As I watched, this horn was waging war [*polemon,* LXX] against the saints and defeating them." This attack is again described in 12:17 and 13:7: "Then the dragon was enraged at the woman and went off to make war against the rest of her offspring . . . [the beast] was given power to make war against the saints and to conquer them." This is the second and final phase of the dragon's persecution of the Christian prophets and saints.

8 Here we have the place of the attack on the witnesses and the place of their death: "The street of the great city, which is figuratively called Sodom and Egypt, where also their Lord was crucified." Verse 8 is both full of meaning and difficult to interpret. At first glance, it seems apparent that John is referring to the actual city of Jerusalem where Christ died. This allusion seems obvious. Yet John's terminology also implies more than this. The city is called the "great city," a designation that refers to Babylon throughout the rest of the book (16:19; 17:18; 18:10, 16, 18–19, 21). Moreover, John's use of the word "city," from the very first occurrence in 3:12, is symbolic. In fact, there are really only two cities in the book, the city of God and the city of Satan, which is later referred to as Babylon. A city may be a metaphor for the total life of a community of people (Heb 11:10; 12:22; 13:14).

Here the "great city" is clearly more than merely Jerusalem, for John says it is "figuratively called Sodom and Egypt." "Figuratively" comes from the Greek word *pneumatikōs,* which BAG (p. 685) says means "spiritually, in a spiritual manner, full of the divine Spirit." Elsewhere in the NT, the word characterizes that which pertains to the Spirit in contrast to the flesh (1 Cor 2:14–15; Eph 1:3; 5:19; Col 3:16; 1 Peter 2:5, etc.). RSV and NEB translate it "allegorically," which is questionable, since there is the Greek word *allēgoreō,* which means precisely that (cf. Gal 4:24); and nowhere else does *pneumatikōs* have this sense. NASB has "mystically." Closer may be Knox, who renders *pneumatikōs* "in the language of prophecy," or Minear's "prophetically" ("Ontology and Ecclesiology in the Apocalypse," NTS, 12 [1966], p. 94, n.1), or Phillips's "is called by those with spiritual understanding."

The spiritually discerning will catch the significance of the threefold designation of this city. It is called "Sodom," which connotes rebellion against God, the rejection of God's servants, moral degradation, and the awfulness of divine judgment (cf. Ezek 16:49). In Isaiah's day the rebellious rulers of Jerusalem were called the rulers of Sodom (Isa 1:10; cf. Ezek 16:46). The second designation is "Egypt." Egypt, however, is a country, not a city. It is virtually certain that by John's day, Egypt had become a symbolic name for antitheocratic world kingdoms that enslaved Israel (K. Jose b. Chalaphta, "All kingdoms are called by the name of Egypt because they enslave Israel" [SBK, 3:812]). The third designation is "the great city, . . . where also their Lord was crucified" (cf. Matt 23:28–31, 37–38; Luke 13:33ff.; 21:20–24).

If, as most commentators believe, John also has Rome in mind in mentioning the "great city," then there are at least five places all seen by John as one—Babylon, Sodom, Egypt, Jerusalem, and Rome. (This one city has become, in the eyes of the spiritually discerning, all places opposed to God and the witness of his servants—Sodom, Tyre, Egypt, Babylon, Nineveh, Rome, et al.) Wherever God is opposed and his servants harassed and killed, there *is* the "great city," the transhistorical city of Satan, the great mother of prostitutes (cf. 17:1ff.). What can happen to God's witnesses in any place is what has already happened to their Lord in Jerusalem. Bunyan's city, called "Vanity Fair," approaches this idea, though not precisely, since John uses actual historical places where this great transhistorical city found its manifestation. Mounce suggests that "the great city in which the martyred church lies dead is the world under the wicked and oppressive sway of Antichrist" (*Revelation,* p. 227). It is curious that in the Greek the singular noun *ptōma* ("body") is used for both witnesses in vv.8–9a, but the plural *ptōmata* ("bodies") is used in 9b. Their dead bodies lie in full public view "in the street."

9–10 People from every nation—Jew and Gentile—will "gloat over" their corpses and refuse them the dignity of burial. To have his dead body lie in view of all was the worst humiliation a person could suffer from his enemies (Ps 79:3–4; Tobit 1:18ff.). Furthermore, the pagan world will celebrate the destruction of the witnesses and the victory over them by exchanging gifts, a common custom in the Near East (Neh 8:10, 12; Esth 9:19, 22). Thus the beast will silence the witness of the church to the glee of the beast-worshiping world. The time of their silence corresponds in days to the time of their witness in years. It denotes only a brief time of triumph for the beast.

11–12 The witnesses now experience a resurrection and an ascension to heaven following their three-and-one-half-day death. In regard to this puzzling passage, it is generally held that Ezekiel's vision of the restoration of the dry bones was in John's mind (Ezek 37:5, 10–12). Just as interpretations of Ezekiel's vision vary, so interpretations of vv.11–12 of Revelation 11 also vary. Some hold that the dry bones vision refers to the spiritual quickening of the nation of Israel (KD, *Ezekiel,* 2:120). Others, following rabbinic interpretation and certain church fathers, understand the descriptions to refer to the physical resurrection of the dead. If the two witnesses represent the witness of the church, then physical resurrection and ascension could be in mind. (The summons "Come up here" followed by "they went up to heaven in a cloud" perhaps points to the Rapture [1 Thess 4:16–17].)

On the other hand, John may be using the figure of physical resurrection to represent the church's victory over the death blow of the beast. In Romans 11:15 Paul uses the figure of resurrection symbolically to depict a great spiritual revival among the Jews in a future day. Here in Revelation 11:12 the reference to the "cloud" may be significant. The "cloud" depicts the divine power, presence, and glory; and yet this is the only instance in the book where strictly human figures are associated with a cloud. This must be significant. The two witnesses share in Christ's resurrection. The cloud is a sign of heaven's acceptance of their earthly career. Even their enemies see them, as they will see Christ when he returns with the clouds (1:7). The events of Christ's return and the ascension of the witnesses seem to be simultaneous. Thus in the two witnesses John has symbolized the model of all true prophets, taking as a central clue the story of Jesus' appearance in Jerusalem and describing the common vocation of appearing in the Holy City (or temple) in such a way that reaction to their work would separate the worshipers of God from the unbelievers in language drawn from the stories of many prophets (Minear, *I Saw a New Earth,* p. 103).

13 The earthquake is God's further sign of the vindication of his servants (cf. 6:12). But unlike the earthquake under the sixth seal, this one produces what appears to be repentance: "The survivors . . . gave glory to the God of heaven." The opposite response in 16:9, "they refused to repent and glorify him," seems to confirm that 11:13 speaks of genuine repentance (cf. 14:7; 15:4). Although Ladd (*Commentary on Revelation,* p. 159) understands the entire chapter as a reference to the conversion of the Jews, since the death, resurrection, and ascension of the two witnesses is more worldwide in scope (vv.9–10), we may infer that the earthquake is also symbolic of a world-wide event. Verse 13 shows that even in the midst of judgment, God is active in the world to save those who repent. If there is such hope in the terrible time of final judgment, how much more now! God has not abandoned the human race, regardless of the recurring waves of unbelief. Neither should we!

14 All the events from 9:13 to 11:14 fall under the sixth trumpet and are called the second woe (see comments on 8:13 and 9:12). Since there are further judgments (woes) mentioned in this chapter, it is natural to see at the sounding of the seventh trumpet (vv. 15–19) the third woe taking place. Its nature is described in the bowl judgments (16:1ff.). Apparently the third woe will come without further delay. Indeed, the seventh trumpet (v. 15) brings us to the final scenes of God's unfolding mystery (10:7).

Notes

1 A. McNicol has recently argued that 11:1–14 represents a Christian response to the fall of Jerusalem. He sees the section as reflecting the post–A.D. 70 conflict between Christians and Jews. "Revelation 11:1–14 and the Structure of the Apocalypse" *Restor Quart* 22/4 (1979), 193–202.

3 David Hill argues that the two prophets represent the messianic remnant that survives the destruction of unbelieving Israel and that bears within its life the continuing testimony of the Law and the Prophets: "In its readiness to proclaim the truth of God in the face of Jewish unbelief, and even to die for that truth, the entire church is being symbolized." Hill also argues that John, the author of Revelation, while identifying himself with the prophets, sees himself as "unique in his community and as standing closer to the tradition of the Old Testament prophets than the function of the New" ("Prophecy and Prophets in the Revelation of St. John," NTS, 18 [1971–72], 401–18).

4. *Sounding of the seventh trumpet*

11:15–19

15The seventh angel sounded his trumpet, and there were loud voices in heaven, which said:

"The kingdom of the world has become the kingdom of
our Lord and of his Christ,
and he will reign for ever and ever."

16And the twenty-four elders, who were seated on their thrones before God, fell on their faces and worshiped God, 17saying:

"We give thanks to you, Lord God Almighty,
who is and who was,
because you have taken your great power
and have begun to reign.
18The nations were angry;
and your wrath has come.
The time has come for judging the dead,
and for rewarding your servants the prophets
and your saints and those who reverence your name,
both small and great—
and for destroying those who destroy the earth."

19Then God's temple in heaven was opened, and within his temple was seen the ark of his covenant. And there came flashes of lightning, rumblings, peals of thunder, an earthquake and a great hailstorm.

15 The seventh trumpet sounds, and in heaven loud voices proclaim the final triumph of God and Christ over the world. The theme is the kingdom of God and of Christ—a dual kingdom eternal in its duration. The kingdom is certainly a main theme of the entire Book of Revelation (1:6, 9; 5:10; 11:17; 12:10; 19:6; 20:4; 22:5). This kingdom involves the millennial kingdom and its blending into the eternal kingdom (chs. 20–22). The image suggests the transference of the world empire, once dominated by a usurping power, that has now at length passed into the hands of its true owner and king (Swete). The present rulers are Satan, the beast, and the false prophet. The announcement of the reign of the king occurs here, but the final breaking of the enemies' hold over the world does not occur till the return of Christ (19:11ff.).

Verses 15–18 are reminiscent of Psalm 2. The opening portion of this psalm describes the pagan nations and kings set in opposition to God and his Messiah (Anointed One). Then there follows the establishment of the Son in Zion as the Sovereign of the world and an appeal to the world rulers to put their trust in the Son before his wrath burns. John does not distinguish between the millennial kingdom of Christ and the eternal kingdom of the Father (but cf. 3:21) as Paul does (1 Cor 15:24–28). This should be viewed as a difference merely of detail and emphasis, not of basic theology. Furthermore, in John's view this world becomes the arena for the manifestation of God's kingdom. While at this point the emphasis is on the future visible establishment of God's kingdom, in John's mind that same kingdom is in some real sense now present; and he is participating in it (1:9).

16–17 As the other features in these verses are anticipatory, so the expression "have begun to reign" looks forward to the millennial reign depicted in chapter 20. Significantly, the title of God found earlier in the book, "who is, and who was, and who is to come" (1:8; 4:8), now is "who is and who was." He has now *come!* God has taken over the power of the world from Satan (Luke 4:6).

18 This passage contains a synopsis of the remaining chapters of Revelation. The nations opposed to God and incited by the fury of the dragon (12:12) have brought wrath on God's people (Ps 2:1–3). For this, God has brought his wrath upon the nations (14:7; 16:1ff.; 18:20; 19:19b; 20:11–15). The time (*kairos*, "season") has now come for three further events: the judgment of the dead (20:11–15); the final rewarding of the righteous (21:1–4; 22:3–5); and the final destruction of the destroyers of the earth (Babylon, the beast, the false prophet, and the dragon) (19:2, 11; 20:10).

In Revelation there are three groups of persons who receive rewards: (1) God's "servants the prophets" (cf. 18:20; 22:9); (2) the "saints" (perhaps the martyrs; cf. 5:8; 8:3–4; 13:7, 10; 16:6; 18:20, 24; or simply believers in every age, cf. 19:8; 20:9); and (3) "those who reverence [God's] name" (cf. 14:7; 15:4). In whatever way these groups are denoted, it is important to note that in Revelation the prophets are specially singled out (16:6; 18:20, 24; 22:6, 9).

19 In the heavenly temple John sees the ark of God's covenant. In the OT the ark of the covenant was the chest that God directed Moses to have made and placed within the holiest room of the tabernacle sanctuary (Exod 25:10–22). He was directed to put in the ark the two tables of the Decalogue—the documentary basis of God's redemptive covenant with Israel (Exod 34:28–29). It is presumed that the ark was destroyed when Nebuchadnezzar burned the temple in 586 B.C. There was no ark in the second temple (Jos. War V, 219 [v.5]).

A Jewish legend reported in 2 Maccabees 2:4–8 indicates that Jeremiah hid the ark in a cave on Mount Sinai until the final restoration of Israel. There is no reason, however, to believe that John is alluding in v.19 to this Jewish tradition, since he is clearly referring to a heavenly temple and ark, which is symbolic of the new covenant established by the death of Christ. As the way into the holiest was barred under the old covenant to all except the high priest, now full and immediate access for all, as well as a perfect redemption, has been secured by Christ's death (Heb 9:11–12; 10:19–22).

In v.19 the kingdom of God is seen retrospectively as having fully come. Yet its coming will be elaborated in chapters 20 to 22. Prospectively, this sight of the ark of the covenant also prepares us for the following chapters, which concern the faithfulness of God to his covenant people. As the ark of the covenant was the sign to Israel of God's loyal love throughout their wilderness journeys and battles, so this sign of the new covenant will assure the followers of Christ of his loyal love through their severe trial and the attack by the beast. "Flashes of lightning, rumblings, peals of thunder" call our attention to God's presence and vindication of his people (cf. comments on 6:12; 8:5).

Notes

15–19 Elisabeth S. Fiorenza has argued that the author of Revelation does not seek to comfort the persecuted Christian community with reference to past and future history (as in the Jewish apocalyptic literature) but with reference to the eschatological reality of God's kingdom. She sees this main theme briefly but precisely expressed in the hymn in 11:15–19 and presents an outline for structuring the whole book around this concept ("The Eschatology and Composition of the Apocalypse," CBQ, 30 [1968], 537–69).

C. *The Seven Signs* 12:1–14:20

In this section there is what might be called a Book of Signs. While no signs (*sēmeia;* cf. comments on 12:1) appear in chapters 1 to 11, at least seven signs are mentioned in chapters 12 to 19 (cf. the seven signs in John 1–11). Three are in heaven (12:1, 3; 15:1); four on earth (13:13–14; 16:14; 19:20). Only one is a sign of good (12:1); the others are omens of evil or judgment from God. These signs explain and amplify previous material (e.g., the beast in 11:7 is more fully described in ch. 13) and also advance the drama to its final acts. More specifically, chs. 12 to 14 contain seven further images though only two are directly identified as signs.

This intermediary section (chs. 12–14), preceding the final bowl judgments (15:1ff.), picks up and develops the theme of the persecution of God's people, which has already appeared (3:10; 6:9–11; 7:14; 11:7–10). Chapter 12 gives us a glimpse into the dynamics of the persecution of God's people under the symbolism of the dragon who wages war on the woman and her children (v.17). Chapter 13 continues the same theme by telling of the persecution of the saints by the dragon-energized beasts. Finally, the section closes with (1) the scene of the redeemed 144,000 on Mount Zion who are triumphant over the beast (14:1–5) and (2) looks at the final hour of judgment on the beast worshipers (14:6–20).

1. *The woman and the dragon*

12:1–17

1A great and wondrous sign appeared in heaven: a woman clothed with the sun,
with the moon under her feet and a crown of twelve stars on her head. 2She was
pregnant and cried out in pain as she was about to give birth. 3Then another sign
appeared in heaven: an enormous red dragon with seven heads and ten horns and
seven crowns on his heads. 4His tail swept a third of the stars out of the sky and
flung them to the earth. The dragon stood in front of the woman who was about
to give birth, so that he might devour her child the moment it was born. 5She gave
birth to a son, a male child, who will rule all the nations with an iron scepter. And
her child was snatched up to God and to his throne. 6The woman fled into the desert
to a place prepared for her by God, where she might be taken care of for 1,260
days.

7And there was war in heaven. Michael and his angels fought against the dragon,
and the dragon and his angels fought back. 8But he was not strong enough, and
they lost their place in heaven. 9The great dragon was hurled down—that ancient
serpent called the devil or Satan, who leads the whole world astray. He was hurled
to the earth, and his angels with him.

10Then I heard a loud voice in heaven say:

"Now have come the salvation and the power and the
kingdom of our God,
and the authority of his Christ.
For the accuser of our brothers,
who accuses them before our God day and night,
has been hurled down.
11They overcame him
by the blood of the Lamb
and by the word of their testimony;
they did not love their lives so much
as to shrink from death.
12Therefore rejoice, you heavens
and you who dwell in them!
But woe to the earth and the sea,
because the devil has gone down to you!
He is filled with fury,
because he knows that his time is short."

13When the dragon saw that he had been hurled to the earth, he pursued the
woman who had given birth to the male child. 14The woman was given the two wings
of a great eagle, so that she might fly to the place prepared for her in the desert,
where she would be taken care of for a time, times and half a time, out of the
serpent's reach. 15Then from his mouth the serpent spewed water like a river, to
overtake the woman and sweep her away with the torrent. 16But the earth helped
the woman by opening its mouth and swallowing the river that the dragon had
spewed out of his mouth. 17Then the dragon was enraged at the woman and went
off to make war against the rest of her offspring—those who obey God's commandments and hold to the testimony of Jesus.

In this chapter there are three main figures: the woman, the child, and the dragon. There are also three scenes: the birth of the child (vv.1–6), the expulsion of the dragon (vv.7–12), and the dragon's attack on the woman and her children (vv.13–17).

1 John sees a dazzling sight—a pregnant woman, "clothed with the sun, with the moon under her feet," and wearing a victor's crown (*stephanos*, cf. 2:10; 3:11; 4:4, 10; 6:2; 9:7; 14:14) of twelve stars. John calls the sight a "great sign" (*mega sēmeion*). This shows that the woman is more than a mere woman. She signifies something. Generally John uses *sēmeion* ("sign") to refer to a miraculous sign that points to some deeper spiritual significance in connection with the event or object (John 2:11, 18, et al.; Rev 12:1, 3; 13:13–14; 15:1; 16:14; 19:20). In classical Greek, the word referred especially to the constellations as signs or omens (LSJ, p. 1593).

The basic plot of the story was familiar in the ancient world. A usurper doomed to be killed by a yet unborn prince plots to succeed to the throne by killing the royal seed at birth. The prince is miraculously snatched from his clutches and hidden away, until he is old enough to kill the usurper and claim his kingdom. In the Greek myth of the birth of Apollo, when the child's mother, the goddess Leto, reached the time of her delivery, she was pursued by the dragon Python who sought to kill both her and her unborn child. Only the tiny island of Delos welcomed the mother, where she gave birth to the god Apollo. Four days after his birth, Apollo found Python at Parnassus and killed him in his Delphic cave. In Egypt it is Set the red dragon who pursues Isis, the pregnant mother of Horus. When the child is grown, he too kills the dragon. These stories were living myths in the first century and were probably known to both John and his Asian readers.

While it is easy to point to parallels between these earlier myths and Revelation 12, the differences are striking enough to eliminate the possibility that John merely borrowed pagan myths. As Mounce points out, "Would a writer who elsewhere in the book displays such a definite antagonism toward paganism draw extensively at this point upon its mythology? As always, John is a creative apocalyptist who, although gathering his imagery from many sources, nevertheless constructs a scenario distinctly his own" (*Revelation*, p. 235). To this argument could be added also the evidence of the patristic testimony of the first eight centuries. Not a single voice was raised in favor of interpreting the woman as the embodiment of a mythological figure (Bernard J. LeFrois, *The Woman Clothed With the Sun* [Roma: Orbis Catholicus, 1954], p. 210). Did he, then, draw more directly on OT parallels? Some cite Genesis 37:9–11, where the heavenly bodies of sun, moon, and eleven stars are associated together in Joseph's vision. Joseph's father, Jacob, and his mother, Rachel (the sun and the moon), together with his eleven brothers (the stars), bow down before Joseph. Yet while the sun, moon, and twelve stars are parallel in both accounts, the other details are quite different. For example, the woman and the child who are central to John's account are totally absent from the Joseph dream. It thus seems highly unlikely that John intended his readers to interpret this chapter from the Genesis material.

Others see a more conscious parallelism between the story and the activities of the emperor Domitian around 83 A.D. After the death of his ten-year-old son, Domitian immediately proclaimed the boy a god and his mother, the mother of god. Coinage of this period shows the mother Domitia as the mother of the gods (Cerea, Demeter, Cybele) or enthroned on the divine throne or standing with the scepter and diadem of the queen of heaven with the inscription "Mother of the Divine Caesar." Another coin shows the mother with the child before her. In his left hand is the scepter of world dominions, and with his right hand he is blessing the world. Still another coin shows the dead child sitting on the globe of heaven, playing with seven stars, which represent the seven planets, symbolic of his heavenly dominion over the world. A recently discovered coin of the same period shows on the obverse, like the others, the head of Domitia; but instead of the child on the reverse, it has the moon and the other six planets, emblematic of the golden age. Stauffer interprets this coin's imagery as representing the imperial Zeus child, who has been exalted to be lord of the stars, who will usher in the age of universal salvation that is to come (Ethelbert Stauffer, *Christ and the Caesars* [London: SCM, 1965], pp. 151–52).

Whereas the coinage of Domitian glorifies the son of Domitia as the lord of heaven and savior of the world, Revelation 12 presents Jesus Christ, the Lord of heaven and earth, as he who will rule all nations with a rod of iron (v.5). Tenney says, "The parallel imagery seems almost too similar to be accidental" (Merrill F. Tenney, *New Testament Times* [Grand Rapids: Eerdmans, 1955], p. 337). From this viewpoint, what John does is to demythologize the contemporary Domitian myth by presenting Christ as the true and ascended Lord of heaven, the coming Ruler and Savior of the world.

Another approach to the source problem in this chapter is to compare the chapter with a passage in the DSS. The Hymn scroll contains this disputed passage:

> She who is big with the Man of distress is in her pains. For she shall give birth to a man-child in the billows of Death, and in the bonds of Sheol there shall spring from the crucible of the pregnant one a Marvellous Counsellor with his might; and he shall deliver every man from the billows because of Her who is big with him (1QH E.3:9–10).

In notes explaining the above translation, Dupont-Sommer indicates that not only is the man-child (also called Marvelous Counselor and firstborn) a reference to Messiah based on Isaiah 9:5–6 but that the "crucible" refers to the suffering of the Messiah. The woman symbolizes the "congregation of the just, the Church of the Saints, victim of the persecution of the wicked," and is also associated with the redeeming work of the Messiah. Dupont-Sommer also notices that in the verses of the hymn that immediately follow, there is a reference to another pregnant woman who represents the community of the wicked. She gives birth to the "Asp" or serpent (from Gen 3), which refers to Satan (*The Essene Writings from Qumran*, tr. G. Vermes [Cleveland: World, 1962], p. 208, nn. 1–5).

Other OT references to the birth of the Messiah through the messianic community (Isa 9:6–7; Mic 5:2) and to the travailing messianic community (Isa 26:17; 66:7) should also be noted. In the OT, the image of a woman is frequently associated with Israel, Zion, or Jerusalem (Isa 54:1–6; Jer 3:20; Ezek 16:8–14; Hos 2:19–20). If the main thrust of Dupont-Sommer's interpretation can be accepted (see Notes, v. 1), this background seems to provide a much closer link to the intended significance of chapter 12 than the other proposed parallels. In any case, there seems to be in chapter 12 a blending of elements from OT concepts, Jewish materials, ancient mythical stories, and possibly the Domitian child myth. Regardless of the sources or allusions, John reinterprets the older stories and presents a distinctively Christian view of history in the imagery of the woman and her children.

Who then *is* the woman? While it is not impossible that she is an actual woman, such as Mary, the evidence clearly shows that she, like the woman in chapter 17, has symbolic significance. At the center of chapter 12 is the persecution of the woman by the dragon, who is definitely identified as Satan (v.9). This central theme, as well as the reference to the persecution of the "rest of her offspring" (v.17), renders it virtually certain that the woman could not refer to a single individual. Thus, even some recent Roman Catholic interpreters have departed from this view (Ford, p. 207; Heidt, p. 85; but for a strong case for Mary as the woman, see LeFrois, *Woman Clothed With the Sun,* esp. pp. 211–35).

Some identify the woman exclusively with the Jewish people, the nation of Israel (Walvoord, p. 188). This view seems to be supported by the reference to the woman giving birth to the Messiah or "male child" (v.5); the twelve stars would refer to the twelve tribes (Gen 37:9–11). The twelve signs of the zodiac were thought by the Jews to represent the twelve tribes; their tribal standards corresponded to the zodiacal names (*Berakoth* 32; cf. Ford, p. 343). (On the floor of the ancient sixth-century synagogue of Beth Alpha [near Gilboa in Israel] lies a mosaic with the crescent moon and the sun and the twelve signs of the zodiac with twenty-three stars scattered around a figure representing the sun god.) While these factors must be taken seriously, there are internal problems with this view. The dragon's persecution of the woman after the Messiah's birth could hardly refer to the devil's attack on the nation as a whole but could apply only to the believing part of the people. The whole intent of the passage is to explain the persecution of the believing community, not the persecution of the nation of Israel as a whole.

Since the context indicates that the woman under attack represents a continuous entity from the birth of Christ until at least John's day or later, her identity in the author's mind must be the believing covenant-messianic community. This group would include the early messianic community, which under John the Baptist's ministry was separated from the larger Jewish community to be the people prepared for the Lord (Mark 1:2–3). Later this group merged into the new community of Christ's disciples called the church, or less appropriately, the new Israel, composed of both Jews and Gentiles. John does not at this point seem to distinguish between the earlier almost totally Jewish community and the one present in his day. Their continuity in identity is so strong that whatever ethnic or other differences they have does not affect his single image representing one entity.

The woman's dazzling appearance like the sun relates her to the glory and brilliance of her Lord (Rev 1:16) as well as to her own light-bearing quality (1:20). With the moon under her feet signifying her permanence (Pss 72:5; 89:37; cf. Matt 16:18) and a crown of twelve stars on her head indicating her elect identity (cf. comments at 7:4ff.), she appears in her true heavenly and glorious character despite her seemingly fragile and uncertain earthly history (vv.13–16). A possible allusion to her priestly nature may be suggested by the cosmic imagery of stars, sun, and moon, figures that Josephus uses in describing the high priestly vestments (Antiq. III, 179–87 [vii. 7]; cf. Rev 1:6; 5:10; see Ford, p. 197). Peter likewise refers to the priestly function of the church (1 Peter 2:5, 9). The church viewed as a woman is found elsewhere in the NT as well as in early Christian literature (2 Cor 11:2; Eph 5:25–27, 32; 2 John 1, 5, with 3 John 9; *Hermas* 5.1.i–ii).

2 The woman is in the throes of childbirth. The emphasis is on her pain and suffering, both physical and spiritual. The meaning of her anguish is that the faithful messianic community has been suffering as a prelude to the coming of the Messiah himself and the new age (Isa 26:17; 66:7–8; Mic 4:10; 5:3). The "birth" (*tiktō*) itself does not necessarily refer to the actual physical birth of Christ but denotes the travail of the community from which the Messiah has arisen (see same word in Heb 6:7 and James 1:15).

3 The second "sign" now appears. It likewise is a heavenly sign and introduces us to the second character, the ultimate antagonist of the woman. The dragon is clearly identified with the "ancient serpent called the devil or Satan" (v.9; cf. 20:2–3). The description of him as an "enormous red dragon" symbolically suggests his fierce power and murderous nature. He is further described as having "seven heads and ten horns and seven crowns on his heads." Except for the exchange of the crowns from the heads to the horns, the same description is used for the beast from the sea in chapter 13 and the beast of chapter 17. There is no way of understanding how the horns fit on the heads. While some have tried to find specific meaning for each of the heads and horns, John probably intends to give no more than a symbolic sense of the whole impression rather than of its parts. It is a picture of the fullness of evil in all its hideous strength. (Compare here the OT references to Rahab and Leviathan: Ps 74:13–14; Isa 27:1; 51:9–10; Dan 7:7; 8:10.) There is more than a coincidental similarity in these descriptions and John's image. The diadem crowns on the heads may indicate fullness of royal power (13:1; 19:12).

4 So great is the dragon's power that his tail can even sweep away a large number of the stars and cast them down to the ground (for "a third," see comments on 8:7). This should probably be understood simply as a figure to represent the dragon's power and not as a reference to Satan's victory over some of the angels. In any event, the stars cast down would, after the analogy of Daniel 8:10, 24, refer to the saints of God who were trampled by Satan and not to fallen angels. Satan has placed himself before the woman, thus expecting certain victory over the messianic child. As Lilje (in loc.) notes, it is through this figure that the church shows her awareness that Satan is always threatening the purposes of God within history. Although the attack of Herod against the children of Bethlehem and many incidents during the life of Jesus—such as the attempt of the crowd at Nazareth to throw him over the cliff (Luke 4:28–39)—must also be included, the greatest attempt to devour the child must certainly be the Crucifixion.

5 This verse records the last element of the story. The messianic child comes, finishes his mission, is delivered from the dragon, and is enthroned in heaven. John again refers to the destiny of the child in once more alluding to Psalm 2:9: "Who will rule all the nations with an iron scepter" (Rev 2:27; 19:15). It is not clear whether John also intends a collective identity in the birth of the male child. Daniel 7:13–14, 27 seems to fuse the individual son of man with the people of God. Likewise in Revelation John seems to alternate between the rule of Christ (1:5; 11:15) and the rule of the saints (1:6; 2:26–27). It is, however, difficult to see how the child as well as the woman could be a group of believers. Nevertheless, many early interpreters such as Tyconius (d.390), Pseudo-Augustine (d.542), Primasius (d.552), Quodvultdeus (d.453), and others understood the male child to be simultaneously Christ and the members of Christ; and even a few (Methodius [d.312]; Venerable Bede [d.735]) saw the child as a reference only to the church (LeFrois, *Woman Clothed With the Sun*, pp. 58–61). Through Christ's resurrection and ascension, the dragon's attempt to destroy God's purposes through the Messiah has been decisively defeated.

6 What is this flight into the desert? Is it a symbolic or an actual historic event? Among those who take it literally, some have understood the reference as the escape of the early Jerusalem Christians to Pella (modern Tabaqat Fahil, about twenty miles south of the Sea of Galilee) in A.D. 66 to escape the Roman destruction of Jerusalem. Pella continued to be an important Christian center even after a large portion of the community returned to Jerusalem in 135. Others refer the event to the future, when a portion of the Jewish people will be preserved through the Tribulation period to await the return of Christ (Walvoord). Other approaches view the desert as a symbol for the hiddenness of the church in the world because of persecution (Swete) or as a symbol of its pure condition (Lilje).

Most commentators, however, understand the wilderness to mean the place of safety, discipline, and testing (Caird, Farrar, Ford). This view is preferable because of the highly symbolic nature of the whole chapter, the symbolic use of "desert" in 17:3 (q.v.), and the parallelism to the Exodus where the children of Israel fled from Pharaoh. All are agreed that the reference here to the flight of the woman is anticipatory of vv.13ff. The intervening verses show why the dragon is persecuting the woman (vv.7–12).

For a discussion of the 1,260 days, see comments at 11:2.

7 All agree that the section beginning with this verse, which describes the battle in heaven between Michael and the dragon (vv.7–12), provides the explanation as to why the dragon has turned on the woman and caused her to flee into the desert for protection (vv.6, 13ff.). The account is in two parts: (1) the battle in heaven between Michael and his angels and the dragon and his angels, which results in the ejection of Satan from heaven to the earth (vv.7–9), and (2) the heavenly hymn of victory (vv.10–12).

As elsewhere in the book, the narrative material can be interpreted only in the light of the hymns. This principle is especially important in vv.7–9, where the victory takes place in heaven as the result of Michael's defeat of the dragon. Were this the only thing told us about the "war in heaven," it might be concluded that the dragon's defeat was unrelated to Jesus Christ. But the interpretative hymn (vv.10–12) says that it was in fact the blood of Christ that dealt the actual death blow to the dragon and enabled the saints to triumph (v.8; cf. 5:9). Does this not suggest that the redeeming work of Christ is here depicted by the cosmic battle of Michael and the dragon as it is elsewhere seen as a loosing from sin (1:5), as a washing of our garments (7:14), and as a purchasing to God (5:9)? The time of the dragon's defeat and ejection from heaven must therefore be connected with the incarnation, ministry, death, and resurrection of Jesus (v.13: Luke 10:18; John 12:31). Christ has appeared in order that he may destroy the works of the devil (Matt 12:28–29; Acts 10:38; 2 Tim 1:10; 1 John 3:8).

Early Jewish belief held the view that Michael would cast Satan from heaven as the first of the last-time struggles to establish the kingdom of God on earth. John, in contrast, sees this event as already having taken place through Jesus Christ's appearance and work. Only the final, permanent blow of Satan's ejection from earth remains (Rev 20:10; cf. Charles, *Commentary on Revelation*, 1: 324). The fact that the battle first takes place in heaven between Michael, the guardian of God's people (Dan 10:13, 21; 12:1; Jude 9), and the dragon shows that evil is cosmic in dimension (not limited merely to this world) and also that events on earth are first decided in heaven. By way of contrast, in the DSS the decisive final battle takes place on earth, not in heaven (1QM 9.16; 17.6–7). The single intent of the passage is to assure those who meet satanic evil on earth that it is really a defeated power, however contrary it might seem to human experience (Ladd, *Commentary on Revelation*, p. 171).

8–9 The triumph of the archangel results in the ejection of the dragon and his angels from heaven to earth. Apparently, prior to this event Satan had access to the heavens and continually assailed the loyalty of the saints (Job 1:9–11; Zech 3:1), but now, together with his angels, he has been cast out (cf. Luke 10:18). Whatever appears to be the earthly situation for God's people now, the victory has already been won. When the battle grows fiercer and darker for the church, it is but the sign of the last futile attempt of the dragon to exercise his power before the kingdom of Christ comes (v.12). The "ancient serpent" who tempted Eve with lies about God (Gen 3:1ff.) is in John's mind the same individual as the "devil" and "Satan." As Farrer says, "It is precisely when Satan has lost the battle for the souls of the saints in heaven that he begins the fruitless persecution of their bodies (Austin Farrer, *A Rebirth of Images: the Making of St. John's Apocalypse* [London: Darce, 1949], p. 142). Satan is also the one who "leads the whole world astray." His power lies in deception, and by his lies the whole world is deceived about God (2:20; 13:14; 18:23; 19:20; 20:3, 8, 10; 2 John 7; cf. Rom 1:25).

10 This anonymous hymn, which interprets the great battle of the preceding verses, has three stanzas: the first (v.10) focuses on the victorious inauguration of God's kingdom and Christ's kingly authority; the second (v.11) calls attention to the earthly victory of the saints as they confirm the victory of Christ by their own identification with Jesus in his witness and death; the third (v.12) announces the martyrs' victory and the final woe to the earth because of the devil's ejection and impending demise.

In the first stanza (v.10), the triumph of Christ is described as the arrival of three divine realities in history: God's "salvation" or victory (7:10; 19:1), God's "power," and God's "kingdom." This latter reality is further identified as Christ's assumption of his "authority." The historic event of Christ's life, death, and resurrection has challenged the dominion of Satan and provoked the crisis of history. At the time of Christ's death on earth, Satan was being defeated in heaven by Michael. As Caird has said, "Michael . . . is not the field officer who does the actual fighting, but the staff officer in the heavenly room, who is able to remove Satan's flag from the heavenly map because the real victory has been won on Calvary" (p. 154).

In times past, Satan's chief role as adversary was directed toward accusing God's people of disobedience to God. The justice of these accusations was recognized by God, and therefore Satan's presence in heaven was tolerated. But now the presence of the crucified Savior in God's presence provides the required satisfaction of God's justice with reference to our sins (1 John 2:1–2; 4:10). Therefore, Satan's accusations are no longer valid and he is cast out. What strong consolation this provides for God's faltering people!

11 This stanza is both a statement and an appeal. It announces that the followers of the Lamb also become victors over the dragon because they participate in the "blood of the Lamb," the weapon that defeated Satan, and because they have confirmed their loyalty to the Lamb by their witness even to death. The blood of the martyrs, rather than signaling the triumph of Satan, shows instead that they have gained the victory over the dragon by their acceptance of Jesus' Cross and their obedient suffering with him. This is one of John's chief themes (1:9; 6:9; 14:12; 20:4).

Verses 12 and 17 lead to the conclusion that only a portion of the martyrs are in view (cf. 6:11). Thus this hymn of victory also becomes an appeal to the rest of the saints to do likewise and confirm their testimony to Christ even if doing so means death. This seems to suggest that in some mysterious sense the sufferings of the people of God are linked to the sufferings of Jesus in his triumph over Satan and evil (John 12:31; Rom 16:20; Col 1:24). Since the martyrs have gotten the victory over the dragon because of the Cross of Jesus (i.e., they can no longer be accused of damning sin, since Jesus has paid sin's penalty [1:5b]), they are now free even to give up their lives in loyalty to their Redeemer (John 12:25; Rev 15:2).

12 Satan has failed. Therefore, the heavens and all who are in them should be glad. But Satan does not accept defeat without a bitter struggle. His final death throes are directed exclusively toward "the earth and the sea." Therefore their inhabitants will mourn, for the devil will now redouble his wrathful effort in one last futile attempt to make the most of an opportunity he knows will be brief (three and one-half years; cf. vv.6, 14).

13–14 The narrative is resumed after the flight of the woman into the wilderness (v.6). Why? Because she is under attack from the defeated but still vicious dragon (vv.7–12). No longer able to attack the male child who is in heaven or to accuse the saints because of the victory of Jesus on the Cross, and banned from heaven, the devil now pursues the woman, who flees into the desert. The word "pursue" was no doubt carefully chosen by John because it is also the NT word for "persecute" (*diōkō*, Matt 5:10 et al.). Since the woman has already given birth to the child, the time of the pursuit by the dragon follows the earthly career of Jesus.

The reference to eagle's wings once again introduces imagery borrowed from the Exodus account where Israel was pursued by the dragon in the person of Pharaoh: "You yourselves have seen what I did to Egypt, and how I carried you on eagles' wings and brought you to myself" (Exod 19:4). As God's people were delivered from the enemy by their journey into the Sinai desert, so God's present people will be preserved miraculously from destruction (cf. Deut 32:10–12; Isa 40:31).

15–16 The serpent spews a floodlike river of water out of his mouth to engulf and drown the woman. The water imagery seems clear enough. It symbolizes destruction by an enemy (Pss 32:6; 69:1–2; 124:2–5; Nah 1:8) or calamity (Ps 18:4). As the desert earth absorbs the torrent, so the covenant people will be helped by God and preserved from utter destruction (Isa 26:20; 42:15; 43:2; 50:2). The dragon-inspired Egyptians of old were swallowed by the earth: "You stretched out your right hand and the earth swallowed them" (Exod 15:12). In similar fashion, the messianic community will be delivered by God's power. Whatever specific events were happening to Christians in Asia in John's day would not exhaust the continuing significance of the passage.

17 This attack of Satan against "the rest" of the woman's offspring seems to involve the final attempt to destroy the messianic people of God. Having failed in previous attempts to eliminate them as a whole, the dragon now strikes at individuals who "obey God's commandments and hold to the testimony of Jesus." To "make war" (*poiēsai polemon*) is the identical expression used of the beast's attack on the two witnesses in 11:7 and on the saints in 13:7. Could this possibly correlate the three groups and indicate their common identity under different figures?

Those attacked are called "the rest of her [the woman's] offspring." Some identify this group as Gentile Christians in distinction from the Jewish mother church (Glasson). Others who identify the mother as the nation of Israel see the "rest" as the believing remnant in the Jewish nation who turn to Christ (Walvoord)—a view that depends on the prior identification of the woman with the whole nation of Israel. Others have suggested that the woman represents the believing community as a whole, the universal or ideal church composed of both Jews and Gentiles, whereas the "offspring" of the woman represent individuals of the community (Jews and Gentiles) who suffer persecution and martyrdom from the dragon in the pattern of Christ (Swete, Caird, Kiddle). The close identification of the seed of the woman as first of all Jesus and then also those who have become his brethren through faith agrees with other NT teaching (Matt 25:40; Heb 2:11–12). While Satan cannot prevail against the Christian community itself, he can wage war on certain of its members who are called on to witness to their Lord by obedience even unto death, i.e., "those who obey God's commandments and hold to the testimony of Jesus" (Matt 16:18; Rev 11:7; 13:7, 15). The church, then, is paradoxically both invulnerable (the woman) and vulnerable (her children) (cf. Luke 21:16–18).

Notes

1 On whether the Qumran Hymn (1QH, III) bears a direct relation to John's image of the woman as the Christian community, see pro Dupont-Sommer, *Writings from Qumran,* pp. 207–8, nn. 1–5; Ford, pp. 204–5; contra William LaSor, *The Dead Sea Scrolls and the New Testament* (Grand Rapids: Eerdmans, 1972), pp. 208–9.

6 The third person plural *τρέφωσιν* (*trephōsin*) may be a Semitism for the simple singular passive, meaning, "she might be taken care of." No plural antecedent fits, and the sense is passive. Such occurrences are found in the OT and possibly also in Rev 11:2, "they will trample," meaning, "the holy city shall be trampled." For this idiom, see Ronald J. Williams, *Hebrew Syntax: An Outline* (Toronto: University of Toronto, 1967), p. 32, par. 160.

7 The infinitive construction *τοῦ πολεμῆσαι* (*tou polemēsai;* NIV, "fought") has been discussed by Charles (*Commentary on Revelation,* 1:322) and G. Mussies (*The Morphology of Koine Greek as Used in the Apocalypse of St. John* [Leiden: E.J. Brill, 1971], p. 96), who both conclude that this is a pure Semitism and should be translated as "Michael and his angels had to fight with the Dragon." Almost all translations fail to catch this nuance, so illuminating to the context.

On the dragon myths of the ancient world, see Bruce Waltke's "The Creation Account in Genesis 1:1–3," BS, 132 (January-March 1975), pp. 32ff.

11 NIV does not translate the connective particle *καί* (*kai,* normally "and") that begins this verse in the Gr. text. The particle could be translated "for" and would, if so rendered, give an additional connection between the defeat of Satan and the death of the martyrs.

2. *The two beasts*

13:1–18

[1]And the dragon stood on the shore of the sea.
And I saw a beast coming out of the sea. He had ten horns and seven heads,
with ten crowns on his horns, and on each head a blasphemous name. [2]The beast
I saw resembled a leopard, but had feet like those of a bear and a mouth like that
of a lion. The dragon gave the beast his power and his throne and great authority.
[3]One of the heads of the beast seemed to have had a fatal wound, but the fatal
wound had been healed. The whole world was astonished and followed the beast.

4Men worshiped the dragon because he had given authority to the beast, and they
also worshiped the beast and asked, "Who is like the beast? Who can make war
against him?"
5The beast was given a mouth to utter proud words and blasphemies and to
exercise his authority for forty-two months. 6He opened his mouth to blaspheme
God, and to slander his name and his dwelling place and those who live in heaven.
7He was given power to make war against the saints and to conquer them. And
he was given authority over every tribe, people, language and nation. 8All inhabitants of the earth worship the beast—all whose names have not been written in the
book of life belonging to the Lamb that was slain from the creation of the world.
9He who has an ear, let him hear.

10If anyone is to go into captivity,
into captivity he will go.
If anyone is to be killed with the sword,
with the sword he will be killed.

This calls for patient endurance and faithfulness on the part of the saints.
11Then I saw another beast, coming out of the earth. He had two horns like a
lamb, but he spoke like a dragon. 12He exercised all the authority of the first beast
on his behalf, and made the earth and its inhabitants worship the first beast, whose
fatal wound had been healed. 13And he performed great and miraculous signs,
even causing fire to come down from heaven to earth in full view of men. 14Because
of the signs he was given power to do on behalf of the first beast, he deceived the
inhabitants of the earth. He ordered them to set up an image in honor of the beast
who was wounded by the sword and yet lived. 15He was given power to give breath
to the image of the first beast, so that it could speak and cause all who refused to
worship the image to be killed. 16He also forced everyone, small and great, rich and
poor, free and slave, to receive a mark on his right hand or on his forehead, 17so
that no one could buy or sell unless he had the mark, which is the name of the beast
or the number of his name.
18This calls for wisdom. If anyone has insight, let him calculate the number of the
beast, for it is man's number. His number is 666.

This chapter forms part of the theme of the persecution of God's people John began to develop in chapter 12. Turning from the inner dynamics of the struggle, chapter 13 shifts to the actual earthly instruments of this assault—viz., the two dragon-energized beasts. In accord with the discussion in chapter 12, we may assume that the beast-related activities constitute the way the dragon carries out his final attempts to wage war on the seed of the woman (12:17). A contest is going on to seduce the whole world—even the followers of Jesus—to worship the beast. As Minear shows (*I Saw a New Earth*, p. 118), John seeks to emphasize three things about the first beast: he shows (1) the conspiracy of the dragon with the beast (vv.3–4); (2) the universal success of this partnership in deceiving the whole world to worship them (vv.3–4, 8); and (3) that the partnership will succeed in a temporary defeat of the saints of God, thus accomplishing the greatest blasphemy of God (vv.6–7a).

Finally, not being able to seduce all the earth alone, the conspirators summon yet a third figure to their aids—the beast from the earth. He must remain loyal to his associates and at the same time be sufficiently similar to the Lamb to entice even the followers of Jesus. He must be able to perform miraculous signs (*sēmeia*) much as the two witnesses did (vv.11ff.; cf. 13:13 with 11:5). As the battle progresses, the dragon's deception becomes more and more subtle. Thus the readers are called to discern the criteria that will enable them to separate the lamblike beast from the Lamb himself (13:11 with 14:1).

Two basic interpretative problems confront the reader. These have led students of the book to different understandings of this chapter: (1) The identification of the beast and his associate—are they personal or some other entity? (2) The time of the beast's rule—is it past, continuous, or still future? In seeking some satisfactory answers to these questions, it may be helpful to first set forth the facts about the beast. He (1) rises from the sea (v.1); (2) resembles the dragon (v.1); (3) has composite animal features (v.2); (4) is dragon empowered (v.2); (5) has one head wounded to death but healed (vv.3–4, 7b–8); (6) blasphemes God and God's people for forty-two months (vv.5–6); (7) makes war against the saints and kills them (vv.7a, 15); and (8) gives to those who follow him his "mark," which is either his name or his number, 666 (vv.16–18).

In addition, there are no fewer than a dozen further references in Revelation to the beast (11:7; 14:9, 11; 15:2; 16:2, 10, 13; 19:19–20; 20:4, 10), excluding the nine references to the scarlet-colored beast in chapter 17, which should probably be included. These further references contain no new information, but 11:7 indicates that the beast rises from the Abyss. Also, 19:19 refers to a coalition of the beast with the "kings of the earth," and 19:20 describes his final end in the lake of fire.

The history of the interpretation of chapter 13 is far too extensive for this commentary to cover. As early as the second century, two different understandings of the Antichrist appeared. Some early interpreters take the position that the Antichrist will be a person, a world deceiver who will reign for the last half of Daniel's seventieth week (Dan 7:25). The Epistle of Barnabas (A.D. 70–100?) warns believers to be alert to the imminent appearing of "the final stumbling-block," who is identified with the "little horn" of Daniel 7:24 (4.3–6, 9–10; ANF, 1:138–39). The Didache (early second century?) refers to a "world deceiver [who] will appear in the guise of God's Son. He will work 'signs and wonders' and the earth will fall into his hands and he will commit outrages such as have never occurred before" (16.4, in Cyril C. Richardson, ed., *Library of Christian Classics*, vol. 1, *Early Christian Fathers*, [Philadelphia: Westminster, 1953], p. 178). Justin Martyr (d.165) likewise looked for the appearance in his lifetime of the Antichrist prophesied by Daniel, who would reign for three and one-half years according to Daniel 7:25 (*Dialogue* 32; ANF, 1:210).

Irenaeus (d.202) gives the first extensive discussion of the Antichrist. He is to be an unrighteous king from the tribe of Dan, the little horn of Daniel 7:8, who will reign over the earth during the last three and one-half years of Daniel's seventieth "week" (Dan 9:27). Irenaeus identifies the Antichrist with the first beast of Revelation 13 and the "man of sin" ("lawlessness," NIV) of 2 Thessalonians 2:3–4, who will exalt himself in the Jerusalem temple (rebuilt) (*Contra Haereses* 5.25.1–5; 5.28.2; 5.30.2; ANF, 1:553, 556–59). This view, with modifications, is followed by Irenaeus's student Hippolytus (d.235), also by Tertullian (d.220) and Victorinus (d.304), and in recent times by many commentators, including Barnhouse, Bruce, Gaebelein, Ladd, Morris, Mounce, Scofield, and Walvoord. In its favor is the more literal reading of 2 Thessalonians 2:1–10 and the natural understanding of the Antichrist as being the personal counterpart to the personal Christ.

On the other hand, from the earliest times some interpreters have understood the Antichrist as a present threat of heresy, depending more on the concept found in the Johannine Epistles (1 John 2:18, 22; 4:3; 2 John 7). Thus Polycarp (d.155), said to be a disciple of the apostle John, understands the Antichrist to be revealed in the docetic heresies of his time (*Philippians* 7.1; ANF, 1:34). Likewise, Tertullian identifies the many false prophets of docetism with the Antichrist but sees these teachers as the forerunners of the future Antichrist, who as the Arch Deceiver will come "in all kinds of counterfeit miracles, signs and wonders" to mislead those who "have not believed the truth but have delighted in wickedness" (2 Thess 2:9–12) (*Against Marcion* 5.16; ANF, 3:463–64).

Luther, Calvin, and other Reformers adopting this general view identified the beast with the papacy of the Roman Catholic Church. Only one recent interpreter, Henry Alford, seems to follow the Reformers in their view. However, other modern commentators adopt the theological heresy interpretation of the Antichrist (Berkouwer, Minear, Newman). In its favor are the references to the Antichrist in the Johannine Epistles and the advantage of seeing the beast as a present threat to the church and not merely as an eschatological figure of the last time. This view also argues that the 2 Thessalonians 2 passage need not be understood as referring to a single future individual (see G.C. Berkouwer, *The Return of Christ* [Grand Rapids: Eerdmans, 1972], pp. 268–71). The issue is difficult to settle with any finality. However, I will develop chapter 13 more in accord with the theological heresy view, while recognizing at the same time that Tertullian's position as stated above is consistent with my position and that the personal future Antichrist view has strong support. (See also the comments at v.11.)

In modern interpretation, as Minear points out, there is almost complete agreement that the "wounded head" (v.3) refers to the Nero redivivus legend. It will be helpful to have Minear's summary of the legend before us:

> Let us look first, then, at the Neronic legend itself. Toward the end of his reign Nero's unpopularity among Roman citizens had assumed high proportions. In 67 and 68 open revolts had broken out against his authority in Gaul and Spain. At length he had been repudiated by the praetorian guard and by the Senate. Fleeing from the city, he had taken refuge in a friend's suburban villa, where he had received word that the Senate had proclaimed him a public enemy and had approved Galba as his successor. Having been warned that pursuing soldiers were approaching his hideout, he had cut his own throat with a sword (June 9, 68). After his death a rumor spread abroad that he had not actually died but had escaped to Parthia, whence he would soon return to regain his throne. This rumor circulated most quickly in the eastern provinces, and assumed strange forms. At one stage, popular expectation envisaged the return of Nero from Parthia, with a huge army subduing all opposition:
>
>> And to the west shall come the strife of gathering war and the exile from Rome, brandishing a mighty sword, crossing the Euphrates with many myriads.
>
> On the basis of this rumor, impostors arose in the east who assumed the name of Nero in the effort to exploit the legend. There are records of at least two such claimants. There seems to have been a later stage in the legend in which Nero's figure has become invested with supernatural status. Now his return from the abyss with hordes of demons is anticipated as an omen of the "last days." Among the oracles of the Sibyl we find an extensive reference to this expectation:
>
>> There shall be at the last time about the waning of the moon, a world-convulsing war, deceitful in guilefulness. And there shall come from the ends of the earth a matricide fleeing and devising sharp-edged plans. He shall ruin all the earth, and gain all power, and surpass all men in cunning. That for which he perished he shall seize at once. And he shall destroy many men and great tyrants, and shall burn all men as none other ever did (vv.361ff.) (*I Saw a New Earth*, pp. 248–49.).

This Neronic interpretation presupposes an identification in John's mind between the sea beast and the Roman Empire, a view espoused in our day by both preterist and not a few preterist-futurist interpreters of Revelation (most recently by Mounce, *Revelation,* pp. 250–51). This in turn usually assumes that Revelation 17 identifies the seven heads of the beast as the successive emperors of the Roman Empire. Yet a question concerning the reliability of this whole Neronic approach must be raised. Minear argues convincingly that the Nero redivivus view will fit neither the facts of history nor the text of Revelation 13 and 17 (*I Saw a New Earth,* pp. 228–60). (See comments at 17:8–9.)

Newman also impressively calls the Nero myth into question. He argues that Irenaeus, the best source for the Domitian dating of the book, never refers either to a Domitian persecution as the background for John's thought or to any Nero-myth interpretation, even though he is attempting to refute the identification of the number 666 with any Roman emperor. Newman concludes that Revelation could just as well be viewed as a theological polemic against some form of Gnosticism than, as popularly held, a political polemic. Newman also challenges the widely held assumption that all apocalyptic literature—and especially the Book of Revelation—must be understood as arising out of some contemporary political crisis for the saints. Little evidence can be cited for more than a selective and local persecution of Christians under Domitian's rule (E.T. Merrill, *Essays in Early Christian History* [London: Macmillan & Co., 1924], pp. 157–73; F.F. Bruce, *New Testament History* [New York: Doubleday, 1972], pp. 412–14; Barclay Newman, "The Fallacy of the Domitian Hypothesis," NTS, 10 [1963], 139–49; G. Edmundson, *The Church in Rome in the First Century* [London: Longmans, Green, 1913]).

Likewise rejecting the beast-equals-Rome hypothesis is Foerster, who points out that rabbinic exegesis up to the first century A.D. identified the fourth beast of Daniel 7 as Edom-equals-Rome. Since the beast of Revelation 13 is a composite that unites all the features of the four beasts of Daniel 7, it therefore cannot be identified with Rome (TDNT, 3:134–35, esp. n.11). An attempt will be made in this exposition to demonstrate that the Rome hypothesis is untenable. This leaves the question open as to whether John sees the Antichrist (or beast) as a person or some more encompassing entity.

1a NIV and most other modern translations include v.1a as the concluding verse of chapter 12 because a variant Greek reading changes the KJV text "I stood" to "he stood" (i.e., the dragon). The latter reading is favored by a majority of textual scholars, though the KJV text may be the original (see Notes). If "he stood" is the correct reading, the sense would be that the dragon, who has now turned his rage on the children of the woman (12:17), stands on the seashore to summon his next instrument, the beast from the sea. But if the text reads "I stood," the sense is that John receives a new vision (cf. 10:1) as he gazes out over the sea in the same manner as Daniel (7:2).

1b–2 The beast (*thērion,* "wild beast") has already been described in 11:7 as rising from the "Abyss" (cf. 17:8). Thus the sea may symbolize the Abyss, the source of demonic powers that are opposed to God (cf. 9:1; 20:1–3), rather than "the agitated surface of unregenerate humanity (cf. Isa 57:20), and especially of the seething caldron of national and social life" (Swete, p. 158). This view agrees with the OT images of the sea as the origin of the satanic sea monsters—the dragon (Tannin), Leviathan

("Coiled One"), and Rahab ("Rager") (Job 26:12–13; Pss 74:13–14; 87:4; 89:10; Isa 27:1; 51:9; cf. also Ezek 32:6–8). The ancient Hebrews demythologized the sea-monster myths to depict the victory of the Lord of Israel over the demonic forces of evil that in various manifestations had sought to destroy the people of God. Thus John later foresees the final day of Christ's victory when there will "no longer [be] any sea" or source of demonic opposition to God and his people (21:1).

John describes the beast in words similar to those he used in 12:3 of the dragon: "He had ten horns and seven heads, with ten crowns on his horns." There is a slight difference here in the matter of the crowns, which may represent some change in the dragon's authority. As previously indicated (cf. comments on 12:3), any attempt to identify the heads or horns as separate kings, kingdoms, etc., should be resisted.

The image of the seven-headed monster is well attested in ancient Sumerian, Babylonian, and Egyptian texts. A cylinder seal coming from Tel Asmar (ancient Eshnunna, some fifty miles northeast of modern Baghdad), dating back to about 2500 B.C., shows two divine figures killing a seven-headed monster with flames arising from its back. Four of its heads are drooping as if already dead. A spear is in the hand of a figure who is striking the fourth head (see Alexander Heidel, *The Babylonian Genesis* [Chicago: University of Chicago, 1942], pp. 107–14, and figs. 15, 16; E.A. Wallis Budge, *The Gods of the Egyptians* [New York: Dover Publications, 1969], 1:278–79).

Courtesy of the Oriental Institute, University of Chicago

THE CHAOS MONSTER

Cylinder seal from Tell Asmar (in ancient Mesopotamia) dated c. 2500 B.C., showing two gods spearing a four-legged, seven-headed hydra, four of whose heads hang dead and three still live and show projected forked tongues; six tongues of flame arise from the monster's back; two worshipers and a star in the field are also seen. See Revelation 12:3-4; 13:1, 3, 14; 17:3, 8-11.

It may be argued that John's beast from the sea is to be connected with Leviathan in the OT. See Psalm 74:14, where the "heads" of the monster are specifically mentioned: "It was you who crushed the heads of Leviathan." The seven heads and ten horns, regardless of the imagery used in Daniel or elsewhere, are not to be separately identified. It is true that Leviathan, Rahab, and the dragon (serpent) in the cited OT texts have a reference to political powers, such as Egypt and Assyria, that were threatening Israel. In the minds of the OT writers, however, the national entities were inseparably identified with the archetypal reality of the satanic, idolatrous systems represented by the seven-headed monster (Leviathan, Rahab, and the dragon) so that the beast represented, not the political power, but the system of evil that found expression in the political entity (Budge, *Gods of the Egyptians,* 1:278). The reason this point is so important is that it helps us see that the beast itself is not to be identified in its description with any one historical form of its expression or with any one institutional aspect of its manifestation. In other words, the beast may appear now as Sodom, Egypt, Rome, or even Jerusalem and may manifest itself as a political power, an economic power, a religious power, or a heresy (1 John 2:18, 22; 4:3).

In John's mind, the chief enemy is diabolical deception; his description therefore has theological overtones, not political ones. This interpretation does not exclude the possibility that there will be a final climactic appearance of the beast in history in a person; in a political, religious, or economic system; or in a final totalitarian culture combining all these. The point is that the beast cannot be limited to either the past or the future.

John further states that this beast had "on each head a blasphemous name." This prominent feature is repeated in 17:3 (cf. 13:5–6). Arrogance and blasphemy also characterize the "little horn" of Daniel's fourth beast (7:8, 11, 20, 25) and the willful king of Daniel 11:36. John alludes to the vision of Daniel but completely transforms it.

In keeping with the Rome hypothesis, many have tried to identify the blasphemous names with the titles of the emperor: "Augustus" ("reverend," "to be worshiped"); *divus* ("deified"); "Savior"; *dominus* ("Lord"). But was this in John's mind? In 2:9 he refers to the blasphemy "of those who say they are Jews and are not," a reference that seems to refer to the fact that some Jews at Smyrna had spoken against the lawful messianic claims of Jesus. They may also have charged the Christians with disloyalty to the empire and thus sided with the pagan officials in persecuting them. Could these Jews be part also of the blasphemous names? In 13:6 the blasphemies are directed against God and are further defined: "to blaspheme God, by blaspheming his name, his temple, those who dwell in heaven" (my translation). Thus the beast challenges the sovereignty and majesty of God by denying the first commandment: "You shall have no other gods before me" (Exod 20:3). Therefore, whatever person or system—whether political, social, economic, or religious—cooperates with Satan by exalting itself against God's sovereignty and by setting itself up to destroy the followers of Jesus, or entices them to become followers of Satan through deception, idolatry, blasphemy, and spiritual adultery, embodies the beast of Revelation 13.

The description John gives of the beast from the sea does not describe a mere human political entity such as Rome. Rather, it describes in archetypal language the hideous, Satan-backed system of deception and idolatry that may at any time express itself in human systems of various kinds, such as Rome. Yet at the same time John also seems to be saying that this blasphemous, blaspheming, and blasphemy-producing reality will have a final, intense, and, for the saints, utterly devastating manifestation.

3 The beast has a fatal wound, but the wound is healed. This results in great, world-wide influence, acceptance, and worship for both the beast and the dragon. Verse 3 is important and requires careful exegesis because of the widespread Nero redivivus viewpoint that is read into the wounded head (see introduction to this chapter). There are a number of features of John's description that are inconsistent with both the Nero redivivus and the Roman Empire interpretations. I am indebted for the following arguments to Newman ("Domitian Hypothesis," pp. 133–39) and to Minear (*I Saw a New Earth*, ch. 5).

1. It should be observed that the wounded "head" of v.3 is elsewhere in the chapter a wound of the whole beast (vv.12, 14). A wound inflicted in a former and rejected emperor is not a wound inflicted on the whole empire. If the reference is to Nero, it is difficult to see how his self-inflicted wound could have wounded the whole empire or how the legendary healing of his throat enhanced the authority of the beast or the dragon's war against the saints.

2. The "wound" unto death or fatal wound, must be carefully examined. In the Greek, the word for "wound" is *plēgē*, which everywhere in Revelation means "plague," in fact, a divinely inflicted judgment (9:18, 20; 11:6; 15:1ff.; 16:9, 21; 18:4, 8; 21:9; 22:18). Elsewhere in the NT the word is used of "beatings" or official "floggings" (Luke 10:30; 12:48; Acts 16:23, 33; 2 Cor 6:5; 11:23). In 13:14 we find that the beast has the plague of the "sword" (*machaira*), which supposedly refers to Nero's dagger. Elsewhere in Revelation the "sword" (*machaira*, or *rhomphaia*) (1) symbolically refers to the divine judgment of the Messiah (1:16; 2:12, 16; 19:15, 21); (2) is the sword of the rider on the red horse and equals divine judgment (6:4, 8); and (3) is a sword used as a weapon against the saints of God (13:10). We are, then, nearer to John's mind if we see the sword, not as referring to an emperor's death, but as the symbol of God's wrath that in some event had struck a death blow to the authority of the beast (and the dragon), yet which had been deceptively covered up or restored (for a probable antecedent, see Isa 27:1).

3. The correct identification, therefore, of the beast's enemy will enable us to understand what event John had in mind in the death blow. Everywhere in the book the only sufficient conqueror of the beast and the dragon is the slain Lamb, together with his faithful saints (12:11; 19:19–21). Furthermore, it is the event of the life and especially the crucifixion, resurrection, and exaltation of Jesus that dealt this death blow to the dragon and the beast (1:5; 5:9; 12:11). This same thought is paralleled by other NT teaching (Luke 10:17–24; 11:14–22; John 12:31–33; Col 2:15). Irenaeus suggests that the wound, so central to the Apocalypse, must be understood as an appeal to Genesis 3:13ff. (*Contra Haereses* 5.25–34).

Yet the same paradox found in chapter 12 also appears here in chapter 13. While the dragon (ch. 12) is, on the one hand, defeated and cast out of heaven, on the other hand, he still has time and ability to wage a relentless war against the people of God. Likewise, the beast (ch. 13) has been dealt a fatal blow by the cross of Christ and yet still has time and ability to wage war against the saints. He appears to be alive and in full command of the scene; his blasphemies increase. What the sea beast cannot accomplish, he commissions the earth beast to do (vv.11ff.). All three—the dragon, the sea beast, and the earth beast—though distinguishable, are nevertheless in collusion to effect the same end: the deception that led the world to worship the dragon and the sea beast and the destruction of all who oppose them.

It is this description that leads to the fourth reason why identifying the beast exclusively with any one historical personage or empire is probably incorrect. In John's description of the beast, there are numerous parallels with Jesus that should alert the reader to the fact that John is seeking to establish, not a historical identification, but a theological characterization (though in this there is no implication against the historicity of Jesus): Both wielded swords; both had followers on whose foreheads were inscribed their names (13:16–14:1); both had horns (5:6; 13:1); both were slain, the same Greek word being used to describe their deaths (*sphagizō*, vv.3, 8); both had arisen to new life and authority; and both were given (by different authorities) power over every nation, tribe, people, and tongue as well as over the kings of the earth (1:5; 7:9; with 13:7; 17:12). The beast described here is the great theological counterpart to all that Christ represents and not the Roman Empire or any of its emperors. So it is easy to understand why many in the history of the church have identified the beast with a future, personal Antichrist.

It is curious that in her commentary on Revelation, Ford refers to Minear's "most challenging argument against this [Nero] theory" (p. 220) without offering any refutation. She then proceeds, contrary to Minear's whole thesis, to try her own hand at another *historical* identification that is even less convincing than the long succession of previous ones (see comments on v.11).

While the references in the Johannine literature may be taken as supporting the view that the Antichrist is manifested in multiple persons and was a reality present in John's day (1 John 2:18, 22; 4:3; 2 John 7), Paul's description in such personal terms of the coming "man of lawlessness" (2 Thess 2:3–4, 8–9) has led the majority of ancient and modern interpreters to adopt the viewpoint that it is a personal Antichrist. Bavinck believes that the solution to the conflict between Paul and John lies in seeing John as describing the forerunners (anti-Christian powers in history) while Paul talks about the day when these powers will be embodied in one king(dom) of the world, the epitome of apostasy (cited by Berkouwer, *Return of Christ*, p. 265). John, however, says that in the false teachers "the antichrist" was actually present (2 John 7). Berkouwer shows that it is not necessary to understand Paul's apocalyptic language as describing a personal Antichrist (ibid., p. 270).

But the question must remain open as to whether John in the Apocalypse points to a *single* archenemy of the church—whether past or future—or to a transhistorical reality with many human manifestations in history. Thus the imagery would function similarly with regard to the image of the woman of chapter 12 or the harlot of chapter 17. If such is the case, this does not mean that John would have denied the earthly historical manifestations of this satanic reality; but it would prevent us from limiting the imagery merely to the Roman Empire or to any other single future political entity.

4 The goal of the dragon and the beast in their conspiracy is to promote the idolatrous worship of themselves. This perversion is further enhanced by the earth beast (vv.12, 15). The means of deception varies because not all mankind is deceived in the same way. People follow and worship the beast because he is apparently invincible: "Who can make war against him?" His only real enemy seems to be the saints of Jesus, whom he effectively destroys (2:10, 13; 12:11; 13:15). But little does he realize that in the death of the saints the triumph of God appears. As they die, they do so in identification with the slain Lamb who through the Cross has decisively conquered the dragon by inflicting on him a truly fatal wound. "Who is like the beast?" echoes in parody similar references to God himself (Exod 15:11; Mic 7:18).

5–6 (See comments on v.1.) The period of the beast's authority is given as "forty-two months," the same period already referred to in 11:2–3; 12:6, 13 (see comments at 11:2).

7 Here, to "make war," as elsewhere in the Apocalypse, does not mean to wage a military campaign but refers to hostility to and destruction of the people of God in whatever manner and through whatever means the beast may choose (study carefully 2:16; 11:7; 12:7, 17; 16:14; 17:14; 19:11, 19; 20:8; 2 Cor 10:4). "To conquer" them refers not to the subversion of their faith but to the destruction of their physical lives (cf. Matt 10:28). As in T.S. Eliot's *Murder in the Cathedral,* (New York: Harcourt, Brace & Co., 1935), their apparent defeat by the beast and his victory turns out in reality to be the victory of the saints and the defeat of the beast (15:2). Messiahlike universal dominion was given the beast by the dragon (Luke 4:4–7; 1 John 5:19).

8 John further identifies the worshipers of the beast as "all whose names have not been written in the book of life belonging to the Lamb" (for a discussion of the meaning of the "book of life," see comments at 3:5; also 17:8; 20:12, 15; 21:27). This contrast further emphasizes the theological nature of the description of the beast. The beast from the earth represents the idolatrous system of worship instigated by the dragon to deceive mankind into breaking the first commandment.

It has been debated whether the words "from the creation of the world" (also 17:8) belong grammatically with "have not been written" or with "that was slain." In other words, is it the Lamb who was slain from the creation of the world, or is it the names that were not recorded in the book of life from the creation of the world? In Greek, either interpretation is grammatically acceptable. But the reference in 17:8 implies that the word order in the Greek (not the grammar) favors the latter view and suggests that John is deliberately providing a complementary thought to 17:8. In the former instance, the emphasis would rest on the decree in eternity to elect the Son as the redeeming agent for mankind's salvation (13:8; 1 Peter 1:20); in the latter, stress lies on God's eternal foreknowledge of a company of people who would participate in the elect Son's redeeming work (17:8). In any event, the words "from the creation of the world" cannot be pressed to prove eternal individual election to salvation or damnation since 3:5 implies that failure of appropriate human response may remove one's name from the book of life. Therefore, we must allow John's understanding of predestination to qualify both earlier rabbinic and Qumran as well as later Christian views. This verse strikes a sharp note of distinction between the followers of the beast and those of the slain Lamb. It also calls for faithful commitment and clear discernment of error on the part of the Lamb's people.

9–10 These verses are both important and difficult. This is the only occurrence in Revelation of the words "he who has an ear, let him hear" apart from their use in each of the messages to the seven churches (chs. 2–3). Here they call special attention to the need for obedience to the exhortation in v.10b. Kiddle feels that v.10 is the focal point of the whole chapter, as it calls on the Christian to display faith and patience in the face of the divinely permitted predominance of evil (p. 248). Most agree that the language of v.10 alludes to Jeremiah 15:2 and 43:11 (LXX 50:11), where the prophet describes the certainty of divine judgment that will come upon the rebels in Israel—they will suffer captivity, famine, disease, and death from the sword. Yet it is difficult to see how Jeremiah's words are appropriate here in this context of an exhortation for believers to be faithful. John's meaning must be different—viz., that as the rebels in Jeremiah's day would certainly encounter the divine judgment, so the faithful to Christ are assured that their captivity and martyrdom are in God's will. (For the textual problem in v.10, see Notes.)

No completely satisfying resolution of the problems in v.10 is available. Since the difficult part (10a) is both preceded by (v.9) and followed by (v.10b) appeals to obedience and loyalty, it seems best to stay with the sense of obedient faithfulness and follow the textual readings that support it. Charles puts it this way: "The day of persecution is at hand: the Christians must suffer captivity, exile or death: in calmly facing and undergoing this final tribulation they are to manifest their endurance and faithfulness" (*Commentary on Revelation,* 1: 355). Paul's statement is similar: "Without being frightened in any way by those who oppose you. This is a sign to them that they will be destroyed, but that you will be saved—and that by God" (Phil 1:28). While the DSS reveal that the Essenes held to an active, violent participation in the final eschatological battle for the elect, and while the then current Zealot holy-war doctrine advocated violent revolution, John seems to call believers here to passive resistance against their enemies. Yet this resistance, which may result in captivity and even martyrdom, seems to contribute to the eventual defeat of evil (cf. Adela Yarbo Collins, "The Political Perspective of the Revelation to John," JBL, 96–2 [1977], 241–56).

11 John sees another (*allo,* "one of a similar kind") beast rising from the earth. This second beast completes the triumvirate of evil—the dragon, the sea beast, and the land beast. The land beast is subservient to the beast from the sea and seems utterly dedicated to promoting not himself but the wounded beast from the sea. Elsewhere the land beast is called the "false prophet" (16:13; 19:20; 20:10). As with the first beast, identification is a problem. That this beast comes from the land rather than the sea may simply indicate his diversity from the first, while other references stress their collusion.

A survey of the history of interpretation reveals in general, as with the first beast, two main lines: the beast either represents a power or a movement, or describes a human being allied with the Antichrist at the close of the age (cf. Berkouwer, *Return of Christ,* pp. 260f.). Early Christian interpreters, such as Irenaeus (second century), who identify the first beast not with Rome but with a personal Antichrist, find in the second beast the "armour-bearer" of the first, who employs the demonic forces to work magic and deceive the inhabitants of the earth (*Contra Haereses* 5.28.2). Hippolytus (third century) identified the second beast as "the kingdom of the Antichrist" (*Christ and Anti-Christ,* ANF, 5:214, par. 48). Victorinus (late third century) speaks of this beast as the false prophet who will work magic before the Antichrist. Victorinus then blurs the identification of the second beast with the first in further remarks (*Apocalypse* 13.11–13). Andreas (sixth century) reports that in his day "some say this [second] beast is the Antichrist, but it seems to others that he is Satan, and his two horns are the Antichrist and the false prophet" (Swete, p. 166).

Calvin and Luther, as well as other Reformers, drawing on earlier traditions, were led to identify this beast with the papacy or specific popes. Berkouwer notes that while the Reformers may have been mistaken as to their actual identifications, they were right in seeing the beast as a present threat and not some entity awaiting a yet future manifestation (*Return of Christ,* pp. 262–63). Most modern commentators, following the Nero redivivus view of the first beast, identify this beast as the priesthood of the imperial cultus (Charles, *Commentary on Revelation* 1:357). Alford and others would extend the symbolism to all ages and see in the second beast "the sacerdotal persecuting power, pagan or Christian," and would call special attention to the Roman papacy, though by no means limiting it to this priesthood (Alf, 4: 679). While recognizing that no view is without problems, the following discussion takes the position that the land beast is John's way of describing the false prophets of the Olivet Discourse (Matt 24:24; Mark 13:22). This identification is consistent with the previously stated view of the sea beast as describing not just a specific political reality but the world-wide anti-God system of Satan and its manifestation in periodic, historical human antichrists. The land beast is the antithesis to the true prophets of Christ symbolized by the two witnesses in chapter 11 (cf. Berkouwer, *Return of Christ,* ch. 9, for a full and helpful discussion of the whole Antichrist issue). If the thought of a nonpersonal antichrist and false prophet seems to contradict the verse that describes them as being cast alive into the lake of fire (19:20), consider that "death" and "Hades" (nonpersons) are also thrown into the lake of fire (20:14).

The reference to the "two horns like a lamb" can be understood as highlighting the beast's imitative role with respect to the true Lamb in the rest of the book (e.g., 5:6ff.; 13:8; 14:1). Could the two horns be in contrast to the two witnesses in chapter 11? Since one of the primary characteristics of this second beast is his deceptive activities (v.14; 19:20), his appearance as a lamb would contribute to the confusion over the beast's true identity. If the land beast represents satanic false teaching and false prophets, their evil is intensified because of its deceptive similarity to the truth. Even though the beast is like the Lamb, in reality he is evil because "he [speaks] like a dragon," i.e., he teaches heresy. Jesus gave such a twofold description of false prophets in the Sermon on the Mount: "Watch out for false prophets. They come to you in sheep's clothing, but inwardly they are ferocious wolves" (Matt 7:15). On the other hand, the lamblikeness may simply be a reference to the beast's gentle outward manner in contrast to his true identity as a fierce dragon.

12 The activity of the land beast is repeatedly described as that of promoting the first beast's worship (v.14). Could this be the kind of activity referred to in the reference to the false prophets in Pergamum and Thyatira seducing the servants of God to idolatry (2:14–15, 20, 24)? NIV misses a nuance by rendering the Greek *enōpion* ("in behalf of") as if the second beast exercised all the authority of the first beast merely as the latter's representative. The preposition *enōpion* occurs no fewer than thirty-four times in Revelation and in every instance means "in the presence of" or "before." The same word is used of the two witnesses in 11:4: "These are the two olive trees and the two lampstands that stand before [*enōpion*] the Lord of the earth." Kiddle points out how this word in such a context indicates "prophetic readiness to do the bidding of God, and with the authority inalienable from divine communion" (p. 255). As the antitheses of the two witnesses, the false prophets derive their authority and ministry from the first beast.

13 One of the strategies the land beast uses to deceive people into following the first beast is the performance of "miraculous signs" (*sēmeion;* see discussion at 12:1). The ability of the Satan-inspired prophets to perform deceiving miracles is attested elsewhere in Revelation and in other parts of the Bible (16:14; 19:20; Deut 13:1–5; Matt 7:22; 24:24; Mark 13:22; 2 Thess 2:9). Distinguishing between the true and false prophets has always been difficult but not impossible. The followers of Jesus must be constantly alert to discern the spirits (1 John 4:1–3).

The reference to "fire . . . from heaven" deserves brief comment. It could refer to the fire that the prophet Elijah called down from heaven (1 Kings 18:38) or to the fire coming out of the mouths of the two witnesses (Rev 11:5). Either reference is preferable to the attempt to see here some indication of the imperial cult priests of Rome. John may intend a deliberate contrast between the true witnesses' use of fire and its use by the false prophets (11:5; cf. Luke 9:54).

A quite elaborate theory was worked out by E. Watson and B. Hamilton that connects the fire of God with the true word of God and the Holy Spirit's witness (such as at Pentecost [Acts 2:3]). The false fire would then be a reference to pseudo-charismatic gifts that create a counterfeit church community whose allegiance is to the Antichrist (cited by Minear, *I Saw a New Earth,* pp. 124–27). (In regard to "the fire . . . from heaven," remember the priests Nadab and Abihu, who offered "unauthorized fire" before the Lord, apparently by their own self-will, and received God's judgment in the form of "fire" that "consumed them" [Lev 10:1–2].) In any case, the reference to fire from heaven indicates that no mighty deed is too hard for these false prophets, because they derive their power from the Antichrist and the dragon. Christ's true servants are not to be deceived by even spectacular miracles the false prophets may perform. Such miracles in themselves are no evidence of the Holy Spirit.

14a Here more must be involved than the deceptions of the imperial priesthood. The quality of the miracles deceives those who follow the beast—viz., "the inhabitants of the earth." "Deceive" (*planaō*) is John's term for the activity of false teachers who lead people to worship gods other than the true and living God (2:20; 12:9; 18:23; 19:20; 20:3, 8, 10; cf. 1 John 2:26; 3:7; 4:6; also Matt 24:11, 24).

14b–15 The second beast orders the setting up of an "image" (*eikōn*) of the first beast. Elsewhere, the worship of the first beast, his "image," and his "mark" are inseparable (14:9, 11; 15:2; 16:2; 19:20; 20:4). The *eikōn* of something is not a mere copy but partakes in its reality and in fact constitutes its reality (TDNT, 2: 389). Most interpreters, following the Roman-emperor exegesis, readily identify the image with the statue of Caesar and refer the "breath" and speaking of the image to the magic and ventriloquism of the imperial priests. But as has been argued earlier (see comments on vv. 1, 11), serious questions can be raised against such an exegesis of John's language, which is much more theologically descriptive than the Roman hypothesis allows. This is not to deny that the imperial worship could be included as one form of the beast worship. But the reality described is much larger and far more transhistorical than the mere worship of a bust of Caesar. John, however, would not deny that these realities have their historical manifestations, for in every age the beast kills those who will not worship his image. In terms reminiscent of the great golden image Nebuchadnezzar made and commanded every person to worship on the threat of death (Dan 3:1–11), John describes the world-wide system of idolatry represented by the first beast and the false prophet(s) who promotes it. John describes this reality as a blasphemous and idolatrous system that produces a breach of the first two commandments (Exod 20:3–5).

In speaking about giving "breath" (*pneuma*) to the image, John implies the activity of the false prophets in reviving idolatrous worship, giving it the appearance of vitality, reality, and power. Curiously, the two witnesses were also said to receive "breath" (*pneuma*) (11:11). The idolatrous satanic system has the power of death over those who worship the true God and the Lamb. The same "image" tried to kill Daniel and his friends, killed many of the prophets of God, crucified the Lord Jesus, put to death Stephen (Acts 7:60), James the apostle (Acts 12:1–2), and Antipas (Rev 2:13). Thus he demonstrated to his followers the apparent healing of his wounded head. To limit the image to the bust of Caesar or to some future statue or ventriloquistic device constricts John's deeper meaning and eliminates the present significance of his language.

The contemporary phenomenon of the Korean religious leader Sun Myung Moon and his official interpreter and prophetess, Young Oon Kim, embody what seems to be a clear example of John's teaching about antichrists and false prophets (cf. Young Oon Kim, *Divine Principle and Its Application* [Washington, D.C.: The Holy Spirit Association for the Unification of World Christianity, 1969]). Moon is being heralded as the "Lord of the Second Advent" by Kim and others. His whole stance clearly embodies heresy and blasphemy and many are being deceived into following him and his teaching (cf. Harry J. Jaeger, Jr., "By the Light of a Masterly Moon," CT [19 December 1975], 13–16). Moon's idolatrous image receives continual breath by worship from his followers.

16 The immediate effect of the worship of the beast involves receiving a mark on the right hand or forehead. By comparing the other passages where the beast, image, mark, and name of the beast are mentioned, it seems clear that the "mark" (*charagma*) is an equivalent expression to the "name of the beast" (13:17; 14:11; also 14:9; 15:2; 16:2; 19:20; 20:4), which is also the "number of his name" (13:17; 15:2).

In Greek *charagma* may refer to a work of art such as a carved image of a god (Acts 17:29), to any written inscription or document, to the "bite" of a snake, to a red "seal" (an impress) of the emperor and other official attestors of documents, or to a "brand" on camels indicating ownership (TDNT, 9: 416; MM, p. 683; Deiss BS, pp. 240–47). No evidence, however, can be cited from the ancient world where a *charagma* is placed on a *person,* let alone on the "right hand" or on the "forehead," though a seal (*sphragis*) was customarily put on slaves and soldiers. This lack of concrete evidence has led Swete, who is committed to the Roman-emperor view, to reject any connection between the *charagma* and a literal mark of the emperor. He argues that as the servants of God receive on their foreheads the impress of the divine seal (7:3; 14:1), so the servants of the beast are marked with the stamp of the beast (p. 170). In other words, the *charagma* is not a literal impress seal, certificate, or similar mark of identification, but it is John's way of symbolically describing authentic ownership and loyalty. Those who worship the beast have his *charagma* or brand of ownership on them, as the followers of Jesus have the brand of God's possession on them. The fact that the Babylonian Talmud prohibits the Jew from wearing the tephillim (prayer scroll) on the forehead or on the hand may lie in the background as to why John uses these two places to describe the idolatrous mark (*Megillah* 24b).

17 Those having the *charagma* ("mark") can "buy or sell," those without it cannot. This statement apparently refers to some sort of socio-economic sanctions that would, of course, affect the social and economic condition of Christians in the world. Earlier, John alluded to certain such conditions. Smyrna was a greatly persecuted church and was "poor" (2:9); Philadelphia was of "little strength" (3:8); those faithful to Christ in the Great Tribulation are seen in heaven as never again hungering (7:16), while the great harlot grows rich and wallows in luxury (18:3). Other NT writers also apparently refer to socio-economic sanctions practiced against Christians (Rom 15:26; Heb 10:34). Such a sanction was more social than political, imposed not by the government but by the communities. When governmental Rome took official notice of an illegal religion, it was always by criminal charges in the courts, not by economic sanctions (Caird, p. 173).

18 In v.17, John indicates that the *charagma* ("mark") is the name of the beast or the number of his name. He now reveals the number of the beast: "His number is 666." The list of conjectures concerning the meaning of the number (or its alternates—see Notes) is almost as long as the list of commentators on the book. Taking their cue from the words "let him calculate the number of the beast," most of these interpreters have tried to play the ancient Hebrew game of gematria or, as it is called by the Greeks, *isopsēphia*. Ancient languages, including Hebrew and Greek, use standard letters from their alphabets as numerical signs. For example, *α* (alpha) in Greek can represent the number one, *β* (bēta) the number two, *ιβ* (iōta bēta) twelve, etc. A series of letters could form a word and at the same time indicate a number. Gematria took many forms and consisted in trying to guess the word from the number or trying to connect one word with another that had the same numerical value. On the walls of Pompeii, there are some graffiti, dated no later than A.D. 79, that illuminate the practice. One reads: "Amerimnus thought upon his lady Harmonia for good. The number of her honorable name is 45 (*με* [mu epsilon])." The key to the puzzle seems to be in the word "Harmonia," which was probably not the girl's actual name but refers to the nine Muses (the goddesses of song and poetry); and 45 is the sum of all the digits from 1 to 9 (E.M. Blaiklock, *The Archaeology of the New Testament* [Grand Rapids: Zondervan, 1970], p. 131). Another runs: "I love her whose number is 545 (*φμε* [phi mu epsilon])" (Deiss LAE, p. 277). In these cases, the number conceals a name, and the mystery is perhaps known for certain only by the two lovers themselves.

Similarly, the Jews (esp. Hasidim) used Hebrew alphabetical numbers to indicate concealed names and mysterious connections with other words of the same numerical value. For example, the Hebrew word *nāḥāš* ("serpent") has the same numerical value as the Hebrew word *māšîaḥ* ("Messiah") (358). From this it was argued that one of the names of the Messiah was "serpent." Some suggest that this may relate to Moses' lifting up the "serpent" in the wilderness (cf. Num 21; John 3:14). (For these and many other examples, see William Barclay, "Great Themes of the New Testament. Part V. Revelation xiii (continued)," ExpT, 70, [1959], 292–96.)

Thus it is not difficult to understand why most commentators have understood John's words "Let him calculate the number. . . . His number is 666" to be an invitation to the reader to play gematria and discover the identity of the beast. This interpretation is not new. Irenaeus (second century) mentions that many names of contemporary persons and entities were being offered in his day as solutions to this number mystery. Yet he cautioned against the practice and believed that the name of the Antichrist was deliberately concealed because he did not exist in John's day. The name would be secret till the time of his future appearance in the world. Irenaeus expressly refutes the attempt of many to identify the name with any of the Roman emperors. He feels, however, that the gematria approach is John's intended meaning but warns the church against endless speculations (*Contra Haereses* 29.30).

Irenaeus's fear was not misplaced. Endless speculation is just what has happened in the history of the interpretation of v. 18, as Barclay has well documented it ("Great Themes," pp. 295–96). Barclay himself (following Charles, perhaps) is quite certain that the only possible solution is to use Hebrew letters, and so he comes up with "Neron Caesar," which equals 666. This identification is linked with the view that the Antichrist would be Nero redivivus (see introduction to 13:1). Yet this use of Hebrew letters requires a spelling for "caesar" that is not normal for the word (*qsr*). However, in a publication of an Aramaic document from the Dead Sea cave at Murabbaat, dated to the second year of the emperor Nero, the name is spelled *nrwn qsr,* as required by the theory (BASOR, 170 [April 1963], 65).

More recently the whole line of Nero redivivus interpretation has been seriously challenged by Minear and others (*I Saw a New Earth,* ch. 5; cf. commentary at introduction to 13:1). In the first place, none of the key words of v. 18—name, number, man, 666—requires the effort to find an emperor (or future political dictator) with a name whose letters will add up to 666. The sheer disagreement and confusion created through the years by the gematria method should have long ago warned the church that it was on the wrong track. After surveying all the evidence, Rühle says, "It may be said that all the solutions proposed are unsatisfactory" (TDNT, 1: 464). If John was seeking to illumine believers so that they could penetrate the deception of the beast as well as to contrast the beast and his followers with the Lamb and his followers (14:1ff.), he has clearly failed—that is, if he intends for us to play the gematria game. How Nero could fit these requirements is, on closer examination, difficult to see. If some Christians of John's time did succumb to Caesar worship, it was due less to their being deceived than to their fear of death. Moreover, several exegetical factors argue strongly for another sense of John's words.

In the first place, nowhere does John use gematria as a method. Everywhere, however, he gives symbolic significance to numbers (e.g., seven churches, seals, trumpets, and bowls; twenty-four elders; 144,000 sealed; 144 cubits for the New Jerusalem, etc.). Furthermore, in 15:2 the victors have triumphed over three enemies: the beast, his image, and *the number of his name,* which suggests a symbolic significance connected with idolatry and blasphemy rather than victory over a mere puzzle solution of correctly identifying someone's name.

John seeks to give "wisdom" (*sophia*) and "insight" (*nous*) to believers as to the true identity of their enemy. Curiously, while Mounce favors the gematria explanation, citing that it is a commonly used device in apocalyptic literature and tended to protect the user against sedition (both assertions made without citing any evidence), he ends his discussion by conceding in the light of the confusion that "it seems best to conclude that John intended only his intimate associates to be able to decipher the number" (*Revelation,* pp. 264–65). A similar use of *nous* and *sophia* occurs in 17:9, where John calls attention to the identity of the beast ridden by the harlot. What John seems to be asking for in both cases is divine discernment and not mathematical ingenuity! Believers need to penetrate the deception of the beast. John's reference to his number will help them to recognize his true character and identity.

The statement "it is man's number" (*arithmos . . . anthrōpou*) further identifies the kind of number the beast represents. Does John mean that the beast is a man, that he has a human name? In 21:17 John uses similar words for the angel: "by man's measurement, which the angel was using." The statement is difficult. How can the measure be both "man's" and at the same time of an "angel"? Kiddle seems to sense the peculiarity of the statement in 21:17 and suggests that John is attempting to call attention to some inner meaning in the number of the size of the height of the wall in respect to the size of the city. The meaning perhaps is a mild polemic against first-century tendencies to venerate angels unduly by stating that both men and angels can understand and enter the future city (see comments at 21:15–21). In any case, the statement "it is man's number" alerts the reader to some hidden meaning in 666. From this it may be concluded that the number of the beast is linked to humanity. Why would it be necessary for John to emphasize this relationship unless he assumed that his readers might have understood the beast to be other worldly without any connection to humanity. Might it be, then, that the statement signifies that the satanic beast, which is the great enemy of the church, manifests itself in human form? Thus as the similar phrase in 21:17 linked the angelic and the human, so here it joins the satanic with the human.

Finally, how are we to understand 666? The best way is to follow Minear (*I Saw a New Earth*, ch. 5) and Newman ("Domitian Hypothesis," pp. 133ff.) and return to one of the most ancient interpretations, that of Irenaeus. Irenaeus proposed (while still holding to a personal Antichrist) that the number indicates that the beast is the sum of "all apostate power," a concentrate of six thousand years of unrighteousness, wickedness, deception, and false prophecy. He states that "the digit six, being adhered to throughout, indicates the recapitulations of that prophecy, taken in its full extent, which occurred at the beginning, during the intermediate periods, and which shall take place at the end." Irenaeus also held that the wound of the beast has reference to Genesis 3:13ff. The Messiah has freed men from this wound by wounding Satan and by giving them the power to inflict wounds on the beast by overcoming his blasphemy (*Contra Haereses* 5.29.30).

The significance of the name of the beast is abundantly clear in Revelation (12:3; 13:1–6; 14:11; 17:3ff.). Wherever there is blasphemy, there the beast's name is found. The number 666 is the heaping up of the number 6. Minear adds, "Because of its contrast with 7 we may be content with an interpretation which sees in 666 an allusion to incompleteness, to the demonic parody in the perfection of 7, to the deceptiveness of the almost-perfect, to the idolatrous blasphemy exemplified by false worshipers, or to the dramatic moment between the sixth and the seventh items in a vision cycle (cf. seals, trumpets, bowls, and kings 17:10)" (*I Saw a New Earth*, p. 258). This interpretation of 666 as a symbolic number referring to the unholy trinity of evil or to the human imperfect imitation of God rather than a cipher of a name is not restricted to Minear. It has been held by a long line of conservative commentators—A.C. Gaebelein (*The Revelation* [New York: Our Hope, 1915]), J.A. Seiss (*The Apocalypse* [Grand Rapids: Zondervan, 1957]), J.F. Walvoord, T.F. Torrance (*The Apocalypse Today* [Grand Rapids: Eerdmans, 1959]), L. Morris, J. Ellul (*The Apocalypse: The Book of Revelation* [New York: Seabury, 1977]), and others.

Notes

1 In many critical editions of the Gr. text, the sentence "And the dragon stood on the shore of the sea" is made v.18 of ch. 12 rather than v.1 of ch. 13 following the reading ἐστάθη (*estathē*, "he stood") instead of ἐστάθην (*estathēn*, "I stood"). The third person reading is well supported and may be correct, though the first person yields good sense and the MS evidence is not such as to eliminate it from consideration. A single letter in the Gr. text makes the difference.

10 A major textual problem in the last half of this verse presents a difficulty to understanding its meaning. The problem involves whether the first reference to the verb ἀποκτείνω (*apokteinō*, "kill") should be read with the majority as ἀποκτενεῖ (*apoktenei*, "will kill," a future indicative) or with A as ἀποκτανθῆναι (*apoktanthēnai*, "be killed," an aorist passive infinitive). KJV, RSV, Phillips, NASB all follow the first reading and render it "If any one kills with the sword." Combining this with the last phrase, the latter part of the verse yields either a warning directed toward Christians for them not to turn to violence and killing to vindicate themselves or a promise of requital to believers that their persecutors will be judged by God.

If, on the other hand, we follow the reading of A (preferred by Bruce M. Metzger [*A Textual Commentary on the Greek New Testament* (New York: UBS, 1971), p. 750] and Charles [*Commentary on Revelation*], 1:355), the translation will be as in NIV (cf. NEB, TEV). This yields the sense that Christians who are destined by God for death must submit to his will and not resist the oppressor. It is an appeal to loyalty. In adopting this reading and sense, Charles points out that the construction in A is the same idiomatic Heb. as that in 12:7 (where see note) and yields this sense: "If anyone must be killed with the sword, with the sword he must be killed." Metzger argues that the majority-text reading reflects an altered text influenced by the retribution idea found in Matt 26:52: "For all who draw the sword will die by the sword." No entirely satisfactory solution is available.

11 A curious interpretation of the first and second beasts is offered by Ford (pp. 227–30). She holds that the first beast is the emperor Vespasian and peculiarly identifies the second beast tentatively with Flavius Josephus, the renegade Jew and historian. While Ford's attempt is not without interesting parallels, it founders chiefly on the fact that she should be the first to suggest it. On such a premise, how could we explain the fact that Josephus's writings were not preserved by Jews but by Christians if he were, in fact, recognized as one of their great enemies?

16 The apocalyptic Pss Sol refers to the "mark of God" on the righteous and the "mark of destruction" on the wicked (15.8).

17 When John says "the name of the beast or the number of his name," the "or" (ἢ [*ē*]) may signify mere interchangeability so that the name and/or the mark are equivalent (BAG, p. 342).

18 Instead of 666, which is strongly supported, one good MS and a few lesser witnesses have 616, which is explained as either a scribal slip or a deliberate alteration to give the numbers necessary for the Gr. "Caesar god" (Deiss LAE, p. 278, n.3), or "Gaios Caesar" (Caligula) (Barclay, "Great Themes," p. 296), or the Latin form of Nero Caesar (Metzger, *A Textual Commentary*, p. 752). Irenaeus strongly deplored this 616 reading as heretical and deceptive (*Contra Haereses* 5.30).

A few MSS read 646 or 747 according to Hoskier (H.C. Hoskier, *Concerning the Text of the Apocalypse*, 2 vols. [London: Bernard Quaritch, 1929], 2:364).

---

3. *The Lamb and the 144,000*

14:1–5

[1]Then I looked, and there before me was the Lamb, standing on Mount Zion, and with him 144,000 who had his name and his Father's name written on their foreheads. [2]And I heard a sound from heaven like the roar of rushing waters and like a loud peal of thunder. The sound I heard was like that of harpists playing their harps. [3]And they sang a new song before the throne and before the four living creatures and the elders. No one could learn the song except the 144,000 who had been redeemed from the earth. [4]These are those who did not defile themselves with women, for they kept themselves pure. They follow the Lamb wherever he goes. They were purchased from among men and offered as firstfruits to God and the Lamb. [5]No lie was found in their mouths; they are blameless.

The two previous chapters have prepared Christians for the reality that as the end draws near they will be harassed and sacrificed like sheep. This section shows that their sacrifice is not meaningless. A glance back at chapter 7 reminds us that there the 144,000 were merely sealed; here, however, they are seen as already delivered. When the floods have passed, Mount Zion appears high above the waters; the Lamb is on the throne of glory, surrounded by the triumphant songs of his own; the gracious presence of God fills the universe (Lilje).

Chapter 14 briefly answers two pressing questions: What becomes of those who refuse to receive the mark of the beast and are killed (vv.1–5)? What happens to the beast and his servants (vv.6–20)?

1 The Lamb standing on Mount Zion is contrasted to the dragon standing on the shifting sands of the seashore (13:1). Although the rapid movement mood of the previous chapters gives way to one of victorious rest (1–5, 13), activity continues because the battle between the dragon and the woman (cf. 12:11) is still going on. Immediately the question arises whether the 144,000 here are the same as those in chapter 7. The only reason for viewing the 144,000 in chapter 7 differently is that here they are described as "firstfruits" and "pure" who "did not defile themselves with women" (v.4). The two-group viewpoint has been defended especially by some Roman Catholic exegetes but has been effectively refuted by other Roman Catholic exegetes (see comments at v.4 and Heidt, pp. 94–95; Ford, p. 234).

The problem of the location of this group of 144,000 is more complex. Mount Zion may refer to the hilly area in southeast Jerusalem, the temple mount, the whole city of Jerusalem, or, as in postexilic days, the whole land of Judah and the whole Israelite nation (ZPEB, 5:1063–65). In the prophetic tradition, Zion came to symbolize the place where the Messiah would gather to himself a great company of the redeemed (Ps 48:1ff.; Isa 24:23; Joel 2:32; Obad 17, 21; Mic 4:1, 7; Zech 14:10). Likewise, in late Jewish apocalyptic literature there is a similar idea: "But he shall stand upon the summit of Mount Zion. . . . And whereas thou didst see that he summoned and gathered to himself another multitude which was peaceable, these are the ten tribes" (4 Ezra 13:35, 39–40; also 4 Ezra 2:42 is similar). Zion may here symbolize the strength and security that belong to the people of God (Swete).

In the seven NT references to Zion, five occur in OT quotations. Of the other two, one is here in Revelation and the remaining reference (Heb 12:22–23) implies a connection between Mount Zion and the church: "But you have come to Mount Zion, to the heavenly Jerusalem, the city of the living God . . . to the church of the firstborn." Some, connecting the reference in Hebrews to the one here in Revelation 14:1, have argued for the heavenly location of the 144,000 (Kiddle). Beckwith's view, by contrast, is significant: "The 'mount Zion, the city of the living God, the heavenly Jerusalem' in Heb 12:22, the 'Jerusalem that is above' in Gal 4:26, denote the perfect archetype or pattern of the earthly, which in Hebrew thought now exists in heaven, and in the end is to descend in full realization: they are not designations of heaven, the place of God and his hosts" (p. 647). For Beckwith and others, Mount Zion refers to the earthly seat of the messianic or millennial kingdom (also Beasley-Murray, Charles, Walvoord). Whether this Mount Zion has any connection (as to locality) with ancient and historical Zion, John does not say. At any rate, that the 144,000 are singing "before the throne" (v.3) is not an objection to seeing them as the earthly Zion; it is not the redeemed who are singing but the angelic harpists (Alf, 4:684).

The 144,000 have on their foreheads the names of the Father and the Lamb, showing that they belong to God, not the beast. In 7:3ff., the elect group has the seal of God on their foreheads, linking them to this group in chapter 14, while the further description that "they follow the Lamb" (v.4) may show their connection with the second group in 7:9ff. (see esp. 7:17: "lead them"). One of the most beautiful and assuring promises in the whole book is that God's servants will have his name on their foreheads (cf. 3:12; 22:4).

Chapter 14 advances the drama a step further than chapter 7. While the members of the multitude are the same, the circumstances in which they are seen have altered (Charles). In chapter 7 the whole company of God's people are sealed (7:1–8), readied for the satanic onslaught, and then a company (a martyred portion?) are seen in heaven serving before the throne of God (7:9ff.); whereas in chapter 14, the whole body of the redeemed is seen (resurrected?) with the Lamb in the earthly eschatological kingdom. The repetition of the reference to the 144,000 may also be a liturgical phenomenon, a chief characteristic of the book—either the repetition of the introit or of antiphons.

The background of the scene (vv.1–5) may reflect John's reinterpretation of Psalm 2, which he had alluded to elsewhere and which describes the battle between the rebellious nations and God, with God suppressing the revolt by enthroning his Son on Mount Zion (Caird). John, however, does not see the warrior-king the writer of Psalm 2 hoped for, but he sees the Lamb and those who repeated his victory over the enemy by their submission (his name on their forehead). Psalm 76 may also be part of the background, where Zion is the symbol of the defeat of God's enemies and the salvation of his people.

2 The "sound" John hears is probably a "voice" (*phōnē*) as in 1:15. It is important to recognize that this voice is not that of the redeemed; it is a loud angelic chorus (cf. 5:11), sounding like "the roar of rushing waters," like "a loud peal of thunder," and like "harpists playing their harps" (1:15; 5:8; 6:1; 19:1, 6; cf. comments on 5:8 and note on 5:9–10). Charles indicates that grammatically the sentence is Hebraistic. Again the scene is liturgical, emphasizing the connection between the earthly victory and the heavenly throne.

3 This "new song" should be related to the "new song" in 5:9, also sung by the angelic choirs (q.v.). It is the song of redemption and vindication. What was seen in chapter 5 as secured for the redeemed by Christ's death (i.e., that "they will reign on the earth" [v.10]) has now been realized on Mount Zion. In the one further reference to a song (*ōdē*) in Revelation, the redeemed "victors" now sing "the song [*ōdē*] of Moses . . . and the song of the Lamb" (15:3), which may also relate to the new song of chapters 5 and 14 (see comments at 15:3). This heavenly example of worship may help us understand and appreciate Paul's references to songs inspired by the Spirit (*ōdais pneumatikais*) and sung in the first-century congregations (Eph 5:19; Col 3:16). Also instructive are the OT references to a "new song" (Pss 33:3; 40:3; 96:1; 144:9; 149:1; Isa 42:10). A "new song," in consequence of some mighty deed of God, comes from a fresh impulse of gratitude and joy in the heart (KD, *Psalms*, 1:402). The angels sing a new song because now the victors themselves have become victorious. We are reminded again of the Passover motif (Exod 15:1ff.).

While the angels sing, only the 144,000 can "learn" the new song, for they alone of earth's inhabitants have experienced God's mighty deed of victory over the beast through their ordeal of suffering and death. Possibly, the word "learn" (*manthanō*) in this context may mean to "hear deeply" (TDNT, 4:407). In the Gospel of John, the word is used in the sense of a deep listening to divine revelation that results in learning: "Everyone who listens to the Father and learns from him comes to me" (John 6:45).

The 144,000 who were "redeemed" or "purchased" (*agorazō*) from "the earth" or "from among men" (v.4) must be the same as those "purchased" (*agorazō*) from all the earth's peoples in 5:9 and those sealed in 7:4–8, who have washed their garments in the blood of the Lamb (7:14ff.).

4 John's most difficult statement about this group is that they did "not defile themselves with women." Does he mean that this group consists only of men who had never married? Or should it be understood as referring to spiritual apostasy or cult prostitution? It is unlikely that "defiled" (*molynō*) refers merely to sexual intercourse since nowhere in Scripture does intercourse within marriage constitute sinful defilement (cf. Heb 13:4). On the other hand, the word "defiled" is found in the Letter of Aristeas (15.2) in connection with the promiscuous intercourse practiced by the Gentiles that defiled them but from which the Jews have been separated by the commandments of God (R.H. Charles, *The Apocrypha and Pseudepigrapha of the Old Testament*, 2 vols. [New York: Oxford, 1913], 2:109). Therefore, the words can refer only to adultery or fornication; and this fact, in turn, establishes "pure" as the meaning of *parthenoi* ("virgins") in this context (NIV is paraphrastic here, but accurately so). In fact, *parthenos* can be used of formerly married persons in this figurative way and is so used of widows by Ignatius (*Smyrna* 13). The same masculine plural word (*parthenous*) is used in the LXX of Lamentations 2:10, which Ford suggests may be in parallel with "the elders of the daughter of Zion" (p. 242).

Kiddle thinks the reference is to actual celibacy, which alone could fit a man to be a sacrificial lamb for God (p. 268; also Glasson, p. 85). Caird connects the purity reference with holy-war regulations for soldiers who were ceremonially unclean because of sexual reasons (Deut 23:9–10; 1 Sam 21:5; 2 Sam 11:11). Each of these views founders because of the assumption that "uncleanness" (*akathartos*) is the equivalent of "defile" (*molyno*). Such an assumption not only fails on linguistic grounds but involves us in a scriptural contradiction, i.e., that the marriage bed is defiling and sinful. It is better, then, to relate the reference to purity to the defilement of idolatry. In fact, John seems to use *molyno* this way elsewhere of cult prostitution (3:4; cf. 2:14, 20, 22).

The group as a whole has remained faithful to Christ; "they follow the Lamb wherever he goes" in obedient discipleship. They are purchased by Christ's blood and offered to God as a holy and pure sacrifice of firstfruits. Surely this symbolically implies that the bride of Christ must be pure from idolatry. Paul, likewise, uses this figure: "I promised you to one husband, to Christ, so that I might present you as a pure virgin to him" (2 Cor 11:2–3).

Those spoken of in v.3 are "firstfruits" (*aparchē*) (v.4) presented to God. The word can have two meanings. It may designate the initial ingathering of the farmer, after which others come. So it may mean a pledge or downpayment with more to follow. Though it is difficult to find this sense of the word in the OT, it seems to be its meaning in several NT references (Rom 8:23; 11:16?; cf. 1 Cor 15:20; 16:15). On the other hand, in the usual OT sense and alternate NT usage, *aparchē* means simply an offering to God in the sense of being separated to him and sanctified (wholly consecrated), where no later addition is made, because the firstfruits constitutes the whole (Num 5:9 [NIV, "sacred contributions"]; Deut 18:4; 26:2; Jer 2:3; James 1:18). That this is John's intended sense is evident from the expression "offered as firstfruits to God."

5 The "lie" that would bring "blame" refers to the blasphemy of the beast worshipers who deny the Father and the Son and ascribe vitality to the beast by believing his heresies and worshiping his image (21:27; 22:15; cf. John 8:44–45; Rom 1:25; 2 Thess 2:9–11; 1 John 2:4, 21–22, 27).

Notes

---

4 The extensive discussion of this passage in Beckwith's commentary is especially helpful (pp. 646ff.).

---

4. *The harvest of the earth*

14:6–20

[6]Then I saw another angel flying in midair, and he had the eternal gospel to
proclaim to those who live on the earth—to every nation, tribe, language and
people. [7]He said in a loud voice, "Fear God and give him glory, because the hour
of his judgment has come. Worship him who made the heavens, the earth, the sea
and the springs of water."
[8]A second angel followed and said, "Fallen! Fallen is Babylon the Great, which
made all the nations drink the maddening wine of her adulteries."
[9]A third angel followed them and said in a loud voice: "If anyone worships the
beast and his image and receives his mark on the forehead or on the hand, [10]he,
too, will drink of the wine of God's fury, which has been poured full strength into
the cup of his wrath. He will be tormented with burning sulfur in the presence of
the holy angels and of the Lamb. [11]And the smoke of their torment rises for ever
and ever. There is no rest day or night for those who worship the beast and his
image, or for anyone who receives the mark of his name." [12]This calls for patient
endurance on the part of the saints who obey God's commandments and remain
faithful to Jesus.
[13]Then I heard a voice from heaven say, "Write: Blessed are the dead who die
in the Lord from now on."
"Yes," says the Spirit, "they will rest from their labor, for their deeds will follow
them."
[14]I looked, and there before me was a white cloud, and seated on the cloud was
one "like a son of man" with a crown of gold on his head and a sharp sickle in his
hand. [15]Then another angel came out of the temple and called in a loud voice to
him who was sitting on the cloud, "Take your sickle and reap, because the time
to reap has come, for the harvest of the earth is ripe." [16]So he that was seated on
the cloud swung his sickle over the earth, and the earth was harvested.
[17]Another angel came out of the temple in heaven, and he too had a sharp sickle.
[18]Still another angel, who had charge of the fire, came from the altar and called in
a loud voice to him who had the sharp sickle, "Take your sharp sickle and gather
the clusters of grapes from the earth's vine, because its grapes are ripe." [19]The
angel swung his sickle on the earth, gathered its grapes and threw them into the
great winepress of God's wrath. [20]They were trampled in the winepress outside the
city, and blood flowed out of the press, rising as high as the horses' bridles for a
distance of 1,600 stadia.

This section forms a transition from the scene of the saints' final triumph (14:1–5) to the seven bowls (16:1ff.), which depict the final judgments on the enemies of the Lamb. As such, it forms a consoling counterpart to the first vision as it assures the 144,000 that God will judge the beast, his followers, and his world-wide system—Babylon.

6–7 The first angel announces that there is still hope, for even at this crucial moment in history God is seeking to reclaim the beast followers by issuing a message appealing to the people of the world to "fear God . . . and worship him." That this appeal is called a "gospel" (*euangelion*) has raised a question. How can it be good news? Yet is not the intent of the gospel message that men should fear God and worship him? Is it not the "eternal" gospel because it announces eternal life (John 3:16)? Could this be John's way of showing the final fulfillment of Mark 13:10? Let us not fail to see how in the NT the announcement of divine judgment is never separated from the proclamation of God's mercy.

The reference to the coming of the hour of judgment (v.7) supports the view that there is chronological progression in Revelation and that not everything described by John is simultaneous (see comments at 15:1). This is the first reference in the book to the "judgment [*krisis*] of God" (16:7; 18:10; 19:2), though the "wrath" (*thymos* or *orgē*) of God, which appears to be a synonymous term (v.19), has been mentioned earlier (6:16–17; 11:18; 14:8, 10; 15:1; cf. 16:1, 19; 18:3; 19:15).

8 In anticipation of a more extended description in chapters 17 and 18, the Fall of Babylon, the great anti-God system of idolatry, is announced. The actual fall does not occur until the final bowl judgment (16:19). There may be in 11:8 a previous allusion to Babylon as the "great city" (cf. 17:18).

9–12 The explicit reference to the certain judgment of the beast worshipers ties this section to chapter 13. Through an OT figure of eschatological judgment, unmixed wine (not diluted with water) in the cup of God's wrath (Ps 75:8; Jer 25:15) and "burning sulfur" (Isa 30:33; 34:8–10; cf. Gen 19:24; Rev 19:20; 20:10; 21:8), John describes God's judgment inflicted on those who refused his truth and worshiped a lie (Rom 1:18, 25). For those who drink Babylon's cup (v.8), the Lord will give his own cup of wrath.

The reference to "torment" (*basanizō;* cf. 9:5; 11:10; 12:2; 20:10) has troubled some commentators since the torment takes place "in the presence . . . of the Lamb" (so Ford, p. 237). Thus Glasson calls the passage "sub-Christian" (p. 86), while Caird only concedes a momentary final "extinction," the force mitigated by the further statement that "the smoke of their torment rises for ever and ever" (v.11), which is more appropriate to cities than individuals. While the view that some recalcitrant individuals will suffer eternal deprivation seems repugnant to Christian sensitivity, it is clear that it is not only John's understanding but that of Jesus and other NT writers as well (Matt 25:46; Rom 2:3–9; 2 Thess 1:6–9).

John's imagery conveys a sense of finality and sober reality. It is not clear whether the imagery points only to permanency and irreversibility of God's punitive justice or whether it also includes the consciousness of eternal deprivation (cf. Rev 20:10; John 5:28–29). Berkouwer wisely says that preaching about hell should never be used as a terror tactic by the church but should always be presented in such a way as to show that God's mercy is the final goal (G.C. Berkouwer, *The Return of Christ* [Grand

Rapids: Eerdmans, 1972], pp. 417–23). C.S. Lewis acknowledges that hell is a detestable doctrine that he would willingly remove from Christianity if it were in his power. But, as he goes on to point out, the question is not whether it is detestable but whether it is true. We must recognize that the reality of hell has the full support of Scripture and of our Lord's own teaching. Indeed, it has always been held by Christians and has the support of reason (*The Problem of Pain* [New York: Macmillan, 1954], ch. 8).

The worshipers of the beast will be unable to rest day and night. Notice the contrast with the saints who will "rest" from their labor (v.13). While the beast worshipers have their time of rest, and while the saints are persecuted and martyred, in the final time of judgment God will reverse their roles (7:15ff.; cf. 2 Thess 1:6–7).

The great test for Christians is whether through patient endurance they will remain loyal to Jesus and not fall prey to the deception of the beasts (see comments at 13:10). They do this by their serious attention to God's Word and their faithfulness to Christ Jesus (1:3; 2:26; 3:8, 10; 22:7, 9; cf. Phil 1:28–30).

13 A fourth voice comes from heaven (an angel's or Christ's?), pronounces a beatitude, and evokes the Spirit's response. This is the second beatitude in Revelation (cf. comments at 1:3). Its general import is clear. But how are the words "from now on" to be understood? Do they mean that from the time of the vision's fulfillment onward (i.e., the judgment of idolators and the 144,000 with the Lord on Mount Zion), the dead will be blessed in a more complete manner (Alford)? Or do they refer to the time of John's writing onward? If the latter, why from *that* time? While either interpretation is grammatically possible, the preceding verse, which implies an exhortation to Christians in John's day, favors the latter view (Beckwith). John expects the imminent intensification of persecution associated with the beast, and the beatitude indicates that those who remain loyal to Jesus when this occurs will be blessed indeed.

Apart from 22:17, this is the only place in Revelation where the Spirit speaks directly (cf. Acts 13:2; Heb 3:7; 10:15). The beatitude is no doubt intended to emphasize the reality of the martyrs' future. Their blessedness consists in "rest" from the onslaught of the dragon and his beasts and the assurance that their toil (*kopos*, cf. 2:2) for Christ's name will not be in vain but will be remembered by the Lord himself after their death (Heb 6:10; cf. 1 Tim 5:24–25).

14–16 After a brief pause to encourage the faithfulness of the saints, John returns to the theme of divine judgment on the world. He does this by first describing the judgment in terms of a harvest (14:14–20) and then by the seven bowl plagues (chs. 15–16). John sees a white cloud and seated on it one resembling a human being ("a son of man"). He has a crown of gold and a sharp sickle, the main instrument of harvest. John clearly wishes to highlight this exalted human figure and his role in the eschatological judgment. The question of the identity of the "son of man" is not unlike the problem of the identity of the rider of the white horse (6:1). The same words *homoion huion anthrōpou* ("like a son of man") are used of Jesus in 1:13, in both places without the definite article. Some have noted the close association of the one "seated on the cloud" with the words "another angel" in v.15 and the similar implications in v.17, that another angel "too" had a sharp sickle, implying that the former figure with the sickle was likewise an angel. Further, if the figure on the cloud is Jesus, how can we account for an angel giving a command to him to reap the earth (v.15).

Though there are difficulties, Charles is no doubt right when he says, "There can be no question as to the identity of the divine figure seated on the cloud. He is described as 'One like a Son of Man.' " Charles shows how Daniel 7 comes to be associated with the person of the Messiah under the title "a son of man" (*Commentary on Revelation,* 2:19). Indeed, it is quite appropriate for John to use the term Son of Man, since in the Gospels that term is most frequently associated with the Messiah's suffering and the glory of the Second Advent as well as with his right to judge the world (Matt 26:64; John 5:27). Both themes are present in the context of Revelation. The imagery of Daniel 7, frequently used in the Apocalypse, links the suffering people of God ("the saints") to the Son of Man who sits in judgment over the kingdoms of the world (cf. Richard N. Longenecker, *The Christology of Early Jewish Christianity* [London: SCM, 1970], pp. 82–93; R.T. France, *Jesus and the Old Testament* [Downers Grove, Ill.: InterVarsity, 1971], pp. 202–5). It should, of course, be remembered that this is a highly symbolic description of the final judgment.

The harvest is an OT figure used for divine judgment (Hos 6:11; Joel 3:13), especially on Babylon (Jer 51:33). Jesus also likens the final judgment to the harvest of the earth (Matt 13:30, 39). He may use the instrumentality of angels or men, but it is his prerogative to put in the sickle. While this reaping may be the gathering of his elect from the earth (so Caird citing Matt 9:37–38; John 4:35–38, et al.), the context favors taking the harvest to be a reference not to salvation but to judgment.

17–20 "Another" angel here has no more necessary connection with the Son of Man than the "another" angel in v.15; it may simply mean another of the same kind of angel mentioned in the succession of personages in the book (cf. 14:6, where no other angel is involved except the one mentioned). This angel (v.17) will gather the vintage of the earth. He is associated with the angel from the altar who has authority over its fire. Though opinion about the identification of the altar is divided, it is the incense altar; and the fire is symbolic of God's vindication of his martyred people (cf. 8:3–5 and comments at 6:9–11).

The divine eschatological judgment is presented in a threefold imagery: the unmixed wine in the cup (v.10), the grain harvest (vv.14–16), and the vintage harvest (vv.17–20). These are best understood as three metaphors describing different views of the same reality, i.e., the divine judgment. Again the OT provides the background for this imagery of divine judgment (Isa 63:1–6; Lam 1:15; Joel 3:13; cf. Rev 19:13, 15). Caird certainly strains the text when he argues that the vintage overflowing with blood does not refer to the enemies of Christ but, connecting the "earth's vine" (v.18) with the new Israel, argues that the vintage must refer to the death of the martyrs of Jesus (p. 192). The reference to the "great winepress of God's wrath" in v.19 should clarify the imagery and leave no doubt that it denotes God's judgment on the rebellious world and not the wrath of the beast on the followers of the Lamb.

The final verse (v.20) is gruesome: blood flows up to the horses' bridles for a distance of about two hundred miles (sixteen hundred stadia). Again the source of the imagery is Isaiah 63:1–6, heightened by John's hyperbole. A similar apocalyptic image for the final judgment on idolators occurs in the pre-Christian Book of Enoch, where the righteous will slay the wicked: "And the horse shall walk up to the breast in the blood of sinners, and the chariot shall be submerged to its height" (1 Enoch 100.1.3, cited in R.H. Charles, *The Apocrypha and Pseudepigrapha of the Old Testament,* 2 vols. [New York: Oxford, 1913], 2:271). Here in Revelation the judgment is not the task of human vengeance but belongs exclusively to the Son of Man and his angelic reapers (cf. Rom 12:19–21). The symbolism is that of a head-on battle, a great defeat of the enemy, a sea of spilled blood. To go beyond this and attempt to find a symbolic meaning of the sixteen hundred stadia or to link the scene to some geographic location (cf. 16:4–6) is pure speculation.

The term "outside the city" requires explanation. It may refer merely to ancient warfare when a besieging army was slaughtered at the city walls, and the blood flowed outside the city. Some think John may have had an actual city in mind and have suggested Jerusalem because of the OT predictions of a final battle to be fought near the city (Dan 11:45; Joel 3:12; Zech 14:4; but cf. Rev 16:16—"Armageddon" is not near Jerusalem; so Beckwith, Ford, Mounce, Swete, etc.). On the other hand, John's symbolic use of "city" in every other reference favors taking the word symbolically in this verse. In Revelation there are only two cities (the "cities" of the seven churches in Rev 2–3 are not called cities), the city of God, which is the camp of the saints, and the city of Satan, Babylon, which is made up of the followers of the beast (Beasley-Murray, Kiddle). There is no way to be really sure of the identity of the city, nor is its identity important. It is sufficient to take it as the same city that was persecuted by the pagans (11:2) and is seen in 20:9, i.e., the community of the saints (Charles).

Notes

---

14 A few of the many who identify the figure on the cloud as Christ are Beckwith, Bruce, Caird, Charles, Ford, France, Ladd, Lilje, Morris, Mounce, Walvoord, and I.H. Marshall ("Martyrdom and the Parousia in the Revelation of John," *Studia Evangelica,* 4 [1968], 337). Others identify the figure with an angel (Glasson, Kiddle, Beasley-Murray).

18 The "sickle" is a δρέπανον *(drepanon)*, which is a "reaping hook" used both for reaping grain and for pruning the vine and cutting off clusters at vintage (Beckwith, p. 664).

20 Some commentators have seen in the number sixteen hundred stadia the approximate length of Palestine from Dan to Beersheba (Ladd, *Commentary on Revelation,* p. 202). Taking four as a universal number and the multiplier forty times four, Victorinus suggested that the number was symbolic, i.e., "throughout all the four parts of the world" (ANF, 7:357).

D. *The Seven Bowls* (15:1–19:10)

It is difficult to know where the divisions should fall in these further visions. Since the last series of sevens in Revelation includes the fall of Babylon under the seventh bowl (16:19), it has seemed appropriate to include the extensive description of the city's fall under the bowl-series division.

Chapter 15, a sort of celestial interlude before the final judgment, is preparatory to the execution of the bowl series described in chapter 16, while chapters 17 and 18 elaborate the fall of Babylon. What has already been anticipated under the three figures of the divine eschatological judgment—the cup of wine (14:10), the harvest of the earth (14:14–16), and the vintage (14:17–20)—is now further described under the symbolism of the seven bowls. In typical Hebrew fashion, each cycle repeats in new ways the former events and also adds fresh details not in the former series.

It is clear that in these final judgments only the unbelieving world is involved; therefore, they are punitive plagues (16:2). Yet even in these last plagues, God is concerned with effecting repentance, though none abandon their idolatry (16:9, 11). But are the faithful still on earth? Verse 2 of chapter 15 locates the whole company of conquerors not on earth but before the throne. So intense are these final judgments that Victorinus argues: "For the wrath of God always strikes the obstinate people with seven plagues, that is, perfectly, as it is said in Leviticus; and these shall be in the last time, when the church shall have gone out of the midst" (ANF, 7:357). It is difficult to support or refute such a view. Farrer also argues that the saints are now gone (Austin Farrer, *A Rebirth of Images: the Making of St. John's Apocalypse* [London: Darce, 1949], p. 155).

My position is that the inclusive series of bowl judgments constitute the "third woe" announced in 11:14 as "coming soon" (so Alford, Beckwith, Ladd, etc.—see comments at 11:14). Since the first two woes occur under the fifth and sixth trumpets, it is reasonable to see the third woe, which involved seven plagues, as unfolding during the sounding of the seventh trumpet, when the mystery of God will be finished (10:7). The actual woe events were delayed till John could give important background material concerning not only the inhabitants of the earth but also the church herself, her glory and shame, her faithfulness and apostasy (12:1–14:20). These last plagues take place "immediately after the distress of those days" referred to by Jesus in the Olivet Discourse and may well be the fulfillment of his apocalyptic words: "The sun will be darkened, and the moon will not give its light; the stars will fall from the sky, and the heavenly bodies will be shaken" (Matt 24:29). Significantly, the next event that follows this judgment, the coming of the Son of Man in the clouds, is the same event John describes following the bowl judgments (19:11).

1. *Preparatory: The seven angels with the seven last plagues*

15:1–8

1 I saw in heaven another great and marvelous sign: seven angels with the seven
last plagues—last, because with them God's wrath is completed. 2 And I saw what
looked like a sea of glass mixed with fire and, standing beside the sea, those who
had been victorious over the beast and his image and over the number of his name.
They held harps given them by God 3 and sang the song of Moses the servant of
God and the song of the Lamb:

> "Great and marvelous are your deeds,
> Lord God Almighty.
> Just and true are your ways,
> King of the ages.
> 4 Who will not fear you, O Lord,
> and bring glory to your name?
> For you alone are holy.
> All nations will come
> and worship before you,
> for your righteous acts have been revealed."

5 After this I looked and in heaven the temple, that is, the tabernacle of Testimony,
was opened. 6 Out of the temple came the seven angels with the seven plagues.
They were dressed in clean, shining linen and wore golden sashes around their
chests. 7 Then one of the four living creatures gave to the seven angels seven
golden bowls filled with the wrath of God, who lives for ever and ever. 8 And the
temple was filled with smoke from the glory of God and from his power, and no one
could enter the temple until the seven plagues of the seven angels were completed.

Chapter 15 is tied closely to chapter 16. Both deal with the seven last plagues of God's wrath. One is preparatory and interpretative, the other descriptive. Chapter

15 is largely oriented to the OT account of the Exodus event and is strongly suggestive of the liturgical tradition of the ancient synagogue. The chapter has two main visions: the first portrays the victors who have emerged triumphant from the great ordeal (vv.2–4); the second relates the appearance from the heavenly temple of seven angels clothed in white and gold who hold the seven bowls of the last plagues (vv.5–8).

1 This verse forms a superscription to chapters 15 and 16. The final manifestation of the wrath of God takes the form of seven angels of judgment and is called a "sign" (*sēmeion*). This is the third explicitly identified heavenly "sign" (cf. the woman and dragon at 12:1, 3). The qualifying adjective "marvelous" (*thaumaston*, cf. v.3) apparently is added because John understood the seven angels to represent the completion of God's wrath, viz., the last plagues. They are awesome as well as final in character. The word *teleō* means to "finish," "to bring to an end," "to accomplish," "to perform" (BAG, p. 818; cf. Rev 10:7; 11:7; 15:8; 17:17; 20:3, 5, 7). While these plagues may be the finale to the whole historical panorama of God's judgments, it would be exegetically preferrable to find a connection of them with events related in Revelation itself. As has already been argued, the first reference to the eschatological judgments is found in 6:17: "For the great day of their wrath has come, and who can stand?" After the interlude of the sealing of the saints from spiritual harm (ch. 7), the seven trumpets are sounded (8:1ff.). The sixth one involves three plagues that kill a third of mankind (9:18). The third woe (11:14) includes the bowl judgments that are called the "last" plagues. From this we may conclude that the trumpets begin the eschatological wrath of God that is finished in the seven bowls.

2 As in 14:1ff., John again focuses his attention on a scene that contrasts sharply with the coming judgment, an indication of his pastoral concern. He sees before the throne the likeness of a sea of glass shot through with fire (cf. 4:6). It is a scene of worship, and its imagery is suitable for depicting the majesty and brilliance of God, which the sea of glass is reflecting in a virtual symphony of color. No further symbolic significance than this needs to be sought here. Firmly planted on (*epi* can also mean "beside," NIV) the sea are those who were "victorious over the beast." They are the same ones who are seen throughout Revelation as having won out over the idolatrous beasts through their faithful testimony to Christ, even to the extent of martyrdom (e.g., 2:7, 11, 26; 12:11; 21:7; cf. 3:21; 5:5). They are the 144,000, the elect of God (7:4; 14:1), the completed company of martyrs (6:11). Note the absence of "received his mark" since mention is made of the equivalent expression "the number of his name" (see comments at 13:17). Suddenly in this dazzling scene the sound of harps and singing is heard.

3–4 The song sung by the redeemed is the "song of Moses, the servant of God and the song of the Lamb"—a single song as vv.3–4 show. The Song of Moses is in Exodus 15:1–18. It celebrates the victory of the Lord in the defeat of the Egyptians at the Red Sea. In the ancient synagogue it was sung in the afternoon service each Sabbath to celebrate God's sovereign rule over the universe, of which the redemption from Egypt reminds the Jew (Joseph Hertz, *The Authorized Daily Prayer Book*, rev. ed. [New York: Block, 1948], p. 100). Such is the emphasis in the liturgical collection of psalms and prophets John quotes from (e.g., "King of the ages"). As the deliverance from Egypt, with its divine plagues of judgment on Israel's enemies, became for the Jew a signpost of God's just rule over the world, so God's eschatological judgment and the deliverance of the followers of the Lamb bring forth from the victors over the beast exuberant songs of praise to God for his righteous acts in history.

Each line in vv.3–4 picks up phrases from the Psalms and Prophets. Compare the following OT words with vv.3–4: "Then Moses and the Israelites sang this song" (Exod 15:1); "your works are wonderful" (Ps 139:14); "LORD God Almighty" (Amos 4:13); "all his ways are just. A faithful God . . . upright and just is he" (Deut 32:4); "who shall not revere you, O King of the nations" (Jer 10:7); "they will bring glory to your name" (Ps 86:9), etc. John may or may not have heard the victors over the beast singing these actual words. But it was revealed to him that they were praising God for his mighty deliverance and judgment on their enemies. His rendering of the song may be drawn from the liturgy of the synagogue and no doubt from the early Christian church. In fact, it is precisely in connection with the ancient Easter liturgy that the church's dependence on the synagogue Passover liturgy is most easily recognizable (Massey H. Shepherd, Jr., *The Paschal Liturgy and the Apocalypse* [Richmond: John Knox, 1960], p. 96). The Exodus background is quite obvious throughout both chapters 15 and 16 (cf. 8:7ff. and see comments at 1:10). On the possible theme of resurrection in the hymn, see Notes.

5–8 A second and still more impressive scene follows. The door to the temple in heaven is again opened (cf. 11:19), and the seven angels dressed in white and gold come out of the temple. In a dignified manner, one of the living creatures gives a bowl to each of the seven messengers. The bowls (*phialē*) are the vessels used in the temple ministry especially for offerings and incense (5:8). *Phialē* translates the Hebrew *mizrāq* (a bowl for throwing liquids) in most instances in the LXX. This might have been a large banquet bowl for wine (Amos 6:6), but more often it was a ritual bowl used for collecting the blood of the sacrifices (Exod 27:3). Golden bowls seem to be always associated with the temple (e.g., 1 Kings 7:50; 2 Kings 12:13; 25:15). *Phialē* in the Greco-Roman world was a broad, flat bowl or saucer used ritually for drinking or for pouring libations (LSJ, p. 1930).

The "smoke" that filled the temple refers to the shekinah cloud first associated with the tabernacle and then with the temple. It symbolizes God's special presence and that he is the source of the judgments (Exod 40:34ff.; 1 Kings 8:10–11; Ezek 11:23; 44:4). His awesome presence in the temple until the plagues are finished (16:17) prohibits even angels from entering it (cf. Isa 6:4; Hab 2:20).

Notes

3 K. Boronicz argues that according to Jewish tradition the doctrine of resurrection is implicitly contained in the Law and is exemplified by the Canticle of Moses (Exod 15:1–18). Revelation 15:3–4 has a prophetic and messianic sense and points to resurrection. In their prophetic symbolism, the Song of Moses and the Song of the Lamb are identical ("*Canticum Moysi et agni*"—Apoc. 15:3, Ruch Biblit, 17 [1964], 81–87). Could this also be the reason why all the early church liturgies included the Song of Moses somewhere in the Easter commemoration and some also included it on other Sundays (Eric Werner, *The Sacred Bridge: Liturgical Parallels in Synagogue and Early Church* [New York: Schocken Books, 1970], p. 142)?

In the ancient synagogue, the Haftorah (prophetic reading) accompanying the Seder on Exodus 15:1ff. was Isaiah 26:1: "In that day this song will be sung in the land of Judah: We have a strong city; God makes salvation its walls and ramparts"; and Isaiah 65:24: "Before they call I will answer; while they are still speaking I will hear." Both prophetic portions are part of the texts called "Consolation of Israel" and emphasize the strengthening of the faith of Israel (Jacob Mann, *The Bible as Read and Preached in the Old Synagogue*, 2 vols. [New York: Ktav, 1971], 1: 431–32). The Song of Moses was apparently not so frequently used in the synagogue but principally in the temple services (Werner, *Sacred Bridge*, p. 141).

6 There is good MS evidence for reading that angels were dressed in λίθον (*lithon*, "stone") instead of λίνον (*linon*, "linen"). But the sense of "stone" is strained and thus both Metzger (Bruce M. Metzger, *A Textual Commentary on the Greek New Testament* [New York: UBS, 1971], p. 756) and Swete argue for *linon* as the preferred reading.

---

2. *Pouring out of the seven bowls*

16:1–21

1Then I heard a loud voice from the temple saying to the seven angels, "Go, pour
out the seven bowls of God's wrath on the earth."
2The first angel went and poured out his bowl on the land, and ugly and painful
sores broke out on the people who had the mark of the beast and worshiped his
image.
3The second angel poured out his bowl on the sea, and it turned into blood like
that of a dead man, and every living thing in the sea died.
4The third angel poured out his bowl on the rivers and springs of water, and they
became blood. 5Then I heard the angel in charge of the waters say:

"You are just in these judgments,
you who are and who were, the Holy One,
because you have so judged;
6for they have shed the blood of your saints and prophets,
and you have given them blood to drink
as they deserve."

7And I heard the altar respond:

"Yes, Lord God Almighty,
true and just are your judgments."

8The fourth angel poured out his bowl on the sun, and the sun was given power
to scorch people with fire. 9They were seared by the intense heat and they cursed
the name of God, who had control over these plagues, but they refused to repent
and glorify him.
10The fifth angel poured out his bowl on the throne of the beast, and his kingdom
was plunged into darkness. Men gnawed their tongues in agony 11and cursed the
God of heaven because of their pains and their sores, but they refused to repent
of what they had done.
12The sixth angel poured out his bowl on the great river Euphrates, and its water
was dried up to prepare the way for the kings from the East. 13Then I saw three
evil spirits that looked like frogs; they came out of the mouth of the dragon, out of
the mouth of the beast and out of the mouth of the false prophet. 14They are spirits
of demons performing miraculous signs, and they go out to the kings of the whole
world, to gather them for the battle on the great day of God Almighty.
15"Behold, I come like a thief! Blessed is he who stays awake and keeps his
clothes with him, so that he may not go naked and be shamefully exposed."
16Then they gathered the kings together to the place that in Hebrew is called
Armageddon.
17The seventh angel poured out his bowl into the air, and out of the temple came
a loud voice from the throne, saying, "It is done!" 18Then there came flashes of
lightning, rumblings, peals of thunder and a severe earthquake. No earthquake like
it has ever occurred since man has been on earth, so tremendous was the quake.

19The great city split into three parts, and the cities of the nations collapsed. God remembered Babylon the Great and gave her the cup filled with the wine of the fury of his wrath. 20Every island fled away and the mountains could not be found. 21From the sky huge hailstones of about a hundred pounds each fell upon men. And they cursed God on account of the plague of hail, because the plague was so terrible.

1 This chapter describes the "third woe" (see comments at introduction to ch. 15) in the form of the outpouring of seven bowl judgments. They occur in rapid succession with only a brief pause for a dialogue between the third angel and the altar, accentuating the justice of God's punishments (vv.5–7). This rapid succession is probably due to John's desire to give a telescopic view of the first six bowls and then hasten on to the seventh, where the far more interesting judgment on Babylon occurs, of which the author will give a detailed account. Again, seven symbolizes fullness, this time fullness of judgment (cf. Lev 26:21). The striking parallelism between the order of these plagues and those of the trumpets (8:2–9:21), though clearly not identical in every detail, has led many to conclude that the two series are the same. The similarity, however, may be merely literary.

Each plague in both series (the trumpets and the bowls) is reminiscent of the plagues on Egypt before the Exodus. The first four in both series cover the traditional divisions of nature: earth, sea, rivers, sky. But in each of the bowls, unlike the trumpets, the plague on nature is related to the suffering of mankind. Furthermore, each bowl plague seems to be total in its effect ("every living thing . . . died" [v.3]), whereas under the trumpets only a part is affected ("a third of the living creatures . . . died" [8:9]). Therefore, it seems better to understand the trumpets and bowls as separate judgments; yet both are described in language drawn from the pattern of God's judgment on Egypt under Moses (see comments at 8:7ff.). The final three plagues are social and spiritual in their effect and shift from nature to humanity.

The question arises whether these descriptions should be taken more or less literally. The answer is probably less literally. But the important point is that they depict God's sure and righteous judgment that will one day be literally and actually done in this world.

2 *The first bowl* has no strict counterpart in the trumpets but recalls the sixth plague of boils under Moses (Exod 9:10–11). As the antagonists of Moses were affected by the boils, so the enemies of Christ who worship the beast will be struck by this plague. Perhaps "painful" sore might be translated "malignant" sore (Swete).

3 *The second bowl* turns the sea into polluted blood (see comments at 8:8). Genesis 1:21 is reversed; all marine life dies (cf. Exod 7:17–21).

4 *The third bowl* affects the fresh waters of the earth, which are essential to human life. They too become polluted as blood (cf. Exod 7:17–21).

5–7 Here the reference to blood calls forth the dialogue between the angel and the altar concerning the logic of the plagues. The blood that sinners drink, which is poured out on them, is just requital for their shedding of the blood of the saints (15:1–4) and prophets (11:3–13; cf. 17:6; 18:20). With blood, God vindicates the blood of the martyrs of Jesus. God's wrath is exercised in recognition of their love. People must choose whether to drink the blood of saints or to wear robes dipped in the blood of the Lamb (Minear, *I Saw a New Earth,* in loc).

8–9 *The fourth bowl* increases the intensity of the sun's heat; it is the exact opposite of the fourth trumpet, which produced a plague of darkness (cf. 8:12). The earth dwellers, instead of repenting of their deeds and acknowledging the Creator, the only act that could even now turn away God's wrath, curse (*blasphēmeō,* "slander," "blaspheme") God for sending them agonizing pain (vv. 11, 21). Yet their problem goes beyond the awful physical pain and is moral and spiritual (cf. Isa 52:5; Rom 1:25; 2:24).

10–11 *The fifth bowl* plunges the kingdom of the beast into darkness. This is not a reference to the fall of the Roman Empire or Caesar worship, though John's words would include this level of meaning. In 2:13, John used the word "throne" (*thronos*) to designate the stronghold of Satan at Pergamum. Thus "the throne of the beast" symbolizes the seat of the world-wide dominion of the great satanic system of idolatry (the Abyss? cf. 20:1). This system is plunged into spiritual darkness or disruption, bringing chaos on all who sought life and meaning in it. Charles seeks to connect this darkness to the darkness and pain caused by the demon-locusts of the fifth trumpet (9:1ff.). But in the trumpet plague the locust-demons are the direct cause of the pain, while the darkness is incidental. This bowl plague, however, though similar to the fifth trumpet, strikes at the very seat of satanic authority over the world; and the darkness is probably moral and spiritual rather than physical (cf. 21:25; 22:5; John 8:12; 12:35–36, 46; 1 John 1:5–7; 2:8–10; Wisd Sol 17:21). Again the terrible refrain is repeated: "But they refused to repent of what they had done."

12–16 *The sixth bowl* is specifically aimed at drying up the Euphrates River and so will allow the demonically inspired kings from the East to gather at Armageddon where God himself will enter into battle with them. The reference to the Euphrates in the sixth trumpet is a striking parallel to the sixth bowl plague (9:14). Thus many identify the two series as different aspects of the same plagues. But while the sixth trumpet releases demonic hordes to inflict death on the earth dwellers, the sixth bowl effects the assembling of the rulers (kings) from the East to meet the Lord God Almighty in battle.

The Euphrates was not only the location of Babylon, the great anti-God throne, but the place from which the evil hordes would invade Israel (see comments at 9:14). Thus, by mentioning the Euphrates by name, John is suggesting that the unseen rulers of this world are being prepared to enter into a final and fatal battle with the Sovereign of the universe. It is a warfare that can be conceived only in terms that describe realities of a primordial and eschatological order, an order that is more descriptive of contemporary actualities than political history (Minear). Thus John does not, in my opinion, describe the invasion of the Parthian hordes advancing on Rome or any future political invasion of Israel (contra Mounce, *Revelation,* p. 12). How could such political groups be involved in the battle of the great day of God Almighty? Instead, in terms reminiscent of the ancient battles of Israel, John describes the eschatological defeat of the forces of evil, the kings from the East.

Further confirmation that these Eastern kings represent the combined forces of evil in the world is John's reference to the three froglike evil (*akatharta,* "unclean") spirits that proceed out of the mouths of the dragon, the beast, and the false prophet. Frogs were considered unclean (*akatharta*) animals by the Jews (Lev 11:10, 41). The background for this figure is not clear but probably relates more to pagan metaphors for evil than to any specific OT references. To the Persian, the frog was the double of Ahriman, god of evil and agent of plagues (Moffatt, EGT, 5:447).

To the Egyptian, the frog was not loathsome, as some suggest, but the symbol of the goddess Heqt, a goddess of resurrection and fertility. But to a Jewish mind, such gods were demons (*daimoniōn*, v.14), Satan's emissaries, and inseparable from idolatry (9:20; 18:2; 1 Cor 10:20–21). These demons produce miraculous signs like the false prophet (13:13–14), and this connects their activity to the deception of the earth's kings. Since these demons come from the "mouths" of the figures, lying and deceptive words are implied (cf. the sword from Christ's mouth that is equal to his word of truth). These kings are summoned to the battle of the great day of God Almighty. It is not necessary to limit John's language to the imperial emperor cult or to the Nero redivivus myth (see introduction to ch. 13). Under the sixth bowl, the kings are only gathered. Not until the seventh bowl do the confrontation and defeat actually occur (19:19–21).

Somewhat abruptly, but not inappropriately so, a warning is issued. Those who worship and serve the Lamb must be constantly vigilant lest their loyalty to him be diverted through the satanic deception (cf. Matt 24:43ff.; 1 Thess 5:2, 4). The Parousia (coming) of Christ is here connected with the judgment of Armageddon and the fall of Babylon. After John has described the latter in more detail (chs. 17–18), he describes the vision of the return of Jesus (19:11–16). In v.15 the third of the seven beatitudes is pronounced (cf. 1:3; 14:13; 19:9; 20:6; 22:7, 14).

Similar to the exhortation given to those in the churches at Sardis (3:2–4) and Laodicea (3:18), the warning about Jesus' coming "like a thief" implies a need for alertness to the deception of idolatry and disloyalty to Jesus. Like a guard who watches by night, the true Christian will remain steadfast and prepared. It is not necessary to relate this warning only to the end time as in the context, since the appeal for the steadfast loyalty of Christians is relevant at any time. Such appeals, however, are associated in the Gospels with the return of Christ (Mark 13:32–37). There is no evidence that John is here reinterpreting the second coming of Christ, seeing that event in the crises of history as Caird suggests (p. 208). Since John's description does not refer to the Roman Empire but to the eschatological judgment, there is no need to resort to any reinterpretation hypothesis.

Many modern interpreters identify Armageddon with the Galilean fortified city of Megiddo and believe that a literal military battle will be fought in the latter days in that vicinity (cf. New Scofield Reference Bible, notes at Judg 5:19 and Rev 16:16; H. Lindsay; Seiss; J.B. Smith; Walvoord). While this sense is not impossible, it is better to take the name as being symbolic. In Hebrew *har* means hill or mountain, while *m*ᵉ*giddôn* (Gr., *magedōn*) could mean Megiddo, a Canaanite stronghold in the Jezreel Plain later captured by the Israelites (Josh 12:21; Judg 5:19). Megiddo, however, is a tell (artificial mound—only seventy feet high in John's day according to Mounce, *Revelation*, p. 301) and not a hill or mountain and is never so designated, though the fact that over two hundred battles have been fought in this vicinity makes the site an appropriate symbol for the eschatological battle (Swete). Neither can it mean Mount Carmel near Megiddo (Lohmeyer), for such a designation is never used and would be totally obscure to the residents of Asia to whom John writes and who probably were for the most part ignorant of Hebrew. Therefore it is better to understand the term symbolically in the same manner as "in Hebrew" in 9:11 alerts us to the symbolic significance of the name of the angel of the Abyss.

Several other possibilities for the meaning of *har m^egiddôn* have been suggested. Rissi derives the word from *har mô'ēd* ("mount of the assembly") and connects this with Isaiah 14:12–15, where the king of Babylon, lifted up in pride, tries to ascend to the "mount of the assembly," i.e., the throne of God (Rissi, *Time and History* pp. 84–85). While the theory is interesting, it rests on a conjectural emendation of the Greek text without any MS evidence and has no direct support from the immediate context (vv.12–16). Another suggestion derives from the Hebrew *har m^egiddô* the phrase "his fruitful mountain," i.e., Jerusalem, and connects the reference to the final battle to be fought near Jerusalem (Joel 3:2; Zech 14:2ff.; cited by Charles, *Commentary on Revelation,* 2:50). Caird (p. 207) mentions a view where *magedōn* (from *'Armagedōn,* "Armageddon") is related to the Hebrew *gādad,* which means "to cut," "attack," or "maraud"; as such with *har* ("mountain") it would mean "marauding mountain" and would be John's variation on Jeremiah's "destroying mountain" (Jer 51:25).

It is surprising that no one has suggested taking *magedōn* as deriving from the secondary sense of the Hebrew *gādad* that means "to gather in troops or bands" (BDB, p. 151). The simple way in Hebrew to make a noun from a verb is to prefix a *ma* to the verbal form. Thus we have *magēd,* "a place of gathering in troops," and the suffix *ô*, meaning "his," yielding "his place of gathering in troops." This is almost equivalent to the expressions in vv.14, 16—"to gather them [the kings] for the battle on the great day of God Almighty"—and would allude to the prophetic expectation of the gathering of the nations for judgment (Joel 3:2, 12). In any case, the name is symbolic and probably does not refer to any geographical location we can now identify, whether in Palestine or elsewhere; but it describes the eschatological confrontation where God will meet the forces of evil in their final defeat. As Mounce states:

> Har-Magedon is symbolic of the final overthrow of all the forces of evil by the might and power of God. The great conflict between God and Satan, Christ and Antichrist, good and evil, which lies behind the perplexing course of history will in the end issue in a final struggle in which God will emerge victorious and take with him all who placed their faith in him. This is Har-Magedon (*Revelation,* p. 302).

Nevertheless, it refers to a real point in history and to real persons who will encounter God's just sentence.

17–21 The seventh bowl is poured out into the air. Nothing further is said about the "air"; rather, John is concerned with the loud voice that cries out, "It is done" (*gegonen*), or, "It has come to pass." With this seventh bowl, the eschatological wrath of God is completed (cf. 6:17; 21:6; John 19:30). Flashes of lightning, peals of thunder, and a severe earthquake occur (cf. 4:5; 8:5; 11:19). These eschatological signs symbolize the destruction of the anti-God forces throughout the world (cf. Heb 12:27). So great is the earthquake of God's judgment that it reaches the strongholds of organized evil represented by the cities of the pagans (*ethnē,* "nations"). Even the great city Babylon, which seduced all the earth's kings and inhabitants (17:2), now comes under final sentence (see comments on 11:8).

The judgment of Babylon will occupy John's attention in chapters 17 and 18. While the catastrophe continues to be described in geophysical terms (islands and mountains disappearing, huge hailstones accompanying a gigantic storm), there is a question whether John intends the destruction to be merely natural or even politico-historical entities or exclusively of the unseen powers of evil. Like the Egyptian plague of hail that further hardened Pharoah's heart, this plague of hail falls on the unrepentant to no avail; they curse God for sending his judgment on them (cf. Exod 9:24). By such language John describes the rising pitch of God's wrath on the rebellious powers of the earth. His words should not be politicized as if he spoke merely of Rome or of some impending historical crisis for the church. He is speaking of the great realities of the end, when God has put down all his enemies.

3. *The harlot and the beast*

17:1–18

[1]One of the seven angels who had the seven bowls came and said to me, "Come,
I will show you the punishment of the great prostitute, who sits on many waters.
[2]With her the kings of the earth committed adultery and the inhabitants of the earth
were intoxicated with the wine of her adulteries."
[3]Then the angel carried me away in the Spirit into a desert. There I saw a woman
sitting on a scarlet beast that was covered with blasphemous names and had seven
heads and ten horns. [4]The woman was dressed in purple and scarlet, and was
glittering with gold, precious stones and pearls. She held a golden cup in her hand,
filled with abominable things and the filth of her adulteries. [5]This title was written
on her forehead:

MYSTERY
BABYLON THE GREAT
THE MOTHER OF PROSTITUTES
AND OF THE ABOMINATIONS OF THE EARTH.

[6]I saw that the woman was drunk with the blood of the saints, the blood of those
who bore testimony to Jesus.
When I saw her, I was greatly astonished. [7]Then the angel said to me: "Why are
you astonished? I will explain to you the mystery of the woman and of the beast
she rides, which has the seven heads and ten horns. [8]The beast, which you saw,
once was, now is not, and will come up out of the Abyss and go to his destruction.
The inhabitants of the earth whose names have not been written in the book of life
from the creation of the world will be astonished when they see the beast, because
he once was, now is not, and yet will come.
[9]"This calls for a mind with wisdom. The seven heads are seven hills on which
the woman sits. They are also seven kings. [10]Five have fallen, one is, the other has
not yet come; but when he does come, he must remain for a little while. [11]The beast
who once was, and now is not, is an eighth king. He belongs to the seven and is
going to his destruction.
[12]"The ten horns you saw are ten kings who have not yet received a kingdom,
but who for one hour will receive authority as kings along with the beast. [13]They
have one purpose and will give their power and authority to the beast. [14]They will
make war against the Lamb, but the Lamb will overcome them because he is Lord
of lords and King of kings—and with him will be his called, chosen and faithful
followers."
[15]Then the angel said to me, "The waters you saw, where the prostitute sits, are
peoples, multitudes, nations and languages. [16]The beast and the ten horns you saw
will hate the prostitute. They will bring her to ruin and leave her naked; they will eat
her flesh and burn her with fire. [17]For God has put it into their hearts to accomplish
his purpose by agreeing to give the beast their power to rule, until God's words are
fulfilled. [18]The woman you saw is the great city that rules over the kings of the
earth."

In an important sense, the interpretation of this chapter controls the interpretation of the whole Book of Revelation. For a majority of exegetes, Babylon represents the city of Rome. The beast stands for the Roman Empire as a whole, with its subject provinces and peoples. The seven hills (v.9) are the seven selected dynasties of Roman emperors from Augustus to Domitian. The ten kings are heads of lesser and restless states, eager to escape their enslavement to the colonizing power. John's prediction of the fall of Babylon is his announcement of the impending dissolution of the Roman Empire in all its aspects. For such a view there is considerable evidence. Babylon was a term used by both Jews and Christians for Rome (2 Baruch 11:1; Sib Oracles 5.143, 158; 1 Peter 5:13; Hippolytus *Christ and Antichrist* 36; TDNT, 1:516). Rome was a great city (v.18), a city set on seven hills (v.9), and by the time of Domitian (A.D. 85) it was notorious for persecuting and killing the saints (v.6). Thus the argument goes. Many scholars of unquestioned competence have been fully convinced of the certainty of these equations.

Yet there is evidence that casts doubt on this exegesis and impels us to look for a more adequate—if also a more subtle—understanding of John's intention. It is simply not sufficient to identify Rome and Babylon. For that matter, Babylon cannot be confined to any one historical manifestation, past or future. Babylon has multiple equivalents (cf. 11:8). The details of John's description do not neatly fit any past city, whether literal Babylon, Sodom, Egypt, Rome, or even Jerusalem. Babylon is found wherever there is satanic deception. It is defined more by dominant idolatries than geographic or temporal boundaries. The ancient Babylon is better understood here as the archetypal head of all entrenched worldly resistance to God. Babylon is a trans-historical reality including idolatrous kingdoms as diverse as Sodom, Gomorrah, Egypt, Babylon, Tyre, Nineveh, and Rome. Babylon is an eschatological symbol of satanic deception and power; it is a divine mystery that can never be wholly reducible to empirical earthly institutions. It may be said that Babylon represents the total culture of the world apart from God, while the divine system is depicted by the New Jerusalem. Rome is simply one manifestation of the total system.

Chapters 17 and 18 form one continuous unit dealing with the judgment on Babylon. The woman is identified as the great city (17:18) whose fall is described in chapter 18. From internal evidence, the identity of Babylon the woman (ch. 17) with Babylon the great city (ch. 18) is so unmistakable that it would be inappropriate to make them different entities. Neither should chapter 17 be viewed as an interpolation, as some have suggested (Mathias Rissi, "The Kerygma of the Revelation to John," Int, 22 [January 1968], 4), simply on the grounds that it seems to be politically specific in the manner of ordinary Jewish apocalyptics (see Introduction: General Nature and Historical Background). While the Roman Empire theory leads more readily to this conclusion, if we reject it, the contents of chapters 17 and 18 are wholly compatible with John's emphasis elsewhere. These two chapters form an extended appendix to the seventh bowl, where the judgment on Babylon was mentioned (16:19). They also expand the earlier references to this city (11:8; 14:8) and look forward by way of contrast to the eternal Holy City (chs. 21–22).

Chapter 17 may be divided as follows: the vision of the great harlot (vv.1–6) and the interpretation of the vision (vv.7–18). In suspenseful literary fashion, John first describes the nature of the harlot and the beast she rides (ch. 17); then he describes her momentous fall in terms drawn from the OT descriptions of the fall of great cities (ch. 18).

1 "One of the seven angels" connects this vision with the preceding bowl judgments, showing that it is a further expansion or appendix of the final bowl action and not an additional event.

John sees a great prostitute (*pornē*) established on many waters. The verse forms a superscription for the chapter. The relationship between prostitution (*porneia*) and idolatry has already been discussed (see comments at 2:14, 20). The prevalence of cult prostitution throughout the ancient world makes this figure appropriate for idolatrous worship. The expressions "abominable things" (17:4) and "magic spell" (18:23) confirm this connection. In the OT, the same figure of a harlot city is used of Nineveh (Nah 3:4), of Tyre (Isa 23:16–17), and frequently of idolatrous Jerusalem (Ezek 16:15ff.). The best background for understanding the language of the chapter is not the history of the Roman Empire or pagan god parallels but the descriptions of Jerusalem the harlot in Ezekiel 16 and 23 and Babylon the harlot in Jeremiah 51. A quick reading of these chapters will confirm the many parallels to John's language.

But the great prostitute (*pornē*), Babylon, that Revelation describes is not any mere historical city with its inhabitants, whether in John's past, present, or future. Rather, this city is the mother of all these historical prostitutes, the archetypal source of every idolatrous manifestation in time and space. Therefore, it is as much a mistake to identify Babylon with Rome (though many scholars do, most recently Mounce, *Revelation,* p. 310) as it is with Jerusalem (so Ford, p. 285). Babylon could equally well be seen in any of these classic manifestations from the past or in modern times—viz., Nazi Germany, Idi Ammin's Ugandan regime, Soviet Russia, Mao's China, British colonialism, or even in aspects of American life (so William Stringfellow, *An Ethic for Christians and Other Aliens in a Strange Land* [Waco: Word, 1973]).

Amazingly, all the harlot-city societies mentioned in Scripture have certain common characteristics that are also reflected in John's description of the great Babylon, in which he merges the descriptions of ancient Babylon and Jerusalem into one great composite. Royal dignity and splendor combined with prosperity, overabundance, and luxury (Jer 51:13; Ezek 16:13, 49; Nah 2:9; cf. Rev 18:3, 7, 16–17); self-trust or boastfulness (Isa 14:12–14; Jer 50:31; Ezek 16:15, 50, 56; 27:3; 28:5; cf. Rev 18:7); power and violence, especially against God's people (Jer 51:35, 49; Ezek 23:37; Nah 3:1–3; cf. Rev 18:10, 24); oppression and injustice (Isa 14:4; Ezek 16:49; 28:18; cf. Rev 18:5, 20); and idolatry (Jer 51:47; Ezek 16:17, 36; 23:7, 30, 49; Nah 1:14; cf. Rev 17:4–5; 18:3; 19:2) are all here. Wherever and whenever these characteristics have been manifested historically, *there* is the appearance of Babylon.

The great prostitute "sits on many waters." This goes back to Jeremiah's oracle against historical Babylon, situated along the waterways of the Euphrates, with many canals around the city, greatly multiplying its wealth by trade (Jer 51:13). While the description alludes to ancient Babylon, it also has a deeper significance, explained in v. 15 as "peoples, multitudes, nations and languages"—figurative for the vast influence of the prostitute on the peoples of the world.

2 Earth's kings and inhabitants committed fornication with the prostitute. This language goes back to references to the harlot cities of the past (e.g., Jer 51:7) and means that the peoples of the world have become drunk with abundance, power, pride, violence, and especially false worship. The expression "kings of the earth" may be in poetic synonymous parallelism (i.e., an equivalent term) with "inhabitants of the earth." If this were so, the exegesis of the former term would be enriched. The evidence for this is not, however, conclusive (cf. 14:8; 17:4–5; 18:3, 9). "The kings of the earth" may describe simply the rulers in contrast to the hoi polloi.

3 John is carried in the Spirit (see comments at 1:10 and cf. 4:2; 21:10) into a "desert." Again the allusion is to ancient Babylon (Isa 14:23; 21:1; cf. Rev 18:2; see comments at 12:6). Caird (p. 213), following more the imagery of 12:6, thinks that John was taken to the desert to be free from the charms and attractions of the whore so that he could understand her exact nature. Yet it is in the desert that he sees the prostitute seated on "a scarlet beast"—scarlet, presumably, because the color symbolizes the beast's blasphemy in contrast to the white-horse rider and those dressed in white, who are faithful and true (19:8, 11, 14). Since this beast is a seven-headed monster, there is no cogent reason against identifying it with the first beast in chapter 13, which is also inseparable from the seven-headed dragon of chapter 12.

4 Dressed in queenly attire (Ezek 16:13; cf. Rev 18:7), the woman rides the beast, swinging in her hand a golden cup full of her idolatrous abominations and wickedness. Note the contrast—beauty and gross wickedness. Her costly and attractive attire suggests the prostitute's outward beauty and attraction (Jer 4:30). The golden cup filled with wine alludes to Jeremiah's description of Babylon's world-wide influence in idolatry (Jer 51:7). Her cup is filled with "abominable things" (*bdelygmatōn*). The *bdelygmatōn* are most frequently associated with idolatry, which was abhorrent to the Jew and likewise to the Christian (21:27). It is the same word Jesus used in referring to Daniel's "abomination that causes desolation" standing in the temple (Mark 13:14; cf. Dan 9:27; 11:31; 12:11). Babylon is the archetype of all idolatrous obscenities in the earth (v.5). "Filth" (*akatharta*, "uncleannesses") is a word frequently associated in the NT with evil (unclean) spirits (e.g., Matt 10:1; 12:43) and also with idolatry (2 Cor 6:17) and perhaps cult prostitution (Eph 5:5).

5 The woman has a title written on her forehead, showing that in spite of all her royal glamour she is nothing but a prostitute. From the writings of Seneca and Juvenal, we know that it was the custom for Roman prostitutes to wear their names in the fillet that encircled their brows (Swete, p. 214). The OT also refers to the peculiar brow of the prostitute (Jer 3:3, "a harlot's brow," NEB).

The first word in the woman's title is "MYSTERY" (*mystērion*, cf. 1:20; 10:7; 17:7). But does the word belong to the name "MYSTERY BABYLON" itself, or is it a prefix before the actual name—viz., "She has a name written on her forehead, which is a mystery, 'Babylon . . .'?" Scholars disagree, but the latter explanation fits better with John's use of *mystērion* as a word denoting a divine mystery or allegory that is now revealed. Furthermore, his use of *pneumatikōs* ("figuratively") before the words "Sodom and Egypt" in 11:8 (q.v.), by which the reader is alerted to a special symbolic significance in what follows, likewise supports this.

No doubt, as Lilje suggests, the specific part of the title that is a divine mystery is that this prostitute is the *mother* of all earth's idolatrous prostitutes (p. 223). She is the fountainhead, the reservoir, the womb that bears all the individual cases of historical resistance to God's will on earth; she is the unholy antithesis to the woman who weds the Lamb (19:7–8) and to the New Jerusalem (21:2–3). Therefore, she cannot be merely ancient Babylon, Rome, or Jerusalem, because these are only her children—*she* is the mother of them all. While at its beginning Babel was associated with resisting and defying God (Gen 11:1–11), it is probably the epoch of the Babylonian captivity of Israel that indelibly etched the proud, idolatrous, and repressive nature of Babylon on the memories of God's people and thus provided for succeeding generations the symbolic image that could be applied to the further manifestations of the mother prostitute.

6 This mother prostitute is also the source of the shed blood of the followers of Jesus, the martyrs referred to throughout the book (6:9; 7:9ff.; 13:8; 18:24). The same mother harlot who had killed the saints of old throughout salvation history is now also responsible for the deaths of the Christians (cf. 2:13). Though there is no direct reference here to Rome or Jerusalem, early Christian readers would understand that whenever they were threatened with death by any temporal power—whether political, religious, or both—they were in reality facing the blood-thirsty mother prostitute God was about to judge and destroy once for all. To be drunk with blood was a familiar figure in the ancient world for the lust for violence (Charles, *Commentary on Revelation,* 2:66; cf. Isa 34:7; 49:26).

7 Verses 7–18 contain an extended interpretation of the vision that parallels the method used in apocalyptic sections in OT prophecy (cf. Zech 1:8ff., etc.; Rev 7:9ff). First the beast is described and identified (vv.7–8), then the seven heads (vv.9–11), the ten horns (vv.12–14), the waters (v.15), and finally the woman (v.18). John's astonishment over the arresting figure of the woman on the beast is quickly subdued by the interpreting angel's announcement that John will be shown the explanation of the divine mystery of the symbolic imagery of woman and beast.

8 Much difficulty in interpreting this section has resulted from incorrectly applying John's words either to the Roman emperor succession (the seven heads), to the Nero redivivus myth ("once was, now is not, and will come up out of the Abyss" [see comments at introduction to ch. 13]), or to a succession of world empires. None of these views is satisfactory for reasons that will be stated below. John's description is theological, not political. He describes a reality behind earth's sovereigns, not the successive manifestations in history. When this is seen to be the case, it is unnecessary to revert to source theories (contra Beasley-Murray, "The Revelation," p. 1300), to interpolation theories (Charles, *Commentary on Revelation,* 2:67; Eller, pp. 165–67), or to other theories in an attempt to relate John's descriptive language to past events.

The beast is the monster from the Abyss, i.e., the satanic incarnation of idolatrous power, described in 13:1ff. (q.v.), mentioned earlier in 11:7, and whose destruction is seen in 19:19–20. John is told that the beast "once was, now is not, and will come up out of the Abyss." This seems clearly to be a paraphrase of the idea in chapter 13 of the sword-wounded beast who was healed (13:3, 14); the language is similar, the astonishment of the world's inhabitants identical, and the threefold emphasis on this spectacular feature is repeated in both contexts (13:3, 12, 14; 17:8 bis, 11).

The play here on the tenses "was, . . . is not, . . . will come" refers to a three-stage history of the beast that requires a mind with wisdom to understand its mystery. Isaiah refers to the chaos monster as "Rahab the Do-Nothing," i.e., the monster thought to energize Egypt is in reality inactive, rendered impotent by the hand of the Lord (Isa 30:7). That John's beast "is not" refers to his defeat by the Lamb on Calvary. To those who worship only the Father and the Son, all other gods are nothing or nonexistent (1 Cor 8:4–6). Satan once had unchallenged power over the earth ("was," cf. Luke 4:6; Heb 2:14–15). Now he is a defeated sovereign ("is not," cf. John 12:31–32); yet he is given a "little time" to oppose God and his people (12:12c; 13:5; 20:3b) before his final sentencing to "destruction" (*apōleia*, v.11; cf. Matt 7:13; John 17:12; Rom 9:22; 2 Thess 2:3). It is this apparent revival of Satan's power and authority over the world after his mortal wound (Gen 3:15) that causes the deceived of earth to follow him.

Note the subtle change in perspective from the way the first reference to the beast is stated (v.8a) to that of the second (v.8b). Whereas the first instance refers to his satanic origin ("out of the Abyss") and his final destruction, a divine revelation to believers, the second simply states how that he was, is not, and yet comes, an unbeliever's view. This twofold viewpoint is paralleled in vv.9–11 where one of the kings "is" (v.10) and an eighth king "is" (v.11); yet the beast "is not" (v.11). There seems to be an intentional double-talk whereby the author seeks to identify theologically the nature of the power that supports the profligate woman.

John's use of the present tense for the beast's coming up out of the Abyss (*anabainein*, cf. 11:7) may suggest a continuing aspect of his character, similar to the use of the present tense to describe the New Jerusalem descending from heaven (*katabainousa;* cf. 3:12; 21:2, 10). That the beast goes into perdition (present tense) may likewise indicate one of his continuing characteristics. There is also a possible parallelism in the expression "once was, now is not, and yet will come" with the divine attributes described in the phrase "who is, and who was, and who is to come" (1:8). On the meaning of the book of life, see comments at 3:5 (cf. 13:8).

9 This and the following verses form the key of the Roman emperor view of the Apocalypse. The woman not only sits on many waters (vv.1, 15), and on the beast (v.3), but she also sits on seven hills. As previously stated, most scholars have no doubt that the seven hills refer to the seven hills of Rome and the seven kings to seven successive emperors of that nation. Mounce states, "There is little doubt that a first-century reader would understand this reference in any way other than as a reference to Rome, the city built upon seven hills" (*Revelation*, pp. 313–14).

Yet there is very good reason to doubt that this interpretation, and its varieties, is the meaning John intended. The following dissenting view is drawn largely from Minear (*I Saw a New Earth*, pp. 237ff.). In the first place, the seven hills belong to the monster, not the woman. It is the woman (i.e., the city [v.18]) who sits upon (i.e., has mastery over) the seven heads (or seven hills) of the monster. If the woman is the city of Rome, it is obvious that she did not exercise mastery over seven successive Roman emperors that are also seven traditional hills of Rome. This introduces an unwarranted twisting of the symbolism to fit a preconceived interpretation. Also, how could the seven hills of Rome have any real importance to the diabolical nature of the beast or the woman? Nor does it help to make the prostitute the Roman Empire and the hills the city of Rome (so Kiddle) since the woman is explicitly identified in v.18 not as the empire but as the city. In fact, nowhere in the NT is Rome described as the enemy of the church.

If it is argued that what is really important in the mention of the seven hills is the identification with Rome, how then does this require any special divine wisdom ("This calls for a mind with wisdom" [v.9])? As Caird (in loc.) remarks, any Roman soldier who knew Greek could figure out that the seven hills referred to Rome. But whenever divine wisdom is called for, the description requires theological and symbolical discernment, not mere geographical or numerical insight (cf. comments at 13:18). Those who follow Charles and argue for a fusing of sources or images to explain the dual reference to the hills and kings simply evade the implications of the incongruity they have created.

In the seven other instances of the word *orē* in Revelation, it is always rendered "mountain," except here in 17:9, where it is translated "hills" (see Notes). Is this a case where previous exegesis has influenced even the best translations (KJV has "mountains")? On the other hand, mountains allegorically refer to world powers in the Prophets (Isa 2:2; Jer 51:25; Dan 2:35; Zech 4:7). It seems better, then, to interpret the seven mountains as a reference to the seven heads or kings, which describe not the city but the beast. The expression "they are also seven kings" seems to require strict identification of the seven mountains with seven kings rather than with a geographic location.

John's use of numbers elsewhere in the book likewise argues against the Roman Empire identification. He has already shown a strong disposition for their symbolic significance—e.g., seven churches, seals, trumpets, bowls, and thunders; twenty-four elders; 144,000 sealed, etc. By his use of seven, he indicates completeness or wholeness. The seven heads of the beast symbolize fullness of blasphemy and evil. It is much like our English idiom "the seven seas," i.e., all the seas of the world. Caird recognizes the patent absurdity of trying to take the symbolic number seven and make it refer to exactly seven Roman emperors. Yet he goes on to explain the seven kings as a reference to an indefinite number of emperors, including Nero redivivus (pp. 218–19). While Caird's view is much more in keeping with John's symbolism, it still labors under the unacceptable assumption that John is identifying the beast with Rome.

10 If the seven heads symbolically represent the complete or full source of evil power and blasphemy, why, then, does John talk about five fallen heads or kings, one existing head or king, and one yet to come? Does this not most readily fit the view of dynastic successions to the imperial throne? To be sure, there have been many attempts to fit the date of Revelation (the then contemporary king would be he who "is") into the emperor lists of the first century (for detailed discussions, see Caird, pp. 217–18; Ford, pp. 289–91). But immediately there are admitted problems. Where do we begin—with Julius Caesar or Caesar Augustus? Are we to count all the emperors or just those who fostered emperor worship? Are we to exclude Galba, Otho, and Vitellius who had short, rival reigns? If so, how can they be excluded except on a completely arbitrary basis? A careful examination of the historic materials yields no satisfactory solution. If Revelation were written under Nero, there would be too few emperors; if under Domitian, too many. The original readers would have had no more information on these emperor successions than we do, and possibly even less. How many Americans can immediately name the last seven presidents? Furthermore, how could the eighth emperor who is identified as the beast also be one of the seven (v. 11)?

Recognizing these problems, others have sought different solutions to John's five-one-one succession of kings. Since the word "king" may also represent kingdoms, Seiss (followed recently by Ladd and Walvoord) has suggested an interpretation that takes the five-one-one to refer to successive world kingdoms that have oppressed the people of God: Egypt, Assyria, Babylon, Persia, Greece (five fallen), Rome (one is), and a future world kingdom (p. 393). While this solves some of the emperor succession problems and fits nicely, it too must admit arbitrary omissions, such as the devastating persecution of the people of God under the Seleucids of Syria, especially Antiochus IV, Epiphanes. This view also suffers in not respecting the symbolic significance of John's use of seven throughout the book. Also, how can these kings (kingdoms) survive the destruction of the harlot and be pictured as mourning over her demise (18:9)? And what logical sense can be made of the fact that the seventh king (kingdom), usually identified with Antichrist, is separate from the eighth king (kingdom), which is clearly identified with the beast (vv. 10b–11)?

A convincing interpretation of the seven kings must do justice to three considerations: (1) Since the heads belong to the beast, the interpretation must relate their significance to this beast, not to Babylon. (2) Since the primary imagery of kingship in Revelation is a feature of the power conflict between the Lamb and the beast and between those who share the rule of these two enemies (cf. 17:14; 19:19), the kind of sovereignty expressed in 17:10 must be the true antithesis to the kind of sovereignty exercised by Christ and his followers. (3) Since the kings are closely related to the seven mountains and to the prostitute, the nature of the relationship between these must be clarified by the interpretation (Minear, *I Saw a New Earth*, p. 240).

If we can see that the seven heads do not represent a quantitative measure but show qualitatively the fullness of evil power residing in the beast, then the falling of five heads conveys the message of a significant victory over the beast. The image of a sovereignty falling is better related to God's judgment on a power than to a succession of kings (-doms) (cf. Jer 50:32; 51:8, 49; Rev 14:8; 18:2).

The imagery of the seven heads presented in 12:3 and 13:1 must be restudied. The ancient seal showing the seven-headed chaos monster being slain (see comments at 13:1b) well illustrates John's imagery here. In that ancient scene, the seven-headed monster is being slain by a progressive killing of its seven heads. Four of the heads are dead, killed apparently by the spear of a divine figure who is attacking the monster. His defeat seems imminent. Yet the chaos monster is still active because three heads still live. Similarly, John's message is that five of the monster's seven heads are already defeated by the power of the Lamb's death and by the identification in that death of the martyrs of Jesus (12:11). One head is now active, thus showing the reality of the beast's contemporary agents who afflict the saints; and one head remains, indicating that the battle will soon be over but not with the defeat of the contemporary evil agents. This last manifestation of the beast's blasphemous power will be short—"he must remain for a little while." This statement seems to go with the function of the ten horns (kings) who for "one hour" (v. 12) will rule with the beast. The seventh king (head) represents the final short display of satanic evil before the divine blow falls on the beast (cf. 12:12c; 20:3c).

11 This verse presents all interpreters with a real difficulty. One of the common interpretations refers the language to the Nero redivivus myth (see comments at introduction to ch. 13)—viz., a revived Nero will be the reincarnation of the evil genius of the whole Roman Empire (Beasley-Murray, "The Revelation," p. 1300). Furthermore, among futurist interpreters there is no agreement as to whether the seventh or the eighth king is the Antichrist. It must be admitted that any king(-dom)-succession hypothesis founders on v. 11. On the other hand, if John has in mind qualitative identification and not quantitative, a theological rather than historical or political sense, the passage may yield further insight into the mystery of the beast.

First, we note the strange (to us) manner in which the sequence of seven kings gives way to the eighth, which is really the whole beast. This pattern of seven-to-eight-equals-one was familiar to the early church. It is a concept those raised in the great liturgical traditions can grasp. The eighth day was the day of the resurrection of Christ, Sunday. It was also the beginning of a new week. The seventh day, the Jewish Sabbath, is held over, to be replaced by the first of a new series, namely Sunday. Austin Farrer has noted how even the whole theme of the Apocalypse is integrally related to this idea. "Sunday is the day of Resurrection. The 'week' with which the Apocalypse deals extends from the Resurrection of Christ to the General Resurrection, when death has been destroyed." He further states the relation between the seventh and eighth:

> God rests from his completed work, but in so resting he initiates a new act which is the eighth-and-first day. We may compare the Gospel once more. On the sixth day Christ conquered, and achieved his rest from the labours of his flesh. But the sabbath-day which follows is in itself nothing, it has no content: it is simply the restful sepulchre out of which, with the eighth and first day, the resurrection springs. (*A Rebirth of Images; the Making of St. John's Apocalypse* [London: Darce, 1949], pp. 70–71).

Each of the series of sevens in the book, except for the seven churches, follows a pattern of the seventh in the series becoming the first of a new series; thus seven to eight equals one. The eighth was the day of the Messiah, the day of the new age and the sign of the victory over the forces of evil (Alexander Schememann, *Introduction to Liturgical Theology* [London: Faith, 1966], pp. 60–64). Shepherd also calls attention to this phenomenon in Revelation (Massey H. Shepherd, Jr., *The Paschal Liturgy and the Apocalypse* [Richmond: John Knox, 1960], pp. 20–21, 80). But does this provide a key to interpret the symbolism of the chaos monster?

Of the three stages of the beast—was, is not, will come—only the last is related to his coming "up out of the Abyss" (v.8). These words appear to be the equivalent of the beast's healed wound (plague) mentioned in 13:3, 14. While, on the one hand, Christ has killed the monster by his death (Gen 3:15; Rev 12:7–9) and for believers he "is not" (has no power), yet, on the other hand, the beast still has life ("one is" [v.10]) and will attempt one final battle against the Lamb and his followers ("the other has not yet come; . . . he must remain for a little while"). In order to recruit as many as possible for his side of the war, the beast will imitate the resurrection of Christ (he "is an eighth king" [v.11]) and will give the appearance that he is alive and in control of the world (cf. Luke 4:5–7). But John quickly adds, for the pastoral comfort of God's people, that the beast belongs to the seven, i.e., qualitatively not numerically (as if he were a former king revived); he is in reality (to the eyes of the saints) not a new beginning of life but a part of the seven-headed monster that has been slain by Christ and, therefore, he goes "to his destruction." While this imagery may seem to us to be unnecessarily obscure, it reveals the true mystery of the beast in a fashion that exposes the dynamics of satanic deception so that every Christian may be forearmed.

12–14 Here John seems to allude to Daniel 7:7, 24. The ten horns are usually understood as either native rulers of Roman provinces, serving under the emperors or native rulers of satellite states, or governors of Palestine. Others see in them a ten-nation confederacy of the future revived Roman Empire (e.g., Walvoord, pp. 254–55). There are good reasons for abandoning these explanations. In the first place, the number ten should—like most of John's numbers—be understood symbolically. Ten symbolizes a repeated number of times or an indefinite number. It is perhaps another number like seven, indicating fullness (Neh 4:12; Dan 1:12; Rev 2:10). Thus the number should not be understood as referring specifically to ten kings (kingdoms) but as indicating the multiplicity of sovereignties in confederacy that enhance the power of the beast.

Second, since these kings enter into a power conflict with the Lamb and his followers (v.14), the kind of sovereignty they exercise must be the true antithesis of the kind of sovereignty the Lamb and his followers exercise. These rulers as well as the beast with which they will be allied can be no other than the principalities and powers, the rulers of the darkness of this world, the spiritual forces of evil in the heavenly realms that Paul describes as the true enemies of Jesus' followers (Eph 6:12). To be sure, they use earthly instruments, but their reality is far greater than any specific historical equivalents (see note on v.14). These "kings" embody the fullness of Satan's attack against the Lamb in the great eschatological showdown. They are the "kings from the east" (16:12–14, 16), and they are also the "kings of the earth" who ally themselves with the beast in the final confrontation with the Lamb (19:19–21).

Finally, there is a link between v.12 and v.11. The ten kings are said to receive authority for "one hour" along with the beast. This corresponds to the "little while" of the seventh king. From the viewpoint of the saints, who will be greatly persecuted, this promise of brevity brings comfort. These kings have "one purpose" (*gnōmē*); they agree to oppose the Lamb. But the Lamb will overcome them because he is Lord of lords and King of kings (cf. Deut 10:17; Dan 2:47; Rev 19:16). He conquers by his death, and those who are with him also aid in the defeat of the beast by their loyalty to the Lamb even to death (cf. 5:5, 9; 12:11)—a sobering thought.

15 On first reading, this verse appears to be out of place. However, closer examination shows that v.16 also refers to the prostitute and the horns. Verse 15 teaches that the influence of the idolatrous satanic system of Babylon is universal (cf. vv.1–2) and embraces all peoples, from the humblest to the kings of the earth.

16–17 On these verses the Roman hypothesis (empire and city) breaks down. For in that view the emperors (the beast and its heads) will turn against the city or empire and destroy her. Swete (p. 222) tries to locate this event in Rome's history and to argue that there is some supporting evidence for it. But the attempt is not convincing. Rather, the attack on the prostitute indicates that in the final judgment the kingdom of Satan, by divine purpose, will be divided against itself. The references to the prostitute being hated by her former lovers, stripped naked, and burned with fire are reminiscent of the OT prophets' descriptions of the divine judgment falling on the harlot cities of Jerusalem and Tyre (e.g., Ezek 16:39–40; 23:25–27; 28:18). The description of the punishment of convicted prostitutes who are priests' daughters (cf. Lev 21:9; the burning with fire is explained by Ford as "a pouring of molten lead down their throats" [p. 55]) is combined with the picture of judgment against rebellious cities (18:8). Caird aptly captures the meaning of John's imagery in v.16: "The ravaging of the whore by the monster and its horns is John's most vivid symbol for the self-destroying power of evil" (p. 221).

In the declaration "God has put it into their hearts to accomplish his purpose" (v. 17), there is another indication of God's use of the forces of evil as instruments of his own purposes of judgment (Jer 25:9–14; cf. Luke 20:18). Nothing will distract them from their united effort to destroy the prostitute till God's purposes given through the prophets are fulfilled (cf. 10:7; 11:18).

18 The "woman" and "the great city" are one. Yet this city is not just a historical one; it is the *great* city, the *mother* city, the archetype of every evil system opposed to God in history (see comments at introduction to ch. 17). Her kingdom holds sway over the powers of the earth. John's concept of the city in Revelation entails much more than a specific historical city even in its political and sociological aspects. The cities in Revelation are communities; they are twofold: the city of God, the New Jerusalem (3:12; 21:2, 10; 22:2ff.), and the city of Satan, Babylon the Great (11:8; 14:8; 16:19; 18:4, 20, etc.). The meaning cannot be confined to Sodom or Egypt or Jerusalem or Rome or any future city. Instead, John describes the real trans-historical system of satanic evil that infuses them all.

Notes

---

1 For Minear's general view, cf. *I Saw a New Earth*, pp. 228–46; idem, "Babylon in the New Testament," IDB, 1:338. While Ford presents five good reasons why Babylon cannot be the city of Rome, she falls into a similar error by identifying the city as Jerusalem (p. 216). But Jerusalem, like Rome, is only one of the multiple manifestations of Babylon in history. Josephus refers to Cleopatra in language very similar to that of the Apocalypse, but as a historical type Jezebel would probably come closer to John's imagery (cf. comments at 2:20; Jos. Antiq. XV, 97 [iv.2]).

Πόρνη (*pornē*, "prostitute") may be either male or female, married or unmarried. The word is generally used of unmarried sexual relations (μοιχεία [*moicheia*] is used for extramarital relations, i.e., adultery and cult prostitution), but it can denote sexual perversions in general, whether among married or unmarried (TDNT, 6:579ff.).

8 Ladd, following Zahn, interprets the play on tenses in a more literal manner, understanding the reference to the beast as the beast that "was" as pointing to the Syrian king Antiochus Epiphanes IV, the great persecutor of the people of God in the days of the Maccabees (c. 167 B.C.) (*Commentary on Revelation*, pp. 230–31). There is some support for this view in Dan 8:9, 21. But the beast that "was" could just as well have been the emperor Vespasian, who ordered Jerusalem destroyed in A.D. 70 by Titus. Or it could also refer to Nero, who undertook an attack on Christians in the city of Rome a short time earlier.

9 Translations that render ὄρη (*orē*) as "hills" include RSV, NEB, TEV, Ph, Knox, NIV; those translating the word as "mountains" include KJV, ASV, NASB. Places in Revelation where ὄρος (*oros*) or *orē* occurs and is translated "mountain(s)" in most all versions are 6:14–16; 8:8; 14:1; 16:20; 21:10. The early Christian work the Shepherd of Hermas (c. 90–140/150) refers to a vision of "twelve mountains" that are interpreted symbolically as the twelve tribes of Israel (*Similitudes* 9.17). The coinage of Vespasian depicts the goddess of the city, Roma, enthroned on the seven hills, with the Tiber and the she-wolf (Ethelbert Stauffer, *Christ and the Caesars* (tr. K. & R. Gregor Smith [London: SCM, 1955], p. 154). One could, however, count at least eight hills in Rome: the Capitol, the Palatine, the Aventine, the Caelian, the Oppian, the Esquiline, the Viminal, and the Quirinal. The Vatican would make a ninth (ZPEB, 5:162).

10 Caird refers to the symbolic significance of the seven heads as indicating not seven specific emperors but a whole line of emperors (pp. 218–19). Why the emperors should then be limited to Rome, Caird does not tell us. He also refers to the well-known Eagle Vision of 4 Ezra 11–12 as support for the emperor succession interpretation of Rev 17:10. However appropriate this interpretation is to Jewish apocalyptic writing, it remains to be demonstrated that John had such an intent in mind. The Jewish visions are more allegorical (language with a specific historical counterpart in mind) than Rev, while Rev is symbolical (language of universal reality having many historical counterparts).

11 In the early church there was an interpretation that took the seven mountains as referring to the seven millennia of world history, a theme current in that period. Thus after asserting that the Sabbath is a type of the millennial reign of Christ, Hippolytus says, "Since, then, in six days God made all things, it follows that six thousand years must be fulfilled. And they are not yet fulfilled, as John says: five are fallen, one is, the other is not yet come (Rev 17:10). Moreover, in speaking of the other he specifies the seventh, in which there shall be rest" (*Commentary on Daniel* 4.23; see note on 20:1).

14 For an enlightening and thorough discussion of the relationship between the angel powers who rule and their earthly agents, see Oscar Cullmann, *The State in the New Testament*, "Excursus: on the most recent discussion of the ἐξουσίαις in Romans 13:1" (New York: Scribner's, 1956), pp. 95–114.

---

4. *The fall of Babylon the Great*

18:1–24

[1]After this I saw another angel coming down from heaven. He had great authority, and the earth was illuminated by his splendor. [2]With a mighty voice he shouted:

"Fallen! Fallen is Babylon the Great!
She has become a home for demons
and a haunt for every evil spirit,
a haunt for every unclean and detestable bird.
[3]For all the nations have drunk
the maddening wine of her adulteries.
The kings of the earth committed adultery with her,
and the merchants of the earth grew rich from her
excessive luxuries."

[4]Then I heard another voice from heaven say:

"Come out of her, my people,
so that you will not share in her sins,
so that you will not receive any of her plagues;
[5]for her sins are piled up to heaven,
and God has remembered her crimes.
[6]Give back to her as she has given;
pay her back double for what she has done.
Mix her a double portion from her own cup.
[7]Give her as much torture and grief
as the glory and luxury she gave herself.
In her heart she boasts,
'I sit as queen; I am not a widow,
and I will never mourn.'
[8]Therefore in one day her plagues will overtake her:
death, mourning and famine.
She will be consumed by fire,
for mighty is the Lord God who judges her.

[9]"When the kings of the earth who committed adultery with her and shared her
luxury see the smoke of her burning, they will weep and mourn over her. [10]Terrified
at her torment, they will stand far off and cry:

" 'Woe! Woe, O great city,
O Babylon, city of power!
In one hour your doom has come!'

[11]"The merchants of the earth will weep and mourn over her because no one
buys their cargoes any more— [12]cargoes of gold, silver, precious stones and
pearls; fine linen, purple, silk and scarlet cloth; every sort of citron wood, and articles
of every kind made of ivory, costly wood, bronze, iron and marble; [13]cargoes of
cinnamon and spice, of incense, myrrh and frankincense, of wine and olive oil, of
fine flour and wheat; cattle and sheep; horses and carriages; and bodies and souls
of men.

[14]"They will say, 'The fruit you longed for is gone from you. All your riches and
splendor have vanished, never to be recovered.' [15]The merchants who sold these
things and gained their wealth from her will stand far off, terrified at her torment.
They will weep and mourn [16]and cry out:

" 'Woe! Woe, O great city,
dressed in fine linen, purple and scarlet,
and glittering with gold, precious stones and pearls!
[17]In one hour such great wealth has been brought to ruin!'

"Every sea captain, and all who travel by ship, the sailors, and all who earn their
living from the sea, will stand far off. [18]When they see the smoke of her burning,
they will exclaim, 'Was there ever a city like this great city?' [19]They will throw dust
on their heads, and with weeping and mourning cry out:

" 'Woe! Woe, O great city,
where all who had ships on the sea
became rich through her wealth!
In one hour she has been brought to ruin!
[20]Rejoice over her, O heaven!
Rejoice, saints and apostles and prophets!
God has judged her for the way she treated you.' "

[21]Then a mighty angel picked up a boulder the size of a large millstone and threw
it into the sea, and said:

"With such violence
the great city of Babylon will be thrown down,
never to be found again.
[22]The music of harpists and musicians, flute players
and trumpeters,
will never be heard in you again.
No workman of any trade
will ever be found in you again.
The sound of a millstone
will never be heard in you again.
[23]The light of a lamp
will never shine in you again.
The voice of bridegroom and bride
will never be heard in you again.
Your merchants were the world's great men.
By your magic spell all the nations were led astray.
[24]In her was found the blood of prophets and of the saints,
and of all who have been killed on the earth."

Chapter 18 contains the description of the previously announced "judgment" (*krima;* NIV, "punishment") of the prostitute (17:1). It is important not to separate this chapter from the portrayal of the prostitute in chapter 17, for there is no warrant for making the prostitute in chapter 17 different from the city in chapter 18 (cf. 17:18). Under the imagery of the destruction of the great commercial city, John describes the final overthrow of the great prostitute, Babylon. He is not writing a literal description, even in poetic or figurative language, of the fall of an earthly city, such as Rome or Jerusalem; but in portraying the destruction of a city, he describes God's judgment on the great satanic system of evil that has corrupted the earth's history. Drawing especially from the OT accounts of the destruction of the ancient harlot cities of Babylon (Isa 13:21; 47:7–9; Jer 50–51) and Tyre (Ezek 26–27), John composes a great threnody that might well be the basis of a mighty oratorio. Here in chapters 17–18 is some of the most beautifully cadenced language in the whole book. John combines the song of triumph and the wailing strains of lamentation into a noble funeral dirge (cf. 2 Sam 1:17–27; Isa 14:4–21; Lam, in its entirety).

First, there is a kind of prelude in which the whole judgment is proclaimed (vv.1–3). Then there comes a call for God's people to separate themselves from the city because the divine plagues are about to descend upon her in recompense for her crimes (vv.4–8). The main movement that expresses the laments for the city's fall is divided into three parts: (1) the lament of the kings of the earth (vv.9–10), then (2) the lament of the merchants who traded with her (vv.11–17), and (3) the lament of the sea captains who became rich from the cargoes they took to the city (vv.18–20). Lastly, the finale sounds the death knell of the life of the city because she deceived the nations and killed God's people (vv.21–24).

1–3 So magnificent is the event about to be enacted that a dazzling angel of glory bears the divine news. Some interpreters have associated this glory with the shekinah glory that, in Ezekiel's vision, departed from the temple because of the harlotry of the Israelites (Ezek 11:23) but later on returned to the restored temple (Ezek 43:2).

In words very similar to those of the prophets who encouraged the people of God as they faced ancient Babylon, the angel announces that Babylon the Great, Mother of all the earthly prostitute cities, has fallen (cf. Isa 21:9; Jer 51:8 with Rev 14:8; 18:2). Again, in words reminiscent of the judgment announced against ancient Babylon when the city would be inhabited only by detestable creatures and evil spirits (Isa 13:19–22; 34:11; Jer 50:39), John hears the same fate announced for this Mother of prostitutes (v.2). "Demons" (*daimoniōn*) are associated elsewhere with idolatry (see comments at 9:20 and 16:14). The "haunt" (*phylakē*) is a watchtower; the evil spirits, watching over fallen Babylon like night birds or harpies waiting for their prey, build their nests in the broken towers that rise from the ashes of the city (Swete). She who was a great city has become a wilderness.

The prostitute city will be judged because of her surfeit of fornication (v.3). Here the same thought of 17:2 is expanded as we hear echoes of the judgments on ancient Tyre and Babylon (Isa 23:17; Jer 51:7; Rev 14:8). One of the great sins of Babylon was her luxury (*strēnos;* cf. at 18:7, 9). Because wealth may lead to pride, the prophets and John view surfeit as a manifestation of Babylon (Rev 18:7; cf. Ezek 28:4–5, 16–18). The close proximity of fornication with luxury may suggest that there is a fornication with Babylon that not only involves idolatry (cult prostitution) but that may be pride in excessive wealth.

4–8 "Come out of her, my people" forms the burden of Jeremiah's refrain concerning Babylon (Jer 50:8; 51:6–9; cf. Isa 48:20; 52:11; 2 Cor 6:17). Even in its OT setting, this was no mere warning to leave the actual city of Babylon, much less here in Revelation. John is burdened to exhort the churches to shun the charms and ensnarements of the queen prostitute (v.7) as her qualities are manifest in the world they live in. Wherever there are idolatry, prostitution, self-glorification, self-sufficiency, pride, complacency, reliance on luxury and wealth, avoidance of suffering, violence against life (v.24), there is Babylon. Christians are to separate themselves ideologically and, if necessary, physically from all the forms of Babylon. Already John has warned the churches of her deceit and snares (chs. 2–3). If they refuse to separate themselves, they will "share in her sins" and also in the divine judgments (NIV, "plagues"). It is not necessary to see this as one last call to repentance addressed to the beast worshipers (Caird). Rather, like the warnings in the letters to the churches (chs. 2–3), it is addressed to professing Christians who were being seduced by Satan through the wiles of the queen prostitute to abandon their loyalty to Jesus. If this occurred, Christ would be forced by their own decision to blot out their names from the book of life and include them in the plagues designed for Babylon when she is judged (cf. 3:5; so Farrer, *Revelation of St. John*, p. 155, n.2).

God will not forget her crimes (*adikēmata*), which are multiplied to the height of heaven (v.5; cf. Gen 18:20–21; Jer 51:9). Her punishment will fit her crimes (v.6; cf. Ps 137:8; Jer 50:15, 29; Matt 7:2). This OT principle of lex talionis is never enjoined on God's people in the NT but, as here, is reserved for God alone (Matt 5:38–42; Rom 12:17–21). "Mix her a double portion from her own cup" (cf. Exod 22:4, 7, 9; Isa 40:2) reflects both the ideas of the severity of God's judgment on those who persistently refuse to repent as well as the truth that God's wrath is related to the outworking of sin (cf. Rom 1:24–32). Verse 7 illustrates the latter point.

Babylon's threefold web of sin is described as satiety ("luxury"), pride ("boasts, . . . sit as a queen"), and avoidance of suffering ("I will never mourn"). The three may be interrelated. Luxury leads to boastful self-sufficiency (Ezek 28:5), while the desire to avoid suffering may lead to the dishonest pursuit of luxury (Ezek 28:18). "I sit as a queen" echoes Isaiah's description of judgment on Babylon (Isa 47:7ff.) and Ezekiel's description of Tyre (Ezek 27:3). As she avoided grief through her satiety, her punishment therefore is grief (*penthos*, "mourning," "sorrow," "misfortune"). Suddenly, "in one day," she will experience what she has avoided by her luxury: "death, mourning and famine." Like ancient Babylon, this queen of prostitutes will become unloved and barren (Isa 47:9). In spite of her many charms (v.23c), she will be powerless to avert her destruction (v.8). The words "consumed by fire" (cf. 17:16) may refer to the destruction of a city (cf. vv.9, 18) or to the OT punishment for prostitution if the woman is a priest's daughter (Lev 21:9). As strong as "Babylon the Great" is, the Lord God is stronger and will judge her.

9–19 Even quick reading of Ezekiel 27 shows that here in these verses John had in the back of his mind Ezekiel's lamentation over the Fall of ancient Tyre. Those who entered into fornication with the great mother prostitute wail over her destruction. In terms drawn from the fall of harlot cities in the past, John describes the end of the great reality of evil, Babylon the Great. While allusions to Rome may seem to appear, it is only because Rome, like Tyre, Babylon, or Jerusalem, is herself a prostitute city; and the characteristics of all these cities are found in the queen mother of prostitutes.

First, the kings of the earth cry out their dirge (vv. 9–10). There is a connection between their adultery with Babylon and their sharing of her luxury, as if sharing her luxury was part of their adultery (cf. Ezek 26:16; 27:30–35). So great is the heat and smoke of her burning that they must stand "far off" (v.10). Though ultimately the kings are all the heavenly powers that rule in the affairs of earthly kings and kingdoms (see comments at 17:10, 14; cf. 1 Cor 2:6, 8), in this extended poetic allegory they are the merchant princes who bewail the collapse of the last great city of man under Satan's rule. The lament "Woe, Woe" (cf. 8:13; 9:12; 11:14; 12:12) is repeated three times in this part of the threnody over Babylon and reflects pain at the suddenness of her downfall ("in one hour," cf. vv.8, 17) and the emptiness of their own existences apart from her.

The merchants wail (vv.11–17). They have most to lose because Babylon the Great was built on luxury. The lists that follow are inventories of exotic items reminiscent of the great Oriental *suks* (marketplaces). Swete has an excellent discussion of the more important items (pp. 230–31). In v.13 "bodies and souls of men" require special mention. "Bodies" (*sōmata*) is a Greek idiom for slaves (cf. LXX of Gen 36:6), while "souls of men" (*psychas*) means essentially the same as bodies (slaves). Thus the whole expression means "slaves, that is, human beings."

The refrain (v.16) also shows the blending of the prostitute image of chapter 17 (dressed in fine linen, etc.; cf. 17:4) and the city image of chapter 18 ("O great city"). The wares are less suitable for Rome than for Asia Minor (Lilje, p. 236).

Finally, in vv.17–19 the sea captains and sailors add their lament because they too suffer irreparable loss because of the city's burning (cf. Ezek 27:28). This language is more appropriate to Tyre as a great port city than Rome, which was inland and had the not-too-distant Ostia as its port. But in any case, it is not John's intent to describe any one city but the great harlot city, the archetype of the earth's evil cities.

20 The threefold lament is balanced by a song of heavenly jubilation. Babylon has also persecuted the church of Jesus (saints, apostles, prophets). Except for the mention of false apostles earlier in the book (2:2), this is the only reference to apostles in Revelation (cf. 21:14). If it is correct to see in v.20 a reference to their being killed (cf. v.24), perhaps John had in mind Herod's martyring of James (Acts 12:1–2) or Rome's killing of Peter and Paul. The picture of Babylon cannot, however, be confined to the political activity of Rome. Therefore, John attributes the deaths of the martyrs to Babylon the Great. It is she who has killed Jesus (11:7–8) and Stephen by the hands of unbelieving Jews (Acts 7:57–60) and the martyr Antipas by the hands of pagan cultists (2:13; cf. Matt 23:34–37).

21–24 The final lament over the fall of Babylon, spoken by an angel, is poignant and beautiful. A mighty angel picks up a huge stone like a giant millstone (four to five feet in diameter, one foot thick, and weighing thousands of pounds) and flings it into the sea. One quick gesture becomes a parable of the whole judgment on Babylon the Great! Suddenly she is gone forever (cf. Jer 51:64; Ezek 26:21). The melancholy recollection of the pulsing life that once filled this great city with the joy of life sounds through these verses "like footsteps dying away in the distance in a desolate city which lies in ruins" (Lilje).

All nations were deceived (*planō*, "led astray") by her "magic spell" (*pharmakeia*, "sorcery"). John has previously used *pharmakeia* in conjunction with "murders," "fornicators," and "thefts" (see comments at 9:21). An element of drugging is involved that results in fatal poisoning (MM, p. 664). With her deceit, Babylon charmed the nations. Compare the similar charge against the harlot city Nineveh for her lies to other nations (Nah 3:4).

In the final verse (24), the great sin of Babylon is cited. She has martyred the prophets and followers of Jesus. John has already mentioned this blood-guiltiness (17:6; cf. 19:2). Elsewhere the death of martyrs is attributed to "the inhabitants of the earth" (6:10), the "beast that comes up from the Abyss" (11:7, 13:7), and the "beast, coming out of the earth" (13:15). In the OT, the city of Jerusalem (Ezek 24:6, 9; cf. Matt 23:37) and Babylon (Jer 51:35) are called cities of bloodshed. In v.24 "the blood . . . of all who have been killed on the earth" refers to all those who in history have been martyred because of their loyalty to the true God. John's word for kill (*sphazō*) is consistently used for martyrs (5:6, 9, 12; 6:4, 9; 13:8). In John's mind, Babylon the Great (v.2) is much more comprehensive than ancient Babylon, Nineveh, Jerusalem, or Rome. She encompasses all the persecution against the servants of God until the words of God are fulfilled (cf. 17:17).

5. *Thanksgiving for the destruction of Babylon*

19:1–5

[1]After this I heard what sounded like the roar of a great multitude in heaven shouting:

"Hallelujah!
Salvation and glory and power belong to our God,
[2]for true and just are his judgments.
He has condemned the great prostitute
who corrupted the earth by her adulteries.
He has avenged on her the blood of his servants."

[3]And again they shouted:

"Hallelujah!
The smoke from her goes up for ever and ever."

[4]The twenty-four elders and the four living creatures fell down and worshiped God, who was seated on the throne. And they cried:

"Amen, Hallelujah!"

[5]Then a voice came from the throne, saying:

"Praise our God,
all you his servants,
you who fear him,
both small and great!"

In stark contrast to the laments of Babylon's consorts, the heavenly choirs burst forth in a great liturgy of celebration to God. In these verses (1–5), we hear four shouts of praise for the Fall of Babylon. First, there is the sound of a great multitude praising God for his condemnation of the prostitute (19:1–2). Then they shout out in celebration of the city's eternal destruction (v.3). Following this, we hear in antiphonal response the voices of the twenty-four elders and the four living creatures (v.4). Finally, a voice from the throne calls on all the servants of God to praise him (v.5).

1–2 The word "Hallelujah" (*hallēlouia*) transliterates the Greek, which in turn transliterates the Hebrew *halᵉlû yāh,* which means "Praise the Lord!" (In v.5, "Praise our God" [*Aineite tō theō hēmōn*] is equivalent to "Hallelujah.") The Hebrew transliteration occurs only in this chapter in the NT (vv.1, 3, 4, 6), but in the LXX it is a frequent title for certain of the psalms (Pss 111:1; 112:1; 113:1, et al.). This phenomenon clearly illustrates the connection of the early church's liturgical worship with the synagogue and temple worship of the first century. These praise psalms formed an important part of the Jewish festival celebrations.

> Hallel is the Jewish song of jubilation that has accompanied our wanderings of thousands of years, keeping awake within us the consciousness of our world-historical mission, strengthening us in times of sorrow and suffering, and filling our mouths with song of rejoicing in days of deliverance and triumph. To this day, it revives on each Festival season the memory of Divine Redemption, and our

> confidence in future greatness (S.R. Hirsch, quoted in Joseph Hertz, *The Authorized Daily Prayer Book,* rev. ed. [New York: Block, 1948], p. 756).

The Hallel is the name especially applied to Psalms 113–118. These psalms are also called "The Hallel of Egypt" because of the references in them to the Exodus. They thus have a special role in the Feast of Passover (M *Pesahim* 10:5–7). The Midrashic sources also unanimously associate the Hallel with the destruction of the wicked, exactly as this passage in Revelation does (Eric Werner, *The Sacred Bridge: Liturgical Parallels in Synagogue and Early Church* [New York: Schocken Books, 1970], pp. 151, 158, 302–3).

The Hallel was most certainly what Jesus and the disciples sang after the Passover-Eucharist celebration, before going out to the Mount of Olives the night before his death (Matt 26:30). This close connection between the Hallel, Passover, and the death of Jesus no doubt explains why all the early church liturgies incorporated the Hallel into the propers for Easter and Easter Week (Massey H. Shepherd, Jr., *The Paschal Liturgy and the Apocalypse* [Richmond: John Knox, 1960], p. 96). This Easter liturgy is the Christian experience of the gospel of redemption from sin, Satan, and death in the victorious triumph of Christ, our Passover. The Paschal liturgy concludes with the celebration of the Eucharistic banquet of Christ, as he holds intimate communion with his church, giving it light and life. Shepherd links the great banquet of vv.7–9 to the Eucharist celebration in the early church. The psalms in the great Hallel (Pss 113:1; 115:13) are unmistakably cited in 19:5. One can hardly read this Hallel section of Revelation without thinking of the "Hallelujah Chorus" in Handel's *Messiah*.

The theme of "salvation" (*sōtēria*) has already been sounded in Revelation in connection with victory or divine justice (7:10; 12:10). God has indeed vindicated the injustice visited on his servants by meting out true justice on the great prostitute, Babylon. She deserves the sentence because she corrupted the earth (cf. 11:18; Jer 51:25) and killed the saints of God (cf. 18:24).

3 The second Hallel supplements the first one. Babylon's permanent end is celebrated in words reminiscent of ancient Babylon's judgment (Isa 34:10).

4 In response to the heavenly Hallels, the twenty-four elders cry out, "Amen, Hallelujah" (cf. comments at 1:7 on Amen, at 4:4 on the elders).

5 This final praise is spoken by a single voice from the throne (cf. 16:17). The voice is probably neither that of God nor that of Christ because of the words "*our* Lord God Almighty reigns" (v.6). Here is a clear reference to the great Hallel Psalms 113 and 115. "Praise our God, all you his servants" reflects Psalm 113:1, while "you who fear him, both small and great" reflects Psalm 115:13 (cf. Ps 135:1, 20). All socio-economic distinctions are transcended in the united worship of the church ("both small and great") (cf. 11:18; 13:16; 19:18; 20:12).

6. *Thanksgiving for the marriage of the Lamb*

19:6–10

[6]Then I heard what sounded like a great multitude, like the roar of rushing waters and like loud peals of thunder, shouting:

"Hallelujah!
For our Lord God Almighty reigns.

[7]Let us rejoice and be glad
and give him glory!
For the wedding of the Lamb has come,
and his bride has made herself ready.
[8]Fine linen, bright and clean,
was given her to wear."

(Fine linen stands for the righteous acts of the saints.)

[9]Then the angel said to me, "Write: 'Blessed are those who are invited to the wedding supper of the Lamb!' " And he added, "These are the true words of God."

[10]At this I fell at his feet to worship him. But he said to me, "Do not do it! I am a fellow servant with you and with your brothers who hold to the testimony of Jesus. Worship God! For the testimony of Jesus is the spirit of prophecy."

6–8 Finally, the cycle of praise is completed with the reverberating sounds of another great multitude. If the multitude in v.1 was angelic, then this one would most certainly be the great redeemed throngs (cf. 7:9). They utter the final Hallel in words reminiscent of the great kingship psalms (93:1; 97:1; 99:1). The first of these psalms is used in the synagogue Sabbath morning and evening services and also in the Armenian church liturgy for Easter Sunday (Werner, *Sacred Bridge*, p. 153). It is also the prelude to Psalms 95–99, which are messianic, and has as its theme the eternal sovereignty of God who will conquer all his enemies (Hertz, *Daily Prayer Book*, p. 362). The Greek verb *ebasileusen* ("reigns"), an ingressive aorist, may better be rendered "has begun to reign."

There is also rejoicing because the "wedding of the Lamb has come, and his bride has made herself ready" (v.7). It is John's way to give us a glimmer of the next great vision at the close of the former one (cf. 21:2, 9). Contrast the prostitute and her lovers in the preceding chapters with the Lamb and his chaste bride ("fine linen, bright and clean").

The bride is the heavenly city, the New Jerusalem (21:2, 9), which is the symbol of the church, the bride of Christ, the community of those redeemed by Christ's blood. The wedding imagery, including the wedding supper, was for the Jews a familiar image of the kingdom of God. Jesus used wedding and banquet imagery in his parables of the kingdom (Matt 22:2ff.; 25:1–13; Luke 14:15–24). The OT used the figure for the bride of Israel (Ezek 16:1ff.; Hos 2:19), and NT writers have applied it to the church (2 Cor 11:2; Eph 5:25ff.). Heaven's rejoicing has signaled the defeat of all the enemies of God. The time of betrothal has ended. Now it is the time for the church, prepared by loyalty and suffering, to enter into her full experience of salvation and glory with her beloved spouse, Christ. The fuller revelation of the realization of this union is described in chapters 21 and 22.

The church's garments are white linen—in marked contrast to the purple and scarlet clothing of the great mother of prostitutes (17:4; 18:16). Linen was an expensive cloth used to make the garments worn by priests and royalty. It has two qualities: brightness and cleanness (cf. 16:6). Bright (*lampros*) is the color of radiant whiteness that depicts glorification (TDNT, 4:27; cf. Matt 13:43). Clean (*katharos*) reflects purity, loyalty, and faithfulness, the character of the New Jerusalem (21:18, 21).

An explanatory interjection, probably added by John, states that "fine linen stands for the righteous acts of the saints." In 15:4, *dikaiōmata* ("righteous acts") describes the manifest deeds of God that relate to truth and justice. The *dikaiōmata* do not imply any kind of meritorious works that would bring salvation. Rather, there is a delicate balance between grace and obedient response to it. The bride is "given" the garments, but she "has made herself ready" for the wedding by faithfulness and loyalty to Christ (cf. 3:4–5, 18). In the parable of the man without a wedding garment, the garment he lacked was probably a clean one supplied by the host but either refused or soiled through carelessness by the rejected guest. The meaning of the clean garment is probably repentance and obedient response to Christ, both of which the Pharisees lacked (Matt 22:11f.; cf. J. Jeremias, *The Parables of Jesus*, rev. ed. [New York: Scribner's, 1963], pp. 188–89). Thus John contrasts the faithful disciples of Jesus, who have been true to God, with those who were seduced by the beast and the prostitute. The bride prepared herself, then, by her obedient discipleship (see comments at 12:11).

9–10 This beatitude is the fourth of seven (1:3; 14:13; 16:15; 20:6; 22:7, 14) in Revelation. In each beatitude there is a subtle contrast to those who are not loyal and faithful followers of the Lamb. The word translated "invited" is *keklēmenoi* ("called"), a form of the verb *kaleō* ("call"), which is used in the NT of the call to salvation (e.g., Matt 9:13; Rom 8:30; 9:24; 1 Cor 1:9; 2 Thess 2:14). However, the word may also mean "invited," with no connotation of election (cf. Matt 22:3, 8; Luke 14:16; John 2:2). The wedding supper began toward evening on the wedding day, lasted for many days, and was a time of great jubilation. Here in Revelation, the wedding is the beginning of the earthly kingdom of God, the bride is the church in all her purity, the invited guests are both the bride and people who have committed themselves to Jesus.

To assure John and his readers of the certainty of the end of the great prostitute and the announcement of the wedding supper of the Lamb, the angel adds, "These are the true words of God" (cf. 1:2; 17:17; 21:5). A similar sentence later seems to give the same assurance for the whole book (22:6).

John, who was himself a prophet and who had received such a clear revelation about idolatry, now falls prey to this temptation. After the final vision, he again slips into idolatry (22:8). Whether John included these references to his own failure because he knew of the tendency toward angel worship in the churches of Asia is not clear. Be that as it may, we need to recognize how easy it is to fall into idolatry. Whenever a Christian gives anyone or anything other than God control of his life, he has broken the first commandment. The "testimony of Jesus" is Jesus' own testimony that he bore in his life and teaching and especially in his death (cf. comments at 1:2, 9; and also the same expression in 6:9; 12:11; 14:12; 20:4). Those who hold to or proclaim this testimony are Christian prophets. Thus "the testimony of Jesus is the spirit of prophecy." The words spoken by the Christian prophets come from the Spirit of God, who is the Spirit of the risen Jesus; they are the very words of God.

Notes

10 See commentary at 1:2 for arguments supporting the identification of Ἰησοῦ (*Iēsou*, "Jesus") in this verse as a subjective genitive and rendering it as "Jesus' witness" (so Caird; Minear, et al.).

IV. Vision of the Return of Christ and the Consummation of This Age (19:11–20:15)

A. *The Rider on the White Horse and the Destruction of the Beast*

19:11–21

[11]I saw heaven standing open and there before me was a white horse, whose
rider is called Faithful and True. With justice he judges and makes war. [12]His eyes
are like blazing fire, and on his head are many crowns. He has a name written on
him that no one but he himself knows. [13]He is dressed in a robe dipped in blood,
and his name is the Word of God. [14]The armies of heaven were following him, riding
on white horses and dressed in fine linen, white and clean. [15]Out of his mouth
comes a sharp sword with which to strike down the nations. "He will rule them with
an iron scepter." He treads the winepress of the fury of the wrath of God Almighty.
[16]On his robe and on his thigh he has this name written:

KING OF KINGS AND LORD OF LORDS.

[17]And I saw an angel standing in the sun, who cried in a loud voice to all the birds
flying in midair, "Come, gather together for the great supper of God, [18]so that you
may eat the flesh of kings, generals, and mighty men, of horses and their riders,
and the flesh of all people, free and slave, small and great."
[19]Then I saw the beast and the kings of the earth and their armies gathered
together to make war against the rider on the horse and his army. [20]But the beast
was captured, and with him the false prophet who had performed the miraculous
signs on his behalf. With these signs he had deluded those who had received the
mark of the beast and worshiped his image. The two of them were thrown alive into
the fiery lake of burning sulfur. [21]The rest of them were killed with the sword that
came out of the mouth of the rider on the horse, and all the birds gorged themselves
on their flesh.

This new vision is introduced by the words "I saw heaven standing open." Earlier John had seen a door standing open in heaven (4:1), the temple in heaven standing open (11:19), and now, in preparation for a great revelation of God's sovereignty, he sees heaven itself flung wide open to his gaze (cf. Ezek 1:1). In one sense, this vision (vv.11–21), which depicts the return of Christ and the final overthrow of the beast, may be viewed as the climax of the previous section (vv.1–10) or as the first of a final series of seven last things—viz., the return of Christ; the defeat of Satan; the binding of Satan; the Millennium; the final end of Satan; the last judgment; and the new heaven, the new earth, and the New Jerusalem.

Early as well as modern interpretation has for the most part seen in 19:11–16 a description of the second coming of Christ—an event to which the NT bears a frequent and unified witness. As for the features of this event, they are variously understood by interpreters.

11 The great vision that begins here reminds us of the first vision of the book (1:12ff.), though its function is entirely different from that of the earlier vision. The whole scene looks alternately to the OT and to the previous references in Revelation to Christ, especially the seven letters (chs. 2–3). So strong are the parallels with chapters 1–3 that Rissi believes that the first section (vv.11–13) of this vision deals with the judgment on the church and the second section (vv.14–16) with the world (Mathias Rissi, *The Future of the World; an Exegetical Study of Revelation 19:11–22:15* [Naperville, Ill.: A.R. Allenson, 1972], p. 19). A white horse with a rider has appeared at 6:1 (cf. discussion in loc.). Both white horses represent conquest or victory, but with that the similarity changes to total contrast: The rider here in chapter 19 is "faithful and true" (cf. 1:5; 3:7, 14) in contrast to the forces of Antichrist with their empty promises and lies. Christ will keep his word to the churches. In contrast to those who pervert justice and wage unjust war, John says of Christ, "With justice [righteousness] he judges and makes war," an allusion to the messianic character described in Isaiah 11:3ff. In only one other place (2:16) is Christ described as making war (*polemeō*), and there the reference is to his judgment of the church. Furthermore, the questions in 13:4, "Who is like the beast? Who can make war against him?" anticipate the answer that Christ alone can do this, while in 17:14 the beast and the ten kings wage war against the Lamb.

Though John uses OT language descriptive of a warrior-Messiah, he does not depict Christ as a great *military* warrior battling against earth's sovereigns. John reinterprets this OT imagery while at the same time inseparably linking Christ to its fulfillment. The close proximity in v.11 of justice and war shows us that the kind of warfare Christ engages in is more the execution of justice than a military conflict. He who is the faithful and true witness will judge the rebellious nations.

12 The reference to the blazing eyes definitely connects this vision with that of chapter 1 (cf. 1:14; 2:18). On his head are not just seven crowns (12:3), or ten (13:1) but many crowns of royalty (*diadēmata*). Perhaps they signify that the royal power to rule the world has now passed to Christ by virtue of the victory of his followers (11:15). All the diadems of their newly won empire meet on his brow (Caird).

So great is Christ's power that his name is known only by himself. Knowledge of the name is in antiquity associated with the power of the god. When a name becomes known, then the power is shared with those to whom the disclosure is made (cf. comments at 2:17). But since two names of Christ are revealed in this vision, "the Word of God" (v.13) and "KING OF KINGS AND LORD OF LORDS" (v.16), it may be concluded that the exclusive power of Christ over all creation is now to be shared with his faithful followers (3:21; 5:10; 22:5). On the other hand, the secret name may be one that will not be revealed till Christ's return.

13 The imagery in this verse has traditionally been related to Isaiah 63:1–6, a passage understood messianically by the Jews and one that John has used in portraying God's wrath in 14:9–11, 17–19. Isaiah pictures a mighty warrior-Messiah who slaughters his enemies. Their life-blood splashes on his clothing as he tramples them down in his anger, as the juice of the grapes splashes on the winetreader in the winepress. But is Christ's blood-dipped robe (v.13) red from his enemies' blood or from his own blood? There are good reasons for accepting the latter (contra Mounce, *Revelation*, p. 345). If the blood is his enemies', how is it that Christ comes from heaven with his robe already dipped in blood before any battle is mentioned? Furthermore, the blood that is always mentioned in connection with Christ in the Apocalypse is his own life-blood (1:5; 5:6, 9; 7:14; 12:11). Caird, however, has no difficulty identifying the blood as that of the saints, which Christ turns into victory over his enemies. But Caird has understood the vintage passage (14:7–20) as a reference to the death of the saints (pp. 242–43).

Admittedly, there is a close connection between the discolored clothing of Christ, the Word of God (to whom the saints bear witness and give their lives), and "the armies of heaven"—i.e., the saints (v.14). Moreover, the word "dipped" (*bebammenon,* from *baptō*) does not fit the imagery of Isaiah 63:2; but it does fit that used in Revelation of believers' garments being washed thoroughly in Christ's blood (7:14; 22:14). The interpretation of the blood as Christ's own is an early one (so Hippolytus, Origen, Andreas; cf. Swete, p. 249). Finally, the sword with which Christ strikes down the nations comes from his mouth and is not in his hand (v.15); and this too is incompatible with battle imagery. In any case, there is sufficient warrant not to press the allusion to Isaiah 63:1–6 too literally.

Applying the expression "the Word of God" (*ho logos tou theou*) to Jesus in a personal sense is peculiar to the Johannine writings (John 1:1, 14; cf. 1 John 1:1). In Revelation "the Word of God" refers to the revelation of God's purpose (1:2; 17:17; 19:9). It is also the message and lifestyle for which the saints suffer oppression and even death (1:9; 6:9; 20:4). The adjectives "true and faithful," which are applied to Christ, are likewise identified with the Word of God (19:9; 21:5; 22:6; cf. 1:5; 3:14; 19:11). Thus Jesus in his earthly life had borne reliable and consistent witness in all his words and actions to the purposes of God and had been completely obedient in doing this. In him the will of God finds full expression. The Word of God and the person of Christ are one.

14 This verse seems somewhat parenthetical because it does not refer directly to Christ's person or his actions. The armies of heaven mounted on white horses are understood by most to be angelic hosts since passages in the OT and NT, though infrequent, speak of the armies or soldiers of heaven as angels (Pss 103:21; 148:2; Luke 2:13; Acts 7:42). Moreover, elsewhere in the NT the coming of Christ is associated with angels (e.g., Matt 13:41; 16:27; 24:30–31). Yet this may not be John's meaning. These soldiers, like their leader, are riding white horses of victory—something hardly true of angels. Their clothing of bright and clean linen is identical to the bride's attire (cf. v.8). Thus it is probably the victors who accompany Christ, either all of them (resurrected and raptured [1 Thess 4:16–17]) or the company of the martyrs. Revelation 17:14 confirms this: "They [the beast and the ten kings] will make war against the Lamb, but the Lamb will overcome them because he is Lord of lords and King of kings—*and with him will be his called, chosen and faithful followers*" (italics added; cf. 15:1–2).

15 There are three OT allusions to the warrior-Messiah in this verse: he strikes down the nations (Isa 11:3ff.); he rules them with an iron rod (Ps 2:9); he tramples out the winepress of God's wrath (Isa 63:1–6). (For the last metaphor, see comments on v.13.) In the first OT allusion, there are significant changes in the imagery. In Revelation the Lamb-Messiah does not wield a sword in his hand, but his sword comes from his mouth (cf. comments at 1:16 and 2:16). This has no exact OT parallel and cannot be accidental, since John emphasizes it so much in Revelation (1:16; 2:12, 16; 19:15, 21). Christ conquers by the power of his word. Yet it is not necessary to see the reference to the sword coming from Christ's mouth as pointing to the expansion of Christianity and the conquest of the nations by their conversion to Christ (so Swete). The scene here is the eschatological return of Christ and his judgment of the nations, not the whole intervening age. Besides, Christ's words are also the instruments of his judgment as well as his salvation (Matt 12:37; John 12:48). On "the rod of iron" and the relationship between "rule" and "shepherd," see comments at 2:27. For the winepress figure, see 14:17ff.

16 This third name of Christ, which all can read, is displayed on that most exposed part of his cloak, the part that covers the thigh, where it cannot escape notice (Swete). The name has already appeared attached to the Lamb (17:14). He is the absolute Lord and King, full of the divine power and authority.

17–18 This section finally brings us to the second last thing (cf. comments at introduction to 19:11–21): the anticipated great confrontation between the beast and his soldiers and the Lamb (vv.17–21; cf. 16:12–16; 17:14). First, there is the summons to the vultures to come to God's great supper and gorge themselves on the slain corpses of the battlefield—a horrible picture of human carnage. The language is borrowed from Ezekiel 39:17ff., which describes the eschatological overthrow of Gog. It may be unnecessary to press the literalness of the description. This battlefield language is designed to indicate that a great victory is about to occur.

19–21 The contrast between the assembling of the beast's might with his kings and their soldiers and the ease by which he is overthrown and captured highlight the beast's powerlessness before his mighty conqueror. The "kings of the earth" refer to the ten horns (kings) of the beast, which is another way of describing the beast's power (see comments at 17:12–14). Both the beast and the false prophet (13:1ff.) are simply seized and thrown into the lake of fire (v.20). Their followers fall before the sword (word) of Christ (v.21). No battle is actually fought. Only the arrangement of the foes and the defeat of the beast is described. Is this accidental? Is John indicating that the battle has already been fought and this is simply the final realization of that previous victory? In chapter 5 the Lamb had overcome (won the victory) by his death (5:5, 9). Further, we are told that there was a battle in heaven, and Satan was cast out and defeated by the blood of the Lamb and the word of his followers' testimony (12:7–9, 11).

There seems to be only one actual battle described in Revelation. Thus these further scenes may be understood as more judicial in character than as literal battlefield descriptions. Because of John's christological reinterpretation, no great eschatological military battle, such as that envisaged in the Qumran War Scroll, will actually be fought. The decisive battle has already been won at the Cross. These armies and the beast are the destroyers of the earth (11:18), who ultimately are the satanic principalities of the world who ally themselves with the human puppets for their idolatrous ends. These have been positionally defeated at the Cross (Col 2:15), but they will finally be stripped of all power at Christ's return. Certainly John would not have denied that Satan and his evil powers are active in the world and that they use historical persons such as a Nero or a Hitler and oppose and harass Christians today.

Although Satan has been dealt a death blow at the Cross (cf. John 12:31; 16:11), he nevertheless continues to promulgate great evil and deception during this present age (cf. Eph 2:2; 1 Thess 3:5; 1 Peter 5:8–9; Rev 2:10). Yet he is a deposed ruler who is now under the sovereign authority of Christ but who for a "little time" is allowed to continue his evil until God's purposes are finished. In this scene of the overthrow of the beast and his kings and their armies, John is showing us the ultimate and swift downfall of these evil powers by the King of kings and Lord of lords. They have met their Master in this final and utterly real confrontation. (On the "lake of fire," see comments at 20:14.)

Notes

---

13 For references to the messianic interpretation of Isa 63:1ff. by the rabbis, see LTJM, 2:730; Swete, pp. 248–49.

The Targum on Gen 49:10ff. has a reference to the warring Messiah whose clothes are discolored with the blood of his enemies (M. McNamara, *Targum and Testament: Aramaic Paraphrases of the Hebrew Bible; A Light on the New Testament* [Grand Rapids: Eerdmans, 1962], p. 141). While this seems to add further evidence to support the view that the blood is from the enemies of Christ, it must still be asked whether John has reinterpreted the figure.

14 For angels accompanying the Messiah in his return, cf. MA Isa 4.14–17. This is probably a Christian document of the first century A.D.

15 While there are no other references in our literature to a sword from the Messiah's mouth, there are references to the destruction of the godless by the mouth of the Messiah, no doubt deriving from Isa 11:4: "He will strike the earth with the rod of his mouth; with the breath of his lips he will slay the wicked." Thus 4 Ezra 13:6, 19 and Pss of Sol 17:10, 45, 49 mention the Messiah in terms such as "He shall destroy the godless nations with the word of his mouth."

19–21 An eschatological military battle is described in both Jewish apocalyptic and Qumran literature (cf. 1 Enoch 90:13–19; 4 Ezra 13:1–13; As Moses 10; Pss Sol 17:23–51; 1QM; 1QH 6.25f.). In these references the war is still to be fought in the future; it involves actual earthly rulers of the godless; and, according to Qumran documents, it will require the military assistance of the godly to effect the defeat of the ungodly. However, this does not seem to be John's view, since Christ alone executes the wrath; and the decisive victory has already been won before the actual eschatological end. Christ *will* really defeat evil once and for all, but not in the literal military sense envisaged by the Jewish apocalyptists.

B. *Binding of Satan and the Millennium*

20:1–6

[1]And I saw an angel coming down out of heaven, having the key to the Abyss and holding in his hand a great chain. [2]He seized the dragon, that ancient serpent, who is the devil, or Satan, and bound him for a thousand years. [3]He threw him into the Abyss, and locked and sealed it over him, to keep him from deceiving the nations any more until the thousand years were ended. After that, he must be set free for a short time.

[4]I saw thrones on which were seated those who had been given authority to judge. And I saw the souls of those who had been beheaded because of their testimony for Jesus and because of the word of God. They had not worshiped the beast or his image and had not received his mark on their foreheads or their hands. They came to life and reigned with Christ a thousand years. [5](The rest of the dead did not come to life until the thousand years were ended.) This is the first resurrection. [6]Blessed and holy are those who have part in the first resurrection. The second death has no power over them, but they will be priests of God and of Christ and will reign with him for a thousand years.

Charles has described this passage as a constant source of insurmountable difficulty for the exegete. Berkouwer has called the Millennium one of the most controversial and intriguing questions of eschatology. He feels that one's view of Revelation 20 is internally connected with the rest of one's eschatology (G.C. Berkouwer, *The Return of Christ* [Grand Rapids: Eerdmans, 1972], p. 291). While the OT and later Jewish literature point forward to a time when the kingdom of God will be manifest in the world, nowhere in Jewish literature is the time of the reign of the Messiah stated to be a thousand years.

The exegesis of the passage leads me to a premillennial interpretation. It should be recognized, however, that there are problems with this view of Revelation 20:1–6, just as there are problems with other views of this difficult portion of the book, and that responsible Christian scholars vary in its interpretation according to their convictions and presuppositions.

For the moment the question of the duration of the reign of Christ (which is equal to the duration of the binding of Satan) may be delayed. The main problem concerns whether the reference to a Millennium indicates an earthly historical reign of peace that will manifest itself at the close of this present age or whether the whole passage is symbolic of some present experience of Christians or some future nonhistorical reality.

In the first place, we may note that the ancient church down to the time of Augustine (354–430) (though not without minor exceptions) unquestionably held to the teaching of an earthly, historical reign of peace that was to follow the defeat of Antichrist and the physical resurrection of the saints but precede both the judgment and the new creation (Jean Daniélou, *The Theology of Jewish Christianity* [Philadelphia: Westminster, 1964]; see note on v.1). To be sure, in the ancient church there were various positions as to the material nature of the Millennium (see comments at v.4), but the true conception of the thousand years was a balance between the worldly aspects of the kingdom and its spiritual aspects as a reign with Christ.

It is well known that the break with this earlier position came with the views of the late fourth-century interpreter Tyconius, an African Donatist, who, partly dependent on the Alexandrian allegorizing of Origen, developed a view of the Millennium based on a recapitulation method of interpretation. In applying this principle, Tyconius viewed Revelation as containing a number of different visions that repeated basic themes throughout the book. Though Tyconius's original work is not available, his exegesis of the Apocalypse can be largely reconstructed through his prime benefactor, Augustine, as well as Tyconius's many Roman Catholic followers. When he came to chapter 20, he interpreted the thousand years in nonliteral terms and understood the period as referring to the church age, the time between the first and second advents of Christ. Tyconius interpreted the first resurrection as the resurrection of the soul from spiritual death to the new life, while the second resurrection was the resurrection of the body at the end of history. The binding of Satan had already taken place in that the devil cannot seduce the church during the present age. Moreover, the reign of the saints and their "thrones of judgment" had already begun in the church and its rulers. Augustine, following Tyconius, "cast the die against the expectation of a millennial kingdom for centuries to come" (H. Berkhof, *Christ the Meaning of History* [Grand Rapids: Baker, 1979], p. 161). The recapitulation method adopted by Augustine continued through the centuries and is not without its modern exponents in both the Protestant and Roman Catholic branches of the church. This is the first main option in modern nonmillennial (or amillennial) interpretations of Revelation 20.

Augustine's approach, however, was not to remain unchallenged. Joachim of Floris (c. 1135–1202) saw in the Apocalypse a prophecy of the events of Western history from the time of Christ till the end. He thought the Millennium was still future in his time but soon to begin. The Franciscans, who followed Joachim, identified Babylon with ecclesiastical Rome and the Antichrist with the papacy. The Reformers followed suit. In modern times, Henry Alford (1810–71) adopted this view.

During Reformation times, still another type of interpretation developed, expounded by a Jesuit scholar named Ribeira (1537–91). He held that almost all the events described in the Apocalypse are future and apply to the end times rather than to the history of the world or contemporary Rome and the papacy. He still, however, held to Augustine's view of the Millennium as the period between the first and second advents of Christ. But at one important point he changed Augustine's view. Instead of the Millennium taking place on earth between the advents, Ribeira saw it as taking place in heaven. It is a reward for faithfulness. When the saints at any time in history are martyred, they do not perish but live and reign with Christ in heaven in the intermediate state before the final resurrection. This is the second main option today for nonmillennialists. John's basic message in Revelation 20 is, according to this viewpoint, pastoral. If Christians face the prospect of suffering death for Jesus, they should be encouraged because if they are killed, they will go to reign with him in heaven. This seems to be the drift of Berkouwer's conclusions (*The Return of Christ*, pp. 314ff.) and earlier those of B.B. Warfield ("The Millennium and the Apocalypse," PTR, 2 [1904], 599–617).

The Augustinian view of Revelation 20 and its variant espoused by Joachim cannot be harmonized with a serious exegesis of Revelation 20 on two important counts. In the first place, it founders on the statements concerning the binding of Satan (vv. 1–3); and, second, it must handle in an absurd fashion the statements about the coming to life of the martyrs, which cannot be exegetically understood as anything other than physical resurrection without seriously tampering with the sense of the words (cf. discussion on vv. 1–4). While it is popular among certain nonmillennialists to view 20:1–6 as a symbolic description of the reward to be granted the martyrs on their entrance into heaven (so Beckwith, Berkouwer, Boer, Schnackenburg), this variation of the Augustinian exegesis, while removing the criticism that the passage refers to the present rule of Christ in the church age, fails to deal seriously with the binding of Satan and other details of the text.

There is yet another view that, though not free of problems, does more justice to the Book of Revelation as a whole and to the exegesis of chapter 20 in particular. This view rejects both the Augustinian interpretation that the Millennium is the rule of Christ during this dispensation and the variant of Joachim that locates the resurrection and the reign of the martyrs in heaven for an interim period before their bodily resurrection and the return of Christ. It likewise rejects the variation of Augustine's view known as postmillennialism or evolutionary chiliasm, which teaches that the forces of Antichrist will gradually be put down and the gospel will permeate and transform the world into an interim of the reign of peace before the return of Christ (see note on v. 1 for representatives of this view). Berkouwer justly criticizes this postmillennial view as exegetically and theologically weak. He then goes on to espouse a totally mystical viewpoint of Revelation 20 that fails to grapple exegetically with the text. For him the millennial language is purely a figure of speech to depict the reality of the hidden triumph of Christ (*Return of Christ*, pp. 208–9). Such a view, however, fails to account for how the reality of the divine kingdom of God has actually invaded history in Jesus Christ.

If eschatological realities are simply mystical, figurative, and pastoral in intent and never impinge on the empirical world, then the Christ event as an eschatological event must likewise be abandoned. Instead, the view espoused in this commentary argues that the Millennium is in history and on the earth as an eschatological reality. Much in the same manner as the kingdom of God was eschatologically present in the life and ministry of Jesus—present, yet still future—so the Millennium is at once the final historical event of this age and the beginning of the eschatological kingdom of Christ in eternity. Oscar Cullmann, one of the principal advocates of this view, states:

> The millennium is future and is, so to speak, the very last part of Christ's lordship, which at the same time extends into the new aeon. Consequently, the thousand-year kingdom should be identified neither with the whole chronological extent of Christ's lordship nor with the present Church. That lordship is the larger concept; it has already begun and continues in the aeon for an undefined length of time. The thousand-year reign, on the other hand, belongs temporally to the final act of Christ's lordship, the act which begins with his return and thus already invades the new aeon (*The Christology of the New Testament* [Philadelphia: Westminster, 1959], p. 226).

This view is called the "end-historical" view. It follows the same chronological sequence as the early church's position, i.e., Parousia—defeat of Antichrist—binding of Satan—resurrection—Millennium—release of Satan—final judgment—new heavens and earth. It differs slightly from earlier chiliasm in viewing the Millennium as an end-historical event that at the same time is the beginning of the eternal reign of Christ and the saints.

The problem as to the limits of the description of the Millennium in Revelation 20–22 is a more difficult question. A group of expositors of varying theological thought (Beasley-Murray, R.H. Charles, Ford, A.C. Gaebelein, Kelly, Zahn) believe that 21:9–22:5, 14–15 belong with 20:1–10 as a further description of the millennial reign, whereas 21:1–5 refers to the eternal state, which follows the final judgment of the dead. This approach is an attempt to harmonize a more literal understanding of certain statements in 21:9ff. with the assumed conditions during the eternal state. For example, according to Beasley-Murray ("The Revelation," p. 1305) the references to nations and kings seem to describe an earthly kingdom better than they describe the eternal condition (21:24, 26); references to leaves "healing" the nations (22:2) seems to describe an imperfect condition better than they describe the perfected eternal state; and, finally, the blessing pronounced on those who come and eat the tree of life while a curse rests on all those outside the city (22:14–15) seems to relate better to the thousand years than to the eternal state when the wicked are in the lake of fire.

Admittedly, this is a possible solution that has the advantage of giving more descriptive content to the millennial reign. This approach, however, suffers from two serious criticisms. First, though it rightly assigns 21:1–5 to the postmillennial New Jerusalem in the context of the new heaven and earth, it arbitrarily assigns 21:9ff. to the millennial New Jerusalem without the slightest hint from the text that this is a recapitulation of 20:1–10. Thus, there is an eternal state New Jerusalem followed immediately by a millennial New Jerusalem, both bearing the same title. This is hardly plausible. Second, this view strongly argues for historical progression in 19:11–21:5; Parousia—defeat of Antichrist—binding of Satan—first resurrection—Millennium—release of Satan—last judgment—new heavens and earth—and then argues for recapitulation in 21:9ff.

It seems best, therefore, despite some problems, to regard the sequence begun at 19:11 as running chronologically through 22:6, thus placing all the material in 21:1ff. after the Millennium. At this point, a suggestion might be offered for further study.

If the Millennium is a true eschatological, historical event like the person, ministry, and resurrection of Jesus, may not 21:1ff. be viewed as the full manifestation of the kingdom of God, a partial manifestation of which will be realized in the thousand-year reign of Christ and the saints, during which Christ will defeat all his enemies, including death (1 Cor 15:23–28)? Some of the same conditions described in 21:1ff. would then, at least in part, characterize the Millennium.

Finally, why the Millennium? There are at least four answers to this question:

1. During the Millennium, Christ will openly manifest his kingdom in world history; the Millennium will provide an actual demonstration of the truthfulness of the divine witness borne by Christ and his followers during their life on earth. It will be a time of the fulfillment of all God's covenant promises to his people.

2. The Millennium will reveal that man's rebellion against God lies deep in man's own heart, not in the devil's deception. Even when Satan is bound and righteousness prevails in the world, some people will still rebel against God. The final release of Satan will openly draw out this hidden evil.

3. The release of Satan after the Millennium shows the invulnerability of the city of God and the extent of the authority of Christ, since the devil is immediately defeated and cast into the lake of fire forever.

4. The Millennium will serve as a long period required to do the general "house-cleaning" needed after the preceding ages of sin, during which sin was prevalent.

1–3 These verses are integrally related to 19:20–21. After the destruction of the beast and his followers and of the false prophet, Satan (the dragon, the ancient serpent) is dealt with. He is thrown into the Abyss to be imprisoned there for a thousand years, which is the third last thing (see comments at introduction to 19:11–21). The Abyss is the demonic abode (see comments at 9:1; cf. 11:7). The angel's mission is to restrain Satan from deceiving the nations—thus the key, the chain, and the violent casting into the Abyss. That this whole action is not a recapitulation of earlier descriptions of Satan is evident from a number of points. In 12:9 (q.v. for the same titles), Satan is "hurled" out of heaven "to the earth," where he goes forth with great fury to work his deception and persecute God's people (13:14; 18:23c). But in 20:1–3, the situation is completely different. Here Satan is cast *out of the earth* into a place where he is kept from "deceiving the nations." The former period of Satan's restriction to earth is described as a "short time" (12:9, 12), while the time here (20:1–3) of his binding is a thousand years. In the earlier references to Satan, he is very active on the earth (2:10, 13; 12:17; 16:13, cf. 1 Peter 5:8); here he is tightly sealed in "prison" (*phylaka*, v.7). The binding of Satan removes his deceptive activity among "the nations" (*ta ethnē*), a term never used to describe the redeemed community (until ch. 21, after Satan's permanent end).

From at least the time of Victorinus (d.c.303), some have interpreted the binding of Satan as the work of Christ in the lives of believers. Thus Satan is "bound" for believers since he no longer deceives them, but he is still "loose" for unbelievers who are deceived (Victorinus *Commentary on the Apocalypse* 20; also Minear, *I Saw a New Earth*, p. 162). This explanation, however, does not take seriously the language of the Abyss and the prison in which Satan is confined, nor does it account for the releasing of Satan after the thousand years. The binding of spirits or angels is mentioned in Isaiah 24:21–23; Jude 6 (cf. Tobit 8:3; 1 Enoch 10:4, 11–12; 88:1–3; Jub 23:29; T Levi 18:12). In all these references there is no question of the spirits being bound in some respects and not in others; it signifies a complete removal as to a prison, usually in the depths of the underworld (Beasley-Murray, "The Revelation," p. 1305).

Mounce's observation is well taken: "The elaborate measures taken to insure his custody are most easily understood as implying the complete cessation of his influence on earth (rather than a curbing of his activities)" (*Revelation*, p. 353).

In only one NT reference is there a question as to the limited binding of Satan. In Mark 3:27 Jesus refers in his parable to the strong man first being bound before his goods can be plundered. The reference is to Satan's being bound by Christ and, according to J. Jeremias, specifically relates to the temptation of Jesus (*The Parables of Jesus*, rev. ed. [New York: Scribner's, 1963], pp. 122–23), or, according to others, to Jesus' exorcisms mentioned in the immediate context. In any case, the binding of Satan by the ministry of Jesus did not totally immobilize the devil but struck him a vital blow. But does the reference in Mark provide a true analogy for the binding of Satan in 20:1–3, as Augustine claimed? A careful examination of Mark 3:27 and Revelation 20:1–3 leads to the conclusion that the two passages are not teaching the same truth. There is a sense in which, according to the Gospel account, Satan is in the process of being bound by the activity of Christ and the kingdom of God; but this is clearly an event different from the total consigning of Satan to the Abyss as taught in Revelation 20:1–3.

Finally, it may be noted that the thousand-year binding of Satan is concurrent with and inseparable from the thousand-year reign of the resurrected martyrs. For a thousand years on this earth, within history, the activity of Satan leading mankind into false worship and active rebellion against God and his people will be totally curbed under the authority of Christ in his kingdom. If that reign is yet future, the binding is future. If the binding refers to an earthly situation—which it clearly does—the thousand-year reign most naturally refers to an earthly situation.

4–6 The fourth last thing (see comments at introduction to 19:11–21) is the thousand-year reign of Christ on the earth. John gives us no picture of life in the Millennium in these verses; they contain only a statement about who will participate in it. He sees thrones, and judges sitting on them. The scene is usually connected with Daniel's vision of the Son of Man (Dan 7:9, 22, 27). In Daniel, justice was done for the saints by the Ancient of Days and they began their kingdom reign. The thought may be similar here. If this is the case, those who sit on the thrones are the angelic court. However, those on the thrones may be the resurrected martyrs who exercise judgmental and ruling functions during the Millennium. This possible reinterpretation of Daniel seems preferable in the light of other NT teaching as well as of Revelation itself (cf. Luke 22:30; 1 Cor 6:2; Rev 2:26). They who were once judged by earth's courts to be worthy of death are now the judges of the earth under Christ.

A more difficult question concerns the identity of those who will rule with Christ. They are the "beheaded" (with an axe, *pelekizō*, elsewhere *sphazō*, "slaughter," cf. 6:9) martyrs who have previously occupied John's attention. The cause of their death is attributed to their faithful witness to Jesus and the word of God (on these terms, see comments at 1:9; cf. 6:9; 12:11). The reference to "souls" (*psychas*) immediately recalls 6:9, where the same expression is used of the slain witnesses under the altar. The word describes those who have lost their bodily life but are nevertheless still alive in God's sight. This term prepares us for their coming to (bodily) life again at the first resurrection. It is a mistake to take *psychas* to imply a later spiritual resurrection or rebirth of the soul as did Augustine and many since (contra Swete, et al.).

These martyrs are also those who did not worship the beast or his image or receive his mark on them (cf. 13:1ff.; 15:2); in a word, they are the followers of the Lamb.

At this point, NIV omits a very important term. Between the description of those beheaded and the description concerning the beast worship in v.4 are the two words *kai hoitines* ("and who"). This construction is capable of bearing two different meanings. It could simply introduce a further qualifying phrase to the identification of the martyrs (so NIV, TEV). But it may also be understood to introduce a second group. There are (1) those who were beheaded for their witness and (2) "also those who" did not worship the beast (so Rissi, Swete; see JB; BV—"and of these also"; NASB—"and those who"). This immediately alleviates a thorny problem, i.e., why only the martyrs should live and reign with Christ. Usually in Revelation the relative pronoun *hoitines* ("who") simply refers to the preceding group and adds some further detail (2:24; 9:4; 17:12); but in one other reference, which alone has the identical introductory terms (*kai hoitines*), the phrase so introduced singles out a special class or group from the more general group in the preceding statement (1:7). Thus the *kai hoitines* clause introduces a special class of the beheaded, i.e., those who were so beheaded because they did not worship the beast, etc. In any case, it seems that John has only the beheaded in mind (cf. 14:13).

But this presents a problem because John has elsewhere indicated that the kingdom reign will be shared by every believer who overcomes (2:26–28; 3:12, 21) and is purchased by Christ's blood (5:10). Also, in 1 Corinthians 6:2–3, Paul clearly speaks of all believers—not just martyrs—exercising judgment in the future. Revelation 5:10 indicates that the kingdom will be a "reign on the earth." Unless only those beheaded by the beast will reign in the Millennium, another explanation is demanded. The pastoral approach would explain John's reference to only the martyrs as a piece of special encouragement to them, while not implying that others would be left out (Beasley-Murray).

I feel somewhat more comfortable with the view expressed earlier (see comments at 6:9)—viz., that the martyrs represent the whole church that is faithful to Jesus whether or not they have actually been killed. They constitute a group that can in truth be described as those who "did not love their lives so much as to shrink from death" (12:11). As such, the term is a synonym for overcomers (chs. 2–3). Thus John could count himself in this group, though he may never have suffered death by the axe of the beast. In 2:11 those who during persecution are faithful to Christ even to the point of death are promised escape from the second death, which in 20:6 is promised to those who share in the first resurrection, i.e., the beheaded (v.4). In fact, a number also of the other promises to overcomers in the letters to the seven churches find their fulfillment in chapter 20 (compare 2:11 with 20:6; 2:26–27 with 20:4; 3:5 with 20:12, 15; 3:21 with 20:4).

The martyrs "came to life." The interpretation of these words is crucial to the whole passage. Since Augustine, the majority of interpreters have taken the words to refer to a spiritual resurrection, or new birth, or to the triumph of the church. Caird, for example, sees the parallel to Christ's resurrection (2:8) but seems to spiritualize Jesus' resurrection and concludes that resurrection for the martyrs "means that they have been let loose into the world" (p. 255). This substitutes some symbolic sense of physical resurrection for the historical event. Others, rightly chastened by a more serious exegesis of the text, hold that the language teaches bodily resurrection but that the whole section (20:1–10) is not to be taken as predicting events within history but is apocalyptic language, figurative of the consolation and reward promised the martyrs (Beckwith, p. 737). Berkouwer's position typifies the mystical and vague language used by nonmillennialists to explain what the passage means:

> We may not tamper with the real, graphic nature of the vision of Revelation 20, nor may we spiritualize the first resurrection. But one question is still decisive: does this vision intend to sketch for us a particular phase of *history?* If one does interpret it this way, it seems to me that he must include the first (bodily) resurrection in his concept of a future millennium. . . . This vision is not a narrative account of a future earthly reign of peace at all, but is the apocalyptic unveiling of the reality of salvation in Christ as a backdrop to the reality of the suffering and martyrdom that still continue as long as the dominion of Christ remains hidden (italics his) (*Return of Christ*, p. 307).

While alleviating the criticism of a spiritual resurrection, Berkouwer fails to take with equal seriousness the language of the thousand-year reign, which is everywhere in the Apocalypse a reign on the *earth* within *history*.

The verb *ezēsan* ("came to life," from *zaō*) is used in v.4 of the martyrs and also in v.5 of the "rest of the dead" who did not come to life till the thousand years were completed. When the context is that of bodily death, *ezēsan* is used in the NT to connote physical resurrection (John 11:25; Acts 1:3; 9:41), though the normal word is *egeirō* ("raise up"). More importantly, Revelation clearly uses *zaō* ("live") for the resurrection of Christ (1:18; 2:8) and also curiously for the sea beast (13:14). John 5:25 is sometimes cited as an evidence that *zaō* refers to spiritual life, not physical resurrection. But a careful reading of the context clearly shows that while John 5:25 does indeed use *zaō* in the sense of spiritual life (as do other NT passages), John 5:29 is definitely referring to physical resurrection and uses the phrase "rise to live" (*anastasin zōēs*, from *zaō*). John plainly says in Revelation 20:5 that "this is the first resurrection" (*anastasis prōtē*). The word *anastasis*, which occurs over forty times in the NT, is used almost exclusively of physical resurrection (Luke 2:34 is the only exception). There is no indication that John has departed from this usage in these verses.

Why does John call this the "first" resurrection? The term *prōtē* clearly implies the first in a series of two or more. John does not directly refer to a second resurrection; a second resurrection is, however, correctly inferred both from the use of *prōtē* and also from the expression "the rest of the dead did not come to life until the thousand years were ended" (v.5). Irenaeus (fl. c.175–c.195) clearly connects John's first resurrection with the "resurrection of the just" (Luke 14:14; Irenaeus *Contra Haereses* 39.3–10). Likewise Justin Martyr held to a physical resurrection before the Millennium (*Dialogue with Trypho* 80) and a general physical resurrection after the thousand years (ibid., 81), though he does not explain whether believers will also participate in the latter. From at least the time of Augustine, the first resurrection was understood as a regeneration of the soul and the second resurrection as the general physical, bodily resurrection of just and unjust (*City of God* 20.9–10). It must, however, be insisted that it is quite weak exegesis to make the first resurrection spiritual and the second one physical, unless the text itself clearly indicates this change, which it does not.

Another response would be to understand "the rest of the dead" who lived not until the close of the thousand years to be all the faithful except the martyrs, plus the entire body of unbelievers (so Mounce, *Revelation*, p. 360). This view, in our opinion, runs aground on the fact that John clearly seems to tie exclusion from the second death with those who are part of the first resurrection, thus strongly implying that those who participate in the second resurrection are destined for the second death.

Therefore, following the lead of the earlier exegesis of Irenaeus, we may understand the first resurrection as being the raising to physical life of all the dead in Christ (cf. 1 Cor 15:12ff; 1 Thess 4:13ff.); this is the resurrection to life of John 5:29 (NIV, "rise to live"). For those who participate in this resurrection, "the second death [the lake of fire (20:14)] has no power over them" (v.6). Therefore, they are "blessed and holy" (the fifth beatitude in Rev; see comments on 1:3) and shall be priests of God and Christ for the thousand years. On the other hand, those over whom the second death will have power must be "the rest of the dead" (v.5), who will be participants in the second resurrection, the "rise to be condemned" of John 5:29 (cf. Acts 24:15).

In the only place other than Revelation 2:11 and 20:6 where the second death is mentioned, it refers to exclusion from physical resurrection (v.14). Likewise, in the Palestinian Targum on Deuteronomy 33:6, the OT *locus theologicus* in rabbinic Judaism for proving the resurrection from the dead, the Targum reads: "Let Reuben live in this world and not die in the second death in which death the wicked die in the world to come." In the Targum the second death means exclusion from the resurrection. Not to die the second death, then, means to rise again to eternal life (cf. M. McNamara, *Targum and Testament: Aramaic Paraphrases of the Hebrew Bible; A Light on the New Testament* [Grand Rapids: Eerdmans, 1962], p. 123).

What now may be said as to the length of the kingdom reign? Nowhere in other literature is the kingdom reign of the Messiah specified as 1,000 years (on 2 Enoch 33, see note on v.6), though estimates of 400, 40, 70, 365, or an indefinite period (*Sanhedrin* 99a) are found. Thus parallels to John's use of 1,000 years must be sought elsewhere. According to Daniélou, the most primitive traditions in Asia relate the 1,000 years to Adam's paradisiacal time span. According to the Book of Jubilees, Adam's sin caused him to die at 930 years of age (Gen 5:5), "seventy years before attaining a thousand years, for one thousand years are as one day [Ps 90:4] in heaven. . . . For this reason [because he ate from the tree of knowledge] he died before completing the years of this day" (Jub 4:29–30). Here the 1,000 years are based on an exegesis of Genesis 2:17 in terms of Psalm 90:4—Adam dies on the day on which he eats the forbidden fruit; but according to Psalm 90:4, a day means 1,000 years, and therefore Adam dies before completing 1,000 years. Daniélou believes this is the origin of John's use of the 1,000 years.

Later, the thousand years began to be associated with the Jewish cosmic-week framework in which the history of the world is viewed as lasting a week of millennia, or seven thousand years. The last day millennium is the Sabbath-rest millennium, followed by the eighth day of the age to come. This idea was then linked interpretatively but inappropriately to 2 Peter 3:8. While early Christian writings, such as the Epistle of Barnabas, reflect this reasoning, it was not, according to Daniélou, the most primitive tradition (*Theology of Jewish Christianity*, pp. 377–404).

Is the thousand years, then, symbolic of a perfect human lifespan or some ideal kingdom environment on the earth? In the first place, the number symbolisms of John in Revelation should not be used to argue against an earthly kingdom. It might be said that the number is symbolic of a perfect period of time of whatever length. The essence of premillennialism is in its insistence that the reign will be on earth, not in heaven, for a period of time before the final judgment and the new heavens and earth. For example, we may rightly understand the 1,260 days (forty-two months) of earlier chapters as a symbolic number, but it still refers to an actual historical period of whatever length during which the beast will destroy the saints. If we look at the time of suffering of the Smyrna Christians, it is "ten days" (2:10), a relatively short time in comparison to a thousand years of victorious reign with Christ. In any case, it is not of primary importance whether the years are actual 365-day years or symbolic of a shorter or longer period of bliss enjoyed by believers as they reign with Christ on earth (cf. 5:10 with 11:15; 22:5).

Notes

1 Some selected bibliographic references on the millennial question may be helpful: Premillennial—Alford, "Revelation," Alf (1884); Tenney, *Interpreting Revelation* (1957); Cullmann, *Christology of the New Testament* (1959); Rissi, *Time and History* (1966); idem, *The Future of the World, An Exegetical Study of Revelation* 19:11–22:15 (Naperville, Ill.: A.R. Allenson, 1972); Walvoord, *The Revelation of Jesus Christ* (1966); Beasley-Murray, "The Revelation," NBCrev. (1970); Ladd, *Commentary on Revelation* (1972); Amillennial—Augustine *The City of God* 20.6–15; Caird, *Revelation of St. John* (1966); Rudolf Schnackenburg, *Present and Future; Modern Aspects of New Testament Theology* (South Bend, Ind.: University of Notre Dame, 1966); G.C. Berkouwer, *The Return of Christ* (1972); Harry Boer, "What About the Millennium?" *The Reformed Journal*, 25 (January 1975), 26–30; idem, "The Reward of Martyrs," *The Reformed Journal*, 25 (February 1975), 7–9, 28; Postmillennial—Lorraine Boettner, *The Millennium* (Philadelphia: Presbyterian and Reformed, 1958); Rousas J. Rushdoony, *The Institutes of Biblical Law* (Nutley, N.J.: Craig, 1973); H. Berkhof, *Christ the Meaning of History* (1979). For background material, see G.R. Beasley-Murray and H. Hobbs, *Revelation: Three Viewpoints* (Nashville: Broadman, 1977); Robert G. Clouse, ed., *The Meaning of the Millennium: Four Views* (Downers Grove, Ill.: InterVarsity, 1977); and Millard J. Erickson, *Contemporary Options in Eschatology. A Study of the Millennium* (Grand Rapids: Baker, 1977). For a helpful historical survey of the origins of millennial thought, see Daniélou, *Theology of Jewish Christianity*.

4–6 Second Enoch 33:1ff. (of doubtful age) is sometimes cited as evidence that the Jews believed in a thousand-year Messianic Age. However, the Jewish cosmic-week explanation for the history of the world did not explicitly connect the Messiah's reign to the seventh-day millennium. Thus there arose a multitude of different year periods assigned to the Messianic Age that would precede the eternal period or age to come.

On the possibility that the first resurrection refers to the intermediate state, see Meredith Kline, "The First Resurrection," WTJ, 37 (1974–75), 366–75; J.R. Michaels, "The First Resurrection: A Response," WTJ, 39 (1976), 100–109; P.E. Hughes, "The First Resurrection: Another Interpretation," WTJ, 39 (1977), 315–18; See also J.S. Deere, "Premillennialism in Revelation 20:4–6," BS, 135 (1978), 58–73.

4 The plural ἐκάθισαν (*ekathisan*, lit., "they sat"; NIV, "were seated") may be another instance of the Semitic idiom where the plural is used for the passive idea (cf. note on 12:6). In this case, the NIV rendering is perfectly justified.

C. *The Release and End of Satan*

20:7–10

[7]When the thousand years are over, Satan will be released from his prison [8]and will go out to deceive the nations in the four corners of the earth—Gog and Magog—to gather them for battle. In number they are like the sand on the seashore. [9]They marched across the breadth of the earth and surrounded the camp of God's people, the city he loves. But fire came down from heaven and devoured them.

[10]And the devil, who deceived them, was thrown into the lake of burning sulfur, where the beast and the false prophet had been thrown. They will be tormented day and night for ever and ever.

7–10 The fifth last thing (see comments at introduction to 19:11–21) is the defeat of Satan. In v.3 the release of Satan after the Millennium was anticipated: "He must [*dei*] be set free for a short time [*mikron chronon;* cf. 12:12, *oligon kairon*]." Why must (*dei*) he once again be released? The answer is so that he can "deceive the nations" throughout the world and lead them into conflict against "God's people." But why should God allow this? Certainly if man alone were prophetically writing the history of the world, he would not bring the archdeceiver back after the glorious reign of Christ 20:4–6. But God's thoughts and ways are not man's (Isa 55:8). Ezekiel's vision of Gog brought out of the land of Magog seems to be clearly in John's mind (Ezek 38–39). Ezekiel also saw an attack on God's people, who had been restored for some time ("after many days" [Ezek 38:8])—i.e., after the commencement of the kingdom age.

In Ezekiel 38–39, Gog refers to the prince of a host of pagan invaders from the North, especially the Scythian hordes from the distant land of Magog. In Revelation, however, the names are symbolic of the final enemies of Christ duped by Satan into attacking the community of the saints. The change in meaning has occurred historically through the frequent use in rabbinic circles of the expression "Gog and Magog" to symbolically refer to the nations spoken of in Psalm 2 who are in rebellion against God and his Messiah (cf. Caird, p. 256, for Talmud references).

If the beast and his armies are already destroyed (19:19ff.), who are these rebellious nations? It may be that the beast and his armies in the earlier context refer to the demonic powers and those in 20:7ff. to human nations in rebellion—not an unlikely solution (see comments at 19:19ff.)—or it may be that not all the people in the world will participate in the beast's armies and thus those mentioned here in v.8 refer to other people who during the millennial reign defected in their hearts from the Messiah. In any case, this section shows something of the deep, complex nature of evil. The source of rebellion against God does not lie in man's environment or fundamentally with the devil but springs up from deep within man's own heart. The return of Satan will demonstrate this in the most dramatic manner once for all. The temporal reign of Christ will not be fulfilled till this final challenge to his kingdom occurs and he demonstrates the power of his victory at the Cross and puts down all his enemies (1 Cor 15:25).

The gathered army, which is extensive and world-wide, advances and in seige fashion encircles the "camp [*parembolē*] of God's people, the city he loves." Most commentators take the expressions camp and city as different metaphors for God's people. The word *parembolē* in the NT refers to either a military camp or the camp of Israel (Acts 21:34, 37; 22:24; Heb 11:34; 13:11, 13). It is a word that reminds us of the pilgrim character of the people of God even at the end of the Millennium, as long as evil is active in God's creation.

The "city he loves" presents more difficulty. According to standard Jewish eschatology, this should refer to the restored and spiritually renewed city of Jerusalem in Palestine (Ps 78:6–8; 87:2; Beckwith, p. 746). A number of modern commentators of various theological opinions have taken this Jewish identification as a clue and have so understood the passage (H. Berkhof, *Christ the Meaning of History*, p. 153; Ladd,

Commentary on Revelation, p. 270; Charles, *Commentary on Revelation*, 2:145). On the other hand, John may have intended to refer merely to the community of the redeemed without any specific geographical location in mind. This would be in harmony with his previous references to the city elsewhere in the book (cf. comments at 3:12; 11:2, 8). There are only two cities or kingdoms in the Apocalyse—the city of Satan, where the beast and harlot are central, and the city of God, where God and the Lamb are central. The city, then, is the kingdom of God in its millennial manifestation; it is the same city that appears in its final, most glorious form in the last chapters (21–22). Wherever God dwells among his people, there the city of God is (21:2–3). Following this understanding of the beloved city in no way weakens the validity of an earthly reign of Christ and the saints.

The swiftness and finality of the divine judgment (v.9) emphasizes the reality of the victory of Christ at the Cross. The fire imagery may reflect Ezekiel's vision of the destruction of Gog (Ezek 38:22; 39:6). Note that unlike the Qumran and Jewish apocalyptic literature, it is God, not the saints, who destroys the enemy (cf. comments at 19:19). The devil is now dealt the long-awaited final and fatal blow (Gen 3:15; John 12:31). The "lake of fire" imagery is probably related to the teaching of Jesus about hell (*gehenna*, Matt 5:22; 7:19; 10:28; 13:49–50; Mark 9:48, et al.). The lake image may be related to certain Jewish descriptions of eternal judgment (cf. 2 Enoch 10:2: "a gloomy fire is always burning, and a fiery river goes forth"). The figure may intensify the idea of the permanency of the judgment (cf. comments at 14:11; also 19:20; 20:14–15; 21:8). That the beast and false prophet are already there does not argue for their individuality (contra Beasley-Murray, "The Revelation," p. 1308) since later in the chapter "death" and "Hades," nonpersonal entities that for the sake of the imagery are personified, are cast into the same lake of fire (20:14).

Notes

---

8 On "Gog," see TDNT, 1: 789–91; Ralph Alexander, "A Fresh Look at Ezekiel 38 and 39," ETS, 17, no. 3 (1974), 157–69. Alexander argues for multiple manifestations of Gog in history and the close parallelism between Ezek 38–39 and Rev 20:7–10.

The Palestinian Targum on Exod 40 refers to the Messiah of Ephraim "by whose hand the house of Israel is to vanquish Gog and his confederates at the end of days" (cited by Ford, p. 356).

D. *Great White Throne Judgment*

20:11–15

[11]Then I saw a great white throne and him who was seated on it. Earth and sky
fled from his presence, and there was no place for them. [12]And I saw the dead, great
and small, standing before the throne, and books were opened. Another book was
opened, which is the book of life. The dead were judged according to what they
had done as recorded in the books. [13]The sea gave up the dead that were in it,
and death and Hades gave up the dead that were in them, and each person was
judged according to what he had done. [14]Then death and Hades were thrown into
the lake of fire. The lake of fire is the second death. [15]If anyone's name was not
found written in the book of life, he was thrown into the lake of fire.

11–15 John describes in vivid pictures the sixth last thing (see comments in introduction to 19:11–21), the final judgment of mankind. Unlike many of the vivid, imaginative paintings based on this vision, here John describes a strange, unearthly scene. Heaven and earth flee from the unidentified figure who sits on the majestic white throne. The language of poetic imagery captures the fading character of everything of the world (1 John 2:17). Now the only reality is God seated on the throne of judgment, before whom all must appear (Heb 9:27). His verdict alone is holy and righteous (white symbolism). It is possible that in Revelation the earth and sky refer more to the religio-political order than to the cosmological one (Caird). Since 20:11–12 makes use of the theophany of Daniel 7:9–10, the one seated on the throne is presumably God himself; but since 22:1, 3 mention the throne of God *and of the Lamb,* it may well be that here Jesus shares in the judgment (John 5:27; R.T. France, *Jesus and the Old Testament* [Downers Grove, Ill.: InterVarsity, 1971], p. 203). God has kept the last judgment in his own hands. This vision declares that even though it may have seemed that earth's course of history ran contrary to his holy will, no single day or hour in the world's drama has ever detracted from the absolute sovereignty of God (Lilje).

But who are the dead (vv.12–13)? Earlier in the chapter, John has mentioned the "rest of the dead" who are not resurrected till the thousand years are completed (v.5). As Mounce observes: "If the first resurrection is limited to actual martyrs, then the judgment of verses 11–15 involves both believer and impenitent. If the second resurrection is of the wicked only, then the judgment is of those who will in fact be consigned to the lake of fire" (*Revelation,* p. 365). While no resurrection is mentioned in vv.11–15, the dead may well be those who did not participate in the first resurrection. Since the second death has no power over those who were raised in the first resurrection (v.6), it may be argued that only those who are the enemies of God—i.e., the wicked dead—stand before this throne (John 5:24). This is by no means a necessary inference, though it is the most satisfying exegesis.

A moment of tension arrives. The books are opened. It is sobering to ponder that in God's sight nothing is forgotten; all will give an account of their actions (v.13). Judgment always proceeds on the basis of works (Matt 25:41ff.; Rom 2:6; 2 Cor 5:10; Heb 4:12–13). The "books" are the records of human deeds (v.12). While in Jewish thought there are references to books of good and evil deeds being kept before God (4 Ezra 6:20; 1 Enoch 47:3), John is probably alluding to Daniel 7:10: "The court was seated, and the books were opened." We are not told whether these books contain both good and evil works or only the latter. John is more concerned about another book, the book of life, which alone seems to be decisive (vv.12, 15; cf. at 3:5; also 13:8; 17:8; 21:27). How can these two pictures be harmonized? In reality there is no conflict. Works are unmistakable evidence of the loyalty of the heart; they express either belief or unbelief, faithfulness or unfaithfulness. The judgment will reveal through the records whether or not the loyalties were with God and the Lamb or with God's enemies. John's theology of faith and its inseparable relation to works is the same as Jesus' and Paul's (John 5:29; Rom 2:6ff.). This judgment is not a balancing of good works over bad works. Those who have their names in the Lamb's book of life will also have records of righteous deeds. The opposite will also be true. The imagery reflects the delicate balance between grace and obedience (cf. comments at 19:6–8).

Three broad places are mentioned as containing the dead: the sea, death, and Hades (v.13). The sea represents the place of unburied bodies while death and Hades represent the reality of dying and the condition entered on at death (cf. 1:18; 6:8).

The imagery suggests release of the bodies and persons from their places of confinement following death; i.e., it portrays resurrection. They rise to receive sentence (John 5:29b). Death and Hades are personified (cf. 6:8) and in a vivid image are cast into the lake of fire to be permanently destroyed (cf. 19:20; 20:10). This not only fulfills Paul's cry concerning the last enemy, death, which will be defeated by the victorious kingdom of Christ (1 Cor 15:16), but also signals the earth's new condition: "There will be no more death" (21:4).

The final scene in this dark and fearful passage is in v.15. From the English rendering it might be inferred that John is doubtful whether anyone will be thrown into the lake of fire. The Greek construction, however, is not so indefinite. John uses a first-class condition, which assumes the reality of the first clause and shows the consequences in the second clause. Thus we might paraphrase the verse: "If anyone's name was not found written in the book of life, and I assume there were such, he was thrown into the lake of fire." When taken seriously, this final note evaporates all theories of universalism or *apocatastasis* (cf. Berkouwer's excellent discussion in *Return of Christ*, pp. 387–423).

Notes

15 The "second death" terminology does not occur in rabbinic teaching in this period, but it is found in the Targum to the Prophets on Isa 65:6, where it is said that the bodies (resurrected) of the wicked are delivered to the second death. This supports the idea of a second resurrection of the unjust that precedes the casting into the second death (cf. Israel Abraham's *Studies in Pharasaism and the Gospels* 2d ser. [New York: Ktav, 1967], pp. 41–49).

V. Vision of the New Heaven and the New Earth and the New Jerusalem (21:1–22:5)

A. *The New Jerusalem*

21:1–27

[1]Then I saw a new heaven and a new earth, for the first heaven and the first earth
had passed away, and there was no longer any sea. [2]I saw the Holy City, the new
Jerusalem, coming down out of heaven from God, prepared as a bride beautifully
dressed for her husband. [3]And I heard a loud voice from the throne saying, "Now
the dwelling of God is with men, and he will live with them. They will be his people,
and God himself will be with them and be their God. [4]He will wipe every tear from
their eyes. There will be no more death or mourning or crying or pain, for the old
order of things has passed away."

[5]He who was seated on the throne said, "I am making everything new!" Then
he said, "Write this down, for these words are trustworthy and true."

[6]He said to me: "It is done. I am the Alpha and the Omega, the Beginning and
the End. To him who is thirsty I will give to drink without cost from the spring of the
water of life. [7]He who overcomes will inherit all this, and I will be his God and he
will be my son. [8]But the cowardly, the unbelieving, the vile, the murderers, the
sexually immoral, those who practice magic arts, the idolaters and all liars—their
place will be in the fiery lake of burning sulfur. This is the second death."

[9]One of the seven angels who had the seven bowls full of the seven last plagues

came and said to me, "Come, I will show you the bride, the wife of the Lamb." [10]And
he carried me away in the Spirit to a mountain great and high, and showed me the
Holy City, Jerusalem, coming down out of heaven from God. [11]It shone with the
glory of God, and its brilliance was like that of a very precious jewel, like a jasper,
clear as crystal. [12]It had a great, high wall with twelve gates, and with twelve angels
at the gates. On the gates were written the names of the twelve tribes of Israel.
[13]There were three gates on the east, three on the north, three on the south and
three on the west. [14]The wall of the city had twelve foundations, and on them were
the names of the twelve apostles of the Lamb.

[15]The angel who talked with me had a measuring rod of gold to measure the city,
its gates and its wall. [16]The city was laid out like a square, as long as it was wide.
He measured the city with the rod and found it to be 12,000 stadia in length, and
as wide and high as it is long. [17]He measured its wall and it was 144 cubits thick,
by man's measurement, which the angel was using. [18]The wall was made of jasper,
and the city of pure gold, as pure as glass. [19]The foundations of the city walls were
decorated with every kind of precious stone. The first foundation was jasper; the
second sapphire, the third chalcedony, the fourth emerald, [20]the fifth sardonyx, the
sixth carnelian, the seventh chrysolite, the eighth beryl, the ninth topaz, the tenth
chrysoprase, the eleventh jacinth, and the twelfth amethyst. [21]The twelve gates
were twelve pearls, each gate made of a single pearl. The street of the city was
of pure gold, like transparent glass.

[22]I did not see a temple in the city, because the Lord God Almighty and the Lamb
are its temple. [23]The city does not need the sun or the moon to shine on it, for the
glory of God gives it light, and the Lamb is its lamp. [24]The nations will walk by its
light, and the kings of the earth will bring their splendor into it. [25]On no day will its
gates ever be shut, for there will be no night there. [26]The glory and honor of the
nations will be brought into it. [27]Nothing impure will ever enter it, nor will anyone
who does what is shameful or deceitful, but only those whose names are written
in the Lamb's book of life.

The seventh last thing (see comments in introduction to 19:11–21) is the vision of the new heavens, the new earth, and the New Jerusalem. Moffatt's striking remark, which captures something of the freshness of this moment in the book, is worth remembering at the outset of the exposition of this incredibly beautiful finale:

> From the smoke and pain and heat [of the preceding scenes] it is a relief to pass into the clear, clean atmosphere of the eternal morning where the breath of heaven is sweet and the vast city of God sparkles like a diamond in the radiance of his presence" (J.B. Moffatt, EGT, 5:477).

Countless productions of art and music have through the ages been inspired by this vision. Cathedral architecture has been influenced by its imagery. John discloses a theology in stone and gold as pure as glass and color. Archetypal images abound. The church is called the bride (21:2). God gives the thirsty "to drink without cost from the spring of the water of life" (21:6). Completeness is implied in the number twelve and its multiples (21:12–14, 16–17, 21) and fullness in the cubical dimension of the city (21:16). Colorful jewels abound as do references to light and the glory of God (21:11, 18–21, 23, 25; 22:5). There is the "river of the water of life" (22:1) and the "tree of life" (22:2). The "sea" is gone (21:1).

Allusions to the OT abound. Most of John's imagery in this chapter reflects Isaiah 60 and 65 and Ezekiel 40–48. John weaves the New Jerusalem vision of Isaiah together with the new temple vision of Ezekiel. The multiple OT promises converging in John's mind seem to indicate that he viewed the New Jerusalem as the fulfillment of all these strands of prophecy. There are also allusions to Genesis 1–3—viz., the absence of death and suffering, the dwelling of God with men as in Eden, the tree of life, the removal of the curse, etc. Creation is restored to its pristine character (cf. Claus Westermann, *Beginning and End in the Bible* [Philadelphia: Fortress, 1972]).

The connection of this vision with the promises to the overcomers in the letters to the seven churches (chs. 2–3) is significant. For example, to the overcomers at Ephesus was granted the right to the tree of life (2:7; cf. 22:2); to Thyatira, the right to rule the nations (2:26; cf. 22:5); to Philadelphia, the name of the city of my God, the New Jerusalem (3:12 and 21:2, 9ff.). In a sense, a strand from every major section of the Apocalypse appears in chapers 21–22. Moreover, almost every major theme and image found in these chapters can be duplicated from Jewish literature (Mathias Rissi, *The Future of the World; an Exegetical Study of Revelation 19:11–22:15* [Naperville, Ill.: A.R. Allenson, 1972], pp. 46–51). But there is in the totality of John's vision a dimension that is clearly lacking in the Jewish parallels. Furthermore, his theology of the Lamb's centrality in the city and the absence of a temple in the New Jerusalem is unique.

In other NT passages, the vision of the heavenly city is described as having the character of eschatological promise. The kingdom reality of the age to come has already appeared in history in the life of Jesus and also in the presence of the Holy Spirit in the church. But the reality is now present only in a promissory way, not in actual fulfillment. Therefore, while the Jerusalem that is from above has present implications for believers (Gal 4:25–31), they are nevertheless, like Abraham, "looking forward to the city with foundations" (Heb 11:10; 13:14). In this sense, the medieval synthesis that made the church on earth and the kingdom synonymous and built its cathedrals to depict that notion was misdirected. John's vision in chapters 21–22 is one of eschatological promise, future in its realization, totally dependent on God's power to create it, yet having present implications for the life of the church in this age.

Outlines of the chapters are necessarily arbitrary because of the familiar Semitic style of doubling back and elaborating on previous subjects. Perhaps 21:1–8 may be seen as a preface or introduction to the vision of the New Jerusalem (21:9–22:6), and this in turn may be seen as followed by the conclusion in 22:7–21.

1 The new heavens and earth were foreseen by Isaiah (65:17) as a part of his vision of the renewed Jerusalem. It is remarkable that John's picture of the final age to come focuses not on a platonic ideal heaven or distant paradise but on the reality of a new earth and heaven. God originally created the earth and heaven to be man's permanent home. But sin and death entered the world and transformed the earth into a place of rebellion and alienation; it became enemy-occupied territory. But God has been working in salvation history to effect a total reversal of this evil consequence and to liberate earth and heaven from bondage to sin and corruption (Rom 8:21). The first heaven and earth refers to the whole order of life in the world—an order tainted by sin, death, suffering, and idolatry (cf. v.4: "the old order of things—death, mourning, crying, pain—has passed away"). John's emphasis on heaven and earth is not primarily cosmological but moral and spiritual. So Peter also speaks of the new heaven and earth, "the home of righteousness" (2 Peter 3:13).

The Greek word for "new" (*kainē*) means new in quality, fresh, rather than recent or new in time (*neos*) (TDNT, 3: 447). That it is a *kainē* heaven and earth and not a second heaven and earth suggests something of an endless succession of new heavens and earth. It is the newness of the endless eschatological ages (2:17; 3:12; 5:9;

cf. Eph 2:7). What makes the new heaven and earth "new" is above all else the reality that now "the dwelling of God is with men, . . . They will be his people, and God himself will be with them and be their God" (v.3). The heaven and earth are new because of the presence of a new community of people who are loyal to God and the Lamb in contrast to the former earth in which a community of idolaters lived.

The sea—the source of the satanic beast (13:1) and the place of the dead (20:13)—will be gone. Again, the emphasis is not geographic but moral and spiritual. The sea serves as an archetype with connotations of evil (cf. comments at 13:1). Therefore, no trace of evil in any form will be present in the new creation.

2–4 The Holy City, the New Jerusalem, occupies John's vision for the remainder of the book. How different is this concept of heaven from that of Hinduism, for example? Here heaven is depicted as a city, with life, activity, interest, and people, as opposed to the Hindu ideal of heaven as a sea into which human life returns like a raindrop to the ocean. First, John sees the city "coming down out of heaven from God"—a phrase he uses three times (3:12; 21:2, 10) in an apparent spatial reference. But the city never seems to come down; it is always seen as a "descending-from-heaven kind of city" (Caird, p. 257). Therefore, the expression stresses the idea that the city is a gift of God, forever bearing the marks of his creation.

Second, John calls the city a "bride" (*nymphē*) (cf. 21:9; 22:17). Earlier he referred to the bride of the Lamb (19:7–8) by a different word (*gynē*), though the reality is the same. The multiple imagery is needed to portray the tremendous reality of the city. A bride-city captures something of God's personal relationship to his people (the bride) as well as something of their life in communion with him and one another (a city, with its social connotations). The purity and devotedness of the bride are reflected in her attire.

The subtitle of the Holy City, "the new Jerusalem," raises a question. The "old" Jerusalem was also called the "holy city" and a "bride" (Isa 52:1; 61:10). Since the Jerusalem from above is the "new" (*kainē*) Jerusalem, we may suppose that it is connected in some manner with the old one so that the new is the old one renewed. The old Jerusalem was marred by sin and disobedience. In it was the blood of prophets and apostles. Still worse, it became a manifestation of Babylon the Great when it crucified the Lord of glory (11:8). The old city always involved more than the mere inhabitants and their daily lives. Jerusalem represented the covenant community of God's people, the hope for the kingdom of God on earth. Thus the OT looked forward to a renewed Jerusalem, rebuilt and transformed into a glorious habitation of God and his people. But the prophets also saw something else. They saw a new heaven and new earth and a Jerusalem connected with this reality. Thus it is not altogether clear precisely what the relationship is between the old and the new, the earthly, restored Jerusalem of the prophets and the Jerusalem associated with the new heaven and earth, the Jerusalem called a heavenly Jerusalem in later Jewish thought (cf. Gal 4:25–31; Heb 11:10; 12:22; 13:14; Rissi, *The Future of the World,* p. 50).

The key to the puzzle must be understood with due respect for the old city. Any exegesis, therefore, that completely rejects any connection with the old city cannot take seriously the name "new" (*kainē*) Jerusalem, which presupposes the old. To speak of the heavenly Jerusalem does not deny an earthly city, as some suggest, but stresses its superiority to the older Jewish hope and affirms the eschatological nature of that hope (TDNT, 5:540–41)—a hope that could not be fulfilled by the earthly Jerusalem, a hope John now sees realized in the Holy City of the future. This city is the church in its future glorified existence. It is the final realization of the kingdom of God.

God's dwelling (*skēnē*) among his people (v.3) is a fulfillment of Leviticus 26:11–13, a promise given to the old Jerusalem but forfeited because of apostasy. As a backdrop for the scene, consider Genesis 3, when man lost his fellowship with God (cf. Exod 25:8; Ezek 37:26–27). Thus the Holy Jerusalem is not only mankind's eternal home but the city where God will place his own name forever. God's presence will blot out the things of the former creation. In a touching metaphor of motherly love, John says that God "will wipe away every tear from their eyes" (cf. 7:17; cf. Isa 25:8). These tears have come from sin's distortion of God's purposes for man. They are produced by death or mourning for the dead, by crying or pain. An enemy has done this to the old order. Now God has defeated the enemy and liberated his people and his creation.

5 Now, for the second time in the book, God himself is the speaker (cf. 1:8). From his throne comes the assurance that the one who created the first heaven and earth will indeed make all things new (*panta kaina*). This is a strong confirmation that God's power will be revealed and his redemptive purposes fulfilled. Since these words are in truth God's words (cf. 19:9; 22:6), it is of utmost importance that this vision of the new heaven and the New Jerusalem be proclaimed to the churches.

6–8 With the same word that declared the judgment of the world finished, God proclaims that he has completed his new creation: "It is done" (*gegonan;* cf. 16:17). The names of God, "the Alpha and the Omega, the Beginning and the End," emphasize his absolute control over the world as well as his creatorship of everything (cf. comments at 1:8 and see 22:13).

To those who thirst for him, God offers the water of life without cost (cf. 7:17; 22:1, 17; John 7:37–39; Rom 3:24). Here salvation is beautifully depicted by the image of drinking at the spring of life. Twice in these last two chapters of Revelation, God offers an invitation to those who sense their need and are drawn toward him. John knows that the visions of God's glory among his people, which he is proclaiming as the Word of God, will create a thirst to participate in the reality of this glory. Nothing is required except to come and drink.

Those who come and drink and remain loyal to Christ as overcomers (*nikaō,* see comments at 2:7, 11, et al.) will inherit all the new things of the city of God. They will be God's children, and he will be their Father. This is the essence of salvation—intimate, personal relationship with God himself, age upon age unending (cf. John 17:3). For John this is really what the heavenly city is all about.

Before John shows us the city, however, he must first confront us with a choice. This choice must be made because there are two cities: the city of God and the city of Babylon. Each has its inhabitants and its destiny. Those who drink from salvation's springs supplied by God himself are true followers of Christ. The "cowardly" (*deilos,* "fearful") are those who fear persecution arising from faith in Christ. Not having steadfast endurance, they are devoid of faith (Matt 8:26; Mark 4:40; cf. Matt 13:20–21). Thus they are linked by John to the "unbelieving" and "vile" (a participial form of the verb *bdelyssomai,* "detest," "abhor," which is used of idolatry [Rom 2:22]). They are called "murderers" because they are guilty of the death of the saints (17:6; 18:24). The "sexually immoral" (fornicators), practitioners of "magic arts, the idolaters and all liars" are those associated with idolatrous practices (cf. 9:21; 18:23; 21:27; 22:15; contrast 14:5). By their own choice, Babylon, not the New Jerusalem, is their eternal home (Caird). Thus this passage is not a picture of universal salvation in spite of man's recalcitrance, though it contains a universal invitation for all who thirst to drink the water of life.

In this section (21:9–22:5), the vision of the New Jerusalem introduced in vv.1–8 is fully described. (For reasons why this section does not describe the millennial kingdom of ch. 20, see comments at introduction to ch. 20.) Verses 9–14 focus on the description of the gates and the walls of the city. This is followed by the action of the angel who measures the city and John's precise mention of the precious stones in the twelve foundations (vv.15–21). Finally, he describes various aspects of the life of the city (21:22–22:5).

9–10 Here the parallelism with 17:1 is clearly deliberate. The bride, the wife of the Lamb, contrasts with the great prostitute. As the prostitute was found to be John's archetypal image for the great system of satanic evil, so the bride is the true counterpart. She is pure and faithful to God and the Lamb, whereas the prostitute is a mockery. To see the prostitute, John was taken to the desert; but now he is elevated by the Spirit to the highest pinnacle of the earth to witness the exalted New Jerusalem (cf. at 1:10; 4:2; 17:3). As his vision will be a reinterpretation of Ezekiel's temple prophecy (Ezek 40–48), like the former prophet, he is taken to a high mountain (Ezek 40:2). For the moment, the author drops the bridal metaphor and in magnificent imagery describes the church in glory as a city with a lofty wall, splendid gates, and jeweled foundations. There is no warrant for thinking of the city descending like a space platform to the mountain or hovering over the earth as some suggest (see comments on v.2).

11–14 In John's description of the city, precious stones, brilliant colors, and the effulgence of light abound. The problem of the literalness of the city has received much attention. If the city is the bride and the bride the glorified community of God's people in their eternal life, there is little question that John's descriptions are primarily symbolic of that glorified life. This in no way diminishes the reality behind the imagery. In the most suitable language available to John, much of it drawn from the OT, he shows us something of the reality of the eschatological kingdom of God in its glorified existence.

Its appearance is all glorious, "with the glory of God" (v.11; cf. Ezek 43:4). The city has a "brilliance" (*phōstēr*, "light-bearer") given it by God's presence that appears as crystal-clear jasper (Isa 60:1–2, 19; Rev 21:23). Jasper (*iaspis*) is mentioned three times in chapter 21 (vv.11, 18–19); earlier in Revelation it refers to the appearance of God (4:3). Jasper is an opaque quartz mineral and occurs in various colors, commonly red, brown, green, and yellow, rarely blue and black, and seldom white. BAG suggests it is an opal (p. 369); others believe it to be a diamond, which is, of course, not quartz but a crystalline carbon. Ginzburg says of it, "This stone changes color even as Benjamin's feelings towards his brothers changed" (cited by Ford, p. 335). Ford thinks the rare and valuable white color is referred to here. Actually, there is no basis for certainty about it.

The wall is very high, its height symbolizing the greatness of this city as well as its impregnability against those described in 21:8, 27. The twelve gates (vv.12–13) are distributed three on each of the four walls (v.13). These may be like the triple gates that can now be seen in the excavated wall of the old Jerusalem. Later John describes the gates as single pearls (v.21). What impresses him at this point about the gates is their angel guards and the inscribed names of the twelve tribes of Israel. The presence of angels proclaims that this is God's city, while the twelve tribes emphasize the complete election of God (cf. comments at 7:4). Here there seems to be a deliberate allusion to Ezekiel's eschatological Jerusalem on whose gates the names of the twelve tribes appear (Ezek 48:30–34). Ezekiel 48:35 says, "The name of the city from that time on will be: THE LORD IS THERE" (cf. Rev 21:3; 22:3–4).

Like the gates, the twelve foundations of the wall have twelve names written on them—in this case the names of the twelve apostles of the Lamb. Foundations of ancient cities usually consisted of extensions of the rows of huge stones that made up the wall, down to the bedrock. Jerusalem's first-century walls and foundation stones have recently been excavated. Huge stones, some of which are about five feet wide, four feet high, and thirty feet long, weighing eighty to one hundred tons each and going down some fourteen to nineteen layers below the present ground level, have been found.

In vv.19–21, John turns to the precious stones that make up the foundations. Here, however, he stresses the names of the twelve apostles. Theologically, it is significant that he brings together the twelve tribes and the twelve apostles of the Lamb and yet differentiates them. This is not unlike what Matthew and Luke tell us that Jesus said (Matt 19:28; Luke 22:30). The earlier symbolic use of twelve (see comments at 7:4), representing in Revelation completeness, implies that it is unnecessary for us to know precisely which twelve will be there. Judas fell and was replaced by Matthias (Acts 1:21–26), but Paul also was a prominent apostle. Furthermore, the number "twelve" is sometimes used to refer to the elect *group* when all twelve are not in view (John 20:24 has ten; 1 Cor 15:5 has eleven; cf. Luke 9:12). The group of apostles represents the church, the elect community built on the foundation of the gospel of Jesus Christ, the slain Lamb. The dual election here depicted admittedly entails some difficulty in identifying the twelve tribes in 7:4ff. with the church as this writer and other commentators have done (see comments at 7:1ff.). Thus some commentators have insisted that the "twelve tribes" refers to an eschatological purpose for the elect Jewish people (Rissi, *The Future of the World,* p. 73; Walvoord, pp. 322–23). It is a puzzling problem.

15–21 The angel measures the city with a golden measuring rod. (The significance of measuring was discussed at 11:1.) The act of measuring signifies securing something for blessing, to preserve it from spiritual harm or defilement. Ezekiel's elaborate description of the future temple and its measuring was to show the glory and holiness of God in Israel's midst (Ezek 43:12). The measuring reveals the perfection, fulfillment, or completion of all God's purposes for his elect bride. Thus the city is revealed as a perfect cube of twelve thousand stadia (12x1000 [about 1,400 miles]). The wall is 144 cubits (about 200 ft.) thick (12x12). These dimensions should not be interpreted as providing architectural information about the city. Rather, we should think of them as theologically symbolic of the fulfillment of all God's promises. The New Jerusalem symbolizes the paradox of the completeness of infinity in God. The cube reminds us of the dimensions of the Most Holy Place in the tabernacle (10x10 cubits [15x15 ft.]) and in the temple (20x20 cubits [30x30 ft.]). John adds that the measurement was both human and angelic (divine): "by man's measurement, which the angel was using" (v.17). This statement is not unimportant. In some sense it shows that both the human and the divine will intersect in the Holy City. Others take v.17 to be John's way of making the reader realize the "disparity" between the city and the size of the wall, thus forcing us to seek a deeper meaning in the angel's measurements (Kiddle).

In vv. 18–21, John describes in more detail the priceless materials of which the city, with its foundations and gates, is made (cf. Isa 54:11–15). The symbolism is not meant to give the impression of wealth and luxury but to point to the glory and holiness of God. The wall of jasper points to the glory of God (4:2–3; see comments at 21:11), while the fabric of the city is pure gold—as clear as glass (v. 21). Such imagery portrays the purity of the bride and her splendor in mirroring the glory of God (cf. Eph 5:27).

The foundation stones are made of twelve precious stones. Here the imagery may reflect three possible sources: (1) the high priest's breastplate (Exod 28:17–20), (2) the jewels on the dress of the king of Tyre (Ezek 28:13), or (3) the signs of the zodiac. The second one, though referring to only nine stones, suggests the splendor of ancient royalty and might be appropriate as a symbol for the glorious kingdom reign in the Holy City. Yet regardless of how one feels about the way some have identified the king of Tyre (Ezek 28:11ff.) with Satan (cf. Feinberg, A.C. Gaebelein, New Scofield Reference Bible), there is something inappropriate about taking this pagan king as symbolic of the future kingdom. Swete and Ford prefer the first option—that of the high priest's breastplate. But while the twelve stones are perhaps the same, the order of their mention is different. This leaves the third option. According to Philo and Josephus, Israel associated these same stones with the signs of the zodiac, and their tribal standards each bore a sign of the zodiac (Caird, p. 276). If we begin with Judah, the tribe of Christ (7:5), the sign is Aries, the Ram, which has the amethyst as its stone. The last sign is Pisces, the fishes, which has jasper as its stone (Charles, *Commentary on Revelation*, 2:167). So the first zodiacal sign agrees with the twelfth foundation and the last zodiacal sign with the first foundation. In fact, the whole list agrees with John's, though in reverse order. This may be a significant device to show John's disapproval of pagan cults. But these matters are uncertain.

The gates are twelve great pearls. Though pearls are not mentioned in the OT, some rabbinic texts refer to gates for Jerusalem hewn out of jewels about forty-five feet square (*Sanhedrin* 100a). As for the one main street of the Holy City, it is like the fabric of the city itself, of pure gold, clear as glass (see comments at 21:18).

22–27 John turns from this beautiful description of the city to the life within it. In antiquity every notable city had at least one central temple. The New Jerusalem not only differs in this respect from ancient cities but also from all Jewish speculation about the age to come. Illuminated by the overflowing radiance of the presence of the glory of God, the Holy City no longer needs a temple (*naos*). Yet paradoxically it has a temple, for the Lord God Almighty and the Lamb are its temple (v. 22). And in another sense, the whole city is a temple, since it is patterned after the Most Holy Place (v. 16). Jewish expectation was centered on a rebuilt temple and the restoration of the ark of the covenant. In his glorious vision, John sees the fulfillment of these hopes in the total presence of God with his purified people, while the Lamb, the sign of the new covenant, is the fulfillment of the restoration of the ark of the covenant (see comments at 11:19; cf. John 4:21, 23). As long as there is uncleanness in the world, there is need for a temple where God's presence and truth are in contrast to the uncleanness. But in the new city no such symbol is needed any longer. In fulfillment of Isaiah 60:19–20, there will be no further need, as in ancient temples, for any natural or artificial lighting because the glory of God will dim the most powerful earthly light into paleness (cf. Zech 14:7). In the earthly tabernacle and temple, there was, to be sure, artificial lighting (the seven-branched lampstand in the OT tabernacle and the temple); yet the Most Holy Place had no such lighting because of the shekinah, the light of God's own presence.

Verses 24–26 present a remarkable picture of "the nations" and "the kings of the earth" entering the city and bringing their splendor (*doxa*, "glory," "honor," "magnificence") into it. John sees a vision of social life, bustling with activity. Elsewhere in Revelation, the nations (*ethnē*) are the pagan, rebellious peoples of the world who trample the Holy City (cf. comments at 11:2; 11:18) and who have become drunk with the wine of Babylon, the mother of prostitutes (18:3, 23), and who will also be destroyed by the second coming of Christ (19:15). The same description applies to the kings of the earth. But there is another use of these terms in Revelation. They stand for the peoples of earth who are the servants of Christ, the redeemed nations who follow the Lamb and have resisted the beast and Babylon (1:5; 15:3; 19:16; 2:26; 5:9; 7:9; 12:5). It is this latter group that John describes figuratively as having part in the activity in the Holy City, the kingdom of God. What this may involve regarding the relation of this life to the future kingdom is not stated.

Life in the age to come will certainly involve continuing activities and relationships that will contribute to the glory of the Holy City throughout eternity. Instead of the nations bringing their precious possessions to Babylon, the harlot city, the redeemed nations will bring these offerings to the throne of God (cf. Isa 60:3ff.). So certain is its perpetual light and security that the gates will never be shut for fear of evil by night (v.25; cf. Isa 60:11). This imagery should not, however, be allegorized as indicating some sort of perpetual invitation to salvation.

One thing is absolutely certain. Nothing impure (*koinos*, "common," "profane") will ever enter the city's gates (v.27). By *koinos* John means ceremonial impurity (cf. at 21:8; 22:15). No idolatrous person may enter. Only those can enter whose names are in "the Lamb's book of life" and who thus belong to him through redemption (cf. 3:5; 20:12, 15). This should not be taken as implying that in the New Jerusalem there will still be unsaved roaming around outside the city who may now and then enter it by repenting (contra Caird). Instead, the exhortation warns present readers that the only way to participate in the future city is to turn one's total loyalties to the Lamb now (cf. 21:7).

Notes

16, 21 Many see a possible allusion to ancient Babylon, which was described in antiquity in language similar to John's. According to Herodotus, Babylon was four-square, magnificent beyond all other cities. As in Revelation, he gives the dimensions of the city in stadia and those of the wall in royal cubits (Herodotus 1.178). Ancient Babylon also had a great street down its center. While these allusions are no more than hypothetical, the similarities are striking.

19–21 Glasson argues that the jewels fulfill the allusion to Isa 54:11–12, which in turn is based on the high priestly breastplate. The city itself is as sacred as the Most Holy Place, and all the inhabitants are named priests of the Lord (Isa 61:6; cf. Rev 1:6)(*The Revelation*, p. 118; see also idem, "The Jewels of Revelation 21:19–20," JTS, 26 (April 1975), 95–99).

B. *The River of Life and the Tree of Life*

22:1–5

[1]Then the angel showed me the river of the water of life, as clear as crystal, flowing from the throne of God and of the Lamb [2]down the middle of the great street of the city. On each side of the river stood the tree of life, bearing twelve crops of fruit, yielding its fruit every month. And the leaves of the tree are for the healing of the nations. [3]No longer will there be any curse. The throne of God and of the Lamb will be in the city, and his servants will serve him. [4]They will see his face, and his name will be on their foreheads. [5]There will be no more night. They will not need the light of a lamp or the light of the sun, for the Lord God will give them light. And they will reign for ever and ever.

1–5 This section continues the description of the Holy City begun in 21:9, but now with the emphasis on its inner life. John returns to his archetypal images from Genesis (1–3) and Ezekiel (40ff.). The paradisiacal quality of the future age is briefly but beautifully described. Here Paradise is regained. As in the OT imagery of the age to come, metaphors of water and light abound (cf. Isa 12:3; Zech 14:7–8). The river of the water of life recalls Ezekiel 47:1ff. (cf. Joel 3:18) and the pastoral scene of Revelation 7:17 (q.v.). In both Testaments water is frequently associated with the salvation of God and the life-imparting and cleansing ministry of the Holy Spirit (Isa 44:3; cf. John 3:5; 4:13–14; 7:37–39; 13:10; 19:34; Titus 3:5). In the new city of God the pure water does not issue from the temple as in Ezekiel but comes from the throne of God, since this whole city is a Most Holy Place with God at its center. Life from God streams unceasingly through the new world.

The tree of life spreads all along the great street of the city (v.2). What was once forfeited by our forebears in Eden and denied to their succeeding posterity is now fully restored (cf. Gen 3:22–24). In Ezekiel's vision these are multiple trees on each side of the river that bear fruit monthly, whose leaves are for healing (Ezek 47:12). Therefore, the tree (*xylon*) John speaks of may be a collective word for Ezekiel's trees. So abundant is its vitality that it bears a crop of fruit each month! Its leaves produce healing for the nations. The imagery of abundant fruit and medicinal leaves should be understood as symbolic of the far-reaching effects of the death of Christ in the redeemed community, the Holy City. So powerful is the salvation of God that the effects of sin are completely overcome. The eternal life God gives the redeemed community will be perpetually available, will sustain, and will cure eternally every former sin.

Thus the curse pronounced in Eden will be removed (v.3; cf. Gen 3:17). This may mean, according to Swete, that no one who is cursed because of idolatry will be in the city (v.15). Instead of Babylon and its servants occupying the earth, the throne of God will be central and his servants will serve him (cf. 2:13). Wherever the throne is in sight, the priestly service of the saints will be perpetual (cf. 1:6). Here our true liturgy is fulfilled (cf. Rom 12:1). Observe John's emphasis on God and the Lamb (21:22–23; 22:1, 3). They share the same glory, the same throne, the same temple significance. The Christology of John's vision is everywhere evident even though stated in functional terms.

With no restriction such as those that pertain to Moses (Exod 33:20, 23) or the high priests (Heb 9:7), the redeemed community will be in Christ's presence, beholding perpetually his glory (cf. Ps 17:15; Matt 5:8; 1 Cor 13:12; 2 Cor 3:18; 1 John 3:2).

Eternal life is perfect communion, worship, the vision of God, light, and victory. Since God and the Lamb are always viewed together, there is no point in saying that the redeemed will see Jesus but not the Father. (Concerning the name on their foreheads, see comments at 14:1.)

A final burst of light engulfs the whole scene, and an announcement that the saints will reign for ever and ever fulfills the first promise of the book (1:6; cf. 5:10; 20:4–6; and see esp. 11:15). The logical sequence as well as the inner relationship of the words "his servants will serve" (v.3) and "they will reign" (v.5) have deep implications for the whole nature of God's kingdom in contrast to that of the satanic Babylon. Surely it is fitting for such a book of prophecy as Revelation to close around the throne, with God's servants both worshiping and ruling.

VI. Conclusion

22:6–21

[6]The angel said to me, "These words are trustworthy and true. The Lord, the God
of the spirits of the prophets, sent his angel to show his servants the things that
must soon take place."

[7]"Behold, I am coming soon! Blessed is he who keeps the words of the prophecy
in this book."

[8]I, John, am the one who heard and saw these things. And when I had heard
and seen them, I fell down to worship at the feet of the angel who had been showing
them to me. [9]But he said to me, "Do not do it! I am a fellow servant with you and
with your brothers the prophets and of all who keep the words of this book. Worship
God!"

[10]Then he told me, "Do not seal up the words of the prophecy of this book,
because the time is near. [11]Let him who does wrong continue to do wrong; let him
who is vile continue to be vile; let him who does right continue to do right; and let
him who is holy continue to be holy."

[12]Behold, I am coming soon! My reward is with me, and I will give to everyone
according to what he has done. [13]I am the Alpha and the Omega, the First and the
Last, the Beginning and the End.
[14]"Blessed are those who wash their robes, that they may have the right to the
tree of life and may go through the gates into the city. [15]Outside are the dogs, those
who practice magic arts, the sexually immoral, the murderers, the idolaters and
everyone who loves and practices falsehood.
[16]"I, Jesus, have sent my angel to give you this testimony for the churches. I am
the Root and the Offspring of David, and the bright Morning Star."

[17]The Spirit and the bride say, "Come!" And let him who hears say, "Come!"
Whoever is thirsty, let him come; and whoever wishes, let him take the free gift of
the water of life.

[18]I warn everyone who hears the words of the prophecy of this book: If anyone
adds anything to them, God will add to him the plagues described in this book.
[19]And if anyone takes words away from this book of prophecy, God will take away
from him his share in the tree of life and in the holy city, which are described in this
book.
[20]He who testifies to these things says, "Yes, I am coming soon." Amen. Come,
Lord Jesus.
[21]The grace of the Lord Jesus be with God's people. Amen.

6 With consummate art, the notes of the introit (1:1–8) are sounded again in the conclusion. So the book ends with the voices of the angel, Jesus, the Spirit, the bride, and, finally, John (v.20). The book is a seamless garment. There are three major emphases in the conclusion: confirmation of the genuineness of the prophecy (vv.6–7, 16, 18–19); the imminence of Jesus' coming (vv.7, 12, 20); the warning against idolatry and the invitation to enter the city (vv.11–12, 15, 17–19). A similar word of assurance (v.6), such as that in 19:9 and 21:5, provides the transition from the glorious vision of the Holy City to the final words of the book. An angel declares that it is "the Lord, the God of the spirits of the prophets," the one from whom the prophets like John receive their message, that assures the readers of the speedy fulfillment of all that has been revealed (cf. 1:1; 10:6–7). John has been the recipient of divine prophecy that will have its immediate consequences (cf. v.10).

7 This first declaration of the imminent coming of Jesus is Jesus' own response to the yearnings of the church (cf. comments at 1:7; 2:25; and esp. 3:11). It is the sixth beatitude in Revelation; and, like the first one (1:3), it is directed toward those who keep (obey) the words of the prophecy (cf. vv.18–19).

8–9 The "I, John" is reminiscent of 1:4, 9. His confession that he "heard and saw these things" and the repetition of the prohibition (19:10) against John's worshiping the angel serve a purpose. No believer, not even one of great spiritual stature as John, is beyond the subtle temptation to worship what is good itself in place of God who alone is to be worshiped.

10–11 These verses stand in contrast to the command given Daniel to seal up his book (8:26; 12:4, 9–10) and in contrast to Jewish apocalypses in general. John's message cannot be concealed because the contents of the vision are needed immediately by the churches. (On the sealing metaphor, see comments at 7:3.) Verse 11 appears at first reading to be fatalistic. Yet on further reflection, the exhortation stresses the imminency of the return of Jesus and the necessity for immediate choices. It echoes the aphorism As now, so always. Far from being an encouragement to remain apathetic, it is evangelistic in spirit. It may also allude to the great ordeal John viewed as imminent. For the unfaithful and wicked, this appeal would be a deep confirmation of their choice, whereas for the faithful, it would alert them to the necessity of guarding themselves against apostasy (cf. Jude 20–21). There is no reason to take this passage as teaching the irreversibility of human choices (contra Swete). Repentance is always a live option as long as a person is living. After death, however, there remains only judgment, not repentance (Heb 9:27).

12–13 This second of three announcements of the imminent return of Jesus in this chapter (cf. vv.7, 20) is associated with the truth of rewards and judgment based on deeds (cf. comments at 20:12; also 11:18). (On the terms Alpha and Omega, etc., see comments at 1:8, 17.)

14 The seventh and last beatitude in Revelation is evangelistic in emphasis (cf. 21:6; 22:11, 17). Strands of the earlier imagery are blended in it. In 7:14 the washing of the robes indicates willing identification with Jesus in his death. It also carries the thought of martyrdom during the great ordeal for the saints (cf. 6:11). Thus it symbolizes a salvation that involves obedience and discipleship, since it is integrally related to the salvation imagery of the tree of life (cf. comments at 22:2) and the gates of the city (cf. 21:25).

15 John has already made it clear that no idolaters can ever enter the city but only those whose names are in the Lamb's book of life (cf. comments at 21:8, 27). Such are "the dogs," i.e., those who practice magic arts, etc.—viz., those who rebel against the rule of God (cf. Deut 23:18, where a dog signifies a male prostitute; Matt 15:26, where "dogs" refers to Gentiles; Phil 3:2–3, where "dogs" refers to the Judaizers). There is no doubt that such people will not be admitted through the gates of the Holy City. They will be in the lake of fire (20:15). But the problem involves what appears to be their present exclusion from the city at the time of John's writing. Are they "outside" now? As has been previously argued in this commentary, the city is future and is not to be identified with the present historical church (see introduction to ch. 21 and comments at 21:2). Only in an eschatological sense can it be maintained that the new city exists in the present.

On the other hand, it is not necessary to place the time of v.15 in the present (contra Caird). There is no verb in the Greek text of the verse. Therefore the time of the action is determined by the context. Since the fulfillment of v.14 lies in the future, the time of v.15 is also most naturally future. The word "outside" is simply a figure that agrees with the whole imagery of the Holy City. It means exclusion. To be outside the city means to be in the lake of fire. Thus it is not necessary either to place the Holy City in the present or to place it in a millennial Jerusalem. The Holy City, as we have previously argued, is a symbol for the future realization of the corporate community of God's people (i.e., the eschatological kingdom of God), and as such it does not have a geographical location other than that it is on the new earth.

16 As in 1:8, 17–20, in this verse Christ addresses John and the churches directly. The "you" is plural in the Greek text. Here Christ's words authenticate the whole Book of Revelation ("this testimony") as being a message to the churches. Therefore, any method of interpreting Revelation that blunts the application of this message in its entirety to the present church must disregard these words of Christ. He is the Messiah of Israel, "the Root and the Offspring of David" (cf. Isa 11:1; see comments at Rev 5:5) and the fulfillment of the promise to the overcomers at Thyatira (see comments at 2:28).

17 The first two sentences in this verse are not an evangelistic appeal but express the yearning of the Holy Spirit and the "bride" (the whole church, cf. 21:9) for the return of Christ. In v.20 John gives us the Lord Jesus' answer: "Yes, I am coming soon." Those who hear (i.e., "him who hears")—viz., the members of the local congregations in John's time—join in the invitation for Christ to return. Then, any in the congregations who are not yet followers of Jesus are invited to come and take the water of life as a free gift (*dōrean*, "freely," cf. Rom 3:24; Rev 21:6). (On the water of life, cf. 21:6; 22:1; also, for the liturgical and eucharistic use of this verse, see comments at v.20.)

18–19 These verses should not be taken as a warning against adding anything to the Bible. Early interpreters understood them as a warning to false prophets not to alter the sense of John's prophecy—i.e., Revelation (so Irenaeus *Contra Haereses* 30.2). Kline has likened the force of these words to the curses pronounced for disobedience in the covenant law codes of the OT period (Meredith Kline, *Treaty of the Great King*

[Grand Rapids: Eerdmans, 1963], p. 44; cf. Deut 4:2; 12:32). Verses 18–19 are a strong warning against any who would tamper with the contents of "this book" (Rev), either textually or in its moral and theological teaching (cf. 1 Cor 16:22). So severe is the danger he is warning against that John says that those who teach contrary to the message of Revelation will not only forfeit any right to salvation in the Holy City but will have visited on them the divine judgments (plagues) inflicted on the beast worshipers.

20 This is the third affirmation (in ch. 22) of Jesus' imminent return and perhaps the response to the longing cry in v.17. John responds to the Lord Jesus' declaration by saying, "Amen. Come, Lord Jesus." These fervent words are part of the liturgy of the early church. They were a prayer used at the close of the meal in the eucharistic liturgy (*Didache* 10.6). Cullmann believes that these words are the earliest expression of the recognition that the Lord's Day (Sunday) is the day of the Resurrection. As Jesus appeared to his disciples alive on the first day of the week, so he was expected to be present in the Spirit at every first-day Eucharist celebration and to appear again at the end, which is often represented by the picture of a messianic meal (Oscar Cullmann, *Early Christian Worship*, [London: SCM, 1953], pp. 13–14). The expression "Come, Lord Jesus" (*erchou, kyrie Iēsou*) is equivalent to the Aramaic *mārānā' 'ᵃṯāh* (Gr. *marana tha*; cf. 1 Cor 16:22, "Come, O Lord," NIV). So in closing Revelation, John alludes to chapter 1, with its reference to the Lord's Day (1:10).

21 A conclusion such as this, while quite unsuitable for a Jewish apocalypse, is wholly appropriate for this prophetic message addressed to the ancient church and, indeed, to the whole body of Christ. The benediction is reminiscent of Paul's usual practice (cf. the final verses of Rom, 1 Thess, Col, et al.). Whether in this benediction we should accept the textual reading "with all" (Bruce M. Metzger, *A Textual Commentary on the Greek New Testament* [New York: UBS, 1971], p. 769) or "with all the saints" (Swete, various MSS) cannot be completely settled. We may, however, agree that nothing less than God's grace is required for us to be overcomers and triumphantly enter the Holy City of God, where we shall reign with him for ever and ever.

Notes

14 Here most of the better textual witnesses read πλύνοντες τὰς στολὰς αὐτῶν (*plynontes tas stolas autōn*, "wash their garments"). Following a number of later minuscule MSS, KJV follows the reading ποιοῦντες τὰς ἐντυλὰς αὐτοῦ (*poiountes tas entylas autou*, "those who do his commands"). The former reading is preferred.

19 While only one or two late Gr. MSS have βιβλίον τῆς ζωῆς (*biblion tēs zōēs*, "book of life") instead of ξύλον τῆς ζωῆς (*xylon tēs zōēs*, "tree of life"), KJV curiously follows this inferior reading, probably because of its presence in the Lat. Vul.